THE
EXPOSITOR'S
BIBLE
COMMENTARY

THE
EXPOSITOR'S BIBLE COMMENTARY

with
**The New International Version
of
The Holy Bible**

IN TWELVE VOLUMES

VOLUME 6
(ISAIAH—EZEKIEL)

ZondervanPublishingHouse
Grand Rapids, Michigan

A Division of HarperCollins*Publishers*

THE EXPOSITOR'S BIBLE COMMENTARY, VOLUME 6
Copyright © 1986 by The Zondervan Corporation
Grand Rapids, Michigan

Requests for information should be addressed to:
Zondervan Publishing House
Grand Rapids, Michigan 49530

Library of Congress Cataloging in Publication Data
(Revised for vol. 6)

Main entry under title:
The Expositor's Bible commentary.

    Includes bibliographies.
    Contents: v. 1. Introductory articles—v. 6. Isaiah-
Ezekiel—[etc.]—v.12. Hebrews-Revelation.
    1. Bible—Commentaries. I. Gaebelein, Frank Ely,
1899- . II. Douglas J. D. (James Dixon) III. Bible.
English. New International. 1976.
BS491.2.E96   220.7'7   76-41334
ISBN 0-310-36480-9 (v. 6)

Printed in the United States of America

97 98 99 00 01 02 /❖ DH/ 17 16 15 14

This edition is printed on acid-free paper and meets the American National
Standards Institute Z39.48 standard.

CONTENTS

Contributors to Volume 6 vi

Preface vii

Abbreviations ix

Transliterations xv

Isaiah 3

Jeremiah 357

Lamentations 695

Ezekiel 737

CONTRIBUTORS TO VOLUME 6

Isaiah: Geoffrey W. Grogan

BD., M.Th., University of London

Principal, Bible Training Institute, Glasgow, Scotland

Jeremiah: Charles Lee Feinberg

Th.M., Th.D., Dallas Theological Seminary; Ph.D., Johns Hopkins University

Dean Emeritus and Professor Emeritus of Semitics and Old Testament, Talbot Theological Seminary

Lamentations: H. L. Ellison

B.A., B.D., Kings College, London

Formerly Lecturer at London Bible College, Cambridge University, and Moorlands Bible College; missionary to Jews in Poland. Deceased

Ezekiel: Ralph H. Alexander

Th.M., Th.D., Dallas Theological Seminary

Associate Professor of Old Testament Language and Exegesis, Western Conservative Baptist Theological Seminary

PREFACE

The title of this work defines its purpose. Written primarily by expositors for expositors, it aims to provide preachers, teachers, and students of the Bible with a new and comprehensive commentary on the books of the Old and New Testaments. Its stance is that of a scholarly evangelicalism committed to the divine inspiration, complete trustworthiness, and full authority of the Bible. Its seventy-eight contributors come from the United States, Canada, England, Scotland, Australia, New Zealand, and Switzerland, and from various religious groups, including Anglican, Baptist, Brethren, Free, Independent, Methodist, Nazarene, Presbyterian, and Reformed churches. Most of them teach at colleges, universities, or theological seminaries.

No book has been more closely studied over a longer period of time than the Bible. From the Midrashic commentaries going back to the period of Ezra, through parts of the Dead Sea Scrolls and the Patristic literature, and on to the present, the Scriptures have been expounded. Indeed, there have been times when, as in the Reformation and on occasions since then, exposition has been at the cutting edge of Christian advance. Luther was a powerful exegete, and Calvin is still called "the prince of expositors."

Their successors have been many. And now, when the outburst of new translations and their unparalleled circulation have expanded the readership of the Bible, the need for exposition takes on fresh urgency.

Not that God's Word can ever become captive to its expositors. Among all other books, it stands first in its combination of perspicuity and profundity. Though a child can be made "wise for salvation" by believing its witness to Christ, the greatest mind cannot plumb the depths of its truth (2 Tim. 3:15; Rom. 11:33). As Gregory the Great said, "Holy Scripture is a stream of running water, where alike the elephant may swim, and the lamb walk." So, because of the inexhaustible nature of Scripture, the task of opening up its meaning is still a perennial obligation of biblical scholarship.

How that task is done inevitably reflects the outlook of those engaged in it. Every Bible scholar has presuppositions. To this neither the editors of these volumes nor the contributors to them are exceptions. They share a common commitment to the supernatural Christianity set forth in the inspired Word. Their purpose is not to supplant the many valuable commentaries that have preceded this work and from which both the editors and contributors have learned. It is rather to draw on the resources of contemporary evangelical scholarship in producing a new reference work for understanding the Scriptures.

A commentary that will continue to be useful through the years should handle contemporary trends in biblical studies in such a way as to avoid becoming outdated when critical fashions change. Biblical criticism is not in itself inadmissable, as some have mistakenly thought. When scholars investigate the authorship, date, literary characteristics, and purpose of a biblical document, they are practicing biblical criticism. So also when, in order to ascertain as nearly as possible the original form of the text, they deal with variant readings, scribal errors, emendations, and other phenomena in the manuscripts. To do these things is essential to responsible exegesis and exposition. And always there is the need to distinguish hypothesis from fact, conjecture from truth.

vii

The chief principle of interpretation followed in this commentary is the grammatico-historical one—namely, that the primary aim of the exegete is to make clear the meaning of the text at the time and in the circumstances of its writing. This endeavor to únderstand what in the first instance the inspired writers actually said must not be confused with an inflexible literalism. Scripture makes lavish use of symbols and figures of speech; great portions of it are poetical. Yet when it speaks in this way, it speaks no less truly than it does in its historical and doctrinal portions. To understand its message requires attention to matters of grammar and syntax, word meanings, idioms, and literary forms—all in relation to the historical and cultural setting of the text.

The contributors to this work necessarily reflect varying convictions. In certain controversial matters the policy is that of clear statement of the contributors' own views followed by fair presentation of other ones. The treatment of eschatology, though it reflects differences of interpretation, is consistent with a general premillennial position. (Not all contributors, however, are premillennial.) But prophecy is more than prediction, and so this commentary gives due recognition to the major lode of godly social concern in the prophetic writings.

THE EXPOSITOR'S BIBLE COMMENTARY is presented as a scholarly work, though not primarily one of technical criticism. In its main portion, the Exposition, and in Volume 1 (General and Special Articles), all Semitic and Greek words are transliterated and the English equivalents given. As for the Notes, here Semitic and Greek characters are used but always with transliterations and English meanings, so that this portion of the commentary will be as accessible as possible to readers unacquainted with the original languages.

It is the conviction of the general editor, shared by his colleagues in the Zondervan editorial department, that in writing about the Bible, lucidity is not incompatible with scholarship. They are therefore endeavoring to make this a clear and understandable work.

The translation used in it is the New International Version (North American Edition). To the International Bible Society thanks are due for permission to use this most recent of the major Bible translations. It was chosen because of the clarity and beauty of its style and its faithfulness to the original texts.

To the associate editor, Richard P. Polcyn, and to the contributing editors— Dr. Walter C. Kaiser, Jr., Dr. Bruce K. Waltke, and Dr. Ralph H. Alexander for the Old Testament, and Dr. James Montgomery Boice and Dr. Merrill C. Tenney for the New Testament—the general editor expresses his gratitude for their unfailing cooperation and their generosity in advising him out of their expert scholarship. And to the many other contributors he is indebted for their invaluable part in this work. Finally, he owes a special debt of gratitude to Dr. Robert K. DeVries, publisher, The Zondervan Corporation, and Miss Elizabeth Brown, secretary, for their assistance and encouragement.

Whatever else it is—the greatest and most beautiful of books, the primary source of law and morality, the fountain of wisdom, and the infallible guide to life—the Bible is above all the inspired witness to Jesus Christ. May this work fulfill its function of expounding the Scriptures with grace and clarity, so that its users may find that both Old and New Testaments do indeed lead to our Lord Jesus Christ, who alone could say, "I have come that they may have life, and have it to the full" (John 10:10).

FRANK E. GAEBELEIN

ABBREVIATIONS

A. General Abbreviations

A	Codex Alexandrinus
Akkad.	Akkadian
א	Codex Sinaiticus
Ap. Lit.	Apocalyptic Literature
Apoc.	Apocrypha
Aq.	Aquila's Greek Translation of the Old Testament
Arab.	Arabic
Aram.	Aramaic
b	Babylonian Gemara
B	Codex Vaticanus
C	Codex Ephraemi Syri
c.	*circa*, about
cf.	*confer*, compare
ch., chs.	chapter, chapters
cod., codd.	codex, codices
contra	in contrast to
D	Codex Bezae
DSS	Dead Sea Scrolls (see E.)
ed., edd.	edited, edition, editor; editions
e.g.	*exempli gratia*, for example
Egyp.	Egyptian
et al.	*et alii*, and others
EV	English Versions of the Bible
fem.	feminine
ff.	following (verses, pages, etc.)
fl.	flourished
ft.	foot, feet
gen.	genitive
Gr.	Greek
Heb.	Hebrew
Hitt.	Hittite
ibid.	*ibidem*, in the same place
id.	*idem*, the same
i.e.	*id est*, that is
impf.	imperfect
infra.	below
in loc.	*in loco*, in the place cited
j	Jerusalem or Palestinian Gemara
Lat.	Latin
LL.	Late Latin
LXX	Septuagint
M	Mishnah
masc.	masculine
mg.	margin
Mid	Midrash
MS(S)	manuscript(s)
MT	Masoretic text
n.	note
n.d.	no date
Nestle	Nestle (ed.) *Novum Testamentum Graece*
no.	number
NT	New Testament
obs.	obsolete
OL	Old Latin
OS	Old Syriac
OT	Old Testament
p., pp.	page, pages
par.	paragraph
Pers.	Persian
Pesh.	Peshitta
Phoen.	Phoenician
pl.	plural
Pseudep.	Pseudepigrapha
Q	Quelle ("Sayings" source in the Gospels)
qt.	quoted by
q.v.	*quod vide*, which see
R	Rabbah
rev.	revised, reviser, revision
Rom.	Roman
RVm	Revised Version margin
Samar.	Samaritan recension
SCM	Student Christian Movement Press
Sem.	Semitic
sing.	singular
SPCK	Society for the Promotion of Christian Knowledge
Sumer.	Sumerian
s.v.	*sub verbo*, under the word
Syr.	Syriac
Symm.	Symmachus
T	Talmud
Targ.	Targum
Theod.	Theodotion
TR	Textus Receptus
tr.	translation, translator, translated
UBS	Tha United Bible Societies' Greek Text
Ugar.	Ugaritic
u.s.	*ut supra*, as above
v., vv.	verse, verses
viz.	*videlicet*, namely
vol.	volume
vs.	versus
Vul.	Vulgate
WH	Westcott and Hort, *The New Testament in Greek*

B. Abbreviations for Modern Translations and Paraphrases

AmT	Smith and Goodspeed, *The Complete Bible, An American Translation*	Mof	J. Moffatt, *A New Translation of the Bible*
ASV	American Standard Version, American Revised Version (1901)	NAB	The New American Bible
		NASB	New American Standard Bible
		NEB	The New English Bible
Beck	Beck, *The New Testament in the Language of Today*	NIV	The New International Version
		Ph	J. B. Phillips *The New Testament in Modern English*
BV	Berkeley Version (The Modern Language Bible)	RSV	Revised Standard Version
		RV	Revised Version — 1881–1885
JB	The Jerusalem Bible	TCNT	Twentieth Century New Testament
JPS	*Jewish Publication Society Version of the Old Testament*		
		TEV	Today's English Version
KJV	King James Version	Wey	*Weymouth's New Testament in Modern Speech*
Knox	R.G. Knox, *The Holy Bible: A Translation from the Latin Vulgate in the Light of the Hebrew and Greek Original*	Wms	C. B. Williams, *The New Testament: A Translation in the Language of the People*
LB	The Living Bible		

C. Abbreviations for Periodicals and Reference Works

AASOR	*Annual of the American Schools of Oriental Research*	BASOR	*Bulletin of the American Schools of Oriental Research*
AB	*Anchor Bible*	BC	Foakes-Jackson and Lake: *The Beginnings of Christianity*
AIs	de Vaux: *Ancient Israel*		
AJA	*American Journal of Archaeology*	BDB	Brown, Driver, and Briggs: *Hebrew-English Lexicon of the Old Testament*
AJSL	*American Journal of Semitic Languages and Literatures*	BDF	Blass, Debrunner, and Funk: *A Greek Grammar of the New Testament and Other Early Christian Literature*
AJT	*American Journal of Theology*		
Alf	Alford: *Greek Testament Commentary*		
		BDT	Harrison: *Baker's Dictionary of Theology*
ANEA	*Ancient Near Eastern Archaeology*	Beng.	Bengel's *Gnomon*
ANEP	Pritchard: *Ancient Near Eastern Pictures*	BETS	*Bulletin of the Evangelical Theological Society*
ANET	Pritchard: *Ancient Near Eastern Texts*	BH	*Biblia Hebraica*
		BHS	*Biblia Hebraica Stuttgartensia*
ANF	Roberts and Donaldson: *The Ante-Nicene Fathers*	BJRL	*Bulletin of the John Rylands Library*
A-S	Abbot-Smith: *Manual Greek Lexicon of the New Testament*	BS	*Bibliotheca Sacra*
		BT	*Babylonian Talmud*
AThR	*Anglican Theological Review*	BTh	*Biblical Theology*
BA	*Biblical Archaeologist*	BW	*Biblical World*
BAG	Bauer, Arndt, and Gingrich: *Greek-English Lexicon of the New Testament*	CAH	*Cambridge Ancient History*
		CanJTh	*Canadian Journal of Theology*
		CBQ	*Catholic Biblical Quarterly*
BAGD	Bauer, Arndt, Gingrich, and Danker: *Greek-English Lexicon of the New Testament* 2nd edition	CBSC	*Cambridge Bible for Schools and Colleges*
		CE	*Catholic Encyclopedia*
		CGT	*Cambridge Greek Testament*

CHS	Lange: *Commentary on the Holy Scriptures*	IDB	*The Interpreter's Dictionary of the Bible*
ChT	*Christianity Today*	IEJ	*Israel Exploration Journal*
DDB	*Davis' Dictionary of the Bible*	Int	*Interpretation*
Deiss BS	Deissmann: *Bible Studies*	INT	E. Harrison: *Introduction to the New Testament*
Deiss LAE	Deissmann: *Light From the Ancient East*	IOT	R. K. Harrison: *Introduction to the Old Testament*
DNTT	*Dictionary of New Testament Theology*	ISBE	*The International Standard Bible Encyclopedia*
EBC	*The Expositor's Bible Commentary*	ITQ	*Irish Theological Quarterly*
EBi	*Encyclopaedia Biblica*	JAAR	*Journal of American Academy of Religion*
EBr	*Encyclopaedia Britannica*		
EDB	*Encyclopedic Dictionary of the Bible*	JAOS	*Journal of American Oriental Society*
EGT	Nicoll: *Expositor's Greek Testament*	JBL	*Journal of Biblical Literature*
EQ	*Evangelical Quarterly*	JE	*Jewish Encyclopedia*
ET	*Evangelische Theologie*	JETS	*Journal of Evangelical Theological Society*
ExB	*The Expositor's Bible*		
Exp	*The Expositor*	JFB	Jamieson, Fausset, and Brown: *Commentary on the Old and New Testament*
ExpT	*The Expository Times*		
FLAP	Finegan: *Light From the Ancient Past*		
GKC	Gesenius, Kautzsch, Cowley, *Hebrew Grammar*, 2nd Eng. ed.	JNES	*Journal of Near Eastern Studies*
		Jos. Antiq.	Josephus: *The Antiquities of the Jews*
GR	*Gordon Review*	Jos. War	Josephus: *The Jewish War*
HBD	*Harper's Bible Dictionary*	JQR	*Jewish Quarterly Review*
HDAC	Hastings: *Dictionary of the Apostolic Church*	JR	*Journal of Religion*
		JSJ	*Journal for the Study of Judaism in the Persian, Hellenistic and Roman Periods*
HDB	Hastings: *Dictionary of the Bible*		
HDBrev.	Hastings: *Dictionary of the Bible*, one-vol. rev. by Grant and Rowley	JSOR	*Journal of the Society of Oriental Research*
		JSS	*Journal of Semitic Studies*
HDCG	Hastings: *Dictionary of Christ and the Gospels*	JT	*Jerusalem Talmud*
		JTS	*Journal of Theological Studies*
HERE	Hastings: *Encyclopedia of Religion and Ethics*	KAHL	Kenyon: *Archaeology in the Holy Land*
HGEOTP	Heidel: *The Gilgamesh Epic and Old Testament Parallels*	KB	Koehler-Baumgartner: *Lexicon in Veteris Testament Libros*
HJP	Schurer: *A History of the Jewish People in the Time of Christ*	KD	Keil and Delitzsch: *Commentary on the Old Testament*
		LSJ	Liddell, Scott, Jones: *Greek-English Lexicon*
HR	Hatch and Redpath: *Concordance to the Septuagint*	LTJM	Edersheim: *The Life and Times of Jesus the Messiah*
HTR	*Harvard Theological Review*	MM	Moulton and Milligan: *The Vocabulary of the Greek Testament*
HUCA	*Hebrew Union College Annual*		
IB	*The Interpreter's Bible*		
ICC	*International Critical Commentary*	MNT	Moffatt: *New Testament Commentary*

MST	McClintock and Strong: *Cyclopedia of Biblical, Theological, and Ecclesiastical Literature*	SJT	*Scottish Journal of Theology*
		SOT	Girdlestone: *Synonyms of Old Testament*
NBC	Davidson, Kevan, and Stibbs: *The New Bible Commentary*, 1st ed.	SOTI	Archer: *A Survey of Old Testament Introduction*
		ST	*Studia Theologica*
NBCrev.	Guthrie and Motyer: *The New Bible Commentary*, rev. ed.	TCERK	Loetscher: *The Twentieth Century Encyclopedia of Religious Knowledge*
NBD	J. D. Douglas: *The New Bible Dictionary*	TDNT	Kittel: *Theological Dictionary of the New Testament*
NCB	*New Century Bible*	TDOT	*Theological Dictionary of the Old Testament*
NCE	*New Catholic Encyclopedia*		
NIC	*New International Commentary*	THAT	*Theologisches Handbuch zum Alten Testament*
NIDCC	Douglas: *The New International Dictionary of the Christian Church*		
		ThT	*Theology Today*
NovTest	*Novum Testamentum*	TNTC	*Tyndale New Testament Commentaries*
NSI	Cooke: *Handbook of North Semitic Inscriptions*		
		Trench	Trench: *Synonyms of the New Testament*
NTS	*New Testament Studies*		
ODCC	*The Oxford Dictionary of the Christian Church*, rev. ed.	TWOT	*Theological Wordbook of the Old Testament*
		UBD	*Unger's Bible Dictionary*
Peake	Black and Rowley: *Peake's Commentary on the Bible*	UT	Gordon: *Ugaritic Textbook*
		VB	Allmen: *Vocabulary of the Bible*
PEQ	*Palestine Exploration Quarterly*		
PNF1	P. Schaff: *The Nicene and Post-Nicene Fathers* (1st series)	VetTest	*Vetus Testamentum*
		Vincent	Vincent: *Word-Pictures in the New Testament*
PNF2	P. Schaff and H. Wace: *The Nicene and Post-Nicene Fathers* (2nd series)	WBC	*Wycliffe Bible Commentary*
		WBE	*Wycliffe Bible Encyclopedia*
		WC	*Westminster Commentaries*
PTR	*Princeton Theological Review*	WesBC	*Wesleyan Bible Commentaries*
RB	*Revue Biblique*	WTJ	*Westminster Theological Journal*
RHG	Robertson's *Grammar of the Greek New Testament in the Light of Historical Research*	ZAW	*Zeitschrift für die alttestamentliche Wissenschaft*
		ZNW	*Zeitschrift für die neutestamentliche Wissenschaft*
RTWB	Richardson: *A Theological Wordbook of the Bible*	ZPBD	*The Zondervan Pictorial Bible Dictionary*
SBK	Strack and Billerbeck: *Kommentar zum Neuen Testament aus Talmud und Midrash*	ZPEB	*The Zondervan Pictorial Encyclopedia of the Bible*
		ZWT	*Zeitschrift für wissenschaftliche Theologie*
SHERK	*The New Schaff-Herzog Encyclopedia of Religious Knowledge*		

D. Abbreviations for Books of the Bible, the Apocrypha, and the Pseudepigrapha

OLD TESTAMENT

Gen	2 Chron	Dan
Exod	Ezra	Hos
Lev	Neh	Joel
Num	Esth	Amos
Deut	Job	Obad
Josh	Ps(Pss)	Jonah
Judg	Prov	Mic
Ruth	Eccl	Nah
1 Sam	S of Songs	Hab
2 Sam	Isa	Zeph
1 Kings	Jer	Hag
2 Kings	Lam	Zech
1 Chron	Ezek	Mal

NEW TESTAMENT

Matt	1 Tim
Mark	2 Tim
Luke	Titus
John	Philem
Acts	Heb
Rom	James
1 Cor	1 Peter
2 Cor	2 Peter
Gal	1 John
Eph	2 John
Phil	3 John
Col	Jude
1 Thess	Rev
2 Thess	

APOCRYPHA

1 Esd	1 Esdras		Ep Jer	Epistle of Jeremy
2 Esd	2 Esdras		S Th Ch	Song of the Three Child
Tobit	Tobit			(or Young Men)
Jud	Judith		Sus	Susanna
Add Esth	Additions to Esther		Bel	Bel and the Dragon
Wisd Sol	Wisdom of Solomon		Pr Man	Prayer of Manasseh
Ecclus	Ecclesiasticus (Wisdom of		1 Macc	1 Maccabees
	Jesus the Son of Sirach)		2 Macc	2 Maccabees
Baruch	Baruch			

PSEUDEPIGRAPHA

As Moses	Assumption of Moses		Pirke Aboth	Pirke Aboth
2 Baruch	Syriac Apocalypse of Baruch		Ps 151	Psalm 151
3 Baruch	Greek Apocalypse of Baruch		Pss Sol	Psalms of Solomon
1 Enoch	Ethiopic Book of Enoch		Sib Oracles	Sibylline Oracles
2 Enoch	Slavonic Book of Enoch		Story Ah	Story of Ahikar
3 Enoch	Hebrew Book of Enoch		T Abram	Testament of Abraham
4 Ezra	4 Ezra		T Adam	Testament of Adam
JA	Joseph and Asenath		T Benjamin	Testament of Benjamin
Jub	Book of Jubilees		T Dan	Testament of Dan
L Aristeas	Letter of Aristeas		T Gad	Testament of Gad
Life AE	Life of Adam and Eve		T Job	Testament of Job
Liv Proph	Lives of the Prophets		T Jos	Testament of Joseph
MA Isa	Martyrdom and Ascension		T Levi	Testament of Levi
	of Isaiah		T Naph	Testament of Naphtali
3 Macc	3 Maccabees		T 12 Pat	Testaments of the Twe
4 Macc	4 Maccabees			Patriarchs
Odes Sol	Odes of Solomon		Zad Frag	Zadokite Fragments
P Jer	Paralipomena of Jeremiah			

E. Abbreviations of Names of Dead Sea Scrolls and Related Texts

CD — Cairo (Genizah text of the) Damascus (Document)

DSS — Dead Sea Scrolls

Hev — Nahal Hever texts

Mas — Masada Texts

Mird — Khirbet mird texts

Mur — Wadi Murabba'at texts

P — Pesher (commentary)

Q — Qumran

1Q, 2Q, etc. — Numbered caves of Qumran, yielding written material; followed by abbreviation of biblical or apocryphal book.

QL — Qumran Literature

1QapGen — Genesis Apocryphon of Qumran Cave 1

1QH — *Hodayot* (Thanksgiving Hymns) from Qumran Cave 1

1QIsa a,b — First or second copy of Isaiah from Qumran Cave 1

1QpHab — Pesher on Habakkuk from Qumran Cave 1

1QM — *Milhamah* (War Scroll)

1QpMic — Pesher on portions of Micah from Qumran Cave 1

1QS — *Serek Hayyahad* (Rule of the Community, Manual of Discipline)

1QSa — Appendix A (Rule of the Congregation) to 1Qs

1QSb — Appendix B (Blessings) to 1QS

3Q15 — Copper Scroll from Qumran Cave 3

4QExod a — Exodus Scroll, exemplar "a" from Qumran Cave 4

4QFlor — Florilegium (or Eschatological Midrashim) from Qumran Cave 4

4Qmess ar — Aramaic "Messianic" text from Qumran Cave 4

4QpNah — Pesher on portions of Nahum from Qumran Cave 4

4QPrNab — Prayer of Nabonidus from Qumran Cave 4

4QpPs37 — Pesher on portions of Psalm 37 from Qumran Cave 4

4QTest — Testimonia text from Qumran Cave 4

4QTLevi — Testament of Levi from Qumran Cave 4

4QPhyl — Phylacteries from Qumran Cave 4

11QMelch — Melchizedek text from Qumran Cave 11

11QtgJob — Targum of Job from Qumran Cave 11

TRANSLITERATIONS

Hebrew

א = '		ד = $\underline{d}$		י = y		ס = s		ר = r
ב = b		ה = h		כ = k		ע = '		שׂ = $ś$
ב = $\underline{b}$		ו = w		ך כ = $\underline{k}$		פ = p		שׁ = $š$
ג = g		ז = z		ל = l		ף פ = $\underline{p}$		ת = t
ג = $\underline{g}$		ח = $ḥ$		ם מ = m		ץ צ = $ṣ$		ת = $\underline{t}$
ד = d		ט = $ṭ$		ן נ = n		ק = q		

(ה)ָ = $â$ (h)		ָ = $ā$		ַ = a		ֵֶ = ^{a}
ֵ = $ê$		ֵ = $ē$		ֶ = e		ֱ = ^{e}
ִ = $î$		ֹ = $ō$		ִ = i		ְ = ^{e} (if vocal)
וֹ = $ô$				ָ = o		ֳ = ^{o}
וּ = $û$				ֻ = u		

Aramaic

' b g d h w z $ḥ$ $ṭ$ y k l m n s ' p $ṣ$ q r $ś$ $š$ t

Arabic

' b t $\underline{t}$ $ǧ$ $ḥ$ $ḫ$ d $\underline{d}$ r z s $š$ $ṣ$ $ḍ$ $ṭ$ $ẓ$ ' $ġ$ f q k l m n h w y

Ugaritic

' b g d $\underline{d}$ h w z $ḥ$ $ḫ$ $ṭ$ $ẓ$ y k l m n s $ṡ$ ' $ġ$ $ṗ$ $ṣ$ q r $š$ t $ṯ$

Greek

α	—	a	π	—	p	αι	—	ai
β	—	b	ρ	—	r	αὐ	—	au
γ	—	g	σ,ς	—	s	ει	—	ei
δ	—	d	τ	—	t	εὐ	—	eu
ε	—	e	υ	—	y	ηὐ	—	ēu
ζ	—	z	φ	—	ph	οι	—	oi
η	—	ē	χ	—	ch	οὐ	—	ou
θ	—	th	ψ	—	ps	υι	—	hui
ι	—	i	ω	—	ō			
κ	—	k				ῥ	—	rh
λ	—	l	γγ	—	ng	ʽ	—	h
μ	—	m	γκ	—	nk			
ν	—	n	γξ	—	nx	ᾳ	—	ā
ξ	—	x	γχ	—	nch	ῃ	—	ē
ο	—	o				ῳ	—	ō

ISAIAH

G. W. Grogan

ISAIAH

Introduction

1. **Background**

   a. **Sources of information**
   b. **The life of Isaiah**
   c. **The international scene**
   d. **The reigns of Uzziah and Jotham**
   e. **The Syro-Ephraimite war**
   f. **The Fall of Samaria**
   g. **Hezekiah and Sennacherib**
   h. **Babylon**

2. **Authorship, Unity and Date**

   a. **The history of criticism**
   b. **The case against its unity**
   c. **The case for its unity**

3. **Theology**
4. **Eschatology**
5. **Messianism and the Servant Songs**

   a. **The thematic approach**
   b. **The contrapuntal approach**
   c. **The programmatic approach**

6. **Structure**
7. **Canonicity**
8. **Text**
9. **Bibliography**
10. **Outline**

The Prophecy of Isaiah is the third longest, complete literary entity in the Bible, being exceeded in length only by Jeremiah and Psalms. Psalms is in a special category as a collection of separate literary units.

Isaiah is at once familiar and neglected. Chapters like 6, 35, 40, and 53 are among the best-known parts of the OT; and there are briefer, well-known sections in chapters like 7, 9, and 61. There are however vast stretches of the book, especially in chapters 13–34, that are virtually unknown to most Christians. Ignorance of any part of Scripture is to be deplored, but this is particularly so with a book that gives such a manifold presentation of Christ. Moreover, a study of the book in its wholeness presents a view of him that is most majestic and moving, one in which the virtually

3

unknown contexts of the well-known passages shed a flood of light on those passages themselves. The NT writers recognized Isaiah's special importance, quoting from and alluding to it frequently. Many of its verses and phrases have passed into common use in literature. For example, there are seventy quotations from Isaiah in the *Penguin Dictionary of Quotations* (J.G. and M.J. Cohen, edd. [Harmondsworth: Penguin Books, 1960]); and Handel used much of Isaiah's language in the *Messiah*.

1. Background

a. *Sources of information*

The Book of Isaiah itself is the major source of information. Additional and supporting material is contained in 2 Kings 15–21 and in 2 Chronicles 26–33. Other contemporary or near-contemporary prophets were Amos and Hosea, both of whom prophesied to the northern kingdom, and Micah, who like Isaiah was a vehicle of God's word to Judah. Assyrian clay tablets are a leading source of material outside the OT. Some Jewish traditions will be mentioned later.

b. *The life of Isaiah*

The opening heading of the book (1:1) places the ministry of Isaiah in the reigns of Uzziah (or Azariah, as he is called in 2 Kings), Jotham, Ahaz, and Hezekiah. We suggest that in fact his ministry continued into the reign of Manasseh. Nothing is known about Isaiah's father, Amoz. Jewish tradition declared him to be of royal stock. While this cannot be substantiated, Isaiah may have been an aristocrat; for he seemed to have easy access to kings (7:3; 37:21–22 et al.). His wife is called "the prophetess" (8:3), which may simply mean she was a prophet's wife, as there is no record of a personal prophetic ministry by her. She was, however, the mother of his two known children, both of whom had names with symbolic meanings (7:3; 8:3, 18), which may account for this description of her.

Isaiah was probably quite young at the time of his vision and call (ch. 6), as his ministry cannot have been shorter than thirty-four years. Some commentators, believing that before his vision he had a close association with the temple and thus absorbed the "holiness" terminology from a knowledge of the priestly rites, think Isaiah may have been a "cult prophet" before he received the personal commission of chapter 6; but this idea is speculative. He seems to have prophesied largely—if not exclusively—in Jerusalem and its environs. It is often assumed from 8:16–17 that the rejection of his warning to Ahaz led to a temporary withdrawal from public ministry and concentration on his disciples. His last datable oracles were in 701 B.C., though the noncanonical *Ascension of Isaiah* states that he was martyred (cf. Heb 11:37) in the reign of Manasseh (who came to the throne in 687 B.C.).

c. *The international scene*

Israel and Judah—under Jeroboam II and Uzziah respectively—enjoyed a period of prosperity during Isaiah's childhood, with little interference from foreign powers. Egypt was weak, while Assyria was occupied with problems elsewhere. The aggressive empire-builder Tiglath-pileser III (known in Babylon as Pul) came to the Assyrian throne in 745 B.C., and the situation quickly changed. Egypt reckoned the small kingdoms in Palestine and Syria to be within her sphere of influence, but Assyria began to carve out a western extension to its empire in that region. Damascus (732 B.C.) and much of Galilee fell to Tiglath-pileser; then Shalmaneser V (727–722 B.C.) and Sargon II (722–705 B.C.) attacked Samaria, the latter taking it in 722 or 721 B.C. In the last decade or so of the century, Egypt began to revive somewhat; and Assyria encountered trouble from Babylon. Because of this Judah and other neighboring states rebelled against Assyria. Sennacherib (705–681) invaded Judah in 701 and subdued it; but God saved Jerusalem, which was to fall over a century later to a resurgent Babylon.

d. The reigns of Uzziah and Jotham

There are some problems in dating of the reigns of the kings of Judah from Uzziah to Hezekiah.[1] Uzziah's death has been variously placed between 747 and 735, the most likely date being around 740. Jotham seems to have been regent for some years before this; and, apparently, several years before his own death (731), he handed over the reins of effective government to his son, Ahaz. Apart from the inaugural vision recorded in chapter 6, there is no material in the book that can be dated with certainty from the reigns of either Uzziah or Jotham. Uzziah had been a godly man till the pride of his latter days (2 Chron 26:16–21), but neither he nor Jotham removed the idolatrous high places.

e. The Syro-Ephraimite war

The threat from Tiglath-pileser brought Syria and Israel into coalition around 734 B.C., and they tried to force Judah to join them. Ahaz was on the throne at the time. Isaiah challenged him to trust in the Lord (ch. 7); instead, Ahaz called on Assyria to come to his aid. Damascus, the capital of Syria, was taken by the Assyrians in 732 and much of Galilee subjugated (2 Kings 15:25–29). Pekah, king of Israel, was murdered by Hoshea, who replaced him and reigned as a virtual Assyrian puppet. Pekah, king of Israel, and Rezin, king of Syria, had inflicted some harm on Judah before the Assyrians brought relief to Ahaz (2 Kings 16:5–9), but more serious still were the religious consequences of the latter's appeal to Assyria (2 Kings 16:10–20).

f. The fall of Samaria

The death of Tiglath-pileser in 727 B.C. raised false hopes of freedom for the little kingdoms on the Mediterranean seaboard. When Ahaz died about a year later (cf. EBC, 1:371), Isaiah uttered a prophecy warning Philistia of the consequences of revolt, and, by implication, counseled Judah against joining her (14:28–32). It was some time later that Hoshea withheld tribute from Shalmaneser V, who for three years besieged Samaria, which was later taken by his successor, Sargon. According to the Assyrians, over twenty-seven thousand Israelites were deported at this time, being settled in the northern parts of the Assyrian empire (ANET, pp. 284–85). For about a decade the area was fairly quiet, Sargon being occupied with wars elsewhere; but then Egypt began to encourage the Philistines and others to form a new coalition against Assyria. This coalition was crushed by Sargon in 711 in a battle on

---

[1]See E.R. Thiele, *The Chronology of the Hebrew Kings* (Grand Rapids: Zondervan, 1977), and G.L. Archer, "The Chronology and Metrology of the Old Testament," EBC, 1:369–71.

the Egyptian border. Judah under Hezekiah stayed out of this, heeding Isaiah's warning (20:1–6).

g. Hezekiah and Sennacherib

Sargon died around 705 B.C. and was replaced by Sennacherib. Immediately there was trouble in different parts of the Assyrian Empire, encouraged by the Ethiopian monarchs who were imparting new vigor to Egypt, and also by Merodach-Baladan (Marduk-apal-iddina) of Babylon. This time, despite Isaiah's warnings (chs. 30–31), Hezekiah became involved and prepared Jerusalem for a siege (22:8–11). The Assyrian army invaded Judah, taking forty-six walled cities and devastating much of the countryside. It invested Jerusalem, but Isaiah encouraged Hezekiah to trust in the Lord; and the city was delivered (37:36). It is unlikely that, as some scholars believe, Sennacherib invaded Judah again in 688. It has, in fact, no support in either the Assyrian or the Babylonian records.

h. Babylon

Merodach-Baladan, a Chaldean prince, took power in Babylon in 721 B.C., declaring it independent of Assyria. Its status under this ruler for the next decade or so is somewhat uncertain, but it is known that Sargon entered Babylon in 711 or 710 without a fight. After Sargon's death, however, Merodach-Baladan became a leader of movements of rebellion against Sennacherib and sought to involve Hezekiah (39:1–2). Sennacherib defeated and deposed Merodach-Baladan; but Babylon revived again during the seventh century, becoming the dominant Mesopotamian power toward the end of that century. This led ultimately to the subjection of Judah to Babylon and to the Fall of Jerusalem in 587. The ensuing Exile fulfilled God's warning to Hezekiah delivered through Isaiah (ch. 39) and forms the background to the following prophecies. However, at least part of chapters 56–66 seems to assume the passage of still more time, with the Exile a thing of the past and the people back in Judah again. Cyrus the Persian, the human instrument of the return, is referred to in chapters 44–45.

2. Authorship, Unity, and Date

a. The history of criticism

The Book of Isaiah has come down to us as a unity, and the name Isaiah son of Amoz is the only one linked with it in any of the Hebrew MSS or ancient versions. Until late in the eighteenth century, only one extant writer questioned the universal assumption that Isaiah wrote the whole book, namely the twelfth-century Jewish commentator Ibn Ezra. He maintained that chapters 40–66 were the work of a prophet who lived late in the Babylonian captivity, and Ibn Ezra quoted an older contemporary, Moses ben Samuel Ibn Gekatilla, as holding a somewhat similar opinion. In the late eighteenth century, soon after Pentateuchal criticism began to get into its stride, the new critical school took an interest in Isaiah. Döderlein and Eichhorn both attributed chapters 40–66 to a prophet of the Exile, who soon was known as "Deutero-Isaiah." This view came to be held very widely in scholarly circles, though its wider dissemination was due largely to George Adam Smith's commentary published in 1890.

A number of leading conservative scholars addressed themselves to the question, and the commentaries by Alexander, Hengstenberg, and Delitzsch are of special importance. These men were Hebraists and exegetes of the highest caliber; and each maintained the Isaianic authorship of the whole book, though Delitzsch later became more open to the "Deutero-Isaiah" hypothesis. J.A. Alexander's work stimulated an interest in the issue at Princeton and, later, at Westminster Seminary, which was to bear fruit in the twentieth century in the works of O.T. Allis and E.J. Young.

The work of Berhard Duhm has influenced all subsequent discussion. In his commentary, published in 1892, he put forward the theory, already being canvassed by some critics, that chapters 56–66 were the work of a postexilic writer, whom he named "Trito-Isaiah." Duhm believed, contrary to many later critics, that Deutero-Isaiah lived, not in Babylon, but in Palestine or Egypt. Important too was his identification of the Servant Songs, which for him were Isaiah 42:1–4; 49:1–6; 50:4–9; 52:13–53:12; and he assigned them to another author. His Trito-Isaiah theory was widely though not quite universally, accepted by critical scholars; less popular was a separate author for the songs. Duhm held too that there was much non-Isaianic material in chapters 1–39; and most scholars from his time denied at least chapters 13–14, 24–27, and 35–39 to the eighth-century prophet.

How then did the Book of Isaiah come into its present form? Duhm believed that a number of oracle collections circulated independently before being gathered into one volume, which was later augmented by the addition, first of all, of chapters 40–55 and then of chapters 56–66. Karl Budde, writing early in the twentieth century, put forward an alternative view. A small collection of Isaiah's prophecies formed a nucleus that received a number of successive expansions over the centuries. Emphasis was placed more and more on the part played by a continuing school of Isaiah's disciples (the idea is based largely on 8:16) and also by a school associated with Deutero-Isaiah, which may have been responsible for collecting together at a later stage the oracles in chapters 56–66, which were increasingly denied a common author. S. Mowinckel held that a school of Isaiah existed for at least two centuries.

C.C. Torrey, for long the *enfant terrible* of biblical criticism, in 1928 attacked the normal critical views of chapters 40–66. He held that the references to Babylon and Cyrus were interpolations that, once removed, enable us to interpret these chapters as the work of a Palestinian writer living towards the close of the fifth century B.C. Torrey's views did not find wide acceptance, though most recent scholars still feel it necessary to deal with points raised by him.

A new factor in critical studies was the rise of form criticism, due chiefly to the work of Hermann Gunkel. Allis (*Isaiah*, p. 47) has well defined this method as "the attempt to determine, to classify, and to trace the history of the various literary types or patterns which are to be found in the Bible and to relate them to similar 'forms' to be found in other literatures." Form criticism discovers such forms as hymns, love-songs, proverbs, oracles, and disputations in the OT, many of which it holds had been used by the OT prophet. Its effect on Isaianic studies has in fact been to accelerate the fragmentizing tendency, especially in chapters 40–55, the one part of the book widely regarded as an original literary unit, even though in this criticism the various small sections are often attributed largely to one person. J. Begrich did much form-critical work on "Deutero-Isaiah"; and S. Mowinckel maintained that the oracles it contains, delivered at first orally, were brought together and linked by the use of catchwords, so that the literary unit produced was in fact quite artificial. The commentary by Westermann represents a more moderate form-critical approach. He holds, for example, that by far the greater part of "Deutero-Isaiah" derives from the prophet himself (p. 30).

The more recent redaction criticism has focused attention on the assumed editor or editors of the prophetic books. As R.E. Clements says, "The book of Isaiah comes to us as a single literary whole, comprising sixty-six chapters, and this given datum of the form of the book must be regarded as a feature requiring explanation."[2] In fact, Clements, in his article, suggests that the prophecies of Deutero-Isaiah were added to the book in order to complement those in Isaiah 1–39, which had given insight into the reasons for the judgments on Judah and Jerusalem. B.S. Childs argues that the phrase "the former things" in 42:9; 43:9, 16–19 et al., refers in fact to the prophecies of Isaiah of Jerusalem.[3] He says, "The nature of the biblical understanding of prophecy and fulfillment is made clear by the canonical form of the book of Isaiah. The Old Testament is not a message about divine acts in history as such but about the power of the word of God. The divine word which proclaims the will of God confirms itself in bringing to completion its promise."[4] W.M. Brownlee, anticipating something of this, pointed out that evidence from 1QIsa (a space of three lines before chapter 34) showed that Isaiah was really a two-volume work but with the division after chapter 33; and he demonstrated that there is a great deal of thematic correspondence between the two parts.[5]

Such recent developments may encourage the hope that the criticism of Isaiah is about to come full circle. Certainly this kind of treatment of the book as a whole is a welcome change, but it is one thing to place emphasis on the theology of the redactor and quite another to accept the work as a whole as the literary expression of the prophecies of Isaiah. A glance at Clements's commentary on Isaiah 1–39 will reveal that, alongside his acceptance of Hermann Barth's theory of a major redaction in the time of Josiah, stands belief in the extreme fragmentariness of the material used by the redactor, with the integrity of passage after passage destroyed.

Another negative development is the line of thought expressed by R.P. Carroll, who applied the psychological theory of "cognitive dissonance" to the prophecies of the OT,[6] including those of the Book of Isaiah. According to this view, prophecies were constantly proved to be in error and so were adapted by later generations in order to fit the actual facts.

Only a realization that the whole book records the prophecies of Isaiah the son of Amoz can secure the authority of its teaching as an important part of the OT preparation for Christ.

b. *The case against its unity*

The case against the unity of the book usually begins with statements about the nature of biblical prophecy. It is said that prophecy is essentially an activity claiming divine inspiration, in which the prophet addresses his contemporaries with a mes-

---

[2]The Unity of the Book of Isaiah," Int 34:2 (April 1982): 117.
[3]*Introduction to the Old Testament as Scripture* (London: SCM, 1979), pp. 311–38.
[4]Ibid.
[5]*The Meaning of the Qumran Scrolls for the Bible* (New York: Oxford University Press, 1964), pp. 247–59.
[6]*When Prophecy Failed* (London: SCM, 1979), pp. 86–128.

sage from God related to their own situation. The claim is made that in Isaiah 40–66 we meet a situation and an audience quite remote from the eighth century. If these chapters had not come down to us as part of the Book of Isaiah, nobody would ever have thought them his. The only personal name mentioned in these chapters—apart from characters from past history like Abraham—is Cyrus, the Persian monarch whose activities made it possible for the people to return from Babylonian exile in the sixth century.

It is said too that there is an important difference in the theology of the two main parts. Isaiah was a preacher of judgment. If he had a hope for the future—and some critics dispute this altogether—it centered in the monarchy and in a remnant that would escape the judgment on the nation as a whole. The message of the section of the book that begins at chapter 40, however, is one of comfort and salvation. There is little interest in the royal house; instead, the mysterious figure of the Servant of the Lord appears. Chapters toward the end of the book show the typical postexilic Jewish preoccupation with matters like the Sabbath and fasting.

The style and vocabulary also seem to change as we move from chapter 39 to chapter 40. Isaiah's style was strongly illustrative. There is less material of this kind after chapter 39. The style becomes very lofty, with a multitude of rhetorical questions and many passages where God is in dispute with the people and argues his case with them.

c. *The case for its unity*

It is clear that the Jews accepted Isaiah's authorship of the later chapters of the book well before the coming of Christ. Ecclesiasticus, written early in the second century B.C., says, "By the spirit of might he [Isaiah] saw the last things,/ and comforted those who mourned in Zion" (Ecclus 48:24). The last clause clearly refers to Isaiah 61:3. The pre-Christian Isaiah scroll from Qumran known as 1QIsaᵃ has the complete text of the book. The only significant gap in the text is that between chapters 33 and 34 (referred to above). Moreover, a few lines of chapter 40 are actually commenced at the foot of a column. Josephus (Antiq. XI, 3–6 [i. 1–2]), writing late in the first century A.D., says that Cyrus read the prophecies about himself in Isaiah and wished to fulfill them. Whether or not this story is true, it shows that Josephus regarded this material as predictive in nature.

More important, however, is the testimony of the NT, which quotes Isaiah—and from different parts (e.g., John 12:37–41)—by name more often than all the other writing prophets combined. It is said that this testimony has little significance because all the NT writers were really doing was identifying the source of their quotations in particular OT books. Although this explanation would fit some of the quotations, there are others that cannot be explained in this way. Each of the named quotations from Isaiah in the Epistle to the Romans is introduced by phraseology using verbs of speech (Rom 9:27, 29; 10:16, 20–21), and those in Romans 10 are from Isaiah 53 and 65. Clearly, Paul believed these chapters to be the work of Isaiah himself.

None of the OT prophetic books is without an opening title in which the prophet's name is given (e.g., Isa 1:1). Isaiah's name is sometimes also mentioned in headings (chs. 2, 7, 13, 20, 37, 38, 39). It is true that there is no reference to him by name in chapters 40–66, but then there is none either between chapters 20 and 37. The opening heading appears to be intended to cover much material because of the reference in it to no less than four kingly reigns; and it would be natural to assume that, like the headings that commence other prophetic books, this was intended to cover the work as a whole. The absence of a heading at the beginning of chapters 40 and 56 is particularly significant. If these circulated initially without headings, they would stand alone among the OT prophets; and if the headings were lost at some time, it seems inconceivable that oral tradition did not preserve the names. The heading to chapter 13 is especially significant, because it links Isaiah with an oracle about Babylon.

The argument from theological difference—never very persuasive—appears still weaker now than it once did; for even staunch advocates of the view that the book comes from more than one author are laying stress on its unifying theological motifs, because of the new interest in the book's redactional unity. For instance Clements says,

> It is not just in chapter 35 that the message of chapters 40–55 is introduced into the earlier part in order to balance out the predominantly threatening note of chapters 1–35. There are earlier summarizing assurances of the return of Yahweh's people to Zion (11:12–16; 19:23; 27:12–13), which are based upon the prophecies from chapter 40 on. Even more strikingly, a promise is made (18:7) that the people of Ethiopia will bring gifts to Yahweh's people in Zion, which must certainly have been taken from the prophetic promise given in Isaiah 45:14.[7]

Although some of these comments assume a relationship between the passages different from what would have been true if they were all the work of Isaiah, they are nevertheless very significant. Without doubt too the whole book has a most exalted doctrine of God. Emphasis on his sovereignty (ch. 6; 24:1–3, 23; 37:15–20; 43:8–11), his holinesss (1:4; 5:16; 30:9–16; 37:23; 48:17–19; 57:15–21), and his hatred of pride (2:11–18; 14:12–15; 37:23–25; 47:8–11; 66:1–3) are not confined to any one section. For these and other theological links, see Eschatology.

A survey of the whole book reveals the high literary quality of so much of its material—in its poetic style, in the wonderful way thought and language are matched to each other, in the plentiful and yet not forced use of devices like assonance and chiasm, and in the use of analogy and anthropomorphism. It is true that there are also passages where the style is somewhat more pedestrian; but there are few of these, and they are not confined to any one part of the book. Variety of style is a characteristic of all great authors who write on diverse themes and over a considerable period of time. If, as is possible, much of chapters 40–55 never had a prewritten form, this in itself may well account for the elevated, flowing style of this part of the book. The prophet has favorite analogies such as that of the burden-bearer (1:4, 14, 24; 46:1–4; 53:4, 11–12) and the branch or the shoot (4:2; 6:13; 11:1; 53:2). The title "Holy One of Israel" is found twelve times in Isaiah 1–39 and thirteen times in the remainder of the book. Its use elsewhere in the OT is infrequent, and its use by Isaiah probably reflects the deep impression made on him by the awesome vision related in chapter 6.

Although we do not approve of Torrey's suggestion that the references to Babylon may be removed from the book quite easily and without detriment to the remaining

---

[7]"Unity of Isaiah," p. 121.

material, this did underline the point that there is very little in the way of Babylonian background. We might expect much more if the author of chapters 40–55 lived there. Of course, it must be said that some writers who accept "Deutero-Isaiah" doubt whether he was resident in Babylon, though their grounds for this doubt can really form part of the argument in favor of the book's unity as the work of the Palestinian resident—Isaiah, son of Amoz.

E.J. Young, having pointed out that the references to trees (41:19; 44:14) are significant because they are native to Palestine, goes on to say, "In 43:14 the Lord speaks of sending *to* Babylon, a passage which is clearly addresssed to those who are not in Babylon. In 41:9 the prophet addresses Israel as the seed of Abraham which the Lord has taken from the ends of the earth" (emphasis his).[8] He also compares the use of such language made by the prophet in 45:22 and 46:11 and then says, "But 52:11 is conclusive. The phrase, 'from thence' clearly shows that this passage was not uttered in Babylon."[9]

It should be particularly noticed that some passages have a quite exceptional emphasis on supernatural prediction (e.g., 25:1–28; 41:21–29; 44:7–8; 46:10–11; 48:3–7). Also, one of the functions of chapter 39 seems to be to show the relevance of chapters 40–66 to the people of Isaiah's day. There were events going on that would ultimately lead to exile in Babylon. The prophecies in these chapters were not addressed to the king whose sinful pride is here treated as a major moral cause of the Exile but to the people as a whole, whose descendants would suffer through it; and it assures them that the long-term purposes of God for them would not be thwarted by it. Only the God of Israel, the people are assured, could make such predictions.

It is in this context that the revelation of the name of Cyrus is given. There is one other instance of the disclosure of a name many generations before a person's arrival on the stage of history (1 Kings 13:2). As Allis (*Isaiah*, pp. 51–80) has shown, the name of Cyrus is revealed in a most impressive way, at the poetic climax of "the poem of the transcendence of the Lord God of Israel" that has a special numerico-climactic structure. It is only the exceptional character of this revelation that can adequately account for the literary phenomenon here. The reader is advised to consult this whole section in Allis.

We conclude that the case for the unity of the book is strong. While it would be too much to say that its rejection is invariably due to a rejection of supernatural prophetic prediction, there is no doubt that this lies behind a great deal of opposition to it. It seems likely that Isaiah lived on into the reign of Manasseh, that during this reign he was unable to function openly as a prophet, but that he committed to writing the revelations he received about the future of his people. No doubt the people in Babylonia, chastened by the hand of their God—and with a new awareness of his sovereignty—would watch events with a deep sense of anticipation; and these prophecies would themselves be instrumental in the hands of God in helping to create that atmosphere of faith and obedience that led to the return. When at last the decree of Cyrus for their return was given and not earlier—for Isaiah had declared that Cyrus was to be the divine agent of this great purpose—they would respond to the divine call, "Depart, depart" (52:11).

---

[8]*Introduction to the Old Testament* (London: Tyndale, 1949), p. 206.
[9]Ibid.

3. Theology

Just as Paul's theology was profoundly molded by Christ's encounter with him on the Damascus Road, so Isaiah's temple vision, recorded in ch. 6, of the thrice-holy God deeply influenced his whole prophetic career and his theology. No doubt much he learned there simply reinforced the instruction he had already received through the regular teaching agencies of the family and the godly community in Israel, but this was all brought vividly to life in a personal encounter in which he was commissioned for divine service.

Isaiah learned some things about God—his holiness, his transcendent separateness, and his incomparable majesty and character. Isaiah's distinctive title for God is "the Holy One of Israel," used twenty-five times in all and felt to be characteristic of his message, even by the people who rejected it (30:11). If we distinguish the majestic holiness and the moral holiness of God, in which he is exalted both as Creator and as the all-righteous One, we can see that, though theoretically distinguishable, they find their true union in his being as revealed here.

Isaiah learned that this God is King, enthroned above all, eternal and deathless, unlike Uzziah and other earthly monarchs. He is also the Lord Almighty, so that the authority of the supreme King is wedded to an omnipotence that enables him to carry out his every purpose. As the almighty King he could use Assyria and Babylon as instruments of his punitive purpose and yet include them also in the great judgments on all the nations (chs. 13–23). In fact, the whole world, as chapter 24 shows, would come under his judgment. He was able too to bring to fruition his purposes for his people, encouraging them with the vision of his sovereign power (chs. 40–66). Isaiah is given a wonderful disclosure of a great King for God's people, who himself bears the name "Mighty God" (9:6).

Isaiah saw that "the whole earth is full of his glory" (6:3); and so it is not surprising that he speaks of God as Creator both of the universe (40:26; 42:5; 48:12–13) and of his people, Israel (43:1, 15). Consistent with this, his prophecies abound in references to the animal and plant creation. He has a vision of the whole earth full of the knowledge of the Lord (11:9) and even of new heavens and a new earth (65:17; 66:22).

Although the God of the whole earth, he has a special relationship to Israel; for he is Yahweh, the LORD, the one who revealed himself in that name to Moses (Exod 3:13–15). Indeed, the phrase "Holy One of Israel" itself expresses the paradox of separateness and yet special relationship to one people. "This people" (6:9–10) and their land (6:12) are never far from Isaiah's thought.

Because this great God is holy, Isaiah's encounter with him gives Isaiah a smarting sense of sin. He is to be the mouthpiece of God, but Isaiah's lips are unclean. The people too have unclean lips; for, though worshiping their God with ritual (1:10–17), fasting (58:1–5), and words (29:13), they were in fact rebellious (1:2–6; 30:1–5 et al.). Many of them even expressed this fundamental rebelliousness in idolatry and syncretistic worship, thus showing their utter blindness (6:10; 29:9–10; 44:18; 45:20). The prophet's scathing denunciations of idolatry (chs. 40–48) reflect not only his own conviction that there is only one God but also his holy intolerance of the sin of idolatry.

Two sins that are singled out for special condemnation are pride and unbelief (e.g., in 2:6–22; 7:1–9); for who in the presence of the holy God, can lift his head high or declare his self-sufficiency or his trust in others, whether "gods" or men?

Like all the eighth-century prophets, Isaiah also condemned injustice (1:16–17; 5:7–8; 26:5–6; 58:6–12); and it is for this reason largely that K. Budde and others have suggested there may be special links between him and Amos.

The prophets have sometimes been accused of Pelagianism, viz., having a doctrine of sin that implies that human beings are perfectly capable, in themselves, of repentance and reformation. Indeed, the prophets did address a call to repentance to their hearers; but, like Jeremiah (e.g., Jer 13:23), Isaiah was made aware of the insensitivity that sin induces in the sinner (6:9–10). Sin is, of course, rebellion against the God who reveals himself; and the prophetic word itself was therefore, though a call to righteousness, also the means through which this hardening process took place. Sin has made the whole people unclean (64:5–7), and the prophet is warned that his own ministry would be rejected. There is a note of hope, however, in his own responsiveness to God's voice and his personal confession of sin.

Sin not only affects the sinner but also his environment. The land—God's own gift to his people—with its cities, houses, and fields, would be ravaged (6:11) by the Assyrians and Babylonians. This would be, as Isaiah was to be shown, "until the LORD has sent everyone far away/and the land is utterly forsaken" (6:12) in the horrors of the Exile, with Israel suffering thus under the Assyrians and Judah and Jerusalem under Babylon. In this way Isaiah's message continues that of the Book of Deuteronomy (cf. Deut 27–28). Isaiah 6:13 also refers to the repetitive nature of divine judgment, reflecting perhaps the message of the Book of Judges, that sin reasserts itself in every new generation and must be punished anew.

Yet the name of the prophet ("Yahweh is Salvation") would lead us to expect a positive note in the inaugural vision and in his message generally, and it is there, for example, in 6:7. The assurance of forgiveness for the penitent is constantly reiterated (1:18–19; 12:1; 30:18–19; 33:24; 38:17; 40:1–2; 43:25; 44:22; 59:20); and, just as the ultimate sacrificial basis of it is suggested in 6:6–7, so it is shown to be grounded in the sacrificial sufferings of God's great Servant (52:13–53:12). But God's purpose is concerned not only with the individual but with the nation, and the remnant (6:13) is the guarantee of the divine veracity and so of the future of the people. In the prophet's teaching about the remnant lies the seed of all that he declares about the future glory of Zion. It was in the temple and so, perhaps, in the context of worship that he saw this vision, and Zion is to be the center of the worship of the true God for the whole world (2:1–4; 45:14, 22–25; 66:18).

Meantime, God has his servants, who are dedicated to doing his will: the seraphim, who extol his holy name (6:2–3), and the prophet, who readily responds to his call (6:8). Israel had been called to this high standing as God's servant (41:8–9; 44:1) but had failed (42:19–20). Cyrus was to perform certain functions for God (44:28; 45:1), but it is the supreme Servant of the Lord who fulfills Israel's destiny of taking light to the nations (42:6; 49:6; 52:14–15) out of his own profound experience of the darkness of suffering and death. Through his work a seed will arise (53:10), answering to the holy seed of his vision (6:13), who as his servants (54:17; 56:5 et al.) will form the nucleus of that society that will reflect in its own glory the glory of the Lord (60:1–3). The interpretation of Isaiah's eschatology will be considered in the next section.

4. Eschatology

The message of Isaiah is strongly eschatological. There are many passages where the prophet deals with the future destiny of Israel and of the Gentiles, a special feature being the range of material that has Jerusalem-Zion as its focus. Passages that relate particularly to a great personal figure of the future, whether he is presented as king or servant, will be treated in our next section, though some reference to them here is inevitable.

a. *Approaches to interpretation*

The Book of Isaiah, like other OT prophetic Scriptures, has been understood in more than one way as far as its eschatology is concerned. Clearly, a high doctrine of Scripture requires us to take the teaching of its every part with great seriousness, and it also requires that we consider the way the NT writers understood it.

Some writers hold to the principle that every prophecy that can be taken literally should be so taken. This does not mean that there is no recognition of figurative language or the wide range of physical analogies used by the writers. It does mean though that Jerusalem is taken to be a geographical location, not a symbol for the church, that the wolf and the lamb lie down together in the Messiah's kingdom as literal animals, and so on.

Others interpret the bulk of the material spiritually, maintaining that the promises made to Israel are to be fulfilled in the church, so that we are not to think in terms of the physical realities themselves so much as the spiritual concepts they were designed to point to. This does not mean, of course, that none of the prophecies are to be taken literally. For instance, Christ did offer his back to those who would beat him (50:6). The key to spiritualization really lies in the formula: For "Israel" or "Jerusalem" read "the church."

In the judgment of the present writer, both these positions have difficulties in the light of the NT. A good case can be made out for the fulfillment of many of the "Israel" prophecies in the church, which is the thesis of O.T. Allis's *Prophecy and the Church*.[10]

But there is an important group of NT passages that can hardly be understood in any other way than in relation to literal Israel and geographical Jerusalem, passages like Matthew 19:28 and Luke 21:24. The most natural interpretation of Romans 11:26–27 takes "all Israel" to be a reference to the earthly nation, and a study of Revelation 20 leads to the conclusion that it is speaking about a thousand-year reign of Christ on earth after his second advent. Of course, those who argue for consistent spiritualization have their own interpretations of these passages, but this writer does not find them convincing. Romans 11:26–27 is particularly important and interesting because it quotes Isaiah 59:20–21 and 27:9. It is also difficult to take the consistently literal position, especially if this means the setting up of a temple and a sacrificial system again after Christ has made the final sacrifice.

b. *The relation of promise to fulfillment*

The intermediate position between the extremes of literalism and spiritualization outlined and advocated above will seem very unsatisfactory to some readers. They

---

[10]Philadelphia: Presbyterian and Reformed, 1964.

may say that as Israel and the church are two quite different realities, it seems inconceivable that they should both be present in the prophecies of the same book and, apparently, without any clear indication of this duality being given in the book itself. There is force in this argument, but one very important point must be borne in mind: the two are not completely distinct, for Jewish Christians belong to both. They enjoy the spiritual fulfillment of these promises; and, by a further manifestation of divine grace, Gentile Christians are also brought into the good of what was promised first to Israel. Promises given in Isaiah about the taking of light, not just to the Jew, but also to the Gentile (e.g., 42:6–7; 49:6–7), have this in view (Acts 13:46–48; 26:19–23). It is only unbelief that stops the Jews from enjoying what can rightly be theirs in Christ.

Another objection made is that it seems that on this basis we can never be certain how a particular part of the eschatological material is to be understood. This objection is, however, formulated in too extreme a way. In many cases the NT gives clear guidance. As suggested above, Acts 13:46–48; 26:19–23 interpret Isaiah 42:6–7; 49:6–7 spiritually; and in Galatians 4:25–27, Paul clearly applies Isaiah 54:1 to "the Jerusalem that is above," the mother of all who by faith are children of Abraham. Isaiah 59:20–21, however, is taken literally, though it should be noted that Romans 11, where the latter is quoted, simply tells us that "all Israel" will be converted and saved, without specifying the mode of its existence as a saved people.

We can of course be sure that when a promise is made of conditions that fall short of perfection—as for instance when life is lengthened but death is not abolished (65:20)—this does not apply to the perfected church but is best related to millennial conditions. Also, pictures of judgment—even universal judgment—that threaten death to most, but not to all unbelievers (24:6–13), most relate not to the ultimate judgment of the second death but to a great judgment on earth. On the other hand, references to "new heavens and a new earth" (65:17; 66:22) presuppose the advent of God's new order, where all will be perfect and which, according to Revelation 21–22, lies beyond the millennium.

There may be passages that present us with continuing problems of interpretation and where it is not plain whether we should understand them literally or spiritually. Perhaps this is what we should expect. We are never promised complete understanding of biblical prophecies before their fulfillment. Their main purpose is to keep us expectant, obedient, and trustful and to provide, in their fulfillment, evidence of the faithfulness of God to his word. In the fulfilled events themselves, God will be seen to be true.

One further possibility must be considered. Might a passage have two or even more meanings? At first sight this might seem an ideal solution to the problem, but is it really? Does God speak ambiguously or equivocally? We expect men to be clear and to say what they mean. Surely God may be expected to have one basic meaning in what he says.[11] This is true, but just as human speech, especially when it is poetical, may suggest further levels of significance beyond the meaning conveyed by the passage in its context, so may the Word of God.

The concept of typology is particularly helpful here. The offices and institutions of Israel provided shadows of which Christ was the substance, and prophecy itself—

---

[11]See the discussion in W.C. Kaiser, Jr., "Legitimate Hermeneutics," in N.L. Geisler, ed., *Inerrancy* (Grand Rapids: Zondervan, 1979), pp. 133–8.

though often pointing to Christ—sometimes does so indirectly by its reference to a person or institution that is a type of him. See the discussion of 7:14–17 below for a suggested example of this. The millennium itself is earthly, and passages that relate primarily to it may also point beyond themselves to the ultimate divine order in the new creation. The church too is imperfect, and its very imperfections are a cry for that perfected new order that God will bring in due course. Thus, both millennial Israel and a profoundly blessed but constantly failing church anticipate what the very inanimate creation itself mutely cries out for (Rom 8:18–25), the coming of God's new universe in which all will bring glory to him.

5. Messianism and the Servant Songs

Each part of the OT presents its own witness to the Christ who was to come, though not all in the same way. There is no OT book—with the possible exception of the Psalter—that is so full and varied in its testimony, and certainly none is so beautifully integrated. To glimpse something of its full beauty and power, we must approach it in three ways.

a. *The thematic approach*

Many themes enter this prophetic literature that are messsianic in the broad sense, that is they witness to the Christ presented in the pages of the NT. We can deal only with some of the more important of these.

The theme of the *Branch* is an important one. God promised Abraham not only a seed but a land (Gen 12:1–3), and this was to be a good land (Deut 11:8–12). If the people were obedient, the land would be fruitful. If they were disobedient, there would be barrenness (Deut 28) and ultimately removal (Deut 29:28). In Isaiah's day the Assyrians had devastated and stripped the Promised Land (1:7–9), and this was only an earnest of fuller judgment (7:23–25). God promised, however, the ultimate blessing of fruitfulness for the land (4:2; see comment there), and this promise is filled out in many wonderful ways later (ch. 35; 41:18–19; 55:12–13).

Yet God's purpose is even more concerned with people than with plants, and so the theme of biological fruitfulness is applied to the people of Israel. This vineyard will become a wasteland (5:1–7); this tree will be felled (6:13). In God's great purpose, however, the vineyard will eventually flourish as never before, filling the whole world with fruit (27:2–6); the holy seed that is Israel's faithful remnant (6:13) will encapsulate the promise of the future. It is not only Israel that is to be reduced to a "stump" (6:13) but the family of Jesse, the royal house of David (11:1), that suffered eclipse in the Exile and thereafter seemed to have been set aside. Out of this stump would come the ultimate fruitful Branch, the messianic King (11:1–5), the source of true fruitfulness for all, his reign bearing fruit in righteousness and peace (11:3–9; 32:1). If, as we shall see, this King is also the Suffering Servant, Isaiah 53:2 takes up this Branch theme again; and the fourth Servant Song reveals that this fullness of life has great cost in suffering and death for him.

The word *Stone* occurs in several important passages. In the OT, God is often called a Rock (e.g., Deut 32:4, 15, 18; Ps 18:2; 61:2), usually with implications of shelter and refuge. In 8:14–15 the prophet turns this familiar figure against the rebellious people. God the Rock is for his people who trust him but against those who refuse to believe, becoming a boulder to trip over in the darkness of sin. In 28:16–17 God promises to lay a tested (or testing) stone in Zion, again for faith. In 32:1–2 the (messianic) King becomes, in effect, a rock of refuge for his people. See the comments on all three passages. So God has committed to the coming One the function of sheltering his people who trust him.

Light is an important concept in Isaiah. The people, forsaking the light of God's word, are in great darkness (8:19–22); but light will in fact come to them in association with the advent of the Messiah (9:1–7). God the Light, like God the Rock, can confront his people with judgment (10:17); but eventually he will turn their darkness to light (30:26; 42:16; 58:8–11). This divine light will shine over Zion, attracting all the nations out of their darkness (60:1–3). This light, coming in Isaiah 9 through the messianic Child, is spread abroad (42:6–7; 49:6, 9), through the Lord's Servant. This suggests then that passages like 60:1–3 and 2:1–4 are implicitly messianic.

The ideas of the branch, stone, and light all move beyond their normal subpersonal uses to provide analogies of the coming One and his work. In the use of the term *Child*, however, we begin at the personal level. The people of Israel are described as sons, reared by God but proving rebellious and so appearing more like the offspring of evildoers (1:2, 4). We are reminded of Deuteronomy, which emphasizes the upbringing of children and prescribes stoning for a rebellious son (Deut 21:18–21). Deuteronomy in fact is at one with Isaiah in its declaration that the Israelites no longer reveal their likeness to God their father (Deut 32:5). Literal children appear on the scene, for it will be a sign of God's judgment that the Israelites will be ruled by children (3:4–5, 12). The prophet's own progeny become signs and portents to Israel, for Shear-Jashub declares God's grace and Maher-Shalal-Hash-Baz his judgment (7:3; 8:1–4, 18). An even more significant child appears in this context—Immanuel, the pledge of God's presence with his people (7:13–14; 8:8–10) for foreshadowing (see comments at 7:13–17) the messianic Child of the fourfold name, the perfect expression of the divine fullness in the messianic King. He is not only the supreme Child, but in his reign every child will find significance and safety (11:6, 8).

What of the messianic *King*? Isaiah had a wide experience of kings (1:1). The Books of Kings used David as the standard of kingship (1 Kings 11:33, 38; 15:3–5 et al.), though his imperfections come clearly into view in the Books of Samuel. There was also a written standard in Deuteronomy 17:14–20; and judged by this, even Hezekiah—especially as he appears in chapter 39—was a failure. In the year his first king died, Isaiah was given a vision of the perfect heavenly kingship, the very throne of Yahweh (ch. 6; cf. also 33:17, 21–22). The universal kingship of heaven leads us on to the earthly kingship of the human yet divine King of Isaiah 9 with the ever-increasing extension of his kingdom (9:6–7) till it becomes universal in the submission of the whole world (11:4, 9–10). His kingship, so unlike that of the empirical kings of Isaiah's time, will be one of perfect righteousness and peace (9:7; 11:3–9), which will include even the animal world. The Servant is said to bring forth justice to the nations and establish it in the earth (42:1, 4; 49:8), which suggests kingly functions and powers. Although a servant of rulers (49:7), the King's great suffering will lead to an overawed hush on the part of earthly kings (52:14–15), and to supremacy of the most absolute kind (52:13) and total victory (53:12) for him. It should be noted that 32:1 and 53:12 suggest the association of others in ruling with the King and the Servant, for the King has his people, the Servant his offspring.

The Servant Songs, presenting God's Servant first identified by Duhm (see p. 7), were held by Duhm to be the work of a different author from "Deutero-Isaiah"; but it is because most modern scholars do treat them as his work that they exclude 61:1–3, held to be the work of "Trito-Isaiah." Accept the unity of the book, and it may be that even 63:1–6 should be included (cf. 61:2 with 63:4). Moreover, the earlier songs should probably be extended beyond the limits set by Duhm—with the first and second reaching at least to 42:7 and 49:9a, the third to the end of chapter 50. An examination of these passages shows the appropriateness of this, and the comment at 48:16 presents the case for seeing a reference to the Servant there. The songs, though clearly forming an identifiable series, have not been arbitrarily introduced to their context; for the servant theme is an important one in Isaiah from chapter 41 onward, with Israel often so-named (41:8–9; 43:10; 44:1–2, 21) and, though often encouraged in such passages, also pronounced a failure (42:18–20). Cyrus too, though not called God's servant, functions for him (44:28–45:7), with the prediction of God's prophetic servants (44:26) and the good of his servant Israel (45:4) as the background and the purpose of his work.

Who then is the servant? The Christian, guided by the use made of the Servant Songs in the NT (e.g., in Matthew 8:17; 12:17–21; John 12:38; Acts 8:30–35 et al.), is likely to immediately say, "Jesus." Certainly there is not a word of the songs that cannot be applied to him, even when the servant is called "Israel" (49:3); for, as Matthew clearly saw, Jesus was the perfect expression of what God intended Israel to be (cf. Matt 2:15 with Hos 11:1–2). Jewish interpreters have identified the servant with Israel as a nation, the faithful remnant, ideal Israel, and various historical characters (including the prophet himself and Jeremiah). Modern scholars have shown the same diversity of outlook. The history of interpretation may be followed in the works of North or Rowley given in the Bibliography.

It is at first a surprise to find that Isaiah 49:6 is applied to Paul and Silas in Acts 13:47, whereas it is apparently applied to Christ in Acts 26:23, and that Isaiah 42:2–3 seems to have influenced the picture of the Christian servant of God in 2 Timothy 2:24–26. In fact, as we have seen already with the branch concept, it looks as if Isaiah is gradually educating his readers as to the deep significance of the servant. Viewed in the light of passages like 41:8–10 and 43:8–10, which form part of its context, the first song could apply to Israel, though in the light of 42:18–20 hardly empirical Israel but perhaps Israel of the future, purged of sin. But 42:6 is a problem, for "the people" here clearly refers to Israel. Perhaps, says the reader, the servant is the faithful remnant, so important in earlier chapters, playing now an important part in underscoring the relationship between the Lord and his people? This seems to be reinforced when we see the servant both identified with and yet distinguished from Israel in the second song (49:3, 5). Certainly in these two songs the servant, even if a group, is personalized; but in the third song the first person singular is dominant. He is taught, he suffers, he is vindicated, and he imparts God's truth to others, who are judged by their attitude to him. There is not, in fact, in the third and fourth songs a single expression necessitating or even suggesting that the servant is a group rather than an individual. Moreover, in chapter 53 his work is unique, for none other in the OT, either within or outside Isaiah, dies as an atoning sacrifice for human sins.

It seems therefore that we have here a kind of pyramid pattern, such as Delitzsch (2:174) discerned in the presentation of the servant. The servant is first of all, outside the songs, Israel; then he is the remnant, the spiritual heart of Israel; then he is an unique person, suffering unjustly at the hands of sinners and yet in fulfillment of the divine purpose of atonement. The earlier songs can be applied to Christians as they share—through his one sacrifice—the glad task of bringing light to the world. They cannot share his atoning work but are called to accept a destiny of suffering for his sake, to proclaim, as he did (61:1–2), his great salvation.

b. The contrapuntal approach

The prophet not only introduces a series of themes that prove eventually to be messianic, but, as we have seen to some extent already, he relates them in a kind of theological counterpoint. This is, of course, a feature of some NT christological passages—for example in Matthew 16:13–20, where terms "Son of Man," "Christ," "Son of the living God," and, perhaps, even "Rock" are all applied to Jesus. John 1 is another passage just crammed full of christological titles. There are many examples of this in Isaiah. For instance, in chapters 8–9 we have the sanctuary (8:14; cf. John 2:19), the stone (8:14) the light (9:2), and the child King (9:7). The kingly theme is interwoven with that of the servant (e.g., 42:4; 52:13; 53:12), while both the king and the servant are endowed with the Spirit of God (11:1–3; 42:1; 61:1). We have already seen how the branch theme interlocks with others. This all gives the impression that some great person is in view, in whom all this material will find its ultimate focus.

c. The programmatic approach

The author of this commentary has attempted to show that Luke 2:25–35 is not only saturated with Isaianic thought and language but that it implies a definite messianic program.[12] The prophecy of Isaiah itself seems also to contain a program, corresponding in many amazing ways to the NT presentation of Christ. Chapters 1–5 present the great spiritual need of the people of Israel. In our Lord's day there was a faithful remnant (cf. Isa 1:9 and Rom 9:29); but, for many, the excessive emphasis on sacrifice had been replaced by a similar phenomenon—Pharisaic legalism. Chapter 6 is related to Christ in John 12:37–41, and we see the condescension of this great divine King in his birth from a virgin (Matt 1:22–23) and in his ultimate destiny of Davidic kingship and universal dominion in chapters 7, 9, and 11, with a glimpse of the Galilean ministry in Isaiah 9:1 (cf. Matt 4:15–16).

Awaiting not only Israel, but also the nations (chs. 13–23)—and indeed the whole world (ch. 24)—is divine judgment for sin, and so all are in dire need of him. After a number of chapters with occasional christological foreshadowings, we hear the voice of the forerunner in Isaiah 40:3–5 (cf. Matt 3:3; Mark 1:3; Luke 3:4–6; John 1:23). In Isaiah 42 his ministry is perhaps viewed from the perspective of his baptism, for v.1, along with Psalm 2:7, is often seen in the words from heaven spoken at that baptism. Matthew 12:18–21 applies the passage to his ministry. Chapter 49, on the other hand, seems to be viewing that ministry in retrospect, for in it he has glorified God and proved to be the true Israel. His ministry to Israel is now to be complemented by a wider ministry to the nations.

In chapter 50 we see that the contents of Jesus' teaching ministry were determined by God through his daily fellowship with him (an emphasis of the Gospel of John); but a personal destiny of shame, fulfilled in the trials, was also revealed.

---

[12]G.W. Grogan, "The Light and the Stone: A Christological Study in Luke and Isaiah," in *Christ the Lord*, ed. H. Rowdon (Leicester: Inter-Varsity, 1982), pp. 151–67.

Earlier passages have spoken of his reign, and the fourth song commences with an emphatic assertion of his coming exaltation. It then expounds his sufferings and death in terms of sacrifice and substitution, before closing with a renewed emphasis on triumph.

Chapters 54–56 remind us of the joyful preaching of the gospel, grounded in the sacrifice and triumph of Christ, in which it is seen as the Good News of God to the barren, the hungry, the thirsty, and the spiritually disadvantaged. Chapter 61 is applied to Christ in Luke 4:17–19. Here he is the representative preacher and so the preacher's ideal. Chapter 62 takes up themes from chapter 61, with the emphasis now more on vengeance than redemption. Christ, as proclaimed in the gospel, must be embraced as Savior or faced as Judge. In chapters 65–66 we are reminded of the Book of Revelation, which also proclaims the advent of a new creation but also, as here, ends on a note of grave solemnity. If he is all that Isaiah has shown him to be, to remain in sin dooms people to the ultimate horror.

6. Structure

Any visitor to the Acropolis can see that aesthetic gifts of a high order may be used in the service of deities that are not worthy of it, but the aesthetic can also be a good servant of the spiritual. This is certainly the case in Isaiah, where language of great beauty is made the vehicle of divine truth. In fact, in parts of the book the language is so sublime that the aesthetically sensitive reader sometimes has to remind himself that all this beauty does not exist for its own sake but that it is the *meaning* of the words that is all-important. There is also a beauty of structure in the book.

Although chronology may have played some part in the arrangement of the oracles, the chief factor appears to be thematic. Moreover, Isaiah's divinely revealed theology (sect. 3), eschatology (sect. 4), and christology (sect. 5) contribute in major ways to that structure, with his concept of God as the most basic factor of all.

As we have seen (p. 12), Isaiah's distinctive designation of God was "the Holy One of Israel," and this stands both for his majesty and character and for his special relationship with an insignificant people in western Asia. This relationship, given the fact of sin, clearly implies grace but cannot deny his holiness, so that the people he has established a special link with—as well as those nations that have no such relationship—must feel the power of his judgment.

In Isaiah's day God's people lived in an area threatened by Assyria, who menaced every nation in the area and who conquered Samaria, the capital of Israel-Ephraim. After Isaiah's death, a political and military shift of power replaced Assyria by Babylonia. Jerusalem, threatened but not taken by Assyria, was overcome by the Babylonians. In chapters 1–35 Assyria is the dominant political background; and in chapters 40–66, Babylonia, while chapters 36–39 provide a transition from the one to the other. Dominating all, however, is Israel's God, whose purposes of judgment and salvation are served by these two powers and by others (notably Cyrus the Persian). In this section of the history of western Asia, the reader is repeatedly reminded of the wider setting, God's purposes of judgment on the whole world (e.g., ch. 24) and his saving purpose for Israel forming the heart of a plan of blessing for the whole world (e.g., chs. 2, 60).

Chapters 1–35, with their focus on God's people against the background of Assyria, may be analyzed in several ways. It is, however, clear that a threefold analysis develops the theme of God's purpose for his people in three variations. Chapters 1–12 focus on Judah and Jerusalem. Their sin and consequent judgment are emphatically delivered, but this already insignificant people is to have a glorious destiny; they are to be the center of the knowledge of God for the whole world. A small remnant and the messianic Child come into focus, and they comprise God's plan to demonstrate his holy control of history. Chapters 13–27 (falling into natural subdivisions, 13–23 and 24–27) focus first on the individual nations of western Asia, beginning with Babylonia (the power yet future) and Assyria (the current power). This section includes both Israelite kingdoms. God decrees judgment on each nation, and this is followed by a picture of universal judgment and an assurance that God's purpose for his people will triumph through their restoration. Chapters 28–35 also fall into two sections (28–33 and 34–35). First of all, we have the solemn reminder (reminiscent of much in chs. 1–12) of the rebellious sin of God's people, especially their failure to hear him and to trust him, but with further reminders also of his purpose to bless them. The last two chapters of this part recapitulate chapters 13–27, showing the judgment of the whole world, while making it clear that this includes particular nations (represented by Edom) and celebrating in glowing praise the triumph of God's redemptive grace for his people. So the reader who has followed the whole sequence of oracles from chapters 1–35 has been taught, by repetition of theme with variation of treatment, the great truths implicit in the phrase "the Holy One of Israel."

Chapters 1–35 emphasize the need for faith and the folly of trust in the flesh. This theme continues in the transitional chapters, 36–39. The mixture of faith and unbelief, so often characterizing God's people, assumes flesh and blood in the person of Hezekiah, so trustful in Jerusalem's great crisis and yet so compromising in his relations with Babylonia. So the scene is set for the chapters to follow.

Chapters 40–66 belong together; yet there is a threefold structure in them, punctuated by warnings to the wicked (48:22; 57:20–21; 66:24). Chapters 40–48 present the people in their future state under Babylonia's domination. Yet the sovereign Holy One of Israel has not forgotten his purpose for the remnant of his people. There is strong emphasis on his uniqueness and his control of history, especially in the advent of Cyrus. Just as God had done in Egypt, so now he would overthrow the deities of the tyrant empire, Assyria. The messianic theme reappears in a new form in the introduction of the Servant of the Lord (ch. 42). Chapters 49–57 are dominated by the Servant and his ministry, not only to Israel but also to that wider world that has been so much in view earlier. Atonement through substitution is described, celebrated, and proclaimed. Chapters 58–66 explore the final issues of salvation and judgment, with the Servant as the supreme agent of both (chs. 61, 63). The ultimate glory of Zion (ch. 60) is to be set in the context of a new creation (ch. 66), but the book ends with the prophetic realism of a warning to the impenitent (66:24).

What is the overarching theme of OT theology? Perhaps it is the covenant. Here in Isaiah, God's special relationship with Israel is presupposed throughout. Perhaps it is the kingdom of God. The whole structure of the book brings out the implications of God's sovereign control of things in the interests of his kingdom. Perhaps it is promise and fulfillment. Here we see time and again the word of divine authority being fulfilled and further fulfillment thereby pledged. Perhaps it is simply God himself, Israel's Holy One. This book is one long exposition of the implications—for Israel and the world—of who and what he is. So this great prophecy—its whole structure unified by its teaching about the Holy One of Isreal, who is true to his word, faithful to his covenant, and pursues the establishment of his kingdom—is a classic disclosure of the very heart of the OT faith.

7. Canonicity

Written prophecies by Isaiah existed by the date of Chronicles, as 2 Chronicles 32:32 shows; and this is usually placed around 400 B.C. Ecclesiasticus, early in the second century, referred to the inspiration of Isaiah; and there is much evidence from Qumran and from Rabbinic sources, as well as from the NT, that the book was regarded as canonical both before and in NT times. The book has always been highly regarded within the church of Christ, especially for its testimony to him.

8. Text

The MT of Isaiah, the only text available till modern times, seems to have been well preserved; for it presents comparatively few major difficulties. The main Greek translation, the LXX, occasionally diverges from it; but only rarely do these divergences alter the meaning of the text in any significant way. The Aramaic Targum sometimes agrees with the LXX but more often with the MT. The Syriac and Vulgate versions, while interesting, are of less value and in general support the MT.

The discovery of two MSS of Isaiah (1QIsa[a] and 1QIsa[b]) at Qumran was an event of major textual importance. Here were two MSS of an important OT book about one thousand years older than the MT, almost certainly to be dated before Christ, and one of them (1QIsa[a]) complete. Particularly important is the fact that they certainly appear to be earlier than the standardization of the text of the OT that, according to the Talmud, took place about A.D. 100. These scrolls show a large measure of agreement with the MT, revealing the extreme care with which the text of the book must have been copied by the scribes over the centuries; but there are occasional interesting agreements with the LXX. The majority of variations from the MT are, however, in spelling, which make no real difference to the text.

For more detailed treatment of this whole question, see W.S. LaSor, "The Dead Sea Scrolls," EBC, 1:395–405, and the references cited there.

9. Bibliography

Books

Alexander, J.A. *Isaiah, Translated and Explained.* 2 vols. New York: John Wiley, 1864.
Allis, O.T. *The Unity of Isaiah.* Philadelphia: Presbyterian and Reformed, 1950.
Cheyne, T.K. *The Book of Isaiah Chronologically Arranged.* London: Macmillan, 1870.
Childs, B.S. *Isaiah and the Assyrian Crisis.* London: SCM, 1967.
Clements, R.E. *Isaiah 1–39.* Grand Rapids: Eerdmans, 1980.
Davies, E.W. *Prophecy and Ethics: Isaiah and the Ethical Traditions of Israel.* Sheffield: J.S.O.T., 1981.
Delitzsch, F. *Biblical Commentary on the Prophecies of Isaiah.* 2 vols. Edinburgh: T. & T. Clark, 1890.
Duhm, B. *Das Buch Jesaia.* Gottengen: Vandenhoeck und Ruprecht, 1922.

Eaton, J.H. *Festal Drama in Deutero-Isaiah*. London: SPCK, 1979.

Erlandsson, S. *The Burden of Babylon: A Study of Isaiah 13:2–14:23*. Lund, C.W.K. Gleerup, 1970.

Gray, G.B. *A Critical and Exegetical Commentary on the Book of Isaiah*. New York: Scribner's, 1912.

Herbert, A.S. *The Book of the Prophet Isaiah*. 2 vols. Cambridge: Cambridge University Press, 1973, 1975.

Jensen, J. *The Use of* tôrâ *by Isaiah: His Debate With the Wisdom Tradition*. Washington: C.B.A.A., 1973.

Jones, D.R. *Isaiah 56–66 and Joel*. London: SCM, 1964.

Kaiser, O. *Isaiah 1–39*. 2 vols. London: SCM, 1974.

Kidner, F.D. "Isaiah." *The New Bible Commentary Revised*. Edited by D. Guthrie and J.A. Motyer. Grand Rapids: Eerdmans, 1970, pp. 588–625.

Kissane, E.J. *The Book of Isaiah*. 2 vols. Dublin: Brown and Nolan, 1941, 1943.

Leupold, H.C. *Exposition of Isaiah*. 2 vols. Welwyn: Evangelical, 1977.

Lindblom, J. *The Servant Songs in Deutero-Isaiah*. Lund: H. & Kan Ohlssons Boktryckeri, 1951.

Mauchline J. *Isaiah 1–39*. London: SCM, 1962.

McKenzie, J.L. *Second Isaiah*. Garden City: Doubleday, 1968.

Muilenburg, J. "The Book of Isaiah: Chapters 40–66." *The Interpreter's Bible*. Edited by G.A. Buttrick. Nashville: Abingdon, 1956, 5:381–773.

North, C.R. *The Suffering Servant in Deutero-Isaiah: an Historical and Critical Study*. London: Oxford University Press, 1948.

_____. *Isaiah 40–55*. London: SCM, 1952.

_____. *The Second Isaiah*. Oxford: Clarendon, 1964.

Orlinsky, H.M., and Snaith, N.H. *Studies on the Second Part of the Book of Isaiah*. Leiden: Brill, 1967.

Rowley, H.H. *The Servant of the Lord*. Oxford: Blackwell, 1965.

Smart, J.D. *History and Theology in Second Isaiah*. Philadelphia: Westminster, 1965.

Smith, G.A. *The Book of Isaiah*. 2 vols. London: Hodder and Stoughton, 1927.

Simon, U.E. *A Theology of Salvation: A Commentary on Isaiah 40–55*. London: SPCK, 1953.

Thexton, S.C. *Isaiah 40–66*. London: Epworth, 1959.

Torrey, C.C. *The Second Isaiah: A New Interpretation*. New York: Scribner, 1928.

Westermann, C. *Isaiah 40–66: A Commentary*. London: SCM, 1969.

Whedbee, J.W. *Isaiah and Wisdom*. Nashville: Abingdon, 1971.

Whybray, R.N. *Isaiah 40–66*. London: Oliphants, 1975.

Young, E.J. *The Book of Isaiah*. 3 vols. Grand Rapids: Eerdmans, 1965, 1969, 1972.

Articles

Driver, G.R. "Isaiah 40–66. Linguistic and Textual Problems." *Journal of Theological Studies* 36 (1935): 396–406.

_____. "Isaiah 1–39. Linguistic and Textual Problems." *Journal of Theological Studies* 38 (1937): 36–50.

_____. "Isaiah 1–39. Textual and Linguistic Problems." *Journal of Semitic Studies* 13 (1968): 36–57.

Roberts, J.J.M. "Isaiah in Old Testament Theology." *Interpretation* 36 (1982): 130–43.

Willis, J.T. "The Genre of Isaiah 5:1–7." *Journal of Biblical Literature* 96 (1977): 337–62.

Young, E.J. "Isaiah 34 and Its Position in the Prophecy." *Westminister Theological Journal* 26 (Nov. 1964—May 1965): 93–114.

10. Outline

I. Oracles Concerning Judah and Jerusalem (1:1–12:6)
  A. God's Charge Against His People (1:1–31)
  B. The Exaltation of God's House and the Extension of His Dominion (2:1–5)
  C. The Day of the Lord (2:6–22)
  D. God's Judgment on Jerusalem and Judah (3:1–4:1)
  E. Zion's Glorious Future (4:2–6)
  F. The Parable of the Vineyard (5:1–7)
  G. Condemnation of Judah's Sins (5:8–30)
  H. The Vision and Call of the Holy One (6:1–13)
  I. The Sign of Shear-Jashub (7:1–9)
  J. The Sign of Immanuel (7:10–25)
  K. The Sign of Maher-Shalal-Hash-Baz (8:1–10)
  L. Isaiah and His Children as Signs and Wonders (8:11–18)
  M. The Light and the Child (8:19–9:7)
  N. The Judgment of Ephraim (9:8–10:4)
  O. The Judgment of Assyria (10:5–19)
  P. The Deliverance of the Lord's Remnant (10:20–34)
  Q. The Davidic King and His Benign Reign (11:1–9)
  R. The Nation and the Nations (11:10–16)
  S. A Song of Joyous Praise (12:1–6)

II. God and the Nations (13:1–23:18)
  A. Prophecy Against Babylon (13:1–14:23)
  B. Prophecy Against Assyria (14:24–27)
  C. Prophecy Against Philistia (14:28–32)
  D. Prophecy Against Moab (15:1–16:14)
  E. Prophecy Against Damascus (and Ephraim) (17:1–14)
  F. Prophecy Against Cush (18:1–7)
  G. Prophecy Against Egypt (19:1–25)
  H. Prophecy Against Egypt and Cush (20:1–6)
  I. Prophecy Against Babylon (21:1–10)
  J. Prophecy Against Edom (21:11–12)
  K. Prophecy Against Arabia (21:13–17)
  L. Prophecy Against Jerusalem (22:1–25)
  M. Prophecy Against Tyre (23:1–18)

III. God and the Whole World (24:1–27:13)
  A. The Judgment of the World (24:1–23)
  B. Psalms and Predictions of Judgment and Salvation (25:1–12)
  C. Praise, Prayer, and Prophecy (26:1–21)
  D. The Restoration of Israel (27:1–13)

IV. God and His People (28:1–33:24)
  A. Woe to Samaria (28:1–29)
  B. Woe to Ariel (29:1–24)
  C. Woe to the Rebellious Children (30:1–33)
  D. Woe to Those Who Seek Help From Egypt (31:1–9)
  E. God's Kingdom and the Triumph of Righteousness (32:1–20)

F. Woe to the Destroyer (33:1–24)

V. God's Purpose of Judgment and Salvation (34:1–35:10)
   A. Judgment on the World—and Edom (34:1–17)
   B. Blessing for God's People (35:1–10)

VI. Isaiah and Hezekiah, Assyria and Babylon (36:1–39:8)
   A. The Deliverance of Jerusalem From Sennacherib (36:1–37:38)
   B. Hezekiah's Illness (38:1–22)
   C. Envoys From and Exile to Babylonia (39:1–8)

VII. The Sole Sovereignty and Sure Promises of the Lord (40:1–48:22)
   A. Good News for Jerusalem (40:1–11)
   B. God the Incomparable (40:12–31)
   C. God the Lord of History for His People (41:1–29)
   D. The Lord's Servant—the Perfect and the Defective (42:1–25)
   E. Grace Abounding and Despised (43:1–28)
   F. Israel's Great God and the Folly of Idolatry (44:1–23)
   G. God's Actions Through Cyrus for Jerusalem (44:24–45:25)
   H. Babylon's Ineffectual Idols and the Lord Almighty (46:1–13)
   I. The Fall of Proud Babylon (47:1–15)
   J. Israel's Stubbornness and God's Purpose of Grace (48:1–22)

VIII. The Gospel of the Servant of the Lord (49:1–57:21)
   A. The Lord's Servant and the Restoration of Israel (49:1–26)
   B. Israel's Sin and the Servant's Obedience (50:1–11)
   C. Listen! Awake! Depart! (51:1–52:12)
   D. The Man of Sorrows and His Vindication (52:13–53:12)
   E. God's Glorious Future for Jerusalem (54:1–17)
   F. The Generosity, Urgency, and Effectiveness of God's Word of Grace (55:1–13)
   G. Salvation Extended to the Disadvantaged (56:1–8)
   H. God's Message to the Wicked (56:9–57:21)

IX. God as Judge and Savior (58:1–66:24)
   A. The True Fast (58:1–14)
   B. Sin, Sorrow, and Salvation (59:1–21)
   C. The Future Glory of Zion (60:1–22)
   D. The Year of the Lord's Favor (61:1–11)
   E. Assured Prayer for Zion's Future (62:1–12)
   F. The Lord the Avenger (63:1–6)
   G. A Psalm of Praise and Lamentation (63:7–64:12)
   H. The Great Final Issues (65:1–66:24)

Text and Exposition

I. Oracles Concerning Judah and Jerusalem (1:1–12:6)

Chapters 1–12, because of their biographical features, have been well called the "Memoirs of Isaiah," though the title is sometimes restricted to a smaller passage, such as 6:1–8:18. Except perhaps for chapter 1, Isaiah's "Memoirs" belong to an early period of the prophet's ministry, during the reigns of Jotham (750–731 B.C.) and Ahaz (735–715 B.C.).

1. *God's Charge Against His People*

1:1–31

¹The vision concerning Judah and Jerusalem that Isaiah son of Amoz saw during the reigns of Uzziah, Jotham, Ahaz and Hezekiah, kings of Judah.

²Hear, O heavens! Listen, O earth!
 For The Lord has spoken:
"I reared children and brought them up,
 but they have rebelled against me.
³The ox knows his master,
 the donkey his owner's manger,
but Israel does not know,
 my people do not understand."

⁴Ah, sinful nation,
 a people loaded with guilt,
a brood of evildoers,
 children given to corruption.
They have forsaken the Lord;
 they have spurned the Holy One of Israel
 and turned their backs on him.

⁵Why should you be beaten anymore?
 Why do you persist in rebellion?
Your whole head is injured,
 your whole heart afflicted.
⁶From the sole of your foot to the top of your head
 there is no soundness—
only wounds and welts
 and open sores,
not cleansed or bandaged
 or soothed with oil.

⁷Your country is desolate,
 your cities burned with fire;
your fields are being stripped by foreigners
 right before you,
 laid waste as when overthrown by strangers.
⁸The Daughter of Zion is left
 like a shelter in a vineyard,
like a hut in a field of melons,
 like a city under siege.
⁹Unless the Lord Almighty
 had left us some survivors,
we would have become like Sodom,
 we would have been like Gomorrah.

¹⁰Hear the word of the LORD,
    you rulers of Sodom;
listen to the law of our God,
    you people of Gomorrah!
¹¹"The multitude of your sacrifices—
    what are they to me?" says the LORD.
"I have more than enough of burnt offerings,
    of rams and the fat of fattened animals;
I have no pleasure
    in the blood of bulls and lambs and goats.
¹²When you come to appear before me,
    who has asked this of you,
    this trampling of my courts?
¹³Stop bringing meaningless offerings!
    Your incense is detestable to me.
New Moons, Sabbaths and convocations—
    I cannot bear your evil assemblies.
¹⁴Your New Moon festivals and your appointed feasts
    my soul hates.
They have become a burden to me;
    I am weary of bearing them.
¹⁵When you spread out your hands in prayer,
    I will hide my eyes from you;
even if you offer many prayers,
    I will not listen.
Your hands are full of blood;
¹⁶ wash and make yourselves clean.
Take your evil deeds
    out of my sight!
Stop doing wrong,
¹⁷ learn to do right!
Seek justice,
    encourage the oppressed.
Defend the cause of the fatherless,
    plead the case of the widow.
¹⁸"Come now, let us reason together,"
    says the LORD.
"Though your sins are like scarlet,
    they shall be as white as snow;
though they are red as crimson,
    they shall be like wool.
¹⁹If you are willing and obedient,
    you will eat the best from the land;
²⁰but if you resist and rebel,
    you will be devoured by the sword."
                        For the mouth of the LORD has spoken.

²¹See how the faithful city
    has become a harlot!
She once was full of justice;
    righteousness used to dwell in her—
    but now murderers!
²²Your silver has become dross,
    your choice wine is diluted with water.
²³Your rulers are rebels,
    companions of thieves;
they all love bribes
    and chase after gifts.

> They do not defend the cause of the fatherless;
> the widow's case does not come before them.
> [24]Therefore the Lord, the LORD Almighty,
> the MIghty One of Israel, declares:
> "Ah, I will get relief from my foes
> and avenge myself on my enemies.
> [25]I will turn my hand against you;
> I will thoroughly purge away your dross
> and remove all your impurities.
> [26]I will restore your judges as in days of old,
> your counselors as at the beginning.
> Afterward you will be called
> the City of Righteousness,
> the Faithful City."
>
> [27]Zion will be redeemed with justice,
> her penitent ones with righteousness.
> [28]But rebels and sinners will both be broken,
> and those who forsake the LORD will perish.
>
> [29]"You will be ashamed because of the sacred oaks
> in which you have delighted;
> you will be disgraced because of the gardens
> that you have chosen.
> [30]You will be like an oak with fading leaves,
> like a garden without water.
> [31]The mighty man will become tinder
> and his work a spark;
> both will burn together,
> with no one to quench the fire."

This chapter fitly opens the book. It vigorously and with many a memorable phrase sums up the teaching, not only of Isaiah, but of the whole prophetic movement. It evinces clear thematic unity, and the noncritical reader is unlikely to detect any disjointedness in thought. To see it as a series of distinct oracles linked by "catchwords" and assembled here to provide a fitting introduction seems hardly necessary, though this view of the chapter is widely held. In fact, chapter 1 abounds in literary devices such as assonance, alliteration, word-order emphasis, and so on (cf. Whedbee on vv.2–3 below). Moreover, material linked by catchwords is not necessarily composite, as a glance at James 1 will reveal. Some of the word-idea links run through much of the chapter. They include not only a theological motif (e.g., rebellion—vv.2, 5, 20, 23, 28) but also a recurrent visual image like burden-bearing, suggested by the reference in v.3 to domestic beasts and developed in vv.4, 14, 24). Such features make oracular unity more likely than the activity of a redactor.

If chapter 1 is, substantially at least, a unity, what is its date? The period of the Syro-Ephraimite threat to Judah (735–732 B.C.) has had its advocates, but most recent scholars favor the time of Sennacherib's invasion (701 B.C.). The description in vv.7–9 of Jerusalem isolated and beleaguered harmonizes so well with Sennacherib's own description (see comment at vv.7–9).

1 Opinions vary as to whether this heading is for chapter 1 or the whole book. Comparison with the openings of Hosea, Amos, Micah, and Zephaniah tends to support the latter, though chapters 40–66 may belong to the reign of Manasseh (see

Introduction, pp. 11–12). The prophet's name means "Yahweh is salvation." Isaiah's father was not the prophet Amos (the names are quite different in Hebrew), and the Jewish tradition of his royal birth is virtually groundless. He certainly had an extensive experience of kings! His knowledge of their imperfections fitted him to be a major channel of God's disclosure of the perfect king. "Vision" (cf. Obad 1; Nah 1:1) suggests to the reader a mode of revelation, but it could be a technical term for an oracle of God, however received.

2–3 These two verses appear to introduce a trial scene. Is the true background ordinary Semitic legal practice or ancient Near Eastern covenant lawsuits? Or are we rather to see here the influence of the wisdom tradition on a prophet? The last is likely only if we isolate these two verses from the rest of the chapter and focus attention on the parable in v.3, for v.2 is not really instruction given to sons (cf. Prov 2:1; 3:1, 11, 21 et al.) but a complaint made against them. The parallel with Deuteronomy 32:1–43 (cf. Mic 6; Ps 50:3–23) suggests that the hearers may well have been reminded of the Sinai covenant by the form of the prophet's address.

Here nature serves the purposes of prophecy. The heavens and earth witness God's complaint against his people, and the ox and the donkey dumbly rebuke Israel's ingratitude. Unreasoning beasts (Prov 7:22) exhibit more sense and appreciation than unthinking Israel (cf. Jer 8:7). As O. Kaiser (in loc.) puts it, "The ox and the ass *know* their masters, that is, they associate with them on terms of trust and obedience" (emphasis his). The words "children" and "they" are both emphatic in the Hebrew underlining the unthinkable character of such filial rebellion.

Whedbee (pp. 42f.) makes this comment:

> Coming on the heels of the opening call to heaven and earth, the two indictments of vv.2b and 3 show the complexity of Isaiah's language. Here he skillfully places two different genres—legal complaint and didactic parable—and two different metaphors—father/son and ass/ox—in a back-to-back position; yet at the same time he implies an inner affinity between the two. . . . The passage is an impressive example of the variety of language Isaiah can tap for his message."

And this is but an earnest of the riches to come!

4 The rich Hebrew vocabulary of words for sin appears here. The prophet's language suggests that guilt is an awful burden; that if paternity is truly revealed in character, then something has gone sadly wrong (cf. Deut 32:5; John 8:39–44); and that the people have added insult to ingratitude. The important phrase "Holy One of Israel" is discussed in the Introduction (p. 12).

5–6 The sinful people were addressed directly here. Their continuance in sin, like all rebellion against God, was utterly irrational. The whole surface of the body politic (i.e., the nation personified) testified to the divine punishment, but the heart remains unchanged. Deuteronomy 28:35 is an instructive parallel. There the condition of the body was due to disease, not to scourging; but the setting of the whole chapter portends just such punishment through a foreign foe as the people were experiencing.

7–9 Using the rich resources of human language, the inspired prophecy replaces metaphor (vv.5–6) by literal statement, which is followed, in turn, by vivid simile. As Isaiah uttered these words, he may well have recalled the divine disclosure of things to come that had been given him at the time of his call (6:11–13). God's word had proved true. City and country were both suffering, for their inhabitants were powerless against the invaders. Sennacherib said of Hezekiah (ANET, p. 288), "Himself I made a prisoner in Jerusalem, . . . like a bird in a cage." Isaiah likened the situation in the land to the roughly made shelters of the farmer's watchmen, standing desolate against the skyline once harvest was over (v.8). Once before southern Canaan had witnessed a scene of utter desolation (Gen 19:24–29), at that time even more thorough. It was the restraining hand of the Lord Almighty (KJV "LORD of hosts," suggestive of comprehensive authority and fullness of resources) that alone saved Jerusalem from sharing the fate of its environs, and the prophet stressed this by placing the names of the two destroyed cities in a position of emphasis (v.9).

10–15 Sodom and Gomorrah—shocking and deeply insulting names to Isaiah's hearers—suggest not only devastation but Gentile sin at its worst; yet the words "LORD" and "our God" have overtones of a covenant relationship unknown to the cities of the plain (v.10). The prophet pressed home his point. Rulers and people had a Sodom-like offensiveness to God, and their ostentatious religious observances only aggravated the situation.

These verses highlight many features of Israel's system of worship. Verse 11 implies an abundance of sacrifices well beyond the divine requirements (cf. Mic 6:6–8). God was nauseated by such a surfeit (cf. Ps 50:12–13), and the words "to me" and "more than enough" suggest the same kind of blasphemous, pagan idea of a god who needs to be fed with sacrifices as Psalm 50 rejects with biting irony.

The temple courts (v.12) felt the heavy tread of the worshiping throng, probably swollen at such times of national crisis; but "trampling" also suggests desecration. This puts the question "Who has asked this of you?" in its true perspective. God rejected "offerings" rendered "meaningless" by hypocrisy (v.13; cf. Jer 7:21–23; Hos 6:6; Amos 5:21–27; Mic 6:6–8). The rendering "your evil assemblies" obscures the studied harshness of the word-combination "iniquity" and "solemn meeting" (KJV). The people have been shown as burdened with guilt (v.4); but here God is shown as burdened with their sacrifices.

The older critical view that Isaiah and other prophets rejected sacrifice as such is now largely abandoned. It is ritual divorced from penitence that God hates. Otherwise, for consistency of interpretation, v.15 must be regarded as a rejection of prayer as such! As it is, this verse—with its references to posture and frequency in prayer—presents the same emphasis on empty externalism we see elsewhere in the passage. Here too we may discern a spiritual link between OT ritualism and the NT Pharisaism (cf. esp. Matt 6:5). Young (*Book of Isaiah*, in loc.) comments:

> The nation . . . had become guilty of idolatry, seeking to worship him as though approaching an idol. He would therefore be to Judah as an idol. The idol could not open its eyes, so he would not open his eyes. The idol could not hear, so he would not hear the multiplied prayer. People who thus sin deserve only an idol. But there was a difference. In reality God was not acting as an idol. He closed his eyes and ears, it is true, but in so doing rejected the worship and prepared to bring judgment upon the worshiper.

16–17 God's true way is announced and the moral note sounded. In view of the alleged Pelagianism of the prophets (viz., that human beings are capable of self-reformation), we should note that v.4 attributes to God the real power to wash away sins (implied too in the promise of v.18)—but the prophets insisted on human responsibility. People are accountable, but the grace and power of fulfillment are God's alone. The prophet's words imply that the reclaimed sinner needs a course of instruction in the ways of God (v.17). This teaching process begins in the call for social justice and defense of the fatherless. Isaiah thoroughly represents eighth-century prophecy (cf. Hos 4:2; Amos 2:6–8; Mic 6:9–12). His rapid-fire style in these two verses underscores the authority and urgency of God's commands to his people.

18–20 The famous call of v.18 has been taken in more than one way by scholars. Many see the words as an offer of total forgiveness, for which vv.19–20 supply the divine conditions. Others understand the language to be ironic and render the second part of the verse as "If your sins are as scarlet, shall they be white as snow? If they are red like crimson, shall they be as wool?" There is still—even on this construction—an element of conditional promise in the passage (v.19), but the general tone becomes distinctly sterner. In fact, the language permits either possibility, though most recent scholars are inclined to the former.

Verses 19–20 summarize the Deuteronomic theology of divine blessing—found in passages like Deuteronomy 28—which underlies much prophetic teaching. They contain a striking play on words. In effect God was saying, "Eat, . . . or be eaten!"

21–23 The rhythm of Isaiah's poetry changes suddenly as he introduces the characteristic "limp" of a Hebrew lament, opening with the exclamation "how!" (v.21); cf. 14:4; 2 Sam 1:19; Ps 137:4; Lam 1:1; 2:1; 4:1; Hos 11:8). Even though there is no explicit threat of judgment till v.24, the sensitive listener would hear the drumbeats of doom in the very sound of the poetic measure.

Did Isaiah view the past through rose-tinted spectacles? Not necessarily, for words like "justice" and "rulers" (cf. also v.26) show that he was thinking primarily of the people's leaders; so the past he had in mind was perhaps the time of David, when Jerusalem first came under Israelite control. Silver and choice wine (v.22) are probably metaphors for the rulers (cf. Jer 6:28, 30; Ezek 22:18), who had become utterly decadent. Cheyne's translation—"rulers are unruly" (p. 40)—preserves the play on words, used also by Isaiah's older contemporary in the northern kingdom (Hos 9:15). Hosea may also be the source of the figure of a harlot for the unfaithful people of God (Hos 1:2 et al.).

24–26 First was the ominous rhythm of the dirge (see commentary at v.21), then came the vivid description of moral corruption (v.23), and here we have a terrifying catena of majestic divine titles (v.24). The first of them—"Lord," meaning "master" —is used of God by Isaiah more than by any other OT writer; and, in its absolute form, as here, it always introduces a note of judgment (cf. 3:1; 10:16, 33 et al.). The second—"the LORD Almighty—often linked with it, indicates supreme power (see commentary at v.9), while the third—"the Mighty One of Israel"—is a somewhat uncommon term suggestive of bulllike strength (Gen 49:24; Isa 49:26; 60:16). Still there was no respite. To complete the verbal build-up, God's message is prefixed by the agitated exclamation "Ah" (cf. v.4).

The burden God bears (cf. v.14) as the result of the meaningless offerings of his "foes" demands relief in judgment. His hand (v.25), so often stretched out against Israel's enemies (Exod 3:20; 15:6; Ps 118:15–16), has turned against his own people (cf. Zech 13:7). His threat of vengenace has taken an unexpected turn, however, for it issues in cleansing rather than destruction. Although so sinful, they were still his people, and his judgments were directed to the removal of their impurities. Verse 25 takes up imagery from v.22, while in v.26 the tone changes further still as God gave a wonderful promise of restoration and renewal. The reader should feel the dramatic quality and the emotional and spiritual power of these three great verses.

27–31 The theme of restoration continues for another verse (its literary setting anticipating the great vision of ch. 2), until the threatening tone returns (v.28). Is Zion's redemption here physical or moral, and does the NIV's "penitent ones" rightly interpret the Hebrew word *šābîm*, which simply means "those who return"? The second question at least should almost certainly be answered in the affirmative, as the contrasting language of v.28 suggests. Redemption terminology is normally used in the OT with a physical connotation and is often so applied to Jerusalem/Zion in other parts of this book (e.g., 35:9–10; 51:10–11; 52:9; 59:20).

Sacred trees played an important part in the Canaanite fertility cult (cf. Deut 12:23; 2 Kings 16:4; Hos 4:13), for deciduous trees like the oak or terebinth may well have symbolized the death and rebirth of the god. The "gardens" (v.29) may be groves of these trees, or, alternatively, (esp. in the light of v.30) places of sacred springs or wells.

Verses 29–30 teach the lesson that a people under judgment may be instructed from the very symbols of their apostasy as to the folly of such departure from the true God, while v.31 imparts the even more important lesson that destruction may come on us from the very thing our sin has brought into being.

Notes

5 עַל מֶה (*'al meh*), rendered "Why?" in most ancient versions (also NIV, RSV, ASV), could mean "On what [part]?" Most commentators reject the Vulgate–NEB reading, for it "destroys the parallelism" (Gray, in loc.); and the former rendering fits the context perfectly, because the chapter contains so much appeal to reason.

7 The NEB margin, following the view of many modern scholars, suggests that סְדֹם (*sᵉdōm*, "Sodom") should be read here instead of זָרִים (*zārîm;* "strangers"). Certainly מַהְפֵּכָה (*mahpēkāh*, "overthrown") is used elsewhere only in reference to the destruction of the cities of the plain (cf. 13:19; Deut 29:23[22MT]; Jer 49:18; 50:40; Amos 4:11), and a scribe could have wrongly transcribed *zārîm* (NIV, "foreigners") from earlier in the verse. Most modern EV do not even give this a place in the margin, and Clements (*Isaiah 1–39*, in loc.) is both difficult to understand and much too dogmatic when he says that the reading in the text "must be regarded as an editor's gloss based upon v.9." The MT reading is perfectly natural. Indeed, a reference to Sodom at this point lessens the dramatic impact of the name, which comes with much greater force in vv.9–10.

8 בַּת־צִיּוֹן (*bat-ṣiyôn*, "daughter of Zion") personifies the city of Jerusalem. It suggests that the hill gave birth to the city, though the concept of geography as the mother of society and so of history seems too sophisticated an explanation of a popular designation.

9 This is no reference to the great doctrine of the remnant (see Introduction, p. 13). Isaiah avoids his usual remnant terminology and uses instead the noun שָׂרִיד (*śārîd*, "survivors").

10 תּוֹרַת (*tôraṯ*, "law") has been understood by some commentators as a reference to the Mosaic Law. Calvin (in loc.) says, "He purposely employed the term *law*, in order to glance at their absurd opinion; because, by imagining that the offering of sacrifices, unaccompanied by faith and repentance, can appease God, they put an absurd interpretation on the law. By these words he reminded them that, by quoting Moses to them, he introduces nothing new and makes no addition to the *law*; that it is only necessary for them to *hear* what the will of God is; and on this subject he will faithfully instruct them" (emphasis his). This in fact approaches the other alternative, that the prophet is referring to the word of God through himself. If the prophet believed himself to be applying the law itself, the two interpretations merge. For possible links with the OT wisdom tradition, see Jensen, pp. 68ff.

13 קְטֹרֶת (*qeṭōreṯ*, "incense") is ambiguous, for it was used of both the smoke of sacrifice and incense proper (cf. Gray, in loc.). The question does not, however, affect the general sense of the passage.

17 The marginal rendering—"rebuke the oppressor"—is possible linguistically and strengthens the tone of the passage still more (cf. Gray, in loc.).

21 The repeated use of צֶדֶק (*ṣedeq*, "righteousness") in vv.21, 26, 27 in relation to Jerusalem is interesting (cf. Heb. 7:1–2). Clements (*Isaiah 1–39*, in loc.) says, "An ancient and strongly felt association appears to have existed between Jerusalem and the concept of *righteousness*. This very probably arose through the use of the word as a divine title" (emphasis his).

26 The juxtaposition of "judges" with "counselors" in consecutive lines suggests a positive attitude towards the institution despite the oracle of judgment against them in 29:13–16. See Whedbee, pp. 139–41, and also the fuller note at 9:6.

31 הֶחָסֹן (*heḥāsōn*, "the mighty man") occurs only here and in Amos 2:9, and in both cases it is connected with trees.

The KJV rendering of פֹּעֲלוֹ (*poʿᵃlô*, "his work") as "the maker of it" is just possible and would require "the mighty man" to refer to the idol. The NIV follows the LXX, which seems to be the more natural rendering.

---

2. The Exaltation of God's House and the Extension of His Dominion

2:1–5

¹This is what Isaiah son of Amoz saw concerning Judah and Jerusalem:

²In the last days

> the mountain of the Lord's temple will be established
>   as chief among the mountains;
> it will be raised above the hills,
>   and all nations will stream to it.

³Many peoples will come and say,

> "Come, let us go up to the mountain of the Lord,
>   to the house of the God of Jacob.
> He will teach us his ways,
>   so that we may walk in his paths."
> The law will go out from Zion,
>   the word of the Lord from Jerusalem.
> ⁴He will judge between the nations
>   and will settle disputes for many peoples.
> They will beat their swords into plowshares
>   and their spears into pruning hooks.
> Nation will not take up sword against nation,
>   nor will they train for war anymore.

> 5Come, O house of Jacob,
> let us walk in the light of the LORD.

1 This heading virtually repeats that with which the book opens, apart from the reference there to the kings. It is not easy to fix the terminus of the material covered by it, but it certainly must have been intended to include chapters 2–4. Isaiah literally saw "the word" (*haddābār;* cf. KJV, RSV et al.), which suggests that the revelation contained both visionary and verbal elements.

2–4 This glorious vision is found, with small variations, in Micah 4:1–3, which, by contrast, concludes with a view of every man sitting in peace under his fruit trees (Mic 4:4). Joel 3:10 contains language clearly parallel with Isaiah 2:4 and Micah 4:3. If we could posit with some certainty—but cannot—an early date for Joel, then the oracle may have originated in a disclosure made to him. Scholars disagree as to whether the oracle was original to Isaiah, original to Micah, or some earlier oracle used by them both, while some, denying unity of authorship in each of the two named books, date the oracle as later than both prophets. If we accept supernatural inspiration, then we cannot exclude the possibility of independent revelation in the case of each prophet. It is worth noting that, apart from its use in Micah 4:4, the statement "for the mouth of the LORD has spoken" is found only in the Book of Isaiah (1:20; 40:5; 58:14). This does not, of course, mean much to those who reject the book's unity; but for the rest of us, this reinforces the majority scholarly opinion that Isaiah was the more likely prophet to have received the oracle. Perhaps Micah began his prophetic ministry within the circle of Isaiah's disciples (cf. 8:16) and became acquainted with the phrase in that way.

"In the last days" (v.2) is a technical eschatological expression; so its introduction here relates the vision to the period when God's purposes will find fulfillment. The NT, making explicit the fact that the Messiah comes twice, applies the phrase both to the period of his first advent (e.g., Acts 2:17; Heb 1:2) and to his second (e.g., James 5:3; 1 Peter 1:5). The context of the oracle in Micah suggests that the first stage of its fulfillment took place in the return from Babylonia (Mic 4:1–10), when ruined Jerusalem (Mic 3:12) would be rebuilt and her temple raised again.

"Temple" (v.2) and "house" (v.3) represent the same Hebrew word (*bêt*); so the NIV's "temple" in v.2 is interpretation. The passage has been rendered in the same way in Micah; so the motive for the variation within the oracle would appear to be stylistic.

The whole of chapter 2 makes extensive use of the language of elevation and abasement to convey dignity and pride on the one hand and lowliness and humiliation on the other. Is this uniformly figurative or are we to take it literally in this small section? There is clearly a figurative element here, picturing nations as streams (cf. Jer 51:44)—flowing upwards! Even if the promised elevation of Mount Zion can be taken literally (the thought occurs elsewhere, viz., Ezek 40:2; Zech 14:10; cf. 68:15–18), its purpose, of course, is to underline its spiritual preeminence as the source of divine teaching for the nations. There is no reference to the messianic King in this passage, but the word "established" reminds us of Psalm 2:6 ("I have installed my King on Zion, my holy hill"). Both the hill and the King are secure because they are in the center of God's purpose for his people.

In Isaiah 1:7 foreigners in Jerusalem's environs greedily strip the fields of their crops. How different the picture here! They now come, not for plunder, but in peace, not to rob, but to learn. The analogy of streams is particularly apt, because the major traditional oppressors of Israel were associated with great rivers—the Nile, the Tigris, and the Euphrates (cf. 8:6–8).

In Isaiah's day "the house of the God of Jacob" was at Jerusalem, not at the original Bethel (*bêt-'el*, "house of God" [Gen 28:16–22]), for Bethel was the site of an apostate shrine (1 Kings 12:28–29). The phrase "God of Jacob" underlines the special relationship of the true God with historical Israel, perhaps including the schismatic northern tribes, while "Zion"-"Jerusalem" represents divinely ordained worship and divinely authorized government. So this passage weds together normal OT particularism with the vision of universal worship and peace, which in different forms recurs often in Isaiah.

In 1:10 the word of God was addressed to rebellious Israelites. Here it is eagerly sought by nations formerly pagan—not for mere information, but for practical obedience. As in 1:10 (cf. Note in loc.), "the law" is paralleled by "the word of the LORD."

The issues that set nations against one another do not disappear automatically but are settled by the supreme Judge, whose decisions are accepted. Thus there is no uneasy calm but peace based on righteousness (cf. 11:1–9; Ps 72). In the abolition of every cause of conflict, war itself disappears; and peace, with its economic consequences (cf. v.4 with passages like 35:1–2), takes its place. The words "swords" and "plowshares" occur in reverse order in Joel 3:10. Clements (*Isaiah 1–39*, in loc.) may be right in suggesting that both prophets are alluding to a common proverb.

5 Isaiah frequently accused God's people of not walking in his ways (42:24; 58:2; 63:17). Micah (4:5) contemplated the idolatry of the nations and expressed, on the part of his people, Judah's determination (probably superficial as far as they were concerned) to walk in the ways of the Lord. Isaiah viewed the future obedience of the nations to the true God as a challenge to the house of Jacob to walk in his ways. The nations are not yet coming to Jerusalem to be taught by the Lord, but Israel already has his word. How unthinkable then that she should continue to walk in darkness! The Christian is faced by the same kind of challenge in Ephesians 5:8–20.

Notes

2–4 Some (e.g., Clements) consider the theology of this passage too advanced for an eighth-century prophet. Herbert considers the arguments for treating it as postexilic to be inconclusive. O. Kaiser thinks it improbable that it is by Isaiah but nevertheless regards it as preexilic. Mauchline defends it as an authentic oracle of Isaiah. The arguments for authenticity are presented in detail by H. Wildberger in "Die Völkerwallfahrt zum Zion: Jes. II 1–5" (VetTest 7 [1975]: 62–81) and in his commentary *Jesaja 1–12* (Neukirchen-Vluyn: Neukirchener Verlag, 1972), pp. 75–90. Jensen (p. 86) declares, "Whether or not one finds Isa 2:2–4 isolated from the rest of the teaching of Isaiah may depend on how one judges the authenticity of passages like 9:1–6 and 11:1–9; for those who accept these oracles as Isaiah's, 2:2–4 presents a picture of future blessedness that is not without analogy in the prophet's thought."

3. *The Day of the Lord*

2:6–22

⁶You have abandoned your people,
  the house of Jacob,
They are full of superstitions from the East;
  they practice divination like the Philistines
  and clasp hands with pagans.
⁷Their land is full of silver and gold;
  there is no end to their treasures.
Their land is full of horses;
  there is no end to their chariots.
⁸Their land is full of idols;
  they bow down to the work of their hands,
  to what their fingers have made.
⁹So man will be brought low
  and mankind humbled—
but do not forgive them.
¹⁰Go into the rocks,
  hide in the ground
from dread of the LORD
  and the splendor of his majesty!
¹¹The eyes of the arrogant man will be humbled
  and the pride of men brought low;
the LORD alone will be exalted in that day.

¹²The LORD Almighty has a day in store
  for all the proud and lofty,
  for all that is exalted
  (and they will be humbled),
¹³for all the cedars of Lebanon, tall and lofty,
  and all the oaks of Bashan,
¹⁴for all the towering mountains
  and all the high hills,
¹⁵for every lofty tower
  and every fortified wall,
¹⁶for every trading ship
  and every stately vessel.
¹⁷The arrogance of man will be brought low
  and the pride of men humbled;
the LORD alone will be exalted in that day,
¹⁸ and the idols will totally disappear

¹⁹Men will flee to caves in the rocks
  and to holes in the ground
from dread of the LORD
  and the splendor of his majesty,
  when he rises to shake the earth.
²⁰In that day men will throw away
  to the rodents and bats
their idols of silver and idols of gold,
  which they made to worship.
²¹They will flee to caverns in the rocks
  and to the overhanging crags
from dread of the LORD
  and the splendor of his majesty,
  when he rises to shake the earth.

²²Stop trusting in man,
    who has but a breath in his nostrils.
Of what account is he?

6–9 I am indebted to Ralph Alexander for pointing out the many links of terminology and idea with Micah 5:10–14, including the exact wording "they bow down to the works of their hands." This thus furnishes a further oracular link between the two prophets (see comment at 2:2–4). The sore trials the people are to pass through will evidence that God has abandoned them (v.6) to their enemies (not absolutely, or forever, as 4:2–6 will show), and this itself is an earnest of the great day of judgment on them.

The causes of this judgment remind us of the divinely given constitution for the kingdom laid down in Deuteronomy 17:14–20, set in a context (Deut 16:18–18:22) of much reference not only to the leadership of the people—which becomes an explicit theme in Isaiah 3—but also to the need for separation from the abominable practices of the nations. The kings of Judah may have been native-born, but this did not prevent the people from being contaminated by foreign religious and semireligious practices.

To "clasp hands" may refer to a gesture symbolizing the striking of a bargain. The people were seeking economic and military self-sufficiency (v.7), so that they need not depend on their God; yet at the same time they were groveling to man-made objects of worship (v.8). Possibly the language here is deliberately evocative of the conditions that prevailed in Solomon's day (1 Kings 10:–11; cf. Deut 17:14–20), to remind the people of the judgment that fell on the land after his death. The principles of God's dealings with them had not changed over the intervening years!

10–11 These verses, plus v.12, remind us of the terrifying words of 1:24. The people had been abasing themselves—but in the presence of dumb idols and not the true and only God. Their action was appropriate, but their object of worship was wrong. Even today in the East, physical abasement is a sign of at least formal respect. Here (v.10) it is terror that motivates this lowliness. The proud are eager to avoid the gaze of God, for his majestic presence drives every rival underground in the frantic and, of course, utterly unavailing search for cover. This picture of the people—enjoying the affluence of the land but turning aside to idols till the Lord establishes his sole right to worship by an act of judgment—is yet another reminder of Deuteronomy (cf. 6:10–15). It is noteworthy, too, that the prophet's call came in the context of an awesome sight of God in his majesty (ch. 6).

12–18 When God acts in judgment, it is often to upset human values so that everything can be seen from the divine perspective. Jerusalem's hill is to be exalted above other greater mountains (v.2), but all that is reckoned great by men will be brought low (v.12). The prophet introduced symbols of pride to engage the imagination. Some commentators (e.g., Clements, O. Kaiser) see this passage depicting a judgment that will sweep over the country from the mountains of Lebanon (v.13) in the north to the ships (v.16) in port at Ezion-Geber on the Gulf of Aqaba. This was certainly the direction from which Israel's enemies normally came into the country.

On the other hand, much of the imagery of this passage could be viewed as

Phoenician. It was in the hinterland of Tyre and Sidon that the cedars grew (v.13); it was there too that the highest mountains (v.14) were found, and the grand designs of stone-masons (v.15) and shipwrights (v.16) were to be seen in its ports. "Every trading ship" is a free translation of "ships of Tarshish" (NIV mg.; cf. Ezek 27:25), and these were based in Phoenicia. This land was notorious as a malign religious influence (v.18), not only on Israel, but also on Judah; for Jezebel's family became part of the dynastic stock of both kingdoms for a while (cf. 2 Kings 8:16–8). It was from this quarter that religious syncretism had come during the previous century, and its features could still stand for alien religion. The main point, of course, is that God's act of judgment would humble every manifestation of human pride.

The repetition of the words "from the dread of the Lord and the splendor of his majesty, when he rises to shake the earth" (vv.10, 19, 21) is awesome indeed and is somewhat reminiscent of the repetition employed by Amos in oracles of judgment (cf. Amos 1:3, 6 et al.; 4:6, 8 et al.).

19–21 The terrifyng revelation of the glory, power, and judgment of the one true God will give human beings—but too late—a proper sense of values (v.19). The silver and gold used to make idols (cf. 2:7–8) are at last recognized as worthless in the light of his glory (v.20). The reference to man-made idols reminds the reader of the deep irony of passages like 44:9–20 and 46:1–7.

22 After the idols have been cut down to size by the revelation of the true God in his judicial majesty, the spotlight of the divine contempt focuses on human beings—through whom the religious infection had taken root (v.6)—whose dignity as creatures made in God's image had been cast away by their groveling before idols made by their own hands (vv.8–9, 20), and whose arrogant pride would be abased before God's disclosure (vv.11, 17–21). Perhaps the reference to breath not only suggests frailty but is also an intentional allusion to Genesis 2:7. So, implied the prophet, you are worshiping gods you have made instead of the God who made you!

Notes

---

6 The NIV renders part of this verse "They are full of superstitions from the East; they practice divination like the Philistines." The NEB, however, has quite a different translation: "for they are crowded with traders and barbarians like the Philistines." The Hebrew of the first clause reads literally, "for they are full from the east." Since the days of Lowth, the father of the modern study of Hebrew poetry, most versions and commentators have supplied "diviners" by comparison with "soothsayers" in the following clause. The NEB, on the other hand, adopts an alternative emendation and understands the whole verse in commercial rather than magical terms. See the brief note in Herbert (in loc.) and the longer technical discussion in Gray (in loc.).

9 "Do not forgive them" may be understood as a word from the prophet to God, seeking perhaps a divine vindication of his message (so most commentators or, less probably, as God's word to Isaiah forbidding him to grant them absolution in the name of the Lord. In either case it probably reflects the word that came to him from God at his call (6:9–10). The NIV mg. gives the alternative translation "not raise them up," which would fit the context well but is a less natural rendering of the Hebrew. IQIsa[a] omits the words altogether.

11 The phrase "in that day" (vv.11, 17, 20) is an OT technical term for the Day of the Lord; and Isaiah's use of it could reflect his awareness of the message of his older contemporary in the north (Amos 5:18–20), who declared that this day of God's judgment would not fall simply on Israel's enemies but on herself.

12 The NIV follows the MT as its stands. The RSV, NEB, and many commentators prefer the LXX, reading the second half of the verse as "against all that is lifted up and high" (RSV). Either could be supported from the context.

16 "Every trading ship" is literally "every ship of Tarshish" (NIV mg.). Tarshish was a Phoenician colony in the western Mediterranean, and the ships named for it were sea-going vessels, though W.F. Albright ("New Light on the Early History of the Phoenician Colonization," BASOR 83 [Oct 1941]: 21f.) has argued that they were essentially ore-carrying vessels. The word translated "vessel" is linked by KB with an Egyptian word meaning "ship."

20 The NEB reads "dung-beetles" for "moles" (KJV; NIV, "rodents"). Herbert (in loc.) says, "The Hebrew word must mean a digging creature, but moles do not inhabit rocky places. This beetle gathers animal droppings as food, rolls the dung into a ball and carries it into a crevice. Known as the scarab, it was venerated in Egypt."

D. *God's Judgment on Jerusalem and Judah*

3:1–4:1

¹See now, the Lord,
   the LORD Almighty,
is about to take from Jerusalem and Judah
   both supply and support:
all supplies of food and all supplies of water,
² the hero and warrior,
the judge and prophet,
   the soothsayer and elder,
³the captain of fifty and man of rank,
   the counselor, skilled craftsman and clever enchanter.

⁴I will make boys their officials;
   mere children will govern them.
⁵People will oppress each other—
   man against man, neighbor against neighbor.
The young will rise up against the old,
   the base against the honorable.

⁶A man will seize one of his brothers
   at his father's home, and say,
"You have a cloak, you be our leader;
   take charge of this heap of ruins!"
⁷But in that day he will cry out,
   "I have no remedy.
I have no food or clothing in my house;
   do not make me the leader of the people."

⁸Jerusalem staggers,
   Judah is falling;
their words and deeds are against the LORD,
   defying his glorious presence.
⁹The look on their faces testifies against them;
   they parade their sin like Sodom;
   they do not hide it.

Woe to them!
They have brought disaster upon themselves.

[10]Tell the righteous it will be well with them,
for they will enjoy the fruit of their deeds.
[11]Woe to the wicked! Disaster is upon them!
They will be paid back for what their hands have done.

[12]Youths oppress my people,
women rule over them.
O my people, your guides lead you astray;
they turn you from the path.

[13]The LORD takes his place in court;
he rises to judge the people.
[14]The LORD enters into judgment
against the elders and leaders of his people:
"It is you who have ruined my vineyard;
the plunder from the poor is in your houses.
[15]What do you mean by crushing my people
and grinding the faces of the poor?"
declares the Lord, the LORD Almighty.
[16]The LORD says,
"The women of Zion are haughty,
walking with outstretched necks,
flirting with their eyes,
tripping along with mincing steps,
with ornaments jingling on their ankles.
[17]Therefore the Lord will bring sores on the heads of the
women of Zion;
the LORD will make their scalps bald."

[18]In that day the Lord will snatch away their finery: the bangles and headbands
and crescent necklaces, [19]the earrings and bracelets and veils, [20]the head-
dresses and ankle chains and sashes, the perfume bottles and charms, [21]the
signet rings and nose rings, [22]the fine robes and the capes and cloaks, the purses
[23]and mirrors, and the linen garments and tiaras and shawls.

[24]Instead of fragrance there will be a stench;
instead of a sash, a rope;
instead of well-dressed hair, baldness;
instead of fine clothing, sackcloth;
instead of beauty, branding.
[25]Your men will fall by the sword,
your warriors in battle.
[26]The gates of Zion will lament and mourn;
destitute, she will sit on the ground.

[4:1]In that day seven women
will take hold of one man
and say, "We will eat our own food
and provide our own clothes;
only let us be called by your name.
Take away our disgrace!"

The solemn melody of divine judgment runs on into this passage, which has so
many links with chapter 2 and which may, in fact, have been part of the same
oracle. It is not always easy to tell where prophetic oracles begin and end, but even

recent criticism displays far too much tendency to divide up prophetic material without real necessity.

The generalized but extremely powerful threats of judgment against everything that would challenge the supreme eminence (cf. 6:1) of the God of Israel have put out of sight for a time the actual forms this sinful arrogance took at the time of Isaiah's prophecy (cf. 2:6–9), but this chapter focuses attention on the contemporary situation. The judgment will, of course, fall on the city and nation; but special attention is directed towards the leaders and the aristcratic women.

1–7 The divine titles in v.1, with their stress on power, lead the reader—and no doubt originally the hearer—to anticipate a strong threat of judgment (cf. 1:24). This comes first of all in summary form (v.1); then it is spelled out in more detail.

Most translations have tried to preserve the alliteration in the Hebrew words that the NIV renders as "supply and support" (v.1). Calvin's Latin *"vigorem et vim"* makes the English reader think of "vim and vigor," but, of course, the phrase is expressive of power directed towards the support of human society. As Calvin (in loc.) says, the clause that the words are found in means "God will take away every help and assistance by which you think that you are upheld, so that nothing whatever may be left to support you."

The reference to famine is brief but ominous (cf. v.7); the prophet concentrated on the removal of responsible and trusted leadership. The application of "supply and support" to these people suggested to Mauchline (in loc.) a parallel with our expression "the pillars of the church." Isaiah brings together many different types of leader (vv.2–7)—the military and the civil, the charismatic and the official, the small and the great, and, moreover, the legitimate and the illegitimate. This final element in particular provides a parallel to a somewhat similar passage in the book of Isaiah's older contemporary in the north, Hosea (Hos. 3:4). The people were showing too great a tendency to put their trust in human beings (2:22). The prophet warned them that the objects of their trust were to be removed. Those traditionally respected—"the old," "the honorable," (v.5)—will be violently replaced by the manifestly inadequate and by the base oppressor.

The situation would in fact reach such a pitch that the mere possession of some outward semblance of wealth or rank would attract the attention of those desperately seeking for someone to bring a measure of order to a situation of chaos. The phrase "this heap of ruins" (v.6) anticipates the later picture of a destitute and defeated city (v.26). O. Kaiser (in loc.) makes a most telling comment: "It is astonishing how realistically the prophet is here able to describe the consequences of a total collapse of the state. Anyone who remembers the months that followed May 1945 in Germany will have the sensation in reading this passage of being carried right back to those days."

8–21 The prophet reminded his readers of the spiritual and moral causes of this anarchy. Judah and its capital city were to reach the brink of total collapse, with disaster to follow, because of insolent and blatant rebellion against the Lord. "His glorious presence" (v.8) is another reminder of chapter 2, especially of v.10. It is true that this may come from an earlier period of Isaiah's ministry than the prophecies in chapter 1, but it may well be that all this human proud and defiant independence of God and his will was going hand in hand with scrupulous religiosity. In fact, vv.10–11 have points in common with the appeal of 1:19–20, including some verbal links. Some writers have noted not only the way this passage reflects the Deuteronomic principle of retribution—which is, of course, extremely common in the prophets—but also some links with the wisdom tradition. Whedbee (p. 89) makes reference to commentators who consider vv. 10–11 a late addition to the Book of Isaiah from someone schooled in wisdom teaching. But we may recognize a link with the wisdom tradition without drawing any such conclusion, for Solomon was two centuries dead when the prophet wrote these words. It is the generalizing tone of the passage that reflects this tradition. Perhaps this, along with the reference to Sodom (v. 9), would stimulate the original hearer to ponder the fate of Sodom and how Abraham prayed for the "righteous" in it (Gen 18–19). There is perhaps an implicit doctrine of the remnant here (see Introduction, p. 13).

Verse 12 takes up the theme of vv. 4–5. By his use of the phrase "my people," Isaiah reminded them of the covenant relationship. Psalm 1, a great wisdom psalm, warns us against walking in the counsel of the wicked (v. 1). This counsel is especially influential and dangerous when it comes from national leadership.

13–15 There are many different points of connection between different parts of the first six chapters of this book. The law-court scene (v. 13) here is reminiscent of chapter 1, while the reference to the vineyard (v. 14) anticipates chapter 5. This brings out the thematic unity of these chapters. The repeated Hebrew word *'am* ("people," vv. 12–15) links these three verses to the end of the previous section.

Many biblical passages show the responsibility of leadership among God's people and the exacting nature of his judgment of the shepherds of his people (e.g., Jer 25; Ezek 34; Zech 10–11; John 10; James 3:1). Not only may leaders take people aside from the right path (v. 12); but, as we have already seen (vv. 5, 12), positions of privilege and responsibility may be used to foster self-interest rather than social good. This forms God's major accusation in this dramatic judgment scene. The great titles that close this section (v. 15; cf. 1:24; 3:1) are a fearsome reminder that God not only has the right to judge his people but also the power to carry his judgment into effect. They cannot possibly escape the consequences of their wrongdoing.

3:16–4:1 If there is still some moral fiber in the women of a rapidly deteriorating society, the situation is not without hope; for it is the women who, through the home, have the most formative influence on the younger generation. The arrogant pride seen in the rulers of Judah was, however, just as evident in its women. Those depicted here are clearly the wealthy, whose rich stores of finery had probably been bought by the plunder taken by their husbands from the poor (cf. v. 14).

In v. 9, the prophet linked the look on the face with a Sodom-like parade of sin, perhaps suggesting that all was not right in the sexual life of the community. This passage moves swiftly from the ostentatious posturing of these women as they parade in the streets of Jerusalem (v. 16) to language that suggests far from seemly attempts to attract male attention (vv. 18–24). The judgment formula "in that day" (vv. 18; 4:1) provides a further link with chapter 2 and introduces a catalog of their adornments and other luxurious paraphernalia. This stands in stark contrast to the repeated phrase "the poor" in vv. 14–15.

It is not always easy to account for a change from poetry to prose in the prophets, and the changes in Isaiah are no exception. Certainly here nothing would seem more appropriate. The women themselves may have waxed eloquent about some of these items at times, but the prophet simply lists them. It is God's judgments that deserve the elevated language of poetry, not the showy baubles human beings so often value and crave.

The judgment would come through enemies who would take the Israelites captive, giving them the rough garb of prisoners of war ("a rope," "sackcloth" [v.24]); and the removal of locks of hair certainly suggests that the city would be taken by the Babylonians, for this was what they did to those taken in war. The reference to "branding" (v.24) is also consistent with an enslavement due to capture.

By a swift and yet appropriate movement of thought, Isaiah for two verses (vv.25–26) turned from the daughters of Zion (the literal meaning of the phrase "the women of Zion" in v.16) to the city herself, referred to in 1:8 as "the Daughter of Zion." The word "your" in v.25 is singular. The city and her gates (v.26) are graphically personified; and for a moment, especially in view of the probable allusions to Babylonian customs with prisoners of war, we could imagine we are reading Jeremiah (cf. Jer 14:2) or Lamentations (cf. Lam 1:1–4; 2:10). Isaiah boldly transports us from his confident predictions to their dire fulfillment. Rationalism would transfer all such passages to the exilic or postexilic periods; but the fact remains that they have come down to us with the name of Isaiah prefixed to them, and attempts to remove them remain unconvincing.

Just as swiftly we return to the women of Jerusalem (4:1). Perhaps those pictured here have been widowed (cf. 3:25) through the violent overthrow of the city. In any case the judgment on the city drastically altered the normal male-female proportions in the population. These concerned women are prepared to forego the normal perquisites of marriage to secure its status—or, at least, to gain the protection of a name. If we find this difficult to understand, it is largely because we live in a society that does not place as high a premium on marriage and child-bearing. The interesting links with 3:7 suggest that the same judgment is in view, or at least one with the same kind of effects on the economy of the country. The leading man could not make proper provision for either subjects or wives. We may recognize both the snare of wealth and the economic consequences that sometimes follow national sin without hardening either into a hard-and-fast rule. God's judgments do not always follow the same pattern—though they always proceed from the same principles, for his nature is unchanging.

Notes

1 Since Duhm, many scholars (e.g., Clements, O. Kaiser) have seen the references to food and water as an editorial gloss, placed here to link the passage with a situation of siege and famine, probably at the Fall of Jerusalem. Mauchline (in loc.), however, declares, "There are at least two reasons for accepting it as authentic: the first is that it would be difficult to account for its later intrusion into a passage which, without it, reads coherently and easily; and, secondly, v.7 supports what is said here, that the land suffered from famine and dire want as well as from social commotions."

3 On "the counselor," see Notes at 1:26 and 9:6.

8 There are some unusual linguistic features here that hardly call for detailed comment. There is a full note of them in Gray (in loc.).

12 Clements (*Isaiah 1–39*, in loc.), among others, follows the LXX and the Targum in reading "usurers" instead of "women" here. Mauchline, however, thinks the concept of exactors

ruling is unlikely and accepts the Hebrew as authentic. As he says (in loc.), "The rule of the queen-mother had been experienced in Judah (cf. II Kings 11:1–16), and was not well-esteemed."

13 The MT reads "peoples"; but the NIV, with most other EV, follows the LXX, because the plural does not make good sense in the context.

18–23 It is not easy to identify all the detailed items here. In fact, there is a difference of opinion among scholars as to the nature of some of them. Among recent commentators, see O. Kaiser (in loc.) and also IDB (1:871) and ZPEB (2:164).

---

5. Zion's Glorious Future

4:2–6

> ²In that day the Branch of the Lord will be beautiful and glorious, and the fruit of the land will be the pride and glory of the survivors in Israel. ³Those who are left in Zion, who remain in Jerusalem, will be called holy, all who are recorded among the living in Jerusalem. ⁴The Lord will wash away the filth of the women of Zion; he will cleanse the bloodstains from Jerusalem by a spirit of judgment and a spirit of fire. ⁵Then the Lord will create over all of Mount Zion and over those who assemble there a cloud of smoke by day and a glow of flaming fire by night; over all the glory will be a canopy. ⁶It will be a shelter and shade from the heat of the day, and a refuge and hiding place from the storm and rain.

Chapters 2–4 exhibit a beautiful balance. Brief but moving passages depict God's future purpose for Jerusalem and enclose a longer passage describing the judgment, making its cause clear. The two pictures of the future hope could hardly be exchanged, for the second refers to the judgment and the need for it in particularly meaningful terms for those who had read the intervening passage. This is just one example of the exquisite order found in Isaiah.

2 The great contrast between this section and the preceding one is accentuated by the fact that both v.1 and v.2 commence with the phrase "in that day." This section itself (4:2–6) contains a note of judgment in v.4; but clearly the Day of the Lord, though basically judgmental, introduces also the salvation that is the sequel and consequence of God's cleansing act.

This verse contains a major *crux interpretum* that introduces us not only to the whole question of the relationship of this passage to its context but also to the right approach to the christological teaching of this book. The question concerns the phrases "the Branch of the Lord" and "the fruit of the land." There are three main views as to their meaning.

1. A majority of modern commentators (e.g., Duhm, Marti, Gray, Procksch, Kaiser, Clements) see both phrases as referring to the renewed fruitfulness of the land, taking the word *ṣemah* ("Branch") to mean "produce," which is quite a proper translation. Similarly, Calvin, rejecting the standard messianic interpretation of his day, understood the verse to signify "a rich supply both of spiritual and earthly blessings." Those arguing that fruitfulness is in view maintain that the two key phrases are related in parallelism; and if the second is botanical, so must the first be. It can be argued also that it fits the general context, with its references to famine (3:1, 7) and devastation through war (3:25–26; cf. 1:7–9, 19–20).

On the other hand, it is asked why this is given the special relationship to the

Lord that the first phrase implies and why its appearance and glory are underlined —instead of its character—as provision for human need? For the first objection, however, the reader should compare Numbers 24:6 and Psalm 104:16, and for the second, Isaiah's own emphasis on the beauty of the renewed land (in passages like 35:1–2 and 60:13).

2. Others say the first phrase refers to the remnant of Israel surviving God's judgment. Among modern commentators who argue for this, Mauchline (in loc.) says that this remnant "will rise as a shoot or branch from the stump of the tree which has been stripped to the ground (cf. 6:13). . . . It . . . will be beautiful and glorious, because it is the righteous remnant and is of God: and the fruit of the land which will spring up in this new day will be their pride and glory." The rest of the passage is said to support this interpretation. But, it must be objected, the remnant is there in v.2 apart from these two phrases. The "branch" and the "fruit" appear to be identical, for the oracle is dominated by identical parallelism and other comparative forms of repetitive phrasing. See 49:3, 6 for a similar difficulty in connection with the attempt to make a straightforward equation of Israel and the servant of God.

3. According to the third view, both phrases apply to the Messiah. This interpretation is very ancient and pre-Christian. The Targum renders "the Branch" as "the Messiah." Most conservative commentators (e.g., Hengstenberg, Delitzsch, Young) have taken at least the first of the two phrases to be messianic. The word ṣemaḥ ("branch") occurs in four verses (Jer 23:5; 33:15; Zech 3:8; 6:12) as a technical messianic designation. It is noteworthy that many of those holding the first interpretation assign the passage to a postexilic date, bringing it into a period when the messianic use of the word had become technical and standard! Young (*Book of Isaiah*, in loc.) thought its use by Isaiah stemmed from his reflection on 2 Samuel 23:5, where the cognate verb ṣamaḥ ("bring to fruition") is used. Psalm 132:17 also uses the verb. Young argued too that the reference in Isaiah 3:12–15 to bad rulers would lead us to expect a reference to a good ruler in the prophet's vision of the future. Many commentators generally sympathetic to the messianic interpretation find it difficult, however, to take the second of the phrases in the messianic sense, for nothing like it is so used elsewhere in the OT.

The Bible's use of technical language reveals a tendency for words and phrases to begin in quite a lowly way but, through their use in various contexts, to gather more connotations and nuances as time goes by. "Branch" is a good example of this (cf. "servant" in chs. 42–53). In this way the depth of God's purpose is progressively revealed. The concept of the branch ("concept" is the right term, because various botanical words are used) begins in Isaiah at the botanical level, which is in view here. The famine and devastation wreaked on the land by their enemies showed the Israelites their dire need of literal fruitfulness. The God of new life therefore promised that the future would be marked by such God-given fruitfulness.

The people's need of life, however, was far greater, embracing the nation's very existence—which was being threatened by its foes. There was need of reassurance that the God of new life would make the remnant of his people fruitful too (cf. comment at 6:13). But their deepest need was for the Messiah; thus, he appears as the ultimate "Branch of the LORD" in chapter 11. The reader familiar with this development will see v.2 in terms of both its meaning in its context and the deeper significance this language was destined to have in the rest of the Book of Isaiah itself. (See the discussion on meaning and significance in W.C. Kaiser, Jr., "Legitimate Hermeneutics," pp. 133–38.) Incidentally, this "branch" theme is later gathered up into both the royal (ch. 11) and the servant (53:2) themes, so that the prophetic picture of God's great purpose is both unified and enriched.

3 This verse finds its explanation in v.4, for the holiness of Jerusalem is due to the Lord's action described there. The recording of the names of Jerusalem's inhabitants may seem at first to be simply a record that they are still alive after the judgments have taken place (cf. 1:9), but the eschatological context suggests that eternal life is in view.

4 Both the women of Jerusalem (3:16–23) and her people generally (1:16–20) needed cleansing, and the Lord promised to do this. What does *rûah* really convey here? The NIV renders it "spirit," while the margin has "the Spirit." The word is rendered "breath," "wind," and "spirit" in the OT and is the regular word used for the Spirit of God. It is used in a context of judgment also in 30:28 (cf. 40:7), where the NIV does not take it as a reference to the divine Spirit. On the other hand, *rûah* is linked with the theme of judgment—though in a much milder context—in connection with the Messiah's ministry in chapter 11. Perhaps we should understand it as "a blast of judgment and a blast of fire" and see it as another example of a term destined for enrichment as the book proceeds (cf. comment at v.2 above).

5–6 In 2:–4 Mount Zion is elevated above the surrounding hills; here (v.5) it is protected by divine symbols reminiscent of the journey out of Egypt (Exod 13:21; 14:19–20). The protective symbols would not move, as they did during the Exodus; for the future Mount Zion is journey's end. The word *bārā* ("create"), used in the creative narrative of Genesis 1, is a favorite later in Isaiah to denote realities brought into being by the Creator in his new and final purpose (cf. e.g., 41:20; 45:8; 48:7; 65:17–18).

The glory thus seen over all Jerusalem, and not just in its temple (cf. 24:23; 60:1–2, 19; Rev 21:23; 22:5), will itself be protected by a canopy, normally used for weddings and royal occasions. The bridal implications of 5:1 might suggest that this was what is in view here. It will protect the city from the natural elements (v.6; cf. 32:2).

The picture in these verses is glorious and certainly has not been completely fulfilled as yet. The returning exiles did not experience such idyllic conditions, though this disappointment is traced by Haggai not so much to the purpose of God as to their own sin (Hag 1:5–9). For the general interpretation of such passages as these, see the Introduction, pp. 14–16.

Notes

3 כָּל־הַכָּתוּב לַחַיִּים (*kol-hakkātûb lahayyîm*, "all who are recorded among the living") is an expression drawn from the recording practices of the Near East (cf. 49:16; Exod 32:32–33; Pss 69:28; 139:16; Jer 22:30; Ezek 13:9; Dan 12:1; Mal 3:16; cf. ZPEB, 1:637; TDNT, 1:619–20).

4 דָּמִים (*dāmîm*, "bloodstains") is in the plural, as in 1:15. In this form it normally suggests blood violently shed.

5 The LXX reads, "Then Yahweh will come on every dwelling place on mount Zion and on her assemblies as a cloud by day." Mauchline (in loc.) favors this as "much nearer to the style of the wilderness narrative of Exodus."

---

6. *The Parable of the Vineyard*

5:1–7

> I will sing for the one I love
>   a song about his vineyard:
> My loved one had a vineyard
>   on a fertile hillside.
> 2He dug it up and cleared it of stones
>   and planted it with the choicest vines.
> He built a watchtower in it
>   and cut out a winepress as well.
> Then he looked for a crop of good grapes,
>   but it yielded only bad fruit.
>
> 3"Now you dwellers in Jerusalem and men of Judah,
>   judge between me and my vineyard.
> 4What more could have been done for my vineyard
>   than I have done for it?
> When I looked for good grapes,
>   why did it yield only bad?
> 5Now I will tell you
>   what I am going to do to my vineyard:
> I will take away its hedge,
>   and it will be destroyed;
> I will break down its wall,
>   and it will be trampled.
> 6I will make it a wasteland,
>   neither pruned nor cultivated,
>   and briers and thorns will grow there.
> I will command the clouds
>   not to rain on it."
>
> 7The vineyard of the LORD Almighty
>   is the house of Israel,
> and the men of Judah
>   are the garden of his delight.
> And he looked for justice, but saw bloodshed;
>   for righteousness, but heard cries of distress.

For exquisite beauty of language and consummate skill in effective communication, this parable is virtually peerless. One difficulty of a literary masterpiece is that a would-be translator who is not the literary equal of the author faces an impossible task. Delitzsch (in loc.) says of this poem, "The fugitive rhythm, the musical euphony, the charming assonances in this appeal, it is impossible to reproduce." It is in fact an outstanding example of the way the inspiring Spirit employed human language to convey the divine message.

The parabolic form and the figure of the vineyard dominate the passage, but there is much diversity within this unity. It starts as a lyric, becomes a courtroom drama, and finally casts the figurative aside to identify Judah as the object of the Lord's judgment.

1–2 Role-play was a device used from time to time by the OT prophets (cf. Zech 11:4–17). Here Isaiah assumed the guise of a folk singer. Did he actually sing the words to a folk tune of the day? Perhaps, or the Spirit may simply have given Isaiah the prophecy in lyrical form. Possibly (cf. Notes) the folk singer was really singing— at least at first—a love song and was identifying with the friend of the bridegroom (the "best man" in our parlance; cf. John the Baptist [John 3:29–30]). If this is so, of course, the bride and groom are depicted figuratively in terms of a vineyard and its owner. The use of "vineyard" for a bride is often found in the Song of Solomon (2:15; 4:16–5:1; 6:1–2; 8:12), and it may have been recognized as a stock metaphor. The constant use of assonance in these verses and the choice even of the more gentle consonantal sounds, especially in the first verse, would probably have induced in the hearers a sense of complacent enjoyment. Not till the last clause of v.2 can we see that this was to be a sad, not a glad, story.

3–4 What a dramatic change! The scene shifts to a courtroom (cf. 1:2–17; 3:13–15), and this time the human hearers are to act as assessors as the owner of the vineyard speaks. The new form suggests, of course, that the "vineyard" has moral responsibility. The more discerning listeners may have the first intimation that the parable may not be for their comfort. It would be interesting to know whether the prophet's use of the "vineyard" analogy in 3:14 pre- or postdated this parable.

5–6 The abandonment of such an unprofitable venture was only to be expected; for who would waste further energy, time, and money? But there was more than this. Definite action—the removal of its hedges and wall (v.5)—would be taken against it. The hidden meaning comes closer to complete unveiling when the last statement of v.6 is uttered. What human owner can control the weather? This is God!

7 The hearers fell into a trap skillfully laid for them. The figurative form is cast off and God's people stand exposed as the guilty objects of his disappointment and his judgment. They have condemned themselves, for the tacit agreement of the hearers to the criticism of the vineyard can be assumed. Thus Nathan secured David's self-condemnation (2 Sam 12:1–14), and perhaps Amos that of Israel (Amos 1:1– 2:16). It is not easy to bring out the powerful play on words in the Hebrew here, though some translators and many commentators have made the attempt. One of the best is from G.H. Box (*The Book of Isaiah* [London: Pitman, 1908], in loc.) "For measures He looked—but lo massacres! For right—and lo riot!"

Notes

1 The description of the Lord as "the one I love" is most unusual. In fact, it is without parallel in the OT; for only if Song of Solomon is to be considered an allegory is there any similar use of endearment terms in relation to God. Attempts at textual emendation here have not generally commended themselves to scholars (cf. Gray, in loc.). The suggestion— which has been popular since Lowth—that the poem begins as a love song is well discussed in Clements (*Isaiah 1–39*, in loc.) and Willis, pp. 337–62.

7. Condemnation of Judah's Sins

5:8–30

⁸Woe to you who add house to house
and join field to field
till no space is left
and you live alone in the land.

⁹The LORD Almighty has declared in my hearing:

"Surely the great houses will become desolate,
the fine mansions left without occupants.
¹⁰A ten-acre vineyard will produce only a bath of wine,
a homer of seed only an ephah of grain."

¹¹Woe to those who rise early in the morning
to run after their drinks,
who stay up late at night
till they are inflamed with wine,
¹²They have harps and lyres at their banquets,
tambourines and flutes and wine,
but they have no regard for the deeds of the LORD,
no respect for the work of his hands.
¹³Therefore my people will go into exile
for lack of understanding;
their men of rank will die of hunger
and their masses will be parched with thirst.
¹⁴Therefore the grave enlarges its appetite
and opens its mouth without limit;
into it will descend their nobles and masses
with all their brawlers and revelers.
¹⁵So man will be brought low
and mankind humbled,
the eyes of the arrogant humbled.
¹⁶But the LORD Almighty will be exalted by his justice,
and the holy God will show himself holy
by his righteousness.
¹⁷Then sheep will graze as in their own pasture;
lambs will feed among the ruins of the rich.

¹⁸Woe to those who draw sin along with cords of deceit,
and wickedness as with cart ropes,
¹⁹to those who say, "Let God hurry,
let him hasten his work
so we may see it.
Let it approach,
let the plan of the Holy One of Israel come,
so we may know it."
²⁰Woe to those who call evil good
and good evil,
who put darkness for light
and light for darkness,
who put bitter for sweet
and sweet for bitter.

²¹Woe to those who are wise in their own eyes
and clever in their own sight.

²²Woe to those who are heroes at drinking wine
and champions at mixing drinks,

23who acquit the guilty for a bribe,
　　but deny justice to the innocent.
24Therefore, as tongues of fire lick up straw
　　and as dry grass sinks down in the flames,
so their roots will decay
　　and their flowers blow away like dust;
for they have rejected the law of the Lord Almighty
　　and spurned the word of the Holy One of Israel.
25Therefore the Lord's anger burns against his people;
　　his hand is raised and he strikes them down.
The mountains shake,
　　and the dead bodies are like refuse in the streets.

Yet for all this, his anger is not turned away,
　　his hand is still upraised.

26He lifts up a banner for the distant nations,
　　he whistles for those at the ends of the earth.
Here they come,
　　swiftly and speedily!
27Not one of them grows tired or stumbles,
　　not one slumbers or sleeps;
not a belt is loosened at the waist;
　　not a sandal thong is broken.
28Their arrows are sharp,
　　all their bows are strung;
their horses' hoofs seem like flint,
　　their chariot wheels like a whirlwind.
29Their roar is like that of the lion,
　　they roar like young lions;
they growl as they seize their prey
　　and carry it off with no one to rescue.
30In that day they will roar over it
　　like the roaring of the sea.
And if one looks at the land,
　　he will see darkness and distress;
　　even the light will be darkened by the clouds.

The eighth-century prophets were at one in condemning the social sins of the affluent society of their day, and this passage is particularly reminiscent of Amos; for he too has "woe" oracles (Amos 5:18; 6:1), and his are often structured with the repetition of a key word or phrase. Moreover, just as in Amos 1–2 the threat of divine judgment came nearer and nearer home—so that it pointed eventually at Israel herself—so the woes here came to rest eventually on the prophet himself in 6:5 (see comment there).

8–10 In an affluent society all do not always profit from the increased wealth. Micah (2:1) in a similar "woe" criticized those who coveted the landed property of others. The horror of the prophets in response to the sin of covetousness in its application to land (cf. 1 Kings 21:17–24) was almost certainly due to their recognition of the Deuteronomic principle—expressed also in the Book of Joshua—that the land really belonged to God and that he had made the various tribes and families stewards of it in perpetuity. O. Kaiser (in loc.) appropriately quotes Leviticus 25:23b as summing up the OT teaching about land. "The land is mine and you are but aliens and my tenants."

The first clause of v.9 reads literally, "The LORD Almighty is in my ears" (cf. 22:14), but the NIV has surely translated in accordance with the intended sense. The rich have coveted and appropriated both house and land, and the judgment of God would descend on each. The NIV supplies a helpful footnote that aids the understanding of v.10, striking a mean between some higher and some lower estimates of the quantities intended. Whatever the measures intended, the main point is clear: there will be a minimal return for a large outlay (cf. Hag 1:5–6).

11–17 There are a number of prophetic passages in which drunkenness is condemned (v.22; 22:13; 28:1–8; Hos 7:5; Joel 3:3; Amos 6:6). Most societies consider early morning drinking a mark of moral degeneracy; for the man who thinks first of drink when he awakes is in its grip, and he cannot pull his weight in the work of the day (cf. Eccl 10:16; Acts 2:13–15). Wealth dubiously gathered (v.8) may well be dissolutely spent. The day that starts with drink ends in musical banquets when wine is drunk well into the night (v.11). They have as little thought as pagan Belshazzar for the acts of the Lord (cf. Dan 5), and like him they will suffer judgment at foreign hands. As in the previous "woe," the penalty is appropriate to the offense; for exile removes them from the land on which they had set their affections, and feasting and drinking would come to an abrupt end. "Lack of understanding" (v.13) relates to the outlook described in v.12b.

"The grave" (v.14) is the NIV's translation of šᵉʾôl ("sheol"), the place of the dead. The midnight revelers, their mouth open for more food and drink, will suddenly find that they have become the food of that hungriest of all monsters—death. Solidarity in punishment means that both "nobles and masses" will suffer the consequences of the sins of the wealthy. In 2 Samuel 24:11–13, each of the punishments offered to David by the Lord involved the people also.

Many commentators consider that vv.14–16 are out of place or are a later addition from the hand of a redactor. For instance, Clements (*Isaiah 1–39* in loc.) places them soon after 587 B.C. Such views are largely due to the absence of a "woe," with the consequent disturbance of the ordered pattern of the passage and, for some commentators, the fact that some of the thought has more in common with the great oracle against the proud in 2:6–22. As we have seen, however, there are connections of both image and message between v.14 and vv.11–13.

Verse 16 is often treated as summing up the connection between holiness and righteousness in Isaiah (See, e.g., N.H. Snaith, *Distinctive Ideas of the Old Testament* [London: Epworth, 1944], pp. 51, 53). God's separateness from human beings is not simply ontological but moral, his holiness not a simple synonym for his majesty (though majesty is an element in it; cf., e.g., Exod 15:11) but the basis in his eternal character of his righteous judgments on sinners. The moral nature of divine holiness finds one of its most awesome expressions in chapter 6.

Verse 17 continues the theme, for it shows the affluent agricultural society of the day (cf. vv. 9–10) reverting to a more thoroughly pastoral one, with the animals taking over the ruins. This suggests incidentally that the various woes of this section are directed against the same people, just as the Beatitudes (Matt 5:1–11) relate to the same people but in terms of different qualities.

18–19 Isaiah was fond of the picture of the burden-bearer (cf. 53:6; 57:10 and comments at 1:4, 14, 24). At this point (v.18) he pictured sinful Judah, not now "loaded with guilt" (1:4), as if it was on their backs, but drawing it as a heavy load behind them. The pictures are different, their import the same. Acceptance of deceit, the big lie (cf. v.20), set their feet on sin's wearying treadmill. Paul used a similar analogy in Romans 6:23. In this way it is implied that sin carries something of its judgment within itself.

Verse 19 sums up the people's sin and exhibits its true nature as cynical rejection of the living God and all his ways. They imply that nothing is happening, a taunt Isaiah himself used against pagan deities in 41:21–24. But the "woe" this section commences with is the prophet's witness to his faith that God will act in judgment on sin—in his own time (cf. 2 Peter 3:3–7). Incidentally, it should be noted that the phrase "the Holy One of Israel" here was probably uttered by them with a curl of the lip, in contemptuous reference to a distinctive note of Isaiah's prophetic message (cf. 30:11–12).

20 This "woe" has a link with the previous one (v.18) for "deceit" is there expounded as skepticism about the ways of God. Unhappily it is an easy journey from such skepticism to the total reversal of values this verse demonstrates, for God is the source of all values; and if we are wrong about him, we can soon be wrong about everything. The Pharisees' rejection of Christ showed itself in the same way, for they attributed the works of the Holy Spirit to Beelzebub (Mark 3:22–29).

21 This verse too may have a link with the previous "woe," for the reversal of values expressed there (v.20) may form the basis for the new "wisdom" of the godless, which is antagonistic to the divine wisdom (cf. 1 Cor 1:17–2:16; 3:18–23). The relationship with earlier "woes' also comes into clearer focus when it is noted that the word $`^a\varsigma^a\underline{t}$ ("plan,"v.19), is often rendered "counsel" or even "wisdom."

22–23 Verse 21 condemned the outlook of those who thought themselves wise, while v.22 exposes the folly of that "wisdom." These men assessed themselves as heroes and champions. In fact, these were not sober judgments, for it was their drink that was talking. They had only the drunkard's courage, so ridiculously subjective as to invite scorn. The situation was even more scandalous when we learn that they occupied positions of great responsibility, needing a clear head and an unweakened moral sense. In the place of justice, they acted corruptly (cf. 1:23; 10:1–2).

24–25 The series of "woes" is over. The last of them was pronounced against evil judges; now the supreme Judge begins to declare sentence. The fire of God will burn them; the hand of God will smite them. In 40:6–8 the prophet likens human life to grass and flowers, doomed to wither and die. Here he uses them as figures of judgment because they are so vulnerable to fire. To those familiar with grassland fires, the illustration suggests comprehensiveness and swiftness as well as the inexorable character of the judgment. The cause spelled out in detail in the preceding woes is summarily expressed as rejection of God's word. The word "law" (tôrāh) is technical enough to suggest a reference to the Mosaic law—the basis of Israel's God-given moral standard—and at the same time general enough to include Isaiah's own authoritative teaching.

Verse 25 seems to refer to a specific judgment not to be regarded as an isolated event but as a manifestation of that divine anger that continued to burn against the people. The mention of mountains shaking and dead bodies lying in the streets would be appropriate if Isaiah had in mind the great earthquake in the days of

Uzziah (Amos 1:1; Zech 14:5). This would be a deeply disturbing memory in the minds of many of his hearers.

26–30 What a gift of vivid description was given to this great prophet! The "still" of v.26a becomes a "movie" almost at once and finally a "talkie" in vv.29–30. The picture makes such an immediate appeal to the imagination that it requires little exposition. The great judgment, anticipated by the earthquake (cf. comment at v.25), is to come through a great army from afar, swift, single-minded, effective, ferocious, and altogether terrifying. "A banner (v.26; cf. 11:10, 12 and esp. 13:2) is raised by God as a rallying-point for his punitive army. He will whistle to them like a beekeeper (see comment at 7:18). The phrase "the ends of the earth" (v.26) is to be taken as hyperbole, for the Assyrians were in view. The references to sea and land in v.30 find their best explanation if we notice that the former occurs in a simile while the latter is literal. The prophet's thought moved from the figure of the roaring lion (v.29) to that of the roaring sea; and then, perhaps, calling to mind the literal sea—which might have been a means of escape from the foe if it had been less turbulent—he declared that there was no hope landward either. The cloud of Assyrian judgment blotted out any light that might have indicated an escape route.

Notes

---

14 The feminine singular termination ה (*āh*, tr. in NIV by "their") is probably a reference to Jerusalem (cf. 3:26).

17 The MT here is difficult. Most commentators and translators accept the LXX reading "lambs" as authentic rather than the Masoretic "strangers" because it fits the parallelism better.

25b–30 Many scholars have raised questions about the positioning of this material (Duhm, Gray, Box, Mauchline, Herbert, O. Kaiser et al.). O. Kaiser, for example, treats 6:1–9:7 as an interpolation. His detailed arguments may be found in his commentary at 9:8–21. It must be said that the text as it stands makes consistently good sense. The metaphor of the hand stretched out in judgment occurs in other passages in Isaiah (cf. 14:26–27; 65:2), and it is not impossible that Isaiah could have used a stylized expression of it in more than one oracle. See further comment at 6:5.

---

8. *The Vision and Call of the Holy One*

6:1–13

¹In the year that King Uzziah died, I saw the Lord seated on a throne, high and exalted, and the train of his robe filled the temple. ²Above him were seraphs, each with six wings. With two wings they covered their faces, with two they covered their feet, and with two they were flying. ³And they were calling to one another:

> "Holy, holy, holy is the Lᴏʀᴅ Almighty;
> the whole earth is full of his glory."

⁴At the sound of their voices the doorposts and thresholds shook and the temple was filled with smoke.
⁵"Woe to me!" I cried. "I am ruined! For I am a man of unclean lips, and I live among a people of unclean lips, and my eyes have seen the King, the Lᴏʀᴅ Almighty."

⁶Then one of the seraphs flew to me with a live coal in his hand, which he had taken with tongs from the altar. ⁷With it he touched my mouth and said, "See, this has touched your lips; your guilt is taken away and your sin atoned for."

⁸Then I heard the voice of the LORD saying, "Whom shall I send? And who will go for us?"

And I said, "Here am I. Send me!"

⁹He said, "Go and tell this people:

" 'Be ever hearing, but never understanding;
    be ever seeing, but never perceiving.'
¹⁰Make the heart of this people calloused;
    make their ears dull
    and close their eyes.
Otherwise they might see with their eyes,
    hear with their ears,
    understand with their hearts,
and turn and be healed."

¹¹Then I said, "For how long, O Lord?"
And he answered:

"Until the cities lie ruined
    and without inhabitant,
until the houses are left deserted
    and the fields ruined and ravaged,
¹²until the LORD has sent everyone far away
    and the land is utter forsaken.
¹³And though a tenth remains in the land,
    it will again be laid waste.
But as the terebinth and oak
    leave stumps when they are cut down,
    so the holy seed will be the stump in the land."

The position of this great passage in the book has aroused much discussion. We might have expected the volume of his collected prophecies to begin with it. The book is not alone, however, in deferring reference to the call of God to a later passage (cf. Amos 7:14–15). In fact, our sense of difficulty may well reflect modern Western individualism, for the Bible teaches that the message is far more important than the messenger (Phil 1:15–18). If Isaiah's oracles are arranged according to a plan determined by the message, then we shall see that the location of this chapter is just perfect (see comment at v.5).

Verse 1 contains a date (one of the book's few references to dates); and it introduces a section written in the first person singular, which may be compared in certain ways with the "we" passages in the Acts of the Apostles. The last instance of this phenomenon is in 8:18; so some commentators take it that the autobiographical section terminates at that point. Others take it as far as 9:7, because of the links of vocabulary and thought that bind these later verses to what preceded them.

1 The date of Uzziah's death has been much disputed (see Introduction, p. 5). Isaiah 14:28–32 is an oracle from the year of the death of King Ahaz, and it has a clear appropriateness to the political situation of that time. We would not be surprised, therefore, to find something similar here; and we can well imagine the spiritual value to the prophet himself of a vision of the almighty King when an earthly reign of over fifty years had come—or was coming—to its end. The vision of

the Lord's transcendence never left Isaiah: the exaltation of Israel's great God is a frequent theme in his oracles (cf., e.g., 2:10–22; 37:16; 40:12–26; 57:15).

Perhaps the last clause of this verse relates to God's immanence, though this depends on the significance of the word "temple" here. Is it the earthly or the heavenly place of worship? Virtually all modern commentators assume the former, though Delitzsch is an important exception. Some of the older commentators who did assume that the earthly temple was intended doubted whether the prophet was physically present in it and thought it possible that he may have been transported there in a vision. Young (*Book of Isaiah*, in loc.) also allows for this possibility: "To insist that Isaiah must have been in the Temple as he received the vision does despite to the visionary character of the message." It is really impossible to be certain, but happily it makes little difference to our understanding of the chapter and its message.

2 This is the only biblical passage where heavenly beings are called "seraphs." It is evident from references in Scripture to angels, archangels, principalities, powers, cherubim, seraphim, etc., that there is a great variety among the heavenly beings created by God. This should occasion no surprise, for the created earth too is the scene of great diversity.

The seraphs are bright creatures, for the word means "burning ones"; yet they hide their faces from the greater brightness and the glory of the Lord. In view of Matthew 22:30, it is best to take the reference to feet literally and not as a euphemism for the sex organs. Covering the feet suggests humility.

3 There is no indication of the number of seraphs seen by Isaiah. Many scholars think that he was present at an act of worship in the temple, perhaps at the New Year, and that the antiphonal singing of the Levitical choir was echoed by the heavenly seraphs of his vision. This is conjectural but cannot be ruled out. The apostle Paul evidently believed that angels are present at Christian worship. It is interesting that the chief passage this idea appears in (1 Cor 11:2–16) deals with veiling and unveiling in the presence of God, referred to also here.

The trisagion, or threefold ascription of holiness (cf. Rev 4:8), has been interpreted in reference to the Trinity since the early fathers. Cautious commentators, including Calvin, are inclined to play this down somewhat. He says (in loc.), "The ancients quoted this passage when they wished to prove that there are three persons in one essence of the Godhead. I do not disagree with their opinion; but if I had to contend with heretics, I would rather choose to employ stronger proofs." It is best for us simply to say that—in the fuller light of the NT—we can see the appropriateness of this threefold expression, which also places added stress on the holiness of the heavenly King. We go to the NT for clear trinitarian teaching and to the OT for hints of it.

The theme of divine holiness is of towering importance in Isaiah (see Introduction, pp. 12–13). This man of God could never forget the disclosure of transcendent purity he encountered when he was called to prophetic service (cf. Ezek 1).

The language of fullness, employing the same Hebrew verb (*mālē'*), occurs three times in these verses (vv. 1, 3, 4), twice in application to the temple and once to the whole earth. So this passage, insisting as it does on the awesome transcendence of the sovereign God, also emphatically teaches his immanence. His transcendence is not remoteness, or aloofness but is known through his presence in his created world and temple. Divine transcendence and immanence are always held in balance in biblical theism. Isaiah himself says later (12:6), "Great is the Holy One of Israel among you."

The word "glory" (*kāḇôd*) is used of God in his manifestation to his creatures. The essence of deity is inscrutable, but something of his glory can be seen if God is pleased to disclose it (Exod 33:17–23; Ezek 1:28). The Targum on Isaiah also employs the word in v.1, with its rendering "I saw the glory of the Lord." In John 12:41, after quoting Isaiah 6:10, John said that Isaiah "saw Jesus' glory and spoke about him." This amazing statement is in fact altogether consistent with the high christology of the NT writers, for Jesus is God incarnate, and the same God is revealed in both Testaments. This might in fact suggest that John understood the trisagion in trinitarian terms.

4 God's power is sometimes manifested in a physical tremor (cf. Exod 19:18; Acts 4:31) and his presence in a cloud of smoke (cf. Isa 4:5; Exod 33:9). So the God who normally hides himself from the senses occasionally made himself known in a form accessible to them, and he ultimately did so in the consummate unveiling of himself in his Son (1 John 1:1–4).

5 The word translated "woe" here (*'ôy*) is different from that used several times in chapter 5 (*hôy*, vv.8, 11, 20, 21, 22), though they are similar in form, pronunciation, and meaning. They are, in fact, synonyms, each possessing various nuances ranging from the threat to the sigh. If this part of the book has been arranged with an eye more to its message than to its chronology, this "woe" may have been viewed as the climax of the series that began at 5:8. The reference in this verse to the people's sin strengthens this possibility, the more so as sins of the tongue have found their place in chapter 5 at least twice (5:18–20) and possibly a third time, for acquittal (5:23) was made known by a pronouncement of the judge. This verse teaches us that in order to be an effective channel for God's penetrating word, the power of that word must be felt in the person's own conscience.

It is true that the lips of the prophet were destined to proclaim God's truth; but if he was in the temple at worship (see comment at v.1), the primary reference may be to the defiled lips of the worshiper (cf. 1:15; 29:13). The people of the OT always felt a deep apprehension at the prospect of seeing God (Gen 32:20; Exod 33:20; Judg 6:22; 13:21–22). This must have been underlined still more for Isaiah as he saw even the unfallen seraphs covering their faces in the presence of the Most High.

6–7 To serve God, Isaiah needed to be a clean instrument. It is the God of burning holiness himself (cf. 33:13–16) who provides this cleansing from the sacrificial altar. There are indications elsewhere in the OT of the purifying efficacy of fire (Num 31:22–23; Mal 3:2). Despite the priestly context of both these passages, however, it is too much to say, with I. Engnell (*The Call of Isaiah*. [Uppsala: A.–B. Lunedquist-ska Bokhandeln, 1949], pp. 31–32), that Israel must have had a regular ritual of cleansing by fire. Is there any connection between the fact that the seraphs are "burning ones" (see comment at v.2) and the fact that the instrument of purification administered to the prophet by one of them burns? Isaiah, like many other OT writers, had a strong etymological awareness, especially in connection with names (cf. 7:3; 8:1–4). He may well have learned from this experience that sinful human beings can join in the worship of the "burning ones" only when purified by the fire of God (cf. 4:4). It is his holiness expressed in sacrifice that burns away sin (cf. 33:13–16).

8 As we have already noted at v.3, biblical teaching presents beautiful balance. This is true in relation to a multitude of themes, and another example occurs here. The message of God to Isaiah in vv.9–10 is strongly predestinarian. How appropriate, therefore, that the verse preceding them should place such emphasis on the prophet's responsibility! He is not coerced into service; rather, his will makes its ready response as a grateful reaction to God's forgiving grace. No doubt Isaiah's very response was itself the product of divine grace, but this is not where the stress falls here. Instead, we see him faced with the challenge to personal commitment.

The plural "us" is often linked theologically with v.3 (see comment in loc.) and interpreted in terms of the Trinity. It is an unusual phenomenon, found elsewhere in the OT only in Genesis (1:26; 11:7). Many modern scholars have taken it to be a reference to a council of heavenly beings. There are, of course, many biblical passages that picture God surrounded by the heavenly hosts. Not one of these, however (unless, of course, the present passage is an exception), suggests that he, the omniscient and all-wise God, called on them for advice or even identified them with him in some way in his utterance. What a pagan king may have attributed to "the decree of the watchers" (Dan 4:17 KJV, but note the way NIV renders this), Daniel called "the decree of the Most High" (Dan 4:24). In a context that speaks both of waters and mountains (and so of nature) and of nations (and so, by implication, also of history), the Lord refutes the notion that he consulted others (40:13–14). The plural, therefore, suggests either the divine majesty or that fullness of his being that was to find its ultimate theological expression in the doctrine of the Trinity. (GKC [par. 124 g, n.2] takes it as a plural of self-deliberation.)

9–10 The suggestion, made by some modern scholars, that this passage was written only after Isaiah had already experienced the people's hardness of heart is based on rationalistic presuppositions. It is of the same order as the idea that our Lord's predictions of his passion were manufactured by the church *ex eventu*. Not only did the Lord Almighty know what would occur, but he planned it; for he is King (vv.1, 5). Some commentators consider the phrase "this people" (v.9) to be contemptuous, but O. Kaiser (in loc.) makes the relevant comment that it is not normally so in the OT (referring to Exod 3:21; 5:22; 17:4; 18:18; Num 11:14; Deut 5:28; Josh 1:2; Mic 2:11; and Hag 1:2). On the other side, however, passages from Isaiah himself, like 9:16 and especially 29:13, do suggest a measure of contempt. It is really not possible to be sure here.

The words of God to Isaiah are quoted in each of the Gospels (Matt 13:14–15; Mark 4:10–12; Luke 8:10; John 12:39–41) and twice by Paul (Acts 28:26–27; Rom 11:8). Each quotation is given as a comment on the rejection of God's word in Christ. The synoptic references are of particular interest; for they all occur in connection with the parable of the sower, which, like this present passage, anticipates widespread failure to make proper response to the words but which also, as here (v.13), shows cause for hope. The holy seed of the vision finds its NT counterpart in the good soil of the parable.

Once again we are impressed by the structure of the book; for this chapter immediately follows and precedes examples of wrong reaction to God's word. In 5:24 it is the people who reject it, and in chapter 7 Ahaz refuses it. Note also the statement that God "is hiding his face from the house of Jacob" in 8:17. Through his prophets of that generation, God warned his rebellious people that both the declaration of the word (Amos 8:11–14) and the grace of repentance in response to it were in the sovereign hand of God the King. We should note also that this hardening judgment was pronounced after centuries of his people's defective hearing of his word, and so it may be seen to be judicial as well as sovereign.

11–12 Delitzsch is probably right in seeing Isaiah's question (v.11) to be related to both the duration and the consequences of his prophetic ministry. The tone of the question is one of lament (cf. Pss 13:2; 74:10; 79:5; 80:4; 89:46; 94:3; Hab 1:2; Zech 1:12). It should not be assumed that the prophets found God's message of judgment easy to utter (cf. Jer 1:6–8, 17; Ezek 2:3–8 et al.). They belonged to the nation they addressed and must often, like Jeremiah, have wept for its sins and its certain judgment (Jer 9:1; 14:17). The opening chapters of the book (as well as later passages in it) record material—from the events of the prophet's day (1:7–9) and from oracles of future judgment (e.g., 3:25–26; 5:8–9, 13, 17)—illustrating these verses.

13 The devastation, great as it was to be, would not be total; but even its survivors would have to submit to further judgment. The illustration from nature, however, introduces an element of hope. God has so ordered the plant kingdom that almost total destruction does not always extinguish life. He has a continuing purpose of life for the remnant of his people (see the important comment at 4:2). The word "seed" in this verse suggests a possible link with the promise given to Abraham that his seed would continue and be blessed by God (Gen 17:1–8; cf. Isa 51:2). The concept of the seed may take its place with "branch" and "servant" as subject to significant development within the Book of Isaiah. (See the extended comment at 4:2.) It is purely biological, for example, at 5:10, 55:10; designates the people as evil and under judgment in 1:4 [NIV, "brood"], 14:20 [NIV, "offspring"], 57:3–4; presents the remnant after judgment here in 6:13; and refers to the "progeny" of the Servant of the Lord in 53:10 [NIV, "offspring"]. Most frequent of all is the concept of the seed of Jacob that is destined for blessing (e.g., 43:5 [NIV, "children"]; 44:3 [NIV, "offspring"]; 54:3 [NIV, "descendants"]; 66:22 [NIV, "descendants"]).

How astounding that God should use the word "holy" (*qōdeš*) of the remnant of his people when it has been used already in v.3 in relation to his own transcendent being! This is condescending grace indeed!

Notes

---

1 שָׂרָף (*śārāp*, "seraph") also appears in Num 21:6, 8; Deut 8:15, and in Isa 14:29; 30:6 in reference to serpents. Young (*Book of Isaiah*, in loc.) says, "More cautious commentators . . . have recognized that the only relationship is to be found in the name." See also "Seraphim," ZPEB, 5:349.

5 נִדְמֵיתִי (*niḏmêtî*, "I am ruined!") has been much discussed. Young's note (*Book of Isaiah*, in loc.) is very helpful, and his discussion of the problems of this whole chapter is particularly full. He acknowledges that it is difficult to determine the force of the verb precisely but sees it as meaning "I have been made to cease, I am cut off, undone, doomed to die."

13 Where the NIV renders "But as the terebinth and oak leave stumps when they are cut down," the NEB translates "Like an oak or a terebinth, a sacred pole thrown out from its place in a hill-shrine." This follows 1QIsa^a plus a conjectural emendation. Other recent translations, like the NIV and the TEV, revert to the MT. See discussions in Young (*Book of Isaiah*, in loc.) and Clements (*Isaiah 1–39*, in loc.). Many modern commentators consider the last clause of the verse a later addition, modifying the picture of total judgment given up to that point; for they follow the RSV in understanding the reference to a stump to relate to the tenth before its final destruction. The omission of this clause in the LXX supports this, but it is present in 1QIsa^a and harmonizes with the general Isaianic remnant doctrine. It should be retained.

---

9. *The Sign of Shear-Jashub*

7:1–9

¹When Ahaz son of Jotham, the son of Uzziah, was king of Judah, King Rezin of Aram and Pekah son of Remaliah king of Israel marched up to fight against Jerusalem, but they could not overpower it.

²Now the house of David was told, "Aram has allied itself with Ephraim"; so the hearts of Ahaz and his people were shaken, as the trees of the forest are shaken by the wind.

³Then the LORD said to Isaiah, "Go out, you and your son Shear-Jashub, to meet Ahaz at the end of the aqueduct of the Upper Pool, on the road to the Washerman's Field. ⁴Say to him, 'Be careful, keep calm and don't be afraid. Do not lose heart because of those two smoldering stubs of firewood—because of the fierce anger of Rezin and Aram and of the son of Remaliah. ⁵Aram, Ephraim and Remaliah's son have plotted your ruin, saying, ⁶"Let us invade Judah; let us tear it apart and divide it among ourselves, and make the son of Tabeel king over it." ⁷Yet this is what the Sovereign LORD says:

" 'It will not take place,
  it will not happen,
⁸for the head of Aram is Damascus,
  and the head of Damascus is only Rezin.
Within sixty-five years
  Ephraim will be too shattered to be a people.
⁹The head of Ephraim is Samaria,
  and the head of Samaria is only Remaliah's son.
If you do not stand firm in your faith,
  you will not stand at all.' "

The section of Isaiah's prophecies that runs from 7:1 through 9:7 has a certain unity, not only in its historical background, but also on account of the children with symbolic names who feature so prominently in it. The "day of Midian's defeat" (9:4), which occurs near its close, perhaps reveals the significance of the whole section. The day of Midian was God's great victory over a mighty horde through a weak human leader commanding a tiny force of soldiers who did not even use proper weapons (Judg 6–7). They were forced to "trust and obey," for there was "no other way" that victory was possible in such a situation. The same lesson of trust in the face of superior foes is taught in these chapters in Isaiah. Through things that are not, God brings to nothing the things that are, so that no flesh may glory in his presence (cf. 1 Cor 1:25–31).

1 For the historical background, see the Introduction, pp. 4–5. It is clear from 2 Kings 15:37 that the alliance of the two northern kings against Judah began before

Jotham died. The challenge to the faith of Ahaz, therefore, came early in his reign and, given a different response from his, could have established him in a relationship of dependent trust on the Lord from the very beginning.

The reference to Uzziah may be purely conventional; or it could form a studied link with 6:1, hinting at the undoubted spiritual connection between the two chapters (see comment at 6:9–10). God's supreme kingship exalts him as sovereign, not only over Judah in the days of its earthly king's demise, but over Rezin, Pekah, and the great Assyrian monarch himself. Chapter 6 predicts unbelief; chapter 7 records its historical manifestation.

2 The designation of Ahaz as "the house of David" (cf. v.13) is most unusual. This phrase perhaps underlines the sin inherent in his fear and in his failure to believe; for the security of David's house, to which he belonged, was guaranteed by the divine word (2 Sam 7). There could be just a hint of the same thought in the picture of the trees shaken by the wind; for forest trees, as distinct from isolated individuals or small clumps, would feel the wind's power without being in serious danger. King and people were alike in their attitude.

3 The name Shear-Jashub is, of course, symbolic, as the NIV margin makes clear (viz., "a remnant will return"). We do not know the age of the boy. If his name was given at birth, its choice may have been determined by the disclosure of the future given to the prophet at his call (6:13). There is a double ambiguity in it. It can suggest either warning or hope and also either physical return from exile or spiritual return to God. Perhaps this ambiguity at both levels was intentional, for all four ideas can be justified from one or more passages in the book. Without doubt the element of warning is prominent in the present context.

The meeting place of prophet and king is precisely located; but, unlike the original readers, we cannot now place it with certainty. The reason for its choice is much clearer. An adequate water supply is imperative for a city under seige. The king was probably satisfying himself as to this or making arrangements for its improvement. He was therefore engaged in an activity directly related to the situation described in v.1 and which provided the setting for God's test of his faith and obedience.

4 How emphatic is Isaiah's exhortation! A verb commanding attention—"be careful" —is followed by three others counseling trust instead of fear. This is further reinforced by the description of the two kings. Their anger may have been fierce, but there was little real fire left in them—they were virtually impotent.

5–6 There is a touch of contempt in the way the personal name of the usurper-elect is omitted (cf. "son of Remaliah" in vv.4–5). "The son of Tabeel" (v.6) cannot be identified with certainty, though, in view of the reference to "the house of David" (v.2), it seems most unlikely that he belonged to the authentic royal line of Judah.

7–9 The message of reassurance in v.7 is clear, and the NIV has brought out the sense by its insertion of the word "only" (not in the Hebrew) in vv.8–9. The rulers of the two small kingdoms to the north were but human beings; they could not stand against the decree of the sovereign Lord (v.7). The parenthetical statement of v.8b has been variously interpreted. It is probably best to view the prophecy as fulfilled in a series of events that included Tiglath-pileser's imminent invasion, the Fall of

Samaria to Sargon II, and eventually the racial mixture introduced to Ephraim by yet another Assyrian emperor, Esar-haddon, just about sixty-five years after this oracle. See Young (*Book of Isaiah*, in loc.) for a fuller discussion of the time reference here.

The verbs translated "stand firm in your faith" and "stand" are closely related in Hebrew. The assonance of these two words makes Isaiah's closing words both striking and memorable. They would have stayed in the mind of Ahaz as a somber summary of the message he had received and rejected (cf. vv.12–13, 17).

Notes

2 נוּחַ (*nûah*, "to rest"; NIV, "allied with") is a favorite with this prophet. It occurs in v.19 ("settle") and pictures foreign soldiers descending on the land like swarms of insects. The marginal rendering ("has set up camp in") may convey the intended sense. The prophet was probably saying that Aram's army had established bases in Israel in the combined advance on Jerusalem.

3 There is a full discussion of the topography of this verse in M. Burrows, "The Conduit of the Upper Pool," ZAW 70 (1958) p. 221–27. See also ZPEB, 5:434–37, and comment at 8:6.

6 טָבְאַל (*ṭābe'al*, "Tabeel") may be Aramean, the LXX spelling, (*ṭābe'al*, lending support to this. In this case he was probably the nominee of Rezin. The name, as spelled by Isaiah, could be an intentional corruption of his real name to produce the mocking sense "Good for Nothing" instead of "God is Good." Such intentional corruption was not uncommon; a modern parallel might be Winston Churchill's drawled pronunciation of "Nazi" to make it approximate to "Nasty"! For documentation, see Clements (*Isaiah 1–39* in loc.).

10. *The Sign of Immanuel*

7:10–25

[10]Again the LORD spoke to Ahaz, [11]"Ask the LORD your God for a sign, whether in the deepest depths or in the highest heights."

[12]But Ahaz said, "I will not ask; I will not put the LORD to the test."

[13]Then Isaiah said, "Hear now, you house of David! Is it not enough to try the patience of men? Will you try the patience of my God also? [14]Therefore the Lord himself will give you a sign: The virgin will be with child and will give birth to a son, and will call him Immanuel. [15]He will eat curds and honey when he knows enough to reject the wrong and choose the right. [16]But before the boy knows enough to reject the wrong and choose the right, the land of the two kings you dread will be laid waste. [17]The LORD will bring on you and on your people and on the house of your father a time unlike any since Ephraim broke away from Judah—he will bring the king of Assyria."

[18]In that day the LORD will whistle for flies from the distant streams of Egypt and for bees from the land of Assyria. [19]They will all come and settle in the steep ravines and in the crevices in the rocks, on all the thornbushes and at all the water holes. [20]In that day the Lord will use a razor hired from beyond the River— the king of Assyria—to shave your head and the hair of your legs, and to take off your beards also. [21]In that day, a man will keep alive a young cow and two goats. [22]And because of the abundance of the milk they give, he will have curds to eat. All who remain in the land will eat curds and honey. [23]In that day, in every place where there were a thousand vines worth a thousand silver shekels, there will be only briers and thorns. [24]Men will go there with bow and arrow, for the land will be covered with briers and thorns. [25]As for all the hills once cultivated by the hoe,

you will no longer go there for fear of the briers and thorns; they will become places where cattle are turned loose and where sheep run.

See introductory note at 7:1-9. Is this section to be viewed as one oracle or should we make a division after v.17? The latter hardly seems necessary, as the remainder of the chapter is most naturally viewed as an exposition of the significance of the concluding clause of v.17. Moreover, there is a link between the curds and honey of v.15 and v.22.

10-11 This oracle probably followed closely on the previous one, for it is related to the same situation. It implies (see esp. the reference to "patience" in v.13) that the earlier prophecy has been rejected or at least treated with noncommittal evasion by the king. If there was even a spark of faith in Ahaz, God was willing to give it an opportunity of expression. He responded to Gideon's repeated request for a sign, even though it followed a clear revelation of his saving will (Judg 6:14, 17-18, 38-40). Once again, as in the day of the Midianite menace (cf. 9:4), a superior foe was threatening the nation. God went even further this time in his patience with human weakness, for he actually offered Ahaz carte blanche, the unrestricted choice of a sign (v.11). Reinforcement of such an overflowing gesture of grace hardly seems conceivable, and yet it is secured by the possessive pronoun "your." This reminds him of his special relationship to God as the chosen people's king (cf. 2 Sam 7:11-16). For further comment on this verse, see comment at v.14.

12 Ahaz made his plans, and they did not include God or his will. Ahaz's reply was a monumental piece of hypocrisy. As O. Kaiser (in loc.) aptly puts it, "There are situations in which outward piety and inward unbelief are identical." Ahaz probably had Deuteronomy 6:16 in mind. It would be good to think that this reveals at least some small attempt earlier in his life to come to grips with this book, which the king was obliged to know and follow (cf. Deut 17:14-20, esp. vv.18-19). Just as Satan was later to quote and misuse Scripture in the temptation of God's Son—to which Jesus gave reply from the very verse Ahaz must have had in mind (Matt 4:6-7)—so here a godless king made an inappropriate and unbelieving allusion to what God had said. It is not testing God to do as he says!

13 Ahaz was still addressed as "house of David" (cf. v.2), with its implication of special promises and also of a continuing dynasty; but here the prophet spoke of "my God" instead of "your God" (cf. v.11). Ahaz may have been the current occupant of the divinely secured throne of David; but it was incumbent on him to hear the divine word through the prophet who, unlike him, was in a sensitive and responsive relationship with God. It was that relationship that made the king's rejection of the prophetic word a trial of God's patience and not simply man's. God was weary of his unbelief (cf. RSV and comment at 1:14).

14-17 This great passage is both important and difficult. We will assume its integrity, for the text has come down to us whole; and a satisfying interpretation of it as a whole can be given. The main interpretations that have been given follow below.

1. The mother is royal, perhaps the queen, and so the child is a royal prince,

perhaps Hezekiah (J. Lindblom, *A Study on the Immanuel Section in Isaiah 7:1–9:6* [*Lund: Gleerup, 1958*], *p. 41*).

2. The mother is Isaiah's wife, and so the child is one of his sons (Clements, *Isaiah 1–39*, in loc.).

3. The prophecy does not refer to a specific mother and child but to mothers in Judah generally, who will give their offspring names symbolizing hope in God (cf. 1 Sam 4:19–22) (O. Kaiser, in loc.).

4. The mother is the Virgin Mary and the child Jesus Christ (cf. Matt 1:22–23). (Young, *Book of Isaiah,* in loc.).

5. The mother is a royal contemporary of the prophet, whose child's name would symbolize the presence of God with his people and who would foreshadow the Messiah in whom God would be incarnate. (J.A. Alexander, in loc.). This view really combines 1 and 4.

Before suggesting a solution, it may be helpful to set out the main facts and problems that a satisfactory interpretation must come to grips with.

1. The mother and child must be seen as a sign to Ahaz. In fact, the reference to the house of David may suggest that the sign will be significant for the whole dynasty.

2. Why did Isaiah use the word ʿ*almāh* (translated "virgin" by the NIV and "young woman" by the RSV), and what is its exact significance here? This has been much disputed. See Notes.

3. Does the Hebrew perfect tense in v.14 mean "will be" (as NIV translates it) or "is" or "has been?" Grammatically all three are possible.

4. Does Immanuel mean "God is with us" or "God with us"? Either is possible.

5. What is the significance of curds and honey (cf. v.22)? Do they suggest plenty and perhaps a secure tenure of the Promised Land (cf. Exod 3:8, 17; Deut 6:3; 11:9; 32:13–15), or, in the context of a developed agricultural society, do they represent a mere subsistence diet? Do they simply designate the normal diet of a recently weaned child? Do they even reflect the mythological diet of Babylonian gods, so suggesting his divinity? To this last suggestion it may be replied that it is doubtful methodology to go outside the OT for an explanation of a phrase if a perfectly good one may be found within it.

6. What does v.15 mean? Is the discrimination in view dietary or moral? What age is in view? Commentators vary in their suggestions between two or three years and twenty!

7. Verses 16–17 appear to relate to historical events that actually took place in the comparatively near future. If this is so, how can the child be simply equated with the Messiah?

8. The chapters that form the context of this passage contain a number of other references to children (7:3; 8:1–5, 18; 9:6–7; 10:19; 11:6, 8). Do any of these passages shed light on the Immanuel prophecy?

9. Why did the LXX translators use the unambiguous word *parthenos* ("virgin") to translate ʿ*almāh*? It is the LXX that is quoted in Matthew 1:23.

10. Can we gain any light from a study of the way Matthew handles other quotations from the OT?

Expressed briefly, the main question is can we find a solution that does full justice to the language of Isaiah and at the same time to Matthew's application of the prophecy to Christ? Number 2 and the Hezekiah version of number 1 might seem at first sight to satisfy the former criterion but not the latter. It is doubtful, however, whether they really satisfy even the former. Neither the queen nor Isaiah's wife was a virgin, and there is no clear OT example of the use of 'almāh for a married woman. It seems to be used consistently to designate a sexually mature but unmarried woman. The LXX translators took it to mean "virgin" (see Notes). There are considerable chronological difficulties in the way of identifying the child with Hezekiah. It seems unlikely that Isaiah's wife would be designated "the prophetess" in 8:3 and yet be indicated so anonymously here. It seems unlikely too that mothers in general would be referred to by a singular noun with the definite article, despite Calvin's (in loc.) somewhat uncharacteristic interpretation of "the boy" (v.16) as a general reference. Moreover, one would normally expect a sign to be more objective and specific than a general return to faith and hope among the people (cf. 8:18; 37:30; 38:7, 22; 55:13 is more general but still objective). If v.14 were not followed by vv.15–17, we could make a straightforward equation of Immanuel with the Messiah; but this context raises major problems. These verses certainly imply a close historical relationship between the child and the political situation of Isaiah's day.

Interpretation 5 above seems the most promising. An unmarried young woman within the royal house would shortly marry and conceive. Her son would be called Immanuel ("God is with us"), probably in ignorance of the prophecy (which may have been given in the presence only of Ahaz) and possibly even as a presumptuous gesture to give the support of a complacent piety to the king's pro-Assyrian policy. Before the child is old enough to eat the characteristic food of the Land of Promise in its solid form (and so, if this is meant, well before the age of moral discretion), the Assyrians would lay waste the lands of Aram and Israel, which they did in 733–732 B.C., only a year or two after the prophecy was given (cf. Introduction, p. 5).

The "sign" of the child, therefore, constitutes an indication that the all-sovereign and all-knowing God has the situation completely in hand, and it rebukes the king's lack of faith in him. It is true that the instrument of this devastation was to be Assyria, the very power Ahaz was courting instead of relying wholly on God. But in fact the events of 733–732 not only heralded the downfall in 722 of Samaria—the capital city of the northern kingdom that was a large part of the domain of the house of David in its earlier days—but within a generation led to the devastation of Judah itself (cf. 1:7).

The prophecy was given to the house of David and not simply to Ahaz ("you" in v.14 is plural). In the fullness of time, the messianic Child would be born of that house. He was to be a symbol of God's salvation of his people, not simply from physical foes like Rezin and Pekah, but ultimately from sin (cf. Matt 1:21). He represents the final purpose of God in his person as well as his work. For he is, in fullness of meaning, God with us; and his mother was a virgin at the time of her conception and not simply, as in the case of the earlier royal mother, at the time of the prophecy. Matthew's concept of fulfillment is very wide-ranging and flexible and embraces many different kinds of corespondence between an OT passage and a NT event (cf. G.W. Grogan, "The New Testament Interpretation of the Old Testament," *Tyndale Bulletin* 18 [1967]:54–59).

It is characteristic of Isaiah to introduce a messianic theme at a somewhat general level before spelling it out in unambiguously messianic terms (cf. comments at 4:2 and 42:1). This interpretation, therefore enables us to see the passage as part of a wider pattern in the book. So, we are contending, Isaiah predicted the coming of a boy who would be a sign from God to his contemporaries and who would foreshadow Christ, in whom the terms of the prophecy—abstracted from its historical situation—would be fulfilled in fullest measure. In terms of his heavenly origin and his destiny of suffering, death, and burial, as well as his exaltation to the highest place, where he fills the whole universe (Eph 4:9–10); the ultimate fulfillment in Christ of the sign given to Ahaz embraces in principle the whole range of options presented to that king (Isa 7:11). It is noteworthy that Matthew's next OT quotation (Matt 2:5–6) comes from a prophecy of Isaiah's contemporary, Micah. This contains mysterious hints of preexistence, makes reference to the child's mother (Mic 5:2–3), gives Bethlehem as the place of birth, and stresses its insignificance, thus providing a possible spiritual link with the Midian-Gideon theme (cf. comment at 9:4).

18–19 The phrase v.17 ends with—"the king of Assyria"—should have struck terror in the heart of Ahaz. History has known few races the equal of the Assyrians for sheer cruelty. An international scene dominated by this mighty and ferocious nation was a sure recipe for sleepless nights in the Fertile Crescent, and the prospect of invasion from that quarter presented the mind with an intolerable thought. Yet such was the fate Ahaz was risking by his course of action! The prophet spelled out the consequences in graphic language.

Whistling for insects (v.18) finds mention in a number of classical texts (for documentation, see Young's note in loc.). To create a universe, God had only to speak; to gather his instruments of punishment, he had only to whistle. In the years that lay ahead, rulers in Judah would look to the Valley of the Euphrates and to Egypt for military help, but God warned Ahaz that both areas were to be viewed as sources, not of support, but of great danger for his people. Lest his reference to bees might maker Ahaz think the invasion is to be somwhat selective and limited in its effect, the prophet pictured them settling in places that were not their normal habitat (v.19). Not since the day of Midian (cf. 9:4) had an invading force been so comprehensively and graphically pictured (cf. Judg 6:1–6).

20 Isaiah passed with ease from one vivid picture to another. The old enemy, Egypt, recedes from the picture so that the spotlight may be turned on the new and even more terrible oppressor that appeared on the northeastern political horizon. Shaving, particularly of the beard, was a way of inflicting shame on a defeated foe (cf. 2 Sam 10:4–5). The word "hired" seems peculiar till we realize that the Assyrians were well paid—in land and booty—for their trouble. It could also be a glancing allusion to the king's own inducement to Assyria to come west, though not against him but against his northern enemies (2 Kings 16:7–8).

21–22 In a passage otherwise dark with judgment, this picture incorporates some element of hope for the future. The judgment will devastate the land, but the survivors will find that small resources will yield adequate provisions (cf. 2 Kings 4:1–7). In this way (cf. 6:13) the purpose of God for his people will continue—if only in a remnant. The fact that "curds and honey" are spoken of in connection with a remnant and with a child who foreshadows the Messiah (see comment at 7:14–17) reinforces other evidence of a divinely purposed link between the two in the prophecies of Isaiah (see comments at 4:2 and 42:1).

23–25 The devastation of the country—caused by human foes who are instruments of the divine judgment—will affect the whole economy of the land and will set civilization back a stage or two. The agricultural economy, symbolized by the vine (v.23), will be replaced by the pastoral, symbolized by cattle and sheep (v.25), and even by the regime of the hunter, symbolized by the bow and arrow (v.24). O. Kaiser (in loc.) doubts that these verses are genuine utterances of Isaiah: "The inartistic threefold reference to 'briers and thorns' does not give the impression of being the work of the prophet, whose language is always so forceful." This comment is subjective, for just the opposite impression was made on at least one reader! If the king carried away in his imagination chiefly a picture of a land covered with briers and thorns, then the message was getting through. Perhaps it was even intended as an emphatic allusion to the threat given in the parable of the vineyard (5:6) if this preceded it chronologically.

Notes

14 The meaning of עַלְמָה *'almāh*, "virgin") has been discussed for centuries. See especially J. Orr, *The Virgin Birth of Christ* (London: Hodder and Stoughton, 1907); J.G. Machen, *The Virgin Birth of Christ* (London: J. Clarke, 1958); and ZPEB, 5:886–89.
The variant readings of the DSS ("and he" or "and they") hardly affect the interpretation of the passage.

18 For the eschatological phrase "in that day" (cf. vv.20–21, 23), see the note at 2:11.

23 The word "shekels" has been inserted by the translators because some word for monetary value is implied, and this seemed the most appropriate to the context.

11. *The Sign of Maher-Shalal-Hash-Baz*

8:1–10

[1]The LORD said to me, "Take a large scroll and write on it with an ordinary pen: Maher-Shalal-Hash-Baz. [2]And I will call in Uriah the priest and Zechariah son of Jeberekiah as reliable witnesses for me."

[3]Then I went to the prophetess, and she conceived and gave birth to a son. And the LORD said to me, "Name him Maher-Shalal-Hash-Baz. [4]Before the boy knows how to say 'My father' or 'My mother,' the wealth of Damascus and the plunder of Samaria will be carried off by the king of Assyria."

[5]The LORD spoke to me again:

[6]"Because this people has rejected
    the gently flowing waters of Shiloah
and rejoices over Rezin
    and the son of Remaliah,
[7]therefore the Lord is about to bring against them
    the mighty flood waters of the River—
    the king of Assyria with all his pomp.
It will overflow all its channels,
    run over all its banks
[8]and sweep on into Judah, swirling over it,
    passing through it and reaching up to the neck.
Its outspread wings will cover the breadth of your land,
    O Immanuel!"
[9]Raise the war cry, you nations, and be shattered!
    listen, all you distant lands
Prepare for battle, and be shattered!
    Prepare for battle, and be shattered!

¹⁰Devise your strategy, but it will be thwarted;
propose your plan, but it will not stand,
for God is with us.

This passage (vv.1–10)—and indeed the whole chapter—has the same general background as chapter 7.

1–2 The word *gillāyôn* (v.1) is broad enough to include both a "scroll" (NIV) and a "tablet" (RSV). What is in view is a large writing surface, its form or material unspecified. Its size strongly suggests it was intended for public display, so that it conveyed a message and could be cited later as evidence when its prophecy was fulfilled. Its somber message of doom was to be interpreted a little later (cf. v.4).

"Maher-Shalal-Hash-Baz" probably means "quick to plunder, swift to the spoil" (NIV mg.). This particular Zechariah is unknown (the name was extremely common), but Uriah the priest is probably the king's ally and instrument in apostasy who is named in 2 Kings 16:11. "Reliable witnesses" need not describe their character so much as their position as people of standing in the community.

3–4 Isaiah's wife is called "the prophetess" (v.3) because she was his wife or because, as the one who bore children with prophetic names, she became involved in the communication of the message of God. It is less likely that she was a prophetess in her own right as there is no other evidence of this. If, as seems probable, the events of vv.1–4 are set out in chronological order (though "then" in v.3 is purely narrative and not sequential in the Hebrew), the time involved—including both the pregnancy and the inarticulate babyhood of the child (v.4)—would be between eighteen months and two years. This would place the inscribed prophecy in 734 B.C., for Damascus was occupied and probably Samaria plundered (cf. 2 Kings 15:29) by Tiglath-pileser III in 732 B.C.

5–8 Here, as he so often did, Isaiah moved from literal statement to vivid picture-language, setting contrasting metaphors side by side; then he suddenly changed the second metaphor to another to bring out a further aspect of the full truth. Naaman had contrasted Jordan with Abana and Pharpar, the rivers of Damascus (2 Kings 5:12), and so had justified his initial rejection of God's way of giving him deliverance from his leprosy. The nation of Judah was more culpable than Naaman, for he had been a Gentile; and the contrast Isaiah used is much more impressive than that used by the Syrian general.

"The gently flowing waters of Shiloah" (v.6) certainly refers to Jerusalem's means of water supply and probably to the channel that conveyed a slow-moving stream of water from the spring Gihon (cf. note at 7:3). It is not impossible that the location of Isaiah's encounter with Ahaz in 7:3 has determined the language here. The challenge to the faith of the king may have been delivered to him at a place that here symbolized the very confidence in God (cf. Ps 46:4–5) that he had rejected. Verse 6 shows in fact that the die was cast and the king and his people were committed to a course of trust in Assyria, not in God.

The NIV's "rejoices over," though a little free, brings out the almost certain meaning of the language. The people were whooping with delight at the prospect of the downfall of the two northern kings.

"The River" (v.7) without further explanation in the OT is always the Euphrates (cf. Josh 24:15). The metaphor is immediately explained as "the king of Assyria with all his pomp," the final phrase of which is seen by Young (*Book of Isaiah*, in loc.) as a genuine Isaianic touch (cf. 10:16; 16:14; 17:3–4). Rivers in flood are viewed ambivalently in areas where this natural phenomenon is important. Normal flooding benefits the ground and its produce; abnormal flooding threatens crops and, if extreme, the lives of the people. This exceptional inundation of foreign troops would move inexorably southward, not respecting the border between Israel and Judah. The deluge would almost—but not quite—submerge the whole nation, for above the neck was the head, Judah's capital, Jerusalem (v.8; cf. 1:7–9). Here again then, in the midst of a terrifying threat of judgment, the remnant theme reminds us of God's continuing purpose and grace (cf. also 7:21–22).

The metaphor suddenly changes. It seems that the Assyrian army is no longer a river in flood but a predator of the sky (cf. Ezek 17; Hos 8:1). But is this really what the prophet meant to convey? The outspread wings could belong to the Lord (v.7), so that the image is one of protection (cf. Pss 17:8; 36:7; 91:4; Matt 23:37) and not judgment, amplifying in this way the promise implicit in "reaching up to the neck." The protection of the capital was the earnest of an ultimate purpose of God for the whole land. So the assurance contained in the name Immanuel (7:14; cf. 8:10) would be justified by events.

9–10 The rebellious confidence of v.6b and the confident taunt of vv.9–10 occupy different worlds. The former belongs to the world of trust in human alliances and weapons, the latter is the exultant cry of faith in God. Its theme is very similar to that of Psalm 2, both passages having messianic overtones. Both generalize rather than specify particular foes, for they state a great principle that is for ever true: God's purpose is proof against all that people or nations—any person or nation—can do. They imply that not only human power (v.9; cf. Ps 9) but also human wisdom (v.10) must fall before the power and wisdom of God (cf. 9:4–6; 1 Cor 1:24–27).

Notes

1 See D.J. Wiseman, "Assyrian Writing-Boards," *Iraq* 17, Part 1 (1955).
"An ordinary pen" could mean just that and no more, or it could mean that the inscription was intended to be read by the common man.
The NIV omits לְ (*le*), normally translated "for," before the name of the boy. The significance of this is uncertain, but most commentators consider it to refer to possession.

6 Young (*Book of Isaiah*), who had an eye and an ear for paronomasia, notes it in מָאַס (*mā'as*, "rejected") and מְשׂוֹשׂ (*meśôś*, "rejoiced"). Isaiah abounds in wordplay of this kind, which could well have been reinforced by voice inflection on the part of the speaker.

9 The word רֹעוּ (*rō'û*—"Raise the war cry" (NIV) and "Do your worst" (mg.)—is difficult in form. Either translation is possible, but there are other options for the translator (cf. Gray, in loc.).

12. *Isaiah and His Children as Signs and Wonders*

8:11–18

[11]The LORD spoke to me with his strong hand upon me, warning me not to follow the way of this people. He said:

[12]"Do not call conspiracy
   everything that these people call conspiracy;
do not fear what they fear,
   and do not dread it.
[13]The LORD Almighty is the one you are to regard as holy,
   he is the one you are to fear,
   he is the one you are to dread,
[14]and he will be a sanctuary,
   and for both houses of Israel he will be
a stone that causes men to stumble
   and a rock that makes them fall.
And for the people of Jerusalem he will be
   a trap and a snare.
[15]Many of them will stumble,
   they will fall and be broken,
   they will be snared and captured."

[16]Bind up the testimony
   and seal up the law among my disciples.
[17]I will wait for the LORD,
   who is hiding his face from the house of Jacob
I will put my trust in him.

[18]Here am I, and the children the LORD has given me. We are signs and symbols in Israel from the LORD Almighty, who dwells on Mount Zion.

Parts of 6:1–8:18 are written in the first person singular, and the first plural occurs in 9:6, so that over three chapters have an autobiographical atmosphere. In the vision in which he was called (6:9–13) and here again, the Lord had spoken directly to the prophet about his ministry.

11 In some way perhaps distinct from but related to the normal process of prophetic inspiration, the hand of the Lord was on the prophet (cf. 1 Kings 18:46 [Heb.]; 2 Kings 3:15; Ezek 1:3; 3:14; Jer 15:17). He was under a special, divine constraint. He may have been troubled at his increasing isolation from the people he was called to address with the word and who persisted in rejecting it (cf. 6:9–10; 8:8).

12–15 A number of conjectural emendations have been suggested to aid our understanding of this passage, but none has commanded general scholarly approval. The text makes excellent sense as it stands and should be approached in its integrity. The NIV margin takes *qešer* in the more formal sense of a treaty, while the text understands it in its more usual sense of a conspiracy. But if God was speaking here of a conspiracy, who was under criticism? The commentators are divided, some taking the verse to be a reference to the political situation Ahaz was involved in through the threat of the two northern kings, others thinking that it was Isaiah and his disciples (v.16; the verbs in v.12 are plural) who were under criticism from the people. If v.12b balances v.12a, the former interpretation is the more likely.

Isaiah and those who welcomed his message ("you" in v.13a is plural; cf. v.18) were to epitomize the response all the people should have made to his message (cf. 7:2), for a deep reverence for God (cf. 29:23) banishes the fear of man. *Miqdāš* ("sanctuary," v.14) comes from the same root as *taqdîšû* ("you are to regard as holy," v.13). God will himself be a holy place in the midst of his people (cf. Exod 40:34–38; John 1:14; Rev 21:3).

The prophet has already shown in his language that he regarded the division of the kingdom as a tragedy of divine judgment (7:17). Both houses will face further judgment from him because of their attitude in the present crisis, though the mention of Jerusalem suggests he had Judah chiefly in mind. Perhaps he took the judgment of apostate Israel for granted.

Isaiah used two analogies to picture this judgment. God is often described in the OT as a Rock (e.g., Deut 32:4, 15, 18; Pss 18:2; 71:3), normally with implications of shelter and refuge. Here the prophet turned this familiar figure against the people. God the Rock is for his people who trust him, but he is against those who refuse to believe. To them he will be either a boulder over which a man falls in the darkness or loose rock at the edge of a ravine. Isaiah has already pictured men under the divine hand of judgment having to become hunters again (7:24); now he speaks of God as the divine hunter, who uses bird-snares and spring-traps as toils for his victims.

The NT writers saw the ultimate, divinely given object of faith to be Christ. Men reveal their attitude to God by their faith in Christ or by their rejection of him; so the NT writers applied this prophecy to him (Matt 21:44; Luke 2:34; Rom 9:33; 1 Peter 2:8). The importance of this passage for the NT is shown by the fact that so many different NT writers quote or allude to it (see also the comments at 28:16).

It is impossible in English to convey the terrifying force of the seven Hebrew words that constitute v.15. All five of the verbs end with the same long vowel, and four of these open with the same letter and follow one another in unbroken sequence. We may essay something like the following: "They will stumble, many of them, they will fall, be smashed, snared, seized." This conveys a little of the sentence's form but does scant justice to its extreme terseness or to its auditory power.

16–17 These verses are often taken to mean that the prophet turned from public ministry for a while to concentrate on those gathered around him who had accepted his message. In this way God's face would be hidden in judgment from the mass of the people. In substance this interpretation must be correct, but it should be recognized that "testimony" and "law" (v.16) may well refer to an actual document, the written record of the prophet's message. O. Kaiser (in loc.) says, "The literal interpretation of a passage must be preferred as long as it can be maintained meaningfully and without artificiality." This written record was literally sealed (cf. 29:11; Jer 32:14)—possibly in the presence of witnesses (cf. 8:1–2)—so that it could not be altered. In view of this, the theory of Carroll and others that the book of Isaiah and other prophetic writings are full of "reinterpretative adjustment of expectations to facts" (Carroll, "Prophecy Failed," p. 112) would, if it were true, introduce into the history of Israel's literature a type of redactor Isaiah would have rejected with horror as no spiritual brother. Incidentally, the DSS have made us familiar with the notion of sealed books.

Hiding the face (v.17) implies judgment (Hab 1:13; of Num 6:25–26; Pss 31:16; 80:3, 7,19). Although persistent rejection of God's word has led to its withdrawal (cf. 1 Sam 28:6; Amos 8:11–13), the prophet, who had welcomed that word and became its channel, reposed confidence in God and in the fulfillment of it. Presumably his prophetic activity ceased for a while, perhaps till after the overthrow of Rezin and Pekah, which would then confirm the word of God through him.

18 Meanwhile, Isaiah and his children with their symbolic names were an eloquent visible message from God. Like Immanuel (cf. 7:14), they were signs pointing beyond themselves to the Lord and his word. O. Kaiser suggests that the words "here am I" are a conscious parallel to 6:8. If this is so, then they demonstrate the prophet's conviction that his establishment of a family with symbolic names was an authentic part of the ministry God called him to.

This section of Isaiah's prophecy raises fascinating questions in view of the way the NT writers used it. First Peter 3:14–15 applies 8:12–13 to Christ in such a way as to show Peter's unqualified acceptance of Christ's deity. The NT teaches that in Christ the sanctuary of God is among his people, for John 1:14 might be translated "the Word became flesh and tabernacled among us"; and the thought occurs in other NT passages (e.g., John 2:19–21; Eph 2:21–22). Admittedly there is no clear evidence that this Isaianic verse was in the minds of the NT writers concerned. It is otherwise with the theme of the stone of stumbling, which is quoted or alluded to with reference to Christ in several passages (e.g., Luke 20:18; Rom 9:32; 1 Peter 2:8; for its use in Nunc Dimittis, see this expositor's "Light and Stone," pp. 151–67).

In this way Isaiah began to weave a darker thread into the messianic tapestry of his book, though his color assumes a lighter shade in 28:16, where the Stone is viewed as the object of faith, not of unbelief as it is here. The NT writers have sometimes been accused of importing christological meaning into passages like this where none was intended, but this is hardly warranted when the passage used occurs in a context where the messianic king is himself described in divine terms (see 9:6–7 and comments there; cf. 7:14). C.H. Dodd (*According to the Scriptures* [London: Nisbet, 1952]) has demonstrated how full of Christ the NT writers saw this part of Isaiah to be.

Young (*Book of Isaiah*, in loc.) has given a conspectus of interpretations of Isaiah 8:16–18, and the reader will discover that the application of these verses to Christ in Hebrews 2:13 has been justified in more than one way. Perhaps it is best to view Isaiah and his disciples here as foreshadowing Christ and his church, especially as Christ himself was a prophet and his disciples, who formed the nucleus of the church, were—like those of Isaiah—themselves a remnant of Israel, committed to God's word in him whom others had rejected. Literally, Israel's children were, so far as we know, but two; figuratively they included his disciples. This would then make this passage somewhat uniform with 7:14–17 as we have interpreted that earlier passage, for in both Christ is presented in type. This would mean then that both the child Immanuel and Isaiah and his children would constitute the same kind of sign (cf. 7:11, 14; 8:18).

Notes

12–14 A comparison of the NIV and the NEB will reveal the extent to which the latter employs conjectural emendation here.

13. *The Light and the Child*

8:19–9:7

> [19]When men tell you to consult mediums and spiritists, who whisper and mutter, should not a people inquire of their God? Why consult the dead on behalf of the living? [20]To the law and to the testimony! If they do not speak according to this word, they have no light of dawn. [21]Distressed and hungry, they will roam through the land; when they are famished, they will become enraged and, looking upward, will curse their king and their God. [22]Then they will look toward the earth and see only distress and darkness and fearful gloom, and they will be thrust into utter darkness.
>
> [9:1]Nevertheless, there will be no more gloom for those who were in distress. In the past he humbled the land of Zebulun and the land of Naphtali, but in the future he will honor Galilee of the Gentiles, by the way of the sea, along the Jordan—
>
>> [2]The people walking in darkness
>>   have seen a great light;
>> on those living in the land of the shadow of death
>>   a light has dawned
>> [3]You have enlarged the nation
>>   and increased their joy;
>> they rejoice before you
>>   as people rejoice at the harvest,
>> as men rejoice
>>   when dividing the plunder.
>> [4]For as in the day of Midian's defeat,
>>   you have shattered
>> the yoke that burdens them,
>>   the bar across their shoulders,
>>   the rod of their oppressor,
>> [5]Every warrior's boot used in battle
>>   and every garment rolled in blood
>> will be destined for burning,
>>   will be fuel for the fire.
>> [6]For to us a child is born,
>>   to us a son is given,
>>   and the government will be on his shoulders.
>> And he will be called
>>   Wonderful Counselor, Mighty God,
>>   Everlasting Father, Prince of Peace.
>> [7]Of the increase of his government and peace
>>   there will be no end.
>> He will reign on David's throne
>>   and over his kingdom,
>> establishing and upholding it
>>   with justice and righteousness
>>   from that time on and forever.
>> The zeal of the LORD Almighty
>>   will accomplish this.

There is undoubtedly a close connection between this section and that preceding it, for the atmosphere of occult darkness in which it opens is due to man's reaction to the hiding of God's face (vv. 17); and the law and testimony of v. 16 recur in v. 20.

19–20 The law strictly forbade necromancy and other occult practices (v. 19; cf. Lev

19:31; 20:6–7; Deut 18:9–14). It was when God no longer spoke to him that Saul sought out a witch (1 Sam 28:6–8), and we have already seen (3:2) that soothsayers had a tolerated place within the nation of Isaiah's day. The words "whisper and mutter" not only describe the low tones the occult practitioners gave their alleged messages in but invite a contrast with the clear and distinct word of prophecy.

Verse 20 introduces the theme of divine light, which is important later in the passage. The true source of light is God's word, for God is himself light (10:17; cf. 1 John 1:5). The dawning light of God within a man provides its own evidence in the way God's word governs his speech, if he professes to be the mouthpiece of God.

21–22 The Assyrian invasions would bring an acute food shortage (cf. 3:1; 7:23–25). Hunger would foster anger, which the Israelites would blame, in part correctly, on their apostate king and, quite wrongly, on their God (v.21; cf. Rev 16:11, 21). As there is none from higher authority, they seek around them alleviation of their distress (v.22). The picture of total darkness here goes even beyond that in 5:30 and is comparable to 60:2, in a context that, like this, also promises new light from the God of grace.

9:1–2 Verse 1 is numbered 8:23 in the MT, the verses following as 9:1, etc., to the end of chapter 9. Verse 1a clearly links up with the end of chapter 8. Despite the fact that Israel had rejected God's word through Isaiah (8:11, 17, 19–20), God has planned to give his people light again, though the timing of this is not specified. The humbling of the lands of Zebulun and Naphtali refers of course to the invasion and annexation of the northern parts of Israel by Tiglath-pileser III in 733/732 B.C. (see Introduction, p. 5). This is made very clear when we consider the other geographical references here, for "the way of the sea" almost certainly refers to Sharon or Philistia, while "Galilee of the Gentiles" is probably Gilead and southeast Syria. The Assyrians carved out three provinces for themselves from these areas. These lands, the first to feel the ominous tread of the warrior's boot (v.5), would be the first to see the new and great light God would focus on Israel (cf. 60:1–3). Matthew rightly saw the fulfillment of this in the ministry of Jesus in Galilee (Matt 4:15–16; cf. Luke 1:79; John 8:12; cf. John 7:52 with its reference to Galilee).

In v.2, as in several of the succeeding verses, past tenses are used to speak of events that, though future, are certain because they are divinely planned and predicted through an authentic prophet of God. These prophetic perfects serve to present faith's faculty of imagination with the assurance of things hoped for (cf. Heb 11:1).

3–5 At this point the atmosphere of great joy that entered the prophecy at v.1, becoming stronger in v.2, turns into exultant praise as the prophet, anticipating the people's own future joy in their God (cf. ch. 12), turned to address him. National enlargement (v.3; cf. 54:1–3) probably presupposes conditions of peace and prosperity under the blessing of God. Both the farmer and the soldier have their times of joy at the climax of their work and these provide illustrations of the joy that is to come to God's people. For the second of these, compare perhaps 53:12.

"The day of Midian" (v.4) has been rightly interpreted by the NIV as the day of Midian's defeat. The Bible is full of pregnant phrases that contain great power of suggestion—and nowhere more so in the OT than in the Book of Isaiah. The appropriateness of this phrase can be clearly seen when we recall the historical situation:

a vast multitude of the enemy swarming all over the land (Judg 6:1–6; cf. Isa 8:7–8); the giving of a sign (Judg 6:17–22; cf. Isa 7:11–14); the emphasis on faith in God and not dependence on man (Judg 7; cf. Isa 7:9; 8:12); and, perhaps, the defeat of great forces through apparently insignificant means (three hundred men in the case of Gideon, and the child of promise here). Most of all, of course, the passage promises total redemption by the Lord. Israel was to be utterly delivered from the oppressor (cf. 10:5; 14:25, and esp. 10:24–27 and comments there).

Isaiah did not picture the resultant peace abstractly but, as is so characteristic of him, in vivid pictures. The boot of the soldier that had tramped across Israel's territory and his garment impregnated with the blood of the dead when he lay down to sleep (v.5) would be as obsolete as the sword (2:4).

6–7 The introductory conjunction "For" is very important here (v.6). All these wonderful events must have an adequate cause. The word "child" is in a position of emphasis. The first person plural "us" suggests a link with 7:14 (see mg. there). Just as the theme of the Branch of the Lord (see extended comment at 4:2) becomes more and more explicitly messianic, so it is with the motif of the child. If the child of Isaiah 7:14–16 (see extended comment there) typifies the ultimate divine Christ, the child of these verses *is* that Christ. It is true that monarchs of the Near East often received exaggerated adulation from their subjects, especially at their enthronement and at subsequent kingdom renewal cermonies. This is not Mesopotamia, however, but Judah, and Hebrew prophecy was founded on truth, not flattery. OT prophets did not hesitate to speak stern words of judgment to their political overlords (cf. e.g., 2 Sam 12:7–12; 1 Kings 21:20–24). To speak to monarchs words that could not be taken at their face value was hardly consistent with their calling.

The passage does not necessarily imply that the child is to be a boy-king. In fact, Isaiah may not have regarded that as a blessing (cf. 3:4, 12). The context says much about children; so the child is spoken of in terms of his birth. The tenderness of the child also suggests a comparison with the defeat of Midian's army by Gideon's small band of men (Judg 6–7), a comparison reinforced by the dual reference to the shoulder (cf. v.4).

It seems likely that the prophet intended us to understand that the child has four names, not five (cf. v.6, text and mg.). The first two suggest divine wisdom and power (cf. 11:2; 1 Cor 1:24), for the word translated "wonderful" has overtones of deity. The last two set forth the ends he accomplished by the exercise of these attributes—his fatherly care of his people and the bringing of peace with all its attendant blessings. In the context this quartet of names comes to its climax with "Prince of Peace," as a glance at vv.4–5 makes clear. Its implications are spelled out in v.7.

The word "increase" combined with the phrase "his [i.e., David's] kingdom" suggest that the prophecy has in view much more than a particularly great king of Judah (cf. 2 Sam 7:12–16). David's kingdom went well beyond this; in fact, its boundary extended far beyond the traditional "Dan to Beersheba" limits of Canaan proper (2 Sam 8). The language of this verse—in which a picture of peace with righteousness comes before the reader—is reminiscent of a pre-Davidic ruler of Jerusalem: Melchizedek (Gen 14:18; cf. Heb 7:2). The harmonious linking of peace and righteousness occurs again, with more detailed exposition, in 11:1–9.

Since the beginning of chapter 7, the prophet has been making the most amazing disclosures in the name of the Lord; and these have come to a great climax in these two verses. The reader is likely to echo the wondering awe of the mother of this child and cry out, "How will this be?" (Luke 1:34). The prophet anticipated such a question in the closing sentence of this oracle. In fact, both the advent of the Messiah and the blessing of his people, the remnant of Israel, are guaranteed by the zeal of the Lord (cf. 37:32).

Notes

9:2 [1MT] צַלְמָוֶת (ṣalmāwet, "the shadow of death") is rendered "land of darkness" in the NIV margin. It is a composite word and may mean either, depending on its division and derivation. Either would be appropriate to the context. See Gray (in loc.) and Young (*Book of Isaiah*, in loc.).

3 [2MT] The MT and 1QIsa read "and not increased their joy." The omission of the negative לֹא (lō᾿) without even marginal comment by the NIV reflects the views of most modern commentators, though Hengstenberg and some others have accepted it as genuine. Probably we should omit it, with the LXX, as a probable corruption of לוֹ (lô, "to him").

6 The rendering "Wonderful, Counselor" (NIV mg.), familiar to us from the KJV and the musical phrasing of Handel's *Messiah*, destroys the symmetry but is not impossible. Young (*Book of Isaiah*, in loc.) has a lengthy note on the translation and interpretation of the names in which he argues that the first three of the four names imply deity.

14. *The Judgment of Ephraim*

9:8–10:4

⁸The Lord has sent a message against Jacob;
    it will fall on Israel.
⁹All the people will know it—
    Ephraim and the inhabitants of Samaria—
who say with pride
    and arrogance of heart,
¹⁰"The bricks have fallen down,
    but we will rebuild with dressed stone;
the fig trees have been felled,
    but we will replace them with cedars."
¹¹But the Lord has strengthened Rezin's foes against them
    and has spurred their enemies on.
¹²Arameans from the east and Philistines from the west
    have devoured Israel with open mouth.

Yet for all this, his anger is not turned away,
    his hand is still upraised.

¹³But the people have not returned to him who struck them,
    nor have they sought the Lord Almighty.
¹⁴So the Lord will cut off from Israel both head and tail,
    both palm branch and reed in a single day;
¹⁵the elders and prominent men are the heads,
    the prophets who teach lies are the tail.

16Those who guide this people mislead them,
and those who are guided are led astray.
17Therefore the Lord will take no pleasure in the young men,
nor will he pity the fatherless and widows,
for everyone is ungodly and wicked,
every mouth speaks vileness.
Yet for all this, his anger is not turned away,
his hand is still upraised.

18Surely wickedness burns like a fire;
it consumes briers and thorns,
it sets the forest thickets ablaze,
so that it rolls upward in a column of smoke.
19By the wrath of the Lord Almighty
the land will be scorched
and the people will be fuel for the fire;
no one will spare his brother.
20On the right they will devour,
but still be hungry;
on the left they will eat,
but not be satisfied.
Each will feed on the flesh of his own offspring;
21 Manasseh will feed on Ephraim, and Ephraim
on Manasseh;
together they will turn against Judah.

Yet for all this, his anger is not turned away,
his hand is still upraised.

10:1Woe to those who make unjust laws,
to those who issue oppressive decrees,
2to deprive the poor of their rights
and withhold justice from the oppressed of my people,
making widows their prey
and robbing the fatherless.
3What will you do on the day of reckoning,
when disaster comes from afar?
To whom will you run for help?
Where will you leave your riches?
4Nothing will remain but to cringe among the captives
or fall among the slain.

Yet for all this, his anger is not turned away,
his hand is still upraised.

Why has an oracle against the northern kingdom been incorporated into the collected prophecies of Isaiah at this point? The threat of Syria and Ephraim/Israel against Judah and the associated Assyrian move against the petty states of the Mediterranean seaboard form the background to everything from the beginning of chapter 7; so such an oracle is not out of place in this setting. Moreover, as some commentators have suggested, the prophecy of the child's universal reign on the throne of David (v.7) would remind the reader of the defection of the northern tribes (cf. 7:17; 11:13).

The oracle stresses God's coming judgment because the northern kingdom was continuing its impenitent rebellion against the Lord. The refrain found throughout this section in (9:12, 17, 21; 10:4; cf. 5:25 and note there) is reminiscent of Amos 1:3, 6 et al.; 4:6, 8–11). To an audience accustomed to the poetic diction of the prophets, it must have sounded as the recurring thunderclap that heralds the fierce storm of judgment. Some time between 734 and 722 B.C. would be an appropriate date for this oracle.

8–12 The word of God has great power, as Isaiah himself recognized (55:10–11; cf. Gen 1:3, 6 et al.). Jeremiah spoke of it as a hammer breaking the rock in pieces (Jer 23:29); here Isaiah viewed its painful descent on Israel, using the same word (*nāpal,* "fall") as occurs in Daniel 4:28 ("happened") with reference to the fulfillment of the word of judgment in the experience of a Babylonian king. The people of Israel would come to know it in the terrors of war.

National pride is usually most arrogant in a capital city. From the heart of the country, Samaria's citizens refused to take the fall of the northern provinces to the Assyrians (cf. 9:1) as more than a temporary setback in the building of a greater and a richer land. In city and garden, the merely adequate that had succumbed to judgment through foreign armies were to be replaced by the superior. Verse 10 could in fact be taken either literally or figuratively. This mood of defiance might seem creditable; but in fact it is an expression of determination of thwart God's punitive will, rather like the construction of the Tower of Babel.

The NIV has moved against the stream of modern versions in accepting the reference to "Rezin's foes" (v.11) as an authentic part of the text. The RSV, for instance, removes the personal name, acknowledging the emendation in the margin. The LXX, in fact, has "adversaries of Zion" instead of "adversaries of Rezin." It is, however, a good canon of textual criticism to accept a harder reading if, despite its difficulty, it still makes sense; and this is the case here. Ephraim may well have discovered that in a foreign alliance you share not only your ally's resources but also his foes. The word "Aramean" (v.12) is applicable more widely than to the citizens of Aram proper, the country over which Rezin reigned; and it could here designate enemies on his borders. In any case, the specific events referred to in vv.11–12 cannot be fully identified. Isaiah was fond of conveying the concept of judgment by using figurative language for eating (v.12a; cf. 5:14; 9:20). The refrain in v.12b (cf. 9:17, 21; 10:4; 5:25) should not be regarded as purely formal and therefore of little consequence. Rather, it presents the fearful thought that the judgment already described does not exhaust the manifestation of God's wrath against his sinful people.

13–17 Verse 13 perhaps surprises the reader till he recalls that the prophet spoke of Israel as the sons of the Lord (1:2). His judgment was both retributive and restorative in purpose when directed against these his people (cf. Hos 2:15; 3:4–5).

In an earlier chapter (3:1–3), Isaiah used and explained figurative language in relation to the national leadership. It is difficult to see why such explanations should be assigned to a later hand and seen as the work of an unimaginative redactor (see Introduction, pp. 6–12). After all, Isaiah was a prophet, and what use is an unsupported analogy to a communicator if there is a danger it will not be understood? Clarity is the first rule of style in any language. His two illustrations here embrace the whole nation, both the honored and the insignificant. Young (*Book of Isaiah,* in loc.) says, "The leaders were in the government, but the false prophets were not at the head of the people. No leaders were they but, following where the leaders led, they simply flattered and fawned, a wagging tail on a dog."

The prophet made it clear that although the nation was being led astray by its leaders and its false prophets (vv.15–16), and the guilt of these was therefore great, nobody was without blame. Even the fatherless and widows (v.17), the socially disadvantaged, must share in the judgment; for the contagion of godlessness had spread through the whole nation. Note the order of the two adjectives "ungodly" and "wicked," suggesting perhaps that the first was the cause of the second (cf. Rom 1:18).

18–21 Both the Bible and experience teach that wickedness unchecked spreads like wildfire, and this is precisely what Isaiah indicated here. The reference to a column of smoke (v.18) may simply serve the purposes of the imaginative grasp of the figure the prophet used; on the other hand, it may suggest that the acrid stench of wickedness reaches the nostrils of God, in which case it provides a transition to the different use of the same analogy in v.19. Here it is not wickedness but divine wrath that causes the blaze. In both cases the undergrowth and the forest trees represent the people. The spreading flame of sin is followed in its turn by the fire of God's judgment, with perhaps just a suggestion of the punishment fitting the crime. The words "briers" and "thorns" are favorites with Isaiah; and he used them together for different purposes (5:6; 7:23–25; 10:17; 27:4), but with enough overlapping significance to give us the impression that in his mind they stood for the consequences of sin (cf. Gen 3:18).

In vv.11–12 the prophet described the attacks made on Israel by her external enemies. From the end of v.19, the more terrible picture of civil war takes over. A study of OT history from the time of the judges reveals many examples of strife within the nation. The tribes of Manasseh and Ephraim should have been particularly close to each other, for they were both descendants of the sons of Joseph (Gen 48). The first civil war in Israel, however, was fought between the Gileadites of Manasseh and the men of Ephraim in the days of Jephthah (Judg 12:1–6). Men who would not unite through a common sympathy were sometimes joined together to pour out their hatred and jealousy against Judah. Both the earlier and later contexts (i.e., v.18–19, 21b) suggest that this civil strife was to be viewed as a judgment from God.

10:1–4 Mauchline (in loc.) fittingly refers to this section as "the accents of Amos," for the OT reader is often reminded of Isaiah's older contemporary here. There is nothing strange about this, for Amos was a southern prophet who addressed the north; and this is the role adopted at this point by Isaiah, for these verses are the conclusion of the oracle against Israel that commenced at 9:8 (see esp. Amos 2:6–7; 5:11–12; 8:4–6).

Many critics (e.g., Clements) consider this section to be part of the series of woes in 5:8–23. Such a view is understandable because of the introductory "woe" (cf. 5:8, 11, 18, 20, 21, 22), but we have already suggested that the true literary and spiritual climax of the sevenfold series is to be found in 6:5 (see comment in loc.). This section not only ends with a refrain that recurs throughout this oracle but also tunes in perfectly with the theme of sin and retribution that sounds throughout the oracle. The Amos parallels also support its present position in an oracle against the northern kingdom.

Verse 1 suggests that the ruling class in Israel had devised a legal system that departed in important respects from the Mosaic standard. The phrase "the oppressed of my people" (v.2) expresses the affront to God's special relationship with the whole people that this evil legislation constituted. It may well have consisted largely in oppressive land laws (cf. 5:8–10). This phrase would suggest to the discerning what v.3 spells out in the clearest of terms, the coming of a day of divine reckoning when possession of ill-gotten wealth would make men the sure objects of wrath.

The picture of cringing prisoners (v.4) is so true in life, for there are few who can walk erect on their way to prison camp after defeat in war. It is possible, too, that Isaiah suggested that they were trying to avoid notice (cf. 2:10, 21) in order to escape death.

The refrain that has occurred at various points in this oracle is truly terrifying in its climactic position. If even physical death does not satisfy the fierce anger of this holy God, what dread punishment lies beyond the grave? It is at this point most of all that we need to recall that no such device as this refrain is ever merely formal when it occurs in the Word of God.

Notes

20 The NIV ("offspring") and most EV and commentators follow the Targum. The MT reading is "arm" (NIV mg.).

15. *The Judgment of Assyria*

10:5–19

5"Woe to the Assyrian, the rod of my anger,
    in whose hand is the club of my wrath!
6I send him against a godless nation,
    I dispatch him against a people who anger me,
to seize loot and snatch plunder,
    and to trample them down like mud in the streets.
7But this is not what he intends,
    this is not what he has in mind;
his purpose is to destroy,
    to put an end to many nations,
8'Are not my commanders all kings?' he says.
9'Has not Calno fared like Carchemish?
Is not Hamath like Arpad,
    and Samaria like Damascus?
10As my hand seized the kingdoms of the idols,
    kingdoms whose images excelled those of Jerusalem
        and Samaria—
11shall I not deal with Jerusalem and her images
    as I dealt with Samaria and her idols?' "

12When the Lord has finished all his work against Mount Zion and Jerusalem, he will say, "I will punish the king of Assyria for the willful pride of his heart and the haughty look in his eyes. 13For he says:

" 'By the strength of my hand I have done this,
    and by my wisdom, because I have understanding.

> I removed the boundaries of nations,
>> I have plundered their treasures;
>> like a mighty one I subdued their kings.
> ¹⁴As one reaches into a nest,
>> so my hand reached for the wealth of the nations;
>> as men gather abandoned eggs,
>> so I gathered all the countries;
>> not one flapped a wing,
>> or opened its mouth to chirp."
> ¹⁵Does the ax raise itself above him who swings it,
>> or the saw boast against him who uses it?
> Asif a rod were to wield him who lifts it up,
>> or a club brandish him who is not wood!
> ¹⁶Therefore, the Lord, the Lord Almighty,
>> will send a wasting disease upon his sturdy warriors;
>> under his pomp a fire will be kindled
>> like a blazing flame.
> ¹⁷The Light of Israel will become a fire,
>> their Holy One a flame;
>> in a single day it will burn and consume
>> his thorns and his briers.
> ¹⁸The splendor of his forests and fertile fields
>> it will completely destroy,
>> as when a sick man wastes away.
> ¹⁹And the remaining trees of his forests will be so few
>> that a child could write them down.

The date of this oracle is not easy to determine, but Carchemish (v.9) was not captured till 717 B.C. This was about two years before the death of Ahaz; so it is possible that the oracle could have been delivered within his reign, as most of the other oracles in chapters 7–12 seem to have been. A date in Hezekiah's reign is also possible, of course. The passage is strongly theological, in the sense that a firm conviction of the sovereignty of the God of Israel underlies it (cf. 6:1). It goes beyond the general sovereignty of God over the rise and fall of world empires—expressed so graphically in 40:23–24—and relates specifically to his use of evil instruments. Isaiah did not deal with the problem this has raised for some believers; it was Habbakuk who confronted this (see esp. Hab 1:12–17). To Isaiah it was enough that God is God (cf. Rom 9:19–21) and that he may use any instrument he desires to fulfill his holy purposes.

5–11 The emotional interjection *hôi* ("woe," v.5) with which v.1 also began (see comment at 6:5) induces in the reader a mind-set that prepares him for the disclosure of Assyria's judgment in vv.12–19. Isaiah tended from time to time to anticipate a God-honoring denouement in this way (see especially 52:13 and its anticipation of 53:12).

This oracle clearly relates in its theme to the preceding one (cf. 9:12, 17, 21; 10:4). God uses instruments to manifest his wrath in the judgment of his people. Assyria was the chief instrument God used in Isaiah's day. The word "godless" (v.6) must have been as shocking as the names "Sodom" and "Gomorrah" (1:10) to those who were fastidious and even excessive in their observance of religious ritual (1:10–17; cf. Mic 6:6–7). In fact, the lack of a specific reference to Judah may even have led Isaiah's hearers to think that he was speaking of some other nation, till the context put his meaning beyond doubt. The prophet's choice of a simile here—"like mud"—

may be due to his conviction that Judah has become spiritually and morally worthless (cf. Matt 5:13).

We have been given a glimpse into the mind of God; now we see the mind of Assyria. The two minds are at one only as to the acts of war themselves, not as to the ultimate purpose of those acts. Assyria and its boastful monarchs certainly had no intention of serving the punitive ends of the God of Israel; rather they sought conquest and territorial expansion for their own glory (v.7; cf. 45:4–5). Verses 8–11 anticipate v.12, with its reference to the king of Assyria, though in fact the cities mentioned in v.9 were overcome by a series of Assyrian monarchs and not just by one. Calno and Arpad (v.9), both in northern Syria, were taken in 738, Damascus in 732, Samaria in 722, and Hamath on the Orontes in 720 B.C. The ancient Hittite city of Carchemish on the upper Euphrates was vanquished in 717 B.C.

The king of Assyria's boastful rhetoric (vv.10–11) must have seemed quite irrefutable to the people of his day. In fact, Samaria had not withstood the might of his armies any more than the pagan cities, and Jerusalem ruled over a smaller kingdom. It was a sad fact that neither the northern nor southern kingdom was without idols (cf. 2:8, 20). What the Assyrian had not realized was the special purpose of God for his people, especially his determination to deliver Jerusalem. The gods of the pagans were mere vanities (cf., e.g., 46:5–13), but Yahweh was the living God (37:4).

12 This verse sums up the theology of this great oracle. God has two ends to fulfill in relation to Assyria. He will punish one nation through her and punish her through another, though the latter nation is not specified nor even hinted at here. The phrase "his work" stands in strong contrast to the expression "my hand" in v.10. This may be God's "strange work" (cf. 28:21–22), but it is his work nevertheless; and Assyria is his agent for its accompaniment. The reference to Mount Zion calls to mind the temple (cf. 2:2; 4:5) and the evidence of religious apostasy it revealed in the time of Ahaz (cf. 2 Kings 16).

All sin comes under the judgment of God, and the arrogance of his unwitting instruments is no exception. Isaiah's special stress on the holiness and majesty of God made it inevitable that he would launch constant attacks on human pride (cf., e.g., 2:11–17; 3:18–4:1; 5:15–16; 9:9–10). Even the pagan Greeks recognized that pride is an affront to deity.

13–14 Clements (*Isaiah 1–39*, in loc.) and other commentators have pointed out that the prophet must have been familiar with the style of Assyrian victory inscriptions, for the words of the king of Assyria here are in that tradition. These inscriptions had only one purpose—the glorification of the monarch. Isaiah has a tendency to introduce direct speech, not only—as so often in the prophets—the words of God, but also those of men (cf. 2:3; 3:6–7; 4:1; 5:19; 8:4, 19: 10:8).

Strength and wisdom (v.13) were widely recognized as vital qualities for anyone in authority, especially for a king. The messianic King has them through the endowment of God's Spirit (11:2; cf. 9:6), but the Assyrian monarch boasted of them as his own. The removal of national boundaries and the consequent mixing of peoples was one of the distinctives of Assyrian policy in the lands they conquered (cf. 2 Kings 17:6, 24). The picture of absolute power and total helplessness that we see in v.14 may have been somewhat exaggerated, but there is no doubt that the might and ferocity of the Assyrians won them many overwhelming victories.

15–19 The illustration of the nest (v.14) is followed by these verses, in which Isaiah moved swiftly from one image to another, almost every word serving the needs of some simile or metaphor. First of all, he developed the thought of v.5; there Assyria is pictured as an instrument of authoritarian chastisement. In v.15 it is not only this but also a tool in the hand of the forester to be used for felling the trees (cf. vv.33–34). In a manner to become very familiar in later chapters (e.g., in 44:9–20; 45:9–13; 46:1–2), Isaiah used logic to expose and to ridicule human sin. The picture of a tool or an instrument breaking loose from the control of its master and exulting in its liberty is familiar to us from a European legend, but the axe here is held by no "Sorcerer's Apprentice" but by the Lord Almighty (v.16).

Inspiration again shakes the kaleidoscope of the prophet's imagination, and two new pictures come into view to convey the judgment of God on the pride of his punitive instruments. The image of a sick man gradually wasting away under a consumptive disease (see note at v.16) and that of vegetation and forest trees destroyed by fire present different aspects of the demise of Assyria. Her enemies wore down her resistance over a period of some years, but the decisive moment ("a single day," v.17) came with the downfall of her capital, Nineveh, which is celebrated as an act of God in the prophecy of Nahum.

The picture of the destroying fire contains two notable features. The first of these is Isaiah's use of the word *kābôd* (rendered "pomp" in v.16 and "splendor" in v.18). God's own unique *kābôd* ("glory" in 6:3) has been revealed to Isaiah. None other may boast of his own splendor in the light of that. The second important feature is particularly striking. The prophet does not tell us simply that the Lord will light the fire of judgment; instead, he declares that "the Light of Israel will become a fire, their Holy One a flame" (v.17). This is a profound spiritual insight, of the same order as that of the Rock of salvation becoming the Stone of stumbling (see comment at 8:12–15). God remains eternally the same, but human beings may experience now one consequence of a particular divine attribute, now another. He is the Light of his people (cf. Ps 27:1), and one day he will be the source of light for all the nations (cf. Isa 2:1–5; 60:1–3); but here that Holy Light is felt by an arrogant conqueror as a fire of judgment. We need to remember that at this time a torch was an agent of both light and heat.

Yet even in the midst of such a description of judgment, there is the slightest suggestion of hope, so characteristic of Isaiah's prophecies (cf. 6:13; 7:3 mg.; 8:8), God planned a devastating judgment for Assyria but, amazingly—for this is not Israel but a Gentile nation—not total obliteration. If Israel was to be left a remnant for the fulfillment of God's purposes for her, so too was Assyria! In this way we are prepared for the astounding revelation given in 19:23–25. Having said this, we must also say that the emphasis in v.19 is still on the judgment.

Notes

13 The RSV and the NEB render "like a bull" instead of "like a mighty one," אַבִּיר (*'abbîr*) may mean either, and either makes good sense in the context. In a passage filled with illustrative language, the simile of a bull would be very much in place.

16 מִשְׁמָן (*mišmān*, "sturdy warriors") literally means "fatness" (cf. 17:4). If it refers to the fat parts of the body rather than to stout warriors, this means that the same image is found in vv.16, 18 (cf. Gray, in loc.).

16. *The Deliverance of the Lord's Remnant*

10:20–34

²⁰In that day the remnant of Israel,
the survivors of the house of Jacob,
will no longer rely on him
who struck them down
but will truly rely on the Lᴏʀᴅ,
the Holy One of Israel.
²¹A remnant will return, a remnant of Jacob
will return to the Mighty God.
²²Though your people, O Israel, be like the sand by the sea,
only a remnant will return.
Destruction has been decreed,
overwhelming and righteous.
²³The Lord, The Lᴏʀᴅ Almighty, will carry out
the destruction decreed upon the whole land.

²⁴Therefore, this is what the Lord, the Lᴏʀᴅ Almighty, says:

"O my people who live in Zion,
do not be afraid of the Assyrians,
who beat you with a rod
and lift up a club against you, as Egypt did.
²⁵Very soon my anger against you will end
and my wrath will be directed to their destruction."
²⁶The Lᴏʀᴅ Almighty will lash them with a whip,
as when he struck down Midian at the rock of Oreb;
and he will raise his staff over the waters,
as he did in Egypt.
²⁷In that day their burden will be lifted from your shoulders,
their yoke from your neck;
the yoke will be broken
because you have grown so fat.
²⁸They enter Aiath;
they pass through Migron;
they store supplies at Michmash,
²⁹They go over the pass, and say,
"We will camp overnight at Geba."
Ramah trembles;
Gibeah of Saul flees.
³⁰Cry out, O Daughter of Gallim!
Listen, O Laishah!
Poor Anathoth!
³¹Madmenah is in flight;
the people of Gebim take cover.
³²This day they will halt at Nob;
they will shake their fist
at the mount of the Daughter of Zion,
at the hill of Jerusalem.

³³See, the Lord, the Lᴏʀᴅ Almighty,
will lop off the boughs with great power.
The lofty trees will be felled,
the tall ones will be brought low.
³⁴He will cut down the forest thickets with an ax;
Lebanon will fall before the Mighty One.

20–23 The eschatological phrase "in that day" (v.20; see comment at 2:11) introduces some verses dominated by the doctrine of the remnant. The phrase also connects these verses with the previous passage. Clements (*Isaiah 1–39*, in loc.) describes them as a kind of midrash (i.e., commentary) on the name Shear-Jashub in 7:3. This is an appropriate description provided we add that it is not simply midrash but actual events that correspond to the symbolic name of Isaiah's son as fulfillment completes promise. In fact, these verses present the reader with a plentitude of allusion to earlier passages of Scripture, from both Isaiah and elsewhere, almost after the fashion of the Book of Revelation.

The words "him who struck them down" (v.20) are exactly the same in the Hebrew (*makkēhû*) as the same phrase in 9:13 [12MT], but here they denote the human instrument of God's wrath rather than God himself (cf. v.5). How incredible that they should put their trust—as Ahaz had done (cf. 2 Kings 16:7–9)—in a nation whose known character could guarantee nothing but rapine and almost inhuman cruelty and refuse to rely on the God who had lavished blessing on them throughout their history! So irrational is man's unbelief.

Verse 21 opens with the phrase *šeʾār yāšûb* ("a remnant will return"), which is identical with the name of Isaiah's son (Shear-Jashub, 7:3). The emphasis in this verse (as distinct from v.22) is positive. God will not utterly destroy his people (cf. also 6:13). There are in fact two symbolic names in the verse, for "Mighty God" is evocative of the description of the messianic King in 9:6. Young reminds us that another eighth-century prophet, Hosea, had written, "Afterward the Israelites will return and seek the LORD their God and David their king" (Hos 3:5). The NT doctrine of the incarnation enables us to understand how relying on the Lord, the Holy One of Israel, can be equated with returning to the messianic King, whose name was "Mighty God." Here then the two great Isaianic doctrines of the remnant and the Messiah come together.

Verse 22 links the remnant doctrine with that which it appeared to negate but which in fact in the purpose of God it guaranteed—the promise to the patriarchs that their seed would be many (cf. Gen 22:17; 32:12). The reader has been prepared for this reminder of the promise by the name Jacob in vv.20–21. The promise, true as it was, could and sometimes did induce complacency (cf. Matt 3:9–10; John 8:33–40), for Satan takes even the Scriptures God gave for man's blessing and interprets them to serve his purposes of error and damnation (cf. Matt 4:6; 2 Peter 3:15–16).

Verses 22b–23 are particularly somber in their tone. God is described by titles of power (cf. comment at 1:24); and this fact—in combination with the reiterated word "decreed"—makes the threatened destruction truly terrifying, for it is sovereign and irrevocable. There is perhaps a hint as to the Mesopotamian origin of the instrument to be used in the word translated "overwhelming," for this uses the same Hebrew verb that is translated in 8:8 as "swirling over." The great Euphrates produced one overwhelming flood of judgment through the Assyrians, who overcame Israel, and another in the Babylonians, who brought Judah's kingdom to its end. These nations were wicked (cf. 10:12; 14:4–6), but God used them as instruments of his righteous purpose of judgment.

Verses 22–23 are cited by the apostle Paul in Romans 9:27–28 (see also his quotation of 1:9 in Rom 9:29), in his great theological treatment of God's purpose for Israel and its relationship to the way its representatives reacted to the gospel of Christ in his day.

24–27 The emphasis on God's power continues as the prophet used the same divine titles as he had used in v.23. This time, however, his power was to be directed rather to the salvation than to the judgment of his people. The section these titles introduce is just as full of allusions to other passages—both within and outside Isaiah—as vv.20–23. Other parts of the country may feel the tread of Assyria's fearful host (v.24; cf. 9:1; 10:28–32), but Zion will be secure (cf. Ps 46). So often in Isaiah's prophecy, Jerusalem/Zion, as the political heart of the country, represents God's continuing purpose for his people.

The references to the rod, the club, and the yoke remind us of 9:4–7, with its promises of defeat for the strong enemy and of the benign government of the Child born to be king. The King is not here, but the deliverance is. Historical parallels are drawn not only with the deliverance from Egypt—an earnest of the new Exodus theme that is to have such a place of importance later in the book—but also with the vanquishing of Midian (cf. 9:4). The death of the two Midianite leaders at Oreb (cf. Judg 7:25) was perhaps the decisive moment in the later stages of the battle, for an army in flight without leaders cannot regroup and counterattack. On both occasions Israel was greatly outnumbered, but her trust in God was shown by him to be well-founded. So would it again!

Verse 25 may be compared with 40:1–2. God's wrath against his people is real; but because they are his people, the foreign scourge—whether Assyria, as here, or Babylon later—would be used against them only for a limited time. God would call a halt and would then punish his unwitting instrument for its sin (cf. 10:12–19).

Once again we encounter one of Isaiah's favorite figures, the bearing of a heavy burden (v.27; see comments at 1:4, 14). Israel was like a slave carrying a heavy burden or like a domestic animal yoked and laden. So there would be an Assyrian captivity, but it would be ended by divine action. "The yoke will be broken because you have grown so fat" may picture Israel as an animal so large that the yoke will not fit it. So she cannot be fully subdued by the enemy (see Notes).

28–32 The processes by which the OT prophets were given their messages are known to us only in part, but we are aware that the vision was one important medium used by the inspiring Spirit (see comment at 1:1). The superbly dramatic appeal to the imagination in these verses suggests a visionary provenance. Perhaps the prophet in his imagination was standing on the city walls looking northward and seeing the inexorable advance of the Assyrian army through places within and just beyond his normal range of sight. For sheer drama these verses have little to equal them in the prophets, except in Nahum. Clements (*Isaiah 1–39*, in loc.) comments, "*Geba* was barely six miles from Jerusalem, and for an attacking force to pitch camp there would indicate complete mastery of the tactical situation, together with confidence that the defenders in Jerusalem were demoralised and powerless" (emphasis his.) Nob was much closer still.

Isaiah 36:2 tells us that the Assyrian army actually came to Jerusalem from Lachish, from almost exactly the opposite direction. Alexander, Young, and others therefore see the description here to be simply an indication that the Assyrian advance through the environs of the capital would be purposeful and swift without necessarily implying that they would pass through every place mentioned. This approach to the passage is not unacceptable, but it is possible that some tactical situation may have arisen that caused the Assyrian army to make a circuit around the city from Lachish, finally approaching it from the north. The history of warfare contains many examples that would furnish parallels. Another suggestion is that Isaiah's words actually apply to an advance against Jerusalem by Sargon during the period of Philistine unrest more than a decade earlier. This too is possible, though insufficient detailed military information exists to make it much more than speculation (see Clements, *Isaiah 1–39,* in loc.).

33–34 After the advance, the counterattack! The Hebrew word *hinnēh* ("see") is often treated as if it is little more than a formal link, much like a simple conjunction. In fact, it is an exhortation to visualize and to take special note. It is well placed here! The divine title of power Yahweh *ṣᵉbāʾôt* ("the LORD Almighty," v.33), so much favored by this prophet, occurs no less than five times in this chapter from 16 onward. This is striking in a section of the prophecy where the mighty and ferocious Assyrian enemy is never far from sight, for it underlines the infinite superiority of the true God over even the greatest of nations.

The Assyrian hosts appear like an advancing forest, making the reader wonder whether this was the source for Shakespeare of the movement of Birnham forest toward Dunsinane in *Macbeth* (act 5, sc. 3). Suddenly the divine Forester begins to attack undergrowth, boughs, whole trees, and even the mighty cedars of Lebanon (v.34; cf. 2:12–18, esp. v.13). The pride of Assyria (cf. v.13) caused it to become an example of the general principle laid down by God in chapter 2—viz., men of pride are always riding for a fall.

Notes

27 The RSV, which assumes that the dramatic advance of the Assyrian army commences in v.27b, translates "He has gone up from Rimmon," instead of "because you have grown fat." This is just one of a number of suggested emendations, but the MT makes sense as it stands and is supported by 1QIsa and the LXX (B).

28–32 For detailed identification of the place names, see ZPEB under the various names, also Clements (*Isaiah 1–39,* in loc.) and Young (*Book of Isaiah,* in loc.). Aiath is possibly a longer form of Ai.

יַפְקִיד כֵּלָיו (*yapqîd kēlāyw,* "they store supplies," v.28) could be translated "he examines his weapons," and this is perhaps even more in keeping with the vigorous dramatic style of these verses. Clements, making this suggestion (*Isaiah 1–39,* in loc.), compares Gen 27:3; Judg 18:11, 16 for this rendering of the noun.

In v.29, 1QIsa has "he goes over the pass," with no alteration of the general sense.

17. *The Davidic King and his Benign Reign*

11:1–9

> ¹A shoot will come up from the stump of Jesse;
>   from his roots a Branch will bear fruit.
> ²The Spirit of the LORD will rest on him—
>   the Spirit of wisdom and of understanding,
>   the Spirit of counsel and of power,
>   the Spirit of knowledge and of the fear of the LORD—
> ³and he will delight in the fear of the LORD.

He will not judge by what he sees with his eyes,
    or decide by what he hears with his ears;
4but with righteousness he will judge the needy,
    with justice he will give decisions
        for the poor of the earth.
He will strike the earth with the rod of his mouth;
    with the breath of his lips he will slay the wicked.
5Righteousness will be his belt
    and faithfulness the sash around his waist.

6The wolf will lie with the lamb,
    the leopard will lie down with the goat,
the calf and the lion and the yearling together;
    and a little child will lead them.
7The cow will feed with the bear,.
    their young will lie down together,
    and the lion will eat straw like the ox.
8The infant will play near the hole of the cobra,
    and the young child put his hand into the viper's nest.
9They will neither harm nor destroy
    on all my holy mountain,
for the earth will be full of the knowledge of the LORD
    as the waters cover the sea.

The messianic theme reappears, having been out of sight since Isaiah 9:7; and it is taken up just at the point where it was left before, because the Davidic throne is implied in the reference to Jesse, David's father, and the effective zeal of the Lord Almighty in the richly empowering Spirit of the Lord.

1–3a Once more the appropriateness of the arrangement of the material in this book makes itself felt. At the end of chapter 10, the axe of divine judgment fell on the forestlike army of Assyria; at the opening of chapter 11, the purpose of divine grace is seen in the growth of a shoot from the stump of Jesse (v.1). Compare Genesis 11, where the migration of the nations under judgment away from Babel is succeeded by the migration of Abraham's family from Ur to Haran at the gracious call of God (cf. Acts 7:2).

The reduction of the Davidic dynasty to a mere stump is a true metaphor for its condition when Christ was born; for, though still in existence, that dynasty had been without royal power for nearly six hundred years. The reference to Jesse—who was of course never king—rather than to David—who was—may point to the total absence of royal dignity in the house of David when the Messiah would come. There was still life in the house though, for God's purpose (cf. 2 Sam 7:16) had not been set aside (cf. Ezek 21:27). The Branch (see comment at 4:2; 6:13) is now fully messianic. God's people need more than the promise of fertile land or of continued national life through the remnant. They need the very incarnation of God's life in the Messiah.

The Assyrian monarch boasted of his own power and wisdom (10:8–14; cf. 14:12–14), but the supreme King will be equipped for his work by the Spirit of the Lord (v.2). There are links between this passage and 9:6, especially in the expression "the Spirit of counsel and of power." The earlier passage shows the King to be divine, while this exhibits his dependence, a combination that requires the Incarnation for its explanation. Solomon, Jesse's grandson—who might have seemed to be the fulfillment of the hope of "great David's greater son," and who was endowed with wisdom by God—might have seemed at first to be an expression of this hope in the earlier history of the people; but he fell far short of the divine ideal expressed in Deuteronomy 17:14–20, because he did not fear the Lord with an undivided heart (cf. 1 Kings 11:1–13). The twofold reference to the fear of the Lord here (vv.2–3a) underlines its importance.

It may be that the basic description "the Spirit of the LORD" followed by three pairs of qualities attributed to the Spirit is intended to add up to a symbolical seven (cf. and contrast the seven "woes" of 5:8, 11, 18, 20, 21, 22; 6:5). If so, the symbolism would suggest that the Messiah was to be perfectly endowed by the Spirit with everything requisite to his kingly task (cf. Rev 5:6).

3b–5 The act of pronouncing judgment in the court is often treated in the OT as the acid test of a wise and incorruptible use of authority (cf., e.g., 5:21–23; Ps 72:1–4). Verse 3b does not mean that right judgment ignores evidence available to the senses but rather that it requires inner qualities of character (cf. John 2:25; 7:24). The word "judgment" has an ominous ring to us; but when used of the poor, it is almost a synonym for salvation (Pss 72:2; 82:2–4). Where there is corruption in the law courts, it is the poor who long for a righteous judge.

The reiterated word "earth" ('ereṣ, v.4) also signifies "land." The rule of the messianic King is to be over Israel but also over the whole world (9:7; cf. 11:10); so it is not easy to tell whether here and in v.9 the narrower or the wider sense is intended. Either would be appropriate. Whichever is meant, we can be sure that the principles he rules the world by will not differ from those operative in the more limited sphere.

In the divine economy, the word is active and powerful (cf. Gen 1:3; Isa 55:10–11), and the Messiah's word of judgment will be utterly effective (cf. John 12:48). He judges as "the Word of God" (Rev 19:13–15). This testifies to his great power (cf. v.2), because, unlike many a monarch, he is well able to execute the judgments he pronounces. In him word and consequent action are virtually one.

In the Near Eastern dress styles, the belt or sash (v.5) was the garment that gave stability to the whole ensemble; and to "gird the loins" (KJV, 1 Kings 18:46; 2 Kings 4:29; 1 Peter 1:13) was to prepare for work. The Messiah would be prepared in character for his work of judgment.

6–9 Biblical eschatology may involve more than the simple restoration of conditions as they were in the unfallen world, but it certainly includes this (cf. Gen 1:26–28; Ps 8; 1 Cor 15:25–28; Heb 2:5–9). It is not now Adam who is to be king of the world but the Second Man, the messianic King. In his reign nature will be at peace with itself and with human kings. There seems no reason to doubt that this is to be understood literally. The whole subject raises fascinating ecological questions that are beyond the scope of this commentary to discuss. We know something of the effects of the Fall on human kings and on plant life (Gen 3:17–18); and we cannot doubt that animal life—bound with the human race and the plants in the unity of a world-wide eco-system—must have been affected also.

The normal prey of the fierce predators need have no fear of them under the Messiah's reign. Young (*Book of Isaiah*, in loc.) points out that the calf is the most vulnerable to the lion and the fatted yearling the most desirable (v.6); yet the prophecy puts them together. The predators will so respect the lordship of human beings, given to them before the Fall (Gen 1:28), that even the little child will command respect and, perhaps, will act responsibly and with benevolence toward the predators like a shepherd leading his flock.

The ecological issues are touched on in v.7, with its implied reference to Genesis 1:30. Any adaptation of the eco-system involved will presumably be a restoration of the world to its unfallen condition. Isaiah 65:25 repeats the thought and some of the language of this passage (see comment there).

Genesis 3 presents the serpent as human beings' first enemy within the animal kingdom. In the light of this fact, v.8 moves even beyond vv.6–7. Normally, venomous snakes will not harm children even when their play temporarily robs the snakes of their access to the world outside their homes, so seeming to constitute a threat to their security and perhaps their life itself. The instinct of self-preservation is very deep in every creature; so this profound scene exhibits peace, trust, and harmony.

As a result of the taming of nature, normally "red in tooth and claw," Mount Zion, the holy mountain of God (v.9), will know a comprehensive peace and security that reminds us of other comprehensive promises in 4:5–6. The breadth of the Messiah's reign (cf. 9:7) means however that the peace and security of Jerusalem will be a microcosm of a much wider blessing. Whatever the meaning of 'ereṣ ("earth") in v.4 (see comment there), it almost certainly refers to the whole world in this passage (cf. Rom 8:19–22) because of the references to the sea here and to the nations in v.10. The conjunction "for" (kî, v.9) is theologically important, because it states the cause of this peace. The restoration of human beings to God that is implied in "the knowledge of God" reverses the alienation introduced by the Fall, so making possible the restoration of their environment to its unfallen condition.

For a discussion of the wider implications of the interpretation of this passage, see the Introduction, pp. 14–16.

Notes

1 גֶּזַע (gezaʿ, "stump") normally refers to the stump of a felled tree (cf. Job 14:8), but contrast Isa 40:24, where it designates a newly planted tree. The parallel here with שָׁרָשִׁין (šorāšin, "his root") tends to support the normal sense.

יִפְרֶה, (yipreh, "will bear fruit") follows the MT, which is supported by 1QIsa. The LXX (B) reading ἀναβήσεται (anabēsetai) implies a reading יִפְרָח (yiprāḥ, "will sprout"). Either would make good sense, the former in terms of identical and the latter of synthetic parallelism.

18. The Nation and the Nations

11:10–16

10In that day the Root of Jesse will stand as a banner for the peoples; the nations will rally to him, and his place of rest will be glorious. 11In that day the Lord will reach out his hand a second time to reclaim the remnant that is left of his people from Assyria, from Lower Egypt, from Upper Egypt, from Cush, from Elam, from Babylonia, from Hamath and from the islands of the sea.

12He will raise a banner for the nations
and gather the exiles of Israel;

> he will assemble the scattered people of Judah
>> from the four quarters of the earth.
> ¹³Ephraim's jealousy will vanish,
>> and Judah's enemies will be cut off;
> Ephraim will not be jealous of Judah,
>> nor Judah hostile toward Ephraim.
> ¹⁴They will swoop down on the slopes of Philistia
>>> to the west;
>> together they will plunder the people to the east.
> They will lay hands on Edom and Moab,
>> and the Ammonites will be subject to them.
> ¹⁵The Lᴏʀᴅ will dry up
>> the gulf of the Egyptian sea;
> with a scorching wind he will sweep his hand
>> over the Euphrates River.
> He will break it up into seven streams
>> so that men can cross over in sandals.
> ¹⁶There will be a highway for the remnant of his people
>> that is left from Assyria,
> as there was for Israel
>> when they came up from Egypt.

10–11 These verses perform a transitional function, for they are linked with vv.1–9 by the word *šōreš* ("root") and with v.12 by *nēs* ("banner"; cf. also 5:26). In 5:26 God raised a banner to summon a nation as one of his instruments of judgment on his people, while here the messianic King has an attractive power that brings the peoples of the world together, just as the Lord himself attracts the nations in darkness to his marvelous light in 60:1–3. In 2:1–4 it was the word of God that had drawing power; here it is the Christ.

The eschatological phrase "in that day" (v.10; see note at 2:11), occurring in both verses, relates this messianic teaching to the end times. Like most of the OT writers, Isaiah had a lively sense of the special importance of the Exodus from Egypt, when God had stretched out his hand to deliver his people. Isaiah looked forward to a time that will see an event comparable with it in redemptive significance (v.11). This will contrast with the Exodus, for those who return will be the remnant of a larger people, while it was the greatly enlarged family of Jacob that left Egypt under Moses. The events will also differ because this time the people will not move together as a body from one point of departure but will come together from many lands and various points of the compass. Instead of going forth under a great leader, they will come together seeking a greater leader still.

The places referred to—with one exception—are located at or near the two great river-systems that have acted as mothers of civilization in the Near East: the Tigris-Euphrates and the Nile. The addition, however, of the phrase "the islands of the sea" is surprising. The word "island" (*'î*) in the plural (*'iyîm*) occurs frequently in Isaiah 40–66 and appears to designate the Mediterranean maritime areas. The only reference to a dispersion of Jews in this area is in Joel 3:6; and, of course, it is by no means agreed that Joel prophesied before Isaiah. We do find a considerable western dispersion in NT times, however, as also today, and this is anticipated here by the Holy Spirit.

12–14 After a brief prose interlude (vv.10–11), the exalted poetry the prophet normally used is resumed. Inventories—whether of geographical areas, as here, or of items of feminine attire, as in 3:18–23—do not generally lend themselves to poetry. Isaiah first summarized the thought of the two prose verses in poetic form, making it clear that by "his people" (v.11) he had Judah primarily in mind, even though "Assyria" might have suggested an application also to Ephraim. The Davidic dynasty had of course been associated exclusively with Judah for many centuries, ever since the division of the kingdom (cf. 7:17). The reference to Assyria finds its explanation however in v.13. There will be a reclamation of northern Israelites as well, and the once-divided nation will be united. It had been torn apart through the sin of a son of David (1 Kings 11:11); it would be reunited under David's greater Son.

David's rule had extended well beyond the bounds of the territory of the Twelve Tribes (2 Sam 8). Ephraim and Judah would make common cause against the Philistines (v.14), taking advantage of their location in the hill country to move down the slopes of the Shephelah, west of the Judean mountains, against the Philistines on the coastal plain. The three neighboring nations to the east and southeast would come under subjection again to Judah. Psalm 2 may well represent the futility of the rebellion of these small nations—as representative of world rebellion—against Judah. This rebellion will now be over.

15–16 The nations mentioned in v.14 were small and insignificant when compared with the great militarist regimes of Egypt and Mesopotamia. God's hand of power will be stretched forth in fulfillment of his purposes for his people in both areas. He had dried up the water of the Red Sea before. He would act again to dry it up—and for the same liberating purpose (v.15). He had used a great wind (Exod 14:21) at the Exodus; he would do so again to bring the people back from Mesopotamia, for the wind would produce there a delta not unlike that at the mouth of the Nile.

The highway promised (v.16) may contain an allusion to Exodus 14:26–29, the dry road through the Red Sea; or it may mean that God will bring them back safely across the desert that stretched between Mesopotamia and the Mediterranean seaboard (cf. 35:8).

Notes

11 פַּתְרוֹס (patrôs, "Pathros," "Upper Egypt") has been identified as that part of Egypt that lies roughly south of Memphis and north of Aswan. It is literally "the southern land."

Cush, which occurs also in 18:1, is Ethiopia and lies just south of Pathros.

Elam lies north of the western end of the Persian Gulf.

Babylonia is properly "Shinar" (NIV mg.), the Babylonian heartland, lying in the southeastern part of the Tigris-Euphrates valley.

Hamath was a Syrian city and small kingdom on the Orontes.

13 צֹרְרֵי (ṣōrᵉrê, "enemies") can also be rendered by the abstract word "hostility" (NIV mg.). The translation "enemies" would mean that "jealousy" would need to be understood as having an objective relationship to "Ephraim's" to preserve the parallelism, whereas the marginal reading would require it to be understood subjectively.

15 In the OT "the River"(NIV mg.) is always the Euphrates. The verse has in view a division of the waters different from that of the Red Sea at the Exodus or of the Jordan at the entry into Canaan. There will be seven shallow streams rather than one deep one.

19. *A Song of Joyous Praise*

12:1–6

¹In that day you will say:

> "I will praise you, O LORD,
>   Although you were angry with me,
> your anger has turned away
>   and you have comforted me.
> ²Surely God is my salvation;
>   I will trust and not be afraid.
> The LORD, the LORD, is my strength and my song;
>   he has become my salvation."
> ³With joy you will draw water
>   from the wells of salvation.

⁴In that day you will say:

> "Give thanks to the LORD, call on his name;
>   make known among the nations what he has done,
>   and proclaim that his name is exalted.
> ⁵Sing to the LORD, for he has done glorious things;
>   let this be known to all the world.
> ⁶Shout aloud and sing for joy, people of Zion,
>   for great is the Holy One of Israel among you."

The first twelve chapters of the Book of Isaiah focus attention on Judah and Jerusalem. Chapter 12 forms a fitting climax and close for this whole section. The preceding chapters have said much about the sins of God's people, warning them of the divine wrath provoked by these sins and the divine judgment that was sure to follow. They have also recorded God's declaration of forgiving grace for the penitent, the challenge to believe, and predictions of a glorious future for God's people. God's great name would be exalted, and his king would reign. Nothing could be more appropriate than a heartfelt psalm of praise to round off this section of the prophecy.

1–3 In chapter 1, the expression "in that day" introduces two verses (10–11) that focus on the Messiah and the remnant—and thus on the great final purposes of God for his people. This psalm of praise (v.1) anticipates the feelings of his people when that great day comes. The eschatological nature of this expression (see note at 2:11), as well as the relationship of chapter 12 to the verses that precede it, further affirm our position that its application cannot be restricted to the return from Babylon but must embrace the final acts in the drama of God's dealings with his people.

The opening words of v.1 and v.4 are identical in English; but, in fact, "you" in v.1 is singular while in v.4 it is plural. Isaiah pictured the nation like a man suffering under God's wrath because of rebellion against God (1:5–6). Once united in sin and its divinely imposed consequences, the nation here engages as a body in one great act of thanksgiving in which—as the change to the plural implies—its every member will joyfully participate.

Isaiah's proclamation of God's forgiveness to the people in Babylonian exile (40:1–5; 43:25) was to be in anticipation of the sweet comfort of pardon they were to know at the very end of their history. The propitiatory basis of this pardon is declared by the prophet in the fourth Servant Song (52:13–53:12).

In view of the contiguity of v.1–2, it would be attractive to interpret the salvation declared in v.2 in spiritual terms, so that it would become a virtual synonym of the forgiveness seen in v.1. This would bring it into line with the normal use of the word "salvation" in the NT instead of with the physical connotation it usually possesses in the Old. The physical and spiritual could be combined here, but there can be little doubt that the prophet had chiefly in mind the deliverance of the people from all their enemies that was to be a consequence of God's forgiving grace. In a later passage, Isaiah extols the comforting salvation of God in close connection with an exhortation to the people to leave the place of their captivity and to return to Jerusalem (52:7–12).

The prophet's language here takes up words from the Song of Moses in Exodus 15, so that Israel's first and final expressions of corporate praise are here brought together. Psalm 118 also praises the Lord as the God of salvation from enemies. The words "The LORD is my strength and my song; he has become my salvation" are identical in the Hebrew to two other verses (Exod 15:2; Ps 118:14), except that instead of the short poetical form Yah, Isaiah has Yah Yahweh (NIV, "The LORD, the LORD" cf. Exod 34:6). The emphasis thus given to the divine name is altogether appropriate because the people's trust in the Lord stands in strong contrast to the unbelief of Ahaz and his trust instead in Assyria (cf. 7:1–9; 2 Kings 16:7–18).

The assertion that God is or has become the salvation of his people goes perhaps a little further than a simple statement that he has effected deliverance for them (see comment at 10:17). It is as if his person has taken color from his work; the person and the work belong together so that the one can hardly be conceived without the other. For a clearer NT parallel, see 1 Corinthians 1:30; but the general concept lies behind a great deal of NT teaching about Christ, perhaps most of all in the way the term "Lamb"—descriptive of his sacrificial work—becomes a designation of his person in the last book of the Bible. To "the song of Moses, the servant of God" is added "the song of the Lamb" (Rev 15:3–4), for salvation receives its deeper meaning through him.

When it is said that he is "my strength and my song" (v.2), the reader is made aware that this God is now everything to his people. The personalizing form of the phrases implies exhaustiveness. Not only do the people rely on him for strength, but they have abandoned all other trust. The prophet had been warned in the inaugural vision of his ministry that the people would be spiritually unresponsive (6:9–10). He had faced the fear and unbelief of Ahaz, their king (ch. 7). Even Hezekiah's faith, real as it was (37:14–20), proved to be imperfect; for he, like Ahaz, had succumbed to the temptation to curry favor with potential military allies (ch. 39). In the future day Isaiah visualized, however, trust in God the Savior would be so complete as to banish all fear.

Not only would the Lord receive all their faith; he would be the sole object of their song of praise. Who will say that this limits it? Other themes may seem narrow but not the praise of earth's Creator and his people's Savior! The redeemed have nothing else to sing about and yet everything to sing about when their song is of him, for every worthy theme is gathered up in him who is supremely worthy.

In v.3, the singular gives place to the plural in anticipation of v.4. Isaiah has already used the imagery of water to symbolize divine supplies that are totally reliable and so can be trusted (8:6). The waters of Shiloah flowing gently and yet constantly into the city are replaced by wells of salvation from which the believing people may keep on drawing with joy. The figure suggests constant recourse on their part and constant provision on his. If v.2 reminds us of Exodus 15 with its glad song of deliverance, v.3 takes us on to Exodus 17, with its provision of water and its rebuke to unbelieving, joyless murmuring.

4–6 For the opening words of v.4, see the comments at v.1 and v.3. This introductory formula is followed in v.4 by three poetic lines, the first two of which are identical in Hebrew with Psalm 105:1. This psalm dwells on Egypt, the Exodus, and the divine provision in the wilderness. This makes us aware of the fact that the second half of chapter 12 is occupied with the same theme as expressed in v.1.

The proclamation to all the nations that the Lord's name is exalted is typical of Isaiah (cf. 2:2–3, 11, 17). So much of the language used in this chapter takes on deeper meaning when read in the light of the NT. The apostolic preachers, identifying Jesus as Lord of all, declared the exaltation of his name and exhorted people to call on him (Acts 2:21, 33; 3:13–16).

With v.5, we find ourselves back in Exodus 15:2, but without the references to horses, horsemen, and the sea—references that focus attention there on the victory of God over Egypt. The truth is that the Exodus—very special as it was to Israel as both the initial and the supreme act of God on her behalf, revealing the power of his arm—will be eclipsed by an even greater disclosure of God's power (Isa 53:1). It will therefore take its place at the beginning of a whole sequence of divine saving acts that may now be celebrated retrospectively in their totality. It would not be enough now that, as in the Song of Moses, the people should praise his name simply in the presence of one another. The whole world must know what he has done so that his name may be exalted in all the earth. This again reminds us of the Acts of the Apostles and of the Great Commission that began to be fulfilled by the apostles.

The universalism of these verses is now modified as is common in the Bible, by a form of particularism. The song being sung was the celebration of God's forgiving grace and saving deeds for his own people, Zion. The pardoning grace of God is the source of many blessings, but none is more wonderful than his presence with his people. That presence was promised and sealed in the child Immanuel (cf. 7:14; 8:10, 18). Here its realization was celebrated and extolled by his people. It is worth noting that the presence of God among his people is no contradiction of his transcendent uniqueness and separateness, expressed in the phrase "the Holy One of Israel." He is distinct but not aloof, for in him holiness and grace find their perfect union.

Notes

1 יָשֹׁב (yāšōḇ, "turn") is a jussive; but the NIV, with other EV, assumes textual corruption here and so translates it as an imperative. Jussives are perfectly natural, however, in an address to God; therefore, yāšōḇ should be rendered "Let your [anger] turn."

2 1QIsaᵃ repeats אֵל (ʾēl, "God") here, perhaps on the analogy of יָהּ יְהֹוָה (YH YHWH, "Yah Yahweh"; NIV, "The LORD, the LORD") later in the verse. Should this represent the true text, it would place even more emphasis than that already present on the totality of Israel's future trust in God alone.

II. God and the Nations (13:1–23:18)

Israel, the chosen people of God, was separated by him from the nations of the world to be his own special people. She did not, however, live her life in isolation but was placed at the most strategic crossroads of the world. In this situation she was brought into contact with many other peoples—especially the world powers of Mesopotamia and the Nile, who could only engage each other in trade or in conflict by taking a route through or very near Israel's territory.

In the time of Isaiah, the international scene was dominated by the cruel and aggressive Assyrians, who were ruled by a succession of ambitious monarchs. Such a situation left a buffer state with only two options: submission or a protective alliance. This formed the general political context for Isaiah's prophetic ministry. Chapters 1–12 relate the kind of message he brought to Judah from the Lord. Foreign foes were instruments of God's judgment on his people for their sins. They were not to seek relief in alliances with little neighbors nor take shelter under the wing of the big aggressor; rather, they were to trust in the Lord himself. His own purposes for his people were sure to triumph in the end, even if—by reason of their own folly—they would experience much chastisement from his hand through the foreign foe.

The international situation brought Judah into contact with virtually all the other states of the Fertile Crescent; and it is most appropriate, not only that oracles declaring the destiny of each should be given to him, but that they should be grouped together at this point. Every one of these states lived under the threat of Assyria and sought their own way of handling it. Each would have to face judgment. If Judah and Jerusalem, God's own people, faced judgment—but not extinction—through Assyria (so chs. 1–12), it is inconceivable that these pagan nations should escape. These judgments were in effect anticipations of those universal judgments that, along with the ultimate deliverance of the sons of Jacob, are set forth in chapters 24–27 as a climax to the oracles against the nations. Thus, the divine holiness revealed to Isaiah in his temple vision in chapter 6 was to be expressed in judgment on Judah, on her neighbors, and on the whole universe.

1. Prophecy Against Babylon

13:1–14:23

¹An oracle concerning Babylon that Isaiah son of Amoz saw:

> ²Raise a banner on a bare hilltop,
>   shout to them;
> beckon to them
>   to enter the gates of the nobles.
> ³I have commanded my holy ones;
>   I have summoned my warriors to carry out my own wrath—
>   those who rejoice in my triumph.
>
> ⁴Listen, a noise on the mountains,
>   like that of a great multitude!
> Listen, an uproar among the kingdoms,
>   like nations massing together!
> The Lord Almighty is mustering
>   an army for war.

⁵They come from faraway lands,
  from the ends of the heavens—
the Lᴏʀᴅ and the weapons of his wrath—
  to destroy the whole country.

⁶Wail, for the day of the Lᴏʀᴅ is near;
  it will come like destruction from the Almighty.
⁷Because of this, all hands will go limp.
  every man's heart will melt.
⁸Terror will seize them,
  pain and anguish will grip them;
  they will writhe like a woman in labor.
They will look aghast at each other,
  their faces aflame.

⁹See, the day of the Lᴏʀᴅ is coming
  —a cruel day, with wrath and fierce anger—
to make the land desolate
  and destroy the sinners within it.
¹⁰The stars of heaven and their constellations
  will not show their light.
The rising sun will be darkened
  and the moon will not give its light.
¹¹I will punish the world for its evil,
  the wicked for their sins.
I will put an end to the arrogance of the haughty
  and will humble the pride of the ruthless.
¹²I will make man scarcer than pure gold,
  more rare than the gold of Ophir.
¹³Therefore I will make the heavens tremble;
  and the earth will shake from its place
at the wrath of the Lᴏʀᴅ Almighty,
  in the day of his burning anger.

¹⁴Like a hunted gazelle,
  like sheep without a shepherd,
each will return to his own people,
  each will flee to his native land.
¹⁵Whoever is captured will be thrust through;
  all who are caught will fall by the sword.
¹⁶Their infants will be dashed to pieces before their eyes;
  their houses will be looted and their wives ravished.

¹⁷See, I will stir up against them the Medes,
  who do not care for silver
  and have no delight in gold.
¹⁸Their bows will strike down the young men;
  they will have no mercy on infants
  nor will they look with compassion on children.
¹⁹Babylon, the jewel of kingdoms,
  the glory of the Babylonians' pride,
will be overthrown by God
  like Sodom and Gomorrah.
²⁰She will never be inhabited.
  or lived in through all generations;
no Arab will pitch his tent there,
  no shepherd will rest his flocks there.
²¹But desert creatures will lie there,
  jackals will fill her houses;
there the owls will dwell,
  and there the wild goats will leap about.

²²Hyenas will howl in her strongholds,
jackals in her luxurious palaces.
Her time is at hand,
and her days will not be prolonged.

¹⁴:¹The LORD will have compassion on Jacob;
once again he will choose Israel
and will settle them in their own land.
Aliens will join them
and unite with the house of Jacob.
²Nations will take them
and bring them to their own place.
And the house of Israel will possess the nations
as menservants and maidservants in the LORD's land.
They will make captives of their captors
and rule over their oppressors.

³On the day the LORD gives you relief from suffering and turmoil and cruel bondage, ⁴you will take up this taunt against the king of Babylon:

How the oppressor has come to an end!
How his fury has ended!
⁵The LORD has broken the rod of the wicked,
the scepter of the rulers,
⁶which in anger struck down peoples
with unceasing blows,
and in fury subdued nations
with relentless aggression.
⁷All the lands are at rest and at peace;
they break into singing.
⁸Even the pine trees and the cedars of Lebanon
exult over you and say,
"Now that you have been laid low,
no woodsman comes to cut us down."

⁹The grave below is all astir
to meet you at your coming;
it rouses the spirits of the departed to greet you—
all those who were leaders in the world;
it makes them rise from their thrones—
all those who were kings over the nations.
¹⁰They will all respond,
they will say to you,
"You also have become weak, as we are;
you have become like us."
¹¹All your pomp has been brought down to the grave,
along with the noise of your harps;
maggots are spread out beneath you
and worms cover you.
¹²How you have fallen from heaven,
O morning star, son of the dawn!
You have been cast down to the earth,
you who once laid low the nations!
¹³You said in your heart,
"I will ascend to heaven;
I will raise my throne
above the stars of God;
I will sit enthroned on the mount of assembly,
on the utmost heights of the sacred mountain.

¹⁴I will ascend above the tops of the clouds;
  I will make myself like the Most High."
¹⁵But you are brought down to the grave,
  to the depths of the pit.

¹⁶Those who see you stare at you,
  they ponder your fate:
 "Is this the man who shook the earth
  and made kingdoms tremble,
¹⁷the man who made the world a desert,
  who overthrew its cities
 and would not let his captives go home?"

¹⁸All the kings of the nations lie in state,
  each in his own tomb.
¹⁹But you are cast out of your tomb
  like a rejected branch;
 you are covered with the slain,
  with those pierced by the sword,
  those who descend to the stones of the pit.
 Like a corpse trampled underfoot,
²⁰ you will not join them in burial,
 for you have destroyed your land
  and killed your people.

 The offspring of the wicked
  will never be mentioned again.
²¹Prepare a place to slaughter his sons
  for the sins of their forefathers;
 they are not to rise to inherit the land
  and cover the earth with their cities.

²²"I will not rise up against them,"
  declares the LORD Almighty.
 "I will cut off from Babylon her name and survivors,
  her offspring and descendants,"
                                    declares the LORD.
²³"I will turn her into a place for owls
  and into swampland;
 I will sweep her with the broom of destruction,"
  declares the LORD Almighty.

This oracle, the "Burden of Babylon" as it is called, has been the focus of much scholarly attention. Many modern scholars have been reluctant to accept it as an authentic utterance of Isaiah, assigning it to the sixth century B.C., shortly before the taking of Babylon by Cyrus the Great of Persia. The whole basis of this scholarly judgment has been called into question. In a masterly study of the passage, Erlandsson argues for the authenticity of the whole series of prophecies against the nations (chs. 13–23) and for the special place of this passage as standing after chapters dealing with Judah's relationship to Assyria and before a series of oracles against nations that were seeking freedom from Assyria's yoke. He demonstrates that it "appears not as an isolated entry in relation to its present context, but from the standpoint of both content and diction, is united to the texts which preceded and follow it" (p. 141). He contends persuasively in his final chapter that the only historical context that is fully appropriate for it is 701 B.C., when the various peoples mentioned in chapters 13–23 were all involved in anti-Assyrian coalitions. The attempt of Babylon to get Judah involved in such a coalition almost certainly lies behind the account in chapter 39.

Erlandsson finally commits himself to a modified form of another view first put forward by Kissane, who held that the bulk of chapters 13–14 consists of an oracle first uttered against Assyria, which a later editor then applied to Babylon, when the latter had become the chief oppressor of Judah. Erlandsson points out that the Assyrian monarch bore also the title "King of Babylon" after the assumption of this title by Tiglath-pileser III in 729 B.C. This involved for most of them the recognition of the Babylonian god Marduk. Sennacherib, who hated all things Babylonian, was an exception.

Erlandsson (p. 163) says:

> The ideology which Babylon represented thus became the official religion in the Assyrian empire, and to a great extent the gods of Babylon superseded the Assyrian gods. But this also meant that revolutionary movements could easily gain a hold in the central city of that kingdom. . . . In an account which, for the most part, portrays how Yahweh will himself intervene and crush the proud Assyrians, the inclusion of the judgment against Babylon in 13:19–22 is not entirely unmotivated. Babylon has offered Judah another way of getting rid of the Assyrians than by relying on Yahweh. But just as certainly as Yahweh will overthrow the proud Assyrians, so will he lay Babylon in ruins and this will take place soon.

Erlandsson's view is much to be preferred to Kissane's, for it takes the text seriously as it stands and moreover as the work of Isaiah. It may be objected that it makes the introduction to it, with its general reference to Babylon, seem strange. Erlandsson (p. 165) points out, however, that there is a parallel phenomenon in 17:1–11, where references to Ephraim and Jacob occur in an oracle concerning Damascus. Ephraim had become involved with Damascus and must share something of its judgment. The same would be true of Assyria and Babylon. Erlandsson (p. 166) says:

> The heading . . . means that, in the text that follows under that heading, namely 13:2–14:27, there are words spoken by the prophet against Babylon. . . . This is exactly the case in 13:19–22 and in the introduction to the epilogue, 14:22b–23. But the rest of the contents also stand in relation to these words of judgment against Babylon, because the clear statement that it is Yahweh himself who will humble the proud and arrogant, 13:2–18, overthrow the proud tyrant, 14:4b–21, and thus crush Assyria and free the people from the Assyrian yoke, 14:24–27, is indirectly a judgment over Babylon which wishes to drive out Yahweh and become the power on which the people will place their hopes.

Jeremiah 50–51 makes use of phraseology and ideas from Isaiah 13–14 and applies them to the fall of the Neo-Babylonian empire (see Erlandsson, ch. 7). In Jeremiah 50:17–18, the prophet declared:

> "Israel is a scattered flock
>   that lions have chased away.
> The first to devour him
>   was the king of Assyria;
> the last to crush his bones
>   was Nebuchadnezzar king of Babylon."

Therefore this is what the LORD Almighty, the God of Israel, says:
"I will punish the king of Babylon and his land
 as I punished the king of Assyria."

Here is the recognition that the kings of Assyria and Babylon, having a common guilt in relation to Israel, would share a common punishment. Jacques Ellul (*The Meaning of the City* [Grand Rapids: Eerdmans, 1970], p. 190) maintains that, as the Book of Revelation shows, there are really only two principles of organization for a society: the Babylonian principle—antagonism toward God—and the Jerusalem principle—submission to his purposes. The Babylonian principle is to be seen right through 13:1–14:27, even if, as Erlandsson suggests, much of it may apply at first to Assyria and its king.

Is it really necessary, however, to transfer almost all of these two chapters to Assyria? The present writer, while grateful for much in Erlandsson's book, does not think so. We may accept that the events of 701 B.C. provided the historical conditions that the inspiring Spirit used in giving this oracle to the prophet, without holding that most of it was fulfilled in the downfall of Assyria. If we accept supernatural foreknowledge in a prophet, his prophecy may be given in one historical era and fulfilled in another. True, Erlandsson never raises rationalistic objections to supernatural prediction; but it could be maintained that his interpretation does not take its possibility sufficiently into account. We will therefore expound the oracle as a prediction of the downfall of the Neo-Babylonian empire and its monarch, uttered by Isaiah at the close of the eighth century, and so intended as a warning to Hezekiah and Judah not to put their trust in coalitions against Assyria inspired by Babylon (cf. ch. 39).

1 The use of a surname or a patronymic, as here, may, in addition to other purposes, serve the end of designating a person with some precision. In view of the denial to Isaiah, son of Amoz, of any part in prophecies concerning Babylon—a denial accepted by the great majority of modern scholars—we may see a special evidential purpose in its use here.

2–5 Isaiah's prophetic greatness lies chiefly in the exalted character and vast range of the themes he declared; but allied to this was an outstanding gift for vivid, memorable communication. In these verses the reader or hearer is presented first with a sight for his eyes and then with a sound for his ears. So the imaginative faculty is pressed to carry more than inward sight, two senses combining to convey a reality so impressive as almost to be tangible.

Imagination's curtain is drawn aside and a bare hilltop is disclosed, surmounted by a banner (v.2). The word *nēs* ("banner") is a favorite with Isaiah (cf. 5:26; 11:12; 18:3; 33:23 ["sail"]; 62:10). A shout and a gesture are added to the banner so that the army will be mustered with urgency. The phrases "a bare hilltop" and "the gates of the nobles" suggest a contrast between the remote areas from which the army comes and the sophisticated urban civilization that they will destroy.

Like the Assyrians (cf. 10:5), this army is the instrument of the Lord. "Holy" (v.3) has no character reference here; but like all words from the root *qdš*, it implies that the persons so designated have been set apart from others, set apart, that is, by the Lord for his purpose of punitive destruction. This is emphasized by the use of the emphatic personal pronoun "I" at the start of v.3.

The single shout of command is replaced by a tumultuous roar (v.4). It is the sound of human voices, yet in such numbers and such volume that words are indistinguishable in the general hubbub. The references to kingdoms, nations, and faraway lands would fit the armies of each of the successive world powers from Assyria through Babylon to Persia; but the mention of the Medes in v.17 plus the use of words like "hilltop" and "mountains" suggest that the army was being massed on the great Iranian plateau. "The ends of the heavens" (v.5) probably refers to the distant horizons and so to the "faraway lands" from which the Medes came. The appropriateness of Isaiah's selection of designations for God can be seen in his use of Yahweh ṣᵉbā'ôṭ ("LORD Almighty"; KJV, "LORD of hosts") here. Clements (*Isaiah 1–39*, p. 115) says, "The five lines in vs. 4–5 show evidence of a masterfully concise but dramatic description which gains additional effect through the pervading rhythm 3 plus 2."

The opening verses of the oracle have made it clear that the armies are the instruments of the Lord and that they are coming to execute his wrathful judgment (vv.3, 5). On whom is this wrath to be visited? The RSV translated kol-hā'āreṣ in v.5 as "the whole earth"; but most modern versions, including the NIV, render it as "the whole country" or "the whole land." If we take v.1 seriously, then the NIV translation is appropriate, particularly in view of the local application implied in v.2.

6–8 The "day of the LORD" (v.6) is a frequent prophetic theme (see note at 2:11), emphasizing the certainty and decisiveness of the Lord's historical judgment in the future. It may be conceived in local or in universal terms. In this chapter it seems to move from the one to the other (see the comments at vv.9, 11). Isaiah was fond of wordplay and the phrase kᵉšōḏ miššadday ("like destruction from the Almighty") is an example of this. The Lord will expound his great name of power in terms of destruction when the day of his judgment dawns.

In vv.7–8 the prophet piled up expression after expression to convey the sense of fear that would overwhelm the objects of God's judgment. The phrase "their faces aflame" (v.8) comes as something of a surprise, for shock normally pales the face. It may be then that the prophet was suggesting that the judgment would be recognized by those who suffer it not simply as a visitation of pain but as a punishment for wrongdoing, bringing a blush to their cheeks.

9–13 At this point this oracle of judgment on a great coming world-power begins to expand to cover the whole world, though the NIV translation of hā'āreṣ as "land" rather than "earth" in v.9 (bringing it into line substantially with the way it is translated in v.5) suggests that it is still local at that point. This translation is however open to question. No doubt it was determined by a felt need of consistency of translation for the same word in vv.5, 9; but the cosmic dimensions of vv.10–13 strongly suggest that verse 9—intimately connected with it—needs to be understood universally also. Matthew 24 shows Jesus, in similar fashion, relating a local judgment that was to fall on Jerusalem to the great events that would usher in his second advent and the end of the age. Every local judgment is meant to stir in human beings a recognition of final accountability.

God created the natural order as an environment for human beings, as Genesis 1 reveals. The Fall disturbed this order, and some indication of this is given in the penalties prescribed by God (Gen 3:14–19). In v.10 we see God's hand of judgment falling on the great heavenly bodies, whose regular motions provide strong support

101

for man's belief in an ordered universe. Their light-giving function (cf. Gen 1:14–19) will be hindered. This language is to be taken up in our Lord's great apocalyptic discourse (Matt 24:29; Mark 13:24–25; cf. Isa 34:4), and the sun hid its face when his own supreme act of sin-bearing took place (Matt 27:45; Mark 15:33; Luke 23:44–45).

It is thoroughly characteristic of Isaiah to mention arrogance and pride as prime targets of God's judgment on the wicked (v.11; cf. 2:11–18; 3:16–24; 10:8–16). Human pride offers a blatant insult to the God who is highly exalted and to whom all his moral creatures should submit in obedient worship. Verse 12 makes it particularly clear that the judgment pictured is universal. As O. Kaiser (in loc.) puts it, "The prophecy makes it impossible for the hearer or reader to imagine that he is unaffected by the coming day of Yahweh."

Verse 13 seems to go even beyond v.10 in depicting the effects of divine judgment on the natural universe. There is to be a general convulsion of the whole created order (cf. 34:4). In this way the instability of the order of things since the Fall will be disclosed (as it is seen in so many of the signs of Christ's coming in Mark 13), thus revealing the need for the eternally stable order of the kingdom of God that Christ's coming will establish.

14–16 The prophet has made no reference to the human agents of God's punitive justice since v.5; and at least since v.10, if not before, it has been abundantly clear that a universal judgment is in view. By definition, such a judgment cannot be humanly executed, for every man and woman is to come under it. The prophet here returns, however, to the more local judgment on Babylon, for it is clear that human agencies of punishment are now being used again. A prediction of the Day of the Lord may expand and then contract again in this way, because each particular judgment foreshadows the great ultimate punishment to fall on the human race as a whole.

Beginning with Tiglath-pileser III, each of the great empires of Mesopotamia followed a policy of transportation and intermingling of peoples. As Babylonia is entered by its conquerors, those living there who have been exiled from their own homelands feel their isolation; and, like hunted or neglected animals, they try to make for home (v.14). Such attempts at survival will be quite fruitless. The bitter enemies of their overlords will make no distinction between the native-born and the unwilling incomer (vv.15–16). This part of the prophecy may well have taken some color from the universal judgment depicted earlier in the chapter, for it shows that the downfall of Babylon will mean the deaths of many from other nations who find themselves within its borders when the blow falls.

17–22 Verse 17 is of special interest because of its reference to the Medes. These Iranian people, who—along with other Aryan tribes—came onto the Iranian plateau about the beginning of the first millennium B.C., were a constant thorn in the flesh of the Assyrian kings; and in 612 B.C. they captured the Assyrian capital, Nineveh. Thus, in Isaiah's day they were a significant factor on the international scene. There was, however, no question of any special antagonism on their part to Babylonia at this time. In fact, the Babylonians were their allies in the eventual sack of Nineveh. By the middle of the sixth century B.C., however, the situation had altered considerably. After a period when there was enmity between the Medes and the Persians (their fellow Aryans), the Medes put their fierce fighting force at the disposal of Cyrus the Persian and were involved with him in the overthrow of Babylonia in 539

B.C. The Medes are probably mentioned here rather than the Persians because of their greater ferocity and also because they were better known to the people of Isaiah's day. According to the Greek historian Xenophon, Cyrus acknowledged that the Medes had served his cause without thought of monetary reward.

Babylon, a very ancient city (cf. Gen 10:10; 11:1–9), seems to have had even in times of decline a special prestige among the peoples of the Near East. This special status was shared also by its leading deity, Marduk, and is well expressed in the phrase "the jewel of kingdoms," which Isaiah gave to it (v.19). Already Babylon was a sure candidate for divine judgment, but the cup of its sin was to become full in the days of its new empire, when it would oppress many nations and destroy Jerusalem and its temple.

If, as Erlandsson maintains (see the general comment at the beginning of this section), this oracle dates from 701 B.C., it is interesting that Isaiah uses the analogy of the overthrow of Sodom and Gomorrah that we find also in 1:9–10, a passage probably dating from the same period. The phrase "Sodom and Gomorrah" (v.19) suggests not only complete destruction but also its moral cause.

As Erlandsson points out, (p. 91), the Assyrian king Sennacherib, who detested Babylon, utterly devastated it in 689 B.C. This was, perhaps, a partial fulfillment of the prophecy given here (vv.20–22), just as some of the messianic prophecies in Isaiah received an anticipatory fulfillment before their final realization in Christ (see comment at 7:14–17). Babylon was quickly rebuilt, and no comparable destruction took place in 539 B.C. The prophecy did find fulfillment, but over a considerable period of time. Darius the Great and Xerxes both issued important decrees of demolition. Alexander the Great apparently had great plans for it, but they did not survive his death; and by the close of the first century B.C., Babylon was utterly desolate. So it is today. The mills of God grind slowly, but they grind exceeding fine. The last sentence of the chapter refers to Sennacherib's act of vengeance that stood at the beginning of the whole process and that, at the time of this prophecy, was to be accomplished within twelve years.

14:1–4a These verses have their own special interest to the Bible student who is sensitive to historical and literary echoes, for they are saturated with allusions to the Exodus from Egypt and the entry into Canaan. The New Exodus theme, which is so important later in the book, is the controlling motif here. The clue to this is given in the words "once again he will choose Israel" (v.1). Clements (*Isaiah 1–39*, in loc.) says: "The entire history surrounding the former election of Israel had been brought to an end with the Babylonian exile. A whole new beginning would have to be made, which would amount to a new act of divine election." The expulsion of Israel from Canaan at the Exile would certainly make it look as if the covenant, so often flagrantly broken by the people, had finally been set aside by God. In fact, however, such was the depth and persistence of his steadfast love that his covenant purpose was never eclipsed by their unfaithfulness. His new choice was really a reaffirmation of the old in the return from Babylonia.

The repeated name "Jacob" is a reminder that—as at the Exodus, so now—it is the God of the patriarchs who is setting his love on the people (cf. Exod 3:6–9). The patriarchs had been given the land by divine promise; so, in the divine purpose, it was already "their own land" as far back as that. O. Kaiser (in loc.) points out that the word *'ᵃdāmāh* ("soil," "land") in the expression "their own land" is used also in Ezekiel 37:14; and he adds, "We may perhaps suggest that this word, which originally referred to the red-brown arable land suitable for cultivation, possessed through its contrast with dismal, uncultivated land the emotive associations of our word 'home', reflecting as in Ezekiel the splendour of the Promised Land."

When Israel left Egypt, there were many other people ("aliens") with them. There were also many aliens within their gates (Exod 20:10; 22:21 et al.). Jethro, Rahab, and other believing Gentiles found a place within the covenant of God with Israel. So it would be again (cf. 56:3–8). Not only so, but the nations in the land would become servants to them (v.2; cf. 60:9–14; 61:5), just as the Gibeonites and others had become in the earlier entry to the land. We can find real parallels to much of this in the actual events of the return from exile, for it was a decree of the Gentile Cyrus that was its immediate human cause (Ezra 1:1–4; cf. Ezra 6:1–12). There are, however, elements of the prophecy that were not fulfilled at this time, especially in the picture of God's people governing their oppressors. No doubt these are properly eschatological, so that the fulfillment at the return from Babylon itself foreshadows God's ultimate purpose for the people (see Introduction, pp. 14–16).

The Christian is also reminded of the fact that there is a spiritual fulfillment of much OT prophecy by the words of v.3. Writing on this verse, O. Kaiser (in loc.) says, "The day on which Yahweh gives rest to the suffering community . . . brings an end to weary toil (cf. Gen 5:29), to the restless turmoil and forced labour (Exod 4:14; 6:9) . . . which is now imposed upon the community that is being directly addressed. When the people are set free . . . the land of their inheritance will be a place of rest, a place where they will remain undisturbed (cf. Deut 12:9f. and 25:19)." Apart from its assumptions about the addressees, this quotation is very apt. This verse reminds us of the teaching of the Epistle to the Hebrews that the true rest for God's people was never found in Canaan but is given only in Christ (Heb 3:7–4:11).

The detailed parallel between the Exodus and the return from the Exile may even embrace v.4, because the Song of Moses, which was an exultant celebration of the Lord's mighty power made known at the Exodus, was at the same time a triumphant assertion of the overthrow of Pharaoh and his hosts (Exod 15).

4b–11 At this point, one of the greatest poems in the whole prophetic corpus commences, running through v.21. Its form is really that of the funeral dirge, with the characteristic limping rhythm of a Hebrew lament, so plaintive and yet ominous to the sensitive ear. The form is appropriate, for it speaks of death (vv.9–11, 15). It is not sung at a funeral, however, for the subject of the song is a tyrant who will be denied proper burial, and the song lacks the pomp a great king would expect as his right at death (vv.18–20). There is a considerable element of irony, so that the whole song becomes a taunt in the guise of a lament.

The subject of this lament is the king of Babylon, the oppressor (v.4); but the reference to the Lord in v.5 is important. Apart from the less direct references of vv.13–14, it is the only place where he is mentioned in the whole poem; yet he dominates it just as much as he does the Book of Esther. It is he whose action is implied in all the passive verbs of the poem. If the oppressor has ceased, it is not simply because of the antagonism and resourcefulness of human foes but rather because God has taken action to bring him low. God does not need to emphasize his part in all this; to mention it is enough to give the reader the true perspective from which to view the events described.

The "unceasing blows" and "relentless aggression" of v.6 conjure up an atmosphere of terror. When a great tyrant reigns in Mesopotamia, all the little nations cower in constant fear, like dogs fearing the boot of a cruel master. How impressive then is the great change intimated in v.7! Just as the calm after the storm heralds the song of shepherds in Beethoven's *Pastoral* Symphony, so the glorious peace that followed the downfall of the Babylonian oppressor becomes the setting for the glad sound of rejoicing.

The pine trees and cedars of v.8 may be literal, figurative, or both. The monarchs of Assyria and Babylon were greedy for wood, and their woodcutters stripped whole districts of their trees. They knew nothing of ecology, but it is doubtful whether they would have heeded its claims if they had. Lebanon, with its magnificent trees, suffered more than most conquered territories at their hands. Just as Mark 13:24–25 can be understood both literally and symbolically, so these trees may refer also to human rulers (cf. 2:13; Jer 22:7; Ezek 17:3; 31:3). They too are safe now.

"The grave" (v.9) is the NIV's translation of $\check{s}e^{\,\jmath}\hat{o}l$ ("Sheol"), the place of the dead (see note at v.15 below). The Babylonian king, though dead, still exists, but now in a different sphere. The picture of the petty kings rising from their thrones to accord a mocking welcome to their oppressor powerfully appeals to the imagination and clearly contains some elements that were never intended to be taken literally. This does not mean, however, that Sheol did not possess objective reality. Its NT equivalent is Hades, and the picture there of the dead man in torment was clearly intended by our Lord to be taken seriously (Luke 16:23).

To rise from one's seat is a token of respect in many cultures. It is probable, therefore, that it indicates not only surprise but also mock homage on the part of those whose submission had been all too real, though unwilling, during their lifetime. They had heard the sound of the Babylonian harpers making music for the king as they were brought trembling into his court. All the pomp and circumstance have disappeared (v.11). His palace would have been replete with soft couches and lush carpets to give him all the comfort he could desire, but the maggots and decomposition had taken over.

12–17 The taunt song continues. Isaiah's prophecies make some use of what has been called "dead mythology," and this may well be an example of this. The language of the myth—known but not, of course, accepted as true by the prophet and his hearers—becomes a vehicle for his thought by supplying the basis of an analogy. Moreover, this passage itself seems to be echoed by the Lord Jesus in Luke 10:18, where language applied here to the king of Babylon is used of Satan. Nothing could be more appropriate, for the pride of the king of Babylon was truly satanic. When Satan works his malign will through rulers of this world, he reproduces his own wicked qualities in them, so that they become virtual shadows of which he is the substance.

To interpret v.12 and the following verses in this way means that the passage points to Satan, not directly, but indirectly, much like the way the kings of the line of David point to Christ. All rulers of international significance whose overweening pride and arrogance bring them to ruin under the hand of God's judgment illustrate both the satanic and the Antichrist principles, for these principles are really one.

Verse 13 reminds us of the Tower of Babel (Gen 11:1–9), though the endeavor to be like God takes us right back to Genesis 3. Here Satan first sought to reproduce in human life his own proud aspirations for equal status with God. The possession of power can, of course, prove disastrous in creating a desire for utter supremacy.

Lord Acton's dictum—"All power corrupts; absolute power corrupts absolutely"—and Milton's somewhat controversial description of Satan as "by merit raised to that bad eminence" both testify to the fact that the one who is fitted for high authority must be aware that, as a result, he faces grave spiritual danger.

The dominant feature of vv. 13–14 is undoubtedly the repetition of the word "I." Only God himself has a right to speak in this fashion (13:11–12; 14:24–25; 41:9–10, 17–19 et al.). The analogy from Canaanite mythology (see comment at v. 12 and also further note below) probably extends to the reference to the sacred mountain. Like the proud figure in the myth, the king of Babylon sought for absolute sovereignty. It is a strange paradox that nothing makes a being less like God than the urge to be his equal, for he who was God stepped down from the throne of his glory to display to the wondering eyes of men the humility of God (Phil 2:5–8).

The leveling power of death is again underlined (vv. 15–16; cf. vv. 9–10). The death of such a great one in worldly terms causes people to think hard. The writer of Ecclesiastes was right: there are more lessons to be learned about the meaning of existence at the place of death than at the place of birth (cf. Eccl 7:1–4). Only God really has the right to make the earth tremble (v. 16; cf. 13:13; 24:1–4). Human tyranny can go too far, and God acts against it from his all-sovereign throne (cf. 40:23–24).

For the references to "the grave" and "the pit," see the note below. For the contrast between heaven and Sheol/Hades as the highest and lowest places in the universe, compare passages like Romans 10:6–7 and Ephesians 4:9–10.

18–21 We know from the Egyptian pyramids and other royal tombs how much stress was put on proper burial—with all the proper rites and ceremonies—in the Fertile Crescent in OT times. How horrifying to a great king of Babylon and to many of his contemporaries would be the prospect of his lying out in the open (v. 19), unburied, his royal body undistinguished and perhaps indistinguishable from those of his soldiers, to be thrown into a common burial pit! What is the cause of such a fate? The great king—like Napoleon, Hitler, and many another—has led many of his people into death on the battlefield to gratify his lust for power. God therefore makes the punishment fit the crime.

The principle of group solidarity in punishment is seen throughout the OT (v. 21; cf. Exod 20:5–6; Num 16:31–35; Josh 7:24–26). In fact, Isaiah states it first of all as a general principle before applying it to the particular situation he has in view here. The reference to the conqueror covering the earth with cities is perhaps a reminder of Genesis 10:8–11, possibly implying that this Babylonian dynasty was following the ways of its great predecessor, Nimrod. Alexander the Great and many other current rulers have sought to perpetuate their names through great city-building enterprises (cf. also Gen 11:4). No throne, no tomb, no progeny, no cities—in all these ways the Lord abases those who seek self-exaltation.

22–23 These verses constitute a kind of appendix to the taunt song. Here the all-powerful divine King (see comment at 1:9) asserts his own intention to act against Babylon. Clearly the language of v. 22 reflects that of vv. 20b–21, but it also goes back to v. 20a. The king of Babylon's sin would bring destruction, not only to his people, but also to his land. He wanted to possess the earth, but in fact the very reverse would take place; for his own land would be possessed—not even by human beings but by owls (v. 23; cf. Ps 102:6)—and it would be covered with pools of stagnant water. The analogy the passage closes with, though based on a most ordinary domestic situation, has an eloquence all its own (cf. 1 Kings 14:10; 21:21; 2 Kings 21:13). The reader can almost hear the woman of the house breathing a sigh of relief as she sweeps the rubbish out her door, knowing that her house is at last clean and fit for human habitation. Rubbish fit only for the broom of judgment—this was God's verdict on mighty Babylon!

Notes

1 מַשָּׂא (maśśāʾ) occurs 12 times in Isaiah in its technical sense of "oracle" (13:1; 14:28; 15:1; 17:1; 19:1; 21:1; 11, 13; 22:1, 25; 23:1; 30:6). It occurs in this sense elsewhere about the same number of times, except for Jer 23:33–38 (where it occurs often), a particularly important passage for understanding it. Despite extensive study, its exact significance is still in doubt. The translations "burden" and "oracle" are both feasible etymologically; and, if the former is correct, it stems from the frequent emphasis on judgment in such utterances. See Erlandsson, pp. 64–65, for comment and documentation.

2 The NIV follows the MT in rendering "beckon to them to enter the gates of the nobles," while the NEB follows the LXX in translating "draw your swords, you nobles." The MT is probably to be preferred. To designate the objects of the Lord's wrath as nobles would be ironic, based on their own self-estimate and suggesting their arrogance (cf. v.11).

13 In Assyrian inscriptions the Medes are frequently described as "the distant-dwelling Medes."

18 The Hebrew of the first clause reads literally "and the bows of the young men are shattered"; many emendations have been proposed, none carrying general conviction with scholars. The text as it stands could refer to the ineffectiveness of Babylon's armies to repulse the Medes.

21–22 The OT contains many problems of zoological identification. צִיִּים (ṣiyîm) cannot be identified with any certainty. It is connected with צִי (ṣî, "desert") and so—here and elsewhere (Isa 23:13; 34:14; Jer 50:39)—may simply designate wild beasts of the desert generally.

אֹחִים (ʾōḥîm, "jackals") is a hapax legomenon. It seems to be connected with the onomatopoeic אָח (ʾāḥ, "ah!") and so to refere to a howling or screeching creature. Palestine's fauna present us with several candidates, as its residents well know!

שְׂעִירִים (śeʿîrîm, "wild goats") are clearly hairy creatures. The apparent use of the word in connection with some kind of demon or satyr in Lev 17:7 has influenced the LXX and most moderns to interpret the reference mythologically, though G.R. Driver ("Lilith," PEQ 91 [1959]:55ff.) contends for a strictly zoological interpretation. Certainly all the other creatures referred to in these verses seem to belong to the animal kingdom.

אִיִּים (ʾiyîm) are probably "hyenas," as here translated, or else "jackals," though the LXX took them to be apes and the Vulgate owls.

תַּנִּים (tanîm) are fairly common in the OT, and the word is rendered variously in the EV. Here it seems likely to be some kind of jackal or wolf. Clements (Isaiah 1–39, in loc.) rightly remarks, "The sense is clear, and is not really dependent upon the precise identity of the species of wild animal that are referred to."

14:4 מַדְהֵבָה (mādhēbāh) is difficult. The NIV and most EV follow the LXX, which presupposes מַרְהֵבָה (marhēbāh; NIV "his fury"), though Erlandsson disputes this. The word in the MT is unintelligible. It does occur several times in the DSS but without ascertainable meaning. See the extended note in Erlandsson (in loc.), who takes it to mean "gold tribute."

12 הֵילֵל (hêlēl, "morning star") has possible links with Akkadian elletu ("Ishtar") and Arabic

hilal ("new moon"). Scholars have shown particular interest in possible connections with the use of the same root in Ugaritic in the Ras Shamra texts from northern Canaan. It is clear enough that in all these Semitic languages the root suggests brightness. In the Ras Shamra polytheism, the morning star attempts to climb beyond all other heavenly bodies to the mountain of the gods in the far north. This would challenge the supremacy of עֶלְיוֹן אֵל (*'ēl 'elyôn*), the Monarch of the gods. He is cast down. It seems likely that elements of the myth, probably well-known throughout Canaan, provide features of the analogy that runs through vv. 12–15. Such an analogy from mythology would be particularly appropriate when applied to the polytheistic Babylonians, whose mythology had many links with that of Ugarit.

13 The language of this verse can be interpreted in terms of the myth (see at v.12 above), with the mount of assembly identified as the northern mountain that is the residence of Ba'al in the Ras Shamra texts. בְּיַרְכְּתֵי צָפוֹן (*beyarketê ṣāpôn*, "on the utmost heights of the sacred mountain") is literally "on the side of the north" (cf. Ezek 38:6, 15; 39:2). It is however associated with Zion in Ps 48:2[3MT], though this too may reflect the language of the myth. The use of such language abstracted from its polytheistic setting is comparable to Paul's use of the language of pagan poets in relation to the true God in Acts 17:28.

15 שְׁאוֹל (*šeʾôl*) and בּוֹר (*bôr*), translated as "grave" and "pit" respectively, are virtual synonyms for the place of departed spirits, the latter developed probably from the place of burial. See articles "Sheol," ZPEB, 5:395, and "Pit," ZPEB, 4:802.

19 The NIV's rendering of כְּנֵצֶר נִתְעָב (*keneṣer nitʿāb*) as "like a rejected branch" makes good sense, conveying an idea not unlike that of 18:5–6 (cf. John 15:6). It is an analogy and so need not be treated as an euphemism for an abortion, as some of the versions have seen it.

---

2. Prophecy Against Assyria

14:24–27

²⁴The LORD Almighty has sworn,

"Surely, as I have planned, so it will be.
and as I have purposed, so it will stand.
²⁵I will crush the Assyrian in my land;
on my mountains I will trample him down.
His yoke will be taken from my people,
and his burden removed from their shoulders."

²⁶This is the plan determined for the whole world;
this is the hand stretched out over all nations.
²⁷For the LORD Almighty has purposed, and who can
thwart him?
His hand is stretched out, and who can turn it back?

This passage has been the subject of much critical interest, many holding it to be incomplete. Some consider it a part of the same oracle as 10:5–15. Erlandsson (pp. 125–27) considers that it should be treated, with vv.22–23, as an epilogue to the Burden of Babylon (see introduction to 13:1–14:23). For him the epilogue is the key to understanding the whole Burden of Babylon, because in his view the burden really deals with both Babylon and Assyria, the Assyrian king having assumed, both politically and religiously, the role of Babylon's ruler. In fact, there was an emotional link between the names "Babylon" and "Assyria" for those who were under threat from Mesopotamia, and this is enough to account for placing this brief oracle at this point.

24–25 Sometimes in Isaiah a divine statement is underlined in some particularly emphatic way (cf. 5:9; 9:7; 37:32), and so it is here. The name of God used here (cf. comment at 1:9) and the statement of his settled purpose (cf. 5:19) combine to assure us that the Assyrian cannot survive. If such a mighty God has designed to crush him, he is doomed indeed. As if to reinforce this certainty still more, God speaks of "my land" and "my mountains" ("my people" is a free translation of the personal pronoun that the RSV simply renders "them").

26–27 The prophetic word here enunciates an important general principle that has been demonstrated so strikingly in the downfall of Assyria. God is sovereign over human history (v.26). All nations will have to submit to his judgment. This principle will be seen in relation to other nations—both small and great—in the oracles that follow. God is not like a man who makes plans and finds he has no power to put them into effect. Perfect wisdom and absolute power find their unity in God.

3. Prophecy Against Philistia

14:28–32

28This oracle came in the year King Ahaz died:

> 29Do not rejoice, all you Philistines,
>   that the rod that struck you is broken;
> from the root of that snake will spring up a viper,
>   its fruit will be a darting, venomous serpent.
> 30The poorest of the poor will find pasture,
>   and the needy will lie down in safety.
> But your root I will destroy by famine;
>   it will slay your survivors.
>
> 31Wail, O gate! Howl, O city!
>   Melt away, all you Philistines!
> A cloud of smoke comes from the north,
>   and there is not a straggler in its ranks.
> 32What answer shall be given
>   to the envoys of that nation?
> "The LORD has established Zion,
>   and in her his afflicted people will find refuge."

28 The heading of this oracle does not in fact establish the year of this prophecy, for there is much uncertainty about the date of the death of Ahaz (see Introduction, p. 5). The Assyrian monarch whose death is implied in vv.29–30 could be Tiglath-pileser III or Shalmaneser V or Sargon II. Although greater chronological certainty could be desired, it would make no real difference to the significance of the oracle.

29–30 The death of a cruel, oppressive monarch is a cause of rejoicing for his subjects, but such celebration is often premature; for that monarch's aggressiveness often characterizes his whole dynasty (v.29).

The prophet's inspired imagination combined two sets of images here. The Assyrian monarchs are likened to a series of reptiles, which is then likened to the succession of root, shoot, and fruit in a plant. In this way the inspiring Spirit used the natural gift of a deeply poetic imagination to vividly and powerfully convey prophetic truth.

Clearly, in the light of v.32, the focus of attention has moved briefly in v.30a from Philistia to Zion. The godliness of the poor and needy and the certainty that God is their helper is often presupposed in the OT (10:2; 11:4; cf. Ps 72:13; Amos 4:1), for the integrity of the godly is rarely profitable in worldly terms. Here God assumes the role of a shepherd to his people (cf. 40:11). The destiny of Philistia is portrayed in stark contrast to this, for famine instead of fresh pasture will be its lot. Leaf, branch, or stem may wither and yet the plant survive, but what hope is there when the root has been destroyed?

31 O. Kaiser (in loc.) says:

> What is one day to happen is as though present to the seer. Thus he already calls upon the gates and city to raise a cry of lamentation because they will be overpowered by the imminent attack. . . . The gate . . . must wail, because the savage mob of the enemy will pour through it into the conquered city. . . . We cannot tell whether the seer was thinking of the watch-fires, signal fires, or what would certainly have produced the most terrifying impression, the clouds of smoke billowing high into the sky from the burning of conquered cities.

32 No doubt the "envoys" were Philistine diplomats sent to Jerusalem to encourage solidarity against the common Assyrian foe. As elsewhere, Isaiah's message encouraged trust in God, not in alliances (cf. 7:1–9; 8:11–15). The word for the envoys is strikingly similar to the great affirmations of faith in Psalm 46.

Notes

---

29 The commentary assumes the broken rod is an Assyrian king and not Ahaz himself, as many earlier and some modern commentators have thought. The reference to the north (v.31) supports the former.

The general reference to a snake followed by the more specific mention of the venomous adder suggests the intensification of aggression and danger. שָׂרָף מְעוֹפֵף (śārāp m^e'ôpēp, "a darting, venomous serpent") may refer to some dragon of popular fancy, but not necessarily. Any swift-moving reptile with a lethal bite or sting would fit the description. In either case the expression brings the series to a climax.

31 The MT's בּוֹדֵד (bôdēd, "straggler") is represented by מוֹדֵד (môdēd, "measure") in 1QIsa[a]. The latter suggests that this great army was beyond counting, but either makes good sense.

---

4. Prophecy Against Moab

15:1–16:14

[1]An oracle concerning Moab:

> Ar in Moab is ruined,
> destroyed in a night!

Kir in Moab is ruined,
    destroyed in a night!
²Dibon goes up to its temple,
    to his high places to weep;
    Moab wails over Nebo and Medeba.
Every head is shaved
    and every beard cut off.
³In the streets they wear sackcloth;
    on the roofs and in the public squares
they all wail,
    prostrate with weeping.
⁴Heshbon and Elealeh cry out,
    their voices are heard all the way to Jahaz.
Therefore the armed men of Moab cry out,
    and their hearts are faint.
⁵My heart cries out over Moab;
    her fugitives flee as far as Zoar,
    as far as Eglath Shelishiyah.
They go up the way to Luhith,
    weeping as they go;
on the road to Horonaim
    they lament their destruction.
⁶The waters of Nimrim are dried up
    and the grass is withered;
the vegetation is gone
    and nothing green is left.
⁷So the wealth they have acquired and stored up
    they carry away over the Ravine of the Poplars.
⁸Their outcry echoes along the border of Moab;
    their wailing reaches as far as Eglaim,
    their lamentation as far as Beer Elim.
⁹Dimon's waters are full of blood,
    but I will bring still more upon Dimon—
a lion upon the fugitives of Moab
    and upon those who remain in the land.

16:1Send lambs as tribute
    to the ruler of the land,
from Sela, across the desert,
    to the mount of the Daughter of Zion.
²Like fluttering birds
    pushed from the nest,
so are the women of Moab
    at the fords of the Arnon.
³"Give us counsel,
    render a decision.
Make your shadow like night—
    at high noon.
Hide the fugitives,
    do not betray the refugees.
⁴Let the Moabite fugitives stay with you;
    be their shelter from the destroyer."

The oppressor will come to an end.
    and destruction will cease;
    the aggressor will vanish from the land.
⁵In love a throne will be established;
    in faithfulness a man will sit on it—
    one from the house of David—

one who in judging seeks justice
and speeds the cause of righteousness.

We have heard of Moab's pride—
her overweening pride and conceit,
her pride and her insolence—
but her boasts are empty.
⁷Therefore the Moabites wail,
they wail together for Moab.
Lament and grieve
for the men of Kir Hareseth.
⁸The fields of Heshbon wither,
the vines of Sibmah also.
The rulers of the nations
have trampled down the choicest vines,
which once reached Jazer
and spread toward the desert.
Their shoots spread out
and went as far as the sea.
⁹So I weep, as Jazer weeps,
for the vines of Sibmah.
O Heshbon, O Elealeh,
I drench you with tears!
The shouts of joy over your ripened fruit
and over your harvests have been stilled.
¹⁰Joy and gladness are taken away from the orchards;
no one sings or shouts in the vineyards;
no one treads out wine at the presses,
for I have put an end to the shouting.
¹¹My heart laments for Moab like a harp,
my inmost being for Kir Hareseth.
¹²When Moab appears at her high place,
she only wears herself out;
when she goes to her shrine to pray,
it is to no avail.

¹³This is the word the LORD has already spoken concerning Moab. ¹⁴But now the LORD says: "Within three years, as a servant bound by contract would count them, Moab's splendor and all her many people will be despised, and her survivors will be very few and feeble."

There are special features of this oracle that make it at once one of the most moving and yet most enigmatic of Isaiah's prophecies. It is poetic literature of a high order. The inspired poet-prophet presents us with graphic pictures of judgment on Moab, sketching them often in the briefest of phrases. What makes the oracle so memorable, however, is not so much its appeal to the eye of the imagination as to the inward ear. Through its verses the anguished wailing of the bereaved and the fugitives touches the heart of the reader. One is reminded of the justice of the judgment; for the godly in every age must take the side of God in his righteous acts of judgment, but the reader is not forbidden to mourn at the consequences of the people's sins. And to his utter astonishment, he discovers that the inspired page is wet too with the tears of the prophet himself! Jeremiah wept for Judah (Jer 9:1), but Isaiah for Moab!

1–4 The small Moabite nation is often mentioned in the OT, sometimes on its own, sometimes with its near neighbor, Ammon. The origin of both nations is traced to

Lot's incest (Gen 19:30–38). It is impossible to determine the exact historical circumstances of this oracle or even to identify the enemy with any certainty; it could have been Assyria or some incursive force of hungry and rapacious nomads from the desert—perhaps Israel (cf. 2 Kings 14:25) or even Judah, though this last seems very unlikely.

It has been pointed out that Isaiah is fond of crowding a number of place-names into a small compass (10:28–32; cf. 23:1–3; 43:3). All the places mentioned in these verses were in Moab. O. Kaiser (in loc.) entitles vv.1–9 "the night raid upon Moab and its consequences." This certainly suits the situation described in v.1. The enemies no doubt had come unheralded. Their predatory purpose fulfilled, they had probably departed as suddenly as they had come. Behind them was a trail of death and destruction. The land was full of weeping people, some gathering at religious shrines to cry to their gods, others in public places to join in corporate displays of weeping. The sounds of such agonized wailing would strike the men of Moab's fighting force with a demoralizing terror.

5–9 Clements (*Isaiah 1–39*, in loc.) is surely right when he rejects O. Kaiser's view (in loc.) that the assurance the prophet gives us that he is deeply moved by the fate of the Moabites is "a stylistic device to re-emphasize the severity of the blow which has struck Moab, rather than an expression of genuine feeling." Moreover, there is not the slightest suggestion that this is ironic. Its emotional content may seem unique, but Isaiah 19 also shows the divine purpose of grace embracing Gentile nations whose record against Israel was far worse than that of Moab.

None of the place names in these verses can be identified with certainty, apart from Zoar (v.5), which is at the southeastern tip of the Dead Sea. It looks as if the general direction of flight for most of the fugitives was southward to Edom. The reference to "the waters of Nimrim" (v.6) seems to suggest that they were the center of a normally fertile area. Perhaps they passed it during the dry season and saw its withered vegetation as a symbol of their own condition (contrast Ps 84:6).

The Moabites were warned that there was no hope of alleviation. This may only have been a night raid, but it was a devastating one and an earnest of further acts of divine judgment. The reference to the enemy as a lion (v.9) reminds us of the reference to Assyria in Amos 3:12, where the ultimate lion of judgment is God himself (cf. Amos 3:4, 8).

We can keep this deeply emotional passage in perspective only if we bear in mind the fact that what it describes is an act of God. This deepens our wonderment at the tears of the prophet. In the NT the provision of propitiation by God's love is all the more wonderful in the light of the demands of his holiness.

16:1–5 The prophetic searchlight, having exposed to view the whole land of Moab with its ruined cities and fleeing, homeless people, becomes a spotlight. It concentrates first on the city of Sela (v.1), the source of the message of vv.3–4a, and then on the fords of Arnon (v.2), where the Moabite refugees, who are the subjects of the message, gather. Sela, normally Edomite, appears to have been in Moabite hands at this time and may even have been the seat of its government. Moab was famous for its great flocks of sheep. The Moabite rulers, in desperation, sent lambs in recognition of the king of Judah's overlordship to support their appeal for asylum for their refugees, many of whom—as in every such situation—would be women with children. How graphic is the prophet's description of their frenzied endeavors to reach safety without harm (v.2)! The shadow of v.3 may well picture Judah as affording protection, like a great rock from the merciless midday sun (cf. 32:2); but it is also possible that it further develops the analogy of the fluttering young birds. These would be easy prey for a predator on the ground, unless the large shadow of the parent bird fell protectingly across them as they moved toward the earth.

Verses 4b–5 are probably the reply sent from Jerusalem to Sela. This passage resembles 14:32 in its triumphant assertion that Jerusalem is a place of security in the purpose of God. These verses have also been understood as continuing the message from Moab to Judah and as constituting a virtual promise on the part of Moab that she would accept the overlordship of the house of David. This latter interpretation is more plausible if the RSV is followed, which renders the verses as follows: "When the oppressor is no more, and destruction has ceased, and he who tramples under foot has vanished from the land, then a throne will be established in steadfast love." Neither rendering does violence to the Hebrew. The comparison with 14:32 makes the former interpretation more likely, for this is the theology of the prophets of Judah, not of Moab.

If the words are addressed from Judah to Moab—or even if they are the prophet's parenthetical assurance to his own people—they are most naturally understood along messianic lines (cf. 55:3). The love and faithfulness referred to are in the heart of God and come to his people on the basis of his promise, such as those of 2 Samuel 7:12–16. The language reminds us somewhat of Isaiah 9:7, and perhaps it is expounding the significance of the fact that there will be no end to the "increase" of the Messiah's government and peace. His righteous government will embrace both Judah and Moab. At one time Moab and Midian were allied against Israel (Num 22:4; 25:1–18). Interestingly, the prophet presents the Messiah's rule as extending over both Midian (9:4–7) and Moab (as here). See also the description of the Messiah's reign of righteousness, faithfulness, and peace in 11:1–9.

6–7 These verses contain the only clear references to the sin of Moab. They save the compassion of this oracle from becoming sentimentalism. Mere sentiment may overlook sin, but true divine compassion does not. A true prophet would be expected to penetrate beyond the misery that results from God's judgment to the offenses against him that caused it, and this Isaiah does here. As is so often the case in this book, pride causes the fire of God's wrath to burn (v.6; cf. 2:11–18; 3:16–24 et al.). Because of pride the Moabites were brought to this sorry pass. Some commentators take this as the Moabite plea for her refugees, but the text does not necessarily imply this.

8–12 Once again the atmosphere of lamentation dominates the prophecy. The prophet visualized the land of Moab as a vast vineyard, with vines spreading to its farthest corners but now trampled underfoot by its enemies (v.8). This passage is reminiscent of the parable of the vineyard (5:1–7). In both passages the figurative element is strong, but the earlier oracle lays special emphasis on God's care for the vineyard and also on the disappointing fruitage. The distinctive features of the parable remind us that Israel, as the people of God, was in a special category; but the common elements of the two passages underline the fact that sin always earns judgment.

In an agricultural community, harvest is a season of great joy (cf. 9:3). In Moab, however, the vineyards would be silent (vv.9–10). The ripened fruit would not be trodden under foot in the wine presses, for judgment through foreign rulers stalked the land.

Once more (cf. 15:5) the prophet's heart was deeply moved by the undoubtedly deserved sufferings of the Moabites (v.11). The skilled and sensitive musician knows what instrument will best carry the feelings of his song to the heart of his hearers, and Isaiah's deep emotions came from the depths of his being with all the pathos of a lament played on a harp. Unhappily, Moab's sufferings had not driven her to the true and living God but to the idol shrines of her god, Chemosh. There could be no help from such a source (v.12).

13–14 There had been earlier prophecies against Moab with the same general import as the oracle just given by the prophet here (cf. Amos 2:1–3). Perhaps this is the meaning of v.13. Alternatively v.13–14 may have been given to Isaiah at a later time than the bulk of chapters 15–16, to which this verse would then apply. We cannot be certain. What is sure is that Isaiah had a very specific disclosure from the Lord as to the time of Moab's judgment. It seems likely—especially in view of the similarity between these verses and 21:16–17—that the prophecy relates to the campaign of Sargon against the tribal peoples of northwest Arabia, for the Assyrian army's route would most naturally go through Moab. This would date the two closing verses of chapter 16 around 718 B.C.

Verse 14 refers either to the contract of a laborer with his master (cf. Gen 29:18; Lev 25:50, 53) or to that of a mercenary soldier with his superior. In either case the point is the same, for the exact calculation of the period is important to the transaction. The prophetic ministry did not require many such timed predictions (though another occurs in 7:8). Their fulfillment would, of course, provide additional clear evidence of their authenticity.

Notes

1 On מַשָּׂא (*maśśā'*, "oracle"), see the note at 13:1.

   Ar seems to have been the capital city of Moab (cf. Num 21:15, 26; Deut 2:9, 18, 29) on the river Arnon, though some have taken it here to be a general reference to the country as a whole. Kir, too, which is קִיר (*qîr*, "walled place" and so "city"), "may refer not to a particular city but to the cities of Moab in general" (O. Kaiser, in loc.). On the other hand, it could be identical with Kir Hareseth (cf. note at 16:7).

2 The Hebrew at the beginning of this verse is difficult, for עָלָה הַבַּיִת וְדִיבֹן (*'ālāh habbayit wᵉḏîḇōn*) really means "the house goes up, and Dibon." Some have taken בַּיִת (*bayit*) to be itself a place name, while others including the RSV, amend it to בַּת (*bat*, "daughter"; cf. note at 1:8). The NIV takes the house to be a temple and assumes the omission of a Hebrew particle or else a somewhat irregular construction. Dibon is just north of the Arnon; Nebo and Medeba are farther north still. For Nebo, see Deut 34:1.

4 Heshbon and Elealeh were also north of the Arnon, while the location of Jahaz (cf. Josh 21:36) is less certain. The first two were outside the Moabite heartland but were in Moabite hands at the time of the oracle.

5 Zoar was near the southeastern corner of the Dead Sea (cf. Gen 13:10; 14:2; 19:22), on the way out of Moab to Edom.

   עֶגְלַת שְׁלִשִׁיָּה *ᶜeglaṭ šᵉlišiyāh*, "Eglath Shelishiyah") can be rendered "Eglath the third," which appears to assume that three places of the same name needed to be thus distinguished. Its location is unknown. For the other place names in this and the following verse, see W. Schottroff, "Horonaim, Nimrim, Luhith und der Westrand des 'Landes Ataroth,'" *Zeitschrift des Deutschen Palastina Vereins* 82 (Wiesbaden, 1966):180ff., and also ZPEB under the various names. It seems that the refugees are here pictured as hurrying southward and southwestward into Edom and perhaps toward southern Judah.

7 נַחַל הָעֲרָבִים (*naḥal hāᵃrābim*, "the Ravine of the Poplars") is probably the Wadi el Hesa, dividing Moab and Edom from each other.

8 Eglaim and Beer Elim cannot be located with full confidence, but the modern sites they are usually identified with are in the Moabite heartland and nearer the Arnon than the border with Edom. The language of this verse leads us to anticipate sites geographically remote from Nimrim in v.6. See ZPEB, 1:506; 2:224.

9 The MT, DSS, some LXX MSS, and the Vulgate render Dimon as Dibon, perhaps conforming it to v.2, though Jerome, the Vulgate's translator, says it was an alternative name for Dibon in his day. However, a different location is not impossible, though identification can only be conjectural.

16: 2 The Arnon was the traditional northern boundary of Moab, but some of the places in chs. 15–16 were north of it and were in Moabite hands at the time.

5 The phrase אֹהֶל דָּוִד (*ʾōhel dāwiḏ*, "house of David"; NIV mg., "tent") is reminiscent of Amos 9:11 (though the Hebrew is different) and may show the influence of the earlier prophet on Isaiah (see Introduction, p. 13).

7 "The men of Kir Hareseth" assumes G.R. Driver's view ("Notes on Isaiah," ZAW 77 [1958]:42–48) that the words translated "the raisin-cakes of Kir-hareseth" in the RSV) are picturesque language for "luxurious dwellers in Kir Hareseth."

Kir is the same as in 15:1, if that is a city. See the note there.

8–9 Sibmah was very close to Heshbon (cf. 15:4 for both Heshbon and Elealeh), and its vines may well have been particularly fine and well-known. Jazer is farther north still and is mentioned to show, with "the desert" and "the sea," how far its vines extended. This is, of course, hyperbole.

11 For Kir Hareseth, see note at v.7.

---

5. *Prophecy Against Damascus (and Ephraim)*

17:1–14

¹An oracle concerning Damascus:

> "See, Damascus will no longer be a city
>   but will become a heap of ruins.
> ²The cities of Aroer will be deserted.
>   and left to flocks, which will lie down,
>   with no one to make them afraid.
> ³The fortified city will disappear from Ephraim,
>   and royal power from Damascus;
> the remnant of Aram will be
>   like the glory of the Israelites,"
>
>   declares the LORD Almighty.
>
> ⁴"In that day the glory of Jacob will fade;
>   the fat of his body will waste away.
> ⁵It will be as when a reaper gathers the standing grain
>   and harvests the grain with his arm—
> as when a man gleans heads of grain
>   in the Valley of Rephaim.
> ⁶Yet some gleanings will remain,
>   as when an olive tree is beaten,

leaving two or three olives on the topmost branches,
four or five on the fruitful boughs,"
declares the LORD, the God of Israel.
⁷In that day men will look to their Maker
and turn their eyes to the Holy One of Israel.
⁸They will not look to the altars,
the work of their hands,
and they will have no regard for the Asherah poles
and the incense altars their fingers have made.

⁹In that day their strong cities, which they left because of the Israelites, will be
like places abandoned to thickets and underbrush. And all will be desolation.

¹⁰You have forgotten God your Savior;
you have not remembered the Rock, your fortress.
Therefore, you set out the finest plants
and plant imported vines,
¹¹though on the day you set them out, you make them grow,
and on the morning when you plant them, you bring
them to bud,
yet the harvest will be as nothing
in the day of disease and incurable pain.

¹²Oh, the raging of many nations—
they rage like the raging sea!
Oh, the uproar of the peoples—
they roar like the roaring of great waters!
¹³Although the peoples roar like the roar of surging waters,
when he rebukes them they flee far away,
driven before the wind like chaff on the hills,
like tumbleweed before a gale.
¹⁴In the evening, sudden terror!
Before the morning, they are gone!
This is the portion of those who loot us,
the lot of those who plunder us.

The heading of this chapter certainly seems to apply to the whole of it; yet there is much in it that relates to Israel rather than to Syria and its capital city, Damascus. This need cause no real problems, for Isaiah 7–8 deals with the Syro-Ephraimite threat to Judah. If two nations are locked together in an alliance and have, at least temporarily, common political and military goals, it is understandable that they should together furnish the subject for an oracle. Ephraim's devotion to the apostate shrines at Bethel and Dan had made her a perpetual rebel against the Lord, but now she became unequally yoked with a pagan nation in an endeavor to coerce Judah into an unholy league against Assyria. This oracle, therefore, certainly appears to belong to the period 735–732 B.C. (see Introduction, p. 5).

1–3 The oracle opens with a call to visualize what God would make of a once-proud city (v.1; cf. 5:7; 25:2). The downfall of Damascus would not be an isolated event, for other cities too would be deserted (v.2). The double conjunction of Ephraim and Damascus and of Aram and the Israelites is striking (v.3). Israel has chosen to accept a close link with Damascus; so she had to accept the consequences of that relationship. A shared purpose involves a shared judgment. The basis of the league between the two nations was chiefly military; and, ironically, it was in military terms that she would suffer, in the loss of her "fortified city." This is no doubt a reference to

117

Damascus, as the fortress that Ephraim herself hoped would protect her from the Assyrians.

The prophet's reference to the "remnant of Aram" may point to petty Aramean states that had taken shelter under the kingdom that had its capital at Damascus, or it may relate to that kingdom itself. The parallelism favors the latter. Damascus, in fact, fell to the Assyrians in 732 B.C., and Samaria, the capital of Israel, fell a decade later. The instrument of these judgments was of course to be Assyria, but the judgments were to be attributed ultimately to the great power of "the LORD Almighty" (see comment at 1:9).

4–6 The repeated phrase "in that day" (v.4; cf. vv.7, 9) underlines the decisiveness of the Lord's judgment on Ephraim. It has an eschatological quality (see note at 2:11), not necessarily in the sense that the events described belong to the period when God's purposes will be consummated, but at least that in these events the great principles of that period cast their shadows before them. In other words, in such judgments God is making an emphatic point about sin and his attitude toward it.

The judgment on Ephraim was to be a devastating one, leaving the people decimated, a remnant so weak and small as apparently to be of no account. The "glory of Jacob" (v.4; cf. v.3) suggests Ephraim's honor, the respect in which others would hold him. He would become subject to a wasting disease, making him perhaps as sorry a sight as if he had been subject to a terrible beating (cf. 1:5–6; 52:14).

Just as in 1:5–9 the picture of a body politic suffering the consequences of sin gives place to one drawn from the harvest, so it is here (v.5), though the wonderful Spirit-controlled imagination of the prophet developed it in a somewhat different way in this context. First he thought in terms of the grain harvest. The reaper's arm encircles and makes taut many stalks of grain so that he can remove their heads by one sweep of his sickle. Fruit trees also will be climbed as far as possible and beaten to gather the great bulk of their fruit (v.6). In each case the farmer endeavors to leave as little as possible for the gleaners, who are allowed by law to gather anything edible that had been missed (Deut 24:19–22). So thorough would judgment be, and yet the destruction would not be total. The phrases "the glory of Jacob" and "the God of Israel" at the beginning and the end of this section constitute a reminder that the God of the patriarchal promises has an ongoing purpose beyond temporal judgment (cf. 6:11–13).

7–8 The judgment on Ephraim would bring a spirit of penitence to at least some of the survivors. The contrast between the phrases "their Maker" (v.7) and "the work of their hands" (v.8) can hardly be other than deliberate and reminds us of 46:1–7. Nothing is more misguided or pathetic than man's attempts to mend the relationship between himself and deity by the work of his own hands. We are all the children of him whose hand took the forbidden fruit, and our own hands are defiled. Such hands cannot construct a way to God. The altars mentioned here may be those of the apostate Yahweh-shrines with their forbidden bull-images at Bethel and Dan. So Mauchline (in loc.) understands this passage: "The return here is to the Holy One of Israel; they no longer pay any respect to forms and images which they have made with their own hands, which means they gave heed to the Second Commandment." It may be, however, that we should read v.8a in the light of v.8b, for "the Asherah poles" (which NIV mg. righty explains as "symbols of the goddess Asherah") reflect the naked paganism of Canaan. The presence of northern Israelites at Hezekiah's celebration of the Passover (2 Chron 30) shows the fulfillment of this prediction.

9–11 The theme of judgment returns. Verse 9 is difficult to translate. The note below takes the matter up in more detail, but we should not miss the fact that the main sense of the verse is clear. When the Israelites came into the land of Canaan many years before, the strong cities of the land were abandoned to them. At this time the Lord was at work for his people, giving them the Land of Promise. However, the situation has changed, and the same cities will be abandoned by the Israelites themselves as they are under the judging hand of God. Here again we see "the Light of Israel" becoming a fire (cf. 10:17 and comments there).

Isaiah had a God-given sense of appropriateness in his choice of titles for God. He was sovereignly using human means to a divine end; so he was "the LORD Almighty" (v.3). He was judging his own people and yet making provision for his purposes for them to survive that judgment; so he was "the LORD, the God of Israel" (v.6). He was turning them away from idolatry to a new faithfulness toward him; so he was "the Holy One of Israel" (v.7). And he was reminding them of his mighty acts of salvation when he brought them at first into the land of Canaan; so he was "God [their] Savior" (v.10; cf. 12:2–3; 33:2; 61:10; 62:11). Their God is also called "the Rock, your fortress"; and this—together with the accusation of ungrateful forgetfulness—recalls Deuteronomy (cf. Deut 5:15; 7:18; 8:2; 31:4, 15, 18) and the lessons of God's gracious acts of deliverance at the beginning of his people's history as a nation.

Verses 10b–11 have been understood in two quite different ways. The NIV, rejecting the translation and interpretation that go back to Cheyne (see Notes), treats these verses in such a way that they are seen to be a further development of the illustrations of judgment given in vv.4–6. Judgment can be pictured as a thorough harvest that leaves only scattered gleanings, but it can also be pictured as disappointing in itself; for even the finest plants, which the grower has searched out in foreign lands and planted in ideal conditions, may come to nothing. Some kind of pestilence is the implied figure of judgment here.

The alternative interpretation seems to be assumed in the RSV, where the NIV's "plant imported vines" becomes "set out slips of an alien god." Perhaps there is an allusion here to the cult of Adonis or Tammuz. This was a fertility cult in which plant cuttings were grown very rapidly, probably by using the best horticultural techniques known at the time. By sympathetic magic the special qualities of the plants were then believed to pass to those who grew them. This understanding of the text is possible, though it does imply that a word for god is the understood noun of which *zār* ("strange," "alien," RSV or "imported," NIV) is the attributive. It would also follow on well from v.8 with its references to paganism.

12–14 Was there ever such a gifted imagination as that of this great prophet? No sooner has the reader's own mind taken in the significance of one picture than another is presented with at least equal vividness. Mauchline (in loc.), says "THE THUNDER OF MANY PEOPLES amassing, reminding us of the opening of Ps. 2, refers generally to the nations, like Syria and Ephraim (7:1ff.) or Assyria (10:5–11), which muster their war-hosts and try, God disregarding, to carry out their plans and satisfy their ambitions" (emphasis his). He is probably right, for the language seems too general to be restricted simply to Assyria, though this may of course be chiefly in view (cf. 8:7). The general nature of the picture is, if anything, underlined by the implied comparison with God's creation ordinance restricting the flow of the waters across the face of the earth (cf. Gen 1:9 and esp. Ps 104:5–9). The God who rules both nature and history employs language taken from his control of the one to give graphic representation to his control of the other.

Now the imagery changes again. The Palestinian farming culture that has already provided illustrations in this oracle—as in many another in Isaiah—returns. The foes are like great rushing torrents (vv. 12–13), but God opposes their waters by his wind (a possible allusion to Exod 14:21?); and they become like chaff blown from the hilltop threshing floor (cf. Ps 1:4; 83:13; Isa 29:5) or like mere dust (cf. Isa 40:15), driven in its blinding grittiness before the advancing storm. The RSV translates *galgal* as "whirling dust," but the NIV's "tumbleweed" is also possible, for the word simply means "something that rolls."

A new thought enters this section of the oracle in v. 14. Not only will God's judgment of the enemies of his people be decisive, it will also be swift. The NIV uses eleven words, to present the graphic contrast (v. 14a); the Hebrew does it in only seven. The view at dusk is presented simply in terms of the overpowering emotion of terror, the prophet leaving the imagination of his hearers to people the scene with countless hosts of pagan soldiers, eager for their prey. In the morning it must all have seemed like a nightmare, for there was not an enemy to be seen! There can be little doubt that God's action against Sennacherib's great army (37:36) is chiefly in view here.

The prophet closes with a general comment based on this singular example of God's care for his people and his city. "This is the portion of those who despoil us, and the lot of those who plunder us." The oracle opened with Damascus, moved on to deal with Ephraim, but at the end it appears clearly that all these events are part of God's plan to keep in safety those who were in Jerusalem—implied but never mentioned—and in the center of his purpose because they were trusting in him.

Notes

1 On מַשָּׂא (*maśśā'*, "oracle"), see the note at 13:1.
2 עָרֵי עֲרֹעֵר (*'ārê 'ᵃrō'ēr*, "the cities of Aroer") are not easy to identify. There was a city of that name on the river Arnon (Deut 2:36) and another near Rabbath-Ammon (Josh 13:25), both probably in Isaiah's day in the territory governed by Moab, not Damascus. Some commentators assume this verse has been misplaced from the preceding oracle against Moab; others, with the RSV ("her cities"), follow the Targum. It is possible, of course, that there may have been cities of this name also in Syria. The place name is rather like a reduplicated version of the common noun so that dittography cannot be ruled out.
5 The NIV, with most other EV, assumes the vocalization קֹצֵר (*qōṣēr*, "reaper") instead of קָצִיר (*qāṣîr*, "harvest") here. The Valley of Rephaim was close to Jerusalem, to the southwest.
9 The RSV follows the LXX in translating "like the deserted places of the Hivites and the Amorites" instead of "like places abandoned to thickets and undergrowth." If this were correct, it would make explicit a parallel with the Israelite conquest of the land that is already implicit (see comment above), but the MT makes adequate sense as it stands and seems authentically Isaianic (cf., e.g., 7:23–25).
10 The theory first put forward by Cheyne is discussed by G. Fohrer (*Das Buch Jesaya*, Band

II [Zurich-Stuttgart: Zwingli Verlag, 1962], in loc.) and R. de Vaux ("The Cults of Adonis and Osiris," *The Bible and the Ancient Near East* [London: Darton, Longman, & Todd, 1971], pp. 210ff. and in most recent commentaries. The Adonis cult is known to us from classical sources and was indigenous to Syria, so that a reference to it would be appropriate in this oracle. This deity was also called Tammuz (cf. Ezek 8:14), and flowers of rapid growth and death were used to represent his short life each spring and summer. See comment above in connection with the translation of the verse. The theory does not require emendation of the text and represents an interesting but unproved possibility.

12–14 See general comments at 18:1–7.

---

6. *Prophecy Against Cush*

18:1–7

¹Woe to the land of whirring wings
    along the rivers of Cush,
²which sends envoys by sea
    in papyrus boats over the water.

Go, swift messengers,
to a people tall and smooth-skinned,
    to a people feared far and wide,
an aggressive nation of strange speech,
    whose land is divided by rivers.

³All you people of the world,
    you who live on the earth,
when a banner is raised on the mountains,
    you will see it,
and when a trumpet sounds,
    you will hear it.
⁴This is what the Lord says to me:
    "I will remain quiet and will look on from my
        dwelling place,
like shimmering heat in the sunshine,
    like a cloud of dew in the heat of harvest."
⁵For, before the harvest, when the blossom is gone
    and the flower becomes a ripening grape,
he will cut off the shoots with pruning knives,
    and cut down and take away the spreading branches.
⁶They will all be left to the mountain birds of prey
    and to the wild animals;
the birds will feed on them all summer,
    the wild animals all winter.

⁷At that time gifts will be brought to the Lord Almighty

from a people tall and smooth-skinned,
from a people feared far and wide,
an aggressive nation of strange speech,
    whose land is divided by rivers—

the gifts will be brought to Mount Zion, the place of the Name of the Lord Almighty.

This oracle is unique in Isaiah 13–23 (except, of course, for ch. 20) in that it does not open with the word *maśśāʾ* ("oracle"). Erlandsson (p. 74) notes that there is some kind of link with 17:12–14, which immediately precedes it. Both passages open with the exclamatory word *hôy*, translated "Oh" in 17:12 and "Woe" in 18:1. This word—whatever its exact significance—usually presages doom. Both passages seem to have chiefly in view the destruction of menacing Assyria. Isaiah 17:12–14 seems in fact to have natural links both with the earlier part of chapter 17 and with chapter 18. Chapter 18 certainly seems to be a later oracle, but the arrangement of material, as so often in this book, shows a keen eye for structure in the one who placed the oracles in literary order. Chapters 18–20 may have been conceived as a unity, for they all deal with Egypt and Cush, which were one at this time. The content of the passage hardly seems to warrant the use of the doom-exclamation with which it begins; for the doom is really pictured as falling on Assyria rather than on Cush, but it perhaps anticipates chapter 20.

Biblical Cush is usually translated "Ethiopia," but the NIV has wisely chosen transliteration rather than translation; for the term designates a much larger area than present-day Ethiopia—an area including the Sudan and Somalia. This somewhat mysterious area, situated at one of the limits of the normal biblical world, had come right into that world in Isaiah's day. It was normally in Egypt's area of influence and, usually, of control; but for a period during the eighth century, Egypt was ruled by an Ethiopian dynasty. The visit of the ambassadors could be placed either during the Philistine revolt against Assyria (around 712 B.C.) or in the period of restlessness after the death of Sargon in 705 (see Introduction, p. 6). Most commentators have difficulty deciding between the two, and it really matters little.

1–3 The phrase "the land of whirring wings" (v. 1) is highly evocative for any hearer or reader who has been in the Nile valley, with its swarms of insects. Onomatopoeia often gives greater power of persistence to a word, and there is a striking example of that here; for the Hebrew *ṣilṣal* ("whirring") as Skinner (in loc.) points out, is closely akin to the Galla word *ṣalṣalya*, used of the tsetse fly.

Ambassadors in OT days were not permanent officials placed by nations in the capital cities of other states with whom they were on friendly terms; rather, they were emissaries sent out on special commissions. There can be no doubt that the purpose here was to foment rebellion against Assyria, which was very much in the interests of the rival power that straddled the Nile valley. The lightness of their papyrus vessels (v. 2) made it possible for them to be carried past rapids and other unnavigable stretches of rivers. The NIV's "sea" literally translates *yām*, while the RSV interpreted it as the Nile. This may well be correct, of course, because the word can be applied to a great river like the Nile. It seems less likely that they would have traveled up the Red Sea from an Ethiopian seaport, especially in such light craft.

The prophet gave charge to the ambassadors. They were to return with all speed to the land they had come from; for their mission, though politically expedient, was spiritually inappropriate and irrelevant, as the later verses of the chapter make clear. J. Skinner (*Isaiah* [Cambridge: Cambridge University Press, 1954], in loc.) says, "While the language breathes the courtly urbanity and respect due to distinguished strangers from a far country, we can easily read between the lines a firm rejection of their overtures. Jehovah, he says in effect, will crush the Assyrian in His own time without human help; and that signal judgment will be a demonstration to Ethiopia and all the world of His supreme Godhead." Even Greeks like Herodotus shared the general admiration felt in antiquity for the tall, handsome, clean-shaven

Nubians of Cush. The military reputation they already possessed had been much enhanced by their recent conquest of mighty Egypt. Israel, remembering its own captivity in Egypt, might well have been particularly impressed.

The message given to the messengers had universal application, for the whole world would reverbate at the trumpet blast heralding mighty Assyria's fall (v.3). The banner and the trumpet (addressing the eye and the ear) represent the call to rally for battle.

4–6 Isaiah often urged his contemporaries to adopt an attitude of quiet faith in their God instead of trusting in alliances with other powers (e.g., 7:4; 30:15). Here it is God himself who is quiet, contemplating calmly the frenzied scene of diplomatic and military activity. When Isaiah commended quiet trust, therefore, he was really calling his hearers to view things from a divine viewpoint (cf. 2 Peter 1:4). As Clements (*Isaiah 1–39*, in loc.) puts it, "The imagery of a calm and pleasant summer evening sums up the serene indifference of Yahweh to the Ethiopian plan."

The second simile of v.4 serves not only to reinforce the first by identical sense-rhythm but also prepares for the disclosure of God's act of judgment described so vividly in v.5. O. Kaiser (in loc.) provides clear information and argues that the divine harvester is here dealing, not with the fruit-bearing branches, but with those that reveal their barrenness by their emptiness (cf. John 15:2, 5). In such circumstances the branches that are valueless to man are left to the local birds and animals who put them to their own use (v.6). This suggests that the fierce Assyrians would themselves become the prey of others.

Clements (*Isaiah 1–39*, in loc.) points out that the Hebrew word *zalzallîm* ("shoots," v.5) "introduces an intentional homophony" on the word *ṣilṣal* ("whirring," v.1). This is certainly possible, especially in the work of a poet-prophet like Isaiah, who was so sensitive to both the meaning and the sound of words. This suggests that Ethiopia, as a similarly barren shoot, would itself fall under the judgment of God.

7 If the comment in the sentence above is correct, vv.6–7 provide an interesting anticipation of the judgment-salvation theme of chapter 19. The very people who, from their position of strength, had sent word to Judah to secure her cooperation in a military venture would come again with gifts for the true God in Zion. This picture (cf. 45:14 and also Pss 68:31; 87:4; Zeph 3:10) is a specific illustration of the general vision in passages like 2:1–4 and 60:1–14 of Zion as the religious center of the whole world.

Notes

1 The NEB renders צִלְצַל כְּנָפָיִם (*ṣilṣal kᵉnāpāyim*) as "sailing ships" instead of "whirring wings," following the LXX and by a linguistic comparison from Arabic. Driver ("Isaiah 1–39," JSS, p. 45) argues for this understanding of the phrase; but the usual translation presents no difficulties and is in line with the prophet's vivid use of language.

2 קַו־קָו (*qaw-qāw*), translated "of strange speech" in the NIV but "mighty" in the RSV, is obscure. See the comment on its use at 28:10. Clements (*Isaiah 1–39*, in loc.), following

Donner, takes it as "most probably an onomatopoeic expression for 'foreign', unintelligible language." The Greek βάρβαρος (barbaros, "barbarian") provides a close comparison.

7. Prophecy Against Egypt

19:1–25

¹An oracle concerning Egypt:

> See, the LORD rides on a swift cloud
>   and is coming to Egypt.
> The idols of Egypt tremble before him,
>   and the hearts of the Egyptians melt within them.

> ²"I will stir up Egyptian against Egyptian—
>   brother will fight against brother,
>   neighbor against neighbor,
>   city against city,
>   kingdom against kingdom.
> ³The Egyptians will lose heart,
>   and I will bring their plans to nothing;
> they will consult the idols and the spirits of the dead,
>   the mediums and the spiritists.
> ⁴I will hand the Egyptians over
>   to the power of a cruel master,
> and a fierce king will rule over them,"
>   declares the Lord, the LORD Almighty.

> ⁵The waters of the river will dry up,
>   and the riverbed will be parched and dry.
> ⁶The canals will stink;
>   the streams of Egypt will dwindle and dry up.
> The reeds and rushes will wither,
> ⁷ also the plants along the Nile,
>   at the mouth of the river.
> Every sown field along the Nile
>   will become parched, will blow away and be no more.
> ⁸The fishermen will groan and lament,
>   all who cast hooks into the Nile;
> those who throw nets on the water
>   will pine away.
> ⁹Those who work with combed flax will despair,
>   the weavers of fine linen will lose hope,
> ¹⁰The workers in cloth will be dejected,
>   and all the wage earners will be sick at heart.

> ¹¹The officials of Zoan are nothing but fools;
>   the wise counselors of Pharaoh give senseless advice.
> How can you say to Pharaoh,
>   "I am one of the wise men,
>   a disciple of the ancient kings"?

> ¹²Where are your wise men now?
>   Let them show you and make known
> what the LORD Almighty
>   has planned against Egypt.
> ¹³The officials of Zoan have become fools,
>   the leaders of Memphis are deceived;
> the cornerstones of her peoples
>   have led Egypt astray.

¹⁴The Lord has poured into them
   a spirit of dizziness;
 they make Egypt stagger in all that she does,
   as a drunkard staggers around in his vomit.
¹⁵There is nothing Egypt can do—
   head or tail, palm branch or reed.

¹⁶In that day the Egyptians will be like women. They will shudder with fear at the uplifted hand that the Lord Almighty raises against them. ¹⁷And the land of Judah will bring terror to the Egyptians; everyone to whom Judah is mentioned will be terrified, because of what the Lord Almighty is planning against them.

¹⁸In that day five cities in Egypt will speak the language of Canaan and swear allegiance to the Lord Almighty. One of them will be called the City of Destruction.

¹⁹In that day there will be an altar to the Lord in the heart of Egypt, and a monument to the Lord at its border. ²⁰It will be a sign and witness to the Lord Almighty in the land of Egypt. When they cry out to the Lord because of their oppressors, he will send them a savior and defender, and he will rescue them. ²¹So the Lord will make himself known to the Egyptians, and in that day they will acknowledge the Lord. They will worship with sacrifices and grain offerings; they will make vows to the Lord and keep them. ²²The Lord will strike Egypt with a plague; he will strike them and heal them. They will turn to the Lord, and he will respond to their pleas and heal them.

²³In that day there will be a highway from Egypt to Assyria. The Assyrians will go to Egypt and the Egyptians to Assyria. The Egyptians and Assyrians will worship together. ²⁴In that day Israel will be the third, along with Egypt and Assyria, a blessing on the earth. ²⁵The Lord Almighty will bless them, saying, "Blessed be Egypt my people, Assyria my handiwork, and Israel my inheritance."

This oracle is of exceptional interest because of its amazing climax: the judgment of God on the Egyptians is followed by their repentance and conversion, by manifestations of God's grace to them, and by their incorporation in the people of God, along with their bitter enemy, Assyria, and the chosen people, Israel, who had suffered so grievously at the hands of both.

A substantial number of commentators, not all conservative, attribute vv. 1–15 to Isaiah. The theme of these verses, after all, relates very well to his message in other passages, warning Judah not to trust to an alliance with Egypt against the Assyrians (cf. 30:1–7; 31:1–3). It is otherwise, however, with vv. 16–25, which have been widely denied to the eighth-century prophet. It is alleged in particular that vv. 18–20 reflect later events, particularly the migration of Jews to Egypt—which was not substantial before Jeremiah's day—and the building of a Jewish temple there around 160 B.C. (see, e.g., Clements, *Isaiah 1–39*, in loc., and O. Kaiser, in loc.). Mauchline (in loc.) and Erlandsson (pp. 76–80) have advanced good arguments on the other side.

Erlandsson concentrates on the linguistic phenomena and general evidence of the complementary nature of the two main sections of the chapter. He calls for "greater care in the matter of assigning very late dates to pronouncements whose function is complementary"; and he goes on to say, "One must not exclude the possibility that vv. 16–25 were appended to the judgment oracle of vv. 1–15 by the prophet himself or his closest disciples" (pp. 79–80).

While Erlandsson questions the late dating of these verses, Mauchline argues persuasively—this time largely on historical grounds—for their unity with the rest of the chapter. He asks, for example, "When . . . was Judah ever a terror to Egypt (v. 17)?" and answers, "Certainly not in the sixth century and not at any time thereafter before the close of the prophetic canon of the Old Testament." He points out that the deliverance of Jerusalem from Sennacherib in 701 must have seemed a divine deliverance. "It was Yahweh triumphant over the mighty gods of Assyria. Egypt had sent an army into Palestine on that occasion and, according to the Assyrian record, it had been defeated at Eltekeh; therefore, themselves humiliated, the Egyptians could claim no share in the humiliation of the Assyrians. Surely there we have circumstances, within Isaiah's lifetime, which are better fitted than any other of later date to evoke the fear of Yahweh and of Judah expressed in vv.16f."

Verses 1–15 have been assigned to various dates during the latter part of the eighth century, but Mauchline's line of reasoning makes it seem more than likely that the whole chapter comes from the period of Sennacherib's invasion.

How Athanasius loved this chapter! He wrote *De Incarnatione* soon after the Edict of Milan, when the persecution of Christians for their faith came to an end within the Roman Empire. He lived and worked in Alexandria and evidently saw in this chapter a prophecy of the triumphs of the gospel of Christ in his native land. He says: "The thing is happening before our very eyes, here in Egypt; and thereby another prophecy is fulfilled, for at no other time have the Egyptians ceased from their false worship save when the Lord of all, riding as on a cloud, came down here in the body and brought the error of idols to nothing and won over everybody to Himself and through Himself to the Father" (*Saint Athanasius on the Incarnation*, translated and edited by a Religious of C.S.M.V. [London: Mowbray, 1970], p. 65).

1–4 The Lord is pictured, in a graphic anthropomorphism, as riding on a swift cloud to Egypt (v.1). Here imagery usually applied to his revelation in nature (cf. Pss 18:10; 104:3) is employed in connection with his interventions in history. Could there be an implied comparison and contrast between the swiftness of the Cushite ambassadors traveling by water in 18:2 and the even greater swiftness of God himself, pictured as coming on the cloud?

Once before this, the God of Israel had judged the gods of Egypt (Exod 12:12; Num 33:4) as well as its people. His appearance on the heavenly horizon fills them both with dread. Their power to resist him is still further diminished by internal division and internecine conflict. In fact, as Herodotus recorded, Egyptian unity— secured by the power of the Cushite dynasty—was destroyed by civil war, with twelve petty kingdoms arising till finally, in the middle of the seventh century, a measure of unity was secured once again under Psammetik I, who had to acknowledge the overlordship of Assyria.

The reader knows that idols and the human agents of paganism can be of no avail to the Egyptians in their predicament, not only because of passages like 2:20–22 and 8:19–22, but also because this oracle itself declares that the Egyptians and their objects of worship will both be overcome by fear (v.1). There is little point in the demoralized turning to the demoralized!

The fierce king of v.4 has been variously identified, but there can be little doubt that the most appropriate application is to Esar-haddon, king of Assyria, who subdued Egypt in 670 B.C. Ferocity was a general characteristic of all the Assyrian monarchs, whose cruelty was proverbial. The Egyptians were not to know this, of course; but their downfall before this monarch would mean the virtual end, not only of their greatness, but even of their independence, for millenniums. Who is this whose power is so great that he can hand over one mighty nation to another? Why, of course, the Lord, the Lord Almighty!

5–10 This passage graphically portrays Egyptian economics, with the total dependence of its industry with the total dependence of its industry on the Nile. Dry up the Nile and, sooner or later, the whole Egyptian economy will grind to a halt. Who can—and will—dry up the Nile, which was a great deity to the Egyptians as well as a great river? Why of course the same God Almighty whose plans to intervene in the history of Egypt had been declared already in vv.1–4! Verse 12 makes this clear.

Again, as in vv.1–4, we are reminded of the events associated with the Exodus, for several of the plagues had involved the judgment of the Nile. The fishing and linen industries (vv.8–10) were very important, and both were completely dependent on the fauna and flora of the Nile.

11–15 Constructive, progressive, and stable rule necessitates the marriage of power and wisdom. These are the characteristics of God's great King (11:1–5), and they are the qualities of God himself. In vv.1–4 he overcame the power of Egypt, and in v.3 we saw him bringing Egypt's wisdom to nought. This theme is now further expounded (cf. 1 Cor 1:20). Every great monarch feels the need of advice from wise counselors, but what if the wisest in the land have nothing but lunacy to offer (v.11)? No matter how ancient nor how exalted as to its source was their lore, it made no difference to their ineptness (cf. Gen 41). The rhetorical question with its taunt at the ineffectual wisdom of paganism is reminiscent of the reiterated mocking questions in other passages (e.g., 41:26; 44:7; 45:20–21). Zoan and Memphis (vv.11, 13) were the two most important cities in Lower Egypt. They are mentioned together because of their administrative importance.

The quaint architectural analogy implicit in the language of v.13b is not peculiar to this verse but is found in a number of OT passages (e.g., Ps 118:22; Zech 10:4). Its use in Isaiah 28:16 is particularly interesting in the light of its use here, for in this passage the leaders who should have given stability to Egypt led her astray, while in the later passage the God of Israel promises a leader who will give true stability to his people. The unifying and stabilizing effect of good leadership may also be in view in the different analogy used in Ephesians 4:16 (cf. v.11). It is instructive too to notice that in Isaiah 28 the folly of the leaders is due to drink and that their confusion here is pictured as if it were the result of drunkenness.

When the prophet says, "The LORD has poured into them a spirit of dizziness," he is of course thinking of a personal spirit (v.14: cf. 1 Sam 16:14; 18:10; 19:9; 1 Kings 22:19–23). It is clear that this spirit comes for moral reasons and as a judgment from God. If we accept that God may use an evil human power in judgment (cf. 10:5), then there is really no difference in principle if he uses an evil spiritual being, as here. Foolish confidence in one's own wisdom may lead not only to failure to produce appropriate counsel but also to walking and causing others to walk along a pathway that leads to disaster. For v.15, see the comment at 9:14–15.

16–17 O. Kaiser and Clements treat the whole passage from v.16 to the end of the chapter as a series of interpolations by later hands. In the opening comment on this chapter, we mentioned the arguments of Mauchline and Erlandsson in favor of an eighth-century date and Isaianic authorship. Clements (*Isaiah 1–39*, in loc.) simply says that these attempts are wrong—without a mention of the arguments themselves or any counterarguments. The fact that this section of the chapter is in prose while the earlier section is poetry tells us nothing about authorship, for there are quite a number of sections of oracles in prose form among the undisputedly Isaianic parts of this book.

Isaiah uses the expression *bayyôm hahû* ("in that day," v.16) forty-two times. This represents a quarter of the instances of its use in the OT and nearly half of its occurrences in the prophets. It lays special emphasis on the time that is in view, and it is often used in eschatological contexts, as here. It occurs also in vv.18, 19, 23, and 24.

Verses 16–17 form a bridge between the first part of the oracle, which is dominated by judgment and the remainder of it, which centers in grace and salvation. They place emphasis on the fear induced in the Egyptians by God's acts of judgment (cf. v.1). We can well see the reason for this, because this fear was a prelude to their repentance. The Exodus account frequently refers to the hand of the Lord and its activities against Egypt (e.g., Exod 8:19; 9:15; 13:3; 9, 16; Deut 4:34). Because God was on Israel's side, her very name became a terror to the Egyptians (cf. Exod 12:33; 15:16; Ps 105:38); so too the mention of Judah would terrorize the Egyptians (v.17). It has been well said that one man with God is a majority, and so one man may be a cause of fear to those who withstand the purposes of God.

18 Much of the debate about this chapter has centered on this verse and the next two. Assuming the accuracy of the majority of the Hebrew MSS, which support the NIV's "The City of Destruction," we will discuss other possible readings in the Notes. The verse as it stands is patient of two different interpretations. It could mean that Jews were then living in Egypt, occupying five of its cities, and so instituting a colony of Yahweh worshipers in this pagan land. Jeremiah 44:1, 15 mentions a number of places in Egypt to which Jews had gone to find refuge from the strife in their own land in the sixth century B.C. It is, of course, possible to take the verse as a prediction of this situation.

On the other hand—and particularly in this context—v.18 could refer to the conversion of Egypt to the worship of the true God. Erlandsson (p. 78), following Kissane, understands it in this way and sees in the five cities an allusion to the original conquest of Canaan by the Israelites. After the capture of Jericho and Ai by Joshua's forces, their first great victory was over the kings of five important Canaanite cities, namely Jerusalem, Hebron, Jarmuth, Lachish, and Eglon (Josh 10). This victory led to the conquest of the whole country. So, Kissane and Erlandsson maintain, the spiritual conquest of Egypt outlined in vv.19–22 starts with the conversion of five cities promised in v.18. This interpretation not only fits the context perfectly but would also furnish a further example of allusion to the Exodus-Conquest period that is such a feature of this oracle.

What then is "the City of Destruction"? The Hebrew *ʿîr haheres* seems like a play on *ʿîr haḥeres* ("the city of the sun"), which is the Hebrew equivalent of Heliopolis, the City of the Sun. The latter is actually read in some of the ancient sources of the text (see Notes). If so, then, the conversion of the people of this stronghold of sun worship is perhaps treated as a major victory, decisive enough and significant enough as a great act of destruction at the time of the Conquest.

19–22 These verses are of great interest because they spell out in detail the circumstances and results of the conversion of the Egyptians. The "altar" (v.19) has sometimes been identified with the Jewish temple built at Elephantiné (modern Aswan) in the sixth or fifth century. There is evidence from Josephus (War VII, 432 [x.3]) that Onias III, when founding the Jewish temple at Leontopolis, appealed to this verse as biblical warrant for the erection of such a temple in Egypt. Although one or more historical fulfillments of such a prediction could be plausibly suggested, it is evident that the final fulfillment of vv. 16–25 has not yet come, unless it is all to be viewed as fulfilled spiritually in the triumphs of the gospel in Egypt (see the Introduction, pp. 14–16 and also the quotation from Athanasius in the introduction to this chapter).

Another echo of the conquest of Canaan is found in the reference to the monument or pillar. Pillars were associated with pagan worship in Canaan and so were prohibited to the Israelites (cf. Deut 7:5; 12:3), but it is clear from v.20 that something quite different is in view. Just as the altars constructed by the patriarchs were witnesses for the true God and his self-disclosure at these places, so various stones and pillars of witness were erected in the days of Joshua (see Josh 4:3, 20–22; 7:26; 8:29; 10:27; cf. also the altar of witness of Josh 22:34 and the great stone of witness in Josh 24:26–27). The pillar-monument here, situated on the border of Egypt, probably symbolizes the claiming of the land for the true and living God, the Lord Almighty.

The analogy of the Conquest continues (v.20b), with a promise that could have come straight out of the Book of Judges (cf., e.g., Judg 3:9, 15). The promise, couched as it is in the language of Judges, appears to be an assurance of deliverance from physical oppressors; but interestingly the savior and defender is singular, while the oppressors are plural. Too much cannot perhaps be based on this grammatical feature, but the language is well fitted to refer to the supreme Savior, the Lord Jesus Christ.

Other possible allusions to the Exodus-Conquest narratives may escape the reader, but it would be difficult to miss the significance of v.21a. One of the major themes of the Exodus story is the knowledge of the Lord that is given in its events. There is, however, a most important distinction drawn between the form that knowledge took for the Israelites and for the Egyptians. The former knew the Lord in the context of his grace to them (e.g., Exod 6:7), the latter knew him as a God of judgment (e.g., Exod 7:5). In fact, it is much more frequently declared that the events will bring the knowledge of God to the Egyptians than it is that they will bring it to Israel. The Lord will reveal himself to Egypt again, but this time in an entirely different way, much more after the pattern of his self-disclosure to Israel; for he will deal with them also on the basis of grace.

The references to sacrifices, grain offerings, and vows (v.21) suggest a comparison with the Mosaic Law, perhaps to make it clear that this is neither an inferior revelation nor a relationship with God of a different kind from that given to Israel. Rather, the Egyptians are to be on equal footing with their erstwhile slaves who had been so gloriously redeemed from their midst. There is an implied rebuke to Israel in the assertion that "they will make vows to the LORD and keep them," which suggests that the basis of their relationship with him is the new covenant (cf. Jer 31:31–34), fulfilled in Christ's death as the ultimate sacrifice (cf. esp. Heb 8:7–9:15).

Verse 22 is a virtual summary of most of the oracle. Isaiah may be indebted to his older contemporary Hosea for the thought and language of this verse (cf. Hos 6:1), but he applies them to Egypt rather than to Israel. The reference to a plague, however, is another clear echo of Exodus. In the time of Moses, the pleas of the Egyptians for the lifting of the plagues were heard through the intercession of Moses, though there was no true penitence in the hearts of Pharaoh and his servants. In terms of this prophecy, however, the plague will bring them to repent-ance, and God will hear their own cries for deliverance.

23 A first-time reader of this oracle, having an awareness of the general background and content of the OT, would become increasingly astonished in reading through this chapter, at least from v.18 onward. The astonishment would reach a new height here at v.23, for the revelation of God's amazing grace to the Gentiles embraces not only the old enemy, Egypt, but the new one, Assyria. Isaiah apparently did not reject this revelation, as Jonah had done at first (Jonah 4:1–3). It is worth consider-ing the spiritual responsiveness that such a revelation would require. In Isaiah's day, Assyria was the one power feared by every little nation in the Fertile Crescent. The calculated brutality of the Assyrians probably made them more of an object of general hatred than any other nation of antiquity. The Egyptians, Babylonians, and Persians were all capable of inhuman acts, but the Assyrian record for callous cruel-ty is difficult to parallel. This amazing verse assured Isaiah's hearers that Egypt and Assyria would drop their long-standing antagonism toward each other and cooper-ate, not only in a great road-building project that would further international com-munication, commerce, and peace, but—abandoning presumably their own distinctive brands of paganism—would come together in the worship of the true God, the God of the little Israelite nation they had both afflicted so sorely!

24–25 It may seem that there is no greater height this oracle could reach; but, if anything, vv.24–25 go further still. Israel, which seems for a time to have been right out of the picture, now takes her place as one member of a trio of godly states. Some of Israel's own titles (cf., e.g., 1:3; 45:11) are applied to her former enemies. This strongly suggests not that the new situation is viewed as a temporary one, soon to give way to a return of old antagonisms and reconversion to paganism, but that the Lord has established a covenant relationship with these nations, perhaps extending to them the new covenant that he promised in Jeremiah to make with his people of Israel and Judah (cf. Jer 31:31–34). (See the Introduction pp. 14–16 for a general discussion of the way such prophecies should be interpreted.)

Notes

1 מַשָּׂא (*maśśā'*, "oracle"), see the note at 13:1.
6 הֶאֱזְנִיהוּ (*he'eznîhû*) is a *hapax legomenon* in this form, and 1QIsa reads וְהִזְנִיחוּ (*wᵉhiznîhû*), assumed by the NIV's "will stink," though the MT too could hardly mean anything else.
9 The 1QIsa reading makes the combers or carders women and the weavers men.
10 The NIV's "the workers in cloth" and the RSV's "those who are the pillars" ("of the land" being understood) assume two different but possible derivations of the same Hebrew word. The former fits the context better.
11 Zoan on the northeastern Nile Delta, known to the Greeks as Tanis, was made Egypt's capital by Rameses II. If the late date for the Exodus is correct, this means that in the same city where Moses confronted Pharaoh, Egyptian wisdom was confounded (cf. Ps 78:12).
13 נֹף (*nōp*) is rightly rendered "Memphis" in the EV. It was the ancient capital of Egypt, situated near modern Cairo.

18 O. Kaiser (in loc.) gives an excellent brief summary of the problems facing the commentator on this verse. As mentioned in the comment above, most Hebrew MSS read עִיר הַהֶרֶס (ʿîr haheres, "the City of Destruction"); but 1QIsa, the Targum, and some Hebrew MSS read עִיר הַחֶרֶס (ʿîr haḥeres, "the City of the Sun"), which must be Heliopolis. Most LXX MSS imply a Hebrew reading עִיר הַצֶּדֶק (ʿîr haṣṣedeq, "the City of Righteousness"). The variety of readings build up into a fascinating textual problem, especially as each of them would make good sense. A good case could be made for a reference to the City of the Sun, for this would show what a signal triumph the Lord was to win over Egyptian paganism. The reading "City of Destruction" could have arisen as a punning taunt. There is a good deal of evidence for this kind of phenomenon in the OT. The pun could, of course, have been in the mind of the prophet, not of a scribe, so that even if we posit something of this sort, it does not necessarily settle the textual issue. In some ways the third reading is the most interesting of all. It suggests an allusion to 1:26 (cf. note at 1:21). In context it may suggest a parallel between this city and Jerusalem, the first and greatest of the five cities of Josh 10 (see comment at v.18). This would fit excellently into such an allusive context but has less support in other ways. The issue cannot be settled with any certainty.

---

8. Prophecy Against Egypt and Cush

20:1–6

> [1]In the year that the supreme commander, sent by Sargon king of Assyria, came to Ashdod and attacked and captured it—[2]at that time the LORD spoke through Isaiah son of Amoz. He said to him, "Take off the sackcloth from your body and the sandals from your feet." And he did so, going around stripped and barefoot.
>
> [3]Then the LORD said, "Just as my servant Isaiah has gone stripped and barefoot for three years, as a sign and portent against Egypt and Cush, [4]so the king of Assyria will lead away stripped and barefoot the Egyptian captives and Cushite exiles, young and old, with buttocks bared—to Egypt's shame. [5]Those who trusted in Cush and boasted in Egypt will be afraid and put to shame. [6]In that day the people who live on this coast will say, 'See what has happened to those we relied on, those we fled to for help and deliverance from the King of Assyria! How then can we escape?'"

This passage is unique in chapters 13–23, for it gives not only an oracle but the circumstances in which it was delivered (see, however, the comment at 14:28). This is perfectly understandable, because—unlike all the other oracles in this section of the book—this was associated with an acted prophecy and so demanded a narrative setting. Its position is very appropriate, for it follows chapters 18–19, which are concerned with the two nations against whom this oracle was given.

1–2 The five Philistine cities were united in a federation, and this union was dominated first by one and then by another of them. The rebellion against Assyria at this time centered in Ashdod. This revolt belongs to the period 713–711 (see Introduction, p. 5) and probably developed in response to events further south. Egypt had been taken over by the Ethiopian dynasty in 715 B.C, and the petty states of Palestine seem to have felt there might be more hope of securing assistance against Assyria. The demise of Ashdod is mentioned in the Assyrian inscriptions and can be accurately dated in 711 B.C.

There has been some discussion of the time references in vv.1–2, especially in the light of v.3. Did Isaiah's acted prophecy begin in 711, as a straightforward reading of the passage would suggest? If so, then the fall of Ashdod and the actions of Isaiah and the prophetic word that explained them constitute together a warning to Judah not to rely on Egypt. This understanding of the passage presents no major difficulties. Most commentators, however, assume that v.2 is a parenthesis or that the time reference there is not intended to be very specific, simply an indication of the general period of the events.

The way Isaiah was clothed (v.2) has suggested to some commentators that the prophet was in mourning at this time, either because of personal bereavement or because of his concern about the nation. At least from the time of Elijah, however, such rough clothing seems to have been associated with the office of the prophet (2 Kings 1:8; Zech 13:4; Mark 1:6). The wording does not preclude the possibility that he was wearing a loincloth (cf. v.4), for strict nakedness would have been religiously and socially unacceptable (cf. Gen 9:20–27).

3–6 The sign was given first and then its significance clarified in a spoken prophecy. The acted prophecy occurs quite frequently in the OT (e.g., 1 Kings 11:29–32; Jer 13:1–11; Ezek 4). It can be viewed as an example of the fact that the OT always treats the human personality as a unity. The God of the OT, too, reveals himself by both deed and word, and these harmonize perfectly. It is important, though, to notice that the act normally requires verbal interpretation before it becomes a true prophecy with specific meaning. The sign was a message to those in Judah who were inclined to put their trust in Egypt (cf. 30:1–5; 31:1–3), especially in its revived strength under its new Ethiopian rulers. In fact, the Egyptian army sent to the help of Judah in 701 was defeated at Eltekeh, and this was the first of a series of disastrous defeats by Assyria in the next few decades.

Verses 5–6 probably refer to different people, those in v.5 being chiefly the leaders of Judah, while v.6 makes reference to the inhabitants of the Palestinian coastal strip. This makes it clear that not only Ashdod but the whole Philistine federation would suffer; and it may even imply that Phoenicia, further north, would be smitten by the Assyrians.

Notes

1 תַּרְתָּן (*tartān*) is translated "supreme commander" in the NIV. It really means "second" and is indirect testimony to the great value the Assyrians attached to military prowess. Their supreme commander was second in status only to the king himself.
2 The NIV ("sandals") and other EV follow the LXX in reading "shoes" rather than "shoe" with the MT, and the former reading now has the support of 1QIsa.

9. Prophecy Against Babylon

21:1–10

¹An oracle concerning the Desert by the Sea:

Like whirlwinds sweeping through the southland,
an invader comes from the desert,
from a land of terror.

²A dire vision has been shown to me:
   the traitor betrays, the looter takes loot.
Elam, attack! Media, lay siege!
   I will bring to an end all the groaning she caused.
³At this my body is racked with pain,
   pangs seize me, like those of a woman in labor;
I am staggered by what I hear,
   I am bewildered by what I see.
⁴My heart falters,
   fear makes me tremble;
the twilight I longed for
   has become a horror to me.

⁵They set the tables,
   they spread the rugs,
   they eat, they drink!
Get up, you officers,
   oil the shields!

⁶This is what the Lord says to me:

   "Go, post a lookout
     and have him report what he sees.
⁷When he sees chariots
   with teams of horses,
riders on donkeys
   or riders on camels,
let him be alert,
   fully alert."

⁸And the lookout shouted,

   "Day after day, my lord, I stand on the watchtower;
     every night I stay at my post.
⁹Look, here comes a man in a chariot
   with a team of horses.
And he gives back the answer:
   'Babylon has fallen, has fallen!
All the images of its gods
   lie shattered on the ground!' "

¹⁰O my people, crushed on the threshing floor,
   I tell you what I have heard
From the Lord Almighty,
   from the God of Israel.

This passage bristles with difficulties for the would-be interpreter; yet, as is so often the case in such circumstances, the main thrust of its message is clear: God would destroy pagan Babylon (v.9). There have been two main schools of interpretation. Some take it that the occasion depicted in the prophet's vision is the downfall of Babylon in 539, when Cyrus the Persian entered the city with his triumphant forces. Cyrus was originally king of Persian lands that were formerly part of Elam, and he had conquered Media a decade or so before his assault on Babylonia. So "Elam" and "Media" in v.2 refer to the multinational army of Cyrus. Some who take this view attribute the prophecy to Isaiah, while others, because of their rejection of supernatural predictive prophecy, attribute it to a writer contemporary with the events it describes.

The main rival of this interpretation relates the passage to the time of Merodach-Baladan, king of Babylon. This king, who is mentioned in Isaiah 39, was known as Marduk-apal-iddina in Babylon. He was prince of Bit Yakin in southern Babylonia. He revolted against Assyria and had himself crowned king of Babylon in 722 B.C., with the support of the Elamites. He reigned during several periods; and after his death, Babylon had further times of independence from Assyria before Senna-cherib's ferocious destruction of it in 689. There had, however, been earlier sackings of the city under Sargon II and Sennacherib, while Merodach-Baladan was alive. This puts not only the prophecy but also its fulfillment in Isaiah's day.

A.A. Macintosh, in a recent special study of Isaiah 21 entitled *Isaiah 21: a Palimpsest* (Cambridge: Cambridge University Press, 1980), takes a mediating view. He contends that this passage is a sort of palimpsest. This term is normally used of a MS the writing has been removed from so that it may be reused. In Macintosh's view, the text of this passage, originally a prophecy connected with Merodach-Baladan, has been worked over to relate it to the later—and for the Jews—much more important fall of Babylon to Cyrus.

Macintosh's theory, however, raises as many problems as it solves and tampers unnecessarily with a chapter that has come down to us in its integrity as part of the Book of Isaiah's prophecies. Erlandsson (pp. 81–92) has made out a very good case for dating the prophecy around 700 B.C. and relating it to Merodach-Baladan's reign in Babylon. The following exposition follows, in general, the main lines of his interpretation.

1a What is "the Desert by the Sea"? It could refer to the desert lands southeast of Babylonia, where Merodach-Baladan's home territory lay. Delitzsch (in loc.) maintained that it was the great plain Babylon stood on. This plain was so divided by lakes and marshy stretches of country that it was appropriate to call it "the sea," as indeed one Greek writer did. The Medieval Jewish commentator Ibn Ezra points out that *yām*, here translated "sea," can also mean "west," and that it is so-called here because it lay to the west of those mentioned in v.2 as laying siege to it. He also maintained that it is called a desert because this was what the Lord was planning to make it when his judgment fell. All three views assert, of course, that it is either Babylon, the city, or Babylonia, the country, that is in view in this heading.

1b–2 The prophet saw in his vision an invader approaching Babylon from the desert lands, through which the invading armies would pass on their way to it. His strongly imaginative mind discerned a similarity between these and the whirlwinds that were liable to move up toward Judah through the Negeb (see Notes).

The prophet then told his hearers that he had been shown a dire vision. The RSV brings out the way noun and verb echo each other in both halves of the poetic parallelism: "The plunderer plunders, and the destroyer destroys." Why is the vision described as a dire one? If the oracle had referred to Cyrus and his attack on Babylon, it might have seemed dreadful at first, because the Jews in Babylon could well have perished in the overthrow of the city. In fact, however, this did not happen, and an application to the time of Merodach-Baladan is certainly feasible. At that time, news of his revolt against Assyria would encourage the Jews in the thought that Assyria might be weakened or perhaps even eventually overthrown by him. The Fall of Babylon would represent a severe setback to such hopes.

Almost all commentators take the words of v.2b as utterances of the Lord, in which he calls on Elam and Media to attack Babylonia. The difficulty with this, however, is that in the time of Isaiah it was much more natural to see Elam and Media as enemies of Assyria and allies of Babylonia. Erlandsson, following Ibn Ezra, gives an interesting solution to the problem, suggesting that v.2 has the battle cries of Babylonia's allies as they launched their attack against Assyria. He then says, "The enigmatic 'I will put an end to all sighs' is perhaps an echo of Marduk-apal-iddina's promise to his partner-in-confederation Hezekiah." This assumes a somewhat different translation from that given in the NIV (see Notes).

3–4 The oracle against Moab (15:5; 16:9, 11) showed the deep distress Isaiah felt when he contemplated the slaughter of human beings, even when these belonged to a nation that was often an enemy of his own people. Clements (*Isaiah 1–39*, in loc.) takes it that this is what these two verses mean. It is, of course, possible that Isaiah's horror came from his own identification with his people so that he felt the deep dismay that came over them with the downfall of their hope in Merodach-Baladan. The latter is perhaps the more likely, because he speaks of fear as well as horror. Mauchline (in loc.) says, "The final part of v.4 can mean that the twilight hour of his days, in which he used to enjoy a period of quiet thought . . . is now filled with foreboding and fear; or the reference may be to the evening of his life, when the prophet had hoped for peace and quiet and now saw that hope shattered."

5 This verse paints a scene of feasting, but where was it enacted? Most commentators assume it took place in Babylon. Herodotus tells us that the taking of Babylon by the Persians in 539 B.C. was so swift that many who were at their wine in the city center did not even know that the outlying parts of the city were in enemy hands.

Erlandsson takes v.5 quite differently. It is the leaders of Judah who are feasting (cf. 22:1–2, 13). The second half of the verse does not in this case depict a sudden change of mood, with agitated preparation for battle, but rather underlines the atmosphere of leisured ease. Arrangements are made for sentry duty, the officers detailed for this using their time on guard to apply oil to the shields to prevent them from cracking when they are struck by the weapons of the foe.

6–10 The prophet had seen a vision; then he heard the word of the Lord. Isaiah was to have a man posted on the lookout (v.6). What was he to expect to see? Any group of riders was to be reported (v.7), for they could be bringing news of what happened in the far country. The lookout was at his post for many days (v.8). His tour of duty wearied him, but his patience was at last rewarded as a lone charioteer appeared on the horizon (v.9). The message he brought was that Babylon, from which the people have been expecting so much, had fallen, presumably to the Assyrians (v.10). There was no trace of the rejoicing that accompanied the fall of that city in chapter 14. If Erlandsson is correct in his interpretation, this is simple to explain; for the prophet was describing the downfall of Babylon, not before the Persians—who were to be the means of return from exile for the Jews—but before the Assyrians, who were still the main "scourge of God" in the Fertile Crescent. The reference to the images of Babylon's gods; and their shattering is perhaps an implied rebuke to Judah's leaders. How could they hope for the blessing of God on an alliance with pagans?

The people of Judah, who had already suffered much at the hands of the Assyrians, are depicted as prostrate—and yet alive—like grain that has fallen—bruised and yet safe—on the threshing floor after the thresher has battered it severely with his flail (v.11). The image underlining their helpless condition was also perhaps intended to convey a note of hope. Judah was not chaff but grain, and the Lord Almighty who had used Assyria to bring the downfall of Babylon was also the God of Israel who would protect his people and fulfill his purposes for them. Their main human hope had gone, but this would leave them free to put their trust in the Lord.

Notes

1 On מַשָּׂא (*maśśāʾ*, "oracle"), see the note at 13:1.

נֶגֶב (*negeb*, "Negeb"), translated "southland" in the NIV, is the tract of land lying south of Judah. It was barren, semidesert country. The NIV's "invader" is not represented in the text.

2 The NIV rightly renders the participle בּוֹגֵד (*bôgēd*) as "traitor" rather than "destroyer" (so RSV, NASB), thus following the correct sense of the verb בָּגַד (*bāgad*, "to betray"; cf. 24:16; 33:1; 48:8). Macintosh (*Isaiah 21*, p. 12) doubts whether the other sense is a valid one at all. He says, "Such a meaning cannot be said to be clearly attested for the verb, and it is not indicated in this verse either by the ancient versions or by the rabbinic commentators."

כָּל־אַנְחָתָה הִשְׁבַּתִּי (*kol- ʾanḥātāh hišbattî*) is translated "I will bring to an end all the groaning she has caused." The last three words are not represented in the text and need not be assumed as required to give good sense, if Erlandsson is correct. See comment above.

10. Prophecy Against Edom

21:11–12

11An oracle concerning Dumah:

> Someone calls to me from Seir,
> "Watchman, what is left of the night?
> Watchman, what is left of the night?"
> 12The watchman replies,
> "Morning is coming, but also the night,
> If you would ask, then ask;
> and come back yet again."

11–12 Our commentary on this short oracle has already commenced, for the heading we have given is itself an interpretation. The NIV margin says, "*Dumah* means *silence* or stillness, a word play on *Edom*" (emphasis theirs). This is almost certainly correct, though some commentators favor a reference rather to an oasis in Arabia: Dumah el Jandal. The latter seems most improbable, however, in view of the name "Seir," which is the rocky, mountainous area in Edom's heartland and which is so often employed as a synonym for Edom itself (cf., e.g., Num 24:18; Judg 5:4).

Cheyne (p. 128) says that for all its practical significance for the prophet's contemporaries and for later generations, this short oracle might just as well not have been written. Yet, as part of the Word of God, it must have both meaning and relevance. It's meaning is perhaps secured if we understand it through the wordplay in its title. God gives light to his people in the midst of perplexing historical circumstances.

The very ministry of Isaiah is evidence of this. It is otherwise, however, with Judah's pagan neighbors. The reply of the watchman (v. 12) is so vague and enigmatic —perhaps even evasive—that it is tantamount to no reply at all. The one certainty is that the night will end in morning but also that this will be followed by another night. Perhaps this refers to the lifting of the oppressive Assyrian overlordship, which would be replaced by another black night, the rule of Babylon.

Notes

---

11 On מַשָּׂא (*maśśā'*, "oracle"), see the note at 13:1.

---

11. *Prophecy Against Arabia*

21:13–17

[13]An oracle concerning Arabia:

> You caravans of Dedanites,
>   who camp in the thickets of Arabia,
> [14] bring water for the thirsty;
> you who live in Tema,
>   bring food for the fugitives.
> [15]They flee from the sword,
>   from the drawn sword,
> from the bent bow
>   and from the heat of battle.

[16]This is what the Lord says to me: "Within one year, as a servant bound by contract would count it, all the pomp of Kedar will come to an end. [17]The survivors of the bowmen, the warriors of Kedar, will be few." The LORD, the God of Israel, has spoken.

13–17 This oracle, or pair of oracles (for some consider vv. 16–17 to be a separate though linked oracle), has often been thought to have close ties with the brief one that precedes it. This would certainly be true if the identification of Dumah with an Arabian oasis proved to be correct. As we have seen, however (cf. comment at v. 11), this presents difficulties in view of the apparent identification of Dumah with Seir. It is noteworthy that Edom was really on the edge of Arabia. Dumah, Tema, and Kedar all occur in Genesis 25:13–16, in the list of Ishmael's descendents. The Dumah referred to there, of course, would be the Arabian one, as Edom was the people of Esau (Gen 25:30).

Macintosh (*Isaiah 21*, pp. 139–43) suggests that vv. 11–17 are really one unit and that vv. 13–17 concern the flight of Edomite refugees to the oases of the Arabian peninsula so that they may find refuge from the enemy from Mesopotamia. This would then provide a parallel with the plight of the Moabites who sought refuge in Judah and in Edom (see commentary at ch. 16). This theory does require a certain amount of textual emendation, and we should always seek to make good sense of a text as it stands before resorting to such alteration.

Sargon II conducted a campaign against the northern Arabian tribes in 715 B.C., and this could well provide an appropriate setting for this oracle. There are armed men (vv. 15, 17) drawn from the various Arabian tribes, but they are no match for the Assyrians and are put to flight. They flee exhausted, parched with thirst, and in need of food. The caravans plying their trade and camping out in the wastelands (v. 13) and the settled town-dwellers of the oases (v. 14) are both urged to provide sustenance for the fugitives. The resistance of the Arab tribes will be short-lived, for their armies will be reduced to a very meagre remnant within twelve months (v. 16). The closing oracle formula (v. 17) probably underlines the fact that this is the judgment of the God of Israel, not simply the interaction of human forces.

Notes

13 On מַשָּׂא (maśśā', "oracle"), see the note at 13:1.

In Ezek 25:13, Dedan has a close association with Edom, and so it seems to have been located in northwestern Arabia.

בַּיַּעַר (bayya'ar) is translated "thickets" in the NIV and the RSV, following the ancient versions (cf. 22:8, "Forest"). Delitzsch (in loc.), pointing out the unsuitability of this in the present context, suggests a link with a cognate Arabic root meaning "rocky terrain," which certainly seems more apt.

The ancient versions presuppose a different pointing of בַּעֲרָב (ba'rab, "concerning Arabia"), reading bā'ereb ("in the evening"), and some modern commentators prefer this. Delitzsch (in loc.) makes the interesting suggestion that, like Dumah (v. 11), the word has a double entendre. This seems very likely. Like Edom, Arabia was destined for a long, dark night.

14 Tema (modern Teyman) was in northwestern Arabia, on one of the most well-watered oases in the peninsula.

16 For the binding of a servant by contract, see the comment at 16:14.

Kedar was an important Arabian tribe, but the word appears as a general reference to the Arabian Bedouin in three passages (42:11; 60:7; Jer 2:10). In this context the wider reference seems appropriate, though the narrower is not impossible.

12. Prophecy Against Jerusalem

22:1–25

¹An oracle concerning the Valley of Vision:

> What troubles you now,
>   that you have all gone up on the roofs,
> ²O town full of commotion,
>   O city of tumult and revelry?
> Your slain were not killed by the sword,
>   nor did they die in battle.
> ³All your leaders have fled together;
>   they have been captured without using the bow.
> All you who were caught were taken prisoner together,
>   having fled while the enemy was still far away.
> ⁴Therefore I said, "Turn away from me;
>   let me weep bitterly.
> Do not try to console me
>   over the destruction of my people."

⁵The Lord, the Lord Almighty, has a day
 of tumult and trampling and terror
 in the Valley of Vision,
a day of battering down walls
 and of crying out to the mountains.
⁶Elam takes up the quiver,
 with her charioteers and horses;
 Kir uncovers the shield.
⁷Your choicest valleys are full of chariots,
 and horsemen are posted at the city gates;
⁸ the defenses of Judah are stripped away.

And you looked in that day
 to the weapons in the Palace of the Forest;
⁹you saw that the City of David
 had many breaches in its defenses;
you stored up water
 in the Lower Pool.
¹⁰You counted the buildings in Jerusalem
 and tore down houses to strengthen the wall.
¹¹You built a reservoir between the two walls
 for the water of the Old Pool,
but you did not look to the One who made it,
 or have regard for the One who planned it long ago.

¹²The Lord, the Lord Almighty,
 called you on that day
to weep and to wail,
 to tear out your hair and put on sackcloth.
¹³But see, there is joy and revelry,
 slaughtering of cattle and killing of sheep,
 eating of meat and drinking of wine!
"Let us eat and drink," you say,
 "for tomorrow we die!"

¹⁴The Lord Almighty has revealed this in my hearing: "Till your dying day this sin will not be atoned for," says the Lord, the Lord Almighty.

¹⁵This is what the Lord, the Lord Almighty, says:

"Go, say to this steward,
 to Shebna, who is in charge of the palace:
¹⁶What are you doing here and who gave you permission
 to cut out a grave for yourself here,
hewing your grave on the height
 and chiseling your resting place in the rock?

¹⁷"Beware, the Lord is about to take firm hold of you
 and hurl you away, O you mighty man.
¹⁸He will roll you up tightly like a ball
 and throw you into a large country.
There you will die
 and there your splendid chariots will remain—
 you disgrace to your master's house!
¹⁹I will depose you from your office,
 and you will be ousted from your position.

²⁰"In that day I will summon my servant, Eliakim son of Hilkiah. ²¹I will clothe him with your robe and fasten your sash around him and hand your authority over

to him. He will be a father to those who live in Jerusalem and to the house of Judah. ²²I will place on his shoulder the key to the house of David; what he opens no one can shut, and what he shuts no one can open. ²³I will drive him like a peg into a firm place; he will be a seat of honor for the house of his father. ²⁴All the glory of his family will hang on him: its offspring and offshoots—all its lesser vessels, from the bowls to all the jars.

²⁵"In that day," declares the LORD Almighty, "the peg driven into the firm place will give way; it will be sheared off and will fall, and the load hanging on it will be cut down." The LORD has spoken.

This chapter divides into two well-defined sections: vv. 1–14 and vv. 15–25. The subjects of the two are different and yet linked. The first section shows us Isaiah's very strong denunciation of Jerusalem's people because of their attitude on the occasion of a deliverance of the city from enemies outside its walls. The second focuses attention on two of the leaders of the people. If we read the first part in the light of chapters 36–37, we may well come to the conclusion that the occasion is the deliverance of the city from Sennacherib. Chapters 36–37 emphasize the divine deliverance that took place in response to the faith of Hezekiah and his people, while this present oracle makes it clear how shallow this faith really was. The picture in chapters 36–37 does not necessarily conflict with what we find here any more than the attitude of the writers of Kings and Chronicles to Josiah's reformation—in which they rejoiced—conflicts with Jeremiah's recognition of the superficiality and shallowness of the spirit of penitence that it was undertaken in.

Both E. J. Young (*Book of Isaiah,* in loc.) and Clements (*Isaiah 1–39,* in loc.) argue that the siege referred to here is that of Nebuchadnezzar, though Young holds the passage to be both Isaianic and predictive, while Clements denies both. The whole discussion in Young is valuable, and the present writer feels that the literary contiguity of vv. 1–14 and 15–25 provides strong evidence for a date in the reign of Hezekiah. See the comments at vv. 15–25 to locate Shebna and Eliakim historically.

1a The expression *gê' ḥizzāyôn* ("Valley of Vision") has been variously understood by commentators, though always in reference to Jerusalem. We do not think of this city as situated in a valley, because of the hills of Zion and Moriah on which it was built; but in fact it is comparatively low, being surrounded by hills (cf. Ps 125:2; Jer 21:13). The phrase may refer to the fact that it was the very place where so many prophetic visions—both Isaiah's and other prophets'—had been received and then given to the people. This would, therefore, intensify the responsibility of her people for their reprehensible attitude.

Many commentators have noted the exceptional sharpness of the prophet's language in these verses. He was deeply disturbed. If we have rightly located the prophecy during the deliverance from Sennacherib, this was late in Isaiah's public ministry; and he poured into this prophecy all the disappointment he had with his own people that must have accumulated throughout the decades he had been prophesying to them. He had been warned that there would be little response (cf. 6:9–10), and he had certainly found this to be true in the days of Ahaz (cf. ch. 7). Perhaps he had hoped for better things under Hezekiah, who was certainly more godly than his predecessor. This would have enabled him to enter into the feelings of the Servant of the Lord as the latter looked back on his own ministry (cf. 49:4).

1b–2a A noisy spirit of excitement came on the whole city, and the flat roofs were thronged with revelers. The people probably went up originally to survey the Assyrians outside the city; but finding them dead (cf. 37:36), they stayed to celebrate (cf. vv. 12–13).

2b–3 These verses present a contrast with vv. 1b–2a. Sennacherib, in his inscriptions, spoke of inflicting a defeat on Hezekiah; and this probably took place during the earlier stages of the Assyrian campaign in Judah (cf. 2 Kings 18:13–16; Isa 1:5–9). Clements (*Isaiah 1–39*, in loc.) considers the reference to the slain in v.2b an ironic comment on the revelers "lying in drunken stupor where, only a short time before, it was feared that they would be killed in battle." This is possible, though the prophet may be thinking of men captured and put to death in the early stages of the campaign. The main point Isaiah was making is not affected, for he was driving home the fact that the people could not glory in themselves, as if they had won a mighty victory. In fact, they were so demoralized at the approach of the enemy that they simply took to their heels and fled.

4–8a Isaiah knew that Jerusalem, delivered by a wonderful act of God's grace, would one day perish at his hand. The people had learned nothing from what had happened. Skinner (*Isaiah*, in loc.) says, "He had expected after the great deliverance, and the fulfillment of his own daring predictions, to see the emergence of the new Israel, the remnant that was to be the nucleus of the Messianic kingdom. Bitter must have been his disenchantment when he saw that the crisis had come and gone, and left the temper of the nation as frivolous, as secular, and as insensible to the divine as it had been before." The spiritual sorrow of the prophet for his people was so deep that he was inconsolable (v.4). As a man of God, of course, he could accept what, as a Judean, he could not welcome; for the destruction of the people that had been revealed to him was the judgment of God.

The Day of the Lord, prophesied in 2:6–22, will fall on Jerusalem. The NIV has brought out the terrifying alliteration and assonance of three consecutive Hebrew words with its translation "tumult and trampling the terror" (v.5). The people were looking down over the walls, gloating over the slain Assyrians. On God's great day those same walls would be battered down by the enemy, and the mountains surrounding the Valley of Vision would echo to the ineffectual wails of Jerusalem's inhabitants.

This prophecy was fulfilled when Nebuchadnezzar took the city in 586 B.C., though history was destined to repeat itself in A.D. 70—when the Romans overcame Jewish resistance and entered Jerusalem to wreak havoc on its people and its buildings. There may have been Elamites and Syrians (from Kir) serving in the army of the Babylonian king (v.6). The mention of them imparts an extra dimension of terror to the oracle, because it pictures the besieging army as an international one.

8b–11 The prophet returned to the situation in Jerusalem, when the Assyrian army appeared on the horizon. By their actions the people had made it very clear to Isaiah that their trust was in human beings rather than in God. A city facing a long siege has many needs. Its defenders need adequate weapons. Jerusalem had, in the Palace of the Forest (v.8), its own royal armory (cf. 1 Kings 7:2–5); and no doubt its staff undertook an urgent check on their supply of swords and spears that day. The walls of the city and especially its defensive towers were in need of repair (v.9), and some of its houses had to be destroyed to obtain stones for this (v.10), for there was neither time nor liberty of access to get stone from the Judean quarries. Any house that was not really needed would have to go. Ahaz, also in unbelief, had busied himself with the water supply of the city (cf. 7:1–3), and the men of Hezekiah's Jerusalem had the same outlook (cf. 2 Chron 32:1–5). A special reservoir was built (v.11), probably to retain, for later use, surplus water from the Pool of Siloam.

God is the maker of history as well as of nature. History, with its series of world-empires and successive judgments (cf. 40:23–24) is all under his almighty hand; and he is the God of Israel, for this people is in special relationship with him. Because of this situation, they should have looked to him with faith. Instead, they were busy trying to find ways of evading the challenge to believe.

12–14 In commenting on 17:10, we noted Isaiah's inspired sense of appropriateness in his choice of titles for God. In view of this, there is something ominous about the use (v.12) of a title of power—"the LORD Almighty,"—instead of one of relationship, like "the God of Israel." The same title is repeated twice in v.14. If the people would not seek his grace in repentance, they would feel his power (cf. 1 Cor 4:21) in a terrifying act of his judgment on their city. The prophet's sense of fitness is outraged by the scene that presents itself to him as he walks through Jerusalem's streets (v.13). They should have been thronged with its people, contrite in spirit, making their way to the temple in a corporate act of penitence. He probably has in mind some time during the siege when all that could be done to prepare for an onslaught by the enemy had been done, and when the people used their leisure in the spirit of the modern saying "You are a long time dead!"

Verse 14 contains one of the Bible's most terrifying sentences, comparable perhaps to the words of Revelation 22:11. The revelers had probably slaughtered the animals used by them for their feasts at Jerusalem's temple. Let them not think though that any sacrifice could be offered to atone for this sin. At the very time when God's promises to protect Jerusalem were being so wonderfully fulfilled, the threat was given that the city would most certainly fall one day before its enemies and that nothing, just nothing, could avert the judgment of God on it.

15–16 Terrifying as this threat of judgment undoubtedly was, it might seem to some to lose something of its horror because it was so general. After all, Jerusalem was a community; and when an act of judgment strikes a group of people, the individual may seek to assure himself that he has simply been caught up in the consequences of other people's sins, for he himself is of course without specific blame. Isaiah allowed no such escape route for the hardened conscience. The spiritual link between vv.1–14 and 15–25 is perhaps underlined by the use of the same great title for God in both sections of it. He is "the Lord, the LORD Almighty" (v.15; cf. v.12). The spotlight of judgment is now directed toward one man, Shebna, the steward of the king's palace (cf. 36:3, 11, 22; 37:2).

The pyramid tombs of the Pharaohs epitomize the desire of prominent people in the ancient Near East to have a grandiose burying place so that they would be the objects of adulation for centuries after their death (v.16). Julius II, in building a splendid tomb for himself, was tarred with the same brush in Michaelangelo's day and proclaimed himself, by this fact alone, unworthy to be a leader of the church of the lowly Savior.

17–19 The NIV's "beware" (v.17) for *hinnēh* ("behold"), though somewhat free, does justice to the purpose of this call to Shebna to visualize the future scene. It is a prospect very different from the one he had planned. The words "O you mighty man" take him at this own estimate of himself. God will show him who it is that has the real power, for God will project him ignominiously out of his office and into another land (vv.18–19). This is surely a reference to Assyria. The splendid tomb, hewn out at his order in some place of prominence, will not then be a witness to his greatness but to his overweening ambition; for he would lie dead in an alien land. He perhaps had paraded through Jerusalem's streets in ceremonial chariots (cf. 2 Sam 15:1; 1 Kings 1:5); but he would now be seen to be, not the glory of his master, the king, but his disgrace.

The contempt felt for Shebna is summed up in the scornful expression "this steward" (v.15; cf. John 8:39), This has led many to suppose that this oracle does not tell us the whole reason for this contempt, that allied to the official's ambition and pride was a political policy (probably pro-Egyptian) that ran counter to Isaiah's mesage for the king and the people to trust only in the Lord. This would certainly explain why this oracle is associated here with the one in vv.1–14.

20–23 Shebna had been riding ostentatiously in his chariots and building a splendid grave for himself, seeking in all this the praise of men. How much better to have God's smile of approval and to be described, in a simple but eloquent phrase, as "my servant" (v.20; cf. 20:3; 42:1; 52:13). Eliakim, who is also—like Shebna—mentioned in 36:3, 11, 22, and 37:2, was to take over Shebna's office and so to be given his ceremonial robes (v.21). See the comment at 36:3 for a discussion of the relative status of the two men at the time of the events recorded there. The word "father" suggests both his authority over the people of Jerusalem and also the provision he would make for them in virtue of his office. Verse 22 is not intended figuratively but literally, for the steward would have the large master key of the palace fastened to the shoulder of his tunic. This passes into symbol in the NT at Revelation 3:7 (cf. Matt 16:19; 18:18).

The simile of v.23 and the metaphor that follows it have different functions. The first may be a tent peg (though its use changes in vv.24–25), giving stability to the kingdom (cf. 33:20). Through him his whole family would advance in social dignity, promoted, as it were, to a seat closer to the throne at the royal table.

It seems probable that Eliakim had a very different policy from that of Shebna, more in line with Isaiah's counsel to trust in God. If so, then, his advice to the king would help to secure a real and not just an apparent strength to the nation in a time of international insecurity.

24–25 The mood of the oracle changes dramatically. The true honor of "my servant" (v.20) is replaced by a satirical picture that reveals almost as much contempt as that shown toward Shebna in vv.15–19. Shebna's great sin was pride, but Eliakim's was nepotism. There was a legitimate honor that would inevitably come to those related to a family head with a high position in the land. Eliakim had, however, been chosen for office because of his own qualities, not theirs. Isaiah played on the double meaning of the Hebrew word _kābôd_, which is translated "honor" in v.23 and "glory" in v.24. It may also signify weight. The peg is not now seen giving strength to the tent but rather fastened to the wall of the palace kitchen with a motley assortment of kitchen vessels hanging from it, the vessels Zechariah perhaps had in mind in his vision of the elevation of the common for holy use (Zech 14:21). The temptations of high office are many, and those who occupy them need the prayers of God's people.

Notes

1 On מַשָּׂא (*maśśā'*, "oracle"), see the note at 13:1.

6 Kir can hardly be identical with "Kir in Moab" (15:1) but rather with that mentioned in three other verses (Amos 1:5; 9:7; 2 Kings 16:9) in each case in connection with Syria. Its location cannot be established with certainty.

9 The NEB translates, "you filled all the many pools in the City of David" instead of "you saw that the City of David had many breaches in its defenses." The former is based on repointing רָאִיתֶם from *re'îtem* ("you saw") to *re'îtem* ("you filled"). This involves understanding בְּקִיעֵי (*beqî'ê*, "breaches") in reference to scooped-out reservoirs. This is quite feasible, but the MT makes good sense, especially as vv.9–10 would then assume an AB-AB pattern, with references to the defenses and the water supply juxtaposed twice.

For the topography of vv.9–11, see the note at 7:3.

11 See the note at 7:3.

13 This verse may quote a current proverb. It is itself quoted in 1 Cor 15:32.

15 Shebna is described as "the secretary" in 36:3. The office he has here seems comparable to the Moslem "grand vizier," the Frankish "mayor of the palace," or the former English "chamberlain." The official in charge of the royal buildings and supplies would certainly have considerable and probably increasing power. See H.J. Katzenstein, "The Royal Steward," IEJ 10 (1960.): 149ff.

---

13. *Prophecy Against Tyre*

23:1–18

[1]An oracle concerning Tyre:

Wail, O ships of Tarshish!
    For Tyre is destroyed
    and left without house or harbor.
From the land of Cyprus
    word has come to them.

[2]Be silent, you people of the island
    and you merchants of Sidon,
    whom the seafarers have enriched.
[3]On the great waters
    came the grain of the Shihor;
the harvest of the Nile was the revenue of Tyre,
    and she became the marketplace of the nations.

[4]Be ashamed, O Sidon, and you, O fortress of the sea,
    for the sea has spoken:
"I have neither been in labor nor given birth;
    I have neither reared sons nor brought up daughters."
[5]When word comes to Egypt,
    they will be in anguish at the report from Tyre.

[6]Cross over to Tarshish;
    wail, you people of the island.

7Is this your city of revelry,
    the old, old city,
whose feet have taken her
    to settle in far-off lands?
8Who planned this against Tyre,
    the bestower of crowns,
whose merchants are princes,
    whose traders are renowned in the earth?
9The LORD Almighty planned it,
    to bring low the pride of all glory
    and to humble all who are renowned on the earth.

10Go through your land;
    the Daughter of Tarshish, like the Nile,
    will no longer be a haven for you.
11The LORD has stretched out his hand over the sea
    and made its kingdoms tremble.
He has given an order concerning Phoenicia
    that her fortresses be destroyed.
12He said, "No more of your reveling,
    O Virgin Daughter of Sidon, now crushed!

"Up, cross over to Cyprus;
    even there you will find no rest."
13Look at the land of the Babylonians,
    this people that is now of no account!
The Assyrians have made it
    a place for desert creatures;
they raised up their siege towers,
    they stripped its fortresses bare
    and turned it into a ruin.

14Wail, you ships of Tarshish;
    your fortress is destroyed!

15At that time Tyre will be forgotten for seventy years, the span of a king's life. But at the end of these seventy years, it will happen to Tyre as in the song of the prostitute:

16"Take up a harp, walk through the city,
    O prostitute forgotten;
play the harp well, sing many a song,
    so that you will be remembered."

17At the end of seventy years, the LORD will deal with Tyre. She will return to her hire as a prostitute and will ply her trade with all the kingdoms on the face of the earth. 18Yet her profit and her earnings will be set apart for the LORD; they will not be stored up or horded. Her profits will go to those who live before the LORD, for abundant food and fine clothes.

History has known a number of small countries—some of them little more than city-states—that have had a disproportionate influence because of their possession of fine harbors and strong commercial instincts and skills. Venice, Genoa, and the cities of the Hanseatic League are examples from the past, while Singapore and the Netherlands, with its great port of Rotterdam, are modern examples. Phoenicia, with its two important ports of Tyre and Sidon, was the maritime commercial state contemporary with much of OT history. Like all Israel's and Judah's neighbors, of course, it was pagan; and the worship of Melkart, the Tyrian Baal, had posed a serious religious threat in the days of Ahab and Jezebel. Mauchline (in loc.) writes, "The Phoenicians, with their accumulated wealth and their blatant materialism, represented the very type of culture against whose vices Amos in particular warned the Israelites." Until the time of the Assyrians, who had designs on the whole Mediterranean seaboard and its hinterland, this small state and its important commercial cities had been left relatively undisturbed by conflict. It certainly merited judgment, however, and would have to experience this at the hands of the Assyrians, just as other states in the area were to face. It was Sennacherib, during the period 705–701 B.C. who turned his attention to Phoenicia, which had been a nominal part of the Assyrian Empire for some time. The country was devastated, and Tyre itself was subjected to a long and bitter siege. It was later also besieged by the Babylonians, the Persians, and the Greeks under Alexander the Great, who virtually destroyed it in 333 B.C. after one of the greatest sieges in history. It may be that the prophecy, in terms of its fulfillment, incorporates elements from some of these later times as well as the time of the Assyrian onslaught on the country.

1–5 The Phoenicians had a number of colonies and dependent trading-stations in the Mediterranean. Tarshish (v.1), probably in Spain (cf. Notes), and some of the cities of Cyprus were among these. Ships making their way back eastward from Tarshish would call at Cyprus before completing their journey to Tyre. At Cyprus they would hear that their harbor had been destroyed; so they could not complete their journey. Sidon (v.2) was the other port that alternated with Tyre as the chief port of the land. The Phoenicians had special commercial links with Egypt and no doubt many a Tyrian or Sidonian vessel would carry large quantities of grain from the fields of Shihor (v.3), in the Nile Valley. These commercial ties with Egypt would be viewed with considerable suspicion by the Assyrians and the rulers of the various world-empires that succeeded them, for Egypt was usually the final major enemy to be overcome before complete mastery of the Fertile Crescent and the eastern Mediterranean could be achieved.

Both vocatives in v.4 apply to Sidon. The sea is personified as the mother of the Phoenicians, and nothing could be more appropriate. With the slaughter of so many Sidonians by Assyria, Sidon had been bereft of her children and was left as if she had never had them. The sadness of the sea is matched by that of Egypt (v.5), whose trading links with Tyre and Sidon and, perhaps, her own danger from the same source gave her sympathy.

6–9 The prophet next turned to the people of the nearest Phoenician colony, Cyprus (cf. v.8 with vv.1–2). They were to take the news farther west to Tarshish (v.6) or even, perhaps, to flee there. The tone of these verses is a shade less mocking than the taunts against Babylon in chapters 13–14. Nevertheless, the prophet pointed to the contrast between Tyre's past gaiety and wide-flung colonization and commercialism (v.7) and its current humbling under the mighty hand of God (v.9). No doubt all the rulers of world empires from Assyria onward would plan to deal with Tyre on their way to other victories; but her downfall was really the work of the Lord, whose counsels ultimately prevail in the affairs of mankind. Isaiah never tired of saying that God was absolutely opposed to human pride in its every form. It is no accident that one of his illustrations of this in 2:13 is "the cedars of Lebanon" that graced the slopes of the mountains behind Tyre and Sidon.

10–12a These verses develop the theocentric theme of vv.6–9. The Phoenicians were warned that their trading links with Tarshish and Egypt should not induce complacency in them in the face of the threat of divine judgment. Had not Jonah found that running away to Tarshish did not enable him to evade the hand of the Lord (Jonah 1:3–4)? That hand (cf. 5:25; 10:4; 31:3)—which had been stretched out over the Red Sea in judgment on the Egyptians in the time of Moses—was stretched out now even over the Mediterranean. No kingdom on its coasts could reckon itself immune from God's righteous wrath.

12b–14 Erlandsson (pp. 99) rightly describes v.13 as a *crux interpretum*. He quotes Buhl as holding that the verse "defies any explanation," Gray as declaring it to be "quite unintelligible," and points out that Fohrer passes over it in silence. Concerning the words "Behold the land of the Chaldeans" (NIV, "Look at the land of the Babylonians"), Clements (*Isaiah 1–39*, in loc.) says, "The phrase is undoubtedly a later addition made after the period of Assyrian domination had passed and re-applying the lament to Tyre in the Babylonian era." There is no need for us to take this view. If we assume that the NIV is correct (see Notes), the verse makes excellent sense in both its literary and its historical contexts. If the prophecy comes from the year 703 or a little after, then it will refer to the ferocious attack of Sennacherib, who had an almost pathological loathing of the Babylonians. If it has to be dated a few years earlier, it could refer to the campaign of Sargon II against the Chaldeans in 710. Both these events predated Sennacherib's attack on Tyre in 701. Neither Tyre nor even Cyprus, across the sea, could be regarded as a haven of safety when Assyria, the instrument of God's wrath (cf. 10:5–11), was on the rampage. Verse 14 picks up language from vv.6, 11 to provide a final lament.

15–18 Many of Isaiah's oracles contain a note of surprise at their end, and so often it is a word of grace (cf. 8:16–9:7; 19:1–25; 42:18–43:13). This however differs from many of the others. Here there is to be a partial reprieve, with a new period of commercial success for Tyre, but with a view not so much to the blessing of her people but to supply the needs of the house of God in Jerusalem.

The period of seventy years (v.15) is familiar to readers of Jeremiah (cf. Jer 25:11–12; 29:10). In the later prophet it refers to the captivity of the Jews in Babylon, while here it applies to Tyre. Erlandsson (p. 102) is surely right when he says, "If one is looking for an interval of seventy years during which Tyre's trade was crippled, the period which immediately comes to mind is that between the years 700 and 630 when Assyria did not permit Tyre to engage in any business activity. When Assyria's hold over Palestine came to an end around 630, most of the western states were enabled to flourish again, especially Judah and Tyre."

A careful study of the symbolic picture of Babylon in the Book of Revelation reveals that it was not only "Babylon" prophecies in the OT that went into the construction of this picture but other oracles also, and especially those against Tyre. The description of the great city as a harlot probably owes something to this present passage. The comparison is appropriate, for the harlot bedecks herself in gaudy finery and enters into a commercial transaction with her clients (v.17). Seaports have always been particularly notorious in connection with prostitution. Tyre was an old, old city (cf. v.7) and so would need to attract her clients now by singing some song associated with her trade.

There is an important link here between the oracles against the nations (which come to their conclusion with this prophecy against Phoenicia) and the range of prophecies that occur later in the book, in the sections often attributed to so-called Deutero-Isaiah and Trito-Isaiah. All three major parts of the book, according to criticism, contain the notion that people from the Gentile nations will come up to Jerusalem, not only to worship (cf. 2:1–5; 49:6–7; 60:1), but also to make their treasures available for the use of the chosen people and in the temple of God (cf. 18:7; 45:14; 49:22–23; 60:9–14). This motif, therefore, gives a further change of tone to the final verse of the oracle. God's ultimate plan for Tyre—as for Ethiopia, Egypt, and Assyria (cf. 18:7; 19:18–25)—is to bring her into line with his central purpose for Israel. Once before, in the days of Solomon, material from Israel's northern neighbor had been used in the service of the temple (cf. 1 Kings 5:1–12); and this will happen again.

Notes

1 On מַשָּׂא (maśśāʾ, "oracle"), see the note at 13:1.
   For "ships of Tarshish," see the note at 2:16. Tarshish is usually identified as Tarsessos, at the mouth of the Guadalquiver in Spain. For other suggestions, see Young (Book of Isaiah, in loc.).
   "Cyprus" translates כִּתִּים (kittîm) and is certainly correct.
2 The island referred to here could be Cyprus, mentioned in v.1, or it could be the small island on which New Tyre had been built. The latter is the more likely, as it forms a sense-rhythm couplet with the next line with its reference to the other seaport of Phoenicia.
8 Why is Tyre called "the bestower of crowns" here? Perhaps it is a reference to the measure of self-government given by Tyre to her various overseas colonies.
9 Instead of the words "to bring low the pride of all glory and to humble all who are renowned on the earth," 1QIsa reads "to humble every proud one, to bring greatness into contempt—all the earth's most honored ones." (cf. BHS).
10 The NIV follows the LXX and 1QIsa, reading עִבְדוּ (ibdû, "work")—instead of the MT's עִבְרִי (ibrî, "Go through")—yielding the sense "Till your land." The particle כ (kᵉ) is then understood slightly differently, so that the whole clause becomes "Till your land as along the Nile."
   The RSV follows the MT in reading מֵזַח (mēzaḥ, "restraint") and so rendering "there is no restraint any more"; but the NIV amends to מָחֹז (maḥōz, "harbor") and translates the Hebrew words as "for you no longer have a harbor." The NIV's rendering would then mean that the people of Tarshish would need to take to agriculture. With the Phoenician harbors no longer available and Egyptian grain no longer coming to their own port, they needed to become internally self-sufficient. The RSV's translation seeks to follow the MT: "Overflow your land like the Nile, O daughter of Tarshish; there is no restraint any more." This suggests that Tarshish, as a Phoenician colony, felt her link with the mother city to be a restraint; and she was encouraged to develop independently. In fact, this makes good sense; so we should probably follow it.
11 "Phoenicia" here is literally "Canaan," which the Phoenicians in fact used to describe their own land. Everywhere else in the OT it is used of the eastern Mediterranean seaboard region generally or else of that part ultimately inhabited by Israel.
15 The words "the span of a king's life" are not easy to understand. Some commentators think they apply to a dynasty rather than to an individual king, while others try to apply them to a paticular monarch. They could mean that the days have been fixed by a king

and so are unalterable, with the implication, possibly, that God is the sovereign who has so decreed matters.

16 The light dance-rhythm employed for the harlot's song contrasts dramatically—and very tellingly—with the limping beat of the lament (cf. comment at 1:21–23) in other parts of the oracle.

III. God and the Whole World (24:1–27:13)

These chapters, often known as "The Isaiah Apocalypse," have for many years been the focus of much scholarly debate. W.R. Millar (*Isaiah 24–27 and the Origin of Apocalyptic* [Missoula, Mont.: Scholars, 1976]) gives a survey of the main points of view that have been advanced concerning these chapters. Crucial to the understanding of any literature, within or outside the Bible, is the question of literary genre. There is no general agreement as to the genre of this part of Isaiah. Millar (p. 21) says, "Within this century, scholars have labelled the literary genre of Isaiah 24–27 as a late post-exilic apocalyptic work, pre-exilic prophetic judgment literature, prophetic eschatology, exilic or early post-exilic proto-apocalyptic and, recently, early apocalyptic."

Basic to much of the discussion is the view that apocalyptic is, in general, later than prophecy; so if this material is to be labeled "apocalyptic," then it must be denied to Isaiah. This is, in fact, very much open to question. Biblical material that is apocalyptic in form—such as Daniel, Joel, and Zechariah 9–14—is often given a late date; and its apocalyptic content is made an important argument for so treating it. This implies a particular view of the chronological relationship between prophecy and apocalyptic. When prophecy and apocalyptic are distinguished, it is usually said that prophecy views the eschatological future in historical terms, with emphasis on particular places and nations, especially those that came into frequent contact with Israel and Judah. Apocalyptic, on the other hand, thinks cosmically and in terms of direct divine intervention in human affairs. Apocalyptic paints the future on a wider canvas than prophecy, with more startling colors but with less specific detail. It is said too that the apocalyptic emphasis on the whole cosmos—as distinct from the narrower world of the international politics of the Fertile Crescent—is a product of wider thinking than characterized the prophets. Moreover, it is often maintained that apocalyptic shows the influence of Persian apocalyptic eschatology, to which Jews were not exposed till the end of the Exile. This is highly questionable.

In fact, the line of distinction between prophecy and apocalyptic can be too rigidly drawn. It is not easy to place chapters 24–27 firmly in the one category or the other. There is a strong universal note in these chapters, but there are also some particular references to peoples and places, so that there is certainly not a complete break with history. Particularly, we note that a number of those mentioned in chapters 13–23 are referred to here (cf. esp. 25:10; 27:12–13). For this and other reasons, some scholars have broken up the unity of chapters 24–27 and treated different parts of this material as coming from different authors and periods. There is, however, a very real internal unity here. (The reader who wishes to pursue these questions in detail should consult especially Millar, *Isaiah 24–27*, and G.W. Anderson, "Isaiah 24–27 Reconsidered," VetTest Supplement 9 [1962]: 118–26.)

This commentary takes the view that the chapters are the genuine work of Isaiah, that they constitute a unity, and that they stand on the border between prophetic eschatology and apocalyptic. It would seem particularly fitting that they should depict the future in cosmic terms without completely losing contact with the histori- cal, because they follow a long series of oracles concerning various nations. If the material in the book has been arranged with great care, as seems to be the case (cf. Introduction, pp. 20–21), then nothing could be more appropriate.

1. *The Judgment of the World*

24:1–23

¹See, the LORD is going to lay waste the earth
  and devastate it;
 he will ruin its face
  and scatter its inhabitants—
²it will be the same
  for priest as for people,
  for master as for servant,
  for mistress as for maid,
  for seller as for buyer,
  for borrower as for lender,
  for debtor as for creditor.
³The earth will be completely laid waste
  and totally plundered.

                    The LORD has spoken this word.

⁴The earth dries up and withers,
  the world languishes and withers,
  the exalted of the earth languish.
⁵The earth is defiled by its people;
  they have disobeyed the laws,
 violated the statutes
  and broken the everlasting covenant.
⁶Therefore a curse consumes the earth;
  its people must bear their guilt.
 Therefore earth's inhabitants are burned up,
  and very few are left.
⁷The new wine dries up and the vine withers;
  all the merrymakers groan.
⁸The gaiety of the tambourines is stilled,
  the noise of the revelers has stopped,
  the joyful harp is silent.
⁹No longer do they drink wine with a song;
  the beer is bitter to its drinkers.
¹⁰The ruined city lies desolate;
  the entrance to every house is barred.
¹¹In the streets they cry out for wine;
  all joy turns to gloom,
  all gaiety is banished from the earth.
¹²The city is left in ruins,
  its gate is battered to pieces.
¹³So will it be on the earth
  and among the nations,
 as when an olive tree is beaten,
  or as when gleanings are left after the grape harvest.

¹⁴They raise their voices, they shout for joy;
  from the west they acclaim the LORD's majesty.

¹⁵Therefore in the east give glory to the LORD;
  exalt the name of the LORD, the God of Israel,
  in the islands of the sea.
¹⁶From the ends of the earth we hear singing:
  "Glory to the Righteous One."

But I said, "I waste away, I waste away!
  Woe to me!
The treacherous betray!
  With treachery the treacherous betray!"
¹⁷Terror and pit and snare await you,
  O people of the earth.
¹⁸Whoever flees at the sound of terror
  will fall into a pit;
whoever climbs out of the pit
  will be caught in a snare.

The floodgates of the heavens are opened,
  the foundations of the earth shake.
¹⁹The earth is broken up,
  the earth is split asunder,
  the earth is thoroughly shaken.
²⁰The earth reels like a drunkard,
  it sways like a hut in the wind;
so heavy upon it is the guilt of its rebellion
  that it falls—never to rise again.

²¹In that day the LORD will punish
  the powers in the heavens above
  and the kings on the earth below.
²²They will be herded together
  like prisoners bound in a dungeon;
they will be shut up in prison
  and be punished after many days.
²³The moon will be abashed and the sun ashamed;
  for the LORD Almighty will reign
on Mount Zion and in Jerusalem,
  and before its elders, gloriously.

This chapter is fundamental to the three that follow it. It speaks of a judgment that is universal. Not only does it make no reference to particular nations or specific historical events, it does not even restrict the judgment to the earth. This means that it sums up all the judgments on particular nations, as predicted in chapters 13–23, and goes beyond them.

1–3 These verses are a fitting introduction to the chapter. They call for inner vision in the opening word "see" (v. 1), so that the prophet is eager for his hearers to share what he has been given (cf. 1:1). Despite the many distinctions that occur in v. 2, these verses are very general in character. A universal judgment on the earth is proclaimed, affecting all its inhabitants, no matter what their status.

There can be no doubt that the word *'ereṣ* here means "earth" and not "land." The parallelism of v. 4 makes this abundantly clear. What kind of disaster does the prophet have in mind here? The Hebrew participle *bôqēq* ("lay waste") signifies emptying, and a second participle, *bôleqāh*, has a similar sense, the two providing a striking example of assonance in true Isaianic fashion.

This emptying is amplified when the prophet says, "He will ruin its face," which the RSV translates, "He will twist its surface." The idea seems to be that of distortion. It may be that the prophet is thinking in terms of an earthquake, so that the inhabitants are scattered by the violence of the tremor. It has also been suggested that he is contemplating an extreme drought (cf. v.7), so that the earth's surface is dried up and cracked. The chapter has a number of points of affinity with our Lord's eschatological teaching in Mark 13 where earthquakes and famine—often caused by drought—are mentioned (cf. Mark 13:8).

Isaiah seems to have had the early chapters of Genesis in mind as he uttered the prophecies of this chapter. At the Tower of Babel judgment, the people were scattered (cf. Gen 11:9); and this was to happen again. God's judgment would be completely indiscriminate, for it would affect all strata of society. The religious, social, and economic relationships of human life would not restrain it (v.2).

The affirmation that God has spoken (v.3) underlines the certainty of the judgments predicted. They are so terrifying and so universal that some such assurance is needed.

4–6 These verses are characterized by a strong moral tone. The true and living God carries out his judgments on moral principles, not as the expression of an arbitrary will. If human kings experience his righteous wrath, it is because their actions and their way of life are contrary to his will.

Some translations of v.4 differ somewhat from the NIV. The RSV, for example, translates "the heavens languish together with the earth" instead of "the exalted of the earth languish." In fact, the word $m^e r\hat{o}m$ ("exalted," NIV; "heavens," RSV) really means "height"; the NIV is to be preferred here. The verse teaches one side of the truth presented in v.2, a truth taught in 2:11–17 and elsewhere in the book.

Modern society is becoming more concerned about the physical pollution of our environment. Isaiah here dealt with the even more tragic and urgent matter of moral pollution, which is as widespread and serious today as it was in the eighth century B.C. The language of v.5 might seem, on the face of it, to be especially appropriate to Israel, because of her possession of the Mosaic Law; but the context here makes it plain that the whole world is in view. Many commentators, including Young and O. Kaiser, see a reference to the Noachian covenant, especially in the phrase "the everlasting covenant," which also occurs in Genesis 9:16. It is possible too that the prophet had Genesis 3 in mind, particularly in view of his reference to the curse in v.6. The world as a whole did not possess the moral commandments of God in written form as in the Mosaic Law; but those laws nevertheless represent the will of God for mankind, and mankind is under judgment for their violation. The word "disobeyed" implies at least some awareness of these moral requirements in the human conscience (cf. Rom 1:18–32; 2:11–16), thus an element of deliberateness in sin.

As suggested already, the curse of v.6 reminds the reader of Genesis 3:17–19. The judgment on the original sin has already been passed, of course, and what is before us in this chapter is an eschatological judgment executed on the whole race after many centuries of disobedience to God. The earth—at the beginning placed under the dominion of the human race—at the beginning, has already been cursed and bears the scars of human folly. Bearing guilt, of course, means suffering its consequences and so experiencing punishment at the hand of God.

7–9 Although this judgment is universal, it appears to be carried out on earth, like many of the judgments in the Book of Revelation; and there will be a remnant of mankind surviving it. (See the Introduction, pp. 14–16, for the general interpretation of this kind of prophecy.) What is the logical and chronological relationship between vv.7–9 and vv.10–13? Are we reading about a further though milder judgment that is to fall on those still left on earth, like the one in 6:12–13, which fell on Judah? This is possible, though it may be that these verses deal with the same judgment as vv.1–6, but in more detailed terms and perhaps in its first stages. The drying up of the world (v.4) certainly relates well to the languishing of the vine.

The Genesis curse had affected the plant world and thus the man whose daily work took him into the fields (Gen 3:17–19). Here the further curse of judgment affects the vines and those who use them to make drink (v.7). The prophet seems to be presenting a scene in which the vineyards are under judgment, so that little wine is available and that which is produced is bitter to the taste. The instrumental music and singing that often accompany bouts of drinking are heard no more (v.8). All the joy seems to have gone out of life (v.9), for the God of judgment is abroad.

10–13 Much has been written about the various references to "the city" in chapters 24–27 (see esp. 25:2–3; 26:5; 27:10–11). There have been many attempts to identify it with some particular city, especially Jerusalem or Babylon or an unnamed Moabite city (cf. 25:10). These attempts are probably all on the wrong track. Clements (*Isaiah 1–39*, in loc.) has well commented:

> There is a complete lack of any specific national reference, and none of the activities which are pursued within the city differentiate it in any special way. It can best be understood, therefore, as a pictorial description of the body of organized human society, a type of "Vanity Fair," which is to be subjected to the divine judgment. When God asserts his will in judgment he will bring to an end the existing human order, so that in a sense every city will be brought to chaos.

These passages, therefore, in a manner consistent with their eschatological setting, help to prepare the way for the symbolic use of Babylon in the Book of Revelation.

The city is in ruins, and the entrances to all its standing houses are blocked. Perhaps this is due to the presence of much rubble in the streets, or else it is because a spirit of fear has gripped the hearts of its remaining inhabitants. They secure themselves within their houses, hoping they will be safe from judgment (cf. 2:19, 21). Those still out in the streets are overtaken by a spirit of gloom, symbolized by the lack of wine (cf. vv.7–9).

Earlier, Isaiah had spoken about the judgment of Ephraim, in league with Damascus, and likened the tiny remnant left after judgment to a few olive berries left on the remotest branches of a tree that had been beaten during harvest, to secure the maximum yield (cf. 17:6). Isaiah used the same image here—but now in relation to the whole world.

14–16a One feature of chapters 24–27 that reminds the reader of the Book of Revelation is the way declarations of coming judgment are interspersed with songs of thanksgiving. The first of these occurs at this point. There has been a great judgment, but God has not made a full end to the earth's population. Those who remain lift up their voices in grateful praise to him (v.14). But who are they? Jews? Gentiles? or both? The verbs of v.14 have no explicit subject; so in grammatical terms the question remains open. It cannot, moreover, be settled for certain in the light of the wider context, for the Book of Isaiah provides other examples both of Jews (12:3–6) and of Gentiles (42:10–13) giving praise to God from the ends of the earth. What favors Gentiles is the reference to "islands of the sea" (v.15), for these are not normally associated in the OT with a Jewish dispersion. In fact, later in the book the phrase often refers to Gentiles considered collectively (cf. 41:5; 42:4, 10 et al.) That the Lord is described as "the God of Israel" must be regarded as neutral or perhaps even as, slightly in favor of a reference to the Gentiles.

What begins as a purely factual statement (v.14) becomes an exhortation (v.15) before emerging again as an affirmation, implying that the exhortation has been heeded. The prophet heard the song first of all in the west. He called on those in the east to blend their voices also in harmony of praise to the Lord. As a result, the praises of the God of Israel ascend on all sides. Perhaps the conversion of Egypt and Assyria (19:23–25) can be taken as an earnest or a symbol of this.

16b–20 The welcome interlude of praise is over. In the perspective of the whole of chapters 24–27, it may be seen as fulfilling a special function. These chapters contain several songs of praise. It is important that this element should be represented in chapter 24, for this chapter is fundamental to the whole section of the book under consideration. A balanced picture of the future in the Bible, as seen most clearly in the Book of Revelation, contains notes of both judgment and salvation; and the most fitting occupation of the redeemed is praise to the Redeemer. But though this is true, we must not overlook the solemn fact that more space is given in Scripture to future judgment—a warning to the heedless—than to future salvation. So the prophet resumed the threatening tone of the earlier part of his oracle.

Before the threats in v.17, however, the prophet lifted his voice, not in praise, but in great sadness. Most modern translations, including the NIV, give the impression that v.16b begins with an adversative particle—"But." This is not the case. The simple narrative conjunction, normally translated "and," is employed; thus, no specific emphasis is laid on a change of mood. This seems strange, for clearly the prophet was crying out in grief. Perhaps he saw his present attitude of sorrow as continuous with the future song of praise to be sung at the ends of the earth, because both were motivated by a desire for the glory of the Lord. To express one's gratitude to God for his grace and to reveal sorrowful concern about the treacherous acts of men is, in both cases, to manifest the character of a godly person.

In Isaiah's day the international scene was dominated by the Assyrians. We tend to think of international law as a comparatively modern phenomenon, but there were conventions and treaties in the international scene of the ancient Near East. Aggression is never welcome; but when it is married to treachery, it is to be doubly feared. The prophet felt a deep horror as he thought about this, and he identified with his people's fear. The words "The treacherous betray! With treachery the treacherous betray!" represent only five Hebrew words. The exceptional paronomasia here can best be appreciated when the words are read aloud: *bōgedîm bāgādû ûbeged bôgedîm bāgādû*. No wonder God told Joshua that the Book of the Law should not depart from his mouth (Josh 1:8)!

Some commentators consider vv.17–18 to continue to describe the effects of Assyrian aggression on the nations. In support of this they point out that the wordplay that characterized v.16 is found in v.17 also. The repetition however of the word *'ereṣ* in vv.17–20 seems to bind them all together. In fact, there is thematic unity even if v.16b relates to the present and the remainder to the future, for the prophet may well be saying that the present Assyrian scourge is to be replaced ultimately by an even greater and more widespread judgment from God. God is the divine Hunter who pursues his guilty prey inexorably to a kill (v.17). There is no escape from the judgment of God (v.18a; cf. Heb 2:1–3).

Frequently in Isaiah's prophecy an image appears for illustrative purposes, then disappears quickly, being replaced by another, then another, and then another. The hearer was therefore without excuse as the revelation of God took up much that was familiar and used it to illuminate and to press home the truth.

The language of the hunt (v.18a) is replaced by that of the flood (v.18b), with allusion to the judgment of the Flood (cf. Gen 7:11). We must not be guilty of insensitive literalism here. In fact, the prophet's language is at two removes from the literal; for we can be certain that neither he nor the author of Genesis actually believed that heaven was fitted out with sluice gates or windows, nor does Isaiah, in any case, seem to be thinking of an actual world-wide flood here. The promise had been given that such a flood—destroying virtually all life—would never happen again (Gen 9:11–17). The language of the Flood was still very appropriate to represent pictorially—which Isaiah was doing here—other great acts of judgment.

The whole earthly order is proved to be unstable (v.19), just as if some colossal earthquake had taken hold of it (cf. Rev 6:12; 21:1). Evidently all that can be shaken is being shaken (cf. Heb 12:26–29). The drunken man and the swaying hut both in their own distinctive ways convey an impression of total instability (v.20). Instability in every realm—physical, international, and religious—is a feature of many of the signs Jesus gave in Mark 13 of his second advent. The calamities that overtake the earth are not merely natural but are traced to their spiritual cause in universal rebellion. Earlier the prophet had used the image of a hut (1:2, 8), though somewhat differently, to describe the divinely ordained effects of rebellion against God. The same basic figure can be used flexibly to teach different lessons.

21–23 The vision of judgment that has already included the whole earth becomes yet wider, for it is seen to encompass the powers of heaven as well as the kings of the earth (v.21). The term ṣᵉḇāʾ ("powers") is sometimes used of the heavenly bodies (34:4; 40:26; 45:12) and sometimes of the angelic armies (1 Kings 22:19; 2 Chron 18:18). To which does the term apply? We might be inclined—on the basis of the use of the word by Isaiah elsewhere—to understand it of the stars here, but the prophet is speaking about punishment; so, despite the reference to other heavenly bodies in v.23, we take it to apply to fallen angels (cf. Eph 6:12). The two sets of powers—in heaven and on earth—are at one in the fact of their rebellion but also in the possession of authority. Rebellion in a subordinate authority is serious, for such a being may well drag others down with him. Isaiah 14 pictures the great king of Babylon descending to Sheol. Here it seems that both the heavenly and the earthly rebels are confined in some kind of prison (cf. 2 Peter 2:4; Jude 6; Rev 20:1–3).

It has been argued that the concluding clause of v.22—"after many days"—refers to the Millennium. Certainly we can at least say that it harmonizes with a premillennial interpretation of Revelation. The spiritual powers of evil are bound in prison during the reign of Christ on earth, after which they—along with the unsaved dead —suffer eternal punishment in the lake of fire. The expression is remarkable because imprisonment might have been taken as a figure for final punishment rather than as its anticipation (see Notes).

The closing verse (v.23) of this chapter contains two notable features. The sun and the moon were created by God to rule the day and the night (Gen 1:16–17). This very expression (cf. Gen 1:28), with its implication of authority, suggests that the term "host" can apply to both heavenly bodies and angelic beings (see comment at v.21) because there is in fact a relationship between them, with parts of the visible universe representing the spheres of authority of unseen heavenly beings. Whether or not this is true, the prophet pictured the two great heavenly bodies hiding their lights in shame when the Lord exercises direct rule in Jerusalem. All other glory is his gift and simply a reflection of his glory, and one day it will be seen that it can be no rival to him (cf. Rev 21:23).

The language of locality in v.23 may be literal or symbolic, in the latter case forming a link with the new Jerusalem of Revelation. The vision of Revelation also shows twenty-four elders, probably representing the redeemed under the old and new covenants, before the throne of God (Rev 4:4). Calvin (in loc.) says, "Then only does God receive his just rights, and the honour due to him, when all creatures are placed in subjection, and he alone shines before our eyes."

Notes

5 חֹק (ḥōq), translated "statutes," is really singular; yet תּוֹרֹת (tôrōt, "laws") is plural. In view of the fact that the two terms often appear as virtual synonyms in the OT (e.g., in Ps 119), the reader is inclined to assume that this is the case here; but the difference of number requires explanation. The singular ḥōq could either contemplate the law as a complete entity (cf. James 2:10–11) or relate to the primeval commandment in Eden. Eschatological and apocalyptic language is appropriate to allude to the early chapters of Genesis. If the latter is its meaning, then the everlasting covenant may not refer simply to the Noachian but to the Adamic covenant, which seems to be presupposed in Rom 5:12–21.

10 The main attempts to identify the ruined city are summarized in Millar, *Isaiah 24–27*, pp. 15–21.

16–17 The comments above make mention of the paronomasia to be found in both verses. Some commentators have used this phenomenon as an argument against the Isaianic authorship of this chapter—or, at least, this part of it—because it seems somewhat heavy and crude. The Book of Isaiah is, in fact, just full of paronomasia of various kinds; and we should remember that in Scripture, style is the servant of the message, not its master. Certainly the wordplay is heavy here, but is this not appropriate to the point being made by the prophet?

22 פָּקַד (pāqaḏ), translated "punished" in the NIV, really means "to visit." It can bear the sense "to visit for deliverance," but more often it refers to punishment; and this fits the context here. It is perhaps significant that few modern commentators—even those to whom the thought of a "larger Hope" would probably be congenial—adopt the alternative rendering. Happily the NIV margin notes this sense ("released"), though the translators were convinced that it should not be in the text.

2. Psalms and Predictions of Judgment and Salvation

25:1–12

¹O LORD, you are my God;
I will exalt you and praise your name,

for in perfect faithfulness
you have done marvelous things,
things planned long ago.
²You have made the city a heap of rubble,
the fortified town a ruin,
the foreigners' stronghold a city no more;
it will never be rebuilt.
³Therefore strong peoples will honor you;
cities of ruthless nations will revere you.
⁴You have been a refuge for the poor,
a refuge for the needy in his distress,
a shelter from the storm
and a shade from the heat.
For the breath of the ruthless
is like a storm driving against a wall
5   and like the heat of the desert.
You silence the uproar of foreigners;
as heat is reduced by the shadow of a cloud,
so the song of the ruthless is stilled.

⁶On this mountain the LORD Almighty will prepare
a feast of rich food for all peoples,
a banquet of aged wine—
the best of meats and the finest of wines.
⁷On this mountain he will destroy
the shroud that enfolds all peoples,
the sheet that covers all nations;
8   he will swallow up death forever.
The Sovereign LORD will wipe away the tears
from all faces;
he will remove the disgrace of his people
from all the earth.

The LORD has spoken.

⁹In that day they will say,

"Surely this is our God;
we trusted in him, and he saved us.
This is the LORD, we trusted in him;
let us rejoice and be glad in his salvation."

¹⁰The hand of the LORD will rest on this mountain;
but Moab will be trampled under him
as straw is trampled down in the manure.
¹¹They will spread out their hands in it,
as a swimmer spreads out his hands to swim.
God will bring down their pride
despite the cleverness of their hands.
¹²He will bring down your high fortified walls
and lay them low;
he will bring them down to the ground,
to the very dust.

This chapter and the two that follow are not easy to analyze. This is at least partly due to the fact that two types of literary genre occur here, the psalm of thanksgiving and the eschatological prophecy. There are, however, unifying concepts that give a kind of oneness to the whole chapter, the most prominent being that of the city; for references to the mountain also have in view the city of Jerusalem crowning Mount

Zion. Chapter 26 also opens with a reference to the city, but a second reference in v.5 proves to be the last; and, as we shall see, other themes integrate that chapter.

We think of the typical OT prophet as characteristically being a descending rather than an ascending mediator; viz., he functions for God manward rather than for man Godward. This is, of course, broadly true—but only broadly, for the prophet Amos, for example, prayed for the people to whom his stern messages of judgment were addressed (Amos 7:2, 5); and Micah was virtually uttering the praises of the God of mercy in the last three verses of his book. None of his predecessors or contemporaries, however—nor even, in fact, his successors among the prophets—include so much praise among his oracles as did Isaiah. Although no song in the Psalter claims him as its author, we must reckon Isaiah a psalmist as well as a prophet. We have already seen this in chapter 12 and will see it again.

1–5 Isaiah's call came to him in the temple (ch. 6), and he must often have joined the worshipers in songs of praise. The language of the Psalms was in his heart; and the inspiring Spirit took phrases from the psalms of David and others and made them, with other language, a new vehicle of inspired praise. Perhaps these verses, given prophetically to Isaiah, like those that open chapter 26, are the future song of Judah. We notice, however, that 25:1 and 26:1 are in contrast; the former uses the first person singular, the latter uses the plural. In the absence of compelling evidence to the contrary, we conclude that Isaiah's inspired praise here was intended to be his own.

The prophet's song of praise is so worded that it may apply almost equally well to his own day or to the eschatological future he has portrayed so vividly in the previous chapter. There is a fitness about this, for God's activities at the End are all of a piece with what he does throughout history; and they provide a climax to the story of his dealings with mankind. All had been done already; and all was yet to be done, just as so many of the signs recorded in Mark 13 of Christ's return are simply, in intensified form, the signs that he has already come in his first advent.

The prophet displayed a sense of personal relationship with God (v.1) that is reminiscent of the psalmists of Israel. The focus of his praise is not simply the acts of God but his faithfulness. Each of the acts of God reveals his attributes and makes us aware of what he is in his perfect character. The word translated "marvelous" is the Hebrew *pele'*, which occurs—along with the verbal noun *yôʿēṣ* ("counselor," which is cognate with the verb translated "planned" here)—in one of the names of the messianic Child in 9:6. The context in the earlier passage speaks of another day of Midian, when the rod of Israel's oppressor would be broken. In the present context Isaiah is giving praise to God after describing his coming judgment on all the earth. The maleficent schemes and actions of men can never overturn God's own sovereign purpose, eternal in conception, declared in his word, and executed in due time.

In our comment at 24:10–13, we accepted the view that references to a city of destruction in chapters 24–27 do not have any particular city in view but are general designations of society organized apart from any reference to God, a concept not unlike "the world" as it so often appears in a depreciatory sense in the NT. Clements (*Isaiah 1–39*, in loc.) has very well said, "The city whose destruction is foretold in 25:1–5 . . . stands as a thematic representation of the forces of evil arrayed against God's faithful people. Whatever may have been drawn, therefore, from the portrayal of the city of Babylon as the centre of such forces of evil, it must be understood

158

as a symbol of representation of the larger reality of world evil and darkness." Each specific city is a manifestation in a particular place and time of the general city-spirit, the determination that life shall be organized for human ends and not for the purposes of God. Such cities had often been brought down, and many would suffer such an overthrow in the future (cf. 40:23–24).

The logical word "therefore" in v.3 should be especially noted. God's judgment of these cities leads the strong and ruthless nations to honor and revere the Lord. Young (*Book of Isaiah*, in loc.) comments, "We must not overlook the profound theological teaching that if the Gentiles are to worship God their own united power must be destroyed. As long as the Gentile nations, represented in Isaiah's day by the Assyrians and Babylonians, sought to control the world and to incorporate the theocracy within their own kingdom, there could be no hope for their salvation. Babylon and all that it represented must first be destroyed." The destruction of every hope in man makes way for penitent hope in God.

The Psalms often extol the God of Israel as the Refuge and Shelter of his people. (See, for example, Ps 61:2–4, where the psalmist used a number of different figures to set forth the truth that God is the safety of his people.) Verse 4 uses three different words, the first of them—"refuge"—repeated, to stress the same thought. Like v.2, this is stated as an accomplished fact—either because it has happened already, or else because, in the purpose and pledge of God, it is as certain as if it has. If these words were written after 701 B.C., then the prophet probably had the deliverance of Jerusalem from Sennacherib in mind.

The "poor" and "needy" (v.4) stand in strong contrast to the "strong" and "ruthless nations" of v.3. Judah had faced the current representative of the spirit of ruthless militarism and imperial aggrandizement. She was, of course, utterly powerless, but she had found that her God had placed his wall of protection around her (see esp. ch. 36–37). He had been her refuge ever since the Exodus from Egypt (Deut 33:27). Contrasting weather conditions provide further illustrations of God's protecting care. Having used these analogies, Isaiah then justified his use and in so doing demonstrated that metaphor has its roots in simile.

Isaiah had a most sensitive awareness of the power of words and the various ways one word may be used to convey somewhat different ideas. He moved easily here from the figure of the shady place to that of the shadow cast by a cloud (v.5), both giving protection from the fierce summer heat, yet in different ways. The raucous battle cries of the foreign armies become a triumph song when God intervenes on behalf of his people, and all is changed.

6–8 Many commentators have pointed out the close connection between v.6 and 24:23. We must not forget that chapters 24–27 constitute a special section within the Book of Isaiah, and that all the diverse parts of it are bound together into one. As the Lord's eschatological purposes unfold, he will reign in glory on Mount Zion. The prophet has already pictured the Gentile nations coming up to that mountain for worship (2:1–4); v.6 gives up a view of the great feast God will prepare for them there. O. Kaiser (in loc.) draws our attention to many points of contrast between the judgment of the earth in chapter 24 and this scene. For instance, the judgment of God takes away the wine; but here it is restored in highest quality. All the adjectives and adjectival phrases in v.6 underline the superb quality of God's provision for the once rebellious nations. The Gentile prodigals find that the fatted calf is killed for them on their return to the Lord.

Verse 7 has been understood in two different ways. It could refer to the blindness of the nations, which in the past caused them to worship false gods and not to acknowledge the Lord. The theme of light from God is important in Isaiah, and in chapter 60 the prophet pictures the shining of a great light over God's people and all the nations moving out of the darkness that covers them and into that light. On the other hand, the prophet could have mourning veils or even a shroud of death (see NIV) in his mind. If this is so, then vv.7–8 are concerned with God's victory over death. Either interpretation seems possible, though the second is perhaps the more likely meaning.

Many modern commentators show a strange reluctance to ascribe to Isaiah a belief in the resurrection of the dead. They tend to delete the opening clause of v.8 as a later addition and to interpret 26:19 as a figure for national renewal, after the fashion of the vision of the valley of dry bones in Ezekiel 37. Clements (*Isaiah 1–39*, in loc.), for example, declares, "The idea of the resurrection of the dead occurs in the Old Testament only as a very late idea (cf. Dan. 12:2)." Yes, if evidence of earlier belief is removed or reinterpreted! This kind of argument can so often be circular.

If the rest of vv.6–8 is attributed to the prophet, there can be no adequate reason —except for a particular theory of the historical development of biblical eschatology —to deny this clause to him, especially if we consider 52:13–53:12 to come from him also (see the Introduction, pp. 6–11). Paul quoted v.8a at 1 Corinthians 15:54 in application to the doctrine of resurrection.

If God is going to deal finally with death and so with the tears occasioned by it, and if vv.6–8 are intended to continue and develop the thought chapter 24 closes with, this raises an important issue of prophetic interpretation. The banishment of death belongs to the final stage of God's great plan, and is associated with the descent from heaven of the New Jerusalem (Rev 21:1–4). This suggests that Mount Zion and Jerusalem in 24:23 are not geographical terms but symbols for the ultimate society. This realizes, therefore, in acute form the question of the relationship between the Millennium and the final state (see Introduction, pp. 14–16 for extended comment on this). It is most unlikely, of course—especially if v.7 is understood as a reference to the removal of spiritual blindness—that vv.6–7—and so also 24:23— may refer to the Millennium but that the prophecy moves on to the final state in v.8.

The disgrace of God's people can be best understood in the light of the later prophecy given in Ezekiel 5:13–17. It lies in the fact that they, who are destined by him for salvation, must suffer judgment at his hands because of their sins. This too will pass away when that day comes. God now stresses that these are his own promises, and so they cannot fail.

9 Once more we hear a song of praise to the Lord (cf. 24:14–16; 25:1–5). It wonderfully expresses the joy in God that comes when patient trust finds its reward in a consummated salvation. Its ideas and language are thoroughly characteristic of this prophet, and different parts of the verse can be paralleled in many different parts of the book (e.g., 8:17; 12:1–6; 30:18; 33:22; 35:1–4, 10; 40:9; 49:25–26; 52:7–10; 60:16; 65:18).

10–12 The destinies of Jerusalem and of Moab are here contrasted. The physical proximity of Mount Zion and the mountains of Moab should not be forgotten. The

Moabite plateau can be clearly seen from Jerusalem, and this might even be included in the prophet's vision of this mountain exalted above all the surrounding hills (2:1–4). Moab, so easily visible, could therefore well represent the surrounding pagan nations. If the purposes of the Lord are to triumph, so that all the nations will find their reconciliation with him and with each other at Mount Zion, it follows that their own pagan and aggressive purposes must be thwarted (see comment at vv. 2–3).

In a powerful anthropomorphic figure, the prophet pictures the Lord's hand resting in blessing on Mount Zion and his feet trampling on Moab in judgment (v. 10; cf. 40:11; 63:3). The following similes are intentionally unpleasant and probably suggest that sin in its vileness reaps a harvest of judgment that is appropriate to it. Some modern commentators find the language quite unacceptable. O. Kaiser, for instance, writes of its "despicable vulgarity," and many accuse the author of vindictive nationalism and hatred of a difficult neighboring nation. If, however, we attribute both this passage and the oracle in chapters 15–16 to Isaiah, it is clear that the prophet was sensitive to Moab's pain, even though he declared the judgment of God against it.

The pride of Moab is symbolized by the high fortified walls (v. 12) that surrounded its cities, making the people think them impregnable. The fall of the cities despite their protective battlement—recalling the Fall of Jericho that could have been seen from the slopes of the Moabite plateau—is just another reminder of the physical symbols of pride that are crowded together in 2:13–18; though obviously the ruin of the walls here is literal. It is also an example of the general judgment threatened in v. 2 on strong fortified towns.

Notes

2 Many commentators, perhaps correctly, assume that מֵעִיר (mēʿîr, lit., "from a city," or "no more a city"), in the first clause of the verse, is textual corruption by dittography because the form occurs again—and with greater apparent appropriateness—later in the verse. They therefore read עִיר (ʿîr, "city") instead.

4 The phrase "like a storm driving against a wall" suggests the ineffectiveness of the assault, because the wall is God's protection of his people.

7 לוֹט (lôṭ, lit., "covering") is boldly translated "shroud" in the NIV. This is unfortunate, as it unnecessarily cuts the knot of a minor exegetical problem (see comment above), which could have been left open by the more general word "covering" (cf. RSV).

11 אָרְבּוֹת (ʾorbôṭ, "cleverness") is a hapax legomenon, though the root occurs occasionally elsewhere in the OT in the sense of "ambush." Driver ("Isaiah 1–39," JTS 38, p. 43) suggests a link with Arabic ʾrbatun ("skill"). The NIV seems to assume some such meaning as the latter.

3. Praise, Prayer, and Prophecy

26:1–21

¹In that day this song will be sung in the land of Judah:

We have a strong city;
 God makes salvation
  its walls and ramparts.
²Open the gates
 that the righteous nation may enter,
  the nation that keeps faith.
³You will keep in perfect peace
 him whose mind is steadfast,
  because he trusts in you.
⁴Trust in the LORD forever,
 for the LORD, the LORD, is the Rock eternal.
⁵He humbles those who dwell on high,
 he lays the lofty city low;
he levels it to the ground
 and casts it down to the dust.
⁶Feet trample it down—
 the feet of the oppressed,
 the footsteps of the poor.

⁷The path of the righteous is level;
 O upright One, you make the way of the
  righteous smooth.
⁸Yes, LORD, walking in the way of your laws,
 we wait for you;
your name and renown
 are the desire of our hearts.
⁹My soul yearns for you in the night;
 in the morning my spirit longs for you.
When your judgments come upon the earth,
 the people of the world learn righteousness.
¹⁰Though grace is shown to the wicked,
 they do not learn righteousness,
even in a hand of uprightness they go on doing evil
 and regard not the majesty of the LORD.
¹¹O LORD, your hand is lifted high,
 but they do not see it.
Let them see your zeal for your people and be
  put to shame;
 let the fire reserved for your enemies consume them.

¹²LORD, you establish peace for us;
 all that we have accomplished you have done for us.
¹³O LORD, our God, other lords besides you have ruled
  over us,
 but your name alone do we honor.
¹⁴They are now dead, they live no more;
 those departed spirits do not rise.
You punished them and brought them to ruin;
 you wiped out all memory of them.
¹⁵You have enlarged the nation, O LORD;
 you have enlarged the nation.
You have gained glory for yourself;
 you have extended all the borders of the land.

¹⁶LORD, they came to you in their distress,
 when you disciplined them,
 they could barely whisper a prayer.
¹⁷As a woman with child and about to give birth
 writhes and cries out in her pain,
 so were we in your presence, O LORD.

¹⁸We were with child, we writhed in pain,
　　but we gave birth to wind.
We have not brought salvation to the earth;
　　we have not given birth to people of the world.

¹⁹But your dead will live;
　　their bodies will rise
You who dwell in the dust,
　　wake up and shout for joy.
Your dew is like the dew of the morning;
　　the earth will give birth to her dead.
²⁰Go, my people, enter your rooms
　　and shut the doors behind you;
hide yourselves for a little while
　　until his wrath has passed by.
²¹See, the Lord is coming out of his dwelling
　　to punish the people of the earth for their sins.
The earth will disclose the blood shed upon her;
　　she will conceal her slain no longer.

Mauchline (in loc.) is surely right when he says of vv.1–19, "These verses are so closely knit together in idea and there is so clear a movement of thought that it seems necessary to regard them as a unity." The movement of thought is, in fact, quite beautiful. The prophet begins by uttering a song of praise, sung by Judah of the future. Its theme is the trustworthiness of God who protects the city of his oppressed people and destroys that of their oppressors (vv.1–6). Next, almost after the manner of the Book of Proverbs, Isaiah meditates on the ways of the righteous and of the wicked (vv.7–11). The Lord has blessed his people, despite their former acknowledgement of the lordship of other deities (vv.12–15). The people had been through a lot but accomplished little blessing for the world, and they confess this (vv.16–18). But the God of grace nevertheless promises them a joyful resurrection to new life (v.19) after the revelation of his wrath against sin (vv.20–21).

1–6 The way chapters 24–27 are punctuated with songs of praise affects this whole section of the prophecy, for even the threats of judgment are seen in the perspective of thanksgiving that God is bringing his own purposes to fruition and that human arrogance and tyranny will not prevail in the end. The theme of the two cities links this passage with chapters 24 and 25. In 25:4, God himself is the refuge of his people, while here (v.1) he gives strength to the city by making salvation its walls and ramparts. The second is not really inferior to the first, for the prophet always thought of such gifts of God as manifestations of what he is in himself (10:17 and comments there). In any case, the idea is expressed again in personal terms v.4. We may conceive the visible gifts of God as distinguishable from himself but not those that are invisible and spiritual.

Every year Jerusalem was the pilgrimage goal for large numbers of people from all parts of the land (cf. Deut 16) as they made their way there to take part in the great feasts. Many of the Psalms, including the "Songs of Ascents" (Pss 120–34), were connected with these pilgrimages. In NT times pilgrims came from all the countries of the Dispersion (cf. Acts 2:5–11). Isaiah may have had some such pilgrimage in mind here. On the other hand, he may have had permanent settlement in view, the city being part physical expression and part symbol for the whole people of God, "the righteous nation that keeps faith" (v.2). The latter seems the more likely.

163

Revelation 21:22–27 may owe something to this passage, though it seems to go beyond it, because it includes the Gentiles (cf. 2:1–4).

Verses 3–4 may be viewed as a beautiful individualization of the thought already conveyed in corporate terms in vv.1–2. The nation that keeps faith is made up of individuals who trust in the Lord, for the new covenant purpose of God provides for a gracious personal knowledge of him for every person included within that covenant (Jer 31:31–34). The gates of the city admit the returning members of the dispersed nation, and its walls symbolize the divine protection; the Lord is himself the protecting Rock in whom the believer may place his trust. Just as there is a place of peace within the city for those who dwell in it with God (cf. Ps 46), so the Lord gives peace to the individual who reposes confidence in him.

Verses 4–5 give two examples of emphasis by repetition. The word šālôm ("peace") is repeated, so conveying the idea that this peace is perfect. "The LORD, the LORD" (NIV) translates Yah, Yahweh, the abbreviated and possibly more ancient form of the divine name (Yah) preceding the normal (Yahweh).

Verses 5–6 take up again the theme of God's judgment on the worldly city (see comment at 24:13–15 and the introduction to 25:1–5). Once again the language of physical elevation is used to suggest pride (cf. 2:12–18). So often an ancient city was built on raised ground so as to gain the maximum military advantage from its physical elevation, which then became the basis for walls, battlements, and other means of defense. This stress on the vertical dimension became part of the typical image of the city for most people. When God judges the pride of the city, he lays it low. In 25:10 the feet of the Lord trample in judgment on Moab; here it is the people who have suffered oppression from it, presumably the people of God, who tread it under foot. This suggests that they share in his victory (cf. Ps 110:2–3; 2 Cor 2:14).

7–11 In v.2 the prophet spoke of the righteous nation and its proper home within the gates of the city of God. Here in v.7 he describes the way of the righteous and contrasts this with the outlook of the wicked in a fashion reminiscent of Psalm 1. The prophetic tradition in Israel was very old; and if the wisdom tradition went back at least to Solomon, then we would expect some spiritual cross-fertilization. Prophetic inspiration did not bypass the whole world and the whole culture in which the prophet lived, and there seems no reason why the Spirit of God should not have taken material from within the wisdom tradition and used this in the interests of prophecy. Both were inspired, and such a use would be similar to the way the NT writers used the writings of the OT, given by the same Spirit of inspiration but in another age.

The thought of v.7 is to be found also in Psalm 27:11, but here there is a profound addition to it. The God of the righteous is himself righteous, and he is described here as yāšār ("upright"). This term does not occur elsewhere in the OT as a divine title, but it is used of God's word (Ps 33:4), his judgments (Ps 119:137), and his ways (Deut 32:4). There are also references to the Book of Jashar (yāšār, the word is exactly the same in Hebrew) in Joshua 10:13 and 2 Samuel 1:18; and this, the Book of the Upright, could take its title from God, the "upright One," who is the source of all righteousness. Physical uprightness or straightness is often the linguistic basis for the moral concept of righteousness, not only in the Bible, but in many other languages. The words also seem to suggest appropriateness of destiny. He who is straight or "on the level" has his path smoothed before him by the God who is upright.

Mišpāṭ almost certainly means "law" rather than "judgment" in v.8, as this fits the context much better. Just as the NT believer looks forward "to a new heaven and a new earth, the home of righteousness" (2 Peter 3:13), so the OT saint, represented here by Isaiah, longed for the coming of a day when God's name would be honored fittingly. The words "we wait for you" show his conviction that such a day would come—and come by the activity of God himself. This passionate longing is not just a deep desire for a better order, a kind of moral Utopia. The whole expectation is personal. It is *God* the prophet longs for (cf. Pss 42:1–4; 63:1; 84:2). This longing possesses him night and day. In a similar way, godly men and women of the church age have yearned for the second advent of Christ.

We earlier alluded (see comment at 1:16–17) to the charge that the prophets were Pelagians before Pelagius, the teacher who saw the grace of God simply as an aid to the self-reformation of man. Verses 9b–10 are in fact much more in line with Augustine's emphasis on the radical nature of both sin and grace. Sin blinds the mind of the sinner so that he sees nothing from a divine perspective, least of all his own sin. It is a function of judgment to teach human beings the seriousness of sin and to show them that God cares deeply about righteousness. Acts 5:1–14 illustrates the operation of this principle. In this respect, the prophet assures us, judgment is more effective than grace. We should not read into this latter term all its NT connotations; for if we did, the statement of Isaiah would be patently untrue. Rather, his statement stresses that the wicked may receive undeservedly many blessings from the hand of God and yet show no more regard for the righteousness that so greatly concerns him. Not only so, but even where general moral conditions are favorable to righteousness (viz., in a time of spiritual revival), the wicked are determined to go their own way. Even now (v.11), God's hand is uplifted, ready to strike them in judgment; but they are totally unaware of it. The prophet identifies himself completely—as the people of God do in Revelation 19:1–5—with the judgment of God on the wicked. We must compassionately seek to bring the gospel to others, but on the day of judgment we must accept his every verdict; for as the Judge of all the earth, he does only what is right.

12–15 From time to time the debt of Isaiah to his older contemporaries—or, at least, his oneness with them in various prophetic themes—is apparent in his work. The present passage is reminiscent of Hosea 14. In v.11—in the context of God's judgment of his enemies—Isaiah spoke about God's zeal for his people. It is as if Isaiah has become suddenly aware of the contrast between God's dealing with Israel and with the nations and is moved to make this confession of the great unworthiness of those who have received such rich blessings from God. Verse 12 suggests that it was written after the singular divine protection of Jerusalem in 701 B.C. Verse 12b is a profound truth that is blessedly destructive of spiritual pride. It would almost fit right into the Pauline Epistles (cf. Phil 2:12–13).

The reiterated name LORD in vv.11–13 (Yahweh in Heb.), in each case taking the primary position in the Hebrew sentence, conveys its own special message. It is the distinctive name of the God of Israel by which he is set apart from every false god. In this way the literary scene is set for the statements of v.13. Obviously this verse does not suggest that the "other lords" had real existence as deities but simply that they were believed to have and that their rule was sinfully acknowledged by the people in past times. A brief survey of the books of Judges and of Kings, for instance, gives many illustrations of this. Most commentators understand the passage somewhat differently, regarding the "other lords" as the various nations that had exercised sovereignty over God's people, and certainly v.14 must refer to human beings. Perhaps it is best for us to think in terms of both false deities and the foreign rulers who regarded themselves as their representatives, the first being emphasized in v.13 and the second in v.14.

The rise and fall of nations and of great empires is a fact of history, and Isaiah saw it to be due to the activity of God in the story of mankind (cf. 40:23–24). Isaiah has already vividly pictured the descent of the king of Babylon into the world of departed spirits in 14:12–21, and now he makes it clear that this is the way all Israel's past oppressors have gone. Young (*Book of Isaiah*, in loc.) warns against misinterpreting the messages of v.14:

> It is a mistake to use this verse to support the position that no general resurrection of the dead is taught here, but only a resurrection of the just. What Isaiah is speaking of is not so much a resurrection, as the fact that those who had once acted as lords over Israel are now dead, and cannot return to life again to afflict the Israelites. He is not denying that in the general resurrection they too shall arise unto everlasting punishment. On that particular subject he is not now speaking. What he is saying, however, is of comfort to the Israelites, for it teaches them that in the kingdom founded on Zion, they shall be free from those who formerly had oppressed them.

In a later passage in the book (54:1–3), Isaiah foretells the expansion of the nation. It was also promised in 9:3, in a context where the coming of the messianic Child is proclaimed. We should, therefore, treat v.15 as predictive, the use of "prophetic perfects" here expressing the prophet's certainty that what God has promised is as sure as if it had taken place already. Isaiah 9:7 contains the intriguing and somewhat enigmatic promise "of the *increase* of his government and peace there will be no end" (emphasis mine). It is worth remembering that the land promised to Israel in Exodus 23:31 was never fully occupied, even in the days of David and Solomon, but that the bounds of the messianic kingdom are to be wider still (cf. Ps 72:8). All this will bring glory to God because it is his act, not theirs (cf. v.12), and because it will result in the showing forth of his glory in areas where paganism formerly held sway.

16–18 The prophet—from the vantage point of the eschatological pinnacle the Spirit of God has transported him to—looks back over earlier days, days that to him, as a man of history, were still in the future. The people would come to the Lord in distress but with great earnestness (v.16). The words "they could barely whisper a prayer" may be more literally rendered as "they poured out a whisper." The verb pertains to the heart, the noun to the lips. Hannah prayed with exceptional earnestness (1 Sam 1:12–16), but it was inaudible to men. Fervor and noise are not necessarily spiritual companions. The phrase "when you discipline them" suggests that the prayer was motivated not only by distress because of foreign oppression but also by sorrow for sin. Perhaps it was the national conversion mentioned in Romans 11:23–32 that was in view.

The experience of childbirth forms the basis for a forceful analogy (v.17). The nation, following in this way the pattern of her ancestor, Jacob, tried to achieve her own salvation, when, in fact, God alone could bring his own purposes for her to birth. Israel was like a woman in labor because of the pains she had suffered, yet unlike her in not giving birth to a child (v.18) All the suffering had been in vain. It was, in fact, to be only through the Servant of the Lord (52:13–53:12), not through Israel's suffering without him, that salvation would be brought to the earth. The NIV's "we have not given birth to people of the world" appropriately continues the analogy and also provides a striking parallel to the penultimate clause. Birth into God's kingdom for the nations (Ps 87:4–7) is God's work alone—through his Messiah-Servant—and beyond the capacity of Israel herself. Only through him who is the true seed of Abraham (Gal 3:16, 28–29) could the nations become his children and so inherit the promise made to him (Gen 12:1–3 et al.) For an alternative interpretation of v.18, see the Notes.

19 This verse is very striking when read, as it should be, in its context. It presents a glorious contrast for Israel not only with the dead and impotent tyrants who have lorded over her in the past (v.14) but also with the strenuous and yet ineffective endeavors of Israel herself to bring forth spiritual fruit (vv.17–18). Because of their reluctance to attribute to Isaiah a belief in physical resurrection (see comment at 25:8), many modern scholars either deny this verse to him, placing it much later, or else interpret it figuratively. If, however, Ezekiel 37 uses the concept of resurrection figuratively, as it clearly does, then we would expect that that concept would be well known in literal terms; and so some awareness of it must have been already given. Why not then through Isaiah?

Is the language in this verse to be understood spiritually, of a rebirth of the nation to a new spiritual life, or literally (*Isaiah*, in loc.) Skinner calls it "a clear intimation of a belief in the Resurrection." Young (*Book of Isaiah*, in loc.) says "The language is not to be taken figuratively." It is quite true that the Book of Isaiah is replete with forceful and graphic imagery, but everything here leads the mind toward a literal interpretation. Certainly there are metaphors here, for the prophet calls the dead to awake and asserts that the earth will give birth to her dead. The metaphorical, however, must always rest on the literal; and it is with the literal that this verse commences: "But your dead will live; their bodies will rise." This verse itself prepared the way for Daniel 12:2, which fills out more fully the destinies of the righteous and the wicked beyond death and subsequent resurrection.

20–21 Verse 20 perhaps anticipates the joyous declaration chapter 40 so memorably commences with. A time will come when God's wrath will have passed by. In this case the wrath is with Israel herself (cf. 40:2); and during the Exile the people are to encourage themselves with the assurance that this judgment on them would come to an end in God's good time. On the other hand, the wrath may be that expressed in God's punishment of the nations, which v.21 relates to. The latter is more likely because there seems to be an allusion to the Passover in v.20. Just as the people of Israel found refuge within the blood-sprinkled doors of their homes (Exod 12), till the wrath of God against Egypt should spend itself, so Israel is told to hide for a while, perhaps in Babylonian exile. Shutting the doors suggests not only safety from danger but also separation from the surrounding pagans, who were under judgment. Israel in exile was called to be a holy people, distinct from her neighbors.

While the people are hidden away in their places, God comes forth from his place for a punitive purpose. Verse 21 is a reminder to us of the general context and of the disclosure of a cosmic judgment given in chapter 24. It also recalls the teaching of v.19. The earth is not only the burial place of many who will desert her at the Resurrection. She has admitted the blood and bodies of many whose deaths have been due to the sins of others, the terrible consequences of the acts of violent men. Places where great human tragedies and horrifying sins have taken place may disclose no evidence of their history to the casual passer-by, but on the day of the Lord's judgment on sin that evidence will appear to the terrified eyes of the perpetrators. Such secrets belong to time, not to eternity.

Notes

3 Clements (*Isaiah 1–39*, in loc.) points out that יֵצֶר (*yēṣer*, "mind") was widely used in the rabbinic writings to express the whole attitude and direction of one's life.

7 מֵישָׁר (*mêšār*) may bear the sense "level" (NIV), but it is more often used figuratively of moral straightness or happiness. The root appears in the literal physical sense, however, in 40:4 and 42:16 and elsewhere outside Isaiah. Possibly the word was deliberately used because of its double meaning.

16 לַחַשׁ (*laḥaš*), though often used of magic spells, properly signifies "whisper," which seems to be the meaning here.

18 יִפְּלוּ (*yippᵉlû*), translated "fallen" in the last clause of the RSV, is rendered "give birth" in the NIV. This latter sense does not occur elsewhere in the OT but is a sense of the cognate Arabic root. The RSV, following the normal sense of the verb, could be correct, in which case Israel is presented here as God's instrument of judgment, deemed ineffective here, on the inhabitants of the world. It seems better to follow the NIV, which integrates the language with the rest of vv.17–18.

19 The MT and 1QIsa both read נְבֵלָתִי יְקוּמוּן (*nᵉḇēlātî yᵉqûmûn*), which is rendered "their bodies will rise," but which actually features the peculiar phenomenon of a singular noun (lit. "my body") with a plural verb (lit., "they will arise"). It seems that the noun views the nation as a collective entity while the verb individualizes it. This suggests that the simple renewal of the nation does not do justice to what the prophet had in mind. It is the resurrection of the nation, but in terms of new life for its individuals.

The reference to the dew suggests the refreshing of the ground so that plants may grow in it, an appropriate image for the new life to be given to the bodily "seed" committed to it.

4. The Restoration of Israel

27:1–13

¹In that day,

the LORD will punish with his sword,
    his fierce, great and powerful sword,
Leviathan the gliding serpent,
    Leviathan the coiling serpent;
he will slay the monster of the sea.

²In that day—

"Sing about a fruitful vineyard;
³I, the LORD, watch over it;
    I water it continually.
I guard it day and night
    so that no one may harm it.
⁴   I am not angry.

If only there were briers and thorns confronting me!
    I would march against them in battle;
    I would set them all on fire.
[5]Or else let them come to me for refuge;
    let them make peace with me,
    yes, let them make peace with me."

[6]In days to come Jacob will take root,
    Israel will bud and blossom
    and fill all the world with fruit.

[7]Has the LORD struck her
    as he struck down those who struck her?
Has she been killed
    as those were killed who killed her?
[8]By warfare and exile you contend with her—
    with his fierce blast he drives her out,
    as on a day the east wind blows.
[9]By this, then, will Jacob's guilt be atoned for,
    and this will be the full fruitage of the removal
        of his sin;
When he makes all the altar stones
    to be like chalk stones crushed to pieces,
no Asherah poles or incense altars
    will be left standing.
[10]The fortified city stands desolate,
    an abandoned settlement, forsaken like the desert;
there the calves graze,
    there they lay die;
    they strip its branches bare.
[11]When its twigs are dry, they are broken off
    and women come and make fires with them.
For this is a people without understanding;
    so their Maker has no compassion on them,
    and their Creator shows them no favor.

[12]In that day the LORD will thresh from the flowing Euphrates to the Wadi of Egypt, and you, O Israelites, will be gathered up one by one. [13]And in that day a great trumpet will sound. Those who are perishing in Assyria and those who were exiled in Egypt will come and worship the LORD on the holy mountain in Jerusalem.

The eschatological-apocalyptic section of Isaiah 24–27 is concerned with God's final purposes in the world. The prophecies recorded here concern the whole world, but they also relate to Israel and her place in the universal purposes of God. Earlier in these chapters, and especially in chapter 24, the emphasis was placed on the nations as a whole; but there is more and more reference to Israel as the chapters proceed, with chapter 26 almost dominated by her. The chapter ends, however, with a reference to the judgment of the nations, and in chapter 27 we are once again reminded of the international context of God's dealings with his people.

1 This fascinating verse presents a graphic picture of God the great Warrior, going into battle against fearsome and monstrous enemies and utterly defeating them. The language used draws on mythology; but this need cause us no serious problems. Writers, whether of Scripture or otherwise, frequently use illustrative material, drawing that material from a wide variety of sources: nature, history, mythology, or literature. The use of mythology here simply shows that Isaiah and his readers knew the mythological stories, not that they believed them. If a modern historian referred to a fierce and aggressive nation as "a great dragon," would his readers assume he believed in the objective existence of such creatures? Surely not!

Every word of this verse could do with comment. The succession of adjectives describing the sword of the Lord stresses the fearsomeness of this weapon and so emphasizes that judgment will be completely effective. Some commentators take it that just as the words "his fierce, great and powerful sword" are to be read as in apposition to "his sword," so "Leviathan the coiling serpent" is in apposition to "Leviathan the gliding serpent." This would mean that the prophet had only two enemies in mind, not three. Others assume that there are two Leviathans here, the first being perhaps a reference to the fast-flowing Tigris where the Assyrian heartland was and the second to the more sluggish and therefore more twisting Euphrates, the great river of the Babylonians. The monster of the sea then becomes Egypt, to complete the trio of Israel's great oppressors. We can hold the latter interpretation and still think of the two phrases as being in apposition, so that the two Mesopotamian enemies are thought of as different manifestations of the same evil power centered in the Tigris–Euphrates basin. This comprehensive statement must have come with real power to assure the people of God (see Notes).

2–6 One of the most memorable passages in the book occurs in 5:1–7. Isaiah's parable of the vineyard there demonstrates that beauty of language and solemnity of theme are not inconsistent with each other. Moreover, his use there of the vineyard for Israel established this word as a symbol. The context here would settle it as a reference to Israel, but the reader is already conditioned to such a reference by the earlier passage. In this way, words and phrases—and the images they convey—come to have technical force so that eventually, in some cases, exceptions to the technical use become rare and even need to be demonstrated.

The repeated phrase "in that day" in vv. 1–2 suggests that the judgment of the enemies of Israel and her own blessing belong to the same general eschatological era. In Isaiah 5, the vineyard is barren and unproductive and is itself threatened with judgment. In the eschatological picture we see here, however, the vineyard is fruitful. The parable began as such a happy song there, to lull the hearers into a complacent mood and so take them unawares with the message of judgment. Here the opening mood is similar, and even its thought follows a somewhat similar pattern. The reader, used to the twist in the tail of the earlier parable, expects to find it repeated here; but once again he is taken by surprise, for this time the opening atmosphere is sustained throughout.

"A fruitful vineyard" (v. 2) is literally "a vineyard of wine." This suggests both comparison and contrast with chapter 5. It compares with the reader's expectation there but contrasts with the prophet's ultimate description. In v. 3 the thought of 5:2 is carried through but expressed quite differently. There is, if anything, even more emphasis on the loving concern of the Lord for this vineyard, and it is made clear that never for one moment does he forget its needs or relax his vigilance, lest it should become a prey to its enemies. The constant watering (v. 3) reminds us of Jeremiah's often repeated assertion that the Lord repeatedly sent his servants the prophets to speak to his people. The vivid literalism of the KJV's "daily rising up early and sending them" (Jer 7:25; 25:4 et al.) has been lost in most modern EV, including the NIV.

The wonderful statement that opens v.4 can really be understood only in the light of the expression "in that day," with which the new parable of the vineyard commences. The prophet was not describing Israel that then was but the Israel that was to be, when the wrath of God was past (cf. 40:2). The hearer or reader, however, with the earlier parable in mind, may well be asking, "But what about the briers and thorns?" These appear in chapter 5 both as part of the judgment of God on the vineyard and as the final evidence of its lack of real fruit. But here God pledges himself to destroy them should any such appear again to threaten his vineyard. Indeed, he appears eager to do this very thing, perhaps as evidence of his covenant faithfulness to his people and his determination to do them good in every possible way. In 10:33–34, God goes into battle against the great trees, lopping the boughs from them with his axe. Here the undergrowth feels the shriveling heat of his anger. The briers and thorns are not explicitly interpreted, but they may represent internal rather than external enemies, paganizers rather than pagans.

Verse 5 is a neglected OT promise of forgiveness to the penitent. In v.4 the God of battles is marching against the briers and thorns with a flaming torch in his hand. He is about to set fire to this rank undergrowth, but before doing so he proclaims the alternative of peace. His action against the briers and thorns is for the protection of his people, but in v.5 the enemies themselves are offered refuge (cf. 25:4) if they will accept his terms of peace. The offer of peace is made most emphatically, with the clause repeated in the Hebrew but with the words in a different order. This serves the purpose of directing the hearer's attention to the words themselves, and so to their meaning and the offer of mercy they contain.

Verse 6 brings the parable to a beautiful climax. It is noteworthy that the prophet does not speak of Judah but of Israel here. He has the whole people in view. The figure of the vineyard disappears, and, instead, Israel is presented as a plant. Perhaps the figure of the vineyard contemplates Israel in the land, whereas the vine lays more stress on the people themselves than the Promised Land God has settled them in—although, of course, it is in the land that Israel takes root.

The picture is at first perfectly normal. The root, the bud, and the blossom depict strong and healthy growth, everything happening in its season. The unexpected comes at the end. This vine will become extraordinarily extensive (cf. 16:8), filling the whole world with its fruit. Perhaps this is an allusion to the fruitfulness and extensive influence of Joseph promised in Genesis 49:22. We can certainly see a spiritual fulfillment of this in the progress of the gospel throughout the world, for the Messiah is himself the true Vine (John 15:1–8) and his disciples the fruit-bearing branches. In this way God's purpose for Israel finds its expression in the supreme Israelite and those who are joined by faith to him. Does this exhaust the fulfillment intended by God? See the Introduction, pp. 14–16, for comment on the interpretation of such passages.

7–11 The interpretation of this passage has been much discussed. Duhm (in loc.) argued for its application to the northern kingdom, and in this opinion he has been followed by many commentators. Although some of the arguments used to support this view are rationalistic, a case can certainly be made out for it without resort to them. The word "Jacob" is used both within this immediate passage (v.9) and in its context (v.6), and this may well suggest that Israel rather than Judah is in mind. The fortified city of v.10 could certainly be Samaria, and the exile of v.8 would then follow its fall. A reference to Judah is not, of course, impossible, especially if we

171

treat the passage as predictive and the past tenses as prophetic perfects. In this case the city would be Jerusalem and the exile in Babylon.

A third possibility, however, suggests itself, which takes into account the fact that so many of the references to cities in chapters 24–27 seem to be general and not specific. (See the comment at 24:10–13 and the introduction to chapter 25.) We may see the reference to Israel (i.e., Jacob) as the designation, not of Israel apart from Judah (that is, the northern kingdom), but of Israel including Judah. The whole people and their judgment are in view. The fortified city stands for each stronghold overcome by the Mesopotamian enemies, and the Exile is the common experience of the whole people. A section of the book whose general subject is so comprehensive (see esp. ch. 24) might be expected to treat the chosen nation as a whole in its concluding chapter. This is the standpoint from which we will view these verses.

The subject of v.7, though unexpressed, is clearly the Lord. The questions of v.7 are rather like those of the imaginary Jewish objector who challenges Paul's thesis in the Epistle to the Romans (e.g., Rom 3:1). There is no doubt that the new parable of the vineyard in vv.2–6 does not tell the whole story of Israel's relationship with God; for he has taken punitive action against his own people, not only against their adversaries. The prophet brings the two together, for example, in 10:5–19. Despite the undoubted fact that God had often to beat his people very severely (e.g., 1:4–9), the implied answer to the question is no. God does make a distinction between his own people and their oppressors. All the chastisement is for a good end and to bring them to repentance (v.9).

By common consent there are real difficulties in v.8. Young (*Book of Isaiah*, (in loc.) gives a helpful comment and translation:

> In this verse and in the ninth Isaiah's purpose is to emphasize with respect to Israel certain points that are necessary for the understanding of the whole picture, namely, that where a terrible burden of judgment has fallen upon the whole earth, Judah suffers but mildly. We would therefore translate, *In measure, in the sending her away, thou does contend with her. By this hard wind he removes her in the day of the east wind*. The thought may then be paraphrased as follows: "By sending Judah away into exile in moderation, thou art trying to contend or reason with her. In a day when the east wind blows, thou does remove Judah by thine own hard wind." (emphasis his).

Except that we see the passage to apply to the whole of Israel, rather than simply to Judah, we will follow this interpretation and give the grounds for it in the Notes.

Characteristically Isaiah refers to judgment as a fierce wind (cf. 4:4 and the comment there; cf. also 41:16). The scorching east wind, driving the hot desert sand before it, was much dreaded (Gen 41:6; Job 27:21–22; Jer 18:17 et al.). Both the Assyrian and the Babylonian enemies came from the east and moved captives from Israel and Judah for exile. In fact, exile, unlike destruction, is punishment tempered by mercy; for there is still life and therefore still hope.

It may seem strange that the language of atonement is used in v.9 in application to the penitence induced by exile rather than in reference to sacrifice. Could Israel then deal with her own sins? If so, why the need for the great self-offering of the Lord's Servant in 52:13–53:12? This present passage and the "Golden Passionale" of the fourth Servant Song seem to be teaching quite different theologies. The doctrinal conflict is, however, more apparent than real. Through exile the nation would come to a penitent awareness of its guilt. The actual objective basis of its reconciliation with God is not so much in view as the practical cause of that reconciliation. The people were removed so that their sins might be removed.

That this is the way the statement about atonement should be viewed becomes clear when we read the whole of v.9; for it is all about a new attitude to the will of God, the product of a penitent heart. Isaiah is in line here with Jeremiah 31:31-34 and Ezekiel 36:24-31. In accordance with Isaiah's great fondness for analogies, language normally applied to objective atonement is applied figuratively to penitent turning to God.

Israel's penitence would show itself especially in the destruction of pagan altars and symbols. (See comment at 7:8 for a detailed interpretation of the various terms used here.) When Israel was being prepared to enter the land of Canaan, she was commanded by God to destroy everything pagan (Exod 34:13; Deut 12:2-3). When God had purified Israel through banishment from the land and the experience of exile, she would return much chastened to carry out this commandment that she failed to do thoroughly enough at the beginning of her sojourn in the land.

It was not, in fact, pagan altars and Asherah poles that lay in ruins in the land at that time. In northern Israel, Samaria and other cities had been devastated by the Assyrians, who had also desolated many cities of Judah (1:7). Jerusalem too would eventually go the same way, through the Babylonians. Isaiah often represents the effects of judgment through war as the virtual reversal of civilization (e.g., 3:4-6; 5:17; 7:23-25). This language is not really figurative but quite literal. When a city is reduced to rubble, the domestic animals, which normally are pastured outside the city, are free to cross the broken walls and roam in the city (v.10). Soon vegetation emerges through cracks in the streets and between the fallen stones. The ghost town will eventually have trees growing in it, and these will feed animals with their bark and supply firewood for the women of the surrounding villages (v.11). Not only was this true of the cities of Israel and Judah when God judged them, but the stones of the cities of once-mighty Rome were used as building materials by the barbarians who took over their territory.

In some respects, as we have already suggested, Isaiah stood in the wisdom as well as in the prophetic tradition. (See the comments at 25:7-11, and see Whedbee, in loc.) His prophecies place emphasis from time to time on the importance of wisdom and discernment and the seriousness of inner blindness. This note is struck, in fact, at the very beginning of the book (cf. 1:2). It was this culpable blindness that caused Israel's exile. The descriptions of God here remind us of later chapters in the book (e.g., 43:1; 44:2). The statement that God does not show compassion or favor to them is not, of course, absolute. It is perhaps a partial yes anwer to the questions of v.7, the main answer to which is no. When the appointed time of their judgment came, God did not show compassion; but later, of course, he would and did.

12-13 These verses are of unusual interest. They bring the great eschatological-apocalyptic section of the book to a wonderful conclusion, but it is important to notice that the two verses do not teach the same truth. They are complementary rather than repetitive. The more unusual of the two is undoubtedly v.12. Here the prophet refers to the traditional boundaries of the Promised Land (cf. comment at 26:15). God will treat this whole large area as one huge grain field. Never throughout its history did a pure Israel exist. There were always foreign and unbelieving elements in it, the two not always coinciding. God's judgment would therefore begin at the land of his own people. If his threshing-floor yields much grain, there

173

will be chaff too. The nation is to be purified, as Ezekiel later promised in Ezekiel 36:24–32, though he speaks of a regathering of the people from alien lands. To this Isaiah now moves.

The figure of the threshing floor is replaced by that of a trumpet (v.13). Beyond the Euphrates is the land of the Assyrians, and beyond the Wadi of Egypt the land it gains its name from. In 2:1–4 and in 60:1–14, Isaiah describes Jerusalem as the focal point the penitent Gentiles would come to, both to hear God's word and to worship him. But not even Israel is there yet, and the prophet declares that the traditional lands of her captivity must yield up her lost and scattered ones so that they may join the worshiping throng at Zion's temple. Like v.6, this is capable of being interpreted at different levels (see Introduction, pp. 14–16).

Notes

1 לִוְיָתָן (liwyātān, "Leviathan") appears in several OT passages (Job 3:8; Pss 74:14; 104:26), where it is clear that a great sea creature is being described. Most scholars consider the creature described under that name in Job 41:1–9 (40:25–29 MT) to be the crocodile. The implication of a plurality of heads in Ps 74:14, however, certainly suggests a mythical creature; and the term as used here is normally linked with the Ugaritic Lotan, the chaos monster destroyed by Baal in the Canaanite creation myth. As indicated in the commentary, the use of such a term does not imply acceptance of Canaanite mythology but simply the knowledge of it, so that the term may be applied figuratively to monstrous enemies of Israel and of God. See ZPEB, 3:912; 4:333–43, and the very balanced note in Young (*Book of Isaiah*, in loc.). For the monster of the sea, see the references to Rahab in Isa 30:7 and 51:9, and especially the comment at the former passage.

2 The words "a fruitful vineyard" are a free translation of כֶּרֶם חֶמֶר (kerem ḥemer, lit., "a vineyard of wine"). This is the reading of BH and 1QIsa, though many commentators favor emending to כֶּרֶם חֶמֶד (kerem ḥemed, "a pleasant vineyard"), read by BHS, LXX et al. Either fits the context.

8 The commentary adopts Young's translation and interpretation of this verse (*Book of Isaiah*). The Hebrew opens with the word בְּסַאסְּאָה (besa'sse'āh), which is a *hapax legomenon*, though the first consonant is probably the common particle בְּ (be, "in"). The word is usually taken to be a contraction of סְאָה סְאָה (se'āh, se'āh, "measure for measure" or "moderately"). Most ancient versions assume something like this. The NIV's "By warfare" follows the LXX. The phrase Young translates as "by sending her away" has a feminine suffix, rather unexpectedly. He suggests, comparing the use of the same verb שָׁלַח (šālaḥ, "to send away") in Isa 50:1, that this conveys a picture of divorce. He thinks therefore that it may not refer to the Exile but to the setting aside of the theocracy for a while. It could surely suggest exile, however; for if the land Israel occupies is peculiarly the Lord's, then the wife is being banished from the marital home.

12 The Hebrew lacks the word "Euphrates," but "the River" in the OT is always the Euphrates unless the context indicates otherwise (cf. Josh 24:15; Isa 8:7).

"The Wadi of Egypt," is the 'El 'Arish, the border between Israel and Egypt (cf. Gen 15:18; 1 Kings 8:65; Ezek 47:15–19).

IV. God and His People (28:1–33:14)

The Book of Isaiah is comparatively simple to analyze into its main divisions, for it has a most beautiful order (see Introduction, pp. 20–22). There is less agreement, however, about the chapters that lie before us than about most other sections of the book. Most writers who recognize overall pattern in the book take chapters 28–32 to be a unity, despite the elements of diversity found in them. Others add chapter 33, while others also add chapters 34–35. Certainly chapters 34–35 form a fitting climax to what has gone before; but just as we treated chapters 24–27, climaxing chapters 13–23, as a sufficiently distinct unit to justify a separate section in our analysis, so we will do with chapters 34–35.

In Psalm 103, the psalmist's thought begins with God's blessings shown to him as an individual, moves out to the blessing of his nation, and ends by reference to the praises of the whole cosmos. There is something of this kind of development in the chapters of Isaiah we have surveyed so far. Judah and Jerusalem are the focus of interest in the first twelve chapters, and then we begin a survey of the nations that formed Judah's political and religious environment. Finally, in chapters 24–27, the prophet's visions encompassed the whole universe, while never neglecting the destiny of his own people. Here we return to "square one" again; and Jerusalem itself—the empirical Jerusalem, that is—is at the center of the picture. That picture will undoubtedly come to include wider elements, but its center is Zion right to the end (see 35:10).

When the Book of Isaiah was divided into chapters, clearly it was noted that at several significant points in this part of it the Hebrew word *hôy* ("woe") occurred; and this was adopted as the clue to the appropriate division of chapters 28–33. This was carried through consistently, except for the division between chapters 31 and 32. We will ourselves, in general, follow this same pattern. The material in those chapters seems to belong to the period of Hezekiah's reign.

1. Woe to Samaria

28:1–29

> ¹Woe to that wreath, the pride of Ephraim's drunkards,
>   to the fading flower, his glorious beauty,
> set on the head of a fertile valley—
>   to that city, the pride of those laid low by wine!
> ²See, the Lord has one who is powerful and strong.
>   Like a hailstorm, and a destructive wind,
> like a driving rain and a flooding downpour,
>   he will throw it forcefully to the ground.
> ³That wreath, the pride of Ephraim's drunkards,
>   will be trampled underfoot.
> ⁴That fading flower, his glorious beauty,
>   set on the head of a fertile valley,
> will be like a fig ripe before harvest—
>   as soon as someone sees it and takes it in his hand,
>   he swallows it.
>
> ⁵In that day the LORD Almighty
>   will be a glorious crown,
> a beautiful wreath
>   for the remnant of his people.
> ⁶He will be a spirit of justice
>   to him who sits in judgment,
> a source of strength
>   to those who turn back the battle at the gate.

⁷And these also stagger from wine
    and reel from beer:
Priests and prophets stagger from beer
    and are befuddled with wine;
they reel from beer,
    they stagger when seeing visions,
    they stumble when rendering decisions.
⁸All the tables are covered with vomit
    and there is not a spot without filth.

⁹"Who is it he is trying to teach?
    To whom is he explaining his message?
To children weaned from their milk,
    to those just taken from the breast?
¹⁰For it is:
    Do and do, do and do,
    rule on rule, rule on rule;
    a little here, a little there."

¹¹Very well then, with foreign lips and strange tongues
    God will speak to this people,
¹²to whom he said,
    "This is the resting place, let the weary rest";
and, "This is the place of repose"—
    but they would not listen.
¹³So then, the word of the LORD to them will become:
    Do and do, do and do,
    rule on rule, rule on rule;
    a little here, a little there—
so that they will go and fall backward,
    be injured and snared and captured.

¹⁴Therefore hear the word of the LORD, you scoffers
    who rule this people in Jerusalem.
¹⁵You boast, "We have entered into a covenant with death,
    with the grave we have made an agreement.
When an overwhelming scourge sweeps by,
    it cannot touch us,
for we have made a lie our refuge
    and falsehood our hiding place."

¹⁶So this is what the Sovereign LORD says:

    "See, I lay a stone in Zion,
    a tested stone,
    a precious cornerstone for a sure foundation;
    the one who trusts will never be dismayed.
¹⁷I will make justice the measuring line
    and righteousness the plumb line;
hail will sweep away your refuge, the lie,
    and water will overflow your hiding place.
¹⁸Your covenant with death will be annulled;
    your agreement with the grave will not stand.
When the overwhelming scourge sweeps by,
    you will be beaten down by it.
¹⁹As often as it comes it will carry you away;
    morning after morning, by day and by night,
    it will sweep through."

The understanding of this message
　will bring sheer terror.
20The bed is too short to stretch out on,
　the blanket too narrow to wrap around you.
21The LORD will rise up as he did at Mount Perazim,
　he will rouse himself as in the Valley of Gibeon—
to do his work, his strange work,
　and perform his task, his alien task.
22Now stop your mocking,
　or your chains will become heavier;
the Lord, the LORD Almighty, has told me
　of the destruction decreed against the whole land.

23Listen and hear my voice;
　pay attention and hear what I say.
24When a farmer plows for planting, does he
　　plow continually?
　Does he keep on breaking up and harrowing the soil?
25When he has leveled the surface,
　does he not sow caraway and scatter cummin?
Does he not plant wheat in its place,
　barley in its plot,
　and spelt in its field?
26His God instructs him
　and teaches him the right way.

27Caraway is not threshed with a sledge,
　nor is a cartwheel rolled over cummin;
caraway is beaten out with a rod,
　and cummin with a stick.
28Grain must be ground to make bread;
　so one does not go on threshing it forever.
Though he drives the wheels of his threshing cart over it,
　his horses do not grind it.
29All this also comes from the LORD Almighty,
　wonderful in counsel and magnificent in wisdom.

It may seem to the reader that our assertion above that Jerusalem is central to chapters 28–35 may require some modification here. It will be seen, however, that Isaiah's prophecies about Ephraim are not simply for the sake of its people but also—and perhaps even more—to point out some salutary lessons to Jerusalem and her rulers (cf. vv. 14–15).

The English stylist G. A. Smith, who was very sensitive to Isaiah's literary qualities but denied its integrity, wrote (in loc.) about this chapter: "This is clearly one of the greatest of Isaiah's prophecies. It is distinguished by that regal versatility of style, which places its author at the head of the Hebrew writers. Keen analyses of character, realistic contrasts between sin and judgment, clever retorts and epigrams, rapids of scorn, and a spate of judgment, but for final issue a placid stream of argument banked by sweet parable—such are the literary forms of this chapter." The original recipients of these oracles, though perhaps not conscious of an outstanding aesthetic experience, would have been gripped by the spiritual content of the words. Nevertheless the one was the vehicle for the other. Great preaching in every age uses forceful logic and vivid imagery to convey spiritual challenge, and Isaiah does this outstandingly here.

1–4 Verse 1 is not easy to translate so as to bring out its meaning clearly in English. Literally it is "Woe to the coronet of pride of the drunkards of Ephraim and to the fading flower of its glorious beauty that is on the head of the fat valley of those who are stunned with wine!" The NIV gives the sense effectively. It has been suggested —and it may well be—that Isaiah had a vision of the alleged spiritual leaders of Ephraim, the northern kingdom (cf. v.7), staggering in their inebriation and wearing some kind of floral wreath on their heads, probably tilted at a jaunty angle. This suggested to him another crowned head, that of the hill on which their capital city, Samaria, was situated. This hill stands in a commanding position at the head of a very fertile valley. Amos also castigated Samaria for its drunken decadence (Amos 4:1; 6:1, 6).

The Assyrian threat appeared on the eastern horizon at a time when the northern kingdom was relatively prosperous. It might have seemed that it was cut off in its prime; but, as this passage shows, the telltale signs of a descent into decay were already present. Flowers there may have been, but they were fading. As Hosea expressed it, with the use of a different image, "His hair is sprinkled with gray, but he does not notice" (Hos 7:9).

A strategically situated city may also be exposed to the elements. A destructive wind from the east (cf. 27:8 and comment there) was no stranger to Israel, though this time it was not the hot "sirocco" coming in from the desert but a strong hail and rain-bearing wind that would normally come from another direction (v.2). The prophet piled up words and phrases to convey the ferocity of the storm. The powerful and strong one is undefined, and the object of its attack is unexpressed; but they are obviously Assyria and Samaria respectively.

At this point (v.3) the language of v.1 reappears. The feet of the Assyrians will tramp through Samaria's streets, and Samaria itself will be trampled on by the great foreign foe. Outside the city walls, figs would be growing. Sometimes a fig would ripen before the normal season, and a traveler—perhaps an Assyrian soldier on his way into the city—would quickly pick and eat it. So suddenly would Samaria's destruction be (v.4).

5–8 Would this judgment on Samaria mean that the people of God would no longer have a coronet to adorn them? The prophet, changing the word "pride" ($g\bar{e}'\hat{u}t$) in v.1 to "glory" ($s^e p\hat{i}r\bar{a}h$) in the phrase translated "glorious crown" (v.5) because of the possibly unfavorable connotation of the former, asserted that this is what the Lord will be to the remnant of his people. Their glorying had a physical focus, but this would be replaced by a spiritual one. Perhaps he had in mind the southern kingdom —so small in comparison with the northern, but with God in her midst—or else the remnant left behind in Israel by the receding Assyrian conquerors, or perhaps even both. A further possibility is that the phrase "in that day" is intended to be understood eschatologically (see note at 2:11), so that the prophet's thought overleaped many intervening centuries to the last days.

The drunkards of v.1 are leaders of the people, such as priests and prophets (cf. v.7). There would probably be judges among them also. The administration of justice requires great wisdom and clear-headedness. The prophet promises that God will himself be a spirit of justice giving wisdom to the judge, and the people's arms will have success against the foe (v.6). We are reminded of 11:1–5, where the spirit of the Lord in all his varied fullness rests on the Messiah, enabling him to dispense justice with righteousness. Isaiah 32:1 associates just rulers with the righteous king.

The remnant would have God as their crown when Samaria, the crown of Ephraim, had been taken by Assyria. But what was that remnant like *now?* Isaiah turned his attention to the leaders of Jerusalem (of v. 14). Such a high destiny and such a low life style! The vivid picture of spiritual guides lacking not only supernatural insight but even common reason—this surely is what "befuddled" suggests—is horrifying. We could wish it were caricature, but prophets declare truth without exaggeration. Nor unhappily is the drunken "minister" unknown to modern Christendom. The realistic description of the environment in v. 8 bears all the marks of eyewitness reporting.

9–10 As the prophet declared the word of God in this drink-dominated setting, his hearers made their response. The NIV is probably right in treating both these verses as a quotation of the words of the drunkards. They felt insulted. Were they not themselves spiritual leaders, well able to teach others? What right had this man to place them in the classroom and teach them the spiritual ABC's? There is something ironic about the reference to milk (v.9) in such a context.

Many commentators have been puzzled by v.10 and have wrestled to make sense of the Hebrew. The truth of the matter seems to be, as the NIV margin suggests, that it is not meant to make sense. Isaiah's words had hardly penetrated the alcohol-impregnated atmosphere that surrounded his hearers. What they picked up were simply a few stray syllables, some of them repeated, like the baby-talk that delights the child but would insult the adult. They mouth this gibberish back at the prophet. The transmitter was as strong and clear as ever; it was the receivers that were at fault. Their judgment, meantime, lay in their failure to hear the word that could have led them back to God; but there was another judgment on its way, most appropriate in its form. Their sin had turned the word of God through Isaiah into a meaningless noise that might just as well have been a foreign language.

11–13 Very well, then, the next message will come through foreigners (v.11). The Assyrian devastation of Judah (cf. 1:5–9) is surely in view. There is a striking aptness about this, because just as the drunkards picked up a few familiar sounds but no connected meaning, so the people of Judah would detect some similarities between the Akkadian of the Assyrians and their own Hebrew (both being Semitic tongues), without being able to understand what was being said. Of course, in reality it was through the Assyrians' swords rather than their words that God would speak his message to Israel.

Was drunkenness the people's main sin? No, for more serious still was their failure to hear God's word offering rest to those who insisted on rejecting it (v.12). The prophet was clearly speaking of the call to faith. This had been refused by Ahaz (cf. chs. 7–8), and attempts to link up with Egypt (cf. 30:1–3; 31:1–5, and the Introduction, pp. 5–6) were contemporary examples of the same sin. Their disobedient refusal of the way of faith in God was therefore a continuing condition preventing the word from getting through to them. The effects of drink may pass off, but unbelief can be a permanent barrier to God's word.

The language of v.13b is strongly reminiscent of 8:14–15, and this very fact conveys a message. On an earlier occasion, in the days of Ahaz, God had pointed out the way of faith and had warned the people against the consequences of rejecting this. Times might have changed, but not the principles of God's dealings with his people. The call to faith then had been accompanied by a warning of the consequences of walking in another way, and those consequences were the same now. It is possible, especially in view of the repetition of the drunkards' syllables from v. 10, that their fall is thought of first of all as a result of their drunken staggering (v. 7); but the range of analogies is then extended to the picture of the hunter's snare. If this is so, the wording is similar to 8:14–15 and the essential message the same, but the imaginative vehicle the message comes through is a little different. The inspired ideation of this prophet is so rich!

14–15 This passage underlines the objectivity of the word of God. Men may have lost their capacity to hear it, but this does not modify its character as God's word one whit. There is no question of its having to become his word in the context of experience. They are commanded to hear it (v. 14), even though it is unlikely to penetrate to their understanding simply because it is his and men are culpable if they do not hear.

In the Book of Proverbs, the scoffer is the worst type of sinner (e.g., Prov 1:22; 29:8; cf. Ps 1:1), for he is utterly contemptuous of the ways of God. There is an element of contempt discernible in the drunken responses of vv. 9–10.

Rejection of God's word and confidence in our own often go hand in hand. Isaiah was not really quoting the "scoffers" (v. 14) in v. 15, of course, but ironically combining their words with his interpretation of their consequences. Clements (*Isaiah 1–39*, in loc.), mentioning O. Kaiser's view (also in loc.) that the political leaders were involved in necromancy, goes on to say, "Yet it is very unlikely that this is the prophet's meaning here. Rather he is using heavily satirical language to characterize the political treaty upon which the leaders pride themselves as an act of political folly which will lead to their doom and death." There can be little doubt that Isaiah had in mind the growing link between Judah and Egypt and the attempt in this way to warn off the Assyrians.

The "overwhelming scourge," as Young (*Book of Isaiah*, in loc.) well notes, contains a mixture of figures; for how can a scourge be said to overflow? The separate elements in this phrase are from 10:26 and 10:22 respectively (cf. also 8:8). The assonance of the two words is very striking (see Notes), and Young draws attention to Delitzsch's perceptive comment (in loc.) that a whip when cracked moves in wavy lines. Perhaps the leaders of Judah had the circumstances of the original Passover in mind. They thought themselves immune, like Israel sheltered beneath sacrificial blood in Egypt (cf. 1:10–17), but there could be no such refuge in that land for them now.

The reference to lies and falsehood may be an attack on that trust in expediency rather than in principle that so often characterizes politicians. It seems more likely, however, that the prophet was not charging them directly with a lack of integrity but rather that his words were still ironic. The assertion that Egypt will effectively come to their aid, which they believed to be sober truth, was in fact a lie. The alternative translation (NIV mg.) of *kāzāb* ("falsehood") as "false gods" (the word is sometimes used in this sense, e.g., Ps 40:5; Amos 2:4) is less likely in this particular context.

16–19 Even a superficial examination of these verses reveals the considerable extent to which—in word and idea—they take up so much of what the prophet has said already in this chapter. The conjunction *lākēn* ("so" or "therefore") v. 16 opens with indicates this logical connection with what God has already said in this oracle.

The further connection, already noted in the comment at v.13, between this prophecy and chapter 8 is also very instructive. In the earlier passage (8:14), the Lord
himself had declared that he would be both a sanctuary—and Judah's sanctuary at
Jerusalem was made of stone—and a stumbling stone for the people of Israel. Faith
would make the difference. Here the stone illustration—having already been developed, by implication, in a negative way in v.13—is presented in an eminently positive fashion.

What then is meant by this stone? Concerning the divergent views held by both
those who accept the MT as it stands and those who follow 1QIsa in reading a
Hebrew participle instead of a finite verb (cf. Notes), O. Kaiser summarized (with
documentation, in loc.):

> It has been identified with the law of Yahweh revealed upon Zion, the Temple
> upon Zion as the refuge of those faithful to Yahweh, the archetypal monarchy set
> up in the person of David, the city of Jerusalem on its hill, the saving work
> begun by Yahweh on Zion, Yahweh's relationship to his people, and even with
> the true community of believers already founded by God. . . . Those who have
> emended the verb into a participle and understood it in a future sense have
> interpreted the statement as referring to Zion as the righteous foundation by
> Yahweh, to the Messiah as the foundation stone of a temple not made with
> hands, faith, the remnant of believers, or very precisely to the statement that
> "He who believes will not waver", as Yahweh's promise.

What then does it mean? Without doubt this passage is of great importance in the
messianic teaching of the prophecies of Isaiah. It is treated as messianic in the NT
and is quoted in application to Christ several times in the apostolic writings (Rom
9:33; 10:11; 1 Peter 2:4–6). It is important, however, for us to see its appropriateness and to seek to determine its precise meaning within its OT context. In 8:14, in
an oracle from the time of Ahaz, the prophet had used the stone analogy in a most
significant way. The Lord himself was calling men to faith. If they responded in
faith, he would be a sanctuary, a holy place, to them. As the altar of God in the
temple was treated as a place of refuge (Exod 21:14; 1 Kings 1:50), so God himself
would be a holy place of refuge for them (cf. Ezek 11:16). If, however, they refused
belief, he would be a stone of stumbling they would fall over. The altar of stone was,
of course, set within a temple of stone, so that both the promise and the threat there
rest on the spiritualizing of the stone.

The context here is very similar. The leadership of Judah was again refused the
way of faith and sought alliance with Egypt. The prophet returned to his previous
image but developed it differently. The stone-built temple is once again a picture of
the God they are to trust in. Instead of reapplying the stone illustration in a threat
(but see v.13b), Isaiah declared God's condemnation of the poor Egyptian makeshift
the rebellious and unbelieving people had constructed as a substitute for faith in
their God. The passage therefore harmonizes perfectly both with its literary and
with its historical contexts. The stone is defined, as we shall see, in terms of the
analogy itself; but the reality of which it is the image is unspecified. A comparison
of the language of 8:14 and the present passage shows us that there the sanctuary
and stone were God himself whereas here the stone is laid by God. If this passage
is a development of the former, then we are bound to ask, "Who, in Isaiah's prophecies, is both God and distinct from him?" The clear answer is "the Messiah," as 9:6
(cf. 7:14) shows. The soundness of this approach is confirmed when we note that

thematic development is a leading feature of Messianism in this book (cf. Introduction, pp. 16–20).

If then the stone is the Messiah, what messianic qualities or functions emerge from the prophet's words? Most modern EV render the verb into English as a present simple or continuous—viz., "I lay" (NIV) or "I am laying" (RSV) (see Notes for discussion of the tense). Zion was itself, of course, the place of the temple and also the place where the leaders of the people lived. The stone is probably defined in a twofold way. First of all, it is a tested or testing stone. If the adjective is taken in an active sense, then it will simply indicate that the foundation stone has been tested for strength and shape. If passive, however, it may well refer to a topstone, shaped by the master mason for placing at the end of the whole building process, so forming a test of trueness of line for the whole edifice. This idea is found in Psalm 118:22 and is applied to Christ in Mark 12:10. He comes as the consummation of the divine building project (sent "last of all," Mark 12:6); and, although rejected by the religious leaders of his day—the spiritual counterparts of the unbelieving leaders here—he was, in fact, God's proof of the soundness of the whole structure of messianic promise. If the prophecy is truly messianic, then it is eschatological; and if eschatological, then the idea of a capstone is most apt. We will take it, therefore, in this sense, though this cannot be established beyond a shadow of doubt.

The testing stone is also "a precious cornerstone for a sure foundation." This clearly points to the stone that is placed on the living rock and that is of special importance also because it is at the junction of two walls. He is "precious" because of his superlative value in the divine plan. The ultimate spiritual sanctuary will find its foundation in him. In the NT God's great "building" is the church. Objectively this is built on Christ, while believers, like Peter, established this foundation for others by confessing and proclaiming him (Matt 16:13–19). Here too there is a call for faith.

If we are right in seeing both topstone and foundation stone here, we have evidence of the freedom of the prophet—and behind him of the inspiring Spirit—in the use of analogies. In architecture the same stone cannot fulfill both purposes; but God gives one great answer to the totality of human need, and that answer is Christ. E.J. Young (*Isaiah 1–39*, in loc.) interprets the passage differently, viewing the testing as God's testing of men. Either view, in fact, makes good sense.

The verb translated "dismayed" (*ḥîš*) literally means "to hasten"; but it can be applied figuratively to emotions, as, for example, in Job 20:2, where it is translated "greatly disturbed," On the other hand, a literal rendering makes good sense because, as Mauchline (in loc.) says, it can suggest a contrast with waiting on God (cf. 8:17; 25:9; 26:8; 30:18; 33:2 et al.).

The architectural language continues into v.17. The first half of this verse may anticipate the thought of v.17b or amplify that of v.16. Divine justice and righteousness may govern the entire building operation, from foundation to capstone, so that the entire edifice of promise and fulfillment is just and true. On the other hand, it may show up as unrighteous and false the flimsy structures of men represented by the refuge or hiding place that the storms of God's judgment will demolish (cf. v.2). Both interpretations are possible, and little depends on a solution. A similar contrast between two buildings—where relationship to Christ and his teaching is the test of true construction—is found in Luke 6:46–49.

Verse 18 too takes up language from earlier verses in the chapter, chiefly from v.15, but also from v.2, so preserving some consistency of figure. It is water that will overflow the hiding place (v.17), sweep by and beat down (v.18), and carry the people away (v.19). Isaiah's pictorial gift enabled him at times to move swiftly from one figure to another, while at others to sustain the same figure through a number of verses and yet with subtle variations and adaptations to clothe the development of his inspired thought.

The judgment will not pass quickly so that relief will soon follow fear. Verse 19 clearly suggests that wave after wave of the enemy will come into Judah, so that the people's hearts will be dominated by fear throughout the whole period. The RSV's translation of v.19—"and it will be sheer terror to understand the message"—is particularly good, providing a kind of rhythmic climax to the whole of vv.14–19. In this way, then, God would speak—through hordes of cruel Assyrian warriors—his message of judgment to his people (cf. v.11, 14), who would not hear the prophet's message (cf. v.9–10 and comment there).

20–22 God's people had made their bed; now they must lie on it (v.20). When they did so, they would discover its inadequacy to provide true rest (cf. v.12). As we have made use of an English proverb, so Isaiah may be using a proverbial saying of his day. In an earlier chapter the prophet had used historical allusion for the comfort of his hearers (cf. 9:6; 10:26 and, to some extent, 1:9). Now such allusions become the vehicle of threats rather than promises. At Mount Perazim and in the Valley of Gibeon (v.21; cf. Josh 10:1–10; 2 Sam 5:17–25), God had "awoken from slumber" (a possible suggestion that the bed and sleep illustration was still in Isaiah's mind) to come to his people's aid against their enemies. "Perazim" means "breaking forth," and this allusion may have been suggested by the waters of judgment in vv.2, 15, 17–19. God's anger against the Philistines, dammed up so long by his people's sin, broke forth and overwhelmed them through David; but that anger, held back again through many a year of grace, would finally burst in a "strange work" of judgment against his own people. Luther, Barth, and others have spoken in general terms of judgment as God's strange work, basing their thought on this verse. It should be remembered, however, that in its context the expression relates to the strange phenomenon of judgment falling on God's own people.

Isaiah's reference to mocking (v.22) should be compared with v.14 and with the comment on vv.9–10. Those destined for judgment are bound with chains, suggesting that there is no way of escape from that destiny. Like Amos earlier (cf. Amos 3:7–8), Isaiah's auditory experience of God made him aware of a terrible judgment to come, in which the whole land will be involved. The devastating Assyrian invasions, culminating in the terrible siege and overthrow of Jerusalem by the Babylonians at a later period, progressively fulfilled this prophecy in line with the terms of v.19.

23–29 Isaiah knew how obtuse and spiritually hard of hearing his listeners were and so, like the Lord Jesus (e.g., Mark 4:3, 9), called on them to pay close attention to his words (v.23). It may be, in fact, that Christ's exceptionally strong call for attention in the parable of the sower reflects the influence of this passage, which is itself replete with agricultural language.

Verses 24–25 consist entirely of a series of rhetorical questions. They are based on the understood but never expressed analogy between the processes of agriculture and the ways of God with men, what Henry Drummond called *Natural Law in the Spiritual World* (London: Hodder and Stoughton, 1897). Nature, as God has created it, contains so many illustrations of spiritual truth that the sensitive and godly observer is forced to conclude that there is divine design in this, just as there is in the phenomenon of typology in OT history. The point made in v.24 is that agriculture requires the farmer to change his activity from time to time. Plowing is needed, but it is not a year-round activity. So God's purposes require him to act differently at different seasons, perhaps sparing Jerusalem in 701 B.C. and destroying it in 586 B.C. Then a farmer does not normally sow all his fields with only one plant variety (v.25). In a mixed farming economy, space is found for a variety of crops. Once again, the variety of God's ways with people is being underlined. The farmer learns such things from God, by a study perhaps of nature (v.26). Why then is man so reluctant to learn from God in spiritual things?

Verses 27–29 take the illustration further. When it comes to harvest time, threshing takes different forms, each form dictated by the type of crop harvested (v.27). More than this, threshing time comes to an end, for the ultimate aim of all this activity is to produce edible food (v.28). Plowing, sowing, threshing, and grinding are all means to this end. So God has his purposes in history, and through a sequence of events he brings them to pass (v.29). God's power ("the LORD Almighty") and wisdom, united in his nature, bring forth a pattern of events in the story of man. Most of the agricultural processes here can suggest pain, perhaps implying therefore that it is possible to find oneself on the wrong side of God's purposes in history and so to experience his judgment. In fact, some such lesson seems to be required by the context.

Notes

10 The interpretation given above is now widely held, for it is difficult to derive proper sense from the Hebrew as it stands. The NIV text is about as near as the translator can get. There seem to be echoes of the Hebrew of v.8, which suggests that the interpretation in terms of broken syllables mouthed by their recipients is correct. G. Fohrer (*Das Buch Jesaya*, in loc.) suggests that the syllables actually used are those a Hebrew mother would use to teach her child the alphabet. This is possible.

11 Paul quoted this verse at 1 Cor 14:21, where he seems to be implying that uninterpreted —and therefore meaningless—glossolalia will simply confirm the unbelieving hearer in his sin and therefore anticipate his judgment. Whether in Isaiah's day, Paul's, or ours, it is meaningful utterance—a message from God addressed to the understanding—that humans need to bring them to the sure foundation of faith.

15 For "grave" the NIV margin has "Sheol," on which see the comment at 5:14.

16 The MT has the Piel perfect יִסַּד (*yissad*, "he has founded"), while 1QIsa^b and the LXX read the Qal active participle יוֹסֵד (*yôsēd* ("founding" or "about to found")). The real problem perhaps lies in the preceding first person pronoun. Young (*Book of Isaiah*, in loc.) helpfully mentions the view of Rashi, the medieval Jewish commentator, that this is a simple case of ellipsis, so that we should follow the MT and read, "Behold! I am he who founds" (cf. NIV's "I lay").

25, 27–28 The various crops mentioned were all common in Palestine. For detailed comment both on the crops and the farming methods referred to here, see E.W. Heaton, *Everyday Life in Old Testament Times* (London: Batsford, 1956), pp. 97–115, and ZPEB, 1:71–78, 1037.

29 The terminological connection between this verse and the messianic passage 9:6 should be

noted. There could be just a suggestion that God is working in history to a messianic end, though it is not possible to assert this categorically.

2. Woe to Ariel

29:1–24

¹Woe to you, Ariel, Ariel,
the city where David settled!
Add year to year
and let your cycle of festivals go on.
²Yet I will besiege Ariel;
she will mourn and lament,
she will be to me like an altar hearth.
³I will encamp against you all around;
I will encircle you with towers
and set up my siege works against you.
⁴Brought low, you will speak from the ground;
your speech will mumble out of the dust.
Your voice will come ghostlike from the earth;
out of the dust your speech will whisper.

⁵But your many enemies will become like fine dust,
the ruthless hordes like blown chaff.
Suddenly, in an instant,
⁶ the LORD Almighty will come
with thunder and earthquake and great noise,
with windstorm and tempest and flames of a
devouring fire.
⁷Then the hordes of all the nations that fight against Ariel,
that attack her and her fortress and besiege her,
will be as it is with a dream,
with a vision in the night—
⁸as when a hungry man dreams that he is eating,
but he awakens, and his hunger remains;
as when a thirsty man dreams that he is drinking,
but he awakens faint, with his thirst unquenched.
So will it be with the hordes of all the nations
that fight against Mount Zion.

⁹Be stunned and amazed,
blind yourselves and be sightless;
be drunk, but not from wine,
stagger, but not from beer.
¹⁰The LORD has brought over you a deep sleep:
He has sealed your eyes (the prophets);
he has covered your heads (the seers).

¹¹For you this whole vision is nothing but words sealed in a scroll. And if you give the scroll to someone who can read, and say to him, "Read this, please," he will answer, "I can't; it is sealed." ¹²Or if you give the scroll to someone who cannot read, and say, "Read this, please," he will answer, "I don't know how to read."

¹³The Lord says:

"These people come near to me with their mouth
and honor me with their lips,
but their hearts are far from me.

Their worship to me
is made up only of rules taught by men.
14Therefore once more I will astound these people
with wonder upon wonder;
the wisdom of the wise will perish,
the intelligence of the intelligent will vanish."
15Woe to those who go to great depths
to hide their plans from the LORD,
who do their work in darkness and think,
"Who sees us? Who will know?"
16You turn things upside down,
as if the potter were thought to be like the clay!
Shall what is formed say to him who formed it,
"He did not make me"?
Can the pot say of the potter,
"He knows nothing"?

17In a very short time, will not Lebanon be turned into a
fertile field
and the fertile field seem like a forest?
18In that day the deaf will hear the words of the scroll,
and out of gloom and darkness
the eyes of the blind will see.
19Once more the humble will rejoice in the LORD;
the needy will rejoice in the Holy One of Israel.
20The ruthless will vanish,
the mockers will disappear,
and all who have an eye for evil will be cut down—
21those who with a word make a man out to be guilty,
who ensnare the defender in court
and with false testimony deprive the innocent of justice.

22Therefore this is what the LORD, who redeemed Abraham, says to the house
of Jacob:

"No longer will Jacob be ashamed;
no longer will their faces grow pale.
23When they see among them their children,
the work of my hands,
they will keep my name holy;
they will acknowledge the holiness of the Holy One
of Jacob,
and will stand in awe of the God of Israel.
24Those who are wayward in spirit will gain understanding;
those who complain will accept instruction."

This chapter presents the second of the "woe" oracles in this section of Isaiah's prophecies (see the general introduction to chs. 28–35). The word *hôy* ("woe") in fact occurs twice in the chapter, at v.1 and v.15; but there is such an intimate link between v.15 and its preceding context that it seems unlikely it is intended to represent the beginning of a fresh oracle. Despite this double use of the word in this chapter, the atmosphere—though solemn—is not one of unrelieved gloom. Not only judgment for Jerusalem but her salvation are promised here.

1–4 The chapter begins with a mystery. What does the reiterated word Ariel mean? The connection of the city with David (v.1) and the reference to Mount Zion in v.8 established its identification with Jerusalem. Why call it Ariel? The last clause of v.2

makes this clear. As the NIV margin says, "The Hebrew for *hearth* sounds like the Hebrew for *Ariel*" (emphasis theirs). Yes, but does this mean that the prophet has invented this name for Jerusalem in order to introduce such a play on words? This seems most ulikely, as paronomasia, which is so common in the OT, loses its force if it loses its naturalness. The name Ariel does possess a certain naturalness if in fact it actually means altar hearth, so that in all four occurrences (two in v.1 and two in v.2) it would bear the same meaning. Its naturalness derives from the fact that Jerusalem was a place of sacrifice, with an altar hearth in the temple where sacrifices were always burning. We will take it that this is the meaning and discuss other possibilities in the Notes.

The NIV margin does not make it clear that the word translated "altar hearth" in v.2 is exactly the same word "Ariel" and not simply like it in sound. The point really is that in this sentence the word clearly is not simply a name but actually *means* something, and what it means in fact is not "hearth" but "altar hearth."

The word *ḥānāh* occurs in both v.1 and v.3. In v.1 it seems preferable to translate "encamped" rather than "settled," so bringing the two verses into line. David, in fact, besieged Jerusalem when it was a Jebusite stronghold. When he took it, it became his capital city. Through many a difficult century in its history it had never been taken again. The true poignancy of the "woe" here lies in the fact that the God who had enabled David to take it would now besiege this city himself, through its enemies (v.5), and cause its destruction by fire just as if the whole city had become an extension of the altar hearth within its temple.

The popular theology of sacrifice in the eighth century B.C. gave it too great a place in the relationship between God and his people, so that religion was conceived to be almost purely external and ritualistic (cf. 1:10–17; 29:13). The point of the ironic exhortations in v.1b is that it was at the festivals of the religious calendar that the Jerusalem altar was busiest. At these times, therefore, given this false popular theology, the people became more and more confirmed in their false assurance that all was well between themselves and God. What a shock awaited them! Verse 3, with its threefold statement that God would become their enemy, is more forceful.

Verse 4 is probably best understood as a development of the statement "she will mourn and lament" in v.2. That penitence of spirit that was so conspicuously absent from the sacrifices her people were making would at last come about through divine chastisement. The language of physical exaltation and abasement is often used by Isaiah in relation to pride and humility (see comment at 22:2–4). Instead of pompous boasting (cf. 28:15), their speech would come as a mere ghostlike whisper from the ground where they lie prostrate. This does not, of course, imply a belief in the real possibility of communications from the dead (see comment at 8:19), for an illustration does not necessarily imply truth in the analogy used but only an acquaintance with it as a concept.

5–8 Here the whole mood of the oracle changes as suddenly and dramatically as the events it depicts. God would judge his people by sending their enemies against their capital city, but he did not intend that city to be taken. The ominous towers and siege works are replaced by fine dust and blown chaff (v.5). These are fit symbols of insubstantiality (cf. 40:15) and judgment (cf. Pss 1:4; 35:5). Those sent in judgment would themselves experience it (cf. 10:5–19). Appearing to be so formidable, they would be cut down to size.

The "many enemies" are further described in v.7 as "the hordes of all the nations." Moreover the coming of the Lord Almighty is described in terms suggestive of a most awe-inspiring intervention. It is questionable whether such language quite fits even the dramatic act of God recorded in chapters 36–37. Perhaps we should see a partial fulfillment of it in these events of 701 B.C. but the ultimate fulfillment in a passage like Revelation 20:8–9 (see Introduction, pp. 14–16). The language (esp. v.6) is so reminiscent of Exodus 19 that it suggests that the God of judgment is also the God of the law, his judgments expressing his concern for righteousness.

Isaiah's illustrations are not only appropriate; they are also true to the common experience of humanity. We all know something of the dream that seems as vivid and compelling as reality itself. The city of Jerusalem, which seemed so real a prize to its attackers, would suddenly be seen to belong to the dream world of military ambition. The phrase "Mount Zion" itself has overtones of stability and divine protection (cf. Ps 48).

9–12 The inaugural vision of Isaiah's prophetic ministry made him aware that as he declared the word of God, many of his hearers—far from being enlightened and coming out of sin-induced blindness into the full light of God—would simply shut their eyes to the truth (cf. 6:9–10). This theme of darkness and light has already received one major exposition in the prophecies (8:16–9:7). The spiritual blindness of the drunken religious leaders has been emphasized in chapter 28. Now the theme occurs again and in a way that suggests a possible allusion to both former passages. The imperatives of v.9 remind us of those in chapter 6 and the references to drink to chapter 28. The professional prophets, whether literally drunk or not, are pictured as stumbling unsteadily through life, unable even to plot their own course— let alone point the way to others. Blindness, drunkenness, and sleep—build up a picture of total inadequacy in the realm of spiritual leadership (vv.9–10).

The whole point of vv.11–12 is that Isaiah's own God-given vision was a closed book to the people of Jerusalem. To the one who could read—perhaps the professional prophet, who knew something of the technical language of prophecy—the vision contained mysteries his eyes were closed to (v.11). He who could not read— perhaps the ordinary inhabitant of Jerusalem—was at once removed further still from understanding (v.12). The seeming advantage of the professional prophet did not really place him ahead of the common man, for neither in fact understood the vision.

13–16 The spiritual blindness of vv.9–12 is an appropriate partner of the externalism and traditionalism of v.13. So often these qualities are associated in godless religion. In 1:15 the God of Israel rejected prayers that were offered in a formalistic spirit. Here the spiritual condition is diagnosed and found to be malign indeed. Verse 13 is quoted by our Lord in Matthew 15:9 with reference to the Pharisees. The spiritual parallel is very striking. In both cases wrong teaching was based on a mishandling of God's true revelation, the sacrificial regulations, and the Mosaic Law as a whole respectively. In each case tradition allied to bad theology resulted in a mishandling of Scripture, and in each the result was a self-justifying complacency in the presence of the most holy God. "Rules taught by men" would apply, of course, not to the Levitical teaching itself, but to the way it was applied by the priests. Human nature does not change through the years but finds different religious as well as nonreligious expressions of its fundamental rebellion against God.

So often in the prophecy of Isaiah the prophet says in effect that the God of Israel who had shown himself to his people in one of his great attributes for their blessing would demonstrate that same quality in an act of judgment (see comments at 10:17 and 28:20–22). He is "wonderful" (*pele'*) and has done wonderful things for his people (Exod 15:11; Ps 77:2, 15; cf. Isa 9:6), but his power to astound them is turned against them. The prophet seems still to have in mind the judgments God has decreed against his people in vv.1–3, and the repetition of the word "woe" in v.15 confirms this. The apostle Paul quoted v.14 in 1 Corinthians 1:19. Isaiah shows great interest in the distinction between worldly and godly wisdom (e.g., 5:21; 11:2; 26:7–10). This makes a verse like v.14 most appropriate in the context of Paul's thought in 1 Corinthians 1.

Negotiations with Egypt to form an anti-Assyrian alliance were probably carried on in secret. If that is in view here in v.15, then Isaiah was implying that the negotiators thought their actions were so clandestine that even the Lord himself was denied access to them. When men's minds are not controlled by the revelation of God, their thoughts of him easily become unworthy of what he really is. The prophet suggested that such people have a completely illogical view of God. Without doubt total depravity so affects the mind that men and women can no longer think God's thoughts after him in any adequate way.

Isaiah anticipates Jeremiah in his use of the illustration of the potter and the clay (v.16; cf. 45:9; 64:8; Jer 18:1–6). Paul too used this illustration in Romans 9:19–21. Each of the three writers made somewhat different points; yet each argued for the sovereignty of God from this analogy. The Assyrian too had boasted of his independence from this sovereign God (10:15).

17–21 Significantly, even when the human mind retreats from logic in its conception of God, God still addresses that mind. The questions of v.16 are therefore followed by a further question in v.17. Translators and commentators have in fact understood this verse in quite different ways. The NIV's rendering—"in a very short time, will not Lebanon be turned into a fertile field/and the fertile field seem like a forest?"—appears to be a promise of blessing for the land. The NEB however presents a picture of natural retrogression: "The time is but short before Lebanon goes back to grassland and the grassland is no better than scrub." The TEV gives, like Psalm 107:33–38, a promise followed by a threat, though these are in reverse order in the psalm.

What then are we to make of v.17? Skinner (*Isaiah*, in loc.), pointing out its resemblance to 32:15, says: "The idea in both passages is the same. Lebanon is here not a symbol of the heathen world-power (as in x.34), but a synonym for forest-land in general, corresponding to 'wilderness' (uncultivated pasture-land) in xxxii.15. The second half of the verse is not a contrast to the first, but a climax. While Lebanon actually becomes a fruitful field, what is now a fruitful field shall then be *counted* no better than a forest" (emphasis his). This transformation of the physical world then becomes the introduction to the eschatological picture presented in the remainder of the chapter. This interpretation best fits the general context.

The former spiritual insensitivity of the people will be a thing of the past (cf. 35:5–6). Isaiah shows a concern for the godly poor (cf. 3:14; 11:4; 25:4). The fact that the reference to them in v.19 is followed by a promise that evil men—especially those who "deprive the innocent of justice" (v.21)—will be cut down certainly suggests that it is the restoration of justice to the oppressed in the messianic kingdom (cf. 11:3-4) that is in view, even though this messianic reference is not made explicit. Once again (see the comment at 26:7-11) we seem almost to be in the Book of Proverbs. For the "mockers" (v.20), see the comment at 28:14, where the same Hebrew word is translated "scoffers." To "have an eye for evil" reminds us of passages like Proverbs 1:11-14; 12:6.

The general picture of malignity rampant presented in v.20 becomes more specific in v.21, where the reader is transported to the court of law. "In court" is literally "in the gate," as the RSV translates it; for this was where justice was dispensed (Deut 21:19-20; Ruth 4:1). Each of the three lines relates to a verbal sin, the clever and specious use of words that perverts justice. The prophets stressed the Lord's hatred of oppression furthered by the manipulation of the courts of justice (see comment at 10:1-4).

22-24 It is sometimes assumed that ths passage is of very late date, many centuries after Isaiah, because of the reference to the redemption of Abraham. It is true that the late noncanonical "Apocalypse of Abraham" makes reference to the way God delivered him from persecution by idolators in Mesopotamia, but this would seem to be natural imaginative extension of the story of a greatly revered ancestor. It is quite unnecessary to read this kind of thing into the simple word "redeemed" here (v.22). Joshua 24:14 links the region "beyond the River" with Egypt as places where the people had served other gods. The language of redemption was regularly applied to the deliverance from Egypt, and there is no good reason why it could not be applied to the exit of Abraham from Ur at the call of God. There may not have been the same human bondage, but in both cases they were under a regime acknowledging other gods. The passage makes much of the people's relationship to their ancestor Jacob, and the mention of Abraham reinforces still more this emphasis on the past. The prophet is probably thinking about the promises made by the God of Israel to the patriarchs and the fact that the prophecies given to him involved their fulfillment.

Most EV obscure the oscillation of grammatical number in vv.22-23. The NIV brings this out in v.22; but the RSV is more accurate in v.23; "For when he sees his children, the work of his hands, in his midst, they will sanctify my name." In the Hebrew grammatical consistency is sacrificed in order to bring out the fact that the prophet has both the patriarch and his descendants in mind. There is such a solidarity between a people and their ancestor that they can be closely identified in this way. The shame of Jacob, when considered in the light of the context, certainly seems to be the dispersion of many of the people of Israel from the land because of their sin (see Deut 28:36-37, 63-64, and comment at Isa 25:8). Their God will bring their scattered children back to the land (v.23). N.H. Snaith (*Notes on the Hebrew Text of Isaiah XXVIII-XXXII* [London: Epworth, 1945], p. 40) comments that v.23a is "a passage which is not as difficult as is generally thought, if it is taken as belonging to the same set of circumstances as xlix.14-25." He is surely correct.

Isaiah's characteristic title for God is "the Holy One of Israel" (see Introduction, p. 12). This holiness sets the God of Israel apart from all other beings, not least the false gods worshiped in the great civilizations of the Fertile Crescent. Thus there is probably a subtle connection between the reference to the redemption of Abraham (from idolatrous Ur and Haran) and the assertion that when scattered Israel will be brought back from the pagan lands of their dispersion they will keep God's name holy. The emphasis on his holiness is very strong. It is as if this is their God's final vindication of his great name at the climax of their history. It is awe inspired by wondering gratitude that will bring about this profound sense of "the godhood of God." It is this deep awareness of God's goodness to them as a nation that will produce a penitent and receptive spirit in those formerly wayward and complaining. God's own light will have dispersed the spiritual darkness the prophet was so conscious of in the people he ministered to, as vv.9–16 reveal (cf. 6:9–10).

Notes

1 אֲרִיאֵל (*ʾarîʾēl*) has been variously understood. Young (*Book of Isaiah*, in loc.) presents the main options in a useful note. Those who reject the meaning given in the comment above, which follows the Targum, usually take it to mean "lion of God," suggestive perhaps of the strength and majesty of this royal city. This would make good sense; and its claims could be strengthened by the reference to David, who made it royal for Israel. On the other hand, the mention of the feasts would tend to support the interpretation given above, as does a reference to "the altar hearth of David" in the Moabite Stone (line 12) and the use of the term in this sense in Ezek 43:15–16. The suggestion of O. Procksch (*Jesaja I* [Leipzig: A. Deichertsche Verlagsbuchhandlung, 1930], in loc.) that Jerusalem, like Mycene, had a lion gate is conjectural and unnecessary.

4 O. Kaiser has a helpful note here (in loc.): "In v.4 he juxtaposes two different conceptions, the first that of a person who has fallen to the ground and begs his conqueror for mercy, and the second that of a dead person who speaks out of the earth like a ghost with a voice reduced to a whisper. This makes clear that the enemy attack which God himself has brought about will bring Jerusalem into the utmost distress and that, rescued [*sic*] to humility (cf. 2:9; 5:15; 20:33) the city will beg its God for deliverance."

5 The MT has זָרָיִךְ (*zārāyik*, "aliens"), but the LXX and the Targum assume זֵדָיִךְ (*zēdāyik*, "enemies"), which is read by 1QIsa; and this is probably correct.

The comment above assumes that the reference to the enemies being like fine dust or blown chaff is descriptive of their judgment. Some commentators however think the similes relate rather to the vast numbers of the foes, just as in God's promises about the growth of Israel it is often likened to the sand on the seashore. If this is so—and it is not impossible—v.5 should be taken with vv.1–4 rather than vv.6–8.

10 The words "the prophets" and "the seers" are in apposition to the phrases they follow. They need not be omitted as glosses, as suggested by Clements et al. Isaiah 28:7 shows their appropriateness.

16 The NIV follows 1QIsa in reading חֹמֶר (*ḥēmer*, "the pot"; lit., "clay") instead of אָמַר (*ʾāmar*, "should say"), which looks like a scribal error in the MT as the same verb occurs earlier in the verse.

17 The reference to Lebanon here may not be to its trees but to the vast areas of mountain slope—impossible to cultivate—that it possessed. See the comment above.

3. Woe to the Rebellious Children

30:1–33

> 1"Woe to the obstinate children,"
>   declares the LORD,
> "to those who carry out plans that are not mine,
>   forming an alliance, but not by my Spirit,
>   heaping sin upon sin;

²who go down to Egypt
   without consulting me;
who look for help to Pharaoh's protection,
   to Egypt's shade for refuge.
³But Pharaoh's protection will be to your shame,
   Egypt's shade will bring you disgrace.
⁴Though they have officials in Zoan,
   and their envoys have arrived in Hanes,
⁵everyone will be put to shame
   because of a people useless to them,
who bring neither help nor advantage,
   but only shame and disgrace."

⁶An oracle concerning the animals of the Negev:

Through a land of hardship and distress,
   of lions and lionesses,
   of adders and darting snakes,
the envoys carry their riches on donkeys' backs,
   their treasures on the humps of camels,
to that unprofitable nation,
⁷ to Egypt, whose help is utterly useless.
Therefore I call her
   Rahab the Do-Nothing.

⁸Go now, write it on a tablet for them,
   inscribe it on a scroll,
that for the days to come
   it may be an everlasting witness.
⁹These are rebellious people, deceitful children,
   children unwilling to listen to the Lord's instruction.
¹⁰They say to the seers,
   "See no more visions!"
and to the prophets,
   "Give us no more visions of what is right!
Tell us pleasant things,
   prophesy illusions.
¹¹Leave this way,
   get off this path,
and stop confronting us
   with the Holy One of Israel!"

¹²Therefore, this is what the Holy One of Israel says:

"Because you have rejected this message,
   relied on oppression
   and depended on deceit,
¹³this sin will become for you
   like a high wall, cracked and bulging,
   that collapses suddenly, in an instant.
¹⁴It will break in pieces like pottery,
   shattered so mercilessly
that among its pieces not a fragment will be found
   for taking coals from a hearth
   or scooping water out of a cistern."

¹⁵This is what the Sovereign Lord, the Holy One of Israel, says:

"In repentance and rest is your salvation,
   in quietness and trust is your strength,
   but you would have none of it.

¹⁶You said, 'No, we will flee on horses.'
  Therefore you will flee!
You said, 'We will ride off on swift horses.'
  Therefore your pursuers will be swift!
¹⁷A thousand will flee
  at the threat of one;
at the threat of five
  you will all flee away,
till you are left
  like a flagstaff on a mountaintop,
  like a banner on a hill."

¹⁸Yet the LORD longs to be gracious to you;
  he rises to show you compassion.
For the LORD is a God of justice.
  Blessed are all who wait for him!

¹⁹O people of Zion, who live in Jerusalem, you will weep no more. How gracious he will be when you cry for help! As soon as he hears, he will answer you. ²⁰Although the Lord gives you the bread of adversity and the water of affliction, your teachers will be hidden no more; with your own eyes you will see them. ²¹Whether you turn to the right or to the left, your ears will hear a voice behind you, saying, "This is the way; walk in it." ²²Then you will defile your idols overlaid with silver and your images covered with gold; you will throw them away like a menstrual cloth and say to them, "Away with you!"

²³He will also send you rain for the seed you sow in the ground, and the food that comes from the land will be rich and plentiful. In that day your cattle will graze in broad meadows. ²⁴The oxen and donkeys that work the soil will eat fodder and mash, spread out with fork and shovel. ²⁵In the day of great slaughter, when the towers fall, streams of water will flow on every high mountain and every lofty hill. ²⁶The moon will shine like the sun, and the sunlight will be seven times brighter, like the light of seven full days, when the LORD binds up the bruises of his people and heals the wounds he inflicted.

²⁷See, the Name of the LORD comes from afar,
  with burning anger and dense clouds of smoke;
his lips are full of wrath,
  and his tongue is a consuming fire.
²⁸His breath is like a rushing torrent,
  rising up to the neck.
He shakes the nations in the sieve of destruction;
  he places in the jaws of the peoples
  a bit that leads them astray.
²⁹And you will sing
  as on the night you celebrate a holy festival;
your hearts will rejoice
  as when people go up with flutes
to the mountain of the LORD,
  to the Rock of Israel.
³⁰The LORD will cause men to hear his majestic voice
  and will make them see his arm coming down
with raging anger and consuming fire,
  with cloudburst, thunderstorm and hail.
³¹The voice of the LORD will shatter Assyria;
  with his scepter he will strike them down.
³²Every stroke the LORD lays on them
  with his punishing rod
will be to the music of tambourines and harps,
  as he fights them in battle with the blows of his arm.

> [33]Topheth has long been prepared;
>   it has been made ready for the king.
> Its fire pit has been made deep and wide,
>   with an abundance of fire and wood;
> the breath of the Lord,
>   like a stream of burning sulfur,
>   sets it ablaze.

This chapter, like the two that precede it, commences with the word *hôy* ("woe") and, also like them, contains promises as well as threats. The people of Jerusalem will have judgments to face, but these will not annul the ultimate purpose of their God to bless them with his salvation.

1 The occasion is still the proposal to enter into alliance with Egypt as a defense against Assyria, whose dark shadow looms menacingly on the eastern horizon. Several commentators have noticed the double entendre in v. 1, though the NIV translation "obstinate" instead of "rebellious" tends to obscure this. The rebellion against Assyria was at the same time a revolt against God. The verb *sārar* is often used of a rebellious son (cf. Deut 21:18, 20; Ps 78:8; Jer 5:23); and the full phrase "rebellious children" reminds us of Isaiah 1:2, though the verb is different there. The Christian reader, noting the parallelism in v. 1, may view its phrasing as establishing that Isaiah had a Trinitarian theology, or, at least, that to him God and his Spirit were one. It is doubtful, however, whether so much an be built on it; for the Spirit may be looked on here simply as the agent of God's will, revealing his purpose to the people through the prophet for their obedience.

The accumulation of sin by the people is probably an allusion to the alliance with Assyria in the days of Ahaz, a device to secure aid against Israel and Syria. This, of course, forms the background to the oracles in chapters 7–9. The political alignment was now different but expressed the same sin—refusal to trust in the Lord and him alone.

2–5 The redemption of Abraham has been mentioned in 29:22. There was a time when he went down through the Negev (cf. v.6) to Egypt without consulting God (Gen 12). Abraham too might have pleaded an adequate reason, for there was famine in the land; but his action had shameful consequences, for both himself and his wife. It is possible too that the reference to a descent to Egypt in both passages may have disapproving as well as topographical significance. The Ethiopian rulers of Egypt had sent ambassadors to her either in 712 or 705 B.C. (see introduction to ch. 18). Here the ambassage moved in the opposite direction, perhaps during the period of Hezekiah's revolt against Sennacherib in the years 703–701 B.C. (see the Introduction, p. 6). The two important towns mentioned (vv.3–4) were both in lower Egypt, though Hanes, in the region of modern Fayyum, was a good deal farther south than Zoan (see comment at 19:11).

The stress of Isaiah on "shame and disgrace" (v.5) is so strong that it may well have some special significance. Perhaps Egypt's failure to send adequate assistance to Judah brought about the fall in disgrace of one of Hezekiah's leading advisers.

6–7 These two verses show us Isaiah's imaginative power. It is characteristic of him not only to visualize Hezekiah's emissaries arriving at Egypt's court but to picture

194

the terrain they had to pass through and the very animals of both the environment and the Judean caravans (v.6). At the end of the journey, too, was an "animal"—Rahab (v.7), the Egyptian dragon. The Negev, to the south of Judah, was inhospitable to travelers; and this may have been the very reason the messengers went this way, avoiding the more public route across the southern Mediterranean Sea. Lionesses and lions occur in reverse order in the Hebrew, perhaps bearing testimony to the well-known fact that—in the case of this animal—"the female of the species is more deadly than the male." The very large number of words for lion in the Semitic group of languages gives some impression of the wildness and danger of much of the Near East in biblical times. The NIV's "darting snakes" renders the same Hebrew word as "darting, venomous serpent" in 14:29. It hardly seems necessary to regard this as a fabulous monster rather than an actual reptile, as many commentators do. If the Negev was tangible, presumably its creatures were too, though granted the stress could be on the danger envisaged and feared by the travelers.

The journey is not only dangerous but costly, for it is expedient to carry a substantial bribe to this powerful potential ally. But was Egypt really all that powerful? Its reputation—no doubt influenced somewhat by the tyrannous exercise of its authority over Israel in the days before the Exodus—was undoubtedly great; and the advent of a new and vigorous regime may well have enhanced it, but Hezekiah was in for a shock. Great powers on the international scene have chosen fearsome animal symbols for themselves, like the lion, the eagle—both single-and double-headed—and the bear. Egypt's designation was not self-chosen. It was identified by others with the mythological Rahab (see ZPEB, 5:27, and comment at 27:1). The NIV's "Rahab the Do-Nothing" (v.7) may owe something to Moffat's striking but somewhat free "Dragon Do-Nothing." There may be an ironic suggestion here that the Judean messengers to Egypt were in more danger from the beasts of the desert than Assyria would be from that notorious supermonster, Egypt! If Assyria was to be shattered, it would be done, as we learn in v.31, by God, not Egypt.

8–11 Prophecy takes two forms, spoken and written. In spoken prophecy only the immediate audience benefits. Written prophecy may reach many more, and not in one generation only. The command to write (v.8) has brought untold blessing and challenge to countless numbers. It may just be the ironic name for Egypt (v.7) that Isaiah is to write, as he wrote the symbolic name of his son on a tablet once before (cf. 8:1). On the other hand, the whole oracle could be in view. The purpose is to secure an objective and visible witness to God's solemn warning. Perhaps the prophet dated it in some way, though the text makes no reference to this. The words "for them" are significant, and vv.9–11 expound the necessity for this written warning.

The prophet repeated his accusation that the people were rebellious children (v.9; cf. v.1 and 1:2). Their words (v.10) to the true prophets of God, like Isaiah himself, were similar in intent to the advice the ungodly priest Amaziah gave Amos: "Get out, you seer! Go back to the land of Judah. Earn your bread there and do your prophesying there. Don't prophesy anymore at Bethel" (Amos 7:12–13). An apostate priesthood and a rebellious people rejected the warnings that came through the true prophet of God. Amaziah would have been quite content had Amos continued to preach the authentic word of God, so long as this was done somewhere else. Isaiah's listeners would listen to him, but only if the content of his message was trimmed to their own desires. But the preacher was to bring a message to his listeners, not to find it among them. The words "way" and "path" (v.11; cf. 26:7–8), with their moral overtones (cf. Ps 1), may be a sarcastic echoing of Isaiah's own message to them, so indicating that prophetic morality was unacceptable to such hearers.

The people's closing command to Isaiah is very striking. His distinctive title for God was "the Holy One of Israel" (see Introduction, p. 12). This title—implying as it did the great demands that relationship to such a God entailed (cf. Amos 3:2)— filled their hearts with loathing. Their ears could no longer tolerate its sound.

12–14 Isaiah's use of the title "Holy One of Israel" here (v.12) is particularly significant. The people had resisted his use of it, but he was not their servant but the Lord's. Nothing would be trimmed to suit their taste. As Young (*Book of Isaiah*, in loc.) says, "The One whom the nation would cause to cease is the One who will cause the nation to cease. He speaks, and his words are an announcement of destruction to come. Yet he gives a reason why this is so, and that reason is found in the people's despising the word that Isaiah had spoken." Our reaction to God's word does not affect that word one whit.

In the context the people's reliance on oppression and deceit is probably to be seen as a reference to Egypt. For Israel Egypt was the oppressor *par eminence*, and at this time her promises of aid were worthless and so must be considered deceitful.

Sin contains the seeds of its own punishment, and Judah's trust in a foreign power rather than in God would bring about her downfall. We have previously commented on Isaiah's gift of illustration and have noted that he sometimes gave a simile or metaphor that was itself followed by a further picture that illustrated the illustration (e.g., 28:4). A small fault may spread, like leaven, and the onlooker may become so accustomed to the bulging wall that he does not detect the worsening of the problem till the collapse comes, and it is too late (v.13). Spiritual and moral deterioration are often like this.

The prophet had to convey not only the suddenness of the judgment but also its completeness. He did this by likening the destruction of the wall to the breaking of an article of pottery (v.14), the disintegration is so complete that nothing of value— even for the most elementary and humble of uses—is found to remain. O. Kaiser (in loc.) helps us make the cultural transference when he says, "In a period when there were no matches or lighters, people would rake through the ashes to find a glowing ember in order to light a new fire, and . . . in a country which was short of water they would be glad to make use of puddles." This prophecy was not, of course, fulfilled in 701 but rather in 586, when Nebuchadnezzar took Jerusalem, and perhaps even more in the destruction of Jerusalem in A.D. 70 (cf. the words of Christ in Mark 13:2).

15–18 Isaiah not only used titles for God, he combined them, and often with striking effect (see comment at 1:24). "The Sovereign LORD" (v.15) translates Adonai followed by Yahweh, thus combining his sovereign authority with his redemptive name. Sovereignty and holiness find expression in vv.16–17 while redeeming grace, joined to these qualities, is seen in vv.15 and 18. The word of God cuts right across ordinary human thinking, for his thoughts are higher than those of men (55:8–9). Those who have learned from God will turn to him in repentant faith, but continued rebellion against him produces panic when the foe appears in all his might. "Repentance" here is literally "returning," and this probably has the same double entendre noted in v.1. In the context of the contemporary political situation, to turn away from trust in Egypt and to return to the Lord were two sides of the same fact. Again the Shear-Jashub theme sounded (cf. comment at 7:3). The Hebrew word translated "your salvation" is emphatic.

Verse 16 has been differently understood. Some—taking the verb *nûs* (twice translated "flee" here) to mean "to make haste"—assume that the prophet overheard the people's boast that they would speed away to the attack on Assyria, using horses obtained from the Egyptians. This is possible; but the verb's normal meaning makes good sense if they are fleeing for Egyptian help, which the prophet characterized as a flight to disaster (v.17). (See Isaiah 8:1–4, where the meaning of Isaiah's son's name conveys the same thought but in somewhat different circumstances.)

The language of v.17a strikes an ominous note. God had promised overwhelming victory to his people if they obeyed him but overwhelming defeat if they were rebellious (Lev 26:7–8; Deut 32:30). The language this threat was couched in is used here. The lonely hill signal—which had served in a promise of God to suggest a fresh rallying of the scattered nation (11:10, 12)—here stands for shattering defeat. The whole army has gone into battle and met its death; the flag-bearer, kept back at the hilltop base in case he was needed for rallying purposes, discovers that he alone is left and so is without function.

The threatening tone of vv.16–17 gives place to an assurance that God is ready and willing to show mercy to his foolish and obstinate people. Verse 18 is easier to understand if we follow the more literal rendering of the RSV: "Therefore the LORD waits to be gracious to you; therefore he exalts himself to show mercy to you. For the LORD is a God of justice; blessed are all those who wait for him." It is precisely because God's justice must be expressed—and therefore punishment must fall on this rebellious people—that the manifestation of his mercy is delayed. As so often in the prophets, God's judgment falls first of all; but a remnant preserved through the judgment experiences the blessings of his grace and the fulfillment of his positive purpose for them. Those who wait for him will be identical with this remnant. The Babylonian exile and the return from it are chiefly in view here.

19–26 The poetic statement of divine grace in v.18 is amplified by the following section in elevated prose. Here (v.19) the God of Israel speaks to his people as if addressing the heart of one person, for singular rather than plural forms are used most of the time. There is a solidarity between the people of Jerusalem that allows that city to be viewed as a single entity, a kind of corporate person, whom God addresses in grace. Here is the marvel of God's immediate response to the penitent's cry. The emphasis on his graciousness conveyed by the Hebrew is well expressed by the NIV's "How gracious . . . !" They were so dull of hearing when he spoke to them (28:7–10; 29:9–10; 30:8–10), but at their cry he comes immediately to meet them in their need. He still hears the cry of repentance today.

Some (e.g., O. Kaiser) take "the bread of adversity and the water of affliction" (v.20) figuratively, after the pattern of Amos 8:11–12, where "famine" is applied to a dearth of the prophetic word. Others (e.g., Young) relate this expression to the food eaten by prisoners of war (cf. 1 Kings 22:27). Either would be appropriate; for the expression probably relates to the Exile, beyond which God would exhibit his grace to them.

The people's penitence would be accompanied by a new responsiveness to his word through the prophetic teachers whose task it was to bring it to them. Rejection of God's word always brings hardness of heart, so that the word cannot be heard as before (cf. 8:16; 29:9–12). There is probably an intentional contrast between v.21 and vv.10–11. The word of God possesses ethical content, keeping God's people to the right path. It also possesses religious content, for their response to it will lead them to purge their land of idolatry. The reference to the silver or golden covering of the wooden idols (v.22) may suggest that the people have come to see that a precious exterior masks a plain interior. The idols, so splendid in appearance, were really worthless at anything but a superficial level. The illustration stresses the repugnance with which they will now be viewed. Worship has given place to its antithesis.

Like so many of his compatriots, Isaiah had a deep attachment to the soil of his own land (v.23). This had its basis, not simply in the natural affection of the patriot for his native land, but in a theology of the land; for it was God's land, given by him to his people and from which he threatened to remove them as a consequence of their persistent sin. The Book of Deuteronomy has this as a major theme (e.g., Deut 1:8, 21–25, 34–40; 3:25–29; 6:10–11; 11:8–17; 28:62–68). The prophet often saw God's blessing therefore in terms of good agricultural weather, increased fruitfulness, and fat cattle (cf. 4:2; 35:1–2 et al.) In the day of God's blessing on the land, even the working animals will live well above subsistence level (v.24).

The reference to the day of great slaughter and the fall of towers (v.25) seems very strange in this context, but perhaps in much the same way that warnings of judgment occur in the midst of the descriptions of ultimate divine blessing (Rev 21–22). The Bible is a realistic book and shows that God's future plan includes judgment for the rebel as well as blessing for the penitent. Young (*Book of Isaiah*, note in loc.) says, "If the reference is to defeat of the Assyrians (Drechsler, etc.) it would point forward to vv.27ff. If it is to the downfall of the Judahites (Delitzsch, etc.) it looks back to vv.16ff and 29:20ff." The former seems the more likely. The choice of the word "tower" is doubly appropriate, for it has military connotations but also suggests haughty pride (cf. 2:15).

In keeping with the general context, the prophet declared that there will be abundant supplies of water from the mountains (v.25). Are the mountains therefore the source of this water or do they themselves benefit from it? The modern town-dweller views hill country quite differently from the country farmer. The one sees its beauty, the other its agricultural barrenness. The language used here suggests that the mountains themselves will enjoy the refreshing waters with all their potential for fruitfulness.

This picture of nature, released fro its present limiting conditions, is taken further still in v. 26. It is difficult to avoid the conclusion that the prophecy has passed beyond anything as yet fulfilled and has located itself in God's eschatological purposes. Both the moon and the sun will be much brighter than at present. The number "seven" is not chosen arbitrarily, for the creation of sun and moon in Genesis 1 occurs in the context of a six-day creation, with divine rest on the seventh. It is as if the fullness of the divine creative energies are channeled to secure the greater radiance of the sun. The people had known severe chastisement from God through the Assyrians (cf. 1:5–9). Now his powers will secure healing where once he had smitten them in wrath (cf. also 40:2).

27–33 During the intertestamental period, Judaism—both in Palestine and in Alexandria—became somewhat embarrassed by the OT anthropomorphisms, as if they presented a picture of God as too much like that humanity he had created. There is no such embarrassment in the work of this prophet. In actual fact, the vivid anthropomorphisms of Isaiah 40 contribute immensely to the impression that that chapter gives us of a living God acting in a very concrete situation on behalf of his people. Here too this kind of language, with its strong visual appeal, is used to describe God, but here not so much as the Redeemer of his people as the Judge of his enemies. The condemned foe is identified in v.31 as Assyria.

The name of the Lord is, of course, a revelation of himself (Exod 3:13–15; 6:2–3). When his name is said to come from afar in judgment, the prophet may be alluding to Mount Sinai, where, in circumstances of awesome splendor (Exod 19), God showed himself in all his holiness to his people.

Verses 27–28 employ four illustrations of the wrath of God. Fire, with all its power to terrify and to destroy, dominates v.27 (cf. 33:14). Hebrews 12:29 makes it clear that, under the new covenant, this quality in God is still experienced by men and should lead them to worship with reverential awe. Fire is replaced by water (v.28). In 8:7–8 the prophet pictured the waters of the great Euphrates overflowing and reaching even to the neck of Judah. In this way God had used Assyria to chastise his people. Now he would himself chastise Assyria, and he uses the same image to state this. The sieve of judgment reveals the spiritual inadequacy of the unrighteous, much as the wind of the threshing floor similarly distinguishes between the light and the heavy (29:5). The figure of the horse with a bit suggests that God will take the arrogant sinner down the road that leads to his destruction.

Verse 29 may appear callous and harsh, but it is important to remember that God's judgments are often his means of salvation. Because Assyria was to be judged, Judah would enjoy God's deliverance. Young (*Book of Isaiah*, in loc.) points out that the great festival in which there was a celebration night was the Passover (Exod 12:42). If there is an intended allusion to this here, the prophet may have expected his hearers to draw the parallel between these two acts of salvation. Certainly it is a pilgrim feast he has in mind. For "the Rock of Israel," see the comment at 26:4.

At certain times the heavens are loud with noise and are the source of God's many demonstrations of his power in nature. Psalm 29 speaks of the voice of the Lord in language strongly reminiscent of a thunderstorm. That kind of language occurs here too. In a thunderstorm there is much to be heard and seen. All this is of course figurative and vigorously presents the judgment of God. The consuming fire links v.30 with v.27. Amid all the noise of the storm, the Lord's arm strikes with many a forceful blow at his adversaries. Judah had been smitten through Assyria (1:3–9; cf. v.26 above), but now the God who had used Assyria would punish her (v.31; cf. 10:5–19).

Verse 32 has been found objectionable by some commentators; but it should be realized that this passage is not unique in Scripture, as a study of Revelation 18–19 will clearly reveal. The truth is that God's people are here portrayed rejoicing at his judgment on sin because they must take his point of view on everything, and because this judgment is at the same time their salvation.

Some places have become symbols of spiritual realities. Zion-Jerusalem is the people of God, Babylon the world in arrogant opposition to God, and Ge-Hinnom (Gehenna) and Tophet God's judgment on sin. Tophet was in the Valley of Hinnom, to the south of Jerusalem (Jer 7:31–32); and there apostate Jews offered their children by fire to the pagan deity, Moloch. Perhaps the prophet is saying here that the king of Assyria himself must pay it. He had dedicated himself to paganism, and now he would suffer for this in terrible judgment from God.

Notes

1 לִנְסֹךְ מַסֵּכָה (linsōk massēkāh, "forming an alliance") is literally "pouring out a drink offering," taken by many—but without clear evidence—to refer to a ritual associated with a covenant. Nevertheless the parallelism and the context together seem to point in the direction of some such explanation.

2 For לָעוֹז (lāʿôz), from עָזַז (ʿāzaz, "to be strong"), we should probably read with the LXX, by repointing, lāʿûz ("take refuge"), represented by the NIV's "look for help."

5 The NIV et al. follow the Qere, הֹבִישׁ (hōbîš, "be put to shame"), instead of the Kethiv, הִבְאִישׁ (hibʾîš, "stink"). The LXX omits this completely.

9 Jensen (pp. 112–20) helpfully explores the background and implications of the phrase יְהֹוָה תּוֹרַת (tôrat YHWH, "the LORD's instruction").

19 The MT of this verse opens: "for a people in Zion shall dwell in Jerusalem." The LXX, Syriac, and Vulgate all presuppose some variation from this. The NIV, with most modern EV, repoints יֵשֵׁב (yēšēb) as yōšēb and translates, "O people of Zion, who live in Jerusalem." This may well be correct, as it makes better sense and does not alter the consonantal text.

20 מוֹרֶיךָ (môreykā, "teachers") is a participle with a pronominal suffix and could be plural, or else singular, as in the RSV's "Teacher." The matter is of comparatively little moment, because in any case the Lord teaches his people through the prophets, who would be designated by the plural.

28 The words translated "rising up to the neck" include the verb יֶחֱעֶה (yeḥeʿeh, basically "to halve"), and all the versions found them difficult. For a conspectus of translations, see (Isaiah XXVIII–XXXII, in loc.).

נָפַת (nāpat) is a hapax legomenon, apparently meaning "sieve."

4. Woe to Those Who Seek Help From Egypt

31:1–9

¹Woe to those who go down to Egypt for help,
  who rely on horses,
who trust in the multitude of their chariots
  and in the great strength of their horsemen,
but do not look to the Holy One of Israel,
  or seek help from the LORD.
²Yet he too is wise and can bring disaster;
  he does not take back his words.
He will rise up against the house of the wicked,
  against those who help evildoers.
³But the Egyptians are men and not God;
  their horses are flesh and not spirit.
When the LORD stretches out his hand,
  he who helps will stumble,
  he who is helped will fall;
  both will perish together.

⁴This is what the LORD says to me:

"As a lion growls,
  a great lion over his prey—

200

and though a whole band of shepherds
    is called together against him,
he is not frightened by their shouts
    or disturbed by their clamor—
so the LORD Almighty will come down
    to do battle on Mount Zion and on its heights.
5Like birds hovering overhead,
    the LORD Almighty will shield Jerusalem;
he will shield it and deliver it,
    he will 'pass over' it and will rescue it."

6Return to him you have so greatly revolted against, O Israelites. 7For in that day every one of you will reject the idols of silver and gold your sinful hands have made.

8"Assyria will fall by a sword that is not of man;
    a sword, not of mortals, will devour them.
They will flee before the sword
    and their young men will be put to forced labor.
9Their stronghold will fall because of terror;
    at sight of the battle standard their commanders
      will panic,"
declares the LORD,
    whose fire is in Zion,
    whose furnace is in Jerusalem.

Like the previous three chapters, this one commences with *hôy* ("woe") but is not entirely threatening in nature, for there are also divine promises.

1–3 Hezekiah had repeated the sin of Ahaz in seeking an alliance with an alien power instead of encouraging his people to put their trust in the Lord. (See the comments at chs. 7–8 and the Introduction, p. 6.) In so doing he showed he had failed to learn from history—for Egypt had proved anything but an ally to Israel in the past—from Scripture—for the attempt to secure horses for cavalry units was against the divine constitution for the king (Deut 17:14–20)—or even from the experience of his father, Ahaz—which could have provided him with a salutary warning.

See the comments at 30:2 for the possible implications of the phrase "go down to Egypt." The Hebrew verb *'āzar* ("to help") occurs four times in these verses, though it should be noted that the concluding line of v.1 translates a different verb (*dāraš*, "to seek, desire") as "seek help." The decision to call for help from a particular source is in fact a value judgment, particularly when there are a number of options open. Judah was showing that—in terms of its protection—it set greater value on Egypt, which the prophet had contemptuously described as "Rahab the Do-Nothing" (30:7), than on the living God. It was not reliance in the power of numbers that had won the great victory over Midian in the days of Joshua, the event Isaiah loved to recall as a paradigm of triumph through reliance on the Lord (see comments at 9:3–5 and 10:24–27).

The statement "yet he too is wise" (v.2) is pregnant with sarcasm. False political wisdom ruled in the courts of Judah. The so-called wise men had themselves used sarcasm when speaking about the Lord's wisdom (5:19; 29:15). The prophet's conviction that divine wisdom would prove all vaunted human sagacity to be wrong was as strong as the apostle Paul's conviction that God's wisdom judged all that passed for wisdom among men (1 Cor 1:18–3:23) (see Whedbee, esp. ch. 4).

"Disaster" (v.2) is literally "evil" (rā') and is, of course, a reference to war (cf. Amos 3:6). This is made the more terrifying by the assertion that God does not retract such threats of judgment. Numbers 23:19 presents the same truth but in terms of blessing rather than of judgment. The poetic parallelism of v.2b is not identical; for the "house of the wicked" (cf. 1:4) is Judah, and "those who help evildoers" are the Egyptians they had appealed to for military assistance.

Comparisons are particularly odious when made between things or people differing in quality. The greatest qualitative distinction exists between the all-sovereign Creator and the universe he originated and rules (v.3). To us "flesh" seems so substantial, because visible and tangible, while "spirit" may seem ethereal. This is partly due to the wide range of connotations that exist for the English word "spirit." Nothing could be further from biblical thinking, as a glance at passages like Zechariah 4:6 and John 3:5–8 will disclose. The invisible source of supernatural, almighty power in God is in an altogether superior class from the apparently strong but actually, in comparative terms, almost infinitely weak men and horses.

The words "when the LORD stretches out his hand" (v.3) are ominous in reference to Egypt; for they have overtones of the Exodus, when all the power of that land was overcome by the Lord (Deut 4:34; 7:19). It is worth remembering too that Egypt at that time was a much more significant world power than in Isaiah's time. Putting Isaiah's thought in v.3b into a figure, the unequal yoke Judah was seeking with Egypt would mean that the fall of the one would bring disaster to the other also.

4–5 The interpretation of v.4 has been much disputed. Everything turns on the identification of the lion. Mauchline (in loc.), giving one of the two main interpretations, says, "The lion represents the Assyrians who have devastated Judah and are ready to devour Jerusalem; the shepherds are the Egyptians who have come to aid Judah and have succeeded only in making an ineffectual noise which has not deterred or troubled the Assyrians."

O. Kaiser (in loc.) well expresses the alternative understanding of this verse:

> The lion will not allow anyone to steal from him what belongs to him. This behavior is compared to Yahweh's descent from heaven to fight upon the hill of Zion (cf. 10:32); thus what Yahweh does and the behavior of the lion correspond. In other words, Yahweh does not allow anyone to steal from him what belongs to him. Jerusalem belongs to him because he has chosen it (cf. Ps. 132:13f.) and therefore he will not allow it to fall into the hands of the attackers, whom we at once recognize as "Assyria."

Amos, whose influence can be seen in Isaiah (see Introduction, p. 13), uses the lion figure of both God (Amos 3:8) and Assyria, the punitive agent of God (Amos 3:12). The way the sentence is structured in the NIV (its protasis-apodosis pattern) assumes that the figure is intended to be understood in terms of God. This in fact reads the Hebrew most naturally. No figure can be pressed to its ultimate limit, and the apparent identification of Jerusalem as the "prey" of the Lord that he protects need imply nothing as to his ultimate intention for it; for it is his protecting activity that is the point to be illustrated.

Verse 5 changes the figure but not the message, though it clarifies the benign intent of God's activity in relation to the capital city of his people. Egypt could give no guarantee of Jerusalem's protection from the Assyrians, but God would make Jerusalem his special care. Young (*Book of Isaiah*, in loc.) says, "These two comparisons complement one another. First, God is compared with a strong lion, bold, unafraid, powerful; then with tender and loving birds which protect their nest. But can tender birds protect their nest? To support the latter comparison we have the first. He who protects is He who is strong as a lion to accomplish His purposes."

In the closing line of v.5 we are reminded of the Exodus allusion in v.3—and also perhaps of the awesome vision in 4:5. The God of the Exodus would protect his people in Jerusalem as he protected them in the wilderness by the pillar of cloud and fire (4:5) and in Egypt itself at the Passover. The NIV uses single quotation marks to suggest this allusion. In fact, the term used is usually applied to the Passover (Exod 12:13, 23, 27; Num 9:4; Josh 5:11; 2 Chron 30:18). Facing Sennacherib and his great hosts, the people of Jerusalem were just as safe as their forebears had been in Egypt on the night of the Passover; for the God who was planning great slaughter of her enemies would once again protect her.

6–7 As a study of chapters 36–37 reveals, the Lord's deliverance of Jerusalem from Sennacherib was a singular demonstration of his reality and power, setting him apart from other deities. The gods of many nations had failed to protect their devotees from the Assyrians, but now the true God showed he was supreme even over the mighty gods of Assyria itself. There had been idolatry among the people of Judah (v.7; cf. 2:8, 20). Isaiah called his people to repentance (v.6) in anticipation of that day when, because of God's singular act of deliverance, the worthlessness of the idols would be recognized. Clearly idolatry was the deep revolt the prophet called them to return from, though of course it had many another manifestation; for ungodliness leads to wickedness (Rom 1:18).

8–9 Isaiah's illustrative gift was very considerable, and he shows a concern here that an analogy should not be taken literally by his hearers. "A sword for the LORD and for Gideon" (Judg 7:20) was not a literal sword at all, and the Lord secured a great victory over Assyria by nonmilitary means, as we see in 37:36–37. The second half of v.8 seems to look beyond this to the ultimate destruction of Assyria by its foes.

"Their stronghold" (v.9) is, literally, "their rock," and the prophet seems to have in view the rocky site of an Assyrian fortress. The picture conveyed is that of a fortress city, perhaps one of the cities in Assyria's heartland, approached by its enemies with their battle standards clearly visible. The sight was so unfamiliar to those who were used to constant victory for their armies that the task of the enemy would be made easy by their demoralization. The description of God, however, takes us back swiftly to Jerusalem, for whose sake Assyria was being judged, and whose temple and its ever-burning altar fire symbolized the presence of God with it.

5. God's Kingdom and the Triumph of Righteousness

32:1–20

¹See, a king will reign in righteousness
and rulers will rule with justice.
²Each man will be like a shelter from the wind
and a refuge from the storm,

like streams of water in the desert
  and the shadow of a great rock in a thirsty land.

3Then the eyes of those who see will no longer be closed,
  and the ears of those who hear will listen.
4The mind of the rash will know and understand,
  and the stammering tongue will be fluent and clear.
5No longer will the fool be called noble
  nor the scoundrel be highly respected.
6For the fool speaks folly,
  his mind is busy with evil:
He practices ungodliness
  and spreads error concerning the LORD;
the hungry he leaves empty
  and from the thirsty he withholds water.
7The scoundrel's methods are wicked,
  he makes up evil schemes
to destroy the poor with lies,
  even when the plea of the needy is just.
8But the noble man makes noble plans,
  and by noble deeds he stands.
9You women who are so complacent,
  rise up and listen to me;
you daughters who feel secure,
  hear what I have to say!
10In little more than a year
  you who feel secure will tremble;
the grape harvest will fail,
  and the harvest of fruit will not come.
11Tremble, you complacent women;
  shudder, you daughters who feel secure!
Strip off your clothes,
  put sackcloth around your waists.
12Beat your breasts for the pleasant fields,
  for the fruitful vines
13and for the land of my people,
  a land overgrown with thorns and briers—
yes, mourn for all houses of merriment
  and for this city of revelry.
14The fortress will be abandoned,
  the noisy city deserted;
citadel and watchtower will become a wasteland forever,
  the delight of donkeys, a pasture for flocks,
15till the spirit is poured upon us from on high,
  and the desert becomes a fertile field,
  and the fertile field seems like a forest.
16Justice will dwell in the desert
  and righteousness live in the fertile field.
17The fruit of righteousness will be peace;
  the effect of righteousness will be quietness
    and confidence forever.
18My people will live in peaceful dwelling places,
  in secure homes,
  in undisturbed places of rest.
19Though hail flattens the forest
  and the city is leveled completely,
20how blessed you will be,
  sowing your seed by every stream,
  and letting your cattle and donkeys range free.

This oracle interrupts the sequence of "woe" oracles that began at 28:1, and which resumes and is concluded with the prophecy that commences in 33:1 (see the general introduction to chapters 28–33). Its purpose in this setting seems to be to encourage the reader to hope in God and the triumph of his kingdom purposes despite the fact that recent chapters have majored somewhat in the judgment of God on his people. Of course, the concluding verses of chapter 31 have prepared somewhat for this.

Many critics reject the Isaianic authorship of vv. 1–8, largely because they seem to owe so much to the wisdom tradition in Israel and so must be treated as nonprophetic and probably as late. Whedbee (p. 16) however asserts: "The recognition is growing that the relationship between wisdom and the prophets is much more complex than was formerly supposed. This is coupled with an increasing awareness that law, prophecy and wisdom are not self contained, isolated categories, but are inter-related in various ways in the history of Israelite society." He gives documentation (pp. 25–26) for those who wish to follow up this matter, though he himself tends to regard this passage as post-Isaianic, but without giving reasons. If, for the OT, David is the supreme psalmist—a fact much more widely recognized today than by nineteenth-century criticism—Solomon is the supreme wise man. If both the prophet and the wise man were under the inspiring influence of the same Spirit and served the same divine ends, it hardly seems necessary to separate their writings so rigidly. We have seen much evidence already of the influence of the wisdom tradition on Isaiah (see comments at 26:7–11).

1–2 Are these verses messianic or do they picture an ideal government in which the whole administrative system of the country is in the hands of righteous men? There is a sense in which the question itself makes a distinction without a difference. Psalm 1 may not be messianic in the strict sense, but it presents a picture of ideal righteousness that never found full expression till the coming of Jesus Christ. It is true that the only explicit reference to the king may be at the beginning of v.1 (but see comments at v.2), but the reader almost inevitably makes a link with the picture of the righteous messianic King given in chapter 11. The Book of Isaiah presents its messianic theme in such a way that there is developnent from one passage to the next, and this passage certainly figures as a development of chapter 11, the new emphasis being on the association of others with the king in his righteous reign (see Introduction, pp. 16–20).

At the opening of chapter 31, the prophet had criticized those at the court who looked to Egypt for help against the Assyrian menace. No doubt the king would have to bear a special responsibility, but clearly the prophet had others at the court in mind as well. Isaiah 1:21–23 gives a black picture of Jerusalem's rulers. The whole sinful scene of government will pass away, and its place will be taken by a righteous king supported by subordinates who share his concern for righteousness and justice. This association of others with a messianic figure is found also in Daniel 7:13–14, 18, and in many NT passages (e.g., Matt 19:28; 2 Tim 2:12; Rev 20:4. The general interpretation of these passages is discussed in the Introduction, pp. 14–16).

Does v.2 refer to the king or to the king and princes together? The NIV gives the impression that it is the latter, with its translation "each man will be. . . ." This is general enough to allow for either interpretation. The parallelism of v.1 suggests that emphasis is being put rather on good government than exclusively on the king himself, in contrast to chapter 11. It seems best then to treat v.2 as an expansion of v.1 as a whole and not simply of its first statement. Government, when it is righteous, affords protection from oppression. The various illustrations drawn from nature are all self-explanatory. In the Messiah's kingdom, both at the national and at the local level, righteousness will reign and fear of the oppressor will belong to the past.

3–7 Isaiah was warned at his call that he would see men shutting their eyes and ears to the truth he proclaimed (6:9–10). When the messianic kingdom comes, this spiritual insensitivity will be no more (v.3). Those who should have had minds made clear by the bright shining of divine truth in them had in fact been befuddled by drink (28:7–10) and had stammered out rash things instead of prophetic truth. This situation too is to be rectified (v.4). It is perhaps significant that the apostle Paul, in a passage where he quoted Isaiah 28:11, also says, "Unless you speak intelligible words with your tongue, how will anyone know what you are saying?" (1 Cor 14:9, 21).

If leaders are blind, their people often share this blindness. A nation gets the leaders it deserves (cf. 3:4–7). The moral sense had been so warped in Judah, as 5:20 shows, that there was failure to recognize the true nature of those who were in positions of leadership. This too would change in the Messiah's kingdom. In v.5 the prophet speaks of the fool and the scoundrel; in vv.6–7 he gives a description of each. In the OT folly often has overtones of godlessness (e.g., Ps 14), and so it has here. If the fear of the Lord is the beginning of wisdom (Ps 111:10; cf. Prov 1:7), then the godless man must be pursuing the wrong way.

Verse 6 presents an appalling picture of a man whose mind is controlled by evil, so that both his own life and his influence with others are evil. The messianic King demonstrates his godly righteousness by his concern for the poor and needy (11:4). The godless fool is utterly unconcerned for their most elementary needs (cf. 58:7).

The prophet next speaks of the scoundrel (v.7), who, if not really the same person, is an even worse character. He stoops to lies and deceit to deprive the poor man of his rights at law. In fact, he is the very man from whom the messianic King will protect the poor (11:4–5). Conduct reveals character (v.8); and this is true of both the noble man, whose day will come in the messianic kingdom, and the scoundrel, who will not enter that kingdom but will face God's judgment.

9–14 Once before, in chapter 3, Isaiah had moved from condemnation of Judah's leaders to strong criticism of the women (v.9). This suggests that certain aristocratic women were exercising an unhelpful influence over their husbands and so must share their judgment. Many an Ananias and Sapphira must face judgment together for complicity in the same sins. In our present passage the stress falls on complacency. This is probably to be explained in terms of the court's pro-Egyptian policy. The women too were relying on Egyptian help for the security of Jerusalem, and so of their homes.

The Book of Isaiah does contain some prophecies with timed fulfillments (e.g., 7:8, 16). This present prophecy was probably uttered a year or so prior to Sennacherib's invasion of Judah, which led to the situation depicted in chapter 1. There it is made clear that both the country and the cities experienced devastation. It is probably the effects of such an invasion that the prophet had in view here, rather than a simple harvest failure (v.10). In this case, its failure is due really to the inability of the people—because of conditions of enemy occupation—to gather the vintage and other ripe fruit. The women are called to mourning (vv. 11–12). It is not their husbands or sons who are dead but their land, but this in itself will produce some of the effects of widowhood; for poverty and malnutrition must surely be their lot.

Isaiah often speaks of "thorns and briers" (v. 13; see comment at 9:18). This also points in the direction of enemy occupation rather than mere harvest failure, for the latter would not account for the generally unkempt condition of the countryside. There is a certain emotional quality attached to the phrase "my people" (cf. 1:3). How sad that the land of God's people, a chosen land for a chosen people, should be reduced to such a lamentable condition! It was, of course, their sin that had caused this.

Do vv. 13b–14 refer to the same act of judgment through the Assyrians or do they go beyond this, describing perhaps the Babylonian capture of Jerusalem and its results? The word *kî* ("yes") in v. 13 has intensive force, suggesting that what follows goes beyond what has already been stated. This could simply indicate that a judgment on dwelling places is felt more immediately and so more forcibly than one on farmland and vineyards, but it could also indicate a later, more intense phase of the divine program of judgment. The latter seems more probable, because the language of these two verses, while employing the singular, suggests that Jerusalem rather than the cities of Judah is in view (see Notes). The devastation caused by Sennacherib's wind would be completed by Nebuchadnezzar's whirlwind.

15–20 The description of judgment suddenly changes to one of blessing. The contrast becomes particularly impressive considering the intentionally illogical words "a wasteland forever, . . . till" (vv. 14–15)! Such a decisive assertion of judgment can only be canceled by an equally decisive manifestation of grace. The condemnation humans live their life under is undoubtedly "forever," because death ushers in their judgment and its eternal consequences; but this condemnation can be canceled by the marvel of justifying grace through faith in Christ.

The reference to the Spirit (v. 15) is most appropriate. If chapter 32 amplifies certain aspects of the messianic prophecy in chapter 11 (see comment at vv. 1–2), we might expect some reference to the Spirit, who has such a place of importance in the earlier chapter. The idyllic picture there is echoed here, but it is particularly significant that the righteous king in v. 1 is accompanied by righteous subordinates. This suggests a wider ministry of the Spirit, not confined simply to the Messiah himself. This is exactly what is now described.

The NT brings together the OT teaching that both the Messiah and his people would know the endowment of the Spirit of God. Here we see an implicit link in Isaiah's own thought. The language of outpouring (v. 15) was destined to be far-reaching, being taken up again by Joel (assuming that Joel is later than Isaiah) in Joel 2:28 and then of course in Acts 2:17–21. As Young (*Book of Isaiah*, in loc. and n.) puts it: "Then there will occur a reversal of the present condition, a renewal that is indeed revolutionary, the very opposite of the condition described in 29:10. No longer will a spirit of sleep be poured out upon the people, but the Spirit from on high, the Spirit that is to be contrasted with mere flesh (31:3), the Spirit who brings rich gifts. . . . It is God's creative Spirit who brings about what amounts to a new creation."

The Introduction (pp. 14–16) discusses whether passages like these should be understood literally or spiritually. There are both literal and figurative dimensions to Isaiah's use of agricultural language. In this particular context, however, a literal interpretation certainly seems the more appropriate, for the judgment that the blessing reverses is certainly physical. Verse 15b should be compared with 29:17. Clements (*Isaiah 1–39*, in loc.) says, "Throughout vv. 15–20 there appears to be an intentional sequence established: prosperity-justice-peace-happiness." As he also says, "Prosperity without justice is a worthless acquisition." The close relationship between righteousness and peace is of course parallel to that seen in 11:4–9.

In discussing v.13 we noted the emotional quality of the phrase "my people," and this may be seen again in v.18. In the former verse God's people experience his hand of judgment on them, his strange work (28:21); but now God is able to bestow on them the blessing that is in his heart for them as his own beloved people. This verse, with its sequence of prepositional phrases, gives emphatic expression to God's promise that he would bring them, through righteousness, into a condition of "quietness and confidence forever" (v.17).

Verse 19 has been understood in three different ways. The RSV translates "and the forest will utterly go down, and the city will be utterly laid low." This is similar in tone, though not in wording, to the TEV, which places the verse in brackets, revealing the translators' awareness that, so understood, it does not seem to fit the immediate context very well. The NEB, on the other hand, takes it quite different-ly, with its rendering "it will be cool on the slopes of the forest then, and cities shall lie peaceful in the plain." The NIV, understanding it along lines suggested by Kis-sane (in loc.), renders "though hail flattens the forest and the city is leveled com-pletely." Each of these translations is possible; but the NIV makes it, with v.20, a fitting conclusion to the oracle, because it sums up its two elements of coming judgment and ultimate blessing.

Verse 20 takes up from 30:23–26 the picture of a plentiful economy based on abundant supplies of water but presents it in an even more desirable form. The amount of produce given by the soil will be so great that the farmer can actually allow his working animals to browse in the fields, rather than feeding them with prepared foodstuff in their stalls.

Notes

10 The NIV's "In little more than a year" translates יָמִים עַל־שָׁנָה (*yāmîm ʿal-šānāh*), which is literally "days on a year" or "days over a year," suggesting either a year or a little more.
12 The NIV's "beat" is in line with the imperative form in 1QIsa, whereas the MT has a difficult masculine participle.
14 עֹפֶל (*ōpel*) and בַּחַן (*baḥan*), translated "citadel" and "watchtower" in the NIV, may be place names. If so, a reference to Jerusalem is established, for Ophel was on Jerusalem's southern edge. See Young (*Book of Isaiah*, in loc.), who brings out also the extensive word play this chapter contains.

6. *Woe to the Destroyer*

    33:1–24

        ¹Woe to you, O destroyer,
          you who have not been destroyed!

Woe to you, O traitor,
  you who have not been betrayed!
When you stop destroying,
  you will be destroyed;
when you stop betraying,
  you will be betrayed.

²O Lord, be gracious to us;
  we long for you.
Be our strength every morning,
  our salvation in time of distress.
³At the thunder of your voice, the peoples flee;
  when you rise up, the nations scatter.
⁴Your plunder, O nations, is harvested as by young locusts;
  like a swarm of locusts men pounce on it.

⁵The Lord is exalted, for he dwells on high;
  he will fill Zion with justice and righteousness.
⁶He will be the sure foundation for your times,
  a rich store of salvation and wisdom and knowledge;
  the fear of the Lord is the key to this treasure.

⁷Look, their brave men cry aloud in the streets;
  the envoys of peace weep bitterly.
⁸The highways are deserted,
  no travelers are on the roads.
The treaty is broken,
  its witnesses are despised,
  no one is respected.
⁹The land mourns and wastes away,
  Lebanon is ashamed and withers;
Sharon is like the Arabah,
  and Bashan and Carmel drop their leaves.

¹⁰"Now will I arise," says the Lord.
  "Now will I be exalted;
  now will I be lifted up.
¹¹You conceive chaff,
  you give birth to straw;
  your breath is a fire that consumes you.
¹²The peoples will be burned as if to lime;
  like cut thornbushes they will be set ablaze."

¹³You who are far away, hear what I have done;
  you who are near, acknowledge my power!
¹⁴The sinners in Zion are terrified;
  trembling grips the godless:
"Who of us can dwell with the consuming fire?
  Who of us can dwell with everlasting burning?"
¹⁵He who walks righteously
  and speaks what is right,
who rejects gain from extortion
  and keeps his hand from accepting bribes,
who stops his ears against plots of murder
  and shuts his eyes against contemplating evil—
¹⁶this is the man who will dwell on the heights,
  whose refuge will be the mountain fortress.
His bread will be supplied,
  and water will not fail him.

17Your eyes will see the king in his beauty
  and view a land that stretches afar.
18In your thoughts you will ponder the former terror:
  "Where is that chief officer?
  Where is the one who took the revenue?
  Where is the officer in charge of the towers?"
19You will see those arrogant people no more,
    those people of an obscure speech,
    with their strange, incomprehensible tongue.

20Look upon Zion, the city of our festivals;
    your eyes will see Jerusalem,
    a peaceful abode, a tent that will not be moved;
  its stakes will never be pulled up,
    nor any of its ropes broken.
21There the Lord will be our Mighty One.
  It will be like a place of broad rivers and streams.
  No galley with oars will ride them,
    no mighty ship will sail them.
22For the Lord is our judge;
    the Lord is our lawgiver;
  the Lord is our king,
    it is he who will save us.

23Your rigging hangs loose:
  The mast is not held secure,
  the sail is not spread.
  Then an abundance of spoils will be divided
  and even the lame will carry off plunder.
24No one living in Zion will say, "I am ill";
  and the sins of those who dwell there will be forgiven.

This oracle is the final one in a series of five, interrupted only by the messianic oracle in chapter 32 (see general introduction to chs. 28–33). It is the only one of the series in which the introductory "woe" is directed, not against the people of God, but a foreign power. Commentators have shown much interest in the structure of the chapter. The school of OT scholarship that goes back through Mowinckel to Gunkel, with its emphasis on the cult, has identified the chapter as a prophetic liturgy (see esp. G. Fohrer [*Das Buch Jesaya*, in loc.] and H. Gunkel, "Jesaia 33, eine prophetische Liturgie," ZAW 42 [1924]:177–208). Although the theory is interesting and can be made out plausibly, it is somewhat speculative; and we will not assume that the chapter is actually cast into this form. What seems certain is that all the material represents an integrated whole. There can be little doubt that its theme is the Assyrian threat to Jerusalem and their departure from it (cf. chs. 36–37).

1 It looks as if the first half of this verse takes up the boasts of the Assyrians, who had been all-victorious for so many years. The second half declares they will be caught in their own trap. Such treatment should be particularly effective in bringing home a sense of guilt to the sinner.

2–4 The people in the city had at last been brought to realize their total dependence on the Lord. These words are best understood as their prayer when the Assyrian army was at the gate. In 30:18–19, the prophet stated that their God would hear them in grace when they called out to him. Isaiah declared, "How gracious he will be when you cry for help!" Here we see his words beginning to bear fruit. This must have been very encouraging after so many years of unresponsiveness to his preaching. Verse 2 has definite points of similarity to the eschatological song in chapter 12, especially v.1–2. Verse 3 is an expression of general confidence in the Lord, with a possible echo of Psalm 68:1. Young (*Book of Isaiah*, in loc.) makes an apt comment on v.4: "Although the prophecy may be taken as the statement of a general truth, namely, that when the enemy has served its purpose, God will intervene and deprive it of its power, one cannot help thinking of the sudden departure of Sennacherib from the land." Joel 1:1–2:10 points up the appropriateness of the image used here.

5–6 Isaiah often uses the language of exaltation and debasement (see comment at 2:2–4). He believed that the Lord alone was fit to be exalted to the highest place, and in chapter 2 he depicted this great God at last given his rightful place when everything that would challenge his supremacy has been debased. Here, however, he presents the complementary truth that the Lord is exalted already (v.5). Eschatological judgment, such as chapter 2 presents, is therefore simply the demonstration in history of that exaltation, though challenged, that is in fact beyond challenge.

This gloriously transcendent God is immanent among his people. There may well be a connection with 32:15–17. There the promise was given that the Spirit of God would be poured out on the people "from on high," suggesting that the exalted throne of God is the source from which God's justice and righteousness will be poured out on his people through the ministry of his Spirit. According to 1:21 (cf. also 1:26), this will in fact be a restoration to the city of a concern for justice that she knew in an earlier day, perhaps under the rule of David (see comments at ch. 1).

In v.6 we find *multum in parvo* ("much in little"), for it is itself "a rich store" and so partakes of the nature of the God who spoke it to the people through his prophet. The major issue in recent chapters (esp. chs. 30–31) has been political security. If the Assyrian officers were below the city walls at the time of this oracle, with all hope of relief from Egypt gone, the words of the prophet are particularly significant. The fact that the words "a rich store of salvation and wisdom and knowledge" are in apposition to "the sure foundation" shows that to the prophet the Lord was all his people needed. This passage strongly reminds us of 1 Corinthians 1:30 and Colossians 2:2–3, in which these blessings in all their riches are made available to God's people in Christ. In the historical context here, the chief thought seems to be that the Lord himself is more than enough to give the people protection from their enemies and wisdom in living as the people of God in the international world.

There is another link with the wisdom tradition (cf. Ps 111:10; Prov 1:7) in the assertion that this rich store becomes available through the fear of the Lord. This reminds us of the association of the fear of the Lord with the messianic King (11:2–3). The word 'fear" may also have been chosen because of the historical situation. The people trusted Egypt and feared Assyria; in fact, God was to be their fear just as the reference to a sure foundation suggests that he too should be their trust.

7–9 Verse 7 introduces a striking contrast, for the prophet focuses attention on the sorry condition of Jerusalem, which led the people eventually to call on their God in penitent faith. Terror grips the hearts of the warriors within the city gates. Those who have been sent out to parley with the enemy return weeping, for their words would not penetrate his hard heart. All normal commerce between communities comes to a halt (v.8; cf. Judg 5:6), and the treaty that apparently existed between Sennacherib and Hezekiah was treated as null and void. The excavations in Hittite territory have confirmed the importance of treaties in the international Near Eastern community in OT times.

The whole land was in mourning (v.9). The northern kingdom had already felt the heavy tread of the conqueror's feet; and the places named suggest that, apart from a divine intervention, Judah would go the same way. If the withering of Lebanon refers to its trees, then this is clearly an indication that what happened was a divine judgment; for its slopes were covered mostly by evergreens, whose leaves do not normally wither. Sharon was one of the most fertile parts of Palestine while the Arabah was dry and arid. O. Kaiser (in loc.) points out that the references to Bashan in Transjordan and Carmel on the west coast give us an impression of the scale of the enemy advance, extending across the whole country. The prophet surveyed places further north and saw the devastation, an earnest of what faced Jerusalem if the Assyrians gained entrance.

10–12 The threefold "now" (v.10) is most reassuring and is particularly impressive in the Hebrew; for the word translated "now" (*attāh*) is forceful—almost explosive —in its sound (see also comments at 43:1 and 44:1). Isaiah had a sensitive feeling for the sound of words as well as their meaning, and the inspiring Spirit put this to good use. The threefold assertion of God's exaltation reminds us also of the thrice-exalted Servant of the Lord in 52:13 (see comments at v.5). The enemy's plan to take Jerusalem would come to nothing, and the prophet used the figure of a pregnancy to bring home its futility (v.11; cf. 26:17–18). Their destruction will in fact be self-induced, for it is the result of their sinful antagonism to God's people. In v.12 it looks as if the prophet has moved briefly from the particular to the general, making a point about the comprehensiveness of judgment when it falls on the nations of the world.

13–16 The judgments of God should have a salutary effect on the people of God, for they underscore his holiness and the impossibilities of sinning with impunity. God speaks, in fact, to the whole world, calling on people to learn from the object lesson provided by his judgment of Assyria. The terms "far away" and "near" (v.13) describe the Gentile nations and Judah respectively (cf. 49:1; 57:19; Acts 2:39; Eph 2:13, 17). The call put in these terms reminds us of God's call to the far off heavens and to the earth Isaiah's recorded prophecies commence with (1:2). God's acts reveal his attributes, in this case his power.

The phrase "the sinners in Zion" (v.14) jars the spirit, for such a situation should not exist. Zion was God's city, the place where there was a concentration of the OT means of grace. This was surely no place for the godless, and yet in every age the godless have lived cheek by jowl with the godly, contemptuous of the things of God that made their presence felt every day.

As this passage develops (v.15), it inevitably reminds us of Psalms 15 and 24, which show the conditions God has laid down for dwelling on his holy hill. The effects of great judgments may have some kinship with those of spiritual revival; for a new sense of God—his power and his holiness—overtakes the sinners in Zion. Like those who heard Peter at Pentecost, these people, cut to the heart, cry out in their conviction of sin (cf. Acts 2:37). The "consuming fire" (v.14) is not hell; it is

God (cf. Heb 12:29)! Yet, in a sense, we may say that those who mistakenly interpret it as hell are not really so wide of the mark. Speaking of judgment, earlier the prophet said, "The Light of Israel will become a fire, their Holy One a flame; in a single day it will burn and consume his thorns and his briers" (10:17).

The cry of the convicted would seem to require a negative answer. No human being can dwell in the presence of such a holy God. Yet the prophet gives his hearers a wonderfully positive reply (v. 15). Time and again he had called his people to faith in God. To find security through the fear of the Lord is to have the key to great spiritual treasure, including that practical wisdom that indicates the way for the individual to walk as well as the right approach to international politics for the leaders (cf. v. 6). This strongly ethical passage reminds us of 58:6–12 and should be compared also with 32:3–8.

The Book of Isaiah, in common with much of Scripture, shows a deep concern about sins of speech (cf. esp. 6:5–7). The man of God will neither speak evil nor listen to it from the lips of others (v. 15). The final line of v. 15 underlines the importance of fleeing from temptation. Verse 16, in the light of its context, promises security and provision to the one who thus dwells with God and walks in righteousness.

17–20 If we are right, that this prophecy was uttered by Isaiah as the Assyrian army threatened Jerusalem, then these words would have been immensely reassuring to the beleaguered people. Commentators seeking to identify the king of v. 17 are divided largely into two groups, for it is hardly possible that the prophet means Hezekiah. The king is either the Messiah or God himself. Young (*Book of Isaiah*, in loc.) and O. Kaiser (in loc.) both present the main evidence, the former arguing that the king is the Messiah while the latter inclines to the alternative interpretation. Good arguments may be advanced on either side, but considerations of poetic structure particularly convince the present writer that the prophet is speaking messianically. It is clear that viewing the land is presented as somehow complementary to seeing the king, and the greatness of the Messiah's earthly dominion has been asserted in passages like 9:7; 11:9–10 (cf. 26:15). In contrast to this embattled city, the only free territory left to God's people, the future king would appear as ruler over a wide empire.

The contrast between v. 17 and 52:14—53:2 is striking, especially in the light of the threefold exaltation of the Servant proclaimed in 52:13. Kingship for the messianic Servant of the Lord comes to its full realization only through his suffering and death.

Isaiah graphically pictures the people in the days of the Messiah reflecting on the past and contrasting their lot then with the blessings they now have (v. 18). They had been the people of a king who had paid tribute to Sennacherib in attempting to buy him off (2 Kings 18:13–16); and Assyrian officials had been seen in the streets of Jerusalem, the financial agents of an avaricious tyrant, no doubt with arrogant mien and gait to match. The earlier prophecy had proved true. God had spoken to this people, in judgment, through men of strange speech (v. 19; cf. 28:11).

At the time the prophet contemplates, however, all this would be a thing of the past, subject still to vivid mental recall, but no longer experienced. The emphasis on sight, whether physical or mental, that has characterized the last few verses continues. Those who have been exhorted to see the king and the wide land of his domain are now called to view his capital city (v. 20), which was also the cultic center

213

of the nation, where its joy in God found its corporate expression at festival time. The enemies will be gone, and peace will reign. The name Jerusalem, whatever its full meaning, certainly includes "peace." It possessed many fine buildings, but we are reminded that its people belonged to a race formerly nomadic by the illustration of the tent firmly fixed. Verse 20 is probably the basis for the further use of the same analogy in 54:2–3, with its vision of a greatly enlarged tent recalling the far-stretching land of v.17 in this chapter.

21–22 One of the chief arguments used by those who understand the king of v.17 to be God himself is that the same word is expressly used of him in v.22. This is true, but the Book of Isaiah has earlier moved swiftly from a vision of the heavenly King in chapter 6 to predictions of the coming messianic King in chapters 7 to 11. Here the sequence is reversed, and the two are brought into even closer literary proximity; but the earlier chapters have served to prepare us somewhat for this, especially in their disclosure that the Messiah is himself divine.

This chapter, so full of compelling imagery, presents a picture of Jerusalem as a kind of Near Eastern Venice or Amsterdam (v.21), or, to place it in its historical context, like the great cities of Egypt or Mesopotamia. Most great civilizations have grown up around important rivers. Israel, in general, and Jerusalem, in particular, were exceptions to this. Indeed, Isaiah remembered the concern for adequate water supplies that had been in the mind of Ahaz when he confronted him on a memorable occasion in the past (7:3). The city would now be amply supplied (cf. Ps 46:4). Just as the prophet hastened to guard against a possible misconception of his imagery once before (see comment at 31:8), so now he makes it clear that such broad rivers would be an unmitigated blessing. Many a city, formerly glad of all the advantages brought to it by its situation on a great river, has cursed its location when that same river has brought an enemy armada into the very heart of it. Gates may keep out an enemy that a waterway may admit. Mighty ships cannot challenge the mighty God (cf. 2:16); the same adjective is used of both.

Verse 21 began with an assertion about the Lord before moving on to statements about Jerusalem. What Jerusalem is depends entirely on what Jerusalem's God is, and this is amplified in v.22. Each of the three brief but impressive statements about God is structured so as to place emphasis on the divine name. All three recall different periods in Israel's history, for the period of the judges was preceded by that of Moses the lawgiver and succeeded by that of the king. All three were savior figures, acting as agents of God to bring deliverance to his people. Their God would now sum up all these functions in himself. How great then would be his salvation! The verse is reminiscent of the way so many functions—discrete and distributed among many human figures in OT days—meet in the NT presentation of Jesus Christ. The introductory word "for" (*kî*) is important, linking a result—peace—with its cause—the presence of the Lord.

23–24 It is quite clear that v.23 takes up again the imagery of the ship from v.21, but who is being addressed by the prophet? Although Drechsler, followed by Young and Clements, argued for an application to Jerusalem, a reference to Assyria seems to fit the context better. If a "mighty ship" (v.21) was feared in Isaiah's day, it was Assyria. Let this ship sail belligerently in the direction of Jerusalem, and its essential instability—making it vulnerable to its foes—will stand revealed. Assyria appeared to be anything but vulnerable, so that the prophet is speaking with

God-given insight. Only God and God's man can penetrate the military facade to the true condition of Assyria. When it falls, its empire will be evenly divided; and even apparently impotent states will find themselves enriched from its plunder.

Verse 24 reminds us that the whole passage is really a description of the future blessedness of Jerusalem. The blessings of God will take both physical and spiritual forms. In Psalm 103:3, the greater blessing of forgiveness is placed first, for the psalm is, only just beginning; here it is placed at the end, to provide a climax for the whole chapter. In Hebrews 10:17–18, the long and full exposition of Christ's priestly and sacrificial work that began at Hebrews 7:1 comes to its triumphant conclusion in the statement that sin has been forgiven. No blessing is greater, none more urgently needed.

Notes

1 We have assumed that the destroyer here is Assyria, but some comentators take it—often on critical presuppositions that deny the chapter, or even parts of it, to Isaiah—to be Babylon, which is not impossible even if we accept Isaiah's authorship. The fact that the destroyer's identity is assumed rather than stated makes it seem more likely in fact that it is the well-known destroyer of the prophet's own day, viz., Assyria.

7 אֶרְאֶלָּם (ʾerʾellām, tr. "brave men") is of uncertain meaning. KB (s.v.) gives three possibilities: "heroes," "priests," "inhabitants." The parallelism makes the first two more likely than the third, but it is impossible to be sure.

8 The NIV, following 1QIsa, reads עֵדִים (ʿēdîm, "witnesses") instead of the MT's עָרִים (ʿārîm, "cities"). Either makes good sense, but the former would then establish identical parallelism as the sense structure of the whole verse.

14 Clements, in *Isaiah 1–39* (in loc.), and also in *God and Temple: the Idea of the Divine Presence in Ancient Israel* (Oxford: University Press, 1965), pp. 73ff., following Gunkel, ("Jesaia 33," pp. 177ff.), maintains that vv.14–16 here follow, like Pss 15:2–5; 24:4, the pattern of a Torah liturgy. Clements (*Isaiah 1–39*, in loc.) says, "The form is based on a question-and-answer pattern used between pilgrims seeking entrance to the temple and the priestly response to this. This response sets out, in a tightly stylised way, the qualities of life of those who would worship Yahweh. Here the prophet has adapted the pattern to deal with the question of *the sinners in Zion*" (emphasis his). Such exegesis is interesting, but Jensen (pp. 25–26) has raised questions about the whole thesis, with special mention of passages like the present one.

18 G.R. Driver ("Isaiah 1–39," JSS, p. 53) takes מִגְדָּלִים (*migdālîm*, "towers") to mean "piles" or "storechests," which would clarify the point of the reference.

V. God's Purposes of Judgment and Salvation (34:1–35:10)

It is widely recognized that these two chapters, in the overall structure of the Book of Isaiah, bear the same kind of relationship to chapters 28–33 as chapters 24–27 do to chapters 13–23. Despite what is said in chapter 34 about Edom, there is a unversality about the references to the judgment to come; and the beautiful picture the prophet has drawn of Israel's future in chapter 35 may be compared with statements of blessing for her given in the earlier passage. This is further evidence of that special attention to structure that is so evident in this book (see Introduction, pp. 20–22).

1. *Judgment on the World—and Edom*

34:1–17

¹Come near, you nations, and listen;
　　pay attention, you peoples!
Let the earth hear, and all that is in it,
　　the world, and all that comes out of it!
²The Lᴏʀᴅ is angry with all nations;
　　his wrath is upon all their armies.
He will totally destroy them,
　　he will give them over to slaughter.
³Their slain will be thrown out,
　　their dead bodies will send up a stench;
the mountains will be soaked with their blood.
⁴All the stars of the heavens will be dissolved
　　and the sky rolled up like a scroll;
all the starry host will fall
　　like withered leaves from the vine,
　　like shriveled figs from the fig tree.
⁵My sword has drunk its fill in the heavens;
　　see, it descends in judgment on Edom,
　　the people I have totally destroyed.
⁶The sword of the Lᴏʀᴅ is bathed in blood,
　　it is covered with fat—
the blood of lambs and goats,
　　fat from the kidneys of rams.
For the Lᴏʀᴅ has a sacrifice in Bozrah
　　and a great slaughter in Edom.
⁷And the wild oxen will fall with them,
　　the bull calves and the great bulls.
Their land will be drenched with blood,
　　and the dust will be soaked with fat.

⁸For the Lᴏʀᴅ has a day of vengeance,
　　a year of retribution, to uphold Zion's cause.
⁹Edom's streams will be turned into pitch,
　　her dust into burning sulfur;
　　her land will become blazing pitch!
¹⁰It will not be quenched night and day;
　　its smoke will rise forever.
From generation to generation it will lie desolate;
　　no one will ever pass through it again.
¹¹The desert owl and screech owl will possess it;
　　the great owl and the raven will nest there.
God will stretch out over Edom
　　the measuring line of chaos
　　and the plumb line of desolation.
¹²Her nobles will have nothing there to be called a kingdom,
　　all her princes will vanish away.
¹³Thorns will overrun her citadels,
　　nettles and brambles her strongholds.
She will become a haunt for jackals,
　　a home for owls.
¹⁴Desert creatures will meet with hyenas,
　　and wild goats will bleat to each other;
there the night creatures will also repose
　　and find for themselves places of rest.

> ¹⁵The owl will nest there and lay eggs,
>> she will hatch them, and care for her young under the
>> shadow of her wings;
>> there also the falcons will gather,
>> each with its mate.

¹⁶Look in the scroll of the Lord and read:

> None of these will be missing,
>> not one will lack her mate.
> For it is his mouth that has given the order,
>> and his Spirit will gather them together.
> ¹⁷He allots their portions;
>> his hand distributes them by measure.
> They will possess it forever
>> and dwell there from generation to generation.

This chapter is remarkable for its combination of the general and the particular, the universal and the local. It reminds us of the Greek word *hekastos* ("each one individually") used in so many descriptions of judgment in the NT.

1–4 Isaiah dramatically apostrophizes the nations of the world here. They cannot hear him, for, presumably, he is speaking in Jerusalem; but his message in fact concerns them all. Such a dramatic apostrophe, addressed to the heavens and the earth, opened the book of his prophecies (1:2). He accumulates words and phrases— "you nations," "you peoples," "earth," "world"—to emphasize the universal scope of his words. This makes the later particular reference to one small state all the more striking.

Such a dramatic address leads us to expect that it will introduce statements, not simply about the nations themselves, but about the sovereign God who addresses them; and so it is. There is to be a great judgment that will manifest the anger of God with them (v.2; cf. Rom 1:18–2:11). It is significant that the prophet refers to the armies of the nations, for national arrogance and cruelty have so often found their focus in aggressive acts by military forces. Israel had in fact been on the receiving end of many such attacks, but divine retribution was coming. Amos, Isaiah's older contemporary, had however proclaimed the judgment of God on all acts of inhumanity by one nation to another, whether or not Israel or Judah was involved (see Amos 1–2 and the Introduction, p. 13). The fearsome description in v.3 is not attractive; it is not meant to be, thus driving home the point that God's wrath will lead to the death of his enemies.

Verse 4 transports us suddenly from earth to the heavens. The ultimate character of this judgment is made clear when we see that it encompasses the entire cosmos, a reminder of the description in 24:21–23. This kind of language is taken up by the apocalyptic passages of the NT (e.g., Matt 24:29; 2 Peter 3:10, and esp. Rev 6:13–14). The way Isaiah illustrates this truth of cosmic judgment from situations familiar to his readers heightens the impression of God's absolute control over all things (cf. 40:12).

5–7 A hearer who failed to feel the force of the contrast presented in v.5 would have to be quite without imagination. God is here the universal Judge, his judgments on the grand scale including even the very heavens (v.5). Then, with great suddenness, the sword of judgment falls on one of the smallest states in the biblical world,

Edom. Edom was a traditional enemy of Israel, and so what we have here probably represents God's judgment on all her foes. It had appropriated territory from Judah during the reign of Ahaz (2 Kings 16:6). The prophecies against the nations recorded in chapters 13–23 do not contain an oracle against Edom, though many of Judah's neighbors are mentioned. Edom has not, however, been overlooked (cf. 11:14). Indeed, its fall was so certain that it was described by the use of the prophetic perfect as "the people I have totally destroyed."

The NIV margin at v.2 makes this a comment on the phrase "totally destroy": "The Hebrew term refers to the irrevocable giving over of things or persons to the LORD, often by totally destroying them; also in verse 5." This had been the position of Jericho in the days of Joshua (see Josh 6:17–21 and NIV mg. there). In some respects cities, persons, and articles thus given over in destruction to the Lord were like sacrifices; for they too were holy to the Lord (Lev 27:28–29). This is probably why v.6 goes on to speak of sacrificial animals. The inhabitants of Edom, under divine judgment, were like sacrificial animals. Like them, the Edomites' fate was death. Yet in one way, it is hardly appropriate to liken the antagonistic Edomites to the comparatively docile domestic animals employed in the sacrificial ritual; so the prophet looked beyond the domestic scene to the herds of wild oxen (v.7) that no doubt roamed parts of Edom's territory as well as the steppes of Bashan further north (Ps 22:12). They too would die.

8–10 The word "judgment" in v.5, sets the slaughter in Edom in a moral context, and this is emphasized in v.8. There are strong links of terminology with the picture of judgment on Edom in chapter 63 (see esp. v.4). Young (*Book of Isaiah*, in loc.), writing of the divine vengeance, says, "It is not mingled with malice and evil as is the case with human vengeance. It is a quality that in God is divine and praiseworthy and in the execution of which God is honoured and glorified." The same may be said of his wrath. This act of vengeance is also to further his purposes for Jerusalem, which, in times of weakness in Judah and strength in Edom, might well have cause to fear a threat from the south. There is an implied comparison with the destruction of Sodom and Gomorrah, a historical judgment that the prophet often uses for purposes of comparison (cf. 1:9–10; 3:9; 13:19), and which is made explicit in Jeremiah 49:17–18.

In commenting on v.10, J.A. Alexander (p. 24) says, "The remarkable gradation and accumulation of terms denoting perpetuity can scarcely be expressed in a translation." Young (*Book of Isaiah*, in loc.), however, makes an attempt; "Night and day it is not quenched; for even its smoke keep ascending. From generation to generation it will burn. For ever and ever there is no one passing through it." Edom's judgment will be so complete, so permanent, that it will be utterly desolate. The final line of v.10 may mean that, not only will Edom be unable to harass Zion herself, but she will not even witness the passage of armies from beyond her borders on their way to attack Judah.

11–15 Isaiah's references to the fauna of his world are always of interest but contain some very uncertain references (see Notes; cf. also the note at 13:21–22). Precise identification of these creatures matters little, for the general thrust of the prophet's thought is clear. Edom will become a desolate place, fit only for creatures of the wild. There may be a hint of contrast with the domestic animals the inhabitants have been likened to in v.6. Just as nomads rejoice to find terrain that has been abandoned by its inhabitants, so the birds and beasts of the wilderness will move into the land whose people have suffered God's judgment.

Verses 11b–12 stand alone in the midst of all these references to wild creatures. Verse 11b employs architectural language in a way we have encountered before—though with reference to Israel—in 28:16–17. What looks at first like a suggestion that Edom, now destroyed, may be reconstructed becomes, in the prophet's paradoxical language, a warning that God is in fact measuring it up rather for destruction. Clements (*Isaiah 1–39*, in loc.) may be right in his suggestion that the references to chaos and desolation here contain "a deliberate reference back to the description of the formless void of the world before God imposed the created order upon it (Gen 1:2)." This is more likely when we recall that the judgment on Edom occurs in a context of universal judgment.

The RSV's translation of the difficult words in v.12 (see Notes) is attractive: "They shall name it No Kingdom There." This provides a kind of parallel to the description of Egypt in 30:7 as "Rahab the Do-Nothing." In any case, the main thought is clear. Just as a measuring line suggests architectural order, so a kingdom suggests social order; but there will be none.

16–17 The opening exhortation of v.16 is noteworthy. What is "the scroll of the LORD"? There have been numerous suggestions, including the Book of Life and also other passages in Isaiah. It seems more than likely, however, as both Young and O. Kaiser recognize, that the prophet is speaking about the prophecy just given. Thus the communication of prophetic oracles to writing has importance because it makes possible later recognition of the veracity of God. What he has said comes to pass because it is he, the God of truth, who has said it. The emphasis of some recent biblical theology on promise and fulfillment as a major biblical theme is a very healthy one, for Scripture is God's witness to his own faithfulness. The Spirit of God puts into effect what his word has promised, and the birds and animals gathering in Edom are mute testimony to the truth of what he has said. Just as God apportioned the world among its human inhabitants (Deut. 32:8), so now he would order the new homes of these creatures in Edom so that each is given his proper place. Even in his judgments—perhaps especially in these—God is concerned that everything should be done in a fitting and orderly way (cf. 1 Cor 14:40).

Notes

6 Bozrah, the Edomite capital, can be identified as modern Buseirah, twenty-seven miles south of the Dead Sea.

11 "Desert owl" translates קָאַת (qāʾat). All kinds of birds have been suggested in identification of this. The NIV gives one of these possibilities.

קִפּוֹד (qippôd, "screech owl") is rendered simply "owl" in 14:23. Some commentators (e.g., Young) reckon it to be the hedgehog or porcupine, but a bird seems more likely here.

יַנְשׁוֹף (yanšôp, "great owl") is particularly difficult to identify.

12 The first part of this verse is difficult, because of a somewhat loose sentence structure. The NIV and the RSV (see comments) represent major options. For fuller discussion, see Young (*Book of Isaiah*, in loc.)

13 For תַנִּים (*tannîm*, "jackals"), see the note at 13:33.

The English "owls" renders בְּנוֹת יַעֲנָה (*benôṭ yaʿⁿāh*, lit., "daughters of the Yaʾanah"), which some have identified with ostriches.

14 The צִיִּים (*ṣiyîm*, "desert creatures"), the אִיִּים (*ʾiyîm*, "hyenas"), and שָׂעִיר (*śāʿîr*, "wild goats") have all been mentioned before in 13:21–22. See Notes there.

15 קִפּוֹז (*qippôz*) is probably an owl (NIV), though it has also been identified as a hedgehog, porcupine, or even a snake.

דַיּוֹת (*dayyôṭ*, "falcons") will certainly be falcons, kites, or vultures.

---

2. Blessing for God's People

35:1–10

¹The desert and the parched land will be glad;
    the wilderness will rejoice and blossom.
Like the crocus, ²it will burst into bloom;
    it will rejoice greatly and shout for joy.
The glory of Lebanon wil be given to it,
    the splendor of Carmel and Sharon;
they will see the glory of the LORD,
    the splendor of our God.

³Strengthen the feeble hands,
    steady the knees that give way;
⁴say to those with fearful hearts,
    "Be strong, do not fear;
your God will come,
    he will come with vengeance;
with divine retribution
    he will come to save you."

⁵Then will the eyes of the blind be opened
    and the ears of the deaf unstopped.
⁶Then will the lame leap like a deer,
    and the mute tongue shout for joy.
Water will gush forth in the wilderness
    and streams in the desert.
⁷The burning sand will become a pool,
    the thirsty ground bubbling springs.
In the haunts where jackals once lay,
    grass and reeds and papyrus will grow.

⁸And a highway will be there;
    it will be called the Way of Holiness.
The unclean will not journey on it;
    it will be for those who walk in that Way;
    wicked fools will not go about on it.
⁹No lion will be there,
    nor will any ferocious beast get up on it;
    they will not be found there.
But only the redeemed will walk there,
¹⁰   and the ransomed of the LORD will return.
They will enter Zion with singing;
    everlasting joy will crown their heads.
Gladness and joy will overtake them,
    and sorrow and sighing will flee away.

Exalted passages of Scripture often suffer at the hands of their readers because they tend not to be read in their contexts. The reader of Romans 8 would profit much from noting the immense change of atmosphere that takes place at the opening of chapter 9. So here the beauty of chapter 35 is enhanced if anything by contrast with the picture of wild desolation that ends chapter 34.

It is taken almost for granted by many critics that this chapter could not be by Isaiah, very largely because of its thematic links with material from the later chapters of the book, so widely denied to him by criticism. This question is discussed in the Introduction, pp. 6–12. The commentary on this chapter will assume that Isaiah is the author of this oracle.

1–2 The prophet speaks of the desert (v.1) but does not indicate its location. The tendency is to assume that it is Judah or Israel-Judah that is in view, but v.8–10 suggest that the prophet is thinking about the exiles returning from Babylon and crossing the many miles of desert lying between Mesopotamia and the Promised Land. In view of the promise that the messianic King would be seen in his beauty as governing a far-stretching land (33:17), it is probably best to think in terms of all the terrain occupied or traversed by God's people, but with Zion (v.10) as the center of the kingdom and the end goal of the returning exiles.

The Greeks used to speak of the music of the spheres. In Job 38:7 God tells Job that at the Creation the morning stars sang together. In these verses nature burst not only into bloom but into song. The very environment of man reflects his own mood of joy at what God has done. If this is the *locus classicus* for this thought in the OT, Romans 8:13–25 occupies the same place in the NT. God's purpose for his people will come to its consummation in a transfigured environment. The familiar "rose" of the KJV has become the "crocus" in the NIV, but many recent writers consider that the asphodel is probably intended.

The prophet does not say that the wilderness will burst into bloom with the crocus but like it (v.2). Probably he has in mind the transformation that comes over a land when winter ends and spring, with its characteristic flowers, suddenly comes with the advent of a few warm days. The whole face of the earth is changed. So will it be with the desert. Lebanon's glory is found of course in its wonderful cedars, while Carmel and the plain of Sharon that runs south from it were also covered with trees and other plant life. In the Bible the glory of God is often manifested in history, but here it is seen in nature. The beauty and splendor of transformed nature will be seen to be a reflection of the beauty and splendor of the Creator and Redeemer (cf. 40:5).

3–4 The prophet returns briefly to his age and the fear that gripped the hearts of so many of his people in the face of the external threat (see esp. 7:2–9). Fear in the heart (v.4) affects the ability of hands to work for God and of feet to walk in his ways (v.3). The command is reminiscent of the often-repeated command of God to Joshua to be strong and very courageous (Deut 31:6–7, 23; Joshua 1:6–7, 9, 18). This could mean then that the returning exiles of v.10 are already in view, needing, as did their distinguished predecessor who led them into the land at the beginning, divine encouragement to make the journey.

The link between chapter 34 and chapter 35 is emphasized, not only by the contrasting pictures of topographical desolation and blessing, but also by the use of *nāqām* ("vengeance") in both 34:8 and here in v.4. Some have found the reference here to divine retributive vengeance a somewhat discordant note in such a context. Biblical realism, however, requires that peace be the result of righteousness (cf. 11:4–9; 32:16–18, and righteousness demands the punishment of sin. Only when God has judged the enemies of his people can his salvation in all its fullness be theirs.

5–7 In view of the frequent references to spiritual blindness and deafness in passages like 6:9–10 and 29:9–12, and the promise that one day spiritual sight and hearing will be restored to the people (29:18), we are at once inclined to interpret v.5—and in harmony with it v.6 in spiritual terms. We must, however, note that Luke 7:18–23 appears to allude to this chapter; and in it our Lord takes the language literally and physically. In fact, we may be able to understand it at more than one level (see Introduction, pp. 14–16), for physical and spiritual sight and hearing have a symbolic relationship; and God's ultimate kingdom in which his people will have glorified bodies and a perfected spirituality will be characterized by both. The healed lame man is likely not only to walk but to leap (cf. Acts 3:8); and, whatever be the first utterance of the loosened tongue, it will certainly give vent to joy (v.6)!

The human world has dominated the picture since v.3, but now renewed nature comes into view once again. It is really the dearth of only one commodity that makes a desert what it is; so it is not surprising that the renewed references to the transformed wilderness are alive with the sound of living streams and gushing springs. This water in fact affects the whole environment. The only sign of life before the water's advent was the jackal or wolf (v.7; see note at 13:22). Such places had little attraction for human beings, but their place would be taken by the characteristic vegetation of lands with abundant water supplies.

8–10 This great passage takes a new turn at this point and begins to remind us even more markedly of chapter 40. In ancient times men did not build roads across stretches of desert. Such an enterprise would have seemed economically stupid as well as involving a criminal waste of life. But this land is desert no longer; so roads across it are appropriate. The prophet concentrates on one highway, with a most exalted name. It is called "the Way of Holiness" (v.8) because its goal is the Holy City of Zion (v.10), but also because it is intended for holy persons. It has been plausibly suggested, for example, by Young (*Book of Isaiah*, in loc.) that this passage may owe some of its imagery to the "holy" ways of antiquity, the roads along which only the ceremonially clean might travel to their temples in fulfillment of cult requirements. Israel's highways were all intended to be roads of pilgrimage, of course, as people went up them at the feasts to meet the Lord in his holy temple. This passage also probably reflects the teaching of Psalms 15 and 24. In the light of 26:7–8, the statement "It will be for those who walk in that Way" is probably to be understood morally, not simply ceremonially. This becomes still more evident if the NIV text is correct (see Notes) in its rendering of the last line of v.8.

Verse 9 makes us aware of the hazardous conditions faced by desert travelers in that part of the world, as the prophet has already shown in 30:6. This road will be free of predators, for it will be restricted to the redeemed. Verse 10 brings the whole oracle to a glorious conclusion. It is repeated in 51:11 and part of it in 61:7. It thus forms a striking link between the three parts of the book into which an earlier criticism divided it, before the more fragmentary criticism that later became popular took over (see Introduction, pp. 6–12).

The most joyous periods of the year for the people of Judah had been the three pilgrim feasts, when they had gone up the highways to Zion singing pilgrim songs. The word "return" (v.10) makes it clear that they are in fact now coming from farther afield, probably not from Babylonia alone, but from all the lands of the Dispersion (see 49:8–26). The note of joy the oracle opens with and which can be discerned through the language of its every part now takes over completely. Sorrow and sighing are denied any place in this revelation of God's purpose of joy for his people (cf. Rev 21:1–4). Had the Book of Isaiah concluded at this point, the reader would have been greedy to be dissatisfied; but there are still more wonders to come, for the greatest oracles of this wonderful book are still in prospect.

Notes

2 In the context the words "they will see the glory of the LORD" appear to refer to the desert and the parched land of v.1. It is possible, however, that the prophet may intend a reference to God's people, who come into view at v.3.

8 There are obscurities in the Hebrew that the NIV translates "it will be for those who walk in that Way," and there is some variety in modern EV at this point. The NIV has the merit of harmony with the context. Its translation "wicked fools" reflects the widespread use of אֱוִיל (ʾewîl, "fool") with connotations of impiety (cf. Job 5:3; Prov 1:7). The NIV margin's "the simple will not stray from it" reflects the less pejorative use of the term of a simpleton (Prov 11:29; 14:3). The moral context here supports the former.

9–10 For the terminology of redemption and ransom, see comments at 43:1, 3.

VI. Isaiah and Hezekiah, Assyria and Babylon (36:1–39:8)

The narrative character of these chapters make them somewhat different from other parts of the book, though there is narrative also in chapters 6–8 and 20. There are oracles of Isaiah here, but they are set in a historical framework. In the overall pattern of the book, they fulfill an important function. Chapters 1–35 have the Assyrian menace as their main historical setting; and, though many other nations are touched, the reader is never allowed for long to forget the dark shadow of that threat in the background. From the beginning of chapter 40, however, exile in Babylon forms the setting of his oracles. These four chapters therefore provide a historical transition, chapters 36–37 looking back to Assyria and chapters 38–39 on to Babylon.

These chapters, apart from small variations, are identical with 2 Kings 18–20, except for the poem of Hezekiah in Isaiah 38:9–20. Most modern scholars consider that the record in Kings is the original and that the Isaiah redactor has inserted material from that book at this point for his own reasons. A good case can, however, be made out for the opposite. The arguments are particularly well put in Young's commentary (*Book of Isaiah*, 2:556–65). Clements (*Isaiah 1–39*, in loc.) summarizes the contrary argument. See also Childs (*Isaiah*, ch.3). This commentary assumes the priority of Isaiah.

1. *The Deliverance of Jerusalem From Sennacherib*

36:1–37:38

[1]In the fourteenth year of King Hezekiah's reign, Sennacherib king of Assyria attacked all the fortified cities of Judah and captured them. [2]Then the king of Assyria sent his field commander with a large army from Lachish to King Hezekiah at Jerusalem. When the commander stopped at the aqueduct of the Upper Pool, on the road to the Washerman's Field, [3]Eliakim son of Hilkiah the palace administrator, Shebna the secretary, and Joah son of Asaph the recorder went out to him.

[4]The field commander said to them, "Tell Hezekiah,

" 'This is what the great king, the king of Assyria, says: On what are you basing this confidence of yours? [5]You say you have strategy and military strength—but you speak only empty words. On whom are you depending, that you rebel against me? [6]Look now, you are depending on Egypt, that splintered reed of a staff, which pierces a man's hand and wounds him if he leans on it! Such is Pharaoh king of Egypt to all who depend on hm. [7]And if you say to me, "We are depending on the LORD our God"—isn't he the one whose high places and altars Hezekiah removed, saying to Judah and Jerusalem, "You must worship before this altar"?

[8]" 'Come now, make a bargain with my master, the king of Assyria: I will give you two thousand horses—if you can put riders on them. [9]How then can you repulse one officer of the least of my master's officials, even though you are depending on Egypt for chariots and horsemen? [10]Furthermore, have I come to attack and destroy this land without the LORD? The LORD himself told me to march against this country and destroy it.' "

[11]Then Eliakim, Shebna and Joah said to the field commander, "Please speak to your servants in Aramaic, since we understand it. Don't speak to us in Hebrew in the hearing of the people on the wall.' "

[12]But the commander replied, "Was it only to your master and you that my master sent me to say these things, and not to the men sitting on the wall—who, like you, will have to eat their own filth and drink their own urine?"

[13]Then the commander stood and called out in Hebrew, "Hear the words of the great king, the king of Assyria! [14]This is what the king says: Do not let Hezekiah deceive you. He cannot deliver you! [15]Do not let Hezekiah persuade you to trust in the LORD when he says, 'The LORD will surely deliver us; this city will not be given into the hand of the king of Assyria.'

[16]"Do not listen to Hezekiah. This is what the king of Assyria says: Make peace with me and come out to me. Then every one of you will eat from his own vine and fig tree and drink water from his own cistern, [17]until I come and take you to a land like your own—a land of grain and new wine, a land of bread and vineyards.

[18]"Do not let Hezekiah mislead you when he says, 'The LORD will deliver us.' Has the god of any nation ever delivered his land from the hand of the king of Assyria? [19]Where are the gods of Hamath and Arpad? Where are the gods of Sepharvaim? Have they rescued Samaria from my hand? [20]Who of all the gods of these countries has been able to save his land from me? How then can the LORD deliver Jerusalem from my hand?"

[21]But the people remained silent and said nothing in reply, because the king had commanded, "Do not answer him."

[22]Then Eliakim son of Hilkiah the palace administrator, Shebna the secretary, and Joah son of Asaph the recorder went to Hezekiah, with their clothes torn, and told him what the field commander had said.

37:1When King Hezekiah heard this, he tore his clothes and put on sackcloth and went into the temple of the LORD. [2]He sent Eliakim the palace administrator, Shebna the secretary, and the leading priests, all wearing sackcloth, to the prophet Isaiah son of Amoz. [3]They told him, "This is what Hezekiah says: This day is a day of distress and rebuke and disgrace, as when children come to the point of birth and there is no strength to deliver them. ⁴It may be that the LORD your God will hear the words of the field commander, whom his master, the king of Assyria, has sent to ridicule the living God, and that he will rebuke him for the words the LORD your God has heard. Therefore pray for the remnant that still survives."

⁵When King Hezekiah's officials came to Isaiah, ⁶Isaiah said to them, "Tell your master, 'This is what the LORD says: Do not be afraid of what you have heard— those words with which the underlings of the king of Assyria have blasphemed me. ⁷Listen! I am going to put a spirit in him so that when he hears a certain report, he will return to his own country, and there I will have him cut down with the sword.' "

⁸When the field commander heard that the king of Assyria had left Lachish, he withdrew and found the king fighting against Libnah.

⁹Now Sennacherib received a report that Tirhakah, the Cushite king of Egypt, was marching out to fight against him. When he heard it, he sent messengers to Hezekiah with this word: ¹⁰"Say to Hezekiah king of Judah: Do not let the god you depend on deceive you when he says, 'Jerusalem will not be handed over to the king of Assyria.' ¹¹Surely you have heard what the kings of Assyria have done to all the countries, destroying them completely. And will you be delivered? ¹²Did the gods of the nations that were destroyed by my forefathers deliver them—the gods of Gozan, Haran, Rezeph and the people of Eden who were in Tel Assar? ¹³Where is the king of Hamath, the king of Arpad, the king of the city of Sepharvaim, or of Hena or Ivvah?"

¹⁴Hezekiah received the letter from the messengers and read it. Then he went up to the temple of the LORD and spread it out before the LORD. ¹⁵And Hezekiah prayed to the LORD: ¹⁶"O LORD Almighty, God of Israel, enthroned between the cherubim, you alone are God over all the kingdoms of the earth. You have made heaven and earth. ¹⁷Give ear, O LORD, and hear; open your eyes, O LORD, and see; listen to all the words Sennacherib has sent to insult the living God.

¹⁸"It is true, O LORD, that the Assyrian kings have laid waste all these peoples and their lands. ¹⁹They have thrown their gods into the fire and destroyed them, for they were not gods but only wood and stone, fashioned by human hands. ²⁰Now, O LORD our God, deliver us from his hand, so that all kingdoms on earth may know that you alone, O LORD, are God."

²¹Then Isaiah son of Amoz sent a message to Hezekiah: "This is what the LORD, the God of Israel, says: Because you have prayed to me concerning Sennacherib king of Assyria, ²²this is the word the LORD has spoken against him:

"The Virgin Daughter of Zion
    despises and mocks you.
The Daughter of Jerusalem
    tosses her head as you flee.
²³Who is it you have insulted and blasphemed?
    Against whom have you raised your voice
and lifted your eyes in pride?
    Against the Holy One of Israel!
²⁴By your messengers
    you have heaped insults on the Lord.
And you have said,
    'With my many chariots,
I have ascended the heights of the mountains,
    the utmost heights of Lebanon.
I have cut down its tallest cedars,
    the choicest of its pines.
I have reached its remotest heights,
    the finest of its forests.
²⁵I have dug wells in foreign lands
    and drunk the water there.
With the soles of my feet
    I have dried up all the streams of Egypt.'

26"Have you not heard?
   Long ago I ordained it.
In days of old I planned it;
   now I have brought it to pass,
that you have turned fortified cities
   into piles of stone.
27Their people, drained of power,
   are dismayed and put to shame.
They are like plants in the field,
   like tender green shoots,
like grass sprouting on the roof,
   scorched before it grows up.

28"But I know where you stay
   and when you come and go
   and how you rage against me.
29Because you rage against me
   and because your insolence has reached my ears,
I will put my hook in your nose
   and my bit in your mouth,
and I will make you return
   by the way you came.

30"This will be the sign for you, O Hezekiah:

"This year you will eat what grows by itself,
   and the second year what springs from that.
But in the third year sow and reap,
   plant vineyards and eat their fruit.
31Once more a remnant of the house of Judah
   will take root below and bear fruit above.
32For out of Jerusalem will come a remnant,
   and out of Mount Zion a band of survivors.
The zeal of the LORD Almighty
   will accomplish this.

33"Therefore this is what the LORD says concerning the king of Assyria:

"He will not enter this city
   or shoot an arrow here.
He will not come before it with shield
   or build a siege ramp against it.
34By the way that he came he will return;
   he will not enter this city,"

                                        declares the LORD.
35"I will defend this city and save it,
   for my sake and for the sake of David my servant!"

36Then the angel of the LORD went out and put to death a hundred and eighty-five thousand men in the Assyrian camp. When the people got up the next morning—there were all the dead bodies! 37So Sennacherib king of Assyria broke camp and withdrew. He returned to Nineveh and stayed there.
38One day, while he was worshiping in the temple of his god Nisroch, his sons Adrammelech and Sharezer cut him down with the sword, and they escaped to the land of Ararat. And Esarhaddon his son succeeded him as king.

A.E. Cundall (*Proverbs—Isaiah 1–39* [London: Scripture Union, 1968], p. 91) writing about the record of events given here, says, "This is history at its best, no dull recital of statistics and dates but an account which enables us to sense the haughty arrogance of the Assyrian and the chilling clutch of despair at the hearts of the Israelites." Whether in the use of many a vivid illustration or in the graphic account of events in which he had participated, Isaiah's God-given facility with words is put to good use.

Historical criticism raises a number of problems about these two chapters. The first concerns the differing accounts given here and in the annals of Sennacherib, the Assyrian king. The differences are comparatively minor and can be explained largely in terms of Assyrian boastfulness, which was proverbial. Every conqueror is tempted to write up his account of his victories with some exaggeration, and the Assyrians had no allegiance to the God of truth to restrain them. A second problem relates to the part played by "Tirhakah, the Cushite king of Egypt" in the story, which seems at this point to be anachronistic. This difficulty has however been greatly reduced by the research of K.A. Kitchen and others, as the note at 37:9 will indicate. It is also said that the account of Hezekiah's surrender to Sennacherib recorded in 2 Kings 18:13–16 cannot be squared with the story here. But the difficulty is only insuperable if we cannot conceive of a monarch deciding to continue his rebellion after a premature gesture of surrender. Finally, it is taken almost for granted by most modern critics that these chapters are constructed from two separate narratives. Isaiah 36:1–37:7, with the addition of 37:37–38, makes up the first narrative and 37:10–36 the second. Chapter 36:8–9 contains the point of transition between the two, though there is some disagreement as to the exact point of connection. E.J. Young (*Book of Isaiah*, 2:540–55) has a most useful appendix in which he examines the difficulties in detail, supporting the unity and accuracy of the whole passage, as well as commenting on the other issues referred to in the present paragraph.

The exposition and notes that follow will attempt to keep these issues in mind and to comment usefully on them, but it should be remembered that the purpose of this series of commentaries is not primarily critical. Readers wishing to follow up these matters in more detail should consult the larger commentaries.

1–3 These events can be dated in the year 701 B.C., which raises a problem about the reference to the fourteenth year of Hezekiah's reign (v.1; see Notes). In his annals Sennacherib declared, "I laid siege to 46 of his strong cities, walled forts and to the countless villages in their vicinity, and conquered (them)" (ANET, p. 288). The NIV translates the familiar "Rabshakeh" of the KJV and RSV as "field commander" (v.2). Second Kings 18:17 refers to the presence of two other Assyrian officials with him. The term means "chief cupbearer," but this must relate to its remote origins. It had become a military title. He was probably second only to the Tartan, or supreme commander, mentioned in 20:1. Lachish, an important fortress city of Judah, guarding the road to Egypt, was captured by Sennacherib; and the siege of it is depicted on an Assyrian bas-relief in the British Museum. The location of the main Assyrian army at this point, because of its strategic position, precluded any possible hope of Egyptian help to Hezekiah.

There can be little doubt that the reference to the aqueduct in v.2 has more than a purely narrative purpose. The reader of Isaiah might already have recalled the attack of external enemies on Judah recorded in chapter 7. Once again, as in the days of Ahaz, Jerusalem was being threatened by her foes. On that earlier occasion, the aqueduct had been the place of decision for a king. Would he trust God or call on Assyria for aid? Much had happened over the more than three decades that separated that event from this; and it was the Assyrian himself who was now the threat, which in itself underlined the folly of Ahaz on that earlier occasion. The foe now was much more powerful than the two allies of the earlier event, and in other ways there were some differences in the circumstances; but the spiritual issue had not altered. At the same spot the kingly son of Ahaz faced the same spiritual issue. How would he react?

The king of Assyria had not come personally but had sent three of his leading men (2 Kings 18:17), and Hezekiah did the same (v.3). In this way he preserved something of his dignity as the monarch.

4–7 Cundall (*Proverbs—Isaiah 1–39*, p. 91 in loc.) gives a brief but exceptionally helpful treatment of the eight-pronged argument of the field commander here. Cundall notes that this man argued that mere words seemed a futile attack against the Assyrian army (v.5); that Egypt was unreliable (v.6); that Hezekiah had, so the Assyrian alleged, insulted the Lord by closing his shrines apart from the Jerusalem temple (v.7); that Judah was unskilled in the use of horses in warfare (vv.8–9); that the Lord had himself sent the Assyrians against Jerusalem (v.10); that Hezekiah's leadership could not be trusted (vv.14–15, 18); that they would be treated well if they surrendered (vv.16–17); and that all other threatened cities had failed to withstand the Assyrian might (vv.18–20). Satan himself could hardly produce a better masterpiece of verbal cajolery.

The grandiose designation of the field commander's master contrasts sharply with the absence even of the word "king" in his own reference to Judah's monarch (v.4). The tone of the speech is therefore insolent from the first, and the opening question shows that it is essentially an attempt to undermine any confidence the people might have. The words "strategy and military strength" (v.5) translate *'ēṣāh ûg ᵉḇûrāh*, rendered "counsel and power" in 11:2. In a sense Hezekiah was the contemporary custodian of the messianic promises, as the dynastic expression "house of David" in 7:13 reminds us. The words of the field commander relayed to Hezekiah may even have encouraged him to trust in the God whose messianic promises were an implicit assurance that his line would continue.

Unknown, no doubt, to the field commander, his words in v.6 tallied exactly with what Isaiah had been saying about the futility of trusting in Egypt (30:3–7; 31:3). His use of a vivid illustration too may have reminded them of the prophet's words, for he so often used analogy to appeal to the mind through the inner eye. No doubt the Assyrians were well aware of Hezekiah's religious reformation (2 Kings 18:3–7). Unlike 2 Kings 18:22, v.7 uses the second person singular, which may represent a purer text; for scribal change from singular to plural is more likely than vice versa, in view of the fact that the field commander refers to Hezekiah here as if he is not addressing him. In fact, of course, the speech, though ostensibly intended for Hezekiah, was so phrased that those who were to relay it to him would ponder its import. The theological misunderstanding shown by the field commander at this point argues for the authenticity of the speech, which many critics have dubbed "a free creation by the author of the narrative" (Clements, *Isaiah 1–39*, in loc.).

8–10 The field commander's offer was sarcastic (v.8). Judah was painfully weak in cavalry and looked to the Egyptian army to supply this lack (v.9; cf. 31:1, 3). He did not at this stage attack the Lord's ability to save his people. That is reserved for later on (v.18–20). He did however imply the anger of the Lord against his people. Verse

10, like v.6, connects with Isaiah's own message; for he constantly taught that the Assyrian armies, wicked as they were, were accomplishing God's purposes of judgment (cf. esp. 10:5–11). Did the field commander actually know the prophecies of Isaiah along this line? Probably not. Rather his assertion seems to be based on the misunderstanding reflected in the words of v.7.

11–12 Aramaic, ultimately to become the common language of Palestine, was at this time the lingua franca of the Fertile Crescent, used normally in diplomatic exchanges, but unintelligible to the mass of the people. The comment by Hezekiah's officials (v.11) perhaps suggests that any confidence they themselves had left was fast ebbing away as a result of this speech (cf. v.22), and they feared its effect on the people. The truculent vulgarity of the field commander's reply again argues for the authenticity of his speech.

13–15 Far from changing the language of his speech, the field commander raised his voice to enable the wider audience to hear more clearly (v.13). He gave at this stage no arguments against faith in the Lord's power to deliver his city (vv.14–15). The field commander had not yet moved from asserting God's unwillingness (v.7, 10) to a contemptuous rejection of his ability (vv.18–20).

16–17 The appeal in v.16 may indicate that there were many from the surrounding villages who had taken refuge within Jerusalem at this time, though the description given here may be a conventional one for family self-sufficiency. The frankness of v.17 is not, at first, easy to understand. The threat of exile was hardly likely to prove an extra inducement to his hearers. A little imagination may supply the answer. The people were actually at the city walls at this time. In the foreground was the Assyrian detachment, including the arrogant speaker himself. Behind them, however, the people could see the devastation these same Assyrians had wrought (cf., e.g., 1:7–9). Where were the vines and fig trees this man was speaking of? They were no more. Perhaps he saw the direction of their eyes and told them the truth for the small element of promise it contained. He would know, of course, that the Assyrian deportation policy was well-known.

18–20 There can be little doubt that this field commander had studied the psychological effects of rhetoric. The reference to exile in v.17 would make the people think about Samaria and its fate twenty years before. Very well, he would exploit this. He gave a list of some of the main places conquered by Assyria, concluding with Samaria (v.19). Each of these had its distinctive gods, but all had proved ineffective against the might of Assyria. Isaiah was himself to declare the gods of paganism—even of Babylonian paganism (46:1–2)—quite ineffective. It would be interesting to know what the field commander understood Samaria's religion to be. Had he realized that, officially at least, Yahweh was the God of Samaria too, he would surely have used this as his crowning argument. This suggests therefore that the Yahwism of the northern kingdom had become so submerged during the final period of its apostate existence that it was no longer recognizable, even by a foe, as the same religion as that practiced by Hezekiah.

The field commander concluded his speech (v.24) with what must have seemed to him to be his punch line. In actual fact, a frontal attack like this on such faith as they had may well have roused his hearers to a greater trust. The Lord had such a wonderful record of delivering his people, going right back to Egypt, that this man was in fact beginning now to tread on thin ice.

21–22 The silence on the wall had apparently been broken only by the request of v.11 (cf. Eccl 3:7).

37:1–4 The attitude of Hezekiah in this crisis is spiritually exemplary. He presented a great contrast with both Ahaz (cf. ch. 7) and his own former attitude (2 Kings 18:14–16). The account in 2 Kings places the visit of the field commander after Hezekiah's first payment of tribute to the king of Assyria at Lachish. Many critics have seen the two as different and irreconcilable accounts of the same event, but this is surely unnecessary. That the king of Assyria should demand tribute and then absolute surrender is not without historical parallel, nor is the change in Hezekiah's attitude inconceivable. Many a believer has been led by the grace of God from conduct inconsistent with his faith to a more confident trust in his God.

Hezekiah went into God's temple (v.1) and sent for God's servant, the prophet (v.2). Hezekiah probably hoped for a reassuring word from the Lord as well as a promise that the prophet would pray. Commenting on v.3, Young (*Book of Isaiah*, in loc.) says, "Whereas on the part of many the day may have been one of distress because of the presence of the Assyrians, for Hezekiah the distress was probably deeper. He saw that the real calamity lay not so much in the presence of a physical enemy as in the displeasure of the Lord that now was being visited upon the nation."

The reference to childbirth (v.3) was probably proverbial. The words "it may be" (v.4) do not betoken lack of faith but rather a realization on the king's part that the people, through their sins, had forfeited any right to expect divine deliverance. Their only hope was in his unmerited favor. Of course, in one sense God would hear the words of the field commander, for he hears everything; but the king was using the verb in that pregnant sense (e.g., cf. Deut 18:19) that implies that action will be taken as a result of what has been heard. There is a sense of sin implicit also in his reference to Yahweh as "the LORD your God," for Isaiah had shown a faithfulness that rebuked both people and king. On the other hand, "to ridicule the living God" and "the remnant" are expressions of hope in God, because of his nature and his purpose for the remnant of his people, so often expressed through Isaiah himself (e.g., 10:20–27).

5–7 Isaiah had once before counseled a king not to be afraid (7:4), but Ahaz had proved unresponsive to the reassuring word of God. The expression "the underlings" (v.6, lit., "the young men") could be an insulting reference to the field commander and the other high officers who had formed the Assyrian delegation. It seems more likely, however—for God's truth does not need to use descriptions that are not really true—that the field commander's words were not the only insults from the Assyrians outside the walls to Judah's God that had assaulted the ears of the inhabitants of Jerusalem.

The NIV's "Listen!" (v.7) treats the Hebrew *hinₑnî* (lit., "Look") as a purely formal command to attend. True, it occurs frequently; but, especially in such a strongly imaginative writer as Isaiah, we would expect that he intended his hearers to visualize what he declared. In an earlier oracle Isaiah had attributed a spirit of dizziness to the Lord (see comment at 19:14). The reference to "a certain report" is often

taken to apply to the report about Tirhakah (v.9). This in fact did not send Sennacherib back to Assyria but rather gave him greater concern to reduce Hezekiah to
submission.

Is v.7 quite irreconcilable with v.36, as so many critics suggest? In fact v.37
records two events, the withdrawal of the threat to Jerusalem and the return to
Nineveh. It is not difficult to imagine that the first was caused by the miracle
recorded in v.36 and the second by a report of trouble elsewhere, perhaps in Babylon. What is more difficult to conceive is that a redactor would place the material
together (see general introduction to chs. 36–37) if it was evident to him that the
accounts could not be reconciled. For the manner of Sennacherib's death, compare
v.38.

8 This detail, which appears to have no relevance to the main message of these two
chapters, is therefore an incidental testimony to the concern for truth of fact that
motivated the author.

9–13 The report of the approach of an Egyptian army gave greater urgency to the
bid to gain Jerusalem (v.9). No military leader welcomes a war on two fronts, even
if his forces are vastly superior to those of both enemies added together. The message—sent by letter as v.14 makes clear—repeats much that the field commander
had said (cf. 36:13–20), except that he attributes deception now to the Lord rather
than to Hezekiah himself (v.10). This is truly devilish, for the first satanic attack on
humanity impugned the veracity of God (Gen 3:1–5). The reader of the NIV gets a
shock at first when he sees the God of Hezekiah designated as "god" (contrast the
RSV), till he recalls that the words come from a pagan and represent his valuation of
the God of Israel. Sennacherib's reference to his forefathers (vv.11–12) shows his
pride in being a member of an all-conquering dynasty. The list of names is longer,
and therefore even more impressive, than that given in 36:19.

14–20 Some critics make much of the Deuteronomic character of this prayer, as if
this means it must have been created by the author—viz., the author of the parallel
passage in 2 Kings (see general introduction to chs. 36–39). But this is to forget that
the kings were given express instructions to study Deuteronomy (cf. Deut 17:14–
20). Hezekiah prayed in similar fashion to the prayer of the early church when Peter
and John had been threatened by the authorities (Acts 4, esp. v.24). His address to
God is theological in the best sense. As "LORD Almighty" (v.16, lit., "Yahweh of
hosts"; see comment at 1:9), he has all power; and, as the sovereign Creator, the
Assyrians are subject to that power. The word "alone" (v.20) is a critical glance at
their paganism. On the other hand, as God of Israel, manifesting his presence
between the cherubim in that very temple, he has a special relationship with his
people and therefore a concern to protect them from their enemies.

True prayer faces facts but interprets them theologically, and this is what Hezekiah did in vv.18–19. Isaiah was often to make the same point about idols in later
oracles (e.g., 44:9–20). The act of salvation he prayed for was to be a revelation of
God to all the kingdoms—acknowledging as they did other gods—that Yahweh
alone was God. This emphasis on the sole deity of the God of Israel also reminds us
of later oracles (e.g., 44:6–8).

21–25 Once more (cf. 36:5–7) God spoke to Hezekiah through Isaiah, but this time

in an oracle that might have taken its place among those against the nations recorded in chapters 13–23 had there not been a special purpose in placing it in its historical context here. Verses 21–22 clearly imply that, even though it was God's purpose
to deliver his people, it was important that Hezekiah prayed. God acts according to
an eternal purpose but in answer to those prayers he has led his people to offer.

The oracle that runs from v.22 to v.29 has been superbly translated in the NIV,
with a feeling not only for the meaning but for the sound of words and also for poetic
form. It is a taunt song with the characteristic "limping" rhythm in Hebrew. In v.22
Jerusalem is represented as a young girl rebuffing with contempt the unwelcome
advances of a churl. Perhaps there is a suggestion that she is betrothed to the Holy
One of Israel, for Isaiah later uses the figure of marriage and divorce in relation to
Israel (50:1). This title for God is, of course, characteristic of Isaiah's prophecies (see
Introduction, p. 12). Characteristic of him too is the emphasis on pride (v.23),
especially the quotation of arrogant words by a foreign monarch (cf. 10:12–14; 14:4,
13–15). In fact, the annals of Sennacherib—in which he records his victories in the
lands west of Assyria—are dominated by the occurrences of the first person singular.
It looks as though the course of his boasting follows that of his conquering marches.
The emphasis here is on the king's ability to overcome any natural obstacle that lay
in his path (v.24). The mountainous, tree-covered terrain of Lebanon could not hold
him back, neither could the waterless lands of southern Palestine and Sinai (v.25).
The streams of the Nile Delta were equally powerless to stop him, for he had but to
tread on them. This final claim, of course, went beyond the facts but was perhaps
made in anticipation of a great victory over Tirhakah (cf. v.9).

26–29 The question "Have you not heard?" (v.26) anticipates the great rhetorical
questions of 40:21, 28 and, as there, draws attention to Israel's God. All the great
conquests of the Assyrians are, in fact, to be ascribed to God, whose instruments
they were. So many of the oracles in the book up to this point have spoken of
judgment on the nations of the Fertile Crescent, including Israel and Judah; and a
great many of them were in fact executed through Assyria. Everything has been
, preordained, and Assyria can boast of nothing. The descriptive words of vv.26a–27
might almost have come from the lips of the Assyrian himself. That they come
instead from God shows that they are true, for without doubt the conquests of this
nation were utterly devastating. There was a ferocity and ruthlessness about them
that the eastern Mediterranean had never seen before, and which has probably not
been surpassed since, at least on the grand scale. The thought of v.27 reappears in
40:24, though with express reference to human agency.

God not only knows all there is to know about his own people (Ps 139) but also
about the Assyrians, and Isaiah expressed this in language that had become standard
(v.28; Deut 28:6; Ps 121:8 et al.). The Assyrians often treated their prisoners like
animals, with the use of the rope and the nose-hook. God would do the same. For
the last line of v.29, compare vv.34, 37.

30–32 In most circumstances Scripture does not encourage us to ask for signs,
though there is an exception in 7:11; but the word is sometimes followed by the sign
given (e.g., in 1 Samuel 10:1–7), as here (v.30). The Assyrian occupation of Judah
had devastated its fields (1:7–8). It would take several years to fully recover. If the
oracle was given at the close of one season, that just about to start would probably
not be normal; for the people would have building as well as agricultural tasks to

perform (32:13–14). The prophecy is therefore consistent with the immediate departure of the Assyrians.

In characteristic fashion Isaiah moved from the literal to the figurative. The remnant (v.31) is pictured as a vine or fruit tree (cf. 27:6). This prophecy relates specifically of course to the deliverance from Sennacherib, its language of a remnant in Jerusalem (v.32) reflecting that of 1:9. God underlines this prophecy and the certainty of its fulfillment in a most impressive manner. The word and sign become a threefold cord when the great affirmation that ends this oracle is spoken. This puts this prophecy on a par with the great messianic oracle of chapter 9, which also closes in the same way (9:7). In fact, the two are linked, for it was of David's line—represented now by Hezekiah—that the Messiah would come and on David's throne—in threatened Jerusalem—that he would reign.

33–35 This brief, trenchant oracle puts the matter clearly and painfully. Far from entering Jerusalem, the Assyrian king would not even subject it to a normal siege (vv.33–34). Sennacherib himself said that he shut up Hezekiah in the city like a caged bird, which tallies well with the vivid descriptions of 1:8, but we should note that the reference to a siege in that earlier chapter is by way of analogy, not of literal statement, so that Sennacherib's further words about raising earthworks were either lies or relate to an earlier occasion. The phrase "for my sake" (v.35) shows that the Lord answers prayer (cf. v.20) and the phrase that follows it, that he keeps his promises (cf. 2 Samuel 7). This is most reassuring, for the word of God and prayer constitute the dual basis of the spiritual life.

36–37 The pace of the chapter undoubtedly quickens from v.33 onward, for a brief oracle is followed immediately by the swift, dramatic record of its fulfillment, The verb used here of the angel of the Lord (yēṣē’, "went out") is used of going forward to battle. The angel of the Lord is a divine figure, at once distinguished from God and yet identified with him. Herodotus, the Greek historian, recorded that one night Sennacherib's army camp was infested by mice (or rats) that destroyed the arrows and shield-thongs of the soldiers. He probably got this tradition from Egyptian sources, and it could well be a somewhat garbled version of the event recorded here. First Samuel 6:4 suggests that the rat, quite appropriately, symbolized plague, which could well have been the means used by the angel of the Lord. Libnah (v.8) might well have been on the way to Egypt; or, of course, the Assyrian might by now have moved further in Egypt's direction. The unexpected and shocking carnage seen by the living next morning is most vividly described in the four Hebrew words that conclude v.36. In a masterpiece of understatement, Young (*Book of Isaiah*, in loc.) comments on v.37, "This was no place for Sennacherib."

38 An interval of twenty years separates v.37 and v.38, but we get the impression that we are meant to understand Sennacherib's death as a further manifestation of divine judgment. His death at the hands of his own progeny is confirmed from Assyrian sources, though each of the two accounts adds something to the knowledge of it we could have obtained from one only. His death when at worship in a pagan shrine should be seen as further evidence of the main thesis of these two chapters, that the God of Israel is the living and true God while all other deities are powerless.

Notes

1 Young (*Book of Isaiah*, 2:540–42) outlines and discusses the main solutions to the problem of Hezekiah's ascension date. The simplest solution is to substitute "twenty-fourth" for "fourteenth" in this verse and its counterpart, 2 Kings 18:13. Conjectural emendation should be adopted only with great caution, but in this case it seems warranted. This was a simple slip for a scribe to make, as Young demonstrates, especially since in the ancient-pointed script the two words would have been even closer in appearance than in the later form. On this see also Gleason L. Archer, *Encyclopedia of Bible Difficulties* (Grand Rapids: Zondervan, 1982), p. 211.

3 For Eliakim and Shebna, see 22:15, 20. Eliakim now occupies Shebna's former office, with the latter reduced to the role of secretary. Joah's name appears nowhere else. The exact nature of each of the three offices is uncertain, but much can be adduced from Egyptian parallels. The first appears to have been a vizier, governing the country in the name of the king. The second was next in line and dealt with the king's personal and state correspondence. The third was the monarch's official spokesman. See R. de Vaux, *Ancient Israel: Its Life and Institutions* (London: Darton, Longman and Todd, 1961), pp. 129–32.

19 For Hamath and Arpad here and in v.13, see the note at 10:9. Sepharvaim could possibly be identical with Sibraim, which Ezek 47:16 locates in Syria, but this is uncertain.

37:9 Tirhakah was not king of Egypt for over a decade from this event. He may have been in charge of its army and have been given this title proleptically by Isaiah or his disciples before the book reached its final form. (cf. K.A. Kitchen, *The Third Intermediate Period in Egypt* [1100–650 B.C.] [Warminster: Aris and Phillips, 1973], pp. 154–72, 387–93; and ZPEB, 5:754–55).

For Cush, see comment at 18:1.

For the MT's וַיִּשְׁמַע (*wayyišma'*, "to learn"), the LXX here and in 2 Kings 19:9 assumed וַיָּשֹׁב (*wayyāšōb*, "and he turned back"). Either is possible, and it is better in such a case to retain the MT.

12 Gozan (cf. 2 Kings 17:6; 18:11) was on the Chaboras, a northern tributary of the Euphrates, east of Haran (Gen 11:31; 12:5 et al.), which itself was on the Belikh, another tributary. Rezeph is probably modern Rusafe, twenty miles south of Haran. Eden, not identical with Eden in early Genesis, lies north and south of the middle Euphrates. Tel Assar may be its capital, Tel Barsip.

13 Hena and Ivvah (cf. 2 Kings 18:34; 19:13) cannot be identified. See note at 36:19 for Sepharvaim and at 10:9 for Hamath and Arpad.

20 The NIV follows 1QIsa and 2 Kings 19:19, probably correctly, in reading "you alone, O LORD, are God" instead of "you alone are the LORD" as in the MT.

25 Once again, as in v.20, the NIV follows 1QIsa and the 2 Kings parallel instead of the MT (which does not have "in foreign lands"). The textual agreement of 1QIsa and 2 Kings must be reckoned strong.

27 Here the 1QIsa and the 2 Kings reading followed in the NIV is supported by some MT and LXX MSS.

38 The god Nisroch is unknown. Young (*Book of Isaiah*, n. in loc.) sees the name as a possibly intentional corruption of Marduk.

---

2. Hezekiah's Illness

38:1–22

¹In those days Hezekiah became ill and was at the point of death. The prophet Isaiah son of Amoz went to him and said, "This is what the LORD says: Put your house in order, because you are going to die; you will not recover."

²Hezekiah turned his face to the wall and prayed to the LORD, ³"Remember, O LORD, how I have walked before you faithfully and with wholehearted devotion and have done what is good in your eyes." And Hezekiah wept bitterly.

⁴Then the word of the LORD came to Isaiah: ⁵"Go and tell Hezekiah, 'This is what the LORD, the God of your father David, says: I have heard your prayer and seen your tears; I will add fifteen years to your life. ⁶And I will deliver you and this city from the hand of the king of Assyria. I will defend this city.

⁷" 'This is the LORD's sign to you that the LORD will do what he has promised: ⁸I will make the shadow cast by the sun go back the ten steps it has gone down on the stairway of Ahaz.' " So the sunlight went back the ten steps it had gone down.

⁹A writing of Hezekiah king of Judah after his illness and recovery:

¹⁰I said, "In the prime of my life
    must I go through the gates of death
    and be robbed of the rest of my years?"
¹¹I said, "I will not again see the LORD,
    the LORD, in the land of the living;
no longer will I look on mankind,
    or be with those who now dwell in this world.
¹²Like a shepherd's tent my house
    has been pulled down and taken from me.
Like a weaver I have rolled up my life,
    and he has cut me off from the loom;
    day and night you made an end of me.
¹³I waited patiently till dawn,
    but like a lion he broke all my bones;
    day and night you made an end of me.
¹⁴I cried like a swift or thrush,
    I moaned like a mourning dove.
My eyes grew weak as I looked to the heavens.
    I am troubled; O Lord, come to my aid!"

¹⁵But what can I say?
    He has spoken to me, and he himself has done this.
I will walk humbly all my years
    because of this anguish of my soul.
¹⁶Lord, by such things men live;
    and my spirit finds life in them too.
You restored me to health
    and let me live.
¹⁷Surely it was for my benefit
    that I suffered such anguish
In your love you kept me
    from the pit of destruction;
you have put all my sins
    behind your back.
¹⁸For the grave cannot praise you,
    death cannot sing your praise;
those who go down to the pit
    cannot hope for your faithfulness.
¹⁹The living, the living—they praise you,
    as I am doing today;
fathers tell their children
    about your faithfulness.

²⁰The LORD will save me,
    and we will sing with stringed instruments
all the days of our lives
    in the temple of the LORD.

²¹Then Isaiah said, "Prepare a poultice of figs and apply it to the boil, and he will recover."
²²Hezekiah had asked, "What will be the sign that I will go up to the temple of the LORD?"

1 The phrase "in those days" employs different words but is similar in meaning to the phrase "at that time," which opens the next chapter. In fact, all these events probably occurred within about two years (see note at v.3). This means then that the time reference in this verse is to be taken very generally. The phrases also indicate a spiritual link between chapters 38 and 39, which will be explored in the exposition to follow. The nature of Hezekiah's illness is not mentioned; neither is it stated that it is punishment for sin. God's command suggests that Hezekiah had a duty to his family and kingdom to arrange their future administration.

Young (*Book of Isaiah,* in loc.) quotes Vitringa, who says, "According to natural causes he (Hezekiah) would have to die, unless with his aid God should intervene beyond the ordinary; God, however, had decided not to intervene, unless at the supplication of the king and the trials of his faith and hope. Moreover, in cases of this kind (Gen 20:3) the condition is not expressed, in order that God may call it forth as voluntary."

2–3 Hezekiah's prayer (v.2) may have been a direct result of putting his house in order, or at least this may have intensified it; for, as a comparison of v.5 with 2 Kings 21:1 shows, he would have been without heir if he had died within three years. Did he turn to the wall to sulk, as Ahab would have done (1 Kings 21:4), or was it to shut out the faces of others while he prayed? Probably the latter. Second Kings 18:5–6 not only confirms Hezekiah's statements about himself (v.3) but shows that his manner of life was grounded in faith in God. It is to be viewed more as pleading implicitly promises like Deuteronomy 7:12–15 than as reliance on his own merits.

4–6 God's description of himself as "the God of your father David" (v.5) itself implies that he is keeping faith with his word, especially, of course, his promises to David in 2 Samuel 7. God is even more concerned about the continuance of David's dynasty than Hezekiah is (see note below on the fifteen added years). Comparison of v.6 and 37:20 suggests that the king's prayer there was based on his word here as well as on the oracle given in 36:6–7.

7–8 Here is another sign of messianic significance (v.7; cf. 7:10–17), for Hezekiah's dynasty was the line of the Messiah. This is given in support of the word (cf. 37:30–32 and comment there). The account in 2 Kings 20 is somewhat longer at this point. The sun had been about to set on the life of Hezekiah but now it would return somewhat, prolonging the day (v.8). Attempts to explain this scientifically or to relate it to some calendrical adjustment—perhaps in conjunction with Joshua's long day (Josh 10)—have not carried full conviction with students of science or chronology. It is best to admit that we do not yet know the explanation but to accept the testimony of the word of God to the fact that a miracle took place.

9–14 The parallel account in 2 Kings does not include this psalm. Verses 10–14 are retrospective, the king recalling his thoughts during his illness (v.9) by the device of self-quotation. A backward glance to our predicament before a divine intervention can be a great stimulus to praise. Verse 10 assumes that a man could normally look forward to a certain probable life span. The reference to gates conveys an image of Sheol (so mg.; see note at 14:15) as a city of the dead. To see God (v.11) probably refers to appearing in his presence in the temple (cf., e.g., 1:12; Ps 42:2; 63:2). The king shows a right sense of priorities when he places this before the continuance of human fellowship. After the tent illustration, he alludes to the weaver rolling up and cutting a finished length of cloth from his loom (v.12). As Clements (*Isaiah 1–39*, in loc.) says, "The images are of objects which suddenly disappear from their expected place." The recurrent statement in vv.12–13 (*mîyôm ʿ aḏ-laylāh*, lit., "from day to night") probably conveys the same idea of suddenness—in the morning perfect health, in the evening, death. Verse 13 seems to refer to a night spent in prayer only to be ended in the morning when God suddenly falls on Hezekiah like a lion.

Here is an almost Job-like appeal to God against God (v.14). The varied cries of Palestine's birds express the varied nature of Hezekiah's many cries to God, now quiet, now shrill, now mournful. The reference to Hezekiah's eyes conveys a picture of concentrated appeal to God and to him alone.

15–20 At this point the tone of the psalm changes dramatically (cf. Ps 22:21–22). The question that opens v.15 implies that the king feels no words of his can do justice to his sense of gratitude to God for his great deliverance. In God word and deed always perfectly correspond. The king has learned humility from this experience, for through it he has come to recognize that another controls the course of his life and the day of his death. The translation difficulties in this passage and especially in v.16 will be noted above. The words "by such things men live" probably refer to the words and deeds of God mentioned in the previous verse. Genesis 1–2 are the best commentary on them. God the Creator is also God the Healer. We may perhaps see the "benefit" of v.17 as his new understanding of God's gracious, forgiving love, expressed in his deliverance from death.

Those commentators, like Young (*Book of Isaiah*, in loc.), who interpret v.18 in terms of Hezekiah's sense of forgiveness of sins are surely right. In other words, the statements he made are to be understood, not as absolute affirmations about the state of man after death—as if, Sadducee-like, Hezekiah believed that fellowship with God could not surmount death. The point is rather that sin merits death. This very thought may have been suggested in fact by his oblique reference to the creation of man, for after that creation came sin and death (Gen 3). The deeper significance of death cries out for the forgiveness of sin, which Hezekiah has himself now experienced. His restoration to health has this as its crowning blessing: he can give thanks to God (v.19). Verse 19b, rendered literally, says, "Father tells children about your faithfulness." If he is speaking in anticipation about his literal children rather than Israel as the children of God, this strengthens the view expressed above (see comment at vv.2–3), that part of his concern lay in his lack of progeny at that time (see 53:10; cf. also Ps 22:30–31).

Verse 20 reminds us that Hezekiah encouraged the singing of the songs of David and Asaph in the temple worship (2 Chron 29:25–30). The NT too shows the glad awareness of salvation being joyfully expressed in song (Rev 5:9–10).

21–22 These verses occur in 2 Kings 20 immediately after the promise that the city would be delivered from the king of Assyria. Of course, 2 Kings does not contain Hezekiah's psalm; so it would be most natural if the writer, dependent on the Book of Isaiah for the facts, inserted these verses in his narrative at that point. Most critics assume that the verses here have become dislocated from their correct position earlier in the chapter. Young (*Book of Isaiah*, in loc.), following J.A. Alexander (in loc.), vigorously contests this. The words of Isaiah and Hezekiah may have been recorded here to satisfy the reader's natural queries about the means of healing and the reason for the sign. Hezekiah is not criticized for asking for a sign. After all, as several commentators point out, Isaiah's two prophecies about him in v.1 and v.5 may have puzzled him by their contradictoriness. He sought not so much confirmation as clarification.

Notes

5 If Hezekiah died in 686 B.C. (cf. ZPEB, 3:149–52), this incident must be dated about 703–701. The former is the probable date of the embassy of Merodach-Baladan and the latter the date of Sennacherib's threat to Jerusalem.

8 It is often assumed that the Hebrew מַעֲלוֹת (*ma'alôt*, "steps") refers here to a sundial in the palace courtyard. There is no other instance of its use in this sense, however, and it probably simply refers to a series of steps and to the play of the shadow of the sun on them.

11 The NIV follows the MT with its repeated יָהּ יָהּ (*Yāh, Yāh*, "the LORD, the LORD"), but the LXX and some Hebrew MSS have a single Yahweh, which could be correct.

The MT reads חָדֵל (*hādel*, "cessation"), which the NIV emends, with most scholars, to חֶלֶד (*heled*, "world"), assuming a simple scribal error.

14 Two of the birds can be identified with fair certainty, but the עָגוּר (*'āgûr*, "thrush") presents problems. It could also be a crane.

15 This contains problems of both translation and interpretation. It could represent the conclusion of Hezekiah's lament, with God's speech and action related to Hezekiah's sickness rather than his cure. The LXX assumes a somewhat different Hebrew text, only part of which corresponds with 1QIsa. The NIV has made good sense of the MT, which should probably be retained.

16 Once again the LXX presupposes textual differences. Young (*Book of Isaiah*, in loc.) gives a literal translation of the MT as follows: "Lord, upon them they live, and as to everything in them is the life of my spirit, and thou wilt recover me and make me live." It can be seen that the NIV makes a brave attempt to render this in good English.

21 Evidence from Ras Shamra shows that figs were used in healing (cf. C.H. Gordon, *Ugaritic Literature* [Rome: Pontifical Biblical Institute, 1949], p. 129). Like the NT use of oil (e.g., James 5:14), the use of means was not reckoned incompatible with divine healing.

3. Envoys From and Exile to Babylonia

39:1–8

¹At that time Merodach-Baladan son of Baladan king of Babylon sent Hezekiah letters and a gift, because he had heard of his illness and recovery. ²Hezekiah received the envoys gladly and showed them what was in his storehouses—the silver, the gold, the spices, the fine oil, his entire armory and everything found among his treasures. There was nothing in his palace or in all his kingdom that Hezekiah did not show them.

³Then Isaiah the prophet went to King Hezekiah and asked, "What did those men say, and where did they come from?"

"From a distant land," Hezekiah replied. "They came to me from Babylon."

⁴The prophet asked, "What did they see in your palace?"

"They saw everything in my palace," Hezekiah said. "There is nothing among my treasures that I did not show them."

⁵Then Isaiah said to Hezekiah, "Hear the word of the LORD Almighty: ⁶The time will surely come when everything in your palace, and all that your fathers have stored up until this day, will be carried off to Babylon. Nothing will be left, says the LORD. ⁷And some of your descendants, your own flesh and blood who will be born to you, will be taken away, and they will become eunuchs in the palace of the king of Babylon."

⁸"The word of the LORD you have spoken is good," Hezekiah replied. For he thought, "There will be peace and security in my lifetime."

This brief chapter is of great importance, because it serves, in the overall plan of the book, to set the scene for the chapters that follow. These chapters—enigmatic to the ordinary reader prior to the reference to Babylon in chapter 43 and perhaps even before the dramatic mention of Cyrus at the close of chapter 44—become clear as to their setting when they are seen to presuppose the fulfillment of the prophecy given in this chapter, which therefore fulfills an indispensable function.

This chapter, perhaps more than any other in the book, tends to reveal the basic presuppositions of commentators. Many place it early in the sixth century and on the sole ground that it purports to predict events that took place then. This then raises the question, Does supernatural prediction really occur? and behind this the even deeper question, What is God's relationship to his creation and to man?

1–2 Merodach-Baladan, known to secular history as Marduk-aplu-idinna, an Aramean, was king of Babylon 721–709 B.C. and again for a brief spell of nine months in 703 B.C. (see ZPEB, 4:191–92). Babylon had known years of greatness in the past and, though now eclipsed by Assyria, was to be great again. Merodach-Baladan's brief success in throwing off the Assyrian yoke was an earnest of this. There was, of course, a political motive for sending his deputation to Hezekiah (v.1). It could have taken place during the closing years of his first period of rule; but, in view of the time references in 38:1 and this verse, it seems likely that it was in 703, only two years before the deliverance of Jerusalem from Sennacherib.

The envoys were taken on a grand tour of the palace and the kingdom (v.2). Hezekiah's glad reception of them may have been due to a desire to be involved in concerted action against Assyria, and the display of his wealth would show he had something to offer as a potential ally.

3–4 Isaiah's inquiry (v.3) may have been a preliminary to the coming of a message from God to him, so that he would himself understand its significance. It is more likely though that its purpose was to emphasize to the king the reason for the prophecy. His conduct had been unbelieving, and there may have been pride in it also. These were the two sins most often condemned by the prophet.

5–7 "The LORD Almighty," the title of God used by Isaiah in v.5 (see comment at 1:24), lays emphasis on the infinite resources used by the Lord in his acts of power. Hezekiah's own resources may have seemed great to him, but those of the Lord were far greater; and they would be used in judgment against Hezekiah's people through the Babylonians. The reference to his fathers (v.6) was perhaps a rebuke to his lack of a sense of stewardship. Through his folly, what others had gathered would be lost. His conduct had been irresponsible in terms of both his ancestors and his descendants (v.7), for the latter would suffer in the judgment to come. There is probably another reason for the reference to his fathers and his descendants. The OT recognizes solidarity in sin and the falling of judgment when the iniquity of a group has come to full expression (Gen 15:16; Dan 8:23; cf. Matt 23:32; 1 Thess 2:16). It was not till Jeremiah, in the days of Babylonia's new empire, that Judah's dynasty was to take its history of sin beyond the point of no return.

Yet even in the midst of this declaration of a coming judgment, there may have been a hint of a continuing purpose of grace, as so often in the stern messages of Isaiah to Judah. Almost certainly Hezekiah was at this time without male progeny (see comment at 38:2–3). Also the phrase "some of your descendants" would leave room for hope.

8 Hezekiah's acknowledgment that God's word was good probably includes a recognition that the judgment was appropriate—because deserved—and that it was not altogether unmixed with grace. Are we then to condemn his final statement as selfish and unfeeling? Probably not. It is more likely to be a thankful recognition that God had not dealt with him personally to the measure of his desert.

VII. The Sole Sovereignty and Sure Promises of the Lord (40:1–48:22)

To move from chapter 39 to chapter 40 is to enter a part of the book (chs. 40–66) that has produced more scholarly literature than any other part of the OT. The number of different views as to authorship, structure, and other related matters of introduction is bewildering; and the debate as to the nature of the Servant Songs (see comment at 42:1–4) and the identity of the servant shows no sign of abating. The Introduction should be consulted for extended discussion of these issues. The view taken here is that the whole book is the work of Isaiah of Jerusalem and that chapters 40–66 consist of oracles given to him by the Spirit of inspiration, thus enabling Isaiah to live in spirit in a future day so that he might be the vehicle of God's message to the people of that day.

Many scholars—whether or not they recognize the integrity of the book—have noted that chapters 40–48 have a certain unity of them. Kidner ("Isaiah," p. 611) has said:

> We emerge in 40:1 in a different world from Hezekiah's, immersed in the situation foretold in 39:5–8, which he was so thankful to escape. Nothing is said of the intervening century and a half; we wake, so to speak, on the far side of the disaster, impatient for the end of captivity. In chs. 40–48 liberation is in the air; there is the persistent promise of a new exodus, with God at its head; there is the approach of a conqueror, eventually disclosed as Cyrus, to break Babylon open; there is also a new theme unfolding, to reveal the glory of the call to be a servant and a light to the nations. All this is expressed with a soaring, exultant eloquence, in a style heard only fitfully hitherto (cf., e.g., 35:1–10; 37:26f.), but now sustained so as to give its distinctive tone to the remaining chapters of the book.

1. Good News for Jerusalem

40:1–11

¹Comfort, comfort my people,
    says your God.
²Speak tenderly to Jerusalem,
    and proclaim to her
that her hard service has been completed,
    that her sin has been paid for,
that she has received from the LORD's hand
    double for all her sins.

³A voice of one calling:
"In the desert prepare
    the way for the LORD;
make straight in the wilderness
    a highway for our God.
⁴Every valley shall be raised up,
    every mountain and hill made low;
the rough ground shall become level,
    the rugged places a plain.
⁵And the glory of the LORD will be revealed,
    and all mankind together will see it.
                For the mouth of the LORD has spoken."

⁶A voice says, "Cry out."
    And I said, "What shall I cry?"

"All men are like grass,
    and all their glory is like the flowers of the field.
⁷The grass withers and the flowers fall,
    because the breath of the LORD blows on them.
    Surely the people are grass.
⁸The grass withers and the flowers fall,
    but the word of our God stands forever."

⁹You who bring good tidings to Zion,
    go up on a high mountain.
You who bring good tidings to Jerusalem,
    lift up your voice with a shout,
lift it up, do not be afraid;
    say to the towns of Judah,
    "Here is your God!"
¹⁰See, the Sovereign LORD comes with power,
    and his arm rules for him.
See, his reward is with him,
    and his recompense accompanies him.
¹¹He tends his flock like a shepherd:
    He gathers the lambs in his arms
and carries them close to his heart;
    he gently leads those that have young.

This passage sets the mood for chapters 40–48. The prophet responds to the command of God to bring a message of comfort to his people.

1–2 The imperatives here are plural, possibly as addressing the prophets generally, though this passage shows us the response of Isaiah. Such a command must have been a great joy to hear, when the prophet had already been fulfilling such a discouraging commission as given in 6:9–13. Imperative or vocational repetition is a characteristic of emotional speech (cf., e.g., Gen 22:11; 2 Sam 18:33; Ps 22:1) and occurs frequently in Isaiah, especially in the chapters that follow (cf. also 29:1). The phrase "my people" (v.1) itself suggests either comfort or rebuke rather than a message of judgment. In close connection with "your God," as here, it is really a covenant term.

Jerusalem is addressed (v.2), for God's saving deeds in Babylon were to make possible a new Jerusalem that would emerge from the ashes of the old. The NIV's "hard service" takes *ṣābāʾ*, not in its usual military sense as "warfare," but as it is used in Job (e.g., Job 7:1). The hard service, of course, is the Babylonian exile. The proclamation of forgiveness, as Young (*Book of Isaiah*, in loc.) says, "is the first intimation of the truth to be more fully revealed in the fifty-third chapter." "Double" appears to be hyperbole used to impress on the people that the chastisement of the exile was really over.

3–5 Like other prophets, Isaiah was given visions (1:1), but he also heard words. An unidentified voice calls (v.3). John the Baptist, to whom the words are applied in the NT, was prepared to be such an unidentified voice (John 1:19–23). It is the ultimate origin and the content of the word of God that matters, not its channel. Isaiah 35:8–10 had spoken of a highway for the returning exiles, implying perhaps that it would traverse the desert (35:1). This is made clear now; and, because it represents God's purpose for his people, it is called his highway.

The verb (*pānnû* ("prepare")) introduces the idea of the removal of obstructions, which is spelled out further in v.4. The whole concept is, of course, figurative, declaring in dramatic fashion that the Lord will let nothing stand in the way of the exiles' return. Young (*Book of Isaiah*, in loc.) interprets it of the people's repentance rather than their journey home to Zion. No doubt coming back often has dual significance in Isaiah, combining the physical and the spiritual (see comment at 7:3), though the verb "to return" does not occur in our present image. John the Baptist's call to repentance does not settle the matter, for the NT fulfillment of an OT passage often moves the concept from the physical to the spiritual. It seems best to consider it physical here but with possible spiritual overtones.

Smart (in loc.) is surely right when he lays all the emphasis on God rather than the exiles. What is in prospect is an amazing new revelation of the glory of the Lord, not now for Israel only (as in her temple, for instance), but for all mankind (v.5; cf. 60:1–3). Isaiah's tendency to add some emphatic statement like "for the mouth of the LORD has spoken" (v.6; cf. 9:7; 37:32) anticipates Christ's "truly I say to you."

6–8 The prophet hears a voice again; and, in response to his request, this is followed by the message he is to give (v.6). Men who are self-sufficient do not respond eagerly to good news from God. The Epistle to the Romans expounds man's need before setting out in its fullness God's answer (cf. also 2 Cor 2:16; 3:4–6). The Exile itself must have made the people aware of their frailty. What unites all human enterprises is their transience. Flowers may look beautiful, but where will they be tomorrow? God is the one-enduring reality in a constantly changing world, and he has himself designed it so. Christ's assertion that the entire universe will prove less endurng than his words (Mark 13:31) may owe something to this passage. The following chapters lay great stress on the enduring word of God.

9–11 Although the reading in the NIV text of v.9 is possible, the marginal rendering

> O Zion, bringer of good tidings,
> go up on a high mountain.
> O Jerusalem, bringer of good tidings

seems much more likely, for the imperatives are feminine, appropriate with "the daughter of Zion" (1:8 et al.). It is Zion who first hears the good news of her God's return and is commanded to climb, like a herald, to some elevated place, to proclaim the news also to her satellite towns. So the NT Good News also spread from Jerusalem to all Judea before going out to all the earth (Acts 1:8).

From v.3 to v.8 the reader has anticipated the coming of the Lord; and he is now described and depicted, with the reiterated call to attention—"see" (v.10). There is a perfect balance of strength and tenderness here. "His arm" suggests Exodus power (Deut 4:34), very appropriate in relation to a return from exile, and due to be most wonderfully expounded later (see 53:1).

Some commentators take "his reward" and "his recompense" to relate to the fact that only God can be rewarded for what has happened, because he has done it, while others take the words to mean that he comes as the righteous judge. The former is possible; and we might expect the latter to find some confirmation in the context, but this seems lacking. Whybray (*Isaiah 40–66*, in loc.) may well be right when he says, "These words . . . refer to the spoils of victory; but in this case the spoils are the rescued exiles, who are in a sense God's 'captives'." All this power is employed with great tenderness on behalf of his people (v.11), leading them back from Babylon to the fold in Jerusalem. The NIV's "Sovereign LORD" (for Adonai Yahweh) in v.10 underscores the idea of a strong and tender Shepherd-King.

2. God the Incomparable

40:12–31

> ¹²Who has measured the waters in the hollow of his hand,
>   or with the breadth of his hand marked off the heavens?
> Who has held the dust of the earth in a basket,
>   or weighed the mountains on the scales
>   and the hills in a balance?
> ¹³Who has understood the mind of the LORD,
>   or instructed him as his counselor?
> ¹⁴Whom did the LORD consult to enlighten him,
>   and who taught him the right way?
> Who was it that taught him knowledge
>   or showed him the path of understanding?
> ¹⁵Surely the nations are like a drop in a bucket;
>   they are regarded as dust on the scales;
>   he weighs the islands as though they were fine dust.
> ¹⁶Lebanon is not sufficient for altar fires,
>   nor its animals enough for burnt offerings.
> ¹⁷Before him all the nations are as nothing;
>   they are regarded by him as worthless
>   and less than nothing.
>
> ¹⁸To whom, then, will you compare God?
>   What image will you compare him to?

¹⁹As for an idol, a craftsman casts it,
and a goldsmith overlays it with gold
and fashions silver chains for it.
²⁰A man too poor to present such an offering
selects wood that will not rot.
He looks for a skilled craftsman
to set up an idol that will not topple.

²¹Do you not know?
Have you not heard?
Has it not been told you from the beginning?
Have you not understood since the earth was founded?
²²He sits enthroned above the circle of the earth,
and its people are like grasshoppers.
He stretches out the heavens like a canopy,
and spreads them out like a tent to live in.
²³He brings princes to naught
and reduces the rulers of this world to nothing.
²⁴No sooner are they planted,
no sooner are they sown,
no sooner do they take root in the ground,
than he blows on them and they wither,
and a whirlwind sweeps them away like chaff.

²⁵"To whom will you compare me?
Or who is my equal?" says the Holy One.
²⁶Lift your eyes and look to the heavens:
Who created all these?
He who brings out the starry host one by one,
and calls them each by name.
Because of his great power and mighty strength,
not one of them is missing.

²⁷Why do you say, O Jacob,
and complain, O Israel,
"My way is hidden from the LORD;
my cause is disregarded by my God"?
²⁸Do you not know?
Have you not heard?
The LORD is the everlasting God,
the Creator of the ends of the earth.
He will not grow tired or weary,
and his understanding no one can fathom.

²⁹He gives strength to the weary
and increases the power of the weak.
³⁰Even youths grow tired and weary,
and young men stumble and fall;
³¹but those who hope in the LORD
will renew their strength.
They will soar on wings like eagles;
they will run and not grow weary,
they will walk and not be faint.

These verses might be taken as a development of the words of proclamation in v.9: "Here is your God!" They also expound more fully the description of an all-powerful yet tender Shepherd-King in vv.10–11, for the incomparable majesty of God set forth in vv.12–26 leads into an assurance that he will give strength to his frail people.

Old Testament form criticism identifies the material in this passage as a series of disputations, taking their form from the argument between two people in which there is some appeal to common ground. Here God reasons with his people on the basis, not of new disclosures about him, but of truths they were already familiar with. Certainly this passage is the *locus classicus* of the rhetorical argument in Scripture.

12–17 It is interesting to compare the mighty questions here with those God put to Job in Job 38:41. In both places God asserts his sole godhood. The use of the magnificent anthropomorphisms in v.12 is so natural after the picture of God as a shepherd (v.11). Such anthropomorphisms do not, as seems to have been thought during the intertestamental period, reduce God to man's level. They simply give vividness to the theological truth of his personality. These questions do not demean God. Rather they magnify him in the eyes of the hearer. R.N. Whybray, in his detailed monograph on vv.13–14 (*The Heavenly Counsellor in Isaiah XI. 13–14* [Cambridge: Cambridge University Press, 1971], p. 10), says, "It is clear that the hypothetical situation here envisaged, only to be denied, is one in which there exists some person or being who gave Yahweh the benefit of his wisdom and experience. This is emphasized by the piling up of verbs meaning 'to teach' with Yahweh as object."

In v.13 the LXX understood *rûaḥ*, (normally "spirit") to mean "mind," as it does in passages like 1 Chronicles 28:12 and Ezekiel 20:32, and as the NIV translates it here. Whybray (*Heavenly Counsellor,* pp. 10–13) argues that this is its probable meaning here. Against this, however, must be set the fact that this passage is about God's creative power, and Genesis 1:2 gives the Spirit a place in this work. We must remember that the Jews in Babylon were to be in the midst of an impressive polytheism. Soon the prophet will commence his attack on idolatry (v.18). Whybray's thesis is that this attack is already introduced here; for—unlike Marduk, the supreme Babylonian deity—the Lord, in his creative work (v.14), takes no advice from other gods, because there are none.

Near Eastern marketplace commerce would take no account of the minute water drop in the measuring bucket or a little dust on the scales when meat or fruit was weighed (v.15). This passage implies the consummate ease of Yahweh's control of history as well as of nature. He had given a sacrificial system but was not, like Babylonia's deities, tied to it; for the most impressive forest land known to the Near East was quite inadequate to furnish fuel or sacrificial animals for a worthy offering to him (v.16).

18–20 The reference to animal sacrifice—visible offerings made to an invisible God (v.18)—leads Isaiah to speak of the spectacular folly of idolatry. In a way much elaborated later (see esp. 44:12–20), he stresses the selection of the best materials and the finest human skills (v.19); but there is a touch of prophetic irony about the stated purpose of all this: "to set up an idol that will not topple" (v.20).

21–24 God is like a father here, gently yet firmly chiding his children for their failure to see the relevance to their situation of God's disclosure in history and nature of the fact that he is sovereign (v.21; cf. Matt 16:8–12). He is supreme over the earth and all its people; he utilizes the majestic heavens he has created to suggest, through their overarching form (v.22), that the universe is a home for him;

and he allows no man, no matter how great, to further his ambitions without limit (v.23). His absolute control over all human life is quite unchallenged. Verses 23–24 represent a great truth of course, not only about individual rulers, but also about world empires.

25–26 Verses 18–20 had contrasted God with the idols that were all too common in Babylonia. Now the same question introduces an implicit contrast with the astral deities that dominated Babylonia on religion (v.25). This passage is antimythological; for it asserts that—far from being deities in their own right—the heavenly bodies are simply the creatures of the one Creator-God, who is also Israel's Holy One. He orders their pattern, knows each in its distinctiveness and upholds them all in their being (v.26; cf. Col 1:17; Heb 1:3). All this had, of course, been revealed to God's people from early times (cf. v.21) in the opening chapters of Genesis.

27–31 The prophet's majestic view of God—stemming, at least in part, from the inaugural vision of chapter 6—is now brought to bear on the people's despondency. The name "Jacob" (v.27) occurs about forty times in Isaiah, about two-thirds of the occurrences being in chapters 40–66. It suggests the unworthiness of the chosen people but also—in this part of the prophecy—brings to mind the ancestor's experience in the story of his descendants (cf. Mal 3:6); for Jacob too had been in exile in (northern) Mesopotamia as a result of his own folly. As God had said to Jacob (Gen 31:13), he was now telling his progeny—to return to the Land of Promise. The language used here suggests that the people were bringing God down to their own level, thinking him either forgetful (v.27) or tired—perhaps because their long history of folly seemed to be never-ending.

The closing verses assert that the God who upholds the stars (v.26) also supports his weary people (vv.29–30). Those who found the journey to Jerusalem from other parts of the land tiring were given strength for it by God (Ps 84:5, 7). The people in Babylon had to travel much farther but could exchange their little strength for his omnipotence. The verb used in v.31a suggests an exchange of strength. The threefold description forms a climax, not its opposite; for the exceptional flying and the occasional running do not require, as does the constant walking, an ever-flowing stream of grace.

Notes

12–31 Westermann (in loc.) brings out the fact that this passage is steeped in the language of the Psalms. Eaton, (p. 43) lists the following affinities: v.16 and Ps 50:8–13; vv.19–20 and Ps 115:4–8; v.22 and Pss 104:2 and 19:4; v.23 and Ps 33:10, 15–16; v.25 and Ps 89: 6–8; v.26 and Pss 147:4 and 8:4; v.27 and Ps 44:24; vv.29, 31 and Pss 33:16–17 and 103:5.

17 The MT's מֵאֶפֶס (*mēʾepes*) is often amended to כְּאֶפֶס (*keʾepes*) with 1QIsa and the LXX, so reading "like nothing" instead of "from nothing." Either is possible.

22 The reference to the circle of the earth is unique, but see the somewhat similar phrases of Job 22:14; Prov 8:27. The expression probably refers to the horizon.

23 Compare Num 13:33 for the reference to grasshoppers.

26 "He who brings out the starry host one by one, and calls them each by name," Whybray

(*Isaiah 40–66*, in loc.) says, "suggests a general marshalling his troops and giving them their orders; . . . none dares fail to be 'on parade'."

---

3. *God the Lord of History for His People*

41:1–29

> ¹"Be silent before me, you islands!
> Let the nations renew their strength!
> Let them come forward and speak;
> let us meet together at the place of judgment.
>
> ²"Who has stirred up one from the east,
> calling him in righteousness to his service?
> He hands nations over to him
> and subdues kings before him.
> He turns them to dust with his sword,
> to windblown chaff with his bow.
> ³He pursues them and moves on unscathed,
> by a path his feet have not traveled before.
> ⁴Who has done this and carried it through,
> calling forth the generations from the beginning?
> I, the LORD—with the first of them
> and with the last—I am he."
>
> ⁵The islands have seen it and fear;
> the ends of the earth tremble.
> They approach and come forward;
> ⁶   each helps the other
> and says to his brother, "Be strong!"
> ⁷The craftsman encourages the goldsmith,
> and he who smooths with the hammer
> spurs on him who strikes the anvil.
> He says of the welding, "It is good."
> He nails down the idol so it will not topple.
>
> ⁸"But you, O Israel, my servant,
> Jacob, whom I have chosen,
> you descendants of Abraham my friend,
> ⁹I took you from the ends of the earth,
> from its farthest corners I called you.
> I said, 'You are my servant';
> I have chosen you and have not rejected you.
> ¹⁰So do not fear, for I am with you;
> do not be dismayed, for I am your God.
> I will strengthen you and help you;
> I will uphold you with my righteous right hand.
>
> ¹¹"All who rage against you
> will surely be ashamed and disgraced;
> those who oppose you
> will be as nothing and perish.
> ¹²Though you search for your enemies,
> you will not find them.
> Those who wage war against you
> will be as nothing at all.
> ¹³For I am the LORD, your God,
> who takes hold of your right hand

and says to you, Do not fear;
   I will help you.
¹⁴Do not be afraid, O worm Jacob,
   O little Israel,
for I myself will help you," declares the LORD,
   your Redeemer, the Holy One of Israel.
¹⁵"See, I will make you into a threshing sledge.
   new and sharp, with many teeth.
You will thresh the mountains and crush them,
   and reduce the hills to chaff.
¹⁶You will winnow them, the wind will pick them up,
   and a gale will blow them away.
But you will rejoice in the LORD
   and glory in the Holy One of Israel.

¹⁷"The poor and needy search for water,
   but there is none;
   their tongues are parched with thirst.
But I the LORD will answer them;
   I, the God of Israel, will not forsake them.
¹⁸I will make rivers flow on barren heights,
   and springs within the valleys.
I will turn the desert into pools of water,
   and the parched ground into springs.
¹⁹I will put in the desert
   the cedar and the acacia, the myrtle and the olive.
I will set pines in the wasteland,
   the fir and the cypress together,
²⁰so that people may see and know,
   may consider and understand,
that the hand of the LORD has done this,
   that the Holy One of Israel has created it.

²¹"Present your case," says the LORD.
   "Set forth your arguments," says Jacob's King.
²²"Bring in your idols, to tell us
   what is going to happen.
Tell us what the former things were,
   so that we may consider them
   and know their final outcome.
²³Or declare to us the things to come,
   tell us what the future holds,
   so we may know that you are gods.
Do something, whether good or bad,
   so that we will be dismayed and filled with fear.
²⁴But you are less than nothing
   and your works are utterly worthless;
   he who chooses you is detestable.
²⁵"I have stirred up one from the north, and he comes—
   one from the rising sun who calls on my name.
He treads on rulers as if they were mortar,
   as if he were a potter treading the clay.
²⁶Who told of this from the beginning, so we could know,
   or beforehand, so we could say, 'He was right'?
No one told of this,
   no one foretold it,
   no one heard any words from you.
²⁷I was the first to tell Zion, 'Look, here they are!'
   I gave to Jerusalem a messenger of good tidings.

²⁸I look but there is no one—
 no one among them to give counsel,
 no one to give answer when I ask them.
²⁹See, they are all false!
 Their deeds amount to nothing;
 their images are but wind and confusion.

Smart (in loc.) opens his exposition of this chapter by saying, "The background against which to read ch. 41 is that which has been created for the reader by ch. 40. If we follow this principle, we permit the prophet himself to be the primary interpreter of his own thought, and instead of prejudging the historical situation, we let it emerge bit by bit as the chapters open out the one from the other." This is a wise comment, even though we differ somewhat from Smart on important exegetical points in this chapter.

1 It is customary for most commentators now to dub this the beginning of a trial-speech, in which—as in 1:2—the scene is a courtroom. We may accept this, of course, if we see it as a purely rhetorical device. In fact, in his dealings with men, God sustains a multiplicity of legal roles; for he is plaintiff, injured party, judge, law-giver, and creator, each role finding its place within his many-sided relationship with sinful men. In chapter 40, the prophet had spoken of God in the third person; here God himself speaks. This kind of oscillation often occurs in the chapters that follow.

Although in form this verse is an address to the nations, the message of the chapter is of course intended for Israel. The discomfiture of the nations and the demonstration that their gods are impotent is intended to encourage God's people to trust in him. The repetition of the phrase "renew their strength" (cf. 40:31) may well be ironic. Perhaps as the exiles renew their strength in the true God, so the nations are ironically exhorted to do the same—but in their man-made deities!

2-4 The Lord directs attention to himself as the true author of great historical events. But who is the mysterious "one from the east" (v.2)? The Talmud—followed by Calvin and, more recently, Kissane and Torrey—identifies this figure with Abraham. Some modern commentators (e.g., Smart) take him to be personified Israel, while others (e.g., Simon) interpret him messianically. It is interesting that a case can be made out for each, though each presents problems. The first two seek support in v.8; the third would provide an introduction to the Servant Songs. Most commentators however have taken this and v.25 to be references to Cyrus, who was to be dramatically named at the close of chapter 44. If, as we have argued in the Introduction (pp. 6–12), this prophecy comes from Isaiah of Jerusalem and not from an unknown prophet of the Exile, and if, as we shall argue (see comment at 44:24–28), the revelation of the name of Cyrus is a moment of great prophetic drama, then we should expect some material at an earlier stage to stimulate the expectations of the reader. The references here and in v.25 fulfill this function admirably, and the language of them is fully appropriate when applied to Cyrus. Abraham's victory over the kings of the east (Gen 14) was of course an earlier example of God's ability to raise up men on the stage of history to accomplish astounding victories, and the reference to him in v.8 may therefore be intentionally suggestive. Every historical conqueror raised up by God is, despite his many faults, a faint shadow of the great ultimate Victor, God's Messiah; and in him Israel is triumphant and her kingdom enlarged (9:2–7).

Cyrus, king of Persia, crossed the Tigris from the east and so entered the Babylonian Empire. He marched swiftly and victoriously against Croesus, king of Lydia, and took his capital, Sardis, in western Asia Minor, having already subdued the Medes in the north (cf. v.25). He could therefore be described as being both from the east and from the north. The references to dust and chaff remind us of 17:13; 29:5, and, in a more recent context, of 40:24. In fact, this reference to Cyrus is a particular example of the general principle stated in 40:23–24. The conquests of Cyrus took him into areas quite unfamiliar to men of his land. The past tenses of these verses should be interpreted as prophetic perfects, describing with vividness what is yet to be. The great conqueror does not hold the center of the prophetic stage for long, however, for he exists and is referred to only to exalt the name of the Lord. Verse 4 declares the absolute sovereignty of God over history—from its beginning, through all its generations, and to its end. No wonder he can predict and raise up Cyrus!

5–7 Places remote from Cyrus's all-conquering route get to hear of what he has done. These verses contain clear allusions to 40:18–20. In the cooperative effort of idol-making, the terrified peoples try to find strength (see comment at v.1). The atmosphere of panic in v.5 seems to disappear, for the pagans have found something akin to Dutch courage. The more gods, the more security—or so they think; but v.29 shows how vain is such trust, as do later passages even more powerfully.

8–10 In Cyrus's day the people of Israel would be in exile in Babylon, itself under threat and eventually to fall to Cyrus. The fear felt by the remote islands (v.5) would be even more natural in their hearts, but these verses are God's answer to his people's fears. Verses 8–9 form a most impressive introduction to the twin exhortations given in v.10, and these are in turn supported within that verse itself by further statements about God.

Verses 8–10 describe Israel in several encouraging ways. The name Israel suggests what God is determined to make of his people (Gen 32:28), while the name Jacob indicates that God loves them and has chosen them despite their demerit (see comment at 40:27). Taking them from the ends of the earth is hyperbole laying stress on the distance of Abraham's journey from Ur to Canaan, undertaken under God's watchful and caring eye. God chose the people for a purpose of service; and so, of course, they cannot perish without that purpose being fulfilled. These people are loved for the sake of beloved Abraham (cf. Deut 7:7–8), to whom God gave great promises (Gen 12:1–3; 17:1–8 et al.). The strength already promised (40:31) would be theirs. The threefold affirmation of strength comes to its consummation in a reference to the righteous right hand of God, a reminder possibly of the tender strength of the Shepherd-King in 40:9–11.

11–16 The four statements of vv.11–12 reiterate the same fact, the repetition being intended to reinforce the assurance of the fearful. The shame (v.11) of course is objective. Those who are put to shame sometimes do not feel it as they ought, because of moral insensitivity. The call to leave their fear—going out so powerfully in vv.8–10—comes yet again, with a reiteration of some of the earlier statements, but also with other encouragements to trust in their God. The assertion "I am the LORD, your God" (v.13) is perhaps a reminder of the impressive opening of the

Decalogue (Exod 20:2) and so is itself suggestive of a new Exodus. This is reinforced in v.14 by the use of *go'ēl* ("Redeemer"; cf. Exod 6:6; 15:13) and made even more emphatic by the phrase "the Holy One of Israel," which stresses his special relationship with Israel (cf. Introduction, p. 12) as well as his own distinctive nature.

The description of Israel in v.14 represents the people's self-valuation, while v.15 shows what God's amazing purpose will make them (cf. 2 Cor 2:16; 3:5–6). North (*Isaiah 40–55*, in loc.) points out that the worm is a "thresher" of the soil. Threshing with a heavy wooden sledge, with stone or iron teeth, was preliminary to winnowing (v.16), which was carried out on hilltops where the wind could carry away the chaff and allow the grain to fall to the ground. The hills are not now the location of the threshing floor but are themselves threshed! In this way the prophet stresses the powerful instrument God would make of this apparently insignificant people. If we read the passage in the light of chapter 40, the mountains and hills will be obstacles to the people's release from exile (cf. 40:4). It seems likely though that the thought goes beyond this, so that every hindrance to God's ultimate purposes in the international scene is overcome through a judgment executed through Israel. A study of Micah 4:10–13, coming from one of Isaiah's contemporaries, supports this exegesis.

17–20 An important key to these verses could be easily overlooked. The provision here described is an answer to prayer (v.17; cf. Ps 107:4–9). The need for water dominates the passage (cf. 32:6–7; cf. also Exod 17:1–7; Num 20:1–13). Through the difficult conditions that would beset the returning exiles, God expresses his total provision for their deepest needs. In the most unlikely places, plentiful supplies will be found, making the whole environment fertile and beautiful (vv.18–19). We may compare and contrast what is said here with the reference to threshing the mountains in vv.15–16. That *must* be figurative, for a literal interpretation is quite inconceivable. Here however, though the picture is wonderful, it is not outside the scope of possible literal fulfillment. It may be understood as three different but connected fulfillments. In relation to the return from exile, it will be figurative, indicating simply that God would supply all that his people needed. In relation to the eschatological future, it may represent a literal transformation of the environment of God's people (cf. Rom 8:18–22). In the light of the NT, it may also relate symbolically to the complete fulfillment of every spiritual need in Christ (see Introduction, pp. 14–16). All this will serve as a revelation of God's power and his grace (v.20).

21–24 The trial scene of v.1 (see comments there) resumes; but it is now the gods of the nations, not the nations themselves, who are called on for evidence. The bracketed phrase (v.22) is understood as addressed either to idolators or to idols. The concept of deity is, in some ways, simple, combining superhuman power and the claim to human worship. It has many implications, however, and ability to predict is one of these. This is the basis of the argument here. If the gods of Babylonia and other nations have objective reality as deities, they should be able to predict the future and also to so interpret history that past and future are seen to be linked in one divinely controlled plan. Verses 23b–24 turn from challenge to utter scorn (cf. 1 Kings 18:27). If prediction is beyond them, let them produce at least some evidence—anything at all—that they exist! They cannot respond; they and their worshipers are beneath contempt.

25–29 If, as we have argued (see comment at vv.2–4), this and the former passage are both about Cyrus; and if, as we have maintained in the Introduction (pp. 6–12), these chapters were written by Isaiah, the context of this passage is most significant. Cyrus was to emerge on the international scene at least a century and a half later. Here then is evidence indeed that what the gods of paganism could not do, the God of Israel could and did do. Here is prediction indeed! North and east ("the rising sun") are combined (v.25), for, considered from the standpoint of Palestine, Cyrus originated in the east and carried out major conquests in the north. For the meaning of the words "one . . . who calls on my name," see the comment at 45:4. The Babylonian idols might have been expected to predict Cyrus's coming, for his activities would greatly concern the people who worshiped them; but they were silent. The prophet pressed home his point with quite exceptional emphasis, for vv.26–29 are given over entirely to different ways of underlining the great contrast between the true God who predicts and the false gods who cannot. The coming of Cyrus was, of course, a message of good tidings for Israel (v. 27; cf. 40:9), because through him would come the release of the exiles.

Notes

2 The NIV text—"calling him in righteousness to his service"— and the NIV margin (and RSV)—"whom victory meets at every step"—both attempt to translate the text as it stands. The key issue is the meaning of צֶדֶק (ṣedeq) here. "Righteousness" is its fundamental sense, but it can also mean "victory." Either makes good sense contextually, but the rest of vv.1–2 are controlled by identical sense-rhythm. This inclines us toward the rendering of the NIV text.

3 The second line can mean that his feet do not touch the ground, thus representing the speed of his conquests (cf. Dan 8:5).

8–10 North (*Isaiah 40–55*, in loc.) writes: "These verses are remarkable for the repetitions of the suffixed endings î (6 times) and îkā (9 times). This is as near to being rhyme as anything in Hebrew poetry. It may not be euphonic but it is nothing if not emphatic, as befits the theme."

14 מְתֵי (mᵉtê, rendered "little" by NIV) has been much discussed. See especially A. Schoors, *I Am God Your Savior* (Leiden: E.J. Brill, 1973), pp. 59–61. Textual emendation is unnecessary, and the NIV can be supported by the use of this word with connotations of numerical weakness in Gen 34:30; Deut 4:27; Jer 44:28.

19 All these trees cannot be identified with certainty. See ZPEB, 2:563–80, and North, *Isaiah 40–55* (in loc.).

21 "Jacob's King" occurs only here in the OT, but compare 44:6.

4. The Lord's Servant—the Perfect and the Defective

42:1–25

1"Here is my servant, whom I uphold,
  my chosen one in whom I delight;
I will put my Spirit on him
  and he will bring justice to the nations.
2He will not shout or cry out,
  or raise his voice in the streets.

³A bruised reed he will not break,
　　and a smoldering wick he will not snuff out.
In faithfulness he will bring forth justice;
⁴　he will not falter or be discouraged
till he establishes justice on earth.
　　In his law the islands will put their hope."

⁵This is what God the Lord says—
he who created the heavens and stretched them out,
　　who spread out the earth and all that comes out of it,
who gives breath to its people,
　　and life to those who walk on it:
⁶"I, the Lord, have called you in righteousness;
　　I will take hold of your hand.
I will keep you and will make you
　　to be a covenant for the people
　　and a light for the Gentiles,
⁷to open eyes that are blind,
　　to free captives from prison
　　and to release from the dungeon those who sit
　　　　in darkness.
⁸"I am the Lord; that is my name!
　　I will not give my glory to another
　　or my praise to idols.
⁹See, the former things have taken place,
　　and new things I declare;
before they spring into being
　　I announce them to you."
¹⁰Sing to the Lord a new song,
　　his praise from the ends of the earth,
you who go down to the sea, and all that is in it,
　　you islands, and all who live in them.
¹¹Let the desert and its towns raise their voices;
　　let the settlements where Kedar lives rejoice.
Let the people of Sela sing for joy;
　　let them shout from the mountaintops.
¹²Let them give glory to the Lord
　　and proclaim his praise in the islands.
¹³The Lord will march out like a mighty man,
　　like a warrior he will stir up his zeal;
with a shout he will raise the battle cry
　　and will triumph over his enemies.

¹⁴"For a long time I have kept silent,
　　I have been quiet and held myself back.
But now, like a woman in childbirth,
　　I cry out, I gasp and pant.
¹⁵I will lay waste the mountains and hills
　　and dry up all their vegetation;
I will turn rivers into islands
　　and dry up the pools.
¹⁶I will lead the blind by ways they have not known,
　　along unfamiliar paths I will guide them;
I will turn the darkness into light before them
　　and make the rough places smooth.
These are the things I will do;
　　I will not forsake them.
¹⁷But those who trust in idols,
　　who say to images, 'You are our gods,'
　　will be turned back in utter shame.

18"Hear, you deaf;
    look, you blind, and see!
19Who is blind but my servant,
    and deaf like the messenger I send?
Who is blind like the one committed to me,
    blind like the servant of the LORD?
20You have seen many things, but have paid no attention;
    your ears are open, but you hear nothing."
21It pleased the LORD
    for the sake of his righteousness
    to make his law great and glorious.
22But this is a people plundered and looted,
    all of them trapped in pits
    or hidden away in prisons.
They have become plunder,
    with no one to rescue them;
they have been made loot,
    with no one to say, "Send them back."

23Which of you will listen to this
    or pay close attention in time to come?
24Who handed Jacob over to become loot,
    and Israel to the plunderers?
Was it not the LORD,
    against whom we have sinned?
For they would not follow his ways;
    they did not obey his law.
25So he poured out on them his burning anger,
    the violence of war.
It enveloped them in flames, yet they did not understand;
    it consumed them, but they did not take it to heart.

In this part of the book, it is not easy to distinguish separate oracles. If, in fact, these chapters were written without prior oral utterance, as some have held (see Introduction, pp. 6–11), then no such analysis is even appropriate. If the Servant Songs are the work of the author of the rest of the work—or even of the rest of chapters 40–55—then this too relieves us of the necessity. Certainly this whole chapter exhibits a point of unity in the servant theme.

1–4 The term "Servant Songs," coined by Duhm, is something of a misnomer, for there is no evidence they were ever sung, but the term has come to stay. For a general discussion of the songs—including their number, their length, and their relationship to their context—see the Introduction, pp. 7, 17–20, where the identity of the servant is also discussed and a particular interpretation of the servant passages as a whole expounded.

The NIV obscures the fact that both v. 1 and 41:29 commence with the word *hēn* ("behold"). Through the prophetic word the reader's eye is directed away from the pagan gods with their images to God's servant. After reading the previous chapter, the reader is inclined to see an immediate link with the description of Israel in 41:8–10, especially as that passage also follows a condemnation of idolatry. It may not be possible completely to identify the servant here with the nation (cf. v.6), but we can certainly say that in him the servant mission of Israel finds perfect expression. As so often in this book, a theme is introduced at a comparatively modest level and rises to an expression truly sublime (see comments at 4:2). There can be little doubt that we are intended to make the identification with Israel to begin with, that we might be gently led to him who is the incarnation of God's mind for Israel (cf. Matt 12:15–21).

The words "in whom I delight" (v.1), confirmed by the reference to faithfulness (v.3), immediately suggest that the servant is either Israel idealized or Israel represented by the ideal Israelite; and these words seem to be reflected in Matthew 3:17 in application to Christ. If the baptism of Jesus was his official initiation into the messianic office, with the descent of the Spirit representing his anointing for the work, the present passage too presents Jesus' ministry in prospect from the perspective of his baptismal inauguration. The gentle nature of his ministry has clearly influenced the picture of the Christian worker given in 2 Timothy 2:24–26, which, with Acts 13:46–48, shows that the NT countenances at least some corporate interpretation of the servant. There are, however, more personal links with the earlier messianic prophecies; for in these the king, anointed by the Spirit, promotes justice (cf. 11:1–5; 32:1). Verses 1 and 4 certainly suggest that even if we cannot completely identify the servant with a king, there is a regal aspect to his work.

Already the element of suffering in the servant's experience, which finds fuller and fuller expression till it achieves dominance in the fourth song (52:13–53:12), is gently suggested in v.4. Others, faced with what he would have to experience, would falter; but his faithfulness sustains him in the pathway of obedient service.

5–7 Duhm limited the first servant song to vv.1–4, but comparison with 49:1–6 (and also with 61:1–3) certainly suggests we should not divide vv.5–7 from the first four verses. Just as Psalm 2 presents the divine address to the messianic King or to Israel's king as foreshadowing him, almost certainly in the context of his kingly inauguration or enthronement, so here, with the ministry of the servant in prospect, God assures him of divine support in the execution of his mission. As Genesis sets redemption in a context of creation, so the picture of God as Creator and Lord of all the universe and of human life given in chapter 40 is summarily expressed here. His relationship to the universe (v.5) is suggestive of almighty power. This power is now channeled for the support of his servant in the doing of his will. If we interpret this passage in terms of its ultimate fulfillment in Jesus, then it was through his earthly ministry with its climax in death that he was "made" a covenant and a light, just as through his sufferings he was perfected in experience for his priestly work (Heb 5:4–10).

Verse 6, with its reference to a covenant of the people, makes us aware of the fact that the servant cannot be simply identified with Israel. He at least represents a group within it, perhaps the faithful remnant (see comments at 4:2), if not an individual. Thus the reader is being gradually educated as to the identity of the true Servant of God. The phrase "covenant of the people" implies a structured relationship between God and those already possessing his revelation, while "a light for the Gentiles" suggests the widening of the scope of this revelation. The covenant reference may be to the new covenant, the special blessings of which were later spelled out in Jeremiah 31:31–34. If it is, it may be viewed as confirming the Abrahamic covenant; for this also spoke of blessing for the nations (cf. Gen 12:1–3 et al.).

Grammatically, v.7 could apply both to the people and the Gentiles, but in fact it looks like an exposition of the light-imparting work of the servant. The whole verse can be so understood, for ancient Near-Eastern prisons were extremely dark; but of course the verse teaches that he gives liberty as well as light (cf. 61:1–2). Freeing captives suggests the conquest of the captors and so kingship (see comment at vv.1–4), while the opening of blind eyes and the enlightenment of the Gentiles introduces a prophetic feature into the work of this Spirit-anointed Servant of God.

8–9 The great assertion "I am the LORD" (v.8) reminds us of 41:13 (cf. comment there) and so makes another link between the servant and Israel (cf. also v.6 and the promise in 41:13, that God would hold the hand of his people). So the reader, sitting in the school of the prophetic Spirit, learns that though the servant may not simply be Israel, he is very closely associated with that people. God acts in the servant's work for his own glory (cf. Eph 1:3–14, and esp. Phil 2:5–11, which contains echoes of the Isaianic servant theme). Chapters 40–48 are particularly emphatic as to the sole deity of the Lord. The servant's work does not detract from his unique glory but rather ministers to it. "The former things" (v.9) could refer to earlier prophecies given through Isaiah and already fulfilled, or the phrase could relate to the entire Israelite prophetic movement and its already fulfilled predictions. The point is that the God who has already proved his word true is able to make known new things. Perhaps he is speaking here of the predicted work of the Servant.

10–13 The voice of praise is often heard in the Book of Isaiah (v.10; cf., e.g., ch. 12). If we take the chapter as a unity, it is natural to see the chief cause of praise to be the work of the Servant. If his ministry is to reach to the islands of the sea (v.10; cf. v.4), then it is not surprising that the whole earth joins in the song. The sea and the desert (v.11) probably find special mention because they are great areas with few people. Even in such places, however, there are islands and oases; and the people who live there are encouraged to join the universal song of praise (v.12). The Bedouin, represented by Kedar, and the inhabitants of rocky Sela will also be involved in this vocal worship. Even from the mountaintops, where perhaps only a wandering shepherd is to be found, singing voices are to be heard.

The song is a new one. Before there can be a new, however, there must be an old; and v.13, recalling perhaps Exodus 15:3–12, suggests that the old song was sung by Israel at its release from Egyptian bondage. If the song is occasioned by the work of the Servant, then he is to achieve a new Exodus, a great victory over the enemies of God. What an amazing paradox, when the gentleness of the Servant (vv.2–3) is pondered! This paradox is even more strikingly expressed in Isaiah 53:1, for "the arm of the LORD" denotes power (cf. also 52:13; 53:12). The nature of the enemies is not indicated here.

14–17 The majestic and terrifying anthropomorphisms of v.13 prepare us for the astonishing picture of v.14. God presents himself in the guise of a pregnant woman, which, as Whybray points out (*Isaiah 40–66*, in loc.), "is reinforced in the Hebrew by a breathless and convulsive style which seems ugly to modern western taste." This proliferation of gutturals and aspirates may seem ugly, but it is most effective oral communication. The long period of gestation—perhaps representing the Babylonian exile—is over; and God, who has seemed inactive, will be at pains to bring forth his people.

Verse 15 means that the Lord will remove obstacles to his people's deliverance (cf. 40:3–4), and the reference to the drying up of the waters may be an intentional allusion to the Exodus. The unfamiliar paths (v.16) recall Abraham, who went out (from Babylonia) not knowing where God would take him. Both the Gentiles and the Israelites need light from God (cf. vv.6–7). Smart, commenting (in loc.) on v.17, says, "To what man gives the worship of his heart is not determined by a consideration of the possible alternatives, with an intelligent weighing of the relative worthiness of the various objects of worship. He worships idols because they promise him more immediate satisfaction than does the worship of an unseen God." But here all such apparent promise that cannot in fact produce results will retreat before the deliverance effected by the true God.

18–20 This passage, depicting Israel as blind and deaf in her sin, stands in stark contrast to vv.1–7, where the perfect Servant of the Lord is depicted. Clearly we have been brought back with a jolt from the future's perfection to the present's lamentable failure. A person who is both blind and deaf can hardly function as a servant at all (v.19), for how will he know what instructions his master has for him? Verse 20 makes it clear that this incommunicado condition is culpable. The faculties are in fact still present, but there is failure to attend. There is a blindness that is of the mind or heart rather than of the eye. Such sinful inability throws the earlier ideal and futuristic picture into high relief.

21–25 Tôrāh ("law") here (v.21) probably means "teaching," so including also the prophetic word. Whether Israel, as God's now useless servant, hears that word or not, God has determined to magnify it. Here the objective greatness of the word of God is presented to us. In contrast Israel in Babylon is anything but great and glorious. Her lot is a sorry one. Not only have the people been plundered, but they are themselves plunder for their enemies. In the perspective of history, the words "with no one to say, 'Send them back' " remind us that before too long Cyrus would say just that.

Verses 23–25 illustrate the blindness of Israel that was the subject of vv.18–19 (cf. 6:9–10). They had failed to learn the spiritual and moral lessons of the Exile, tracing the calamity of it to their own rebellion against God. Herein lay their obtuseness. The occurrence of the first person plural in v.24 makes us aware that the prophet himself is an exception to the condemnation from God he has pronounced on the people. He has spiritual perception and moral sensitivity even if they have not. In this way he anticipates in his own person the Servant of the Lord he has so beautifully portrayed at the start of the chapter.

Notes

1 Young (*Book of Isaiah*, n. in loc.) says, "The combination of *spirit* and *upon him* is found elsewhere only in 11:2–4. This is clearly a Messianic characteristic" (emphasis his).

4 The verbs translated "falter" and "be discouraged" take up words from similar roots in v.3, translated "bruised" and "smoldering," but chiastically. He will have compassion on the broken and the weak and will himself be kept strong in the face of adversity.

6 Young (*Book of Isaiah*, in loc.) comments: "To say that the servant is a covenant are embodied in, have their root and origin in, and are dispensed by him. . . . Moses was a mediator of the covenant, but the servant *is* the covenant" (emphasis his).

11 For Kedar, see 21:16–17. Sela means "rock" and so is often identified with Petra, though this cannot be established with certainty.

13 Of course this verse could be interpreted of the victories of Cyrus that would gain release for Israel rather than of the work of the Servant. Either is possible, and the "exodus" of the return from Exile itself foreshadowed, like the original Exodus, the work of Jesus, the Servant of the Lord (cf. Luke 9:31, where "departure" is ἐξοδος [*exodos*]).

19 מְשֻׁלָּם (*meš̆ullām*, tr. "the one committed to me") is a word of uncertain meaning. For a conspectus of translations and conjectural emendations, see Muilenburg (in loc.). Young (*Book of Isaiah*, in loc.) also has a useful note.

---

5. Grace Abounding and Despised

43:1–28

¹But now, this is what the LORD says—
  he who created you, O Jacob,
  he who formed you, O Israel:
"Fear not, for I have redeemed you;
  I have summoned you by name; you are mine.
²When you pass through the waters,
  I will be with you;
and when you pass through the rivers,
  they will not sweep over you.
When you walk through the fire,
  you will not be burned;
  the flames will not set you ablaze.
³For I am the LORD, your God,
  the Holy One of Israel, your Savior;
I give Egypt for your ransom,
  Cush and Seba in your stead.
⁴Since you are precious and honored in my sight,
  and because I love you,
I will give men in exchange for you,
  and people in exchange for your life.
⁵Do not be afraid, for I am with you;
  I will bring your children from the east
  and gather you from the west.
⁶I will say to the north, 'Give them up!'
  and to the south, 'Do not hold them back.'
Bring my sons from afar
  and my daughters from the ends of the earth—
⁷everyone who is called by my name,
  whom I created for my glory,
  whom I formed and made."

⁸Lead out those who have eyes but are blind,
  who have ears but are deaf.
⁹All the nations gather together
  and the peoples assemble.
Which of them foretold this
  and proclaimed to us the former things?
Let them bring in their witnesses to prove they were right,
  so that others may hear and say, "It is true."
¹⁰"You are my witnesses," declares the LORD,
  "and my servant whom I have chosen,
so that you may know and believe me
  and understand that I am he.
Before me no god was formed,
  nor will there be one after me.

¹¹I, even I, am the LORD,
and apart from me there is no savior.
¹²I have revealed and saved and proclaimed—
I, and not some foreign god among you.
You are my witnesses," declares the LORD, "that I am God.
¹³   Yes, and from ancient days I am he.
No one can deliver out of my hand.
When I act, who can reverse it?"
¹⁴This is what the LORD says—
your Redeemer, the Holy One of Israel:
"For your sake I will send to Babylon
and bring down as fugitives all the Babylonians,
in the ships in which they took pride.
¹⁵I am the LORD, your Holy One,
Israel's Creator, your King."

¹⁶This is what the LORD says—
he who made a way through the sea,
a path through the mighty waters,
¹⁷who drew out the chariots and horses,
the army and reinforcements together,
and they lay there, never to rise again,
extinguished, snuffed out like a wick:
¹⁸"Forget the former things;
do not dwell on the past.
¹⁹See, I am doing a new thing!
Now it springs up; do you not perceive it?
I am making a way in the desert
and streams in the wasteland.
²⁰The wild animals honor me,
the jackals and the owls,
because I provide water in the desert
and streams in the wasteland,
to give drink to my people, my chosen,
²¹   the people I formed for myself
that they may proclaim my praise.

²²"Yet you have not called upon me, O Jacob,
you have not wearied yourselves for me, O Israel.
²³You have not brought me sheep for burnt offerings,
nor honored me with your sacrifices.
I have not burdened you with grain offerings
nor wearied you with demands for incense.
²⁴You have not bought any fragrant calamus for me,
or lavished on me the fat of your sacrifices.
But you have burdened me with your sins
and wearied me with your offenses.

²⁵"I, even I, am he who blots out
your transgressions, for my own sake,
and remembers your sins nor more.
²⁶Review the past for me,
let us argue the matter together;
state the case for your innocence.
²⁷Your first father sinned;
your spokesmen rebelled against me.
²⁸So I will disgrace the dignitaries of your temple,
and I will consign Jacob to destruction
and Israel to scorn.

The whole chapter expounds the redemptive grace of the Lord toward his people, grace that is highlighted at the end by reference to the people's sin (cf. Kidner, "Isaiah," in loc.).

1–7 The words "but now" (v.1) link this chapter with chapter 42, where the prophet declared the consequences of Israel's refusal to obey the law of their God. Here Isaiah declares they will experience God as their Redeemer (cf. 44:1; Rom 3:21; Eph 2:13). These verses are controlled by the repeated exhortation not to be afraid (vv.1, 5). The names "Jacob" and "Israel" together suggest God's grace to an unworthy people and his great purpose for them. His names and titles are reassuring, for all those in v.3 imply a special relationship between God and his people, while his activities on their behalf—such as creation (out of "nothing" in Egypt) redemption, and protection—demonstrate his loving concern, made explicit in v.4.

God promises his people that he will gather them from every quarter, the passage making many allusions to the Exodus. The waters and the rivers look back to the Red Sea and the Jordan, and the fire perhaps points to Daniel 2 (v.2; cf. Ps 66:6, 12). The nation's preciousness to him suggests a filial relationship (v.4; cf. Exod 4:22–23), which becomes individualized in v.7 (cf. Deut 14:1). As the firstborn of Israel were ransomed by substitution at the Passover and subsequently (Exod 13:14 –16), so God would ransom Israel as his own firstborn, so called in Exodus 4:22–23. The statement "I am the LORD, your God" (v.3) would remind every Jewish reader of Exodus 20, where the divine description is followed by the words "who brought you out of Egypt, out of the land of slavery" (Exod 20:2). So, learning from this significant past event, they could rest in his promise to bring them again into their own land, this time from every point of the globe. Fear is banished as God's nature, his activities, and his promises to his people are considered.

8–13 The atmosphere of the prophecy changes from comfort to challenge. Once again the reader is transported to a courtroom (cf. 1:2; 41:1, 21). Israel and the nations are in court together. What is being examined is the Lord's claim to uniqueness, to sole deity. First of all, it is stated that only he can foretell (v.9; cf. 41:25–29). He alone is divine, and this always has been and always will be the truth. From his dealings with Israel in the past—as Revealer and Savior of his people (v.12) and Judge of others, at a time (presumably the Exodus) when the people's trust was in him alone and not, as often later, partly in foreign deities—it is clear that he alone is God and Savior (v.11).

Israel appears in these verses as God's witness (vv.10, 12). Other nations can give no witness for their own impotent deities, but Israel has so much to declare; for the Lord's wonderful works have been done before her and on her behalf. Yet, sadly, though she is God's chosen servant, she is blind, deaf (cf. 42:18–20), and a failure. To make matters worse, her choice by him was with a view to intelligent faith in him, which should have made her most articulate and effective as a witness for him.

14–15 The comforting tone of the opening verses of this chapter is now resumed, and along with it some of the reassuring descriptions of the Lord (cf. vv.1, 3). The generalized promise of vv.5–7 gives place to a specific reference to Babylon, the first express mention of it since chapter 39. Despite textual and translation problems in v.14, it is clear that Babylon is to be judged. Again there is a piling up of titles and descriptions of the Lord (v.15).

16–21 The fundamental principles of the divine activity are changeless, but the outward shape of that activity alters with the changing needs of God's people. We are meant to reflect on the past with gratitude and stimulated faith but not to allow it to stereotype our expectations from God. Here God affirms—in detail and with emphasis on the deadly efficiency of his deeds—that he was the God of the Exodus (vv.16–17), but he also asserts the wonderful freshness of his new act in prospect (vv.18–19). He had made a way through the waters; now he would make a new way—through the desert! Water, formerly a barrier, would now be a blessing, with God as its source. The abundant provision for men would be enjoyed by the wild creatures also (v.20). This would perhaps be an earnest of the regeneration of creation promised elsewhere in Isaiah (cf. 11:6–9; 65:25). Verses 20b–21 suggest that election is not only for privilege but for the praise of God (cf. Eph 1:4–6).

22–28 Once more the mood changes, and comfort gives place to accusation (see comment at v.1). The Lord's past acts of grace should have evoked gratitude from his people, but they have offered him sins instead of sacrifices. Both ritualistic excess of sacrifices (vv.23–24; cf. 1:2–17) and shameful neglect of them testify to a deep spiritual malaise in the nation. No doubt different sections of the populace thus showed their spiritual need in different ways.

It is significant that both here and in chapter 1 the assurance of forgiveness of sins (v.25) is given in the context of sacrifice. This casts much doubt on the view that in Israel priest and prophet represented conflicting concepts of religion. The ultimate in sacrificial—and therefore priestly—teaching is given in 52:13–53:12, where there is full forgiveness through the Servant's sacrifice. There is much in vv.22–25 to remind us—either by comparison or by contrast—of chapter 1; and the double use of the word "burdened" certainly recalls this theme in the earlier chapter (see comments at 1:4, 14, 24). The verb ʿāḇaḏ here actually means "to enslave" or "to burden a slave with toil." The appropriate has been doubly replaced by the unexpected—on God's side by his incredible grace, and on Israel's by her unthinkable ingratitude.

Verse 26 also evokes memories of 1:18, where the divine urge to forgive is expressed in the language of the courtroom, with a call for settlement of the issue. Here God speaks to establish the guilt of his people, for without a recognition of this they would never come for forgiveness. The first father (v.27) could be Adam, Abraham, or Jacob; but most commentators favor the last. Little depends on it, for the basic meaning of the verse is that from its beginning and throughout its history the nation has been characterized by sin, even on the part of its spiritual elite. Not only would that elite be disgraced, but the whole people would suffer destruction at God's hands.

The word translated "destruction" (ḥērem, v.28) is well explained in the NIV margin: "The Hebrew term refers to the irrevocable giving over of things or persons to the LORD, often by totally destroying them." This is what Israel did, by God's command, to pagan Jericho. Again we recall chapter 1 with its reference to Sodom (cf. 1:9–10), for it implies that God will treat Israel as if she is pagan, so far away from him has she fallen. We should remember also, of course, that Isaiah's opening vision assured him that even devastating judgment for Israel would leave a tiny remnant in whom God's purposes would find ultimate fulfillment (cf. 6:11–13).

Notes

2 North (*Isaiah 40–55*, in loc.) says, "The assurance that flames will *not* now scorch is intended as a contrast with the flames that *did* scorch (xlii.25)" (emphasis his).

3 The three place names here are almost equally appropriate whether the Exodus or the return from Exile is in view; for, as North (*Isaiah 40–55*, in loc.) says, "Cush and Seba correspond roughly to Upper Egypt and the Lower Sudan." Both were within Egypt's sphere of influence through much of her history and could therefore be thought of as sharing her fate. A comparison with 15:14 suggests that it is primarily the return from exile that is in view; for Ambyses, successor to Cyrus, conquered Egypt. Thexton comments, "The prophet intends the fabulous wealth and extent of these far-off regions to signify the depth of Yahweh's concern for His people, and His readiness to 'pay any price' for their redemption."

14 The NIV translates the difficult second half of this verse fairly literally. It appears to refer to the trading of Babylon by Cyrus (cf. esp. 45:4 with the words "for your sake" here). The text does not require emendation, for בׇּאֳנִיּוֹת רִנָּתׇם (*bō'ᵒniyôt rinnātām*, lit., "in the ships of their joyous shout") surely suggests pride (cf. 2:16). The ships of the Chaldeans would be used by Israel's conquerors to transport them as captives.

20 For תַּנִּים וּבְנוֹת יַעֲנָה (*tannîm ûbᵉnôt ya'ᵃnāh*, "the jackals and the owls"), see note at 34:13.

22–24 Young (*Book of Isaiah*, in loc.) points out that the negative occurs seven times in these verses and that "me" after the first of these is emphatic. The passage does not teach that the sacrificial system was not divinely originated but rather that it was not intended to be a burden but a blessing.

קׇנֶה (*qāneh*, tr. "fragrant calamus," botanically named *acorus calamus*) is used in the manufacture of incense.

6. Israel's Great God and the Folly of Idolatry

44:1–23

1"But now listen, O Jacob, my servant,
  Israel, whom I have chosen.
2This is what the LORD says—
  he who made you, who formed you in the womb,
  and who will help you:
 Do not be afraid, O Jacob, my servant,
  Jeshurun, whom I have chosen.
3For I will pour water on the thirsty land,
  and streams on the dry ground;
 I will pour out my Spirit on your offspring,
  and my blessing on your descendants.
4They will spring up like grass in a meadow,
  like poplar trees by flowing streams.
5One will say, 'I belong to the LORD';
  another will call himself by the name of Jacob;
 still another will write on his hand, "The LORD's,'
  and will take the name Israel.
6"This is what the LORD says—
  Israel's King and Redeemer, the LORD Almighty:
 I am the first and I am the last;
  apart from me there is no God.
7Who then is like me? Let him proclaim it.
  Let him declare and lay out before me

what has happened since I established my ancient people,
and what is yet to come—
yes, let him foretell what will come.
⁸Do not tremble, do not be afraid.
Did I not proclaim this and foretell it long ago?
You are my witnesses. Is there any God besides me?
No, there is no other Rock; I know not one."

⁹All who make idols are nothing,
and the things they treasure are worthless.
Those who would speak up for them are blind;
they are ignorant, to their own shame.
¹⁰Who shapes a god and casts an idol,
which can profit him nothing?
¹¹He and his kind will be put to shame;
craftsmen are nothing but men.
Let them all come together and take their stand;
they will be brought down to terror and infamy.

¹²The blacksmith takes a tool
and works with it in the coals;
he shapes an idol with hammers,
he forges it with the might of his arm.
He gets hungry and loses his strength;
he drinks no water and grows faint.
¹³The carpenter measures with a line
and makes an outline with a marker;
he roughs it out with chisels
and marks it with compasses.
He shapes it in the form of man,
of man in all his glory,
that it may dwell in a shrine.
¹⁴He cut down cedars,
or perhaps took a cypress or oak.
He let it grow among the trees of the forest,
or planted a pine, and the rain made it grow.
¹⁵It is man's fuel for burning;
some of it he takes and warms himself,
he kindles a fire and bakes bread.
But he also fashions a god and worships it;
he makes an idol and bows down to it.
¹⁶Half of the wood he burns in the fire;
over it he prepares his meal,
he roasts his meat and eats his fill.
He also warms himself and says,
"Ah! I am warm; I see the fire."
¹⁷From the rest he makes a god, his idol;
he bows down to it and worships.
He prays to it and says,
"Save me; you are my god."
¹⁸They know nothing, they understand nothing;
their eyes are plastered over so they cannot see,
and their minds closed so they cannot understand.
¹⁹No one stops to think,
no one has the knowledge or understanding to say,
"Half of it I used for fuel;
I even baked bread over its coals,
I roasted meat and I ate.
Shall I make a detestable thing from what is left?
Shall I bow down to a block of wood?"

²⁰He feeds on ashes, a deluded heart misleads him;
    he cannot save himself, or say,
    "Is not this thing in my right hand a lie?"

²¹"Remember these things, O Jacob,
    for you are my servant, O Israel.
I have made you, you are my servant;
    O Israel, I will not forget you.
²²I have swept away your offenses like a cloud,
    your sins like the morning mist.
Return to me,
    for I have redeemed you."

²³Sing for joy, O heavens, for the LORD has done this;
    shout aloud, O earth beneath.
Burst into song, you mountains,
    you forests and all your trees,
for the LORD has redeemed Jacob,
    he displays his glory in Israel.

1–5 Once again, as in 43:1, after a strong affirmation of divine judgment, God says, "But now." Verses 1–2 take up again much of the phraseology of the earlier oracle (q.v.). The name Jeshurun (v.2) is found in Deuteronomy 32:15; 33:5, 26, and, like Israel, provides a contrast in meaning with Jacob, as there can be little doubt that it means "the Upright One." Jacob, of course, means "Deceiver" (cf. Gen 27:36; 32:28). It may suggest that the Jacob-Israel name combination, so common in chapters 41–49, is used with due awareness of the special sense of each, as if to designate the people as sinful and yet as the object of the Lord's gracious purpose of redemption.

Commenting on v.3, Whybray (*Isaiah 40–66*, in loc.) notes that "there is a general agreement among the commentators that unlike other passages (e.g. 41:18) which use similar language, these promises of abundant rain do not refer to miracles which will occur during the promised journey through the desert but are metaphorical, denoting the conferring of a blessing." This means, of course, that v.3a is being read in the light of v.3b, which seems entirely appropriate. Numerous progeny are often treated in the OT as a sign of God's blessing (cf., e.g., Gen 15:5; 127:3–5), and spiritual progeny are evidence of God's blessing on his suffering Servant (53:10). The two analogies are as apt as they are clear.

Prophecy is full of surprises, common theological motifs suddenly giving way, as here, to a startling thought. Isaiah is almost Pauline at this point, for the Gentile converts of v.5 seem like an (adopted?) extension of the children of Israel to whom v.4 refers. The statement "I will pour out my spirit" (v.3) reminds us of Joel 2:29, with its fulfillment at Pentecost and the Gentile evangelization that followed it. North (*Isaiah 40–55*, in loc.) says, "The passage is remarkable as being perhaps the earliest in which what we call the church is conceived of as a community transcending the boundaries of race." Verse 5 probably refers to the mark of a master on the hand of a slave (cf. 49:16).

6–8 The expression "This is what the Lord says" (v.6), though a standard prophetic formula, should not be regarded as purely formal. Here it is most apt as introducing verses in which God's perceptive word is proclaimed. The piling up of divine titles is characteristic of this part of Isaiah (cf. 43:14; 44:24; but also 1:24). Although

Yahweh is the God of his own special people, he is also sovereign over all history and so holds sole title to the designation "God." He is incomparable (v.7; cf. 40:25), especially in his power to interpret the past and predict the future. The statement "I established my ancient people" (v.7), the phrases "the first" (v.6) and "long ago" (v.8), and the use of the title "Rock" from Deuteronomy 32 all evoke memories of the Exodus, assuring the people that the first Exodus was the guarantee of the second.

9–20 Many modern scholars think the style, the somewhat "labored" irony, and the sheer length of this passage raise doubts about its authorship; and they deny it to the prophet who wrote the bulk of these chapters. The ideas in it can be paralleled again and again however in chapters 40–48. Comments on style are so often subjective, so that Simon (in loc.) can call this passage "a masterpiece." Schubert was a great composer, but what to one music critic is the "heavenly length" of the first movement of his Ninth Symphony to another is excessive exposition of its musical themes. The language Isaiah uses rests on the border line between poetry and prose, so that it cannot be put firmly into either genre. This is not however uncommon in the prophets.

The passage commences with theological statements in vv.9–11, which form an introduction to the imaginative construction of the scene in the idol-maker's shop. The workmen share the worthlessness of their images. Whether viewed singly or collectively, they are nothing and must suffer discrediting and judgment.

Isaiah's imaginative gift is pressed into the service of his inspired satire. Neoplatonism and Brahmanism, in their different ways, have attempted to provide an intellectual framework and justification for idolatry. Isaiah will have none of this, because he is jealous for the glory and sole Godhead of the God of Israel. Whether the medium be iron (v.12) or wood (v.13), the enterprise deserves nothing but ridicule. God-given strength and skill are being misused, and sin has deprived the idolater of any sense of what is fitting. He uses a tree that is dependent on God's rain for its growth and uses it for two purposes—to make a fire for warmth and a god for worship! Here is the *reductio ad absurdum* of idolatry, for sin has blinded the mind (vv.18–20). Right from his call (6:9–10), Isaiah was aware of the blinding effects of sin. The words "he feeds on ashes" translated literally mean "he herds ashes," a ridiculous activity suggested perhaps by the ashes remaining after the idolater's fire has burned itself out.

21–23 The call to remember (v.21) probably embraces both the vast contrast between the true God and the idols and also the earlier reminders of his activity and power to predict revealed in the past history of his people. The promise of 43:25 is repeated, but now the people's sins are likened to passing phenomena of the sky, blotting out the sun for a while (v.22). This does not mean that their sins are not serious, but it does mean that God has determined to deal with them in forgiveness. Here is a rare OT juxtaposition of forgiveness and redemption (cf. Ps 130:8). The command to return implies the objectivity of God's redemptive provision, to which the people are called to react in penitence. This objective work is so wonderful that the whole universe, once called to witness God's indictment of his people's sin (1:2), is now called on to share their exuberant joy at his redemption. Clearly the glory he displays is the glory of his grace (cf. 1:6).

265

Notes

---

4 Commenting on כְּבֵין חָצִיר (*keḇên ḥāṣîr*, "like poplar trees" in NIV; so 1QIsa, LXX), North (*Isaiah 40–55*, in loc.) says: "It is now certain that the difficult Heb. *ben* in this passage is not the preposition 'between' but the 'ben- tree' . . ., a species of *moringa* remarkable for the intense greenness of its leaves. The word is found in Arabic, Aramaic-Syriac, and Akkadian."

7 The RSV's "from my placing an eternal people and things to come" gives the literal sense. (The NIV has "since I established my ancient people,/ and what is yet to come.") The conjectural emendation suggested by some (cf. BHS mg.) is not really needed because, though the construction seems somewhat harsh, the MT's meaning is clear enough and fits the context.

12 מַעֲצָד (*ma'aṣāḏ*), found elsewhere only in Jer 10:3, is rendered here as "tool" in a verse dealing with an ironworker; but in fact the exact significance of the word is still unknown.

14 Isaiah is fond of grouping flora and fauna (cf., e.g., 13:21–22; 28:25; 30:6).

---

7. God's Actions Through Cyrus

44:24–45:25

24"This is what the LORD says—
your Redeemer, who formed you in the womb;

I am the LORD,
who has made all things,
who alone stretched out the heavens,
who spread out the earth by myself,

25who foils the signs of false prophets
and makes fools of diviners,
who overthrows the learning of the wise
and turns it into nonsense,
26who carries out the words of his servants
and fulfills the predictions of his messengers,

who says of Jerusalem, 'It shall be inhabited,'
of the towns of Judah, 'They shall be built,'
and of their ruins, 'I will restore them,'
27who says to the watery deep, 'Be dry,
and I will dry up your streams,'
28who says of Cyrus, 'He is my shepherd
and will accomplish all that I please;
he will say of Jerusalem, "Let it be rebuilt,"
and of the temple, "Let its foundations be laid."'

45:1"This is what the LORD says to his anointed,
to Cyrus, whose right hand I take hold of
to subdue nations before him
and to strip kings of their armor,
to open doors before him
so that gates will not be shut;
2I will go before you
and will level the mountains;
I will break down gates of bronze
and cut through bars of iron.

³I will give you the treasures of darkness,
　　riches stored in secret places,
so that you may know that I am the LORD,
　　the God of Israel, who summons you by name.
⁴For the sake of Jacob my servant,
　　of Israel my chosen,
I summon you by name
　　and bestow on you a title of honor,
　　though you do not acknowledge me.
⁵I am the LORD, and there is no other;
　　apart from me there is no God.
I will strengthen you,
　　though you have not acknowledged me,
⁶so that from the rising of the sun
　　to the place of its setting
men may know there is none besides me.
　　I am the LORD, and there is no other.
⁷I form the light and create darkness,
　　I bring prosperity and create disaster,
　　I, the LORD, do all these things.

⁸"You heavens above, rain down righteousness;
　　let the clouds shower it down.
Let the earth open wide,
　　let salvation spring up,
let righteousness grow with it;
　　I, the LORD, have created it.

⁹"Woe to him who quarrels with his Maker,
　　to him who is but a potsherd among the potsherds on
　　　　the ground.
Does the clay say to the potter,
　　'What are you making?'
Does your work say,
　　'He has no hands'?
¹⁰Woe to him who says to his father,
　　'What have you begotten?'
or to his mother,
　　'What have you brought to birth?'

¹¹"This is what the LORD says—
　　the Holy One of Israel, and its Maker:
Concerning things to come,
　　do you question me about my children,
　　or give me orders about the work of my hands?
¹²It is I who made the earth
　　and created mankind upon it.
My own hands stretched out the heavens;
　　I marshaled their starry hosts.
¹³I will raise up Cyrus in my righteousness:
　　I will make all his ways straight.
He will rebuild my city
　　and set my exiles free,
but not for a price or reward,
　　says the LORD Almighty."

¹⁴This is what the LORD says:

　　"The products of Egypt and the merchandise of Cush,
　　and those tall Sabeans—

267

they will come over to you
and will be yours;
they will trudge behind you,
coming over to you in chains.
They will bow down before you
and plead with you, saying,
'Surely God is with you, and there is no other;
there is no other god.' "

15Truly you are a God who hides himself,
O God and Savior of Israel
16All the makers of idols will be put to shame and disgraced;
they will go off into disgrace together.
17But Israel will be saved by the LORD
with an everlasting salvation;
you will never be put to shame or disgraced,
to ages everlasting.

18For this is what the LORD says—
He who created the heavens,
he is God;
he who fashioned and made the earth,
he founded it;
he did not create it to be empty,
but formed it to be inhabited—
he says:
"I am the LORD,
and there is no other.
19I have not spoken in secret,
from somewhere in a land of darkness;
I have not said to Jacob's descendants,
'Seek me in vain.'
I, the LORD, speak the truth;
I declare what is right.

20"Gather together and come;
assemble, you fugitives from the nations.
Ignorant are those who carry about idols of wood,
who pray to gods that cannot save.
21Declare what is to be, present it—
let them take counsel together.
Who foretold this long ago,
who declared it from the distant past?
Was it not I, the LORD?
And there is no God apart from me,
a righteous God and a Savior;
there is none but me.

22"Turn to me and be saved,
all you ends of the earth;
for I am God, and there is no other.
23By myself I have sworn,
my mouth has uttered in all integrity
a word that will not be revoked:
Before me every knee will bow;
by me every tongue will swear.
24They will say of me, 'In the LORD alone
are righteousness and strength.' "
All who have raged against him
will come to him and be put to shame.

²⁵But in the Lᴏʀᴅ all the descendants of Israel
will be found righteous and will exult.

This great passage, with its two explicit references to Cyrus, has attracted much scholarly discussion. For many modern scholars it represents the strongest argument for "Deutero-Isaiah," for they cannot conceive of supernatural predictive prophecy of such detail. Yet it cannot be denied that the context for such predictions is the most appropriate in the whole Bible; for Isaiah 40–48 says more about the Lord's power to predict than any other passage (see Introduction, pp. 6–11).

God assures his people that he plans to rebuild Judah, Jerusalem, and his temple, that this will become possible through the pagan Cyrus, and that the ultimate issue of the divine acts through Cyrus is that people everywhere will acknowledge God's uniqueness (44:24–45:8). His sovereign choice of such a vehicle is unchallengeable and the coming of Cyrus absolutely certain (45:9–13). God will vindicate Israel as his people in the eyes of pagan peoples subdued by Cyrus (45:14–17). This will herald a final challenge to paganism, the offer of salvation to people everywhere, and the ultimate submission of the whole world to his sovereign rule (45:18–25).

24–28 Torrey's suggestion (in loc.) that both references to Cyrus should be excised as later interpolations, though followed by few commentators, is nevertheless referred to by many of them. How then can we account for the virtual ignoring of Allis's highly significant study (*Isaiah*, pp. 62–80) of these verses by almost all but conservative scholars? Allis demonstrates that vv. 24–28 are a "poem of the transcendence of the God of Israel." He shows that the poem is most carefully constructed and that a study of its form shows most clearly that the revelation of the name of Cyrus comes at its dramatic climax. This is particularly appropriate if the poem comes from Isaiah of Jerusalem, for it emphasizes the role of the prophets in prediction. The NIV has beautifully translated it, conveying much of its poetic form to the English reader while remaining true to the meaning of the text, a combination often difficult to achieve.

The assertion "This is what the Lᴏʀᴅ says" (v.24) punctuates this section of the prophecy (cf. 45:1, 11, 18). The Lord is first designated as his people's Redeemer. This is the character in which he will act on their behalf. The phrase "who formed you in the womb" links this passage with 44:1, and so argues its integrity with the rest of Isaiah 40–48. The simple yet important affirmation "I am the Lᴏʀᴅ" is a reminder of Exodus 20:2 (cf. comment at 43:11); and it introduces a series of prepositional phrases, quite unparalleled in the OT. These are translated, quite legitimately, as relative clauses in the NIV and the EV generally.

These phrases build up into a most powerful doctrine of the past activities of the God of Israel, and they employ themes that have already found prominent place in the prophecy since the beginning of chapter 40. He is the sole creator (v.24; cf. 40:12, 22, 26, 28; 42:5), the sole revealer of the future (vv.25–26a; cf. 41:4, 26–29; 44:7–8, 25–26); the sole guarantor of a new day for Jerusalem and Judah (v.26b; cf. 40:2, 9). The meaning of v.27 is disputed, but Young is probably correct in interpreting this and the next verse along the lines of Jeremiah 23:7–8 and so seeing it as a reference to the Exodus. Young (*Book of Isaiah*, in loc.) writes: "just as at the first exodus the power of God was exhibited in the safe passage of the nation through the Red Sea waters, so now, in the deliverance from the world power, represented by

Babylon, that power will again be seen, and whatever may stand in the way will be completely removed."

There have already been allusions to Cyrus (cf. comments at 41:2, 25), but these have not named him; for his name has been held back for this great moment of poetic-prophetic climax. Only in 1 Kings 13:2 do we find anything quite comparable in the OT, though Isaiah 52:13–53:12 could hardly be made more wonderfully specific by the mention of the name of Jesus. Only a little less dramatic than the name is the description of Cyrus as "my shepherd" (v.28), for this was a pagan foreigner. It is true that Hammurabi, king of Babylon—more than one thousand years before Cyrus—called himself "the shepherd that brings good"; but the term would remind the people of the shepherd-role of their own kings—especially of David (cf. 2 Sam 5:2)—and also of the anthropomorphic description of God in 40:11. The lost sheep were to be rounded up and returned to their true fold in Judah by this foreigner, who would make possible the rebuilding of Jerusalem and the very temple—the sacred temple—of Israel's God. This oracle gives the first explicit reference in the Book of Isaiah to God's plans to rebuild the city.

45:1–7 The last five verses of chapter 44, for all their majesty, contain only one main statement, which is one of the simplest that is grammatically possible: "I am the LORD" (v.24). All else leads into or amplifies this great affirmation. It is repeated in vv.3, 5, and 6. This is surely significant in an address to a pagan king. "His anointed" (v.1) and "my shepherd" (44:28) explain each other; for both, though possessing wider areas of application, meet in the concept of a divinely chosen and divinely employed king. There is precedent for the divine anointing of a non-Israelite king, though in one passage only (1 Kings 19:15–16). Although the living God normally employed Israelites for such purposes, he is sovereign and may use whom he will.

In these verses some of God's promises to Israel are echoed (cf. 40:4; 41:13; 43:1). Because in God's purpose Cyrus functions for Israel, he comes into the good of some of God's promises to that people. He would enjoy great triumphs over his enemies and would find their fortified cities no obstacle to his advance (v.1). Herodotus (1. 179) wrote of Babylon: "There are a hundred gates in the circuit of the wall, all of bronze with bronze uprights and lintels." The reference to great wealth in v.3 could refer equally well to the treasures of Lydia—the riches of whose ruler, Croesus, were proverbial—or to Babylon, and in fact Cyrus overcame both. That all these victories were for the sake of little Israel is one of the ironies of God's control of history. What to man is laughable is nevertheless true, for God's ways are not our ways.

We have noted that Cyrus has been introduced already, though not by name, in chapter 41 (see comments at 41:2, 25). The prophet declared that Cyrus calls on the Lord's name (41:25). Here too it is said that God's support of Cyrus has as its purpose that he might know that Israel's God is the Lord. Yet twice over it is denied that Cyrus acknowledges him. In the Cyrus Cylinder (see EBC, 1:238), the king attributes his victories to Marduk, god of Babylon; yet in Ezra 1, Cyrus is quoted as asserting that the Lord had given him dominion. Clearly Cyrus used the names of deities without any sense of exclusiveness. Josephus (Antiq. XI, 5 [i.2]) recorded that "these things Cyrus knew from reading the book of prophecy which Isaiah had left behind two hundred and ten years earlier."

A universal note is struck in v.6. Young (*Book of Isaiah*, in loc.) says: "We need not necessarily assume that this purpose would be immediately accomplished. Cyrus was raised up that the Jews might return to Palestine and that Christ might then be born in Bethlehem, and that when redemption had been accomplished and its message proclaimed there might be a universal acknowledgment that the God of Israel is the true God."

The general assertions of absolute monotheism in vv.5–6 are underlined by the specific affirmations of v.7. There are three in all, the first related to the universe as such, the second to human society, and the third summing up. Genesis seems to imply—if it does not expressly teach—the creation of darkness as well as light by God (Gen 1:1–5). Although it is said in Genesis that the light is good, there is no suggestion that the darkness is evil, for it too has its function (cf. Ps 104:19–24). The words šālôm and rā' (rendered "prosperity" and "disaster") are, literally, "peace" and "evil." The latter is well interpreted in terms of Amos 3:6. So the God who created darkness that is not itself evil—though it is sometimes used to symbolize it—and who brings disaster as a punishment for sin, is supreme over all. Isaiah has already shown that God brings calamitous judgment on men because of their sins (cf., e.g., 10:5–12). Westermann (in loc.) roundly declares, "If the creator of evil and woe is God, there is no room left for a devil." But this is to go far beyond what the verse says. It is an attack on polytheistic dualism, in which there is at least division of labor and often conflict among the deities. It probably does not confront Zoroastrian dualism directly, for there is no clear evidence that Cyrus shared this belief with some of his successors.

8 This verse, following close on v.7, suggests that the prophet had Genesis 1 in his mind. The heavens and the earth, called on first to witness the rebellion of God's people (1:2) and then to praise God for redeeming them, are now addressed in ecstatic apostrophe. The inspired poetic imagination of the prophet sees the processes by which vegetation grows on the earth as symbols of God's saving work (cf. Heb 6:7). The God of creation and the God of redemption are one God, and so the one may be used to illustrate the other.

Righteousness and salvation are closely linked here, as so often in this part of the book (cf. 46:12–13; 51:5–6, 8; 56:1–2; 59:17; 61:10; 62:1; 63:1). God's righteous order of the future is to include the manifestation of his salvation. In Pauline theology the righteousness of God is seen in the gospel (cf., e.g., Rom 1:16–17; 3:21–22 et al.); for through the bearing of sin by Christ, God's righteous wrath against sin has been fully manifested and sinners are given, by his grace, a righteous standing with God (Rom 3:25–26).

9–10 The style of these verses recalls Isaiah 5 with its series of woes (see comment at 5:8). The point at issue in the quarrel (v.9) is probably God's disclosure to his people that he would deliver them through pagan Cyrus. We cannot accuse God of using inappropriate means to achieve his ends. Isaiah was particularly gifted in portraying sin as ridiculous and illogical, as he does here with the illustrations of the discarded scraps of pottery and the lump of clay in the hands of the potter (cf. Jer 18:1–6). Verse 10 implies an *a fortiori* application to God the Creator (cf. Rom 9:20–21).

11–13 There is a clear, if implicit, reference to Cyrus in v.13 (NIV supplies "Cyrus" for MT's "him"); and this passage establishes him as a subject of prediction, not simply of description *ex eventu*. The reference to the children and the work of his hands are chiastic allusions to vv.9–10. The coming of Cyrus, though still future, is as certain as the existence of God's created universe. Not only is Jerusalem to be rebuilt (cf. 44:26–28), but its people will be freed from their exile, and that without any financial inducement to Cyrus. The latter fact therefore underscores still further the divine origin of all these events.

14 This verse anticipates chapter 60. In 43:3 the Persians are promised Egypt, Cush, and Seba (see comments there), while here their people are seen submitting to Israel. Two different stages of their history are, of course, in view. Despite their chains, the language suggests the people will voluntarily submit, and that for the best of reasons—recognition of Israel's God and him alone. Young (*Book of Isaiah*, in loc.) says, "Paul evidently reflects upon this language when he says, '. . . and declare that God of a truth is in you' (1 Cor 14:25)." (For a general discussion of the interpretation of such passages, see the Introduction, pp. 14–16.)

15–17 The startling disclosures just made prompt this prophetic exclamation of wonderment. The conversion of the Gentiles involves the discrediting of idolatry (v.16) and the salvation and vindication of God's ancient people (v.17). The final phrase of v.17 makes it clear that this is no momentary thing but a permanent vindication of them by their God.

18–19 In this section of the prophecy, the introductory formula "This is what the LORD says" (v.18) introduces some utterances of grandeur about God himself. He created the universe as an environment for man; and so, it is implied, his work is to be discerned in history as well as in nature. Perhaps he does hide himself, for revelation is his sole prerogative; but when he does speak, his word is clear and true, enabling his people—called to seek him—to find him in truth (v.19).

20–21 After the disclosure about Egypt, Cush, and Seba in v.14, the prophet called on the remnant of humanity left after all history's wars and upheavals (v.20). There is to be a last challenge to paganism. Only the Lord predicted the coming of Cyrus and the righteous salvation of Israel. He has established forever his claim to be recognized as the only God there is (v.21).

22–25 Another amazing disclosure is made here; for the God whose actions discredit paganism calls the discomfited idolators, not for the judgment they so richly deserve, but for salvation—if only they will turn to him (v.22; cf. 1 Thess 1:9–10)! God's great decree has been announced that all humanity shall come to acknowledge his sovereignty (v.23). There are definite echoes of v.23 in Philippians 2:10–11, with implications concerning the deity of Jesus all the more impressive because of the emphatic monotheism of the context here. All will not be saved, but all must acknowledge the Lord as God alone (v.24). Under his ultimate sovereignty there will be both judgment for the rebel and salvation for God's people.

Notes

24–28 Some commentators who accept the Deutero-Isaiah theory (e.g. North) are impressed with the literary form of this without drawing the conclusion Allis (*Isaiah*, pp. 62–80) so well contends for, that the form serves the interests of dramatic predictive disclosure. See the comment above.

45: 2 הָדוּרִים (*hᵃdûrîm*, "mountains" in NIV) is a word of uncertain meaning, but the translation fits the context and the imagery of the prophet in similar passages (cf., e.g., 40:4).

4 The title of honor will be "My shepherd" (44:28) or "My anointed" (cf. v.1), or will have a more general reference to an honored place in the working out of God's purposes in history.

8 In this verse "righteousness" is first צֶדֶק (*ṣedeq*) and then צְדָקָה (*ṣᵉdāqāh*), masculine and feminine respectively, but virtual synonyms.

13 The context determines that Cyrus is the subject here (cf. esp. 44:26–28), since only the pronoun is actually used.

14 Some commentators repoint the MT's second person plural pronouns so that they are masculine and so may refer to Cyrus, rather than feminine, referring to Israel. This keeps the MT inviolate but is unnecesary in view of the parallel with chapter 60. Most of those who follow this emendation attribute this chapter to Deutero-Isaiah but chapter 60 to Trito-Isaiah.

18–19 תֹּהוּ (*tōhû*), translated "empty" and "in vain" here, occurs also in Gen 1:2. It is very doubtful whether support for the idea of a catastrophe between Gen 1:1 and Gen 1:2 with a consequent voiding of the universe should be sought or can be found here.

8. Babylon's Ineffectual Idols and the Lord Almighty

46:1–13

¹Bel bows down, Nebo stoops low;
  their idols are borne by beasts of burden.
The images that are carried about are burdensome,
  a burden for the weary.
²They stoop and bow down together;
  unable to rescue the burden,
  they themselves go off into captivity.
³"Listen to me, O house of Jacob,
  all you who remain of the house of Israel,
you whom I have upheld since you were conceived,
  and have carried since your birth.
⁴Even to your old age and gray hairs
  I am he, I am he who will sustain you.
I have made you and I will carry you;
  I will sustain you and I will rescue you.

⁵"To whom will you comapre me or count me equal?
  To whom will you liken me that we may be compared?
⁶Some pour out gold from their bags
  and weigh out silver on the scales;
they hire a goldsmith to make it into a god,
  and they bow down and worship it.
⁷They lift it to their shoulders and carry it;
  they set it up in its place, and there it stands.
From that spot it cannot move

Though one cries out to it, it does not answer;
it cannot save him from his troubles.

8"Remember this, fix it in mind,
take it to heart, you rebels.
9Remember the former things, those of long ago;
I am God, and there is no other;
I am God, and there is none like me.
10I make known the end from the beginning,
from ancient times, what is still to come.
I say: My purpose will stand,
and I will do all that I please.
11From the east I summon a bird of prey;
from a far-off land, a man to fulfill my purpose.
What I have said, that will I bring about;
what I have planned, that will I do.
12Listen to me, you stubborn-hearted,
you who are far from righteousness.
13I am bringing my righteousness near;
it is not far away;
and my salvation will not be delayed.
I will grant salvation to Zion,
my splendor to Israel.

1–2 All references so far made in the prophecy or Isaiah to pagan deities or idols have been general. Here, appropriately, where Cyrus and his victories are much in view, Isaiah named the two great gods of Babylon; Bel (also called Marduk) and Nebo (v.1) familiar to us from the compound names Belshazzar and Nebuchadnezzar. In chapter 45 Isaiah declared that every knee will bow to the Lord, and here he pictures the gods of great Babylon stooping low in humiliation. We noted earlier that Isaiah was fond of the imagery of burden-bearing (see comments esp. at 1:4, 14, 24). Here he applies it first to the gods of Babylon and then, in vv.3–4, to the Lord. The idols are taken from their places of honor and placed on the backs of animals, bundled off perhaps first in flight and then to captivity (v.2). It is true (see comment at 45:1–7) that Cyrus attributed his victories to Marduk, but there can be little doubt that those who heard of the downfall of Babylon would see in this a colossal defeat for her gods. P. Volz (*Jesaia II* [Leipzig: A. Deichertsche Verlagsbuchhandlung, 1932], in loc.) has suggested that the tiredness of the animals is calculated to underline still further the impotence of the gods. They have become a liability to both man and beast.

3–4 How different is the Lord's relationship to his people! No contrast could be greater. His people do not carry him; rather he bears them, and moreover he always has done so and always will. This passage is an inspired affirmation of the only worthy concept of deity, that of the true eternal God, over against the gross inadequacies and irreverences of paganism. The verbs used here—repeating and underlining over and over again the fact that he is the God who carries his people—give place suddenly and dramatically at the end of v.4 to a new one. The God of their history promises to rescue them. The work of Cyrus was to be viewed as God's great work of deliverance.

5–7 Isaiah has already proclaimed the Lord's uniqueness in ringing rhetorical questions (cf. 40:18, 25); and he repeats this, most aptly here (v.5), for that uniqueness has been singularly demonstrated in the overthrow of Babylon's gods. Not in their downfall alone, but at every point in their history, the idols' paltry character vividly contrasts with the Lord's unique majesty. The poor values of man determine their idols' materials. The whole process, from the preparation through the commissioning of the workmen and the transportation of the idols to their eventual worship, is quite unavailing; for they are powerless to hear, to speak, or to save.

8–13 This part of Isaiah concentrates largely on consolation and encouragement, but the prophet was a realist and knew from experience that there was much unbelief among the people. They approached the prophecies of Cyrus and his work with skepticism. The Lord calls them to consider the history of his relationship with his people (vv.8–9). This illustrates the important fact that faith has objective reference and so is a response to revelation, to truth about God declared by God himself. The people's whole history had demonstrated his sole deity and especially his power to predict (v.10). He asserts it again: from the east (v.11; cf. 41:2), Cyrus will swoop on his victims, as suddenly as the descent of an eagle or a falcon from the sky. Whether they believe it or not (v.12), it will happen; for in this way the Lord would fulfill his saving purpose for Israel. The term "Zion" here (v.13) should be noted; it is a reminder of the promises of 44:26–28.

Notes

1–2 A number of commentators (e.g., Westermann, Whybray) note the rapid rhythm of these two verses, expressive for the writer and inducing in the reader a feeling of excitement.

In this context the three long vowels of הֲלָכָה (*hālāḵāh*, "go"), as North (*Isaiah 40–55*, in loc.) points out, emphasize weariness. We might compare the sentence "so strode he back slow to the wounded king" in Tennyson's "Morte d'Arthur."

11 עַיִט (*ʿayiṭ*, "bird of prey") is found also in 18:6, but its promise meaning is unknown. It was probably a type of eagle, falcon, or vulture.

9. The Fall of Proud Babylon

47:1–15

¹Go down, sit in the dust,
  Virgin Daughter of Babylon;
sit on the ground without a throne,
  Daughter of the Babylonians.
No more will you be called
  tender or delicate.
²Take millstones and grind flour;
  take off your veil.
Lift up your skirts, bare your legs,
  and wade through the streams.
³Your nakedness will be exposed
  and your shame uncovered.
I will take vengeance;
  I will spare no one."

⁴Our Redeemer—The LORD Almighty is his name-
   is the Holy One of Israel.

⁵"Sit in silence, go into darkness,
   Daughter of the Babylonians;
no more will you be called
   queen of kingdoms.
⁶I was angry with my people
   and desecrated my inheritance;
I gave them into your hand,
   and you showed them no mercy.
Even on the aged
   you laid a very heavy yoke.
⁷You said, 'I will continue forever—
   the eternal queen!'
But you did not consider these things
   or reflect on what might happen.

⁸"Now then, listen, you wanton creature,
   lounging in your security
and saying to yourself,
   'I am, and there is none besides me.
I will never be a widow
   or suffer the loss of children.'
⁹Both of these will overtake you
   in a moment, on a single day;
loss of children and widowhood.
They will come upon you in full measure,
   in spite of your many sorceries
   and all your potent spells.
¹⁰You have trusted in your wickedness
   and have said, 'No one sees me.'
Your wisdom and knowledge mislead you
   when you say to yourself,
   'I am, and there is none besides me.'
¹¹Disaster will come upon you,
   and you will not know how to conjure it away.
A calamity will fall upon you
   that you cannot ward off with a ransom;
a catastrophe you cannot foresee
   will suddenly come upon you.

¹²"Keep on, then, with your magic spells
   and with your many sorceries,
   which you have labored at since childhood.
Perhaps you will succeed,
   perhaps you will cause terror.
¹³All the counsel you have received has only worn you out!
   Let your astrologers come forward,
those stargazers who make predictions month by month,
   let them save you from what is coming upon you.
¹⁴Surely they are like stubble;
   the fire will burn them up.
They cannot even save themselves
   from the power of the flame.
Here are no coals to warm anyone;
   here is no fire to sit by.
¹⁵That is all they can do for you—
   these you have labored with
   and trafficked with since childhood.

Each of them goes on in his error;
there is not one that can save you.

We experience a sense of fitness when we find that an oracle about the downfall of Babylon's gods is followed immediately by a proclamation of the Fall of Babylon herself. It was fitting that the discomfiture of the one should involve the fall of the other, for there was solidarity between them.

1–4 The prophet's inspired imagination continues to overleap the years separating his own day from the close of the Babylonian exile. He addresses the proud capital city with irony as "my lady Babylon" (Thexton, in loc.). She is to be dethroned and made to sit in the dust (v.1). It may be that there are three analogies here, following one another in swift succession: (1) she is the beggar, sitting in the dust; (2) she is the slave, divesting herself of the gentlewoman's veil and accepting the hard grind of manual labor (v.2a); and (3) she is the fugitive, needing to tuck in her skirts to enable her to cross streams (vv.2b–3), abandoning of necessity the decorum that befitted her former station. It is possible, however, that the prophet envisages Babylon simply as a slave and that she crosses the streams on her master's business.

The Lord declares all this to be an expression of his impartial punitive justice, and the prophet follows this by asserting that the judgment is to be understood in the context of his holy and redemptive purpose for Israel. Westermann (in loc.) helpfully comments on v.4 that Isaiah's addition of the phrase "Yahweh of hosts ['the LORD Almighty' in the NIV] is deliberate; he was thinking of the importance attaching to the heavenly bodies in Babylon (v.13), but they are no more than the creatures of God, who obey his command (40:26)."

5–7 The prophet's interjection in v.4 is parenthetical, for the direct address from God is now resumed. From the blare of world publicity and the glare of the palace lights to the silence of obscurity (v.5)! Babylon's dominion was not only over the southern Mesopotamian heartland of her empire but also over many petty kingdoms she had vanquished. The prophecy recognizes that the Babylonian destruction of Judah and the exile of its people was to be understood as a divine punishment (v.6; cf. 39:5–7 and, for the same principle 10:5–6, 12). Babylon, however, went too far, and it has been suggested that the condition of the exiles may have worsened toward the close of their captivity. It is characteristic of Isaiah to underline not only man's inhumanity to man, in which Amos had anticipated him (cf. Amos 1:3, 6, 9, 13; 2:1, 6–8; 4:1; 5:11; 8:4–6), but also pride as a major cause of Babylon's judgment (v.7; cf. esp. 13:19; 14:13–15).

8–11 The accusation of self-sufficient pride already leveled at Babylonia is further expounded. This pleasure-loving lady of leisure will soon find herself a childless widow (v.8), her widowhood robbing her of the possibility of further family. Isaiah has already made it plain that sorcery and other ways of trafficking with the forbidden supernatural realm were a cause of God's judgment on his people (v.9; 2:6; 8:19). For the Babylonians, sorcery also induced a mood of complacency (v.10), because the people relied on their magicians to predict the coming of the enemy and to defeat him. In Babylonia the intellectual and the magical were intertwined, the wise man being instructed in all the arts of the supernatural.

12–15 The NIV has very well interpreted the changes of tone to be found in this section, each verse having its own atmosphere. First, in v.12 the prophet taunts Babylonia sarcastically. Such a rag bag of spells and magic arts she has accumulated! Could it be that there is an outside chance of success? "Not a hope!" the prophet implies. Then in v.13 he exhorts the experts with the horoscopes to provide deliverance. Babylonia, with its astral deities, was the natural home of the astrologer and his kin. The prophet identifies for a moment with the people, besieged with advice from such men and yet with no hope of a remedy for future calamity. In v.13 he says, "Let them save you"; and in v.14 he boldly asserts, "They cannot even save themselves."

Verse 14 is dominated by an illustration. The coming of the great judgment is likened to a consuming fire, and the tone of sarcasm returns in the second half of the verse. They should not mistake the meaning of the illustration. This is fire as an enemy, not as a friend. The whole history of Babylon's long flirtation with astrology is bluntly dismissed in v.15. All this effort, all this expenditure, and at the end—nothing! Those who have turned from the living God to the daily horoscope in our own society would do well to heed this passage.

Notes

1 For the description of a city as a בַּת (*bat*, "daughter"), see the note at 1:8.

The NIV margin—"Or *Chaldeans*; also in verse 5"—gives the literal rendering for "Babylonians"; but of course the two terms are virtual synonyms, Babylonia being originally the locational and Chaldean the ethnic designation.

10. Israel's Stubbornness and God's Purpose of Grace

48:1–22

1"Listen to this, O house of Jacob,
    you who are called by the name of Israel
    and come from the line of Judah,
you who take oaths in the name of the LORD
    and invoke the God of Israel—
    but not in truth or righteousness—
2you who call yourselves citizens of the holy city
    and rely on the God of Israel—
    the LORD Almighty is his name:
3I foretold the former things long ago,
    my mouth announced them and I made them known;
    then suddenly I acted, and they came to pass.
4For I knew how stubborn you were;
    the sinews of your neck were iron,
    your forehead was bronze.
5Therefore I told you these things long ago;
    before they happened I announced them to you
so that you could not say,
    'My idols did them;
    my wooden image and metal god ordained them.'
6You have heard these things; look at them all.
    Will you not admit them?

"From now on I will tell you of new things,
of hidden things unknown to you.
⁷They are created now, and not long ago;
you have not heard of them before today.
So you cannot say,
'Yes, I knew of them.'
⁸You have neither heard nor understood;
from of old your ear has not been open.
Well do I know how treacherous you are;
you were called a rebel from birth.
⁹For my own name's sake I delay my wrath;
for the sake of my praise I hold it back from you,
so as not to cut you off.
¹⁰See, I have refined you, though not as silver;
I have tested you in the furnace of affliction.
¹¹For my own sake, for my own sake, I do this.
How can I let myself be defamed?
I will not yield my glory to another.
¹²"Listen to me, O Jacob,
Israel, whom I have called:
I am he;
I am the first and I am the last.
¹³My own hand laid the foundations of the earth,
and my right hand spread out the heavens;
when I summon them,
they all stand up together.

¹⁴"Come together, all of you, and listen;
Which of the idols has foretold these things?
The Lord's chosen ally
will carry out his purpose against Babylon;
his arm will be against the Babylonians.
¹⁵I, even I, have spoken;
yes, I have called him.
I will bring him,
and he will succeed in his mission.

¹⁶"Come near me and listen to this:

"From the first announcement I have not spoken in secret;
at the time it happens, I am there."

And now the Sovereign Lord has sent me,
with his Spirit.

¹⁷This is what the Lord says—
your Redeemer, the Holy One of Israel:
"I am the Lord your God,
who teaches you what is best for you,
who directs you in the way you should go.
¹⁸If only you had paid attention to my commands,
your peace would have been like a river,
your righteousness like the waves of the sea.
¹⁹Your descendants would have been like the sand,
your children like its numberless grains;
their name would never be cut off
nor destroyed from before me."

> [20]Leave Babylon,
>   flee from the Babylonians!
> Announce this with shouts of joy
>   and proclaim it.
> Send it out to the ends of the earth;
>   say, "The LORD has redeemed his servant Jacob."
> [21]They did not thirst when he led them through the deserts;
>   he made water flow for them from the rock.
> he split the rock
>   and water gushed out.
>
> [22]"There is no peace," says the LORD, "for the wicked."

The integrity of this chapter has been denied, especially on account of its "abrupt alternations of mood" (Whybray, *Isaiah, 40–66*, in loc.). It should however be remembered that the generally comforting tone of chapters 40–48 is punctuated by such passages as 40:21, 27–28; 42:18–25; 43:22–28; 45:9; 46:8–12. A degree of oscillation between comfort and rebuke therefore is characteristic of this section of the book. Whybray admits that there are plenty of unifying themes.

1–6a The call to attend (v.1; cf. vv.12, 14, 16, 18) introduces God's charge that his people are stubborn skeptics. They are untrue both to their national names and to their religious profession. The name "Israel" means "he struggles with God" (Gen 32:28 [NIV mg.]; cf. Rom 9:6) and "Judah" means "praise". (Gen 49:8; cf. Rom 2:28–29). The people were proud too of their citizenship in the place God had set apart for himself (cf. 52:1 and also 1:21, 26). The reality beneath these verbal symbols however was lacking. God's own name was used in solemn religious vows and in prayer, not in true faith manifested in righteousness, but in presumptuous reliance on mere profession. Isaiah often calls for faith in God, but faith requires proper biblical definition, as James recognized (James 2:14–26). Let them recall that he is also the Lord Almighty (v.2), implying that he may use this great power to bring judgment on them (cf. 1:9, 24 and comments there).

Not only were the people stiff-necked and brazen in their attitude toward God's word (v.4), but they had a chronic tendency to attribute his acts to other gods (v.5; cf. Hos 2:8). The adjectives "wooden" and "metal" reflect the prophet's contempt for idols (cf. 44:19). Let them admit that he is the God of prophecy and fulfillment and therefore true to his word (v.6a).

6b–11 From things foretold "long ago" (vv.3, 5), the divine word proceeds to reveal new things (v.6b)—the work of Cyrus (vv.14–16) and the Servant of the Lord (vv.16; 49:1–7). The word *bārā'* ("create"), used in Genesis 1 of God's creative word, is used in v.7 to underline the fact that what God has declared is as certain as if it is already fulfilled (cf. Heb 1:1).

Israel is rebellious (v.8; cf. 1:2). God did not reveal these things earlier, for he knew how cynically she would react. Her ear was shut to his glad tidings, while, Isaiah will show, the Servant's would be open to accept his destiny of suffering (50:4). There may be an implied contrast between vv.9, 11 and vv.1–2 (see earlier comments). The people were untrue to their own name, but—it is strongly emphasized—God would vindicate his own. Rebellious and treacherous they might be, but they would always find him true, upholding the honor of his great name and therefore restraining the full outpouring of his wrath on the people of the promises.

12–16 The renewed call to listen (v. 12; cf. v. 1) may mark this as a separate oracle. It is more likely however that it underlines the importance of the three great facts here declared. First, God speaks of himself, his self-existence, his lordship over all history from its beginning to its consummation (v. 12), and his creation and present control of all that is (v. 13). Then he speaks a word about Cyrus, whom he calls "the LORD's chosen ally" (v. 14; cf. 44:28; 45:1). This makes explicit for the first time that Cyrus's work would bring down Babylonia (v. 15; cf. 14:13–23).

Finally (v. 16) another speaker mysteriously enters the prophecy. This verse has a number of features that have mystified commentators, who have been puzzled particularly by its final couplet. Young, Kidner, and other conservative commentators have argued that the new speaker introduced here (or in the whole verse) is in fact God's Servant, the Servant of the songs. He is clearly not simply the Lord, and the phrase "Sovereign LORD" recurs in 50:4–5, 7, 9, in the context of the third Servant Song. Unlike the first and fourth songs, where it is God who speaks about him, here, as in the second and third, he himself speaks. Perhaps he is introduced here because Cyrus's work is in fact simply a type of harbinger of the much greater deliverance he would bring to God's people (see esp. the comment at 53:1).

Grammatically "the Spirit" (v. 16) could be either a second subject or a second object, but it is almost certainly the latter. North (*Isaiah 40–55*, in loc.) says, "In the Old Testament the spirit never sends but is always sent." The NIV's rather free rendering is probably intended to leave both options of interpretation open.

17–19 Every sensitive teacher knows the pain of heart that comes when he pours himself out for students who prove to be unteachable. Israel proved to be like that (cf. v. 8); and God expresses his deep concern for them, because they are themselves the losers. Here is one of the Bible's great cries from the very heart of God (cf. Gen 3:9; Deut 5:28–29; Ps 81:13–14; Hos 11:8; Luke 13:34–35). The language used does not, in fact, exclude all possibility of penitent amendment, as if all hope had gone. The similies speak of abundance; and the whole passage stresses the contingent nature of God's blessings, even some of these that have been the subject of his own promises (v. 19; cf. Gen 22:17). Divine grace can of course so work within the heart that promises seemingly uncertain of fulfillment are made sure by the regenerative work of the Spirit.

20–22 This most dramatic passage anticipates the call given in 52:11–12. The military-style command is explicit and urgent and is associated with a call to all the earth to praise God for his redeeming grace to Israel. The "shouts of joy" (v. 20) were of course perfectly natural, and those who have suffered internment in prison camps in our own day know how deep such joy can be. Verse 21 suddenly moves from the future to the past, for the people's confidence in God as their redeemer from Babylonia was to be based on his redeeming love demonstrated at the Exodus and his care of his people during their journey through the wilderness. In such a context v. 22 may seem harsh, but the prophet was a realist and knew the unbelief many of the people would view this vision with; for, as he has shown earlier in the chapter, their skepticism was endemic. Acts of salvation are not for the stubbornly wicked and unbelieving but for those who have faith (cf. Rev 22:14–15).

Notes

1 "The line of Judah"—מִמֵּי יְהוּדָה (*mimmê yᵉhûḏāh*)—is literally "the waters of Judah," which could be a euphemism for semen; or else—after the model of Deut 33:28; Ps 68:26 (lit., "fountain of Israel")—Judah is pictured as the spring the stream of the people took its rise from. Conjectural emendation is not needed.

4 Some commentators point out that the language here is more characteristic of Ezekiel, but this could suggest the dependence of the later prophet on the earlier and need not imply the work of another hand.

8 The active verb פִּתְּחָה (*pittᵉḥāh*, "open"), though unusual, should be retained as giving emphasis to the fact that their deafness was culpable.

10 The words "though not as silver" are difficult. In their context they probably mean that God had chastened the people in a way that could be likened to the methods used for refining silver but that, because of their obstinacy, the desired results had not been achieved. For Egypt as the furnace of affliction, see Deut 4:20; 1 Kings 8:51; Jer 11:4.

14 The NIV inserts "the idols" to make explicit what is clearly implicit here (cf. 41:22).

16 The call to attend here may be compared with 49:1 and raises the possibility that the whole verse, not just its closing couplet, may relate to the Servant. It would make the reference less abrupt but no less impressive. It also suggests a possible contrast between speaking in secret here and being concealed in God's quiver in the later passage, suggesting perhaps that the latter should be understood relatively not absolutely.

VIII. The Gospel of the Servant of the Lord (49:1–57:21)

Those who distinguish between Deutero- and Trito-Isaiah normally terminate the work of the former at the end of chapter 55. We do not, however, accept the author division or fragmentation of the book (see Introduction, pp. 6–12). In many respects chapters 49–57 form a better division within the book. If the remaining chapters constitute a further special section, then the repetition of the words of 48:22 in 57:21 and the similar theme that concludes the whole book may be intentional structural markers in a book chracterized by its order (see Introduction, pp. 20–21).

1. *The Lord's Servant and the Restoration of Israel*

49:1–26

¹Listen to me, you islands;
  hear this, you distant nations:
Before I was born the LORD called me;
  from my birth he has made mention of my name.
²He made my mouth like a sharpened sword,
  in the shadow of his hand he hid me;
he made me into a polished arrow
  and concealed me in his quiver.
³He said to me, "You are my servant,
  Israel, in whom I will display my splendor."
⁴But I said, "I have labored to no purpose;
  I have spent my strength in vain and for nothing.
Yet what is due me is in the LORD's hand,
  and my reward is with my God."

⁵And now the LORD says—
  he who formed me in the womb to be his servant

to bring Jacob back to him
and gather Israel to himself,
for I am honored in the eyes of the Lord
and my God has been my strength—
⁶he says:
"It is too small a thing for you to be my servant
to restore the tribes of Jacob
and bring back those of Israel I have kept.
I will also make you a light for the Gentiles,
that you may bring my salvation to the ends
of the earth."

⁷This is what the Lord says—
the Redeemer and Holy One of Israel—
to him who was despised and abhorred by the nation,
to the servant of rulers:
"Kings will see you and rise up,
princes will see and bow down,
because of the Lord, who is faithful,
the Holy One of Israel, who has chosen you."

⁸This is what the Lord says:

"In the time of my favor I will answer you,
and in the day of salvation I will help you;
I will keep you and will make you
to be a covenant for the people,
to restore the land
and to reassign its desolate inheritances,
⁹to say to the captives, 'Come out,'
and to those in darkness, 'Be free!'

"They will feed beside the roads
and find pasture on every barren hill.
¹⁰They will neither hunger nor thirst,
nor will the desert heat or the sun beat upon them.
He who has compassion on them will guide them
and lead them beside springs of water.
¹¹I will turn all my mountains into roads,
and my highways will be raised up.
¹²See, they will come from afar—
some from the north, some from the west,
some from the region of Aswan."
¹³Shout for joy, O heavens;
rejoice, O earth;
burst into song, O mountains!
For the Lord comforts his people
and will have compassion on his afflicted ones.

¹⁴But Zion said, "The Lord has forsaken me,
the Lord has forgotten me."

¹⁵"Can a mother forget the baby at her breast
and have no compassion on the child she has borne?
Though she may forget,
I will not forget you!
¹⁶See, I have engraved you on the palms of my hands;
your walls are ever before me.
¹⁷Your sons hasten back,
and those who laid you waste depart from you.

18Lift up your eyes and look around;
  all your sons gather and come to you.
As surely as I live," declares the LORD,
  "you will wear them all as ornaments;
  you will put them on, like a bride.

19"Though you were ruined and made desolate
  and our land laid waste,
now you will be too small for your people,
  and those who devoured you will be far away.
20The children born during your bereavement
  will yet say in your hearing,
'This place is too small for us;
  give us more space to live in.
21Then you will say in your heart,
  'Who bore me these?
I was bereaved and barren;
  I was exiled and rejected
Who brought these up?
  I was left all alone,
  but these—where have they come from?' "

22This is what the Sovereign LORD says:

"See, I will beckon to the Gentiles,
  I will lift up my banner to the peoples;
they will bring your sons in their arms
  and carry your daughters on their shoulders.
23Kings will be your foster fathers,
  and their queens your nursing mothers.
They will bow down before you with their faces
    to the ground;
  they will lick the dust at your feet.
Then you will know that I am the LORD;
  those who hope in me will not be disappointed."
24Can plunder be taken from warriors,
  or captives rescued from the fierce?

25But this is what the LORD says:

"Yes, captives will be taken from warriors,
  and plunder retrieved from the fierce;
I will contend with those who contend with you,
  and your children I will save.
26I will make your oppressors eat their own flesh;
  they will be drunk on their own blood, as with wine.
Then all mankind will know
  that I, the LORD, am your Savior,
  your Redeemer, the Mighty One of Jacob."

For general discussion of the so-called Servant Songs and their interpretation, the reader should see the Introduction, pp. 7, 17–20. This is the second of the songs, though, as we have suggested at 48:16, this passage is anticipated not only by chapter 42 but also by that verse.

1–7 Although a collective interpretation of this passage is not impossible and is naturally suggested by a consideration of v.3, a straightforward application to Israel is ruled out by vv.5–7. The (probably intended) result is that the reader is forced by the material itself to face the question Who is this?

If—as we suggested in the introduction to chapter 42—the first song can be viewed as contemplating the ministry of Jesus the Servant in prospect from the perspective of his baptism, this second song seems to be looking back on that ministry from its close. The distant nations are to benefit from his work; so he calls them to listen (v.1). This itself harmonizes with the prophetic ministry he was predestined to (cf. Jer 1:4–5). Isaiah's illustrative gift can be seen in v.2, where the penetrating character of the Servant's message is likened to two sharp weapons, while the implications of the second are developed to bring out a further point. Concealment in the quiver suggests, as does v.1 more literally, an eternal purpose manifest at the appropriate time (cf. 1 Peter 1:20).

Isaiah 42:18–20 presented Israel as the deaf and blind servant of the Lord, and 44:21–23 assures us that nevertheless God intends to display his glory in Israel his servant. Here (v.3) that promise is reiterated. Matthew saw Jesus as the expression of God's mind for Israel, as his quotation of Hosea 11:1 in Matthew 2:15 makes clear; and the Gospel of John asserts that God's glory is revealed in him (e.g., John 1:14; 2:11). Jesus, even more than Nathanael, is "a true Israelite, in whom there is nothing false" (John 1:47).

The close of the ministry of Jesus saw the great crowds of Galilean days no longer thronging him, the official religious leaders plotting his death, and the disciples forsaking him in the face of danger; but God would reward him (v.4; cf. Heb 12:2).

Verse 5 makes it clear that the Servant is not Israel per se, for he has a ministry to Israel. The people may despise him (v.7), but God honors him. Honor is shown in the range of his ministry, for through it he will in fact be brought to great honor before the world's kings and princes. The phrase "and now" suggests the transition from the limited ministry of the Gospels to the more extensive proclamation of his gospel through the apostles in Acts. The words of v.6—"it is too small a thing"— suggest an estimate of his person or of his work or of perhaps both. The restoration of the remnant—mentioned often in Isaiah (e.g., 11:10–16)—is to be expounded later in this chapter. Israel has light but needs restoration, while the Gentiles need both light and salvation. The church's mission to the Gentiles is to be viewed in the context of the mission of Jesus himself (cf. John 20:21) and is to the uttermost parts of the earth (Matt 28:19; Mark 16:15; Luke 24:47; Acts 1:8).

Accordingly Paul and Barnabas could apply the words of v.6 to themselves (Acts 13:46–47). The Nunc Dimittis, on the other hand, applies this verse to Jesus himself (Luke 2:32). This means that we have NT warrant for interpreting this second song both individually and collectively, with the second emerging out of the first.

Verse 7 prepares for the third and fourth songs. The unique servant's ministry was in fact rejected by the nation (cf., e.g., Rom 9–11). Great as he was, he came as a subject, not only of God himself, but of earthly rulers such as Augustus, Tiberius, and Herod. As a result of his work, the highest of men and women would not only stand in respect and perhaps amazement but, even more appropriately, would bow low in worship and submission.

8–12 Although the opening words of v.8 certainly appear to mark a new beginning, almost a fresh oracle, they present a contrast with v.7. So often, especially in the Acts of the Apostles, it is said in the NT that the Christ rejected and crucified by men was raised and thus vindicated by God (e.g., Acts 2:23). The favor of God to the unique Servant is of course merited, but the quotation of v.8 in 2 Corinthians 6:2

shows that in Christ we share not only his service (see comment at v.6) but also his acceptance (cf. Eph 1:6).

The background to the expression "the time of my favor" (v.8) is probably the Day of Jubilee in Leviticus 25:8–55 (cf. 61:1–2 and the comments there). For the covenant reference, see the comment at 42:6. The context here suggests that part of the Servant's work is to establish the aspects of the Abrahamic and possibly the Mosaic covenants that related to the land of Canaan. Children and a land were major blessings of the covenant with Abraham (Gen 12:2–3); the first is mentioned in 48:19 and the second here. The Servant would be a kind of second Joshua (the Hebrew equivalent to the Greek "Jesus"). The land would be repeopled by freed captives (v.9a).

The new conditions of the people are beautifully described in vv.9b–12. They are first pictured like sheep finding abundant pasture in a formerly barren land (the "desolate heritages" of v.8). In this land they will find food, water, and shelter (v.10). They will be guided by a compassionate shepherd (cf. Ps 23). These verses are echoed and applied to Christ in Revelation 7:16–17. The pastoral imagery now disappears and is replaced by assurances of suitable road conditions (v.11) and of a return from every quarter (v.12), already familiar to us from earlier passages (cf. 35:8; 40:3–4; 42:16; 43:5–7). The application of such passages is discussed in the Introduction, pp. 14–16.

13–21 The news of deliverance from Babylonia was to be proclaimed with joy to the ends of the earth (48:20); now the heavens and the earth, in true Isaianic fashion, are called to praise the Lord (v.13; cf. 1:2; 44:23). The note of comfort chapter 40 opened with returns, but now the prophet confronts the people's discouragement. Verse 14, like 40:9 (cf. also 44:26–28), speaks not of Israel but of Zion. At the time of the return from the Exile, the Holy City would be in ruins, its walls reduced to rubble. The Lord assures her that he has not forgotten her. He uses two telling illustrations. Mother love (v.15) is proverbial in every culture; God's love for this city and its people went well beyond this. Verse 16 may have tattooing in view (see KD, 2:269; but cf. Lev 19:28). The walls of Jerusalem would not even exist at the time of the return, but those people that had been and were yet to be were engraved on the hands of God.

Abraham had been told to lift up his eyes to look at the Land of Promise (Gen 13:14); now Zion was to look up to see her restored citizens coming from every quarter (v.18). In another beautiful image God pictures Zion as proudly putting on her citizens, like a bride her jewels. In fact, the numbers coming would be so great that the city could not house them all (v.19). Young (*Book of Isaiah*, in loc.) well sums up vv.20–21: "Zion regarded herself as a widow; as a matter of fact her Husband, the Lord, had not forsaken or forgotten her. The children who will one day crowd to her are legitimate children, begotten through a lively faith."

22–23 Earlier in the chapter, the Servant is told that kings and princes will give him respect and submission. His people will have their share also; for not only will the Gentile nations rally to God's banner (v.22) tenderly bringing the exiled Israelites with them (cf. 11:10–12), but their exalted monarchs, with all the gentle care of parents, will also do obeisance (v.23). There will be a recognition of the special place of Israel. The Lord had made himself known to Israel at the Exodus (Exod 6:7, et al.). God will not fail his people who trust in him (cf. 28:16).

24-26 Echoes of the Exodus constantly appear in this part of Isaiah. Those who read the question of v.24 will certainly have recalled that this is exactly what God did when he delivered his people from Egypt, the house of bondage (v.25). Moreover on that occasion not only did God make himself known to Israel but also to the Egyptians, and the greater redemption from oppression promised here will also lead to a wider recognition that God is—but this time by all mankind. Verse 26a is a graphic and gruesome way of indicating the utter desperation of the enemies of Israel, overcome with hunger and thirst, in contrast to Israel's promised condition (vv.9-11).

Notes

3 This is the most difficult verse in the Servant Songs for the individual interpretation. Many commentators have argued against the authenticity of the word "Israel" here, but the evidence against it is weak unless it be thought impossible for the Servant to be Israel and to have a mission to Israel at the same time. The Introduction (pp. 17–20) suggests a solution that treats the text seriously.

7 בְּזֹה־נֶפֶשׁ (bᵉzōh-nepeš, "despised" in NIV) is literally "a despising of soul." 1QIsa et al. read בְּזוּי־נֶפֶשׁ (bᵉzûy-nepeš, "despised of soul"), which may be correct.

12 סִינִים (sînîm) has long puzzled commentators, some taking it to refer to China. 1QIsa reads סוניים (swnyym), which is close to סְוֵנִים (sᵉwēnîm), a conjectural emendation often accepted by commentators. This would mean the people of Syene or Aswan (cf. Ezek 29:10; and is followed by the NIV 30:6). Jeremiah (44:1) refers to Jews in his day living in this area of Lower Egypt.

17 The NIV's "your sons" follows the MT's בָּנָיִךְ (bānāyik), while 1QIsa and some versions repoint it as bōnayik ("your builders"). Either is possible, for in either case there could be intentional paronomasia.

2. Israel's Sin and the Servant's Obedience

50:1-11

¹This is what the LORD says:

> "Where is your mother's certificate of divorce
> with which I sent her away?
> Or to which of my creditors
> did I sell you?
> Because of your sins you were sold;
> because of your transgressions your mother was sent away.
> ²When I came, why was there no one?
> When I called, why was there no one to answer?
> Was my arm too short to ransom you?
> Do I lack the strength to rescue you?
> By a mere rebuke I dry up the sea,
> I turn rivers into a desert;
> their fish rot for lack of water
> and die of thirst.
> ³I clothe the sky with darkness
> and make sackcloth its covering."

⁴The Sovereign Lord has given me an instructed tongue,
   to know the word that sustains the weary.
He wakens me morning by morning,
   wakens my ear to listen like one being taught.
⁵The Sovereign Lord has opened my ears,
   and I have not been rebellious;
   I have not drawn back.
⁶I offered my back to those who beat me,
   my cheeks to those who pulled out my beard;
I did not hide my face
   from mocking and spitting.
⁷Because the Sovereign Lord helps me,
   I will not be disgraced.
Therefore have I set my face like flint,
   and I know I will not be put to shame.
⁸He who vindicates me is near.
   Who then will bring charges against me?
   Let us face each other!
Who is my accuser?
   Let him confront me!
⁹It is the Sovereign Lord who helps me.
   Who is he that will condemn me?
They will all wear out like a garment;
   the moths will eat them up.

¹⁰Who among you fears the Lord
   and obeys the word of his servant?
Let him who walks in the dark,
   who has no light,
trust in the name of the Lord
   and rely on his God.
¹¹But now, all you who light fires
   and provide yourselves with flaming torches,
go, walk in the light of your fires
   and of the torches you have set ablaze.
This is what you shall receive from my hand:
   You will lie down in torment.

Here, as in chapter 42, the true Servant of God appears in a context speaking of rebellious Israel, named also as God's servant in the earlier passage (42:19). Here, as in 49:3, 6, the Servant is the perfect expression of God's mind for Israel. The imperfect servant, though not so named, appears in vv. 1–3 and 11, and the perfect in vv. 4–10.

The chapter provides an interesting study in the prophet's use of questions. In v. 1 Isaiah queries assumptions made by his hearers; in v. 2 he uses questions to level accusations at them; in vv. 8–9 his questions are exclamatory and exultant expressions of faith; and in v. 10 they suggest a reply enabling him to identify a particular group among his hearers.

1–3 The figures of divorce and debt set forth Israel's conception of the Lord's relationship to her (v. 1). Exiled, she assumes that he has cast her off (cf. 40:27); but God her husband (cf. Jer 31:32) has not divorced her nor sold her to pay off his debts; for he, the Creator, has none. The cause of the Exile was simply sin on Israel's part; and, it is implied, if she returns to God, he will restore her.

Verse 2 rebukes Israel's unbelief. Through the prophets God has called to the people but found no answering response of obedient faith (cf. 48:8). Their unbelief had closed the book of redemptive history—with its lessons—to them. The end of this verse clearly refers to the Exodus; see especially the reference to "my arm" (cf. Exod 15:16; Deut 26:8; Ps 77:15). "A mere rebuke" suggests how simple an act of deliverance is for him. The argument from history is reinforced from nature, itself affected by the events associated with the Exodus. The judgment on the Nile and the clothing of the sky's naked brightness with darkness (v.3; cf. 45:7) are fit symbols of God's power to judge Israel's enemies.

4–9 Smart (in loc.) says of chapter 50:

> We sense an increasing tension as we read it, an ominous note foreshadowing rejection, bitter conflict, and deep suffering. It is a kind of forecourt of chapter 53, and we are not likely to see far into the later chapter unless we interpret the earlier one rightly, just as the story of the cross in the Gospels discloses its profound significance only to the reader who has grasped something of the nature of the conflict in which Jesus' mission involved him with the religious and political forces of his time.

Although there is no explicit reference to the Servant here (but see v.10), there are many links with the other songs and also—through the first person singular and the use of the expression "the Sovereign LORD," (v.4)—to 48:16. This divine title (Adonai Yahweh) also binds this song together, occurring in four of six verses.

At once the reader is conscious of a contrast with vv.1–3. Here is response to God's word (cf. v.2 and 42:18–20). The second song stresses the penetrating power of the word the Servant transmits (49:2), while this shows its pastoral effectivenes (cf. Matt 11:28–30 and Isa 40:27–30). As Thexton (in loc.) says, "The Servant of God has the 'trained tongue' and the 'trained ear'. The 'training' is not, however, the gaining of a technique, but the practice of discipleship." He waits on God in the morning watch (cf., e.g., Mark 1:35). the word he speaks comes from the God who sent him (cf. John 7:16–18).

Israel is rebellious (cf. 1:2; 48:8), but the Servant is responsive even when a destiny of suffering and shame is the subject of God's word to him (v.5). As God's Servant, he does not draw back but "offers" his body to the tormentors (v.6). Perhaps not even in chapter 53 are we more conscious of the gospel story (cf. Matt 26:67; 27:30; Mark 15:19; Luke 22:63). A combination of pain and shame introduce the Servant's conviction that the disgrace these suggest must yield place to a glorious vindication (cf. 52:13; 53:12). His face, cruelly assaulted, will not flinch before suffering (v.7; cf. Luke 9:51, where the RSV translates, "he set his face"). Even in this, however, though the individualization reaches a high point (see Introduction, pp. 17–20), we are reminded of the picture of afflicted Israel in Psalm 129. Herbert (in loc.) reminds us of other comparisons, when he writes: "There are many points of resemblance to Jeremiah's confessions (cf. Job 30f.) and the psalms in which the individual cries out to God for help, e.g. Ps 22." The Servant is the innocent sufferer *par eminence*.

God helps Israel (43:2, 5; 44:2) and Cyrus (45:1, 5); he will also help his unique Servant (v.8; cf. 43:1). The NT preaching constantly emphasizes the vindication by God through resurrection of the despised and suffering Jesus (Acts 2:23–24; 3:15; 13:29–30 et al.). Here, however, there is no indication of the form the divine vindication takes. The setting of vv.8–9 is clearly forensic, and the trials of Jesus in the Gospels make this peculiarly appropriate. He too could confront his enemies with the challenge "Can any of you prove me guilty of sin?" (John 8:46). For the analogy v.9 closes with, see the comment at 51:6, 8.

10–11 Many modern commentators deny the integrity of these verses with the rest of the chapter, attributing them to a later hand, largely because they seem alien to a prophet of consolation. But Smart (in loc.) is surely right when he speaks of "the appropriateness of the verses as the conclusion of a chapter in which the gulf between the Servant and Israel in its unbelief has become distressingly wide. If the prophet's message of hope was met with a solid wall of scorn and rejection, as the chapter seems to suggest, it is not surprising that an actual division should have begun to be apparent between those who fear the Lord and obey the voice of his Servant and those who heap upon the Servant only ridicule and humiliation." The people who obey are, in fact, identifying themselves with the Servant's own attitude (cf. v.5) and so expressing their reverential fear of God (cf. Deut 18:15–18; Luke 9:34–35). This fear is not one that makes men hide (cf. 2:10–11, 19–21) but draws them to God in faith.

Verse 10b perhaps calls for repentance, for it speaks of walking in darkness and offers, by implication, light from God through the word of the Servant (cf. John 12:44–45).

The modern reader needs to remember that before the advent of modern science, a source of light was also a source of heat; so the analogy of v.11 develops that which brings v.10 to its close. It may be compared with 10:17 and furnishes a striking link in imagery between parts of the book so often attributed to two distinct authors (see Introduction, pp. 6–11). It also reminds us of 1:29–31, teaching as it does that the wicked man will be caught in his own trap. For verses 10–11, compare also Psalm 2:10–12.

Notes

1 This verse alludes to the divorce legislation of Deut 24:1–4.
11 The NIV follows the AV and the RSV in assuming אוֹר (*'ôr*, "light"), rather than the MT's אוּר (*'ûr*, "flame"), which seems fully appropriate and should be retained. As Whybray (*Isaiah 40–66*, in loc.) puts it, "MT is correct: those who have started the fire will be caught by it and will find themselves unable to escape its flames." Then, "unable to escape from it, the arsonists will writhe in agony on the ground." The fire then will be either their rebellion in general or some special manifestation of it, perhaps in despising and persecuting the Servant.

3. Listen! Awake! Depart!

51:1–52:12

¹"Listen to me, you who pursue righteousness
and who seek the LORD;

Look to the rock from which you were cut
 and to the quarry from which you were hewn;
²look to Abraham, your father,
 and to Sarah, who gave you birth.
When I called him he was but one,
 and I blessed him and made him many.
³The Lord will surely comfort Zion
 and will look with compassion on all her ruins;
he will make her deserts like Eden,
 her wastelands like the garden of the Lord.
Joy and gladness will be found in her,
 thanksgiving and the sound of singing.

⁴"Listen to me, my people;
 hear me, my nation;
The law will go out from me;
 my justice will become a light to the nations.
⁵My righteousness draws near speedily,
 my salvation is on the way,
 and my arm will bring justice to the nations.
The islands will look to me
 and wait in hope for my arm.
⁶Lift up your eyes to the heavens,
 look at the earth beneath;
the heavens will vanish like smoke,
 the earth will wear out like a garment
 and its inhabitants die like flies.
But my salvation will last forever,
 my righteousness will never fail.

⁷"Hear me, you who know what is right,
 you people who have my law in your hearts:
Do not fear the reproach of men
 or be terrified by their insults.
⁸For the moth will eat them up like a garment;
 the worm will devour them like wool.
But my righteousness will last forever,
 my salvation through all generations."
⁹Awake, awake! Clothe yourself with strength,
 O arm of the Lord;
awake, as in days gone by,
 as in generations of old.
Was it not you who cut Rahab to pieces
 who pierced that monster through?
¹⁰Was it not you who dried up the sea,
 the waters of the great deep,
who made a road in the depths of the sea
 so that the redeemed might cross over?
¹¹The ransomed of the Lord will return.
 They will enter Zion with singing;
 everlasting joy will crown their heads.
Gladness and joy will overtake them,
 and sorrow and sighing will flee away.

¹²"I, even I, am he who comforts you.
 Who are you that you fear mortal men,
 the sons of men, who are but grass,
¹³that you forget the Lord your Maker,
 who stretched out the heavens
 and laid the foundations of the earth,

291

that you live in constant terror every day
   because of the wrath of the oppressor,
   who is bent on destruction?
For where is the wrath of the oppressor?
¹⁴   The cowering prisoners will soon be set free;
   they will not die in their dungeon,
   nor will they lack bread.
¹⁵For I am the LORD your God,
   who churns up the sea so that its waves roar—
   the LORD Almighty is his name.
¹⁶I have put my words in your mouth
   and covered you with the shadow of my hand—
I who set the heavens in place,
   who laid the foundations of the earth,
   and who say to Zion, 'You are my people.' "
¹⁷Awake, awake!
   Rise up, O Jerusalem,
you who have drunk from the hand of the LORD
   the cup of his wrath;
you who have drained to its dregs
   the goblet that makes men stagger.
¹⁸Of all the sons she bore
   there are none to guide her;
of all the sons she reared
   there was none to take her by the hand.
¹⁹These double calamities have come upon you—
   who can comfort you?—
ruin and destruction, famine and sword—
   who can console you?
²⁰Your sons have fainted;
   they lie at the head of every street,
   like antelope caught in a net.
They are filled with the wrath of the LORD
   and the rebuke of your God.
²¹Therefore hear this, you afflicted one,
   made drunk, but not with wine.
²²This is what your Sovereign LORD says,
   your God, who defends his people:
"See, I have taken out of your hand
   the cup that made you stagger;
from that cup, the goblet of my wrath,
   you will never drink again.
²³I will put it into the hands of your tormentors,
   who said to you,
   'Fall prostrate that we may walk over you.'
And you made your back like the ground,
   like a street to be walked over."

⁵²:¹Awake, awake, O Zion,
   clothe yourself with strength.
Put on your garments of splendor,
   O Jerusalem, the holy city.
The uncircumcised and defiled
   will not enter you again.
²Shake off your dust;
   rise up, sit enthroned, O Jerusalem.
Free yourself from the chains on your neck,
   O captive Daughter of Zion.

3For this is what the LORD says:

"You were sold for nothing,
and without money you will be redeemed."

4For this is what the Sovereign LORD says:

"At first my people went down to Egypt to live;
lately, Assyria has oppressed them.

5"And now what do I have here?" declares the LORD.

"For my people have been taken away for nothing,
and those who rule them mock,"
declares the LORD.
"And all day long
my name is constantly blasphemed
6Therefore my people will know my name;
therefore in that day they will know
that it is I who foretold it.
Yes, it is I."

7How beautiful on the mountains
are the feet of those who bring good news,
who proclaim peace,
who bring good tidings,
who proclaim salvation,
who say to Zion,
"Your God reigns!"
8Listen! Your watchmen lift up their voices;
together they shout for joy.
When the LORD returns to Zion,
they will see it with their own eyes.
9Burst into songs of joy together,
you ruins of Jerusalem,
for the LORD has comforted his people,
he has redeemed Jerusalem.
10The LORD will lay bare his holy arm
in the sight of all the nations,
and all the ends of the earth will see
the salvation of our God.

11Depart, depart, go out from there!
Touch no unclean thing!
Come out from it and be pure,
you who carry the vessels of the LORD.
12But you will not leave in haste
or go in flight;
for the LORD will go before you,
the God of Israel will be your rear guard.

The sensitive reader of Scripture becomes aware in its pages, not only of the communication of truth, but also of differences in emotional tone and atmosphere. The climax of the servant theme and, indeed, of the christological theme generally in this book (see Introduction, pp. 16–20) is being prepared for in this passage. There is a sense of impending climax, like that to be found in certain other OT passages (e.g., Gen 44, Exod 19, and Job 37), and this is marked by certain literary features.

This section of the prophecy contains an unusual number of imperatives; and there are several series of verbs and their synonyms, so that there is a call to listen (51:1, 4, 7, 21; 52:8), to awake (51:9; 52:1; cf. 51:17), to look (51:1–2, 6), and, finally, to depart (52:11). Some of these commands occur in immediately doubled form (always an indication of emotion in a writer or speaker); and once the imperative is threefold, though in this case it is addressed to God, not man (51:9). There are rhetorical questions (51:9–10, 12–14; 52:5); allusions to chapter 40, itself sure to have roused much feeling in its first readers (cf. esp. 52:7, 9 and 40:1, 9); and also many great statements about God and promises of what he will do. There are in fact many allusions to earlier parts of Isaiah in this section, and all this encourages in the discerning reader an anticipation of a great climax.

1–3 The prophet calls for maximum attention (v.1), the concentration of both the literal ear and also the eye of the imagination (cf. Mark 4:3, where "listen" is, literally, "listen, look!"). His call is, in other phraseology, to those who fear the Lord (50:10). The people are to reflect on their origins, for this will encourage them as they await his deliverance from Babylonia. The Lord had brought this nation into being from such small beginnings, in fulfillment of his promises; and so, it is implied, he is able still to translate his word into events.

The Jewish Midrash on v.1 reads as follows: "When God looked on Abraham who was to appear, he said, 'Behold, I have found a rock on which I can build and base the world,' therefore he called Abraham a rock" (SBK, 1:733). Cullmann has suggested that this passage and its midrashic interpretation may lie behind Matthew 16:18, with Peter—representing the apostles as the first Christian believers—paralleling Abraham's place as father of the faithful, but for the new covenant. Just as Abraham's faith in God was a pattern for the OT community that succeeded him (and, of course, for Christians, too), so that of Peter and his fellow apostles in Christ would lead to the building of the church (see O. Cullmann, *Peter, Disciple, Apostle, Martyr* [London: SCM, 1953]. p. 193).

God's promise to Abraham included a land as well as a people (cf. Gen 17:1–8). The capital city of that land is now in ruins and its environs reduced to a wasteland, but God will comfort her (v.3; cf. 40:1–9) by transforming her land and giving her a voice to praise him. Genesis has been in view in the reference to Abraham and Sarah (v.2); and it is mentioned again when the prophet alludes to the Garden of Eden, an allusion incidentally that was clearly meaningful to the first readers of the prophecy.

4–6 The NIV uses the word "my" nine times in these verses, presenting a most vivid impression of the personal activity of God on behalf of his people. The Lord will in fact manifest his own righteousness to those who are pursuing it (v.5; cf. v.1). He declared at 2:3–4 that his law would go out to the nations, creating justice among them. The first Servant Song shows that the Servant is the mediator of this divine justice (42:1). Here we see that the law, justice, righteousness, and salvation are all to be widely disseminated throughout the nations. This particular combination of terms certainly suggests that there is going to be a thorough reordering of human life among the nations on the basis of God's own character, revealed in his law, expressed in his righteousness, and taking the form of salvation. Salvation and righteousness are clearly closely parallel ideas here, providing a background for the Pauline doctrine of salvation as righteousness (e.g., Rom 1:16–17). Whether passages such as this are to be understood in terms of international relations or are to be taken as pictures of spiritual salvation—or both—is taken up in the Introduction (pp. 14–16).

The prophet calls on Israel—already addressed at the beginning of v.4—to consider the universe. The heavens and the earth that seem to be so stable are in fact less enduring than the salvation God has promised (cf. Mark 13:31).

7–8 These verses open with a call identical in substance, though not in language, with v.1. Here, as in vv.4–5, there is a close link between righteousness and the law of God; for the law publishes God's right way for men. The heart is where God's law should be (cf. Deut 30:14), and, of course, the new covenant pledges that it will be written there (Jer 31:31–34). The prophet assumes that the righteous in the land will experience antagonism from the wicked, which can be copiously illustrated from the Psalter and finds its ultimate illustration in human antagonism to the Christ-Servant of God. Like the visible universe (v.8; cf. v.6), wicked men will perish. The only abiding realities in God's new order are his own righteousness and salvation. Verse 8b repeats this assurance from v.6.

9–11 Characteristically, prophets stand facing the people, addressing them for God. They must often have prayed however for those to whom they were sent (cf., e.g., 1 Sam 7:8, Amos 7:1–6). Here Isaiah prays wonderfully, with great urgency expressed in the threefold cry, "Awake!" (v.9). God had given wonderful promises to his people. The prophet had been the inspired channel of these and now cries to God for their fulfillment. A new revelation of the power of his arm had been promised (cf. v.5 and the comment at 50:2). This had already been manifested in the destruction of Egypt's power, for Rahab and the monster are symbols of that land (see comment at 30:7). Here is praying indeed, in which God's great deeds in the past (v.10) are made the basis of prayerful confidence in his power to act again for his people. Once before the people had entered the Land of Promise with joy, and so they would again (v.11; cf. v.3).

12–16 God here begins to answer his people's cry, expressed through the prophet in the previous three verses. He rebukes the people for their lack of faith (v.12). As he had been telling them ever since the opening of chapter 40, he is going to make himself known to them as their divine Comforter. The repeated "I" serves to heighten the contrast between "the LORD their Maker" (v.13) and the "mortal men" they were afraid of (cf. 40:6–8). Who are the oppressors mentioned here? Presumably they are the Babylonians, though there is of course an important general principle here also.

The cowering prisoners (v.14) are either the people as a whole or, perhaps, a group of hostages imprisoned as surety of the good behavior of the remainder. If the Exile did become more severe toward its close, v.14 may reflect the fears of the people that death or extreme starvation would overcome them before their release.

Verse 16 is apparently an allusion to the Servant of the Lord (cf. 49:2), another indication that he is to be found outside the Servant Songs (cf. 48:16). Verse 16 closes with references to both God's creative work, in which he estasblished the cosmos, and that special work he had pledged himself to on Zion's behalf.

17–20 Chapter 40 opened with a declaration that the God of punitive wrath would reveal himself also as the God of comfort. The references to his wrath here are appropriate therefore in a context that speaks also of his comfort (cf.12). The repeated imperative of v.17 must surely be the divine call to Jerusalem that answers the call of the prophet to God (cf. v.9). The illustration of a cup, containing the awful wrath of God and so potent in its effects that those who drink it would be totally overcome by it, is a bold one and is echoed in the Gospels in relation to Christ's substitutionary sufferings (cf., e.g., Mark 10:38).

Such a person is, of course, unable to walk steadily without a guide; but Jerusalem's sons (v.18), sharing her drunkenness, lie prostrate in the streets. The "double calamities" (v.19) remind us of 40:2. Here the figure of inebriation gives way first to the general—"ruin and destruction"—and finally to the specific—"famine and sword"—this last pair probably representing the two calamities intended. God thus metes out his judgment through nature and men.

21–23 In v.19 the prophet asks, "Who can comfort you?" Here the Lord gives the answer. The cup of his wrath, justly placed by him in Israel's hand, is now to be removed in mercy and transferred to her oppressors. The barbaric practice referred to in v.23 is well documented in the ancient Near East, featured especially, but not exclusively, in Assyrian inscriptions.

52:1–2 The cry "Awake, awake!" (v.1), addressed first to God (51:9) and then to Jerusalem (51:17), comes again as a clarion call to that city, but this time in more exultant tones. Comparison of these verses with chapter 47 makes it clear that they are a development of the theme of transferred punishment seen in 51:21–23. Babylon is to be debased, and Jerusalem exalted. The strength Jerusalem is to put on is of course the power of her God (cf. 40:28–31; 51:9; but also Judg 6:12–16; Ps 84:5, 7). Her garments typify not only armored might but also probably priestly beauty, fitting in view of her new God-given holiness, having now a reality formerly lacking (cf. 48:2). The exclusion of the uncircumcised and the defiled should not be read as the product of a harsh nationalism but as a reminder that the alien had so often entered Jerusalem either to conquer or to pollute its worship or both (cf. Ps 79:1). Verse 2 especially reminds us of chapter 47; for, instead of Babylon, Zion is now to be enthroned in queenly splendor, a gloriously free city.

3–6 Verse 3 preserves in brief compass three important truths. Jerusalem was, in fact, handed over to Babylonia by God himself—as a punishment, of course. Yet those who were given her paid nothing and so were owed nothing. So God would act again but this time in redemption, not punishment. So the word "redeemed," normally implying cost, does not have this connotation here.

Verses 4–5 trace a history of oppression and a sequence of oppressors, with Babylonia, it is implied, to be added to Egypt and Assyria. The divine soliloquy in v.5 dramatically presents the question of the appropriate divine action in this new situation faced by his people. All three tyrant nations scoffed at the God of Israel (cf., e.g., 36:20) with constant blasphemy. The expression "in that day" (v.6) points forward to a period in which God will act decisively for his people in vindication of his name (see note at 2:11). The prediction would be called to mind when it was fulfilled, thus establishing the true and exclusive deity of the God of Israel (cf. 45:21).

7–10 Thexton (in loc.) says, "In imagination the prophet sees the runner speeding across the hills to the Holy City, and being greeted joyously by its watchmen, through whom the news of the coming salvation spreads through the whole city." This exultant passage contains echoes of 40:1–11. There Jerusalem was given good news about her God, who would come with power and yet gentleness. Here the prophet brings together a number of important themes, virtually identifying peace, salvation, and the kingdom of God, and so reminding us of the NT revelation that Christ's work secures these and every other blessing for God's people. How fitting this is just prior to the fourth Servant Song (52:13–53:12), in which the sufferings of God's Servant are described and their significance expounded! (See the Introduction, pp. 14–16, for a general discussion of the interpretation of passages like this.)

Verse 9 reminds us that Zion here is the ruined city of the future. Faith can claim the promises with joyous songs, rejoicing in God's comfort and redemption. The reference to God's holy arm (v. 10) takes us back to 51:9, and it is part of God's answer to his prophet's prayer (see comment there and at 53:1). This powerful act of salvation will be as public as the deliverance from Egypt.

11–12 The doubled imperatives of this passage now become more urgent. Yet, urgent as the call is, the departure from Babylonia is not to be a pressured flight, unlike that from Egypt (Exod 12:33, 39). Interestingly, Babylonia—for it is surely in view—is described, not as "here," but as "there," (v. 11), indicating that the prophet is in Judah and not Babylonia (see Introduction, pp. 6–12).

Ceremonial purity is important, especially for the priests who transported the holy temple-vessels (cf. 2 Kings 25:14–15; Ezra 1:5–11). It is clear, incidentally, that the purpose-of God includes the rebuilding of the temple. The most comforting word of all comes at the end, for God promises that—just as at the Exodus—he would protect this holy procession from both the front and the rear (cf. Exod 13:21–22; 14:19–20).

Notes

3 Whybray (*Isaiah 40–66*, in loc.) writes: "The wonderful garden which God had once given to man to inhabit (Gen 2:8–9) has become in the OT a symbol of the ideal pastoral or agricultural existence (cf. Gen 31:10; Ezek 31:8–9; Joel 2:3). Here, however, and also in Ezek 36:35, we have the additional idea of a 'Paradise Regained': the promise of the Return of a Golden Age."

4 The word לְאֹם (*le'ōm*, "nation") is never elsewhere applied to Israel, considered separately, in the OT. Genesis 25:23 supplies some precedent however, and the term is certainly appropriate and should be retained rather than following the few Hebrew MSS that have the plural (cf. KD, 2:283).

9 It is quite unnecessary to assume, with some commentators (e.g., Whybray) that this is a direct reference to the Tiamat myth rather than a symbolic reference to Egypt. Verses 9–10 read very naturally as dealing with two aspects of the same Exodus event (see quotations from Young, *Book of Isaiah*, at v. 10).

10 Young (*Book of Isaiah*, in loc.), commenting on the word translated "deep" in the NIV, says: "The designation *tehôm* . . ., which usually signifies the primeval ocean, need not possess that connotation here. It serves simply to point out that the sea is a great deep of water, a formidable and (to man) impossible obstacle to cross. What to man was a *tehôm*, the arm of the Lord made to be dry."

13 Thexton's perceptive comment on this verse deserves special mention. Part of it reads

thus: "A reminder to God that He is God (verses 9–10) may indicate one's own failure to remember that very thing (verse 13). . . . So the reply of verses 12–13 is a quiet affirmation: 'Yes, I *am* the God you have described. Why will you not really accept the implications of what you yourself have said of Me? If you do, you will know how absurd it is to fear anything mortal man can do, and you will know that your promised redemption is sure indeed.' "

16 The MT reads literally "to plant the heavens," which as Skinner and Young suggest, would relate the verse to the new heavens and new earth predicted in 65:17; 66:22. The NIV, with many commentators, seems to follow the conjectural emendation לִנְטוֹת (*linṭôt*, "stretching out") instead of לִנְטֹעַ (*linṭōaʿ*, "planting"). The former verb occurs also in v.13, where the NIV translates "stretched out" instead of "set" as here; so possibly the translators have freely translated here rather than emended the text. The absence of a footnote may suggest this.

18 The comment above assumes that Babylonia's sons could not help her because they shared her drunkenness. "Fainted" (v.20) would support this. Many commentators take it, however, that v.20 pictures them as suffering death at the hands of the Babylonians, with the antelope analogy supporting this. It is possible, of course, that v.20 commences with the inebriation analogy before moving to that of the captured antelope.

19 The NIV follows 1QIsa and the versions. Its note translates the MT as "how can I." The former fits the parallelism better, though the MT is not impossible.

20 תְּאוֹ (*teʾô*, "antelope") occurs only here and in Deut 14:5.

52:2 The NIV follows the MT here in translating "shake off your dust; rise up, sit enthroned, O Jerusalem," while the RSV has "shake yourself from the dust, arise, O captive Jerusalem," based on a conjectural emendation, supported by the versions. Whybray (*Isaiah, 40–60*, in loc.) is surely right in saying, "There is no reason to reject the Heb. Jerusalem is told first to arise from the dust and then to take her seat on a throne. The word *šebiyyāh*, 'captive' already occurs once in the verse, and a repetition of it is unlikely."

5 Here the NIV quite properly follows the Qere in translating "what do I have here?" in place of the difficult Kethiv. "Whom do I have here?" It also follows 1QIsa, Aquilla, and the Vulgate in emending the MT's יְהֵילִילוּ (*yehêlîlû*, "wail") to יְהַלְלוּ (*yehallēlû*, "mock" or "boast"). The emendation affects also the interpretation of "those who rule them." If they are represented as wailing, they must be the rulers of Jerusalem at the time Jerusalem was captured by the Babylonians, whereas if they mock, they will be the Babylonian rulers. Either appears possible, with the latter perhaps seeming more appropriate, but the former doing justice to the MT as it stands.

7 Thexton (in loc.) remarks, "There is a splendid artistry in its urgent, tumbling phrases, so that by the end of the verse we feel a sense of tremendous expectancy as the herald at last declares his message—'*Thy God reigneth!*' " (emphasis his).

---

4. The Man of Sorrows and His Vindication

52:13–53:12

13See, my servant will act wisely;
    he will be raised and lifted up and highly exalted.
14Just as there were many who were appalled at him—
    his appearance was so disfigured beyond that
        of any man
    and his form marred beyond human likeness—
15so will he sprinkle many nations,
    and kings will shut their mouths because of him.
For what they were not told, they will see,
    and what they have not heard, they will understand.

^{53:1}Who has believed our message
  and to whom has the arm of the L<small>ORD</small> been revealed?
²He grew up before him like a tender shoot,
  and like a root out of dry ground.
He had no beauty or majesty to attract us to him,
  nothing in his appearance that we should desire him.
³He was despised and rejected by men,
  a man of sorrows, and familiar with suffering.
Like one from whom men hide their faces
  he was despised, and we esteemed him not.

⁴Surely he took up our infirmities
  and carried our sorrows,
yet we considered him stricken by God,
  smitten by him, and afflicted.
⁵But he was pierced for our transgressions,
  he was crushed for our iniquities;
the punishment that brought us peace was upon him,
  and by his wounds we are healed.
⁶We all, like sheep, have gone astray,
  each of us has turned to his own way;
and the L<small>ORD</small> has laid on him
  the iniquity of us all.

⁷He was oppressed and afflicted,
  yet he did not open his mouth;
he was led like a lamb to the slaughter,
  and as a sheep before her shearers is silent,
  so he did not open his mouth.
⁸By oppression and judgment, he was taken away.
  And who can speak of his descendants?
For he was cut off from the land of the living;
  for the transgression of my people he was stricken.
⁹He was assigned a grave with the wicked,
  and with the rich in his death,
though he had done no violence,
  nor was any deceit in his mouth.
¹⁰Yet it was the L<small>ORD</small>'s will to crush him and cause him
      to suffer,
  and though the L<small>ORD</small> makes his life a guilt offering
he will see his offspring and prolong his days,
  and the will of the L<small>ORD</small> will prosper in his hand.
¹¹After the suffering of his soul,
  he will see the light of life, and be satisfied;
by his knowledge my righteous servant will justify many,
  and he will bear their iniquities.
¹²Therefore I will give him a portion among the great,
  and he will divide the spoils with the strong,
because he poured out his life unto death,
  and was numbered with the transgressors.
For he bore the sin of many,
  and made intercession for the transgressors.

The interpreter who has meditated on the third Servant Song in chapter 50 and then moves on to the fourth song feels somewhat as a godly high priest must have felt when he moved from the Holy Place into the Most Holy Place on the Day of Atonement. In fact, however, the very designation of these passages as a series of "songs" (which they almost certainly were not) is particularly unhelpful at this point.

This fourth song is to be seen in its full glory, not only in the light of the NT interpretation of it, but also in terms of the context in which it comes to us in. We have already commented, in introducing 51:1–52:12, that this earlier passage builds up an atmosphere of excitement, as if to prepare for a revelation of special significance. It should also be noted that the important phrase "the arm of the LORD" in 53:1 is anticipated in 51:9 and 52:10. There is also, as we shall note, an important relationship to the chapters that follow it.

The vast majority of commentators hold that the fourth song extends from 52:13 to 53:12, but an important minority group of scholars (e.g., Lindblom, Orlinsky, Smart, Snaith, Whybray) denies the integrity of 52:13–15 with chapter 53. The merit of this minority view is that it emphasizes the links these three verses have with the remainder of chapter 52, thus stressing the importance of the context. Orlinsky, for example, in his monograph "The So-called 'Servant of the Lord' and 'Suffering Servant' in Second Isaiah" (in Orlinsky and Snaith, *Second Part of Isaiah*, pp. 21–22), writes: "The entire chapter—actually the theme begins already in chapter 51 preceding—is a proclamation and exhortation to Zion-Jerusalem to prepare for the triumphant return of the exiles, a triumph even greater than the Exodus from Egypt. . . . It is with this dramatic proclamation that our section is to be associated: God's degraded servant, His people Israel, will astonish everyone by the great restoration that he will achieve."

Orlinsky's point is not undermined if we question the communal interpretation he gives the servant; for, if we do interpret the servant as an individual here, he nevertheless expresses and fulfills God's own mind for Israel. What in fact Orlinsky and others have probably succeeded in doing is establishing the connections of these verses with the earlier part of chapter 53 without really disproving their function as the opening of the fourth song. It is only if we insist on a separation of the songs from their context that the question of oracular unity becomes of major importance.

A great deal has been written on the interpretation of the songs in general and the fourth song in particular. The chief views are still probably best surveyed in North's *Suffering Servant in Deutero-Isaiah*. The view adopted in this commentary is made clear in the Introduction (pp. 17–20). Whatever may be said about the earlier songs, we take it that this one is to be understood exclusively in individual terms, fulfilled in Jesus. It is readily granted that the principles of obedience to God's will whatever the cost, in which the cross is taken up by the disciple of Jesus, apply to individual Christians and to the church as a whole. The atoning significance of the sufferings of the Servant, outlined in this passage, are however peculiar to Jesus the unique Servant.

Kidner ("Isaiah," in loc.) has well outlined the beautiful structure of this passage, which, incidentally, provides one argument for treating it as an entity. He says, "The poem, unusually symmetrical, is in five paragraphs of three verses each. It begins and ends with the Servant's exaltation (first and fifth stanzas); set within this is the story of his rejection in sections two and four, which in turn form the centrepiece (vv. 4–6) where the atoning significance of the suffering is expounded. God and man, reconciled, share the telling (see the 'my' and 'I' of the outer sections, and the 'we' and 'our' of 52:1–6)."

The text of this great passage presents a good many difficulties. In fact, North (*Isaiah 40–55*, in loc.) declares:

No passage in the Old Testament, certainly none of comparable importance, presents more problems than this. . . . In the period following Duhm textual emendation was freely resorted to; . . . but even before the discovery of the Qumran scrolls textual critics were becoming more cautious and conservative. . . . In a responsible translation like the RSV only two variants from the *textus receptus* are recognized. The prevailing attitude now is that it does not follow that because an LXX reading. . . . is more easily intelligible than the MT, it is without more ado to be accepted.

North's words, written in 1964, still hold true as a survey of most more recent commentaries will reveal. Because there are so many problems, it would seem best for us to take the NIV at its face value here and to reserve all textual, translation, and the more thorny interpretation problems for the footnotes.

13–15 Once again, as in 42:1, God draws attention to his servant (v.13). If we relate v.13 to its earlier context, we may see this as a concern that the reader should not simply rejoice in the wonder of the new Exodus. Wisdom consists largely in determining desirable ends and devising practical means to achieve them. The Servant's wisdom was deeply self-denying, for it meant accepting ends determined by God and willingly shouldering a burden of untold suffering to make them possible. Here God's wisdom and man's decisively part company (cf. 1 Cor 1:17–25). The threefold assertion of the Servant's exaltation is most emphatic, whether or not we spell it out in terms of resurrection, ascension and session, or second advent. The predicted exaltation is most reassuring for the reader as he approaches predictions of shame and suffering (v.14).

The NIV has well presented the striking comparison that occurs in vv.14–15, where many observers of the Servant have a double experience of astonishment, the first mingled with horror and the second, at least for those responding in faith, with joy. The theme of suffering and subsequent glory, so common in the NT in application to Christ (e.g., in the Acts of the Apostles and in 1 Peter), is here presented from the standpoint of the impression made on the onlooker. The strong word translated "appalled" finds its justification in the words that follow, for the sight disclosed is of such exquisite suffering that the Servant's bodily appearance seemed hardly human. We need not assume from this that the experience being described is purely physical, for deep inner experiences of anguish demonstrate their presence by their effects on the face and form of the sufferer.

The word "sprinkle" has priestly-sacrifical overtones (see Notes; cf. Exod 29:20–21; Lev 16:14–15), preparing us for further sacrificial language later in the passage. In common with everything else in these three verses, "sprinkle" would relate to the consequences of the Servant's sufferings rather than to the sufferings themselves. It would also relate his sacrificial work to the world in general, not simply to Israel. His exaltation gives him complete supremacy over all; and kings will fall silent in his presence, astonished, over-awed, deeply respectful (cf. Job 29:7–10), and eager perhaps to see and hear rather than themselves to speak in the presence of such an unprecedented revelation. In Romans 15:21 Paul applies v.15 to the preaching of the gospel in virgin and largely Gentile territory. Note the striking reversal here of the discouraging words of Isaiah's commission (6:9–10).

53:1–3 The intimate link between v.1 and the closing verse of the last chapter can hardly be missed and poses a difficulty for those who would divorce the end of chapter 52 from this chapter (see comments at the introduction to this passage). The two astonishing events of 52:14–15—the appalling suffering of God's own wise Servant who deserved none of it and the subsequent elevation of one so dishonored by men—would in fact produce incredulity in many hearing the report of these things. God's way of doing things often does not seem to make sense to men (cf. 55:8–9; 1 Cor 1:18–31). The cross is, however, where God's power resides; and here is the ultimate answer to the prophet's prayer of 51:9, anticipated by its foreshadowing in the new Exodus of 52:10. John 12:37–41 joins this verse with Isaiah 6:10 in illustration of the rejection of Jesus by many of the Jews of his day.

Who are the speakers in v.1? Are they Gentiles—or Israelites, possibly speaking through the prophet as their representative? It is not necessary to take a collective view of the Servant to feel the power of the arguments for the former. His work was to have wide-ranging application (cf. 42:6; 49:6). In the context it would seem natural that the nations and kings (52:15), at first struck dumb by the astounding revelation, should then speak in response to it. The "arm of the Lord" is the disclosure of his power. So this revelation answers the prophet's representative prayer in 51:9 (see comment there).

Verse 2 echoes and yet contrasts with 4:2 (see comment there). The whole verse suggests that the Servant would be confronted with adverse conditions from his youth. In fact, Jesus could not be explained in terms of his human environment, which in his day was dominated by a legalistic Judaism almost devoid of the refreshing moisture of God's word truly understood and applied. Verse 2b implies that his true intrinsic beauty was hidden from people because they looked at him entirely from a human standpoint, in which case there are interesting comparisons and contrasts with 1 Samuel 16:5–13, where "a shoot from . . . Jesse" (cf. Isa 11:1) is chosen to be king. The principle that human appearance is irrelevant to God's choice is more radically applied here than in the choice of David. It is possible, on the other hand, that these words apply to the Servant, not in terms of his normal appearance, but that which was produced by his sufferings (cf. 52:14).

Verse 3 develops the thought of v.2, for the onlookers moved from failure to desire him to despising and rejection, refusing even to look at him (cf. perhaps Num 21:8–9; John 3:14–16). The words translated "sorrows" and "suffering" really mean "pains" and "sickness." They occur again in v.4a. What does this imply? Kidner ("Isaiah," in loc.) writes that they "might suggest to the reader either a sick man or one sick at heart, as in Jer 15:18. But there is another category, that of the physician's voluntary involvement; for he is also a man of pain and sickness in the sense that he gives himself to these things and their relief. This is the sense defined in Mt 8:17, quoting Isa 53:4."

There is another possibility. The concept of punishment finds many analogies in Isaiah's prophecies, from the whipping of the body politic in 1:5–6 to the inebriated helplessness of 51:17–20. Could not this sickness be another? In this case the punitive nature of the Servant's sufferings is indicated before the vicarious nature of them is made clear in v.4.

4–6 This central stanza of the fourth Servant song has a number of general characteristics. The first is the frequency of the first person plural. This occurs of course several times in vv.1–3 as well. Who are the speakers here? Probably the amazed onlookers of the first stanza, who appear from 52:15 to be predominantly, if not exclusively, Gentiles. Then there is the frequency of nouns and verbs suggesting both pain and punishment. The passage also emphasizes the sins of the onlookers, with one of the most vivid analogies—even in this illustration-saturated book—given in v.6. Here is a picture of the willful and yet purposeless waywardness of sin, with probably a suggestion that this is an offense against love as well as holiness, for the divine Shepherd is a tender, loving image in the Bible (cf. esp. 40:11). This aimless yet determined wandering is marvellously conveyed in the music of Handel's *Messiah*, with its jerkily wandering melody, and likewise, in total contrast, the deeply moving affirmation of atonement of great cost with which the verse ends.

It is that costly atonement that provides the dominant theme of this stanza. Verse 4a views our punishment figuratively in terms of the visitation of disease (see comments at v.3), while v.4b shows the onlookers coming to the grievously wrong conclusion that the Servant was suffering for his own sins at the hand of God. Verse 5 shows that they have now accepted for themselves the objective fact declared in v.4a. Piercing and crushing are both appropriate terms for the Crucifixion, the first literal and the second figurative; and both are aptly summed up as "wounds" later in the verse. Peace and healing view sin in terms of the estrangement from God and the marring of the sinner himself that it causes. Verse 6 may well derive its language from the Day of Atonement ritual (cf. Lev 16:21–22); for as God was the Author of the ritual (cf. Lev 17:11), the high priest was simply his agent for transferring the sins of the people symbolically to the scapegoat.

Finally, we should note the element of conversion conveyed in vv.4–5. The onlookers put aside their premature judgment on the matter and accept that the sufferings of the Servant were not only penal but also substitutionary. Kidner ("Isaiah," in loc.) notes "the expressions, *all we . . . we all*, which give the verse an identical beginning and end in the Hebrew; grace wholly answering sin" (emphasis his).

7–9 Thexton (in loc.) has given an admirable précis of these verses: "Meekly and without protest the Servant accepts sentence to death and suffers execution. Although innocent, he is given a felon's grave." The term "oppressed" (v.7) was appropriate in relation to the trials and death of Jesus; for all those who tried him—Pilate, Herod, Annas, and Caiaphas—had a measure of human authority and misused it when they condemned him or, washing their hands of him, allowed others to take him to the place of death. In it all, he had a quiet and uncomplaining bearing (cf. esp. 1 Peter 2:23), which suggests not only comparison but also contrast with Jeremiah (cf. Jer 11:18–20; 12:1–3). Writing on v.7b, Simon (in loc.) says, "This new David (cf. Ezek 34:23) gives his life for the sheep who, strangely, are his murderers. He combines both the initiative and the submissiveness of the priest-shepherd and the victim-sheep. Thus he transmutes what might have been merely the murder of a good person into a holy and abiding Messianic sacrifice."

The phrase "by oppression and judgment" (v.8) is, formally, somewhat like the earlier expression "iniquity and solemn assembly" (1:13 RSV; "evil assemblies," NIV), in that the two nouns present concomitant aspects of the same fact. The judgment was in fact employed as an instrument of oppression. It seemed as though he must die without issue, which was regarded as a great misfortune or worse in that society. The phrase "cut off" strongly suggests not only a violent, premature death but also the just judgment of God (cf., e.g., Gen 9:11; Exod 12:15), not simply the oppressive judgment of men. H.R. Minn (*The Servant Songs* [Christchurch; Presbyterian Bookroom, 1966] p. 23) points out that the versions support the MT in reading "my people"; then he goes on to say, "If this is allowed to stand—and why should it not?—there is a distinction between the people and the Servant. They are not identical" (see Introduction, pp. 17–20).

Verse 9 presents an enigma, a striking prediction fulfilled in due time, and a transition to the final stanza, which describes the Servant's vindication. The enigma consists in the apparent juxtaposition of "the wicked" and "the rich," the former more appropriate to his rejection and the latter to his ultimate vindication. We are forced to conclude that the parallelism is not synonymous but antithetical, the first line indicating the human intention and the second the divinely ordained intervention and transference. This in fact was strikingly fulfilled in the burial of Jesus (Matt 27:57–60). Simon (in loc.) writes:

> By a very simple manipulation of the text we may read a less dramatic account according to which he was thrown into a common grave with the wicked and evil-doers. But though this emendation may claim to restore an obvious Hebrew parallelism the simplification seems altogether regrettable here. The ancient commentators wisely retained the word "rich," which has become troublesome only to modern minds. . . . By retaining the unconventional "rich" and rejecting the easier "evil-doers" we follow a sound principle. "Rich" must have been there from the start; it may have become "evil-doers" whereas the reverse is impossible. The paradox should be taken quite seriously.

The Servant's gentle ingenuousness is asserted at the close of the stanza.

10–12 The NIV text gives the word "yet" twice in this chapter, the previous occurrence being in v.4. Both verses present reassessment that means the balancing of one partial truth with another, thus giving a full picture. In v.4 penal suffering is balanced—and so interpreted—by substitution; here man's unjust treatment of the Servant is balanced—and also interpreted—by God's saving purpose in the Servant's sufferings. Verse 10a is almost shocking in its apparent presentation of arbitrary disregard for personal righteousness, but then the reader recalls the substitutionary nature of those sufferings, already declared in vv.4–6 and to be referred to again later in this stanza. At once God is seen not to be harsh but astonishingly gracious.

Verses 10b–11, as rendered in the NIV, remind us of 52:14–15; for after suffering comes vindication, suggesting perhaps at the same time the completion of the Servant's atoning work in his death and the opening of a new life beyond that death. The guilt offering may have special overtones of completeness for it involved restitution as well as an offering to God (cf. Lev 5). Nothing then remained to be done; the work was complete.

Verse 11a (cf. Notes), with its contrast of "suffering" and "light," certainly makes us think of the Resurrection, which is still more clearly suggested by the earlier words "prolong his days." In fact, the words "he will see his offspring and prolong his days" seem to stand in intended contrast with the second and third lines of v.8. There is a parallel here with Psalm 22, which has so much in common with this passage, where a sufferer now vindicated declares, "Posterity will serve him" (Ps 22:30).

Some commentators take the words "by his knowledge" with the preceding clause; but, as Young points out, the Masoretic accentuation, representing of course the Jewish traditional understanding, links it with the words that follow it. If this is so, are we to take the pronominal suffix to be subjective, as in the NIV text ("by his knowledge") or objective, as in the NIV margin ("by knowledge of him")? Young (*Book of Isaiah,* in loc.) well expresses the contextual argument for the latter: "In this context the servant appears, not as a teacher, but as a saviour. Not by his knowledge does he justify men, but by bearing their iniquities." We are saved, not simply by revelation, but by redemptive suffering, the latter being the teaching of the context of this verse. In this case, then, it is the experimental knowledge of faith that is in view; and we have here an important background for the Pauline doctrine of justification through the blood of Christ, appropriated by faith.

The adjective "righteous" and the verb "will justify," coming from the same Hebrew root (*ṣdq*), are placed next to each other in the Hebrew, as if to stress their relationship. Calvin stressed that the obedience of Christ was the chief circumstance of his death. His righteousness and therefore his innocence of sin furnished a basis for his substitution. The final clause of v.11, with its reminder of v.6 (see comments there), states the objective grounds of this justification, which is of course a new position before God, the righteous Judge, on the basis of what the Servant has achieved in his sufferings and not of what we have ourselves done or will do.

The opening statement of v.12, reminding many commentators of Philippians 2:9, shows God honoring the Servant for his faithful work and the Servant in turn distributing the spoils of battle to others. In fact it introduces a new note into the passage; for 52:13, to which in other ways it answers, contains no military language. The NT however does; and Christ's work there is presented as a victory over spiritual foes, resulting in a distribution of the spoil to those made strong in him (cf., e.g., Eph 4:8; 6:10–17). J. Jeremias (in W. Zimmerli and J. Jeremias, *Servant of God* [London: SCM, 1957], p. 97), L.S. Thornton (*The Dominion of Christ* [Westminster: Darce, 1952], pp. 91–95), and others have argued that the words *heauton ekenōsen* ("made himself nothing") in Philippians 2:7 are a translation from a Semitic original meaning "he poured himself out" and are based on this verse. Thornton further points out that the clause can in fact be completed by the words "to death" from v.8. Here, in both passages, is the ultimate in self-abnegation in dedication to the will of God.

The last three clauses of v.12 sum up the matter. The Servant was numbered with the transgressors, not only in the outward circumstances of his death (Mark 15:27 NIV mg), but as a general description of the meaning of his sufferings (Luke 22:37). Innocent, he was charged with human sins and so bore their penalty. Beyond this, as the Epistle to the Hebrews proclaims, he has an intercessory ministry based on the finality of his sufferings. This means that even when vindicated by God, he is still concerned to minister to his people.

In 44:28 the name "Cyrus" is solemnly and dramatically revealed long before his coming. Our present passage speaks so eloquently of the work of Christ that even the inclusion of his name could add but little more to the extent of its disclosure of him.

Notes

13 יַשְׂכִּיל (*yaśkil*, "will act wisely") can also mean "will have success," "will prosper" (NIV mg., RSV). This latter sense is less common, but it would give this line a sense parallel with the one that follows it. Thus either rendering can be well supported.

14 עָלֶיךָ (ʿāleykā, "at you," NIV mg.) is usually amended to עָלָיו (ʿālāyw, "at him"), with the Syriac and the Targum (so NIV). Lindblom, North et al. argue for retention as the harder reading and as consistent with oscillation between second and third persons found elsewhere in Hebrew poetry.

There could be a line missing after line 1, completing the sense rhythm; but in the absence of textual evidence this is purely conjectural. Young (see his discussion in *Book of Isaiah*, in loc.) construes vv.14–15 differently, so that there is still a protasis-apodosis construction, but a different one. The unusual nature of the poetic structure here may be intentional, to compel attention to the exceptionally important theme.

15 יַזֶּה (yazzeh) is often denied the sense of "sprinkle" (so NIV) on syntactical grounds, though E.J. Young (*Studies in Isaiah* [Grand Rapids: Eerdmans, 1955], pp. 199–206) argues persuasively for it and for a priestly-sacrificial meaning. C.R. North (*Isaiah 40–55*, in loc.)—following H.S. Nyberg ("Smärtonas man. En studie till Jes. 52:13–53:12," *Svensk Exegetisk Arsbok* 7 [1942]:47)—argues that it does have this meaning. North, however, interprets it in terms of a decontamination ritual, perhaps for a leper (cf. n. at 53:3), translating, "so shall many nations guard against contagion by him," and interpreting the shutting of the mouth in line with this. This seems unlikely in the light of v.15b, which suggests a positive revelation and therefore a contrast with the horror of v.14, not a further exposition of it. Most commentaries now in fact take the verb to be from a Hebrew root cognate with the Arabic *nazāʾ* ("to leap)," with the sense "to cause to leap in amazement"). North (in loc.) argues against this; but the LXX seems to support it, while other Greek versions do not. The sense "startle" is perhaps slightly more likely, giving a better contrast with "appalled" (v.14) and a better parallel with "shut their mouths."

2 The theory—usually associated with OT scholars of the Scandinavian school, like Nyberg ("Smärtonas man," pp. 5–82) and I. Engnell, "The Ebed Yahweh Songs and the Suffering Messiah in 'Deutero-Isaiah,'" BJRL 31 (1948):54–93—that the language here shows the influence of the mythology and cult of Tammuz—the dying and rising vegetation god—is rejected by most scholars as being largely conjectural and as having insufficient objective basis. See especially E.R. Yamauchi, "Tammuz and the Bible," JBL (1965):283–90.

3–4 Some modern scholars suggest that the Servant is presented here as a leper. Certainly נָגוּעַ (nāgûaʿ, "stricken") is used in connection with leprosy in 2 Kings 15:5, but this does not constitute full proof; nor does the use of נֶגַע (negaʿ, "skin disease," from the same root) in Lev 13:2–3 et al., because 2 Kings 15:5 uses a different noun. There is however support from rabbinic sources. In such a picturesque writer as Isaiah, it is possible that he identified the Servant as a leper metaphorically to picture his social isolation and substitutionary sin-bearing.

5 Most commentators—even those who deny the presence of penal substitution elsewhere in the OT—agree that it is the meaning of this passage, though some argue against this (see, e.g., Whybray, *Isaiah 40–66*, in loc.).

8 מֵעֹצֶר וּמִמִּשְׁפָּט לֻקָּה (mēʿōṣer ûmimmišpāṭ luqqāh) is translated "by oppression and judgment he was taken away"; but all three main Hebrew words are uncertain in meaning, and the particle מִן (min), with which the first two words begin, has a wide range of meanings. The NIV text (cf. RSV) is interpreted in the comments above. The words could also mean "after arrest and judgment he was taken away," or "by oppression and without judgment he was taken away"; and there are several other possibilities. The general sense however is very clear. The Servant was the victim of a grave miscarriage of justice. See the major commentaries for further details.

The next clause is also difficult. NIV takes דּוֹרוֹ (dôrô) to mean "descendants," as in Num 9:10. Driver ("Isaiah 40–66," p. 403) suggested connections with Accadian and Arabic roots with the sense "plight." So, as Whybray (*Isaiah 40–66*, in loc.) says, the clause could mean "but who gave a thought to his plight?" Either rendering would suit the context. So also would the NIV mg., which takes dôrô in another possible sense and treats three-quarters of the verse—instead of its second clause only—as a question.

10 The NIV text expresses the intention of the second person singular (cf. mg.). Such oscillation between second and third persons is common in prophecy.

11 The KJV's "He shall see of the travail of his soul, and shall be satisfied" follows the MT. The NIV, apart from the bracketed words inserted to complete the sense, follows the LXX and 1QIsaᵃ and is now generally assumed to be correct.

---

5. God's Glorious Future for Jerusalem

54:1–17

¹"Sing, O barren woman,
    you who never bore a child;
burst into song, shout for joy,
    you who were never in labor;
because more are the children of the desolate woman
    than of her who has a husband,"

                says the LORD.

²"Enlarge the place of your tent,
    stretch your tent curtains wide,
    do not hold back;
lengthen your cords,
    strengthen your stakes.
³For you will spread out to the right and to the left;
    your descendants will dispossess nations
    and settle in their desolate cities.

⁴"Do not be afraid; you will not suffer shame.
    Do not fear disgrace; you will not be humiliated.
You will forget the shame of your youth
    and remember no more the reproach
        of your widowhood.
⁵For your Maker is your husband—
    the LORD Almighty is his name—
The Holy One of Israel is your Redeemer;
    he is called the God of all the earth.
⁶The LORD will call you back
    as if you were a wife deserted and distressed in spirit—
a wife who married young,
    only to be rejected," says your God.
⁷For a brief moment I abandoned you;
    but with deep compassion I will bring you back.
⁸In a surge of anger
    I hid my face from you for a moment,
but with everlasting kindness
    I will have compassion on you,"
    says the LORD your Redeemer.
⁹"To me this is like the days of Noah,
    when I swore that the waters of Noah would never again
        cover the earth.
So now I have sworn not to be angry with you,
    never to rebuke you again.
¹⁰Though the mountains be shaken
    and the hills be removed,
yet my unfailing love for you will not be shaken
    nor my covenant of peace be removed,"
    says the LORD, who has compassion on you.

¹¹O afflicted city, lashed by storms and not comforted,
    I will build you with stones of turquoise,
    your foundations with sapphires.
¹²I will make your battlements of rubies,
    your gates of sparkling jewels,
    and all our walls of precious stones.
¹³All your sons will be taught by the LORD,
    and great will be your children's peace.
¹⁴In righteousness you will be established;
    Tyranny will be far from you;
        you will have nothing to fear.
    Terror will be far removed,
        it will not come near you.
¹⁵If anyone does attack you, it will not be my doing;
    whoever attacks you will surrender to you.

¹⁶"See, it is I who created the blacksmith
    who fans the coals into flame
    and forges a weapon fit for its work.
And it is I who have created the destroyer to work havoc;
¹⁷ no weapon forged against you will prevail,
    and you will refute every tongue that accuses you.
This is the heritage of the servants of the LORD,
    and this is their vindication from me,"

                                        declares the LORD.

Herbert (in loc.) writes: "The change of mood between Isa 53 and 54 is abrupt. Yet . . . it is appropriate. The Servant's task is seen to be fulfilled. Nothing can be added to that. But . . . the incredible triumph of Isa 53:10–12 issues into the hymn of praise in 54:1–10, welcoming the dawn of the New Age."

1–3 The only appropriate response to a great work of God is joyous praise, which is exactly what we find here, not for the first time (cf., e.g., 12:5; 26:1; 35:10; 42:10–11), nor for the last (cf. 61:10–11).

This passage is anticipated in 49:14–23 and also in 50:1–3, that is, in the bulk of the material that stands between the second and third Servant Songs. Now the theme is taken up finally and definitively when the Servant's work has been fully accomplished. This certainly suggests that his sufferings and triumph provided the basis for the reconciliation of Israel and the mission to the Gentiles that are joyously proclaimed here.

In the OT culture childlessness was a deeply shameful state (v.1; cf., e.g., 1 Sam 1). As the prophet has already indicated in 50:1, there has been no divorce between God and his people. After the temporary separation of the Exile, Israel would bear more children than in earlier days. Paul applied this promise to the Jerusalem that is above (Gal 4:27) and so to the church. For the wider issues of interpretation this raises, the Introduction, (pp. 14–16) should be consulted.

A figure is taken from nomadic life (v.2), suggesting that the promises to Abraham and his nomadic family (e.g., Gen 12:1–3; 28:13–14) are in the prophet's mind. The family tent must be enlarged and in consequence will need to be strengthened. The probable allusion to Genesis 28 finds confirmation, as Whybray (*Isaiah 40–66*, in loc.) notes, when we find the verb translated "spread out" (v.3) used there also. He mentions too that the phrase "dispossess the nations" (*yāraš haggôyim*), occurs elsewhere in the OT only in Deuteronomy and always in reference to the conquest of

Canaan by Israel. This suggests therefore that the primary reference is to the gradual expansion of the little postexilic community in Judea; however it is possible to interpret it more broadly.

4–8 The figure of the restored wife continues to dominate the passage. People often fear disgrace as much as or even more than physical danger (v.4). The shame of their youth will be either Egyptian bondage (cf. Hos 11:1) or, less likely, affliction under the Assyrians; and the widowhood is of course the Exile. In v.5 the prophet encourages them to think of the one who is the husband of his people. No less than six titles and descriptions are brought together here, all building up a picture of a God of immense power and overflowing grace. He is both able and willing to restore them to himself and to their land. The husband analogy occurs also in Jeremiah 31:31–34, in the context of the new covenant promise there.

Illustrations serve many purposes in Scripture, but it is important to bear in mind their limitations. God is no more to be thought of as a deserting husband (vv.6–7) than as an unjust judge (Luke 18:1–8), though both figures teach spiritual lessons. The repeated phrase "for a (brief) moment" contemplates the Exile—which must have seemed so long to the people themselves—as a mere episode in contrast to God's everlasting kindness that will embrace them (v.8).

9–10 The writer to the Hebrews lays special stress on the great assurance the oath of God gives us (Heb 6:14–20; 7:20–28). Illustrating his theme from both history and nature, the prophet compares God's oath to the great postdiluvial promise of Genesis 8:22, which itself related to the natural environment of man and so suggested the reference to the mountains. Even the visible universe, dominated for the Judean by the hills of his native land, would prove less enduring than God's love, guaranteed by his word (cf. Mark 13:31). A relationship between persons is given added strength by its formalizing in covenant terms. The beautiful Hebrew word *ḥeseḏ* (the love that is unswervingly loyal to a covenant) is here rendered "unfailing love."

11–15 The expression "covenant of peace" (cf. Ezek 34:25–31) in v.10 is expounded here (see esp. v.13). God's covenant with his people implies that he will protect them, as a husband does his wife. In fact, the marriage analogy is still present; and it has been suggested by Eaton (p. 85) that "the adornment of Zion with jewels and eye-cosmetic . . . may relate to her preparation as a royal bride of Yahweh." Certainly Revelation 21:10–27—which is based on this passage—presents the New Jerusalem in the context of v.2, which reads, "I saw the Holy City, the new Jerusalem, coming down out of heaven from God, prepared as a bride beautifully dressed for her husband."

This covenant of peace may not be identified with the new covenant of Jeremiah 31:31–34, but it has important links with it; for in it the people—not only collectively but distributively—will know God through his personal instruction. Thus v.13 can be quoted and applied to Christ and his disciples (cf. John 6:45). The swift movement of thought from stones to children may reflect a pun found also in the NT, as Simon (in loc.) suggests: "Like John the Baptist in the Gospels he puns on the assonance in Hebrew of stones and children (*'avanim-banim*, cf. Matt 3:9)." The city that has for so long known iniquity and the judgment through enemies that God visited on her (vv.14–15) will then be true to its name, a place of peace, resulting from its new righteousness. There is no reference to the Messiah, but the juxtaposition of righteousness and peace reminds us of 9:7; 11:1–9. All this will of course be under God's new regime, not foreign or domestic tyranny. Yet perfect and effectively protected as the city is, there will still be evil intent on its destruction, suggesting the Satan-inspired antagonism faced by the church, the city of God, in the NT (see Introduction, pp. 14–16).

16–17 These verses both amplify and contrast with v.15. There God promises that he will not send attackers against his people (contrast this with 10:5–12), while here he declares that destructive nations are created by him. The point here, of course, is that this means they are in his absolute power and so are employed or restrained under his sovereign hand. Not only physical assault but moral accusation will be repulsed, for Israel's righteousness (v.14) is from him. The people then enter their heritage (Deut 4:21). The term "servants" (pl.) is of such frequent occurrence in so-called Trito-Isaiah (chs. 56–66) that it links parts of the book ascribed by many scholars to two different authors (see Introduction, pp. 6–12). "Servant" in the singular occurs twenty times from chapters 41–53; but in chapters 54–66—since the supreme Servant and his unique act of divine service has been revealed, and he has made the singular use of the word forever his own—it never occurs again in the singular in this book, contrary to KJV.

Notes

8 שֶׁצֶף (*šeṣep*, "surge") is a *hapax legomenon*. North (*Isaiah 40–55*, in loc.) mentions the suggestion that it is connected with *šāṣap* ("to cut," "to slash"), so indicating a momentary fit of anger. He himself prefers the suggestion, implied in the RSV, that it should be emended to *šeṭep* ("flood"), thus providing a bridge to v.9. It is preferable to retain the MT if, as here, it makes sense.

11–12 פּוּךְ (*pûk*, "turquoise") appears also in 2 Kings 9:30; Jer 4:30, where it is an eye cosmetic (see comment by Eaton in commentary); but in 1 Chron 29:2 it is apparently a setting for stones, which looks more likely here. The various stones referred to in these verses cannot be identified with certainty.

6. The Generosity, Urgency, and Effectiveness of God's Word of Grace

55:1–13

> ¹"Come, all you who are thirsty,
>   come to the waters;
> and you who have no money,
>   come, buy and eat!
> Come, buy wine and milk
>   without money and without cost.
> ²Why spend money on what is not bread,
>   and your labor on what does not satisfy?
> Listen, listen to me, and eat what is good,
>   and your soul will delight in the richest of fare.
> ³Give ear and come to me;
>   hear me, that your soul may live.
> I will make an everlasting covenant with you,
>   my faithful love promised to David.

⁴See, I have made him a witness to the peoples,
    a leader and commander of the peoples.
⁵Surely you will summon nations you know not,
    and nations that do not know you will hasten to you,
because of the Lord your God,
    the Holy One of Israel,
for he has endowed you with splendor."

⁶Seek the Lord while he may be found;
    call on him while he is near.
⁷Let the wicked forsake his way
    and the evil man his thoughts.
Let him turn to the Lord, and he will have mercy on him,
    and to our God, for he will freely pardon.

⁸"For my thoughts are not your thoughts,
    neither are your ways my ways,"

                                              declares the Lord.

⁹"As the heavens are higher than the earth,
    so are my ways higher than your ways
    and my thoughts than your thoughts.
¹⁰As the rain and the snow
    come down from heaven,
and do not return to it
    without watering the earth
and making it bud and flourish,
    so that it yields seed for the sower and bread
        for the eater,
¹¹so is my word that goes out from my mouth:
    It will not return to me empty,
but will accomplish what I desire
    and achieve the purpose for which I sent it.
¹²You will go out in joy
    and be led forth in peace;
the mountains and hills
    will burst into song before you,
and all the trees of the field
    will clap their hands.
¹³Instead of the thornbush will grow the pine tree,
    and instead of briers the myrtle will grow.
This will be for the Lord's renown,
    for an everlasting sign,
    which will not be destroyed."

In introducing this passage, Kidner ("Isaiah," in loc.) says, "This call to the needy is unsurpassed for warmth of welcome even in the N.T. The chapter builds up twice to a climax, first in vv.1–5, then, over a still greater range, in vv.6–13."

For those commentators who hold that "Deutero-Isaiah" wrote chapters 40–55 of the book, this chapter is the climax of his work; and they point for example to the emphasis on the divine word that also comes at the beginning of his prophecies (cf. 40:1–11). This chapter would certainly figure as a climax, but the realistic recognition of sin and continued rebellion, which characterizes some of the later chapters, and the prediction of a new heaven and earth (65:17; 66:22), which goes even further than the vision of this chapter, make us realize that God has still more to say through his prophet to his people.

1–5 Many commentators hear the voice of the Near Eastern water vendor in v.2, while others discern the accents of personified wisdom (Prov 9:1–6). Either would be appropriate, for Isaiah was a master of illustrations from nature and contemporary culture. Moreover, as Whedbee has shown, at least for the chapters acknowledged to be by Isaiah of Jerusalem, he had definite contact with the Israelite wisdom tradition. We may in fact discern overtones of both. The water carrier is also a wise counselor.

Young (*Book of Isaiah*, in loc.) has pointed out that the introductory word *hôy*, which lies behind the first instance of the English "Come" in v.1 ("ho" in KJV), "is mainly an attention-getting device, but it expresses a slight tone of pity." Young goes on to say, "The prophet is an evangelist with a concern for the souls of men and a realization of their desperate condition without the blessings that the servant has obtained."

The water vendor is, of course, part of the normal commercial scene in the Near East; but God through the prophet offers the people in Babylon not only water but more costly drinks and invites them too to a banquet (Luke 14:15–24). Verse 2, with its mildly chiding tone, probably alludes to the people's preoccupation with settling down in Babylon. As Thexton (in loc.) puts it: "They had been in Babylon for many years—some for the whole of their life. They had grown roots, acquired property and commercial interests, were prosperous and secure. The prophet does not plead or argue, but throws into the quiet pool of their complacency a disturbing pebble, as he asks: 'Does all this really satisfy you? Is this what you are for?'" He speaks with urgency, "Listen, listen." (See the comment introducing 51:9–52:12.)

A substantial group of modern commentators (e.g., Westermann, Whybray) consider that in vv.3–5 God promises his people that he will take the Davidic covenant (2 Sam 7:8–16) away from the royal line and give it to the people as a whole, thus perhaps putting it on a par with the Abrahamic and Mosaic covenants. But Eaton (pp. 87–88) points out: "If the author had intended to make a fundamental change in the Davidic doctrine . . . he would surely have needed to be more explicit. . . . The nation is to be blessed within the radius of the Davidic covenant, but the destiny of the royal house remains. . . . It would be a poor sort of eternity that the covenant would have, if its heart were taken out!" This passage, which constitutes an important link with the promises of a Davidic Messiah given earlier in the book, is quoted by Paul in Acts 13:34 with reference to the resurrection of Christ, through whose risen kingship the promises of this passage receive their eternal and therefore their final fulfillment.

During the reign of David, Israel's kingdom reached its greatest extent. David, as a faithful worshiper of the Lord, was therefore a witness to God's truth to all the peoples in his empire, as well as being their leader. He therefore anticipated in himself the prophetic and kingly functions of the Messiah. In God's future for his people, as here depicted, the empire would be wider still (cf. 9:7). The far parts of the earth will come up to Zion (cf. 2:1–5; 60:1–14), because she will attract them by the beauty her God has given her (cf. 54:11–12).

6–7 The call of vv.1–3 is echoed here but with a stronger moral emphasis. Earlier the folly of self-willed waywardness was stressed, while here it is its wickedness. Verse 6 implies both a promise and a warning. There is urgency in this call, for the time is not unlimited (cf. 61:2). Both in his life style and in the attitudes that lie behind it, the sinner is wrong; and so repentance must touch the inner man as well as the outward deeds (cf. Matt 5:21–22, 27–28). The call here is not simply uttered to the people as such, as in chapter 54, but to the individual. The promise of God's pardon is assured (cf. 1:16–20; 44:22 et al.).

8–13 Verses 8–9 do not refer simply to the inscrutable character of God's ways and thoughts; for, in the light of v.7, it is clear that there is a stress on the moral difference. God's thoughts and ways are in fact governed by righteousness—his righteousness—and his effective word therefore accomplishes a moral purpose, the reclamation of the sinner from the error and wickedness of his ways. The reference to heaven and earth is very characteristic of Isaiah.

Verse 10 shows an awareness of the ceaseless round of nature but also of the purpose of it, which was hidden, at least for a time, from the Preacher in Ecclesiastes 1:5–7. The whole food-producing process is encapsulated within v.10, the only important factor excluded being the actual sowing of the seed. This latter is featured in the parable of the sower (Mark 4:1–20), which has some features in common with this passage (cf. also Heb 6:7–8). The passage teaches the efficacious nature of God's word and of the grace that works through it (v.11). Here, as in Henry Drummond's book-title (London: Hodder and Stoughton, 1897), we may discern "Natural Law in the Spiritual World"; for the world of nature, designed by God, often furnishes illustrations of spiritual truth.

With God's conditions of repentance having been fulfilled and the people's return to the Lord having made possible a return to the land (see comment at 7:3), the prophet can speak of their joyous and peaceful journey (v.12). He moves from the literal joy and peace to the metaphorical mountains and hills and then back again to the literal; for v.13 probably refers to the regeneration of the land, though this in turn may symbolize spiritual fruitfulness. All this will serve to bring glory to God, pointing beyond itself to his eternal grace and power.

Notes

13 The נַעֲצוּץ (na'ᵃṣûṣ, "thornbush") occurs only here and in 7:19. For בְּרוֹשׁ (bᵉrôš, "pine trees"), see the note at 41:19. סִרְפַּד (sirpaḏ, "briers") is a *hapax legomenon*, rendered "nettle" by North (*Isaiah 40–55*, in loc.), who rightly says, "Some such mean and noxious weed is required by the parallel 'camel-thorn' and the contrasting 'myrtle'."

7. *Salvation Extended to the Disadvantaged*

56:1–8

¹This is what the LORD says:

"Maintain justice
 and do what is right,
for my salvation is close at hand
 and my righteousness will soon be revealed.
²Blessed is the man who does this,
 the man who holds it fast,
who keeps the Sabbath without desecrating it,
 and keeps his hand from doing any evil."

³Let no foreigner who has bound himself to the LORD say,
"The LORD will surely exclude me from his people."
And let not any eunuch complain,
"I am only a dry tree."

⁴For this is what the LORD says:

"To the eunuchs who keep my Sabbaths,
who choose what pleases me
and hold fast to my covenant—
⁵to them I will give within my temple and its walls
a memorial and a name
better than sons and daughters;
I will give them an everlasting name
that will not be cut off.
⁶And foreigners who bind themselves to the LORD
to serve him,
to love the name of the LORD,
and to worship him,
all who keep the Sabbath without desecrating it
and who hold fast to my covenant—
⁷these I will bring to my holy mountain
and give them joy in my house of prayer.
Their burnt offerings and sacrifices
will be accepted on my altar;
for my house will be called
a house of prayer for all nations."
⁸The Sovereign LORD declares—
he who gathers the exiles of Israel:
"I will gather still others to them
besides those already gathered."

Just as chapters 40–55 are widely denied to Isaiah and ascribed to an unknown exilic author, generally designated "Deutero-Isaiah," so chapters 56–66 are often denied to both and viewed as the work either of a single author, "Trito-Isaiah," prophesying after the return from exile, or to a group of postexilic prophets. There are still some, however, who see the chapters as part of Deutero-Isaiah's work, while those who maintain the traditional conservative view treat the whole book as the work of Isaiah of Jerusalem (see Introduction, pp. 6–12).

Whatever our view on the question of authorship, there can be little doubt that there is a change in geographical perspective. The people addressed in chapters 40–55 are being encouraged to return from the Babylonian captivity, whereas in the chapters in prospect they are in the land of Canaan. That land was "a place of corruption (56:9–59:15a) and devastation (63:7–64:12)" (Kidner, "Isaiah," in loc.), so that neither the moral standards of God nor the great hopes of the people found true realization in it. Everything cried out for something more; and, of course, it was never intended that the great promises given earlier in the book should find perfect fulfillment in the postexilic community but in an altogether new order. They are therefore confronted with their own failures and stimulated afresh both to turn to God and to hope in him.

1–2 Many scholars point to the verbal links with 46:13 here and yet also to the difference in atmosphere of the two verses. In the earlier passage God chastised his people for their unrighteous unbelief and failure to accept his word promising them an imminent salvation. Here, however, it is their general life style and their failure to keep his law (cf. v.1 with 51:4), symbolized by the Sabbath, that are under attack. Young (*Book of Isaiah*, in loc.), pointing out that righteousness by works is not being taught here, goes on to say, "Smart also maintains that this verse moves in the direction of the later Judaism, in which God's coming salvation is made to depend upon the nation's keeping of the law. That, however, is not what the verse teaches. Men are to do righteousness, not in order that God's salvation may come, but because it is already near." Compare the call for repentance of both John the Baptist and Jesus himself in view of the imminence of the kingdom of God (Matt 3:1–2; 4:17; cf. Isa 40:3).

The benediction formula, characteristic of but not peculiar to the wisdom literary genre (cf. Ps 1:1; 119:1; Prov 8:32, 34; but also Isa 30:18; 32:20), names the Sabbath-keeper as a truly happy man. The NIV, which preserves the poetic variation of "man" to "son of man" in successive lines in 51:12, has opted for a more prosaic identity of translation in v.2. Is the ideal here presented a negative one? Only if the Sabbath itself is viewed in terms simply of the prohibition of work and not positively, in terms of opportunities of worship and of spiritual, mental, and physical renewal. The negative that brings v.2 to its close is balanced by the positive exhortations in v.1: "Maintain justice and do what is right." Westermann (in loc.) writes: "During the exile the Sabbath had become a badge denoting membership of the community that worshipped Yahweh." So, from now on, "whether one holds to Yahweh or not is a matter for the individual to decide for himself, and the most conspicuous sign of decision is observance of the Sabbath."

3–8 The worship system of Israel, which was centered in the temple and was always important, was to be underlined by the work of Haggai and Zechariah, who lent all their prophetic authority to supporting the rebuilding enterprise in Jerusalem. Ezra and Nehemiah too, of necessity, emphasized the particularism of the Jewish faith. Inevitably some who lived in the land would feel excluded; and, of course, passages like Deuteronomy 23:1–8 banned eunuchs and some foreigners from participation in the worship system. The prophet has a word of comfort for them, showing that the blessing pronounced in v.2 did not contain built-in racial or physical limitations.

Verse 3 speaks of the proselyte and the eunuch. The prophet engages with the sense of insecurity that must often have plagued proselytes. If even native-born Israelites could still have guilty consciences despite the offering of sacrifices (cf. Heb 9:9), how much more the "incomer"! The eunuch would have felt even more insecure, for his very place in the ongoing life of God's people was simply an episode. The family had great importance in the religio-cultural emotions of Israel. A dry tree bears no fruit; a eunuch begets no children.

For each group God has an authoritative word of consolation through the prophet. This word need not be viewed as a cancellation of Deuteronomy 23 but rather as eschatological and so belonging to the new order of the future. In this way there is a "practical translation of the missionary vision of chs. 40–55 into modest terms, in the concern shown for the *eunuch* and the *foreigner*, outsiders in the midst of Israel" (Kidner, "Isaiah," in loc., emphasis his). Faithfulness to the Lord— expressed in keeping the Sabbath law (v.4), because it pleases him and therefore is surely done out of love for him (cf. v.6)—will give the eunuch a secure place in God's temple. (It should be noted that the Sabbath is treated in Exod 31:12–17 as a sign of the covenant, as it appears to be also here.) We can hardly imagine that the prophet is speaking literally when he refers to a memorial in the temple (v.5). There may even be a suggestion of eternal life in the closing affirmation of v.5. The six marks of the foreigner (v.6) provide a beautiful description of true godliness, with love as its great dynamic, the very antithesis of Pharisaic legalism.

In one of Isaiah's greatest visions (2:1–4), the people of the nations come up to Jerusalem to worship in the house of the Lord. There it is their eagerness that is highlighted, while here it is the divine initiative. The very one whose purpose involves gathering his own scattered people will include the foreigners too in the great pilgrimage to Jerusalem. The Court of the Gentiles was a kind of symbol and earnest of this, and it was from this that Christ expelled the sharp-practicing traders, saying, " 'Is it not written: "My house shall be called a house of prayer for all nations"? But you have made it "a den of robbers" ' " (Mark 11:17; cf. John 2:16). These Gentiles would not come simply on sufferance or as mere observers but as full participants, offering sacrifices alongside the Jews. (For discussion of the interpretation of this, see the Introduction, pp. 14–16.)

Notes

---

5 The MT reads "I will give him an everlasting name." The NIV follows 1QIsa[a] here in using the plural.

---

8. *God's Message to the Wicked*

56:9–57:21

> [9]Come, all you beasts of the field,
>   come and devour, all you beasts of the forest!
> [10]Israel's watchmen are blind,
>   they all lack knowledge;
>   they are all mute dogs,
>   they cannot bark;
>   they lie around and dream,
>   they love to sleep.
> [11]They are dogs with mighty appetites;
>   they never have enough.
>   They are shepherds who lack understanding;
>   they all turn to their own way,
>   each seeks his own gain.
> [12]"Come," each one cries, "let me get wine!
>   Let us drink our fill of beer!
>   And tomorrow will be like today,
>   or even far better."
>
> [57:1]The righteous perish,
>   and no one ponders it in his heart;
>   devout men are taken away,
>   and no one understands
>   that the righteous are taken away
>   to be spared from evil.

²Those who walk uprightly
    enter into peace;
    they find rest as they lie in death.

³"But you—come here, you sons of a sorceress,
    you offspring of adulterers and prostitutes!
⁴Whom are you mocking?
    At whom do you sneer
    and stick out your tongue?
Are you not a brood of rebels,
    the offspring of liars?
⁵You burn with lust among the oaks
    and under every spreading tree;
you sacrifice your children in the ravines
    and under the overhanging crags.
⁶The idols, among the smooth stones of the ravines are
        your portion;
    they, they are your lot.
Yes, to them you have poured out drink offerings
    and offered grain offerings.
    In the light of these things, should I relent?
⁷You have made your bed on a high and lofty hill;
    there you went up to offer your sacrifices.
⁸Behind your doors and your doorposts
    you have put your pagan symbols.
Forsaking me, you uncovered your bed,
    you climbed into it and opened it wide;
you made a pact with those whose beds you love,
    and you looked on their nakedness.
⁹You went to Molech with olive oil
    and increased your perfumes.
You sent your ambassadors far away;
    you descended to the grave itself!
¹⁰You were wearied by all your ways,
    but you would not say, 'It is hopeless.'
You found renewal of your strength,
    and so you did not faint.

¹¹"Whom have you so dreaded and feared
    that you have been false to me,
and have neither remembered me
    nor pondered this in your hearts?
Is it not because I have long been silent
    that you do not fear me?
¹²I will expose your righteousness and your works,
    and they will not benefit you.
¹³When you cry out for help,
    let your collection of idols, save you!
The wind will carry all of them off,
    a mere breath will blow them away.
But the man who makes me his refuge
    will inherit the land
    and possess my holy mountain."

¹⁴And it will be said:

"Build up, build up, prepare the road!
    Remove the obstacles out of the way of my people."
¹⁵For this is what the high and lofty One says—
    he who lives forever, whose name is holy:

"I live in a high and holy place,
    but also with him who is contrite and lowly in spirit,
to revive the spirit of the lowly
    and to revive the heart of the contrite.
[16]I will not accuse forever,
    nor will I always be angry,
for then the spirit of man would grow faint before me—
    the breath of man that I have created.
[17]I was enraged by his sinful greed;
    I punished him, and hid my face in anger,
    yet he kept on in his willful ways.
[18]I have seen his ways, but I will heal him;
    I will guide him and restore comfort to him,
[19]   creating praise on the lips of the mourners in Israel.
Peace, peace, to those far and near,"
    says the LORD. "And I will heal them."
[20]But the wicked are like the tossing sea,
    which cannot rest,
    whose waves cast up mire and mud.
[21]"There is no peace," says my God, "for the wicked."

Some modern scholars, accepting in general terms a threefold analysis of the book (see Introduction, pp. 6–12), nevertheless regard this passage as preexilic, though not necessarily as Isaianic. The sins in view here kept on recurring in Israel's history, so that the question of date cannot be easily settled by reference to the content of the passage. If we accept the unity of the book, the matter becomes a question of the readers chiefly intended to profit by the oracle. If they are postexilic, this would reveal the continued presence of pagan syncretism, though, of course, it may be that this was chiefly to be found among those who had never been in Babylon.

9–12 These verses remind us of earlier verses in Isaiah (see 5:11–12, 22) and later ones in Ezekiel (Ezek 3:16–21; 34:1–6). The people are viewed, implicitly, as the flock of God. The prophet, as God's mouthpiece, likens the enemies of Israel to wild beasts lurking in field and forest and ironically calls them to feast on the sheep (v.9). The watchmen—which almost certainly include false prophets (cf. Jer 6:17; Ezek 3:17; 33:2–7) and also perhaps other leaders of the people—belong properly to a different picture, that of a city in danger; but they are soon translated into the dominant scene as dogs, set to watch the sheep (v.10). Blindness, muteness, indolence, and self-seeking greed describe different aspects of their culpable ineffectiveness. When the analogy moves from the dogs to the shepherds (v.11), the same characteristics can be seen. Verse 12 graphically represents the drunkard's careless abandon (cf. 22:13) and inebriated optimism.

57:1–2 Thexton (in loc.) comments:

It is one thing to see righteous men perishing and to doubt in consequence either the justice or the power of God. With this problem the biblical writers are frequently concerned, and most notably in the Book of Job. But when the suffering or downfall of good men causes no heart-searching, raises no problems, demands no explanation, it means that though religious observance may survive, faith in God has given place to a practical atheism. . . . It is from this basic atheism that there spring all the other evils and abuses of which the prophet speaks.

Verse 1 has an unexpected twist to its thought at the end, suggesting the rewarding of the righteous after death and leading into v.2. A man lying dead may seem to a distant observer to be resting. He is, indeed, if he is righteous.

3–10 It almost seems in vv.3–13 that the people are on trial and are charged, found guilty, and sentenced, though this judicial setting is less obvious than in 1:2–20. The words of v.3 and v.4b are intentionally insulting, not to the parents, but to the children. This was a conventional way of indicating undesirable qualities (cf. 1 Sam 20:30). Sorcery (cf. 2:6) and adultery in combination point to pagan fertility rites. Those who practiced them apparently did so quite blatantly and with many a mocking gesture against the true prophet of God sent to chastise them in his name (v.4; cf. 30:9–11).

The pagan rites of Canaan, featuring sacred trees (v.5; cf. 1:29–30), pandered to the sexual appetites of the worshipers. During the reign of Ahaz (cf. 2 Kings 16:3–4) and—if he saw it—of Manasseh (2 Kings 21:2–9), Isaiah must have been deeply grieved by the pagan child-sacrifices practiced in the land. The references to ravines, crags, and stones are obscure but no doubt reflect aspects of paganism.

At v.6 the verbs change from plural to singular, so that the people are pictured collectively as an adulterer or a prostitute. The place where adultery was committed was "a high and lofty hill" (v.7; cf. Jer 2:20), referring to the pagan high places. The analogy could refer either to the temple or to domestic houses, but there may be an implied comparison with the prostitute's sign of her trade. The sensitive Israelite reader would, of course, remember that it was the word of God—and, most aptly, the assertion that there is only one God—that was to be inscribed on the doors (v.8; cf. Deut 6:4–9).

Molech (v.9), god of the Ammonites, is associated with child-sacrifice (Lev 18:21; 2 Kings 23:10) in the OT (see Notes). The olive oil and perfumes could be offerings, or else they belong to the picture of the prostitute. The apostate people did not pursue their paganism as a kind of leisure activity but went to great lengths (v.10). They had courted the gods of nations far away and indulged too in necromancy. Weariness had not however induced them to give up. Verse 10 might represent an ironic comparison with 40:27–31 and even perhaps a suggestion that there was a wicked, supernatural source this strength was derived from.

11–13 Isaiah is fond of rhetorical questions, and those of v.11 are followed by irony in v.12 and by mocking challenge in v.13a. The section closes with a message of comfort for the man of faith. The people had forgotten who he was (v.11; cf. v.15), for otherwise how could they fear the petty deities of the pagans more than their great and holy God? The references to righteousness and works are of course ironic. Verse 13 reminds us of the prophet's onslaught on idolatry in chapters 40–48, and it should be compared also in its language with 40:6–8, 24. The best exposition of the closing promises is Psalm 37.

14–21 The note of comfort for the faithful, expressed in v.13b, prepares us for these verses. The urgent imperatives of v.14, so characteristic of certain passages in this prophecy (esp. 51:9–52:12), echo 40:3, the second allusion to that chapter in this passage (cf. comment at vv.11–13). The great call for repentance in 55:6–7 finds expression in this picture of spiritual road-building requiring the removal of obstacles.

The wearied but unrepentant sinner somehow finds renewal of his strength to continue in sin (v.10); but here those "crushed and bowed down"—as Thexton (in loc.) literally renders the words translated "contrite and lowly" (v.15)—are revived in the presence of the exalted, living, and holy God (cf. ch. 6). The urgent call to bustling activity in v.14 contrasts strikingly with the eternal calm of v.15, and we are reminded of the sublime statement of Ephesians 1:3, made to Christians deeply involved in the workaday world. The Lord is not here pictured—as Epicurean philosophy depicted the gods on Mount Olympus—in detached unconcern for the world but active in reviving the spirits of his dispirited people.

In vv.16–18 we seem to once again encounter allusions to chapter 40, as a glance at 40:1–2, and 27 discloses. There is also an echo of Genesis 6:3. These verses reveal the righteous anger and the amazing grace of God and also the awful persistence of man's rebellion against him. The unmerited nature of God's favor has rarely been expressed more beautifully than in v.18. The passage does not suggest that there is to be grace for the determinedly impenitent, for the "mourners" of v.19 are probably identical with the dispirited of v.16, properly chastened and restored to God, but hardly daring to hope for comfort from him (cf. Matt 5:4). Isaiah's language here may reflect that of Hosea, his older contemporary in the northern kingdom (Hos 6:1–2; 11:3; 14:2, 4). Once more the prophet employs a reiterated word—"Peace, peace"—to make a point. Possibly, as some commentators suggest, he thus uses the familiar conventional word of greeting to emphasize that there is a welcome home for the wayward. The far and the near here may simply be home-dwelling and dispersed Israelites respectively (cf. 11:11–12; 43:5–7; 56:8), or it may include also the foreigners. Certainly its language can appropriately include these, as the quotation in Ephesians 2:17 shows.

This passage ends with the same warning to the recalcitrant as the prophet gave in 48:22 but with the addition of a telling illustration. In a book so well structured as this, it may mark what was for the prophet or compilers the end of a particular section of prophecies (see Introduction, pp. 20–22).

Notes

10 The word "Israel" is not in the text but is obviously needed. In fact, it may well look back to v.8, showing, as Young (*Book of Isaiah*, in loc.) points out, that no new beginning is being made here.

57: 5 Whybray (*Isaiah 40–66*, in loc.) points out the unusual spelling of אֵלִים (*'ēlîm*, "oaks") and suggests that in fact it may refer to "the Els," i.e., the Canaanite gods. The prophet is no doubt using a play on words, because of the association of sacred trees with Canaanite polytheism.

6 חֵלֶק (*ḥēleq*, "smooth") is an attributive without an expressed noun, "stones" being conjectural. For other suggested translations, see W.H. Irwin, "'The Smooth Stones of the Wady'? Isaiah 57, 6," CBQ 21:1 (Jan 1967):31–40.

8 This verse has been the subject of many conjectural emendations, the more important of which are gathered together in Whybray (*Isaiah 40–66*, in loc.) The NIV makes good sense without emendation—but with rather free translation at some points.

9 The NIV text repoints מֶלֶךְ (*melek*, "king") as *mōlek* (i.e., "Molech"). The MT is not impossible, as it would line up the thought with the reference to ambassadors later in the verse.

17 See also the reference to greed in 56:11, suggesting oracular unity.

19 There are difficulties of syntax here. Young (*Book of Isaiah*, in loc.) suggests that the "fruit of the lips" (lit. Heb.; NIV, "praise on the lips") is in fact the message of peace to those who are far and near. The introductory formula "says the Lord" will then probably introduce the promise of healing.

IX. God as Judge and Savior (58:1–66:24)

These chapters, while confronting realistically the fact of human sin, present God's final purposes of both judgment and salvation and thus make us aware of both his justice and his grace.

1. *The True Fast*

58:1–14

¹"Shout it aloud, do not hold back.
Raise your voice like a trumpet.
Declare to my people their rebellion
and to the house of Jacob their sins.
²For day after day they seek me out;
they seem eager to know my ways,
as if they were a nation that does what is right
and has not forsaken the commands of its God.
They ask me for just decisions
and seem eager for God to come near them.
³'Why have we fasted,' they say,
'and you have not seen it?
Why have we humbled ourselves,
and you have not noticed?'

"Yet on the day of your fasting, you do as you please
and exploit all your workers.
⁴Your fasting ends in quarreling and strife,
and in striking each other with wicked fists.
You cannot fast as you do today
and expect your voice to be heard on high.
⁵Is this the kind of fast I have chosen,
only a day for a man to humble himself?
Is it only for bowing one's head like a reed
and for lying on sackcloth and ashes?
Is that what you call a fast,
a day acceptable to the Lord?

⁶"Is not this the kind of fasting I have chosen:
to loose the chains of injustice
and untie the cords of the yoke,
to set the oppressed free
and break every yoke?
⁷Is it not to share your food with the hungry
and to provide the poor wanderer with shelter—
when you see the naked, to clothe him,
and not to turn away from your own flesh and blood?
⁸Then your light will break forth like the dawn,
and your healing will quickly appear;

then your righteousness will go before you,
and the glory of the LORD will be your rear guard.
⁹Then you will call, and the LORD will answer;
you will cry for help, and he will say: Here am I.
"If you do away with the yoke of oppression,
with the pointing finger and malicious talk,
¹⁰and if you spend yourselves in behalf of the hungry
and satisfy the needs of the oppressed,
then your light will rise in the darkness,
and your night will become like the noonday.
¹¹The LORD will guide you always;
he will satisfy your needs in a sun-scorched land
and will strengthen your frame.
You will be like a well-watered garden,
like a spring whose waters never fail.
¹²Your people will rebuild the ancient ruins
and will raise up the age-old foundations;
you will be called Repairer of Broken Walls,
Restorer of Streets with Dwellings.

¹³"If you keep your feet from breaking the Sabbath
and from doing as you please on my holy day,
if you call the Sabbath a delight
and the LORD's holy day honorable,
and if you honor it by not going your own way
and not doing as you please or speaking idle words,
¹⁴then you will find your joy in the LORD,
and I will cause you to ride on the heights of the land
and to feast on the inheritance of your father Jacob."
The mouth of the LORD has spoken.

Although this oracle may have been intended especially for the postexilic community, there are a number of features that remind us of the eighth-century prophets. There is the emphasis on social righteousness and also particular phrases, as a comparison of v. 1 with Hosea 8:1 and Micah 3:8 will reveal. An eighth-or early seventh-century provenance is therefore perfectly feasible. It also has links with Zechariah 7, where the prophet underlines the harmony of his teaching with that of the earlier prophets, presumably including Isaiah. Its teaching also has links with the Sermon on the Mount (Matt 5–7).

1–3a The prophet has already exposed the empty ritualism of the people in chapter 1. Here he concentrates on one religious activity—fasting. A trumpet call (v. 1) is intended to rouse the hearers to action, but it must be clear and unambiguous (cf. 1 Cor 14:8). There is no mistaking the message here. The people showed outward evidence of wanting to do God's will, probably by consulting priests and prophets (v. 2). They were prepared too to show their earnestness by enduring the minor inconvenience of fasting (v. 3a). What did a little abstinence matter if they could retain their basic life style of disobedient rebellion against the moral demands of their God? Such empty externalism reappears in every age and culture, and it is significant that the prophet's earlier condemnation of it in chapter 1 comes hot on the heels of his indictment of their rebellion in vv. 2–5 of that chapter.

3b–5 Through his prophet God exposes the people's hypocrisy (v. 36). Clearly their fasting was not spiritually motivated. Apparently they made the fast easier by idleness and made up for lost time by getting their laborers to work all the harder. Fasting undertaken as a duty can produce an edgy, irritable community, especially in difficult climatic conditions; and v.4a probably reflects this. Prayers offered with this kind of background would never reach the heavens (v.46). The humbling v.5 refers to (cf. also v.3) seems to be a synonym for fasting. Sackcloth and ashes also suggest the extravagant expression of humiliation.

6–9a The questions of vv.6–7, following immediately on those of v.5, serve to point up the people's separation of religious observance and social righteousness, a theme the eighth-century prophets never tired of expounding. There was oppression (cf. Jer 34:8–22) and poverty in the land. The prophet even has to appeal to the claims of blood relationship, such a pitch had insular selfishness reached.

Young (*Book of Isaiah*), commenting on v.8, recalls the references to light in the promises of 9:2 (cf. 60:1–3) thus: "In these first two clauses the emphasis falls upon speed. Elsewhere Isaiah uses the verb *break forth* of the hatching of eggs (59:5) and of water gushing forth (35:6). The word seems to suggest suddenness, swiftness, and novelty. In the Near East the light of day follows almost immediately upon the darkness of night" (emphasis his). God also pledges restoration of health, protection, and access to himself in prayer. Verse 8b recalls 52:12. "Light" perhaps encapsulates all this, for in these chapters it suggests fullness of divine blessing (cf. 59:9; 60:1).

9b–12 Isaiah develops the same basic theme again but with some variations. Oppression is emphasized by repetition, and there is also a reference to character assassination. Verse 10 suggests that social concern is not just to be seen in an isolated episode, but it is to be a way of life for God's people. We are to spend not just our money but ourselves (cf. 2 Cor 12:15). The promise of v.8 is taken still further. The glorious dawn will issue in an even more glorious midday. In this light life that is fully provided for and strong—always refreshed (cf. Jer 31:12) and ever refreshing others—can flourish under God's blessing (v.11). An intended postexilic readership seems in view in v.12, though of course this does not necessarily imply postexilic authorship (see Introduction, pp. 6–12).

13–14 Herbert (in loc.) suggests that the association of "sabbath" with self-mortification in Leviticus 16:31 may account for the inclusion of these verses in this chapter. There is no need, however, for us to detach them from the rest of it. Moreover, as Ralph Alexander pointed out (in a personal communication), the Sabbath here could represent the entire Mosaic covenant and the blessings to be enjoyed in following it (see comment at 56:3–8). Kidner's fine comment ("Isaiah," in loc.) is worth full quotation:

> Lest it should seem that philanthropy is all, these verses describe the strictness and the gladness of the sabbath-keeping God desires. If fasting is to be an opportunity to show love to our neighbour, the sabbath should express first of all our love of God (though both the foregoing passage and the sabbath practice of Jesus insist that it must overflow to man). It will mean self-forgetfulness (v.13a) and the self-discipline of rising above the trivial (v.13b). But to people of this spirit God can safely give great things (v.14).

2. *Sin, Sorrow, and Salvation*

59:1–21

¹Surely the arm of the LORD is not too short to save,
    nor his ear too dull to hear.
²But your iniquities have separated
    you from your God;
your sins have hidden his face from you,
    so that he will not hear.
³For your hands are stained with blood,
    your fingers with guilt.
Your lips have spoken lies,
    and your tongue mutters wicked things.
⁴No one calls for justice;
    no one pleads his case with integrity.
They rely on empty arguments and speak lies;
    they conceive trouble and give birth to evil.
⁵They hatch the eggs of vipers
    and spin a spider's web.
Whoever eats their eggs will die,
    and when one is broken, an adder is hatched.
⁶Their cobwebs are useless for clothing;
    they cannot cover themselves with what they make.
Their deeds are evil deeds,
    and acts of violence are in their hands.
⁷Their feet rush into sin;
    they are swift to shed innocent blood.
Their thoughts are evil thoughts;
    ruin and destruction mark their ways.
⁸The way of peace they do not know;
    there is no justice in their paths.
They have turned them into crooked roads;
    no one who walks in them will know peace.

⁹So justice is far from us,
    and righteousness does not reach us.
We look for light, but all is darkness;
    for brightness, but we walk in deep shadows.
¹⁰Like the blind we grope along the wall,
    feeling our way like men without eyes.
At midday we stumble as if it were twilight;
    among the strong, we are like the dead.
¹¹We all growl like bears;
    we moan mournfully like doves.
We look for justice, but find none;
    for deliverance, but it is far away.

¹²For our offenses are many in your sight,
    and our sins testify against us.
Our offenses are ever with us,
    and we acknowledge our iniquities:
¹³rebellion and treachery against the LORD,
    turning our backs on our God,
fomenting oppression and revolt,
    uttering lies our hearts have conceived.
¹⁴So justice is driven back,
    and righteousness stands at a distance;
truth has stumbled in the streets,
    honesty cannot enter.

¹⁵Truth is nowhere to be found,
and whoever shuns evil becomes a prey.

The LORD looked and was displeased
that there was no justice.
¹⁶He saw that there was no one,
he was appalled that there was no one to intervene;
so his own arm worked salvation for him,
and his own righteousness sustained him.
¹⁷He put on righteousness as his breastplate,
and the helmet of salvation on his head;
he put on the garments of vengeance
and wrapped himself in zeal as in a cloak.
¹⁸According to what they have done,
so will he repay
wrath to his enemies
and retribution to his foes;
he will repay the islands their due.
¹⁹From the west, men will fear the name of the LORD,
and from the rising of the sun, they will revere
his glory.
For he will come like a pent-up flood
that the breath of the LORD drives along.

²⁰"The Redeemer will come to Zion,
to those in Jacob who repent of their sins,"
declares the LORD.

²¹"As for me, this is my covenant with them," says the LORD. "My Spirit, who is
on you, and my words that I have put in your mouth will not depart from your
mouth, or from the mouths of your children, or from the mouths of their descendants from this time on and forever," says the LORD.

The prophet who could speak words of great comfort and encouragement could
also confront his hearers with their sins and make them face unpleasant spiritual and
moral facts. In chapter 57 he condemned adulterous paganism, in chapter 58 hypocritical fasting, while here it is chiefly injustice that calls forth his condemnation.
Each of these chapters speaks about prayer. In chapter 57 it was not answered
because it was not addressed to the true God (57:13); in chapter 58 because the
petitioners are hypocrites (58:4); while here, in vv. 1–2, it is because of their sins and
particularly, as later verses indicate, their injustice.

This passage, like much else in chapters 56–66, is often ascribed to "Trito-Isaiah"
(see Introduction, pp. 6–12); but, despite this, many modern commentators see
plenty of links with earlier parts of the Book of Isaiah. For example, Herbert (in loc.)
likens it to Isaiah 24–27, "in which prophetic word and community response are
interwoven."

1–8 The vivid anthropomorphisms of vv. 1–2 ("arm" . . . "ear" . . . "face"), following
on from the reference to "the mouth of the LORD" in the previous verse, remind us
of chapter 40. Here however they come in a very different context, stressing condemnation rather than comfort. God is addressing people who have anticipated
some kind of divine intervention and have prayed for it, but whose life style reveals
all too clearly that their desire and prayer are not directed toward the establishment
of God's rule on earth; for they are themselves rebels against that rule.

The people are guilty particularly of social injustice. In words reminiscent of 1:15, the prophet moves from the worst effects of legal oppression—viz., unjust condemnation to death (v.3)—to the false witness that produced such a verdict (v.4), and ultimately to the state of deep social and moral apathy that was the cause of such a situation. He then employs two figures taken from man's basic needs of food and clothing (vv.5–6). The metaphors seem to imply that what these evil people produce seems at first wholesome and constructive, only to be revealed for what it really is later. In fact, the illustration of the gossamer that is useless for clothing implies that evil is ultimately counterproductive, not only for its victims, but for its perpetrators. Sin is self-destructive.

The prophet does not indicate that he is condemning any particular class among the people, though perhaps he has chiefly in mind those in whose hands the administration of justice is placed (cf. 5:22–23). Because Isaiah's words are not only strong but general, Paul could quote them in his general indictment of human sin in Romans 3:15–17. Several commentators have pointed out that the image of the moral life as a walk—so common in Scripture—dominates vv.7–8. "The way of peace" finds its definition at the end of v.8, making it clear that the prophet is speaking, not about the results of their conduct for others, but for themselves (cf. 57:20–21).

9–11 Here there is a sudden change from the third to the first person; and the people, accused and condemned in the earlier verses, now begin to face their own sins, or, at least, the consequences of them. The justice and righteousness he speaks of here (v.9) are God's, to be manifested on behalf of his people. The contrast with 58:10–11 should be noted; compare also 8:19–22. Such darkness is declared—in Deuteronomy 28:15, 29—to be caused by disobedience to God. For the sorrowful sounds of v.11, see 38:14.

12–15a A new and much deeper note is now sounded. Hatred of the consequences of sin and its destructive effects on one's own life are not necessarily evidence of true repentance. It is when we face sin as rebellion against the holy God who loves us that we begin to see it, in some degree, as he sees it. The prophet may be identifying with the people, expressing himself what he knew should be their own penitence. His thought employs much of the available Hebrew vocabulary for sin (vv.12–13; cf. 1:2–4). From recognition that all has been committed in his sight, he moves to confess that all was against him. In v.9 the people recognize that divine justice, that saving justice in which God delivers his oppressed people, is far away, while here they acknowledge that social justice is excluded from their society (v.14), along with truth (v.15), again probably largely truth of witness (cf. vv.3–4 and the comment there). The situation is so serious that the good man is at risk in such a society.

15b–18 Paul's quotation of vv.7–8 in Romans 3:15–17 is in a context (Rom 3:18–20) that presents sin against the background of the wrath of God against it. Here is that wrath manifesting itself. The intervention probably applies to those who are willing to take the part of the oppressed. The salvation reference is made to would then be God's saving activity on behalf of those unjustly treated (v.17; cf. 49:24–26). God goes to war against sin; and this passage becomes a model for Paul's description of the Christian armor employed by God's people in their struggle against the devil, master of the realm of sin (Eph 6:10–17). For the zeal of the Lord, compare 9:7; 37:32. In the final line of v.18, it becomes clear that the enemies God will do battle against evil in Gentile lands as well as in Israel.

19–21 The chapter that began with such a picture of a nation utterly depraved by its sin moves now to a glorious climax in the grace of God.

Verse 19 has been variously translated and interpreted (see Notes). As rendered by the NIV, it means that God's acts of judgment will cause men over all the world to reverence him, the second part of the verse presenting a further statement of the overflowing wrath of God against his foes. Coming in judgment to the world, he will however come in quite a different character to Zion, but only when she repents. Paul aptly uses v.20 in support of his hope of Jewish repentance in Romans 11:25–27, where the word modification is accounted for by the LXX. The NT shows that God has given two covenant gifts to his church—the Word made flesh in Christ and the Holy Spirit (cf. Gal 4:4–7). These two gifts are here pledged (v.21)—at least in their anticipatory forms—as eternal gifts. The word in the mouth may suggest personal reading (cf. Josh 1:8), for completely silent reading is a product of a more sophisticated society; or it could suggest that the word given and appropriated is now to be proclaimed.

Notes

5 צִפְעוֹנִי (ṣip‘ônî, "vipers") cannot be identified with certainty. The word occurs also in 11:8.
19 The NIV margin "When the enemy comes in like a flood, the Spirit of the LORD will put him to flight"—supplies a subject for the first clause and interprets רוּחַ יְהֹוָה (rûaḥ YHWH) as the "Spirit of the LORD," which of course is its most frequent OT sense. There is a helpful discussion of this verse in Young (*Book of Isaiah*, in loc.).

3. *The Future Glory of Zion*

60:1–22

> [1]"Arise, shine, for your light has come,
>   and the glory of the LORD rises upon you.
> [2]See, darkness covers the earth
>   and thick darkness is over the peoples,
> but the LORD rises upon you
>   and his glory appears over you.
> [3]Nations will come to your light,
>   and kings to the brightness of your dawn.
> [4]"Lift up your eyes and look about you:
>   All assemble and come to you;
> your sons come from afar,
>   and your daughters are carried on the arm.
> [5]Then you will look and be radiant,
>   your heart will throb and swell with joy;
> the wealth on the seas will be brought to you,
>   to you the riches of the nations will come.
> [6]Herds of camels will cover your land,
>   young camels of Midian and Ephah.

And all from Sheba will come,
   bearing gold and incense
   and proclaiming the praise of the LORD.
[7]All Kedar's flocks will be gathered to you,
   the rams of Nebaioth will serve you;
they will be accepted as offerings on my altar,
   and I will adorn my glorious temple.

[8]"Who are these that fly along like clouds,
   like doves to their nests?
[9]Surely the islands look to me;
   in the lead are the ships of Tarshish,
bringing your sons from afar,
   with their silver and gold,
to the honor of the LORD your God,
   the Holy One of Israel,
   for he has endowed you with splendor.

[10]"Foreigners will rebuild your walls,
   and their kings will serve you.
Though in anger I struck you,
   in favor I will show you compassion.
[11]Your gates will always stand open,
   they will never be shut, day or night,
so that men may bring you the wealth of the nations—
   their kings led in triumphal procession.
[12]For the nation or kingdom that will not serve you
     will perish;
   it will be utterly ruined.

[13]"The glory of Lebanon will come to you,
   the pine, the fir and the cypress together,
to adorn the place of my sanctuary;
   and I will glorify the place of my feet.
[14]The sons of your oppressors will come bowing before you;
   all who despise you will bow down at your feet
and will call you The City of the LORD,
   Zion of the Holy One of Israel.

[15]"Although you have been forsaken and hated,
   with no one traveling through,
I will make you the everlasting pride
   and the joy of all generations.
[16]You will drink the milk of nations
   and be nursed at royal breasts.
Then you will know that I, the LORD, am your Savior,
   your Redeemer, the Mighty One of Jacob.
[17]Instead of bronze I will bring you gold,
   and silver in place of iron.
Instead of wood I will bring you bronze,
   and iron in place of stones.
I will make peace your governor
   and righteousness your ruler.
[18]No longer will violence be heard in your land,
   nor ruin or destruction within your borders,
but you will call your walls Salvation
   and your gates Praise.
[19]The sun will no more be your light by day,
   nor will the brightness of the moon shine on you,

for the LORD will be your everlasting light,
    and your God will be your glory.
20Your sun will never set again,
    and your moon will wane no more;
the LORD will be your everlasting light,
    and your days of sorrow will end.
21Then will all your people be righteous
    and they will possess the land forever.
They are the shoot I have planted,
    the work of my hands,
    for the display of my splendor.
22The least of you will become a thousand,
    the smallest a mighty nation.
I am the LORD;
    in its time I will do this swiftly."

This chapter depicts the future glory of Zion, which is identified in v.14, and it is anticipated by the last three verses of the previous chapter. Most commentators take it to be a unity, except for v.12, the status of which will be discussed in the notes.

In 2:1–5 Jerusalem is distinguished by its elevation. There it is the center from which the divine message goes out to all the world, and so people of other nations come up to worship at the temple. In 42:6; 49:6–7, the servant of the Lord has a ministry to the nations, who in 52:14–15 are astonished by both his sufferings and his subsequent exaltation.

It is only when our present chapter is treated in isolation from these earlier passages, especially from 52:13–53:12, and assigned to a different author (see Introduction, pp. 6–12) that it can be said that it sets forth "resurrection without death, triumph without travail, conquest without a cross" (Thexton, in loc.). Such criticisms are not made of chapters 54 and 55, as they could easily have been, simply because of their literary unity with chapter 53. But, on the assumption of the book's unity of authorship, chapter 60 rests as much on the sufferings of that chapter as they do.

If it can be said that the NT teaches not only substitutionary atonement through the sufferings of Christ but also the church's identification with him in suffering for the will of God, and that the latter element is not represented here, then we must say that there is a place for presenting the glorification by God of his people as a pure gift, as this underlines his unmerited favor. It is the glory of the Lord that makes this vision what it is, for Zion's glory is seen to be simply the reflection of his. For the general interpretation of the chapter, see the Introduction, pp. 14–16.

1–3 In 52:1–2 God calls Zion to awake and to sit on her throne. This passage goes further, calling her to shine with the divine glory (v.1). Impenetrable darkness covers the whole earth (v.2), and it once enveloped Israel when she was not walking in the light with her God (cf. 8:19–22; 59:9–10). The wonderful spotlight now shining on Zion's hill is really the divine glory that is situated above Jerusalem, whereas in the wilderness journeys it preceded and followed God's people (see Exod 14:19–20; Isa 52:12; 58:8, but esp. 4:5–6). His glory, so situated, would act like the sun, not only giving light, but causing the city itself to radiate it (cf. v.5). This light of God would have great power of attraction. The combination of "nations" and "kings" (v.3) reminds us of 52:15; and this, along with the use of chapter 60 in Revelation 21 and the linking of the glory of God and the Lamb in Revelation 21:22, prompts us to think of the divine glory here as that of the risen Christ-Servant-Lamb.

4–9 God told Abraham to lift up his eyes and look at Canaan, which he and his seed were to possess (Gen 13:14–17). Here Zion is told to look and see her dispersed children coming from other lands (v.4). She glows with the radiance of God's glory and with the joy of a fulfilled hope (v.5). There are also streams of pilgrims from the far parts: wealthy sea-faring peoples like the Phoenicians and merchants from the deserts of Arabia. They all come with appropriate gifts: the gold, incense, and lambs all finding their place in the decoration and worship of the temple (vv.6–7; cf. Matt 2:1, 11). As Kidner ("Isaiah," in loc.) points out, the priestly-sacrificial terms of v.7 preclude a purely literal interpretation, in the light of passages like John 4:21–26; Hebrews 10:1; 13:10–16. This passage, unfulfilled before the coming of Christ, can hardlly teach literal sacrifice, when his sacrifice has fulfilled the entire OT system of offerings (see Introduction, pp. 14–16).

The questions of v.8, with their vivid imagery, are echoed by the Christian reader. Psalm 87 predicts that foreigners will be registered among the citizens of Zion. Isaiah 19:23–25 places Egypt and Assyria alongside Israel as God's people. Do the sons of Zion here include foreigners or are they simply the dispersed of Israel returning on Gentile ships (v.9)? Probably we should opt for the latter interpretation, though the former is not impossible in the context.

10–12 Throughout much of her history, Jerusalem had been subject to assault from foreign enemies. It was foreigners, the Babylonians, who destroyed her walls; and other foreigners, the Romans, would do so again. Like other Near Eastern cities, Jerusalem's gates would have been shut every night as a protection against sudden attack. All this reflected the judgment of her God that was so often on her. Now she would be the object of his grace (cf. 40:1–11). Jerusalem will receive both the service and the wealth of the nations and their monarchs, and no opposition to her will be tolerated by her God (vv.11–12). Any fulfillment of this after the Exile was only partial. The Persians made possible the rebuilding of the walls but did not do it themselves (v.10). Its true fulfillment lay beyond the OT era altogether.

13–14 Although this goes beyond anything realized in history, it will take up into itself elements from the past. Just as Lebanon supplied wood for the building of Solomon's temple (1 Kings 5), so it would again (v.13; cf. Ezek 40–42). The nations that had come against Jerusalem in such a scornful spirit (see esp. chs. 36–37) would now do obeisance to her as the city of her God (v.14). The term "Holy One of Israel" is found in each of the three main parts Isaiah is often divided into and serves as an important link running through the book (see Introduction, pp. 12–13).

15–22 The exultant tone of this chapter is sustained right to its end. The city so oppressed by some (v.14) had been avoided by others (v.15). Perhaps her smaller near neighbors are in view. Now foreigners and their monarchs will love and cherish her, delighting to supply her needs. This is because the LORD will be revealing himself to her in all the glory of his grace, as indicated by the catena of titles used in v.16, each of which has covenant implications. "The Mighty One of Jacob," of course, is also a reminder of the sinfulness and guile of Israel's ancestor, so underlining God's unmerited favor.

In v.17 the merely adequate is replaced by the valuable. Its reference is probably more general than that of vv.6–7, where the materials are all related specifically to the needs of the temple. Once again peace and righteousness, those heavenly twins, are found together (cf. 54:13–14). The beautifully poetic description leads on, in v.18, first of all to literal statements about the absence of violence, and then to further abstractions, symbolizing God's action on Zion's behalf and her own reaction to this. There may be just an implicit reference to the meaning of the name "Judah," which is "praise."

Verses 19–20 supply important background for Revelation 21–22. Genesis 1:14–19 —probably deliberately attacking pagan worship of the heavenly bodies (see G. Von Rad, *Commentary on Genesis* [London: SCM, 1961], in loc.)—describes the sun and the moon as mere lamps made by God for lighting the earth. The Lord himself, whose glory set over the city gives the latter its special glory in this chapter, is in fact replacing his creatures—the sun and the moon—with himself. This symbolizes the fact that God's people, in his community, will always know his presence and the revelation and joy that come from him. This constant fullness of divine light will transform everything, including all the imperfections ("sorrows") of life.

Verse 21 reminds us of the declarations in Revelation 21–22 that only those cleansed of sin may have any part in God's city. His promise to Abraham (Gen 17:8) will be fulfilled. The "shoot" illustration, which has appeared at so many significant points in this book (4:1; 6:13; 11:1; 53:2) is found again. God's splendor is in fact displayed in the growth and fruitage of this despised shoot, as a study of this theme in the passages quoted above will show. In the present passage, of course, the shoot is Israel (see Introduction, p. 16). Verse 22 really develops it, for the tiny shoot is seen here in its fullest development. The second half of v.22 grounds these promises in God's great name—Yahweh. It is perhaps hinted that the fulfillment of this prophecy will be somewhat remote in time from its utterance. Once the events of the end time begin, however, the total realization of God's plan for Jerusalem will come to speedy fulfillment.

Notes

6 Midian, referred to historically in 9:4; 10:26, was an Arabian merchant people. Ephah is unknown except for the reference to Ephah, son of Midian, in Gen 25:4. Sheba occurs fairly often in the OT and appears to be in southwestern Arabia. Its wealth was proverbial (1 Kings 10:10; Ps 72:10, 15).

7 For Kedar, see note at 21:16. Nebaioth (cf. Gen 25:13; 28:9) is usually identified with Nabataea in northern Arabia.

9 For Tarshish, see the note at 2:16.

12 Some commentators (e.g., Muilenburg, Westermann, Herbert) dispute the integrity of this verse with the rest of the chapter, on the grounds of its prose form and its supposed inappropriateness in the context. The former consideration is not decisive, and the latter seems subjective. It goes beyond what is said in vv.10–11 but builds on this. If a scribe could be conceived as doing this, why not the prophet himself?

13 For the trees mentioned here, see the note at 41:19.

16 The RSV's "you shall suck the breast of kings" is more literal than NIV's "and be nursed at royal breasts" (cf. 49:23). The picture is strange only if we assume always a straightforward correspondence between an analogy and what it illustrates. Here the application of

the analogy is complicated by the fact that a nation's resources were viewed as summed up in its king, not its queen.

---

4. The Year of the Lord's Favor

61:1–11

¹The Spirit of the Sovereign Lord is on me,
because the Lord has anointed me
to preach good news to the poor.
He has sent me to bind up the brokenhearted,
to proclaim freedom for the captives
and release from darkness for the prisoners,
²to proclaim the year of the Lord's favor
and the day of vengeance of our God,
to comfort all who mourn,
³ and provide for those who grieve in Zion—
to bestow on them a crown of beauty
instead of ashes,
the oil of gladness
instead of mourning,
and a garment of praise
instead of a spirit of despair.
They will be called oaks of righteousness,
a planting of the Lord
for the display of his splendor.

⁴They will rebuild the ancient ruins
and restore the places long devastated;
they will renew the ruined cities
that have been devastated for generations.
⁵Aliens will shepherd your flocks;
foreigners will work your fields and vineyards.
⁶And you will be called priests of the Lord,
you will be named ministers of our God.
You will feed on the wealth of nations,
and in their riches you will boast.

⁷Instead of their shame
my people will receive a double portion,
and instead of disgrace
they will rejoice in their inheritance;
and so they will inherit a double portion in their land.
and everlasting joy will be theirs.
⁸"For I, the Lord, love justice;
I hate robbery and iniquity.
In my faithfulness I will reward them
and make an everlasting covenant with them.
⁹Their descendants will be known among the nations
and their offspring among the peoples.
All who see them will acknowledge
that they are a people the Lord has blessed."

¹⁰I delight greatly in the Lord;
my soul rejoices in my God.
For he has clothed me with garments of salvation
and arrayed me in a robe of righteousness,

> as a bridegroom adorns his head like a priest,
> and as a bride adorns herself with her jewels.
> ¹¹For as the soil makes the sprout come up
> and a garden causes seeds to grow,
> so the Sovereign LORD will make righteousness and praise
> spring up before all nations.

Is there a fifth Servant Song here? Many—especially of the older—commentators have thought so, though most modern commentators do not favor this. They view the speaker as the prophet himself, though there are other views. Herbert (in loc.), for example, takes the speaker to be Zion personified. What is clear is that Christ identified the speaker with himself in Luke 4:17–21 (cf. also Luke 7:22), though this does not prove that this is a Servant Song; for he could have seen himself as the supreme prophet, just as the writer to the Hebrews saw him and his people antici-pated in Isaiah and his disciples (Heb 2:13; cf. Isa 8:17–18). There are however a number of links with the Servant Songs. Compare the language of v.1 with 42:1, 7, and 49:9; of v.2 with 49:8; and the use of the expression "Sovereign LORD" (ᵃḏōnāy YHWH) in 50:4, 7, 9.

It could also be significant that this passage clearly reflects, as we shall show, the Year of Jubilee legislation, and that that year began on the Day of Atonement (Lev 25:9). This would provide a link with the sacrificial teaching of 52:13–53:12. Kidner ("Isaiah," in loc.) says, "Our Lord could quote this passage at the outset of His career because He had already accepted, in His baptism and temptation, the role of suffering Servant, and with it the cross. Those are the 'benefits of His passion'; His miracles spoke the same language." We will therefore take it that there is a theologi-cal development here that makes this passage rest on Isaiah 53, just as the preaching of the gospel in Acts rested on the atoning sacrifice presented in the Gospels.

1–3 These verses present a picture of a man anointed by the Spirit of God, espe-cially for the task of preaching (v.1; cf. 1 Kings 19:15–16). He proclaims glad tidings (cf. 40:9; 41:27; 52:7). His anointing with the Spirit of God provides a link with both the kingly and the servant prophecies of this book (11:1; 42:1). Both earlier pictures refer to a ministry through speech (11:4; 49:2). If he is both King and Servant, then already within the Book of Isaiah that union of the two in Jesus Christ is anticipated.

Those benefiting from the preacher's message are described as the poor, the brokenhearted (cf. Ps 147:3), the captives, and the prisoners. The poor may be literal, but the word probably has overtones of piety as well as poverty (e.g., Pss 40:17; 72:12–14). The brokenhearted appear again as those who mourn and grieve. They could be mourning for sin (cf. 57:15) or over the destruction of Jerusalem, though this was itself punishment for sin. If it is the latter, then the comfort refer-ence is made to is that given in chapter 40. The poor and the mourners reappear in the Beatitudes of Jesus (Matt 5:3–4). The captives and the prisoners are likely to be the Exiles (cf. 42:22; 49:9; 51:14), so that the overtones of a New Exodus are still present.

The first two lines of v.2 are important. The term gôᵓēl ("Redeemer") does not appear in this passage, but in the OT the Year of Jubilee—when slaves were set free and land was returned to its original owners—was closely linked with the legislation providing for the kinsman-redeemer (Lev 25); and the same word was used of the avenger of blood (e.g., Num 35:12). Moreover the Hebrew word translated "freedom" in v.1 is *dᵉrôr*, a technical term for the Jubilee release in the OT (cf. Lev 25:10, 13; 27:24; Jer 34:8–10; Ezek 46:17). God presents himself here then both as the Savior and as the Judge. It is often felt to be significant that Jesus, in quoting these verses, stopped before the reference to the day of vengeance. Herbert has however raised a question mark about this, pointing out that Jesus did include the idea of divine vengeance in Luke 18:7–8. Herbert (in loc.) says, "Jesus, like any other rabbi, quoted enough to call the whole passage to mind."

The threefold bestowal, promised in v.3, expresses the same basic idea in different ways. Ashes were symbolic of deep sorrow; and the crown, oil, and garment all suggest preparations for joyous festival.

The "oaks of righteousness" are an allusion to 60:21 but with the thought now individualized. If Matthew 15:13 is based on this, then it is because the Pharisees were too concerned for the display of their own righteousness and not the glory of the Lord.

4–9 There are echoes here of the previous chapter, and like that this passage seems to go beyond the OT era for its fulfillment as much of its detail does not fit the return from Exile (see Introduction, pp. 6–12). At Sinai God had described his people as "a kingdom of priests" (Exod 19:6). This ideal, never fully realized in their history, would now come to pass (v.6). As the Levitical priests were released for their distinctive work because others labored and provided for them, so is Israel's place among the nations to be. It should be noted that this implies that her priestly ministry is for the nations' benefit.

The laws of inheritance, so closely linked to the Jubilee regulations, provided for a double inheritance for the firstborn (Deut 21:17). Previously, perhaps because privilege brings greater responsibility, Israel had received double punishment (40: 2); now, as God's "firstborn" among the nations (Exod 4:22–23; cf. Ps 89:27), she has a double portion in her land (v.7). Probably this means that the "land flowing with milk and honey" (Exod 3:8, 17 et al.) was itself reckoned to be of double value.

The land will be restored to God's people because those who had taken it had no right to it, and the Lord is a God of justice. The everlasting covenant (v.8), preceded by a reference to the divine faithfulness, probably undergirds the existing covenants; so it is evidence of God's integrity. The reference to their blessing among the nations (v.9) may suggest that it is the Abrahamic covenant (cf. Gen 12:1–3) rather than the Davidic (cf. Isa 55:3) that is chiefly in view.

10–11 The speaker in these verses is probably personified Zion, who expresses her unbounded joy in God. The analogy of clothing (v.10), already employed in v.3, appears again. Its appropriateness is due to the fact that clothing often expresses either status or mood—or both. Paul uses the same kind of language in relation to Christian salvation, for example, in Romans 13:14 and Ephesians 4:22–24.

The final verse of the chapter (v.11) reminds us of 55:10–11. If it is an intentional allusion, then it will support the theme of God's faithfulness (v.8). God's faithful word will secure the growth of righteousness and praise in his people, which will be publicly displayed, as at a bridal feast, before all the nations.

Notes

1 פְּקַח־קוֹחַ (pᵉqaḥ-qôaḥ, "release . . . for the prisoners") is preceded by אֲסוּרִים (ᵃsûrîm, "captives"). Some Hebrew MSS, including 1QIsaᵃ, take the former phrase to be one word, meaning "opening." The root פקח (pqḥ) is regularly used of opening the eyes, and the LXX apparently reads סַנְוֵרִים (sanwērîm, "blind"). This accounts for the quotation in Luke 4:18: "recovery of sight for the blind."

3 פְּאֵר (pᵉʾēr, "crown" or "ornamental headdress") and אֵפֶר (ʾēper, "ashes") not only have the same consonants, though in a different order, but also "e" vowels. This wordplay would not be lost on the hearers, especially as it could be highlighted in the pronunciation.

8 The NIV's "iniquity" follows the LXX and other versions in repointing עוֹלָה (ʿōlāh, "burnt offering") to ʿawlāh ("iniquity"), which makes better sense, unless 1:13 (see comment there) provides some precedent in this book.

5. Assured Prayer for Zion's Future

62:1–12

¹For Zion's sake I will not keep silent,
    for Jerusalem's sake I will not remain quiet,
till her righteousness shines out like the dawn,
    her salvation like a blazing torch.
²The nations will see your righteousness,
    and all kings your glory;
you will be called by a new name
    that the mouth of the Lord will bestow.
³You will be a crown of splendor in the Lord's hand,
    a royal diadem in the hand of your God.
⁴No longer will they call you Deserted,
    or name your land Desolate.
But you will be called Hephzibah,
    and your land Beulah;
for the Lord will take delight in you,
    and your land will be married.
⁵As a young man marries a maiden,
    so will your sons marry you;
as a bridegroom rejoices over his bride,
    so will your God rejoice over you.

⁶I have posted watchmen on your walls, O Jerusalem;
    they will never be silent day or night.
You who call on the Lord,
    give yourselves no rest,
⁷and give him no rest till he establishes Jerusalem
    and makes her the praise of the earth.
⁸The Lord has sworn by his right hand
    and by his mighty arm:
"Never again will I give your grain
    as food for your enemies,
and never again will foreigners drink the new wine
    for which you have toiled;
⁹but those who harvest it will eat it
    and praise the Lord,
and those who gather the grapes will drink it
    in the courts of my sanctuary."

> ¹⁰Pass through, pass through the gates!
>   Prepare the way for the people.
> Build up, build up the highway!
>   Remove the stones.
> Raise a banner for the nations.
>
> ¹¹The Lord has made proclamation
>   to the ends of the earth:
> "Say to the Daughter of Zion,
>   'See, your Savior comes!
> See, his reward is with him,
>   and his recompense accompanies him.' "
> ¹²They will be called the Holy People,
>   the Redeemed of the Lord;
> and you will be called Sought After,
>   the City No Longer Deserted.

Herbert (in loc.) declares, "There is a quality of splendid impatience in this chapter, an impatience which is uninhibited within the assurance that God hears and answers." This, of course, assumes that the speaker is the prophet, though some commentators argue that he is probably the Lord, pointing out that here God breaks the silence so often referred to in this book (see 18:4; 42:14; 57:11; 65:6). Young (*Book of Isaiah*) and Whybray (*Isaiah 40–66*) give arguments for this interpretation. Certainly a real case can be made out for this, though the Lord is spoken of in the third person many times in this chapter. In view of this, and also because the prophet has before appeared interceding for the people (cf. 51:9), we will assume that it is he who speaks here.

1–7 Here the prophet takes his place among the great men of prayer in the OT. He has received a vision of Jerusalem, living in the good of all God's promises and shining with the glory of her God (ch. 60), and he now prays with persistence and deep feeling for that day to come. The most-assured praying rests on the promises of God. For an OT example of this, see Genesis 32:9–12. As in chapter 60, Jerusalem will be a spectacle for the whole world to see. So often in the OT a new name (v.2) is the pledge of divine action to change the status or character of a person (cf., e.g., Gen 17:5, 15). Zion's new name will emerge in vv.4, 12 and will reflect the grace of God to her, for "the mouth of the Lord" in Isaiah is associated with utterances of grace (cf. 40:5; 58:14). Once again Zion will enjoy an intimate relationship with her God.

The theme of the wife, separated from her husband because of her sin and yearning for reconciliation and home, often appears in this book from chapter 49 onward. It emerges again in vv.4–5. In fact, the promise that she would be a crown for her God, "the city walls having the appearance of a tiara" (Whybray, *Isaiah 40–66*, in loc.), may reflect the idea that a wife, especially a queen, should be an adornment to her husband (v.3). The Servant of the Lord is a delight to him (42:1); so is she to be. From a NT perspective, of course, we can view this in terms of the church's acceptance in Christ (see Introduction, pp. 14–16 for general discussion).

Verse 5 presents as strange an analogy as that in 60:16 (see comment there). In both cases there seems to be an intentional breach in the normal application of the analogy, perhaps in the interests of vivid impression. Such analogies puzzle us, but we do not forget them! Moreover, Jones (in loc.) points out that "the metaphor serves the thought, not the thought the metaphor." There is, of course, a very real sense in which loyal citizens may be said to be married to their city. For an alternative interpretation resting on conjectural emendation, see the Notes. The analogy of the bride and groom reminds us of Revelation 21:2, 9; 22:17, chapters much influenced by this part of Isaiah.

Verse 6 reminds us that the vision of vv. 1b–5 inspires the prophet in his praying, and that prayer continues here. If the speaker is the prophet, not God (see general introduction to this chapter), the watchmen here may be his fellow prophets (cf. Ezek 3:17), or the godly in general, protecting the city from the ravaging forces of evil by their prayers. If however he is God, then the watchmen could still be the godly at prayer, fulfilling a function analogous to the *mazkîr* (see Notes). Of course true prayer begins as well as ends at the throne of God, if it is guided by the Spirit of God. We have here the language of accommodation (cf. Ps 44:23), for God really needs no reminding; but he does graciously involve others, through prayer, in the fulfillment of his great purposes. This passage may well furnish part at least of the OT background to the parables of importunate prayer told by our Lord (Luke 11:5–10; 18:1–8).

8–9 These words are particularly assuring to Zion's prayer-watchmen. The solemn oath of God underlines his faithfulness (v.8; cf. Isa 54:9; Heb 6:13–20; 7:20–28), and the fact that he has sworn by his mighty arm stresses his ability to carry out his word; for his arm is the executor of the divine will, its power in salvation already wonderfully demonstrated (cf. 53:1). Through much of her history, Zion had been subject to assault from her enemies and had been robbed of her food supplies, either by marauding armies (1:7–8) or as the payment of taxes to foreign overlords. God had warned her that disobedience would bring this about; but now, through his own gracious action, she is righteous (62:1), and the Lord promises that this will never occur again. The temple courts would in fact be thronged with worshipers offering the harvest firstfruits to the Lord and rejoicing before him (v.9; cf. Deut 14:22–26; Isa 9:3).

10–11a Here phraseology is gathered up from a number of previous utterances (see esp. 40:3; 48:20; 49:22; 52:11; 57:14). For the doubled imperative (v.10), see the comments at 51:9. There is to be a massive pilgrimage to the city. So a road-building and road-clearing project is to be undertaken, with the banner and a proclamation (v.11a) providing visible and audible signals to the nations of its completion; for, as chapter 60 shows, they will be instrumental in enabling the dispersed to return, and many of them will themselves come.

11b–12 For v.11b, see especially 40:10–11. Here is salvation in its final stage, the fulfillment of all that has gone before. Verse 12 takes up and develops the theme of v.4, rather in the way that the name of 7:14 is given further exposition in 9:6. All these names bring out different aspects of God's grace to his people (cf. Hos 1). The first goes back to the beginnings of their history as a nation (Exod 19:6). Then too they first knew what it was to be the Lord's redeemed people, but before the consummation this experience will have been filled out with other wonders of redeeming grace. Jerusalem's destiny as the wife of the Lord will find completest fulfillment because he has sought to win her from her sin and restore her to everlasting married fellowship with himself.

Notes

4 The meanings of the names Hephzibah and Beulah are given in the NIV margin as "my delight is in her" and "married" respectively.
5 Some commentators emend בָּנָיִךְ (bānāyiḵ, "your sons") to בֹּנֵךְ (bōneḵ, "your Builder"; so NIV mg.), but it is doubtful whether this is necessary (see comment above).
6 Whybray (Isaiah 40–66, in loc.) expounds the view that הַמַּזְכִּרִים (hammazkîrîm, "you who call on"; RSV, "you who put . . . in remembrance") is connected with the מַזְכִּיר (mazkîr, "recorder"; 2 Sam 8:16; 1 Kings 4:3; Isa 36:3), with an assumed etymology from the verb זָכַר (zāḵar, "remember"), and says, "If this is so, Yahweh as a great king is here seen as having recorders among his heavenly courtiers, one of whose functions was to see that the programme of duties to which he was committed did not go by default." He agrees, however, that neither the meaning of the word nor the functions of the office is entirely clear. There are too many imponderables for us to espouse this interpretation.

6. The Lord the Avenger

63:1–6

> ¹Who is this coming from Edom,
>> from Bozrah, with his garments stained crimson?
> Who is this, robed in splendor,
>> striding forward in the greatness of his strength?
>
> "It is I, speaking in righteousness,
>> mighty to save."
>
> ²Why are your garments red,
>> like those of one treading the winepress?
> ³"I have trodden the winepress alone;
>> from the nations no one was with me.
> I trampled them in my anger
>> and trod them down in my wrath;
> their blood spattered my garments,
>> and I stained all my clothing.
> ⁴For the day of vengeance was in my heart,
>> and the year of my redemption has come.
> ⁵I looked, but there was no one to help,
>> I was appalled that no one gave support;
> so my own arm worked salvation for me,
>> and my own wrath sustained me.
> ⁶I trampled the nations in my anger;
>> in my wrath I made them drunk
>> and poured their blood on the ground."

1–6 Is it possible, as has been suggested, that this is a sixth Servant Song? Verse 4 and 61:2 show that there is a thematic link at least with chapter 61, and if that chapter is a Servant Song (see comments there), then we conceive this also to be one. Does the strong emphasis on divine wrath make this impossible? Only if we deny that the God of the Servant Songs is the God of the OT generally, for he is a God of both wrath and grace. Isaiah 53:6, 10 clearly imply that there was divine necessity as well as divine grace in the sacrificial death of his Servant. If the Servant's death and vindication were unique divine acts, then it is apt that the series should come to its close with an assurance of judgment on those who continue in rebellion.

The oracle is most dramatic. The only OT passage that in any way resembles it is the account of Joshua's encounter with the angelic captain of the Lord's host (Josh 5:13–6:5). There too, as here, there are two questions and two answers; and there is a similar anxious inquiry: "Are you for us or for our enemies?" Westermann (in loc.) comments on the "consummate artistry" in our present passage. The city watchman or sentry peers anxiously out at a solitary and majestic figure who appears on the scene, his garment spattered with crimson (v.1). When he first comes into view, it is clear that he is coming from the direction of Bozrah, Edom's capital. That Edom means "red" (cf. Gen 25:30 n.) is particularly apt in this context. Is this fearsome figure who has been executing judgment on Edom now coming to judge Jerusalem (cf. Amos 1:11–12; 2:4–5)? The answer makes it clear, albeit indirectly, that this is the Lord himself. In fact, the element of indirectness, with its overtones of mystery, if anything underlines the divine nature of the warrior (cf. 59:17–18). It is clear too that he comes to his people, not as their judge, but as their righteous Savior.

As the figure draws nearer, the watchman directs a question to him, perhaps still with a measure of apprehension. The winepress metaphor (v.2) has no relevance to atonement but only to judgment (cf. Rev 14:19–20; 19:11–16), though atonement itself involves the bearing of the wrath of God. The Book of Revelation clearly takes this passage to be fulfilled in Christ as the Judge of the world, and his title "the Word of God" there is probably reminiscent of the reference to speech at the close of v.1. Jones (in loc.) says, "God's speech is also action." The Lord declares that he has executed the judgment himself alone (v.3; cf. 44:24; 59:16). This strongly suggests that the passage looks beyond historical judgments—in which God uses one nation to punish another—to the eschatological day of God's wrath.

The day of vengeance and the year of redemption (v.4) belong together to the same complex of ideas, involving the $g\bar{o}^{\,\prime}\bar{e}l$ ("redeemer"; see comment at 61:1–3). God's act of judgment against Edom is clearly conceived to be a putting right of the wrongs done to Zion (see 34:8–15), especially when the Edomites took advantage of Judah's weakness after the Fall of Jerusalem to the Babylonians (Lam 4:21–22; Ezek 25:12–14; 35:1–15). Thus, as at the Exodus from Egypt and also at the return from Exile—preceded as it was by the judgment on Babylon through the Persians—judgment and redemption would be effected through the same events.

Verse 5 reminds us of Revelation 5 and the search for someone to open the Book of Destiny, with its revelation of the ultimate judgments. This in fact testifies to the universality of sin. Verse 6 widens the judgment, making it clear that Edom is simply an appropriate example of the judgment of God on the nations. In many prophetic passages, in fact, Edom appears to represent Gentiles under divine judgment (see comment at 34:5–7). For the reference to drunkenness as a picture of the divine wrath, see the comments at 51:22–23.

Thexton (in loc.) comments on this passage as follows: "While the vision taken as a whole is suggestive of Christ's work as Judge, there are none the less certain features of it which do anticipate His work as Savior." He instances Christ's solitariness in his work of saving his people from their enemies, the fact that the Cross stands for the judgment of the world as well as its salvation, and that "the destruction of mankind's most implacable enemies is both the aim and the fruit of his sacrifice" (ibid).

7. *A Psalm of Praise and Lamentation*

63:7–64:12

[7]I will tell of the kindnesses of the LORD,
    the deeds for which he is to be praised,
    according to all the LORD has done for us—
yes, the many good things he has done
    for the house of Israel,
    according to his compassion and many kindnesses.
[8]He said, "Surely they are my people,
    sons who will not be false to me";
    and so he became their Savior.
[9]In all their distress he too was distressed,
    and the angel of his presence saved them.
In his love and mercy he redeemed them;
    he lifted them up and carried them
    all the days of old.
[10]Yet they rebelled
    and grieved his Holy Spirit.
So he turned and became their enemy
    and he himself fought against them.

[11]Then his people recalled the days of old,
    the days of Moses and his people—
where is he who brought them through the sea,
    with the shepherd of his flock?
Where is he who set
    his Holy Spirit among them,
[12]who sent his glorious arm of power
    to be at Moses' right hand,
who divided the waters before them,
    to gain for himself everlasting renown,
[13]who led them through the depths?
Like a horse in open country,
    they did not stumble;
[14]like cattle that go down to the plain,
    they were given rest by the Spirit of the LORD.
This is how you guided your people
    to make for yourself a glorious name.

[15]Look down from heaven and see
    from your lofty throne, holy and glorious.
Where are your zeal and your might?
    Your tenderness and compassion are withheld from us.
[16]But you are our Father,
    though Abraham does not know us
    or Israel acknowledge us;
you, O LORD, are our Father,
    our Redeemer from of old is your name.
[17]Why, O LORD, do you make us wander from your ways
    and harden our hearts so we do not revere you?
Return for the sake of your servants,
    the tribes that are your inheritance.

¹⁸For a little while your people possessed your holy place,
    but now our enemies have trampled down
        your sanctuary.
¹⁹We are yours from of old;
    but you have not ruled over them,
    they have not been called by your name.

⁶⁴:¹Oh, that you would rend the heavens and come down,
    that the mountains would tremble before you!
²As when fire sets twigs ablaze
    and causes water to boil,
come down to make your name known to your enemies
    and cause the nations to quake before you!
³For when you did awesome things that we did not expect,
    you came down, and the mountains trembled before you.
⁴Since ancient times no one has heard,
    no ear has perceived,
no eye has seen any God besides you,
    who acts on behalf of those who wait for him.
You come to the help of those who gladly do right,
    who remember your ways.
But when we continued to sin against them,
    you were angry.
    How then can we be saved?
⁶All of us have become like one who is unclean,
    and all our righteous acts are like filthy rags;
we all shrivel up like a leaf,
    and like the wind our sins sweep us away.
⁷No one calls on your name
    or strives to lay hold of you;
for you have hidden your face from us
    and made us waste away because of our sins.

⁸Yet, O Lᴏʀᴅ, you are our Father.
    We are the clay, you are the potter;
    we are all the work of your hand.
⁹Do not be angry beyond measure, O Lᴏʀᴅ;
    do not remember our sins forever.
Oh, look upon us, we pray,
    for we are all your people.
¹⁰Your sacred cities have become a desert;
    even Zion is a desert, Jerusalem a desolation.
¹¹Our holy and glorious temple, where our fathers
        praised you,
    has been burned with fire,
    and all that we treasured lies in ruins.
¹²After all this, O Lᴏʀᴅ, will you hold yourself back?
    Will you keep silent and punish us beyond measure?

Since the start of chapter 60, Isaiah's prophecies have majored in the theme of Zion's exaltation, the final fulfillment of all God's purposes for her. What effect would the reception of such visions have on the man who received them? No doubt they would fill him with a deep, almost agonized longing for their fulfillment, especially if he was passing through a period of intense, God-given awareness that Judah's sin was going to bring devastating judgment through the Babylonians. Just as the Spirit of God used such moods in the psalmists to produce many an impassioned lamentation, so he did also with Isaiah. Indeed, this passage is really a psalm of communal lamentation, wherein the prophet's identification with the nation becomes the means by which he expresses the deep longing of the most spiritually sensitive in it. Such prayers were part of the prophetic ministry, as we see many times in the life of Moses and also in passages like 1 Samuel 12:19–25; Jeremiah 15:1; Amos 7:1–6; and we have already overheard the prophet engaging in prayer on the people's behalf (e.g., 6:11; 25:1–5; 51:9–10; 59:9–15; 62:1).

7–10 The repeated word "kindnesses" in v.7 is the Hebrew *hesed*, the love that is faithful to the covenant ("steadfast love," RSV). It is altogether fitting that the prophet should commence with praise, for God has never failed to honor his covenant promises even though his people have so often proved untrue to him. There is a threefold reference to his deeds, for it is in them that his faithfulness has revealed itself. Verses 8–10, using language of accommodation (cf. Calvin, in loc.), present a picture of God as a disappointed Father, facing the fact that his sons have rebelled against him (cf. 1:3–6). This does not, of course, deny his omniscience or even the sovereignty of his purpose but expresses for the reader that Israel's rebellion ought never to have been and was an offense against love as well as holiness.

God, declaring himself to be his people's Father (v.8; cf. Exod 4:22–23), promised to save them from Egypt, declaring that he knew their afflictions (Exod 3:7–10). Verse 9 is one of the most moving expressions of the compassionate love of God in the OT, reminding the reader of some of the great passages in Hosea, Isaiah's older contemporary. There are Trinitarian overtones in the passage, for "the angel of his presence"—in whom the Lord is personally present—is apparently a reference to Exodus 23:20–23, in combination with Exodus 33:12–14; and "his Holy Spirit" (cf. Num 11:17, 25–29)—who can be grieved (cf. Eph 4:30)—is clearly personal (cf. 48:16 and comments there). The latter expression is found elsewhere in the OT only in Psalm 51:11 and similarly in a moral context. The people's rebellion brought God into conflict with them, as he had threatened (Exod 23:21; cf. ch. 32).

11–14 A wistful note enters the psalm. The prophet, still dwelling on the past deeds of God for his people, suggests in his questions that things have changed since "the days of old" (v.11). A comparison with the somewhat similar passage in 51:9–10 will reveal a difference of tone. The focus of attention is still the events of the Exodus period, when the nation came into being. Moses, like David, was taken from pastoring the flock to leadership of Israel, thus symbolizing the self-forgetful care God expects in those in authority over his people. The right arm of Moses (v.12) symbolized and was accompanied by the right arm of God, for the Exodus was an act of divine power (see comments at 51:9; 52:10; 53:1).

The two analogies of v.13–14 point to the conditions of the crossing of the Red Sea and the Jordan respectively. The people found the sea bed—and perhaps the wilderness afterwards—easy to negotiate; and, descending from the plateau of Moab to the Jordan and across it, they were like a herd of cattle being led into green pasture. The word "rest" is reminiscent of passages like Deuteronomy 12:10 and Joshua 21:44, though Hebrews 3–4 teaches that there is a deeper rest available in Christ.

15–19 The wistful note that began to be sounded in the last few verses now becomes explicit, and the characteristics of a communal lamentation appear clearly. In his prayer at the consecration of the temple, Solomon had called on God to hear his people's cry from his heavenly dwelling-place (1 Kings 8:44–53), and Isaiah has shown a personal awareness of God as exalted in his holiness (e.g., ch. 6; 57:15).

This exalted God has pledged his zeal in the cause of his people (9:7; 37:32); but now, as he foresees the temple and its ruin, the prophet identifies with the people's cry for mercy.

In v.16 we have the first two of three references to God as Father (cf. also 64:8). Kidner ("Isaiah," in loc.) says that this repeated plea "gives this prayer its special intensity, as the sense of estrangement struggles with that of acceptance." In fact, the sense of relationship with God as seen here goes even deeper than national solidarity. It is the deepest fact of the people's life.

Verse 17 makes us think of Isaiah's commission and the warning he had then (cf. 6:9–13), that through his verbal ministry the people would become hardened in sin. The prayer perhaps alludes also to the hardening of Pharaoh's heart in the Exodus story, which has provided so much background to the thought here. It recognizes that God has established that moral law in which sin hardens the heart and does so by divine design (cf. Rom 1:18–32). The word "return" may suggest the return of the shekinah glory to the temple as the symbol of God's dwelling among his people (cf. Ezek 43:6–12). Certainly v.18 implies that their sense of alienation from him is not unconnected with the destruction of their sanctuary. There is a deep sense of special election in v.19.

64:1–7 The longing for renewed blessing expressed in the closing verses of the previous chapter is now poured out in the passionate outburst of v.1. The Exodus had been followed by the great revelation at Sinai, when the mountain trembled at the presence of God (Exod 19:16–19). On that occasion God descended on the mount (Exod 19:18). Here the prophet graphically conceives of the very heavens being rent by Israel's God in his eagerness to be once more in the midst of his people. The illustration of v.2 of course sets forth the judgment of God. Pharaoh and the Egyptians had learned the power of God's name at the Exodus (Exod 13:3, 18). The Sinai revelation had made God's people tremble; this new disclosure of him would terrify the nations of the world.

What was God like, this God of the Exodus and Sinai who revealed himself to his people? He was the God of the unexpected (v.3), for in so many of the plagues the ordinary course of nature was interrupted. He was a unique God, for all other so-called deities are impotent. Paul used the words of v.4 in 1 Corinthians 2:9, in the conviction that God still acts on behalf of those who wait on him. He was also a God of righteousness, caring about the obedience of his people to his laws. It is this ethical quality in him—and therefore an element of his nature as true to that early revelation as his saving grace manifested in the Exodus—that is revealed over against the sins of his people.

Verses 5–7 present a many-sided doctrine of sin, remarkably full for an OT passage. Sin is a continual practice; it is defiling, it is destructive, and it creates a barrier between God and man—both from man's side, for we do not want to pray, and from God's, because he will not hear us. It is God himself who has determined that it shall have these results (cf. v.7 with 63:17). No wonder the people cry out, "How then can we be saved?" (v.5).

8–12 Verse 8 quite suddenly moves from the thought of God as the moral governor to whom his people are responsible to the Father who brought them into being. Both Jeremiah (Jer 18:1–6) and Paul (Rom 9:19–21) develop the analogy of the potter and the clay; and both do so in contexts that, as here, present God as sovereign in the realm of sin and judgment. The people cast themselves on the mercy of God, calling on him to remember, not their sins, but their standing as his people (v.9). Because the land is itself holy, so all its cities are, though the prophet lays special emphasis on the desolation of Jerusalem (v.10). There is an appeal to the fact that the land is his, and that it was to him the praises of earlier generations had been offered in the temple he had set apart for that purpose, before the people state their own deep sense of loss, "All that we treasured lies in ruins" (v.11).

The final verse (v.12) implores God to intervene and bring to his people that forgiveness and salvation that has been promised over and over again in this book, especially since chapter 40. What response did God make to this prayer? The two closing chapters of the prophecy will show us.

Notes

7 N.H. Snaith ("Isaiah 40–66: A Study of the Teaching of the Second Isaiah and Its Consequences," in Orlinsky and Snaith, *Second Part of Isaiah*, p. 235), following L.E. Browne, holds that in this whole psalm the writer "is speaking on behalf of a group who are being denied a place among the People of God," in fact, that it expresses the heart-cry of the Samaritans, who were being denied their rightful place by the Jews who had come back from the Exile. The theory is ingenious, but hard evidence for it is lacking. Theologically, vv.7–8 are important for the whole psalm because they place the situation in a covenant context and therefore already anticipate a continuing purpose of God for his people.

9 "He too was distressed" (lit., "there was distress to him") follows the Qere לוֹ (*lô*, "to him")—rather than the Kethiv לֹא (*lō'*, "not")—with most EV, but against 1QIsa (contrast also NEB). Young (*Book of Isaiah*, in loc.) appeals to Judg 10:16 as theological support for the Qere reading.

פָּנָיו (*pānāyw*, "his presence") is literally "his face."

11 The NIV text reads "then his people recalled"; the margin gives the alternative: "But may he recall." In fact, the NIV text involves altering the verbal form to the plural, which reads more naturally, though the singular does make sense, despite the awkwardness of an abrupt change from God to the people for the questions.

In the phrase "Moses and his people," the conjunction appears to have fallen out of the text, but the NIV supplies it.

"The shepherd" follows the LXX and the Targum. The MT has the plural, which cannot be ruled out, for it may include Aaron and perhaps others. The text of this verse certainly seems to have suffered in transmission. For further comment, see Whybray (*Isaiah 40–66*, in loc.).

18–19 These verses too contain translation problems. The issues are somewhat complex. Young (*Book of Isaiah*, in loc.) presents other possibilities and McKenzie (in loc.) conjectural emendations. The NIV and the RSV agree as to the meaning of v.18—despite differences of wording—and are probably right, while they render v.19 a little differently, with both renderings being feasible.

64: 1 Our verse numbering in this chapter follows the EV; the MT numbering is different.

4–5 Young (*Book of Isaiah*, in loc.) has a special note on the textual difficulties of these two verses. Again the NIV and the RSV represent basic agreement on the thrust of the passage and without emending the text (see also S.H. Blank, " 'And all our Virtues'—An Interpretation of Isaiah 64, 4b–5a," JBL 71 [1952]: 149–54).

6 טָמֵא (*tāmē'*, "unclean") is a technical term for ritual impurity, and בֶּגֶד עִדִּים (*beged 'iddîm*) means "menstrual cloth."

8. *The Great Final Issues*

65:1–66:24

> ^{1}"I revealed myself to those who did not ask for me;
>   I was found by those who did not seek me.
> To a nation that did not call on my name,
>   I said, 'Here am I, here am I.'
> ^{2}All day long I have held out my hands
>   to an obstinate people,
> who walk in ways not good,
>   pursuing their own imaginations—
> ^{3}a people who continually provoke me
>   to my very face,
> offering sacrifices in gardens
>   and burning incense on altars of brick;
> ^{4}who sit among the graves
>   and spend their nights keeping secret vigil;
> who eat the flesh of pigs,
>   and whose pots hold broth of unclean meat;
> ^{5}who say, 'Keep away; don't come near me,
>   for I am too sacred for you!'
> Such people are smoke in my nostrils,
>   a fire that keeps burning all day.
>
> ^{6}"See, it stands written before me:
>   I will not keep silent but will pay back in full;
>   I will pay it back into their laps—
> ^{7}both your sins and the sins of your fathers,"
>   says the LORD.
> "Because they burned sacrifices on the mountains
>   and defied me on the hills,
> I will measure into their laps
>   the full payment for their former deeds."

^{8}This is what the LORD says:

> "As when juice is still found in a cluster of grapes
>   and men say, 'Don't destroy it,
>   there is yet some good in it,'
> so will I do in behalf of my servants;
>   I will not destroy them all.
> ^{9}I will bring forth descendants from Jacob,
>   and from Judah those who will possess my mountains;
> my chosen people will inherit them,
>   and there will my servants live.
> ^{10}Sharon will become a pasture for flocks,
>   and the Valley of Achor a resting place for herds,
>   for my people who seek me.
>
> ^{11}"But as for you who forsake the LORD
>   and forget my holy mountain,
> who spread a table for Fortune
>   and fill bowls of mixed wine for Destiny,
> ^{12}I will destine you for the sword,
>   and you will all bend down for the slaughter;
> for I called but you did not answer,
>   I spoke but you did not listen.

You did evil in my sight
and chose what displeases me."

¹³Therefore this is what the Sovereign Lord says:

"My servants will eat,
but you will go hungry;
my servants will drink,
but you will go thirsty;
my servants will rejoice,
but you will be put to shame.
¹⁴My servants will sing
out of the joy of their hearts,
but you will cry out
from anguish of heart
and wail in brokenness of spirit.
¹⁵You will leave your name
to my chosen ones as a curse;
the Sovereign Lord will put you to death,
but to his servants he will give another name.
¹⁶Whoever invokes a blessing in the land
will do so by the God of truth;
he who takes an oath in the land
will swear by the God of truth.
For the past troubles will be forgotten
and hidden from my eyes.
¹⁷"Behold, I will create
new heavens and a new earth.
The former things will not be remembered,
nor will they come to mind.
¹⁸But be glad and rejoice forever
in what I will create,
for I will create Jerusalem to be a delight
and its people a joy.
¹⁹I will rejoice over Jerusalem
and take delight in my people;
and sound of weeping and of crying
will be heard in it no more.
²⁰"Never again will there be in it
an infant who lives but a few days,
or an old man who does not live out his years;
he who dies at a hundred
will be thought a mere youth;
he who fails to reach a hundred
will be considered accursed.
²¹They will build houses and dwell in them;
they will plant vineyards and eat their fruit.
²²No longer will they build houses and others live in them,
or plant and others eat.
For as the days of a tree,
so will be the days of my people;
my chosen ones will long enjoy
the works of their hands.
²³They will not toil in vain
or bear children doomed to misfortune;
for they will be a people blessed by the Lord,
they and their descendants with them.
²⁴Before they call I will answer;
while they are still speaking I will hear.

²⁵The wolf and the lamb will feed together,
    and the lion will eat straw like the ox,
but dust will be the serpent's food.
They will neither harm nor destroy
    on all my holy mountain,"

            says the LORD.

^{66:1}This is what the LORD says:

"Heaven is my throne,
    and the earth is my footstool.
Where is the house you will build for me?
    Where will my resting place be?
²Has not my hand made all these things,
    and so they came into being?"

           declares the LORD.

"This is the one I esteem:
    he who is humble and contrite in spirit,
    and trembles at my word.
³But whoever sacrifices a bull
    is like one who kills a man,
and whoever offers a lamb,
    like one who breaks a dog's neck;
whoever makes a grain offering
    is like one who presents pig's blood,
and whoever burns memorial incense,
    like one who worships an idol.
They have chosen their own ways,
    and their souls delight in their abominations;
⁴so I also will choose harsh treatment for them
    and will bring upon them what they dread.
For when I called, no one answered,
    when I spoke, no one listened.
They did evil in my sight
    and chose what displeases me."

⁵Hear the word of the LORD,
    you who tremble at his word:
"Your brothers who hate you,
    and exclude you because of my name, have said,
'Let the LORD be glorified,
    that we may see your joy!'
    Yet they will be put to shame.
⁶Hear that uproar from the city,
    hear that noise from the temple!
It is the sound of the LORD
    repaying his enemies all they deserve.

⁷"Before she goes into labor,
    she gives birth;
before the pains come upon her,
    she delivers a son.
⁸Who has ever heard of such a thing?
    Who has ever seen such things?
Can a country be born in a day
    or a nation be brought forth in a moment?
Yet no sooner is Zion in labor
    than she gives birth to her children.
⁹Do I bring to the moment of birth
    and not give delivery?" says the LORD.

> "Do I close up the womb
>   when I bring to delivery?" says your God.
> ¹⁰"Rejoice with Jerusalem and be glad for her,
>   all you who love her;
> rejoice greatly with her,
>   all you who mourn over her.
> ¹¹For you will nurse and be satisfied
>   at her comforting breasts;
> you will drink deeply
>   and delight in her overflowing abundance."

¹²For this is what the LORD says:

> "I will extend peace to her like a river,
>   and the wealth of nations like a flooding stream;
> you will nurse and be carried on her arm
>   and dandled on her knees.
> ¹³As a mother comforts her child,
>   so will I comfort you;
> and you will be comforted over Jerusalem."

> ¹⁴When you see this, your heart will rejoice
>   and you will flourish like grass;
> the hand of the LORD will be made known to his servants,
>   but his fury will be shown to his foes.
> ¹⁵See, the LORD is coming with fire,
>   and his chariots are like a whirlwind;
> he will bring down his anger with fury,
>   and his rebuke with flames of fire.
> ¹⁶For with fire and with his sword
>   the LORD will execute judgment upon all men,
>   and many will be those slain by the LORD.

¹⁷"Those who consecrate and purify themselves to go into the gardens, following the one in the midst of those who eat the flesh of pigs and rats and other abominable things—they will meet their end together," declares the LORD.

¹⁸"And I, because of their actions and their imaginations, am about to come and gather all nations and tongues, and they will come and see my glory.

¹⁹"I will set a sign among them, and I will send some of those who survive to the nations—to Tarshish, to the Libyans and Lydians (famous as archers), to Tubal and Greece, and to the distant islands that have not heard of my fame or seen my glory. They will proclaim my glory among the nations. ²⁰And they will bring all your brothers, from all the nations, to my holy mountain in Jerusalem as an offering to the LORD—on horses, in chariots and wagons, and on mules and camels," says the LORD. "They will bring them, as the Israelites bring their grain offerings, to the temple of the LORD in ceremonially clean vessels. ²¹And I will select some of them also to be priests and Levites," says the LORD.

²²"As the new heavens and the new earth that I make will endure before me," declares the LORD, "so will your name and descendants endure. ²³From one New Moon to another and from one Sabbath to another, all mankind will come and bow down before me," says the LORD. ²⁴"And they will go out and look upon the dead bodies of those who rebelled against me; their worm will not die, nor will their fire be quenched, and they will be loathsome to all mankind."

These two chapters are not only the end of the book but also its climax. In them the eschatology reaches its zenith, for the promise of new heavens and a new earth (65:17; 66:22) not only goes beyond anything else in the book but even the speculative imagination could not conceive any greater reality. At the same time, the spiritual challenge to the reader and the ultimate issues of destiny are presented with great power.

It must also be said however that the Christian reader sometimes leaves a perusal of these chapters with a sense of disappointment. So much of the book has ministered Christ to him, but where is his beloved Savior in these closing chapters? Surely here if anywhere he would be set forth in all his glory! Yet he does not seem to be present in a single verse here. If, however, the chapters be read, not in isolation from the rest of the book, but as a concluding study, it will appear that there are a number of passages that call to mind the earlier strongly christological passages. In fact, Christ is as truly present here as God is in the Book of Esther.

Chapter 64 is an impassioned prayer in which the people, represented by the prophet, state their sense of relationship to God but also make frank confession of their sins, crying to him for mercy. Can these chapters be regarded as God's answer? Thexton (in loc.), among others, says they cannot, because in chapter 64 the prophet confesses sin on behalf of the whole people, while here it appears that the community is divided into two groups—the penitent and the impenitent. True, but does this really affect the matter? A man of deep spiritual sensitivity may—like Daniel (Dan 9) or Ezra (Ezra 9)—take the burden of a whole community's sins on his heart and confess those sins with a depth of feeling that may be shared, in fact, by very few of his compatriots. Isaiah, at his call, had confessed not only his personal sin but that of his people generally (6:5). We will then treat these chapters as God's answer to the prayer of chapter 64.

1–5 At once we encounter a major difference in interpretation, in which the bulk of modern commentators diverge sharply from the traditional interpretation that is still taken by most conservative scholars. Paul applies vv. 1–2 to the Gentiles in Romans 10:20–21. Many modern commentators, however, hold that this is misapplication— or at best the reapplication—of the prophetic words to a similar but not identical situation, for they take both verses to apply properly to the Jews. The RSV translates "I was ready to be sought by those who did not ask for me; I was ready to be found by those who did not seek me." The Hebrew construction is Niphal *tolerativum*: "I permitted myself to be sought"; but, as Kidner ("Isaiah," in loc.) points out, this construction always refers to actual events, not simply to an attitude. He says, "Nowhere else does this construction imply a non-event." The NIV is somewhat disappointing when it translates "to a nation that did not call on my name," following the LXX and the Targum, but not the MT, which reads "to a nation that was not called by my name." We therefore take it that v. 1 applies to the Gentiles and v. 2 to the Jews. This then reminds us of the work of the Messiah, through whom the knowledge of the Lord will fill the earth (11:9), and especially of the Servant of the Lord, whose work will savingly enlighten the nations (42:6) through his sufferings and exaltation (52:15).

Verse 2 presents God's hands held out in love, "all day long," meaning perhaps throughout Israel's history, but finding obstinate rejection of his ways (cf. 64:5). "Imaginations" may refer to the sinful product of the unsanctified imagination in idols. "Continually" in v. 3 seems to answer to "all day long" in v. 2, with the thought that the people's sinful insults to God were as constant and long-standing as his own gracious overtures to them. The catalog of sins in v. 3–4 reminds us in some ways of the sins of Revelation 21:8; 22:15, which lead to the second death and thus exclude those who practice them from the Holy City. For "offering sacrifices in gardens," see the note at 1:29. "Burning incense on altars of brick" must, because of its context, be pagan, though its exact significance is unknown. The first half of v.4 refers to the forbidden practice of necromancy (cf. 57:9; Deut 18:9–13), while v.4b probably refers to flagrant disregard of the laws about unclean meats that, even if occurring within the context of Yahweh worship, show a rebellious outlook.

There is a tone of irony in v.5a. Paganism has its "holy" men; and these, in their fancied sanctity, instill fear in others lest they should come too close to them and be harmed. These descriptions of sin begin to give place to the assurance of punishment at the close of the verse (cf. Deut 32:22; Jer 17:4).

6–7 The introductory "see" (v.6) is a call to attention. God has those sins written before him (cf. Rev 20:12). The people's prayer (64:12) is answered, but not in the way they would hope for. In responding to our prayers, God always keeps within the spiritual and moral structure he has himself established. His judgment on a nation often awaits the full term of its sin (Gen 15:16; Dan 8:23; Matt 23:32; 1 Thess 2:16; cf. Rev 14:15). The mountain shrines were centers of idolatrous worship (cf. 57:7; Jer 3:6 et al.).

8–10 Here again is the important doctrine of the remnant, which played such a big part in earlier chapters of the prophecy and has important links with the Messiah (see Introduction, pp. 16–17). In much the same way, Paul modified the concept of a rejecting and rejected Israel in Romans 9–11. The vineyard of Israel, so unproductive (5:1–4), has nevertheless produced some genuine grapes; and these are recognized (v.8). They are the servants of God (see comment at 54:17). In them the promises to "the chosen people" (v.9) find their fulfillment, for this remnant is "my people who seek me" (v.10). Those who had received the great OT revelation had a responsibility to seek the Lord on the basis of it, while those who had never known its light would receive it through a new divine initiative (v.1).

Sharon was beautiful and fertile; but Achor had an ominous sound, for it symbolized the judgment of God on his people (Josh 7:24–26). Hosea, Isaiah's older contemporary, had however presented the divine promise: "I will give her back her vineyards,/and will make the Valley of Achor a door of hope" (Hos 2:15).

11–12 Here God turns to the rebels among his people. The reference to the holy mountain (v.11) refers to the forsaking of the worship of the Lord at his temple. This true worship involved the offering of items connected with the people's food and drink. Instead these were being presented to pagan deities (see Notes). First Corinthians 10:21–22 probably alludes to this passage. Verse 12 recalls v.2 (cf. also 55:1–7).

13–16 The term "Sovereign LORD" (*ᵃḏōnay YHWH*) was characteristic of two passages picturing the Servant of the Lord (48:16; 50:4–5, 7, 9). Here (vv.13, 15) the term occurs again, providing a link between the Servant and the servants, similar perhaps to that between the Messiah and the remnant in the earlier part of the book. Revelation 22:3, 6 refers to the "servants of God" in the final vision of the Bible. Those addressed in these verses as "you" are, of course, the same rebels God speaks to in vv.11–12.

In Revelation God's people are promised food, drink, and table fellowship (Rev 2:7, 17; 3:20; 21:6; 22:2, 17). As there, so also here, those still in their sins will be excluded from the joy of it all; and their name will be a byword among God's people for the curse of God. The true servants of God will have a new name (v.15; cf. Rev 2:17), perhaps the name of their God (Rev 3:12), the "God of truth" (v.16; cf. Rev 3:14). This name is unique to this passage in the OT and so appropriate to a description of the eschatological climax in which all God's promises will be fulfilled and his truth demonstrated. The final promise of v.16 takes its significance from the fact that the nation's troubles had been the result of its sins. This full and free forgiveness would be achieved through the sacrifice of God's Servant (ch. 53).

17–25 The great promise, with its introductory call to special attention—"Behold, I will create new heavens and a new earth" (v.17; cf. Rev 21:1)—consists of only seven words in Hebrew; yet its implications are staggering. The whole created order is to be renewed. Great and new as this promise is, the reader does not come to it competely unprepared, for it builds on passages like 11:1–9 and chapter 24. For those whose imagination cannot cope with the macrocosm, the prophet indicates that Jerusalem too is to be created anew (v.18). Young (*Book of Isaiah*, in loc.) reminds us of 63:9. The God who had identified with his people in their affliction would now do so in their joy also (v.19). The former sorrows will be over (cf. Rev 21:4).

The picture given in v.20, taken literally, promises greatly extended but not infinite life; yet v.19 declares that weeping will be banished! This suggests that we are meant to dwell on the positive blessings outlined in v.20 and not on their negative implications. On the other hand, if we take the references to death seriously, we have here a blessed but not ideal state, not quite parallel therefore to the whole of Revelation 21:4 (for fuller comment, see Introduction, pp. 14–16).

The people's state of blessedness is portrayed largely in terms reminiscent of the "godly materialism" of Deuteronomy (vv.21–23; cf. also 62:8–9). The greatest of all the blessings they will know, however, will be a relationship with God in which there is complete harmony between their prayer and his will, between his desire to provide and their dependence on him to give (v.24). Verse 25, taken almost entirely from 11:6–9, is a reminder that these blessings come only through the Messiah, while the words "dust will be the serpent's food" (alluding to Gen 3:14) remind us that the overthrow of Satan, the great serpent (Rev 20:2), is the result of the work of the woman's offspring (Gen 3:15).

66:1–2a There was a reference to Jerusalem in 65:18–19 and to its holy mountain (65:11) but no express mention of the temple. What place is that to have in God's new order? These verses could mean that this great God, who could not be contained in the whole of the old created order (cf. 1 Kings 8:27), could have no appropriate temple at all. But the postexilic temple was built at his command; so the passage must mean rather that no edifice made by human hands could be more than a symbol; and the symbol could, as Stephen made clear, come to be cherished above the reality (Acts 7:44–54).

2b–4 Isaiah 57:15 refers to God's heavenly dwelling and the fellowship he offers to the contrite and lowly in spirit. There is therefore a particular aptness about the placing of v.2b here. At Sinai, where the sacrificial system was given but before its details were made known, God's people trembled when the Ten Commandments were heard (Exod 20:18–21). Here it is clearly a humble, sensitive reverence for God's word that is in view. This thought governs v.3, where the teaching is even stronger than in 1:10–20. The most sacred exercises of true God-given religion are like the worst of sins when they are divorced from humility of spirit. Verse 4 repeats the thought of 65:12. This is all the more striking in the light of the context of the words in chapter 65, for there it is paganism that forsakes the holy mountain of God that is being condemned. Paganism that sets aside God's word and ritualism that obeys it in the letter only and not the spirit are alike abominations to the Lord.

5–6 Once more the word of God passes from his enemies within Israel (vv.3–4) to his servants. Kidner ("Isaiah," in loc.) says, "The intolerance in v.5 was acted out, almost to the letter in Jn 9:24, 34. It is one of the earliest allusions to purely religious persecution and theological hatred." The words in the second half of the verse are, of course, uttered in irony. Verse 6 certainly implies that in some sense (see comment at 1) God accepted the Jerusalem temple as his, for it was from there that he revealed his wrath against his enemies. The Christian reader finds his mind irresistibly drawn to our Lord's cleansing of the temple (see comment at 56:7).

7–11 In 54:1–3, just after the fourth Servant Song, Zion was told to rejoice and to prepare her tent for a great influx of inhabitants. This is emphasized again, with special stress on the suddenness of it. The questions of v.9 are really making the point that God promises not only a speedy but a complete work, with Zion's family deeply satisfied in their mother.

12–16 In 8:6–8, in one of his most graphic images, Isaiah pictured Assyria—the cruelest enemy Israel and Judah ever had to face—flooding the whole country like an immensely spreading inundation from the Euphrates. He had then gone on to promise endlessly increasing peace as the result of the Messiah's reign (9:7). Now the analogy of the over-flowing river is applied to that peace (v.12), the nations coming up, not now in devastating conquest, but in peace and with their wealth (cf. 48:18; 60:11).

From the thought of Zion's children as nursed by her, the thought moves to God as the mother of his people (v.13). This is dramatic and surprising, for in earlier chapters God has been represented as the husband and Zion as the wife (e.g., 54:5). Once again, then, the prophet demonstrates the freedom of inspiration in its use of illustrative language (see comments at 60:16 and 62:5). Here the purpose is to make it clear that the Lord is the real source of those blessings mediated to Zion's children through her. The same flexibilty is shown in v.14, where grass is not a symbol of human frailty (cf. 40:8) but rather of nourishment under the blessing of God. In this way God's power will be shown in grace to his servants but in wrath to his enemies. The manifestation of his wrath is expressed especially in terms of fire, which, like the whirlwind and the sword, has great destructive potential (vv.15–16). As Young (*Book of Isaiah,* in loc.) points out, the apparently universal language of v.16 is probably to be understood of the people of Israel, because the context limits it in this way.

17–21 The book that has been largely poetical throughout ends in prose. To understand v.17, it should be remembered that it is possible to consecrate oneself to a false god. The prophet clearly has in view those described in 65:3–5. For the phrase "the one in the midst of," see the Notes. In v.18 "their actions and imaginations" refers to the Jews and their departure from the true God (cf. 65:2). Isaiah had seen the glory of the Lord in the temple (ch. 6), where it had also been revealed to him that the people of Israel would not accept his message. Frequently, during the course of his prophecy, he has seen the light of God going forth and the Gentiles being attracted to it (e.g., 2:1–4; 42:6; 49:6; 60:1–3). Now he expresses their promised knowledge of God in terms reminiscent of his own inaugural vision.

Young (*Book of Isaiah*, in loc.), commenting on v.19, points out that the precise language used here of a sign is used in Exodus 10:2 and Psalm 78:43 of a miracle and interprets it of Christ. Kidner ("Isaiah," in loc.) suggests that Matthew 12:38–40—with its reference to Christ crucified and risen—relates to this. The survivors are the Jewish remnant, and they go out to many a foreign country to proclaim the glory of the true God. The beautiful picture in v.20 is based on the Levitical system of offerings. The Gentiles will bring the dispersed remnant to the temple, just as if the Gentiles themselves were Israelites and the members of the dispersion were the offerings they would bring to present to the Lord. It is not impossible grammatically that the words of v.21 apply to the Gentiles, which, in this case, would anticipate the Pauline teaching that there is no barrier to blessing or to privilege in Christ (e.g., Gal 3:28–29). It seems more likely, however, that they apply to priests and Levites selected from among the regathered brothers mentioned in v.20.

22–24 God here makes the greatest and most comprehensive of all his promises: the guarantee of his pledges to his people. He further affirms that the wider vision of the worship of all mankind will also find its fulfillment. This is expressed in terms of the old God-given Jewish system of special days and Sabbaths for worship and, with many other aspects of these two final chapters, raises important questions of interpretation (see Introduction, pp. 14–16). The prophecy ends on a note of the starkest realism. It pictures vividly the lessons to be learned from the eternal judgment of God on sinners for their rebellion against him. It should be noted that this judgment will have the approval of men. This reminds us of the awesome "Hallelujah!" of Revelation 19:1. God's people must agree with all he says, for he is God.

Notes

4 The NIV's "keeping secret vigil" assumes, with the NEB, the repointing of בַּנְצוּרִים (*bann⁰-*
ṣûrîm, "in hidden places") to *banniṣṣûrîm*, though, of course, both expressions require interpretation. The esoteric element in much religion makes either possible.

The NIV's "broth" follows the Qere, 1QIsaᵃ, the LXX, and the Targum in reading מְרַק (*m⁰raq*) instead of the Kethiv פְּרַק (*p⁰raq*, "fragment").

11 "Fortune" and "Destiny" translate הַגַּד (*haggad*) and הַמְנִי (*hamnî*), which, as Whybray says (*Isaiah 40–66*, in loc.), conceal the names of the Syrian god Gad, personifying good luck, and Meni, "a god of fate, possibly identical (though masculine) with the Arabian goddess Manât," mentioned in the Qu'ran.

66: 13 The NIV's "her child" in fact translates אִישׁ (*îš*, "a man"). Young (*Book of Isaiah*, in loc.) comments, "Not only as children sucking the mother's breast does God comfort His people, but also as a mother comforts her grown son. . . . The mother's love for her offspring remains firm throughout life and thus forms a natural comparison for the divine comfort (cf. 40:1)."

17 The NIV, following the Kethiv, renders אַחַר אַחַד בַּתָּוֶךְ (*'aḥar 'aḥad battāwek*) as "following the one in the midst of," suggesting an illicit rite, conducted by a group with a leader, such as that described in Ezek 8:7–11. Volz (*Jesaia II*, in loc.) sees a reference to a mystery cult, so dating the verses extremely late. This is quite unnecessary.

18 The LXX reading, given in the NIV margin, makes little substantial difference, except that it weakens the link between Israel's sin and the wider purpose of God suggested in the Hebrew.

19 For "Tarshish," see the note at 2:16. פוט (*pûṭ*, "Put") follows the LXX (B), rather than the unknown פול (*pûl*, "Pul") of the MT. The NIV's "Lydians" is, literally, "Lud." Put and Lud occur also in Ezek 27:10; 30:5, the first being in Africa (cf. Gen 10:6) and perhaps also the second, which could however be Lydia in Asia Minor. The NIV text therefore represents possibilities, not certain identifications. Tubal and Greece are mentioned in Ezek 27:13, the former almost certainly being the Tiberanoi of northeast Asia Minor mentioned by Herodotus.

24 A comparison with Jer 7:32–8:3 strongly suggests the prophet has the Valley of Hinnom, or Gehenna, in mind. Mark 9:48, in its context (vv.42–49), applies this to eternal punishment.

JEREMIAH

Charles L. Feinberg

JEREMIAH

Introduction

1. General
2. The Person of Jeremiah
3. Date and Authorship
4. Historical Setting
5. Literary Form and Structure
6. Theological Emphases
7. Special Problems
8. Bibliography
9. Outline

1. General

Almost without exception, Bible students consider Jeremiah to be one of the foremost OT prophets. With good reason he has been called a sublime figure. He was the most autobiographical of all the prophets, and we know more about him than any other OT prophet. Highest praise has been given him; in fact, he has been credited with the survival of his people after the Fall of Jerusalem in 586 B.C., a veritable savior of the Jews (so Bright). Nonetheless, this man of God is one of the most misunderstood of the great OT leaders.

Some expositors have judged Jeremiah's prophecy to be the most difficult in the OT. Many passages have eluded the comprehension of diligent commentators. Jeremiah, it has been claimed with some justification, is the least read and least understood of all OT books because it reveals no clear arrangement and demands so much extrabiblical, contemporary history for its understanding. Not surprising, then, while many commentaries have been written on the Book of Isaiah, Jeremiah has suffered from neglect. In Germany, however, some of the most eminent Semitic scholars have engaged in thorough study of the book; and scholars in other countries have more recently labored to correct the imbalance.

The Book of Jeremiah is longer than Isaiah or Ezekiel, and the Minor Prophets combined are about a third shorter. The claim has been made that it is the longest book in the Bible (if 1 and 2 Samuel, Kings, and Chronicles are reckoned as separate books) and the most valuable book in the OT (so Elliott-Binns). Judgments will vary here, but no one can deny the book's great exegetical interest, its valuable light on the subject of the decline and fall of the Judean kingdom, and its vast influence on theological thinking in subsequent ages. Among the Apocrypha are *The Letter of Jeremiah* and *The Book of Baruch*. The Syriac version (so also the Gr.) has an *Apocalypse of Baruch*.

The three divisions of the Hebrew canon are Law, Prophets, and Writings. The Prophets section is divided into the Former Prophets (Joshua, Judges, Samuel, Kings) and the Latter Prophets (the books designated as Major and Minor Prophets with the exception of Lamentations and Daniel). In the English and Greek versions, the Book of Jeremiah appears after Isaiah and before Lamentations and Ezekiel. Many MSS of the OT place it at the head of the Latter Prophets, seemingly indicating that at one time the book had the first place in the order of the Latter Prophets. This suggests a solution to the problem of ascription of authorship in Matthew 27:9.

2. The Person of Jeremiah

a. *His background*

Jeremiah's name, not uncommon in Israel, is of disputed meaning. It has been rendered "Yahweh [the LORD] hurls" (cf. Exod 15:1), "the LORD founds," "the LORD establishes," or "the LORD exalts." His name may well reflect his parents' hopes for him and the nation, in which case the last rendering would be preferable. Jeremiah's relation to so many political events makes it strange that his name appears nowhere in Kings or Chronicles. The prophet's native home was the Levitical town of Anathoth in the territory of Benjamin. The name is preserved in the modern Anata, which is located in the vicinity of the ancient site. Some, however, equate the nearby Ras el-Harrubeh, which is about two miles northeast of Jerusalem, with Anathoth (cf. Josh 21:17–19; 1 Kings 2:26–27; cf. also ZPEB, 1:155–56).

Any study of the person of Jeremiah makes one immediately aware of his uniqueness. His life is unlike any other in Scripture. In his day he was unquestionably the greatest spiritual personality in Israel. Elements of the natural and the supernatural mingle in him in an unparalleled way. His was not a happy life, at least outwardly, for it was marked by constant sadness; his expressions of sorrow are classic. There is general agreement that Jeremiah's personality is more clearly portrayed than that of any other prophet. To study him carefully is to ascertain the meaning and ministry of the prophet of God. Only he among the prophets shows his personal feeling as he proclaims God's message; thus he has been referred to as the most psychological of the prophets and at the same time the most interesting as a man. Many are agreed that his greatest contribution to posterity is his personality: by birth a priest; by grace a prophet; by the trials of life a bulwark for God's truth; by daily spiritual experience one of the greatest exponents of prophetic faith in his unique relation to God; by temperament gentle and timid, yet constantly contending against the forces of sin; and by natural desire a seeker after the love of a companion, his family, friends, and, above all, his people—which were all denied him.

Jeremiah's life—private and public—is openly displayed in his book. His brave actions, his tenderheartedness toward his coreligionists, his deep emotional and spiritual struggles before God—all these and more are clearly presented. His disappointments and sufferings were undeniably as poignant as those of any other Jewish prophet. He reminds one of Hosea, who heralded the Fall of Samaria as Jeremiah heralded the Fall of Jerusalem. His life may be characterized as being one long martyrdom.

Jeremiah the son of Hilkiah was of a priestly family, but nothing indicates that he ever exercised a priestly ministry. Some scholars (cf. IOT, p. 802, n.2) hold that his father was the Hilkiah who found the "Book of the Law" in the temple (2 Kings 22:8). Jeremiah's father was probably a descendant of Abiathar, the sole survivor of the priests of Nob (1 Sam 22:20). After ministering under David, Abiathar was exiled by Solomon to Anathoth, where he had property (1 Kings 2:26). Furthermore, had his father been high priest, Jeremiah would have lived in Jerusalem, would have been designated by the proper title, and would have belonged to the line of Zadok, not Ithamar. That he was from Anathoth further accounts for the fact that in Josiah's day Jeremiah was not so well known as Huldah the prophetess (2 Kings 22:14–20). That Jeremiah was a man of means may be inferred from his purchase of the field in 32:6–15.

Jeremiah was born at Anathoth about 646 B.C. and died, probably in Egypt, not long after 586. He was called to the prophetic office in 626 (1:2; 25:3) and served in it for more than forty years. The Lord did not permit him to marry (16:2). Though his public ministry was long and checkered, there is no indication that he ever had any disciples; and his closest companion was his faithful secretary and scribe, Baruch the son of Neriah.

As stated above, Jeremiah was called to his ministry in 626 B.C., in the thirteenth year of Josiah's reign (1:2), and preached in Jerusalem until the Fall of Judah in 586 (cf. 7:2; 22:1; 27:1–2; 32:1). After the decline of the kingdom, he labored for some time among the survivors in Judah and later among the Jews who had fled to Egypt (chs. 40–44). His call included both Israel and the other nations of his time (1:10). The call was both simple and direct (1:4–5), but the prophet's reaction differed markedly from Isaiah's (Isa 6) and Ezekiel's (Ezek 1). Expositors differ about the age of Jeremiah at the time of his call. He was probably about twenty, though na'ar ("child," 1:6–7) is difficult to define chronologically because this Hebrew noun only conveys the concept of relative age.

b. His public ministry

Jeremiah's ministry was carried on in a politically, socially, morally, and spiritually chaotic era. The glorious days of reformation under Hezekiah in the eighth century were eclipsed by the long, ungodly reign of Manasseh, who along with his fealty to the Assyrian monarchs maintained a syncretistic worship for his people. Jeremiah did not hide his hatred for the religious apostasy and social injustices of Manasseh. In this spiritual declension priests and prophets alike were implicated.

When Jeremiah began to preach, the godly Josiah had begun his reforms to wipe out idolatry from his kingdom. The content of the prophet's preaching confirms his full support of Josiah's reforms and calls for a truly repentant return to the Lord. Tragically, the people of Judah had already become so ungodly that they were no longer responsive to calls to return to God. But in grace the Lord continued to plead with Judah through Jeremiah. From the beginning of his ministry, Jeremiah never deviated from the position that Judah and Jerusalem were to be destroyed by a nation from the north and the people carried into captivity (4:5–9; 6:22–26). The threatening invasion of the northern enemy gave urgency to his warnings.

With Jehoiakim's rule (608 B.C.), Jeremiah again began public ministry. In the famous temple address (chs. 7, 26), he indicated that only faithfulness to God could guarantee the nation's security; otherwise the temple would be destroyed. He aroused bitter opposition to himself and his message from all segments of the nation, including his own family. Sad and despairing because of the rejection of his message, he yet loved, prayed for, and agonized over his people. No greater and truer Jewish patriot ever preached the truth to them. Even when the Lord forbade him to pray for them, he continued to intercede. At times he felt that God himself had forsaken him. He even cursed the day of his birth. Jehoiakim was so enraged with Jeremiah's denunciatory messages that he cut the scroll of his prophecy to pieces and burned it. So Jeremiah became a fugitive from the king's wrath. In the fourth year of Jehoiakim's reign (according to Hebrew reckoning [25:1], or in the third year according to Babylonian computation [Dan 1:1]), Nebuchadnezzar of Babylon first invaded Judah. He had defeated Pharaoh Neco of Egypt at the Battle of Carchemish (605 B.C.), an event of unsurpassed importance because it settled the question of world supremacy in that day. After Egypt's defeat, Jeremiah counseled that it was futile and contrary to God's will to resist Nebuchadnezzar. One can imagine the unpopular nature of this message. Thereafter Jeremiah's life was one of uninterrupted misunderstanding and persecution.

Under Zedekiah's rule, Jeremiah fared no better, though this king was not so violently opposed to him as Jehoiakim had been. But Zedekiah was weak, vacillating, and in constant fear of his powerful nobles. Jeremiah had some ministry to the king, but it bore little if any fruit. When the Judean kingdom fell to him in the eleventh year of Zedekiah's reign, Nebuchadnezzar appointed Gedaliah governor of Judah (40:1–6). Soon after his appointment the governor was assassinated by a descendant of the Davidic house (41:1–2), Ishmael son of Nethaniah. The remnant in Mizpah, against Jeremiah's protests, fled to Egypt from the wrath of Babylon (vv.16 –18). Jeremiah and Baruch were compelled to accompany them (42:1–43:7). At the end of his ministry, Jeremiah was at Tahpanhes (i.e., Tell Defenneh, Daphnae) in Egypt, where he both predicted Nebuchadnezzar's conquest of Egypt (43:8–13) and denounced the idolatry of the Jews there (ch. 44). Beyond this nothing is known of Jeremiah's life.

Such in general outline was the public ministry of Jeremiah. He had encountered more opposition from more enemies than any other OT prophet. Much of it stemmed from the fact that, unlike Elisha, Isaiah, and others, who urged the nation to withstand their enemies and promised God's help, Jeremiah continually preached one theme: unconditional surrender. Had not the Lord protected him, he would have been martyred.

Nothing certain is known of the time, place, or manner of Jeremiah's death. According to 44:29–30, Jeremiah was still alive around 570 B.C. (Pharaoh Hophra [Apries] reigned 588–569). By an unusual providence the prophet who fought all his life against Egypt was forced to end his days there as a captive. A late, unattested tradition, mentioned by Tertullian, Jerome, and others, claims that the men of Tahpanhes stoned Jeremiah to death. There is a rabbinical account of his deportation with Baruch to Babylon by Nebuchadnezzar at the time of the conquest of Egypt and of his death there, but this is unconfirmed.[1]

Singularly, this great man of God, so little heeded by his own people, has been accorded great respect after death. Alexandrian Jews especially have held him in profound regard (cf. 2 Macc 2:1–8; 15:12–16; see also Matt 16:14). That later Jews saw in him their intercessor partially explains this.

c. His prophetic profile

Probably no writer on Jeremiah has failed to mention certain resemblances between him and the Lord Jesus Christ. There are a number of parallels. The life of no

---

[1]*Seder Olam Rabba* c.26.

other prophet has so close an analogy to the earthly life of our Lord. Jeremiah has been rightly called the most Christlike of the prophets. Certain disciples saw in Jesus of Nazareth the prophet Jeremiah returned to life (Matt 16:14). Here are some analogies between Jesus and Jeremiah.

1. Their historical settings were similar. Jerusalem was about to fall; the temple was soon to be destroyed; religion was buried in formalism; there was need for emphasis on the spiritual life. Outwardly the life of Jeremiah closely resembled that of our Lord.

2. Both had a message for Israel and the world.

3. Both were conscious of the world of nature about them and used many figures from it.

4. Both came from a high tradition: Jeremiah from a priest-prophet background, Christ from the divine-kingly planes.

5. Both were conscious of their call from God.

6. Both condemned the commercialism of temple worship and did so in a similar way (7:11; Matt 21:13).

7. Both were accused of political treason.

8. Both were tried, persecuted, and imprisoned.

9. Both foretold the destruction of the temple (7:14; Mark 13:2). Two great external catastrophes struck the OT theocracy: Nebuchadnezzar's destruction of Jerusalem and its temple and Titus's similar destruction of them. Of the first Jeremiah was the prophet; of the latter, Christ himself (Matt 24).

10. Both wept over Jerusalem (9:1; Luke 19:41).

11. Both forcefully condemned the priests of their day.

12. Both were rejected by their kin (12:6; John 1:11).

13. Both were tenderhearted. Jeremiah was so much like the Man of Sorrows that the rabbis identified Jeremiah with the Suffering Servant of Isaiah 53.

14. Both loved Israel deeply.

15. Both knew the meaning of loneliness (15:10; Isa 53:3).

16. Both enjoyed unusual fellowship with God. One of the unique features of Jeremiah's life was that he could be so free and honest in communion and conversation with God (20:7; cf. John 11:41–42).

3. Date and Authorship

For some years a number of scholars have held to the supposed Scythian invasion of Judah as the background of the early prophecies in the book (see IOT, p. 803, n.6), thus calling into question the historical accuracy of Jeremiah. Their position can be summarized as follows: What Jeremiah originally thought to be a Scythian threat to Judah turned out to be the Babylonian invasion. The older position had been that between 630 and 624 B.C. the Scythians, proto-Russians or proto-Turks, came south along the Mediterranean coast and penetrated as far as Egypt. To counter this position, other scholars have maintained that the Scythians did not attack Judah (ibid.), for no traces of any such invasion are demonstrable. Much depends on the handling of the relevant material from Herodotus (1.103–5), the chronicler of the Persian wars. If the Scythians are to be understood as the Umman Mauda of the Babylonian Chronicle, then their role in international affairs would seem to date from events in 612–610 B.C. Evidence suggests that in 612 B.C. the Scythians did join the Babylonians and Medes under Cyaxares in the downfall of Nineveh (so Bright).

Actually, the passages in Jeremiah on the enemy from the north fit much better what is known of the Babylonians than of the wild Scythians. Many scholars have now abandoned the Scythian view. The evidence for a Scythian invasion of Judah about 625 B.C. is far from compelling. In fact, Herodotus does not actually connect the Scythians with Judah. Besides, there are several biblical facts that do not concur with Herodotus's account: (1) the reference to "an ancient and enduring nation" (5:15); (2) the use of "chariots" (4:13); the army's capture of "cities of Judah" (4:16; 6:6); their battle array in regular ranks (6:23); their love of Jerusalem (4:30). The present writer agrees with the position that the enemy in view in Jerusalem is Babylon throughout.[2]

Scholars have extensively discussed the origin of the Book of Jeremiah and held differing opinions about it. Several ingenious suppositions have been proposed, but none is completely satisfactory. Broadly speaking, scholars are divided into two groups as to their view of the origin of the book: (1) those who think Jeremiah wrote very little of it and assign the major part of it to other writers; (2) those who assign the entire book to Jeremiah (ch. 52 is treated separately) through the secretarial aid of Baruch (i.e., he was to Jeremiah what Luke was to Paul).

The first group favors a division of the book into three sources: (1) messages dictated by Jeremiah; (2) a biography of Jeremiah, probably by Baruch; and (3) various contributions from redactors and later authors. Three types of material were early identified: (1) prose discourses, (2) biographical prose, and (3) poetical prophecies (so Duhm). The second school holds that the prophet dictated his messages to Baruch, his secretary (36:17–18; 45:1).

Internal evidence indicates that the first written material of the book was done in the fourth year of Jehoiakim's reign (605 B.C.; cf. 36:1–2). In addition, passages like 29:1; 30:2; and 51:60 appear to compel the conclusion that prophecies apart from those contained in Baruch's scroll were immediately recorded. The scroll burned by Jehoiakim was replaced with additions (36:32). Apparently through the first score of years of his ministry, Jeremiah had kept notes of his messages, which were put into writing at God's command (36:2). The burned scroll was replaced and the material gradually added to. The entire book was probably gathered together shortly after Jeremiah's death (c. 586 B.C.). It seems reasonable that Jeremiah edited his work during the Captivity. The conclusion appears inescapable that Baruch's rewritten scroll was the basis for Jeremiah's written prophecies. The book bears marks of having been gathered together by one person at one time. For example, many of its parts are interdependent. Arguments for different, multiple editings and changes are highly subjective and inconclusive. (For further discussion of this, see 5. Literary Form and Structure, also, see 7. Special Problems.)

---

[2]See also R. Vaggione, "Over all Asia? The Extent of the Scythian Domination in Herodotus," JBL 92 (1973): 523–30.

4. Historical Setting

a. *Prophetic background*

Just as the eighth century B.C. saw a galaxy of prophets in Israel, so did the end of the seventh and the first half of the sixth centuries. The contemporary prophets were Zephaniah (Zeph 1:1), Obadiah (Obad 11–14, if one holds, as this writer does, that the prophet was speaking of the destruction of 586 B.C.), the prophetess Huldah (2 Kings 22:14; 2 Chron 34:22), all in Judah, and Ezekiel (Ezek 1:1–3) and Daniel (Dan 1:1) in Babylon. Especially close is the relationship between Jeremiah and Ezekiel; some eighteen clear points of contact between them have been demonstrated (so Elliott-Binns). It is probable that Nahum and Habakkuk were also contemporaries of Jeremiah. It is of interest that three of the four major prophets in the English canon were related to captivities: (1) Daniel to that in Jehoiakim's time (Dan 1:1), (2) Ezekiel to that in Jehoiachin's time (Ezek 1:1–3), and (3) Jeremiah to that in Zedekiah's time (1:1–3).

Most commentators feel that Jeremiah was greatly influenced by the prophecies of those who preceded him, especially those of Hosea. Some have also suggested that Jeremiah had a strong influence on the psalmists, and parallel concepts and expressions have been pointed out to substantiate this. This could be true, however, only of the psalmists who wrote in the exilic and early postexilic periods.

b. *Historical background*

1) *Events*

To understand Jeremiah's prophecy requires close scrutiny of his times because of (1) the critical events in the political world of his day—events in which Judah was directly affected—and (2) the number of kings in Judah who reigned during his career and with whom he had close contact. Jeremiah was a national and international figure. A general chronological table will help us visualize the historical background of his book.

> 639–609 B.C.—the reign of Josiah
> 609 B.C. (3 months)—the reign of Jehoahaz
> 609–597 B.C.—the reign of Jehoiakim
> 597 B.C. (3 months)—the reign of Jehoiachin
> 597–586 B.C.—the reign of Zedekiah
> 586 B.C.—the Fall of Jerusalem
> 586(?) B.C.—the assassination of Gedaliah

Events of significance during this period are as follows:

> 626 B.C.—the call of Jeremiah
> 612 B.C.—the Fall of Nineveh
> 609 B.C.—the death of Josiah at Megiddo
> 605 B.C.—the Battle of Carchemish and the Fall of the Assyrian Empire
> 605 B.C.—the first siege of Jerusalem by Nebuchadnezzar (Daniel exiled to Babylon)
> 597 B.C.—the second siege of Jerusalem
> 588–586 B.C.—the final siege of Jerusalem, beginning the Babylonian captivity

Nabopolassar, the father of Nebuchadnezzar and conqueror of Assyria, came from Chaldea, a province in the southern part of Babylonia, and reigned from 625 to 605 B.C. Nebuchadnezzar (more properly Nebuchadrezzar), the most famous of the Babylonian monarchs, ruled from 605 to 562 B.C.

The times of Jeremiah are among the most important in OT history; thus details are essential. Because of their great significance, they are the best-documented times in all Israel's history. The Book of Jeremiah is so filled with historical, biographical, and autobiographical material that his life can be synchronized with dates and known events to a degree unparalleled in the writings of other prophets.

The world in Jeremiah's day was in commotion and revolution. During Jeremiah's ministry, Judah was under the domination of Assyria, Egypt, and then Babylonia. During the more than four decades of his service, five epochal events occurred: (1) the dissolution of the Assyrian Empire after the death of Ashurbanipal (669– c. 630 B.C.); (2) the fall of the empire (612 B.C.); (3) the emergence of the Babylonian Empire under the Chaldeans; (4) the defeat of Egypt, Assyria's confederate, by the Chaldeans and Medes at Carchemish (605 B.C.); and (5) the Fall of Jerusalem with the destruction of the Solomonic temple (586 B.C.).

Geographically and politically Judah was in a vulnerable position in the power politics of Egypt and Assyria. In the eighth century B.C., Isaiah had warned against trusting Egypt (Isa 30:1–7) and had keenly evaluated the threat of Assyria (Isa 37). By God's protection the kingdom of Judah had escaped Sennacherib's forces. But from the godly reign of Hezekiah, the nation declined to the lowest spiritual depths under the godless rule of Manasseh (2 Kings 21:9–15; 24:3–4). If Jeremiah was called in his early twenties, he lived in the reigns of Manasseh and Amon. Under Manasseh's long, apostate reign of fifty-five years, the reforms of his godly father, Hezekiah, were forgotten. Judah was then under Assyrian power; so to please his overlords, Manasseh introduced syncretistic elements into the temple worship at Jerusalem. The northern kingdom (Israel) already exiled (722 B.C.), the remnant residing there had embraced mixed elements in their faith (2 Kings 17:28). During the reigns of Esarhaddon and Ashurbanipal, the Assyrian power conquered Egypt; but the latter regained strength under Psammetik I (664–609 B.C.), so that Judah found herself balancing off one great power against the other.

2) Rulers

a) *Josiah*. Josiah came to the throne when a boy of eight. Politically, Assyria was under strong opposition from Babylon, fighting to survive. This gave Judah more freedom to throw off Assyrian elements in her worship. In 633 B.C., Josiah sought the Lord (2 Chron 34:3); his reforms began in 629 B.C. (2 Chron 24:36); and in 623–622 B.C., the Book of the Law was found in the temple (2 Kings 22:3–8; 2 Chron 34:8–15). The reforms are detailed in 2 Kings 22–23; though widespread and well inaugurated, they did not last, as is evident from Jeremiah's ceaseless condemnation of the nation's sins. Jerusalem was made the only authorized center for worship.

In 609 B.C., Pharaoh Neco of Egypt joined Assyria to strengthen them. Josiah, though he had been warned by Neco, interfered and lost his life at the Battle of Megiddo (2 Kings 23:29; 2 Chron 35:20–24). But Babylon, stronger than Egypt, dominated the world scene under Nabopolassar of Chaldea, ruler of Babylonia by 625 B.C. and the destroyer of Nineveh in 612 B.C. His son, Nebuchadnezzar II, succeeded him and reigned for forty-three years, having defeated Egypt at the Battle of Carchemish on the Euphrates River in 605 B.C. (46:2; 2 Chron 35:20). Thereafter Babylon was master of the world. For years Jeremiah steadily counseled against Judah's involvement in world politics. When the people refused his counsel, he repeatedly entreated them to surrender to the superior forces of Babylon, who at that time were an instrument for carrying out God's will.

b) *Jehoahaz*. Distraught over the calamitous death of godly Josiah, the people took matters into their own hands and set Jehoahaz (Shallum [22:11]), son of Josiah, on the throne. In three months of rule he manifested an anti-Egypt and pro-Babylon policy, for which he was summarily deposed by Pharaoh Neco (2 Kings 23:31–33), who took him to Egypt and imposed tribute on the country. In his place Neco set on the throne Eliakim, oldest son of Josiah and half-brother of Jehoahaz (2 Kings 23:34, 36), changing his name to Jehoiakim (2 Kings 23:30–35; 2 Chron 36:1–4).

c) *Jehoiakim*. The reign of this king was the time of Jeremiah's greatest trial and opposition. Politically, king and prophet were diametrically opposed, the king favoring Egypt and Jeremiah counseling submission to Babylon. Spiritually, the two were even farther apart. Jehoiakim has been characterized as the worst and most ungodly of all Judah's kings. He has been labeled a blood-thirsty tyrant, an inveterate enemy of the truth. He cared nothing for the worship of the God of Israel, exacted exorbitant taxes, used forced labor without pay, and had no regard for the word or prophet of God (22:13–14; ch. 36). In Jehoiakim's eleven-year reign, the Battle of Carchemish took place (cf. 46:2). It was an event of permanent significance, for it marked the transfer of power over the Middle East from Egypt to Babylon. This defeat was the final blow to Egypt's aspirations and guaranteed the Chaldeans the supremacy of the West. It was the turning point of the period and had important consequences for Israel's future. The Babylonians made Jehoiakim their vassal and exiled a number of Jewish nobles (2 Kings 24:1), among them Daniel (Dan 1:1). Some scholars consider this first taking of Jerusalem by Nebuchadnezzar the beginning of the seventy years of Judah's exile in Babylon (25:11); with it the dissolution of the Davidic kingdom had begun (so KD). Jehoiakim sponsored idolatry and had no concern for the widespread social injustice in his realm (22:13–19; 2 Kings 23:37). Of all the kings under whom Jeremiah prophesied, Jehoiakim was the most inveterate foe of the message and messenger of God (cf. 26:20–23; 36:20–26). In 598–597 B.C., he revolted against Babylon but was unsuccessful, thus adding to Judah's problems (2 Kings 24:1–5). In Jehoiakim's time, Jeremiah was persecuted, plotted against, maligned, and imprisoned. The king destroyed his written prophecies, but the prophet did not swerve from his divine commission (cf. 11:18–23; 12:6; 15:15–18; 18:18; 20:2; 26:10–11, 24; 36:23). Jehoiakim died violently in Jerusalem in 598–597 B.C., in the eleventh year of his rule, as Jeremiah had predicted (22:18–19). The Chronicler records Jehoiakim's deportation to Babylon under Nebuchadnezzar (2 Chron 36:6–7; see also Dan 1:1).

d) *Jehoiachin*. Jehoiakim was succeeded by his son Jehoiachin (also called Jeconiah and Coniah [22:24 mg., 28 mg.; 24:1 mg.]), who reigned only three months (cf. 2 Kings 24:8). But this teen-age king ruled long enough to reveal himself as a wicked monarch, whom Jeremiah strenuously denounced (22:24–30). Jehoiachin's father's rebellion against Babylon forced Nebuchadnezzar to besiege Jerusalem in 597 B.C., when Jehoiachin capitulated (2 Kings 24:12). He was exiled to Babylon with many of Judah's upper class (among them the prophet Ezekiel [Ezek 1:2]), and the temple was plundered (2 Kings 24:10–16). Jehoiachin was a prisoner in Babylon for thirty-seven years (52:31–34). He was released by Evil-Merodach, son and successor of Nebuchadnezzar (2 Kings 25:27–30). Strangely, the Jews long held a hope of his restoration to the Davidic throne; and Ezekiel refers to him, not to Zedekiah his successor, as king.

e) *Zedekiah.* Among the many accomplishments of the great Nebuchadnezzar were king making and name changing. After the exile of Jehoiachin, Nebuchadnezzar set on the Judean throne Mattaniah, a son of Josiah, full brother of Eliakim and uncle of Jehoiachin, and changed his name to Zedekiah (2 Kings 23:34; 24:17; 2 Chron 36:10; Jer 1:3), a fact confirmed by the Babylonian Chronicle. Indeed, archaeological confirmation for this period is abundant from both the Babylonian Chronicle and the Lachish Letters. Moreover, the chronology of the last quarter of the seventh century B.C. has been well illuminated by D.J. Wiseman.[3] What was the situation in Judah at the outset of Zedekiah's reign? Clearly a series of sieges and deportations with changes in rulers had depleted the small kingdom of some of its best minds. Zedekiah, weak, vacillating, deficient in personality, found it beyond him to exert effective governing leadership. A puppet of Babylon, to whose king he had sworn fealty in the name of the God of Israel, he was checkmated in every decision by the pro-Egyptian policy of his officials.

Zedekiah's relationship with Jeremiah was closer than any previous Judean king, with the probable exception of the godly Josiah. But he was powerless to protect Jeremiah from the vicious designs of the nobles and to follow the God-given counsel Jeremiah ceaselessly reiterated about submitting to Nebuchadnezzar. In the fourth year of his reign, Zedekiah had plotted rebellion against Babylon with a confederacy of the kings of Edom, Moab, Ammon, Tyre, and Sidon (27:3–11). This was their object in sending representatives to Jerusalem. The plot was denounced by Jeremiah and ultimately came to nothing. Perhaps Zedekiah's visit to Babylon that same year was intended to assure Nebuchadnezzar of his loyalty (51:59).

The end, however, was not far off. In the ninth year of his reign (588 B.C.), Zedekiah conspired with Pharaoh Hophra (Apries) against Nebuchadnezzar. Babylon responded with an invasion of Judah, which ended when the city fell in the summer of 586 B.C. (2 Kings 24:20–25:7; 2 Chron 36:17; Jer 38:28–39:10). Throughout the siege, Jeremiah urged Zedekiah to surrender (21:1–10; 34:1–5, 17–22; 37:3–10, 16–17; 38:14–23). At one point the approach of the Egyptian army compelled the withdrawal of Babylon's forces, but the siege was resumed (37:1–10). Meanwhile, because of the cowardly attitude of Zedekiah, Jeremiah was mistreated by his enemies in Judah (37:11–21; ch. 38). The destruction of Jerusalem at this time, annually observed in mourning among Jews the world over on the ninth of the month Ab, was the greatest judgment of God on Israel in the OT. Zedekiah, captured as he tried to escape, his sons slain before him, and his eyes blinded, was carried to Babylon with a company of his subjects.

After the destruction of the city and temple, the king of Babylon appointed Gedaliah governor of Judah. After a brief period (which, in the absence of evidence, could be three months or a few years), Gedaliah was murdered by a scion of the Davidic house, possibly at the instigation of pro-Egyptian sympathizers. Fearing reprisal from Babylon, the survivors of this tragedy fled to Egypt, taking Jeremiah and Baruch by force with them. So was completed a cycle begun with deliverance

---

[3]*Chronicles of Chaldean Kings (626–556 B.C.) in the British Museum* (London: British Museum, 1956).

from Pharaoh by Moses centuries before. Strange, too, that Jeremiah, who counseled throughout his ministry against confidence in Egypt, should end his earthly days there against his will. Thus an important era in the theocracy in Israel was ended. The destruction of the sanctuary at Shiloh had closed the Age of the Judges. The destruction of Solomon's temple marked the end of the period of the monarchy in Israel. The fall of the second temple by Titus (A.D. 70) was the catastrophic close of Israel's occupation of her land till modern times.

5. Literary Form and Structure

Like the origin of the book, the order or arrangement of its prophecies poses problems. No commentator, ancient or modern, has seriously posited a chronological arrangement of its prophecies. It is too much, however, to conclude that the book is a hopeless maze. A book may be arranged topically rather than chronologically. Indeed, its order may be a combination of both. The difficulty of determining which method prevails calls for close research. Even a cursory reading will show that some prophecies of Zedekiah's reign precede those of Jehoiakim's time. Though chapter 39 records the Fall of Jerusalem, the oracles of chapters 46–51 against the nations were largely delivered before the city fell. In any event, the question of the book's arrangement does not affect at all the inspiration of the text (cf. Gen 2:2 and 2:7–9; cf. also a harmony of the Gospels). The task of the commentator and student is to handle the book in its given order without being entirely occupied with rearranging the text, though observations must, of course, then be made on the chronological order. For this commentary, the chronological arrangement has, on the whole, been subordinated to considerations of subject matter. Chapters 37–44, on the other hand, are chronologically consecutive.

A suggested historical arrangement of the prophecies is as follows:

Reign of Josiah	chs. 1–6
Reign of Jehoahaz	nothing (cf. 22:10–12)
Reign of Jehoiakim	7:1–13:17; 13:20–20:18; 25–26; 35–36; 45:1–46:12; 47; 48(?); 49
Reign of Jehoiachin	13:18–19; chs. 22–23(?)
Reign of Zedekiah	chs. 21; 24; 27–34; 37–44; 46:13–28; 50–52(?)

In discussing the style of the book, many have repeated the estimate of Jerome, who felt that Jeremiah, though no less inspired than the other prophets, was more rustic (*rusticior*) in his writing. But not all students of the prophecy agree with this. The fact that Jeremiah may not attain the heights of elegance, majesty, or sublimity of Isaiah is no valid basis for disparaging or patronizing Jeremiah's style, as some have done. The leading characteristic of his style is a certain simplicity. His writing is direct, vivid, unornamented, incisive, and clear. Though not the lofty language of Isaiah, it has its own attractiveness. There is an unstudied truthfulness as the prophet's most intimate thoughts come pouring out of his anguished soul.

Prominent in Jeremiah's style is the note of sorrow. With good reason he has been called the "weeping prophet." The plight of his people never left him, and he could not respond to it dispassionately. Among his writings are some of the most tender and sympathetic passages in the Bible. When he denounces, he does so with real anguish of soul. A vein of sorrow and sadness runs throughout the book. Touch the work where you will, and it will weep (cf. 9:1).

Students of the prophecy observe Jeremiah's fondness for repetition, even triplicity. This is so both in the prose and in the poetic portions. That the prophet frequently repeats himself is understandable in view of the sameness of the message God commanded him to preach. The people kept on in the same sins, and Jeremiah did not alter the penalty God required him to pronounce against them. If his style is occasionally monotonous, it is a style that reflects the tragic mood of his message. He leaves his readers with an inescapable impression of the monotony of sin and of its inevitable judgment.

Unquestionably, Jeremiah was a reverent student of Scripture; thus he leaned heavily on earlier portions of the OT. He was familiar with the Pentateuch, especially Deuteronomy. Some sixty-six passages from Deuteronomy find an echo in Jeremiah's eighty-six references to the book (so Zunz). Jeremiah's writing shows affinities with Job and the Psalter (cf. Pss 22, 31, 35, 38, 40, 55, 69, 71, 88). Most commentators remark at length on the influence of Hosea on Jeremiah. Because of the sorrows of their lives, they have been called the martyr prophets. Though there are relationships in words and thought between Jeremiah and Hosea, these should not be overstressed. The figure of husband and wife (for the Lord and Israel) is not the sole property of Hosea; it is found more than once in Isaiah also, to say nothing of the extended allegory in Ezekiel 16.

As to form, the book contains both prose and poetry in practically equal portions. This is surprising to one who has always read the book in the KJV and ASV texts, but a glance at the prophecy in the RSV, NEB, NASB, JB, and NIV will reveal the large amount of poetry in the work (so also Isaiah and other prophets). Jeremiah's poetry is lyrical; indeed, some would call him the greatest lyrical poet of all the prophets. His poetry consists of tender elegies, full of pathos. He has been termed "the poet of the heart."[4] He uses imagery and figures with dramatic effect. He makes much use of anthropomorphisms. His similes are from everyday life: potter, almond rod, caldron, girdle, wine bottles, and others. Jeremiah also used symbols (ch. 19; 28:10; 43:8–10), symbolic actions (chs. 25, 32), visions (ch. 24), the spoken word, and the written word. Reference has already been made to his biographical notations and autobiographical material.

Lastly, even a single reading of the book will reveal the prophet's acute sensitivity to nature. An observant naturalist, he lived close to nature and used examples from it to illuminate his messages (4:23–26; 18:14; cf. also 2:23–25; 4:7, 11–13).

6. Theological Emphases

The dominant elements of Jeremiah's message are of paramount significance for his day and ours. What was it that sustained him throughout a lifetime of grief and opposition? Simply this: he had an undying confidence in God and his promises (18:7; 29:14; 32:1–15). The two focuses of his life and ministry were God—his goodness, his claims on man, his requirements of repentance and faith—and his wayward people—their welfare, physically and spiritually.

Jeremiah enjoyed a high concept of God as Lord of all creation (27:5). The gods of

---

[4]So Carl H. Cornill, *The Prophets of Israel* (Chicago: Open Court, 1897), pp. 97–99.

the nation are nonentities (10:11 [the only verse in the book in Aramaic], 14; 14:22). God knows the malady of the human heart (17:9–10); yet he loves his people deeply (31:1–3), longing to bless those who trust him (17:7). Idolatrous worship and heartless, impenitent service are alike an abomination to him (19:4–6; 14:12). No greater insult can be offered God than to represent him under the form of dead idols. Idolatry was the special sin Jeremiah tirelessly preached against. Three kinds of falsehood stirred him: (1) false security that refused all calls for repentance, (2) false prophets who lulled the people into dangerous complacency, and (3) the false worship of idols (so Overholt). Worship was tendered Baal, Moloch, and the Queen of Heaven (Ishtar). Images of these deities were even placed in the temple (32:34; cf. 7:31; 19:5; 32:35; 44:18–19).

Immorality always accompanies idolatry. In Jeremiah's time moral corruption was widespread and social injustices abounded (5:1–9; 7:1–11; 23:10–14). Priests and prophets were as culpable as the rest of Judah (6:13–15). Yet the nation carried out its religious rites. But God was not to be placated with these merely external services. Jeremiah preached that judgment was inescapable. God had already used drought, famine, and foreign invaders (14:1–6; 4:11–22); he would yet bring the culminating visitation through Nebuchadnezzar (25:9). But God's love and faithfulness to his covenants would not permit the judgment to be fatal or final. There was a future hope. Jeremiah foretold the return from captivity in Babylon (25:11; 29:10) as well as the doom of Babylon itself (chs. 50–51). He did not hesitate to give Israel's hope tangible manifestation (32:1–15).

Jeremiah also had a ministry to the nations (1:5, 10). He saw Nebuchadnezzar as God's agent in the events of that day (27:6). He warned the other nations against resisting Nebuchadnezzar (27:1–11). In God's name he demanded righteousness of all nations (chs. 46–51). He voiced God's concern for the welfare of all peoples (29:1–14, esp. v.7).

Probably the outstanding emphasis in Jeremiah's ministry was the priority of the spiritual over everything else. He saw how secondary the temporal features of Judah's faith were. He saw his coreligionists trusting (1) an outward acceptance of the covenant of the Lord (11:1–5), (2) circumcision (9:25–26), (3) the temple (7:1–15), (4) the sacrificial system (6:20; 7:21–23), (5) outward possession of the law of Moses (8:8), (6) false prophecy (23:9–40), (7) prayer (11:14; 15:1), (8) the throne (22:1–9), and (9) the ark (3:16). Jeremiah preached more about repentance than any other prophet (so Hyatt). His overarching concern at all times was the condition of the individual heart. His exposition of the new covenant is outstanding in Scripture (31:31–34). The NT shows us how deeply this truth entered into the work of our Lord.

As for the distant future, Israel will return in penitence to the Lord (32:37–40). Messiah will rule over her in justice and righteousness (23:5–8). The remnant of the nations will enjoy blessing at that time (3:17; 16:19).

As for messianic prophecy, Jeremiah does not describe messianic times in detail. Moreover, the person of the Messiah is not so prominent in his book as in Isaiah, Micah, Zechariah, or Daniel. But it does contain some significant messianic passages: (1) the proclamation of a revelation of God that will outshine the ark of the covenant (3:14–17); (2) the disclosure of a new covenant (31:31–34); (3) the realization of the Mosaic ideal (Exod 19:6) with the fulfillment of the Davidic covenant (33:14–26).

The lasting value of Jeremiah's book lies not only in the allusions (between forty and fifty of them) in the NT (over half are in Revelation) but also in its being a wonderful handbook for learning the art of having fellowship with God. Here is personal faith at its highest in the OT, a veritable gateway to understanding the deeper meaning of the priesthood and the monarchy under the Davidic dynasty (23:1–8; 33:14–18). Indeed, the abundance of bright promises for the nation in chapters 30–33 has led commentators to designate this portion The Book of Consolation. The most famous passage in Jeremiah's prophecy deals with the new covenant (31:31–34). He does not speak of personal resurrection but of the restoration of Israel.

Because Jeremiah is so unlike any other OT prophet, and because his writings are so inextricably bound up with his life and thought, the student of his prophecy must consider in depth the inner life and characteristics of this man of God, some elements of which have already been lightly touched on. Besides the features of his natural abilities, his emotions, his motivation, and his personal relationship to the Lord, there are the so-called Confessions of Jeremiah, his dialogues with the Lord, his imprecations on his enemies, and especially his prayer life. No OT prophet has disclosed more of his heart and spiritual yearnings than he. Though he was gentle and timid (but never effeminate as some have charged), because of the call and commission of God he adamantly held to his duty. He could not be swayed. No one in Judah was more patriotic; yet he never allowed himself to gloss over Judah's sin. His was a lonely and isolated life; though he longed for human fellowship and love, all his life he was denied a family and close friends. In spite of his deep love for his people, he was divinely compelled to proclaim almost monotonously their suffering and national doom. His fellowship with God was particularly deep and intimate. At times this was so frank that many modern students of his book feel he borders on the blasphemous, or at least on the irreverent.

We often forget that Jeremiah was a man of exceptional courage, unwaveringly determined to proclaim God's truth though the entire nation oppose him. Such a stance he maintained at great mental and physical cost. Imagine his agony of heart and mind when he saw his people undeviatingly headed for catastrophe, felt himself powerless to avert it, and was all the while experiencing the relentless opposition of those for whose benefit he was prophesying. These trials and temptations molded him into one of the greatest spiritual giants of all time. Because of his innate timidity, he was prone to discouragement and despair, a state in which he expressed himself so frankly in the autobiographical portions of the book. Note that the Lord gave him no signs or miracles to confirm the validity of his predictions. At one period of his life Jeremiah had decided to resign his commission (20:8–9), but the divine compulsion would not let him do it. God had promised to make him an iron pillar and a bronze wall and did not default on his word.

It was apparently quite natural for Jeremiah to carry on extended dialogues with the Lord. These dialogues are valuable principally because they show how Jeremiah (and other prophets under similar conditions) kept separate his personal consciousness and the message of God (cf. 12:1–6; 14:7–15:21).

Some expositors have expressed their horror at Jeremiah's calls for revenge on his enemies; for them this is the chief blot on his life. But these imprecations are explicable on the same basis as those in the Psalms and should be understood as involving no feeling of personal vindictiveness. Jeremiah knew he was God's messenger; therefore, those who attacked him were arraying themselves against God. Jeremiah's intense fidelity to his God and his longing for the triumph of divine righteousness show that his curses were not so much personal as uttered for the vindication of the glory of the Lord. The OT saints, moreover, had no clear revelation of future retribution (cf. Job, who pleads incessantly for vindication in this life).

Nothing is more revealing of a man of God than his prayer life. Jeremiah lived, worked, and wept in an atmosphere of prayer and openness before the Lord. He was so committed to prayer for his wayward people that God had to proscribe such activity by him (7:16; 11:14; 14:11). And he included himself in his prayers: 11:18–20; 12:1–4; 15:10, 15–18; 17:14–18; 18:19–23; 20:7–11, 14–18—passages known as the Confessions of Jeremiah. In them are the most unreserved statements of any prophet in Israel. Other prophets narrate their experiences, but the OT has few parallels to these self-disclosures. In them Jeremiah stands in all his human frailty, his love for his people, and his utter devotion to the will and call of God.

Jeremiah had faith in the Lord and in his ultimate purpose for Israel and the nations. In spite of impending disaster on Judah, he found solid ground for confidence. Through all his denunciations he saw God's final aim to bless his people, whether the remnant in the land or the exiles in Babylon (29:1–14; 32:1–15). His prophecies of Israel's restoration are among the most glowing in the Bible (3:14–18; 30:18–22; 31:1–14; 33:10–13).

Jeremiah manifested a complete frankness with God, concealing from him no emotional reaction and no fear. He even questioned the Lord's dealings with him and others (12:1; 15:10–18; 20:7). Moreover, he was able to love all men (17:7–8). He enjoyed the devotion of Baruch (36:32), the friendship of the high priest Zephaniah (29:24–32), merciful deliverance at the hands of Ebed-Melech the Ethiopian (38:7–13), and the respect of King Zedekiah (38:14–28).

Jeremiah had an intense and unrelenting hatred of sin. On whatever level of society it was committed, he rebuked it in scathing words. He scrutinized the political, social, moral, and spiritual life of the people. Prophets, priests, kings, nobles— even relatives—could expect no favoritism from him (cf. 5:1–5; 13:1–14; 23:1–4; 22:13–19).

Jeremiah displayed faith in the indestructibility of Judah, though in his day the nation was headed for judgment. Babylon was irresistible because of the purpose of God, but this never meant total extinction of the nation (30:11, 18–22; 31:35–37; 33:19–26). Though considered a traitor by his contemporaries, he had more faith in the nation's future existence than his accusers did (chs. 32 and 37; see also 25:11; 29:7–14).

7. Special Problems

Chapter 52 calls for special treatment. With the exception of conservative scholars, practically all other scholars deny Jeremiah's authorship of chapters 50 and 51 as well as chapter 52. The argument against the former chapters is that they are so diametrically opposite to all the recorded messages and ministry of Jeremiah that he could not have written them. The problem will be dealt with in the exposition. Chapters 50 and 51 are not, however, to be treated with the last chapter. Since the last chapter carries the history on to about 560 B.C., it has been denied to Jeremiah by both conservative and liberal scholars (cf. 51:64). Since chapter 52 agrees so closely with 2 Kings 24:18–25:30, in all probability it was taken from the same source as the historical account.

Often the argument for denying Jeremiah's authorship of parts of the book is based on presuppositions of the Wellhausen school, which conservative scholars do not admit here any more than they do in the Pentateuch. This denial has led to the conclusion that the text has not always been well preserved, that the versions are not always helpful, and that emendations have to be resorted to (so Bewer). On the other hand, all known Hebrew MSS of Jeremiah contain substantially the same text. It is possible to trace the MT back to the end of the first century A.D. Contemporary scholars are sure that the Hebrew text of Jeremiah is well preserved (so Bright). Some scholars deny the integrity of the Hebrew text because of its wide divergences from the Greek translation of the OT, the Septuagint (LXX), i.e., the Alexandrian version, begun in the third century B.C. and completed sometime in the second century B.C.

Anyone who has carefully researched the many phases of the LXX is bound to admit that, in spite of all his extended labors, many complex problems remain in the Greek translation of Jeremiah.[5] In Jeremiah the LXX text differs more widely from the Hebrew than in any other part of the OT. There are great differences in Job, Esther, Proverbs, and Daniel; but still greater ones are in Jeremiah. The Greek is shorter by one-eighth than the Hebrew—about twenty-seven hundred words. Moreover, the oracles against the nations (chs. 46–51) are placed after 25:13 in the LXX, with a change in sequence also. The differences are in omissions, additions, transpositions, alterations, and substitutions.[6]

The LXX is quite free and does not always grasp the meaning of the Hebrew text. Undeniably there are cases where the Greek may more correctly reflect the original text. On the whole, however, the Hebrew text is held to be much superior to the Greek. The absence of an extant definitive text for any of the ancient versions of the OT places the OT textual critic at a disadvantage. How can so many divergences be explained? Most of the omissions in the Greek seem to demand a shorter form of the Hebrew text. The discoveries of the DSS at Qumran have revealed MS fragments of both the longer and the shorter forms of the text.[7] The Hebrew MS (4QJerb) follows the shorter text appearing in the LXX. This has confirmed a tentative judgment, long held by textual critics, that there was more than one recension of the Book of Jeremiah. It best explains the existing difficulties.

8. Bibliography

There is a formidable array of extant works on the Book of Jeremiah. The bibliography below is highly selective and includes fewer than half the works consulted and used. Among them are volumes that represent various theological positions.

Books

Ball, C.J. *The Prophecies of Jeremiah*. New York: A.C. Armstrong, 1903.
Bewer, Julius A. *The Book of Jeremiah*. 2 vols. New York: Harper and Brothers, 1955.
Blank, Sheldon H. *Jeremiah: Man and Prophet*. Cincinnati: H.U.C., 1961.
Blayney, Benjamin. *Jeremiah and Lamentations*. Oxford: Clarendon, 1810.
Bright, John. *Jeremiah*. Garden City, N.Y.: Doubleday, 1965.

---

[5]So Sidney Jellicoe, *The Septuagint and Modern Study* (Oxford: Clarendon, 1968).
[6]So G.C. Workman, *The Text of Jeremiah* (Edinburgh: T. & T. Clark, 1889), pp. 18–181.
[7]So E. Lipinski, "Jeremiah," *Encyclopedia Judaica*, vol. 9 (Jerusalem: Keter, 1971), pp. 1346–59.

Broadbent, E.H. *Jeremiah*. London: Pickering and Inglis, n.d.

Calvin, John. *Commentaries on the Book of the Prophet Jeremiah*. Translated and edited by John Owen. 3 vols. Edinburgh: Calvin Translation Society, 1852.

Cheyne, Thomas K. *Jeremiah: His Life and Times*. London: Nisbet, 1888.

Clarke, Adam. *Clarke's Commentary: Jeremiah*. Vol. 4. New York: Abingdon-Cokesbury, n.d.

Cowles, Henry. *Jeremiah*. New York: D. Appleton, 1869.

Cundall, Arthur E. *Jeremiah*. Grand Rapids: Eerdmans, 1969.

Cunliffe-Jones, H. *The Book of Jeremiah*. New York: Macmillan, 1961.

Driver, S.R. *The Book of the Prophet Jeremiah*. London: Hodder & Stoughton, 1906.

Elliott-Binns, L.E. *The Book of the Prophet Jeremiah*. Westminster Commentaries. London: Methuen, 1919.

Francisco, Clyde T. *Studies in Jeremiah*. Nashville: Convention, 1961.

Freedman, H. *Jeremiah*. London: Soncino, 1961.

Frost, S.B. "The Book of Jeremiah." In *The Interpreter's One-Volume Commentary on the Bible*. Edited by C.M. Laymon. Nashville: Abingdon, 1971.

Gordon, Thomas C. *The Rebel Prophet. Studies in the Personality of Jeremiah*. New York: Harper, 1932.

Habel, Norman C. *Concordia Commentary: Jeremiah*. St. Louis: Concordia, 1968.

Harrison, R.K. *Jeremiah and Lamentations*. Downers Grove, Ill.: InterVarsity, 1973.

Henderson, E. *The Book of the Prophet Jeremiah*. Andover, Mass.: W.F. Draper, 1868.

Hyatt, James P. *Jeremiah, Prophet of Courage and Hope*. New York: Abingdon, 1958.

Jensen, Irving L. *Jeremiah, Prophet of Judgment*. Chicago: Moody, 1966.

Kinsler, F. *Inductive Study of the Book of Jeremiah*. Guatemala: Presbyterian Seminary, 1971.

Laetsch, Theodore. *Jeremiah*. St. Louis: Concordia, 1952.

Leslie, Elmer A. *Jeremiah*. Nashville: Abingdon, 1954.

Lewis, Howell E. *The Book of the Prophet Jeremiah*. London: Religious Tract Society, 1924.

Lofthouse, W.F. *Jeremiah and the New Covenant*. London: J. Clarke, 1925.

Meyer, F.B. *Jeremiah, Priest and Prophet*. London: Morgan & Scott, 1911.

Morgan, G.C. *Studies in the Prophecies of Jeremiah*. New York: Revell, 1931.

Myers, Jacob M. "The Book of Jeremiah." In *Old Testament Commentary*. Edited by H.C. Alleman and E.E. Flack. Philadelphia: Muhlenberg, 1948.

Orelli, C. von. *Prophecies of Jeremiah*. Edinburgh: T. & T. Clark, 1889.

Overholt, Thomas W. *The Threat of Falsehood: A Study in the Theology of the Book of Jeremiah*. Naperville, Ill.: A.R. Allenson, 1970.

Payne Smith, R. *Jeremiah. Speaker's Commentary*. Vol. 5. London: John Murray, 1975.

Peake, A.S. *Jeremiah*. The Century Bible. Edinburgh: T.C. and E.C. Jack, 1910.

Skinner, John. *Prophecy and Religion, Studies in the Life of Jeremiah*. Cambridge: University Press, 1922.

Smith, George A. *Jeremiah*. 4th ed. New York: Harper and Brothers, 1929.

Streane, A.W. *Jeremiah and Lamentations*. Cambridge: University Press, 1881.

Welch, A.C. *Jeremiah: His Time and His Work*. Oxford: Clarendon, 1928.

Journals

Anderson, Bernhard W. "The Lord Has Created Something New: A Stylistic Study of Jer. 31:15–22." *Catholic Biblical Quarterly* 40 (1978): 463–78.

Holladay, William L. "Jeremiah 2:34b—A Fresh Approach." *Vetus Testamentum* 25 (1975): 221–25.

———. "The Identification of the Two Scrolls of Jeremiah." *Vetus Testamentum* 30 (1980): 452–67.

Kutsch, Ernst. "Das Jahr der Katastrophe: 587 V Chr: Kritische Erwägunen zu Neueren Chronologischen Versuchen." *Biblica* 4 (1974): 520–45.

Lemche, N.P. "Manumission of Slaves—The Fallow Year—The Sabbatical Year—The Jobel Year [Jer 34:8–20]." *Vetus Testamentum* 26 (1976): 38–59.

Levenson, Jon D. "On the Promise to the Rechabites." *Catholic Biblical Quarterly* 38 (1976): 508–41.

Lindars, Barnabas. "Rachel Weeping for Her Children: Jeremiah 31:15–22." *Journal for the Study of the Old Testament* 12 (1979): 47–62.

Manahan, Ronald E. "An Interpretive Survey: Audience Reaction Quotations in Jeremiah." *Grace Theological Journal* 2 (1980): 163–83.

Rubinger, Naphtali J. "Jeremiah's Epistle to the Exiles and the Field in Anathoth." *Judaism* 26 (1977): 84–91.

Selms, Adriaan van. "Telescoped Discussion as a Literary Device in Jeremiah." *Vetus Testamentum* 26 (1976): 99–112.

Smith, Morton. "Veracity of Ezekiel, the Sins of Manasseh, and Jeremiah 44:18." *Zeitschrift für die Alttestamentliche Wissenschaft* 1 (1975): 11–16.

Wimmer, Donald H. "The Sociology of Knowledge and 'The Confessions of Jeremiah.'" *Society of Biblical Literature: Seminar Papers* 13 (1978): 393–406.

9. Outline

I. Prophecies From the Reign of Josiah (1:1–20:18)
  A. The Call and Commission of Jeremiah (1:1–19)
    1. The title (1:1–3)
    2. The call of Jeremiah (1:4–10)
    3. The vision of the almond rod (1:11–12)
    4. The vision of the boiling caldron (1:13–19)
  B. Warnings of Judgment on Judah's Sins (2:1–6:30)
    1. God's controversy with Judah (2:1–37)
        a. Israel's ingratitude (2:1–8)
        b. Israel's idolatry (2:9–19)
        c. Israel's immorality (2:20–28)
        d. Israel's irrationality (2:29–37)
    2. A call to repentance (3:1–25)
        a. Judah, the faithless wife (3:1–5)
        b. Judah worse than Israel (3:6–10)
        c. The call to return (3:11–14a)
        d. Future blessing (3:14b–18)
        e. Israel's disobedience (3:19–20)
        f. Exhortation to repentance (3:21–25)
    3. The invasion from the north (4:1–31)
        a. The call to genuine repentance (4:1–4)
        b. The enemy on the way (4:5–18)
        c. The agony of Jeremiah (4:19–22)
        d. The cosmic catastrophe (4:23–26)
        e. The desolation of the land (4:27–31)
    4. Judah's total corruption (5:1–31)
        a. The bill of particulars (5:1–9)
        b. Denial of the Lord's activity (5:10–13)
        c. The judgment described (5:14–19)
        d. Israel's willful ignorance and rebellion (5:20–31)
    5. The siege and fall of Jerusalem foretold (6:1–30)
        a. The approach of the invaders (6:1–5)
        b. The siege of Jerusalem (6:6–8)
        c. The fall of the city (6:9–15)
        d. The cause for judgment (6:16–21)
        e. The terror of the enemy forces (6:22–30)
  C. Jeremiah's Temple Address (7:1–10:25)
    1. No refuge in the temple (7:1–34)
        a. Misplaced confidence (7:1–7)
        b. Indifference to godly living (7:8–11)
        c. The example of Shiloh (7:12–15)
        d. Worship of the Queen of Heaven (7:16–20)
        e. Obedience better than sacrifice (7:21–26)
        f. Reception of Jeremiah's message (7:27–28)
        g. Lament over Judah's desolation (7:29–34)
    2. Remonstrance with Israel (8:1–22)
        a. Desecration of the graves (8:1–3)

      b. Obduracy of Israel in idolatry (8:4–7)
      c. Penalty for Judah's falsity (8:8–13)
      d. The invading army (8:14–17)
      e. The sorrow of Jeremiah (8:18–22)
  3. Sin and punishment (9:1–26)
      a. The prophet's lament (9:1–2a)
      b. The glaring sins of the day (9:2b–9)
      c. The judgment threatened (9:10–16)
      d. The universal lamentation (9:17–22)
      e. The ultimate good (9:23–24)
      f. Not privilege but morality (9:25–26)
  4. Denunciation of idolatry (10:1–25)
      a. The folly of idolatry (10:1–5)
      b. The majesty of God (10:6–16)
      c. Exile for sinning Israel (10:17–22)
      d. Prayer for the nation (10:23–25)
D. Signs to Awaken Repentance (11:1–20:18)
  1. The broken covenant (11:1–23)
      a. The violation of the covenant (11:1–13)
      b. Inadequacy of sacrifices (11:14–17)
      c. Plot against Jeremiah's life (11:18–23)
  2. Punishment and promise (12:1–17)
      a. The prosperity of the wicked (12:1–6)
      b. Punishment on the ungodly (12:7–13)
      c. Promise for the repentant nations (12:14–17)
  3. Corruption of the nation's life (13:1–27)
      a. The marred linen belt (13:1–11)
      b. The wine of God's wrath (13:12–14)
      c. Warning against pride (13:15–17)
      d. Tragedy in the royal house (13:18–19)
      e. Captivity and shame of Judah (13:20–27)
  4. Drought and impending exile (14:1–22)
      a. The critical drought (14:1–6)
      b. The confession of the nation (14:7–9)
      c. The Lord's answer in judgment (14:10–12)
      d. The doom of the false prophets (14:13–16)
      e. The grief of Jeremiah (14:17–18)
      f. Prayer of confession and plea for help (14:19–22)
  5. Impending judgment and Jeremiah's complaints (15:1–21)
      a. Prayer unavailing for Judah (15:1)
      b. The punishment determined (15:2–9)
      c. Jeremiah's complaint (15:10–11)
      d. The inevitable judgment (15:12–14)
      e. Jeremiah's charge against the Lord (15:15–18)
      f. God's rebuke and encouragement (15:19–21)
  6. Bane and blessing (16:1–21)
      a. The loneliness of Jeremiah (16:1–9)
      b. The cause of the judgment (16:10–13)

       c. Restoration to the land (16:14–15)
       d. Complete retribution (16:16–18)
       e. The nations in blessing (16:19–20)
       f. The goal of the punishment (16:21)
   7. Man's deceitful heart (17:1–27)
       a. Israel's ineradicable sin (17:1–4)
       b. The way of cursing and blessing (17:5–8)
       c. Humanity's desperate heart condition (17:9–13)
       d. Jeremiah's plea for vindication (17:14–18)
       e. Sabbath observance (17:19–27)
   8. The parable of the potter (18:1–23)
       a. The message of the potter (18:1–12)
       b. The fickleness of Judah (18:13–17)
       c. The plot against Jeremiah (18:18–23)
   9. The destruction of Jerusalem (19:1–15)
       a. The clay jar at Hinnom (19:1–5a)
       b. The imminent calamity (19:5b–9)
       c. The destruction of Judah (19:10–13)
       d. The message summarized (19:14–15)
 10. The lament of Jeremiah (20:1–18)
       a. Pashhur's persecution of Jeremiah (20:1–6)
       b. Jeremiah's inescapable call (20:7–10)
       c. Prayer for God's vindication (20:11–13)
       d. Jeremiah's curse on the day of his birth (20:14–18)

II. Prophecies From the Reigns of Jehoiakim and Zedekiah
   (21:1–39:18)
   A. The Trials and Conflicts of Jeremiah (21:1–29:32)
      1. Zedekiah's dilemma (21:1–14)
         a. The embassy from Zedekiah (21:1–7)
         b. The choice of ways (21:8–10)
         c. Exhortation to the Davidic dynasty (21:11–14)
      2. Messages to the Davidic kings (22:1–30)
         a. Exhortation to justice (22:1–9)
         b. The fate of Shallum (Jehoahaz) (22:10–12)
         c. The condemnation of Jehoiakim (22:13–23)
         d. The rejection of Coniah (Jehoiachin) (22:24–30)
      3. Messiah the King (23:1–40)
         a. Godless leaders versus David's Righteous Branch
           (23:1–8)
         b. Condemnation of the false prophets (23:9–12)
         c. False prophecy in Samaria and Jerusalem (23:13–15)
         d. Characteristics of lying prophecy (23:16–22)
         e. Lying versus true prophets (23:23–32)
         f. The burden of the Lord (23:33–40)
      4. The good and the bad figs (24:1–10)
         a. The vision of the baskets of figs (24:1–3)
         b. The explanation of the good figs (24:4–7)
         c. The meaning of the bad figs (24:8–10)

5. Prophecy of the Babylonian captivity (25:1–38)
   a. Israel's rejection of the prophetic ministry (25:1–7)
   b. Prediction of the Exile (25:8–11)
   c. Judgment on Babylon (25:12–14)
   d. The cup of God's wrath (25:15–29)
   e. Judgment on all the world (25:30–38)
6. Consequences of the temple address (26:1–24)
   a. The temple address (26:1–6)
   b. The arrest, trial, and condemnation of Jeremiah (26:7–11)
   c. Jeremiah's defense (26:12–15)
   d. The release of Jeremiah (26:16–19)
   e. The murder of Uriah (26:20–24)
7. The yoke of Babylon (27:1–22)
   a. The message to the ambassadors (27:1–11)
   b. The address to King Zedekiah (27:12–15)
   c. The warning to the priests and people (27:16–22)
8. Hananiah against Jeremiah (28:1–17)
   a. Hananiah's contradiction of Jeremiah (28:1–4)
   b. Jeremiah's appeal to the past (28:5–9)
   c. Hananiah's response (28:10–11)
   d. Jeremiah's stronger pronouncement (28:12–14)
   e. Prediction of Hananiah's death (28:15–17)
9. Jeremiah's letters to the exiles (29:1–32)
   a. Introduction (29:1–3)
   b. The letter of Jeremiah (29:4–19)
      1) Warning against false prophets (29:4–9)
      2) The seventy-year exile (29:10–14)
      3) A "second letter" of Jeremiah (29:15–19)
   c. Denunciation of the false prophets Ahab and Zedekiah (29:20–23)
   d. Condemnation of Shemaiah (29:24–32)
B. The Book of Consolation (30:1–33:26)
   1. Trial and triumph for Israel (30:1–24)
      a. Return from captivity (30:1–3)
      b. "The time of Jacob's trouble" (30:4–7)
      c. Freedom from bondage to oppressors (30:8–11)
      d. Israel's wounds healed (30:12–17)
      e. Rebuilt Jerusalem and her ruler (30:18–22)
      f. Judgment then blessing (30:23–24)
   2. The new covenant (31:1–40)
      a. God's mercy for Ephraim (31:1–6)
      b. The restoration of Israel in joy (31:7–14)
      c. Israel's lamentable present (31:15–22)
      d. Judah's bright future (31:23–26)
      e. National increase under Messiah (31:27–30)
      f. God's new covenant (31:31–34)
      g. The perpetuity of Israel (31:35–40)

3. The manifestation of faith (32:1–44)
   a. The setting for Jeremiah's act of faith (32:1–5)
   b. The Lord's command (32:6–8)
   c. The purchase (32:9–15)
   d. Jeremiah's doubts and prayer (32:16–25)
   e. The Lord's answer (32:26–35)
   f. Promises of restoration (32:36–44)
4. The righteous reign of the Davidic Ruler (33:1–26)
   a. The exhortation to call on the Lord (33:1–3)
   b. The certainty of the Fall of Jerusalem (33:4–5)
   c. Days of return and rejoicing (33:6–13)
   d. Restoration of royalty and priesthood (33:14–22)
   e. Confirmation of the promises (33:23–26)
C. Messages and Events Before the Fall of Jerusalem
   (34:1–39:18)
1. Zedekiah and the mistreated slaves (34:1–22)
   a. The warning to Zedekiah (34:1–7)
   b. The perfidy against the slaves (34:8–11)
   c. The sin of the nation (34:12–16)
   d. The Lord's retribution for the perfidy (34:17–22)
2. The faithfulness of the Recabites (35:1–19)
   a. Jeremiah's test of the Recabites (35:1–5)
   b. The Recabites' loyalty to Jonadab (35:6–11)
   c. The rebuke to Judah (35:12–17)
   d. The Recabites' reward (35:18–19)
3. Jehoiakim's penknife and God's Word (36:1–32)
   a. The dictation of the scroll (36:1–8)
   b. The public reading (36:9–10)
   c. The reading to the officials (36:11–19)
   d. The reading to Jehoiakim (36:20–26)
   e. The prophecies rewritten (36:27–28)
   f. The condemnation of Jehoiakim (36:29–31)
   g. The prophecies recorded again (36:32)
4. Resolute Jeremiah and weak Zedekiah (37:1–21)
   a. Zedekiah's request (37:1–5)
   b. Jeremiah's reply (37:6–10)
   c. The charge of treason against Jeremiah (37:11–15)
   d. Jeremiah in the dungeon (37:16–21)
5. Confined in a cistern (38:1–13)
   a. The accusation against Jeremiah (38:1–4)
   b. Jeremiah in the cistern (38:5–6)
   c. The rescue of Jeremiah (38:7–13)
6. Counsel to the king (38:14–28)
   a. Zedekiah's secret interview with Jeremiah
      (38:14–23)
   b. The officials' inquiry (38:24–28)
7. The Fall of Jerusalem (39:1–18)
   a. The capture of the city (39:1–3)

   b. The fate of Zedekiah (39:4–8)
   c. The release of Jeremiah (39:9–14)
   d. The commendation of Ebed-Melech (39:15–18)
III. Ministry of Jeremiah After the Fall of Jerusalem (40:1–45:5)
   A. Ministry to the Survivors in Judah (40:1–42:22)
      1. Gedaliah the governor (40:1–16)
         a. The release of Jeremiah (40:1–6)
         b. Gedaliah's assurances (40:7–10)
         c. The return of the fugitives (40:11–12)
         d. The warning of Gedaliah (40:13–16)
      2. The atrocities of Ishmael and the flight to Egypt (41:1–18)
         a. The assassination of Gedaliah (41:1–3)
         b. The massacre of the pilgrims (41:4–10)
         c. The escape of Ishmael (41:11–15)
         d. The flight to Egypt (41:16–18)
      3. Warning against going to Egypt (42:1–22)
         a. The inquiry of the remnant (42:1–6)
         b. The Lord's answer to Jeremiah's question (42:7–17)
         c. Further penalties for settling in Egypt (42:18–22)
   B. Ministry in Egypt (43:1–44:30)
      1. The flight to Egypt (43:1–13)
         a. The warning flouted (43:1–7)
         b. Jeremiah's prophecy in Egypt (43:8–13)
      2. Condemnation of Ishtar worship (44:1–30)
         a. Exhortation to heed past experience (44:1–10)
         b. Warning of punishment (44:11–14)
         c. The stubborn persistence in idolatry (44:15–19)
         d. Condemnation of the remnant's stubbornness (44:20–30)
   C. The Message to Baruch (45:1–5)
      1. Baruch's complaint (45:1–3)
      2. The response of the Lord (45:4–5)

IV. Prophecies Concerning the Nations (46:1–51:64)
   Caption for the Prophecies Against the Nations (46:1)
   A. Concerning Egypt (46:2–28)
      1. The defeat of the Egyptian army (46:2–6)
      2. The humbling of Egypt's pride (46:7–12)
      3. The coming of Nebuchadnezzar (46:13–19)
      4. The Fall of Egypt (46:20–26)
      5. Blessing on Jacob (46:27–28)
   B. Concerning Philistia (47:1–7)
   C. Concerning Moab (48:1–47)
      1. Desolation of the Moabite cities (48:1–10)
      2. The proud complacency of Moab (48:11–19)
      3. The downfall of Moab (48:20–28)
      4. The pride of Moab (48:29–39)
      5. The terror caused by the invader (48:40–47)

D. Concerning Ammon (49:1–6)
E. Concerning Edom (49:7–22)
F. Concerning Damascus (49:23–27)
G. Concerning Kedar and Hazor (49:28–33)
H. Concerning Elam (49:34–39)
I. Concerning Babylon (50:1–51:64)
   1. Babylon's doom announced (50:1–10)
   2. Babylon's sin and judgment (50:11–16)
   3. Consolation to Israel (50:17–20)
   4. God's vengeance on Babylon (50:21–28)
   5. Babylon's arrogance (50:29–32)
   6. Israel's Kinsman-Redeemer (50:33–40)
   7. The permanence of Babylon's doom (50:41–46)
   8. The Lord's vengeance on Babylon (51:1–14)
   9. The omnipotent Lord and impotent idols (51:15–26)
  10. The nations summoned (51:27–33)
  11. Babylon's defenses useless (51:34–44)
  12. Warning to Israel to flee Babylon (51:45–48)
  13. The certainty of Babylon's fall (51:49–53)
  14. The completeness of Babylon's destruction (51:54–58)
  15. The mission of Seraiah (51:59–64)
V. Historical Supplement (52:1–34)
A. The Fall of Jerusalem (52:1–11)
B. Results of the Fall (52:12–27a)
C. Nebuchadnezzar's Captives (52:27b–30)
D. Evil-Merodach's Kindness to Jehoiachin (52:31–34)

Text and Exposition

I. Prophecies From the Reign of Josiah (1:1–20:18)

A. *The Call and Commission of Jeremiah* (1:1–19)

1. *The title*

1:1–3

> ¹The words of Jeremiah son of Hilkiah, one of the priests at Anathoth in the territory of Benjamin. ²The word of the LORD came to him in the thirteenth year of the reign of Josiah son of Amon king of Judah, ³and through the reign of Jehoiakim son of Josiah king of Judah, down to the fifth month of the eleventh year of Zedekiah son of Josiah king of Judah, when the people of Jerusalem went into exile.

1–2 These verses serve as the title for the entire book. They name the man through whom God gave the prophecies and refer to his home (v.1), the period of his main labors, and the chief national event of his times (v.2). The more usual formula for the title of a prophecy is "the word of the LORD." Here the term "words" (*dᵉbārîm*) has a connotation broad enough to include both the prophecies and the events of Jeremiah's life. The more usual expression follows in v.2. Jeremiah was a priest by birth but a prophet by calling. The territory of Benjamin bordered Judah on the south, Ephraim on the north. The tribe of Benjamin gave Israel its first king (Saul) and the great apostle to the Gentiles (Paul). The date indicated in v.2 is not that of Jeremiah's birth, as a few have surmised, but of his call to service, namely, 626 B.C. (cf. 25:3 for confirmation). The call of God came five years before the important reforms of Josiah (2 Kings 22–23).

3 The terminus of Jeremiah's ministry omits the events after the Fall of Jerusalem because most of his ministry had already been completed. The reason the names of Jehoahaz and Jehoiachin are omitted is probably that their reigns lasted so short a time (three months each). Here, then, in Jeremiah's ministry was a service for God of more than two decades and possibly half a century. The Exile to Babylon occurred in the fifth month (Ab) of 586 B.C. (2 Kings 25:4–10).

Notes

1 The name "Jeremiah" (יִרְמְיָה [*yirmᵉyāh*] and the longer form יִרְמְיָהוּ [*yirmᵉyāhu*]) is an imperfect from either the root רָמָה (*rāmāh*, "to hurl") or רוּם (*rum*, "to be high"; causative, "to exalt") with a theophorous ending. It is not an unusual name in the OT; it appears in 2 Kings 23:31; 1 Chron 5:24; 12:4, 10, 13; Neh 10:2; 12:1, 12; Jer 35:3; 52:1, besides the many references to the prophet. It also appears in Lachish Letter 1 (Harry Torczyner et al., *The Lachish Letters* [London: Oxford University Press, 1938], p. 27) and on a seal discovered at Beth Shemesh (Elihu Grant and G. Ernest Wright, *Ain Shems Excavations* V [Haverford: Haverford College, 1939], p. 80).

2. *The call of Jeremiah*

1:4–10

4The word of the LORD came to me, saying,

5"Before I formed you in the womb I knew you,
before you were born I set you apart;
I appointed you as a prophet to the nations."

6"Ah, Sovereign LORD," I said, "I do not know how to speak; I am only a child."
7But the LORD said to me, "Do not say, 'I am only a child.' You must go to everyone I send you to and say whatever I command you. 8Do not be afraid of them, for I am with you and will rescue you," declares the LORD.
9Then the LORD reached out his hand and touched my mouth and said to me, "Now, I have put my words in your mouth. 10See, today I appoint you over nations and kingdoms to uproot and tear down, to destroy and overthrow, to build and to plant."

4 Though brief, this verse is the heart of the prophetic experience. Jeremiah's call came not in a vision but by hearing the divine word. Unless the verse denotes inspiration by God, words are meaningless. Compare Jeremiah's call with that of Amos (Amos 7:10–17); contrast it with that of Isaiah (Isa 6) and Ezekiel (Ezek 1:1–2:8).

5 In order for Jeremiah to know that his commission was by divine decree, the Lord explained his motivation in accomplishing his purpose through him. Observe the four actions of God toward his prophet: God knew, formed, consecrated, and appointed him. It was indeed encouraging for Jeremiah to know that God had specifically equipped him to carry out his commission. The knowing was not mere cognition but a sense of relationship (Amos 3:2) and approval (Ps 1:6). God's claim on his life was prior to all other relationships, as with the Servant of the Lord (Isa 49:1–5), the psalmist (Ps 139:13–16), and Paul (Gal 1:15). Jeremiah's consecration was his being set apart for a definite spiritual purpose. Here is a biblical coupling of God's foreknowledge and his sanctifying his servant. The emphasis is on the divine initiative and sovereign choice. In this respect Jeremiah was appointed a prophet for a world-wide ministry. This refutes the idea that the work of God's servants was always provincial (cf. 25:15–29; chs. 46–51). God is the Lord of the nations. Jeremiah's service, unlike that of Moses, Elijah, and Elisha, was similar to that of Isaiah, Ezekiel, Amos, and others who spoke oracles to various nations.

6 Jeremiah, struck with terror over the magnitude of the task, pled his youth and inexperience (cf. Moses [Exod 4:10]). The Hebrew word for "child" does not connote a precise definition of age, but we may infer from the length of his ministry that Jeremiah must have been about twenty at the time of his call. He patently did not seek the office on his own. Realizing that ability in public speaking was essential to the prophetic office, he stated his lack of eloquence. But what God required for Jeremiah's ministry, which was to be so sad and denunciatory, was a tender heart able to sympathize with the condemned. Little could the young man know how difficult, hopeless, and heartbreaking his task would be.

7–8 God never makes a mistake in choosing his servants (v.7). He empowers all he calls and provides the encouragement and help they need. Moreover, God's promise of his presence would dispel Jeremiah's fear, another source of his hesitation (v.8). He would be mercilessly opposed and persecuted, but the Lord would preserve him from the attacks of his enemies and give him the moral courage he would so greatly need.

9 As tangible evidence that he had empowered Jeremiah, in a spiritual experience God touched Jeremiah's mouth. Thus he was inspired to speak God's truth, and thus the impartation of the divine message was indicated to him. From then on Jeremiah's words would be truly God's, and he would actually become a mouthpiece for God (cf. Isa 6:7).

10 Now follows the content of Jeremiah's message in one of the most important passages in the book. The purposes of God in Jeremiah's ministry are twofold: destructive and constructive. God's word is accompanied with power so that the prophet will accomplish these objectives (Isa 55:10–11). For Jeremiah's ministry, the emphasis is undoubtedly on its destructive element; four verbs are used to express this, whereas two verbs indicate its constructive and restorative element. God's appointment brings with it his commitment of authority to carry out his goals for his prophet.

Notes

---

5 The noun נָבִיא (*nābî*, "prophet") occurs over three hundred times in the OT. It is said to be related to the Akkadian *nabū* ("to call," "to appoint"). Thus the term, with its passive force, denotes one who is called, appointed (so Albright, KB et al.).

The root of the verb "formed" (יָצַר, *yāṣar*) means "to shape," as a potter does to clay (cf. the creation of Adam [Gen 2:7–8]).

6 The word נַעַר (*naʿar*) is rendered "child" in KJV, RV, ASV, NEB, JB, and NIV. In English this translation can be misleading. It has been translated "youth" in AmT, RSV, and NASB. It is true that the Hebrew word can mean "child" (cf. Moses in the ark of bulrushes [Exod 2:6]). But it also means "young man" (cf. the men in Abraham's army [Gen 14:24]). It is used of Absalom at the time of his rebellion (2 Sam 18:5). The meaning also appears to be that concept of relative age—i.e., youthful. LXX is noncommittal, rendering it νεώτερος (*neōteros*, "too young"; cf. TDNT, 4:897).

---

3. The vision of the almond rod

1:11–12

> [11]The word of the LORD came to me: "What do you see, Jeremiah?"
> "I see the branch of an almond tree," I replied.
> [12]The LORD said to me, "You have seen correctly, for I am watching to see that my word is fulfilled."

11–12 Two visions were granted Jeremiah evidently to authenticate his call. They were probably shown to him shortly after his call. Both visions are uncomplicated and are explained; both relate to judgment. The first vision was that of an almond tree (v.11), which blossoms in January when other trees are still dormant. It is a harbinger of spring, as though it watches over the beginning of the season. So the Lord is watching to bring judgment on Israel's sins. What former prophets had said would come, was about to happen. Judgment was imminent. God was prepared to act because he was aware of world conditions. The "branch" (*maqqēl*) symbolizes judgment here, which was soon to overtake Israel (cf. Mic 6:9). God keeps his word promptly and works toward an early fulfillment (v.12). Notice this early use of nature by Jeremiah.

Notes

11–12 These verses contain a play on words (paronomasia) that is lost in English but is vital for the force of the vision. The "almond tree" is שָׁקֵד (*šāqēd*) and God is "watching" (*šōqēd*) over his word to fulfill it.

4. *The vision of the boiling caldron*

1:13–19

13The word of the LORD came to me again: "What do you see?"

"I see a boiling pot, tilting away from the north," I answered.

14The LORD said to me, "From the north disaster will be poured out on all who live in the land. 15I am about to summon all the peoples of the northern kingdoms," declares the LORD.

"Their kings will come and set up their thrones
in the entrance of the gates of Jerusalem;
they will come against all her surrounding walls
and against all the towns of Judah.
16I will pronounce my judgments on my people
because of their wickedness in forsaking me,
in burning incense to other gods
and in worshiping what their hands have made.

17"Get yourself ready! Stand up and say to them whatever I command you. Do not be terrified by them, or I will terrify you before them. 18Today I have made you a fortified city, an iron pillar and a bronze wall to stand against the whole land—against the kings of Judah, its officials, its priests and the people of the land. 19They will fight against you but will not overcome you, for I am with you and will rescue you," declares the LORD.

13–14 The word "again" (*šēnît*, lit., "a second time") shows that the visions are closely related (v.13). The first deals with the time of the judgment; the second, with the direction and nature of the coming disaster. A "boiling pot" can only signify calamity. It is not stated that the pot was facing toward the north but that it was "tilting away from the north," that is, facing toward the south, where its contents would be poured out. It would strike from Babylon. Though Babylon is located east of Judah, her armies—and all invading armies from Asia—would invade Palestine from the north because of the impassable Arabian desert. The first declaration of disaster in the book is found in v.14. It will engulf the entire land of Judah. The invasion will issue in victory for the enemy.

15–16 The "northern kingdoms" (v.15) mentioned suit a Babylonian invasion under Nebuchadnezzar rather than a Scythian invasion (cf. Introduction: Date and Authorship). The setting up of the thrones at the gates of Jerusalem, the place of public business, implies complete subjugation. (The fulfillment is recorded in 39:3.) Thus from the outset of his ministry Jeremiah is a preacher of judgment. As Isaiah speaks of the salvation of the Lord, Ezekiel of the glory of the Lord, and Daniel of the kingdom of the Lord, so Jeremiah incessantly proclaims the Lord's judgment (v.16). The cause of Judah's punishment is stated in three clauses, which describe her idolatry.

17–19 In the remainder of the chapter, Jeremiah is given strong encouragement for his hard task (v.17), because his message would be neither welcome nor popular with his people. To fulfill his duties nothing less than utter commitment to God and to his strength would suffice. With God, Jeremiah would be invincible (v.19). In his darkest hours these words sustained him mentally, emotionally, and spiritually. He is commanded to prepare vigorously for action. He would need to rely on a triple defense (v.18) against his fourfold enemy. Kings, officials, priests, and people—all opposed him at one time or another. Who loves a preacher of judgment (cf. 2 Tim 4:3–4)? The secret of spiritual victory is given in v.19. Jeremiah is assured success on the condition of faith in God. He ultimately prevailed over all his enemies; and his prophecies were verified, attesting him to be a true prophet of the Lord.

Notes

14–15 A strange view has been propounded by Welch (pp. 97–131, esp. 129–31), that the OT references to the foe from the north are not to a historical person but have universal and apocalyptic overtones, referring actually to the Antichrist.

B. *Warnings of Judgment on Judah's Sins* (2:1–6:30)

There is general agreement that chapters 2–6 form a connected message, coming probably from Josiah's reign and in the early years of Jeremiah's ministry (3:6). They show at once how little it was in Jeremiah's mind to excuse Judah's sin. The major themes in these five chapters are (1) God's indignation against moral and social sin, (2) his love for his people and land, (3) the certainty of doom on the unrepentant nation, and (4) salvation for the believing.

1. *God's controversy with Judah* (2:1–37)

No sooner had Jeremiah been appointed to the prophetic office than the Lord's message of condemnation began to sound out in Judah. It reminds one of Isaiah's great arraignment of the nation (Isa 1) more than a century before. The focal emphases in this chapter are (1) the sacred love of God for his people and (2) their love of idols.

a. *Israel's ingratitude*

2:1–8

¹The word of the LORD came to me: ²"Go and proclaim in the hearing of Jerusalem:

" 'I remember the devotion of your youth,
how as a bride you loved me
and followed me through the desert,
through a land not sown.
³Israel was holy to the LORD,
the firstfruits of his harvest;
all who devoured her were held guilty,
and disaster overtook them,' "

declares the LORD.

⁴Hear the word of the LORD, O house of Jacob,
all you clans of the house of Israel.

⁵This is what the LORD says:

"What fault did your fathers find in me,
that they strayed so far from me?
They followed worthless idols
and became worthless themselves.
⁶They did not ask, 'Where is the LORD,
who brought us up out of Egypt
and led us through the barren wilderness,
through a land of deserts and rifts,
a land of drought and darkness,
a land where no one travels and no one lives?'
⁷I brought you into a fertile land
to eat its fruit and rich produce.
But you came and defiled my land
and made my inheritance detestable.
⁸The priests did not ask,
'Where is the LORD?'
Those who deal with the law did not know me;
the leaders rebelled against me.
The prophets prophesied by Baal,
following worthless idols."

1–2 In order to show the nation how far the people had departed from the Lord, Jeremiah reminds them of the time of their deliverance from Egypt. Like a devoted bridegroom, the Lord informs them he still remembers their love as his true bride (v.2). The imagery is that of Hosea 1–3. Some writers believe this verse refers to God's love for Israel. If so, this is a strange way of expressing it; the text is stating what it is in his people that God recalls. It is true that the word for "devotion" (*ḥesed*, "kindness") is not usually employed of man's attitude toward God, but there is an extension of meaning here because of the marriage figure and the concept of reciprocity (cf. Isa 54:5). Proof that Jeremiah is speaking of Israel's love for God is shown by her following him in the wilderness at the time of their marriage, the

387

period of her faithfulness and devotion to the Lord. Warmth, love, and purity marked her first relationship with her covenant God. Apart from the golden-calf incident (Exod 32:1–29), Israel's failures in the wilderness came from lack of faith rather than outright apostasy.

3 The earliest bond between God and Israel was not only a fragrant remembrance to him but also a sad contrast to her deep plunge into apostasy. In those early favored days, Israel was set apart as sacred to God, his very firstfruits, because she was the first nation to worship the true God (cf. Exod 19:5–6; Amos 6:1). The firstfruits were the portion of the harvest that belonged to God, and this could not be eaten by the people. Only the priest and his family were allowed to eat the firstfruits. No strangers could do so (Lev 22:10, 16).

Verse 3b means that no nation was to trouble Israel because she was dedicated to the Lord. To disobey this prohibition was to incur the wrath of God as in the unauthorized eating of firstfruits.

4–5 Because of the covenant relationship, Israel was and still is under divine protection (v.4; cf. Gen 12:1–3). But what happened to that beautiful union between the Lord and his people? The answer is now addressed to the entire nation. The strange question in v.5 is intended to awaken the people's consciences. Its only logical answer is that the change in relationship of Israel to God was not his fault but theirs. They had broken the marriage covenant by their infidelity in going after impure lovers. A play on words in v.5b (*hebel* ["vanity," "worthlessness"] with *yehbālû* ["became vain, worthless"]) reveals how worshipers become like the objects they worship. The translations "empty," "vain," or "worthless" correctly convey the idea that the Lord regards idols as without substance or reality (cf. 1 Kings 16:13; 1 Cor 8:4). Jeremiah levels as scathing denunciations against idols as any prophet; idolatry was Israel's chief and besetting sin. In a sense Jeremiah's whole book is an elaboration of what 1:16 says of this sin. Near-Eastern treaties show that *hᵃlōḵ 'aḥᵃrê* (Heb., "to walk after"; NIV, "followed") meant "to serve as a vassal" (cf. IOT, pp. 24–26). How base was the ingratitude of the Lord's favored nation!

6–7 Again and again Scripture demonstrates that to be thoughtless is to be thankless (cf. Ps 103:1–2). Israel's attention is directed to the multiplicity of benefits the nation enjoyed at God's hand; yet the people were unmindful of his presence in their midst (v.6). They had forgotten the wilderness experiences and the dangers the Lord had graciously brought them through. They were brought to a "fertile land" (v.7), literally, "a land of Carmel," a Carmel land, one well cultivated and productive. But how did the people respond? By their idolatry and immoral practices they defiled God's land. Although God gave Israel the land, he has never relinquished his own ultimate ownership of it. In the truest sense, the land was a stewardship to Israel from the Lord.

8 What part did the leaders of the nation play in Judah's departure from God? Could they not have stemmed the tide? Unfortunately, the leaders are included in the indictment. They misled the people. Jeremiah singles out three (or four) groups of leaders as being directly responsible for Judah's spiritual defection. God had set apart the priests and Levites to teach the people his will recorded in Scripture. The tribe of Levi was entrusted with this task (Deut 33:10; Mal 2:7). Instead, the priests were wholly indifferent to God and to his will. Because they dealt with the law, the priests and Levites had well-prescribed regulations for the life of the nation. But in Jeremiah's time they acted as if they did not know the Lord at all.

What of the civil authorities? They were no better. The "leaders" (Heb., "shepherds")—i.e., temporal rulers, kings—were adept in violating the law of God. In the ancient Orient, the title "shepherd" was current for rulers (so often in the Bible, e.g., 23:4). The prophets were probably the most culpable. Their high duty was to proclaim the will of God and bring the sinful people back to the Lord. They were some of Jeremiah's worst enemies. The priests and prophets were a particular grief to him because he was a priest by birth and a prophet by calling. It was his lifelong trial to incur the persistent enmity of both groups. The false prophets, instead of speaking by God's empowerment, spoke for Baal. The reference to Baal here and elsewhere in the prophecy is to idols in general. Properly speaking, Baal (meaning "lord" or "master"), whose personal name was Hadad, was the chief male object of Canaanite (Phoenician) worship. As a nature god, he was the master of storm and fertility; his worship was cruel, degenerate, and unconcerned for human life. Idolatry is always worthless, devoid of any objective reality. In the Hebrew there is an indirect play on words, "worthless" (lō'-yôʿilû, "do not profit") approximating Belial (beliyaʿal, i.e., "without profit").

Notes

2 One of the most meaningful terms in the OT is חֶסֶד (ḥeseḏ), translated variously as "kindness" (KJV, ASV), "affection" (JB, JPS), "devotion" (NASB, NEB, RSV, NIV), and ἔλεος (eleos in LXX, meaning "mercy"). It has been defined as "the self-devoting, nestling love of Israel to its God" (KD). Too often it has been pressed into a rigid legal view in connection with a fixed covenant. It must remain more free and spontaneous (TDNT, 9:381–82), being related to χάρις (charis, "grace").

3 "Firstfruits" is an important OT and NT doctrine. The usual Hebrew word is בִּכּוּרִים (bikkûrîm); the one used here is רֵאשִׁית (rēʾšît), meaning "beginning," "chief." For Israel it signifies that she was God's chosen nation to bring blessing to all other nations (Exod 4:22). In the NT the church is now a firstfruit for blessing to the nations (James 1:18). The concept is extended to include Christ as the firstfruits in resurrection (1 Cor 15:20), since he is the pattern of the resurrection of the godly.

b. *Israel's idolatry*

2:9–19

9"Therefore I bring charges against you again,"
                                            declares the LORD.
"And I will bring charges against your children's children.
10Cross over to the coasts of Kittim and look,
    send to Kedar and observe closely;
    see if there has ever been anything like this:
11Has a nation ever changed its gods?
    (Yet they are not gods at all.)
But my people have exchanged their Glory
    for worthless idols.

¹²Be appalled at this, O heavens,
  and shudder with great horror,"

                                      declares the LORD.

¹³"My people have committed two sins:
  They have forsaken me,
    the spring of living water,
  and have dug their own cisterns,
    broken cisterns that cannot hold water.
¹⁴Is Israel a servant, a slave by birth?
  Why then has he become plunder?
¹⁵Lions have roared;
  they have growled at him.
  They have laid waste his land;
    his towns are burned and deserted.
¹⁶Also, the men of Memphis and Tahpanhes
  have shaved the crown of your head.
¹⁷Have you not brought this on yourselves
  by forsaking the LORD your God
  when he led you in the way?
¹⁸Now why go to Egypt
  to drink water from the Shihor?
And why go to Assyria
  to drink water from the River?
¹⁹Your wickedness will punish you;
  your backsliding will rebuke you.
Consider then and realize
  how evil and bitter it is for you
when you forsake the LORD your God
  and have no awe of me,"
                  declares the Lord, the LORD Almighty.

9–12 Having shown clearly the nation's deep ingratitude, Jeremiah now presents the Lord's expostulation with his people under the figure of a court case. "Bring charges" (v.9) is a legal term for a plaintiff's (in this instance, God) introducing his case in court (*rîḇ;* cf. Job 33:13; Isa 3:13; 49:25). The subject of the controversy is Judah's unparalleled idolatry. Because there is a moral continuity in the nation, the people and their children are included. The heart of the contention is clearly stated (vv.10–11). God's people have forsaken their living and true God, whereas even nations with nature gods, actually nonentities, stay loyal to their worthless deities. So Judah is exhorted to investigate from Kittim to Kedar to verify the indictment. Kittim, the Phoenician town Kition in Cyprus (modern Larnaca), gave its name to the whole island; then by extension the name was used for the islands and coasts of the west (cf. Gen 10:4; Ezek 27:6 mg.). Kedar was the name of an Arab desert tribe; then it came to represent people of the eastern desert (Gen 25:13). Thus the nation is urged to observe conditions from west to east, in short, anywhere.

Mark the horror and amazement of the prophet at the enormity of Judah's apostasy (v.11)! The people have acted more faithlessly than the pagans. God has not changed, but Judah has—and for what? The Lord himself was her glory (Ps 106:20; Rom 1:23). So incredible has this apostasy been that nature is called on to react to it (v.12). The heavens themselves are summoned as a witness in the Lord's litigation against his people (cf. Deut 32:1; Isa 1:2). Again Jeremiah uses a play on words—this time in his apostrophe to the heavens (*šōmmû šāmayim,* "Be astonished, O heavens"). Because inanimate nature so consistently obeys God's commands, it is pictured as astounded at Judah's actions. To heighten the effect, Jeremiah uses three strong verbs—*šōmmû* ("Be astonished"; NIV, "Be appalled"), *śā'ărû* ("Be agitated"), *ḥārbû* ("Be devastated"; NIV idiomatically renders the last two verbs "shudder with great horror").

13 Like a lawyer, Jeremiah summarizes his charges: Judah's sin was compounded by rejection of truth and reception of error. The pagan nations had committed the one sin of idolatry, often exchanging one superstition for another. But Judah had exceeded them in disobedience in renouncing her own real God to serve nobodies. Jeremiah's figures are singularly vivid and apt. His nation's God is called the "spring of living water," the source of life (cf. Ps 36:9)—a metaphor often used in Scripture of God, salvation, and Christ (cf. Isa 12:3; 55:1; John 4:10–14; 7:37–39). Water was a rare luxury in Palestine, and water from perennial sources was cherished. On the other hand, cisterns, though needed and used because of seasons of insufficient supply, could only store rain water. The thousands of them uncovered in archaeological digs attest their importance. At best, cisterns often yielded stagnant water; at worst, they cracked and allowed the water to seep out. Dead gods cannot impart life.

14 Sin inevitably brings its own punishment, and to this fact Jeremiah now turns. By two forceful questions the Lord points out the consequences of disobedience. What a strong contrast with the early condition of Israel set forth in v.3! A slave or homeborn servant was the master's permanent property (Exod 21:1–6). The answer to both questions is strongly negative. Since that is so, why, then, has Israel become "plunder" to her enemies, as though her Lord could not protect her? Freed from Egyptian bondage, Israel has enslaved herself by her sins, this time to Assyria and Egypt. Some writers seek to specify the oppressor as Assyria, which had already exiled the northern kingdom. This cannot be denied, but the text need not be so restricted. It speaks of any and all the enemies of the nation. Notice the *a fortiori* force of the questions: If a man protects his property, be he slave or homeborn servant, how much more would God do so when the object of his care is his son (Exod 4:22)? Verse 17 gives us the answer.

15 To specify how Israel became plunder, Jeremiah reminds the people of the depredations of Assyria and Egypt. The lion, a symbol of Babylon, was also a figure of Assyria; so the reference here could well be to the Assyrian conquest of the Ten Tribes in 722–721 B.C. (2 Kings 15:19–20, 29; 17:4–26) and to Assyria's hostility to Judah also (Isa 10:24–32). But Egypt would not stop at exploiting Judah as well; for as Egypt was no help to the northern kingdom against the Assyrians, so it would be no help in Jeremiah's day against the threat of Chaldean power (37:7).

16 The Egyptian cities were Judah's allies on whom she depended. Memphis was the ancient capital of Lower Egypt; Tahpanhes (the modern Tell el-Defenneh) was the Greek Daphne, a fortified city on the northeast border of Egypt, southwest of Pelusium. They "shaved" (another reading of the verb renders it "fed on," "grazed") the crown or scalp of the nation's head. Perhaps there is a reference here to Egypt's attack on Jerusalem during Shishak's reign, in the time of Rehoboam, son of Solomon (1 Kings 14:25–28). But it is more tenable to understand the reference to Josiah's death at the hands of the Egyptians under Neco (2 Kings 23:29). Thus both

Assyria and Egypt were detrimental to Judah because they led not only to political slavery but religious disobedience as well.

17–19 With great courage Jeremiah states the cause of the impending judgment (v.17). The responsibility for it rests solely on the nation. The people will have to live with the fruit of their evil ways. God's leading was forsaken; so doom would come. Remonstrating with them further, Jeremiah asked whether they had learned nothing from the useless and dangerous game of power politics. Courting Egypt or Assyria was never in Judah's best interests. The figure of water looks back to v.13. "Shihor" ("Black River") is the Nile (v.18), so called because of its muddy appearance from the black deposit of soil after the annual inundations (cf. Isa 23:3). "The River" is the Euphrates, standing for the nations of Mesopotamia—here the Assyrians.

In Jeremiah's day there were two chief political parties, a pro-Egyptian one and a pro-Assyrian one. Of what help would godless nations be to Judah? Ultimately, her doom would be sealed, not by the presence or absence of treaties with allies, but by her defection from the Lord (v.19). The final cause of her calamity would be the hand of God, not the nations he used to punish her. Her great lack was the reverential fear of the Lord.

Notes

12 Hebrew verbs uniformly emphasize the concrete. The translation "shudder" is a rendering of שַׂעֲרוּ (śaʿᵃrû), a denominative verb that literally denotes "let your hair stand on end."

c. *Israel's immorality*

2:20–28

> 20"Long ago you broke off your yoke
>   and tore off your bonds;
>   you said, 'I will not serve you!'
> Indeed, on every high hill
>   and under every spreading tree
>   you lay down as a prostitute.
> 21I had planted you like a choice vine
>   of sound and reliable stock.
> How then did you turn against me
>   into a corrupt, wild vine?
> 22Although you wash yourself with soda
>   and use an abundance of soap,
>   the stain of your guilt is still before me,"
>   declares the Sovereign LORD.
> 23"How can you say, 'I am not defiled;
>   I have not run after the Baals'?
> See how you behaved in the valley;
>   consider what you have done.
> You are a swift she-camel
>   running here and there,

²⁴a wild donkey accustomed to the desert,
    sniffing the wind in her craving—
in her heat who can restrain her?
Any males that pursue her need not tire themselves;
    at mating time they will find her.
²⁵Do not run until your feet are bare
    and your throat is dry.
But you said, 'It's no use!
I love foreign gods,
    and I must go after them.'

²⁶"As a thief is disgraced when he is caught,
    so the house of Israel is disgraced—
they, their kings and their officials,
    their priests and their prophets.
²⁷They say to wood, 'You are my father,'
    and to stone, 'You gave me birth.'
They have turned their backs to me
    and not their faces;
yet when they are in trouble, they say,
    'Come and save us!'
²⁸Where then are the gods you made for yourselves?
    Let them come if they can save you
when you are in trouble!
For you have as many gods
    as you have towns, O Judah."

20 Along with Israel's idolatry went unbridled immorality of long standing. Commentators who read the text "I have broken" understand Jeremiah to be speaking of God's liberation of Israel from the Egyptian yoke of bondage. In keeping with the context of this chapter, it seems more harmonious to take the verb "broke off" as implying that long ago they had thrown off all restraint (so LXX and Vul.). In a powerful metaphor, Jeremiah pictures idolatry as adultery. Canaanite worship chose high hills and luxuriant trees to carry out its licentious rites. Judah rebelled against God's service and became a spiritual harlot. Although Jeremiah is speaking primarily of spiritual uncleanness, it must not be forgotten that sexual immorality of the lowest order was always a part of this so-called worship. The latter part of v.20 explains the figure in the early portion (cf. Hos 4:10–14).

21 In this verse Jeremiah changes to the figure of viniculture. God had planted Israel a choice vine, one of completely reliable stock (cf. Isa 5:1–7; Ezek 17:1–10; Hos 10:1; see also John 15:1–8). It was literally a "Sorek Vine," bearing a high-quality red grape cultivated in Wadi al-Sarar, located between Jerusalem and the Mediterranean Sea (cf. Gen 49:11). Even though it had been planted correctly, the result was corrupt, rotten branches alien to the genuine stock.

22–25 These verses show graphically how incorrigible the people had become in their wickedness. Judah's sins were so deeply ingrained that they were ineradicable. Soda is natron, a mineral alkali; soap is a vegetable alkali (v.22). Outer cleanliness could not hide the people's inner defilement. No amount of outward reform could please God. Sin is more than skin deep. In spite of their record, the people defended themselves by brazenly denying wrongdoing (v.23). How could they claim innocence when they were carrying on their vile worship of Baal in the Valley of Hinnom with their child sacrifices? Shamelessly, like a young she-camel that has not foaled runs around to find satisfaction, impelled by uncontrolled instinct, so Judah went to extremes of idolatry, chasing after ever-new objects of worship. Modesty and self-control have gone. As a wild donkey in heat sniffs at the wind to find a male (v.24), so the people sought out idols; the idols did not need to woo them. Jeremiah pleads with them not to run their feet bare nor their throats dry in their lust for strange gods (v.25). But they reply that they are determined to do so in spite of God's warnings.

26–28 These verses underscore the senselessness of idolatry. The nation is warned that the people are doomed to shame in their idolatry, like a thief caught in the act (v.26). The condemnation rests on the same leaders as in v.8. In the OT prophets, Baal worship is called "shame." Jeremiah quotes words of idolatrous adoration. What a disgrace that they should give idols the glory that is God's as Creator! Some think the references in v.27 are to the ritual use of standing stones and wooden pillars; others, to primitive rites of worship of trees and stones. Having turned completely from the Lord, the people have descended to these depths. But in the hour of their trouble, they find out the worthlessness of their idols and appeal to God for deliverance. In time of trial, people somehow feel that they have a claim on God's help. The irony of v.28 is bitter; yet it is meant to lead the people to realize the senselessness of trusting nonentities. Their false gods were as numerous as their towns (cf. 11:13).

Notes

20 The KJV renderings of "I have broken" for שָׁבַרְתִּי (šāḇartî) and "[I have] burst" for נִתַּקְתִּי (nittaqtî) do not serve the context of the passage. The forms are archaic, with yod paragogic for the second feminine singular, obviously mistaken by the Masoretes for the first person (cf. GKC, par. 44h, n.1), so also v.34: "You did not catch them." NIV and other modern translations give the correct meaning. LXX and Vulgate render "thou" in v.20.

d. *Israel's irrationality*

2:29–37

> ^{29}"Why do you bring charges against me?
> You have all rebelled against me,"
>
> declares the LORD.

> ^{30}"In vain I punished your people;
> they did not respond to correction.
> Your sword has devoured your prophets
> like a ravening lion.

> ^{31}"You of this generation, consider the word of the LORD:

> "Have I been a desert to Israel
> or a land of great darkness?
> Why do my people say, 'We are free to roam;
> we will come to you no more'?

³²Does a maiden forget her jewelry,
  a bride her wedding ornaments?
Yet my people have forgotten me,
  days without number.
³³How skilled you are at pursuing love!
  Even the worst of women can learn from your ways.
³⁴On your clothes men find
  the lifeblood of the innocent poor,
  though you did not catch them breaking in.
Yet in spite of all this
³⁵ you say, 'I am innocent;
  he is not angry with me.'
But I will pass judgment on you
  because you say, 'I have not sinned.'
³⁶Why do you go about so much,
  changing your ways?
You will be disappointed by Egypt
  as you were by Assyria.
³⁷You will also leave that place
  with your hands on your head,
for the LORD has rejected those you trust;
  you will not be helped by them."

29–31 In spite of all she has done, Judah thinks she has a case (*rîḇ*, same verb as in v.9) against God (v.29). She found fault with God because she could not manipulate him to her pleasure. She murmured at his judgments and chastisements, though the fault was hers. God's visitations were unavailing (v.30). Those who sought to lead her back to godliness were slain, as in Manasseh's reign and also in Jehoiakim's (2 Kings 21:16; Jer 26:20–23). In seeking to turn Judah from her irrational ways, Jeremiah thunders, "You of this generation" (Heb., "O generation—you") (v.31). Do the people think God to be like a wilderness to them, unable to sustain and nourish their needs? A land of thick darkness with all kinds of imagined dangers? What has moved them to rebel against him, to wander at will? With this as their intention, all moral control and decency are lost (v.33).

32–33 The rhetorical question (v.32) focuses attention on the fact that though God is Judah's great adornment, she had forgotten him, though no bride would forget her wedding attire. Contrast this with her state as described in v.2. The number of different Hebrew words in the OT (cf. Isa 3:18–22) used for ornaments shows they were in common use. Oriental women take pride in wearing many of them. Judah was without gratitude for God's gifts to her. So abandoned was she that she could even teach wicked women new methods of seduction (v.33). She used all kinds of artifices to make herself desirable to her lovers and cared nothing for God's love.

34–37 All scholars find the text of v.34 difficult. The first half is quite clear; it shows that social sins inevitably follow spiritual declension, so that the poor are oppressed. The historic reference could be to Manasseh's reign, but surely not exclusively so (cf. Amos 2:6–8; 4:1; 5:10–12). It was not as if there was no justification for the taking of life; in the case of housebreaking, the law permitted it (Exod 22:2–3). But there was no such warrant here; the victims were the innocent poor. The difficulty lies in the last words of the text, which are lame and anticlimactic in KJV and ASV. The rendering of RSV, NASB, and NIV joins the words with v.35; thus the force of the passage is that in spite of all these wicked actions, the nation considered itself innocent—the height of irrationality. Judah's argumentative self-justification will do nothing to avert the visitation of God. It is always easy to justify oneself, no matter how sinful one's life. From Adam on, human beings have been experts at such self-justification.

Jeremiah now returns to Judah's determination to make allies to bolster her position in the political world. In the long run, both Egypt and Assyria will disappoint her (v.36); no alliance will work out to the nation's benefit. The omnipotent God will overrule all her overtures to her shame, disappointment, and grief (v.37).

Notes

36 Jeremiah in the first instance was referring to Ahaz's reign when he robbed the temple to gain help from Tiglath-Pileser III of Assyria, but to no avail (cf. 2 Chron 28:16–21). The prediction regarding Egypt was fulfilled to the letter in Zedekiah's reign, when Judah looked to Egypt for help in raising Nebuchadnezzar's siege of Jerusalem, but in vain (37:7). As stated above, chapters 2–6 belong in the early part of Jeremiah's ministry. One of the proofs is the mention of Egypt (2:16, 18, 36).

2. A call to repentance (3:1–25)

The prophecies through chapter 6 are in all probability a condensation of those Jeremiah gave during Josiah's reign. The theme (ch. 2) of the faithless wife of the faithful God is continued in chapter 3, which contains repeated invitations for Judah to repent of her ways (vv.1, 7, 10, 12, 14, 19, 22).

a. Judah, the faithless wife

3:1–5

> ¹"If a man divorces his wife
>   and she leaves him and marries another man,
> should he return to her again?
>   Would not the land be completely defiled?
> But you have lived as a prostitute with many lovers—
>   would you now return to me?"
>
>   declares the LORD.
> ²"Look up to the barren heights and see.
>   Is there any place where you have not been ravished?
> By the roadside you sat waiting for lovers,
>   sat like a nomad in the desert.
> You have defiled the land
>   with your prostitution and wickedness.
> ³Therefore the showers have been withheld,
>   and no spring rains have fallen.
> Yet you have the brazen look of a prostitute;
>   you refuse to blush with shame.
> ⁴Have you not just called to me:
>   'My Father, my friend from my youth,
> ⁵will you always be angry?
>   Will your wrath continue forever?'
> This is how you talk,
>   but you do all the evil you can."

1 The chapter has an unusual beginning because the first word in the Hebrew text is *lēʾmōr* ("and saying"). Many have been the attempts to explain this construction, even going back to 2:37 to join the word with the concept of the Lord's rejection. But this is forced, too far removed, and unnecessary. Probably the words "The word of the LORD came to me" have been omitted by an early copyist. The LXX and Syriac omit the word *lēʾmōr* altogether. The Lord is questioning the nation on the basis of the law of Moses. Deuteronomy 24:1–4 forbade the remarriage of a man with his divorced wife, even if her second husband had died or divorced her. This law evidently did not apply to a man whose wife was forcibly taken from him (cf. 2 Sam 3:14–16 [David and Michal]). The purpose of the law was to curb the husband's arbitrary use of his right to divorce his wife. But with the Lord's people, the case was different on more than one count. They had not been divorced at all but had played the harlot. Furthermore, they had sought out not one lover (god) but many. It is perhaps too much to say that the Lord did not recognize the claim of both Egypt and Assyria on Israel as their wife; but since Israel had left God for pagan lovers, God would abide by the law of divorce, relinquishing his right to receive her back (so Streane).

Much depends on the understanding of the last clause in v.1 as to how the questions in this verse are to be answered. Scholars are clearly divided on the issue, and the reason is understandable. The verb "return" (*šôḇ*) in the last line of v.1 is an infinitive that may allow for more than one rendering. If the verb is taken as an imperative, then the Lord is calling the nation to penitence in spite of the gravity of her sins. If the clause is interpreted as a question, then the sense is "Would you now return to me [in spite of all you have done]?" (so NIV; see also GKC, par. 113cc, which suggests that an infinitive beginning a narrative can be rendered as a jussive; e.g., "Let her return to me!"). The second view would then emphasize the legal prohibition of the restoration of the union. Judah, unfaithful in the marriage relationship, had no right to return to the Lord. In short, her pollution because of idolatry would make a reconciliation difficult, if not impossible. The broken bond was irreparable.

It is hard to see, however, how the Lord would be declaring a reconciliation impossible when, throughout the remainder of the chapter, he is pleading for that very thing in urging Judah to repent. Even the question form of the last clause can be understood to impress Judah that it would be no light thing, considering her many offenses, for God to reclaim her. God is not indignantly rejecting the possibility of her return. We must never forget that God, as he wills, exercises grace beyond the law. Ruth was a Moabitess and was excluded from Israel (cf. Deut 23:3); how then does she become the ancestress of David and of the Lord Jesus? God operated by grace beyond the law. So God was ready to forgive Judah in spite of all her past failures. Legal claims to the contrary, God calls Judah to the solution to her predicament—namely, repentance. Some interpreters maintain that Jeremiah never held out hope to the nation. Apart from chapters 30–33, this chapter proves the opposite.

2 But God's people must see that their return to the Lord does not permit continuance in sin. Their abandonment to idolatry was notorious. They had waited for lovers by the way (cf. Tamar [Gen 38:14, 21]) as marauding Bedouin bandits of the desert waited for passersby to plunder. Their desire for idolatry was insatiable. Again, immoral practices were an integral part of the pagan fertility cult. Since God could not tolerate such disobedience, he chastised his people. As Moses had warned, sin would cause the withdrawal of God's prosperity of the land.

3 The rains were vital in a dry land. The early rains fell about October/November and the latter rain (for the maturing of the crops) fell in March/April (cf. Deut 11:10–17). But because of the nation's impudence, the discipline was ineffective. Natural providences that were meant to bring the nation to repentance were without success.

4–5 Instead of truly turning to the Lord, the people felt that a mere avowal of allegiance to him would suffice (v.4). Some point out that the avowal came at the time of the drought. But the preferable view is that the nation claimed that from now on—that is, in the days of Josiah's reform—the Lord would be their sole guide and companion. The term "father" ('ab) was sometimes used by a young wife of her husband. The Hebrew word 'allûp denotes a husband and companion ("friend," NIV, RSV; "guide," KJV). But the reformation was more apparent than genuine. The people's crying to God was empty lip service because they continued in their wickedness (v.5). Did they think a pretense of obedience to God would insure his favor? Moreover, they were building on false hopes that God's anger would not last; so they persisted in wickedness to the limit of their power, evidently convinced that God's wrath would subside regardless of what they did.

b. Judah worse than Israel

3:6–10

> 6During the reign of King Josiah, the LORD said to me, "Have you seen what faithless Israel has done? She has gone up on every hill and under every spreading tree and has committed adultery there. 7I thought that after she had done all this she would return to me but she did not, and her unfaithful sister Judah saw it. 8I gave faithless Israel her certificate of divorce and sent her away because of all her adulteries. Yet I saw that her unfaithful sister Judah had no fear; she also went out and committed adultery. 9Because Israel's immorality mattered so little to her, she defiled the land and committed adultery with stone and wood. 10In spite of all this, her unfaithful sister Judah did not return to me with all her heart, but only in pretense," declares the LORD.

6 In order to show the gravity of Judah's spiritual condition, Jeremiah compares it with that of exiled Israel, the northern kingdom. The captivity of the Ten Tribes should have been a warning to Judah, but the example had been lost on her. See the extended allegory on the same subject in Ezekiel 23. In spite of her sins, Judah considered herself favored beyond the possibility of judgment on her. How vividly this shows that Josiah's reformation was superficial and short-lived! In v.6 Jeremiah uses strong language, calling the northern kingdom "faithless Israel" (i.e., "backsliding Israel," so KJV). She had become apostasy personified. The Hebrew word for backsliding (mᵉšubāh) is used in nine of its twelve OT occurrences in Jeremiah. Thus Judah had learned nothing from the tragic fate of Israel, whose apostasies had led her into exile.

7–10 Furthermore, it was not as though the Lord had not shown patience with the northern kingdom, for he had waited for her to repent (v.7). But she did not. And Judah, called in v.10 "unfaithful" (KJV, "treacherous"; RSV, "false"), witnessed these dealings and their consequences but remained unmoved. The Lord used the metaphor of divorce (v.8) to describe the captivity for Israel (cf. Deut 24:1–3). If anything, Judah tried to outdo her sister, Israel. Idolatry and immorality seemed trivial to her; she gave herself to idols of stone and wood (v.9; cf. 2:27), with all their base fertility rites. In Canaanite religion the main emphasis was on fertility and sex. Worship was entered into in order to insure the fertility of the land, the animals, and the people. Sacred prostitution was practiced widely. Among the sacred objects were stone altars and the sacred tree or grove (so G.E. Wright, "The Archaeology of Palestine," *The Bible and the Ancient Near East*, ed. G.E. Wright [London: Routledge and Kegan Paul, 1961], pp. 73–112).

The Hebrew word underlying NIV's "mattered so little" in v.9 is *qōl*, whose root (*ql*) can mean either "light" (so KJV; NASB, "the lightness of") or "voice," "sound" (so KD, CHS). In view of the context, where the gravity of idolatry does not weigh heavily on Judah, the latter seems preferable, i.e., that Judah's immorality only sounded before God but went unnoticed by Judah herself. To make matters worse, Judah pretended repentance (v.10) under the reforms of Josiah (cf. 2 Kings 23; 2 Chron 34–35). Such falsity could not hoodwink God. Apostasy Israel and Treachery Judah were spiritual sisters, and the latter was worse than the former.

Notes

9 Verse 8 seems clearly to require that the subject of v.9 be Judah (so KJV, ASV, RSV, NASB, KD, CHS). But v.10 seems to require that the subject of v.9 be Israel (so NIV). The insertion by NIV of "Israel" is unhappy, for the word does not appear in the Hebrew. Confusion arises because both kingdoms are seen as feminine.

c. *The call to return*

3:11–14a

[11]The LORD said to me, "Faithless Israel is more righteous than unfaithful Judah. [12]Go, proclaim this message toward the north:

" 'Return, faithless Israel,' declares the LORD,
    'I will frown on you no longer,
for I am merciful,' declares the LORD,
    'I will not be angry forever.
[13]Only acknowledge your guilt—
    you have rebelled against the LORD your God,
you have scattered your favors to foreign gods
    under every spreading tree,
    and have not obeyed me,' "

declares the LORD.

[14]"Return, faithless people," declares the LORD, "for I am your husband."

399

11 In this section and the next, Jeremiah proclaims to the northern kingdom of Israel both a call to repent and a promise of restoration. First he gives a summary statement that in view of what has been said has only one logical conclusion: Apostate Israel is more righteous than treacherous Judah (cf. Ezek 23:11). The northern kingdom did not have the example of judgment before her as Judah did; therefore Israel is less guilty. Also, only one of Israel's kings (viz., Jehoahaz) is said to have sought the Lord, and that only when in distress because of the Syrian invasion (2 Kings 13:1–5). Furthermore, Judah had greater privileges with a divinely appointed king and a revealed priestly service, together with the example of the kingdom of Israel.

12–13 The Lord is calling Israel to return (v.12), for there is still hope for her. This call is directed toward the north, that is, toward Assyria, where the Ten Tribes had been for about a century. It must be remembered that not all of the northern kingdom had been carried away; a remnant was left that mingled with the expatriated Assyrians to form the Samaritans. God promises not to retain his anger toward Israel, for though less guilty than Judah, she has no claim on restoration. It is all of grace. Such a call to return was meant to provoke Judah to jealousy. Mark well that Israel, contrary to many erroneous views, was not assimilated into the surrounding nations (cf. James 1:1).

Judah must recognize that the prerequisite for pardon and blessing was acknowledgment of her sins (v.13). There must be no palliation of them but a confession that she has scattered her favors among foreign gods, all the while heedless of God's voice.

14a Again the Lord summons Israel to return. The context is one of tenderness and regard for the intimate relationship between the Lord and his people. The ground of the plea is still the indissoluble marriage bond entered into at Sinai with the nation. Actually, a double figure is employed: Israel is both son and wife. Strangely enough, some writers (cf. KD) have taken the verb *bāʿaltî* ("I am a husband") and rendered it "to master, despise, act tyrannically," pointing to its usage in cognate languages. But the meaning of a Hebrew usage must be determined within the bounds of the OT, no matter how much light—and it is considerable—is available from extrabiblical sources. In the OT *bāʿaltî* means "to possess," hence "to marry." There is also a play on the word "Baal" here (cf. Hos 2:16–17). Restatement of the marriage bond indicates acceptance with God.

Notes

11 Notice the number of occurrences of "faithless" in the chapter. Much in this section turns on the word שׁוּב (*šûb*), which in variations means "turn away" (apostatize), "turn back" (repent), "backsliding(s)" (participle form or noun form from same verb). When used of repent, it has the same force as the Greek μετανοία (*metanoia*, lit., "a change of mind").

12 A number of errors cluster around the concept of the "ten lost tribes." This is an inaccurate phrase and is without scriptural foundation (James 1:1). If it means that the identity of the northern tribes is lost, then this holds true for the southern tribes as well. Only identity has been lost; all Twelve Tribes are scattered around the world. (See the excellent footnote in the New Scofield Reference Bible, p. 446.)

The idiomatic clause "I will frown on you no longer" signifies that God would not look with disfavor on them (cf. for the concept Gen 4:5; also cf. the English expression "dejected countenance").

An unusual characterization of God is referred to in חָסִיד (ḥāsîd, "merciful"). This adjective is found of God only here and in Psalm 145:17. It is the word from which Hasidim is derived. This modern Jewish sect stems from Poland (c. 1750) and is characterized by mysticism and a strong opposition to rationalism.

---

d. Future blessing

3:14b–18

> I will choose one of you from every town and two from every clan and bring you to Zion. ¹⁵Then I will give you shepherds after my own heart, who will lead you with knowledge and understanding. ¹⁶In those days, when your numbers have increased greatly in the land," declares the LORD, "men will no longer say, 'The ark of the covenant of the LORD.' It will never enter their minds or be remembered; it will not be missed, nor will another one be made. ¹⁷At that time they will call Jerusalem The Throne of the LORD, and all nations will gather in Jerusalem to honor the name of the LORD. No longer will they follow the stubbornness of their evil hearts. ¹⁸In those days the house of Judah will join the house of Israel, and together they will come from a northern land to the land I gave your forefathers as an inheritance.

14b In vv.14b–18 the reunion and restoration of both kingdoms are set forth. The Lord promises that even if those who return to him are few, he will bring them back to Zion. We must not press the passage into a NT setting and make this the inclusion of the Jews into the church of this age. Jeremiah is saying that the paucity of their numbers will not hinder the Lord's purpose for them. The word "clan" is not to be understood in the restricted sense of a "family" (so KJV, RSV) but of a people or tribe. Compare the narrow and broad use of the term in English where the human family refers to the totality of mankind. No matter how small, a remnant will return; God's message of pardon is ultimately on the basis of individual response to him.

15 Once back in the land, the nation will need godly rulers; and this the Lord promises them. These shepherds (leaders [2:8; 23:4]) will govern with knowledge, i.e., in the fear of the Lord. In contrast to the corrupt leaders of Jeremiah's day, these rulers, like David, will conform to the mind and will of God. There is here no inference of perfection on the leaders' part. Moreover, in this context all is literal and nonsymbolic (cf. chs. 30–31). In the time of their restoration to the land, the Lord's people will increase greatly (cf. 23:3; Ezek 36:11; Hos 1:10 [2:1 MT]). The phrase "in those days" (vv.16, 18) clearly refers to messianic times (cf. 30:24; 21:27, 29, 31, 33, 38).

16 In that era of blessing, no one will even mention the ark of the covenant of the Lord. For an OT prophet to make such a statement was an unparalleled example of boldness. The thought is that the worship of God will need no visible aids, for God will dwell among his people; and all nations will be drawn to them. The ark will not be recalled with heartfelt longing. It was the center of the religious life of God's people and the place where the high priest offered the blood of the sacrifice on the Day of Atonement. Verse 16b shows that the old economy was to be dissolved. The old covenant, of which the ark was a central feature, was to give way to another—a preview of 31:31–34. The ark will not be restored because it will no longer be necessary as a symbol of God's presence. The times of ceremonial emphasis will pass away. The actual glory of God in the midst of his people will be sufficient, and therefore the typical glory will not be missed.

What was the history of the ark? The first mention is in Exodus 25. It was in Solomon's temple (1 Kings 8:6). The last historical reference to it is in 2 Chronicles 35:3. It was probably taken to Babylon in 586 B.C. Strangely enough, it is not mentioned among the spoils listed in 52:17–23. It was lost in 586 B.C. and never found or replaced.

17 In the same vein, Jeremiah predicts that Jerusalem will be known as the throne of God. The ark of the tabernacle and temple represented God's throne on earth (Exod 25:22; 1 Sam 4:4; also called God's footstool in 1 Chron 28:2; Ps 99:5). Neither Israel nor the nations will then be misled into idolatry. Israel purged of idolatry will be a witness and blessing to all the nations (Ps 67). That the ark would be lost and not replaced was so incredible to Jewish commentators that they have admitted great perplexity concerning Jeremiah's prediction. One of them, Abarbanel, expressed the opinion that the promise was bad since it uprooted the whole law, and he wondered how it could be that Scripture referred to it as good.

18 United to God in holiness of life, the two long-divided parts of the nations will finally be reunited to dwell in the land promised to the patriarchs (cf. Ezek 37). In summary, the elements of the promise are godly leaders, absence of outward elements of worship, the dwelling of God's presence with them, a godly life, a successful witness to the nations, and a unified nation.

Notes

16 With the return of the Jews to Palestine and the establishment of the State of Israel in 1948, questions are frequently asked about the ark of the covenant. As has been stated in the exposition, the ark disappeared after the Fall of Jerusalem in 586 B.C. The reference to the ark in Rev 11:19 is not pertinent here.

e. *Israel's disobedience*

3:19–20

> [19]"I myself said,
>
> > " 'How gladly would I treat you like sons
> > and give you a desirable land,
> > the most beautiful inheritance of any nation.'
> > I thought you would call me 'Father'
> > and not turn away from following me.

²⁰But like a woman unfaithful to her husband,
   so you have been unfaithful to me, O house of Israel,"
                                          declares the LORD.

19–20 From this point to the end of the chapter, there is an extended dialogue between God and Israel. In these verses the purpose or ideal of God for his people and their response to it are stated. God's love and favor met with Israel's ingratitude and disobedience. His intention was to give them a place as if they were sons (v.19). As a daughter, Israel was to receive an inheritance like that of sons, an event that was contrary to Hebrew practice (cf. Num 27:1–8). The legacy was the land of Palestine. But they would match their words with their deeds. They will enter into the promise only when they practice what they profess. But again they disappointed all expectations and committed treachery (v.20). What a contrast between God's hopes for them and what happened! From the rosy prospects of the future, Israel must be called back to the dark present.

f. Exhortation to repentance

3:21–25

²¹A cry is heard on the barren heights,
   the weeping and pleading of the people of Israel,
because they have perverted their ways
   and have forgotten the LORD their God.

²²"Return, faithless people;
   I will cure you of backsliding."

"Yes, we will come to you,
   for you are the LORD our God
²³Surely the ¸idolatrous¸ commotion on the hills
   and mountains is a deception;
surely in the LORD our God
   is the salvation of Israel.
²⁴From our youth shameful gods have consumed
   the fruits of our fathers' labor—
their flocks and herds,
   their sons and daughters.
²⁵Let us lie down in our shame,
   and let our disgrace cover us.
We have sinned against the LORD our God,
   both we and our fathers;
from our youth till this day
   we have not obeyed the LORD our God."

21 Now the prophet turns to the nation's avowal of repentance. Where they had so flagrantly carried on their idolatries, the people now lament for their transgressions. Since their sin was public and prominent, so would their cries of penitence be (cf. 31:15 for some words of their cries).

22–23 In response to their genuine repentance (v.22), the Lord promised to heal the wounds his people had acquired in their apostasy (cf. 30:17; 33:6; Hos 14:4). Their answer showed the depth and reality of their penitence; they accepted the

Lord's offer of pardon. Once more the way to ruin and the way of deliverance are stated (v.23). Idolatry with its wild and clamorous excesses is the way of death (cf. the priests of Baal at Mount Carmel [1 Kings 18:26–29]), but the way of salvation and life is in the Lord (Ps 3:8; Jonah 2:9).

24–25 Jeremiah goes on to portray the destructive consequences of the people's idolatry. At last they are convinced that idolatry has been their undoing. The "shameful" thing (v.24, the article is emphatic in the Hebrew) is Baal, the god of shame. In 11:13 Baal and shame are identified, so also Jerub-Besheth for Jerubbaal (2 Sam 11:21) and Ish-Bosheth for Ishbaal (2 Sam 2:8). How costly their idolatry was in terms of property and even more in terms of the sacrifices of their sons and daughters! And the malady was of long standing. So at the end of the chapter, we see the nation robbed of her vigor, possessions, and dignity, totally cast down by her sin and willing to endure the grief it has caused. As mourners lie down in dust and cover themselves with it, so the nation lies prostrate on the ground (v.25).

3. The invasion from the north (4:1–31)

The preceding chapter closed on a note of confession on the part of the people, following the Lord's brief appeal for them to return to the Lord and his promise to heal their backsliding (3:22). But vv.1–4 of this chapter show that the reform under Josiah was only superficial. More, much more, was needed.

a. The call to genuine repentance

4:1–4

> ¹"If you will return, O Israel,
>   return to me,"
>
> declares the LORD.
>
> "If you put your detestable idols out of my sight
>   and no longer go astray,
> ²and if in a truthful, just and righteous way
>   you swear, 'As surely as the LORD lives,'
> then the nations will be blessed by him
>   and in him they will glory."

³This is what the LORD says to the men of Judah and to Jerusalem:

> "Break up your unplowed ground
>   and do not sow among thorns.
> ⁴Circumcise yourselves to the LORD,
>   circumcise your hearts,
>   you men of Judah and people of Jerusalem,
> or my wrath will break out and burn like fire
>   because of the evil you have done—
>   burn with no one to quench it."

1–2 The people's cry of anguish (3:24–25) is now answered by the Lord with an assurance of blessing when they do return to him. There is a vast difference between perfunctory repentance and heartfelt restoration to God. If Judah would truly repent, it must be to God alone (v.1). Furthermore, they must really rid themselves of their detestable things, their idols. Evidently they had not yet done this. Moreover, if the people will remain steadfast (on their oath in the name of the Lord) in the essential qualities of truth, justice, and righteousness, then their example will profoundly affect the nations (v.2). Judah's conversion will herald blessing for the nations. To swear by God's name involves recognition of him as Lord. Oaths in the name of other gods were not to be sworn by them. When the nations are being blessed, the Abrahamic blessing is being realized (cf. Gen 12:3; 18:18; 22:18; 26:4; 28:14; see also Isa 2:3; Zech 8:20–23). The very name of Israel will become a formula of blessing.

3–4 Jeremiah now uses two figures to show the nation's need of spiritual renewal: one from agriculture and the other from physiology. He exhorts the people of Judah to break up their neglected and untilled hearts, which had become as hard as an uncultivated field (v.3). No farmer will sow seed on unplowed ground. So the plow of repentance and obedience was needed to remove the outer layer of weeds and thorns that had resulted from idolatry. Otherwise, thorns would choke the newly sown seed (Hos 10:12). The very foundations of the nation's spiritual life needed tending, even restructuring.

Again, Jeremiah calls for repentance—this time under the figure of circumcision (v.4). The hard encrustation on their hearts must be cut away. Nothing less than removal of all natural obstacles to the will of God would suffice. Outward ritual must be replaced by inward reality (cf. Deut 10:16; Rom 2:28–29). The heart was involved because outward worship was valueless unless the inner life was given over to God. Their hearts must be spiritually receptive. The only other alternative to obedience was to experience the fitting wrath of God. Jeremiah everywhere underscores the necessity for the new heart as in the prophecy of the new covenant (ch. 31).

b. *The enemy on the way*

4:5–18

> [5]"Announce in Judah and proclaim in Jerusalem and say:
>   'Sound the trumpet throughout the land!'
> Cry aloud and say:
>   'Gather together!
> Let us flee to the fortified cities!'
> [6]Raise the signal to go to Zion!
>   Flee for safety without delay!
> For I am bringing disaster from the north,
>   even terrible destruction."
>
> [7]A lion has come out of his lair;
>   a destroyer of nations has set out.
> He has left his place
>   to lay waste your land.
> Your towns will lie in ruins
>   without inhabitant.
> [8]So put on sackcloth,
>   lament and wail,
> for the fierce anger of the LORD
>   has not turned away from us.
>
> [9]"In that day," declares the LORD,
>   "the king and the officials will lose heart,
> the priests will be horrified,
>   and the prophets will be appalled."

¹⁰Then I said, "Ah, Sovereign LORD, how completely you have deceived this people and Jerusalem by saying, 'You will have peace,' when the sword is at our throats."

¹¹At that time this people and Jerusalem will be told, "A scorching wind from the barren heights in the desert blows toward my people, but not to winnow or cleanse; ¹²a wind too strong for that comes from me. Now I pronounce my judgments against them."

¹³Look! He advances like the clouds,
    his chariots come like a whirlwind,
  his horses are swifter than eagles.
    Woe to us! We are ruined!
¹⁴O Jerusalem, wash the evil from your heart and be saved.
    How long will you harbor wicked thoughts?
¹⁵A voice is announcing from Dan,
    proclaiming disaster from the hills of Ephraim.
¹⁶"Tell this to the nations,
    proclaim it to Jerusalem:
  'A besieging army is coming from a distant land,
    raising a war cry against the cities of Judah.
¹⁷They surround her like men guarding a field,
    because she has rebelled against me,' "

                              declares the LORD.

¹⁸"Your own conduct and actions
    have brought this upon you.
  This is your punishment.
    How bitter it is!
    How it pierces to the heart!"

5–6 The remainder of the chapter is occupied with vivid portrayals of the invasion of the land, the siege of Jerusalem, the devastation of the land, and the decimation of the population. So certain is the judgment that Jeremiah sees the imminent invasion as already present. From v.5 on, the prophet is explicit in his warnings to the nation of calamity from the north (cf. 4:5–7, 13–17; 5:15–17; 6:1–6, 22–23; also 1:13). Since the siege is imminent, the people are warned to take refuge. The trumpet signals the danger (Amos 3:6). The fortified cities were the refuge for the fleeing rural population. The signal to point the way to Zion was well advised because the city was so strongly fortified. What was the "disaster from the north" (v.6)? Many have taken it to be a reference to a Scythian invasion. But the difficulty is that the Scythians never invaded Judah, and the descriptions of the invading army do not fit the Scythians (see Introduction: Date and Authorship). The descriptions do, however, tally with what is known of the Babylonians. Older expositors (Hyatt, Orelli, Volz) understood the enemy to be the Babylonians; more recent expositors (Bewer, Eissfeldt) have taken the messages in 4:5–6:30 to refer to the Scythians. Jeremiah, so the argument runs, believed that the campaigns of the Scythians (c. 625 B.C.) were the intended instrument of God's wrath on sinning Israel. When, however, the stroke did not fall, the prophet finally saw that the Babylonian invasion was meant. Most recently many have relinquished the Scythian invasion view. Indeed, the whole concept of such an invasion arose from an antisupernatural basis against predictive prophecy. We suggest that the reference is clearly to the Babylonian invasion under Nebuchadnezzar, specifically named later in the book.

7–9 In describing the invaders, Jeremiah shows poetic skill and deep feeling and uses vivid imagery. He compares the foe to a "lion" (v.7), a "scorching wind" or sirocco (v.11), and watchers or besiegers (v.16). The lion represented the Assyrians and Babylonians (here the latter). Lions in enamel have been removed from the Processional Way of Babylon (cf. Dan 7 for the figure). So great was the Babylonian military prowess that the other nations feared it. For Judah the power of Babylon would mean disaster to the land, its cities, and its citizenry (cf. 43:5–7). The prophet encourages the people to lament (v.8), for there is no possibility of averting or escaping the visitation. Unrepentant, the nation could only expect doom. Until their sins received their merited punishment, the blow could not be deflected from them. In the hour of distress, the very ones who should encourage the nation—king, princes, priests, and prophets—will be devoid of courage (v.9). The reference to their "losing heart" is not to a failure in understanding but rather to failure in stamina and valor. This failure is well illustrated by the Lachish Letters of the final siege of Jerusalem in 588–586 B.C.

10 This verse has received more attention and occasioned more differences of interpretation than almost any other passage in the book. At first reading, it appears that Jeremiah is blaming God for deceiving the nation (so Bright). In the light of James 1:13, such action is impossible for the God of Scripture. The difficulty is not resolved by attributing the deception to the prophet's attempt to mislead the people by speaking God's message to them, for at no time had Jeremiah prophesied that Jerusalem would have peace. His message was always the opposite. Some have tried to explain the difficulty by reading with the LXX "And they said" instead of "Then said I," so making the words a quotation of the false prophets (so Cheyne, Hyatt). But there is too little support for such a textual reading; the same is true for reading "they" instead of "you." One view suggests that the words are the prophet's, spoken in a time of deep depression. Actually, it was the false prophets who constantly deceived the people with false promises of peace and prosperity regardless of their ways.

The solution lies in the way the Jews spoke of evil in a world ruled by a righteous and holy God. God is said to do what he permits (so Streane). Scripture often omits second causes and relates all to God as the First Cause (cf. Exod 9:12; Eph 1:11; 2 Thess 2:11; particularly pertinent is 1 Kings 22:21–23). Jeremiah was so emotionally moved at this point that it is probably better not to understand his remarks as an ironical reference to the false prophets, as some writers have done (so Calvin, Frost). In short, the false prophets had spoken deceptively to the people; they had misled the people into false hopes; and God had permitted it all. Instead of peace, destruction faced Judah. The rendering "throat" for the Hebrew *nepeš* ("breath," "soul") is well attested in Ugaritic (cf. Isa 5:14; also, KB, s.v.).

11–18 In a sense v.10 is parenthetical, for the prophet continues his portrayal of the invading army in vv.11–18. With the approach of the enemy, the news will be carried by messengers in the way shown here. The foe is likened to the "scorching wind" (v.11) from the desert that withers vegetation and brings discomfort to mankind. For winnowing and cleansing, a much less vehement wind is needed. Its purpose is not to sift but to judge (v.12); it does not separate good from bad but takes all away. All will happen at God's command. In v.13 Jeremiah uses vivid metaphors—"clouds," "whirlwind," "eagles"—to depict the Babylonian army, with its chariots and war horses. For a similar use of the cloud metaphor, see Ezekiel 38:16. No wonder the people cry out that they are ruined.

Amazingly enough, even at that late hour there was still opportunity for repentance. Prophecies of judgment are conditional; obedience to God reverses the threat of judgment. But there must be inner cleansing, even of the thought life, if disaster is to be averted. The Lord's patience is wearied with Judah's continued unfaithfulness; so he asks (v.14) how long their minds will be centered on wickedness. The need for repentance is urgent. The foe is near; there is little time left to return to God. Dan (v.15) was the northern boundary of the land; Mount Ephraim was the northern border of Judah, not far from Jerusalem. The invaders are making rapid progress. So unprecedented is the fate that will now overtake God's people that the nations are called on to witness the judgment soon to fall on Judah. Resistance has not availed against the invaders; so they are finally seen besieging the capital, Jerusalem (v.16). As watchmen guard their fields from predatory animals, so Jerusalem will be surrounded to cut off any who would escape (v.17). All has come on her because of her own wickedness and rebellion (v.18). The calamity is bitter to bear because the people now realize that they have brought it on themselves. Their wounds are serious, reaching to the heart.

Notes

5 "Cry aloud" translates קִרְאוּ מַלְאוּ (*qir'û mal'û*), where the verb מָלֵא (*mālē'*, "to fill") is used adverbially to give the literal sense of "a full or loud voice."

c. *The agony of Jeremiah*

4:19–22

> [19]Oh, my anguish, my anguish!
> I writhe in pain.
>
> Oh, the agony of my heart!
> My heart pounds within me,
> I cannot keep silent.
> For I have heard the sound of the trumpet;
> I have heard the battle cry.
> [20]Disaster follows disaster;
> the whole land lies in ruins.
> In an instant my tents are destroyed,
> my shelter in a moment.
> [21]How long must I see the battle standard
> and hear the sound of the trumpet?
>
> [22]"My people are fools;
> they do not know me.
> They are senseless children;
> they have no understanding.
> They are skilled in doing evil;
> they know not how to do good."

19–22 These verses have been variously interpreted as (1) the words of the Lord, (2) the words of the nation, or (3) the words of Jeremiah. Undeniably the Lord was affected by the agony of his people. Certainly the nation would express its agony at their plight. But it appears in keeping with the immediate and broad context of the entire book to understand the words as expressing Jeremiah's personal involvement with the calamity of his people. Much is surely lost of the prophet's thoughts and feelings if these passages are denied an individualistic frame of reference. The scene is so real to him that he cries out in physical pain (v.19). His profound emotion affects him physically. His personal anguish over the impending destruction is inescapable (v.20). So wholesale is the destruction that Jeremiah cannot suppress his deep sympathy with those he must denounce in obedience to the Lord's commission. Though he was accused of treason later, how can anyone reasonably deny the patriotism and love of Jeremiah for his people? Some of the people may have felt the invasion and destruction deeply, but no one felt these more keenly and clearly than the prophet. Fellowship with God and obedience to his service always sharpen the sensibilities of his servants. Thus the prophet agonizes in soul and can scarcely endure the scene of judgment on his people. He longs to know the end of the travail (v.21); so the Lord answers that the trial will continue as long as they persist in disobeying him. Their trouble is that they have no fellowship with the Lord in doing his will (cf. Hos 4:1). Their moral values are completely reversed: they major in evil and minor in good (v.22).

d. *The cosmic catastrophe*

4:23–26

> 23I looked at the earth,
>   and it was formless and empty;
>   and at the heavens,
>   and their light was gone.
> 24I looked at the mountains,
>   and they were quaking;
>   all the hills were swaying.
> 25I looked, and there were no people;
>   every bird in the sky had flown away.
> 26I looked, and the fruitful land was a desert;
>   all its towns lay in ruins
>   before the LORD, before his fierce anger.

23–26 Commentators have been unstinting in praise of this beautiful vignette, and rightly so. It has been acclaimed one of the most forceful passages in all prophetic literature (so Cornill, *Prophets of Israel*). For vividness, simplicity, directness, breadth of reference, and gravity of subject matter, the verses are unique in Scripture. From a contemplation of Israel's calamity, the prophet is led by the Spirit who inspired him to witness (mark the fourfold reference to his seeing) cosmic catastrophe (v.23). Chaos engulfs the physical world. It is the story of Genesis 1 in reverse. It may be taken to describe the coming Day of the Lord (so Bright). All nature is upheaved and no area of life—geological, terrestrial, celestial, human, ornithological, horticultural, and demographical—is left untouched (vv.24–26). The apocalyptic overtone is unmistakable.

Notes

23 Verses 23–26 are the finest lyrical portion in the entire prophecy. In order to show how thoroughgoing the judgment on Israel will be, Jeremiah recalls the original chaos of Gen 1:2, with its phrase תֹהוּ וָבֹהוּ (*tōhû wāḇōhû,* "formless and empty") repeated here, as though the work of creation had been cancelled out. Sin is catastrophic in its consequences. (See also Bruce K. Waltke, *Creation and Chaos* [Portland, Oreg.: Western Conservative Baptist Seminary, 1974], pp. 20–28.)

e. The desolation of the land

4:27–31

27This is what the LORD says:

> "The whole land will be ruined,
>> though I will not destroy it completely.
> 28Therefore the earth will mourn
>> and the heavens above grow dark,
> because I have spoken and will not relent,
>> I have decided and will not turn back."

> 29At the sound of horsemen and archers
>> every town takes to flight.
> Some go into the thickets;
>> some climb up among the rocks.
> All the towns are deserted;
>> no one lives in them.

> 30What are you doing, O devastated one?
>> Why dress yourself in scarlet
>> and put on jewels of gold?
> Why shade your eyes with paint?
>> You adorn yourself in vain.

> Your lovers despise you;
>> they seek your life.

> 31I hear a cry as of a woman in labor,
>> a groan as of one bearing her first child—
> the cry of the Daughter of Zion gasping for breath,
>> stretching out her hands and saying,
> "Alas! I am fainting;
>> my life is given over to murderers."

27 Again, Jeremiah must impress his hearers with the actuality of the coming doom. What literary genius he shows in returning to the same theme, yet without boring his listeners! The thrust of the passage is that the die is cast, and nothing can reverse the decree. Jeremiah now puts in prophetic discourse what he saw in spirit. A ray of hope is held out: though the calamity will be real enough, the Lord will not allow it to accomplish the complete dissolution of the nation. There will be no reenactment of Sodom and Gomorrah's destruction (cf. Lev 26:44; Isa 6:13; Amos 9:8; Mic 5:6–7; for wording, see Jer 5:10, 18; 30:11; 46:28). God is committed to preserving a remnant of his people.

28-31 Because God purposes grace toward the nation, let none of the people presume that judgment would not fall. The decision was irrevocable; the fulfillment came in 586 B.C. For this destruction of the land, the very heavens and earth will mourn (v.28). The Babylonians took over the military strategy of the Assyrians, becoming adept bowmen (v.29). Archaeological monuments give much evidence that the Babylonians were a people of archers. Before such an adversary the only course will be to escape to the rocky hills; the whole city of Jerusalem will be deserted. The desperate condition of Israel is finally pictured under the figure of a harlot who even in her desperate hour still tries to allure the enemy by her wiles (v.30). Her "lovers" (lit., "paramours") will be unimpressed and will despise her. Jeremiah depicts her final agonies under the figure of a miscarriage of a first child with the mother in her final gasps for breath (v.31). Though undeserving, the nation will not find Jeremiah deaf to her agonizing cries. The courtesan will be murdered by her lovers, but the prophet enters completely into her plight.

Notes

30 In order to allure her enemies (former paramours) from their murderous intentions, Judah seeks to improve her appearance by well-known coquettish devices. One of these is enlarging the eyes with paint. The verb קָרַע (*qāra'*) means "to rend"; here it indicates her zeal in seeking to enlarge (NIV, "shade") her eyes to excess. This was done by the use of black mineral powder (antimony, stibium), as the Egyptian women did in ancient days and as Arab women—and many women in the western world—do today (cf. 2 Kings 9:30; Ezek 23:40).

The word translated "lovers" is not the usual Hebrew one for illicit lovers. It is the masculine plural participle of עָגַב (*'āgab*, "to have inordinate affection, lust"; BDB, s.v.). This unusual verb is used only here and in Ezek 23:5, 7, 9, 12, 16, 20, where Samaria and Jerusalem are personified as harlots. The lovers here are not idols but foreign nations.

4. Judah's total corruption (5:1-31)

This chapter reveals Jerusalem under moral investigation. It may be viewed as a theodicy. A superficial reading of the earlier chapters of the prophecy might lead one to conclude that the nation has been charged with all it has been guilty of. But the depths of her sin against the Lord must be reviewed at length. The nation must come to a much fuller realization of her ingrained sin. The desperately low spiritual state of the nation must be brought under the searchlight of God's scrutiny. Moreover, her sin must be judged in view of her continued refusal to heed the Lord's gracious calls to repent and so avert disaster. What a telling portrayal of unrelieved apostasy the chapter gives us!

a. The bill of particulars

5:1-9

> [1]"Go up and down the streets of Jerusalem,
>   look around and consider,
>   search through her squares.

If you can find but one person
  who deals honestly and seeks the truth,
  I will forgive this city.
2Although they say, 'As surely as the LORD lives,'
  still they are swearing falsely."

3O LORD, do not your eyes look for truth?
  You struck them, but they felt no pain;
  you crushed them, but they refused correction.
They made their faces harder than stone
  and refused to repent.
4I thought, "These are only the poor;
  they are foolish,
for they do not know the way of the LORD,
  the requirements of their God.
5So I will go to the leaders
  and speak to them;
surely they know the way of the LORD,
  the requirements of their God."
But with one accord they too had broken off the yoke
  and torn off the bonds.
6Therefore a lion from the forest will attack them,
  a wolf from the desert will ravage them,
a leopard will lie in wait near their towns
  to tear to pieces any who venture out,
for their rebellion is great
  and their backslidings many.
7"Why should I forgive you?
  Your children have forsaken me
  and sworn by gods that are not gods.
I supplied all their needs,
  yet they committed adultery
  and thronged to the houses of prostitutes.
8They are well-fed, lusty stallions,
  each neighing for another man's wife.
9Should I not punish them for this?"
  declares the LORD.
"Should I not avenge myself
  on such a nation as this?"

1–3 Some have suggested that these words are Jeremiah's and not the Lord's (so Cunliffe-Jones, Freedman). Nevertheless, Jeremiah's words were so truly those of God that the distinction is only academic. He is not preaching his own thoughts but the Lord's. The accumulation of synonyms in v.1 shows how thorough the search was to be. Investigation, full and impartial, must always precede indictment on a legal bill of particulars. The object of the search was to find one righteous person. For such a person who practiced justice and made truth (faithfulness) the goal of his life, the Lord promised to pardon Jerusalem. What an exposé of the extent of the city's wickedness! There may be an allusion here to Abraham's intercession for Sodom (Gen 18:23–33; for an even more pessimistic word, see Jer 15:1–4). Although Jeremiah's statement was justified, we should not take it too literally. Obviously some godly people like Josiah, Baruch, Zephaniah, and Jeremiah himself were living in Jerusalem. But the words certainly applied to the mass of the populace. In short, corruption was so widespread that exceptions were not significant (cf. Ps 14). The reference to those who said, "As surely as the LORD lives," does not mitigate the severity of Jeremiah's statement. Their oath was not a judicial one but a spurious profession of piety. They used the most binding and the right form of oath, but their conduct showed it to be perjury (v.2). Even God's severe chastisements made no difference in their lives. Some interpreters have tried to restrict v.3 to Josiah's death at Megiddo, but the terms are too general to limit the meaning in this way.

4–5 Jeremiah thought of extenuating circumstances for the plight of his people (v.4). The population was generally poor; their poverty kept them from opportunities of learning the way of the Lord. In his disappointment, the prophet had thought that the situation might be different among the nation's leaders. But a higher station in life does not mean greater piety (v.5). The great had thrown off all restraint, placing themselves above the law (probably the Mosaic Law). The great and learned were no more open than the poor and ignorant. All classes were alike implicated. Judgment must follow.

6 Jeremiah uses three predators—"a lion," "a wolf," and "a leopard"—to portray the imminent judgment. Some expositors believe these beasts are literal beasts; others believe they represent nations that have from time to time harassed Israel; still others believe the beasts symbolize the Babylonians. Although none of these views does violence to the text, it is preferable in the light of the broad context of the prophecy to hold the last. The lion represents strength, the desert wolf ravenousness, and the leopard swiftness—all traits of the Babylonians. (Dante refers to these three predators in the first canto of the *Inferno* [30–55].)

7–9 Here we have God's reasoning with his people to convince them of the justice of his judgments. In a sense the entire chapter is a theodicy. God's bounty to the people evoked not gratitude but a greater desire for idolatry. Material blessings only made them feel secure in their sins. The reference in v.7 is to idolatry ("not gods"); v.8 underscores the immorality that always accompanies it. Apostasy and adultery are a horrendous pair. Publicly and unashamedly the people thronged to the prostitutes' house, that is, the idol temple (the noun is singular in Hebrew); but as v.8 shows, their actions were not confined to apostasy but included physical immorality. Orgiastic rites accompanied the idolatry of Jeremiah's times. Idolatry, now as then, always opens the door to immorality. Notice how largely this chapter is concerned with the social sins of the people. In v.9 the Lord asks the nation whether he is not punishing them justly.

Notes

7 It has been suggested (so Orelli) that the translation "fed them to the full" (KJV, ASV, RSV, JPS, NEB [substantially], NASB, JB, AmT; so also LXX, Vul., and Syr.; NIV has "supplied all their needs") does not fit the context. Instead of שָׂבַע (śāḇaʿ, "to satisfy"), the preference is for שָׁבַע (šāḇaʿ, "to make swear") in the causative, with reference to Exod 24:3 and other occasions, explaining why the breaking of the covenant at Sinai is likened to adultery (cf. Jer 2:2). But from the rest of the verse, carnal infidelity is clearly indicated (cf. also v.8b).

The verb יִתְגֹּדָדוּ (yitgōdāḏû) is rendered "to assemble themselves in troops" (KJV), "trooped" (RSV), or "thronged" (NIV). The verb may also mean "to slash themselves" as in

Canaanite cult practices (cf. 1 Kings 18:28; for the same verb in funeral rites, see Deut 14:1). This latter translation is a possibility because the verb in the text is not followed by a preposition in the Hebrew.

---

b. *Denial of the Lord's activity*

5:10–13

> 10"Go through her vineyards and ravage them,
>   but do not destroy them completely.
> Strip off her branches,
>   for these people do not belong to the Lord.
> 11The house of Israel and the house of Judah
>   have been utterly unfaithful to me,"
>
> declares the Lord.
>
> 12They have lied about the Lord;
>   they said, "He will do nothing!
> No harm will come to us;
>   we will never see sword or famine.
> 13The prophets are but wind
>   and the word is not in them;
>   so let what they say be done to them."

10 The result of such ungodliness must be the outpouring of the divine wrath. Thus the Lord now gives the people over to the attacks of their foes. The call is from God to Israel's enemies (cf. v.15). The Lord is prepared to have his vineyard destroyed (cf. for the same figure Isa 5:1–7; Ezek 17:1–6). The branches are to be stripped off because they are fruitless and no longer belong to the Lord. But because God has not forgotten that he promised Abraham an eternal nation, he will not allow the complete destruction of his people. Some expositors believe that the negative expression *kālāh ʾal-taʿᵃśû* ("do not destroy them completely") is not authentic, but this view lacks MS authority. Furthermore, the immediate context that speaks of stripping away the branches is a full pruning, not a complete desolation. Only the branches are involved, not the root or stock. Moreover, the broad context and the other prophets reveal that God always intended a remnant of his people to survive.

11–12 In presenting the reason for the punishment he has just announced, Jeremiah includes both parts of the nation—Israel and Judah (v.11). Although the destruction will not be absolute, it is amply warranted. Treacherously, the people have tried to minimize the Lord's warnings. First of all, they have brazenly lied about him. They have scornfully said, "He will do nothing!" (v.12). God, they thought, would not bring calamity on them. The Lord is not, they assume, responsible for either their blessing or their trials; so they claim to have nothing to fear. When told that disaster is impending, their response is that God will do no such thing (cf. Zeph 1:12). So they deny God's intervention and even his interest in their ways. They were practical atheists.

13 In the second place, the people rejected the validity of God's word given through his prophets. How did they do this? They claimed that the Spirit in the prophets of the Lord was only wind. There is a play here on the Hebrew word *rûaḥ*, which can mean "wind" or "spirit" (cf. the same usage of the Greek *pneuma* in the NT). The prophets believed they had the Spirit of the Lord; the people claimed the prophets had only wind. Thus the people denied the inspiration of the message of God through Jeremiah. To label a prophet of God "wind" ("windbags," so Mof) is the ultimate in irreverence. And the people had the effrontery to say that the judgment the prophets threatened would descend on the prophets themselves.

c. *The judgment described*

5:14–19

¹⁴Therefore this is what the LORD God Almighty says:

"Because the people have spoken these words,
I will make my words in your mouth a fire
and these people the wood it consumes.
¹⁵O house of Israel," declares the LORD,
"I am bringing a distant nation against you—
an ancient and enduring nation,
a people whose language you do not know,
whose speech you do not understand.
¹⁶Their quivers are like an open grave;
all of them are mighty warriors.
¹⁷They will devour your harvests and food,
devour your sons and daughters;
they will devour your flocks and herds,
devour your vines and fig trees.
With the sword they will destroy
the fortified cities in which you trust.

¹⁸"Yet even in those days," declares the LORD, "I will not destroy you completely. ¹⁹And when the people ask, 'Why has the LORD our God done all this to us?' you will tell them, 'As you have forsaken me and served foreign gods in your own land, so now you will serve foreigners in a land not your own.' "

14 Because the people denied the validity of the Lord's word to his prophets, the Lord determined to make that word a fire in Jeremiah's mouth to consume them. What they considered to be nothing more than wind, God would energize like fire. Though spoken by Jeremiah, they are still God's words. In order to make this important pronouncement, the solemn, august name of God is used (YHWH *ʾelōhê ṣᵉḇaʾ ôṯ*)—"the LORD God of hosts" (KJV, RSV et al.); "the LORD God Almighty" (NIV; cf. Jer 2:19 [cf. Preface to NIV, p. ix]; cf. also TEV rendering). God is the self-existent One, Commander of all the armies of heaven and earth. Here is expressed God's power over all created intelligences in the universe, a reference to the armies of Israel (Exod 7:4), the heavenly hosts (Ps 103:21), and the stars (Isa 40:26). God's word is never to be trifled with.

15–16 Here Jeremiah addresses the whole nation ("house of Israel") as he begins to describe the invading enemy (v.15). At this time Josiah exercised some rule over the remnant of Israel in the north (2 Kings 23). The repetition of "nation" heightens the force of the statement. The description of the foe is both accurate and detailed. Five of their characteristics are given: (1) distant, (2) ancient, (3) enduring, (4) unintelligible in speech, and (5) deadly in war. Though they are not named, the description points to the Babylonians. Distance would be no obstacle to the invaders because of their persevering and determined nature. The coming of a distant nation had already been predicted by Moses (cf. Deut 28:49). The invaders would be an enduring (lit., "perennial"), hardy people, used to war. The foe would be an ancient nation, for the national entity (to which the Chaldeans were later joined) was founded by Nimrod (cf. Gen 10:10; 11:31). An ancient nation could not be the Scythians, for Herodotus (4.5) stated: "The Scythians say that theirs is the youngest of all nations." Jeremiah emphasizes that the enemy would speak a language Israel did not understand. This meant that the invaders would be the more fearful and unfeeling because they would not respond to cries for mercy. In ancient times lack of ability to communicate was always a source of fear (Deut 28:49; Isa 28:11). Finally, they would be invincible because their quivers would be filled with death-dealing arrows, always bringing more destruction (v.16). Every arrow could be depended on to slay someone.

17–18 Having so explicitly described the invaders' power, Jeremiah paints a vivid picture of the devastation they will wreak on the land. Four times he uses the verb *'ākal* ("devour"), with a compound direct object in each case. A final blow is added to loss of harvest, children, flocks, herds, vines, and trees—viz., the impoverishment and demolition of the fortified cities (v.17). Yet, in accord with v.10, the destruction will not be total (v.18). God's punishments are not vindictive but are meant to be restorative of the sinner. God must, and does, preserve a remnant according to his pledged word.

19 There is a direct relation between the nation's sin and its punishment—viz., recompense in kind, lex talionis (Deut 28:47–48). The Exile is foretold. Because the people worshiped foreign gods in the Lord's land, they would have to serve foreign overlords in a foreign land. It was useless for them to inquire, as if they were blameless, why judgment had descended on them. The root of all their difficulties was their slippage into idolatry.

d. *Israel's willful ignorance and rebellion*

5:20–31

> 20"Announce this to the house of Jacob
>   and proclaim it in Judah:
> 21Hear this, you foolish and senseless people,
>   who have eyes but do not see,
>   who have ears but do not hear:
> 22Should you not fear me?" declares the LORD.
>   "Should you not tremble in my presence?
> I made the sand a boundary for the sea,
>   an everlasting barrier it cannot cross.
> The waves may roll, but they cannot prevail;
>   they may roar, but they cannot cross it.
> 23But these people have stubborn and rebellious hearts;
>   they have turned aside and gone away.
> 24They do not say to themselves,
>   'Let us fear the LORD our God,
> who gives fall and spring rains in season,
>   who assures us of the regular weeks of harvest.'
> 25Your wrongdoings have kept these away;
>   your sins have deprived you of good.

26"Among my people are wicked men
   who lie in wait like men who snare birds
   and like those who set traps to catch men.
27Like cages full of birds,
   their houses are full of deceit;
  they have become rich and powerful
28   and have grown fat and sleek.
  Their evil deeds have no limit;
   they do not plead the case of the fatherless to win it,
   they do not defend the rights of the poor.
29Should I not punish them for this?"
  declares the LORD.
  "Should I not avenge myself
  on such a nation as this?

30"A horrible and shocking thing
  has happened in the land:
31The prophets prophesy lies,
  the priests rule by their own authority,
  and my people love it this way.
  But what will you do in the end?"

20–21 This double exhortation (v.20) is addressed to hearers concerned for their nation. Such a call (the reference covers both Jacob and Judah) to "announce" and "proclaim" (note the double imperatives) the word of God occurs nowhere else in the book. What weighty announcement are they to make? They are to proclaim that moral blindness and deafness have kept the people from realizing their perilous state. What a rebuke to their stupidity! The words Jeremiah uses in v.21 refer to idols in Psalm 115:5–6. Here they refer to the people who had become like the idols they worshiped. The language is purposely blunt to awaken the people to their dangerous condition. How can they be so obtuse concerning the truth that God is Creator, Provider, and Judge?

22 God is to be adored and served because he controls the raging sea, the mightiest force in creation. Moreover, he does so by the most unlikely of restraining forces, the sand. Though made up of such small, shifting particles, the sand can and does set a bound to the violence of the sea. If God can restrain the sea, surely he can restrain the invader. Since even the turbulent sea obeys God's commands, Israel is senseless to rebel against him (cf. Job 38:8–11; Ps 104:5–9).

23–25 Although the sea remains within its appointed limits, Israel has revolted against the Lord (v.23). The people have overstepped God's moral limits. Furthermore, they are blind to their dependence on God's providence (v.24). They do not see the hand of the Lord even in the balance of rain for harvest and his withholding it in times of his displeasure. Here is another reason for them to reverence the Lord—gratitude for his gifts. The "regular weeks of harvest" are the seven weeks between the Feast of Passover and the Feast of Weeks (Lev 23:15–16). As Creator, God has control over the rain as he does over the sea (cf. Deut 11:10–17). The withholding of seasonal rains was attributable to their sinfulness (v.25).

26–29 Jeremiah now specifies the wicked deeds of the people. Three classes are arraigned before the divine justice: the rich oppressors of the poor (vv.26–28), the

417

lying prophets, and the time-serving priests (v.31). Widespread social injustices cry out for God's judgment. The wicked rich have acquired their wealth by deceit and heartless oppression of the poor and helpless. As a fowler snares birds by devices, so the people accumulate wealth by deceit. The trap (v.26) was probably a clapnet as represented on Egyptian monuments. In those days fowlers would place several tame birds in a cage (v.27); when the wild birds saw them, they lighted on the cage, falling into the snare. The heartless aristocracy had wealth enough but were not satisfied. Prosperity did not bring piety with it (Deut 32:15; Ps 73:7). In fact, they excused their wicked deeds on the flimsiest grounds. They could not have troubled themselves less over whether the cause of the orphan was maintained (v.28). As in v.9, so in v.29 and with even greater force, Jeremiah asked whether for sins like theirs, the people could possibly believe God would overlook inevitable judgment.

30–31 Now Jeremiah, standing aside, as it were, and viewing the moral wreckage, exclaims over the astonishing and horrible things transpiring in the land (v.30). Those who should have been the chief moral backbone of the nation had treacherously denied the Lord's commitment to them. The leaders had become misleaders. Foremost among the guilty were the false prophets (v.31), whose rosy predictions led the nation to its final doom in 586 B.C. Next to them were the spineless priests who ruled "by their own authority" (lit., "at their direction"; cf. 1 Chron 25:2; 2 Chron 23:18 for this idiom). So the chapter closes with the tragic statement that those entrusted with the spiritual welfare of the nation were unworthy of their positions. Worse yet, the people were so unaware of the issues that they acquiesced in all that their leaders did. The rampant evil did not trouble the people, who had come to accept it and favor it. They preferred indulgent leaders who made few, if any, moral demands. The people had lost all sense of moral values and did not realize they were being duped. They cherished their false security. But the final question is, In the time of retribution, when the calamity would strike, then what would they do? Then where would their hope and confidence be?

Notes

24 The "regular weeks of harvest" were the seven weeks from Passover to Pentecost. Barley harvest came soon after Passover; wheat was not ready to harvest till Pentecost (cf. Exod 34:22; Lev 23:15–16). In Israel rain was always considered a gift of God (Acts 14:17). The climate in Palestine is dependent on the rain in fall and spring and on the dew in summer. Though the Jews were exiled from the land for centuries, the liturgy of the orthodox synagogue includes a "counting" ritual (סְפִירָה, *sepîrāh*), which is recited daily between Passover and Pentecost. Dew is so important in the Holy Land that the orthodox prayers include "petition for dew" (תְּפִלַּת טַל, *tepillat ṭal*).

31 The usual rendering for יִרְדּוּ עַל יְדֵיהֶם (*yirdû 'al yedêhem*, "rule by their authority") has been altered by a few to the clause "they have descended on their hands," in the sense of joining hands with them (so Blayney). This appears to suit the context less well than the first reading. It takes the verbal form from יָרַד (*yārad*, "to go down, descend") rather than רָדָה (*rāḏāh*, "to rule").

418

5. *The siege and fall of Jerusalem foretold* (6:1–30)

The striking feature of this chapter is its rapidity of movement leading to the gathering storm of invasion soon to engulf the capital and the land. It has been called a chapter of alarms; it begins on a note of impending doom and concludes with the utter rejection of the people.

a. *The approach of the invaders*

6:1–5

> 1"Flee for safety, people of Benjamin!
>   Flee from Jerusalem!
> Sound the trumpet in Tekoa!
>   Raise the signal over Beth Hakkerem!
> For disaster looms out of the north,
>   even terrible destruction.
> 2I will destroy the Daughter of Zion,
>   so beautiful and delicate.
> 3Shepherds with their flocks will come against her;
>   they will pitch their tents around her,
>   each tending his own portion."
>
> 4"Prepare for battle against her!
>   Arise, let us attack at noon!
> But, alas, the daylight is fading,
>   and the shadows of evening grow long.
> 5So arise, let us attack at night
>   and destroy her fortresses!"

1–3 The chapter may be divided into five sections, each marked by the declarative "This is what the LORD Almighty says" (vv.6, 9) or "This is what the LORD says" (vv.16, 21, 22). The doom is so near that Jeremiah sees the invasion as already in progress. The attack, as he has already said, comes from the north. Jeremiah calls the people to flee for safety. In 4:5–6 he advised Judah to flee to Jerusalem. Now the city is no longer safe; it is soon to undergo a siege. The way to safety is only by flight (v.1). The people could never plead that they had not been fully warned. The reason the people of Benjamin are mentioned is that geographically Jerusalem belonged to the territory of Benjamin. It was settled by Judeans and Benjamites (cf. 1 Chron 9:3), separated by the Valley of Hinnom. Moreover, Jeremiah was a Benjamite and had strong ties with his own tribesmen.

Two means of warning the people are mentioned: the trumpet call and the fire signal. Tekoa, twelve miles south of Jerusalem, was the home of the prophet Amos (cf. 2 Sam 14:2; Amos 1:1). In the Hebrew there is a play on words here between "Tekoa" (*teqôa'*) and "sound [*tiq'û*] the trumpet." Tekoa was the last town in Judah on the edge of the desert. The "signal" or "beacon" (*maś'ēt*) was to show the way. This uncommon word is found in Lachish Letter 4, line 10 (Torczyner, *The Lachish Letters*, p. 79; cf. also Judg 20:38–40). Such fire signals were used in military communication. Beth Hakkerem (lit., "house of the vineyard") has been identified by some with 'Ain Karim, west of Jerusalem. The site is mentioned only here and at Nehemiah 3:14. Others believe it is Frank Mountain, three miles northeast of Tekoa. It should probably be identified with modern Ramat Rahel, a village in Israel whose ruins (*Khirbet Salih*) have been identified with Beth Hakkerem (so H.G. May, ed., *Oxford Bible Atlas* [London: Oxford University Press, 1962], pp. 63, 73, 77, 120, 136). The people are to flee south because invasion threatens from the north. The disaster is personified; it "looms" or looks down on its prey.

Destruction is to fall on Zion, pictured as a beautiful and delicate woman (v.2). By a sudden change of figure, a characteristic of Jeremiah's style, the invaders are portrayed as shepherds and their armies as flocks (v.3; cf. 12:10 for the same figure). They denude the land, everyone tending (devastating) "his own portion" (lit., "what has been assigned him"). This is not a picture of a horde of nomads trying to starve the city (contra Frost).

4–5 Jeremiah next presents a consultation of the enemies of Judah. Their speech reveals haste, impatience, and thirst for destruction. The army will brook no delay in taking the city. The call to prepare (lit., "sanctify," i.e., set apart to the deity) for battle (v.4), as elsewhere in the OT, included offering sacrifices and performing religious ceremonies because Israel had a religious view of war (Deut 20:2–4) and considered it a sacred service undertaken in the Lord's name (cf. 1 Sam 25:28). Though the enemy here is the Babylonian army, the Babylonians too had a religious concept of war.

So eager is the enemy to destroy Jerusalem that they decide to make a surprise attack at noon, when soldiers would normally be resting. But the light is fading; so they must make a night attack (v.5). They will be satisfied with nothing less than the utter destruction of Jerusalem's fortresses.

Notes

2 The verb דָּמָה (*dāmāh*) means "to be like" in the simple Qal stem, but only in the intensive Piel stem does it have the significance of "likening, compared to" (so KJV, "I have likened"). Here the context demands a translation of "to destroy" (so NIV).

b. *The siege of Jerusalem*

6:6–8

⁶This is what the LORD Almighty says:

> "Cut down the trees
>   and build siege ramps against Jerusalem.
> This city must be punished;
>   it is filled with oppression.
> ⁷As a well pours out its water,
>   so she pours out her wickedness.
> Violence and destruction resound in her;
>   her sickness and wounds are ever before me.
> ⁸Take warning, O Jerusalem,
>   or I will turn away from you
> and make your land desolate
>   so no one can live in it."

6–8 The Lord appears to be leading the assault against Jerusalem by using the enemy as his agent of judgment. The early preparations for the siege include felling trees for bulwarks and building siege works (v.6; cf. Deut 20:20). Mounds of earth were also heaped up to make them level with the walls to facilitate entry into the city. Again, the Lord reminds the people that the cause of judgment lay in Judah. Jerusalem, blessed of God for some four centuries, is now characterized as oppressive. Just as a well keeps its water cool and fresh, so Judah seems incapable of anything but sin (v.7). The cry of the oppressed (cf. 20:8) is regularly heard in Jerusalem. All her troubles come from her persistence in sin. The Lord sees the people's spiritual sickness as unchanged (cf. v.14). But in his infinite grace he warns them before it is too late (v.8). While there is still a ray of hope, he warns the people of the doom awaiting their continued defiance in their sin. Reluctant to part from his people, the Lord must issue another call to repent.

c. The fall of the city

6:9–15

⁹This is what the LORD Almighty says:

> "Let them glean the remnant of Israel
> as thoroughly as a vine;
> pass your hand over the branches again,
> like one gathering grapes."

¹⁰To whom can I speak and give warning?
Who will listen to me?
Their ears are closed
so they cannot hear.
The word of the LORD is offensive to them;
they find no pleasure in it.
¹¹But I am full of the wrath of the LORD,
and I cannot hold it in.

> "Pour it out on the children in the street
> and on the young men gathered together;
> both husband and wife will be caught in it,
> and the old, those weighed down with years.
> ¹²Their houses will be turned over to others,
> together with their fields and their wives,
> when I stretch out my hand
> against those who live in the land,"

declares the LORD.

¹³"From the least to the greatest,
all are greedy for gain;
prophets and priests alike,
all practice deceit.
¹⁴They dress the wound of my people
as though it were not serious.
'Peace, peace,' they say,
when there is no peace.
¹⁵Are they ashamed of their loathsome conduct?
No, they have no shame at all;
they do not even know how to blush.
So they will fall among the fallen;
they will be brought down when I punish them,"

says the LORD.

9 Once more Israel is viewed in the figure of a vineyard (cf. 5:10). A thorough gleaning, a complete devastation, awaits them. The Lord authorizes the enemy even to search out the remnant to take them captive—viz., the enemy will not be satisfied with one invasion but will repeat it. It may be that the northern tribes are implied by the main gathering of grapes. Judah, left as a remnant, is now also to be gleaned. The enemy leader is exhorted to pass over the branches repeatedly, lest any grapes be overlooked.

10 Responding to the nation's unbelief, Jeremiah identifies himself with the Lord in speaking of the people's obtuseness to his word. In fact, they regard it with contempt. To warn them further is useless; their ears are "closed" (*ārlāh*, "uncircumcised"). The metaphor is used in the OT of lips and constantly of the heart (cf. 4:4). But this is its only application to the ears (cf. Acts 7:51 for "uncircumcised hearts and ears"). They resolutely refuse to listen to God. Here is the first hint of the lack of response of the nation to Jeremiah's message.

11 Regardless of success or failure, Jeremiah's duty was to preach the Lord's message. Whether the people listened or not, he was divinely compelled to voice the Lord's indignation. Full of the divine wrath, he is commanded to pour it out on everybody—children, young men, married couples, the elderly—all are involved in the city's doom. Even the children and the aged, usually the special objects of God's care, are to be shown no mercy. The wrath was evoked by the sins now set forth: greed (v.13), deceitful prophecy (vv.13–14), loathsome deeds and shamelessness (v.15), obduracy (vv.16–17), rejection of the law (vv.18–19), and worthless sacrifices (v.20). (For the figure of the cup of God's wrath, see also 25:15.)

12–13 With the conquest of Jerusalem, houses, fields, and wives also will be violently given away to others (v.12). This is exactly what Moses had warned about (cf. Deut 28:30). (Verses 12–15 are repeated in 8:10–12.) The entire gamut of society covets gain (v.13). Because of their greed the people will lose everything. The blame lay largely with the priests and prophets who held out false hopes to the people regardless of the way they lived. Those whose integrity should have been exemplary practiced deceit.

14–15 Another sin was false optimism, listening to baseless promises of peace when there was no ground for it. The priests and prophets, physicians of no value ("they dress the wound of my people as though it were not serious"), misled the people (v.14). Only superficially did they heal the wound (lit., "the breach") between God and Judah. Their stock in trade was constant babbling that all was well (cf. Mic 3:5), making nothing (so LXX) of the people's heinous sin. (When the OT speaks of peace, it often connotes more than the absence of war and refers to material and spiritual prosperity.)

Lulled into complacency, the people lost all sense of shame for their abominable deeds (v.15). Insensitive to wrong, they were so hardened in sin that their hearts were no longer open to the message of truth. As for those who misled them, they were to share the fate of the nation they duped.

d. *The cause for judgment*

6:16–21

¹⁶This is what the LORD says:

"Stand at the crossroads and look;
  ask for the ancient paths,
ask where the good way is, and walk in it,
  and you will find rest for your souls.
  But you said, 'We will not walk in it.'
¹⁷I appointed watchmen over you and said,
  'Listen to the sound of the trumpet!'
  But you said, 'We will not listen.'
¹⁸Therefore hear, O nations;
  observe, O witnesses,
  what will happen to them.
¹⁹Hear, O earth:
  I am bringing disaster on this people,
  the fruit of their schemes,
because they have not listened to my words
  and have rejected my law.
²⁰What do I care about incense from Sheba
  or sweet calamus from a distant land?
Your burnt offerings are not acceptable;
  your sacrifices do not please me."

²¹Therefore this is what the LORD says:

"I will put obstacles before this people.
  Fathers and sons alike will stumble over them;
  neighbors and friends will perish."

16–17 The reason for the people's judgment is their straying from the ancient ways of the patriarchs into the ways of idolatry. Jeremiah pictures travelers who have lost their way; when they arrive at crossroads, the moment calls for clear decision (v.16). To go one way can mean death; to go another, life. The ancient paths and the good way are the same; they are the way of repentance, reconciliation, fear, and love of God. They were the ways of the Mosaic tradition. Here, by the way, is ample refutation of the view that the prophets were mainly, if not wholly, innovators in their messages. (The contrast in ways is found also in 18:15 and 23:12.) The result of walking in the way of obedience was peace and rest of soul. Our Lord may well have had this passage in mind in his words in Matthew 11:28–29 (cf. also Isa 28:12). How did the people respond to Jeremiah's words? They refused to walk in the ancient paths. The Lord even sent prophets as watchmen (v.17) to warn them of impending danger (cf. Ezek 3:17; 33:7). The nation obeyed neither the admonition in v.16 nor the message of the prophets (v.17). God always gives ample warning of coming judgment. The people's disobedience was threefold: (1) they were unfaithful to the covenant bond with God (v.16—"We will not"); (2) they were unheeding of the warnings of the true prophets (v.17—"We will not"); and (3) they rejected the law (v.19).

18–20 Now (v.18) God calls on the nations and all the earth to see how fully his people deserve their punishment. Ordinarily *'ēḏāh* ("congregation," KJV, RSV) refers in the OT to Israel, but here it must mean the Gentiles; so NIV translates the word "witnesses." The Gentiles are being alerted to what is to happen to Judah. They will witness the righteous consequences of Judah's wicked deeds—her public humiliation (v. 19). Strangely enough, when the Lord informs man that his heartless worship is unacceptable, he turns to more of the same as though quantity can substitute for quality. When sin is not forsaken, sacrifices are useless. This does not mean that Jeremiah was against sacrifices per se; he was only against unethical sacrifices. Offerings are worthless when the heart is not right in making them. Incense (v. 20) came from Sheba, southwest of Arabia. Cane or calamus probably came from India and was used in making the holy anointing oil (Exod 30:23). These ingredients of worship were costly because they were brought from a great distance. But they were of no value when they were part of heartless, godless offerings. In themselves, sacrifices were never efficacious; all the prophets who speak of them as used in heartless worship deny them validity (cf. Isa 1:11–13; Jer 7:21–23; Hos 6:6; Amos 5:21–27; Mic 6:6–8). Jeremiah's statement is all the more remarkable since he was a priest by birth.

21 The last verse of this section has been erroneously understood as saying that God placed stumbling blocks in the nation's way to bring about her eternal doom. But this is not at all the meaning. Jeremiah is referring to the Babylonians who were the instruments to bring about Judah's physical destruction; they were not agents to effect her moral fall. The stress is on the general operation of God's moral law (cf. James 1:13–15). In contrast to the rest promised in v. 16, which they rejected, the people will meet with destruction that will engulf them all—from father to son and neighbor to friend. All will suffer the consequences of their wicked acts.

e. *The terror of the enemy forces*

6:22–30

22This is what the LORD says:

> "Look, an army is coming
> from the land of the north;
> a great nation is being stirred up
> from the ends of the earth.
> 23They are armed with bow and spear;
> they are cruel and show no mercy.
> They sound like the roaring sea
> as they ride on their horses;
> they come like men in battle formation
> to attack you, O Daughter of Zion."

> 24We have heard reports about them,
> and our hands hang limp.
> Anguish has gripped us,
> pain like that of a woman in labor.
> 25Do not go out to the fields
> or walk on the roads,
> for the enemy has a sword,
> and there is terror on every side.
> 26O my people, put on sackcloth
> and roll in ashes;
> mourn with bitter wailing
> as for an only son,
> for suddenly the destroyer
> will come upon us.

27"I have made you a tester of metals
    and my people the ore,
that you may observe
    and test their ways.
28They are all hardened rebels,
    going about to slander.
They are bronze and iron;
    they all act corruptly.
29The bellows blow fiercely
    to burn away the lead with fire,
but the refining goes on in vain;
    the wicked are not purged out.
30They are called rejected silver,
    because the LORD has rejected them."

22–23 In order to arouse the nation to repentance, Jeremiah underscores the terror of the coming enemy by adding details to the portrayal in 5:15–17. The direction, "the north," from which the enemy will come is again given (v.22). They will come from the remote parts of the then-known earth. The prophet describes their weaponry, their cruelty, their vigor, their speed, and their readiness for war against Zion (v.23; cf. 50:41–43). The portrayal cannot be applied to the Scythians (so KD). In their cruelty the Babylonians remind us of the Assyrians (Jonah 3:8). To burn prisoners in a furnace (29:22; Dan 3:11), impale them, and flay them alive were common occurrences in Babylonian wars. Their shouts in battle were like the roaring sea. The war horses seem to have been new to the nation, which was used to the war chariots of the Egyptians rather than to cavalry.

24–26 Jeremiah describes Judah's response to the news of the invading Babylonians. As one of the people, he expresses his emotions and theirs at the report that the enemy was actually attacking. There is no power in the people to resist; they are limp (v.24). Because "there is terror on every side" (v.25, a favorite expression of Jeremiah; cf. 20:3 mg., 10; 46:5; 49:29), the people are warned not to go in undefended places, for to do so would mean death. Their trials are likened to the pain of childbirth (v.24b; cf. 4:31) and the death of an only son (v.26), leaving no one to carry on the family name (cf. Amos 8:10; Zech 12:10). Among Jews death is always viewed as a calamity; and when an only son dies, it means the end of "immortality" for the parents, and the blow is unbearable. The destroyer will come suddenly on Judah; though they had been repeatedly warned, the people will find themselves unprepared because of their faith in false hopes.

27–30 The last verses of the chapter focus on the nation's incorrigibility. So that no one may think God has not given the people every chance, he is willing to have them tested for any merit or worth that may be in them (v.27). Therefore he informs Jeremiah that he is to act as a tester and assayer of the moral worth of Judah. Using a superlative, Jeremiah evaluates them as the rebellious of the rebellious, i.e., "hardened rebels" (v.28). They are entirely of inferior metal—bronze and iron, not silver and gold (Ezek 22:18–22). And though the refining process is thoroughly carried out (v.29), there is no valuable residue to reward the labors of the refiner. In antiquity lead was put with silver in a crucible; when heated, the lead, acting as a flux, oxidized and carried off the alloy. But here the ore is so impure that the alloys are not removed. The labors of Jeremiah are in vain. As refuse silver, they are rejected by the Lord (v.30). There is a play on words: rejected silver, they are rejected of the Lord. Three truths emerge from the passage: (1) the nation rejected God; (2) God has rejected the nation; and (3) men count the nation as refuse. So judgment is inevitable.

Notes

23 The "spear" is usually understood to be a javelin. 1QM from Qumran indicates that כִּידוֹן (kîḏôn) was a sword like the Roman *gladius* (cf. Y. Yadin, *The Scroll of the War of the Sons of Light Against the Sons of Darkness* [New York: Oxford University Press, 1962], pp. 124–31).

27 Both KJV and JPS translate "a tower and a fortress" for בָּחוֹן (bāḥôn) and מִבְצָר (mibṣār). ASV has "a trier and a fortress." NASB chooses "an assayer and a tester." NIV renders "a tester of metals and my people the ore." "Tower and fortress" are not in accord with the context of testing and refining metals. For the first noun (bāḥôn), all ancient translations (except the Targum) and modern commentators agree on "trier," "prover," rather than "tower." In harmony with this position, mibṣār may be better translated "assessor" (NASB, RSV) or "tester of metals" (NIV), reading the second noun as the Piel participle mᵉḇaṣṣēr ("an assessor"; so Harrison).

C. *Jeremiah's Temple Address* (7:1–10:25)

1. *No refuge in the temple* (7:1–34)

Chapters 7–10, known as the temple address(es), were not necessarily delivered on a single occasion. Jeremiah's address (ch. 7), which he delivered standing at the gate of the temple, has been called one of the majestic scenes of history. One of the crucial events in his ministry, it undoubtedly initiated the unrelenting opposition he experienced during the remainder of his life. According to 26:1, Jeremiah delivered it early in Jehoiakim's reign (c. 609–605 B.C.); and chapter 26 records the consequences of the address. The time was not long after the death of Josiah. The entire discourse seemed to run counter to Josiah's attempt to centralize worship at the temple in Jerusalem and appeared to blast hopes inculcated by the earlier prophets, Isaiah among them. Josiah's reform promised a restoration of God's blessing and not the calamity of the temple and the dissolution of the commonwealth. In Isaiah's day the repentance of godly Hezekiah and the people issued in God's removal of the Assyrian threat in one night (Isa 37:36). But the spiritual decline of the nation proved irreversible in Jeremiah's time. In spite of points of similarity between chapters 7 and 26, some interpreters have contended that they are not to be identified but could have been delivered on different occasions (so Laetsch). But Jeremiah liked to repeat his own words, and he might well have spoken more than once on the same theme (so G.A. Smith). The scholarly consensus that unites chapters 7 and 26 is doubtless correct. The temple-gate address is an eloquent attack on the people's confidence in the temple as insuring Jerusalem's inviolability from all enemies. The emphasis on ethical issues is paramount.

a. *Misplaced confidence*

7:1–7

> ¹This is the word that came to Jeremiah from the LORD: ²"Stand at the gate of
> the LORD's house and there proclaim this message:
> " 'Hear the word of the LORD, all you people of Judah who come through these
> gates to worship the LORD. ³This is what the LORD Almighty, the God of Israel,
> says: Reform your ways and your actions, and I will let you live in this place. ⁴Do
> not trust in deceptive words and say, "This is the temple of the LORD, the temple
> of the LORD, the temple of the LORD!" ⁵If you really change your ways and your
> actions and deal with each other justly, ⁶if you do not oppress the alien, the
> fatherless or the widow and do not shed innocent blood in this place, and if you do
> not follow other gods to your own harm, ⁷then I will let you live in this place, in the
> land I gave your forefathers for ever and ever.' "

1 Jeremiah spoke at a critical time. The nation was shocked by Josiah's death, the
removal of Jehoahaz, and the imposition of Jehoiakim as king by Pharaoh Neco.
With Jehoiakim a religious reversal took place in the nation. Canaanite rites were
reappearing in Judah. The temple address was Jeremiah's first public sermon and,
as has been said above, the source of all his later opposition from various groups in
the nation. Through it he made lasting enemies and may have been excluded from
the temple because of it (36:5). It was a thoroughgoing denunciation of the worship
of the day. The deliverance of Jerusalem in 701 B.C. in Hezekiah's reign had
become almost legendary and led to the idea that Jerusalem was inviolable because
of the sanctuary (cf. 2 Kings 18:13–19:37). Jeremiah spoke during a lull in hostile
political activity. Doubtless, many were ready to attribute the respite to the glory of
the temple.

2–3 The immediate occasion of Jeremiah's address may have been one of the three
pilgrimage festivals (Deut 16:16). The "gate" (v.2) was the one that connected the
outer and inner courts. The place suggested is the Eastern Gate; some identify it
with the New Gate (cf. 26:10; 36:10). Jeremiah's position insured him a wide hearing. It was doubly significant that Jeremiah's attack on the superstitious attitude
toward the temple was uttered at that very place. Verse 3 states the theme of the
sermon. It was a simple, direct, unmistakable message: Repent if you expect to
remain in your native land (v.7; cf. Deut 7:12–15). The people must change their
settled habits and way of life.

4 With great courage Jeremiah warned the people against believing the deceptive
words of false prophets ascribing talismanic power to the temple. The threefold
repetition of the false prophets' words expresses emphasis even to the superlative
degree (cf. Isa 6:3). In effect they were saying, "These buildings are assuredly the
temple of the Lord!" And they were saying this at a time when the temple was made
central by Josiah's reforms in 621 B.C. The people were using these words like a
magical incantation. The words were true, but what the people inferred from them
was entirely erroneous. The temple had become a kind of fetish and object of faith
(cf. the use of the ark [1 Sam 4:3]). The basis for this was (1) the promise of an
eternal dynasty to David (cf. 2 Sam 7:11–14) and (2) the choice of Zion as God's
earthly abode (cf. Ps 132:13–16). Therefore no harm could come to the temple. The
false prophets continually assured the people of the personal intervention of God in

case of any danger to the temple and Zion. But Jeremiah thundered that the temple without godliness was a delusion.

5–7 Jeremiah had called for the people to repent; now he turns to the prescription for their remaining in the land. Profession and conduct must be in accord (v.5), or all their efforts will be unavailing. The way of blessing, then as now, is to give spiritual and moral principles the first place in life. Four things (v.6) are stressed: (1) justice; (2) concern for the alien, fatherless, and widow; (3) avoidance of judicial murders; and (4) abandonment of idolatry. Idolatry, the root of their problems and their first national sin at Mount Sinai, comes last for emphasis. Nothing less than spiritual renewal would insure continuance in the land God had given their fathers in perpetuity (v.7; cf. Deut 14:29; 24:19–21; chs. 28–30). As always, acceptance with God depends not on ceremonial observances but on true piety.

b. *Indifference to godly living*

7:8–11

> ⁸But look, you are trusting in deceptive words that are worthless.
> ⁹" 'Will you steal and murder, commit adultery and perjury, burn incense to Baal and follow other gods you have not known, ¹⁰and then come and stand before me in this house, which bears my Name, and say, "We are safe"—safe to do all these detestable things? ¹¹Has this house, which bears my Name, become a den of robbers to you? But I have been watching! declares the LORD.

8–10 Now the prophet turns to the woeful spiritual state of the people. They were trusting in deceptive words (v.8; cf. v.4) that veneered their sins (cf. 2 Tim 4:3–4). They were guilty (v.9) of violating five of the Ten Commandments (Exod 20; Deut 5); the Decalogue was still valid and binding on them all. All these violations were going on at the same time that they expressed confidence in the temple. All the verbs except the last one (in v.9) are in the infinitive absolute form in Hebrew, showing strong emphasis on the actions themselves. The description may even be understood as expressing great indignation at the evil practices that their attendance at the temple was meant to atone for (v.10; so Orelli). The people felt that going to the temple granted them release from guilt; it was as though they had an indulgence to go on sinning (cf. Eccl 8:11). Ignoring God's ethical demands, they rested in ceremonial rites.

11 Ultimately the people were treating the temple, the house of God, as robbers do their dens. It was a temporary refuge till they sallied forth on another foray. Limestone caves in Palestine were used as robbers' dens; so Jeremiah's metaphor was clear to his hearers. Here was nothing less than corruption of the best and the holiest. The Lord, having seen the situation, will deal with it accordingly (cf. Isa 56:7 and Matt 21:13; Mark 11:17; Luke 19:46).

c. *The example of Shiloh*

7:12–15

> ¹²" 'Go now to the place in Shiloh where I first made a dwelling for my Name, and see what I did to it because of the wickedness of my people Israel. ¹³While

you were doing all these things, declares the LORD, I spoke to you again and again, but you did not listen; I called you, but you did not answer. ¹⁴Therefore, what I did to Shiloh I will now do to the house that bears my Name, the temple you trust in, the place I gave to you and your fathers. ¹⁵I will thrust you from my presence, just as I did all your brothers, the people of Ephraim.' "

12 Shiloh, the modern *Seilûn* (possibly about one mile from the ancient site), was on the main highway between Jerusalem and Shechem. The Mosaic tabernacle was set up there after the conquest of Canaan (cf. Josh 18:1; 22:12; Judg 21:19; 1 Sam 1:9, 24). It was the abode of the ark and tabernacle during the era of the judges. In Saul's reign the tabernacle was at Nob (cf. 1 Sam 21:1–2). At Shiloh, Israel went into idolatry (1 Sam 4:1–11); so the ark was captured by the Philistines at the Battle of Ebenezer. The Bible gives no historical account of the destruction of Shiloh. Jeremiah's references to its destruction (cf. also 26:6, 9) have been confirmed by excavations of the site, which revealed a city destroyed by the Philistines about 1050 B.C., probably after the Battle of Ebenezer. The dig was carried out by the Danish Palestine Expedition. Their findings confirmed Psalm 78:60–64. Shiloh was to the judges what Jerusalem was to the kings. Jeremiah was a descendant of the Eli family; so the tragedy had personal implications for him. The destruction of Shiloh did not necessarily mean the demolition of the tabernacle, because it was still in existence at Gibeon in David's time (cf. 1 Chron 21:29), at the commencement of Solomon's reign. The sanctuary at Shiloh proved the falsity of the claim that the Lord was unalterably committed to an earthly temple and its preservation regardless of the moral state of the people.

13–15 Because they had committed the sins mentioned in v.9, the Lord had earnestly and continuously entreated the people through his prophets, but without response (v.13). By a strong anthropomorphism, Jeremiah portrays the Lord as "rising up early and speaking" (lit. Heb.; NIV, "I spoke to you again and again"). This expression is a favorite with Jeremiah (cf. v.25; 11:7; 25:3–4; 26:5; 29:19; 32:33; 35:14–15; 44:4; it does not occur elsewhere in the OT). Again Jeremiah makes it plain that the people trusted the temple of God instead of the God of the temple (v.14). God is never dependent on any particular place of worship. For Jeremiah's hearers, this was unheard of heresy. The outcome of Judah's ways would soon be exile, as it had been for Ephraim (Israel), the northern kingdom, in 722–721 B.C. (v.15). This was the message that inflamed Jeremiah's hearers and earned him their lasting hatred and opposition almost to the point of martyrdom.

Notes

12 Shiloh was eighteen miles north of Jerusalem. The site was not resettled after its destruction in the eleventh century B.C. until about 300 B.C. (cf. Hans Kjaer, "The Excavation of Shiloh 1929," *Journal of the Palestine Oriental Society*, 10 [1930]: 87–174).

d. *Worship of the Queen of Heaven*

7:16–20

> ¹⁶"So do not pray for this people nor offer any plea or petition for them; do not plead with me, for I will not listen to you. ¹⁷Do you not see what they are doing in the towns of Judah and in the streets of Jerusalem? ¹⁸The children gather wood, the fathers light the fire, and the women knead the dough and make cakes of bread for the Queen of Heaven. They pour out drink offerings to other gods to provoke me to anger. ¹⁹But am I the one they are provoking? declares the LORD. Are they not rather harming themselves, to their own shame?
>
> ²⁰" 'Therefore this is what the Sovereign LORD says: My anger and my wrath will be poured out on this place, on man and beast, on the trees of the field and on the fruit of the ground, and it will burn and not be quenched.' "

16–18 Now (v.16) the Lord explicitly forbids the prophet to intercede for his people (cf. 11:14; 14:11–12). They were so obdurately sinful that praying for them was futile. What was particularly abominable to the Lord was the worship of the Queen of Heaven by the entire populace (vv.17–18). This goddess was probably the Assyro-Babylonian Ishtar (cf. also 44:17—the goddess of love and fertility; she was the planet Venus (so Cunliffe-Jones). It appears she was worshiped mainly by women (cf. ch.44, esp. vv.15–19). A female deity is foreign to OT theology; so the implication is that this cult was of non-Hebraic origin. Such worship was probably initiated by Manasseh (2 Kings 21:1–9) and reintroduced into Judah by Jehoiakim. This obscene idolatry was practiced not only privately but also by whole families, including the children. The "cakes" have been described as round and flat, resembling the moon (so CHS, p. 94). Also, the people offered libations to other gods.

19–20 If they thought they were spiting God (v.19), the people were grossly insensate. They would bear both spite and shame as consequences of their sins. Moreover, sin affects all realms of nature (v.20; cf. Rom 8:20–22). Devastation would fall on man, beast, trees, and produce of the soil.

Notes

18 Some fifty-two MSS and certain commentators prefer to read an א (') after the first syllable of מְלֶכֶת (*m^eleket*, "queen"), giving the meaning of "work," i.e., the host or stars of heaven, without a particularization of one deity. Apart from the context here and in 44:17–19, the fact is that Ishtar was known by the Babylonian title *sharrat shamê* ("Queen of Heaven"), goddess of the planet Venus. LXX is inconsistent in rendering στρατία (*stratia*, "army") here but βασιλίσσα (*basilissa*, "queen") in the parallel passage in 44:17–19, 25 = LXX 51:17–19, 25.

e. *Obedience better than sacrifice*

7:21–26

> ²¹" 'This is what the LORD Almighty, the God of Israel, says: Go ahead, add your burnt offerings to your other sacrifices and eat the meat yourselves! ²²For when I brought your forefathers out of Egypt and spoke to them, I did not just give them

commands about burnt offerings and sacrifices, 23but I gave them this command: Obey me, and I will be your God and you will be my people. Walk in all the ways I command you, that it may go well with you. 24But they did not listen or pay attention; instead, they followed the stubborn inclinations of their evil hearts. They went backward and not forward. 25From the time your forefathers left Egypt until now, day after day, again and again I sent you my servants the prophets. 26But they did not listen to me or pay attention. They were stiff-necked and did more evil than their forefathers.' "

21 This part of Jeremiah is one of the most disputed and misunderstood in the entire book. Having been prohibited from interceding for the nation, Jeremiah had revealed the punishment awaiting Judah's idolatry. Would more sacrifices help them? To this question Jeremiah now addresses himself. Undoubtedly he spoke the words of this verse ironically and contemptuously. The purpose is to show how totally erroneous was Judah's concept of sacrifices. Because they have missed the true meaning of the Lord's worship, they may even eat the sacrifices intended only for the Lord because he cares for none of them. He calls them mere flesh. In other words, they could multiply their offerings as much as they liked because all of them were worthless.

22 The most controversy centers around this verse because it appears to invalidate the whole sacrificial system. Certain critics have understood it to mean that the law of sacrifices was not given by Moses but was introduced centuries later—a position that is part of the elaborate system that denies the Mosaic authorship of the Pentateuch. In order to treat the question adequately, one must understand the sense of the Hebrew text. In it a rhetorical negation is used to point up antithesis between v.22 and v.23 more emphatically (cf. Deut 5:3). Moreover, the negative in Hebrew often supplies the lack of the comparative—i.e., without excluding the thing denied, the statement implies only the prior importance of the thing set in contrast to it (Hos 6:6). In short, the Hebrew idiom permits denial of one thing in order to emphasize another (cf. for a NT parallel Luke 14:26). The idiom does not intend to deny the statement but only to set it in a secondary place (so Frost).

That the OT sacrifices were non-Mosaic cannot be valid: (1) sacrifices are mentioned in 33:18, also 6:20; 7:21; 14:12; and 17:26; (2) Hosea and Amos, ministering before Jeremiah's time, mention sacrifices; and (3) frequent condemnation of heartless worship with sacrifices implies that sacrifices were a well-established institution in Israel (so Streane). Here Isaiah 1:11–15; Hosea 6:6; Amos 5:21–25; and Micah 6:6–8 should be carefully considered. Judah had left out the main element: obedience to God. In view of the passages just cited, and in view of the Pentateuchal legislation, sacrifices were always meant to be of secondary importance to obedience and godliness. Neither Jeremiah nor any other prophet decried sacrifices as such. They meant that moral law is always paramount to the ritual law. It is significant that when Leviticus 6–8 is read in the synagogue, this passage in Jeremiah is read as the concluding portion, called the Haphtorah (so Freedman).

23–26 Actually, God had not spoken at Sinai of sacrifices but only of obedience (v.23)—and this even before the law was given (Exod 19:3–6). Jeremiah's words show that he had in mind in v.23 the giving of the Ten Commandments. Among these there were no directions for sacrifices; they dealt solely with spiritual and moral matters. The OT order was first obedience and worship of God and then institution of sacrifices (cf. Ps 51:16–19). In Judah, as Jeremiah shows, the whole sacrificial system was invalidated on the ground that it was not carried out in true faith (v.24). Obedience always was and would be the dominant consideration (so Cundall). And this very element was the one so conspicuously absent in the nation, whether in Moses' time or in the time of Jeremiah (v.25). Indeed, in spite of Jeremiah's consistent warnings, Judah did worse than her fathers (v.26).

Notes

22 The translation "about burnt offerings" for עַל דִּבְרֵי עוֹלָה (*'al diḇrê 'ôlāh*) could better be "for the sake of burnt offerings" (BDB, s.v.). This would strengthen the position taken by this writer on vv.22–23; namely, that at the Exodus, God's whole intent in his covenant relationship with his people was not for sacrifices but for obedience.

f. Reception of Jeremiah's message

7:27–28

27"When you tell them all this, they will not listen to you; when you call to them, they will not answer. 28Therefore say to them, 'This is the nation that has not obeyed the LORD its God or responded to correction. Truth has perished; it has vanished from their lips.' "

27–28 Just as the Lord had said at Jeremiah's call (ch. 1) that he would experience opposition, so now he informs Jeremiah that the nation would not listen to him (v.27; cf. Isa 6:9–10). He would have no greater success in his ministry than did his predecessors. The nation was preeminent in this respect: the people continually disobeyed the voice of the Lord, their very own God (v.28). That faith must be joined with works was lost to them; so the time of Jeremiah was a sad epilogue to Judah's history.

g. Lament over Judah's desolation

7:29–34

29"Cut off your hair and throw it away; take up a lament on the barren heights, for the LORD has rejected and abandoned this generation that is under his wrath.
30" 'The people of Judah have done evil in my eyes, declares the LORD. They have set up their detestable idols in the house that bears my Name and have defiled it. 31They have built the high places of Topheth in the Valley of Ben Hinnom to burn their sons and daughters in the fire—something I did not command nor did it enter my mind. 32So beware, the days are coming, declares the LORD, when people will no longer call it Topheth or the Valley of Ben Hinnom, but the Valley of Slaughter, for they will bury the dead in Topheth until there is no more room. 33Then the carcasses of this people will become food for the birds of the air and the beasts of the earth, and there will be no one to frighten them away. 34I will bring an end to the sounds of joy and gladness and to the voices of bride and bridegroom in the towns of Judah and the streets of Jerusalem, for the land will become desolate.' "

29 The prophet's attention now turns to the Valley of Hinnom, the center of the cult of infant sacrifice, introduced by Ahaz and Manasseh (2 Kings 16:3; 21:6), abolished by Josiah (2 Kings 23:10), but later revived under Jehoiakim. The command to cut off the "hair" (lit., "crown"; cf. KB, s.v.; NASB mg.) is in the feminine in Hebrew, showing that the city (cf. 6:23—"O Daughter of Zion") is meant. The charge stems from the fact that the Nazirite's hair was the mark of his separation to God (Num 6:5). When he was ceremonially defiled, he had to shave his head. So Jerusalem because of her corruption must do likewise. Her mourning is because the Lord has cast her off. Because of her sin, the chief mark of her beauty must be cast away as polluted and no longer consecrated to the Lord.

When Israel encountered bereavement, defeat in war, or awareness of God's displeasure, the people would lament, lying on the ground, pouring dust on their heads, tearing their clothes, beating their breasts, and cutting off their hair. Now they were to lament on the "barren heights," for the place of their idolatries was to be the place of their mourning. Their lament would be heard at a distance. For that generation was the one on which God's wrath would be poured out.

30–32 The people had brazenly introduced their idols in the temple, as though to defy God to his face (v.30; cf. 2 Kings 21:5; 23:4–7; Ezek 8). This was their crowning insult to God. Furthermore, they had set up high places (altars) in Topheth (v.31a), which was near the eastern end of the southern part of the Valley of Hinnom. The etymology of Topheth is uncertain, but it may have originally signified "fireplace" from the Aramaic. It was pointed with the Hebrew vowels of *bōšet* ("shame"), a name for Baal. Hinnom may have been the name of the original owner of the area.

The Hinnom Valley was a place of idolatrous sacrifices as well as the area for the debris and rubbish of the city. The rabbis saw it as a symbol of the place of future punishment, calling it Gehenna (cf. Matt 5:22). Here the idolatrous nation burned their children to appease the fire god, Molech. This passage reveals that the children were not merely made to pass through an ordeal by fire; they actually burned up. God disclaims any connection with this hideous practice (v.31b). Now their pagan sanctuary was to become their cemetery (v.32). This heartless worship was clearly proscribed by the law of Moses (Lev 18:21; 20:2–5). Since they so flagrantly disobeyed God, therefore where their children were slaughtered, they themselves would be slaughtered. The slaughter of the coming doom of the city will be so great that Topheth will have to be used for burial, thus changing the name of the place to The Valley of the Slaughter (the definite article being used).

33–34 So complete will the desolation of the land be that no one will be there to drive the birds of prey from the carcasses (v.33). The ancients dreaded being left unburied after death (Deut 28:26; Isa 18:6). The highest indignity for the dead was to leave the body unburied. The chapter closes on the tragic note that all joy—even that of marriage (v.34)—will be removed from Judah.

2. *Remonstrance with Israel* (8:1–22)

The early verses of this chapter are so closely connected with the preceding one that many commentators treat vv.1–3 with chapter 7. That they belong to the sermon at the temple gate is clear from the phrase "At that time" (v.1). Chapter 7 closes with a picture of unrelieved carnage and with dead bodies denied decent burial. But more was in store.

a. *Desecration of the graves*

8:1–3

> [1]" 'At that time, declares the LORD, the bones of the kings and officials of Judah, the bones of the priests and prophets, and the bones of the people of Jerusalem will be removed from their graves. [2]They will be exposed to the sun and the moon and all the stars of the heavens, which they have loved and served and which they have followed and consulted and worshiped. They will not be gathered up or buried, but will be like refuse lying on the ground. [3]Wherever I banish them, all the survivors of this evil nation will prefer death to life, declares the LORD Almighty.' "

1–3 Even the remains of the long dead would be desecrated (v.1). The invaders would not be satisfied until the bones of the leaders as well as of the people of Jerusalem were exhumed. Various explanations have been suggested for this barbarous action, probably the best being that it was the ultimate insult, as much as to say that the people of Judah were incapable of guarding the remains of their ancestors from desecration. This practice of violating the dead was not unknown in ancient warfare (cf. Amos 2:1). It adds to the funereal atmosphere to have the word *'aṣmôt* ("bones") mentioned five times in the Hebrew text of this passage. A number of commentators also believe the graves were vandalized for plunder. Excavations in Egypt and Babylon show that this was common. The dead, especially kings and prominent leaders, were buried with treasures. At any rate, what an end vv.1–3 portray for those who so eagerly practiced idolatry with the hope of getting help from their gods!

Jeremiah elaborates on the fate of the dead. Their bones will be scattered in the open air under the sun to hasten their disintegration (v.2) and will be exposed like refuse (v.3). All the stages of Judah's worship of idols are detailed (v.2) in five verbs ("loved," "served," "followed," "consulted," "worshiped") to reveal the people's great zeal in doing so. Jeremiah is purposely diffuse in his language. Later he speaks of unburied corpses as becoming dung (cf. 16:4). The heavenly bodies the people worshiped will be helpless to hinder the desecration heaped on their dead followers (v.2). The statement is derisive and exposes the worthlessness of astrology (so Bright).

In spite of the violation heaped on their dead compatriots, the survivors will prefer death to life (v.3) because of the many trials they are yet to suffer at the hands of their captors (so Bewer). The banished are the whole nation of Israel (cf. 3:14), and the places where they have been driven are the countries outside Palestine (cf. Lev 26:36–39; Deut 28:65–67).

b. *Obduracy of Israel in idolatry*

8:4–7

> [4]"Say to them, 'This is what the LORD says:
>
>> " 'When men fall down, do they not get up?
>> When a man turns away, does he not return?
>> [5]Why then have these people turned away?
>> Why does Jerusalem always turn away?

> They cling to deceit;
>> they refuse to return.
> ⁶I have listened attentively,
>> but they do not say what is right.
> No one repents of his wickedness,
>> saying, "What have I done?"
> Each pursues his own course
>> like a horse charging into battle.
> ⁷Even the stork in the sky
>> knows her appointed seasons,
> and the dove, the swift and the thrush
>> observe the time of their migration.
> But my people do not know
>> the requirements of the LORD.' "

4–5 Yet again the Lord in his grace would reason with Judah concerning her sin, seeking to lead her to repentance. In a series of questions throughout this eighth chapter, God remonstrates with his people. First, he shows how contrary to nature is their apostasy. If a man falls down, he instinctively tries to rise as soon as possible (v.4). If he turns from the right way, he returns to it at the earliest opportunity. But Judah is different from others (v.5); her misconduct is unique. Having fallen into idolatry and having strayed from the path of obedience, she manifests no desire to either rise or return. In vv.4–5 there is an extended play on the word šûḇ ("to turn," "turn away," "return"). It is too late to repent. The nation is incorrigible in her apostasy. Judah shows no desire to correct her ways but holds tenaciously to her deceitful idolatry.

6–7 God waited for the people to amend their ways; he listened in vain for some word of repentance and confession of guilt (v.6). They acted mindlessly. As a war horse rushes into battle, they impetuously followed their own way regardless of the consequences. The figure stresses their determination to keep on in sinning. Even subhuman creatures (v.7) know how to follow their instincts better than Judah follows the way of the Lord. Migratory birds recognize and follow the seasons of their migration instinctively. The stork, dove, swift, and thrush regularly return to Palestine every spring. They know more about God's appointed way for them than Judah knows about God's appointed way for her (cf. Isa 1:1–3). Man, created so much higher than the lower creation, drifts so much farther than it does when he loses his moorings in God.

Notes

6 The participial form שׁוֹטֵף (šôṭēp) in the sense of "rushing headlong" is used primarily of streaming water (cf. Isa 30:28; 66:12; Ezek 13:11, 13). Only here is it employed of a running (NIV, "charging") horse.

c. *Penalty for Judah's falsity*

8:8–13

> [8] 'How can you say, "We are wise,
> for we have the law of the LORD,"
> when actually the lying pen of the scribes
> has handled it falsely?
> [9] The wise will be put to shame;
> they will be dismayed and trapped.
> Since they have rejected the word of the LORD,
> what kind of wisdom do they have?
> [10] Therefore I will give their wives to other men
> and their fields to new owners.
> From the least to the greatest,
> all are greedy for gain;
> prophets and priests alike,
> all practice deceit.
> [11] They dress the wound of my people
> as though it were not serious.
> "Peace, peace," they say,
> when there is no peace.
> [12] Are they ashamed of their loathsome conduct?
> No, they have no shame at all;
> they do not even know how to blush.
> So they will fall among the fallen;
> they will be brought down when they are punished,
>
>   says the LORD.
> [13] 'I will take away their harvest,
>
>   declares the LORD.
> There will be no grapes on the vine.
> There will be no figs on the tree,
> and their leaves will wither.
> What I have given them
> will be taken from them.' "

8–9 In spite of her willful ignorance of the law of God, the nation boasts of her wisdom. The chief offenders were the priests and false prophets. Apparently they thought that having the law meant they had all the wisdom they needed. Denying God's word by their deeds, they still boasted of its presence with them (cf. Rom 2:17–23). To make matters worse, the "scribes" (v.8) so manipulated the law of God as to falsify its message. They interpreted it in such a way as to assure the people that they could sin with impunity. These deceitful scribes were not mere copyists but men who knew the law. They twisted it to make it mean what they wanted it to. Here in v.8 is the first mention in the OT of scribes as a separate class. First Chronicles shows that they were formed into families or guilds (cf. also 2 Chron 34:13). To them were committed the study and exposition of the law. They were the predecessors of the postexilic scribes in Judaism, mentioned in the NT. This does not mean that all scribes were ungodly. Ezra, for example, was an eminent and pious scribe. Incidentally, the presence of scribes demands that there must have been a law by this time (contrary to the view of some OT scholars), in which they were experts (cf. 2 Chron 34:13). In v.8 there is an appeal to reason, as there is an appeal to conscience in v.12. As a result of the people's delusion about their wisdom, they will not heed the word of the Lord. The answer to the question in v.9 is that there is no wisdom when God's word is rejected (cf. Prov 1:7).

10–12 Since God is a God of righteousness and holiness, he must visit on Judah the punishment he has warned them of. These three verses repeat what has already been stated in 6:12–15. Dwelling so constantly on the same theme, Jeremiah shows his literary genius in not repeating his own words more often. God ordered him to repeat the truth to impress it on the minds of the people. But the people, refusing to listen to God's word, were misled by false prophets and deceitful priests.

13 The remainder of chapter 8 depicts the doom of the land and the people. The passage from 8:13 to 9:23 is the lectionary portion in the synagogue on the ninth of Ab, the day of the destruction of the temple. The failure of the vintage and the harvest is a frequent OT metaphor of complete devastation. When God's judgment strikes, nothing will be left; the desolation of the land and the people will be complete. God will withdraw all his gifts. Since the nation bore no fruit morally, the dissolution of its commonwealth was imminent.

d. *The invading army*

8:14–17

> 14"Why are we sitting here?
>   Gather together!
>   Let us flee to the fortified cities.
>   and perish there!
>   For the LORD our God has doomed us to perish
>   and given us poisoned water to drink,
>   because we have sinned against him.
> 15We hoped for peace
>   but no good has come,
>   for a time of healing
>   but there was only terror.
> 16The snorting of the enemy's horses
>   is heard from Dan;
>   at the neighing of their stallions
>   the whole land trembles.
>   They have come to devour
>   the land and everything in it,
>   the city and all who live there."
>
> 17"See, I will send venomous snakes among you,
>   vipers that cannot be charmed,
>   and they will bite you,"
>
>   declares the LORD.

14–15 The invasion by the northern enemy is now going on. Those in the rural areas will ask themselves why they should stay where they live (v.14), exposing themselves to the enemy's cruelties. They will exhort one another to flee to the fortified cities for greater protection and longer survival. Alas, even if they flee to the fortified cities, these, like poisoned water, will be their ruin. "Poisoned water" recurs in 9:15 and 23:15, again with a penal significance. There is no reference in v.14 to the drought described in 14:1–6. The people find to their dismay that the opposite of what they looked for has come on them (v.15). The false prophets had purveyed only false hopes.

16–17 Now Jeremiah graphically describes the invasion of the enemy, who had already come from the north. Dan, in the far north of the land and bordering on Phoenicia, would feel the invasion first. So many would be the enemy's horses (v.16) that their sound would shake the earth and they would desolate the land. Suddenly the figure for the invader changes to that of serpents (v.17) that cannot be charmed away (Ps 58:4–5). The invader will be irresistible.

e. *The sorrow of Jeremiah*

> 8:18–22

> ¹⁸O my Comforter in sorrow,
>   my heart is faint within me.
> ¹⁹Listen to the cry of my people
>   from a land far away:
> "Is the LORD not in Zion?
>   Is her King no longer there?"
>
> "Why have they provoked me to anger with their images,
>   with their worthless foreign idols?"
>
> ²⁰"The harvest is past,
>   the summer has ended,
>   and we are not saved."
>
> ²¹Since my people are crushed, I am crushed;
>   I mourn, and horror grips me.
> ²²Is there no balm in Gilead?
>   Is there no physician there?
> Why then is there no healing
>   for the wound of my people?

18–19 From v.18 through 9:1 we have Jeremiah's moving lament for his people. Though his predictions are coming true, he does not gloat over those who opposed him. Rather, he is thoroughly heartbroken (v.18). He agonizes over the Fall of Jerusalem. He had lived in a state of tension between his love for his land and countrymen and his fidelity to God's commission for him. Now he foresees Judah's captivity and the distress of her exile. Forlorn and distraught, the exiles wonder why they have been conquered and degraded. How could this happen when the Lord their King was surely in Zion? They are trying to harmonize their theology with their deplorable condition. Why have they not been delivered? The King referred to (v.19) is not the Davidic ruler but God. God answers their question with one of his. Why have they gone on defying him with their idolatries when they were constantly warned of his judgment on them (cf. Mic 3:11)?

20 Jeremiah drives home another truth by using the figure of the harvest. Harvest of barley, wheat, and spelt came in April, May, and June; harvest of summer fruits like figs, grapes, and pomegranates came in August and September, and of olives in October. If these were not provided, no fruit was garnered for the winter. Some writers believe that v.20 is speaking of actual food for the coming year. This is scarcely possible in light of the last clause of the verse. It was a proverbial saying meaning the people had lost every opportunity given them by God, and now they were entirely without hope. One favorable time after another went unheeded. The time is past, of course, when either Egypt or other allies can come to their aid (so Calvin). Their hope is all gone.

21–22 In spite of his denunciations, Jeremiah does not hesitate to identify himself with his people (v.21). Their hurt (lit., "breaking"; NIV, "crushed") hurts him so deeply that he is filled with mourning and dismay. In a final metaphor (v.22), Jeremiah asks why, since there is balm in Gilead (for which that region is famous) and physicians to apply it, the nation's malady has not been healed. The balm referred to is the resin or gum of the storax tree. It was used medicinally (cf. Gen 37:25; Jer 46:11; 51:8; Ezek 27:17). The prophet is distressed because he knows that though there is a remedy for the people, they have not availed themselves of it. Gilead is a mountainous region of Palestine east of Jordan and north of Moab; so the remedy is not far away. But Judah's sickness is not healed (lit., "come up" again, as skin grows over a healing wound). The plaintive question "Is there no balm in Gilead?" has become proverbial.

Notes

18 The text is difficult, especially the beginning of the verse. The first word מַבְלִיגִיתִי (*mabligîtî*) is rendered "comfort myself" (KJV, ASV), "beyond healing" (NASB, RSV), "sorrow overtakes me" (JB), and "O my Comforter" (NIV). The meaning of the word is lost and has been restored from an Arabic root (*baliğa*), meaning "to shine" as the rising sun, hence "comfort." It has been suggested that the word in Jeremiah is a noun from בָּלַג (*bālag*), with the sense of "hilarity," "exhilaration," thus giving the translation "My exhilaration within me is sorrow" (so Henderson et al.). To divide the word into two, as some propose, gives no better sense (cf. KB, BDB, s.v.).

3. *Sin and punishment* (9:1–26)

Verse 1 of chapter 9 is v.23 of chapter 8 in the Hebrew text. Many expositors rightly feel that it fits better at the end of chapter 8. It is from utterances like this that Jeremiah has been called "The Weeping Prophet," a term confirmed by his moving poems in Lamentations. Henderson considers v.1 the most pathetic in the book.

a. *The prophet's lament*

9:1–2a

> [1]Oh, that my head were a spring of water
>   and my eyes a fountain of tears!
> I would weep day and night
>   for the slain of my people.
> [2]Oh, that I had in the desert
>   a lodging place for travelers,
> so that I might leave my people
>   and go away from them;

1–2a These words remind us of Romans 9:1–5 and 10:1. (See also David's grief [2 Sam 18:33] and our Lord's lament over Jerusalem [Matt 23:37].) Jeremiah's metaphors show the depths of his grief. The destruction to be visited on the nation would be so thoroughgoing that he would weep day and night. The "fountain" is a reservoir or well rather than a spring. The "slain" of this verse are those in need of a physician in 8:22. Their sickness has ended in death.

Some scholars think that the ideas in v.1 and those in v.2a are too different to have come from the same source. But the difference can be explained psychologically. Two strong emotions gripped Jeremiah: great sympathy for his people and utter revulsion against their many sins. The life of the people was so corrupt as to make it impossible for Jeremiah to live among them. Even a lonely lodging in the desert was preferable to the soul anguish he experienced in the midst of his people (cf. David in Ps 55:6–8).

b. *The glaring sins of the day*

9:2b–9

> for they are all adulterers,
>   a crowd of unfaithful people.
> ³"They make ready their tongue
>   like a bow, to shoot lies;
> it is not by truth
>   that they triumph in the land.
> They go from one sin to another;
>   they do not acknowledge me,"
>
>   declares the LORD.
>
> ⁴"Beware of your friends;
>   do not trust your brothers.
> For every brother is a deceiver,
>   and every friend a slanderer.
> ⁵Friend deceives friend,
>   and no one speaks the truth.
> They have taught their tongues to lie;
>   they weary themselves with sinning.
> ⁶You live in the midst of deception;
>   in their deceit they refuse to acknowledge me,"
>
>   declares the LORD.
>
> ⁷Therefore this is what the LORD Almighty says:
>
> "See, I will refine and test them,
>   for what else can I do
> because of the sin of my people?
> ⁸Their tongue is a deadly arrow;
>   it speaks with deceit.
> With his mouth each speaks cordially to his neighbor,
>   but in his heart he sets a trap for him.
> ⁹Should I not punish them for this?"
>   declares the LORD.
> "Should I not avenge myself
>   on such a nation as this?"

2b The blatant sins Jeremiah describes are literal. Society was shot through and through with wickedness. The first sin in this bill of indictment was universal adultery. As the prophet has already shown, the reference is to their spiritual adultery of idolatry, with which gross immoralities were carried out. *In toto* the people were a treacherous assembly. The Hebrew word *ʿaṣeret* ("crowd") is used for solemn assemblies on pilgrimage feasts. They had fallen far short of that concept. The several sins of the tongue are noteworthy (cf. Ps 12; James 3:1–12).

3 The picture here is vivid: the tongue is the bow and the lying is the arrow. The people are consummate liars (cf. v.5; also Ps 64:3–4). To "make ready" is literally "to tread" because one placed his foot on the bow to fit it with an arrow. Unwearied, the people went from one sin to another. They were valiant, but not for truth. They used their power and influence, not for helping their countrymen, but for oppressing the poor and needy. They had completely abandoned moral and social standards. Mutual trust had vanished. The inner cohesiveness of the nation had broken down. Judah was laden with deceit. At the same time Jeremiah was in anguish over the people's sufferings, he was appalled at the depth of their departure from the Lord. Willful ignorance of God was the root of their sin. They did not care to know or recognize him (Rom 1:28).

4–5a When a nation lacks spiritual dedication, human relations become insecure (v.4). People will try to exploit one another. Even the godly succumb to suspicion. Society itself is threatened when mutual confidence is lost. Even homes and families in Judah were split by mistrust (cf. the parallel in Mic 7:5–6). The unity of the nation was threatened from within. The covenant of God with his people required brotherly love, but their conduct violated this. They went to great pains to deceive one another (v.5a).

5b–6 To show the unnaturalness of their wickedness, Jeremiah says that the people trained their tongues contrary to their proper function (v.5b). Lying takes more effort than speaking the truth, but they were willing to endure the drudgery of sin. They persisted in their wrongdoing. Their desire to do evil exceeded their power and strength. The words of v.6 are addressed to the whole nation, not solely to Jeremiah. Deceit was the very atmosphere of their life. They lived in it and would rather cling to their deceptive ways than recognize God and abandon their godless deeds. Verse 3 states that they did not know God; now we are told that they flatly refused to know him. In a world ruled by a Moral Governor, their woes inevitably stemmed from this recalcitrance.

7–9 The prophet returns to the metaphor of refining metals (v.7; cf. 6:28–30). But now the process will go on in the fiery furnace of affliction and will aim to remove the dross, not by lead, but by suffering. The Lord is still seeking to purge, not exterminate, his people (cf. Mal 3:3, where the Hebrew word for refining is the same as here). Reasoning with them, the Lord asks how else he could deal with their sinful ways. No other choice was left him. What other action was open to him? The passage underscores the inevitability of judgment in view of God's righteousness. He still yearns over Judah, for he addresses the nation as *bat-ʿammî* ("the daughter of my people"; NIV, "my people"). Again, the prophet emphasizes their deceitful dealings (v.8). Their tongues are death dealing; deceit is second nature to them. Even when their conversation appears to be cordial, in their hearts they are scheming to ensnare their neighbors. In v.9 the Lord repeats like a refrain the word in 5:9, 29.

Notes

8 KJV renders שׁוּחָט (Kethib, *šôḥuṭ* [where *āw* contracts to *ô;* cf. GKC, par. 7e]; Qere, שָׁחוּט, *šāḥûṭ* [where *uw* contracts to *û*]) as "shot out." ASV, NASB, RSV, JB, NEB, and NIV translate the term as "deadly arrow." JPS has "sharpened." The text has an active participle and the marginal reading has the passive of the same verb. The active form has the force of "killing," "murdering," hence, "deadly." The marginal reading occurs only with זָהָב (*zāhāb*, "gold"), as in 1 Kings 10:16–17; 2 Chron 9:15, which may denote gold beaten thin. Thus the meaning "pointed" or "sharpened" is derived (so Syr., Aram.). It appears better to hold to the reading of the NIV and others—viz., "deadly arrow."

c. *The judgment threatened*

9:10–16

10I will weep and wail for the mountains
    and take up a lament concerning the desert pastures.
They are desolate and untraveled,
    and the lowing of cattle is not heard.
The birds of the air have fled
    and the animals are gone.

11"I will make Jerusalem a heap of ruins,
    a haunt of jackals;
and I will lay waste the towns of Judah
    so no one can live there."

12What man is wise enough to understand this? Who has been instructed by the LORD and can explain it? Why has the land been ruined and laid waste like a desert that no one can cross? 13The LORD said, "It is because they have forsaken my law, which I set before them; they have not obeyed me or followed my law. 14Instead, they have followed the stubbornness of their hearts; they have followed the Baals, as their fathers taught them." 15Therefore, this is what the LORD Almighty, the God of Israel, says: "See, I will make this people eat bitter food and drink poisoned water. 16I will scatter them among nations that neither they nor their fathers have known, and I will pursue them with the sword until I have destroyed them."

10–11 This section details Judah's punishment. A suggested date for the section has been the time of the Chaldean invasion of Judah in 602 B.C. (so Hyatt), recorded in 2 Kings 24:1–2; but there is no evidence for separating this invasion from the one treated thus far. Jeremiah is seen as prepared for mourning in the hour of disaster (v.10). The pastures in the Judean wilderness will be burned up because there will be no one to water and care for them. The land will be devastated and its inhabitants exiled. All will be so desolate that the cattle will disappear, and even the birds will abandon the land. So complete will the devastation be that only scavengers will remain (v.11).

442

12–16 Once more the Lord tries to show the people the cause of their ruin. The catechetical style is for emphasis. The Lord challenges any of the wise of the nation to state the cause of their calamities (v. 12). It is not a challenge for just any wise man but for one with the wisdom of prophetic inspiration (so Henderson). Only such a true prophet could rightly diagnose the fatal disease. The wise will see by God's enlightenment that departure from God must always lead to punishment. In v. 13 God himself answers the question in v. 12. The nation had violated the law given at Sinai and constantly proclaimed by the true prophets; the people repeatedly ignored God's call to walk in conformity with his revealed will. Instead, they had followed a path to destruction. It was their defection from God that had brought along with it their flagrant social injustices.

In vv. 14–15, Jeremiah sets forth cause and effect. The cause of the nation's problems was an insubordinate spirit that led the people into idolatry—their undoing from the wilderness period to that hour. Their sinful practices were handed down from one generation to another. In the metaphor "bitter food" (la ʿanāh, "wormwood") and "poisoned water" (mê-rōʾš, "water of gall"), the first is a plant with very bitter juice, the second a poisonous bitter herb. They represent the bitter suffering in the fall of the kingdom and the Babylonian exile. These visitations had already been threatened in Moses' time (cf. Lev 26:33; Deut 28:64), especially in relation to Israel's future dispersion. The annihilation (v. 16) does not include the whole nation but only its ungodly members. Repeatedly, Jeremiah shows there will be no complete decimation of the people (cf. 4:27; 5:18; 30:11).

d. *The universal lamentation*

9:17–22

> [17]This is what the LORD Almighty says:
>
>> "Consider now! Call for the wailing women to come;
>>> send for the most skillful of them.
>> [18]Let them come quickly
>>> and wail over us
>> till our eyes overflow with tears
>>> and water streams from our eyelids.
>> [19]The sound of wailing is heard from Zion:
>>> 'How ruined we are!
>>> How great is our shame!
>> We must leave our land
>>> because our houses are in ruins.' "
>
> [20]Now, O women, hear the word of the LORD;
>> open your ears to the words of his mouth.
> Teach your daughters how to wail;
>> teach one another a lament.
> [21]Death has climbed in through our windows
>> and has entered our fortresses;
> it has cut off the children from the streets
>> and the young men from the public squares.
>
> [22]Say, "This is what the LORD declares:
>
>> " 'The dead bodies of men will lie
>>> like refuse on the open field,
>> like cut grain behind the reaper,
>>> with no one to gather them.' "

17–18 This section describes the people's expulsion from their land. It has been called a poem on "Death the Reaper" and acclaimed as perhaps the most brilliant prophetic elegy in the OT (so Skinner). The "wailing women" (v.17) were professionals employed to arouse relatives and others at funerals to outward display of their grief (v.18). They used plaintive cries, baring their breasts, flailing their arms, throwing dust on their heads, and disheveling their hair (2 Chron 35:25; Eccl 12:5; Amos 5:16; Matt 9:23). This practice was not peculiar to the Jews; it prevailed among the Greeks and Romans and still exists among certain peoples today. (The writer witnessed such a display in 1959 in Lebanon.)

19–21 As the people go into captivity, their wailing sounds out from Jerusalem (Zion, v.19). Jeremiah gives the words of the women's dirge. The demand for their services will be so great that they will have to teach others how to mourn (v.20)— particularly their daughters and neighbors. Death will penetrate into the homes of poor and rich alike (v.21). Even children and young men will die in public places. A number of interpreters believe that the death referred to is the result of pestilence. But the passage need not be limited to this. The invading army could do the killing.

22 Here we see Death as the Grim Reaper. The custom was for a reaper to hold in his arm what a few strokes of his sickle had cut. Then he put it down, and behind him another laborer then gathered it into bundles and bound it into a sheaf. So death was to cover the ground with corpses, but the carcasses would lie there unburied because of the paucity of survivors and the great number of dead. The wages of sin is always death (Rom 6:23).

e. *The ultimate good*

9:23–24

23This is what the LORD says:

"Let not the wise man boast of his wisdom
　or the strong man boast of his strength
　or the rich man boast of his riches,
24but let him who boasts boast about this:
　that he understands and knows me,
that I am the LORD, who exercises kindness,
　justice and righteousness on earth,
　for in these I delight,"

declares the LORD.

23–24 Now Jeremiah speaks of three things in which men of the world trust: wisdom, strength, and riches (v.23). But these cannot ward off disaster and the Lord's displeasure. Men's wisdom is not like God's wisdom (cf. Ps 111:10; Prov 1:7; 9:10). Their might is not the moral strength of righteousness. Their wealth is not the spiritual riches immune to theft or corrosion. Then as now the scholar, athlete, warrior, and financier were highly esteemed. Such persons are prone to trusting in their own resources. Wisdom, strength, or riches cannot help the worldly. If these fall short in the time of need, what will avail? Our highest good is to know God (v.24), not just intellectually or philosophically, but in spirit and in his true character. This is the true and lasting wisdom. The source of our highest blessing is the knowledge of God (John 17:3). The path of God's approval is clear (cf. 1 Cor 1:31; 2 Cor 10:17). Observe how the ethical qualities in v.24 follow a true knowledge of God. God manifests lovingkindness (cf. 2:2)—a readiness to manifest grace and mercy; justice—a proper evaluation of the rights of men; and righteousness—the absolute essential of all faith and worship. (See Hos 5:4; 6:3; 8:2 for knowing God; Mic 6:8; 7:18 for the activities that please the Lord.)

f. *Not privilege but morality*

9:25–26

> 25"The days are coming," declares the LORD, "when I will punish all who are circumcised only in the flesh— 26Egypt, Judah, Edom, Ammon, Moab and all who live in the desert in distant places. For all these nations are really uncircumcised, and even the whole house of Israel is uncircumcised in heart."

25–26 As the two preceding verses warned against trust in human achievements, these verses condemn faith in religious privileges. The paradox (an oxymoron, lit., "circumcised in uncircumcision") shows that circumcision is in itself as valueless as sacrifice, temple, or any other outward form of religious practice (v.25). If Judah has the rite of circumcision only in the flesh, she is no different from the pagans who have only an external sign and no inward faith. Judah cannot plead the virtue of her covenant sign when she does not possess what it stands for (cf. Rom 2:25–29). The nations enumerated in v.26 practiced circumcision but not of the heart. Outward rites are unavailing; the condition of the heart is paramount. Notice with whom Judah is placed—what degradation! According to Herodotus (2.36–37, 104), Egypt practiced circumcision. Joshua 5:9 implies that the rite was practiced there. Egypt is mentioned first because Israel was so prone to confide in them. Edom seems to have abandoned the practice till it was imposed on them by John Hyrcanus (Jos. Antiq., XIII, 257–58 [ix.1]; 318–19 [xi.3]). The Arab tribes, recognized by their peculiar tonsure, were, along with those already mentioned, the objects of Nebuchadnezzar's attack (cf. 49:28–33). The Babylonian Chronicle refers to a campaign in 599–598 B.C. (so Bright).

Notes

26 The translation of קְצוּצֵי פֵאָה (q⁽ᵉ⁾ṣûṣê pēʾāh) in ASV, substantially the same in NASB, JPS, and JB, is "that have the corners of their hair cut off." KJV has "that are in the utmost corners"; and NEB has substantially the same with "who haunt the fringes of the desert," as does NIV with "who live in the desert in distant places" and adds in a footnote "desert and who clip the hair by their foreheads." Some modern interpreters take the latter renderings, understanding the words to be a geographical notation of the isolated dwelling of the Arab tribes. The first renderings (so all the ancient versions) see here a reference to a certain style of hair. The Hebrew may be rendered "corner-clipped" (cf. 25:23 mg.; 49:32 mg.). Certain Arab tribes practiced this cutting of the hair of their temples in honor of Bacchus, the god of wine (Herod. 3.8). Israel was forbidden on religious grounds to follow this practice (cf. Lev 19:27; Deut 14:1).

4. Denunciation of idolatry (10:1–25)

The greater portion of this section is devoted to a condemnation of idolatry. It is reminiscent of Isaiah 40:18–20; 41:7; 44:9–20; 46:5–7, other classic passages on the emptiness of idolatry. Jeremiah shows his firsthand knowledge of idol worship, both Canaanite and Babylonian. Scholars generally hold that this passage was meant to dissuade Judah from idolatry in view of her removal from her country to Babylon. This, however, is only partially true because the people were already worshiping idols while in their own land. The first sixteen verses have been called a psalm to conclude the prophetic collection in chapters 8–9, just as Habakkuk 3 concludes that prophecy (so Frost). This is a possibility. Certainly vv. 1–16 are a sarcastic polemic against idol worship. Once men lose their awareness of God, they do not thereby lose their need of God. So they substitute the false worship for the true. Idolatry is the result. Along with the similar passages in Isaiah, vv. 1–16 constitute one of the basic passages on idolatry in the whole Bible. The presupposed historical setting is that of the Exile, either 597 B.C. or 586 B.C. (so Habel), with the later date probably being preferable.

a. The folly of idolatry

10:1–5

Hear what the LORD says to you, O house of Israel. ²This is what the LORD says:

> "Do not learn the ways of the nations
>   or be terrified by signs in the sky,
>   though the nations are terrified by them.
> ³For the customs of the peoples are worthless;
>   they cut a tree out of the forest,
>   and a craftsman shapes it with his chisel.
> ⁴They adorn it with silver and gold;
>   they fasten it with hammer and nails
>   so it will not totter.
> ⁵Like a scarecrow in a melon patch,
>   their idols cannot speak;
> they must be carried
>   because they cannot walk.
> Do not fear them;
>   they can do no harm
>   nor can they do any good."

1–2 The message is addressed to the house of Israel (v.1), which includes the whole nation, not just the Ten Tribes already in exile for more than a century. Those who remained in the land still retained the customs of their heathen neighbors before them (v.2). The purpose of Jeremiah's words was to warn the people against being influenced to fall in with the cultic customs of the pagan nations in worshiping their gods. Idol worship was attended by elaborate ritual, motivated by demonic power, and accompanied by moral looseness. Thus it was a constant temptation. The signs of the heavens referred to are not the sun, moon, and stars, or signs of the zodiac, meant by God to be signs (Gen 1:14), but unusual phenomena like eclipses, comets, and meteors, which were supposed to portend extraordinary events. They struck terror in the hearts of those who worshiped the superhuman power in the stars. They were supposed to predict evil. Both the Egyptians and the Babylonians were addicted to astrology. Idolatry that involves the heavenly bodies displeases God as much as the worship of man-made idols.

3–5 Now (v.3) Jeremiah turns to the absurdity of idolatry. All idols are vanity (lit., "breath"—that which is without substance). The worthlessness of worshiping them is proved by the worthlessness of the pagan gods. The prophet's description of idol making has its parallel in Babylonian inscriptions (so Bewer). Jeremiah details every stage of the making of these worthless images. The first stage (v.3) is the cutting down of a tree from the forest; the second stage, its shaping with an axe; the third, adorning the idol with precious metals; the fourth, fastening the idol in place (v.4). The final stage (v.9) is dressing the idol in royal apparel. There is an exquisite touch of sarcasm in the mention of fastening the idol with nails. The mighty god has to be kept from tottering. Even after the image is secured, it has no more value than a scarecrow (v.5). Immovable, it has no power of speech to comfort the needy soul; it cannot walk to come to the aid of the harassed; instead, it is a burden to be carried. Incapable of moral decisions, it cannot counsel troubled souls. Archaeological research tells us that idols were carried about in the religious processions of Babylon (Isa 46:7). They were just so much cumbersome baggage.

Notes

5 The Hebrew term תֹּמֶר (tōmer) is rendered "palm tree" in KJV and ASV (margin has "pillar"). RSV and NASB have "scarecrows in a cucumber field" (so also JB, NEB); NIV has "scarecrow in a melon field." The point of comparing a palm tree with an idol was the uprightness and smoothness of the palm; there are no branches except at the top. An attempt to reconcile "pillar" and "scarecrow" has been made by suggesting the resemblance of a scarecrow to a pillar (so Freedman). But the same imagery of an idol and a scarecrow in a field is found in the apocryphal Ep Jer (v.70). Another explanation sees the idols as phallic pillars. In Greek and Roman religions, such pillars represented the male generative power personified as a god and regarded as protecting vineyards and gardens.

b. *The majesty of God*

10:6–16

> 6No one is like you, O Lord;
> you are great,
> and your name is mighty in power.
> 7Who should not revere you,
> O King of the nations?
> This is your due.
> Among all the wise men of the nations
> and in all their kingdoms,
> there is no one like you.
> 8They are all senseless and foolish;
> they are taught by worthless wooden idols.
> 9Hammered silver is brought from Tarshish
> and gold from Uphaz.

What the craftsman and goldsmith have made
is then dressed in blue and purple—
all made by skilled workers.
¹⁰But the LORD is the true God;
he is the living God, the eternal King.
When he is angry, the earth trembles;
the nations cannot endure his wrath.

¹¹"Tell them this: 'These gods, who did not make the heavens and the earth,
will perish from the earth and from under the heavens.' "

¹²But God made the earth by his power;
he founded the world by his wisdom
and stretched out the heavens by his understanding.
¹³When he thunders, the waters in the heavens roar;
he makes clouds rise from the ends of the earth.
He sends lightning with the rain.
and brings out the wind from his storehouses.

¹⁴Everyone is senseless and without knowledge;
every goldsmith is shamed by his idols.
His images are a fraud;
they have no breath in them.
¹⁵They are worthless, the objects of mockery;
when their judgment comes, they will perish.
¹⁶He who is the Portion of Jacob is not like these,
for he is the Maker of all things,
including Israel, the tribe of his inheritance—
the LORD Almighty is his name.

6–8 Here the prophet contrasts the majesty of God with the uselessness of idols (v.6). Indeed, this section (vv.1–16) is full of contrasts between God and gods. Man-made idols cannot walk or stand unaided, but the true God is great in himself and in his power. To attempt to compare him with other gods or creatures shows woeful ignorance of his true character and attributes. Furthermore, in ancient times pagan nations had their own nationally restricted deities; but the Lord God of Israel is King (v.7), sovereignly ruling and wisely administering the affairs of the nations. Worship is due him by right and due no one else. Men at the highest point of their reasoning could never approximate, let alone comprehend, the blessed God of the universe (1 Cor 1:21). From a wooden idol no spiritual benefit or instruction can be expected (v.8). The Hebrew for the second clause of v.8 is literally "an instruction of vanities is the tree itself." Instruction from idols is no more valuable than the idol itself. No human skill can turn wood into an intelligent creature. All the wise men among the pagan are foolish because their gods from which they receive instruction are no more than wood. Idolatry has no redeeming feature whatever.

9 At this point Jeremiah speaks of the origin of idols. Silver was obtained from Tarshish—viz., Tartessus, either southern Spain or the island of Sardinia (so Cunliffe-Jones; cf. Ezek 27:12; Jonah 1:3). Spain was rich in silver, iron, tin, and lead—all of which were sent to Tyre. Gold was brought from Uphaz, whose location is unknown. It is mentioned only here and in Daniel 10:5 (Heb.). The Syriac, Targum, and Theodotion versions read Ophir, a gold-producing region on the southwest coast of Arabia (cf. 1 Kings 9:28; 10:11; Isa 13:12). Blue (violet) and purple were obtained from the murex, a Mediterranean shellfish. These pigments were costly and were used in the curtains of the tabernacle (Exod 25:4). In spite of all the workmanship lavished on them, idols are still the work of human hands. Everything connected with them is made by puny man.

10 In a telling contrast, Jeremiah presents the distinctive attributes of the God of the universe. He is the true God, that is, God in truth, literally God who is truth. He is alive and the everlasting King, whose power is manifest in the earthquake and whose wrath the nations endure (cf. 1 Thess 1:9). This verse contains a threefold contrast with idols: (1) They are false; he is true. (2) They are dead; he is living. (3) They are transitory and subject to destruction; he is eternal.

11 This is the only verse in the book in Aramaic, a cognate language to Hebrew. A number of interpreters consider the verse to be an interpolation or gloss of some copyist. It should, however, be remembered that Aramaic was the lingua franca of the day; so the pagan idolators would be able to read the judgment of God on their idolatry. The truths enunciated thus far in this section are that (1) Israel is not to imitate the nations around her, (2) idols are powerless, and (3) God's power is infinite.

12–16 This section is repeated in 51:15–19. It dwells on the theme of the might of the true God, especially in nature, and his relationship to Israel, particularly in his covenant promises. Both the power and the wisdom of God (contrasted with the impotence and foolishness of idols) are clearly manifested in the creation of the heavens and the earth (v.12; cf. Ps 135). Indeed, every thunderstorm witnesses to the omnipotence of God (v.13). The living God is not imprisoned in nature as pagan religions hold. The incredibly potent lightnings are also his work. Before these wonders of nature, people unenlightened by revelation are without knowledge (v.14). Every idolater will ultimately be ashamed when the nothingness of idols is revealed (v.15). For a thinking person to engage in idol making and worship is no less than a degrading of his God-given endowments. The prophet's final word on idols is that they are not only worthless but also a work of mockery, worthy only of being ridiculed. In essence, instead of helping their devotees in time of need, idols will themselves be destroyed. On the other hand, Israel's God is totally distinct from idols (v.16); instead of being made, he is the Maker and Creator of all the universe. Moreover, he is still faithful to his covenant promises, though his people have rejected him (cf. the parallel passage 51:19). Though he is Lord of all, yet he has a special portion or inheritance in Israel. As we come to the end of this classic passage, we should remember this: The Babylonian exile accomplished what everything else failed to do. It cured the nation Israel of idolatry, making the people witnesses of the one true God in every country where they were scattered (so Broadbent).

Notes

11 Because this verse is in Aramaic, a number of expositors reject it as a gloss. But all the versions have it. Furthermore, it fits the context splendidly. No one has ever explained why an interpolator would introduce it here. It was a proverbial saying; so it was given in the language of the people (so Streane). The best explanation appears to be that it is in Aramaic so that the exiles could use these very words as a reply to solicitations by the Chaldeans to join in their idol worship. It is interesting that two different words are used for "earth," both found in the Assuan (Egypt) Papyri.

---

c. Exile for sinning Israel

10:17–22

> ¹⁷Gather up your belongings to leave the land,
>   you who live under siege.
> ¹⁸For this is what the LORD says:
>   "At this time I will hurl out
>   those who live in this land;
>   I will bring distress on them
>   so that they may be captured."
>
> ¹⁹Woe to me because of my injury!
>   My wound is incurable!
> Yet I said to myself,
>   "This is my sickness, and I must endure it."
> ²⁰My tent is destroyed;
>   all its ropes are snapped.
> My sons are gone from me and are no more;
>   no one is left now to pitch my tent
>   or to set up my shelter.
> ²¹The shepherds are senseless
>   and do not inquire of the LORD;
> so they do not prosper
>   and all their flock is scattered.
> ²²Listen! The report is coming—
>   a great commotion from the land of the north!
> It will make the towns of Judah desolate,
>   a haunt of jackals.

17–18 In respect to continuity of thought, vv.1–16 are parenthetical. In vv.17–25 the subject that was interrupted at 9:22 is resumed, thus concluding the temple sermon. The suggested date for the passage (vv.17–25) is 598–597 B.C., during the siege under Jeconiah. The portion is a dialogue between Jeremiah and personified Jerusalem. The people of Judah are addressed as they are told of impending exile. Now the doom of the city is at the very gates; so they had better gather up their bundles from the ground (v.17) because they are to be cast out of the land (v.18). Only distress awaits them.

19–22 A new era was to begin for the nation! On other occasions when the nation was invaded, the enemy took spoils and imposed tribute. But this time invasion would result in expatriation. This means for Jeremiah an almost unbearable burden; so on behalf of the nation he laments the catastrophe (v.19). The people now recognize and admit that they have merited the divine judgment. They are resigned to God's punishment. Jerusalem is next seen (v.20) as a tent-dwelling mother, deprived of her children and home. None is left to rebuild the destroyed land. The blame is placed on the leadership of the nation (v.21; cf. 2:8). Doom is near; the report has it that the army of the enemy is approaching (v.22).

d. *Prayer for the nation*

10:23–25

> ²³I know, O LORD, that a man's life is not his own;
> it is not for man to direct his steps.
> ²⁴Correct me, LORD, but only with justice—
> not in your anger,
> lest you reduce me to nothing.
> ²⁵Pour out your wrath on the nations
> that do not acknowledge you,
> on the peoples who do not call on your name.
> For they have devoured Jacob;
> they have devoured him completely
> and destroyed his homeland.

23–25 Jeremiah pleads the constitutional mental and moral weakness of man in extenuation of his predicament. Man can never direct his life so as to achieve blessing without God's help (v.23; cf. Ps 37:23; Prov 16:9; 20:24). No one can decide the course of his life. God is in ultimate control. True to his office, Jeremiah as the prophet of God acts as an advocate for his people. He prays that Judah will not be called on to suffer more than she can endure. He admits her merited punishment but pleads for it to be kept within limits (v.24). God should show a measure of mercy so that destruction will not come. It is in this context that the last petition (v.25) is to be understood. Some scholars think that Jeremiah's attitude toward the nations at this point is unlike that of his attitude elsewhere (so Smith). But he is not praying out of malice or revenge but is appealing to God's justice (cf. the parallel passage in Ps 79:6–7). The nations had been moved by a spirit of vindictiveness and out of proportion to what God had intended. They wanted to destroy Israel utterly. Notice the fury of the verbs in the second part of v.25. This verse is recited annually at the Passover service of the Jews. The enemies of Israel and the executors of God's wrath would one day experience his scourge also. This was fulfilled even in that century. Nebuchadnezzar was punished with insanity. His grandson Belshazzar was slain in his revelry. The empire was finally conquered by the Medo-Persians. Jeremiah's prayer was not that of a nationalistic Jew against hated Gentiles. It was a plea that God might destroy Judah's enemies before they could carry out their wicked aim to destroy God's people (so Laetsch). Thus closes this whole great section (chs. 7–10). Its undying message is that God seeks reality in life and worship, and no kind of ritual can ever be a substitute for piety.

D. *Signs to Awaken Repentance* (11:1–20:18)

1. *The broken covenant* (11:1–23)

Chapters 11 and 12 (some add ch. 13) form a unit because there is no break between them. Since this section is not dated, scholars differ as to the historical setting. Some, recognizing that Jeremiah is condemning Judah for disobeying the law of Moses, hold that the time must be in Jehoiakim's reign, when there was a retrogression from the reformation in Josiah's reign. Others hold, and their view represents a consensus of expositors, that the historical setting was the reign of Josiah with his reformation, which proved to be only superficial. This position is preferable. The date might even have been soon after the discovery of the Book of the Law before the reform became widespread (v.6; cf. 2 Kings 23). Many take this section as teaching that in sponsoring Josiah's reforms Jeremiah itinerated as he urged the people to follow the ideals of the reformation. Later, however, he became disillusioned with the superficial nature of the movement (so Hyatt). Others question this interpretation. Chapters 11–20 contain material that is more autobiographical and more narrative than that in the previous chapters. In this section (chs. 11–20) we find the prophet's "confessions," in a sense a private diary (see Introduction: Theological Emphases). The section now under consideration constitutes a mixed anthology without a planned structure, as in chapters 1–7 (so Frost). The main emphasis of chapter 11 is an admonition to be faithful to the covenant.

a. *The violation of the covenant*

11:1–13

> ¹This is the word that came to Jeremiah from the LORD: ²"Listen to the terms of this covenant and tell them to the people of Judah and to those who live in Jerusalem. ³Tell them that this is what the LORD, the God of Israel, says: 'Cursed is the man who does not obey the terms of this covenant— ⁴the terms I commanded your forefathers when I brought them out of Egypt, out of the iron-smelting furnace.' I said, 'Obey me and do everything I command you, and you will be my people, and I will be your God. ⁵Then I will fulfill the oath I swore to your forefathers, to give them a land flowing with milk and honey'—the land you possess today."
>
> I answered, "Amen, LORD."
>
> ⁶The LORD said to me, "Proclaim all these words in the towns of Judah and in the streets of Jerusalem: 'Listen to the terms of this covenant and follow them. ⁷From the time I brought your forefathers up from Egypt until today, I warned them again and again, saying, "Obey me." ⁸But they did not listen or pay attention; instead, they followed the stubbornness of their evil hearts. So I brought on them all the curses of the covenant I had commanded them to follow but that they did not keep.'"
>
> ⁹Then the LORD said to me, "There is a conspiracy among the people of Judah and those who live in Jerusalem. ¹⁰They have returned to the sins of their forefathers, who refused to listen to my words. They have followed other gods to serve them. Both the house of Israel and the house of Judah have broken the covenant I made with their forefathers. ¹¹Therefore this is what the LORD says: 'I will bring on them a disaster they cannot escape. Although they cry out to me, I will not listen to them. ¹²The towns of Judah and the people of Jerusalem will go and cry out to the gods to whom they burn incense, but they will not help them at all when disaster strikes. ¹³You have as many gods as you have towns, O Judah; and the altars you have set up to burn incense to that shameful god Baal are as many as the streets of Jerusalem.'"

1–3 The initial charges were not directed to Jeremiah alone (v.1) because the imperatives are in the plural. The commands are not to the people, nor to the priests as the teachers of the law, but to the prophets of the time (v.2). Surprisingly, much discussion has gone on among expositors as to which covenant is meant in v.3— whether the one made with the nation at Sinai or the one promulgated by Josiah. Yet surely the account in 2 Kings 22–23 makes it clear that the godly king was not introducing a new covenant but only calling for a reaffirmation of the old Mosaic covenant, as did other of the prophets aside from Jeremiah. Moreover, there is no room for doubt as to which covenant is meant, in view of what the immediately following verses say. Jeremiah even repeats the very curse pronounced on those who violated the Lord's covenant with Moses (cf. Deut 11:28; 27:26; 28:15–19; 29: 20–21). Ancient Near Eastern treaties contained both benedictions and curses for adherence or nonconformity to them.

4–5 The time of the promulgation of the Mosaic covenant is seen as being the whole Exodus period (v.4). The iron-smelting furnace refers to the hardships the Israelites underwent in Egypt (cf. Deut 4:20). What the Lord was seeking was an obedient people for his very own, a people who would rejoice in their intimate relationship and fellowship with him. Too, the Lord had in mind his gracious promises to the patriarchs, which he wished to fulfill (v.5). "A land flowing with milk and honey" symbolizes the fertility of the land. Outside the Pentateuch, this figure (now revived in modern Israeli songs) occurs only here, in 32:22, and in Ezekiel 20:6, 15. Jeremiah reminds the nation that she was still in possession of the Promised Land. His own answer to the pronouncement of the curse was "Amen," indicating his acquiescence in God's arrangement (cf. Deut 27:15–26). He testified to the justice of the Lord's announcement and his own consent to it. In vv.3–5 there is a summary of the spiritual essence of the covenant as in 7:23. The Lord's dealings with Israel have always been on clearly defined covenant grounds (so Myers). There were renewals of and restorations to the covenant under Elijah, Hezekiah, and Josiah. But these were always temporary.

6–8 On the basis of v.6, a number of scholars have suggested that Jeremiah accompanied Josiah in journeying to "the towns of Judah" in order to promote the destruction of idolatry in the land (cf. 2 Kings 23:15, 19). Actually, there was no need for the prophet to take a preaching tour "in the towns of Judah," for the expression is proverbial for length and breadth of the country (so Freedman). Moreover, the Lord's command to Jeremiah in 25:15–29 about making the nations drink the Lord's cup of wrath did not require him to itinerate among them. Judah's response to the Lord's command is given in vv.7–8, which reveal faithlessness and breach of the covenant. In spite of the Lord's loving exhortation through his prophets, the people followed their own ways in violating the law of God. In fact, the nation had already suffered (in the exile of the ten northern tribes to Assyria) some of the penalty for their infractions of the covenant; the remainder of the judgment was soon to be realized in the coming visitation on Judah (cf. Lev 18:28; 20:22; Deut 29:28).

9–13 Some have understood these verses to refer to Jehoiakim's reign when the people reverted to their former apostasy (v.10). But such a change in historical setting is not necessary. Jeremiah divulges an existing conspiracy against the covenant of God (v.9). It was not the outcome of hasty impulse but of settled policy. One suggestion has been that the Hebrew word *qeŝer* may be better translated "revolt" because "conspiracy" seems to convey the idea of political action. This is not a necessary conclusion. The conspiracy need not have been a formal one, though the people willed to assent to it. There was general though secret resistance to Josiah's policy of reform. The people had determined not to follow in the way of the Lord but in the wicked ways of their fathers (v.10). The "forefathers" (lit., "first fathers") were probably those who lived during the wilderness wanderings and during the time of the judges. Josiah's heart was right with the Lord, but true piety never comes by osmosis. People must submit individually to God and his ways. Of their own accord, Josiah's generation broke the covenant the Lord made with the nation. The only possible result was inescapable judgment (v.11). Not only would their worthless gods be impotent to help them (v.12), but the Lord also refused to help them. The hour of his patience has passed.

Once more Jeremiah stresses the impotence of the people's idols. The people's appeals to the idols will, as always, go unheeded. Not that they had a paucity of idols; their gods were, Jeremiah says (v.13), as numerous as their towns; every city had its own tutelary god. It was said of ancient Athens that it was easier to find the image of a god there than a man. The "shameful god" referred to is Baal, as in 3:4 (cf. also 2:28). In spite of and contrary to Josiah's reforms, these secret practices went on throughout the land (so Streane).

b. Inadequacy of sacrifices

11:14-17

14"Do not pray for this people nor offer any plea or petition for them, because I will not listen when they call me in the time of their distress.

15"What is my beloved doing in my temple
as she works out her evil schemes with many?
Can consecrated meat avert ˌyour punishmentˌ?
When you engage in your wickedness,
then you rejoice."

16The LORD called you a thriving olive tree
with fruit beautiful in form.
But with the roar of a mighty storm
he will set it on fire,
and its branches will be broken.

17The LORD Almighty, who planted you, has decreed disaster for you, because the house of Israel and the house of Judah have done evil and provoked me to anger by burning incense to Baal.

14-15 Because the nation's wickedness had passed the limit of God's patience, Jeremiah is again forbidden (cf. 7:16) to intercede for his people (v.14). Their guilt had come to a climax (cf. Exod 32:10; 1 John 5:16). Their cries for help would go unanswered because they were not repentant. The text of v.15 is obscure, and many interpreters have despaired of translating it intelligibly. All are agreed, however, that its thought parallels 7:10-11, 21-23. Apparently the people had gone to the temple to pray and offer sacrifices. "My beloved" refers to Judah. The prophet is repeating the worthlessness of sacrifices without godliness and concern for social righteousness. Sacrifices ("the consecrated meat") will not avert the doom. Actually, all the people have is defiled meat (cf. Hag 2:12). In their hypocrisy they have tried to hide their apostasy by their temple sacrifices. How, then, can the people think they have a right to rejoice? They cannot because God cannot be deceived.

16-17 Jeremiah goes on to compare the nation to a beautiful green olive tree (v.16) —viz., the way the Lord saw it and wanted it to be. Olive trees are common in Palestine, as elsewhere in the Near East. But Judah had become so barren that she must suffer the flames of judgment. The same figure is the basis of Paul's key passage about the relation of Jew and Gentile in Romans 11:17–24. God's ideal for the nation was for it to remain green and beautiful; but, because of the barrenness of sin, it must be destroyed. Some have interpreted the storm as symbolizing an invading army. It is probably better to take the words, as most scholars do, as a reference to a storm with lightning that struck down a tree. The judgment is clearly determined for both parts of the nation (v.17). Baalism has been their spiritual and political ruin.

Notes

15 The Hebrew of the entire verse is difficult and the solutions suggested mystifying. The original is corrupt; for (1), as it stands, it yields no intelligible meaning; and (2) the ancient versions indicate other readings. Briefly, some of the problems are a masculine plural adjective modifying a feminine noun without agreement with what precedes or follows, a singular noun and its construct followed by a plural verb, Masoretic punctuation that yields no good meaning, an archaic ending on one of the nouns that is hard to explain, and an adverb before the final verb that seems out of harmony with the sense. BHS has a number of suggestions, but they have too little support from the MSS. KJV and ASV render the passage the same way; NASB, RSV, and NIV diverge after the first question.

c. Plot against Jeremiah's life

11:18–23

18Because the LORD revealed their plot to me, I knew it, for at that time he showed me what they were doing. 19I had been like a gentle lamb led to the slaughter; I did not realize that they had plotted against me, saying,

"Let us destroy the tree and its fruit;
let us cut him off from the land of the living,
that his name be remembered no more."
20But, O LORD Almighty, you who judge righteously
and test the heart and mind,
let me see your vengeance upon them,
for to you I have committed my cause.

21"Therefore this is what the LORD says about the men of Anathoth who are seeking your life and saying, 'Do not prophesy in the name of the LORD or you will die by our hands'— 22therefore this is what the LORD Almighty says: 'I will punish them. Their young men will die by the sword, their sons and daughters by famine. 23Not even a remnant will be left to them, because I will bring disaster on the men of Anathoth in the year of their punishment.' "

18–20 Here is the first of Jeremiah's personal crises to be mentioned in the book. Its context is the portion called, as has already been said, The Confessions of Jeremiah. In them are disclosed deepest spiritual agonies. In this instance the plot against his life (v.18) by his fellow citizens of Anathoth could well have been an aftermath of his temple address (ch. 7). Moreover, they may have resented his support of Josiah's reforms, with its abolition of local sanctuaries—something that would have been hard for the priests of Anathoth to swallow. It appeared to them that in exalting the Jerusalem priesthood, Jeremiah was further degrading that of Anathoth, which had suffered obloquy since King Solomon's time. The plot was hatched in secret; so Jeremiah suspected nothing (v.19). The Lord had to reveal it to him. Rejecting God and his message, the nation was not afraid to reject his messenger. That his family, friends, and fellow citizens in his native town could conspire to assassinate him was something difficult to bear (cf. Isa 53:7). God disclosed not only the plot to Jeremiah but also the very words the conspirators said. Unsuspecting and trusting, he was to be murdered in the full vigor of his life. Because he was unmarried (16:2), and thus had no progeny, even his memory would be eradicated. Both he and his work (called here "fruit") were to be obliterated. Destroying a tree with its fruit was proverbial of total destruction.

In v.19 the people speak, in v.20 the prophet speaks, and in vv.21–23 the Lord speaks. In order to understand v.20 (and the passage has troubled many expositors), we must realize Jeremiah is praying, not for his own, but for God's vengeance on the plotters. Jeremiah is utterly open to the Lord and has entrusted his case to him who knows perfectly all human emotions, thoughts, and desires. This kind of prayer (recall how Jeremiah wanted to intercede for the nation when God forbade it) came from the conviction that his enemies were God's enemies. He was depending on the Lord to deal with them, and the Lord did.

21–23 The Lord answered Jeremiah's request by indicating his intention to vindicate him. The people had threatened Jeremiah with death if he continued to preach in the Lord's name (v.21). That note of authority galled them. They tried to suppress God's message. It will be recalled that Anathoth was the home of the priestly house of Abiathar, a friend of David. The house was deposed by Solomon, who supplanted it with the house of Zadok. Anathothites resented Jeremiah's favoring the deposition of the sanctuaries other than Jerusalem. This seemed to them like siding with Zadok against their own ancestor Abiathar. Furthermore, being priests, they doubtless hated his castigation of empty priestly ritual. Their punishment would come at the siege of Jerusalem (v.22). Death would prevail inside and outside the city. The young men of military age would die in battle, the rest by famine. The threat of no remnant (v.23) must be understood only of Jeremiah's enemies, for according to Ezra 2:23 some men of Anathoth returned to postexilic Judah (so Harrison). The year of their visitation was that of Nebuchadnezzar's conquest of the land. Anathoth was near the beleaguering armies and was thus more exposed to the carnage of war than Jerusalem.

2. *Punishment and promise* (12:1–17)

Many commentators join vv.1–6 of this chapter with 11:18–23, and indeed their subject matter is related. Out of the context of the opposition to his ministry he suffered in his hometown of Anathoth, Jeremiah deals with the question of the prosperity of the wicked, which has been called the great problem of the OT (cf. Job, David in Ps 37, Asaph in Ps 73, and Habakkuk). Jeremiah's perplexity, and that of others like him, is understandable because the OT does not offer full information on life after death. Only through the NT revelation, especially that of the resurrection of Christ (1 Peter 1:3–5), can the problem be placed in its true perspective.

a. *The prosperity of the wicked*

12:1–6

You are always righteous, O LORD,
  when I bring a case before you.
Yet I would speak with you about your justice:
  Why does the way of the wicked prosper?
  Why do all the faithless live at ease?
²You have planted them, and they have taken root;
  they grow and bear fruit.
You are always on their lips
  but far from their hearts.
³Yet you know me, O LORD;
  you see me and test my thoughts about you.
Drag them off like sheep to be butchered!
  Set them apart for the day of slaughter!
⁴How long will the land lie parched
  and the grass in every field be withered?
Because those who live in it are wicked,
  the animals and birds have perished.
Moreover, the people are saying,
  "He will not see what happens to us."
⁵"If you have raced with men on foot
  and they have worn you out,
  how can you compete with horses?
If you stumble in safe country,
  how will you manage in the thickets by the Jordan?
⁶Your brothers, your own family—
  even they have betrayed you;
  they have raised a loud cry against you.
Do not trust them,
  though they speak well of you."

1–2 The problem of the prosperity of the wicked in the light of God's righteousness is not directly solved here or elsewhere in Scripture. The only final answer is faith in the sovereign wisdom and righteousness of God. Some interpreters see in Jeremiah's questions (v.1) a measure of impatience. He is still deeply troubled by the treachery of his fellow citizens of Anathoth. He acknowledges at the outset that God is righteous—a fact basic to all theistic thinking. Jeremiah refuses in principle to question the justice of God, but he still has questions about the success of the wicked in the light of his own trials. Even in the light of the NT, believers today are troubled by similar doubts. In a spirit of holy familiarity, Jeremiah would reason or argue the case with the Lord. The wicked he refers to are not just those of Anathoth but the wicked in general. Aware only of temporal rewards and punishments, OT saints continually probed the problem. With true discernment Jeremiah realizes that prosperity is not accidental but goes back to God's general grace in providing human needs (cf. Matt 5:45; Luke 6:35). He uses the figure of a fruit-bearing tree (v.2). The wicked, instead of thanking the Lord for his goodness and worshiping him, are actually hypocrites, mouthing pious phrases without reality in their hearts (cf. Isa 29:13).

3 Now Jeremiah contrasts the state of his heart and life with that of the wicked. Their hatred of him was uncalled for. He speaks of his intimate fellowship with the

457

Lord. The Lord knows that he is not speaking hypocritically. In strong language Jeremiah asks the Lord to deal with his enemies as they deserve. In asking him to "set them apart [i.e., 'sanctify them'] for the day of slaughter," Jeremiah is comparing the wicked to animal sacrifices. Though the wicked have been "planted" in the land (v.2), they will be utterly destroyed from their place.

4 Some scholars think v.4 is misplaced. However, it carries forward the thought begun in v.1. Jeremiah is describing some consequences of the prosperity of the wicked in Judah. The ungodly are a curse to the nation. God sends punishment, and the righteous suffer with the wicked. The drought does not negate what Jeremiah said in v.1 about the Lord's righteousness, because calamities like those he is describing affect the godly more than the wicked. The ungodly rich usually escape them. The land, beasts, and even birds suffer along with man. If the pronoun "he" near the end of v.4 refers to God, then it is the height of wickedness in claiming that he is morally indifferent to the sin of the rich. This is practical atheism. Most scholars think the people are mocking Jeremiah's predictions and claiming they will never be realized. At least, he will perish before they do.

5–6 The Lord's answer to Jeremiah's complaint is meant to teach him that he is too impatient. He would have to suffer even more. What he had endured in Anathoth would be insignificant compared with the trials he had yet to undergo. What would he do then (cf. 36:26; 38:4–6)? His confrontation with the men of his own town has made him realize the magnitude of the task he has undertaken. He cannot turn to his family for help because they were part of his difficulty. God now challenges him to greater courage and faith for greater trials in the future. In spite of his problems, up to this point his situation has been like that of a dweller in a peaceful land. The language in v.5 is proverbial. It is an *a fortiori* argument. "The flooding of the Jordan" (cf. NIV mg.) refers to the annual overflow of the Jordan in time of harvest (Josh 3:15) and earlier (April and May) that filled the Ghor (cf. ZPEB, 2:710). With the flooding of the valley, the beasts of prey were driven from their haunts along the river bank. The reference here is probably to the jungle of the Jordan (NIV, "the thickets of the Jordan"), the land adjacent to the river covered with bushes and heavy undergrowth and inhabited by wild beasts (cf. 49:19; 50:44; Zech 11:3). Second Kings 6:2 implies an area of wooded character.

To give Jeremiah a glimpse of how serious matters would become, the Lord grants him a new disclosure (v.6). The threefold "even" in the Hebrew (KJV and RSV have two "evens," NIV one) is for emphasis. Even his own family cannot be trusted, for they will raise a hue and cry after him as though he were a criminal fleeing from justice. Nor will they be open and aboveboard; they will use threats and blandishments to obscure their true intentions toward him.

Notes

4 The LXX translates the Hebrew word אַחֲרִיתֵנוּ (*ahᵃrîtēnû*, "our end"; NIV, "what happens to us") as ὁδοὺς ἡμῶν (*hodous hēmōn*, "our ways") by slight textual emendation, but this is not helpful. The present text is intelligible as it stands.

5 Contrary to the belief of some, the reference to "a safe country" is not a reference to death.

The passage was meant to prepare Jeremiah for more trying days ahead of him. Expositors give different translations of the verse. Some, following B and ℵ of the LXX, add "not" before "safe" (so Morgan). JB accepts the insertion; but, though it makes good sense, the negative is not to be preferred. KJV, ASV, JPS render it substantially the same: "In the land of peace, wherein thou trustedst." RSV has "a safe land."

NASB, RSV, and NEB translate בָּטַח (bāṭaḥ, "trust") as "fall down" or "fall headlong"; NIV has "stumble." This rendering comes from taking the meaning of the Arabic cognate baṭaḥa ("to fall down"). This was suggested as early as the tenth century B.C. and has been favored by some modern scholars. (See Prov 14:16, where the verb can have the same meaning [so Hyatt].)

---

b. *Punishment on the ungodly*

12:7–13

> 7"I will forsake my house,
>   abandon my inheritance;
>   I will give the one I love
>   into the hands of her enemies.
> 8My inheritance has become to me
>   like a lion in the forest.
>   She roars at me;
>   therefore I hate her.
> 9Has not my inheritance become to me
>   like a speckled bird of prey
>   that other birds of prey surround and attack?
>   Go and gather all the wild beasts;
>   bring them to devour.
> 10Many shepherds will ruin my vineyard
>   and trample down my field;
>   they will turn my pleasant field
>   into a desolate wasteland.
> 11It will be made a wasteland,
>   parched and desolate before me;
>   the whole land will be laid waste
>   because there is no one who cares.
> 12Over all the barren heights in the desert
>   destroyers will swarm,
>   for the sword of the LORD will devour
>   from one end of the land to the other;
>   no one will be safe.
> 13They will sow wheat but reap thorns;
>   they will wear themselves out but gain nothing.
>   So bear the shame of your harvest
>   because of the LORD's fierce anger."

7–8 The Lord, not Jeremiah, is still speaking. The verb forms are prophetic perfects, viewing future events as though already fulfilled. Judgment for breaking the covenant is in view. Scholars are generally agreed that the historical background of this passage was probably the events recorded in 2 Kings 24:1–2, when Jehoiakim revolted against Babylon after three years of submission. Nebuchadnezzar dispatched Chaldean, Syrian, Moabite, and Ammonite soldiers against Judah. Dates for these events range from about 602 B.C. to 598 B.C. The Lord's lament over the nation's devastation contains an abundance of figures: "house," "inheritance," "the one I love" (v.7); "a lion" (v.8); "a speckled bird of prey" (v.9); "vineyard," "field" (v.10). Having warned Judah of the consequences of disobedience, the Lord now abandons her utterly to her enemies. Notice the threefold "my": "my house," "my inheritance," "my beloved" (Heb.). It was difficult for the Lord to punish his own guilty but beloved people. As ever, his judgment was tempered with love. Thus abandoned by their Lord, the people were incapable of resisting their foes. They were surrendered to the enemy because they as fiercely as a lion opposed the Lord (v.8). They had become his declared enemy; raising their voices against him shows the violence of their rebellion. In saying that he hates his people, the Lord is declaring that he has withdrawn his love and protection from them. He forsook them as though he hated them, and this was a greater agony for him than for them.

9 The first part of this verse is in question form, as if picturing God in "pained astonishment" at the situation. The question requires an affirmative answer. Some interpreters consider the "speckled bird" a hyena, following the LXX; but others agree with KJV, ASV, NASB, RSV, and NIV. Speckled birds are unusually colored birds, which are attacked by other birds, who will not allow a strange bird among them. As birds attack unfamiliar birds, so the Lord's people, who are different from other nations, will be attacked by them. Ancient seals have been discovered inscribed with roosters, showing that chickens were known in Jeremiah's day (so Frost). The Lord invites the wild beasts (Babylon and her allies) to devour the land.

10–13 The Lord's great love for his land is reflected in his three endearing designations of it (v.10). The shepherds, who have devastated his vineyard, Israel (cf. Isa 5:1), are the heads of the invading army (cf. 6:3). They have done what they wished, heedlessly breaking through and trampling the well-tended area. It is impossible to see here, as some have suggested, mere nomads with their flocks trampling vineyards (so Cowles). Though the desolation has been thoroughgoing, no one considers the causes that have brought such judgment. There is a splendid example of assonance in the Hebrew text of v.11, with its six sibilants—*śāmāh lišmāmāh* ("it will be made a wasteland"), *š^emēmāh nāšammāh* ("[it] will be laid waste"), *'iš śām* ("[no] man places [it to heart]"; NIV, "no one cares"). The "sword of the LORD" (v.12) in the hand of the Lord's agents will do its work throughout the country. Apparently the enemies will invade from the east. As far as Judah is concerned, nothing has turned out successfully for her people. In spite of all their labors in the field, they gain nothing (v.13). They reap the opposite of what they expect. Their crops are a failure (cf. 14:3–4). In fact, the harvests are so poor that even the farmers are ashamed of them. The Lord had not prospered them at all.

c. *Promise for the repentant nations*

12:14–17

> ¹⁴This is what the LORD says: "As for all my wicked neighbors who seize the inheritance I gave my people Israel, I will uproot them from their lands and I will uproot the house of Judah from among them. ¹⁵But after I uproot them, I will again have compassion and will bring each of them back to his own inheritance and his own country. ¹⁶And if they learn well the ways of my people and swear by my name, saying, 'As surely as the LORD lives'—even as they once taught my people to swear by Baal—then they will be established among my people. ¹⁷But if any nation does not listen, I will completely uproot and destroy it," declares the LORD.

14–17 In this section we have an anticipation of the prophecies in chapters 47–49. In prophesying to the nations, Jeremiah was fulfilling his commission (1:10). The nations (Syria, Moab, Ammon) were to be punished by the same enemy that punished Judah, namely, Babylon. The Lord identifies himself with Judah when he calls the surrounding peoples "my wicked neighbors" (v.14). They, too, for their evil ways will experience deportation from their lands. This is part of the answer to the prophet's complaint concerning the prosperity of the wicked. But this is not the end of the matter; these nations are promised future blessing after the Lord has chastened them as his people have been punished. A millennial setting is in view in vv.15–16. Repatriation is promised for Israel and the nations, who have learned of God from his people, just as Israel formerly learned the worship of idols through these nations. Notice that the basis of the predicted blessing is repentance and faith. (For the restoration of the foreign nations, see 48:47 and 49:6.) If the pagans adopt the worship of God in truth, they will be incorporated into God's people. Israel will lead in godliness as she formerly did in idolatry. There will be a remnant among the nations (cf. Gen 12:1–3; Rom 11:15). But the members of the remnant will have to make a genuine avowal of God as their own (cf. 4:2). Then the nations with Israel will know peace in the Messianic Age (so Freedman). When they were in the midst of the nations (vv.7, 9), it was to God's people's detriment; when the nations are in the midst of God's people, it will be to the nations' spiritual blessing. The chapter closes with the alternative to faith and is a warning to all (v.17). For unbelief there will be doom. Here, as always, prophecy is ethically conditioned.

3. *Corruption of the nation's life* (13:1–27)

Some expositors hold that the five sections in this chapter (vv.1–11, 12–14, 15–17, 18–19, 20–27) have no common theme. These warnings do, however, reiterate the subjects on which Jeremiah has been preaching: sin and punishment. As to a date for the chapter, opinions vary between a time after the Battle of Carchemish in 605 B.C., in the reign of Jehoiakim (so Hyatt), and the reign of Jehoiachin, chiefly because of the reference to him and the queen mother in v.18, about 597 B.C.

a. *The marred linen belt*

13:1–11

> ¹This is what the LORD said to me: "Go and buy a linen belt and put it around your waist, but do not let it touch water." ²So I bought a belt, as the LORD directed, and put it around my waist.
> ³Then the word of the LORD came to me a second time: ⁴"Take the belt you bought and are wearing around your waist, and go now to Perath and hide it there in a crevice in the rocks." ⁵So I went and hid it at Perath, as the LORD told me.
> ⁶Many days later the LORD said to me, "Go now to Perath and get the belt I told you to hide there." ⁷So I went to Perath and dug up the belt and took it from the place where I had hidden it, but now it was ruined and completely useless.
> ⁸Then the word of the LORD came to me: ⁹"This is what the LORD says: 'In the same way I will ruin the pride of Judah and the great pride of Jerusalem. ¹⁰These wicked people, who refuse to listen to my words, who follow the stubbornness of their hearts and go after other gods to serve and worship them, will be like this belt—completely useless! ¹¹For as a belt is bound around a man's waist, so I bound the whole house of Israel and the whole house of Judah to me,' declares the LORD, 'to be my people for my renown and praise and honor. But they have not listened.'"

1–7 This passage has occasioned an unusual amount of comment. Was the act a real one? If it was actually done, what place is referred to in v.4? If it was a vision, of what value would it have been to the people Jeremiah preached to? Moreover, some hold variants of these views. The chief problem with the literal view is that the distance to the Euphrates (Perath)—and two round trips were made—would require Jeremiah to walk hundreds of miles. The passage has been called an acted oracle.

The arguments for the literal view are as follows:

1. The act would have to be witnessed to be of value as a message to the people (so Bright). This would not be possible in a prophetic vision.

2. The language supports the literal sense.

3. Jeremiah was away from Jerusalem for part of Jehoiakim's reign, and his absence could account for Nebuchadnezzar's kind feeling toward him because of previous personal acquaintance (39:11–12).

4. "Perath" (v.4) should be understood as an abbreviation of Ephrata (the initial letter has been omitted), the original name of Bethlehem, about six miles south of Jerusalem. Then it would be easy for Jeremiah to carry out the command literally. (A variation of this view will be discussed at v.4.)

There are, on the other hand, good expositors who believe in a nonliteral explanation. For them all was enacted in a vision (so Calvin). As stated above, the chief argument for the symbolic view is the great distance involved; and this should not be minimized. With able scholars on both sides and with a number of imponderables involved, a dogmatic interpretation is unwarranted. This writer somewhat prefers the literal view. But neither position is without difficulties.

What was the act and what was its significance? This is paramount. Jeremiah was charged to buy a linen belt, place it around his loins or waist, but not to put it in water (v.1). Bright (p. 94) sees the "linen belt," not as a sash or outer band over the garments, but as the usual undergarment, i.e., a short skirt worn about the hips, reaching midway down the thighs. It was to be of linen for two reasons: (1) Linen would easily rot; skin or leather would not. (2) The original cleanliness spoke of Israel's purity when first in fellowship with the Lord. Also, the linen belt would recall Israel's priestly calling (priests wore only linen) and character (cf. Exod 19:6). After wearing it for a while (v.2), Jeremiah was commanded (v.3) to hide it in a crevice of the rock (v.4) at the Euphrates (KJV, RSV, NIV mg.), and he did so (v.5). After many days, he was ordered to go to the rock and retrieve the belt he had buried (v.6). It was ruined and worthless (v.7) because it had been close to the moisture of the river. Why the Euphrates? The purpose of the trip may have been to underscore the influence of Mesopotamia in corrupting the nation religiously, beginning with ungodly Manasseh (2 Kings 21). Also, there may be an allusion to the coming Babylonian exile (so Cundall).

If one assumes token journeys are indicated here (cf. Ezek 4), then the suggestion adopted by many is that the destination intended is Parah (NIV, "Perath"), the modern 'Ain Farah, about three miles northeast of Anathoth, mentioned in Joshua 18:23 (cf. the LXX rendering, "Pharan"). Some have pointed out that there are rocks at this place, which are not on the banks of the middle or lower Euphrates (so Bewer). For this reason some settle for a place in the Carchemish region.

8–11 Now the prophet explains the transaction and the aptness of this acted oracle (v.8). A linen belt was used because just as it is placed closely about the body, so the nation Israel was brought into intimate relationship with her gracious Lord. The ruination of the garment teaches that idolatry corrupts anyone who engages in it (v.9). Idolatry had corrupted Israel from her loyalty to God and made her worthless (v.10). Instead of clinging to her God in faith and love (v.11), she destroyed herself.

b. *The wine of God's wrath*

13:12–14

> [12]"Say to them: 'This is what the LORD, the God of Israel, says: Every wineskin should be filled with wine.' And if they say to you, 'Don't we know that every wineskin should be filled with wine?' [13]then tell them, 'This is what the LORD says: I am going to fill with drunkenness all who live in this land, including the kings who sit on David's throne, the priests, the prophets and all those living in Jerusalem. [14]I will smash them one against the other, fathers and sons alike, declares the LORD. I will allow no pity or mercy or compassion to keep me from destroying them.' "

12–14 Possibly at a drinking feast, Jeremiah took occasion to utter a proverbial saying about jars (KJV, RSV, NIV, "wineskins") and wine, which was probably a platitude concerning the hope of continued prosperity. The jar was the largest earthenware container for storing wine (Isa 30:14). The largest found in excavations hold almost ten gallons. When Jeremiah used the pun of filling (vv.12–13), the wine drinkers mocked his banal remark, which he immediately gave a serious turn (v.14). Jeremiah pointed out that the people were the jars and were to be filled with the wine of God's wrath against their sin. He had turned their saying into a prediction of disaster.

Four groups are singled out for the judgment: the kings, the priests, the false prophets, and the people (v.13). Jeremiah had several kings in mind; they would all be the objects of God's judgment. His mention of David's throne may possibly have been meant to stress how far they had fallen from the standard of worship in David's day. All the people will be filled with mental intoxication, a symbol of helplessness and confusion. Canaanite worship was characterized by drunkenness. In the nation's drunkenness, the male portion of the population, who should have defended the land against the invaders, will be colliding and dashing one against another. Here Jeremiah anticipates the truth elaborated in 25:15–28; 51:7 (cf. also Ps 60:3; Isa 51:17–18; Ezek 23:31–34; Rev 16:19; 17:2). Three times the Lord declares that he will show no pity on the nation.

c. *Warning against pride*

13:15–17

> [15]Hear and pay attention,
>   do not be arrogant,
>   for the LORD has spoken.
> [16]Give glory to the LORD your God
>   before he brings the darkness,
> before your feet stumble
>   on the darkening hills.
> You hope for light,
>   but he will turn it to thick darkness
>   and change it to deep gloom.

¹⁷But if you do not listen,
      I will weep in secret
  because of your pride;
  my eyes will weep bitterly,
    overflowing with tears,
  because the LORD's flock will be taken captive.

15–17 Pride, the sin of Satan, has infected the human family before the Tower of Babel and ever since. Jeremiah warns the people against pride in their spiritual privilege (v.15). Proud of their favored position before God as his chosen people, they refused to heed his message through his prophets. The scene in this section is that of a weary traveler on a mountain caught in the dark night, "the darkening hills" (v.16) being literally "the twilight hills." The statement "Give glory to the LORD your God" is an OT idiom for "Confess your sins" (cf. Josh 7:19; John 9:24). To do so would avert the evil about to come on the nation. But Jeremiah knew their obstinate ways; they would not listen. Firm in declaring the truth of God without fear or favor, he was nonetheless tender in his compassion and grief over their obduracy, which would yet lead them into captivity. He took no delight in the prospect of their misery (v.17).

Notes

16 The antithesis between light and darkness is an important one from Gen 1 to Rev 22. It involves (1) the natural darkness of the unregenerate heart (cf. Eph 4:18); (2) the deliberate darkness of the sinner who willfully turns from the light (cf. John 3:19–20); and (3) the judicial darkness imposed by God on inveterate sinners (Jer 13:16; 2 Thess 2:11–12).

d. *Tragedy in the royal house*

    13:18–19

¹⁸Say to the king and to the queen mother,
  "Come down from your thrones,
  for your glorious crowns
    will fall from your heads."
¹⁹The cities in the Negev will be shut up,
  and there will be no one to open them.
  All Judah will be carried into exile,
    carried completely away.

18 Here the Lord commands Jeremiah to address the king and queen mother— King Jehoiachin and his mother, Queen Nehushta, who were carried away to Babylon in the second deportation under Nebuchadnezzar in 597 B.C. (cf. 2 Kings 24:8, 12, 15). The address is an exhortation to humility in view of their impending loss of sovereignty. Pride was characteristic of the royal house. Because kings practiced polygamy, their mothers were highly influential (cf. 1 Kings 2:19; 15:13; 2 Kings 10:13). This was all the more true of Jehoiachin and his mother because he was only

464

eighteen when he began his short reign of three months; so she probably had much influence over him. She is mentioned again—but not by name—in 22:26 and 29:2. Both the king and his mother were unreceptive to the message of God.

19 Unlike the invasion of Sennacherib (2 Kings 18:13), Nebuchadnezzar will strike the cities of the South, the Negev, which is the barren area in the south of Judah (Josh 15:21–32). Though the Negev is farthest from Jerusalem, it too will feel Nebuchadnezzar's might—an evidence of the total extent of Judah's captivity. The cities will be in ruins with no one to clear them. The statement that "all Judah" will be exiled is rhetorical exaggeration, since only some leaders and skilled workmen were taken to Babylon at that time (597 B.C.). Yet they represented the whole nation.

Notes

18 To the ordinary reader, the different translations of מַרְאֲשׁוֹתֵיכֶם (*mar'ašôtêkem*) can be mystifying. KJV has "your principalities"; ASV, "your headtires"; NASB, "from your heads"; and RSV and NIV, "crowns." As the word is pointed in the MT, it is a *hapax legomenon*. Most scholars change the pointing to read "from your head" in following LXX, Vulgate, and Syriac versions (cf. M.J. Dahood, "Two Textual Notes on Jeremiah," CBQ 23 [1961]: 462, who prefers a plural form of "head" [so NASB] found in Ugaritic [*rašt*]). In that case alteration of the term would be unnecessary.

e. *Captivity and shame of Judah*

13:20–27

20Lift up your eyes and see
  those who are coming from the north.
Where is the flock that was entrusted to you,
  the sheep of which you boasted?
21What will you say when the LORD sets over you
  those you cultivated as your special allies?
Will not pain grip you
  like that of a woman in labor?
22And if you ask yourself,
  "Why has this happened to me?"—
it is because of your many sins
  that your skirts have been torn off
  and your body mistreated.
23Can the Ethiopian change his skin
  or the leopard its spots?
Neither can you do good
  who are accustomed to doing evil.
24"I will scatter you like chaff
  driven by the desert wind.
25This is your lot,
  the portion I have decreed for you,"

declares the LORD,

"because you have forgotten me
  and trusted in false gods.
26I will pull up your skirts over your face
  that your shame may be seen—

465

> ²⁷your adulteries and lustful neighings,
>   your shameless prostitution!
> I have seen your detestable acts
>   on the hills and in the fields.
> Woe to you, O Jerusalem!
>   How long will you be unclean?"

20–21 This section describes the Captivity; vv.22–27 give its cause. Jerusalem is addressed under the figure of a shepherdess who has abandoned her flock (v.20). She is called on to account for the sheep entrusted to her. She has been derelict in duty and has misled her flock. Those "coming from the north" are again the Babylonians. Jerusalem was responsible for protecting the entire nation. For her unfaithfulness to the Lord's flock, Jerusalem will have to endure subjection to the very powers she has helped to gain control. There may be reference here to her foreign policy that courted Egypt and Babylon, especially the latter, when Judah was tributary to Neco of Egypt. Though she toadied to both, Judah would be dominated by them (v.21). Judah had tried to make binding alliances with Babylon on more than one occasion (cf. 4:30). Ultimately, she was the one who made the Babylonians her masters by invoking their aid against Egypt instead of trusting the Lord.

22 When Judah is in agony as a mother in childbirth, she will ask why she is suffering. Continuance in sin has deadened the nation's conscience. She does not feel she is suffering justly. The shameful way the conquerors will treat the people will be like the shaming of a prostitute (v.26; Hos 2:3, 10). Exposure of the secret parts (here euphemistically described as tearing off the skirt and mistreating the body) was the public disgrace heaped on prostitutes.

23 Using a famous proverb, Jeremiah points out that Judah is so far beyond change that her repentance would be like a suspension of nature's laws. God still invites people to repent. But with Judah sin was so ingrained that there was no hope of repentance. Here is a classic example of loss of freedom of the will through persistent sinning. Sin becomes natural. Jeremiah is speaking of the force of habit, not denying freedom of choice (cf. John 8:34). The passage shows how difficult it is for anyone to liberate himself from the innate tendency to sin (cf. Gen 6:5; Jer 17:9). Obviously Jeremiah is stating the case radically. He does not mean to rule out any response to the working of God in people's hearts to bring them to repentance, as v.27 shows.

24–27 Because of the nation's persistent sin, the Lord will subject the people to a process of winnowing—a familiar scene to them, for they had often seen the strong wind from the Arabian desert carry off the useless stubble. None of the things described in vv.24–27 is accidental; they are God's judgment on Judah for forgetting him and trusting in "the [the article is in the original] lie" (so Heb.; NIV, "false gods"), specifically, Baal (v.25). Judah's retribution will be to know the full measure of disgrace (v.26). Verse 27 is a recapitulation of Judah's sins. The "neighings" are a bestial figure for illicit love (cf. 5:8; 50:11). The last question—"How long will you be unclean?"—shows that there is still opportunity for Judah to repent. The Lord does not close the door on a future return from idolatry. He still wishes the nation will repent in time and escape punishment. Two strong emotions struggled in Jeremiah: (1) the certainty of disaster for the nation and (2) the hope that it might yet be averted.

Notes

21 KJV translates אַלֻּפִים (*allupîm*) as "chiefs." ASV has "friends" (so RSV), whereas NASB renders "companions" with "chieftains" in the margin. The meaning of this word determines the translation of the verse. At times the word means the captain of a thousand, a chiliarch (cf. Gen 36:15; Zech 9:7). The term also means a member of the same family or class, hence a familiar friend (cf. Prov 16:28; Mic 7:5). Now it is clear that since the Babylonians could not be tribal chiefs in Judah, there is no basis for the general sense of chiefs or princes. The sense of friend, ally (so NIV), or confidant alone remains (so Payne Smith). Those whom Judah had been courting were yet to be her masters and tyrants.

4. Drought and impending exile (14:1–22)

Chapters 14 and 15 belong together. They are autobiographical and full of Jeremiah's grief for the future of his people. They also relate to the drought. Without chronological references it is difficult to date passages like these. One scholar dates them in the fourth year of Jehoiakim; another suggests a time early in Jehoiakim's reign. Even references to invasions and exile cannot help to date the material before us because there were three invasions of Judah and as many deportations. Nor can one identify the material with a particular crisis in the life of the nation. The drought here is probably later than that mentioned in 3:3 and 12:4 because this drought is connected with war (vv. 17–18).

2. The critical drought

14:1–6

¹This is the word of the LORD to Jeremiah concerning the drought:

²"Judah mourns,
   her cities languish;
they wail for the land,
   and a cry goes up from Jerusalem.
³The nobles send their servants for water;
   they go to the cisterns
   but find no water.
They return with their jars unfilled;
   dismayed and despairing,
   they cover their heads.
⁴The ground is cracked
   because there is no rain in the land;
the farmers are dismayed
   and cover their heads.
⁵Even the doe in the field
   deserts her newborn fawn
   because there is no grass.
⁶Wild donkeys stand on the barren heights
   and pant like jackals;
their eyesight fails
   for lack of pasture."

1 The portion begins with an unusual formula, literally, "That which was the word of the LORD to Jeremiah" (cf. 46:1; 47:1; 49:34). This is its first use in the OT. The Hebrew word for "drought" (*baṣṣārôt*) is in the plural, which may indicate an intensive plural or point to a series of droughts. Rainfall in Palestine is never overabundant. A year of drought can cause suffering. Unlike Egypt and Mesopotamia, Palestine depends on seasonal rainfall. Droughts were common in Palestine (cf. Gen 12:10; Ruth 1:1; 2 Sam 21:1; 1 Kings 8:37). In Israel a drought was never viewed as a chance occurrence. Drought had been threatened for disobedience (Deut 28:23–24) and was part of the covenant curses. The Lord's purpose in sending the drought was to bring the nation to repentance.

2–4 Jeremiah vividly portrays the distress of humanity and the animals. The entire country suffers anguish from the lack of water (v.2). The drought extends to the city. The nation is clothed in black to express its mourning. The capital cries out for help. Nor are the nobles immune (v.3)! When they send their servants (lit., "little ones") to the cisterns for water, they return with empty vessels. Rain water was stored for time of need, but the supply has long been exhausted. In their mourning the people cover their heads, as though to shut out the painful sight. The famine afflicts city, country, humanity, and animals. The ground is "cracked" (*ḥattāh*, lit., "dismayed"). By poetic license the verb transfers human emotions to inanimate objects. The farmers cannot work the soil and, hence, cannot expect a harvest. They, too, are in deep mourning (v.4).

5–6 It is sad for irrational creatures to have to suffer because the people have incurred God's displeasure. The doe (v.5), known for her care for her fawns (noted by ancient writers), no longer is able to care for her offspring. The wild donkeys (v.6), known for their hardiness and ability to survive on very little, will be greatly debilitated. Even on the bare heights they will gasp for breath. Also, instead of the usual sharpness of sight, they lose the power of vision in their agony. The imagery throughout this portion reflects Jeremiah's poetical ability.

b. *The confession of the nation*

14:7–9

> 7Although our sins testify against us,
>   O LORD, do something for the sake of your name.
> For our backsliding is great;
>   we have sinned against you.
> 8O Hope of Israel,
>   its Savior in times of distress,
> why are you like a stranger in the land,
>   like a traveler who stays only a night?
> 9Why are you like a man taken by surprise,
>   like a warrior powerless to save?
> You are among us, O LORD,
>   and we bear your name;
>   do not forsake us!

7 Expositors differ about whose confession this is. It is conceivably Jeremiah's, but he usually expresses his intercession personally and uses singular pronouns. But the portrayal of the nation's agony is incomplete if the people are not making their own confession. Some expositors think that the people are more concerned about the Lord's not intervening on their behalf than about the gravity of their sins. There is, however, a good case for the contrary position. In this verse the people acknowledge their apostasy and sin, which deserve only death. But they plead on solid ground—viz., that the Lord's honor may be exhibited to the pagan nations. Because there is no merit in Judah, the Lord's work in the people's behalf will reveal his nature as a God of compassion.

8–9 So Jeremiah entreats the Lord not to disappoint his people's hope in him. When he calls the Lord the "Hope of Israel" (v.8), Jeremiah is using one of his favorite expressions (cf. 17:7 [NIV, "confidence"], 13; 50:7; cf. Paul's use of it in Acts 28:20; Col 1:27; 1 Tim 1:1). The people ask the Lord why he is as a stranger or traveler with no interest in the country he is only passing through. Why should the Lord do so to his people? Others may disclaim any responsibility for the land, but surely not the Lord God of Israel! If he is their Hope and Deliverer in times of distress, why does he not now act as such in their behalf? The Lord is not powerless (v.9); so why should he hesitate like one paralyzed by fright? His presence was still among his people in the ark, the temple, and the sacred worship. Furthermore, the people plead the covenant, for they are called by the Lord's name. So they pray that the Lord will not forsake them.

c. *The Lord's answer in judgment*

14:10–12

¹⁰This is what the LORD says about this people:

> "They greatly love to wander;
>   they do not restrain their feet.
> So the LORD does not accept them;
>   he will now remember their wickedness
> and punish them for their sins."

¹¹Then the LORD said to me, "Do not pray for the well-being of this people. ¹²Although they fast, I will not listen to their cry; though they offer burnt offerings and grain offerings, I will not accept them. Instead, I will destroy them with the sword, famine and plague."

10–12 The Lord's reply explains his chastisements. Because his people have kept on in their wickedness, they were punished for their ungodliness. Apparently the Lord considered the nation lacking in true penitence. They were constantly wandering after foreign gods (v.10); because the people rejected him, he was rejecting them. For the third time Jeremiah is forbidden to pray for the people (v.11; cf. 7:16; 11:14). They were beyond help because of their determined disobedience. Intercession was an important prophetic function, but Jeremiah was not permitted to intercede at that fateful time (cf. 1 Sam 7:8; 12:19). Worse visitations than the drought would overtake the people—viz., the sword, famine, and pestilence (v.12). The combination of these three appears seven times in the book. Neither fasting nor sacrifices would avail to recover God's favor, as long as the people were bent on idolatry. External marks of repentance are useless, since the Lord seeks above all else reality, truth in the heart.

d. *The doom of the false prophets*

14:13–16

> [13]But I said, "Ah, Sovereign LORD, the prophets keep telling them, 'You will not see the sword or suffer famine. Indeed, I will give you lasting peace in this place.'"
>
> [14]Then the LORD said to me, "The prophets are prophesying lies in my name. I have not sent them or appointed them or spoken to them. They are prophesying to you false visions, divinations, idolatries and the delusions of their own minds. [15]Therefore, this is what the LORD says about the prophets who are prophesying in my name: I did not send them, yet they are saying, 'No sword or famine will touch this land.' Those same prophets will perish by sword and famine. [16]And the people they are prophesying to will be thrown out into the streets of Jerusalem because of the famine and sword. There will be no one to bury them or their wives, their sons or their daughters. I will pour out on them the calamity they deserve."

13 Here the false prophets are blamed for the plight of the nation. They lulled the people into unwarranted complacency (v.13), which led them to believe all was well and would continue to be well. As a mitigation of the nation's sin, Jeremiah pleads that the false prophets have misled the people. But he does not excuse their sin. What about the false prophets? Why did they appear on the scene of the nation's history, especially in Jeremiah's day? In fact, he said more about them than any other prophet did. First of all, the appearance of a prophet in Israel with a message from the Lord was a sign that the nation was not walking in the Lord's will. Recall how the first prophecy in the Bible appears in a setting of failure (cf. Gen 3:15). Prophets were revivalists, calling the people back to God. They denounced sin; so their messages were not welcome to the ungodly. The true prophet was never really popular any more than he is today (cf. 2 Tim 4:3–4). Thus there arose alongside the true prophets of God false prophets—self-seeking, profiteering, and zealous for popularity, but with no authoritative word from God. Since Jeremiah's message was a heartbreaking one of almost unrelieved judgment, it gave the false prophets an ample excuse to speak. In those desperate times, they preached deliverance and peace; so the people would not believe in the imminence of judgment. They promised "lasting peace" (lit., "peace of truth"), the very opposite of Jeremiah's true message. Imagine the confusion with their babel of bright promises over against Jeremiah's thundering message of doom. They were false, lying prophets because the Lord never sent them, even though they claimed his authorization.

14–16 Verse 14 points out the four methods by which the false prophets practiced their deception. The Lord's retribution on the lying prophets will be their endurance of the very punishment they would not predict (vv.15–16). The people should have known that the Lord punishes sin, and they should not have believed the false prophets. The judgment of the nation is spoken of here because the people were willing to be deceived.

e. *The grief of Jeremiah*

14:17–18

> [17]"Speak this word to them:

> " 'Let my eyes overflow with tears
> night and day without ceasing;
> for my virgin daughter—my people—
> has suffered a grievous wound,
> a crushing blow.
> ¹⁸If I go into the country,
> I see those slain by the sword;
> if I go into the city,
> I see the ravages of famine.
> Both prophet and priest
> have gone to a land they know not.' "

17–18 Jeremiah shows the hardened nation his grief in seeing their coming ruin. He grieves over both war and famine. Jeremiah cannot view the people's distress dispassionately (cf. 9:18; 13:17). He calls Judah "the virgin daughter—my people" (v.17) because she had been jealously kept from the idolatrous nations, as virgins are guarded in Oriental households. Now the prophet describes the conditions in the land after the Fall of Jerusalem. The blame still falls on the false prophets and godless priests (v.18), who must be exiled to a foreign land.

Notes

18 The verb סָחַר (sāḥar) is translated "to go about, travel about," in the sense of trading. (NIV has "have gone to a land.") In modern Hebrew it means "to go about as a merchant." In the Syriac it denotes "to go about as a beggar, be a beggar." In what sense is the passage here to be understood concerning the activity of "both prophet and priest"? The renderings vary. RSV has it in the sense of plying a trade as a merchant (cf. Gen 34:10,21; 42:34), reading "both prophet and priest ply their trade through the land." The concept appears to be that they traffic as usual in spite of the people's distress (so Hyatt). KJV, ASV, JPS, and NASB have substantially the same reading, i.e., "go about in the land." A freer translation is "they wandered off to a land with which they were unfamiliar" (so Harrison). JB has "even prophets and priests plough the land; they are at their wit's end," a translation difficult to defend on many grounds. AT and NEB are substantially alike: "go begging round the land." BHK suggests in the margin the rendering "have been dragged to a land that they know not" (cf. 15:3). But there is no textual or MS authority for this conjecture (so Bright). It seems best to adhere to the KJV, ASV, and NASB rendering.

f. *Prayer of confession and plea for help*

14:19–22

> ¹⁹Have you rejected Judah completely?
> Do you despise Zion?
> Why have you afflicted us
> so that we cannot be healed?
> We hoped for peace
> but no good has come,
> for a time of healing
> but there is only terror.

> ^{20}O LORD, we acknowledge our wickedness
>   and the guilt of our fathers;
>   we have indeed sinned against you.
> ^{21}For the sake of your name do not despise us;
>   do not dishonor your glorious throne.
> Remember your covenant with us
>   and do not break it.
> ^{22}Do any of the worthless idols of the nations bring rain?
>   Do the skies themselves send down showers?
> No, it is you, O LORD our God.
>   Therefore our hope is in you,
>   for you are the one who does all this.

19–22 Here is further lament and another appeal for divine aid. The nation pleads its own case with the Lord. The questions are more intense. The people cannot believe that the Lord has irretrievably cast them off (v.19). Now they freely admit that all their hopes and prospects have been blasted. They also admit the basis of their woes: their wickedness (v.20). How genuine their words were time would tell. They acknowledged the sinfulness of their ancestors. In desperation they plead three reasons for the Lord to help them in spite of their sins: (1) his reputation in the earth, (2) his temple, and (3) his covenant (v.21). The throne of God's glory is Zion, especially the temple (cf. 2 Kings 19:15; Ps 99:1). Still haunted by the drought (v.22), they declare their belief that neither idols nor the heavens by themselves can give rain. Only God can do this. He alone can end their trials, and they expect him to help them out of their difficulties. The Talmud states: "Three keys have not been entrusted to an agent (but are kept in God's hand): the keys of birth, rain and resurrection" (*Sanhedrin* 113a; so Freedman).

5. *Impending judgment and Jeremiah's complaints* (15:1–21)

Many expositors link the first four verses of chapter 15 to chapter 14. Actually, the break between chapters 14 and 15 should be disregarded. The mood in this chapter intensifies as Jeremiah elaborates on the Exile. In fact, he plumbs the depths of despair so deeply as to lead him to say some things the Lord rebukes.

a. *Prayer unavailing for Judah*

15:1

> ^{1}Then the LORD said to me: "Even if Moses and Samuel were to stand before me, my heart would not go out to this people. Send them away from my presence! Let them go!"

1 The Lord refuses to avert judgment from his people; his decision to punish them is irreversible. Therefore the continued intercession of Jeremiah or of any others cannot succeed. The people's incorrigibility has placed them beyond the power of prayer. Moses and Samuel, exemplary intercessors for Israel, would have been unable to move the Lord from his decision (cf. Exod 32:11–14, 30–34; Num 14:13–23; Deut 9:18–20, 25–29; 1 Sam 7:5–9; 12:19–25; cf. also Ps 99:6–8). The Lord commands that the nation be sent from his presence. No longer can he tolerate them; nor does he want Jeremiah to keep reminding him of them. Nevertheless, the command in v.1 is not absolute and final but rather conditional.

b. *The punishment determined*

15:2–9

2"And if they ask you, 'Where shall we go?' tell them, 'This is what the LORD says:

" 'Those destined for death, to death;
those for the sword, to the sword;
those for starvation, to starvation;
those for captivity, to captivity.'

3"I will send four kinds of destroyers against them," declares the LORD, "the sword to kill and the dogs to drag away and the birds of the air and the beasts of the earth to devour and destroy. 4I will make them abhorrent to all the kingdoms of the earth because of what Manasseh son of Hezekiah king of Judah did in Jerusalem.

5"Who will have pity on you, O Jerusalem?
Who will mourn for you?
Who will stop to ask how you are?
6You have rejected me," declares the LORD.
"You keep on backsliding.
So I will lay hands on you and destroy you;
I can no longer show compassion.
7I will winnow them with a winnowing fork
at the city gates of the land.
I will bring bereavement and destruction on my people,
for they have not changed their ways.
8I will make their widows more numerous
than the sand of the sea.
At midday I will bring a destroyer
against the mothers of their young men;
suddenly I will bring down on them
anguish and terror.
9The mother of seven will grow faint
and breathe her last.
Her sun will set while it is still day;
she will be disgraced and humiliated.
I will put the survivors to the sword
before their enemies,"

declares the LORD.

2–4 Should the nation ask where the people were to go, the answer is that each will proceed to the punishment allotted him by the Lord (v.2). If they think they are only going to be banished, they are tragically mistaken. Their destination will be death by disease (cf. 14:12), warfare, or famine. It will also be exile. Then, as if the judgments specified in v.2 were insufficient, the Lord speaks of "four kinds of destroyers against" the people (v.3). The first will destroy the living; the other three will mutilate and consume the dead. For the corpse of a man to be dragged on the ground and then become carrion for bird and beast was too horrendous for an Israelite to contemplate. It was the ultimate in desecration of the dead. It has been carried over into Revelation 6:1–8. When the Lord refers to making the people an object of horror to all kingdoms of the earth (v.4), he apparently has in view more than the generation of Jeremiah's time. Manasseh's sin is presented as a root cause of Judah's captivity—not as if the nation's suffering was the direct result of his sins. He had contributed to the moral decline of the nation, but the people had imitated his ways when he brazenly led Judah into idolatry (cf. 2 Kings 21:3–7, 10–15; 23:26–27; 24:3–4).

5–7 No.one will pity Jerusalem when the Lord forsakes her (v.5). She will be left desolate without anyone caring. These conditions could be the result of one of the previous Babylonian invasions of the land. Because the people repeatedly rejected the Lord and his worship by slipping back into apostasy (v.6), he will no longer be merciful to them. As a farmer winnows the wheat to remove the chaff (v.7), so the Lord will disperse the people from their cities—"the city gates" standing for the whole country. The population will be decimated. The cause of all this is the refusal of Judah to be truly repentant.

8–9 To the Lord's grief, Judah's widows will be more numerous than the sand of the seas (v.8), an amazing comparison (cf. 2 Chron 28:6). Even the mothers of warriors will not escape the destroyer, because Judah will be defenseless through the loss of her valiant sons in battle. Many take the reference to "mothers" figuratively of Jerusalem, and this is surely correct. The enemy will strike at noonday—suddenly and unexpectedly (cf. 6:4). To have seven sons is a Hebrew picture of complete happiness, but the mother in v.9 has had her happiness pass all too soon. Because of the blessing of abundant offspring, she might have considered herself secure. But she is seen breathing out her soul, or gasping for breath, i.e., her throat gasps (cf. 4:10). Any survivors of the Fall of Jerusalem will suffer the same end as those already slain.

c. *Jeremiah's complaint*

15:10–11

> ^{10}Alas, my mother, that you gave me birth,
> a man with whom the whole land strives and contends!
> I have neither lent nor borrowed,
> yet everyone curses me.

^{11}The LORD said,

> "Surely I will deliver you for a good purpose;
> surely I will make your enemies plead with you
> in times of disaster and times of distress."

10–11 In his overwhelming despondency the prophet laments his life's work and his lot (v.10). This is one of Jeremiah's most moving confessions. He was complaining of loneliness. His greatness lay in his sensitive nature that felt acute pain for his people and their doom. The hopelessness of the nation's situation and his own difficulties of his position weighed on him. He is lapsing into self-pity. This is one of the saddest cries in the book. It must have been uttered at a time when he was experiencing great opposition, probably during Jehoiakim's reign. He feels deeply his alienation from the nation he loves. He wishes he had not been born. Notice his tenderness in addressing his mother. He is like one constantly in a lawsuit with his people. Borrowing and lending are proverbial reasons for disagreement and tense relations between people. The populace was cursing him because he attacked their sins so unsparingly. Passages such as this show that the prophets were not supermen but fully human, neither impassive nor automata. Now the Lord responds to Jeremiah's complaint and gives him personal assurance (v.11). The Hebrew of v.11 (and also v.12) is difficult. The force of the verse is that God promises vindication for Jeremiah against his enemies as well as strength for his ministry, the objective of which is only good. In times of distress, even his enemies will come asking for his intercession (cf. 21:1–6; 37:3; 42:1–6).

Notes

10 The last two words כֻּלֹּה מְקַלְלֹונִי (*kullōh mᵉqallawnî*, "everyone curses me") have occasioned some difficulty. The last word in the original is entirely abnormal. The term *kullōh* has been rendered in KJV, ASV, NASB, and RSV as "all of them" or "every one of them" and in NIV as "everyone," according to the Qere (marginal reading) כֻּלֹּו (*kullô* for *kullām*). The best explanation for the final word is to understand it as a *forma mixta* or conflate.

11 More difficulty has centered around this verse than any in chapter 15. The term שֵׁרִותֶךָ (*šēriwtēkā*) has been understood as a noun and as a verb. KJV translates it as a noun: "It shall be well with thy remnant." This seems to be the least likely translation, because the word is not written correctly (a letter must be assumed as having been dropped out), and the obvious force appears to be verbal rather than nominal. Even those who agree on a verbal form are not in accord on the final translation. RSV has a divergent rendering: "If I have not entreated thee for their good." This with the remainder of the verse gives no good principal clause; so RSV has decided on an exclamatory sentence. BHS's margin reveals the multiplicity of opinions. ASV prefers "I will strengthen thee for good"; JPS, "I will release thee for good"; NEB is substantially as ASV; JB agrees with ASV in the footnote; NASB renders "I will set you free for purposes of good." NIV has "I will deliver you for a good purpose." The area seems to be restricted to rendering the verb as from שָׁרָה (*šārāh*, "to set free, release") or from שָׁרַר (*šārar*, "to establish, strengthen"). Taking into account the context in which the prophet in his despair of life needs undergirding to go on with his ministry, the preferable translation would be that of strengthening him for good, that is, with the objective of his accomplishing the good he has been called to perform. Thus NIV and NASB provide acceptable translations.

d. The inevitable judgment

15:12–14

> 12"Can a man break iron—
>   iron from the north—or bronze?
> 13Your wealth and your treasures
>   I will give as plunder, without charge,
> because of all your sins
>   throughout your country.
> 14I will enslave you to your enemies
>   in a land you do not know,
> for my anger will kindle a fire
>   that will burn against you."

12–14 This passage clearly predicts the Exile. But v.12 is so difficult that some scholars claim it is a gloss. Bronze is an alloy of copper and tin. Unusually hard iron was available from the region of the Black Sea; it probably came from Chalybes in Pontus on the Black Sea coast. This iron was famous for being harder than all other iron and was like steel. What is the purpose of the question here? The sense is that as little as men can break iron, Judah will not be able to sustain an attack from the power in the north, i.e., the Chaldeans (so Calvin et al.). The query demands a negative answer. Because Judah will not be able to withstand the northern enemy, her wealth and treasures will be freely carried off by the adversary. God's wrath against their sin will not be satisfied till all is plundered (v.13) and taken to Babylon (v.14).

Notes

14 According to some scholars the verb וְהַעֲבַרְתִּי (wᵉhaʿᵃbartî; KJV, "And I will make to pass over") is probably a corruption for וְהַעֲבַדְתִּי (wᵉhaʿᵃbadtî, "I will make you serve" [so Plumptre]). NIV follows this textual change—"I will enslave you." This brings it in harmony with a parallel passage in 17:4; also, there are some twenty-seven MSS that have this reading. Either reading gives an acceptable text. A word of caution is in order, however, regarding claims of a corrupt text. This must be done only on good grounds lest it become a gateway for free emendations, from which the OT has suffered at the hands of well-meaning scholars.

e. Jeremiah's charge against the Lord

15:15–18

> ¹⁵You understand, O LORD;
>   remember me and care for me.
>   Avenge me on my persecutors.
> You are long-suffering—do not take me away;
>   think of how I suffer reproach for your sake.
> ¹⁶When your words came, I ate them;
>   they were my joy and my heart's delight,
> for I bear your name,
>   O LORD God Almighty.
> ¹⁷I never sat in the company of revelers,
>   never made merry with them;
> I sat alone because your hand was on me
>   and you had filled me with indignation.
> ¹⁸Why is my pain unending
>   and my wound grievous and incurable?
> Will you be to me like a deceptive brook,
>   like a spring that fails?

15–16 On the basis of his loyalty to the will of the Lord, Jeremiah pleads for divine help. (Verse 15 is linked in thought with v.10.) He prays that vengeance will be meted out by the Lord on those who have opposed his prophet. Jeremiah does not want the Lord to be patient with his enemies and withhold vengeance on them till he is gone. Jeremiah wants vindication in this life (cf. Job). For the OT saints, future life was an uncertain quantity because it was not yet clearly revealed by the Lord (so Bewer). In effect, then, Jeremiah is pleading that God will not be so lenient with his persecutors as to give them time to destroy him. In a striking figure he recalls his first reception of God's message and how he made it his own (v.16). (For a similar figure, see Ezek 2:8–3:3 and Rev 10:9–10.) It symbolizes the assimilation of God's revealed truth. Jeremiah was every inch a chosen servant of the Lord. His chief delight was in God's word.

17–18 Jeremiah describes his solitariness in the midst of his people (v.17). Because he sided with God, he was cut off from the joys of those around him. He was filled with God's indignation against their sin. It greatly pained him to be out of step with his contemporaries. The hand of God was on him; the constraint of God's truth weighed on his spirit. The rhetorical question in v.18 implies that for the moment Jeremiah gave way to despair. He was so deeply and continuously wounded that he wanted to know whether God had abandoned him and had proved unreliable. After all, his own family had betrayed him. The "deceptive brook" was a familiar figure to all his readers (cf. Job 6:15–20). In Palestine many brooks have water only after a downpour. At other times a traveler may be disappointed if he looks for water in them (contrast 2:13). In his distraught state, Jeremiah charged the Lord with failure to fulfill his promises to strengthen him in his resistance against his enemies (1:18–19).

f. God's rebuke and encouragement

15:19–21

19Therefore this is what the LORD says:

> "If you repent, I will restore you
>   that you may serve me;
> if you utter worthy, not worthless, words,
>   you will be my spokesman.
> Let this people turn to you,
>   but you must not turn to them.
> 20I will make you a wall to this people,
>   a fortified wall of bronze;
> they will fight against you
>   but will not overcome you,
> for I am with you
>   to rescue and save you,"
>
> declares the LORD.
> 21"I will save you from the hands of the wicked
>   and redeem you from the grasp of the cruel."

19–21 In this amazing passage Jeremiah recorded the Lord's greatest rebuke in the hour of his despair and his hasty accusation of his Lord (v.19). In it the Lord tells Jeremiah that if he gives up his doubts and reproaches and avoids worthless statements and holds to worthy ones he may continue to be his prophet and mouthpiece (Exod 4:16). Jeremiah himself will have to undergo the refining process so that he can cleave to precious words, not vile, worthless ones. The end of v.19 has a play on

477

words: "turn," "not turn." He must lift his people and not let them drag him down to their level. His only hope is to trust more fully in God and be faithful to the message whatever response it brings. He need not trim it to suit them; rather, they will be won over by his firm stand (v.20). Then God promises assurance and personal victory. Verses 19–21 are practically a recommissioning of Jeremiah (cf. 1:18–19). He will be kept from the power of the violent wicked (v.21). There were such men in Judah, and they finally assassinated Gedaliah, the governor of Judah after the Fall of Jerusalem (cf. 41:1–3). This word of encouragement was sufficient for the prophet's need; and though opposition to his message mounted perilously, he never again complained to the Lord as he did in vv.10, 15–18.

6. *Bane and blessing* (16:1–21)

Again, the chapter division is illogical, since 16:1 through 17:18 are a unit. The date for this passage is probably the fourth year of King Jehoiakim (2 Kings 24:1–2). Jeremiah had complained of his loneliness in chapter 15, but the Lord promises him no relief. Verse 17 of chapter 15 is elaborated and in relation to Judah's political and spiritual state. Two sections of the passage deal with doom and two with bright promises for the future.

a. *The loneliness of Jeremiah*

16:1–9

> ¹Then the word of the LORD came to me: ²"You must not marry and have sons or daughters in this place." ³For this is what the LORD says about the sons and daughters born in this land and about the women who are their mothers and the men who are their fathers: ⁴"They will die of deadly diseases. They will not be mourned or buried but will be like refuse lying on the ground. They will perish by sword and famine, and their dead bodies will become food for the birds of the air and the beasts of the earth."
>
> ⁵For this is what the LORD says: "Do not enter a house where there is a funeral meal; do not go to mourn or show sympathy, because I have withdrawn my blessing, my love and my pity from this people," declares the LORD. ⁶"Both high and low will die in this land. They will not be buried or mourned, and no one will cut himself or shave his head for them. ⁷No one will offer food to comfort those who mourn for the dead—not even for a father or a mother—nor will anyone give them a drink to console them.
>
> ⁸"And do not enter a house where there is feasting and sit down to eat and drink. ⁹For this is what the LORD Almighty, the God of Israel, says: Before your eyes and in your days I will bring an end to the sounds of joy and gladness and to the voices of bride and bridegroom in this place."

1–2 All but the last three verses of chapter 16 are prose. Undoubtedly, the Lord's command (v.1) for Jeremiah not to marry (v.2) was an emotional shock for him. Celibacy was unusual, not only in Israel, but throughout the Near East. Among the Jews marriage was viewed as man's natural state (cf. Gen 1:28; 2:18; Deut 7:14). And in NT times nonmarriage was exceptional (Matt 24:19; 1 Cor 7:26). The desire to perpetuate the family name led to almost universal marriage in Israel. Jeremiah's dedication to his prophetic service allowed him no time for family life or for participation in the usual joys and sorrows of his countrymen. His compliance with the

Lord's command not to marry shows his complete submission to the divine will and underscores the woes predicted for the nation. His being denied a wife and children would be a warning that the family life of the nation was to be disrupted. "This place" (v.2) was Jerusalem and Judah. Recall the price Jeremiah had already paid for his ministry—isolation from his countrymen (15:10), loneliness (15:17). And now not only is he forbidden to marry, but he is also not allowed to participate in funerals (v.5) or times of joy (v.8). It was almost a sentence of social excommunication.

3–4 The Lord tells Jeremiah that the sorrows of parents will be increased (v.3). Children will die of "deadly diseases" (lit., "deaths of sicknesses")—epidemic diseases (v.4). The number of deaths will be so great that there will be no time for mourning or burial. Moreover, the results of war and famine are detailed in v.4.

5–9 Jeremiah is not to mourn over the carnage in the land (v.5). Private sorrow will be exceeded by the national doom and mourning. Abstinence from mourning would be a sign of universal disease and death on a universal scale. Not to show grief was abnormal and was cause for criticism. The rituals for the bereaved—even for those who lost a father or mother—would not be permitted. So Jeremiah will be denied the blessing of serving the sorrowing. He will have to refrain from mourning because the Lord will no longer prosper his people or bestow his grace on them. Death will overtake nobles as well as common people (v.6). There will be no time to perform the pagan practices of mourning the people. To cut themselves and make themselves bald were actions strictly forbidden in the law of Moses (Lev 19:28; 21:5; Deut 14:1); but these were evidently often practiced in Israel and Judah (41:5; 47:5; Ezek 7:18; Amos 8:10; Mic 1:16). In time of death, fasting was usual (cf. 1 Sam 31:13; 2 Sam 3:35; Ezek 24:17). In the evening, however, food and drink were provided by friends (v.7), since the food and drink in the home of the mourner had become ceremonially unclean because of the dead body (Hos 9:4). As for the cup of consolation, in later Judaism it was a special cup of wine for the chief mourner (cf. Prov 31:6). Moreover, the prophet was also commanded to abstain from the joys of the people (v.8). This was meant to show the imminence of the calamity that awaited them. He could have little joy at marriage festivities when he remembered the threat hanging over them all. Nor were they to think that the doom was far off; it would happen in their lifetime (v.9).

Notes

5 The word מַרְזֵחַ (*marzēaḥ*) means "a shrill sound." In Amos 6:7, the only other biblical reference, it is applied to revelry. Because the context does not favor such a rendering, scholars translate it "mourning" here, as in the Aramaic Targum.

7 KJV renders יִפְרְסוּ לָהֶם (*yiprᵉsû lāhem*) as "men tear themselves for them in mourning." ASV and NASB translate "break bread for them in mourning," with which JPS, RSV, JB, and NEB agree. NIV has "offer food to." LXX has pointed *lāhem* ("themselves") as *leḥem* ("bread"). In view of the mention of the cup, there is strong backing for the latter rendering, followed in this commentary.

b. *The cause of the judgment*

16:10–13

> 10"When you tell these people all this and they ask you, 'Why has the LORD decreed such a great disaster against us? What wrong have we done? What sin have we committed against the LORD our God?' 11then say to them, 'It is because your fathers forsook me,' declares the LORD, 'and followed other gods and served and worshiped them. They forsook me and did not keep my law. 12But you have behaved more wickedly than your fathers. See how each of you is following the stubbornness of his evil heart instead of obeying me. 13So I will throw you out of this land into a land neither you nor your fathers have known, and there you will serve other gods day and night, for I will show you no favor.' "

10–13 Jeremiah's withdrawnness would mystify his people; so he would have to explain it. He was prepared to spell out the cause of their miseries and the reason for the Babylonian exile (v.10). Aided by the false prophets, the people had become complacent in their sinning. They continued to be deceived and were blind to the true cause of their plight—apostasy (v.11). How unaware they were of the magnitude of their sin (cf. 5:19 for the substance of this passage)! The prophet explains that they would be exiled for their lapses into idolatry and indicts the nation—first its fathers, then the present generation—for forsaking the Lord (v.12). In fact, the latter outdid their ancestors in evil. As always, with greater responsibility comes severer punishment. Let none think it was their fathers' sins that brought judgment on them; it was their own wicked ways (cf. Ezek 18). With great force (so Heb.) the Lord was going to "throw" them out of their land into an unknown land (v.13). While they may have known of the land, it was unknown to them by the actual experience of living. There Jeremiah ironically assures them that they will have the opportunity of indulging their desire for pagan worship day and night. And the Lord would completely withdraw his favor from them.

c. *Restoration to the land*

16:14–15

> 14"However, the days are coming," declares the LORD, "when men will no longer say, 'As surely as the LORD lives, who brought the Israelites up out of Egypt,' 15but they will say, 'As surely as the LORD lives, who brought the Israelites up out of the land of the north and out of all the countries where he had banished them.' For I will restore them to the land I gave their forefathers."

14–15 Judgment is never God's last word (v.14). Some scholars think vv.14–15 were transferred here from 23:7–8. But they are not an interpolation because the prophets often tempered condemnation with promise so that the godly among the people might not be overwhelmed by despair. After exile will be repatriation. The Exodus from Egypt will pale in significance before the people's deliverance from Babylon and from world-wide dispersion (v.15). The future Exodus will be greater than the past one. The regathering is the final one in the consummation of Israel's national history in the last days. The reference to "all the countries" shows that the prophet was predicting a restoration from a general dispersion after the Exile (so Bewer). The return will be through God's gracious faithfulness to the covenant he made with the patriarchs regarding the land (Gen 12:1–3, 7).

d. *Complete retribution*

16:16–18

> ¹⁶"But now I will send for many fishermen," declares the Lord, "and they will catch them. After that I will send for many hunters, and they will hunt them down on every mountain and hill and from the crevices of the rocks. ¹⁷My eyes are on all their ways; they are not hidden from me, nor is their sin concealed from my eyes. ¹⁸I will repay them double for their wickedness and their sin, because they have defiled my land with the lifeless forms of their vile images and have filled my inheritance with their detestable idols."

16–17 Before the repatriation there will be deportation. In these two verses we have the thorough nature of the threatened calamity. There will be no escape from the coming judgment of the Lord. Part of the threat in v.13 concerning the throwing out of Israel is now elaborated. The figures of fishing and hunting do not refer, as many older writers thought, to the restoration and conversion of Israel. The participants are not Cyrus, Zerubbabel, Ezra, Nehemiah, and others, who aided in the return to the land after the Exile. The passage deals, rather, with the scattering of the nation out of the land. The content of vv.16–17 clearly shows this. The hunters and fishermen are the pagan conquerors who were to be God's instruments for chastising Israel. No one will escape the invaders. To seek to hide from God will be futile. Jeremiah is not speaking of two periods of divine visitation. He is simply indicating that in the day of reckoning there will be no place to find refuge, either in the rivers and lakes or in the air (cf. for the figure Ezek 12:13; Amos 4:2; Hab 1:15; see also Amos 9:2–4). Verse 17 makes clear that v.16 refers to an emptying of the land, not a regathering of the exiles. The Lord knows all the nation's acts; none of the people's deeds has escaped his notice. But first, before they can be restored, the people must undergo retribution for their iniquity.

18 The double penalty has been understood by some scholars to mean double punishment (so Peake)—i.e., it has placed the nation under the burden of exonerating the Lord for his harsh punishment, as though his judgment was in excess of what the nation deserved. But this is invalid, because it does not harmonize with the biblical doctrine of God. The word *mišneh* ("double") cannot be understood outside the context of the Hebrew viewpoint, which used the term to express ample, full, complete punishment (cf. Isa 40:2) (so Harrison, KD). According to an Alalakh (in the plain of Antioch in Syria) tablet, the word may be better rendered "proportionate" (so Wiseman, cited in Harrison); so the punishment will be commensurate in full with the offense. Nothing is more defiling than idolatry. As corpses pollute, so do idols. The "lifeless forms" may refer to either the animals offered to idols or the idols themselves (so NIV), likened to a polluted body (cf. Lev 26:30; Num 19:11).

e. *The nations in blessing*

16:19–20

> ¹⁹O Lord, my strength and my fortress,
>   my refuge in time of distress,
> to you the nations will come
>   from the ends of the earth and say,

> "Our fathers possessed nothing but false gods,
> worthless idols that did them no good.
> ²⁰Do men make their own gods?
> Yes, but they are not gods!"

19–20 Jeremiah next worships the Lord for the restoration of Israel and the drawing of the Gentiles to him. He expresses the hope that the nations will finally turn from idolatry and confess the emptiness of such worship. The threefold "my" (v.19) expresses the Lord's sustaining of Jeremiah in his loneliness. So unprecedented will the divine retribution be that even idolatrous nations will respect the name of the Lord. What an admission from idolaters that their idols are only lies! So the nations will come to the Lord, not by human persuasion, but spontaneously and voluntarily (cf. Isa 2:1–4; 45:14; Zech 8:20–23). Without doubt the picture is messianic. It is best to take v.20 as a continuation of the declaration of the enlightened nations. Even they will see the folly of idolatry. Can people be so senseless as to think idols are gods made by them?

f. The goal of the punishment

16:21

> ²¹"Therefore I will teach them—
> this time I will teach them
> my power and might.
> Then they will know
> that my name is the LORD."

21 Once and for all, the Lord will manifest his hand and might—viz., the severe trials incurred by disobedience to his word and his will. Expositors are divided as to whether the Jews or the Gentiles are meant here. Actually, what is said will apply to both; there is no need to exclude either one (cf. Ezek 36:23; 37:14). All will vindicate God's unique glory. God is who he claims to be.

Notes

21 The Hebrew verb יָדַע (yāḏaʿ, "to know") is used three times in this verse. The Hebrews, aware of its pedagogical value, never avoided repetition in the interests of mere style. The first use is מוֹדִיעָם (môḏîʿām, "I will teach them"), the participle conveying the force of habitual action. The second is אוֹדִיעֵם (ʾôḏîʿēm, "I will teach them"), the imperfect emphasizing the continuing stages of his instruction. The third is וְיָדְעוּ (wᵉyāḏᵉʿû, "and they will know"), the perfect (with waw consecutive) signifying the result of the teaching (so NIV).

7. Man's deceitful heart (17:1–27)

Verses 1–18 continue the denunciations of the sins of the nation (ch. 16). As a whole, chapter 17 has no central theme but gathers together important aphoristic or proverbial sayings on the issues of life, sin, and the way of the curse and blessing. Attempts have been made to date the chapter, but they are generally unsatisfactory because of the lack of chronological data. LXX omits vv.1–4, but this is hardly significant.

a. *Israel's ineradicable sin*

17:1–4

> ¹"Judah's sin is engraved with an iron tool,
>   inscribed with a flint point,
> on the tablets of their hearts
>   and on the horns of their altars.
> ²Even their children remember
>   their altars and Asherah poles
> beside the spreading trees
>   and on the high hills.
> ³My mountain in the land
>   and your wealth and all your treasures
> I will give away as plunder,
>   together with your high places,
>   because of sin throughout your country.
> ⁴Through your own fault you will lose
>   the inheritance I gave you.
> I will enslave you to your enemies
>   in a land you do not know,
> for you have kindled my anger,
>   and it will burn forever."

1 When Jeremiah says that Judah's sin is "engraved" on the people's hearts and on their altars with "an iron tool" or "a flint point," he means that their sin is indelible. Thus God's judgment is inescapable. Sin, especially idolatry, had become an integral part of Judah's life. It had been etched on their very natures and on their temple worship (cf. Exod 27:2). (The reference to "the horns of their altars" may be to the altars of Baal.) Iron tools were used in cutting inscriptions on stone (cf. Job 19:24). Ancient inscriptions almost defy the ravages of time, as the Hammurabi Stela, Moabite Stone, or the Behistun Inscription. The "horns of the altars" were the metal projections from the four corners. In the temple rituals sacrificial blood was sprinkled for expiation on the four horns of the altar (Lev 16:18). What a perversion to have sin ineradicably engraved on the heart where the new covenant belongs (31:31–34) and on the very places where solemn expiation was made for the sins of the people!

2–4 Verse 2 is difficult because there is no finite verb. Two views have been suggested: (1) as men remember their sons with longing, so they yearn for their idol altars (so NASB); (2) the children in Judah will be so steeped in idolatry by their parents that the desire for it will emerge at the slightest provocation. Probably the latter position (cf. NIV) is preferable as being in accord with the broad context. Asherim were poles placed beside the altars in Canaanite worship; they were proscribed in the Mosaic Law (Deut 16:21). They represented the sacred tree (*asherah*), part of the Baal cult and a symbol of the Canaanite goddess ʿAthtart (cf. note at 44:17). Thus long continuance in idolatry is implied. For such iniquities the nation will lose (v.3) all its wealth to its enemies.

Some scholars have had difficulty with the expression "mountain in the land," an obvious reference to Zion or Jerusalem. But it is addressed this way because of its eminent position as the center of the country (so Streane). Moreover, Jerusalem is called "rocky plateau" in 21:13. In this case plateau does not have to denote level land but the surrounding countryside. Jeremiah further elaborates on the loss of the nation's inheritance. The people have outraged the Lord's patience; so through their own fault (v.4), they will be separated from their land. The verb *šāmaṭ* ("lose") is the root of the noun "sabbatic year" (Exod 23:11; Deut 15:1-2; NIV has "seventh year"). Some have therefore suggested that because Judah did not keep these appointments with the Lord, he will enforce her observance of them by removing her into captivity. It is better, however, to understand the verb in a general sense, since the context here points out idolatry, not the nonobservance of sabbatic years, as the cause of the Exile. (Second Chronicles 36:21 is not referring to this passage of Jeremiah but rather to 25:11 and 29:10.)

Notes

3-4 These verses are difficult and some emendations have been suggested. Jeremiah 15:13-14 offers some help. As stated in the introduction to this section, vv.1-4 are omitted in the LXX; so there is no aid available from that source. It is too much to emend here בָּמֹתֶיךָ (*bāmōṯeyḵā*, "your high places") to בִּמְחִיר (*bimḥîr*, "with a price"; NIV, "without charge") in order to bring the passage into conformity with 15:13 (so Syriac).

The suggestion to read יָדְךָ (*yāḏeḵā*, "your hand") for וּבְךָ (*ûḇeḵā*, "your own") has merit since it is supported by the LXX and the Vulgate and conforms to the Hebrew idiom. The resultant reading would then be "You will let drop your hand" (cf. RSV).

b. The way of cursing and blessing

17:5-8

[5]This is what the LORD says:

> "Cursed is the one who trusts in man,
>   who depends on flesh for his strength
>   and whose heart turns away from the LORD.
> [6]He will be like a bush in the wastelands;
>   he will not see prosperity when it comes.
> He will dwell in the parched places of the desert,
>   in a salt land where no one lives.
>
> [7]"But blessed is the man who trusts in the LORD,
>   whose confidence is in him.
> [8]He will be like a tree planted by the water
>   that sends out its roots by the stream.
> It does not fear when heat comes;
>   its leaves are always green.
> It has no worries in a year of drought
>   and never fails to bear fruit."

5-8 The main concept of the broader context (vv.5-13) appears to be that of permanence. Many interpreters have seen as the background of vv.5-8 Judah's constant international alliances in the perilous game of power politics. This was undeniably a constant temptation (Isa 31:3). The nation was prone to rely on Egypt, Babylon, and others. But when a passage is as general as this one, it is rash to try to particularize and to dogmatize about its details. For example, able expositors are divided on whether the reference in v.5 is to Jehoiakim, who expected help from Egypt when he revolted against Nebuchadnezzar (2 Kings 24:1), or to Zedekiah, who attempted to gain Egypt's help against Babylon. It is best, however, to understand vv.5–8 as emphasizing the need of reliance on God alone in all life's circumstances. The one who trusts man is mentioned in vv.5–6; the one who relies on God is referred to in vv.7–8. The results of choices are clearly spelled out: a curse on trust in mere man (v.5), a blessing on reliance on the Lord (v.7). Where one depends on man, spiritual life cannot thrive; that person is like the dwarf juniper of the desert (v.6). Its leaves are not refreshed by rain; so it is both stunted and starved. This is the lot of the person foolish enough to trust in mere man.

On the contrary, the person who trusts in the Lord is blessed indeed (v.7). He need fear no circumstance in life. Again, the figure of a tree is used (v.8). The blessed man is firmly "planted" (*šāṭûl*, which is not the ordinary verb for "plant," i.e., *nāṭaʻ*) where there is abundance of water. Growth and fruitfulness, therefore, are assured (cf. Ps 1:3 for parallel imagery).

Notes

---

5 The English versions have generally not reflected the different words translated "man." KJV, ASV, RSV, JB, and NEB render "man" for גֶּבֶר (*geḇer*) and אָדָם (*ʼāḏām*). The first Hebrew term (used here in v.5) thinks of man in his strength over against children, women, or noncombatants in battle; the noun is related to the verb that means "to be mighty, prevail." The second noun refers to man in the general sense of "mankind," i.e., human being. The word בָּשָׂר (*bāśār*), translated here as "flesh," indicates man's frailty over against God's omnipotence. NASB and NIV both preserve the distinction.

---

c. Humanity's desperate heart condition

17:9–13

> ⁹The heart is deceitful above all things
>   and beyond cure.
>   Who can understand it?
> ¹⁰"I the LORD search the heart
>   and examine the mind,
>   to reward a man according to his conduct,
>   according to what his deeds deserve."
>
> ¹¹Like a partridge that hatches eggs it did not lay
>   is the man who gains riches by unjust means.
>   When his life is half gone, they will desert him,
>   and in the end he will prove to be a fool.
>
> ¹²A glorious throne, exalted from the beginning,
>   is the place of our sanctuary.

> [13]O Lᴏʀᴅ, the hope of Israel,
>   all who forsake you will be put to shame.
> Those who turn away from you will be written in the dust
>   because they have forsaken the Lᴏʀᴅ,
>   the spring of living water.

9 If there is such blessing in trusting God, then why do people so generally depend on their fellow humans? Why is it that the blessed are not more numerous than the cursed? The answer lies in the innate depravity of the human heart (v.9). The source of all human difficulty is the human heart (cf. Prov 4:23). In OT usage the heart signifies the total inner being and includes reason. From the heart come action and will. Notice the connection between "heart" and "deeds" in vv.9–10. Some think v.9 is a personal confession of the depths of Jeremiah's heart (so Cundall); others refer the text to Jehoiakim or Zedekiah. Actually, the passage best fits all humanity. The human heart is more deceptive (*'āqōb*, "tortuous," "crooked") than anything else. It is desperately corrupt and, humanly speaking, incurable. The word *'ānuš* actually means "sick"; so NIV's "beyond cure" is correct. The word is translated in 15:18 and 30:12 as "incurable." Who on earth can plumb the depths of the heart's corruption and sickness? Even its owner does not know it.

10–11 The rhetorical question in v.9 is answered in v.10. It is the Lord who knows the whole truth about the heart, and he will deal with all of us justly, according to our deeds. Many commentators have said that Jeremiah's reference to the partridge (v.11) shows his ignorance of this bird's habits and his acceptance of a popular misconception. Some scholars try to explain the reference by claiming that the notion of the partridge's hatching other birds' eggs might have been inferred from the large number of eggs the partridge lays. But this explanation is hardly convincing. Others believe the partridge Jeremiah referred to is different from the one known in the Occident (so Clarke). Still another suggestion is that the noun *qōrē'* may mean some type of sand grouse, because partridges do not hatch the eggs of other birds. This explanation seems preferable. At any rate, the meaning of the passage is clear: ill-gotten gain is, like a bird with young she has not hatched, soon lost (cf. Prov 23:5). The brood forsake their foster mother. It is interesting that though the partridge is the most common game bird in Palestine (so Elliott-Binns), it is referred to only twice in the OT (here and 1 Sam 26:20). The person who wearies himself to accumulate wealth unjustly is a moral and spiritual fool (cf. Ps 14:1).

12–13 In these verses Jeremiah extols the majesty of God. True permanence, since unjustly gained riches are fleeting, is found only in the Lord. His sanctuary and throne—between the cherubim (Ps 80:1)—refer to Jerusalem (v.12). Unlike riches soon lost is the eternal throne of God. That throne demands both reward and punishment. It is the fixed center of the universe and an endless source of comfort to the believer. In God's purpose it has been so from time immemorial. Those who forsake the Lord will suffer shame (v.13), for a life "written in the dust" instead of in the Book of Life (cf. Exod 32:32; Luke 10:20; Rev 20:12; 21:27) results from having forsaken the fountain of living waters (cf. 2:13). Those who do so are as unenduring as names written on the dust.

Notes

9 The term אָנֻשׁ (*'ānuš*) is translated "desperately wicked" (KJV), "exceedingly corrupt" (ASV), "desperately corrupt" (RSV), "perverse" (JB), "desperately sick" (NASB, NEB), and "beyond cure" (NIV). The last three versions are closest to the original. The simple passive participle is from the verb אָנַשׁ (*'ānaš*, "to be weak, sick"). To think of the heart as desperately wicked, which many other passages emphasize, is not to get the exact force of the Hebrew word here. It signifies, rather, "gravely ill," "dangerously sick," and even "incurable." LXX has misread the text, taking the participle for the noun אֱנוֹשׁ (*'enōš*, "man," in his weakness), and has translated καὶ ἄνθρωπός ἐστιν (*kai anthrōpos estin*, "and he [it] is man"), a rendering scarcely forceful or instructive.

13 The usual interpretation of this verse is that the names of apostates will be written in the dust, erased, and forgotten. M.J. Dahood, in "The Value of Ugaritic for Textual Criticism," *Biblica* 40 (1959): 164–66, judges from the Ugaritic that the Hebrew term אֶרֶץ (*'ereṣ*, "earth"; NIV, "dust") is the underworld. The sense then would be that they will be scheduled for death (so Bright).

---

d. Jeremiah's plea for vindication

17:14–18

> ¹⁴Heal me, O LORD, and I will be healed;
>   save me and I will be saved,
>   for you are the one I praise.
> ¹⁵They keep saying to me,
>   "Where is the word of the LORD?
>   Let it now be fulfilled!"
> ¹⁶I have not run away from being your shepherd;
>   you know I have not desired the day of despair.
>   What passes my lips is open before you.
> ¹⁷Do not be a terror to me;
>   you are my refuge in the day of disaster.
> ¹⁸Let my persecutors be put to shame,
>   but keep me from shame;
> let them be terrified,
>   but keep me from terror.
> Bring on them the day of disaster;
>   destroy them with double destruction.

14–15 From time to time the unwelcome nature of Jeremiah's prophecies drove him to plead for divine help. The Lord was his only hope and cure (cf. v.9). So Jeremiah prayed on the basis of his Lord's known faithfulness. Only the Lord can heal and save (v.14). The prophet's desire for healing and salvation undoubtedly includes moral and spiritual ills as well as deliverance from his enemies. Some place vv.14–18 in Josiah's time, but there is little to base this on. Jeremiah's coreligionists taunt him and scoff at him daily because his predictions are not fulfilled (v.15). They criticize him for being a false prophet (Deut 18:22). This was doubly difficult for him to bear because he had prayed the Lord to refrain from meting out his judgment on Judah. Scoffing, the mockers declare, "Let it [the word of the LORD] now be fulfilled" (cf. the parallel in Isa 5:19). The passage indicates that the Fall of Jerusalem had not yet occurred; if Jeremiah's prophecies had already been fulfilled, the people would not have asked their derisive question. God's continued long-suffering led the prophet's enemies to demand a visible confirmation of the word he preached.

16 So Jeremiah sets forth a threefold vindication of his ministry: (1) he has not refused to follow God's will; (2) he has not hoped for their doom; and (3) all his utterances were fully known to God (so Cowles). Moreover, he had not tried to relinquish his ministry because of the suffering it involved. The word "shepherd" usually refers to a king, but here it refers to Jeremiah as a leader of the people. His enemies accused him of wanting disaster to overtake the nation. But he never wanted his threatenings in proclaiming the Lord's message to be fulfilled. He took no delight in predicting doom. One need only look at chapter 40 to see his attitude after the Fall of Jerusalem and to verify his claim that he had not desired disaster. "The day of despair" is the day of the fall of the city, when the predicted woes would come on it. Furthermore, the Lord knows everything Jeremiah preached and also his prayers that the doom might be averted.

17-18 The "terror" (v. 17) Jeremiah fears was that the Lord might confound him and desert him before his enemies. He wants the Lord's protection and prays that his loyalty to him may not be the cause of his ruin. If the Lord will not encourage him, then he is doubly bereft of comfort. For the vindication of God's truth, he needs to be proved right. It is this that pervades his prayers for vengeance (so Cunliffe-Jones). There is no contradiction between v. 18 and v. 16 because the people in view are not the same. By "double destruction" is meant full, complete destruction (cf. comments at 16:18).

Notes

---

16 Most English versions render the first clause similarly (KJV, ASV, NASB, JPS, and NIV), vocalizing the radicals מרעה (*mrʿh*) as *mērōʿeh* ("from a shepherd"). A slight change in MT's vocalization yields *mērāʿāh* ("from evil, calamity," etc.). Following this, RSV and JB introduce the word "evil"; NEB has "disaster"; BV, "calamity"; and AT, "trouble." The context appears to favor "shepherd."

---

e. *Sabbath observance*

17:19-27

> [19]This is what the LORD said to me: "Go and stand at the gate of the people, through which the kings of Judah go in and out; stand also at all the other gates of Jerusalem. [20]Say to them, 'Hear the word of the LORD, O kings of Judah and all people of Judah and everyone living in Jerusalem who come through these gates. [21]This is what the LORD says: Be careful not to carry a load on the Sabbath day or bring it through the gates of Jerusalem. [22]Do not bring a load out of your houses or do any work on the Sabbath, but keep the Sabbath day holy, as I commanded your forefathers. [23]Yet they did not listen or pay attention; they were stiff-necked and would not listen or respond to discipline. [24]But if you are careful to obey me, declares the LORD, and bring no load through the gates of this city on the Sabbath, but keep the Sabbath day holy by not doing any work on it, [25]then kings who sit on David's throne will come through the gates of this city with their

officials. They and their officials will come riding in chariots and on horses, accompanied by the men of Judah and those living in Jerusalem, and this city will be inhabited forever. [26]People will come from the towns of Judah and the villages around Jerusalem, from the territory of Benjamin and the western foothills, from the hill country and the Negev, bringing burnt offerings and sacrifices, grain offerings, incense and thank offerings to the house of the LORD. [27]But if you do not obey me to keep the Sabbath day holy by not carrying any load as you come through the gates of Jerusalem on the Sabbath day, then I will kindle an unquenchable fire in the gates of Jerusalem that will consume her fortresses.' "

19–23 These verses show that prophecies of doom were always ethically conditioned. Sabbath observances would certainly counteract tendencies toward idolatry (so Freedman). The way of blessing was still open for Judah. This passage, however, has troubled interpreters who recall Jeremiah's preaching against Jerusalem, the ark, the temple, the sacrifices, and rites (3:16; 7:14, 21–22; 14:12) but now see his emphasis on the Sabbath. They find an inconsistency here. The verses have, therefore, been attributed to a postexilic scribe (cf. Neh 10:31; 13:15–22). But we must recognize that the Sabbath was a vital part of the Decalogue and was the touchstone of Israel's contractual, covenant relationship with God (so Habel; cf. Exod 20:8–11; 31:13; Ezek 20:12). Because Jeremiah was against insincere worship, we have no ground for thinking he would oppose sincere religious practices (so Frost).

The "gate" (v.19) where the Lord commanded Jeremiah to deliver his message was surely not the main gate of the palace (contra Bewer) but one where a number of the people could be found. It is not clear which gate is specifically meant, but this verse and v.29 lead us to think that it must refer to one of Jerusalem's gates. Being for the laity, it was distinct from the gate of the priests and Levites. Obviously it was one of the temple gates. In v.19 the kings referred to are successive kings of Judah; those in v.20, however, appear to be the king and his princes, i.e., his royal house. The passage makes sense only if we understand that the people habitually violated the Sabbath. They used it to conclude the work of the week and to prepare for the coming week's work. Contrary to the express word of Moses, the Sabbath had been chosen by the people to bring their produce in from the country, since they worked the fields during the week (v.21). This must not continue. The people carried burdens out of their homes in exchange for the produce brought into the city (v.22; cf. Neh 13:15–18). The prohibition of labor on the Sabbath was so general that later on it became encrusted with absurd restrictions, which the Lord Jesus assailed in the Gospels. The people's response to Jeremiah's preaching was highly negative (v.23).

24–27 Now the blessings on obedience follow. It has been suggested that the Sabbath is used here by metonymy (part for the whole), i.e., the Sabbath and the other laws (so JFB). But v.27 refutes this because it again specifies the observance of the Sabbath "day" (for parallels, cf. Isa 56:2–6; 58:13–14). In summary, the Sabbath (1) recognizes God as Creator, which is a witness against idolatry, and (2) marks the special covenant relationship between God and Israel. If obedience is forthcoming (v.24), the blessings are distinctive. First, the continuance of the Davidic dynasty is assured (v.25). Second, Jerusalem will be settled and continue perpetually. Third, the temple will again be the center of worship for the nation (v.26). Thus Judah is assured the promise of peace, prosperity, and permanence through her native dynasty and the authorized priesthood.

The several regions of Judah are mentioned (v.26); these were still possessed by Judah and Benjamin. The land of Benjamin was north of Judah. The lowland or Shephelah (NIV, "western foothills") was the low hills stretching toward the Philistine maritime plain, west and southwest of Judah, and was the center of agriculture. The hill country was the central region, with the wilderness of Judah stretching down to the Dead Sea. The Negev was the arid South (cf. Josh 15:21–32). The offerings the people were to bring are divided into blood offerings (two) and bloodless offerings (two). The incense mentioned here (lᵉḇōnāh, "frankincense") was not the incense offering (cf. Exod 30:7–9) but was one of the ingredients added to the offerings. The list concludes with the thank offerings, which were the principal class of the peace offerings (šᵉlāmîm; cf. Lev 7:11).

The passage concludes with the price of disobedience (v.27), though God's yearning heart would yet keep his people from destruction. Fire is a symbol of destruction throughout the Bible (cf. Amos 1:3–2:5; for similar wording, cf. 21:14; 49:27; 50:32).

8. The parable of the potter (18:1–23)

Most expositors consider chapters 18–20 a unit, dating from the early years of Jehoiakim's reign. The potter's house (vv.1–12) is the most familiar of Jeremiah's figures and is found elsewhere in Scripture and in many languages and literatures (cf. Job 10:9; 33:6; Ps 2:9; Isa 29:16; 45:9; 64:8; Rom 9:20–21; Rev 2:27; cf. also Ecclus 38:29–30). In this passage we have a true but mysterious blending of the divine sovereignty and human responsibility. The Lord used the potter to illustrate how he deals with humanity.

a. The message of the potter

18:1–12

> ¹This is the word that came to Jeremiah from the LORD: ²"Go down to the potter's house, and there I will give you my message." ³So I went down to the potter's house, and I saw him working at the wheel. ⁴But the pot he was shaping from the clay was marred in his hands; so the potter formed it into another pot, shaping it as seemed best to him.
> ⁵Then the word of the LORD came to me: ⁶"O house of Israel, can I not do with you as this potter does?" declares the LORD. "Like clay in the hand of the potter, so are you in my hand, O house of Israel. ⁷If at any time I announce that a nation or kingdom is to be uprooted, torn down and destroyed, ⁸and if that nation I warned repents of its evil, then I will relent and not inflict on it the disaster I had planned. ⁹And if at another time I announce that a nation or kingdom is to be built up and planted, ¹⁰and if it does evil in my sight and does not obey me, then I will reconsider the good I had intended to do for it.
> ¹¹"Now therefore say to the people of Judah and those living in Jerusalem, 'This is what the LORD says: Look! I am preparing a disaster for you and devising a plan against you. So turn from your evil ways, each one of you, and reform your ways and your actions.' ¹²But they will reply, 'It's no use. We will continue with our own plans; each of us will follow the stubbornness of his evil heart.' "

1–4 Far too many have misunderstood this parable because they have seen God in the light of an arbitrary sovereign, whereas the deeper level of meaning speaks of God's grace that underlay the coming disaster on Judah. Jeremiah speaks of the

Lord in strongly anthropomorphic terms to accommodate our human inability to comprehend the divine mystery of God's ways—viz., that he always acts in grace in keeping with his spiritual laws. The command (v.1) came to Jeremiah to go down to the pottery, where it was the Lord's intention to give him a message for the people (v.2). So he went there from the temple that was in the upper part of the city. Pottery was one of the earliest of all trades. The potter's house was probably on the slopes of the Valley of Hinnom (south of Jerusalem), where water and clay were found. Here the prophet was to be taught the principles of the divine government. In this parable they are set in a national perspective that reveals the sovereignty of God. At the pottery Jeremiah saw what was already very familiar to him (v.3). The potter was making a vessel on the wheels, the upper and lower discs made of stone or wood. The lower one was worked by the foot of the potter and was attached by an axle to the upper one, on which the clay was worked. The process is clearly described in Ecclesiasticus 38:29–30. The discs were in a horizontal position. As happened frequently in the daily life of a potter, the clay did not turn out right (v.4). Often in throwing the clay, some defect would become evident. The potter then rolled the clay into a lump to begin his task again to make a more suitable product. The chief point here is the power the potter had over the clay. The clay was in his hand and under his control. The defects were in the clay, not the hand of the potter. The potter's perseverance must not be overlooked at this point in this passage.

5–10 Now Jeremiah is taught the meaning of the figure (v.5). The infinite power of the Lord is compared with that of the potter over his clay (v.6). Just as the potter remade the clay to conform to his purpose, so the Lord's will and power continue to mold the nation until it is conformed to his plan. The Lord will never be defeated even if Judah turns from his way for them. There is a conditional element in his dealings with his people (vv.7–10). Repentance can always change the Lord's decree of judgment. His threatenings are never unconditional (v.8). The parallel between humanity and the clay must not be carried too far. Human "clay" is not passive. Upon a person's repentance God can rework him or her into a vessel of honor. The position is not one of absolute fatalism (blotting out man's freedom), nor is it one where God's sovereignty is wholly dependent on man's choice. Ultimately, no man is free. But God in his mysterious working in human life has ordered it so that humanity may choose. In this passage the point is neither denial or affirmation of human freedom.

Verses 7–10 show that in his rule over the nations, God treats all of them with grace. He does not exercise his omnipotence arbitrarily or capriciously but conditions everything ethically. Though the parable is meant principally for Judah (v.11), God deals similarly with all nations. All people are given the opportunity to repent and conform to God's purpose. When the Scriptures speak of God's relenting or repenting, we must understand this in the light of Numbers 23:19. When used of God, repentance never means what it does for man; it is a strong anthropopathism. It must always undergo redefinition (cf. 4:28; 15:6). It is impossible for God to repent as people do, for God has never done wrong. He does act differently toward men and women when they turn from disobeying him to obeying him (26:3; cf. also the case of Nineveh [Jonah 3:4–11]). In short, with God repentance is not a change of mind but is his consistent response according to his changeless nature to the change in the nation's conduct. So in this parable the prophet is holding out the opportunity for Judah to repent.

11–12 The call to repent is given in v.11 and the response of the people in v.12. Jeremiah now applies the parable of the potter to his nation. Responsibility clearly rests on them. When the Lord says he is "preparing" (*yôṣēr*) calamity for Judah (v.11), the Hebrew verb is the same as the word for potter; so there is a play on words. The word is deliberately chosen to suggest this relationship (so Freedman). The threatened calamity is the Exile. With the issues so clearly presented, what was the nation's reaction? The people claim it was hopeless to try to dissuade them from their ways (v.12; cf. 2:25). Having gone too far to turn back, they condemned themselves. Their obduracy showed how deep-seated their love of idolatry was. What a disheartening response for Jeremiah to receive after all his pleading!

b. *The fickleness of Judah*

18:13–17

13Therefore this is what the LORD says:

> "Inquire among the nations:
>   Who has ever heard anything like this?
> A most horrible thing has been done
>   by Virgin Israel.
> 14Does the snow of Lebanon
>   ever vanish from its rocky slopes?
> Do its cool waters from distant sources
>   ever cease to flow?
> 15Yet my people have forgotten me;
>   they burn incense to worthless idols,
> which made them stumble in their ways
>   and in the ancient paths.
> They made them walk in bypaths
>   and on roads not built up.
> 16Their land will be laid waste,
>   an object of lasting scorn;
> all who pass by will be appalled
>   and will shake their heads.
> 17Like a wind from the east,
>   I will scatter them before their enemies;
> I will show them my back and not my face
>   in the day of their disaster."

13 Even the nations about Judah would have to attest to the revolting nature of her acts (v.13). Her willfulness in forsaking the Lord was without parallel in the ancient world (cf. 2:9–13; 5:20–25; 8:7). The horror is heightened by calling her a virgin. She had been hedged about by the Lord to preserve her sanctity.

14 This verse is unusually obscure (cf. NIV mg.). It seems farfetched to hold that the prophet is saying that the covenant was as binding and lasting as the phenomena of nature mentioned in v.14 (contra Myers). There has been no preparation in the text for a comparison with the covenant. Furthermore, it is equally strange to hold that Jeremiah is asking why any reasonable person would leave a farm always watered by melted snows from Lebanon in order to take a rocky one instead (contra Clarke). This kind of interpretation treats the passage too freely. The basic thought appears to be that Jeremiah is asking questions that underscore the constancy of nature. The snow from Lebanon and cold running water are dependable, but Judah has proved herself fickle in the extreme. Her conduct has been wholly unnatural. The questions anticipate negative replies. Lebanon (*lᵉḇānôn*, lit., "white mountain") has permanent snow cover and so regularly provides moisture. Cold water does not evaporate quickly. Nature does not change its course, but Judah has. Nature's reliability puts to shame Judah's instability.

15–17 Since v.14 is parenthetical, v.15 looks back to v.13. The appalling sin the people committed was idolatry in spite of a clearly defined path for their blessing. They forgot their Lord; they were misled by their false prophets, false priests, and false gods. The nation had lost its way. The ancient paths were those of blessing through obeying the Lord (cf. 6:16). The contrast is between a rough track in the country and an elevated causeway. The result of the nation's apostasy will be the desolation of her land (v.16). This condition will be so shocking that the land will be "an object of lasting scorn" (*šᵉrîqāh*, lit., "hissing," "whistle"; cf. 19:8). The hissing will be more in amazement than in ridicule. Men will shake their heads at the nation's uncommon stupidity. The Lord himself will scatter the people as the east wind (v.17), the sirocco from the desert east-southeast of Palestine. When the Lord says he will show them his back and not his face, he means that his face will be hidden from them. But this is the very treatment Judah has given him (cf. 2:27). His "face" indicates his favor (Num 6:24–26).

Notes

14 A number of emendations of this seemingly cryptic verse have been suggested. The initial verb עָזַב (*'āzaḇ*, "leave") is strange in relation to its subject—the snow of Lebanon. What is the force, moreover, of the "rocky slopes"? Some expositors have proposed for מִצּוּר שָׂדָי (*miṣṣûr śāday*, lit., "from the rock of the field") a change in the second noun to שִׂרְיוֹן (*śiryôn*, "Sirion"), the Phoenician name for Mount Hermon (cf. Deut 3:9; cf. also Ps 29:6; Ugaritic II AB 6:19, 21 [UT, p. 142]). Hermon, some ninety-one hundred feet above sea level, is usually covered with snow all year (so Hyatt et al.). The proposed change is interesting but not compelling in view of the absence of MS and version confirmation.

c. *The plot against Jeremiah*

18:18–23

¹⁸They said, "Come, let's make plans against Jeremiah; for the teaching of the law by the priest will not be lost, nor will counsel from the wise, nor the word from the prophets. So come, let's attack him with our tongues and pay no attention to anything he says."

¹⁹Listen to me, O LORD;
    hear what my accusers are saying!
²⁰Should good be repaid with evil?
    Yet they have dug a pit for me.
Remember that I stood before you
    and spoke in their behalf
    to turn your wrath away from them.

²¹So give their children over to famine;
    hand them over to the power of the sword.
Let their wives be made childless and widows;
    let their men be put to death,
    their young men slain by the sword in battle.
²²Let a cry be heard from their houses
    when you suddenly bring invaders against them,
for they have dug a pit to capture me
    and have hidden snares for my feet.
²³But you know, O LORD,
    all their plots to kill me.
Do not forgive their crimes
    or blot out their sins from your sight.
Let them be overthrown before you;
    deal with them in the time of your anger.

18–20 Unable to tolerate Jeremiah's drastic preaching, the leaders of Judah decided to hound him to death. Their opposition is spelled out: (1) slandering him and turning a deaf ear to his words (v.18), (2) digging a pit for his soul (vv.20, 22), (3) setting snares for his feet (v.22), and (4) planning to slay him (v.23). The very three groups he had to condemn were in the forefront of the plot against him (cf. 11:18–23; 12:6; 15:10–11, 15–21 for other conspiracies against him). They boasted that because they had priests to instruct them in the law, wise elders to counsel them in the affairs of daily living, and (false) prophets to give them the word (supposedly from God), they had no need for Jeremiah. They could not conceive of a time when such ungodly leaders would be unable to fulfill their functions. So their aim now was to silence Jeremiah after they had rejected his message (v.12). They were certain that his words would not be fulfilled. Why should they listen to him and thereby reject the advice of all their other leaders?

By a charge of treason, the leaders of Judah hoped to effect Jeremiah's downfall. His messages against Judah's policies provide ample basis for accusing him of treason. So he pleads with the Lord to pay attention to him and to hear his enemies' plots (v.19). In so doing, he was using the same words as his foes but now in the affirmative sense (v.20). He wanted his prayers answered. Verses 19–23 give Jeremiah's reaction to his enemies' conspiracies against him. Some scholars labeled this passage Jeremiah's harshest and bitterest prayer for vengeance (so Hyatt et al.). With transparent honesty, he bares his heart. These imprecations are best understood in the light of the following: (1) Jeremiah's enemies were not merely personal ones but enemies of God and his truth (so the imprecatory psalms), and his was not a vindictive cry for personal revenge; (2) life after death and retribution in the afterlife were not clearly revealed in OT times; and (3) Jeremiah delivers the people judicially to the course they have chosen for themselves (v.15; cf. Matt 23; Gal 5:12).

What cut the prophet to the quick was the manner in which his countrymen repaid good with evil. He had only sought their good and had even interceded for them when the Lord forbade him to do so (cf. 14:7–9, 21). Their response is described by the metaphor of digging a pit to trap wild beasts.

21–23 The imprecations in this section are not leveled against the entire nation but only against Jeremiah's enemies. The words are admittedly strong because these leaders had incited the people against him, the Lord's prophet. Invaders will do their deadly work, in the wake of which other forms of death will come (v.21). Not only will calamity strike people outside the city, but even their own houses will provide them no security (v.22). Here is the outcry of the prophet's wounded heart (v.23). He realized the depth of the resentment and hatred toward him. Their plans had been concealed, but the Lord knew every secret plot against him (cf. the parallel in Ps 141:9–10). For Christians in similar situations, the norm is in Matthew 5:44 and Romans 12:20. Even then it was personally enjoined in Proverbs 25:21–22. There is a basic distinction between personal and judicial vengeance.

9. The destruction of Jerusalem (19:1–15)

Chapters 19 and 20, part of the literary unit of chapters 18–20, are closely linked, as 20:1 shows. Although a date as late as the reign of Zedekiah has been suggested for chapter 19 (so JFB), scholars generally agree on a date in the early part of Jehoiakim's reign. To be more precise, a date after Nebuchadnezzar's victory at Carchemish has been favored because of the mention of Babylon in 20:1–6. The episode in 20:1–2 could not have occurred in the time of Josiah. In chapter 19 we have another of Jeremiah's symbolic acts (for the first one, cf. 13:1–11), and 20:1–6 gives us the first account of bodily harm to the prophet. He delivers his message in two places, in the Valley of Hinnom and in the court of the Lord's house; and its theme is the destruction of Judah in that generation. Chapter 19 differs from the previous one. There the potter's wet clay vessel could be shaped; here the clay jar is so worthless that it is destroyed. As long as the clay vessel was in a pliable state, it could be reworked. Once baked, it was not possible to reshape it; it would have to be broken.

a. The clay jar at Hinnom

19:1–5a

> ¹This is what the LORD says: "Go and buy a clay jar from a potter. Take along some of the elders of the people and of the priests ²and go out to the Valley of Ben Hinnom, near the entrance of the Potsherd Gate. There proclaim the words I tell you, ³and say, 'Hear the word of the LORD, O kings of Judah and people of Jerusalem. This is what the LORD Almighty, the God of Israel, says: Listen! I am going to bring a disaster on this place that will make the ears of everyone who hears of it tingle. ⁴For they have forsaken me and made this a place of foreign gods; they have burned sacrifices in it to gods that neither they nor their fathers nor the kings of Judah ever knew, and they have filled this place with the blood of the innocent. ⁵ªThey have built the high places of Baal to burn their sons in the fire as offerings to Baal—' "

1 The Lord commanded Jeremiah to buy a clay jar. It was a receptacle for water. The Hebrew noun *baqbuq* ("clay jar") is onomatopoeic, sounding like the gurgling of outpouring water. Jars that have been excavated range from four to ten inches in height. Because of the jar's narrow neck, it could never be repaired. Jeremiah was to take with him the elders of the people and of the priests to lend solemnity to the occasion (cf. 2 Kings 19:2). The elders were the civil and religious leaders of the nation and should have been best qualified to understand the message. They were probably chosen to go with Jeremiah because they had lived under Josiah's reformation. They need not be linked with the twenty-four courses arranged by David (1 Chron 24:1–4) (contra Clarke). The prophet is about to act out the final stage of Judah's spiritual hardness. There can come a time in a people's history when constant opposition to God's will must result in their overthrow. Whereas chapter 18 taught the sovereignty and patience of God, this passage treats the irreversible judgment about to fall on Judah.

2 The prophet was specifically told where to go and the way to take. He was to go to the Valley of Hinnom by way of the Potsherd Gate. Because of its proximity to the potter's house (18:1) and the dumping of potters' waste outside it, one gate of Jerusalem became known as the Potsherd Gate (*ḥarsît*, the Hebrew word occurs only here). It led to the Valley of Hinnom. Because it had been connected with child sacrifice, Josiah had made the valley a garbage dump for Jerusalem (2 Kings 23:10). Its rubbish fires constantly smoldered. The NT Gehenna ("hell") is a corruption by the Jews for "Ge [valley of] Hinnom." The Targum calls the Potsherd Gate the Dung Gate. Many scholars agree with this and think it is the gate mentioned in Nehemiah 2:13; 3:13–14; and 12:31. The KJV translation "east gate" comes from equating the Hebrew word with the archaic word for "sun" (*ḥeres;* cf. Job 9:7), hence, east gate. Jerome preferred a connection with the word for "earthenware," which is probably correct. There is a link between the name of the gate and the action Jeremiah performed.

3–5a Jeremiah's denunciatory words (vv.4–5a) are addressed to the kings and the people (v.3). He used the plural "kings" because the message was not only to the reigning king but to the whole dynasty that was responsible for the apostasy. The place of the calamity is Jerusalem; the disaster will be such that all who hear of it will be stunned. The metaphor of tingling ears was associated with threatened punishments (cf. 1 Sam 3:11; 2 Kings 21:12). The sins that brought on the Lord's judgment are now enumerated (vv.4–5). By forsaking the Lord and cleaving to idolatry, the people "made this a place of foreign gods"; i.e., they have treated their land as foreign by making foreign gods at home in it. They made it an alien place by "denationalizing" it so that it appeared no longer Israelite (so Bright). According to v.4, they brought many innovations into their idolatry. Moreover, this kind of worship desensitized their moral nature (cf. 2 Kings 21:16), for they shed the blood of innocent people (not children, who are mentioned in the next verse). One of the most debased forms of idolatry involved child sacrifice (v.5). It was practiced in the worship of Baal and Molech (cf. 32:35). Verses 5–6 are almost identical with 7:31–32.

Notes

3 LXX adds וְהַבָּאִים בַּשְּׁעָרִים הָאֵלֶּה (*wᵉhabbāʾîm biššᵉʿārîm hāʾēlleh,* "and those who enter these gates") after יֹשְׁבֵי יְרוּשָׁלָיִם (*yōšᵉbê yᵉrûšālāyim,* "people of Jerusalem"), following the pattern of 17:20; 22:2.

b. *The imminent calamity*

19:5b–9

> [5b] 'something I did not command or mention, nor did it enter my mind. [6]So beware, the days are coming, declares the LORD, when people will no longer call this place Topheth or the Valley of Ben Hinnom, but the Valley of Slaughter.
> [7] 'In this place I will ruin the plans of Judah and Jerusalem. I will make them fall by the sword before their enemies, at the hands of those who seek their lives, and I will give their carcasses as food to the birds of the air and the beasts of the earth. [8]I will devastate this city and make it an object of scorn; all who pass by will be appalled and will scoff because of all its wounds. [9]I will make them eat the flesh of their sons and daughters, and they will eat one another's flesh during the stress of the siege imposed on them by the enemies who seek their lives.' "

5b–7a By a strong anthropopathism, the Lord indicates that the enormities the nation committed in sacrificing children had never been enjoined on them or spoken of and had never even entered into his mind (v.5b). It was totally alien to and opposed to his will. For these terrible violations of his law, the Lord would bring down such drastic destruction that the place called Topheth (cf. 7:32), or the Valley of the Son of (Ben) Hinnom, would have its name changed to the Valley of Slaughter (v.6; cf. vv.11–15; Isa 30:33). Because the valley had water, an invading force would besiege it first; and its defenders would suffer casualties in trying to hold it. In saying that the Lord would "ruin" the plans of Judah (v.7a), Jeremiah used the Hebrew word *bāqaq* ("to make empty," "to pour out"), a play on the Hebrew word *baqbuq* ("jar"), which is from the same root (cf. NIV mg.). The Lord would make their plans fall to the earth (so Orelli). He would empty them of wisdom that could shield them and their country from the enemy. Some think that at this point Jeremiah emptied the water from the jar (so Harrison; cf. 1 Sam 7:6; 2 Sam 14:14).

7b–9 The tragic prospect facing the nation included death for the people at the hands of their enemies and consumption of their carcasses by birds and beasts (v.7b). After the horrors and carnage of war had been perpetrated on the nation, passersby would "scoff" (*yišrōq*, "hiss") in scorn at the havoc (v.8). The word rendered "wounds" (*makkôt*) is used elsewhere of pestilences and literally means "blows," thus referring to the people's calamities. Verse 8 is substantially the same as 18:16. As in many wars, famine will run rampant. The calamity will be so great that the people will be reduced to cannibalism; their distress of that hour will overcome natural affection (v.9). This prediction was literally fulfilled in 586 B.C., in the Babylonian invasion under Nebuchadnezzar, and again in A.D. 70, when Titus destroyed Jerusalem (cf. Lev 26:29; Deut 28:53–57; 2 Kings 6:28–29; Lam 2:20; 4:10).

Notes

5b LXX omits וְלֹא דִבַּרְתִּי (*wᵉlōʾ dibbartî*, "or spoke of"; NIV, "or mention"), probably because of 7:31; 32:35; but cf. 14:14.

8 The verse makes striking use of assonance. לִשְׁרֵקָה (lišrēqāh, "hissing"; NIV, "an object of scorn") conveys the sound of whistling as men do in amazement, scorn, or shock (cf. 18:16).

9 LXX omits נַפְשָׁם וּמְבַקְשֵׁי (ûmᵉbaqšê napšām, "and those that seek their lives"), but cf. 19:7; 21:7; 22:25; 34:20; 34:21; 38:16; 44:30; 46:26; 49:37. Variations between MT and LXX may be explained from translation technique, omission of doublets on their second occurrence, deliberate omission, or a different *Vorlage*.

---

c. *The destruction of Judah*

19:10-13

> ¹⁰"Then break the jar while those who go with you are watching, ¹¹and say to them, 'This is what the LORD Almighty says: I will smash this nation and this city just as this potter's jar is smashed and cannot be repaired. They will bury the dead in Topheth until there is no more room. ¹²This is what I will do to this place to those who live here, declares the LORD. I will make this city like Topheth. ¹³The houses in Jerusalem and those of the kings of Judah will be defiled like this place, Topheth—all the houses where they burned incense on the roofs to all the starry hosts and poured out drink offerings to other gods.' "

10–13 After this message of doom, Jeremiah was commanded to break the jar in the sight of the elders who accompanied him (v. 10; cf. Ps 2:9). This was another illustrated oracle (cf. 13:1–11). The gravity of Jeremiah's act lay in the fact that it not only illustrated the Lord's acts but inaugurated them, so to speak. This was more than dramatization; it was seen as actually activating the Lord's word of destruction (v. 11). This explains Pashhur's violent reaction and persecution in 20:1–6. By his act Jeremiah was attacking the very existence of the nation. In the Near East, it is still the practice to break a jar near a person who has done wrong to one and voice the hope that he will be similarly broken (so Freedman). The Egyptian practice of writing on clay vessels the names of enemies and breaking them at a sacred place has been suggested as a parallel (so Hyatt). Such action was intended to bring about the downfall of the enemies. So Jeremiah vividly portrayed the fate of the nation. The thrust of this acted oracle was to show the irrevocability of the nation's ruin. They knew of no way to mend a broken jar, which could only be thrown away. So Judah will be rejected because she failed to repent. There is a clear distinction between the acted oracle in this chapter and that of the potter's house. Clay can be shaped and reshaped, but broken jars are cast away.

In Judah's downfall, the dead will be so numerous that even unclean Topheth will have to be used for their burial (v. 11). Topheth was a place of uncleanness (cf. 7:31), made such by the detestable idolatry practiced there. So the homes in Jerusalem would be defiled by corpses just as their idolatries had made Topheth even more a place of defilement (v. 12; cf. 33:5; 2 Kings 23:10). Even the roofs of their houses had become places of religious corruption (v. 13). The flat Oriental roofs were used for various activities (cf. Judg 16:27; 1 Sam 9:26; Neh 8:16; Acts 10:9), among them idolatry (cf. 32:29; 2 Kings 23:12; Zeph 1:5). On their roofs the people worshiped the starry host of heaven, a form of idolatry brought from Mesopotamia, where it had flourished. At Ras Shamra, tablets (esp. *The Legend of Keret*, pp. 39, 45) have been found with a ritual for offerings on the housetops to the heavenly bodies.

Notes

11 LXX omits וּבְתֹפֶת יִקְבְּרוּ מֵאֵין מָקוֹם לִקְבּוֹר (*ûbᵉtōpet yiqbᵉrû mēʾên māqôm liqbôr*, "They will bury the dead in Topheth until there is no more room"). P. Volz (*Der Prophet Jeremiah* [Leipzig, 1922], ad loc) suggests that these words have intruded into the text, possibly from their original place at the end of v.6 (cf. also 7:31–33).

d. The message summarized

19:14–15

> ¹⁴Jeremiah then returned from Topheth, where the LORD had sent him to prophesy, and stood in the court of the LORD's temple and said to all the people, ¹⁵"This is what the LORD Almighty, the God of Israel, says: 'Listen! I am going to bring on this city and the villages around it every disaster I pronounced against them, because they were stiff-necked and would not listen to my words.'"

14–15 Because these two verses are in the third person, many writers believe that they are from Baruch's memoirs. In the court of the temple area (v.14), to which the prophet had returned from Hinnom, Jeremiah repeated his message of doom. Its summary gave the meaning of the act he had just carried out. The crisis is pictured as rapidly approaching. The reference to "the villages around it" (v.15) is strange; the Hebrew is literally "this city and all its cities." The reference is probably to Jerusalem and the cities of Judah (cf. 34:2). The text may point to the suburbs or environs, but the usual wording is not here (cf. Notes). The cause of the nation's calamity was the people's stubborn refusal to listen to the Lord's warnings. "Stiff-necked" is a figure taken from unruly oxen who resist the yoke. In Stephen's defense he accused his people of the same sin (cf. Acts 7:51).

Notes

14 An emendation has been proposed (so Volz, *Jeremiah*) for MT's מֵהַתֹּפֶת (*mēhattōpet*, "from Topheth") to מֵהַפֶּתַח (*mēhappetaḥ*, "from the entrance"; i.e., from the entrance of the gate). In favor of the suggestion is the fact that it calls for minimal change in the consonantal framework of the word. However, it appears that vv.11–13 adequately account for the text as it is.

15 הָעִיר (*hāʿîr*, "the city") and כָּל־עָרֶיהָ (*kol-ʿāreyhā*, "all her cities") seems strange; but the intended meaning, as in other passages in OT prophecy, is Jerusalem and the cities of Judah. The usual expression would be וּסְבִיבוֹתֶיהָ (*ûsᵉbîbôteyhā*, "and her surroundings").

10. The lament of Jeremiah (20:1–18)

The prophet's symbolic actions in the Valley of Hinnom and his words in the temple court could not have gone unnoticed. This section carries the narrative forward and shows the consequence of what Jeremiah did and said. It has usually been placed in the reign of Jehoiakim.

a. Pashhur's persecution of Jeremiah

20:1–6

> ¹When the priest Pashhur son of Immer, the chief officer in the temple of the
> LORD, heard Jeremiah prophesying these things, ²he had Jeremiah the prophet
> beaten and put in the stocks at the Upper Gate of Benjamin at the LORD's temple.
> ³The next day, when Pashhur released him from the stocks, Jeremiah said to
> him, "The LORD's name for you is not Pashhur, but Magor-Missabib. ⁴For this is
> what the LORD says: 'I will make you a terror to yourself and to all your friends;
> with your own eyes you will see them fall by the sword of their enemies. I will
> hand all Judah over to the king of Babylon, who will carry them away to Babylon
> or put them to the sword. ⁵I will hand over to their enemies all the wealth of this
> city—all its products, all its valuables and all the treasures of the kings of Judah.
> They will take it away as plunder and carry it off to Babylon. ⁶And you, Pashhur,
> and all who live in your house will go into exile to Babylon. There you will die and
> be buried, you and all your friends to whom you have prophesied lies.' "

1 Among the listeners to Jeremiah's words in the temple court was Pashhur, son of
Immer, the deputy or executive priest entrusted with the responsibility for maintaining order through the temple police he had charge of (cf. 29:25–26). He was not
the Pashhur referred to in 21:1 and 38:1 (cf. 1 Chron 9:12). The mention in 29:25–26
of another person in the same position suggests that Pashhur was taken captive to
Babylon in 597 B.C. (cf. 2 Kings 24:15). The date of the prophecy of chapter 19
might have been the occasion of the Babylonian victory over Egypt at the Battle of
Carchemish (605 B.C.). That prophecy may have been the reason Jeremiah was
denied access to the temple (cf. 36:1–3). Pashhur was a fairly common name; so we
cannot be certain that the Pashhur in this chapter was the father of Gedaliah (38:1).
Immer was the sixteenth priestly family that returned to Jerusalem after the Exile
(1 Chron 24:14). Jeremiah was a threat to the authority of the overseer priest,
especially since this priest added prophecy to his duties (cf. the actions of Amaziah
at Bethel [Amos 7:10–17]).

2 Angered beyond control, Pashhur "struck" (*yakkeh*) Jeremiah (NIV, "had Jeremiah beaten") with his open hand (cf. Matt 26:67; Acts 23:2). Many expositors believe Pashhur ordered Jeremiah to be beaten with forty stripes less one (cf. Deut
25:3). In any event, this is the first recorded instance of violence done to Jeremiah.
Notice that "the prophet" stands in apposition to "Jeremiah," as if to indicate the
sacrilege of Pashhur's act. For him Jeremiah's words were intolerable. His ministry
was becoming a political threat to those who were supposedly concerned for the
nation's security. The "stocks," where the prophet was confined, were intended not
only for restraint but also for torture. The stocks, which were used for false prophets
(cf. 2 Chron 16:10), held the feet, hands, and neck so that the body was almost
doubled up (cf. 29:26). The Hebrew word for "stocks" (*mahpēket̠*) means "causing
distortion." Jeremiah was put in the stocks at the Upper Benjamin Gate—the northern gate of the upper temple court. It was one of the most conspicuous places in the
city.

3 The next morning Pashhur released Jeremiah only to find that he had not changed
his message and to hear the judgment for the indignity done the Lord's prophet.
Scholars have looked for an etymology of the name "Pashhur" in cognate Semitic

languages, but their attempts have not been entirely successful. Some have suggested that the name cannot be etymologically explained (so Orelli). The translation most often given for "Pashhur" is "ease," "tranquillity." Be that as it may, Jeremiah now gave Pashhur a new name—"Magor-Missabib" (*māgôr missābîb*), meaning "terror on every side." From that time he would be "Mr. Terror All Around." Among the Hebrews it was customary to change names of persons and places in response to changing circumstances—e.g., Abram-Abraham (Gen 17:5); Jacob-Israel (Gen 35:10). The new name Magor-Missabib may have been suggested by Psalm 31:13 ("terror on every side," i.e., *māgôr missābîb*). This compound name is found five times in Jeremiah—6:25; 20:3, 10; 46:5; 49:29 (also in Lam 2:22). Elsewhere *māgôr* ("terror") is found only in Isaiah 31:9. The name symbolized the terror Pashhur would be to himself and to those about him as a consequence of what the Babylonians would instill in the people of Judah.

4 Jeremiah interprets the new name in this verse. For his opposition to the word of God through his prophet, Pashhur was to be exiled to Babylon and die there. This was God's punishment for the calamity Pashhur had helped bring on the land by opposing the truth of God. This is the first time in the book that the king of Babylon is specifically mentioned as the conqueror of Judah. Some believe this dates the prophecy after the Battle of Carchemish (605 B.C.), where Nebuchadnezzar was victorious. When the Exile happened, it would be evident how Pashhur, in misleading the people, was responsible for the disaster. Some have thought that Pashhur was the head of the pro-Egyptian party in Judah, but this cannot be proved. At any rate, his policy would bring judgment on him and on all he had persuaded to follow it.

5–6 Furthermore, Babylonians would plunder the land of its wealth and all its products (v.5). Both Pashhur and his family would suffer in the Fall of Jerusalem and would die in exile (v.6). Apparently Pashhur had not only given the false prophets license to lie but, though a priest, had falsely assumed the prophetic office. For this he was worthy of death. He was probably exiled in 597 B.C. (the captivity of Jehoiachin) because later (29:25–26) Zephaniah had taken over Pashhur's temple position.

Notes

2 The "Upper Gate of Benjamin" was built by Jotham (2 Kings 15:35). The Jerusalem Talmud claims that "the upper gate" was one of the seven names of the Eastern Gate of the temple. The name "Benjamin," however, shows it was on the north side of the temple area.

b. *Jeremiah's inescapable call*

20:7–10

> [7]O LORD, you deceived me, and I was deceived;
> You overpowered me and prevailed.
> I am ridiculed all day long;
> everyone mocks me.

> 8Whenever I speak, I cry out
> proclaiming violence and destruction.
> So the word of the LORD has brought me
> insult and reproach all day long.
> 9But if I say, "I will not mention him
> or speak any more in his name,"
> his word is in my heart like a burning fire,
> shut up in my bones.
> I am weary of holding it in;
> indeed, I cannot.
> 10I hear many whispering,
> "Terror on every side!
> Report him! Let's report him!"
> All my friends
> are waiting for me to slip, saying,
> "Perhaps he will be deceived;
> then we will prevail over him
> and take our revenge on him."

The remaining verses of this chapter have occasioned much comment and difference of interpretation, perhaps as much as any portion of the book. All admit that they are unusual in revealing Jeremiah's inner feelings. They are the last of his so-called confessions and have been called his saddest and bitterest complaints (so Hyatt). At the same time, the passage has been recognized as one of Jeremiah's most significant self-disclosures (so Frost). Indisputably, it is one of the most impressive passages in all the prophetic books. What makes it so significant is that it reveals not only much about Jeremiah but also about the whole range of canonical prophecy, with its profound convictions, conflicts, and certainties. As has often been recognized, Jeremiah's doubts and agonies of soul are not expressed publicly. Nowhere in Scripture is a prophet's sense of divine compulsion to his mission so clearly expressed (cf. Amos 3:8; 1 Cor 9:16). Jeremiah never doubted the reality of his call and never lost his identity under God.

7 The verb "deceived" is so bold and offensive to religious sensibilities that some have tried to soften it by translating it "persuaded" or "enticed" so that the verse does not seem to verge on blasphemy. In its intensive form (as here), the verb *pāṯāh* means "to seduce," as a virgin is seduced (cf. Exod 22:16; 1 Kings 22:20–22). To be sure, Jeremiah is not accusing God of lying or misrepresentation; but what he calls seduction is the divine compulsion on his spirit. He is claiming that the Lord overpersuaded him to be a prophet. He pleads that, though the Lord overcame his resistance to his call (1:4–10) and he believed the Lord's promises, he has now been abandoned to shame. We must remember, however, that the Lord had clearly informed Jeremiah of the difficulties he would face (1:18). Understandably, he could not have conceived of the magnitude and viciousness of the opposition, but the Lord had not lied to him. He complains that God had seized (so the Heb.) and overpowered him. The statement that the Lord had prevailed shows that his prophets did not speak by their own will. Jeremiah's message was so unpopular that he was continually mocked and laughed at. This was doubtless in Jehoiakim's reign. The mockery was so blatant because Jeremiah's prophecies were so long in being fulfilled. As the doom of the nation approached, he felt the Lord had overpersuaded

him in calling him to the prophetic office when he did not realize all it involved. So he clearly speaks like a man overtaxed and overwrought. Who of us can feel justified in censuring him for what he said here?

8–9 In v.8 the verb *zā·aq* ("cry out") speaks of a cry of complaint and *qārā'* ("proclaim") a cry of protest. In summary form, Jeremiah sets forth the gist of his messages: "violence and destruction." This is not so much a statement of what he himself experienced; rather, his message was consistently one of doom and annihilation (cf. 28:8). "Violence and destruction" was the cry of the attacked, and Jeremiah's prophecies were about coming disaster. The burden became so heavy that Jeremiah finally decided he would no longer serve as a prophet (v.9). But he found out the impossibility of denying his call. He learned that it was irreversible and that God's word was irrepressible. Though he arouses opposition from his enemies, he can find no other satisfaction than in preaching God's truth. His own propensities would have led him to a different calling; but once he was called by the Lord, the divine compulsion, which never left him, marked him out as a true prophet. It is just as dangerous not to go when called by the Lord as it is to run without being called (so Clarke). For Jeremiah the word of God was a reality, not the product of his thinking. It demanded expression in spite of opposition and derision. So great was this compelling force of the revelation that he never doubted its reality.

10 Now Jeremiah amplifies the reason he was so determined to resign his prophetic office. He includes some of the sayings he has overheard his enemies using. The defaming is that of people whispering in twos or threes apart. The "many" may mean a crowd (cf. Exod 23:2). They mimick him with the phrase "Terror on every side!" Because he had used it so many times, they now make it a nickname for him. Their plots were intolerable to his sensitive soul. They plotted to report him for treason by beguiling him into unguarded words that could be construed as treasonable (cf. 26:11). Even his trusted friends waited for him to make a misstep. Some have pointed out that with this outpouring of his anguish, Jeremiah's ministry in a sense closed. It was during the fourth year of Jehoiakim that the die was cast. All Jeremiah could do from this time forward was to seek to alleviate something of the judgment that was certain to come on the nation.

c. Prayer for God's vindication

20:11–13

> ¹¹But the LORD is with me like a mighty warrior;
>   so my persecutors will stumble and not prevail.
> They will fail and be thoroughly disgraced;
>   their dishonor will never be forgotten.
> ¹²O LORD Almighty, you who examine the righteous
>   and probe the heart and mind,
> let me see your vengeance upon them,
>   for to you I have committed my cause.
>
> ¹³Sing to the LORD
>   Give praise to the LORD!
> He rescues the life of the needy
>   from the hands of the wicked.

11-13 This is Jeremiah's prayer and hymn of praise for the Lord's protection and vindication. This was the hope that encouraged him. A new calm enabled him to withstand all criticism and physical sufferings. His ultimate confidence was the Lord's presence as a warrior striking his foes with dread (v.11). Their defeat—never to be forgotten—is as certain as if it had already happened. The Lord, who tests his own and knows all their innermost thoughts, is Jeremiah's champion (v.12). Verse 12 is substantially the same as 11:20. Praise bursts forth from his grateful heart as Jeremiah contemplates the prospect of his ultimate vindication. His circumstances had not changed, but now he could sing for joy (v.13). The genuineness of this verse has been questioned; but in view of the fluctuations common to human emotions, it is entirely credible.

d. Jeremiah's curse on the day of his birth

20:14-18

> ¹⁴Cursed be the day I was born!
> May the day my mother bore me not be blessed!
> ¹⁵Cursed be the man who brought my father the news,
> who made him very glad, saying,
> "A child is born to you—a son!"
> ¹⁶May that man be like the towns
> the LORD overthrew without pity.
> May he hear wailing in the morning,
> a battle cry at noon.
> ¹⁷For he did not kill me in the womb,
> with my mother as my grave,
> her womb enlarged forever.
> ¹⁸Why did I ever come out of the womb
> to see trouble and sorrow
> and to end my days in shame?

14 Because this passage is enveloped in such gloom and despair immediately after the triumphant words of vv.11-13, expositors have labored to explain the quick transition and contrast. Some think the passage was accidently transposed. But as we have already seen, sudden transitions are frequent in Jeremiah. Others have even attributed these words to Pashhur. Still others claim that the words can be explained as sentiments that passed through the mind of the prophet from time to time during his unproductive ministry. Actually, however, none of these proposals is valid. The solution to the problem lies in the working of the human mind. The transition and contrast are psychologically understandable in view of the constant pressures on Jeremiah. Feeling an utter failure after being in the stocks, he wished he had never been born. The passage is emotionally authentic because he was being prepared for the greatest blow of all—the destruction of the beloved city of Jerusalem. The experience of Jeremiah at this time shows how difficult the task of God's servants can be and how readily available the grace of God is to sustain them in their darkest hours. Jeremiah's response was normal for one caught between two inescapable contrarities: faithfulness to the message of God and love for his sinful countrymen. Unquestionably, this whole section contains some of the deepest psychological insights into the prophet's heart (so Myers).

15-17 Jeremiah's wish that he never had been born is reminiscent of Elijah's cry when pursued by Jezebel after his victory at Mount Carmel (1 Kings 19:1–3). But Jeremiah held no real animus against the man who brought news of his birth; his cry is strictly rhetorical (v.15). In the East, the messenger who brings news of a son's birth is rewarded. Notice that the prophet did not curse his parents; the law of Moses condemned this (Exod 21:17). The towns referred to in v.16 are Sodom and Gomorrah, a standing example throughout the OT of God's condign punishment on ungodliness. The outcry in the morning represents a call for help when under attack; the shout of alarm or trumpet blast is an alarm of war (cf. 4:19). Jeremiah wishes his mother's womb had been at once his birthplace and his grave (v.17). The translation "enlarged forever" is literally "an eternal conception" (*h*ᵃ*rat ʿôlām*).

18 As the last of Jeremiah's "confessions," this verse portrays the burden he had to bear without interruption. In his outward ministry he never wavered, but to fulfill his ministry was to spend himself totally (so Frost). The shame he refers to is that of his inability to avert the catastrophe threatening his people. It is clear that Jeremiah had no revelation of life after death or of the resurrection of the dead. Later, the truth of his predictions was all too evident; so the ridicule against him ceased.

Notes

16 To אֲשֶׁר־הָפַךְ יְהוָה (*ᵃšer-hāpak* YHWH, "which the LORD overthrew"), LXX adds ἐν θυμῷ (*en thymō*, "in anger"; cf. Deut 29:23; Job 9:5).

II. Prophecies From the Reigns of Jehoiakim and Zedekiah (21:1–39:18)

A. *The Trials and Conflicts of Jeremiah* (21:1–29:32)

1. *Zedekiah's dilemma* (21:1–14)

Chapter 21 moves on to the reign of Zedekiah (597–586 B.C.) and begins a new division of the book. Chapters 21–45 differ from chapters 1–19 in that they abound in references to time, place, and persons. In particular, chapters 21–23 contain a series of messages Jeremiah delivered during the reigns of Jehoahaz, Jehoiakim, Jehoiachin, and Zedekiah. In fact, Frost suggests that the three chapters be characterized as comments on kings. Scholars generally agree that chapter 21 should be dated 588 B.C., when the Babylonians were advancing against Jerusalem but not yet besieging it at close range (vv.4, 13). This was the ninth year of Zedekiah's eleven-year rule. The siege lasted one and a half years (cf. 52:1, 4–7). Chronologically, this chapter should come between chapters 37 and 38. Zedekiah was a vassal king elevated by Nebuchadnezzar (cf. 2 Kings 24:17). The uncle of Jehoiachin, Zedekiah respected Jeremiah but did not have the moral courage to do what he knew was right. He was weak and vacillating, and his reign was made all the more difficult because the Jews still considered Jehoiachin (taken captive in 597 B.C.) as their true king and looked for his early return from exile (cf. 28:4). The personal interplay between Jeremiah and Zedekiah in the years before the Fall of Jerusalem is one of the most remarkable features in the book (cf. 37:3–10; 38:14–18; so Cunliffe-Jones). In the unfolding of God's plan, chapters 21–29 are of vital importance because they foretell "the times of the Gentiles" (Luke 21:24).

a. *The embassy from Zedekiah*

21:1–7

> ¹The word came to Jeremiah from the LORD when King Zedekiah sent to him Pashhur son of Malkijah and the priest Zephaniah son of Maaseiah. They said: ²"Inquire now of the LORD for us because Nebuchadnezzar king of Babylon is attacking us. Perhaps the LORD will perform wonders for us as in times past so that he will withdraw from us."
>
> ³But Jeremiah answered them, "Tell Zedekiah, ⁴'This is what the LORD the God of Israel, says: I am about to turn against you the weapons of war that are in your hands, which you are using to fight the king of Babylon and the Babylonians who are outside the wall besieging you. And I will gather them inside this city. ⁵I myself will fight against you with an outstretched hand and a mighty arm in anger and fury and great wrath. ⁶I will strike down those who live in this city—both men and animals—and they will die of a terrible plague. ⁷After that, declares the LORD I will hand over Zedekiah king of Judah, his officials and the people in this city who survive the plague, sword and famine, to Nebuchadnezzar king of Babylon and to their enemies who seek their lives. He will put them to the sword; he will show them no mercy or pity or compassion.' "

1–2 At the approach of the siege of Jerusalem, Zedekiah, in great consternation, sent a deputation to Jeremiah. The situation was so desperate that the king and his court officials were now willing to consult Jeremiah about the future. The king, at this point more weak than wicked, had more respect for the prophet than Jehoiakim ever had. The members of the deputation were high officials. Pashhur (v.1) is not the Pashhur referred to at 20:1 but the important official of that name mentioned in 38:1. Zephaniah was the successor of Jehoiada the priest (29:25–26; 37:3; 52:24) and was second in rank to the high priest. He was slain by Nebuchadnezzar at Riblah; he and Pashhur opposed Jeremiah's views of the political prospects of the nation. (Compare Zedekiah's embassy to Jeremiah with that of Hezekiah's to Isaiah during an earlier siege of Jerusalem [cf. 2 Kings 19:2; Isa 37:2].) Verses 1–2 are a fulfillment of 15:11. Zedekiah, depending on Pharaoh Hophra of Egypt, had foolishly rebelled against Nebuchadnezzar. Now he is terrified at what his breach of fealty to Nebuchadnezzar had brought on him. Zedekiah wanted both Jeremiah's intercession and the Lord's intervention (cf. a similar appeal in 37:3–10).

The purpose of the embassy is clearly stated. They hoped that Jeremiah would pray for the Lord's intervention by lifting the siege of Nebuchadnezzar (Nebuchadrezzar; cf. Notes). Zedekiah wanted an oracle that would reveal the future, showing, perhaps, that the invader and his army would withdraw from the city and the land. He was evidently thinking of the times of Hezekiah (2 Kings 18–19), Jehoshaphat (2 Chron 20), and the judges. Zedekiah wanted Jeremiah's prayers and fully expected deliverance from God, though he uttered no syllable of repentance or desire to do God's will. Nebuchadnezzar, it will be recalled, was the son of Nabopolassar, who put him in command of the forces against Egypt and Judah at Carchemish when he was crown prince. Upon his father's death, he returned to Babylon to succeed to the throne.

3–4 In answer to Zedekiah's request, Jeremiah did not equivocate (v.3). Instead of the one oracle Zedekiah desired, God gave him three: one to King Zedekiah, one to the people, and one to the royal Davidic house, all found in the remainder of this chapter. For the nation there was no word of hope. The people could expect no help from God in averting the Fall of Jerusalem; in fact, the Lord himself would also fight against them. The Babylonians were to conquer them as the instruments of God's judgment; since this is what the invading Babylonians were, it would be impossible to turn them back. All Judah's resistance and all their stratagems would prove useless. The reference to turning the weapons of war against them (v.4) means that their defense of Jerusalem would fail. The Babylonians (Chaldeans) were originally a seminomadic tribe living between northern Arabia and the Persian Gulf. In the tenth century B.C., the Assyrians gave the name *Kaldu* to the area formerly known as the "Sea-Land" (so Harrison). Later, "Chaldea" was used to include Babylonia as a whole (cf. Ezek 23:23; Dan 3:8). When the text indicates that the Babylonians were besieging them, the meaning is "closing in on you," "blockading you," or "pressing you hard" (so Bright) because the actual siege had not yet begun, as stated above. But the defenders would be driven inside the city when they could no longer fight outside it.

5 To compound Judah's misery, the Lord himself was to fight against her; thus it was too late for the request for Jeremiah's intercession. The metaphor of the outstretched hand and mighty arm had been used many times (Deut 4:34 et al.) of God's miraculous intervention on Israel's behalf in Egypt. But now it is used to express God's opposition to his people. Their doom was inevitable and the defeat total. Jerusalem would be crowded with refugees who, with their cattle, will have fled from the surrounding areas.

6–7 During a siege, an epidemic is always a threat. A fearful plague (v.6) would weaken the people. Then the Lord would deliver Zedekiah into the invaders' hands. Slaughter awaited Judah. The prediction about Zedekiah and his court (v.7) was literally fulfilled in 586 B.C. (cf. 52:9–11, 24–27). The idiom "put them to the sword" means to slay ruthlessly, mercilessly, without quarter. The fate of Zedekiah, his sons, and many Jewish nobles is clear in the OT. Though Zedekiah was not slain, he died of grief in exile as a blinded, deposed monarch (34:4; 2 Kings 25:6–7; Ezek 12:13). The three expressions in the last clause of v.7 give the contemplative, negative, and positive phases of benevolence (so Elliott-Binns).

Notes

2 The spelling "Nebuchadrezzar" is more in accord with the inscriptions excavated in Babylon than is "Nebuchadnezzar." The latter spelling is probably a Hebraized one. A number of transliterations of the name have been given; probably the preference should be for the Akkadian *Nabū-kudurri-uṣūr*, meaning, "Nebo, do thou protect the crown." Although Jeremiah uses the spelling with *n*, the customary usage is that which occurs here. The exceptions are 27:6, 8, 20; 28:3, 11, 14; 29:1, 3.

b. *The choice of ways*

21:8–10

> 8"Furthermore, tell the people, 'This is what the LORD says: See, I am setting before you the way of life and the way of death. 9Whoever stays in this city will die by the sword, famine or plague. But whoever goes out and surrenders to the Babylonians who are besieging you will live; he will escape with his life. 10I have determined to do this city harm and not good, declares the LORD. It will be given into the hands of the king of Babylon, and he will destroy it with fire.' "

8–10 This section is not part of Jeremiah's answer to the king's deputation. It is difficult to determine the time of this message. The setting of the way of life and that of death before the people (v.8) is reminiscent of the words of Moses (cf. Deut 30:19). But there is a difference: here it refers to escape from physical death in the Fall of Jerusalem; in Deuteronomy it referred to spiritual deliverance. Jeremiah's counsel was for the people to submit to Babylon (v.9). Total warfare called for unconditional surrender if they were to be spared. Theirs was the choice. To speak of his nation in this way was a terribly difficult duty for Jeremiah, and it was the reason they called him a traitor. But his motive was more than patriotism; it was the declared will of God. In 38:17–18 Jeremiah also advised giving in to the Babylonians. Again he was charged with treachery (cf. 37:13–14), a charge proved false after the capture of the city when he chose to remain in the devastated land (cf. 40:6).

Though Jeremiah was actually counseling desertion, which was ordinarily treason, as a prophet of God, he spoke with an authority higher than even that of a king. This made him most unpopular with the nation as a whole, which was in a life-and-death struggle with a powerful invader. Yet some people did take his advice (cf. 39:9; 52:15). The idiomatic expression "escape with his life" is literally "his soul will be to him for booty" (cf. 38:2; 39:18; 45:5). All that was promised the nation was bare survival. Those who surrendered would have to realize they would lose all but their lives. As for Jerusalem itself, it was doomed (v.10); the Babylonians, tired of repeated rebellions, would burn it.

c. *Exhortation to the Davidic dynasty*

21:11–14

> 11"Moreover, say to the royal house of Judah, 'Hear the word of the LORD; 12O house of David, this is what the LORD says:
>
> > " 'Administer justice every morning;
> > rescue from the hand of his oppressor
> > the one who has been robbed,
> > or my wrath will break out and burn like fire
> > because of the evil you have done—
> > burn with no one to quench it.
> > 13I am against you, ˌJerusalem,ˌ
> > you who live above this valley
> > on the rocky plateau,
>
> > > declares the LORD—
>
> > you who say, "Who can come against us?
> > Who can enter our refuge?"
> > 14I will punish you as your deeds deserve,
>
> > > declares the LORD.

> I will kindle a fire in your forests
> that will consume everything around you.' "

11–12 This message, directed to the royal house (v.11), relates to a time when there was still a possibility of escape through repentance and righteous living. Continuance in blessing was possible through uprightness and social justice. The monarch and his court officials were to administer justice in the morning. In the narrower sense, the call was to the king and his family; in the wider sense, to the entire court. It was fitting for Jeremiah to address the royal family because administering justice (v.12) was the prerogative of the king and not of all. To avoid the heat of the day, court was held in the morning (cf. 2 Sam 4:5). The emphasis here is on diligence and persistence. The king and his court were to mete out justice promptly and expeditiously. These were basic, not unusual, demands made on monarchs. Even at that late hour deliverance on these godly conditions was not impossible. It is possible that the Lord was not urging righteousness as if the people could escape punishment entirely, but as the prerequisite for its mitigation (so JFB).

13–14 The addressee here is undoubtedly Jerusalem, since the feminine gender is used. Because of past deliverances when the city had been spared from capture for about two centuries, the people were caught up in a wholly unwarranted confidence in the city's invincibility. Complacent in their sins, in their pride the people asked, "Who can come against us?" (v.13). The answer was that God would do so in judgment. They could not claim immunity from punishment on any other ground than obedience to God's will. Some take the reference to "forests" (v.14) literally of forests that covered a larger area than in later times (cf. Ps 132:6—$\acute{s}^e d\hat{e}$-$y\bar{a}^{\cdot}ar$ ["the fields of the wood"; NIV, "fields of Jaar"]; also 1 Sam 7:2—$qiryat\ y^e{}^{\cdot}ar\hat{\imath}m$ ["city of forests"; NIV, "Kiriath Jearim"]; 1 Sam 23:15—$\hbar\bar{o}r\check{s}\bar{a}h$ ["forest"; NIV, "Horesh"]). Figuratively, "forests" was used of the royal palace (1 Kings 7:2; 10:21). The prophets had a keen eye for natural beauty, and a forest connoted grandeur and stateliness. Thus this reference to forests has been equated with the entire city of Jerusalem (so Streane et al.)

Notes

13 Regarding the qualified "Jerusalem" in the early part of this verse, some expositors feel that it is not clear who is addressed and that the mention of "this valley" is directed against an unknown place. The context suggests that Jerusalem is intended, but the city is not located on a rock or in a valley (so Freedman). Others maintain that neither designation suits Jerusalem. Still others speculate whether the words may originally have had reference to some other location, such as Moab (cf. 48:8, 21, 28). This is a remote possibility and does not explain why the phrases should have been transposed to this passage. Did not Jeremiah, his amanuensis, or Ezra and his scribes notice this supposed displacement? This position creates more problems than it solves.

It has also been proposed that there is an analogy with cherubim in 1 Sam 4:4 and 2 Sam 6:2, where the same verbal construction as in v.13 occurs. The sense would then be that Jerusalem sits *above* the valley. In reply to the claim that "rock of the plain" (KJV, RSV) is not suitable for Jerusalem, it can be shown that the Hebrew may be rendered "level rock" or "rock of the level place," since מִישׁוֹר (*mîšôr*) denotes "plateau" (so Bright) (cf. Ps 27:11 ["straight path"]; 143:10 ["level ground"]). It would refer, then, to the level "rocky plateau" (so NIV) on which Jerusalem stood. The valley could be the Tyropoen, between Mount Zion and Mount Moriah, an appropriate designation in that the royal residence was located on Mount Zion (so Henderson). Edward Robinson, the early archaeologist, understood the "rocky plateau" to be Mount Zion, where there is a level tract of considerable extent. Finally, because the city was surrounded by high hills, it could appropriately be called a valley (Isa 22:1). Thus the words of the text are explicable.

---

2. Messages to the Davidic kings (22:1–30)

Once more Jeremiah gives us a cluster of prophecies (chs. 22–23), linked not by chronology but by similar themes. Chapter 22 deals with the temporal leaders of the nation; chapter 23 with the Messiah contrasted with the false spiritual leaders. Both the temporal leaders (the kings) and the spiritual leaders (the prophets, apart from Jeremiah) were responsible for the national calamity. There are two views as to the date of chapter 22. Some scholars date it in the reign of Zedekiah because they believe that the fate of his three predecessors was held up as a warning to him. But the majority of interpreters hold, in the light of vv.13–18, that the chapter, with its oracles about four kings of Judah, belongs to Jehoiakim's reign.

a. Exhortation to justice

22:1–9

¹This is what the LORD says: "Go down to the palace of the king of Judah and proclaim this message there: ²'Hear the word of the LORD, O king of Judah, you who sit on David's throne—you, your officials and your people who come through these gates. ³This is what the LORD says: Do what is just and right. Rescue from the hand of his oppressor the one who has been robbed. Do no wrong or violence to the alien, the fatherless or the widow, and do not shed innocent blood in this place. ⁴For if you are careful to carry out these commands, then kings who sit on David's throne will come through the gates of this palace, riding in chariots and on horses, accompanied by their officials and their people. ⁵But if you do not obey these commands, declares the LORD, I swear by myself that this palace will become a ruin.'"

⁶For this is what the LORD says about the palace of the king of Judah:

"Though you are like Gilead to me,
    like the summit of Lebanon,
I will surely make you like a desert,
    like towns not inhabited.
⁷I will send destroyers against you,
    each man with his weapons,
and they will cut up your fine cedar beams
    and throw them into the fire.

⁸"People from many nations will pass by this city and will ask one another, 'Why has the LORD done such a thing to this great city?' ⁹And the answer will be: 'Because they have forsaken the covenant of the LORD their God and have worshiped and served other gods.'"

1–5 The Lord commanded Jeremiah to go down, evidently from Mount Zion, to the palace south of it (v.1; cf. 26:10; 36:12). The words were directed to the ruling king and his court (v.2) and are a strong exhortation to practice justice. The Lord demands that the Davidic throne make justice its primary responsibility (v.3). The king was to be addressed publicly in the midst of his court. There is no question that the sins mentioned were present in the reigns of most Judean kings, but in Jehoiakim's time they were especially rife (cf. 2 Kings 23:35). Inequities and oppression of the needy abounded in his reign. However, God never desires the death of the wicked but wants them to repent and live. Thus the prophet holds out blessing for obedience, a blessing that means nothing less than the continued prosperity of the Davidic dynasty (v.4), with the people settled securely in the land. On the other hand, the penalty is also specified (v.5)—namely, desolation of the house of David and of the land. To emphasize the truth and solemnity of the occasion, the Lord swore by himself (cf. 49:13; 51:14; Gen 22:16; Isa 45:23; Amos 6:8; Heb 6:13–18). There could be no stronger ratification of a declaration from God.

6–9 These four verses give a clear picture of desolation. Are they referring to the Davidic dynasty or to the royal palace? Those who take the first view are driven to allegorizing the text by seeing the regions and trees as princes and leaders. But most expositors favor the second position, which is preferable. Gilead and Lebanon in the north are mentioned (v.6) because they were regions famous for their beautiful forests. Moreover, the cedars of Lebanon were largely used in the construction of Solomon's palace (cf. 1 Kings 5:6, 8–10; 7:2–5; 10:27). The cedar columns were like trees of Gilead and Lebanon in their loftiness and magnificence (so KD). Those who destroy this grandeur will be God's instruments of judgment (v.7). Even the surrounding nations will realize that the fall of Jerusalem and its palace are the work of the Lord. Furthermore, they will also know the cause of the judgment (v.8). The covenant (v.9) they violate will not be the Davidic covenant of 2 Samuel 7 (contra Habel) but, rather, the initial covenant at Sinai referred to recurringly in the earlier portion of the book. The extensive devastation will be a lesson to the nations on the perils of idolatry.

b. The fate of Shallum (Jehoahaz)

22:10–12

> 10Do not weep for the dead ⌊king⌋ or mourn his loss;
> rather, weep bitterly for him who is exiled,
> because he will never return
> nor see his native land again.

11For this is what the LORD says about Shallum son of Josiah, who succeeded his father as king of Judah but has gone from this place: "He will never return. 12He will die in the place where they have led him captive; he will not see this land again."

10–12 Jeremiah tells the nation at large that they need not mourn the death of the godly king Josiah (v.10), who had been slain at the Battle of Megiddo in 609 B.C. (cf. 2 Kings 23:29–35; 2 Chron 35:25; Zech 12:11). It had become customary among God's people to sing dirges for departed rulers. But now they were to reserve their weeping for Josiah's son Shallum-Jehoahaz (v.11), who was to be forever exiled from the land. The fate of the slain Josiah was better than that of his son who was exiled to Egypt and died there (v.12; cf. 2 Kings 23:34). Scholarly opinion is divided as to whether he reaped the consequences of his father's encounter with Pharaoh Neco, or whether his short reign was enough for him to reverse his father's godly policies (cf. 2 Chron 36:1–4). Jehoahaz was the first ruler of Judah to die in exile. Shallum— his private, preregnal name—was elevated by the people to the throne following the tragic death of his father (cf. 1 Chron 3:15). This arrangement did not meet the pleasure of Pharaoh Neco, who after three months deposed Jehoahaz and exiled him to Egypt. His older brother Eliakim, whose name Neco changed to Jehoiakim, was chosen by Neco to succeed Jehoahaz. Jehoahaz is contrasted with his father Josiah to highlight the tragic condition of the young king. Mourning would be more in place for him than for his departed father, Josiah.

c. *The condemnation of Jehoiakim*

22:13–23

> 13"Woe to him who builds his palace by unrighteousness,
>   his upper rooms by injustice,
> making his countrymen work for nothing,
>   not paying them for their labor.
> 14He says, 'I will build myself a great palace
>   with spacious upper rooms.'
> So he makes large windows in it,
>   panels it with cedar
>   and decorates it in red.
>
> 15"Does it make you a king
>   to have more and more cedar?
> Did not your father have food and drink?
>   He did what was right and just,
>   so all went well with him.
> 16He defended the cause of the poor and needy,
>   and so all went well.
> Is that not what it means to know me?"
>   declares the LORD.
> 17"But your eyes and your heart
>   are set only on dishonest gain,
> on shedding innocent blood
>   and on oppression and extortion."

18Therefore this is what the LORD says about Jehoiakim son of Josiah king of Judah:

> "They will not mourn for him:
>   'Alas, my brother! Alas, my sister!'
> They will not mourn for him:
>   'Alas, my master! Alas, his splendor!'
> 19He will have the burial of a donkey—
>   dragged away and thrown
>   outside the gates of Jerusalem."
>
> 20"Go up to Lebanon and cry out,
>   let your voice be heard in Bashan,
> cry out from Abarim,
>   for all your allies are crushed.
> 21I warned you when you felt secure,
>   but you said, 'I will not listen!'
> This has been your way from your youth;
>   you have not obeyed me.

²²The wind will drive all your shepherds away,
  and your allies will go into exile.
Then you will be ashamed and disgraced
  because of all your wickedness.
²³You who live in 'Lebanon,'
  who are nestled in cedar buildings,
how you will groan when pangs come upon you,
  pain like that of a woman in labor!"

13–14 The prophecy against Jehoiakim is the most scathing of all Jeremiah's messages against kings. Verses 13–14 address him in the third person; in vv.15–17 he is addressed in the second person; in v.18 he is addressed by name. Though a son of the godly Josiah, Jehoiakim was the opposite of his father in temperament, action, and attitude toward God. There was constant conflict between the prophet and the king (609–597 B.C.). Jeremiah does not mince matters in stating the enormity of Jehoiakim's injustice and oppression. He mixed injustice with luxury (v.13). The building mania, common among Oriental monarchs, had siezed him. What aggravated the condition of the nation was that, while he was paying heavy tribute to Neco, Jehoiakim decided to build and beautify his palace by forced, unpaid labor (cf. 2 Kings 23:34–35). Forced labor without wages was in direct violation of the law of Moses (cf. Lev 19:13; Deut 24:14–15). His tyrannical, covetous ways precisely emulated those of Manasseh (cf. 2 Kings 24:3–4). The appointments of his palace were sumptuous indeed (v.14). Jeremiah's reference to the people as the neighbors of the king shows how God regarded the sovereign-subject relationship in Israel (so Hyatt).

15–16 Here Jehoiakim is contrasted with his father, Josiah, just as earlier Jehoahaz had been contrasted with his godly predecessor Josiah (vv.10–12). Scathingly, Jeremiah asks Jehoiakim (v.15a), "Does building palaces of cedar make you a king?" (so Driver). He had mistaken fine buildings as the mark of a true king. Kingly rule entails more than luxurious buildings. There follows a splendid commendation of Josiah (15b–16), who held to true values. He enjoyed the normal comforts of life but never made ostentation his goal. He knew how to enjoy life without extortion or oppression. He was no ascetic but did not make it his ambition to rival Solomon in building. Actually, for Josiah to do justice and righteousness was food and drink. Therefore, he received the blessing and commendation of God because he was deeply concerned for justice and showed this concern in helping the needy and afflicted. His deeds reflect true kingly piety (v.16)—viz., to love God so much that he would not allow any of his subjects to be neglected in their hour of need. Fellowship with God is evidenced in social justice. Josiah showed himself acquainted with God's nature by doing his will.

17 But Jehoiakim had a contrary spirit, and with splendid irony Jeremiah points out what Jehoiakim excelled in. His motivation was covetousness. This led him to practice oppression and extortion in order to pile up dishonest gain. Finally, he did not stop at "shedding innocent blood." This biblical expression has a twofold force. It may mean that Jehoiakim persecuted the innocent after rendering unjust decisions on them (so Hyatt), or it may mean that he had innocent persons slain. For an instance of the latter meaning, see 26:20–23, where the prophet Uriah was extradited from Egypt and then put to death, a glaring example of Jehoiakim's tyranny.

18–19 Following this exposé of Jehoiakim's evil ways, the intrepid prophet told him of the disgraceful death that awaited him. Twice Jeremiah says that there will be no mourning for Jehoiakim (v.18). The references to brother and sister (the latter inapplicable to Jeremiah) show by parallelism that his kin will not grieve for him. Verse 18b implies that he will not be lamented by subjects or friends. He will be buried without any royal funeral ceremonies. All this stands in striking contrast with the widespread and continued lamentation for Josiah (cf. 2 Chron 35:24–25). Jehoiakim would not be missed, and his passing would not even be marked by the normal courtesies—a great indignity for a king. But the most shocking part of Jeremiah's denunciation was that Jehoiakim would be buried with a donkey's burial (v.19); that is, his body would be left to the beasts and birds (cf. 36:30). This meant no burial at all. He would be thrown outside the gates of Jerusalem, as though to insure that he would no longer pollute the city in death as he had done in life. He died in 597 B.C.

20 The consensus of commentators dates this section probably in 597 B.C. It is a call to mourning. Jeremiah is calling on his contemporaries (included in Jerusalem, for the verbs are in the feminine gender) to mourn the disastrous results brought on the land by the foolish international policy of Jehoiakim. The occasion was probably the eve of Nebuchadnezzar's expedition against Judah. The regions mentioned—Lebanon, Bashan, and Abarim—represent the land in its entirety, from north to northeast to southeast. The invaders would overrun the whole land. Abarim refers to the regions beyond the Jordan, that is, the mountains of Moab (including Mount Nebo), east of the Dead Sea (cf. Num 27:12; Deut 32:49). Scholars differ widely about the identity of the "allies" (*me'ahabîm*, lit., "lovers," "paramours") in vv.20, 22. Some claim they are Jerusalem's faithful patriots, such as Ezekiel the prophet (so Bewer). Others hold that the leaders of the nation are probably intended (so Cunliffe-Jones). Still others see them as Egypt and other nations Jehoiakim relied on for aid against the Babylonians. All three views are held by reputable scholars. The last one, however, is preferable because of the immediate context (v.22, where there is a contrast with the nation's leaders—"your shepherds") and the broad context (cf. 4:30); so NIV translates the word as "allies," not "lovers."

21–23 Jeremiah now emphasizes the nation's practice of disobedience (v.21). And the people all persisted in their willfullness in spite of God's blessing on them in times of prosperity (NIV, "when you felt secure"). The winds of adversity and invasion will carry off their leaders and allies alike (v.22). There is a play on words in the first verb in v.22 (*tir'eh*, "feed," "consume"; KJV, "eat up"; ASV, "feed"; NASB, "sweep away"; RSV, "shepherd"; NIV, "drive away"); the first clause may be rendered "depasture your pastors." Jeremiah's next figure for the nation's doom is that of childbirth (v.23; cf. 4:31; 6:24; 13:21). "You who live in Lebanon" refers to the king and his nobles in their cedar palaces. Jerusalem considered herself secure, like the eagles nesting in the cedars of Lebanon (cf. 21:13).

Notes

19 Some scholars have questioned the actual fulfillment of prophecy in this verse. They point to 2 Kings 24:6, which says that Jehoiakim died ("rested with his fathers") and so infer that he was buried in the customary manner. But the prophecy of this verse is reiterated in 36:30. Notice that 2 Kings does not state that Jehoiakim was "buried" with his fathers. Resting, sleeping, or being gathered with the fathers is not tantamount to burial with the fathers. They are two different concepts, as is seen in 2 Kings 15:38 and 16:20. It is true that sleeping or resting with the fathers usually means burial in the family burial place, but it is often used of death in general, as will be seen. That there is no recorded fulfillment of v.19 is not a valid argument against the prophecy, for neither is there any record of Jeconiah's burial. We do know that in the third year of his reign the Exile began (cf. 2 Kings 24:1; 2 Chron 36:6; Dan 1:1–2). This was the first deportation, the one in which Daniel and his friends were included (cf. Dan 1:1–6).

Several solutions to the problem have been offered, and all are plausible. It has been suggested that Jehoiakim received a hurried burial during the siege; then, when the Babylonians conquered Jerusalem, his body was disinterred and cast out. According to Herodotus (3.16), Cambyses so treated the body of the Egyptian Amasis (so Elliott-Binns). Another solution assumes that there was a palace revolt in which the king was assassinated and his body thrown over the wall to show the Babylonians that the Jews did not favor the king's policy of revolt (so Cundall). Yet another solution is that Jehoiakim may have had a proper burial but that the body was later exhumed by the Babylonians or the Jews (so Hyatt). W.F. Albright ("The Seal of Eliakim and the Latest Preexilic History of Judah, With Some Observations on Ezekiel," JBL [1932]: 90–91) believed that Jehoiakim received no funeral, his body having been thrown outside the gates of Jerusalem, possibly after a palace uprising. Finally, we should note that 2 Kings 24:6 does not invalidate a literal fulfillment because the same wording is used of Ahab's dishonorable death (cf. 1 Kings 21:19; 22:30–38, 40).

---

d. The rejection of Coniah (Jehoiachin)

22:24–30

> ²⁴"As surely as I live," declares the LORD, "even if you, Jehoiachin son of Jehoiakim king of Judah, were a signet ring on my right hand, I would still pull you off. ²⁵I will hand you over to those who seek your life, those you fear—to Nebuchadnezzar king of Babylon and to the Babylonians. ²⁶I will hurl you and the mother who gave you birth into another country, where neither of you was born, and there you both will die. ²⁷You will never come back to the land you long to return to."
>
> ²⁸Is this man Jehoiachin a despised, broken pot,
>   an object no one wants?
> Why will he and his children be hurled out,
>   cast into a land they do not know?
> ²⁹O land, land, land,
>   hear the word of the LORD!
> ³⁰This is what the LORD says:
> "Record this man as if childless,
>   a man who will not prosper in his lifetime,
> for none of his offspring will prosper,
>   none will sit on the throne of David
>   or rule anymore in Judah."

24–27 Verses 24–30 deal with the condemnation of Jehoiachin (Coniah, cf. NIV mg.). Coniah (the name occurs only in Jer 22:24, 28; 37:1) is the abbreviated form of Jeconiah and alternate form of Jehoiachin, which is probably his throne name (cf.

515

Jehoahaz-Shallum [v.11]). The son and successor of Jehoiakim (v.24), Jehoiachin was exiled in 597 B.C. (cf. 2 Kings 24:8–17; 25:27–30). After a reign of three months over Judea, he was imprisoned for thirty-seven years in Babylon. His punishment was mitigated, according to 52:31–34. He is mentioned under the name of *Ya'u-kin* in ration tablets between 595 and 570 B.C.; these were unearthed near the Ishtar Gate in Babylon and are known as the Weidner Tablets (so Harrison). Coniah's full name (Jeconiah) means "the LORD will establish," but permanence and stability were not his portion because of his wickedness.

The signet (v.24) of a king was very valuable because it was used to authenticate official correspondence and documents. Jeremiah declared that even if Jehoiachin was as dear to God as a signet ring on God's right hand (and he was not), he would be torn off for his misdeeds. (See Hag 2:23 for the same figure used of Jehoiachin's grandson Zerubbabel.) Jehoiachin and his mother (Nehushta [2 Kings 24:8]) would suffer exile and die in Babylon despite the promises of the false prophets (vv.25–26; cf. 52:31–34). They both went into the second captivity and never returned (v.27). Ezekiel and Mordecai were in this same group of exiles (Ezek 1:1–2; Esth 2:5–6).

28–29 As though this fate was not enough, Jeremiah predicts severe judgment into the distant future. Three questions (v.28; NIV combines the first two) show Jehoiachin's rejection by the Lord. They expect affirmative answers, but Jeremiah's concern is for the Davidic line rather than for Jehoiachin personally. He is likened to a broken earthenware pot, undesirable and worthless. His descendants are mentioned because children were born to him in captivity. There was apparently a desire to restore Jehoiachin from Babylon to replace Zedekiah (cf. 28:1–4; 29:1–32). Before he makes a final pronouncement on Jehoiachin, Jeremiah calls three times on the "land" (v.29) to hear the word of the Lord. The repetition implies strongest emphasis, solemnity, and intensity (cf. 7:4), not extreme affection (contra Freedman). The whole nation was to be impressed by the fate of Jehoiachin.

30 The command to "record" relates to a register of citizens (cf. Isa 4:3); the figure is that of a census list. Jehoiachin had seven sons (cf. 1 Chron 3:17; Matt 1:12), but none succeeded him on the throne. Cuneiform inscriptions from Babylon list amounts of oil given Jehoiachin and his sons. Matthew's genealogy includes Jehoiachin but shows only who Jesus' legal father was, not his natural one. Luke traces Jesus' parental line through Nathan, a son of David, not through Solomon. Zerubbabel, grandson of Jehoiachin, though governor of Judah in 520 B.C., never ruled as king, nor did any other descendant of his. Jehoiachin's uncle, Zedekiah, reigned after him but died before him (cf. 52:10–11). Jehoiachin was thus the last of the Judean kings. In him the royal line became extinct. So chapter 23 goes on to speak of the new King to be raised up by the Lord (cf. 23:5–6).

3. Messiah the King (23:1–40)

This chapter is linked to Jeremiah's denunciation of the godless kings of Judah. The three already mentioned in chapter 22 are included along with Zedekiah. The date is probably in the time of Zedekiah's reign, which may also account for the fact that of the five monarchs (including godly Josiah) he is not mentioned by name. The parallel passage is Ezekiel 34:1–6.

a. *Godless leaders versus David's Righteous Branch*

23:1–8

> [1]"Woe to the shepherds who are destroying and scattering the sheep of my pasture!" declares the LORD. [2]Therefore this is what the LORD, the God of Israel, says to the shepherds who tend my people: "Because you have scattered my flock and driven them away and have not bestowed care on them, I will bestow punishment on you for the evil you have done," declares the LORD. [3]"I myself will gather the remnant of my flock out of all the countries where I have driven them and will bring them back to their pasture, where they will be fruitful and increase in number. [4]I will place shepherds over them who will tend them, and they will no longer be afraid or terrified, nor will any be missing," declares the LORD.

> [5]"The days are coming," declares the LORD,
>   "when I will raise up to David a righteous Branch,
> a King who will reign wisely
>   and do what is just and right in the land.
> [6]In his days Judah will be saved
>   and Israel will live in safety.
> This is the name by which he will be called:
>   The LORD Our Righteousness.

> [7]"So then, the days are coming," declares the LORD, "when people will no longer say, 'As surely as the LORD lives, who brought the Israelites up out of Egypt,' [8]but they will say, 'As surely as the LORD lives, who brought the descendants of Israel up out of the land of the north and out of all the countries where he had banished them.' Then they will live in their own land."

1–2 The "shepherds" on whom Jeremiah pronounced woe are not only kings but all the leaders of Judah (v.1). They were the civil leaders and also the spiritual leaders, the prophets and priests. Homer reportedly said that all kings are shepherds of the people (so Morgan). In Zedekiah's reign the court officials exercised inordinate influence on policy because of his weakness (cf. 38:5). The leaders were guilty of gross dereliction of duty. By oppression and shedding innocent blood, they destroyed the flock; those who were not destroyed were scattered to wander without protection. So the leaders were guilty of the very things the shepherds are charged with preventing. By leading the nation into idolatry and so into the Babylonian captivity, the leaders had scattered the people. Moreover, contrary to the duty of shepherds to lead and feed the flock, they had driven the flock away. The doom on the people would not leave their leaders unscathed. By a play on words, Jeremiah uses the double sense of the Hebrew word *pāqad* ("to care for," "to chastise"): the shepherds had "not bestowed care on" the flock; so God would "bestow punishment on" them in judgment (v.2).

3–4 Just as the scattering of the people was literal, so will the regathering be (v.3). The promise of restoration presupposes the Exile. The return from dispersion had already been announced in 3:15–18. Now it is God himself who does the work of the true shepherd, regathering the sheep from all countries. Here a world-wide dispersion is in view, not just in Assyria and Babylon. What the shepherds did in driving the people away is now attributed to the Lord because he ultimately carried out the penalty brought on the people by their own sins and by the sins of their leaders (shepherds). The people will be returned to their own pasture. Moreover, God will replace the faithless shepherds with faithful ones (v.4). They will rule in godliness under the ideal King (vv.5–6). A number of commentators understand the godly shepherds to be Zerubbabel, Ezra, Nehemiah, the Maccabees, and others; but these do not exhaust the meaning of the passage because of the world-wide dispersion that is in view. The fulfillment awaits eschatological times (cf. Matt 19:28). The hour when assured peace will be Israel's and none will be missing or lost has not yet come. It has been strangely suggested that here Jeremiah was announcing a revocation of the promise to David in 2 Samuel 7:12–16 (so Payne Smith). But this is impossible, because the Davidic covenant has eternal and divine implications as shown by this very passage—i.e., vv.5–6.

5 The reference to good shepherds (v.4) leads on to a prediction of the Messiah, the Davidic King par excellence. Here is the high point of the promise for faithful rulership. A number of scholars question whether these verses (1–8) are a genuine oracle of Jeremiah. They feel messianism was not a significant element in Jeremiah's thought. But how can we know this when the concept of messianism is found here, in 33:15–16, and other passages (3:15–18; 31:31–34) presuppose it? Though Jeremiah has few direct references to the messianic King, this is surely such an instance (so Frost, Hyatt). The formula "days are coming" is a messianic formula; Jeremiah uses it to direct special attention to what is stated. The phrase is used fifteen times in the book. In contrast to the troublous times of Jeremiah's day, there will be a time of blessing ahead. The promise is centered in David in view of the covenant in 2 Samuel 7:8–16.

After Jeremiah has denounced the faithless shepherds of the nation and has predicted the coming of good shepherds, he describes as a climax the incomparable rule of the King Messiah, the "Branch." This designation has much in common semantically with "seed" (Gen 3:15), the Davidic "son" (2 Sam 7), and the "servant of the LORD" (Isa 42–53). In each case there is a general reference to a number of individuals; but by a process of strict selection and narrowing down, the seed, the son, and the servant ultimately find highest fulfillment in the Lord Jesus the Messiah, "the Seed of the Woman," "the Son of David," and "the Servant of the LORD." The Lord was thus superintending the historical process in such a way that his ultimate choice unmistakably was Jesus of Nazareth (cf. KD).

It is clear that the term "Branch" is symbolic of the Messiah because the adjective modifying it is a quality of persons and not plants. The shoot or sprout is a scion of the stock of David. "Branch" has a collective meaning when used horticulturally but not when used symbolically (so KD). (On "Branch," see J.G. Baldwin, "Şemaḥ as a Technical Term in the Prophets," Vet Test 14 [1964]: 93–97.) Furthermore, the collective sense cannot be permitted here because (1) "a King who will reign" cannot refer to a number of kings; (2) "The LORD Our Righteousness" (v.6) cannot speak of a series of monarchs; and (3) the parallel passages refer to one person (cf. 30:9; Ezek 34:23–24; 37:24; for the use of Branch [lit., "sprout"] for the Messiah, cf. Isa 4:2; Jer 33:15; Zech 3:8; 6:12). Moreover, he will reign as a true king, not as a puppet like Zedekiah and his immediate predecessors. He will execute justice and righteousness like his ancestor David (cf. 2 Sam 8:15; for Messiah, see Ps 72:2). In contrast to the inequities and injustices common to the Davidic kings, the Messiah's reign will be diametrically the opposite.

6 Now Jeremiah dilates on the benefits that will come to Messiah's people from his reign. First, he will rule over a reunited nation; both Judah and Israel will be restored (cf. Ezek 37:19). Second, he will bring salvation to his people. The verb "saved" (yāša') denotes spiritual not physical deliverance (cf. same verb in Isa 45: 22). Third, peace and security will characterize Messiah's righteous rule. Much diversity of opinion surrounds the interpretation of the last half of v.6. One group of scholars sees the name, not as that of a scion of David, but of the nation as a whole. They find support in 33:16, where the name is given to Jerusalem. That it is a symbolic surname (not for actual use but as an ideal inscription or objective characterization) is readily admitted (so CHS). A number of commentators emphasize that the name stands in vivid contrast to the name Zedekiah, which means "The LORD is my righteousness," a declaration that his life so fully belied. This King who is "The LORD Our Righteousness" will be righteousness in actuality. Other scholars see here the name of the Messiah and that of none other. It would, they believe, be totally out of keeping with the context for Jeremiah to be speaking of a Davidic descendant and then without warning or preparation to turn to a name for Jerusalem. The usage of a noun with a name for deity has more than one attestation in the OT (cf. Gen 22:14; Exod 17:15; Judg 6:24; cf. also Isa 7:14; 9:6). Finally, the Jews understood the name in v.6b to be that of the Messiah. The Targum reads, "The Messiah of the righteous," or "The Messiah of righteousness." Even the majority of Jewish commentators rejected the reading "And this is the name by which the Lord will call him: Our righteousness," because it is opposed to the Hebrew accents (cf. Abenezra on the passage). They acknowledged the two words to be the name of the Messiah.

A word of caution must be introduced here. At this point the concept of forensic imputed righteousness with all its implications, as elaborated in the NT, must not be injected. It is sufficient that Messiah is presented as the righteous King, as deity, and as redeeming his people.

7-8 That which is directly and inseparably related to the messianic hope is the national restoration of Israel (cf. 16:14-15). The future restoration of the people will exceed anything in the past. It will surpass the deliverance from Egypt. The Exodus (v.7) will pale into insignificance in comparison with the future ingathering of the nation from world-wide dispersion (v.8). The inauguration of the new Exodus cannot be equated with the return of Israel under Cyrus in the last decades of the sixth century B.C. (cf. Isa 11:11-12).

Notes

4 Just as there was a play on the word פָּקַד (pāqad, "to care for," "to chastise") in v.2, so now there is a continuation with the meaning "missing."

5 צֶמַח (ṣemaḥ, "shoot") in Jeremiah's day (here and 33:15) and later (Zech 3:8; 6:12) had the technical meaning of the Davidic, messianic King. This King's reign will be effective (cf. הַשְׂכִּיל [hiśkîl, "to do wisely"] here with יַשְׂכִּיל [yaśkîl, "he will do wisely"] of Isa 52:13).

6 It has been suggested that the mention of צַדִּיק (ṣaddîq, "righteous") with צֶמַח (ṣemaḥ, "Branch") in v.5 and now the occurrence of יהוה צִדְקֵנוּ (YHWH ṣidqēnû, "The LORD Our Righteousness") strongly favor a play on the name Zedekiah (צִדְקִיָּהוּ, ṣidqiyyāhû), which was given him for his original name (Mattaniah) by Nebuchadnezzar (2 Kings 24:17). What motivated Nebuchadnezzar to change the name, as Pharaoh Neco did in the case of Elia-

519

kim (2 Kings 23:34), can only be conjectured. It is possible that in such cases the dominant king wanted to display his own authority.

Because יהוה צִדְקֵנוּ (YHWH *ṣidqēnû*, "The LORD Our Righteousness") are joined by a conjunctive rather than a disjunctive accent, they are not to be separated and read apart. Thus the position that takes the words to be a proper name is strengthened.

---

b. *Condemnation of the false prophets*

23:9–12

⁹Concerning the prophets:

> My heart is broken within me;
>   all my bones tremble.
> I am like a drunken man,
>   like a man overcome by wine,
> because of the LORD
>   and his holy words.
> ¹⁰The land is full of adulterers;
>   because of the curse the land lies parched
>   and the pastures in the desert are withered.
> The ˻prophets˼ follow an evil course
>   and use their power unjustly.
> ¹¹"Both prophet and priest are godless;
>   even in my temple I find their wickedness,"
>
>   declares the LORD.
> ¹²"Therefore their path will become slippery;
>   they will be banished to darkness
>   and there they will fall.
> I will bring disaster on them
>   in the year they are punished,"
>
>   declares the LORD.

9 The remainder of this chapter gives Jeremiah's classic denunciation of the false prophets. Because the tension between Jeremiah and the false prophets was greatest during Zedekiah's reign, this section may well be dated from that reign (so Bright). Jeremiah more than any other OT writer speaks of false prophets (cf. 2:8; 5:30–31; 6:13–14; 8:10–11; 14:13–15; 18:18–23; 26:8, 11, 16; 27:1–28:16 and here). Their characteristics were that (1) they used God's name without authorization, (2) they were of low moral character, (3) they spread false hopes and promises among the people, (4) the source of their messages was their own minds or those of other false prophets, and (5) they were never called of God (so Hyatt). To this H. Wheeler Robinson (*Inspiration and Revelation in the Old Testament* [Oxford: Clarendon, 1946], pp. 187–88) adds "popularity seekers" (vv.17–18) and "plagiarist" (v.38). Other prophets also denounced these misleaders of the people (cf. Isa 28:7–13; Ezek 13:1–16; Mic 3:5–12). Let us not think that Jeremiah took his condemnation of the false prophets lightly. It cost him tremendous emotional and physical stress. He was disturbed and shocked at the enormity of their offenses and was so overcome with the trauma of it that he could only liken himself to a drunken man. He showed no vindictiveness against those who tried to nullify his life's work, only heartbrokenness. Next to the ungodly kings, the false prophets were most responsible for bringing about the nation's ruin. When Jeremiah contrasted their evil ways and words with the holy words of God, it was more than he could contemplate without deep agony of soul.

10 As always, immorality directly led to godlessness. The influence of the false prophets on the nation was totally evil; the people followed the evil ways of their leaders. The adultery referred to is not just the spiritual unfaithfulness of breaking the covenant with God but refers to the gross immorality of these godless men, whose ways could never lead to repentance. The curse on violation of the laws of God was manifest in a drought. Their use of their power was perverted. Only in doing wrong were they strong.

11–12 Furthermore, the false prophets had accomplices—namely, the priests (v. 11). Instead of drawing the people to God, the priests were part of the national corruption. Their wickedness reached into the house of God itself; it was either greed like that of Eli's sons or idolatry as in Manasseh's day (cf. 1 Sam 2:12–17, 22; 2 Kings 21:5; 23:12; Ezek 8:6, 10, 14, 16). The penalty for such sin would be spiritual blindness. Slippery paths (v. 12) symbolize the punishment of falling into perilous life situations (cf. Pss 35:6; 73:18). The imagery of darkness parallels 13:16.

c. *False prophecy in Samaria and Jerusalem*

23:13–15

> ¹³"Among the prophets of Samaria
>   I saw this repulsive thing:
> They prophesied by Baal
>   and led my people Israel astray.
> ¹⁴And among the prophets of Jerusalem
>   I have seen something horrible:
> They commit adultery and live a lie.
> They strengthen the hands of evildoers,
>   so that no one turns from his wickedness.
> They are all like Sodom to me;
>   the people of Jerusalem are like Gomorrah."

¹⁵Therefore, this is what the LORD Almighty says concerning the prophets:

> "I will make them eat bitter food
>   and drink poisoned water,
> because from the prophets of Jerusalem
>   ungodliness has spread throughout the land."

13–15 Jeremiah now particularizes the evils done by the false prophets of Samaria and Jerusalem. The prophets of the northern kingdom were devoted to Baal and seduced the people from worshiping God (v. 13). The prophets of the southern kingdom were worse (v. 14), having learned nothing from the sinful deeds and tragic consequences of their counterparts in the north. The Samaritan prophets prophesied by a false god, but the Jerusalem prophets were worse in misusing God's name and committing moral outrages. Polluted by adultery, their lives were a libel of true worship. By advocating idolatry and living in immorality, by being indifferent to good and encouraging evil, they hardened the nation against repentance. The result was that the Jerusalem prophets had no influence for godliness. In God's sight all the people of Jerusalem had become as bad as those of Sodom and Gomorrah, and the prophets were the instigators to the people's sin. God's only recourse was to punish the prophets, and this he declares in unequivocal terms. Because they had poisoned the nation's spiritual springs, the Lord was to inflict drastic judgment on them—portrayed by "bitter food" (*laʿᵃnāh*, "wormwood"; i.e., strong smelling and bitter tasting) and "poisoned water" (v.15). Instead of piety, only pollution resulted from the false prophets' labors.

d. *Characteristics of lying prophecy*

23:16-22

16This is what the LORD Almighty says:

> "Do not listen to what the prophets are prophesying
> to you;
> they fill you with false hopes.
> They speak visions from their own minds,
> not from the mouth of the LORD.
> 17They keep saying to those who despise me,
> 'The LORD says: You will have peace.'
> And to all who follow the stubbornness of their hearts
> they say, 'No harm will come to you.'
> 18But which of them has stood in the council of the LORD
> to see or to hear his word?
> Who has listened and heard his word?
> 19See, the storm of the LORD
> will burst out in wrath,
> a whirlwind swirling down
> on the heads of the wicked.
> 20The anger of the LORD will not turn back
> until he fully accomplishes
> the purposes of his heart.
> In days to come
> you will understand it clearly.
> 21I did not send these prophets,
> yet they have run with their message;
> I did not speak to them,
> yet they have prophesied.
> 22But if they had stood in my council,
> they would have proclaimed my words to my people
> and would have turned them from their evil ways
> and from their evil deeds."

16-17 Verses 16-22 detail the failures of the false prophets. The crux of the matter is in v.16. The source of their messages and the cause of the Lord's condemnation are these: Their messages originated with them and thus lacked any real authority (cf. v.18). The origin of their prophecies showed that they were deficient in the all-important prerequisite for true prophecy. When they deceived the people with empty hopes by self-devised messages, they showed that their words had not come from the mouth of the Lord. The heart of false prophecy was that it always held out false hope. Therefore the false prophets led the sinning nation into false security that prevented moral transformation. Because they continually denied any future evil or calamity, they have been called the "success prophets" (so Myers). Their messages of peace and prosperity at any price marked them out as false (v.17). True prophets were burdened by necessary messages of doom (cf. 28:8-9).

18 What was the demarcating feature between false and true prophets? Verse 18 clearly presents it in the form of two questions, the answer to which not one of the false prophets could give. What is the meaning of standing in the council of the Lord? According to the Eastern custom, ministers or royal servants remained standing during deliberations (so Henderson). The picture is that of a group of friends in close consultation (cf. Ps 25:14). Because archaeological research has found that in Near Eastern polytheism there was the concept of a council or assembly of supernatural beings presided over by the deity, a number of scholars have declared that such is the case here. This need not be so. A concept or belief found in one civilization or culture is not ipso facto proof that such a belief must have existed in the culture of the Bible. Other factors must be considered, especially the general context and teaching of Scripture. This reveals that the council concept was an integral part of monotheism and was based on the Lord's desire to share his truth with his trusted servants (cf. v.22; Amos 3:7). The reason for the false prophets' corruption was that they had not gone to *the* fountainhead for their message. Anyone who had had intimate dealings with the Lord could not follow the ways of the lying prophets (cf. v.22).

19–20 These verses occur almost verbatim in 30:23–24. They contain the burden of the Lord's purpose for the nation made known in his council. The tempest of the divine wrath was soon to burst upon the impenitent wicked (v.19). When that judgment finally falls, there will be no mistaking the Lord's intention. Often the phrase "in days to come" (v.20) refers to the Lord's vindication of his word and his deeds in messianic times. Here, however, it can hardly mean this. The force of the phrase is that when the judgment comes, events will show the nation the truth of Jeremiah's words and warnings.

21–22 Because Jeremiah's message was relentlessly opposed by the false prophets, he had to express God's displeasure against them and their deceitful works. He showed clearly that no prophet of God can ever derive his message from observing the times he lives in. Graphically, Jeremiah points out how the words of the lying prophets were wholly unauthorized (v.21). Their call was merely from themselves. They never received a divine commission (cf. v.32); yet they ran, with their false messages, eagerly and energetically trying to accomplish their own objectives. No words could more emphatically state the falsity of their lives and ministry. On the other hand, if they had been in the intimate circle where God divulges his plans to his faithful followers, i.e., in his council, they would have uttered God's truth to his needy people (v.22). The result would have been the repentance of the nation and their restoration to godliness. A proof of the true prophet was his desire to win others to the way of godliness in which he himself was walking. The results of his ministry were indicators of the genuineness of his call and message.

e. *Lying versus true prophets*

23:23–32

²³"Am I only a God nearby,"

declares the LORD,

"and not a God far away?

²⁴Can anyone hide in secret places
so that I cannot see him?"

declares the LORD.

"Do not I fill heaven and earth?"

declares the LORD.

²⁵"I have heard what the prophets say who prophesy lies in my name. They say, 'I had a dream! I had a dream!' ²⁶How long will this continue in the hearts of these lying prophets, who prophesy the delusions of their own minds? ²⁷They think the dreams they tell one another will make my people forget my name, just as their fathers forgot my name through Baal worship. ²⁸Let the prophet who has a dream tell his dream, but let the one who has my word speak it faithfully. For what has straw to do with grain?" declares the LORD. ²⁹"Is not my word like fire," declares the LORD, "and like a hammer that breaks a rock in pieces?

³⁰"Therefore," declares the LORD, "I am against the prophets who steal from one another words supposedly from me. ³¹Yes," declares the LORD, "I am against the prophets who wag their own tongues and yet declare, 'The LORD declares.' ³²Indeed, I am against those who prophesy false dreams," declares the LORD. "They tell them and lead my people astray with their reckless lies, yet I did not send or appoint them. They do not benefit these people in the least," declares the LORD.

23–24 The questions in this section are meant to point out that the Lord cannot be circumscribed as though the false prophets could escape his notice. God is not a localized deity whom it is easy to avoid; he is inescapable (cf. Ps 139:7–10). God is both immanent and transcendent, omniscient and omnipresent. The false prophets cannot hide from God's judgment. In v.24, Jeremiah elaborates on the query in v.23. An omnipresent and omniscient God cannot be deceived and surely has heard the lies of the false prophets.

25–26 This section contains a strong contrast between dreams and the word of God. The repetition in v.25 expresses the assumed solemnity of the false prophets. Jeremiah is not denying that dreams were a legitimate method of divine revelation (cf. Gen 37, 41; Num 12:6; 1 Sam 28:6; Dan 2:7; Joel 2:28; Zech 1:7–6:8). But some of the false prophets relied on their dreams as the origin of their inspiration. Authentic prophetic dreams there undoubtedly were, but here was a channel of revelation easily abused and counterfeited (v.26). The deceivers knew just how to trick the gullible, but the omniscient Lord was aware of their lies.

27–29 The impunity of the falsifiers will not last. They were having the same baneful effect on the contemporaries of Jeremiah as Baal worship had had on an earlier generation (v.27). As so often in the OT, the result is viewed as the purpose. When the lying prophets prophesied, the Lord was banished from the hearts of the nation. The truth of God and mere dreams were so different in essence that they had to be kept separate (v.28). If a prophet had a dream, he was to relate it as a dream and nothing more. Dreams of the false prophets were to the word of God as chaff to wheat. Words of the false prophets have no value; those of the true messengers of God are as wheat, as food for believers. So Jeremiah presents the qualities of the true word. God's truth is like fire (v.29) in contrast to the useless, powerless words of the false prophets. It is penetrating, purifying, and consumes evil. Jeremiah himself had experienced this (cf. 5:14; 20:9). Moreover, God's word is full of power like a hammer strongly wielded (cf. Heb 4:12–13). His message does not lull men in their sins; it crushes the heart to bring it to repentance. The true word convicts and converts; it neither amuses nor entertains.

30–32 Jeremiah describes three classes of false prophets. Three times he declares that the Lord is against the false prophets; each verse begins with a statement of the opposition of God to the godless seers. The first group of lying prophets are those who misappropriate the prophecies of the true prophets, giving them out as their own (v.30). To their lies they add plagiarism; their words were not original but stolen from others. Here was spiritual bankruptcy indeed! A second group are accused of using their tongues as the main weapon in their deceptions. They use their tongues too freely (v.31). They "wag" (*lāqaḥ*, lit., "take") them to introduce their lies by the formula of the true prophets: "The Lord declares." They did this to give their words a ring of authenticity. They merely pretended divine authorization. The last group included those with whom national interests were paramount (v.32). Their words—true or not—must, they felt, lift national morale. No wonder the prophet refers to their speech as empty talk.

Notes

---

23 An interesting parallel is found in the fourteenth century B.C. Hymn to Aten (Aton) of Egypt: "Thou hast made the distant sky in order to rise therein, in order to see all that Thou dost make" (ANET, p. 371).

27 שְׁמִי (*šemî*, "my name") is more than a matter of nomenclature. It encompasses God's personality and essence.

28 This verse, though making a distinction between a prophet's dream and God's word, does not intend to deny the validity of prophetic dreams (cf. Dan 7:1–2, 15; 8:1–2, 15; 10:1, 7). From vv.25–27 it is clear that the dreams referred to are those of the false prophets.

31 In וַיִּנְאֲמוּ נְאֻם (*yinᵃmû neᵓum*), the verb *nāᵃam* ("speak as a prophet") is a *hapax legomenon*, whereas the passive participle *neᵓum* used substantively is frequent among the prophets. The play on words (paronomasia) may be rendered "utter an utterance," "oracle an oracle," or "declare a declaration" (cf. NIV). The verb may be denominative. The false prophets use counterfeit phraseology to give the impression of divine authority.

---

f. The burden of the Lord

23:33–40

> [33]"When these people, or a prophet or a priest, ask you, 'What is the oracle of the Lord?' say to them, 'What oracle? I will forsake you, declares the Lord.' [34]If a prophet or a priest or anyone else claims, 'This is the oracle of the Lord,' I will punish that man and his household. [35]This is what each of you keeps on saying to his friend or relative: 'What is the Lord's answer?' or 'What has the Lord spoken?' [36]But you must not mention 'the oracle of the Lord' again, because every man's own word becomes his oracle and so you distort the words of the living God, the Lord Almighty, our God. [37]This is what you keep saying to a prophet: 'What is the Lord's answer to you?' or 'What has the Lord spoken?' [38]Although you claim, 'This is the oracle of the Lord,' this is what the Lord says: You used the words, 'This is the oracle of the Lord,' even though I told you that you must not claim, 'This is the oracle of the Lord.' [39]Therefore, I will surely forget you and cast you out of my presence along with the city I gave to you and your

fathers. [40]I will bring upon you everlasting disgrace—everlasting shame that will not be forgotten."

33–34 For many this is a difficult section to interpret; it can be understood, though with difficulty, if the reader studies the passage on the basis of the English text only. It is important, however, to realize that there is here a play on the word "oracle" (*maśśā'*). Furthermore, *maśśā'* had a primary meaning from which was derived an important secondary meaning. In the first instance, *maśśā'* comes from the simple verb *nāśā'* ("to lift, lift up"), with the noun denoting a "burden" in the physical sense. By usage the word came to mean that which was placed as a burden on the heart of a prophet, having already been such on the heart of God. Thus it referred to a threatening prediction or "oracle" (cf. Zech 9:1; 12:1). Now the interpretation of the passage becomes clearer. Jeremiah indicates that the people, the priests, and the prophets (v.33) had begun to use this important word mockingly and derisively. They would ask Jeremiah, "What is the oracle [burden] now?" "What is the heavy word from the Lord now?" (so Cundall). The answer in KJV, ASV, and NASB is stated either in an interjectional or interrogative style: "What burden?" or "What burden!" NIV has "What oracle?" It is much better to follow LXX, Vulgate, and RSV and translate it "You are the burden!" This requires no change of consonants in the Hebrew text but only another division of them. Otherwise, the sign of the accusative in the original is hard to explain. Not only were the lying prophets the burden, but the Lord immediately indicated that he would unburden himself of them (v.34). The word of God is ultimately not the burden on them, but they are a burden to the Lord.

35–37 Moreover, because the false prophets derisively called the word of the Lord a burden, when they themselves were a constant burden to him (v.35), the word "oracle" ("burden") was forbidden them. Since they misused the word, they were no longer to use it in their prophecies (v.36). So Jeremiah's contention was that, since all the prophets of his day were using this phrase in their oracles, such frequent and overdone usage destroyed the force of the words (so Francisco). Their use of the word showed irreverence and impenitence. Interestingly enough, though the term "oracle" was used by canonical prophets (e.g., Isa 13:1; Nah 1:1; Hab 1:1; Zech 9:1; Mal 1:1), Jeremiah never used it of his own prophecies because it had become the hallmark of the lying prophets. Punishment would now follow their use of the word. Jeremiah even points out how they should inquire about a message from God (v.37). There were clear alternatives to "oracle" ("burden") they could use. What lying prophets spoke in jest will be found to be heavy indeed. Their mockery of the word will weigh them down and crush them. This is the penalty for misusing a great word for their own purposes and not God's. (The thought of v.35 is repeated in v.37.)

38–40 The last three verses of the chapter deal with the penalty for ignoring the Lord's admonition. The result of the false prophets' pointless mockery (v.38) of God's oracles against them will be that they will live to fulfill them. False prophecy had assumed such proportions that drastic measures had to be taken to eliminate it (v.39). The horrifying prospect of being utterly forgotten of God loomed before the lying prophets (v.40).

4. The good and the bad figs (24:1–10)

This chapter belongs to the same period as chapters 22 and 23, namely, in the reign of Zedekiah. Its date is fairly well indicated by the chronological reference in v.1. The time was after—perhaps not long after—Nebuchadnezzar had deported King Jeconiah and his skilled laborers to Babylon in 597 B.C. This was the captivity Ezekiel was involved in. It carried off the better element of the nation, those who would be useful to Nebuchadnezzar in his building projects and would not participate in a siege against his invading forces (cf. 2 Kings 24:14–16).

Objection has been raised against the whole chapter on the ground that it is not in keeping with Jeremiah's attitude as already set forth and elaborated later in the book (so Hyatt). The arguments are (1) the portrayal in chapter 5 of all in Jerusalem as wicked; (2) Jeremiah's position in chapter 29 toward the exiles in Babylon; (3) Jeremiah's estimate of Jehoiachin in 22:24–30; (4) his opinion of Zedekiah as weak rather than evil (chs. 37–38); and (5) Jeremiah's own decision in 586 B.C. to stay in Jerusalem rather than go to Babylon (39:13–14; 40:1–6). These difficulties can be cleared away if one realizes that Jeremiah is comparing the exiles in Babylon with the remnant left in the land, not in an absolute, but in a comparative sense. Moreover, with the final captivity ahead for those who remained in the land, rebuke was eminently in order for the complacent remnant in Jerusalem.

a. The vision of the baskets of figs

24:1–3

> ¹After Jehoiachin son of Jehoiakim king of Judah and the officials, the craftsmen and the artisans of Judah were carried into exile from Jerusalem to Babylon by Nebuchadnezzar king of Babylon, the LORD showed me two baskets of figs placed in front of the temple of the LORD. ²One basket had very good figs, like those that ripen early; the other basket had very poor figs, so bad they could not be eaten.
>
> ³Then the LORD asked me, "What do you see, Jeremiah?"
>
> "Figs," I answered. "The good ones are very good, but the poor ones are so bad they cannot be eaten."

1–3 In these verses the vision is revealed; in the remainder of the chapter it is explained. The purpose of the vision was to declare that those who went into exile with Jehoiachin would be better off than those left behind in Jerusalem; those who escaped the deportation would naturally think just the opposite. The emphasis is on the poor caliber of leadership left in Judah in contrast to the able men now in Babylon (cf. 52:28). In v.1 the verb "showed" ($r\bar{a}\bar{a}h$) in the causative stem is used of supernatural disclosure (cf. Amos 7:1, 4, 7). The vision of v.2 resembles the one in Amos 8:1–3. Some expositors believe the baskets were set before the temple as an offering. First, we must remember that Jeremiah saw them in a vision, not in reality. Second, bad figs could not be offered to the Lord (cf. Deut 26:2). Fig trees in Palestine produce fruit three times a year (so F.H. Wight, *Manners and Customs of Bible Lands* [Chicago: Moody, 1953], p. 200). The first-ripe figs are especially juicy and are considered a delicacy; they ripen in June (cf. Isa 28:4; Hos 9:10). The question the Lord asked Jeremiah (v.3) was meant to focus attention on the vision and its explanation.

Notes

1 The Hophal participle מוּעָדִים (*mûʿādîm*, "placed") is rare, occurring only once more (Ezek 21:21 [16 Eng.]). The meaning is "set" or "directed." Many scholars read the Qal active participle עוֹמְדִים (*ʿômᵉdîm*, "standing") or מָעֳמָדִים (*moʿᵒmādîm*, a noun occurring only in Ps 69:3 in the sense of "standing ground," "foothold"; cf. BDB, KB). The footnote in BHK suggests the latter reading with the indication of the agreement of the versions. It is difficult, however, to see how the proposed changes add anything to the meaning of the passage.

Because the noun מַסְגֵּר (*masgēr*, "artisan") derives from the common verb סָגַר (*sāgar*, "to shut, close"), LXX has rendered it τοὺς δεσμώτας (*tous desmōtas*, "the bound ones," "prisoners"). The translation "artisans" (here and 29:2) is to be preferred, for all those previously mentioned in the verse ("officials," "craftsmen") were equally prisoners of Nebuchadnezzar.

b. *The explanation of the good figs*

24:4–7

⁴Then the word of the LORD came to me: ⁵"This is what the LORD, the God of Israel, says: 'Like these good figs, I regard as good the exiles from Judah, whom I sent away from this place to the land of the Babylonians. ⁶My eyes will watch over them for their good, and I will bring them back to this land. I will build them up and not tear them down; I will plant them and not uproot them. ⁷I will give them a heart to know me, that I am the LORD. They will be my people, and I will be their God, for they will return to me with all their heart.'"

4–7 This passage identifies the good figs and holds out some comprehensive promises of future blessing: (1) constant prosperity from the Lord, (2) restoration to their own land, (3) permanent establishment in that land, (4) spiritual turning to the Lord in genuine conversion. The passage explicitly says that the good figs are the exiles of 597 B.C. under Jehoiachin (v.5). The word "good" refers not to the character of the exiles but to their circumstances. They were not taken to Babylon for their piety and godliness. But the Lord promised them that he would look with favor on them (v.6). His feeling of concern for them was manifested in their exemption from the horrors of the Fall of Jerusalem in 586 B.C. and their being cured of their idolatry. These exiles prospered in Babylon (cf. 2 Kings 25:27–30; Jer 29:4–7). Jeremiah's evaluation of them was the very opposite of the opinion prevalent among the people of the land. To those yet in the land, the very fact that they escaped exile was an evident token that God was favorable to them. But the influence of men like Daniel must have helped the exiles. The full force of vv.4–7 may, however, relate to the generality of the Lord's blessings. The verbs in v.6 remind us of those in 1:10; they recur throughout the prose sections of the book.

After purification in Babylon, the exiles will return, whereas those left in Jerusalem will be slain at the destruction of the city. What appeared in 597 B.C. to be all disaster, the Lord will overrule for good. Judgment will have its intended result. Jeremiah was right: the future of the nation lay with its exiled portion. Physical restoration to the land would be followed by spiritual renewal (v.7). God foretold their reinstatement into the original covenant (cf. 31:31–34)—an event in the distant future.

Notes

---

7 The people will return to the Lord with their לֵב (*lēḇ*, "heart"), which stands for their whole mind and will. The OT prophets delight to dwell on Israel's wholehearted return to the Lord in fulfillment of the Abrahamic covenant (cf. Jer 29:13; 31:33; Ezek 36:26–27; 37:13–14, 27–28; Zech 13:9).

---

c. The meaning of the bad figs

24:8–10

> 8"'But like the poor figs, which are so bad they cannot be eaten,' says the LORD, 'so will I deal with Zedekiah king of Judah, his officials and the survivors from Jerusalem, whether they remain in this land or live in Egypt. 9I will make them abhorrent and an offense to all the kingdoms of the earth, a reproach and a byword, an object of ridicule and cursing, wherever I banish them. 10I will send the sword, famine and plague against them until they are destroyed from the land I gave to them and their fathers.'"

8 The bad figs represent Zedekiah and his courtiers, and for them a bleak future is prophesied. Jeremiah's estimate of those who remained in the land coincided with that of Ezekiel (cf. Ezek 11:5–6, 14–21; 33:24). Jeremiah did not mean that those in exile were intrinsically better than the remnant in Judah but that the purpose of God in his unmerited favor promised them a bright future. Those who remained with Zedekiah were yet to be scattered in disgrace. (Notice Jeremiah's letter [29:1–14] to the self-complacent in exile.) The reference to those living in Egypt (v.8) has been variously understood. To understand them as those involved in the events of chapters 43 and 44 is to leap too far ahead in the narrative of the book. A number of scholars suggest that those living in Egypt were Jews who were deported with Jehoahaz to Egypt by Pharaoh Neco (cf. 2 Kings 23:31–34). Others suggest that they were emigrants who were opposed to the Babylonian domination of Judah or fled to Egypt at the first approach of Nebuchadnezzar. Another proposal is that they were fugitives from Judah who went to Egypt during various wars. Since details are lacking, it is impossible to rule out any of these possibilities. Archaeological research does, however, reveal that those who remained in Egypt set up a rival temple later on; the Elephantiné Papyri confirm a Jewish colony with a temple in Egypt before 525 B.C. (so Myers et al.).

9–10 The doom awaiting the Jews in Judah and Egypt is now detailed. The new exiles will witness the same privations as the previous ones had. The people had failed to repent. Those left behind became more hardened in their wickedness. The broad prediction in v.9 surely looks beyond the imminent Babylonian exile to a world-wide dispersion. The prophecy of v.10 was fulfilled in part in the Fall of Jerusalem in Nebuchadnezzar's day (cf. Deut 28:25, 37) but more so in the siege of Jerusalem by the Roman emperor Titus in A.D. 70 (cf. Matt 23:38).

5. *Prophecy of the Babylonian captivity* (25:1–38)

This chapter deals with a time of national and international ramifications. In 605 B.C. (some say 606), the Babylonians defeated the Egyptians at the Battle of Carchemish, thus bringing to an end the domination of Palestine by Pharaoh Neco of Egypt. Carchemish was one of the decisive battles of the world because it affected the course of history in western Asia. Through it Jeremiah was enabled by the Lord to see the working out of the divine purposes of judgment on Judah by means of Babylon. Some scholars hold that this chapter belongs chronologically between chapters 35 and 36 (so Clarke). It was written at the time when Jeremiah dictated his messages to Baruch (36:1–4). Not only is chapter 25 important historically, geographically, and prophetically, it is also remarkable for the abundance of its ideas, the variety of its figures, and the diversity of its style in treating the same theme of sin, repentance, and judgment. It is without parallel in world literature.

a. *Israel's rejection of the prophetic ministry*

25:1–7

> ¹The word came to Jeremiah concerning all the people of Judah in the fourth year of Jehoiakim son of Josiah king of Judah, which was the first year of Nebuchadnezzar king of Babylon. ²So Jeremiah the prophet said to all the people of Judah and to all those living in Jerusalem: ³For twenty-three years—from the thirteenth year of Josiah son of Amon king of Judah until this very day—the word of the LORD has come to me and I have spoken to you again and again, but you have not listened.
>
> ⁴And though the LORD has sent you all his servants the prophets again and again, you have not listened or paid any attention. ⁵They said, "Turn now, each of you, from your evil ways and your evil practices, and you can stay in the land the LORD gave to you and your fathers for ever and ever. ⁶Do not follow other gods to serve and worship them; do not provoke me to anger with what your hands have made. Then I will not harm you."
>
> ⁷"But you did not listen to me," declares the LORD, "and you have provoked me with what your hands have made, and you have brought harm to yourselves."

1 This prophecy is precisely dated to show its extraordinary significance. The fourth year of Jehoiakim synchronizes with the first year of Nebuchadnezzar (cf. 36:1; 45:1; 46:2), namely, 605 B.C. This verse and Daniel 1:1 are not in conflict. Archaeology has shown that there were two methods of chronological reckoning in the Near East—by accession year and by nonaccession year. Judah used the first method; Babylon, the second (so Harrison; cf. Edwin R. Thiele, *The Mysterious Numbers of the Hebrew Kings* [1951; rev. ed., Grand Rapids: Eerdmans, 1965], pp. 6–7, 17 et al.). The first year of Nebuchadnezzar marked his first invasion of Judah with his allies (cf. 2 Kings 24:1–2). It also began an important era in redemption history—the Times of the Gentiles (cf. Luke 21:24)—because his reign began the succession of the four great kingdoms that exercised world dominion (cf. Dan 2, 7). The emphasis in vv.1–7 rests on Israel's continued disobedience. Jeremiah's purpose was to lead the nation to reconsider her past sinful ways and to alert her to the future. The Lord's patience with Israel had at last been exhausted.

2–7 That Jeremiah could address all in Jerusalem and Judah shows that he was still able to move about freely and speak publicly (v.2; cf. 36:1, 5, 26). Sad indeed it must have been for Jeremiah to look back on twenty-three years of faithful, earnest ministry for the Lord and then to have to pronounce it a failure as far as Judah was concerned (v.3). Nineteen years under Josiah and four under Jehoiakim (Jehoahaz and Jehoiachin ruled only three months each) did not suffice to turn Judah to repentance; she would not hear. It was now about the middle of Jeremiah's career (cf. 1:2–3), and more difficult days lay ahead. Moreover, in his grace the Lord had sent some other godly prophets contemporary with Jeremiah to warn Judah of the impending disaster (v.4). There were Uriah, Zephaniah, and Habakkuk. At the heart of the message of all true prophets was the appeal to God (v.5), lest the nation jeopardize the blessings of God and the privilege of living in the Promised Land. Above all, the people were repeatedly exhorted to forsake the senseless worship of idols (v.6); but their response was always the same—persistent obstinacy (v.7).

Notes

1 The first year of Nebuchadnezzar was a significant year in the history of redemption and of the world (cf. Dan 2–4 with Luke 21:24). The great Jewish commentator Rashi (A.D. 1040–1105) wrote: "In this year their exile was finally decreed; yet before it was actualized, Jeremiah was bidden to make one more appeal to the people that they might repent and avert their doom" (cited in Freedman).

b. Prediction of the Exile

25:8–11

8Therefore the LORD Almighty says this: "Because you have not listened to my words, 9I will summon all the peoples of the north and my servant Nebuchadnezzar king of Babylon," declares the LORD, "and I will bring them against this land and its inhabitants and against all the surrounding nations. I will completely destroy them and make them an object of horror and scorn, and an everlasting ruin. 10I will banish from them the sounds of joy and gladness, the voices of bride and bridegroom, the sound of millstones and the light of the lamp. 11This whole country will become a desolate wasteland, and these nations will serve the king of Babylon seventy years."

8–9 Because of Israel's determined disobedience (v.8), the Lord had his agent of judgment ready to inflict the merited judgment (v.9). That agent was Nebuchadnezzar and his followers. The reference to "peoples of the north" has been variously explained. These people have been interpreted as being the allies of the king of Babylon, the many nations comprising the Babylonian Empire, subunits or divisions of a tribe, a political unit, or the Babylonians in general. Perhaps the last is the best interpretation because it best suits the context. Nebuchadnezzar is designated three times (here; 27:6; 43:10) as the Lord's servant. (See the parallel usage for Cyrus [Isa 44:28; 45:1].) The characterization of Nebuchadnezzar as the Lord's servant shows the magnitude of the work committed to him. It was not so much that God's pleasure was on him but that as the Lord's instrument he was to execute the divine plan for Judah and the nations. He was unconsciously doing God's will by devoting whole populations to destruction (haḥᵃramtîm, lit., "I will put them under the ban"), whether Judah or the surrounding nations.

10–11 Specifically, Jeremiah points out the domestic effects of invasion (v.10). Normal life will be totally disrupted. The land will be shorn of its inhabitants. All joy and domestic work would go. Sounds of normal human activity would cease. In v.11, Jeremiah for the first time indicates the duration of the captivity in Babylon, i.e., seventy years (cf. 29:10). Most interpreters—both liberal and conservative—believe the seventy years of captivity are a round number, i.e., a normal life span (cf. Ps 90:10; Isa 23:15). It has been suggested that they were the years between 587 and 520–515 B.C. (cf. Zech 1:12), or the period from 587 to 538 B.C. (cf. 2 Chron 36:20–23; so Bright). Another proposal for the Captivity is 598 to 538 B.C., again a round number (so Hyatt).

On the other hand, there are many who take the number of years to be precise, namely, from the fourth year of Jehoiakim (the first year of Nebuchadnezzar) to the end of the Babylonian dynasty with the coming of Cyrus (cf. 2 Chron 36:21–22; Ezra 1:1–3). They hold that the reckoning must be precise because Daniel (cf. 9:1–2) went to Babylon with the first deportation and knew that he had been there seventy years. Furthermore, the number of years involved in the period of the seventy heptads of years in Daniel 9:24–27 is based on the years of the Captivity (so Henderson). Defenders of the precise period of seventy years offer a choice between 605 B.C. (or 606) and 536 B.C., when resettlement took place under Zerubbabel and Joshua; or 586 B.C., the beginning of the Babylonian captivity, and 516 B.C., the year of the completion of Zerubbabel's temple (so Archer et al.).

Of the two options for the precise-dating view, the former appears more tenable in view of the period of the three deportations, dating from Jehoiakim's reign to Jehoiachin's to Zedekiah's. One conservative authority (KD) has even spelled out the years of the New Babylonian Empire: Nebuchadnezzar (605–562 B.C., forty-three years), Evil-Merodach or Amel-Marduk (562–560 B.C., two years), Neriglissar or Nergal-šarri-uṣur (560–556 B.C., four years), Labashi-Marduk (556 B.C., nine months), and Nabonidus or Nabunaid (556–539 B.C., seventeen years), with one year between the siege of Jerusalem by Nebuchadnezzar and the death of his father, Nabopolassar, and two years of Darius the Mede, a total of sixty-nine and three-quarter years. But there seems to be no need to go to such lengths to arrive at a precise date (contra KD, who unnecessarily introduce a symbolic significance in the number, i.e., seven for perfection in God's works and ten for earthly completeness).

c. Judgment on Babylon

25:12–14

> ¹²"But when the seventy years are fulfilled, I will punish the king of Babylon and his nation, the land of the Babylonians, for their guilt," declares the Lord, "and will make it desolate forever. ¹³I will bring upon that land all the things I have spoken against it, all that are written in this book and prophesied by Jeremiah against all the nations. ¹⁴They themselves will be enslaved by many nations and great kings; I will repay them according to their deeds and the work of their hands."

12–14 The same divine principles that worked against Judah's sin will also be effective against Babylon (v.12). Its rule was terminated by the Medes and Persians under Cyrus (c. 536–535 B.C.). The threat of everlasting desolation probably looks beyond the near future to a far-distant day (so Cunliffe-Jones). Babylon was not to be punished for carrying out God's will but for her own sins (cf. 50:11–13; Isa 13:19). It is clear that God used Babylon, not because of her merit, but because of Israel's sin. After the first half of v.13 (to the word "book"), LXX inserts the material in chapters 46–51 in a different order from the Hebrew text. As already shown (see Introduction: Special Problems, pp. 15–16), LXX followed a different textual tradition, which cannot be proved to be of superior quality (so Harrison). Verse 14 indicates that Babylon will receive retribution in kind (cf. 50:29; 51:24). The "many nations" and "great kings" refer to the Medes and Persians with their many allies or tributary kings under Cyrus the Great. They would impose forced labor on the once-invincible Babylonians.

d. *The cup of God's wrath*

25:15–29

> ¹⁵This is what the LORD, the God of Israel, said to me: "Take from my hand this cup filled with the wine of my wrath and make all the nations to whom I send you drink it. ¹⁶When they drink it, they will stagger and go mad because of the sword I will send among them."
>
> ¹⁷So I took the cup from the LORD's hand and made all the nations to whom he sent me drink it: ¹⁸Jerusalem and the towns of Judah, its kings and officials, to make them a ruin and an object of horror and scorn and cursing, as they are today; ¹⁹Pharaoh king of Egypt, his attendants, his officials and all his people, ²⁰and all the foreign people there; all the kings of Uz; all the kings of the Philistines (those of Ashkelon, Gaza, Ekron, and the people left at Ashdod); ²¹Edom, Moab and Ammon; ²²all the kings of Tyre and Sidon; the kings of the coastlands across the sea; ²³Dedan, Tema, Buz and all who are in distant places; ²⁴all the kings of Arabia and all the kings of the foreign people who live in the desert; ²⁵all the kings of Zimri, Elam and Media; ²⁶and all the kings of the north, near and far, one after the other—all the kingdoms on the face of the earth. And after all of them, the king of Sheshach will drink it too.
>
> ²⁷"Then tell them, 'This is what the LORD Almighty, the God of Israel, says: Drink, get drunk and vomit, and fall to rise no more because of the sword I will send among you.' ²⁸But if they refuse to take the cup from your hand and drink, tell them, 'This is what the LORD Almighty says: You must drink it! ²⁹See, I am beginning to bring disaster on the city that bears my Name, and will you indeed go unpunished? You will not go unpunished, for I am calling down a sword upon all who live on the earth, declares the LORD Almighty.' "

15–16 This powerful passage records either a vision or a figure of speech. It is a message about God's wrath on Judah and the nations. LXX connects these verses with chapters 46–51, which deal with the oracles against the nations. It is not that the nations will be given a potion to help them endure the force of God's fury but that the cup (v.15) symbolizes his wrath. As the agent of God's fury, Nebuchadnezzar would be victorious over the nations. There is no need to believe that Jeremiah actually took a cup and went to these nations, because stupefying judgments are figured here. The cup is a common figure in Scripture to signify God's wrath (cf. 49:12; 51:7; Job 21:20; Ps 60:3; Isa 51:17, 22; Ezek 23:31; Mark 10:39; 14:36; John 18:11; Rev 14:8, 10; 16:19; 18:6). It is also a well-known symbol of God's blessing (cf. Pss 16:5; 23:5; Luke 22:17, 20; 1 Cor 10:16; 11:24–25). With the mention of the sword in v.16, fact replaces the figure. The horrors of war will drive the nations mad.

17–18 But how did Jeremiah take the cup and make all the nations drink it (v.17)? Did he journey to the several kings or give the cup to the ambassadors who were in Jerusalem, as some have suggested? Of course not! The cup is not a physical cup but the wrath of God, and the drinking is not physical. Jeremiah declared the Lord's judgment on the nations through Babylon as his instrument. The roster of the nations that will suffer judgment begins with Jerusalem and Judah. All the nations named in chapters 46–51 except Damascus are included. The list runs from south to north, from Egypt to Persia. The kings of Judah include Jehoiakim, Jehoiachin, and Zedekiah. The sins of Judah and her kings had been most offensive to God because Judah was so highly privileged. So they are the first to be mentioned. The words "as they are today" (v.18) may have been inserted by Jeremiah after the fulfillment of the prophecy.

19–22 Following Judah, Egypt is listed (v.19) because Pharaoh Neco instigated the alliance against the Babylonians. "All the foreign people" (v.20) have been understood as being the mercenaries who joined the Egyptian forces, or foreigners in general, or some of the Egyptians of mixed blood. We do not have sufficient data to be certain just who they were (cf. Herod. 2.152, 154). Uz (cf. Job 1:1) was east or northeast of Edom (so Bewer). The Philistine pentapolis, except for Gath, is mentioned next; by this time it had lost its importance (cf. 2 Chron 26:6; Amos 6:2; so Orelli). Jeremiah speaks of the remnant of Ashdod because the city was destroyed by Psammetik I (663–609 B.C.) after a siege of twenty-nine years (so Hyatt; cf. Herod. 2.157). Ashdod was rebuilt in Nehemiah's day (Neh 13:23). Edom, Moab, and Ammon (v.21), all blood relations of Israel, were in Transjordania. The main Phoenician cities, Tyre and Sidon (v.22), are named as objects of Babylon's wrath. The coastlands were the Phoenician colonies in the Mediterranean, which some have identified with Cyprus (so Payne Smith).

23–25 The Lord's judgment, begun with Israel, moves inexorably on to other nations. Now northern Arabian tribes are mentioned (v.23). Dedan, a son of Abraham by Keturah, lived southeast of Edom (cf. Gen 25:3). Tema (modern Teima, about 250 miles southeast of Edom in Arabia) was a son of Ishmael (cf. Gen 25:15; Job 6:19). Buz represents a tribe descended from Nahor, brother of Abraham (cf. Gen 22:21), who lived in northern Arabia. The last referred to are the Bedouins of the Arabian desert (v.24; cf. 9:26; 49:23). They are followed by the inhabitants of the portion of Arabia contiguous to Palestine. The "foreign people" may refer to many tribes of Arabia that had intermarried with Cushite elements. The location of Zimri (v.25) is unknown, though the name does appear elsewhere (Num 25:14; 1 Kings 16:9–20; 2 Kings 9:31; 1 Chron 2:6; 8:36; 9:42). Perhaps Zimri is to be connected with Zimran, a son of Abraham by Keturah (cf. Gen 25:2). He lived in a region between Arabia and Persia. Elam and Media were lands east of the Tigris River. The first was northeast of the Persian Gulf, about 200 miles east of Babylon, and is here representative of all Persia. It was known as Elymais by the Greeks. Media was north and west of Persia. The arm of Babylon was to reach afar to the Caspian Sea, ultimately encompassing a world-wide dominion (cf. Dan 2:38; 4:22).

26 Finally Jeremiah reaches the culminating point of the prophecy—viz., the judgment of Sheshach. Who is meant here? The name occurs only in Jeremiah. One view is that Sheshach was the name of a dynasty of the second millennium B.C., possibly from the same area as the Chaldeans. But it seems quite improbable that this was known to the Hebrews as late as Jeremiah's times (so Hyatt). Following Jerome, many hold that the name is a cipher (code) that stands for Babylon. The cipher is known as *Atbash,* a system of secret writing that substituted the last letter of the Hebrew alphabet for the first, the next to the last for the second, and so through all the Hebrew consonants (cf. v.12; 51:1, 41, where the Chaldeans are meant under "Leb Kamai"). For example, Sheshach, which has three consonants in Hebrew, is a code for Babylon in this manner: sh = b (*bis*) and ch (or k) = l. The phrase "after all of them" indicates that Babylon's judgment too will come finally. An objection to the cipher explanation is that in chapter 25 Jeremiah has already mentioned Babylon by name. Why then use a code to hide its identity? However, Jeremiah might have resorted to the code name while Nebuchadnezzar was at the gates of Jerusalem.

27-29 This passage underscores the inevitability of the judgment Jeremiah has been describing (v.27). The same divine governmental principles apply to the other nations just as they do to Israel. The meaning of the cup metaphor (v.28) is set forth. In a series of staccato commands, the Lord addresses all the aforementioned nations. They must be reduced to utter helplessness. Should any nation be so foolish as to seek to resist the will of God through Babylon, it will be futile. With irresistible logic God asks, as it were (v.29), "If Israel suffers, will you nations escape?" It will be impossible for any people to escape destruction for their sins. This *a fortiori* argument also occurs in Ezekiel 9:6 and even more clearly in 1 Peter 4:17.

Notes

15 Hebrew grammar does not allow כּוֹס הַיַּיִן הַחֵמָה הַזֹּאת (*kôs hayyayin hahēmāh hazzō't*) to be translated "the cup of the wine of wrath" (NIV, "this cup filled with the wine of my wrath"), for it would require the construct יֵין (*yên,* "wine of ") (so Syr., Vul.). Literally, the phrase reads "the cup of wine, this wrath." A possibility would be to understand the nouns as in apposition, thus, "this cup of wine [that is], this cup of wrath." Bright (p. 161) says: "The origin of the figure is uncertain. It may lie (Weiser) in an old sacral tradition having to do with passing judgment (Ps lxxv.8f [7f.E]), perhaps in the practice of ordeal (cf. Num v.11-31), which required a person suspected of crime to drink a noxious potion, with disastrous results to him if guilty. Or is it merely a 'knockout drop' (to render insensate) given to a person marked for execution to render him incapable of struggle?" (cf. Zech 12:2, though the phrase is סַף רַעַל (*sap ra'al,* "basin," "bowl of reeling"). Symbolic use indicates an apportionment from God to man, whether in wrath (as here) or in joy (Ps 23:5).

e. *Judgment on all the world*

25:30-38

³⁰"Now prophesy all these words against them and say to them:

" 'The LORD will roar from on high;
    he will lift his voice from his holy dwelling
    and roar mightily against his land.
He will shout like those who tread the grapes,
    shout against all who live on the earth.
31The tumult will resound to the ends of the earth,
    for the LORD will bring charges against the nations;
he will bring judgment on all mankind
    and put the wicked to the sword,' "

                      declares the LORD.

32This is what the LORD Almighty says:

"Look! Disaster is spreading
    from nation to nation;
a mighty storm is rising
    from the ends of the earth."

33At that time those slain by the LORD will be everywhere—from one end of the earth to the other. They will not be mourned or gathered up or buried, but will be like refuse lying on the ground.

34Weep and wail, you shepherds;
    roll in the dust, you leaders of the flock.
For your time to be slaughtered has come;
    you will fall and be shattered like fine pottery.
35The shepherds will have nowhere to flee,
    the leaders of the flock no place to escape.
36Hear the cry of the shepherds,
    the wailing of the leaders of the flock,
    for the LORD is destroying their pasture.
37The peaceful meadows will be laid waste
    because of the fierce anger of the LORD.
38Like a lion he will leave.his lair,
    and their land will become desolate
because of the sword of the oppressor
    and because of the LORD's fierce anger.

30–33 In vivid poetry Jeremiah restates vv.27–29. Turning from the metaphor of the cup, he uses the metaphor of the lion (v.30; cf. v.38). Like a lion's roar, the Lord's voice sounds from heaven against his own fold—the Holy Land and its people. Again, judgment begins with Judah. Suddenly the imagery shifts to a vintage scene, which was always attended with shouts of rejoicing (cf. Isa 9:3; 16:10). The shouting symbolizes a war cry; here it becomes the shout of the Lord treading down the nations (cf. Isa 63:3; Rev 14:19–20; 19:15). The noise (v.31) is like the trampling of an army; it is the crash of war (cf. Amos 2:2). Again changing the figure, Jeremiah portrays a lawsuit (v.31; cf. 2:9; 12:1) in which God is both prosecutor and judge of all the nations. Then he takes another metaphor of judgment from nature (v.32)—namely, that of a tempest (i.e., Nebuchadnezzar). Nation after nation will fall under the domination of Babylon. Then in plain prose (v.33), Jeremiah describes the appalling scene of the multitudes of unburied dead.

34–38 At once Jeremiah reverts to poetry, as he returns three times to the shepherd metaphor for the leaders of the nation (cf. vv.34, 35, 36). In each instance the shepherds are called "leaders of the flock"—in short, the elite of the nation. They are to weep, wail, and cover themselves as thickly with dust as though they had rolled in it (v.34). The hour of reckoning has come so that only slaughter and dispersion remain for them. Jeremiah, great writer that he is, moves from the figure of a flock of sheep to that of "fine pottery" smashed by a fall. Some interpreters have found difficulty with this figure. RSV, following LXX, by a slight change in consonants translates the figure "like choice rams" instead of "like fine pottery" on the ground that the ram figure fits the context better than the pottery one. But this is conjectural and has no MS authority. Moreover, other versions have the usual reading. Also, in 22:28 Jeremiah used the pottery figure of Coniah. Although rams fit the context of shepherds and flock, the emendation goes poorly with the verb "fall." Flight from the calamity will be out of the question (v.35). The leaders will be inconsolable because with the decimation of the flock their pastures will be destroyed (v.36). Even the peaceful land will suffer the ravages of the Lord's anger (v.37). In v.38 Jeremiah returns to the lion metaphor. As a lion abandons a den that has been destroyed, so the Lord will abandon his own land after he has devastated it with the sword of the oppressive invader.

Notes

30–38 These verses are denied Jeremiah by some (so Hyatt) because the language is said to be too apocalyptic for him and the poetry less original than would be expected of Jeremiah. In view of the wide range of style and subject matter in Jeremiah's prophecies, it is overly subjective to deny him this portion.

34 A suggested reading for וּתְפוֹצוֹתִיכֶם (ûtᵉpôṣôtîkem, lit., "and I will break you in pieces"; NIV, "you will . . . be shattered") is ûtᵉpûṣōtêkem ("and your dispersions [are at hand]").

38 The phrase חֲרוֹן הַיּוֹנָה (ḥᵃrôn hayyônāh, "anger of the oppressor") troubled translators and interpreters alike. The Hebrew text is difficult with its double use of the word "anger." A score of Hebrew MSS, the LXX, Vulgate, and Targum read חֶרֶב (ḥereb, "sword") for ḥᵃrôn. Thus with hayyônāh (Qal act. part. used substantively and collectively), the reading is "the sword of the oppressor(s)" (so NIV).

6. *Consequences of the temple address* (26:1–24)

Chapters 26–45 combine incidents in the life of Jeremiah. Some are autobiographical (cf. the first personal pronoun); others are biographical (cf. the third personal pronoun). This chapter (26) gives us the setting of the temple address (7:1–20). Almost all commentators connect that address with the one in chapter 26, even though some say that no relationship is demanded since Jeremiah often repeated material in his messages and frequently spoke in the temple (so KD). But the affinities between chapters 7 and 26 are too many and too minute for them not to relate to the same address. Here in chapter 26 the emphasis is on the results of the temple address and on a brief summary of it. In a sense, the first verses of this chapter give us a condensation of chapters 7–10. The heart of the temple address was that unless Judah repented, Jerusalem would be as Shiloh. By his specific warnings, Jeremiah had incurred the wrath of the false prophets and their followers. And later on when he predicted the seventy years' captivity, they tried to bring about his death.

a. *The temple address*

26:1–6

> ¹Early in the reign of Jehoiakim son of Josiah king of Judah, this word came from the LORD: ²"This is what the LORD says: Stand in the courtyard of the LORD's house and speak to all the people of the towns of Judah who come to worship in the house of the LORD. Tell them everything I command you; do not omit a word. ³Perhaps they will listen and each will turn from his evil way. Then I will relent and not bring on them the disaster I was planning because of the evil they have done. ⁴Say to them, 'This is what the LORD says: If you do not listen to me and follow my law, which I have set before you, ⁵and if you do not listen to the words of my servants the prophets, whom I have sent to you again and again (though you have not listened), ⁶then I will make this house like Shiloh and this city an object of cursing among all the nations of the earth.' "

1–3 The Lord gave the prophet specific orders as to where and when he would address the nation and what he would say to them. The date in v. 1 is chronologically earlier than that of 25:1. Most modern expositors connect the beginning of Jehoiakim's reign with his accession year, a date of 609–608 B.C. (so Bright et al.). To give the greatest publicity to his message, Jeremiah was charged to stand in the outer court (v. 2; cf. 19:14), where the people assembled. It was doubtless a feast day when the people from the towns of Judah came together for worship. Furthermore, Jeremiah was not to omit a word of his message for fear of the consequences of his preaching. Nor was he to trim it to suit the feelings of his hearers. Notice how the words "perhaps . . . each will turn from his evil way" (v. 3) show that the repentance the Lord demands is always an individual matter. Predictions of divine judgment are conditional. The true repentance of the people of Judah at any time before the hour of doom would have been met by God's willingness to relent from his threatened punishment.

4–6 Here we have a kind of précis of the longer address in chapter 7. Perhaps because of their very succinctness, vv. 4–6 convey a clearer note of pleading than chapter 7 does. In the précis three things stand out: (1) the necessity of obeying God's law (v. 4) if the coming punishment is to be averted; (2) Jeremiah's alignment with other prophets in Judah who had preached repentance or judgment (v. 5); and (3) the unrelieved gravity of the sentence on the temple and on the city of Jerusalem (v. 6). Shiloh was not far from Jerusalem; the people could see the evidences of its destruction (c. 1050 B.C.)—a destruction that overtook it even though it had been the first resting place of the ark of the covenant in the land. Even worse, Jerusalem and Judah would become notorious among the nations as an example of God's execration. Debased before the nations, Jerusalem would be an object lesson of the consequences of incurring God's wrath. What a contrast to the promise in Genesis 12:3!

Notes

---

1 The phrase רֵאשִׁית מַמְלְכוּת (*rēʾšîṯ mamlᵉḵûṯ*, "early in the reign") is not a vague expression in the Akkadian *rēš šarrūti*, which is a technical designation for the time between a king's accession and the following New Year, when his first regnal year was reckoned (so Bright).

---

b. *The arrest, trial, and condemnation of Jeremiah*

26:7–11

> [7]The priests, the prophets and all the people heard Jeremiah speak these words in the house of the LORD. [8]But as soon as Jeremiah finished telling all the people everything the LORD had commanded him to say, the priests, the prophets and all the people seized him and said, "You must die! [9]Why do you prophesy in the LORD's name that this house will be like Shiloh and this city will be desolate and deserted?" And all the people crowded around Jeremiah in the house of the LORD.
>
> [10]When the officials of Judah heard about these things, they went up from the royal palace to the house of the LORD and took their places at the entrance of the New Gate of the LORD's house. [11]Then the priests and the prophets said to the officials and all the people, "This man should be sentenced to death because he has prophesied against this city. You have heard it with your own ears!"

7–9 The people listened in hushed respect till Jeremiah had finished speaking (v.7), shocking though his words were. Even the priests and false prophets did not interrupt him. LXX calls these prophets (vv.7–8, 11, 16) "pseudoprophets." But once Jeremiah had concluded, the pent-up fury of the crowd broke loose (v.8). He was arrested and the death penalty pronounced on him. The priests, prophets, and people refused to believe his seemingly incredible prediction (v.9). For them it was blasphemy and false prophecy—both of which were crimes punishable by death in accordance with the law of Moses (cf. Deut 18:20). It is clear that the priests and false prophets were at the forefront of the opposition to Jeremiah. They were angered because they had consistently promised immunity to the city and sanctuary, relying on God's past deliverances as in Hezekiah's day (cf. Isa 37:36–37).

10–11 So great was the tumult around Jeremiah that the court officials, hearing of the mob's fury, hurried from the palace to the temple (v.10). It was indeed a timely move because the tumult could easily have led to Jeremiah's death. So the officials took their places where trials were held (cf. 2 Kings 15:35)—viz., at the "New Gate" (perhaps the Upper Gate built by Jotham [cf. 20:2]). The priests and false prophets, with their vested interest in the situation, were the leaders of the opposition against Jeremiah. Acting as the prosecution, they announced the verdict beforehand (v.11). It was (literally trans'ated) "A judgment of death belongs to this man!" Although Jeremiah had spoken against both the temple and the city, his accusers referred only to his words against the city. This gave their charge a political slant and appealed to those who heard the message.

Notes

9 The fall of Shiloh to the Philistines is clearly stated in 1 Sam 4:10, but apart from Ps 78:60–61, where the wording is "abandoned the tabernacle of Shiloh," the Scriptures are silent on the destruction of Shiloh (Arabic Seilûn) in the inheritance of Ephraim. Archaeology has supplied the information for the lacuna here, through the labors of Danish archaeologists, who place the destruction of the city about 1050 B.C.

539

10 The "New Gate" is identified in the Targum on Jeremiah as "the gate of the house of the temple of the Lord, the eastern."

---

c. *Jeremiah's defense*

26:12–15

> ¹²Then Jeremiah said to all the officials and all the people: "The LORD sent me to prophesy against this house and this city all the things you have heard. ¹³Now reform your ways and your actions and obey the LORD your God. Then the LORD will relent and not bring the disaster he has pronounced against you. ¹⁴As for me, I am in your hands; do with me whatever you think is good and right. ¹⁵Be assured, however, that if you put me to death, you will bring the guilt of innocent blood on yourselves and on this city and on those who live in it, for in truth the LORD has sent me to you to speak all these words in your hearing."

12–13 The prophet defended the message directly, courageously, and appropriately. Nowhere in the book does he appear in a better light than here. He did not trim his message. He did not cower and beg for mercy. His defense was always the same: God had sent him to deliver the controversial message (v. 12). Jeremiah stated the source of his message. He did not deny the truth he had preached; instead, he stressed its origin and authority. Their contention would have to be with God, for it was solely his message (cf. Acts 5:39). Then, probably quite unexpectantly, Jeremiah called them to repentance (v. 13). He was not a man to be diverted from the central issue, and he stuck to it with unswerving fidelity. He clearly informed the leaders and the people that there was still time for repentance. Though from the death of Josiah till the Fall of Jerusalem conditions in Judah varied little if at all, yet Jeremiah unwearyingly held out the only hope God offered his sinful people.

14–15 In the hour of trial, Jeremiah's courage and fidelity to God shone brightly. He did not plead for his life (v. 14). He recognized the ability of his enemies to carry out the death sentence against him but warned them of the consequence of killing him (v. 15). He knew that he faced imminent death; but he also knew that he had done no wrong, let alone committed any capital crime (cf. Matt 27:24–25; Acts 5:28).

d. *The release of Jeremiah*

26:16–19

> ¹⁶Then the officials and all the people said to the priests and the prophets, "This man should not be sentenced to death! He has spoken to us in the name of the LORD our God."
>
> ¹⁷Some of the elders of the land stepped forward and said to the entire assembly of people, ¹⁸"Micah of Moresheth prophesied in the days of Hezekiah king of Judah. He told all the people of Judah, 'This is what the LORD Almighty says:
>
> > " 'Zion will be plowed like a field,
> > Jerusalem will become a heap of rubble,
> > the temple hill a mound overgrown with thickets.'
>
> ¹⁹"Did Hezekiah king of Judah or anyone else in Judah put him to death? Did not Hezekiah fear the LORD and seek his favor? And did not the LORD relent, so

that he did not bring the disaster he pronounced against them? We are about to bring a terrible disaster on ourselves!"

16–19 The prophet's honesty and conviction by the Spirit gripped the hearts of the civil officials and the people (v. 16). They sided with Jeremiah against the priests and false prophets. The judges and people were freer of prejudice than the religious leaders. They saw in Jeremiah what he claimed to be: God's spokesman. To the shame of the priests, the laymen alone realized the prophet was bound to preach what the Lord had committed to him. At this point the elders of the land added their confirmation to what had been expressed in v. 16. The term "elders" (v. 17) did not designate official status but only the fact that they were men of advanced age. They cited as a precedent the case of Micah (v. 18) in the days of Hezekiah (eighth century B.C.). A direct citation like this occurs nowhere else in the prophetic literature (cf. Mic 3:12; see also 2 Kings 18:3–6). Micah had lived more than a century before. He also prophesied about the destruction of the temple. As in law cases, citing a precedent carried weight. The reference to this prophecy turned the tide for Jeremiah.

Micah was a native of Moresheth, identified by Eusebius as a village east of Eleutheropolis (so Streane), about twenty-three miles southwest of Jerusalem. It is possible that Micah was as influential in the reforms of Hezekiah as Isaiah was (cf. 2 Kings 18:3–6). Micah's warning message bore fruit. Hezekiah and his people heeded the Lord's words and turned to him instead of threatening Micah's life (v. 19). Thus the calamity was averted from Judah in that day. The people saw the possibility of averting judgment by repenting.

The argument from precedent was successful. Though it is not explicitly stated, Jeremiah was acquitted by the civil leaders. They saw the enormity of the guilt that would be incurred by mistreating the Lord's messenger.

Notes

19 וַיְחַל אֶת־פְּנֵי יהוה (*wayᵉḥal 'et-pᵉnê* YHWH) is a vivid anthropomorphism for seeking the Lord's favor (so NIV) that literally means "and he will stroke the face of the LORD."

e. *The murder of Uriah*

26:20–24

20(Now Uriah son of Shemaiah from Kiriath Jearim was another man who prophesied in the name of the LORD; he prophesied the same things against this city and this land as Jeremiah did. 21When King Jehoiakim and all his officers and officials heard his words, the king sought to put him to death. But Uriah heard of it and fled in fear to Egypt. 22King Jehoiakim, however, sent Elnathan son of Acbor to Egypt, along with some other men. 23They brought Uriah out of Egypt and took him to King Jehoiakim, who had him struck down with a sword and his body thrown into the burial place of the common people.)
24Furthermore, Ahikam son of Shaphan supported Jeremiah, and so he was not handed over to the people to be put to death.

20–24 Some scholars think that Jeremiah's accusers quoted this incident to justify what they intended to do to the prophet (so Freedman). The passage can scarcely be the words of Jeremiah's opponents because there is no introductory formula. We do not know when the events here narrated took place. Not all faithful preaching had the same results as Jeremiah's. Uriah's situation turned out differently, and he paid for his preaching with his life. But for the Lord's intervention, this could have been Jeremiah's fate also (cf. 36:26). Jeremiah did not, however, run from his mission.

God does not always grant immunity to his servants. Uriah (mentioned only here) was a true prophet (v.20) from Kiriath Jearim, a town identified with Karyet-el-Enab, seven miles northwest of Jerusalem on the road to Jaffa (cf. Josh 9:17; 1 Sam 7:2). His message agreed with Jeremiah's preaching. When Jehoiakim and his military leaders heard Uriah's words, their intense hatred of the truth sought an outlet in slaying Uriah; but he escaped to Egypt, the natural refuge for fugitives from Palestine (v.21). At this time rights of extradition prevailed between Egypt and Judah because Jehoiakim was a vassal of Egypt. International treaties in the ancient Near East called for extradition; it was part of vassalage terms imposed by Egypt. The head of the embassy to implement the extradition was Elnathan (v.22). Perhaps this was the Elnathan of 2 Kings 24:8, grandfather of Jehoiachin and father-in-law of Jehoiakim—a man of status (cf. 36:12, 25). If so, his father, Acbor, was one of the deputation in 2 Kings 22:12.

Once extradited, Uriah was slain and dishonored by burial in a common cemetery, not in a family sepulcher (v.23). He was denied due process of law and the elementary right of burial with his ancestors. For OT prophets assassination was infrequent (cf. 1 Kings 18:13; 2 Chron 24:20–22). That Jehoiakim had no part in Jeremiah's case may mean it occurred early in his reign, before he gained influence over the civil leaders. Even though Jeremiah had been acquitted, he was still in danger. Ahikam (v.24), an official under Josiah (cf. 2 Kings 22:12, 14) and father of Gedaliah, governor of Judah under Nebuchadnezzar after the Fall of Jerusalem in 586 B.C. (cf. 39:14; 40:13–41:3; 2 Kings 25:22), espoused his cause. And Ahikam's prominence helped secure Jeremiah's release.

Notes

20 It is a mistake to think that true prophets preached their messages without the cooperation of contemporary fellow prophets. As in Isaiah's day, when Hosea, Micah, and Amos also ministered, so in his day Jeremiah was not the sole voice for God. Unfortunately, Uriah fled to Egypt, which gave his enemies ground for an accusation of sedition, an offense punishable by death. We are not to conclude that the events of vv.20–23 were recited in defense of Jeremiah's preaching, hence the parentheses in the English text. The Israeli archaeologist Tur Sinai (formerly Torczyner) identified Uriah with an unnamed prophet mentioned in Ostracon III of the Lachish Letters (cf. D.W. Thomas, ed., *Documents from Old Testament Times* [New York: Thomas Nelson, 1958], pp. 214–15). But without more evidence, the equation cannot be sustained (so Harrison).

7. The yoke of Babylon (27:1–22)

Most scholars believe that chapters 27–29 are linked in background and contents. Chapters 27–28 attack the false optimism of the prophets of Judah and are dated by the majority of scholars in the fourth year of Zedekiah (594–593 B.C.). Foreign envoys were coming to Jerusalem to promote a confederacy against Nebuchadnezzar. Neighboring countries were apparently trying to involve Judah in a rebellion against Babylon, an enterprise encouraged by the false prophets at Jerusalem. The contemplated rebellion failed because of Nebuchadnezzar's forthright action. Chapters 27–29 were written to dispel the erroneous view that Babylon was just a passing power, not to be reckoned with. From 51:59 we may infer that Zedekiah was called to Babylon to explain what part he had in the unsuccessful plot against Nebuchadnezzar.

a. The message to the ambassadors

27:1–11

> ¹Early in the reign of Zedekiah son of Josiah king of Judah, this word came to Jeremiah from the LORD: ²This is what the LORD said to me: "Make a yoke out of straps and crossbars and put it on your neck. ³Then send word to the kings of Edom, Moab, Ammon, Tyre and Sidon through the envoys who have come to Jerusalem to Zedekiah king of Judah. ⁴Give them a message for their masters and say, 'This is what the LORD Almighty, the God of Israel, says: "Tell this to your masters: ⁵With my great power and outstretched arm I made the earth and its people and the animals that are on it, and I give it to anyone I please. ⁶Now I will hand all your countries over to my servant Nebuchadnezzar king of Babylon; I will make even the wild animals subject to him. ⁷All nations will serve him and his son and his grandson until the time for his land comes; then many nations and great kings will subjugate him.
>
> ⁸" ' "If, however, any nation or kingdom will not serve Nebuchadnezzar king of Babylon or bow its neck under his yoke, I will punish that nation with the sword, famine and plague, declares the LORD, until I destroy it by his hand. ⁹So do not listen to your prophets, your diviners, your interpreters of dreams, your mediums or your sorcerers who tell you, 'You will not serve the king of Babylon.' ¹⁰They prophesy lies to you that will only serve to remove you far from your lands; I will banish you and you will perish. ¹¹But if any nation will bow its neck under the yoke of the king of Babylon and serve him, I will let that nation remain in its own land to till it and to live there, declares the LORD." ' "

1 In this verse most MSS read "Jehoiakim" (so also KJV, ASV [but cf. mg.]). This, however, is obviously a scribal error for Zedekiah. Three Hebrew MSS, the Syriac, and the Arabic versions read "Zedekiah." That the name Jehoiakim is a later interpolation is clear from vv.3, 12, 20, and 28:1. The interpolation may reflect an attempt to bring v.1 into conformity with 26:1. All of v.1 is lacking in the LXX, which differs widely from the Hebrew text in this chapter and the next one.

2 With Judah on the verge of revolt against Babylon, God spoke to Jeremiah and commanded him to make a yoke and place it on his neck. Some have suggested that he merely did this in a vision; if so, the force of the message was largely lost. But there is no reason to deny that Jeremiah really did what the Lord commanded. The yoke, similar to that used for oxen, was made of wooden bars held together by leather thongs. According to 28:10, Jeremiah was wearing the yoke when Hananiah challenged him. A yoke was a symbol of submission, servitude, and captivity (cf. 1 Kings 22:11; Ezek 7:23).

3 There is no need to insist that Jeremiah made a yoke for each king named in this verse and had the ambassadors deliver the yokes any more than there is to insist that the cup of wrath (ch. 25) was passed around among the nations. It is clear that Jeremiah actually wore the yoke in public, because Hananiah broke it (28:10–11). As has already been said, Jeremiah did not make duplicate yokes to be sent to the kings represented in the conclave (contra Freedman et al.). He did, however, convey to the kings the message of the yoke. Their envoys had assembled to plan how to shake off the yoke of Babylon; so the yoke symbol was highly appropriate. Jeremiah required great courage to stand against these envoys as well as his own countrymen, but Jeremiah was exercising his commission as a prophet to the nations (cf. 1:10). Smaller nations often revolted against their Mesopotamian conquerors, often with the help and prodding of Egypt, but they seldom did it with success. Through Jeremiah the Lord is charging them all that it is his will for them to submit to Nebuchadnezzar for their own good. The enumeration of the kings is from south (Edom, Moab, Ammon) to north (the Phoenician cities of Tyre and Sidon). The rebellion of the smaller nations may have been activated by the accession of Psammetik II as Pharaoh of Egypt. (For an acted parable similar to Jeremiah's yoke, see Isa 20.)

4–7 The message the envoys took back to their kings (v.4) was that the sovereign Creator of the universe had the right to give the dominion of earth to whomever he pleased (v.5). Revolt was futile and wrong because God had appointed Babylon to execute his purpose of judgment. Resistance, then, was useless because Nebuchadnezzar was God's instrument (cf. Isa 44:28 for God's use of Cyrus). To resist the known will of God is always spiritual suicide. Nebuchadnezzar's dominion was vast, extending even to the animals of the field (v.6). As to its duration, Babylonian rule would extend from Nebuchadnezzar to the third generation (v.7). It passed from him to Evil-Merodach and Belshazzar (52:31; Dan 5:1, 30). Thus the Babylonian threat was not to be only temporary, as the false prophets glibly promised. When the appointed time came for the termination of Babylonian supremacy, the rulers of Persia, Media, and contiguous areas finally overthrew it. God is Creator of the universe and Administrator in the affairs of the nations.

8–11 Here Jeremiah points out the danger of disobedience to this program of God. The meaning of the yoke is explained in v.8. Those resisting the Babylonian power, as the coalition was planning to do, would be punished by the threefold stroke of sword, famine, and plague—well-known results of war. Above all, the prophecies of the false prophets were not to be trusted, for they were dealing in lies that would only lead the nation to disaster. Moved by the knowledge of God's message and its authority, Jeremiah did not shrink from opposing the whole array of false leaders in all the countries (so Cundall). The five kinds of foretellers mentioned in v.9 all helped forward the policy of rebellion. They represented various pagan methods of prognostication among the heathen. The result for Judah would be deportation (v.10), a policy the Assyrians had used for Israel and one the Babylonians would use for Judah. In time of national crisis, religious fakers always flourish because many people want to hear only comforting messages, which may often be untrue (cf.

2 Tim 4:3–4). But nations that obey God will remain in peace in their lands and will prosper (v.11).

Notes

6 The term עַבְדִּי (*'aḇdî*, "my servant") has several possible connotations: (1) a servant of God as a prophet (Num 12:7–8); (2) all Israel (Isa 42:19); (3) the remnant in Israel (Isa 41:8–10); (4) a godly individual, not necessarily of Israel (Job 1:8); (5) the Messiah, the Servant par excellence (Isa 42:1; 49:3; 50:4–9; 52:13–53:12); (6) a scion of the Davidic dynasty (Hag 2:23); and finally, (7) even unbelieving rulers, who also derive their authority from God— e.g., Cyrus (Isa 45:1) and Nebuchadnezzar (Jer 27:6)—and are his instruments to carry out his will (cf. Rom 13:1). Interestingly, in the LXX *'aḇdî* is either omitted or altered whenever it refers to Nebuchadnezzar (cf. 27:6; 43:10).

7 בְּנוֹ וְאֶת־בֶּן בְּנוֹ (*bᵉnô wᵉ'eṯ-ben bᵉnô*, "his son and the son of his son"; NIV, "his son and his grandson") is not Jeremiah's way of indicating the length of the Babylonian dynasty. The emphasis is rather on the comparatively long period of time of the Babylonian captivity, which should underscore the falsity of the prediction (v.16) of the near restoration of the articles of the Lord's house.

b. The address to King Zedekiah

27:12–15

¹²I gave the same message to Zedekiah king of Judah. I said, "Bow your neck under the yoke of the king of Babylon; serve him and his people, and you will live. ¹³Why will you and your people die by the sword, famine and plague with which the LORD has threatened any nation that will not serve the king of Babylon? ¹⁴Do not listen to the words of the prophets who say to you, 'You will never serve the king of Babylon,' for they are prophesying lies to you. ¹⁵'I have not sent them' declares the LORD. 'They are prophesying lies in my name. Therefore, I will banish you and you will perish, both you and the prophets who prophesy to you.' "

12–15 The warning already extended to the envoys of the nations is now directed to Zedekiah (v.12). Here we have the meaning of the yoke (v.2) for the Davidic king. The thrust of the message is Zedekiah's submission to the Babylonians. He was a weak and ambivalent ruler who could never carry through a resolve to follow the Lord wholly. The reference to "necks" (Heb. pl.) relates to both king and people. Zedekiah is exhorted not to choose the way of resistance and disobedience, which can only bring disaster with it (v.13). So powerful was the influence of the false prophets at this time that the king had to be counseled to ignore their lying pronouncements (v.14). God never sent them; they predicted lies; the result of their advice could only be exile for the nation (v.15). To underestimate the power of a lie in times of national distress is sheer folly.

c. The warning to the priests and people

27:16–22

¹⁶Then I said to the priests and all these people, "This is what the LORD says: Do not listen to the prophets who say, 'Very soon now the articles from the LORD's

house will be brought back from Babylon.' They are prophesying lies to you. ¹⁷Do not listen to them. Serve the king of Babylon, and you will live. Why should this city become a ruin? ¹⁸If they are prophets and have the word of the LORD, let them plead with the LORD Almighty that the furnishings remaining in the house of the LORD and in the palace of the king of Judah and in Jerusalem not be taken to Babylon. ¹⁹For this is what the LORD Almighty says about the pillars, the Sea, the movable stands and the other furnishings that are left in this city, ²⁰which Nebuchadnezzar king of Babylon did not take away when he carried Jehoiachin son of Jehoiakim king of Judah into exile from Jerusalem to Babylon, along with all the nobles of Judah and Jerusalem— ²¹yes, this is what the LORD Almighty, the God of Israel, says about the things that are left in the house of the LORD and in the palace of the king of Judah and in Jerusalem: ²²'They will be taken to Babylon and there they will remain until the day I come for them,' declares the LORD. 'Then I will bring them back and restore them to this place.' "

16–18 So vital was the message of Jeremiah at this time that it had to be repeated to the priests and people also (v.16). The false prophets were holding out baseless hopes that the temple vessels taken to Babylon were soon to be returned. This was a powerful incentive for Judah to revolt against the Babylonians, but Jeremiah reiterated the necessity of submitting to Nebuchadnezzar (v.17). The prophets of "peace" thought that their words would be more effective if they referred to details like the temple objects. The vessels were originally made by Solomon but were doubtless added to through the years by gifts from the people (cf. 1 Kings 7:15, 23, 27, 48–50). Some were carried away in the deportation of Jehoiakim (cf. 2 Chron 36:5–7), and even more were carried away in 597 B.C. (cf. v.20; 2 Kings 24:13). Instead of these vessels being returned "shortly," as the lying prophets claimed, the vessels remaining in the temple would be carried off too (cf. v.22; 2 Kings 25:13). In fact—and here Jeremiah places the false prophets under a severe test—if the prophets who were predicting a speedy return of the vessels taken to Babylon were indeed what they claimed to be, they could serve the nation best by praying that the vessels still in the temple would not be taken to Babylon. Some interpreters see an element of sarcasm in v.18. Of course, history reveals that the temple vessels were taken to the land of exile.

19–22 Of all the temple appointments, three are mentioned here as well as elsewhere (v.19; cf. 52:17). The pillars were made of bronze and were placed in front of the temple; their names were Jakin and Boaz (cf. 1 Kings 7:15–22). Before being taken away to Babylon, they were actually broken into pieces because they were too large to take intact. The Sea was a large cast basin, supported on the backs of twelve cast oxen, and used for the washings of the priests (cf. 1 Kings 7:23–26). There were also stands to support the lavers (cf. 1 Kings 7:27–37; 2 Chron 4:6), and the stands were on wheels. All of these remaining vessels would be taken to Babylon also, Jeremiah prophesied (vv.20–21). The hope the false prophets held out was impossible of fulfillment and hence not from God. To the prediction of the carrying away of all these things, the Lord added a promise that they would be restored (v.22) in the day that he would execute judgment on Babylon. And the vessels actually were returned to Jerusalem by Cyrus at the beginning of his reign (c. 536 B.C.; cf. Ezra 1:7–11).

Notes

16 The Hebrew term כְּלִי (*k*ᵉ*lê*, "articles") is as broad and as difficult of precise rendering as the Greek ὅπλα (*hopla*). Suggestions for translation have been "objects," "utensils," "ornaments," "sacred treasures." Some readings indicate too much; others too little. "Articles" (NIV) fits well the demands of the context.

18 It has long been noticed and remarked upon that the בֹאוּ (*bō'û*, "be taken"; finite form of the verb) after לְבִלְתִּי (*l*ᵉ*biltî*, "not"), instead of the usual בֹא (*bō'*, lit., "come"; the infinitive), is unusual and contrary to grammatical usage. Older commentators have suggested the reading לְבִלְתִּי יָבֹאוּ (*l*ᵉ*biltî yābō'û*, "in order that they may not come"). Such a reading is probable in view of the fact that only a simple haplography is called for (after *l*ᵉ*biltî*).

8. Hananiah against Jeremiah (28:1–17)

Chapter 28 continues without a break in the narrative of chapter 27 (cf. the phrase "in the same year" [28:1]), which shows that Jeremiah was still wearing the yoke. Again there are some divergences between the Hebrew text (MT) and the Greek (LXX). The chapter tells about the confrontation of the prophets Jeremiah and Hananiah.

2. Hananiah's contradiction of Jeremiah

28:1–4

¹In the fifth month of that same year, the fourth year, early in the reign of Zedekiah king of Judah, the prophet Hananiah son of Azzur, who was from Gibeon, said to me in the house of the LORD in the presence of the priests and all the people: ²"This is what the LORD Almighty, the God of Israel, says: 'I will break the yoke of the king of Babylon. ³Within two years I will bring back to this place all the articles of the LORD's house that Nebuchadnezzar king of Babylon removed from here and took to Babylon. ⁴I will also bring back to this place Jehoiachin son of Jehoiakim king of Judah and all the other exiles from Judah who went to Babylon,' declares the LORD, 'for I will break the yoke of the king of Babylon.'"

1 Some interpreters have been troubled by the mention of the fourth year of Zedekiah as the "beginning of his reign" (lit. Heb.; NIV, "early in the reign"; LXX omits this), which lasted eleven years. But according to Jewish usage, the date was indeed the beginning of his rule, for the Jews divided periods of time into halves: beginning and end (Henderson, p. 171). It means simply "in the first half of his reign."

Hananiah the prophet, whom the LXX calls a false prophet, seized an opportunity when the temple was frequented by the people, either at the celebration of the new moon or a Sabbath, to contradict what Jeremiah had just said (cf. ch. 27). Apart from this chapter, we know nothing of Hananiah, whose name was a common one. He has been characterized as a fanatical nationalist prophet who was sincerely wrong. He was a native of Gibeon, the modern el-Jib, five miles northwest of Jerusalem. It was one of the priestly cities; so, like Jeremiah, Hananiah may have been a priest (cf. Josh 21:17). The year was 594–593 B.C., and the fifth month places the episode in the summer.

2–3 Hananiah had the temerity to use the same introductory formula as Jeremiah, implying a claim for inspiration similar to his. The form of the Hebrew verb *šābartî* ("I will break") in v.2 is the prophetic perfect, which emphasizes the certainty of a future event or promise. The yoke refers to the one Jeremiah had just made. Flatly contradicting Jeremiah's God-given counsel of submission, Hananiah predicted a return of the captives and the temple vessels within two years, emphasizing the time element by putting it first (v.3). This mention of two years was meant to bolster the credibility of his false prophecy. He paid no attention to the warning in 23:31. That the prophecy was never fulfilled showed its falsity (cf. Deut 18:21-22). The Babylonian Chronicle indicates that Nebuchadnezzar was quelling a revolt in Babylon at the time. This may have acted as a spur to Hananiah's optimism.

4 Perhaps Hananiah saw approval on the faces of his hearers because he went even further. He predicted that Jeconiah would be restored from exile (v.4), a contradiction of Jeremiah's prophecy in 22:24-27, which was fulfilled in 52:31-34. Hananiah's prediction showed he favored Jeconiah over the vacillating Zedekiah because he may have thought that the former would resist Nebuchadnezzar better. To make his message more uplifting, he made a most sweeping prediction of the return of all the Judean exiles. One can well imagine the confusion created in the minds of the populace by the spectacle of the false prophet's denying the central elements in the message of the true prophet of God.

Notes

1 The reading אֵלַי (*'ēlay*, "to me") is found both in the MT and the versions. Because Jeremiah is spoken of in the third person elsewhere in this chapter, it has been suggested that the Hebrew is an abbreviated writing for אֶל יִרְמְיָה (*'el yirmᵉyāh*, "to Jeremiah"), corresponding to the first personal pronoun appearing in 27:2 (so Bright). The conjecture has little to recommend it.

חֲנַנְיָה (*ḥᵃnanyāh*, "Hananiah") is called a prophet because he was known as such to the people, though he had never been commissioned of God. The Talmud (*Sanhedrin* 89a) claimed his false predictions resulted from an unfounded deduction: since Jeremiah had predicted the fall of Elam (49:34-39), a subject state of Babylon, Hananiah concluded that the prophecy doubtless would apply even more certainly to Babylon. Such reasonings are never tantamount to a direct word from God to his prophets, especially when they run counter to the Lord's word already given his authenticated messenger (22:24-27).

b. *Jeremiah's appeal to the past*

28:5-9

> [5]Then the prophet Jeremiah replied to the prophet Hananiah before the priests and all the people who were standing in the house of the LORD. [6]He said, "Amen! May the LORD do so! May the LORD fulfill the words you have prophesied by bringing the articles of the LORD's house and all the exiles back to this place from Babylon. [7]Nevertheless, listen to what I have to say in your hearing and in the hearing of all the people: [8]From early times the prophets who preceded you and me have prophesied war, disaster and plague against many countries and great kingdoms. [9]But the prophet who prophesies peace will be recognized as one truly sent by the LORD only if his prediction comes true."

5–9 Jeremiah's response (v.5) to Hananiah was immediate. Many interpreters believe it was spoken ironically. His "Amen" (v.6) revealed how deeply he desired Judah's good. He was just as concerned for the nation as Hananiah was. As a man of God, he sincerely desired the captives' return and that Hananiah's prediction be true. But notice that Jeremiah did not begin his reply with "Thus says the LORD." So while he longed for the captives' return, he knew that a prophecy of success, especially at that time, needed confirmation. Fulfillment was what counted (cf. Deut 13:1–5; 18:20–22). So in fidelity to his call, Jeremiah had to deal with the facts (v.7). He reminded Hananiah of the words of the true prophets who had preceded both Hananiah and him (v.8). Hananiah's words contradicted their predictions just as much as they contradicted those of Jeremiah. The former prophets also spoke in warning messages because of the sinful condition of the people they ministered to. Jeremiah showed that, in view of the nation's long spiritual declension, prophecies of disaster were not new. He made it clear that the fulfillment of a prophecy remained the best proof of its truthfulness (v.9); this was the time-honored criterion of true prophecy. The scope of the prophetic activity was comprehensive, reaching to many lands and many kingdoms, small and great. In the contest between Hananiah and Jeremiah, antecedent probability was in favor of a prophet who spoke in agreement with the true prophets of the past. The trouble with the false prophets was that they always predicted prosperity unconditionally and without need of repentance. It is always less popular to predict calamity rather than prosperity; so the presumption of truth rests with the prophet of calamity. At this time Jeremiah evidently had no specific message from God against Hananiah.

Notes

8 More than a score of MSS (along with the Vulgate, *de fame*) read רָעָב (*rāāḇ*, "famine") instead of רָעָה (*rāāh*, "disaster") as more in conformity with the usual formula in parallel passages for predicted trials for disobedience.

c. *Hananiah's response*

28:10–11

> [10]Then the prophet Hananiah took the yoke off the neck of the prophet Jeremiah and broke it, [11]and he said before all the people, "This is what the LORD says: 'In the same way will I break the yoke of Nebuchadnezzar king of Babylon off the neck of all the nations within two years.'" At this, the prophet Jeremiah went on his way.

10–11 Because of Jeremiah's incontrovertible argument, Hananiah resorted to force. A visual prophecy like the yoke made a great impression on the people. So Hananiah took the yoke from Jeremiah's neck and smashed it (v.10), to show that Nebuchadnezzar's power would be shattered in two years (v.11). Once more Hananiah presumed to use the introductory formula of the true prophets. Instead of waiting for the fulfillment of his prediction, he acted violently to capture the people's attention and mask his own confusion. In doing so, he may have hoped to reverse the impact made by Jeremiah's making and wearing the yoke (cf. the act of Zedekiah, son of Kenaanah [1 Kings 22:24]). There has been much discussion as to why Jeremiah left without replying. He could have been waiting for a time when emotions had cooled off. Also, he was doubtless waiting for further instructions from the Lord. Actually, there was no need for haste because it would take two years to see whether or not Hananiah's prediction came true. And Jeremiah may have left without answering Hananiah so as not to confuse the people.

Notes

10 We should expect the suffix of the verb וַיִּשְׁבְּרֵהוּ (*wayyišberēhû,* "and he broke it") to be in the feminine because of מוֹטָה (*môṭāh,* "yoke"), but the agreement is to עֹל (*'ōl,* "yoke," "servitude"; cf. v.4), a concept that permeates the whole passage.

11 Some expositors are at a loss to state whether Jeremiah concluded his remarks and the confrontation out of cowardice (because Hananiah's message would be preferable to his, since it was more pleasing to the hearers) or disgust (because the false prophet had lowered the high office of prophet to the level of pleasing people). It was for neither of those reasons. He left because (1) he knew his own message was truly from God, and (2) he was convinced that God would vindicate his own message by verification by future events (Deut 18:22; also Jer 28:9).

d. *Jeremiah's stronger pronouncement*

28:12–14

¹²Shortly after the prophet Hananiah had broken the yoke off the neck of the prophet Jeremiah, the word of the LORD came to Jeremiah: ¹³"Go and tell Hananiah, 'This is what the LORD says: You have broken a wooden yoke, but in its place you will get a yoke of iron. ¹⁴This is what the LORD Almighty, the God of Israel, says: I will put an iron yoke on the necks of all these nations to make them serve Nebuchadnezzar king of Babylon, and they will serve him. I will even give him control over the wild animals.' "

12–14 The Lord's answer through Jeremiah did come a short time later (v.12). To one who had falsified the Lord's reiterated intentions for Israel, it was an emphatic rebuttal. By breaking the yoke, Hananiah had raised false hopes of successfully resisting the invaders—hopes that were only to make their lot harder. In the Hebrew the plural *môṭōṯ* ("yokes"; "yoke-bars," RSV; "yoke," KJV, NIV) reflects the several parts of which the yoke was made. By breaking it, Hananiah had alleviated the pain of the yoke. But Jeremiah replied that the people were exchanging the wooden yoke of submission for the inflexible iron yoke of servitude in Babylon (v.13). (Not only were the people to suffer more; but, as 38:17–23 shows, Zedekiah's fate was more severe than that of Jehoiakim or Jehoiachin.) Hananiah's actions would have no influence whatever on God's declared purpose. Human devices cannot circumvent God's will. They can only aggravate the situation. Whereas for Hezekiah to resist Assyria in 701 B.C. was an act of faith, for Judah to rebel against Babylon in Jeremiah's time was an act of disobedience. Not only will all the nations serve Nebuchadnezzar (a fact stated twice; cf. 27:7; 28:14), but his dominion would extend over all the wild animals (v.14, cf. 27:6).

e. Prediction of Hananiah's death

28:15–17

> 15Then the prophet Jeremiah said to Hananiah the prophet, "Listen, Hananiah! The LORD has not sent you, yet you have persuaded this nation to trust in lies. 16Therefore, this is what the LORD says: 'I am about to remove you from the face of the earth. This very year you are going to die, because you have preached rebellion against the LORD.'"
> 17In the seventh month of that same year, Hananiah the prophet died.

15–17 Perhaps after an interval of only a few days, Jeremiah received a word from the Lord against Hananiah. First, the Lord said that he had not sent Hananiah (v.15). Second, Hananiah had misled Judah into believing lies. In the Hebrew there is a telling play on words in vv.15–16: because the Lord had not sent Hananiah (lō'-šelāḥªkā, "he has not sent you"), yet he went; therefore, the Lord would remove him (mešallēḥªkā, "sending you") away from the earth, that is, he would die. Hananiah had set a time limit of two years for the realization of his prediction. But the Lord did not choose to wait that long. He decreed that Hananiah was to die that very year, and he died in two months (cf. v.1 and v.17) after his wicked prophecy. He had to die because in opposing Jeremiah he instigated rebellion against the Lord. Rebelling against a servant of the Lord was tantamount to rebelling against God himself. The Jews knew the penalty for apostasy (cf. Deut 13:1–5); Ezekiel saw it carried out in his day against Pelatiah (cf. Ezek 11:13), and in the infant church Peter saw it executed on Ananias and Sapphira (Acts 5:1–11). Jeremiah's prophecy was authenticated in the death of Hananiah, which discredited him as a fraud. Thus the authority of the true prophet was vindicated. Observe the high cost of false prophecy. These events only served to accredit Jeremiah's ministry. Why did God wait for two months before punishing Hananiah? Perhaps in his grace God wanted to give him ample time to think about and retract the bold falsehood.

9. Jeremiah's letters to the exiles (29:1–32)

Because the time reference in v.2 is indefinite, various dates for this chapter have been proposed. They range from 597 B.C. (the year of the deportation of Jehoiachin) through 595, 594, and 593 B.C., down to 587 B.C. On balance, the chapter may be placed a few years after the exile of 597 B.C.

More important than the precise date are the contents of the chapter. In it we have the first letter recorded in the Bible (vv.4–23). (For other OT letters, see 2 Chron 21:12–15; 30:1, 6–9; 32:17; Ezra 1:2–4; 4:9–22; 5:7–16; 6:3–12; 7:12–26.) In addition, chapter 29 refers briefly to other letters (vv.15–19, 25–32).

The historical situation of the chapter was that in 597 B.C., some three thousand Jews had been exiled with Jehoiachin, among them a number of priests and prophets along with the royal household. In Jerusalem, Jeremiah heard that some exiled false prophets were predicting an early fall of Babylon and an early restoration of the exiles to Judah. Jeremiah's letters warned the exiles against this deception and urged them to wait patiently for God's time.

a. *Introduction*

29:1-3

> [1]This is the text of the letter that the prophet Jeremiah sent from Jerusalem to the surviving elders among the exiles and to the priests, the prophets and all the other people Nebuchadnezzar had carried into exile from Jerusalem to Babylon. [2](This was after King Jehoiachin and the queen mother, the court officials and the leaders of Judah and Jerusalem, the craftsmen and the artisans had gone into exile from Jerusalem.) [3]He entrusted the letter to Elasah son of Shaphan and to Gemariah son of Hilkiah, whom Zedekiah king of Judah sent to King Nebuchadnezzar in Babylon. It said:

1-2 Who were the "surviving elders" (v.1) to whom Jeremiah's letter was sent? One suggestion is that the word *yeṭer* ("remnant"; NIV, "surviving") means "chief" here (so Harrison). Although the word has this sense in some contexts, it is not demanded here. The common rendering (e.g., "surviving") is harmonious with the historical setting. Jeremiah rightly felt he still had a God-given responsibility for the "surviving elders," who were clearly those who had not succumbed to the rigors of the deportation. The suggestion has been made that resistance to the Babylonian rule had issued in the death of many elders (so Freedman). Though it is impossible to be completely certain of what had happened, it is clear that some form of community organization like that in Judah had been continued in the Exile. Verse 1 says that the letter was directed not only to the elders but to all the exiles. The "queen mother" (v.2) was Nehushta (cf. 13:18; 2 Kings 24:8). The craftsmen and artisans were deported to help King Nebuchadnezzar beautify Babylon.

3 Jeremiah gave his letter to an embassy whom Zedekiah sent to Nebuchadnezzar. The embassy's purpose is not stated. According to one view, it reflected the desire of the many who wanted to bring Jehoiachin back to Jerusalem and restore him to the throne he had held for three months (cf. 28:4). But it would have been strange indeed for such an aim to have Zedekiah's approval. Another view is that the embassy may have been sent with tribute and assurance of Zedekiah's loyalty to Nebuchadnezzar. This is more probable, as is the view that the embassy was sent to exonerate Zedekiah of any complicity in the plot to rebel against Babylon. At any rate, only by Zedekiah's permission could Jeremiah have sent his letter to the exiles. The members of the embassy were Elasah son of Shaphan and Gemariah son of Hilkiah. The first, probably a brother of Ahikam (cf. 26:24), agreed with Jeremiah and would have been welcome in Babylon. The other was probably a son of Josiah's high priest Hilkiah (cf. 2 Kings 22:3-4). Babylon probably permitted communication between Judah and the exiles. The exiles were just as subject to false prophets as the people in Jerusalem were. Also, they might have been expected to heed Jeremiah's words (cf. 24:5-7). The false hope of a quick end to the Exile would only have nullified the disciplinary effects of the Exile.

Notes

2 In modern Hebrew usage, הַגְּבִירָה (hagg^ebîrāh, "the queen mother"; cf. 13:18) has the force of "lady." Protocol of the ancient Near East gave the queen mother a prominent place (cf. 1 Kings 2:13–20; 15:2, 10; 22:42; Dan 5:10). She was especially important in this instance, since Jehoiachin was only eighteen years old (2 Kings 24:8–15).

סָרִיסִים (sārîsîm, "eunuch"; NIV, "court officials") is a usual title for royal officials of unspecified duties (cf. 52:25; 1 Sam 8:15).

b. The letter of Jeremiah (29:4–19)

1) Warning against false prophets

29:4–9

> ⁴This is what the LORD Almighty, the God of Israel, says to all those I carried into exile from Jerusalem to Babylon: ⁵"Build houses and settle down; plant gardens and eat what they produce. ⁶Marry and have sons and daughters; find wives for your sons and give your daughters in marriage, so that they too may have sons and daughters. Increase in number there; do not decrease. ⁷Also, seek the peace and prosperity of the city to which I have carried you into exile. Pray to the LORD for it, because if it prospers, you too will prosper." ⁸Yes, this is what the LORD Almighty, the God of Israel, says: "Do not let the prophets and diviners among you deceive you. Do not listen to the dreams you encourage them to have. ⁹They are prophesying lies to you in my name. I have not sent them," declares the LORD.

4–7 Do we have in this chapter a word-for-word record of Jeremiah's main letter and the other subsidiary letters? Probably not, though we certainly have the gist of what was written. Underlying the main letter is the assumption that, though he had deported the exiles, Nebuchadnezzar was only the agent of the Lord. Ultimately the Lord himself had brought about the Exile (v.4). Since the Lord's will was behind it, for Judah the part of wisdom was submission. Verses 5–7 are so remarkable for their advice to the exiles that they are without parallel in the literature of antiquity (esp. v.7). The exiles were to settle in Babylon and live normal lives there, even praying for their captors (cf. Matt 5:43). They would have considerable freedom in their exile. Instead of expecting an early return to their homeland, they were to settle down in Babylon and even to work and pray for its peace and prosperity. Otherwise, their influence would be negligible and their exile all the more galling. What unusual advice for Jeremiah to give his exiled countrymen! History shows that in all the centuries of their world-wide dispersion, the Jews have tried to follow this pattern. They have identified themselves with the country of their residence, while at the same time looking toward eventual restoration to their native land. Jeremiah's exhortations show that the Babylonian stay would be an extended one. His advice to build homes there (v.5) implies they had not yet been in Babylon a long time. The freedom allowed them implies they were neither slaves nor prisoners in their new land. Any feeling that they should not build homes in a foreign, unclean land was thus dispelled (cf. Hos 9:1–9; Amos 7:17; so Bewer). The wives Jeremiah encouraged them to marry (v.6) were Jewish, not foreign (cf. Deut 7:3). The seed of Abraham must continue according to the divine promise (cf. Gen 12:1–3). Unique in ancient literature was Jeremiah's command for them to pray for their pagan captors. The city referred to in v.7 was any of the Babylonian cities. Throughout the centuries the precepts enjoined here have been followed by the Jews in dispersion. To this day they pray in their worship on the Sabbath and on festivals for the rulers under whom they are living. Cyrus had asked for the prayers of the people (cf. Ezra 6:10; also 1 Macc 7:33).

8–9 Again Jeremiah warned the exiles not to trust false prophets (v.8). In Babylon, as in Judah, false prophecy was flourishing (cf. vv.15, 21). The theme was always the same: a speedy return to the homeland. Rosy predictions were the stock in trade of the falsifiers. Some scholars interpret v.8 to teach that some exiles in despondency had asked some prophets to supply them with dreams because of the use of the causative in the verb *ḥālam* ("to dream"; NIV, "dreams you encourage them to have"). Probably the versions (LXX, Syr., Vul.) are more accurate here in translating the simple stem "they dream." Such deceptive dreams could only work havoc among the exiles. The deceivers must not be trusted because they had never been commissioned by the Lord (v.9).

Notes

5 It is interesting that Jeremiah did not mention trade and commerce, an area in which the Jews through the centuries of later world-wide dispersion have excelled. Numerous factors, such as the prohibition that hindered them from owning land, kept them from cultivating the soil. However, in the first century A.D., Josephus could write: "As for ourselves, we neither inhabit a maritime country, nor delight in such intercourse with other men as arises from it; but the cities we dwell in are remote from the sea, and as we have a fruitful country to dwell in, we take pains in cultivating it" (*Contra Apion* I, 60 [12]).

2) *The seventy-year exile*

29:10–14

> ¹⁰This is what the LORD says: "When seventy years are completed for Babylon, I will come to you and fulfill my gracious promise to bring you back to this place. ¹¹For I know the plans I have for you," declares the LORD, "plans to prosper you and not to harm you, plans to give you hope and a future. ¹²Then you will call upon me and come and pray to me, and I will listen to you. ¹³You will seek me and find me when you seek me with all your heart. ¹⁴I will be found by you," declares the LORD, "and will bring you back from captivity. I will gather you from all the nations and places where I have banished you," declares the LORD, "and will bring you back to the place from which I carried you into exile."

10–11 Jeremiah now presents a beautiful prophecy of encouragement to the exiles. The Lord's ultimate purpose for his people calls for blessing. The length of the Exile is again given as seventy years (v.10; cf. 25:11). The seventy years are "for Babylon" because Jeremiah is linking the duration of Nebuchadnezzar's kingdom with the termination of the Exile. The "gracious promise" is that of the exiles' restoration to Judah (cf. 27:22). Moreover, the Lord assures them that despite their surmise as to his lack of concern for their plight, he had not forgotten them. Regardless of appearances to the contrary, the Lord was not denying them hope for the future; it would not be realized immediately or in the near future. Jeremiah's words "hope and a future" (v.11) are literally "an end and a hope," which is a hendiadys (a figure in which a complex idea is expressed in two words linked by a coordinating conjunction) and means "a hopeful end." This word from the Lord was surely more heartening to the exiles' spirits than the false prophets' promises of quick deliverance.

12-14 The remainder of this section stresses the nature of the hopeful future. The Lord says that he can and will be entreated of the exiles (v.12). The promises, however, are contingent on their wholehearted repentance (v.13). Then the Lord will listen to them and will make himself accessible to them. In v.14 the declaration "I will gather you from all the nations and places where I have banished you" looks far beyond the Jews' return from Babylon to their future restoration from worldwide dispersion.

3) A "second letter" of Jeremiah

29:15-19

> 15You may say, "The LORD has raised up prophets for us in Babylon," 16but this is what the LORD says about the king who sits on David's throne and all the people who remain in this city, your countrymen who did not go with you into exile— 17yes, this is what the LORD Almighty says: "I will send the sword, famine and plague against them and I will make them like poor figs that are so bad they cannot be eaten. 18I will pursue them with the sword, famine and plague and will make them abhorrent to all the kingdoms of the earth and an object of cursing and horror, of scorn and reproach, among all the nations where I drive them. 19For they have not listened to my words," declares the LORD, "words that I sent to them again and again by my servants the prophets. And you exiles have not listened either," declares the LORD.

15-19 Many expositors believe these verses to be out of place. They feel that Jeremiah would scarcely have written so critically of Zedekiah in a letter carried by his ambassadors. This objection is based on the assumption that vv.4-23 constitute a single letter. But why could not vv.15-19 be a second letter written at a subsequent time and inserted parenthetically here? Some take these verses to be a marginal gloss, but they are too long for that. Their omission in the LXX perhaps shows that the translators could not understand their connection with the rest of the chapter. Yet it can be shown that the verses do fit the context. The situation was doubtless something like this: The exiles asked why Jeremiah insisted on an exile of seventy years when their prophets in Babylon were telling them the very opposite (v.15). Jeremiah replied that the false prophecies would be shown to be lies and their perpetrators would perish. For the Jews to depend on the pronouncements of the deceivers was the highest folly. Actually, the Jews still in Jerusalem were soon to experience grievous judgments for their persistence in disobeying the Lord.

Again, it must be emphasized that vv.15-19 were probably part of a second letter not sent by the king's embassy (v.3) because the king in v.16 is Zedekiah, who was yet destined for exile. "This city" was Jerusalem. The false prophets made much of the fact that in Jerusalem a Davidic king still ruled and argued from this that the Exile would soon end. But those still in Judah were to undergo the calamities of war and were likened to vile figs of the worst sort (v.17; cf. 24:1–10). For the thought and language of v.18, compare 19:8; 24:9; 25:18; and 42:18. And even in exile, the grace of God was seen in raising up Ezekiel in the exile in 592 B.C. (cf. Ezek 1:2–3). The change in pronoun in v.19b (from "they" to "you"), though harsh to our ears, was a natural one. It also reveals the care the Jews took in transmitting the text of Scripture. Once more the Lord states that he is the Author of the Exile.

c. Denunciation of the false prophets Ahab and Zedekiah

29:20–23

> ²⁰Therefore, hear the word of the LORD, all you exiles whom I have sent away from Jerusalem to Babylon. ²¹This is what the LORD Almighty, the God of Israel, says about Ahab son of Kolaiah and Zedekiah son of Maaseiah, who are prophesying lies to you in my name: "I will hand them over to Nebuchadnezzar king of Babylon, and he will put them to death before your very eyes. ²²Because of them, all the exiles from Judah who are in Babylon will use this curse: 'The LORD treat you like Zedekiah and Ahab, whom the king of Babylon burned in the fire.' ²³For they have done outrageous things in Israel; they have committed adultery with their neighbors' wives and in my name have spoken lies, which I did not tell them to do. I know it and am a witness to it," declares the LORD.

20–23 This paragraph shows that Jeremiah was well informed about conditions in Babylon (v.20). Two false prophets, Ahab and Zedekiah—of whom nothing more is known than that they had famous names and were deceitful and grossly immoral (v.23)—are singled out as examples of the heinousness of false prophesying (v.21). They were probably condemned as guilty of treason against the Babylonian crown. Like Hananiah, these false prophets would become object lessons of the Lord's wrath. In vv.21–22 there is a play on words in the Hebrew in "Kolaiah," father of Ahab, "curse," and "burned" (lit., "roasted") (see Notes). Babylon used burning as a punishment (cf. Dan 3:6, 20, 23).

Notes

21–22 There is a word-play on the name קוֹלָיָה (qôlāyāh, "Kolaiah") as related to קְלָלָה (qᵉlālāh, "curse") and the verb קָלָה (qālāh, "to burn, roast").

d. Condemnation of Shemaiah

29:24–32

> ²⁴Tell Shemaiah the Nehelamite, ²⁵"This is what the LORD Almighty, the God of Israel, says: You sent letters in your own name to all the people in Jerusalem, to Zephaniah son of Maaseiah the priest, and to all the other priests. You said to Zephaniah, ²⁶'The LORD has appointed you priest in place of Jehoiada to be in charge of the house of the LORD; you should put any madman who acts like a prophet into the stocks and neck-irons. ²⁷So why have you not reprimanded Jere-

miah from Anathoth, who poses as a prophet among you? [28]He has sent this message to us in Babylon: It will be a long time. Therefore build houses and settle down; plant gardens and eat what they produce.'"

[29]Zephaniah the priest, however, read the letter to Jeremiah the prophet. [30]Then the word of the LORD came to Jeremiah: [31]"Send this message to all the exiles: 'This is what the LORD says about Shemaiah the Nehelamite: Because Shemaiah has prophesied to you, even though I did not send him, and has led you to believe a lie, [32]this is what the LORD says: I will surely punish Shemaiah the Nehelamite and his decendants. He will have no one left among this people, nor will he see the good things I will do for my people, declares the LORD, because he has preached rebellion against me.'"

24–28 After castigating the two false prophets for their deceit and their profligacy (v.23), Jeremiah pronounces the Lord's condemnation on Shemaiah the Nehelamite (v.24), a false prophet who presumed to order a member of the priesthood in Jerusalem to silence Jeremiah. Of Shemaiah nothing more is known than what we have in this passage. We do not know whether "Nehelamite" has reference to his family or his birthplace. The background of Shemaiah's letter is clear. Jeremiah's letter understandably angered the false prophets in Babylon. Shemaiah, who was one of them, wrote the deputy priest Zephaniah to silence Jeremiah. Instead, Zephaniah read Shemaiah's letter to Jeremiah, who replied in a message predicting the doom of Shemaiah for denying Jeremiah's authority (v.27). The false prophets had apparently overlooked the promises Jeremiah had given (vv.10–14).

In v.25 the plural "letters" is used for the singular (cf. 2 Kings 19:14; 20:12). Zephaniah was the chief warden in charge of police regulations of the temple (cf. 21:1; 37:3; 52:24). The text of Shemaiah's offensive letter is in vv.26–28. On his own initiative he displaced Jehoiada the priest (cf. 2 Kings 11:4) with Zephaniah (so Harrison). Although in that day insanity may have been considered as an aberrant gift of prophecy (cf. 1 Sam 19:20–24; 2 Kings 9:11), the charge of madness (v.26) was an insult to Jeremiah. The "neck-irons" were an iron collar that held the head immovable while the prisoner was in the stocks (cf. 20:2). Knowing nothing of Jeremiah's divine call, Shemaiah had accused him of usurping authority as a spokesman for God (v.27). Shemaiah's anger was centered on Jeremiah's letter to the exiles (v.28), which was diametrically opposed to the lies of the false prophets.

29–32 After Zephaniah had read the letter to Jeremiah (v.29), the Lord told him (v.30) to send a letter to all the exiles (v.31), unmasking Shemaiah's hypocrisy and announcing his punishment, which was twofold: (1) he would have no descendants, and (2) he would not see the blessings on the Lord's people that Jeremiah had been predicting (v.32). Shemaiah had forfeited the privilege of participating in the restoration to the homeland.

Notes

26 Why the word פְּקִדִים (peqidîm, "officers"; NIV, "to be in charge") is in the plural is unknown. Certainly the verse indicates a low view of the prophetic office.

B. *The Book of Consolation* (30:1–33:26)

1. *Trial and triumph for Israel* (30:1–24)

Expositors generally agree that chapters 30–33 constitute a group of prophecies. The section has been called "The Book of Consolation" and has been variously interpreted. Some scholars believe these prophecies to be the work of an editor who lived after the time of the so-called Second Isaiah, possibly in the time of Ezra and Nehemiah (so Hyatt). Others consider the whole section to be non-Jeremianic; others believe it contains some prophecies by Jeremiah. Estimates as to the date of chapters 30–33 vary from the early days of Jeremiah's ministry under Josiah to a time after the Fall of Jerusalem. A number of scholars feel that the section relates in a large part only to the restoration of the northern kingdom.

Verse 1 of chapter 32 gives us the historical background of these prophecies (cf. 33:1). Jerusalem was in the final period of an eighteen-month siege by the Babylonians. Other Judean cities had already capitulated to them. The temporary intervention of Egypt (cf. 37:4–5) failed to stem the tide of events, and Jerusalem remained disillusioned and helpless. The remarkable feature of chapters 30–33 is that, though written during a time of deep distress for Jerusalem, they foretell a glorious future for the nation (cf. the latter part of 1:10). Up to this point in the book, Jeremiah's prophecies have mostly been threatening and gloomy, despite some bright glimpses (cf. 2:1–3; 3:14–17; 16:14–15; 23:1–8; 24:4–7). Now in chapters 30–33 the prophetic outlook changes. This is all the more striking since chapters 32 and 33 (probably chs. 30–31 also) were given in the tenth year of Zedekiah, when the final blow was about to fall. The overall theme is that Israel will not perish as a nation. As has already been said, some interpreters deny these chapters are Jeremiah's. But a valid basis for their marked departure from the tenor of the previous chapters is that Jeremiah is occupied not with the near future but with the distant consummation of Israel's history. He was in prison, the city in dire straits by famine and disease; yet it was then that he spoke words of greatest comfort. He predicted the permanence of the nation, the coming of the Gentiles to the truth, the institution of God's new covenant of redemption, and the rule of the Davidic King over cleansed Zion. These chapters amply refute the superficial charge that Jeremiah was only a pessimist.

a. *Return from captivity*

30:1–3

> ¹This is the word that came to Jeremiah from the LORD: ²"This is what the LORD, the God of Israel, says: 'Write in a book all the words I have spoken to you. ³The days are coming,' declares the LORD, 'when I will bring my people Israel and Judah back from captivity and restore them to the land I gave their forefathers to possess,' says the LORD."

1–3 These verses constitute the introduction to chapters 30–31 and in all probability for chapters 32–33 as well (so Harrison). They strike the hopeful theme of the nation's restoration. Here is a clear and unequivocal statement of return to the land. The Lord commanded Jeremiah to write these hopeful prophecies in a book (vv. 1–2) in order to insure their permanence at a time when so many in the nation were being exiled. Also, his activities may have been restricted at this time. These prophecies, then, were not to be spoken, as were most of Jeremiah's prophecies; but they were to be written so that they could be read. Obviously "the book" (v.2) was not to contain all we now have in the Book of Jeremiah, not even all he spoke to this time.

First of all, the words "the days are coming" (v.3) look toward eschatological times (cf. 3:16; 16:14; 23:5; 31:27, 31). Jeremiah is contemplating the distant, not near, future of the nation. This statement, which strikes the keynote of the section, restricts the material involved to "The Book of Consolation" in chapters 30–33. To bring back any people from captivity indicates a restoration of their fortunes, which is the emphasis of this section. The good news was the promise of the people's restoration to and their possession of their homeland, a message of glorious hope in that gloomy hour. Moreover, we must not forget that this hope relates to Israel and Judah, not to one without the other (cf. v.10).

Notes

3 The English versions generally translate שְׁבוּת . . . וְשַׁבְתִּי (wᵉšabtî . . . šᵉḇûṯ) "I will turn the captivity" (cf. ASV) or "I will bring back from captivity" (cf. RSV, NASB, JB, NAB, NIV). This sense accords well with the theme of chapters 30–33. However, there are instances— e.g., Job 42:10 (with regard to his misfortunes); Ezek 16:53 (a prediction concerning Sodom)—where captivity is not in view. In such cases a derived meaning such as "reverse or restore the fortunes" fits well (cf. BDB, s.v.).

b. *"The time of Jacob's trouble"*

30:4–7

⁴These are the words the LORD spoke concerning Israel and Judah: ⁵"This is what the LORD says:

" 'Cries of fear are heard—
terror, not peace.
⁶Ask and see:
Can a man bear children?
Then why do I see every strong man
with his hands on his stomach like a woman in labor,
every face turned deathly pale?
⁷How awful that day will be!
None will be like it.
It will be a time of trouble for Jacob,
but he will be saved out of it.' "

4–6 Here the prophet speaks of the whole nation over which David and Solomon ruled (v.4). Strangely, some see in these verses only the political upheavals that finally destroyed the Babylonian power and liberated the Jews. Such a view does not do justice to the eschatological direction of the passage. Jeremiah is stating that before the just-mentioned promise of restoration can be fulfilled, the nation must be severely disciplined, but not to the extent of final calamity. The words "fear" and "terror" (v.5) not only point to war in contrast with peace but, as will presently be seen, have further implications. The awful terror that will come can be compared only with the travail of a mother in childbirth (v.6), a figure of extreme distress (cf. 4:31; 6:24; 13:21; 22:23; 49:24; 50:43).

7 Interpretations of this verse differ widely. These are that the passage is referring to (1) the immediate situation, (2) the whole period of the Captivity, and (3) the time of tribulation in the end time before Israel's final restoration. Whatever their stance, most expositors favor either (1) or (3). Those who hold the first view understand "that day" (vv.7–8) to mean the day of the capture of Babylon, with emphasis on the terror caused by the approach of Cyrus. It is not readily clear why such a situation would be so horrendous for God's people. Actually, Cyrus would be considered their liberator from those who took them captive. In the light of the immediate context and what follows, the preferable position is to assume that the reference is to the Day of the Lord. "That day" was not one immediately at hand. It is not the day of the destruction of Jerusalem but the day of God's comprehensive judgment. The present is not to be excluded, but it is swallowed up in the future. That day was to be marked by great calamities. In a sense the fall of Babylon was only the opening scene of the extended drama. Yet it is vitally important to remember that v.7 speaks of Jacob's trouble, not Babylon's. The prophetic Scriptures are replete with references to this unique time of Jacob's distress; e.g., "There is none like it" (cf. Matt 24:21 with the earlier prediction in Dan 12:1; cf. also 46:10; Isa 2:12–21; 13:6; 34:1–8; Ezek 30:3; Joel 1:15; 2:1–2, 11; Amos 5:18–20; Mic 1:2–5; Zeph 1:2–3:8; Zech 14:1–8, 12–15 among others). Notice that the travail will issue in both physical and spiritual deliverance (cf. Zech 12:10–13:1) and that liberation will be such that never again will Israel be enslaved by any nation. This could never be said of any deliverance to this present hour; it must refer to eschatological times.

Notes

7 The phrase הַיּוֹם הַהוּא (hayyôm hahû', "that day") is frequently used in the prophetic Scriptures to introduce information concerning the Day of the Lord, a significant eschatological theme. This passage is important (1) in linking Israel with that time, (2) in portraying the excruciating agony of the experience, and (3) in stating unequivocally Israel's deliverance from it. The concept of an eschatological time of tribulation for Israel is absent from rabbinical commentaries, understandably so. But it is strangely treated in some Christian works as well (cf. Cunliffe–Jones, p. 190).

c. *Freedom from bondage to oppressors*

30:8–11

> 8" 'In that day,' declares the LORD Almighty,
> 'I will break the yoke off their necks
> and will tear off their bonds;
> no longer will foreigners enslave them.
> 9Instead, they will serve the LORD their God
> and David their king,
> whom I will raise up for them.

10" 'So do not fear, O Jacob my servant;
    do not be dismayed, O Israel,'

declares the LORD.

'I will surely save you out of a distant place,
    your descendants from the land of their exile.
Jacob will again have peace and security,
    and no one will make him afraid.
11I am with you and will save you,'
    declares the LORD.
'Though I completely destroy all the nations
    among which I scatter you,
    I will not completely destroy you.
I will discipline you but only with justice;
    I will not let you go entirely unpunished.' "

8-9 Only in the most preliminary way may "the yoke" (v.8) refer to bondage to Nebuchadnezzar; what is meant is total liberation from all foreign oppressors. This can be effected only by the glorious intervention of Israel's messianic King (cf. Ezek 34:23; Hos 3:5). After the yoke of foreign rule has been broken, the benevolent yoke of their King will be gladly assumed by the godly in Israel and Judah (cf. Matt 11:28-30). Notice the pairing of "the LORD their God" with "David their king" (v.9). It is significant that in the prophetic Scriptures a resurrection of David himself is not predicted as antecedent to the rule of his Son, the Lord Jesus Christ, on the Davidic throne. The person indicated here is the future ideal King, the so-called second David (cf. "last Adam" and "second man" [1 Cor 15:45-47]). The messianic regent is a scion of the house of David (cf. Ezek 37:24-25). The Targum, though interpretative, is correct in identifying this ideal King as "Messiah, the son of David." Among the Jews the name David came to be used of royalty, much as Pharaoh, Caesar, or Czar, but only in the highest and final sense.

10-11 This passage closes with promises of return, peace, freedom, and permanence. The nation is referred to as Jacob, God's servant, a title of honor (v.10; cf. Isa 41:8; 44:1-2). God's people are to be regathered from all the lands of their dispersion. The picture of quiet and ease is that of sheep lying undisturbed in their pastures (so Driver). Now Jeremiah makes a telling distinction between the fate of God's people and that of their oppressors: the oppressors may be removed finally from the scene of history, but God's people never (v.11; cf. 4:27; 5:10, 18; 46:28). This is not partiality on God's part, for he will not overlook his people's sins. They can no more sin with impunity than any other persons or nation. The Lord *must* chasten them and he will do so with justice, not capriciously. It is no wonder that Isaiah refers to Israel (i.e., Israel and Judah) as an eternal nation; for whereas Ammon, Assyria, Edom, Moab, and others no longer exist, Israel is present throughout the world, even though in the divine chastening of dispersion.

Notes

9 The force of the prophecy דָּוִד מַלְכָּם (dāwiḏ malkām, "David their king") is best understood as a contrast ("instead") to the burdensome yoke (in v.8 the pronominal suffix וֹ [ô, "his"] in

עֻלּוֹ [*'ullô*, "his yoke"] is to be taken as collective for all oppressors). Since the promise in v.8 is also unlimited as to time—וְלֹא ... עוֹד (*weˡ lō'* ... *'ôd*, "no longer")—the compelling conclusion is that fulfillment must be sought in eschatological times. Notice that (1) service is involved, (2) God and the people's king are to be served equally, and (3) the promised monarch is God's gift to his people. Is the king here literally David or the ideal (messianic) King as in Ezek 37:24? The Targum (Schocken ed.) reads in Jer 30:9 מְשִׁיחָא בַּר דָּוִד מַלְכְּהוֹן (*meˡ šîḥā' bar dāwid malkehôn*, "Messiah, Son of David their king").

---

d. Israel's wounds healed

30:12–17

12"This is what the LORD says:

" 'Your wound is incurable,
 your injury beyond healing.
13There is no one to plead your cause,
 no remedy for your sore,
 no healing for you.
14All your allies have forgotten you;
 they care nothing for you.
I have struck you as an enemy would
 and punished you as would the cruel,
because your guilt is so great
 and your sins so many.
15Why do you cry out over your wound,
 your pain that has no cure?
Because of your great guilt and many sins
 I have done these things to you.

16" 'But all who devour you will be devoured;
 all your enemies will go into exile.
Those who plunder you will be plundered;
 all who make spoil of you I will despoil.
17But I will restore you to health
 and heal your wounds,'

                                        declares the LORD,

'because you are called an outcast,
 Zion for whom no one cares.' "

12–15 Jeremiah now turns to the serious condition of Israel. His purpose is to show that her punishment was well deserved. The pronouns in v.12 are in the feminine, referring to the nation. Her wounds were, apart from God, incurable—literally, "It is ill with your bruise" (cf. 10:19; 14:17; 15:18). Doubtless, the wounds are those she has received from her enemies because of her flagrant sins. Because God's people have transgressed so grievously (v.14), no one can defend them (v.13); moreover, there is no hope of their recovery. Jeremiah mingles his figures of speech: he sees Israel as a defendant in a lawsuit and as one suffering from a fatal wound. All her antagonists have the upper hand as they accuse her before God. The first clause of v.13 reflects the legal process. Then Jeremiah shifts to medicine (v.15). What made her trial the harder to bear was that Israel's allies had left her in the lurch. Her punishment clearly stemmed from the Lord because sin was at the root of all her calamities. Furthermore, she had no right to complain of her punishment since she amply deserved it.

16–17 The prophet goes on to contrast Israel's mistreatment by her supposed lovers with the Lord's actions on her behalf. Because his people have undergone judgment and have acknowledged their guilt, God pronounces retaliation in kind on their enemies (v.16). It is the principle of measure for measure, the well-known lex talionis. The future blessings begin with judgments on Israel's oppressors. God will heal her and afflict her enemies. The Babylonians who devoured the nation will in turn be devoured by the Medes and Persians. So it has been throughout redemption history: those who have treated God's people ill have to reckon with God as avenger (cf. Gen 12:1–3). Again, the promise of restored health (v.17) precedes any action the Lord may take against Israel's foes. In their contempt, the enemies of God's nation called her an outcast, for whom no one cared. The figure is that of a woman put away by her husband (cf. Isa 62:4). Why did the Lord consider this treatment of his nation so great an offense? Because the words and actions of the enemies revealed their disregard of God and his expressed purpose for his people. Ultimately, calling them an outcast impugned God's faithfulness to his elect people.

e. Rebuilt Jerusalem and her ruler

30:18–22

18"This is what the LORD says:

" 'I will restore the fortunes of Jacob's tents
and have compassion on his dwellings;
the city will be rebuilt on her ruins,
and the palace will stand in its proper place.
19From them will come songs of thanksgiving
and the sound of rejoicing.
I will add to their numbers,
and they will not be decreased;
I will bring them honor,
and they will not be disdained.
20Their children will be as in days of old,
and their community will be established before me;
I will punish all who oppress them.
21Their leader will be one of their own;
their ruler will arise from among them.
I will bring him near and he will come close to me,
for who is he who will devote himself
to be close to me?'

declares the LORD.

22" 'So you will be my people,
and I will be your God.' "

18–20 Days of rich blessing are ahead. Here we have details of the nation's restoration. These verses deal with Jerusalem rebuilt, repopulated, and governed by a native prince responsive to the Lord. It also shows us the nation experiencing the blessings of renewed fellowship with the Lord. The "tents" and "dwellings" (v.18), now desolate, do not refer to the people's temporary housing in Babylon (contra

JFB) but to the wretched condition of their houses in their homeland. Jerusalem will be rebuilt on its original location. The word "ruins" is the well-known term *tēl* ("tell," "mound," "heap"), now used by Arabs for the ruined mounds of Palestine, the remains of ancient cities. Jerusalem and its buildings are probably intended. There are those who understand "palace" to refer to the "temple," but the meaning is that the city will be settled by a king, with all that pertains to such a residence (so Streane). Furthermore, along with material prosperity will come joy and honor so long denied the people (v.19). Out of the city and palace will flow praise and merriment. Instead of degradation and insignificance, the people will grow in numbers and in the esteem of the nations as the Lord honors them. The children of Jacob (v.20) will enjoy prosperity like that in the heyday of the monarchy under David and Solomon. The congregation—the people as a whole—will be established under God's oversight.

21–22 Embedded in this passage so full of promise is one of the most beautiful of the messianic predictions in the OT. First, the nation will be blessed by a native, not a foreign, ruler (v.21). This was surely a prophecy of strong consolation in view of the nation's imminent subservience to a foreign power. The coming ruler will not be an exotic plant but will come from native soil (cf. Zech 6:12). Second, he will have the privilege of approach to God. Usage in the OT shows that this means priestly position and ministry (cf. Ps 110:4; Zech 6:13). The verbs convey this. The ruler will need no mediator. Thus he will be greater than even David and Solomon. Like Melchizedek he will have a dual role. No man can take to himself the office of priesthood (cf. Heb 5:4). In fact, it was dangerous for even a king to do so (cf. Jeroboam in 1 Kings 12:26–33; 13:1–6; and Uzziah in 2 Chron 26:16–20). In order to emphasize the importance of access to God, Jeremiah by a rhetorical question shows that it is no light thing to approach God. This was permitted only to the priests and, on the Day of Atonement, only to the high priest. The question implies a negative answer. Here is a reiteration of the promise to restore the Davidic line (cf. v.9). Because there is no reference here to a king, some have strangely proposed that v.21 indicates the abrogation of the Davidic kingship (so Payne Smith). But in the light of both this context and OT prophecy as a whole, this position cannot possibly be maintained. The Targum, though interpretative, is correct in its rendering "Messiah shall be revealed to them out of their own midst." And no one would "devote himself [lit., 'has been surety for his heart'] to be so close" to God on his own initiative. Immediately (v.22) Jeremiah turns to the result of Messiah's ministry— viz., the old covenant is renewed. The nation will be restored to the position of fellowship and worship that God intended for her. The people will be seen to be God's people, not only de jure, but de facto.

Notes

18 The Hebrew תֵּל (*tēl*, "mound" of a ruined city) corresponds to the Arabic *tell*. New towns in the Near East were frequently built on the ruins of the previous settlements. Notice how *tēl* (*tell*) formed a part of place names: Tel Aviv (Ezek 3:15), Tell el-Amarna (in Egypt), Tel Assar (2 Kings 19:12), Tel Melah, and Tel Harsha (Ezra 2:59).

f. Judgment, then blessing

30:23–24

> ²³See, the storm of the LORD
>   will burst out in wrath,
> a driving wind swirling down
>   on the heads of the wicked.
> ²⁴The fierce anger of the LORD will not turn back
>   until he fully accomplishes
>   the purposes of his heart.
>   In days to come
>   you will understand this.

23–24 Before there can be blessing, judgment must be meted out to the guilty. Such a passage as this is inserted at this point lest the careless be given false security in their sins. In spite of promises of hope, God's moral purposes always remain the same. The last two verses of this chapter repeat 23:19–20. God is behind the judgment to be executed by Nebuchadnezzar. Jeremiah uses the figure of a sudden storm (v.23) to describe it. The Lord does his work of redemption by his power displayed in judgment. The blessings Jeremiah has been speaking of are only for the godly. The reference to "the days to come" (v.24) appears to point to a time after the judgment has passed.

2. The new covenant (31:1–40)

In chapter 30 the restoration of Judah is foretold; here that of Israel is predicted. The messages of hope and restoration, it will be recalled, carry through chapter 33. The dominant themes in this chapter are the restoration of God's people and the new covenant. The whole nation is addressed in v.1, then the Ten Tribes in vv.2–22, then Judah in vv.23–26, then both Israel and Judah in vv.27–40 (so KD).

a. God's mercy for Ephraim

31:1–6

> ¹"At that time," declares the LORD, "I will be the God of all the clans of Israel, and they will be my people."
> ²This is what the LORD says:
>
> > "The people who survive the sword
> >   will find favor in the desert;
> > I will come to give rest to Israel."
>
> ³The LORD appeared to us in the past, saying:
>
> > "I have loved you with an everlasting love;
> >   I have drawn you with loving-kindness.
> > ⁴I will build you up again
> >   and you will be rebuilt, O Virgin Israel.
> > Again you will take up your tambourines
> >   and go out to dance with the joyful.
> > ⁵Again you will plant vineyards
> >   on the hills of Samaria;
> > the farmers will plant them
> >   and enjoy their fruit.

> ⁶There will be a day when watchmen cry out
>   on the hills of Ephraim,
> 'Come, let us go up to Zion,
>   to the LORD our God.'"

1–2 Verse 1 of this chapter is v.25 of chapter 30 in the MT, while v.2 of this chapter is 31:1 in the MT. The time reference with which the verse begins refers to the "days to come" of 30:24, that is, the Messianic Age. Although vv.1–6 deal primarily with the northern kingdom, the designation "clans of Israel" must be allowed to comprehend the Twelve Tribes in light of the promise to the whole nation in 30:22 (so KD). Jeremiah dilates on the grace of God (v.2) revealed to the northern tribes. There are two views of the words "the people who survive the sword." One applies them to the Exodus and the wilderness wanderings; the other applies them to the return of the Ten Tribes from Assyrian captivity, perhaps also including the later captives from Babylon. Although no one can deny the analogy to the Exodus, the majority of interpreters, who apply the words to the survivors of the Captivity, are probably right in view of the mention of the sword. The Lord is continuing the grace he showed his people in the desert wanderings (cf. 2:1–3). The desert is thus a figure for the land of the Exile in contrast to their homeland. As of old, the Lord in his infinite grace is concerned about finding rest for his troubled, weary people. What he did by the pillar of cloud and the pillar of fire in the desert, he was willing to do for the returning exiles.

3–4 In vv.3–6, one of the most beautiful poems in his book, Jeremiah cites the declaration of the people (v.3)—"The LORD appeared to us [lit., 'to me']." Again, referring to the analogy of the Exodus, the people recall the unparalleled love, grace, and comfort God had extended to them "in the past" (lit., "from afar"). Here Jeremiah underscores the Lord's inexhaustible patience—the basic concept of his constantly wooing his people and drawing them to himself. What comfort was theirs in the recognition of such perpetual love! Addressing Israel as a virgin (v.4), unsullied before God, Jeremiah implies that the Lord sees her just as appealing as in the time of her departure from Egypt (cf. 2:1–3; Hos 2:14–23). Grace blots out all the failures of the past. Both rebuilding and joy are promised the northern kingdom. Contrasted with the sorrow of the Exile (Ps 137:1) is the use of tambourines at dances in times of rejoicing (cf. Exod 15:20). In ancient times dancing was often a religious exercise (cf. 2 Sam 6:14).

5 Amplifying the thought of restoration, Jeremiah says that the hills of Samaria will be planted with vineyards. Essentially an occupation in time of peace, viniculture is often interrupted by war. But in the time Jeremiah is looking forward to, those who plant grapes will enjoy (lit., "make common") the fruit of their labors—i.e., use it as common food. The law of Moses did not permit the Hebrews to eat the fruit of the first three years. Fruit of the fourth year was given to God, but it could be redeemed and eaten as common food (cf. Lev 19:23–25; cf. also Deut 20:6; 28:30). Thus Jeremiah's reference to the vineyards implies that Israel will be settled in her land and enjoying it under normal conditions.

6 Even more glorious is Jeremiah's prediction that watchmen will direct those of Ephraim (the northern kingdom) to go up to Zion to worship the Lord there. Some interpreters believe v.6 to be a later addition to the book, but this is not tenable. In the OT the temple in Zion is always considered the *only* authorized sanctuary. Besides, Jeremiah is nowhere opposed to sincere temple worship. According to Jewish tradition watchers were appointed for the appearance of the moon, from which their months were counted. Here the watchmen on the hills of Samaria are to show the northern kingdom how to go up to Jerusalem to keep the feasts, as the pilgrimage feasts were annually observed in ancient times (cf. Deut 16:16). This will mark the end of the disruption of the kingdom of Solomon in 930 B.C. Ephraim's condition in blessing will be permanent because Jeroboam's misleading them from the Lord's sanctuary will be a thing of the past, when they return to Zion. The breach of many centuries will at last be healed.

b. *The restoration of Israel in joy*

31:7–14

⁷This is what the LORD says:

> "Sing with joy for Jacob;
>   shout for the greatest of the nations.
> Make your praises heard, and say,
>   'O LORD, save your people,
>   the remnant of Israel.'
> ⁸See, I will bring them from the land of the north
>   and gather them from the ends of the earth.
> Among them will be the blind and the lame,
>   expectant mothers and women in labor;
>   a great throng will return.
> ⁹They will come with weeping;
>   they will pray as I bring them back.
> I will lead them beside streams of water
>   on a level path where they will not stumble,
> because I am Israel's father,
>   and Ephraim is my firstborn son.
>
> ¹⁰"Hear the word of the LORD, O nations;
>   proclaim it in distant coastlands:
> 'He who scattered Israel will gather them
>   and will watch over his flock like a shepherd.'
> ¹¹For the LORD will ransom Jacob
>   and redeem them from the hand of those stronger
>   than they.
> ¹²They will come and shout for joy on the heights of Zion;
>   they will rejoice in the bounty of the LORD—
> the grain, the new wine and the oil,
>   the young of the flocks and herds.
> They will be a well-watered garden,
>   and they will sorrow no more.
> ¹³Then maidens will dance and be glad,
>   young men and old as well.
> I will turn their mourning into gladness;
>   I will give them comfort and joy instead of sorrow.
> ¹⁴I will satisfy the priests with abundance,
>   and my people will be filled with my bounty,"

declares the LORD.

7–9 This section (vv.7–14) emphasizes joy at the end of the Exile. With five verbs ("sing," "shout," "proclaim," "praise" [NIV combines "proclaim" and "praise" into "make your praises"], "say") Jeremiah celebrates the great salvation provided for Israel (v.7). It has been suggested that "greatest [lit., 'head'] of the nations" be emended to "top of the mountains" (so Hyatt). This is wholly unnecessary and contrary to Jeremiah's intent, for elsewhere Israel is more than once designated in a similar way (cf. Deut 26:19; Amos 6:1). She will be restored to her rightful position. Moreover, in his answer the Lord promises a return, not only from the north country, but ultimately from all parts of the earth (v.8). Notice the affinities in style and thought with the latter parts of Isaiah. And from the restoration Jeremiah is describing, none will be excluded. The blind, the lame, the pregnant women—even those in labor, for whom the journey would be especially burdensome—will be included. The picture is one of universal participation. Furthermore, the return will be accompanied by weeping and tears of repentance (v.9). Weeping for their sin and rebellion will then be overshadowed by the joy of return. Repentance, as always, issues in salvation. As the people give themselves to prayer, the Lord will lead them by streams of water, a metaphor of refreshment (cf. Isa 41:18; 43:20; 49:10). All this tenderness and concern for Ephraim (Israel) stems from the original elective purpose of God declared in Exodus 4:22 (cf. Deut 32:6). The designation of firstborn in Exodus 4:22 included the whole nation, whereas here it is transferred to Ephraim, the head of the Ten Tribes. Ephraim is mentioned before Judah (vv.23–26) because the Ten Tribes were in exile much longer and, humanly considered, were less likely to be delivered. The prophet could with warrant call Ephraim the firstborn, for Joseph actually received the birthright of the firstborn, which was forfeited by the sin of Reuben (cf. 1 Chron 5:1–2). Sonship in the OT includes the concept of paternal love and care on a national scale, rather than the NT concept of personal membership in the family of God by the Spirit.

10–14 These five verses contain additional promises to Israel. The word is to be spread afar that the Lord has regathered Israel (v.10). The nations will be told that it was the Lord who exiled his people and that it is he who restores them. The figure of shepherd and flock portrays the dual concepts of tenderness and concern. Just as the Lord alone was responsible for Israel's chastisement, so now it is he alone who will regather them. The Lord will ransom Israel, that is, deliver the people from foreign bondage under the power of a pagan world ruler (v.11). Promises are heaped one upon another—predictions of joy, return to Jerusalem, nature transformed, and a new prosperity (v.12). Israel will be ransomed, redeemed, rejoicing, and restored. When the people come to Zion, they will find every need supplied. God's "bounty" (lit., "goodness") includes material blessings as the text shows. Never again will God's people sorrow as they did in the time of their Exile (v.13). So great will be the prosperity bestowed on them that the priests will be satiated because of the many sacrifices brought by the worshipers (v.14; cf. Lev 7:34). With abundant harvests, the portions of the priests will increase.

c. *Israel's lamentable present*

31:15–22

¹⁵This is what the LORD says:

"A voice is heard in Ramah,
   mourning and great weeping,
Rachel weeping for her children
   and refusing to be comforted,
   because her children are no more."

16This is what the LORD says:

"Restrain your voice from weeping
   and your eyes from tears,
for your work will be rewarded,"

                        declares the LORD.
   "They will return from the land of the enemy.
17So there is hope for your future,"

                        declares the LORD.
   "Your children will return to their own land.
18"I have surely heard Ephraim's moaning:
   'You disciplined me like an unruly calf,
   and I have been disciplined.
Restore me, and I will return,
   because you are the LORD my God.
19After I strayed,
   I repented;
after I came to understand,
   I beat my breast.
I was ashamed and humiliated
   because I bore the disgrace of my youth.'
20Is not Ephraim my dear son,
   the child in whom I delight?
Though I often speak against him,
   I still remember him.
Therefore my heart yearns for him;
   I have great compassion for him,"

                        declares the LORD.

21"Set up road signs;
   put up guideposts.
Take note of the highway,
   the road that you take.
Return, O Virgin Israel,
   return to your towns.
22How long will you wander,
   O unfaithful daughter?
The LORD will create a new thing on earth—
   a woman will surround a man."

15 From glowing predictions of tenderness and joy, Jeremiah now turns back to the sad conditions of his day. He pictures Rachel at Ramah weeping disconsolately for the loss of her children. She was an ancestress of the northern tribes of Ephraim and Manasseh (through Joseph), as well as of Benjamin in the south. Undoubtedly, she is lamenting the exile of her children in 722–721 B.C. Some place the incident later at 586 B.C. The first is preferable because it relates specifically to the captivity of the northern kingdom. This, however, need not rule out her weeping for the Exile yet predicted, which occurred in 586 B.C. Ramah was a town five miles north of Jerusalem, the very place where exiles were gathered before deportation to Babylon (cf.

40:1). Rachel weeping is a poetical figure looking forward to her seeing her posterity carried off into exile. Jeremiah himself was in a camp for exiles in Ramah (cf. 40:1). She who had so longed for children (cf. Gen 30:1) is cruelly bereaved of them, but God purposes to restore them.

16–17 The Lord bids Rachel to stop mourning because now she can comfort herself by the promise of her children's return. Twice it is said that they will return (vv. 16–17). The "work" to be "rewarded" includes bearing, rearing, sorrowing over, and praying for her children (so Bewer). As they were a source of grief to her, now they will be a joy on their return from exile.

Much discussion among expositors has centered on the interpretation of this reference to Rachel and even more on the quotation of this prophecy to Herod's slaughter of the innocents recorded in Matthew 2:17–18. The first aspect of the problem, the meaning of Jeremiah's prediction, has already been treated. But how can this prophecy be fulfilled in Matthew's reference? First, it must be stressed that Matthew's method of quoting an OT reference does not automatically imply a direct fulfillment (cf. "The Old Testament in the New Testament," EBC, 1:617–27). For proof see the immediate context in Matthew 2:15, where Hosea 11:1 in its original context unmistakably speaks of the nation Israel but by analogy and higher fulfillment (called by some "compenetration") refers to Christ. Similarly, that which related to Israel in original revelation (v. 15) is by analogy ("typological fulfillment," so KD) used in speaking of Herod's atrocities. In both cases God will overrule the nation's sorrow for her ultimate joy.

18–20 It is one thing to hear of Rachel's concern for Ephraim, but what was his attitude? Ephraim expressed godly sorrow for his sins (vv. 18–19). He prayed for the Lord to help restore him. In grief over his own waywardness, he reviewed the Lord's dealings with him. He admitted that he has been brought under control by the chastisement of the Lord. At last he recognized the need for repentance before restoration. He was formerly like an untrained calf, refractory and in need of training. Through the Lord's judgments he learned discipline. As earlier in this book, Jeremiah plays on the words for "turn . . . return" (NIV, "restore . . . return"; cf. note at 30:3). Once he was chastened and became submissive to the providences of the Lord, Ephraim smote his thigh (*yārēk;* but NIV, "breast," so KJV, RSV et al.) in grief and sorrow (v. 19). The Spirit of God had done his effective work so that Ephraim recognized the shame his earlier sinful life brought on him. Finally we have the Lord's answer to Ephraim's confession of need. His fatherly concern for the prodigal Ephraim is beautifully expressed (v. 20). Divine love will not be denied Ephraim in spite of his sin. As the Lord had to denounce the sins of his people many times, he recalls his intimate relationships with them. Fatherly tenderness prevails over childish recalcitrance (cf. David and Absalom [2 Sam 13:37–39]). In the Hebrew, "my heart yearns for him" is strongly anthropopathic (lit., "my bowels sound"). Ephraim is forgiven.

21 Jeremiah now addresses the returning exiles of the northern kingdom. They are to make ample preparation for their homeward journey. The succession of imperatives shows the urgency of their preparation for return. It was the custom of caravans to set up pillars, poles, and heaps of stones to guide them. So the exiles are told to mark out the old route, to set up signs to help them find their way back. They are to pay heed to the way they went into exile in order to be able to retrace their steps (so Streane). The imperatives admonish them not to delay their return by wavering.

22 The second half of this verse is one of the most disputed in the entire book. Interpretations vary greatly and are often mutually exclusive. Many scholars admit that a satisfactory solution is not attainable; no interpretation has been accepted by a majority of scholars. The verse is difficult because the background is lacking. One view sees here a prophecy of the Virgin Birth of the Lord Jesus Christ. This is an ancient interpretation, coming from the church fathers; but it is rejected by the majority of interpreters. It is based on the concept of the Lord's creation of "a new thing," obviously something miraculous, and the idea of a woman in some way controlling a man (so Broadbent, Streane et al.). This view is invalid for the following reasons.

1. The word "woman" (*nᵉqēbāh*, lit., "a female") does not even have the definite article (cf. Isa 7:14).
2. The word "woman" cannot be made to mean a virgin. In fact, it is a most general word for woman in contradistinction to man.
3. The verb *sābab* ("surround") is poles apart from the idea of conceiving.
4. The interpretation is ill suited to the context. How does it flow from its context? Granted that the word "virgin" occurs in v.21 and earlier in v.4; but it is plain that these references are to Israel, not an individual. The interpretation is reverent, but not possible.

Other solutions do not fare much better. Some propose that the "new thing" is a woman who protects a man. Thus it describes a physically weaker partner surrounding and sustaining a stronger one (so Harrison). A second proposal is that "Virgin Israel" returns to the Lord (so Hyatt). A third one is that the words refer to the security Israel will enjoy so that the women will be able to protect the nation in case of attack, allowing the men to be occupied with their work (so Cundall). A fourth view is that, though the Lord has embraced the woman Israel in love, the latter days will witness a situation in which the woman Israel will seek after and embrace her lover, the Lord (so Jensen). A fifth view suggests that the woman will propose marriage to the man; that is, Israel will seek union with the Lord. This requires the translation "a female will turn into a man"—viz., she becomes of manly character, no longer hesitant in returning to God but resolute in doing so (so Freedman). A sixth view is that Israel will overcome the power of the Gentiles (so H.A. Ironside, *Notes on the Prophecy and Lamentations of Jeremiah* [New York: Loizeaux Brothers, 1946], ad loc.). Finally, some interpret the verse to mean that Israel, weak as a woman, becomes superior to the strong Babylonians (so Calvin, though he agrees with the Fathers that it refers to the Virgin Birth). With such an abundance of interpretations, it is foolhardy to be dogmatic about the meaning of these puzzling words. On the whole, it seems best to take them as a proverbial saying about something amazing and hard to believe. The meaning is beyond present solution (so Bright et al.).

Notes

15 In this verse Rachel, ancestress of the tribes of Ephraim, Manasseh, and Benjamin, is pictured as mourning over her children who have been taken into exile. Her weeping is

connected with Ramah, but discussion has centered on the question as to the reason for this site. According to Joshua 18:25, Ramah lay between Gibeon and Beeroth, five miles north of Jerusalem. Ramah is mentioned as the birthplace and home of Samuel (cf. 1 Sam 1:19; 25:1) in Mount Ephraim. Ramah was also the place from which the exiles were sent to Babylon (cf. 40:1). Uncertainty as to the exact location of Ramah has been voiced by some scholars (cf. E.G. Kraeling, *Rand McNally Bible Atlas* [New York: Rand McNally & Co., 1956], p. 184; it is clear that Ramah in northwest Galilee is ruled out; cf. ibid., maps VI, VII, VIII, IX, and X). Many claim that Ramah was the site of Rachel's tomb (so Bewer et al.). The traditional site of her tomb, five miles south of Jerusalem, is then claimed to be a wrong identification of the place mentioned in Gen 35:16–20. First Sam 10:2 is adduced as proof that Rachel's tomb was in that vicinity. This does not harmonize with Gen 35:16–20 or 48:7. The modern er-Ram (five miles north of Jerusalem) is in the territory of Benjamin. Since Christian times, however, the tomb of Rachel has been located about a mile north of Bethlehem, as required by the Genesis passages. This has been explained as a traditional site influenced by the quotation in Matt 2:16–18 and the slaughter of the innocents.

How can the locations be harmonized? Two options are open.

1. A.P. Stanley (HJP, 1:63) suggests: "After the allotment of the country to the several tribes, the territory of the Benjamites was extended by a long strip far into the south to include the sepulchre of their beloved ancestress."

2. A second option is so simple that many have overlooked it. Ramah in Benjamin is probably meant. But notice that the text states nothing of the grave of Rachel. Her lamentation is heard at Ramah, the most elevated border-town of the two kingdoms, and the cry would easily reach to Judah (so KD, Orelli).

---

d. *Judah's bright future*

31:23–26

> 23This is what the LORD Almighty, the God of Israel says: "When I bring them back from captivity, the people in the land of Judah and in its towns will once again use these words: 'The LORD bless you, O righteous dwelling, O sacred mountain.' 24People will live together in Judah and all its towns—farmers and those who move about with their flocks. 25I will refresh the weary and satisfy the faint."
>
> 26At this I awoke and looked around. My sleep had been pleasant to me.

23–25 Jeremiah, after painting a magnificent picture of Ephraim's return and blessing, now addresses Judah with words of strong assurance and with promises similar to those given Ephraim. When the southern kingdom and her cities are restored, the old greeting of those visiting Jerusalem will be heard once more (v.23). "O sacred mountain" refers to the temple mount and Jerusalem as a whole (cf. Ps 2:6; Isa 66:20). The city will again be characterized by her righteousness (cf. Isa 1:21). Once spiritual things are cared for, temporal things will be provided (v.24). Judah's cities will not be abandoned by their inhabitants, and those settled in them will enjoy tranquillity and prosperity without fear of marauders or invading armies. Indeed, every individual need will be amply met (v.25).

26 Jeremiah goes on to give his own response to the bright promises of the millennial time under Messiah. Many expositors take v.26 to be an insertion by a later writer because they find difficulty in reconciling it with 23:25, where Jeremiah disparaged dreams. But it is not difficult to discern that Jeremiah in 23:25 was speaking only of the false dreams of false prophets. He never, however, denied that dreams might be a true means of revelation (cf. the dreams of Jacob, Joseph, Pharaoh, Nebuchadnezzar et al.). The truths he had been communicating had been given him in a supernatural dream during a sleep that may have been ecstatic. Elsewhere in the OT the revelatory state compared to the normal state is likened to sleep (cf. Dan 10:9; Zech 4:1). Jeremiah's sleep was sweet because the truths he received in them were comforting foreviews of future glory for God's people (contrast the disappointing dreams in Isa 29:8; cf. Prov 3:24).

e. National increase under Messiah

31:27–30

27"The days are coming," declares the LORD, "when I will plant the house of Israel and the house of Judah with the offspring of men and of animals. 28Just as I watched over them to uproot and tear down, and to overthrow, destroy and bring disaster, so I will watch over them to build and to plant," declares the LORD. 29"In those days people will no longer say,

'The fathers have eaten sour grapes,
and the children's teeth are set on edge.'

30Instead, everyone will die for his own sin; whoever eats sour grapes—his own teeth will be set on edge."

27–30 Because invasions and deportations had taken man and beast from the land, the Lord used Jeremiah to portray a dramatic renewal of the land through resowing the country with man and beast (v.27; cf. Ezek 36:8–11; Hos 1:11; 2:23). That messianic times are in view is clear from the formula "The days are coming" (cf. 30:3). What a contrast to the condition of the land with its population and cattle decimated by the captivities! Once their chastisement and suffering are over, the Lord will refashion his people and his land. He prefers to build rather than destroy (v.28; cf. 1:10). Verses 29–30 reflect the bitterness of the exiles who traced their predicament to the sins of their parents and ancestors. They felt that God was judging them unjustly for circumstances they were not responsible for. The popular proverb is also used by Ezekiel (cf. Ezek 18:2–4). One would think that in light of Deuteronomy 24:16 no one would claim that children pay for the sins of their parents. The proverb may have been suggested, though erroneously so, by Exodus 20:5–6. The altogether sufficient answer to the fatalistic despair voiced by the proverb is that in the suffering of Israel individual responsibility is clear. Each man and woman was personally responsible; so none could claim exculpation.

f. God's new covenant

31:31–34

31"The time is coming," declares the LORD,
"when I will make a new covenant
with the house of Israel
and with the house of Judah.
32It will not be like the covenant
I made with their forefathers

when I took them by the hand
  to lead them out of Egypt,
because they broke my covenant,
  though I was a husband to them,"
                     declares the LORD.
33"This is the covenant I will make with the house of Israel
  after that time," declares the LORD.
"I will put my law in their minds
  and write it on their hearts.
I will be their God,
  and they will be my people.
34No longer will a man teach his neighbor,
  or a man his brother, saying, 'Know the LORD,'
because they will all know me,
  from the least of them to the greatest,"
                     declares the LORD.

"For I will forgive their wickedness
  and will remember their sins no more."

Expositors of all shades of conviction have written in glowing terms of the significance of this portion of the book. It has been acclaimed as one of the most important passages in the entire OT, signally validated against hypercritical doubts and theories (so Bewer et al.). It is beyond dispute that the passage has had tremendous influence on NT doctrine. Many expositors maintain that the concept of the new covenant is Jeremiah's greatest contribution to biblical truth.

At this point an outline of the remainder of the chapter, detailing the fullness of Jeremiah's revelation, will be useful:

1. The time of the covenant (v.31)—"The time is coming"
2. The Maker of the covenant (v.31)—the LORD (vv.3, 20, 32, 35)
3. The name of the covenant (v.31)—"new" (Rom 11:27; Heb 8:6–13; 10:14–18; also Matt 26:26–28; Mark 14:22–24; Luke 22:19–20; 1 Cor 11:23–25)
4. The parties of the covenant (v.31)—"house of Israel" and "house of Judah" (cf. Ezek 37:15–19; Rom 9:4–5—the nation of the covenants)
5. The contrasted covenant (v.32)—not like the old covenant: based on merit and works, susceptible of infraction, no enablement (nonfulfilling), did not give life (Gal 3:21)
6. The nature of the covenant (vv.33–34)—not dependent on external law nor human interpretation; law written on the heart; gives intimate knowledge of and fellowship with God, forgiveness of sins, and peace of heart
7. The immutability of the covenant (vv.35–37)—the unchanging purpose of God reflected in the fixed order of nature
8. The physical aspects of the covenant (vv.38–40)—rebuilt Jerusalem in holiness and permanence
9. The Guarantor of the covenant (vv.31–40)—"declares the LORD" or "the LORD says" (nine times), as though to swear by himself (cf. Heb 6:17–18).

31 This mountain-peak OT passage stands in a real sense as the climax of Jeremiah's teaching. Every one of its phrases and clauses is vital. Jeremiah wrote the passage while he was shut up in the court of the guard. The passage begins with the attention-arresting "Behold" (*hinnēh*, so KJV, RSV et al.; untranslated in NIV). The words "the time is coming" have already been used by Jeremiah; they are an es-

chatological formula that places the prophecy in messianic times in the Day of the Lord, the consummation period of the nation's history (cf. v.27). The promise relates to a "new covenant" and is a prediction of a radical change in God's economy (i.e., his dealing with humanity). Thus when Jeremiah foretold a new covenant, by implication the Mosaic covenant became the old one (cf. Heb. 8:13). Moreover, the new covenant is an eternal one. National covenants do not die because of old age. The old covenant spoke of a great physical deliverance from Egypt through the blood of lambs and the power of God; the new covenant proclaims a great spiritual deliverance from sin and death through the efficacious blood of the Lamb of God and the power of God. The Passover Feast memorialized the first; the Lord's Supper memorializes the second.

Jeremiah explicitly presents the parties to the covenant: the Lord, the house of Israel, and the house of Judah. Notice that the covenant brings to mind the cleavage of the nation into two kingdoms, but notice also that both parts of the nation are included. The whole covenant is for the whole nation. Significantly, the new covenant will be with God's chosen people, as was the old. It could not be made with the church because no former (old) covenant had been made with her (so Ironside, *Prophecy and Lamentations of Jeremiah*).

Does this mean that believers today have no part in this new covenant? Surely not, for the same death of Christ that implemented the new covenant for Israel does so for all sinners for all time. The testimony of the entire NT is too clear on this point to be misunderstood. Because Israel rejected the covenant in the first advent, Gentiles availed themselves of its provisions (cf. Rom 9:30–33); and Israel will yet ratify it at the climax of her history (cf. Zech 12:10–13:1). Thus it is correct to say that all believers in Christ are by virtue of this covenant grafted into the stock of Abraham (cf. Rom 11:16–24).

Does this mean that another covenant needs to be made for either Israel or Gentiles? Obviously not, since both share redemption by faith in the blood of the new covenant. Writing to Hebrews of his time, and there were believing Hebrews among them, the writer of the Epistle to the Hebrews makes clear how the new covenant now avails for both (cf. Heb 8; see also Eph 3:1–7). Does this mean that all the blessings promised Israel may now be appropriated by believers? Does this efface the distinction between Israel and the church? The answer to these questions is a resounding no! The NT is careful to state in each instance what elements in the blessings promised Israel may be transferred to the common enjoyment of Israel and the church. It is neither warranted nor in harmony with Scripture to go beyond this.

Some ask how the new covenant can apply to the church when it was to be negotiated with Israel and Judah. The historical argument is insurmountable: when the new covenant was inaugurated (see the gospel accounts), there *was* no church, nor could there be until the resurrection of Christ (cf. Eph 1:22–23). Furthermore, although Jeremiah 31 does not state it, the making of the new covenant was inextricably bound up with the crucifixion of Christ for all mankind. When Israel refused to enter into the covenant (cf. Isa 53; Matt 22:1–10; Luke 14:15–23), God having but *one* way of salvation for all ages of history, the offer of redemption (the procuring means of the covenant) went out to all people. Although the church is not explicitly seen in the OT, the salvation of non-Jews is predicted more than once (cf. Isa 49:1–7, esp. v.6). It is the new truth of the NT that redeemed Jews and Gentiles (the "new man" of Eph 2:15) constitute the church of this age. Salvation is possible only through the death of Christ, and this is the basis of the new covenant. All sinful mankind is thus in view in this covenant. Finally, Israel as a nation will ratify the covenant after the "full number of the Gentiles has come in" (Rom 11:25–27).

32 Jeremiah points out in this verse that the new covenant is built on the fact of Israel's failure under the old covenant. Because the old covenant was a legal one ("If you do . . . I will do"), it was incumbent on both parties to the covenant (contract) to maintain its provisions. This Israel did not do, for the people broke the first commandment before Moses descended from Sinai. Jeremiah does not repudiate or depreciate the Mosaic covenant any more than Paul does (cf. Rom 7:12; 8:3–4). The fault lay with the people and their sin; *they* broke the covenant. Thus the new covenant must supersede the old. If the old covenant had not been broken, then what need was there for the ministry of Jeremiah or any of the OT prophets? All were commissioned by God to call the nation to repent of her transgressions of the Mosaic Law (cf. v.32; 11:10; 32:40; Ezek 37:26). The day when the covenant was made with the "forefathers" refers to the whole period of the Exodus (cf. 7:22). "I took them by the hand" is a tender nuance of paternal love and concern (cf. Hos 11:3–4). The blame for breaking the covenant rested wholly on Israel and Judah, for there was no fault in God; he had ever been as faithful to them as a faithful husband to his wife. This marriage relationship was the very basis on which God expected obedience to and fidelity in the covenant.

33 Once more Jeremiah stresses the nature of the covenant as a national, not an individual, covenant. The parties to it are the same as those in v.31. The time factor is again stated; it is "after that time"—i.e., after the return from exile. Instead of changing his covenant relationship to his people because they broke the covenant, in his grace God finds a way whereby they will not break the new covenant. How can this be done? God will write the law within them; on their heart he will inscribe it. The old covenant had been engraved in stone. The new covenant will include a revolutionary change in will, heart, and conscience. It will be an internal rather than an external covenant. Here is a contrast to the writing on the tables of stone (cf. Exod 19:3–8; 24:3–8; 31:18; Deut 4:13; 29:1–29; 2 Cor 3:3). The law now becomes a principle of life (cf. Rom 8:1–4). It will become part of the nature of God's people; it will be instinctive. The core of the new covenant is God's gift of a new heart (cf. Ezek 36:25–27). Herein lies the sufficient motivation for obeying God's law. Basic to obedience is inner knowledge of God's will coupled with an enablement to perform it, all founded on the assurance that sins are forgiven. Permanence is also a feature of this covenant (cf. vv.35–37). Since the inward dynamic was absent in the old covenant, it could not be effective. There must be an inner force, a new power.

Some have claimed that there is nothing in this passage to suggest that the new covenant would differ in character from the old (so Freedman). On the contrary, the entire transaction implies the new birth set forth in the gospel. The regenerate spirit is the source of all godly action. The "heart" includes man's emotional, ethical, and intellectual life (so Peake). The goal of the covenant is that relation between God and his people that was repeatedly emphasized from Abraham's time on. In this connection it is instructive to examine once more Ezekiel's doctrine of the new heart (cf. Ezek 11:19; 18:31; 36:26) and John's doctrine of regeneration (cf. John 1:10–13; 3:1–16).

Is it not strange, however, that so many believers today yearn for laws and rules, putting themselves under the economy of the old covenant, which Jeremiah, Christ, and the apostles warned was not capable of fulfillment? No wonder the new covenant is a missionary message for the world! Its nature is individual, internal, and universal. The reason Jeremiah emphasized the national factor (cf. vv.31–33) was that he wanted to stress the origin of the covenant and to sharpen the contrast between the new covenant and the old covenant, which was made with Israel only at Sinai.

34 One of the grand features of the new covenant is that it affords a clear apprehension of God and his will by believers without human mediation. God will be known instinctively and his will performed spontaneously (cf. Isa 54:13; John 6:45). Experience of God will be direct, not dependent on external instruction. The knowledge spoken of is not theoretical knowledge transmitted by religious instruction. It is rather knowledge of God based on a heart experience of divine grace and imparted by the Holy Spirit with assurance that the believer has been received into the family of God through the forgiveness of sins (so KD). This knowledge does not militate against or render unnecessary religious instruction. (See the NT teaching concerning teachers in 1 Cor 12:28–29 and Eph 4:11–12.) There will be direct access to God for both Jew and Gentile. A vital feature of the old covenant was human mediation (cf. Exod 20:19). In the new one there is immediate access to God through Christ, our High Priest (cf. Heb 4:16; 10:19–22). The firsthand knowledge of God will be completely fulfilled in the coming kingdom (so Cunliffe-Jones). For the present it does not mean that every believer will be self-sufficient and independent of others. But it does indicate that all will have their own experience of God without resort to others. "The least of them" is very broad in meaning and includes "the least" in intellectual ability, in influence or position, in moral capacity—all are included in the comprehensive scope of the phrase.

Finally, the climax of this wonderful section comes in the revelation that the basis of the new covenant is forgiveness of sin. Thus gratitude for forgiveness will issue in spontaneous obedience. The new covenant does not envision sinlessness but forgiveness of sin resulting in restoration of fellowship with God. The foundation of the new covenant (after which the NT itself is named) is the absolute and complete forgiveness of all sins. Notice that the covenant shows no dependence on law, temple, sacrifices, ark, human priesthood, nation, or country. The old covenant did not, could not, and was never intended to save anyone. The last clause of v.34 states that what grace forgives, divine omniscience forgets. In summary, the enunciation of the new covenant, which differs so much from the old, focuses on its permanence and its sustaining principle that evokes gratitude for the forgiveness of sin. The overarching emotion is love, not fear. The goal in both covenants is the same (so Peake): "I will be their God, and they will be my people" (cf. v.33 with Exod 29:45; Lev 26:12).

Notes

32 The translation "I was a husband to them" (NIV, NASB; "I was their husband," RSV) is paralleled in practically all the English versions. However, NEB translates "I was patient with them" (on what basis is not clear), and AmT renders "I had to reject them." Why the great disparity? The Hebrew verb בָּעַל (bāʿal, "to marry, rule over") with its noun baʿal ("owner," "lord," "husband") is well known in Semitic languages and in Hebrew of differ-

ent periods. The variant reading comes from the LXX, which rendered the verb with ἠμέλησα (*ēmelēsa*, "to neglect, be unconcerned about, disregard"), a translation followed by the Syriac. By altering the Hebrew from בָּעַלְתִּי (*bā'altî*, "I was a husband") to גָּעַלְתִּי (*gā'altî*, "I abhorred, loathed"), the meaning is achieved. What complicates the matter is that the LXX is quoted word for word in Heb 8:9. A translation of "abhorred" is too strong for the Greek word. It must be pointed out that in Jer 3:14 the LXX has "I will be your lord [i.e., 'husband']." In 31:32 the Syriac agrees with the LXX, but in 3:14 it translates "I have pleasure in you." The Vulgate is more consistent, having in 3:14 *ego vir vester* and in 31:32 *ego dominatus sum eorum*. Most scholars see no need for emendation since the MT is satisfactory. It is altogether likely that the Greek translators of the LXX had another Hebrew word in their text. The NT Greek text (UBS, Nestle et al.) follows the LXX because it does no violence to the sense of the passage or the purpose of the sacred writer.

g. *The perpetuity of Israel*

31:35–40

35This is what the LORD says,

> he who appoints the sun
>> to shine by day,
> who decrees the moon and stars
>> to shine by night,
> who stirs up the sea
>> so that its waves roar—
> the LORD Almighty is his name:
>
> 36"Only if these decrees vanish from my sight,"
>> declares the LORD,
> "will the descendants of Israel ever cease
>> to be a nation before me."

37This is what the LORD says:

> "Only if the heavens above can be measured
>> and the foundations of the earth below be searched out
> will I reject all the descendants of Israel
>> because of all they have done,"
>
>> declares the LORD.

38"The days are coming," declares the LORD, "when this city will be rebuilt for me from the Tower of Hananel to the Corner Gate. 39The measuring line will stretch from there straight to the hill of Gareb and then turn to Goah. 40The whole valley where dead bodies and ashes are thrown, and all the terraces out to the Kidron Valley on the east as far as the corner of the Horse Gate, will be holy to the LORD. The city will never again be uprooted or demolished."

35–37 Of what value is an eternal covenant if certain parties to it are limited in life span? But such is not the case with the new covenant, for it is made with an eternal people. The permanence of the nation is illustrated from the fixed arrangements in nature (v.35). The survival of Israel through the centuries can be explained only on supernatural grounds (v.36; cf. 33:20, 25). Scripture knows no greater guarantee for the validity and permanence of the covenant than that stated here. As unchangeable as the laws of nature is God's covenant with the deathless nation. The concept of nation carries with it geographical location, government, and other ethnic features to be fully realized in the end time. In short, it is utterly impossible that Israel should cease to be a nation before God (v.37). National existence is assured, regardless of how God may have to deal with individuals in the nation. God regards his promises rather than their demerits.

38–40 The same eschatological formula—"The days are coming"—that has pervaded this chapter is reiterated once more (v.38). Since a literal nation must have an actual geographical location in which to reside, it is now revealed that the capital, Jerusalem, will be rebuilt and expanded—yes, the very city that Jeremiah was before long to see destroyed by the Chaldean army. This disclosure is not an anticlimax, as some suggest. A renewed covenant demands a renewed Jerusalem. It will be greatly enlarged and permanently settled. The rebuilding is not for themselves or for secular purposes but for the glory of the Lord. It will be dedicated and separated to him (cf. v.40).

The rebuilding of the city will encompass the four corners of the capital (cf. Zech 14:10). The Tower of Hananel was the northeast corner of the city (cf. Neh 3:1; 12:39; Zech 14:10). The Corner Gate probably refers to the one at the northwest corner of the city wall (cf. 2 Kings 14:13; 2 Chron 26:9). The locations of Gareb and Goah are unknown (v.39); conjecture places Gareb on the western side of Jerusalem and Goah toward the Valley of Hinnom on the south. There are no clues to the sites. The valley of the corpses and ashes (v.40) is generally understood to be the Valley of Hinnom (cf. 7:31). It has been suggested that the fields are quarries. The Kidron flows east of Jerusalem (cf. 2 Sam 15:23). The Horse Gate is apparently at the southeast corner of the temple courts (so Bewer; cf. Neh 3:28 with 2 Kings 11:16; 2 Chron 23:15). Thus even the polluted areas would be sanctified to the Lord.

In strong language the section closes with the affirmation that the city will be invincible forever. A permanent nation calls for a permanent capital. The rebuilding of the city envisioned here cannot be that effected in Nehemiah's day because (1) the contextual considerations demand the end time for Israel (cf. "days are coming" [vv.27, 31]) and (2) the temple rebuilt by Zerubbabel was thrown down thereafter and again destroyed (cf. Matt 24:1–2; Luke 21:20–24). Finally, in the broader context of prophecy, this passage will not permit an interpretation that applies it to a spiritual, heavenly, or symbolic Jerusalem. If that were possible, why is it so full of literal detail?

3. The manifestation of faith (32:1–44)

Jeremiah's faith in the Lord's words of restoration in chapters 30–31 is now put to the test. This chapter is important as showing the reality of Jeremiah's faith in the Lord's promises of the nation's restoration. The time was the second year of the siege of Jerusalem—588–587 B.C. (the latter year is the more likely). The siege had begun in Zedekiah's ninth year (cf. 39:1), but the Babylonians had withdrawn on hearing of the approach of the Egyptian army (cf. 37:5). Jerusalem fell in August of the following year, 586 B.C. (so Hyatt et al.). The reference to "the eighteenth year of Nebuchadnezzar" is in accord with the chronology indicated by 25:1 and 52:12.

At this point a long section of the book begins. In chronology it is more cohesive than the preceding parts of the book. Some scholars place this chapter after chapters 37–38. Chapter 32 deals with what happened during the years before the capture of

Jerusalem, the destruction of the city, and the incidents that immediately followed. What Jeremiah did at that time showed his faith in the nation's restoration to the land after the Captivity. It was indeed a dark time. Jerusalem was undergoing its final siege, and Jeremiah himself was in prison. But it was also just the time for a heroic example of faith.

a. The setting for Jeremiah's act of faith

32:1-5

> ¹This is the word that came to Jeremiah from the LORD in the tenth year of Zedekiah king of Judah, which was the eighteenth year of Nebuchadnezzar. ²The army of the king of Babylon was then besieging Jerusalem, and Jeremiah the prophet was confined in the courtyard of the guard in the royal palace of Judah.
> ³Now Zedekiah king of Judah had imprisoned him there, saying, "Why do you prophesy as you do? You say, 'This is what the LORD says: I am about to hand this city over to the king of Babylon, and he will capture it. ⁴Zedekiah king of Judah will not escape out of the hands of the Babylonians but will certainly be handed over to the king of Babylon, and will speak with him face to face and see him with his own eyes. ⁵He will take Zedekiah to Babylon, where he will remain until I deal with him, declares the LORD. If you fight against the Babylonians, you will not succeed.'"

1-2 This entire chapter moves within the framework of the OT law of redemption (cf. Lev 25). Verses 1-5 describe the times in which Jeremiah carried out his great act of faith. The tenth year of Zedekiah was 587 B.C., the second year of the final siege of Jerusalem (cf. 2 Kings 25:8). The siege of Jerusalem was at an advanced state. The outlook was dark, the situation desperate. Verse 2 tells of Jeremiah's imprisonment; vv.3-5 give the reason for this. Chapter 37 shows us that Jeremiah had not yet been imprisoned during the siege of Jerusalem by the Babylonians and the raising of that siege by the approach of the Egyptian army (cf. 37:4-12). During the temporary raising of the Babylonian siege, when he tried to leave the city to go to the land of Benjamin, Jeremiah was taken and thrown into a dungeon on the pretense that he was defecting to the Babylonians (37:11, 16). He remained there a good while until Zedekiah ordered him to appear before him to be questioned about the outcome of the war. When he told Zedekiah that he would be captured by Nebuchadnezzar (37:17), Jeremiah then lamented about the difficulty of his own imprisonment (37:20) and begged not to be put back into the dungeon. So Zedekiah ordered him (37:21) to be moved to the "courtyard of the guard" (v.2), where he stayed until the city fell (38:13, 28; 39:14). He was shut up at the request of the officials (38:4-6) and at Zedekiah's command. The courtyard of the guard, probably a stockade (cf. Neh 3:25), was the part of the palace area set apart for prisoners. (Friends could visit them there.) The soldiers who guarded the palace were quartered there.

3-5 There is no contradiction between v.3 and 37:15. Verse 3 is a general account without details. The officers had confined Jeremiah in Jonathan's house (37:15), but Zedekiah had moved him into the palace (37:21). Even though Zedekiah witnessed the fulfillment of Jeremiah's predictions, he was angry enough to imprison him, as if this could alter what was happening. Such is the irrationality of unbelief. Zedekiah, then, is ultimately responsible for Jeremiah's imprisonment. Zedekiah should have known by this time that Jeremiah's message was not his own. Yet he found fault with the prophet's predictions because they were wholly unfavorable to the country and to Zedekiah himself. In plain, unequivocal terms Jeremiah foretold Zedekiah's fate. Some scholars have considered this reference to the Lord's judgment (vv.4–5) to be ambiguous because they do not think it was necessary at this time to divulge to Zedekiah what was in store for him (so Streane). Most scholars believe that v.4 speaks of the Lord's punishment of Zedekiah. The context appears to support this view. All that is intended by the passage, however, appears to be Zedekiah's death, for he was never released from Babylon (so Freedman et al.).

Notes

1–15 This passage is valuable, not only for the light it throws on Lev 25 and Ruth 4, but also because it contains incidental proof of the falsity of the charge recorded in Jer 37:11–14. Would the prophet have defected in view of (1) the demonstration of his faith in buying land for future occupancy, (2) his repeated statements to Zedekiah that there was no escape from Babylonian Exile except through capitulation to Nebuchadnezzar, and (3) his later refusal to live in Babylon when invited by the captors of the city?

b. *The Lord's command*

32:6–8

> ⁶Jeremiah said, "The word of the LORD came to me: ⁷Hanamel son of Shallum your uncle is going to come to you and say, 'Buy my field at Anathoth, because as nearest relative it is your right and duty to buy it.'
> ⁸"Then, just as the LORD had said, my cousin Hanamel came to me in the courtyard of the guard and said, 'Buy my field at Anathoth in the territory of Benjamin. Since it is your right to redeem it and possess it, buy it for yourself.'
> "I knew that this was the word of the LORD."

6–7 Throughout this chapter Jeremiah is giving his own report of events. Verses 6–7 relate to the Lord and Jeremiah; vv.8–10 to Hanamel and Jeremiah. His God-given hope for the future is now to have an opportunity for expression. Jeremiah's purchase of the field from Hanamel, his cousin (v.7), was meant to encourage the people regarding their return from captivity and to show Jeremiah's firm faith in their future despite their desperate situation. Because of the siege, Hanamel might well have been in financial straits. The Lord told Jeremiah in advance (v.6) that his cousin Hanamel would come to him. That Hanamel did so was in accordance with the law in Leviticus 25:23–28 (cf. Ruth 4:1–6).

Family property must not pass into the hands of an outsider (v.7). The purpose of this law was to keep property in the family and preserve the bond between the family and their property. For the seller this was duty; for the relative or kinsman-redeemer it was a right. Thus such a transaction is spoken of as the duty of redemption and the right of preemption. Hanamel was evidently childless (so Freedman). The passage reveals that the ancient laws of land tenure were still followed in Judah in spite of its apostasy. In addition to the general law for all Israel, these land-tenure

laws would in Jeremiah's time have special relevance to alienation of property belonging to priestly families—property that should not pass into nonpriestly hands.
The situation is all the more dramatic since the field Jeremiah was to buy had
already been captured by the invading Babylonians.

8 Here was a public test of Jeremiah's prophecies about the future blessing of the
land. Hanamel was able to visit Jeremiah because the siege was not yet a tight one.
His request for his cousin to buy the field seemed preposterous with the enemy at
the gates of Jerusalem and exile certain. Of what use could the field be to Jeremiah?
Some have suggested that Hanamel offered Jeremiah the field to see whether he
would back his glorious prophecies of Judah's future with his actions. But the episode is too natural and unaffected to be interpreted like that. When Hanamel came,
Jeremiah knew that the Lord was behind the offer. He had not doubted the Lord's
word and had its confirmation in vv.6-7. Now he realized all the meaning of the
purchase in relation to the nation's future.

c. *The purchase*

32:9-15

> ⁹"So I bought the field at Anathoth from my cousin Hanamel and weighed out for
> him seventeen shekels of silver. ¹⁰I signed and sealed the deed, had it witnessed,
> and weighed out the silver on the scales. ¹¹I took the deed of purchase—the
> sealed copy containing the terms and conditions, as well as the unsealed copy—
> ¹²and I gave this deed to Baruch son of Neriah, the son of Mahseiah, in the
> presence of my cousin Hanamel and of the witnesses who had signed the deed
> and of all the Jews sitting in the courtyard of the guard.
> ¹³"In their presence I gave Baruch these instructions: ¹⁴'This is what the LORD
> Almighty, the God of Israel, says: Take these documents, both the sealed and
> unsealed copies of the deed of purchase, and put them in a clay jar so they will
> last a long time. ¹⁵For this is what the LORD Almighty, The God of Israel, says:
> Houses, fields and vineyards will again be bought in this land.'"

9-11 Jeremiah's faith sustained him in what appeared to be the inevitable loss of his
money. We do not know the source of his income, nor can we speculate about the
adequacy or inadequacy of the price (v.9) or about the size of the field. These details
are not important. The transaction was carried out with legal precision (v.10). This
is the only account in the Bible of a purchase of this kind. Before the introduction
of coinage about the sixth century B.C., payment in financial transactions was made
by weighing out quantities of gold or silver (cf. Gen 23:16). Signing, sealing, and the
presence of witnesses were necessary for legalizing a transaction like the one between Hanamel and Jeremiah. Two copies of the deed were made (v.11), one for
security and the other for future reference in proving that the agreed-on terms had
not been tampered with. All the conditions of the sale were carefully specified.
Deeds were probably executed on papyrus with the writing in cursive Hebrew,
known from the Lachish Letters of that time. Similar illustrative material has been
found at Elephantiné in Egypt. The title deeds went to the buyer. The practice of
sealing deeds throws light on the metaphor of the seven-sealed scroll (Rev 5:1),
which was the title deed to the world purchased by Christ.

12-14 The deed (in duplicate) was given Baruch, the trusted confidant and secretary of Jeremiah, for preservation from loss or mutilation. Up to this point, Baruch had kept himself in the background. Now (v.12) we have the first mention of him in the book. The sale was made as public as possible (v.13); secret transactions were avoided. Moreover, the publicity stressed and disseminated the message implicit in Jeremiah's purchase of the field. The documents were stored in clay jars to insure their permanence (v.14). Such storage jars have been found at Elephantiné (Egypt) and Qumran (Palestine); the Dead Sea Scrolls (written on leather) have survived in earthenware jars for over two thousand years. Usually the jars were sealed with pitch.

As for Jeremiah's transaction, it is obvious that after the Exile the deeds would be of great value to the owners. Here, then, is an instance of ancient title insurance. The transaction (as many commentators have pointed out) has something of a parallel in Livy (26.11) and Florus (2.6), who say that when Hannibal was encamped before the gates of Rome, the site of his camp was auctioned in the city and bought at the customary price. (The double deed was also a Babylonian and Egyptian custom.)

15 Finally, Jeremiah stated that his purchase of the field symbolized the restoration of Israel to her land after the Captivity. This afforded comfort to the beleaguered people of Judah. Jeremiah had availed himself of the opportunity the Lord had given him of showing his full confidence in the prophecy that had been revealed to him by the Lord.

d. *Jeremiah's doubts and prayer*

32:16–25

16"After I had given the deed of purchase to Baruch son of Neriah, I prayed to the LORD:

17"Ah, Sovereign LORD, you have made the heavens and the earth by your great power and outstretched arm. Nothing is too hard for you. 18You show love to thousands but bring the punishment for the fathers' sins into the laps of their children after them. O great and powerful God, whose name is the LORD Almighty, 19great are your purposes and mighty are your deeds. Your eyes are open to all the ways of men; you reward everyone according to his conduct and as his deeds deserve. 20You performed miraculous signs and wonders in Egypt and have continued them to this day, both in Israel and among all mankind, and have gained the renown that is still yours. 21You brought your people Israel out of Egypt with signs and wonders, by a mighty hand and an outstretched arm and with great terror. 22You gave them this land you had sworn to give their forefathers, a land flowing with milk and honey. 23They came in and took possession of it, but they did not obey you or follow your law; they did not do what you commanded them to do. So you brought all this disaster upon them.

24"See how the siege ramps are built up to take the city. Because of the sword, famine and plague, the city will be handed over to the Babylonians who are attacking it. What you said has happened, as you now see. 25And though the city will be handed over to the Babylonians, you, O Sovereign LORD, say to me, 'Buy the field with silver and have the transaction witnessed.' "

16 Some expositors have taken the position that this section (vv.16–25) is irrelevant to the context (so Hyatt). Others have seen a need on Jeremiah's part for confirmation of the transaction. Still others feel that Jeremiah slipped into an attitude of doubt (so Freedman). Given all the circumstances and the tension of the political and military situation, such an attitude would be understandable. Jeremiah may have longed for some reconciliation of the purchase with his prophecies of Jerusalem's destruction. There was the possibility that his hearers would accuse him of changing his position on the fate of Judah. He could hardly believe the promises the Lord had commanded him to proclaim (so Bright). So he had misgivings when he thought it over later on. Although he had explained the meaning of the episode (v.15), he was still troubled by its improbabilities; furthermore, he also longed for reassurance for the people.

17–25 As far as the prayer itself is concerned, it has been highly praised; one writer has even said that it contains the outline of a theology (so Cunliffe-Jones). In it Jeremiah deals with the Lord's grace to Israel throughout her long history.

First, Jeremiah begins at the place where all theology should begin—viz., the person and works of God (v.17). He acknowledges the power of God in creation. (In his reply the Lord uses the very words of Jeremiah [cf. vv.17, 27].) Second, Jeremiah speaks of the boundless grace of God to man and the truth of the divine retribution for sin (v.18). Grace does not disregard the righteousness of God. Divine retribution is likened to a harvest laborer's putting his pay into the folds of his children's garments (NIV, "into the laps of his children"; cf. Luke 6:38). Third, Jeremiah magnifies the wisdom of God, who in his omniscience surveys all the deeds of men in order to dispense absolute justice (v.19). Fourth, Jeremiah sees the wonderful works the Lord did on behalf of Israel in Egypt as harbingers of mercies he continued to show them "to this day" (v.20). Fifth, Jeremiah summarizes the Lord's gracious dealings from the Exodus through the conquest (v.21) and Israel's settlement in the land (v.22). Finally, in spite of this outpouring of God's love to them, Israel decided to live in disobedience to his will, thus bringing on themselves the calamities they were experiencing (v.23).

The "siege ramps" (v.24) were earthworks used in capturing a city. The Babylonians had already reached the city walls. As the Lord had foretold, the enemy had ample weaponry. The siege was successful, the city was doomed, and there was no hope of escape. The Lord's long and patient warnings were coming true. The fall of the city and the divine command for Jeremiah's purchase of land seemed irreconcilable (v.25). The incongruity was plain. Why buy the field when it would soon be lost to the Babylonians? Yet in spite of the dire circumstances, God had commanded Jeremiah to buy the field and to do it publicly. It was a situation calling for faith in and obedience to the word the Lord had given him to proclaim. So Jeremiah prayed for illumination rather than for confirmation of his understanding of the purpose of God.

Notes

16–25 It has been suggested that this passage—except for vv.24–25—is not original. The reasons given are (1) it is mainly irrelevant to the situation, as though negating the force of the transactions in vv.1–15, and (2) its form is more liturgical than ejaculatory or expostulatory, which the context would appear to require (so Hyatt). But the objections fail altogether to take into account the emotional and psychological factors that entered into the prophet's prayer. Surely the range of Jeremiah's literary ability would not exclude its presence here.

17 The verb פָּלֶא (*pālā'*, "wonderful," "difficult"; NIV, "too hard") here and in v.27 is used in a context of great solemnity. Judah is on the verge of dissolution; yet God commands Jeremiah to buy land from his relative. Such a transaction would require a miraculous, wonderful operation of God. The prophet by faith affirms his assurance that nothing is too wonderful, too hard, for the Lord. What Jeremiah asserted in faith, God actually did for him (v.27; see also Isa 9:5 [6 Eng.]).

---

e. The Lord's answer

32:26–35

> 26Then the word of the LORD came to Jeremiah: 27"I am the LORD, the God of all mankind. Is anything too hard for me? 28Therefore, this is what the LORD says: I am about to hand this city over to the Babylonians and to Nebuchadnezzar king of Babylon, who will capture it. 29The Babylonians who are attacking this city will come in and set it on fire; they will burn it down, along with the houses where the people provoked me to anger by burning incense on the roofs to Baal and by pouring out drink offerings to other gods.
>
> 30"The people of Israel and Judah have done nothing but evil in my sight from their youth; indeed, the people of Israel have done nothing but provoke me with what their hands have made, declares the LORD. 31From the day it was built until now, this city has so aroused my anger and wrath that I must remove it from my sight. 32The people of Israel and Judah have provoked me by all the evil they have done—they, their kings and officials, their priests and prophets, the men of Judah and the people of Jerusalem. 33They turned their backs to me and not their faces; though I taught them again and again, they would not listen or respond to discipline. 34They set up their abominable idols in the house that bears my Name and defiled it. 35They built high places for Baal in the Valley of Ben Hinnom to sacrifice their sons and daughters to Molech, though I never commanded, nor did it enter my mind, that they should do such a detestable thing and so make Judah sin."

26–29 The Lord's reply to Jeremiah's prayer was reassuring (v.26). As impossible as a bright future for Jeremiah and his people might seem, it was not outside the range of the Lord's power (v.27). Though all seemed futile, the Lord had to be reckoned with. It was as if the Lord were asking Jeremiah if he believed his own words in v.17. The omnipotent God is the source of confidence for believers in all ages. So the Lord's assurance came to Jeremiah in the very words he had used (cf. v.17). There follows a divine summary of the nation's punishment. The people's sins had made judgment inescapable. Nebuchadnezzar's capture of Jerusalem was the inevitable retribution for persistent idolatry (v.28). The homes the Lord had given his people had been used for the degenerate worship of Baal. The burning of the city was the penalty Judah would have executed on the Babylonians according to the Mosaic Law (cf. Deut 13:12–16). That the people practiced their idolatry on the rooftops (v.29; cf. 19:13) shows their brazen defiance of the Lord's repeated warnings.

30–33 The nation's stubborn resistance to the Lord's will had characterized the people from the beginnings ("their youth") of their national existence (v.30), which 2:2 places at the Exodus (cf. Exod 32). The reference to the work of their hands probably includes not only their idols but also their deeds in general—their whole ethical conduct. This was what aroused God's wrath in punishing them (v.31). In sweeping condemnation Jeremiah declares the long-standing character of their idolatry, even from Jebusite days—viz., "from the day it was built." Actually, Solomon completed the building of the city, and he was the first of all Israel's kings to fall into idolatry. At the first the idolatrous Canaanites had built Jerusalem, which was indeed a source of irritation to the Holy God of Israel. All the inhabitants of the city, from the highest to the lowest, were implicated in the sin (v.32), unwilling to be taught and to be turned from their wicked practices (v.33).

34–35 The height of the nation's impiety was reached when the people set up their idols in the temple of God himself (v.34). Their obscene symbols had been removed during Josiah's reforms. But they were reintroduced in the years of apostasy after Josiah's reign (cf. 7:30; 2 Kings 23:4, 6; Ezek 8:3–11). Molech worship (v.35) included human sacrifice; so along with gross idolatry went child sacrifice (cf. 19:1–13). So abhorrent was this practice that the Lord by a strong anthropomorphism says that it had never entered his mind that his favored people would stoop so low.

Notes

31 Jeremiah was not implying by אֲשֶׁר בָּנוּ אֹתָהּ (*ašer bānû 'ōtāh*, "which they built it"; NIV, "it was built") that Jerusalem was built by Israel, for it had been built and inhabited by the Jebusites from whom David captured it. The verb בָּנָה (*bānāh*, "to build") may denote an original building or later addition or enlargement (cf. Josh 19:50; Judg 21:23; and esp. Josh 6:26 with 1 Kings 16:34, though in the last reference a different verb is used).

33 The word מוּסָר (*mûsār*, "instruction"; NIV, "discipline") has a variety of doctrinal implications, such as chastening, instruction, and correction. It is parallel to the NT concept of child training. Israel refused to obey her God as a recalcitrant child balks at parental correction. In rabbinical phraseology *mûsār* is commonly used for moral and ethical instruction.

f. Promises of restoration

32:36–44

[36]"You are saying about this city, 'By the sword, famine and plague it will be handed over to the king of Babylon'; but this is what the LORD, the God of Israel, says: [37]I will surely gather them from all the lands where I banish them in my furious anger and great wrath; I will bring them back to this place and let them live in safety. [38]They will be my people, and I will be their God. [39]I will give them singleness of heart and action, so that they will always fear me for their own good and the good of their children after them. [40]I will make an everlasting covenant with them: I will never stop doing good to them, and I will inspire them to fear me, so that they will never turn away from me. [41]I will rejoice in doing them good and will assuredly plant them in this land with all my heart and soul.

[42]"This is what the LORD says: As I have brought all this great calamity on this people, so I will give them all the prosperity I have promised them. [43]Once more fields will be bought in this land of which you say, 'It is a desolate waste, without men or animals, for it has been handed over to the Babylonians.' [44]Fields will be bought for silver, and deeds will be signed, sealed and witnessed in the territory

of Benjamin, in the villages around Jerusalem, in the towns of Judah and in the towns of the hill country, of the western foothills and of the Negev, because I will restore their fortunes, declares the LORD."

36–42 The flow of the argument has been (1) judgment (vv.28–29), (2) the causes of the judgment (v. .30–35), and (3) the restoration (vv.37–44). The Lord views the "city" (v.36) as representing the whole kingdom. Jeremiah now turns to the ultimate condition of Judah—one that will be glorious indeed. The people will be restored to their land, and the country will again be prosperous. After the punishment, a godly remnant will return from exile to security and normal activity. The mention of "all the lands" (v.37) presupposes a world-wide dispersion. The new covenant is reiterated (vv.38–40) because the prophets looked forward to more than just a physical return of the people (cf. 31:32). The covenant bond between God and his people will be renewed, and they will walk in righteousness. This relationship is at the heart of the covenant in the past and in the future. Material and spiritual blessings go hand in hand. Moreover, the nation will be characterized by unity of purpose and life, not by the wicked ways the people have followed. They will show singleness of purpose in both thoughts and acts devoted to the Lord. The reference to inner disposition and outward expression again points to the new covenant with its promise of a new heart. Unity always characterizes the Messianic Era (cf. Zeph 3:9; Zech 14:9; John 10:16). The covenant will never again be broken (cf. Isa 55:3; Ezek 37:26). Moreover, the promise of restoration—"assuredly plant them" (v.41)—is just as certain as the predictions of punishment. Whatever God foretells, he makes good (v.42).

43–44 Finally, in the last two verses, Jeremiah returns to the main theme of this chapter. His transaction was an example to be universally followed in the future restoration (v.43). What he did will be repeated by many others in that coming day. A population increase after the decimation of warfare and exile is implied. In v.44 Jeremiah mentions several specific places in the land to show that the Lord's promise covers the whole country (cf. 17:26 for the various geographical divisions of the country). Benjamin may have been mentioned first because of the property of Jeremiah at Anathoth.

Notes

40 In the light of Heb 8, בְּרִית עוֹלָם (*bᵉrît ʿôlām*, "an everlasting covenant") can only refer to that already explicated in chapter 31. It is noteworthy that this covenant emphasizes divine enablement and uninterrupted obedience to the Lord.

In view of the Lord's clear statement, "I will inspire them to fear me," it is curious that a rabbinical axiom states, "Everything is in the hands of Heaven [God] save the fear of Heaven." The text literally understood does not eliminate the will of man from the ethical teaching of the Bible (contra Freedman).

41 Nowhere else in the OT is the phrase בְּכָל לִבִּי (*bᵉkol libbî*, "with all my heart") used of God.

4. *The righteous reign of the Davidic Ruler* (33:1–26)

This chapter concludes the Book of Consolation (chs. 30–33). The remainder of Jeremiah deals with Jerusalem's final siege and destruction and with the ultimate results of the prophecies against the nations. It also contains additional promises of future blessing. The theme of chapter 33 is the restoration of Jerusalem and the reestablishment of its worship. The date and occasion are the same as in chapter 32. Once more the Lord gives Judah light in her darkest hours.

a. *The exhortation to call on the Lord*

33:1–3

> ¹While Jeremiah was still confined in the courtyard of the guard, the word of the LORD came to him a second time: ²"This is what the LORD says, he who made the earth, the LORD who formed it and established it—the LORD is his name: ³'Call to me and I will answer you and tell you great and unsearchable things you do not know.'"

1–3 The time reference in v.1 links this chapter to the preceding one; this new message probably came to Jeremiah soon after the Lord spoke to him about the field (ch. 32). He was still imprisoned in the courtyard of the guard, where the elders and officers of the king could consult him. But the word of God was not bound (cf. 2 Tim 2:9). The pronouncements now to be given Jeremiah are weighty; so the Lord underscores their veracity by affixing his eternal name to them (v.2). He himself is surety for the program he is unfolding. So he invites Jeremiah to ask him for remarkable disclosures. It is a call for him to test the Lord. (We must ask before we receive [cf. Matt 7:7].) The things to be revealed are "unsearchable" (*bāṣûr*, lit., "inaccessible") because they are beyond the grasp of human knowledge (v.3). The participial adjective *bāṣûr* is used of the strongly fortified cities of Canaan in Deuteronomy 1:28 ("walled up"); here it refers to matters so far beyond human insight that they require divine revelation. Some scholars have suggested that by changing one Hebrew consonant (*bāṣûr* to *nāṣûr*) the participial adjective can be read "hidden" and brought into conformity with the reading "hidden" of Isaiah 48:6 (so Bewer). Actually, *bāṣûr* is as serviceable and understandable as the suggested emendation. The things under consideration are the truths concerning the restoration of the nation and Jerusalem.

Notes

3 The Hebrew וּבְצֻרוֹת (*ûbeṣurôt*, "and unsearchable things") with the remaining words of the verse ("you do not know") remind us of Isa 48:6, where the reading is נְצֻרוֹת (*neṣurôt*, "hidden things"). Six Hebrew MSS and the Targum (with its וּנְטִירָן [*ûneṭîrān*]) prefer "hidden things." It is true that *beṣurôt* is used of fortified, inaccessible cities. However, it is known that physical concepts can be extended to the mental or spiritual realm; thus KB translates *unfassbare Dinge* ("incomprehensible things"). The more difficult MT is to be preferred. The inscrutable things are those of this chapter (and indeed all the consolatory predictions in chs. 30–33) that relate to Israel's national restoration along with the hope of the reinstitution (for her) of the Davidic monarchy and the Levitical priesthood.

b. *The certainty of the Fall of Jerusalem*

33:4–5

> 4"For this is what the LORD, the God of Israel, says about the houses in this city and the royal palaces of Judah that have been torn down to be used against the siege ramps and the sword 5in the fight with the Babylonians: 'They will be filled with the dead bodies of the men I will slay in my anger and wrath. I will hide my face from this city because of all its wickedness.' "

4–5 These verses show that all the efforts of the king and his people to save Jerusalem will be futile. Theirs was a lost cause. "The houses . . . and the royal palaces of Judah" (v.4) were not demolished by the enemy but by the besieged people of Jerusalem who used them for defense against the Babylonians. But whatever measures were taken to defend the city would be useless. "The dead bodies" (v.5) refers to the defenders of Jerusalem, not to the Babylonians (contra RSV). The opposition of Judah to the invaders could not change the situation, for God had withdrawn his favor from his people because of their wickedness.

c. *Days of return and rejoicing*

33:6–13

> 6"'Nevertheless, I will bring health and healing to it; I will heal my people and will let them enjoy abundant peace and security. 7I will bring Judah and Israel back from captivity and will rebuild them as they were before. 8I will cleanse them from all the sin they have committed against me and will forgive all their sins of rebellion against me. 9Then this city will bring me renown, joy, praise and honor before all nations on earth that hear of all the good things I do for it; and they will be in awe and will tremble at the abundant prosperity and peace I provide for it.'
> 10"This is what the LORD says: 'You say about this place, "It is a desolate waste, without men or animals." Yet in the towns of Judah and the streets of Jerusalem that are deserted, inhabited by neither men nor animals, there will be heard once more 11the sounds of joy and gladness, the voices of bride and bridegroom, and the voices of those who bring thank offerings to the house of the LORD, saying,
>
> > "Give thanks to the LORD Almighty,
> > for the LORD is good;
> > his love endures forever."
>
> For I will restore the fortunes of the land as they were before,' says the LORD.
> 12"This is what the LORD Almighty says: 'In this place, desolate and without men or animals—in all its towns there will again be pastures for shepherds to rest their flocks. 13In the towns of the hill country, of the western foothills and of the Negev, in the territory of Benjamin, in the villages around Jerusalem and in the towns of Judah, flocks will again pass under the hand of the one who counts them,' says the LORD."

6–9 Past trials will yet be turned into blessings. So Jeremiah sets forth promises of prosperity. These promises include those of health, restoration, joy, and peace. The word "health" (*ªrukāh*) in v.6 is literally "new flesh" (cf. 8:22). In other words, the Exile will have a healing effect. The wounds of the nation will be bound up in peace and security. God will repair the losses and rebuild the land that had been destroyed. The restoration of Judah and Israel (v.7) must refer to the latter days because the captivity of Israel did not end after seventy years. Judah and Israel will be restored as the one kingdom they were before the division of the kingdom under Rehoboam. Far more important than any territorial restitution will be the pardon and cleansing the Lord now promises (v.8). Once more the vital element of the new covenant is reiterated (cf. 31:34; 50:20). The future for the Jews will be so glorious that the nations will stand in awe of them and tremble at their greatness (v.9). Thus Jerusalem, with its former state reversed, will be made holy.

10–11 Jeremiah sees the land and Jerusalem as already desolate (v.10). The tense of the verb *ḥārēḇ* ("it is waste"; NIV, "desolate") shows that Jerusalem had already fallen. But it will arise. For Jerusalem and Judah there will be joy in worship in the temple (v.11). This verse is the closing part of the benediction in the Jewish marriage ceremony today. Joy and gladness will not only mark the relationships of God's people but will also mark their worship in his temple. The liturgical words were those used by the Levitical singers in the temple service (Ps 106:1) and showed that the temple would be rebuilt and the ministry restored as in preexilic days. Joy will be accompanied by security.

12–13 The reference to shepherds with their flocks (v.12) points to the future time of peace, tranquillity, and prosperity. In ancient Israel and Judah, shepherds counted their sheep as they came to the fold at night (v.13). So in the restored and united kingdom, the shepherds will count their sheep in peace. There may be an allusion here to Leviticus 27:32. Strangely, the Targum has a messianic interpretation here and substitutes the word "Messiah" for "the one who counts them."

d. *Restoration of royalty and priesthood*

33:14–22

14" 'The days are coming,' declares the Lord, 'when I will fulfill the gracious promise I made to the house of Israel and to the house of Judah.

15" 'In those days and at that time
I will make a righteous Branch sprout from David's line;
he will do what is just and right in the land.
16In those days Judah will be saved
and Jerusalem will live in safety.
This is the name by which it will be called:
The Lord Our Righteousness.'

17For this is what the Lord says: 'David will never fail to have a man to sit on the throne of the house of Israel, 18nor will the priests, who are Levites, ever fail to have a man to stand before me continually to offer burnt offerings, to burn grain offerings and to present sacrifices.' "
19The word of the Lord came to Jeremiah: 20"This is what the Lord says: 'If you can break my covenant with the day and my covenant with the night, so that day and night no longer come at their appointed time, 21then my covenant with David my servant—and my covenant with the Levites who are priests ministering before me—can be broken and David will no longer have a descendant to reign on his throne. 22I will make the descendants of David my servant and the Levites who minister before me as countless as the stars of the sky and as measureless as the sand on the seashore.' "

14 This beautiful passage (vv.14–26) is not in the LXX and has therefore been suspect to many commentators. The promises in these verses have been called hyperbole; those who voiced them have been called wrong in their predictions but right in their optimism and faith (so Frost). So the verses are judged to be non-Jeremianic with the passage as a whole probably coming from a later editor (so Hyatt). Other scholars are equally convinced that the passage is in the right place. But this passage is perfectly compatible with the revelation in chapter 23 and with chapters·30–33. As a whole, Jeremiah is declaring that monarchy and priesthood, interrupted by the Exile, will coexist permanently. He proclaims the perpetuity of the Davidic dynasty and the Levitical priesthood without equivocation. The predicted restoration ("the days are coming") is not, however, to be looked for in the immediate time of the return from the Captivity. Only in a limited and preliminary way were these promises fulfilled in Zerubbabel and Sheshbazzar after the Captivity (cf. Ezra 1:8; 2:2; also 2:40–54; 8:15–20). Ultimately, they are combined in the highest sense in Christ (cf. Ps 110:4) and are yet to be fulfilled in the reign of Messiah on earth.

15 The good word the prophets announced is found in many other passages (cf. 16:15; 23:3; 29:10; 32:37; Hos 1:10; 2:15; 6:11; Amos 9:14; Mic 7:9; Zeph 3:10). It comprises the entire panorama of glorious promises made to both parts of the nation. "Those days" are the messianic times (cf. 23:5–6). The passage undeniably parallels the great prophecy of Messiah in 23:1–8. The wording is not identical, but the parity of ideas is unmistakable. It is through the Lord Messiah, the righteous One, that the restoration and attendant blessings will be realized. Jeremiah's picture of the coming Messiah, though not so replete as Isaiah's, is nonetheless varied and unique. Jeremiah pictures the coming Messiah as (1) the spring of living waters (2:13); (2) the good Shepherd (23:4; 31:10); (3) the righteous Branch (here and 23:5); (4) the Redeemer (50:34); (5) The LORD Our Righteousness (23:6); (6) David the king (30:9); and (7) the Agent of the new covenant (31:31–34) (so Harrison).

16 Salvation and safety are in store for Judah and Jerusalem because of the presence of justice and righteousness personified. The name given the Messiah in 23:6 is here given to Jerusalem. This has troubled a number of expositors because there is an apparent contradiction between the two passages. One expositor has denounced the translation "she shall be called" (KJV, ASV, NASB et al.) as both ignorant and impious (so Clarke). The suggestion he gives is to take the pronominal suffix in *lāh* ("to her") as masculine after the analogy of Aramaic. Then instead of "to her" the reading is to be "to him" (*lô*), according to the Aramaic, Vulgate, Syriac, and one or two MSS. This is supposed to bring the passage into agreement with 23:6. Some have even suggested that *lāh* be read as an archaic masculine ending *lōh*. But these are measures of desperation that will not stand up under textual criticism nor fit the immediate or larger context. Are there not parallel uses of the Lord's name being linked to Jerusalem (Ezek 48:35) and being given to his altar (Judg 6:24) by Gideon? Most scholars agree that the name "The LORD Our Righteousness" refers to Jerusalem. She can have the same name as the Messiah because she reflects that righteousness the Messiah bestows on her (so KD). Jerusalem will then be the embodiment of the nation's ideal in the Messiah (so Bewer). The city will be marked by righteousness (cf. 2 Cor 5:21).

There is, however, no need to allegorize the name of the city as though it were the NT church. On what grounds could the impartation of such a concept be justified here? Jerusalem will be called by his name because she will partake of his nature, which has been graciously imparted to her. She has the same name as Messiah because of the mystical oneness between them (so JFB; cf. Rom 16:7; 1 Cor 12:12, where the church is identified with "Christ").

17-18 Because of a misinterpretation of vv.17-18, some have claimed that they contradict the facts of history. If one sees in them a constant presence and succession of Davidic rulers and Levitical priests, then, of course, history does not validate this interpretation. But the passage claims no such thing. It says only that David's dynasty will never cease. Temporary interruption is only apparent, not true cessation. David's Scion still lives. The permanence of the royal and priestly lines is forcefully stated. In the highest sense Christ as King-Priest will, of course, fulfill these promises (cf. Ps 110:4). But in the priestly realm the primary emphasis is on Levi's line, which must not be confused with Christ's priesthood after the order of Melchizedek. Nor can one fall back on the notion that a partial fulfillment of v.17 may be seen in Zerubbabel, then in the Maccabees, and finally at the Second Advent. To introduce the Maccabees into the discussion is wholly erroneous because they were of the Hasmonean (descended from Levi) dynasty, not the Davidic dynasty. To put it plainly, Jeremiah predicts that David will never lack a descendant to occupy his throne. In that sense his dynasty will never be permanently cut off (cf. Luke 1:32-33).

Monarchy and priesthood were the two bases of the OT theocracy. When these appeared to be most in danger of extinction in Jeremiah's day, we find their continuance couched in sure and irrevocable terms. What *is* affirmed of the monarchy in v.17 is promised the priesthood in v.18. The Levitical priesthood is assured a permanent ministry (cf. the promise to Phinehas in Num 25:13). As legitimate priests, they will serve the Lord.

A discrepancy has been suggested between vv.17-19 and the new covenant (so Habel). In the latter (31:31-34) we have a clear statement that, because of the Lord's immediate and instinctive knowledge of all people, the traditional channels of mediation between God and man would no longer be needed. Those who accept this "discrepancy" fail to see that they introduce an inconsistency in this age also; for in this time of the fulfillment of the new covenant, there still is, on the basis of their argument, need for a NT priesthood. The difficulty is a real one for those who deny an earthly reign of Christ at the end of earthly history because they do not differentiate between the temporal and eternal states. Too many expositors apply a dual hermeneutic to passages like vv.14-26.

19-22 What has been stated in 31:35-37 as a guarantee of the new covenant is now used to illustrate the certainty of the continuance of the monarchy and priesthood. The greater the promises, the stronger the assurances that they will be fulfilled. The certainty of the prophecies is riveted in God's order in nature, and the prophecies themselves are linked with the unfailing regularity of the natural order (vv.20-21). A nullification of the covenant is an impossibility. Just as the covenant with Noah (cf. Gen 8:22) is kept, so the covenant with David (cf. 2 Sam 7) and that with Levi (Num 17) will also be kept. Moreover, the Lord adds a promise of a great increase in the descendants of David and the Levites (v.22); what was originally stated of the entire nation is here specifically applied to them (cf. Gen 15:5; 22:17).

Notes

14–16 The connection between this passage and 23:5–6 is unmistakable; however, even a cursory reading of both passages will reveal minor variations. What is puzzling is that the name given the Branch in 23:6 ("The LORD Our Righteousness"), indicated by שְׁמוֹ ($š^emô$, "his name") and יִקְרָאוֹ ($yiqr^e'ô$, "he will be called"), is here transferred to Jerusalem (in 23:6 it was "Israel"). Nevertheless, three Hebrew MSS, the Syriac, and the Vulgate (with its *vocabunt eum*) read יִקְרָאוּהוּ ($yiqrā'ûhû$, "they will call him"). Furthermore, it is possible to point the לָהּ ($lāh$, lit., "to her," the preposition with the third feminine pronominal suffix) in the masculine. Finally, should both be called by the same name, there is a parallel case in Rev 21:2, 9–10, where the New Jerusalem and the Bride are described. Now it is without argument that the New Jerusalem (the city) and the Bride of the Lamb are neither identical nor coextensive. Rather, the intent appears to be to indicate the chief resident(s) in the city, namely, the Bride.

17–26 This passage has been a *crux interpretum* for expositors. It is especially difficult for those who hold an amillennial position in eschatology. The only resort for them is in allegorization of the text or the use of a dual hermeneutic. Simply stated, the passage assures that just as the Davidic covenant (2 Sam 7) is guaranteed by God's promise, so is the Levitical priesthood. But whereas the amillennial system can find room for the Son of David to reign now and in the future by transferring the earthly throne to the heavenly one at the Father's right hand, it is not so easy to find Levitical priests with their ministrations in the same framework. Strangely, Hengstenberg and Jahn consider that the promises, literally understood, would be a *threat* instead of a blessing, "since the support of such a multitude of royal and priestly persons would be an intolerable burden to the state" (cited by Henderson).

A few questions are in order here.

1. If the promises here are to be understood symbolically, this at once prejudges the disposition of the sacrifices in Ezek 40–48, the interpretation of Isa 66:21–23, and the treatment of Zech 14:16–19. How are these passages to be handled?

2. Why is there any need to inject the church and her religious privileges into Israel's age?

3. What is to be done with Mal 2:4, which promises a continuing covenant with Levi?

4. Does not Ezek 21:26–27 join turban (= mitre), representative of priesthood, with crown, which unmistakably points to monarchy, both finally resting in the Messiah?

5. Is it not the part of safe interpretation not to mix the millennial and temporal with that which is eternal and restricted to the church?

Having interpreted himself into a corner, Henderson, who has frankly stated, "We are shut up to the spiritual interpretation of the passage," informs us: "As the literal Jews are introduced in the twenty-fourth verse in their national character, it is more natural to consider what is here said of the seed of Jacob and of David in the same light, than to take the terms in a spiritual acceptation, though, from the exigency of the case [*sic!*], we are compelled to put this construction upon them, ver. 22" (pp. 201–2). No one can ride two horses (cf. interpretations of this passage) at the same time unless they are going in the same direction.

e. *Confirmation of the promises*

33:23–26

[23]The word of the LORD came to Jeremiah: [24]"Have you not noticed that these people are saying, 'The LORD has rejected the two kingdoms he chose'? So they despise my people and no longer regard them as a nation. [25]This is what the

LORD says: 'If I have not established my covenant with day and night and the fixed laws of heaven and earth, [26]then I will reject the descendants of Jacob and David my servant and will not choose one of his sons to rule over the descendants of Abraham, Isaac and Jacob. For I will restore their fortunes and have compassion on them.' "

23–24 The reproach that the nation had suffered from her neighbors and even the unbelieving in her midst will be removed. There are three views as to the meaning of "two families" (v.24; NIV, "kingdoms"): (1) Israel and Judah, (2) Jacob and David (v.26), and (3) Jacob and Levi (the two families that had the monarchy and priesthood). Although there are some scholars who refer vv.21–22 to the regal and sacerdotal families, the great majority correctly understand them to refer to the two kingdoms of the Hebrew nation. This points to a time when the nation will still be divided as in Rehoboam's time. Who are the authors of the statement in v.24? It is not the taunt of the pagan nations because the words "these people" are never used of any besides Israel. The verb "chose" (*bāḥar*) occurs only here in Jeremiah as referring to God's choice of Israel (cf. Exod 19:5–6; Amos 3:2). Certain Jews, discouraged by the times, thought that without freedom and a government of their own they were no longer a nation (cf. Rom 11:1). The fear and lament of the people showed that they considered that God had forsaken them utterly and finally.

25–26 Of what use would the greatest national promises be if the nation were not in existence to enjoy them? The Lord guarantees his people that, despite all thoughts to the contrary, he will make good every promise (v.25). They will certainly return from exile. They are undeniably the eternal nation. The Lord will allow no one to impugn his covenant promises to Israel. The threefold mention of the patriarchs (v.26) points to the whole chain of promises repeatedly given them. Nature will utterly collapse before God will go back on the slightest promise to his people.

C. Messages and Events Before the Fall of Jerusalem (34:1–39:18)

1. Zedekiah and the mistreated slaves (34:1–22)

Jeremiah is unique among the prophetic writings because the fulfillment of its central oracles about the Lord's judgment on Jerusalem and the Babylonian captivity is set forth more than once in its pages. Chapters 34–38 are largely occupied with Jeremiah's experiences during the siege of Jerusalem. Like other portions of the book, they are not in strict chronological order. Most of the events they narrate took place in the reigns of Jehoiakim and Zedekiah, shortly before the Fall of Jerusalem in 586 B.C. Chapters 34–38, largely biographical, cover the siege of Jerusalem; chapter 39, its fall; and chapters 40–44, events after the fall.

a. The warning to Zedekiah

34:1–7

[1]While Nebuchadnezzar king of Babylon and all his army and all the kingdoms and peoples in the empire he ruled were fighting against Jerusalem and all its surrounding towns, this word came to Jeremiah from the LORD: [2]"This is what the LORD, the God of Israel, says: Go to Zedekiah king of Judah and tell him, 'This is

what the LORD says: I am about to hand this city over to the king of Babylon, and he will burn it down. ³You will not escape from his grasp but will surely be captured and handed over to him. You will see the king of Babylon with your own eyes, and he will speak with you face to face. And you will go to Babylon.

⁴" 'Yet hear the promise of the LORD, O Zedekiah king of Judah. This is what the LORD says concerning you: You will not die by the sword; ⁵you will die peacefully. As people made a funeral fire in honor of your fathers, the former kings who preceded you, so they will make a fire in your honor and lament, "Alas, O master!" I myself make this promise, declares the LORD.' "

˙ ⁶Then Jeremiah the prophet told all this to Zedekiah king of Judah, in Jerusalem, ⁷while the army of the king of Babylon was fighting against Jerusalem and the other cities of Judah that were still holding out—Lachish and Azekah. These were the only fortified cities left in Judah.

1–2 This section (vv.1–7) stresses the certainty of the Babylonian capture of Jerusalem. In view of this certainty, it would have been wise for Zedekiah to surrender. The warning in vv.1–3 amplifies that in 32:3–4. Jeremiah's faithfulness in delivering it led to his imprisonment. Jeremiah set clear choices and their consequences before Zedekiah. This passage may be dated 589–588 B.C. (39:1–2; 2 Kings 24:20–25:1; so Cunliffe-Jones). The siege actually lasted from 588–586 B.C. Daniel 3:2–4 and 4:1 show the vast extent of the neo-Babylonian empire. Soldiers came from subject countries to join in the siege (cf. 2 Kings 24:2). Nebuchadnezzar's army had to be formidable because Egypt was hostile to him. His assault on Judah and Jerusalem was still in the early phase because the Judean cities were only being threatened at this time, and Jeremiah was not yet in prison. Since cities like Lachish and Azekah (v.7) were not yet captured and Jerusalem was still free (v.2), the date was early in the final invasion, probably in Zedekiah's ninth year (so Streane). As v.22 shows, the Babylonians, who had temporarily retired from the siege (37:5), would return to finish the destruction of Jerusalem.

3 This verse discloses the fate of Zedekiah in the siege. The Lord's message to him was that he was not to be led astray by the temporary respite in the siege; the situation was actually hopeless. As for Zedekiah, there would be no escape; he would have to face the invader (32:4). The mention of a face-to-face confrontation with Nebuchadnezzar shows something of the fear he inspired. Zedekiah could not escape the consequences of his treason in breaking his covenant with Nebuchadnezzar. He would have to answer personally for it. This prophecy and the prophecy in Ezekiel 12:13 are reconciled by the fact that after his confrontation with Nebuchadnezzar, Zedekiah was blinded and taken to Babylon (52:11).

4–5 Through Jeremiah the Lord counseled Zedekiah to surrender. The Lord promised him that he would not be slain (v.4) but would die in captivity. Unlike Jehoiakim (cf. 22:18–19), Zedekiah would die a natural death. Nuances here and elsewhere imply that Jeremiah felt kindly toward Zedekiah. The "funeral fire" (v.5) does not refer to cremation, which was not practiced by the Hebrews, but to the custom of burning spices at royal funerals (cf. 2 Chron 16:14; 21:19). The lamentation "Alas, O master!" (equivalent to "Alas, your Majesty!") was normally used of mourning for a king (cf. 22:18). Some scholars claim that this prophecy was not fulfilled because Zedekiah was blind and died in Babylon (cf. 39:7; 52:8–11; Ezek 12:13); thus the prophecy was conditional. But it is not impossible that the exiled Jews in Babylon would be permitted to show their customary respect at the death of their Davidic king. The authority for the promise is the Lord himself.

6–7 Speaking so boldly to the king was hazardous, but Jeremiah feared only God (v.6). At the time of this prophecy the only cities that remained uncaptured were Jerusalem, Lachish, and Azekah (v.7). The latter two had been fortified by Rehoboam (2 Chron 11:5, 9); both were southwest of Jerusalem—Lachish, thirty-five miles; Azekah, fifteen miles—not far from the Philistine border. Since their fall was necessary to the capture of Jerusalem, they marked the southern limit of Nebuchadnezzar's invasion. Lachish is the modern Tell ed-Duweir; Azekah, the modern Tell ez-Zakariyeh (so Kraeling, *Rand McNally Bible Atlas:* Lachish, p. 316; Azekah, p. 138). The Lachish Letters give a vivid picture of these events. The twenty-one ostraca (broken, inscribed pottery) date from the time of this invasion. Letter 4 reads: "We are watching for the smoke signals of Lachish . . . because we do not see Azekah." This indicates that Azekah had already fallen. Lachish capitulated soon after this.

Notes

---

5 The "funeral fire [מִשְׂרְפוֹת, *miśrᵉpôt*] in honor of your fathers" is not to be confused with the funeral pyre so well known in India. Cremation has never been a prevailing custom among the Jews. Exceptions can be found where cremation was added to the death penalty (cf. Josh 7:15, 25; see also 1 Kings 13:2; 2 Kings 23:20). In case of an epidemic, cremation was carried out; such is the inference from Amos 6:10. As to the burning of kings and nobles, the Mishnah (*Abodah Zarah* 1:3) states, "Every death which is accompanied by burning is looked upon as idolatry." The Talmud records the custom of making a funeral pyre of the bed (not the body) and other articles as an honor to the dead (*Sanhedrin* 52b; so Freedman). The case of Saul is an exception; the cremation can probably be explained as a method whereby no further indignity could be inflicted on the dead.

---

b. *The perfidy against the slaves*

34:8–11

> ⁸The word came to Jeremiah from the LORD after King Zedekiah had made a covenant with all the people in Jerusalem to proclaim freedom for the slaves. ⁹Everyone was to free his Hebrew slaves, both male and female; no one was to hold a fellow Jew in bondage. ¹⁰So all the officials and people who entered into this covenant agreed that they would free their male and female slaves and no longer hold them in bondage. They agreed, and set them free. ¹¹But afterward they changed their minds and took back the slaves they had freed and enslaved them again.

8–10 When the siege became more severe, Zedekiah made a covenant with the people to liberate their Hebrew slaves (v.8). The Hebrew law concerning slavery (cf. Exod 21:1–11; Lev 25:39–55; Deut 15:12–18) apparently had fallen into disuse. The covenant did not follow the letter of the law because it liberated all the slaves no matter how long they had served (vv.9–10). It was ratified most solemnly in the temple (cf. vv.18–20).

Expositors differ about the reasons for the covenant. It may have been made because under the continuing threat of invasion the poor—unable to freely work outside the city—were faced with starvation or slavery. Now that invasion appeared imminent, liberation of slaves would mean a lessening of the burden on the owners. Perhaps the covenant was an attempt at reform and was made in the hope that it would lead to the Lord's blessing. More probably the covenant was made with the thought that the liberated slaves would join in defending the city.

11 When the siege was temporarily lifted through the intervention of their Egyptian allies, the Jews forced the liberated slaves back into former bondage. This was not only a shameful repudiation of their solemn covenant but a flagrant violation of Deuteronomy 15:12; it also profaned the Lord's name, in which they had made the covenant. The incident has been aptly called "panic piety" (so Lewis). Recall how often the eighth-century prophets Isaiah, Micah, Hosea, and Amos denounced social injustices against slaves. To reimpose slavery on those who had been freed showed that the covenant had not been motivated by compassion, justice, and obedience to the Lord's command.

c. The sin of the nation

34:12–16

> ¹²Then the word of the LORD came to Jeremiah: ¹³"This what the LORD, the God of Israel, says: I made a covenant with your forefathers when I brought them out of Egypt, out of the land of slavery. I said, ¹⁴'Every seventh year each of you must free any fellow Hebrew who has sold himself to you. After he has served you six years, you must let him go free.' Your fathers, however, did not listen to me or pay attention to me. ¹⁵Recently you repented and did what is right in my sight: Each of you proclaimed freedom to his countrymen. You even made a covenant before me in the house that bears my Name. ¹⁶But now you have turned around and profaned my name; each of you has taken back the male and female slaves you had set free to go where they wished. You have forced them to become your slaves again."

12–14 With telling effect, the Lord reminds the people that their ancestors had been slaves in Egypt (vv.12–13). Who, then, should have more compassion on slaves than those who were obligated to keep the Passover, the annual celebration of Israel's release from Egyptian slavery? Part of the law given at Sinai dealt (as has already been pointed out) with Hebrew slaves, and this the people in Jerusalem had now disobeyed. In v.14 the words "sold himself" reflect the Near Eastern custom of voluntary slavery for economic reasons. As stated above, the covenant Zedekiah made did not exactly fit the law in Deuteronomy 15:1, 12, because it required the immediate liberation of all slaves, not just those who had served six years. Thus the law did not cover this case (so Bewer). The "seventh year" is the year of liberation; the Hebrews counted both the first and the last years in calculating time periods, a custom that sheds light on the time Christ was in the tomb.

15–16 The sin of Zedekiah and his people was especially serious because they had made the covenant of freedom in the house and name of the Lord (v.15). In contrast to earlier generations, they had decided to obey the law of releasing Hebrew slaves. Their covenant was not only a civil and economic act but a religious one as well. Their perfidy had profaned the Lord's name (v.16), in which they had sworn this covenant. Zedekiah was already notorious for breaking his pledged word (cf. Ezek 17:11–21) to Nebuchadnezzar on ascending the throne of Judah.

d. *The Lord's retribution for the perfidy*

34:17–22

> ¹⁷"Therefore, this is what the LORD says: You have not obeyed me; you have not proclaimed freedom for your fellow countrymen. So I now proclaim 'freedom' for you, declares the LORD—'freedom' to fall by the sword, plague and famine. I will make you abhorrent to all the kingdoms of the earth. ¹⁸The men who have violated my covenant and have not fulfilled the terms of the covenant they made before me, I will treat like the calf they cut in two and then walked between its pieces. ¹⁹The leaders of Judah and Jerusalem, the court officials, the priests and all the people of the land who walked between the pieces of the calf, ²⁰I will hand over to their enemies who seek their lives. Their dead bodies will become food for the birds of the air and the beasts of the earth.
> ²¹"I will hand Zedekiah king of Judah and his officials over to their enemies who seek their lives, to the army of the king of Babylon, which has withdrawn from you. ²²I am going to give the order, declares the LORD, and I will bring them back to this city. They will fight against it, take it and burn it down. And I will lay waste the towns of Judah so no one can live there."

17–22 In v.17 there is pungent play on the Hebrew word *derôr* ("liberty" or "release"). NIV puts it most effectively: "freedom." Since they had not actually given the slaves freedom, God ironically declares that the people themselves would be freed—freed from his protecting hand. The guilty would be freed for doom and destruction. Because they had enslaved their brothers and sisters, they were to be subjected to their enemies. The ancient method of making a covenant is indicated in v.18 (cf. Gen 15:9–17). As in the Assyrian inscriptions, the intention was that, as they passed through the pieces of the divided sacrifice, they invoked on themselves a curse that, if they broke the covenant, they would be cut in pieces like the sacrificial calf (so Driver et al.). The Hebrew way of referring to making a covenant by saying "cut a covenant" obviously goes back to Genesis 15:9–17. Notice how large a number of the people (v.19) had contracted to release slaves. The heinousness of their sin is underlined by the punishment decreed for them (v.20). The Babylonians had only temporarily lifted the siege to meet Pharaoh Hophra (v.21; cf. 37:5, 7–10). The Lord assured Zedekiah and the people that the destruction would finally be consummated (v.22), and the Babylonians did return and destroy the city.

Notes

18–19 There is a difference of opinion on the etymology of the important word בְּרִית (*berît*, "covenant"). Some relate it to the Akkadian *burru*, which denotes "to establish a legal situation by testimony with an oath." Others connect it with the Akkadian *birtu*, which means "a fetter." Yet another view holds that the word is to be traced to the root *brh*, the food and eating involved in the covenant meal. Certain OT theologians (notably Eichrodt) believe that the idea of covenant is the dominant theme of the OT (TWOT, 1:128–29). In recent times much research, evangelical and otherwise, has been carried on with reference to this subject (cf. the work of George Mendenhall, D.J. McCarthy, M.G. Kline, and J. Barton Payne among others [for adequate bibliography, see TWOT, 1:128–30]). As to the procedure in covenant making, Gen 15 and Jer 34 are determinative. A well-known and often cited record is that between Assur-nirari V and Mati'-ilu of Agusi. The former, standing before a divided ram, declared: "This head is not the head of the ram, but the head 'of Mati'-ilu, his sons, his nobles, and the people of his land. If Mati'-ilu violates this oath, as the head of this ram is struck off . . . so will the head of Mati'-ilu be struck off" (TDNT, 2:117, n.49).

19 A סָרִיס (sārîs, "court official") is not necessarily a eunuch but is a court or state official (cf. Gen 37:36; 1 Sam 8:15; Jer 52:25). The origin of the Hebrew term is traced to the Assyrian ša rēši (ša rîši), denoting "the captain at the [king's] head." Eunuchs were excluded by Mosaic Law (Lev 22:24; Deut 23:1). It has been claimed that Jezebel (1 Kings 22:9) may have introduced the practice of employing eunuchs (cf. 2 Kings 8:6; 9:32) (TWOT, 2:634–35). Rabbinical Judaism has always discountenanced celibacy. Marriage was an undebatable obligation; thus, there is only one known celibate rabbi, Ben 'Azzai, and he was severely criticized by other rabbis (TDNT, 2:767).

---

2. The faithfulness of the Recabites (35:1–19)

The events of this chapter (which, along with ch. 36, precede chs. 32–34 chronologically) occurred at the close of Jehoiakim's reign. The Babylonians and Syrians were ravaging Judah (cf. v.11; 2 Kings 24:2). Like a flashback, chapters 35–36 interrupt the narrative flow of chapters 32–44 and take the reader back some seventeen years to the fourth year of Jehoiakim's reign—a time when the Babylonians and Syrians had driven many in Judah, the Recabites among them, to take refuge in Jerusalem. The dates given for chapter 35 vary from 606 B.C. (so Cheyne) to 602 B.C. (so Cunliffe-Jones) to 598 B.C. (so Cundall, Freedman, Bewer). The fourth year of Jehoiakim's reign (cf. 36:1) would appear to place it about 606 B.C.

a. Jeremiah's test of the Recabites

35:1–5

> ¹This is the word that came to Jeremiah from the LORD during the reign of Jehoiakim son of Josiah king of Judah: ²"Go to the Recabite family and invite them to come to one of the side rooms of the house of the LORD and give them wine to drink."
>
> ³So I went to get Jaazaniah son of Jeremiah, the son of Habazziniah, and his brothers and all his sons—the whole family of the Recabites. ⁴I brought them into the house of the LORD into the room of the sons of Hanan son of Igdaliah the man of God. It was next to the room of the officials, which was over that of Maaseiah son of Shallum the doorkeeper. ⁵Then I set bowls full of wine and some cups before the men of the Recabite family and said to them, "Drink some wine."

1–2 Chapter 35 has a single objective: to contrast the obedience of the Recabites with the disobedience of Judah. The episode is a rebuke to the nation for their unfaithfulness to God. "The Recabite family" (v.2) refers to their tribe or clan, since they were nomads (cf. vv. 3, 5, 18). They were a separatist group, stemming from Jonadab (or Jehonadab, c. 840 B.C.; cf. 2 Kings 10:15–23). Desiring to return to the simplicity of the nomadic life, they banned all sedentary occupations. As relations of the Kenites, they were kindred of Jethro, Moses' father-in-law (cf. Judg 1:16; 1 Chron 2:55). Their ancestor Jonadab was prominent in purging the northern kingdom of Baal worship in the time of Jehu (c. 840 B.C.). The Recabites lived in the southern deserts (1 Sam 15:6) and in Israelite territory (Judg 4:17; 5:24). With the fall of the northern kingdom, they moved south into Judah. According to some scholars, they were proselytes of the gate (so JFB). Like the Nabataeans of a later time (cf. *Diodorus Siculus* 19.94), they gave up vine growing. The "side rooms" were probably anterooms of the temple used for storage and available to the Levites (cf. 1 Chron 28:12; so Freedman). This chapter must not be interpreted in such a way as to imply that God necessarily approved of the restriction Jonadab placed on his descendants, the Recabites. Nor is it per se a temperance lesson, despite its use for that purpose by some Sunday school quarterlies. Rather, what God commended was the fidelity of the Recabites to their convictions (cf. also F.S. Frick, "The Recabites Reconsidered," JBL 90 [1971]: 279–87).

3–5 Jeremiah's testing of the Recabites was commanded by the Lord. We know essentially nothing of the persons mentioned in vv.3–4, except for Maaseiah, who was probably the father of Zephaniah the priest (cf. 21:1; 29:25; 37:3). He was in charge of the money given for the temple repair (cf. 2 Kings 12:10). Jaazaniah was probably the leader of the group. The name, not uncommon in Jeremiah's day, has been found on a seal (c. 600 B.C.) at Tell en-Nasbeh. The leaders were brought into the house of the Lord in order to publicize the message that was to follow (v.4). "The sons of Hanan" (a prophet of God) were probably his disciples. He appears to have been in sympathy with Jeremiah. The three leaders (cf. 52:24; 2 Kings 25:18) probably had charge of the inner and outer court of the temple and the entrance door. They ranked next to the high priest and his deputy (so Streane). Jeremiah put wine before the Recabites and invited them to drink (v.5).

Notes

2 The Recabites (הָרֵכָבִים, *hārēḵāḇîm*), the root of whose name suggests "charioteer," have already been mentioned in the historical books of the OT (cf. 2 Kings 10:15, 23). The present chapter in Jeremiah has nine references to the ancestor and his family (clan). The progenitor of the tribe charged his descendants to live a nomadic life, probably hoping to keep them from the lax living and allurements to idolatry that plagued Israel in city life. Scripture portrays their ancestor as a zealot for God and an energetic force in extirpating Baal worship from Israel in the reign of Jehu (2 Kings 10:15–23). A confused and unlikely story is related by Hegesippus, repeated by Eusebius, concerning the martyrdom of James the Just, who, when questioned by the scribes and Pharisees, gave an unexpected witness to the messiahship of Jesus. The account continues: "And while they were thus stoning him one of the priests of the sons of Rechab, the son of Rechabim [the Heb. pl. of the previous name], to whom Jeremiah the prophet bore witness, cried out saying, 'Stop! what are you doing? The Just is praying for you.' And a certain man among them . . . took the club with which he used to beat out the clothes, and hit the Just on the head, and so he suffered martyrdom" (Eusebius *Ecclesiastical History* 2.23.14–18).

b. The Recabites' loyalty to Jonadab

35:6–11

⁶But they replied, "We do not drink wine, because our forefather Jonadab son of Recab gave us this command: 'Neither you nor your descendants must ever drink wine. ⁷Also you must never build houses, sow seed or plant vineyards; you must never have any of these things, but must always live in tents. Then you will live a long time in the land where you are nomads.' ⁸We have obeyed everything our forefather Jonadab son of Recab commanded us. Neither we nor our wives nor our sons and daughters have ever drunk wine ⁹or built houses to live in or had vineyards, fields or crops. ¹⁰We have lived in tents and have fully obeyed everything our forefather Jonadab commanded us. ¹¹But when Nebuchadnezzar king of Babylon invaded this land, we said, 'Come, we must go to Jerusalem to escape the Babylonian and Aramean armies.' So we have remained in Jerusalem."

6–11 The Recabites could not be tempted to disregard the commands of their ancestor (v.6), called "father" (*'āḇ*; NIV, "forefather") in the broad Semitic sense of ancestor. This prohibition was apparently meant to help them escape the defiling Baal worship, which was accompanied by the carousing that often goes with city life. Viniculture could not be carried on under nomadic conditions; so it was banned (v.7). Wine drinking, so common in the ancient Near East, was an integral part of Canaanite religious worship. The restrictions imposed by Jonadab went far beyond abstinence from wine and grape growing and led to an austere and nomadic lifestyle. For over two hundred years this tribe had obeyed their forefather's command (vv.8–9). Their lifestyle resembled that of the Nazirites (cf. Num 6:1–21). During their desert wanderings, the Hebrews had no wine. As has already been said, it was not the asceticism of the Recabites that Jeremiah commended but their fidelity to Jonadab (v.10). His restrictions were a protest against social and religious decay in the nation that resulted from increasing urbanization. With the invasion of Nebuchadnezzar and the Syrians, the Recabites were forced to seek refuge in Jerusalem (v.11); but this did not compel them to drink wine. They could no longer live in tents in the open country.

c. The rebuke to Judah

35:12–17

¹²Then the word of the LORD came to Jeremiah, saying: ¹³"This is what the LORD Almighty, the God of Israel, says: Go and tell the men of Judah and the people of Jerusalem, 'Will you not learn a lesson and obey my words?' declares the LORD. ¹⁴'Jonadab son of Recab ordered his sons not to drink wine and this command has been kept. To this day they do not drink wine, because they obey their forefather's command. But I have spoken to you again and again, yet you have not obeyed me. ¹⁵Again and again I sent all my servants the prophets to you. They said, "Each of you must turn from your wicked ways and reform your actions; do not follow other gods to serve them. Then you will live in the land I have given to you and your fathers." But you have not paid attention or listened to me. ¹⁶The descendants of Jonadab son of Recab have carried out the command their forefather gave them, but these people have not obeyed me.'

¹⁷"Therefore, this is what the LORD God Almighty, the God of Israel, says: 'Listen! I am going to bring on Judah and on everyone living in Jerusalem every disaster I pronounced against them. I spoke to them, but they did not listen; I called to them, but they did not answer.'"

12–17 These verses drive home the purpose of the Recabite episode. Jeremiah probably spoke these words (vv. 12–13) in one of the temple courts. They were meant to shame the people of Judah and Jerusalem for the way they had treated the Lord. Notice the telling contrasts between the Recabites and Judah.

1. The Recabites obeyed a fallible leader (v. 14); Judah's leader was the eternal God (cf. Mal 1:6).

2. Jonadab gave his commands to the Recabites only once; God repeatedly sent his messages to his people (v. 15).

3. The restrictions that bound the Recabites did not deal with eternal issues; God's messages to his people had eternal as well as temporal implications.

4. The Recabites obeyed the commands of Jonadab for about three hundred years; the Lord's people constantly disobeyed (v. 16).

5. The loyalty of the Recabites would be rewarded; for their disloyalty God's people would be punished (v. 17).

Notes

15 The phrase הַשְׁכֵּם וְשָׁלֹחַ (haškēm wᵉšālōah) is well translated by "again and again" (NIV). Literally, it is "rising [early] and sending"; by a vivid anthropomorphism the phrase indicates the energy, patience, and perseverance of God in commissioning his prophets to call Israel to repentance. Jeremiah uses the expression eleven times (7:13, 25; 11:7; 25: 3–4; 26:5; 29:19; 32:33; 35:14–15; 44:4). The first verb in the phrase שָׁכַם (šākam) is denominative with the concept of loading the backs of beasts (early in the morning).

d. *The Recabites' reward*

35:18–19

> ¹⁸Then Jeremiah said to the family of the Recabites, "This is what the LORD Almighty, the God of Israel, says: 'You have obeyed the command of your fore-father Jonadab and have followed all his instructions and have done everything he ordered.' ¹⁹Therefore, this is what the LORD Almighty, the God of Israel, says: 'Jonadab son of Recab will never fail to have a man to serve me.'"

18–19 In promising to bless the Recabites for their fidelity (v. 18), God did not commend all aspects of their lifestyle (cf. 32:1–15 on land tenure). The expression "serve me" ('ōmēd lᵉpānay, lit., "stood before me") has been variously understood (v. 19). It is a technical term for the privilege of service, used of prophets (1 Kings 17:1), priests (Num 16:9), and kings (1 Kings 10:8). The term usually involves service in the temple but may not connote that here (so Laetsch). Some scholars think the promise in v. 18 was literally fulfilled in the Recabites' being in some way incorporated into the tribe of Levi. The Targum of Jonathan has "Shall not want a man ministering before me," i.e., serving as a Levitical priest. But the promise may be a general one because 'ōmēd lᵉpānay was used of patriarchs (Gen 19:27), of Moses and Samuel (Jer 15:1), and of the nation worshiping the Lord (7:10). Many reports are extant, however, of the continued existence of the Recabites in the East (so Streane et al.).

Notes

19 Because the clause לֹא יִכָּרֵת אִישׁ (lōʾ yikkārēt ʾîš, "will never fail to have a man") is so prominent in the promises of 33:17–18 with reference to the dynasty of David and the Levitical priests in eschatological times, the temptation has been strong to see this promise realized in the future messianic kingdom. Furthermore, it is suggested that, because the phrase עֹמֵד לְפָנַי (ʿōmēḏ lipnê, "to stand before") is employed, it indicates service in a priestly office. Actually, no more is to be read into the passage than longevity for the descendants of Jonadab (Jehonadab) and their service (in a general sense) to the Lord (cf. Gen 41:46, where Joseph was before Pharaoh). In the Middle Ages and modern times, travelers in the Near East have claimed to find tribes claiming to be Recabites, but credence is to be reserved until further proof is forthcoming.

3. Jehoiakim's penknife and God's Word (36:1–32)

This chapter contains a unique description of the writing of a substantial portion of God's Word. We learn from it how Jeremiah's prophecies were written down after he had spoken them. In those days dictating to a secretary was common. Taking dictation was then, as now, a specialized skill. Jeremiah dictated his book in Jehoiakim's fourth year; when the first copy was destroyed (cf. vv.23, 32), a new one with additions was produced. Certain scholars think that the strange order of material in Jeremiah as we have it today may be attributed to the way it was composed—i.e., it was originally a shorter work that grew through many revisions to its present size. This concept, however, should be used with care, for some scholars have a tendency to let subjective insights shape their interpretations. This chapter may have been put at this place in the book to point to Jeremiah's relations with the kings who reigned near the end of his ministry. The date of the chapter is the fourth year of Jehoiakim—viz., 605 B.C. This was a year of highly significant events: the Battle of Carchemish, the defeat of Pharaoh Neco, the subjugation of Jehoiakim to Nebuchadnezzar (for details, see Introduction: Historical Setting). Events before and after the siege of Jerusalem are covered in chapters 36–44.

a. The dictation of the scroll

36:1–8

¹In the fourth year of Jehoiakim son of Josiah king of Judah, this word came to Jeremiah from the LORD: ²"Take a scroll and write on it all the words I have spoken to you concerning Israel, Judah and all the other nations from the time I began speaking to you in the reign of Josiah till now. ³Perhaps when the people of Judah hear about every disaster I plan to inflict on them, each of them will turn from his wicked way; then I will forgive their wickedness and their sin."

⁴So Jeremiah called Baruch son of Neriah, and while Jeremiah dictated all the words the LORD had spoken to him, Baruch wrote them on the scroll. ⁵Then Jeremiah told Baruch, "I am restricted; I cannot go to the LORD's temple. ⁶So you go to the house of the LORD on a day of fasting and read to the people from the scroll the words of the LORD that you wrote as I dictated. Read them to all the people of Judah who come in from their towns. ⁷Perhaps they will bring their petition before the LORD, and each will turn from his wicked ways, for the anger and wrath pronounced against this people by the LORD are great."

⁸Baruch son of Neriah did everything Jeremiah the prophet told him to do; at the LORD's temple he read the words of the LORD from the scroll.

1–3 The year (v.1) is the same as in 25:1. The way the events are narrated in the chapter implies the presence of an eyewitness—doubtless Baruch, Jeremiah's secretary. The Lord commanded Jeremiah to write on a scroll all the messages he had received from the Lord from the beginning of his ministry under Josiah "till now" (v.2), i.e., the fourth year of Jehoiakim (cf. 25:1–3; 30:2). (These were undoubtedly the messages Jeremiah had spoken to the people.) This was the first time they were written down; a prodigious feat of memory would have been required. The command was probably carried out partly by transcribing parts of records and partly by drawing on Jeremiah's memory of his prophecies over some twenty years of ministry (so Streane). In Jeremiah's time, scrolls were of either papyrus or parchment fastened to a wooden roller at one or both ends. (Book form—sheet upon sheet—dates only from early Christian times.) The writing was arranged in columns parallel to the rollers. (Our word "volume"—from the verb "to roll up"—goes back to this form of book.) The contents of the scroll are generally but not precisely specified; they probably included a summary of Jeremiah's messages from 626–605 B.C. (so Harrison). The written word might be more successful than the preached word. The impending capture of Jerusalem added weight to the hope that the Lord's warnings through his prophet might yet be effective. The purpose of all Jeremiah's prophecies of judgment was to spur the nation to repentance (v.3), hence the conditional nature of the warnings (cf. 18:8; 26:3).

4–8 Baruch, the prophet's secretary (already mentioned in 32:12–13), came from a prominent family (v.4; cf. 45:1; 51:59). Jeremiah was inspired to dictate to Baruch from memory, probably with the aid of notes he had made (so Bewer). (That he dictated to Baruch should not, however, be taken to mean that God, who inspired him and the other biblical writers, used them in the same way. Biblical inspiration is not to be equated with dictation.) The dates in this chapter (vv.1, 9, 22) show that a number of months passed between the dictation and public reading of what was written. Jeremiah was "restricted" ('āṣûr, lit., "shut up") from going to the temple (v.5). (It has been conjectured that this was because of ritual uncleanness on his part, but the time was too long for that [cf. v.1 with v.9].) The authorities had probably forbidden him to speak there because of his unpopular temple address (cf. 7:1–15; 26:1–7). In 33:1 and 39:15 the verb 'āṣar means "confined" or "imprisoned," but it cannot have that precise meaning here (cf. vv.19, 26). With Nebuchadnezzar on the march against Jerusalem, Jeremiah's message could no longer be considered harmless. Because he could not go to the temple, he had Baruch act as his agent. To guarantee a good hearing of his written messages, Jeremiah chose a fast day when the people would be assembled in the temple (v.6). After the Exile, fast days were specified (cf. Zech 7:3, 5; 8:19), but earlier they were called in time of emergency (cf. Joel 2:12, 15). Some public calamity, perhaps a drought, had occasioned this fast. Internationally, it was a most opportune time for a fast because Jeremiah saw the significance of Egypt's defeat by the Babylonians at Carchemish in 605 B.C. There was a feeling that turning to the Lord (v.7) in a public fast might avert the judgment that had been conditionally predicted (v.8).

Notes

2 מְגִלַּת־סֵפֶר (meḡillaṯ-sēper) was a "book-scroll" made of skins (smoothed for such use) or papyrus. The modern book (codex) came into use about the first century A.D. It has been claimed (so Hitzig) that מְגִלָּה (meḡillāh, "scroll," "roll") was a term not used before the time of Jeremiah (but see Ps 40:8 for the identical phrase). Herodotus states that from the earliest period the Ionians wrote on goat and sheep skin; so even Moses could have used such materials (so Henderson).

6 The reference to בְּיוֹם צוֹם (beyôm ṣôm, "a fast day") and then added mention in v.9 cannot apply to the Day of Atonement because (1) the former is too indefinite and (2) the latter falls on the tenth day of the seventh month (Lev 16:29; 23:27), not the ninth month. Both cases come under the category of days of fasting announced during times of special national distress, here because of the terror of Nebuchadnezzar's victories. Since fasts, other than Atonement, were apparently not on fixed dates, a fast was chosen for the reading in order to take advantage of the crowds then assembled.

b. *The public reading*

36:9–10

⁹In the ninth month of the fifth year of Jehoiakim son of Josiah king of Judah, a time of fasting before the LORD was proclaimed for all the people in Jerusalem and those who had come from the towns of Judah. ¹⁰From the room of Gemariah son of Shaphan the secretary, which was in the upper courtyard at the entrance of the New Gate of the temple, Baruch read to all the people at the LORD's temple the words of Jeremiah from the scroll.

9 The "fifth" year was 604 B.C., and the "ninth" month was about December. The year was reckoned from spring (April), not from the fall (September/October). The fast was not that of the seventh month stated in the Law (cf. Lev 16:29; 23:27) but possibly one specially designated because of the first capture of Jerusalem in 605 B.C. (Jerusalem would again be invaded in 597 and 586 B.C.) The ninth month was the one in which the Babylonians sacked the Philistine city of Ashkelon. These events may have decided Jehoiakim's shift of allegiance from Egypt to Babylon. Notice it was the people, not the king, who proclaimed the fast. The public reading was the first of three readings that day (cf. vv.10, 15, 21). Because of the repeated readings, it is probable that only certain portions were read.

10 Gemariah was the son of Shaphan, Josiah's secretary of state (cf. 2 Kings 22:3, 8, 12). This Gemariah was the brother of Ahikam, a friend of Jeremiah (cf. 26:24); he was not the Gemariah mentioned in 29:3. Shaphan's family was evidently a noble, godly one. Gemariah was a common name in the seventh century B.C. and occurs in Letter 1 of the Lachish Letters. He permitted Baruch to use his room in the temple's inner court. Evidently Baruch stationed himself at the door to Gemariah's room so that what he read could be heard by the assembled people.

c. *The reading to the officials*

36:11-19

> ¹¹When Micaiah son of Gemariah, the son of Shaphan, heard all the words of the LORD from the scroll, ¹²he went down to the secretary's room in the royal palace, where all the officials were sitting: Elishama the secretary, Delaiah son of Shemaiah, Elnathan son of Acbor, Gemariah son of Shaphan, Zedekiah son of Hananiah, and all the other officals. ¹³After Micaiah told them everything he had heard Baruch read to the people from the scroll, ¹⁴all the officials sent Jehudi son of Nethaniah, the son of Shelemiah, the son of Cushi, to say to Baruch, "Bring the scroll from which you have read to the people and come." So Baruch son of Neriah went to them with the scroll in his hand. ¹⁵They said to him, "Sit down, please, and read it to us."
>
> So Baruch read it to them. ¹⁶When they heard all these words, they looked at each other in fear and said to Baruch, "We must report all these words to the king." ¹⁷Then they asked Baruch, "Tell us, how did you come to write all this? Did Jeremiah dictate it?"
>
> ¹⁸"Yes," Baruch replied, "he dictated all these words to me, and I wrote them in ink on the scroll."
>
> ¹⁹Then the officials said to Baruch, "You and Jeremiah, go and hide. Don't let anyone know where you are."

11-15 It was in Micaiah's father's chambers that Baruch read the scroll for the first time (cf. v.10). Micaiah doubtless felt that what Baruch had read affected the public interest (v.11); so he told the officials about it (vv.12-13). When they had heard what was in the scroll, their response was immediate (v.14); and they asked that it be read to them (v.15). Of the officials mentioned, Jehudi (v.14), otherwise unknown, must have been an important person, since his ancestry is traced back to the third generation. Cushi (lit., "Ethiopian") does not necessarily imply Ethiopian descent, because the prophet Zephaniah (cf. Zeph 1:1) was a son of Cushi and of Hebrew descent (so Freedman). Observe the interest and respect the officials had for the message of the scroll. The way they addressed Baruch (vv. 15, 19) implies that they favored him and Jeremiah. Baruch assumed the sitting position of an Oriental teacher (cf. Luke 4:20).

16-19 The reading showed the officials truths so diametrically opposed to the hopes and assurances of the king that they were stricken with fear (so KD). They believed the prophecies and may have feared for the lives of Baruch and Jeremiah as well as their own. Jehoiakim was no champion of the truth. Not in the sense of informers, but because of the terrifying contents of the book, they felt that the king should hear the message (v.16). The scroll contained such bold announcements at a time of crisis and struggle for the nation's existence that they felt it imposed a solemn responsibility on them. Not wishing to appear before the king as uninformed, they asked Baruch how the scroll had come to be written (v.17). Artlessly, he told them precisely how he had written down what Jeremiah had dictated (v.18). He had only put down the words; in no sense was he a collaborator or an editor. Realizing the potential danger involved, and knowing the king's character, the officials showed their concern for the safety of Jeremiah and Baruch (v.19). Later on (cf. v.25) they even risked the king's displeasure. Their concern for safety was a wise precaution in view of what had happened to Uriah (cf. 26:20-23).

Notes

14 Because his great-grandfather was a Cushite, it has been conjectured that יְהוּדִי (*yᵉhûdî*, "Jehudi") was a subordinate official (cf. Deut 23:9 [8 Eng.]) who had become a naturalized Jew as the first of his family (so Orelli et al.). It is quite unusual for one to be named with three generations; therefore, some have inferred two men are meant here: Jehudi and Shelemiah. The Hebrew text is simple and will not allow such a bifurcation. Moreover, the prophet Zephaniah (Zeph 1:1) is also named with four generations, and his father's name was Cushi. There appears to be no need to assume naturalization in either case.

18 The word בַּדְּיוֹ (*baddᵉyô*, "in ink") is a *hapax legomenon* and implies that Baruch merely performed the mechanical work as an amanuensis. The ink was made by mixing soot or lampblack with a liquid.

d. *The reading to Jehoiakim*

36:20–26

²⁰After they put the scroll in the room of Elishama the secretary, they went to the king in the courtyard and reported everything to him. ²¹The king sent Jehudi to get the scroll, and Jehudi brought it from the room of Elishama the secretary and read it to the king and all the officials standing beside him. ²²It was the ninth month and the king was sitting in the winter apartment, with a fire burning in the firepot in front of him. ²³Whenever Jehudi had read three or four columns of the scroll, the king cut them off with a scribe's knife and threw them into the firepot, until the entire scroll was burned in the fire. ²⁴The king and all his attendants who heard all these words showed no fear, nor did they tear their clothes. ²⁵Even though Elnathan, Delaiah and Gemariah urged the king not to burn the scroll, he would not listen to them. ²⁶Instead, the king commanded Jerahmeel, a son of the king, Seraiah son of Azriel and Shelemiah son of Abdeel to arrest Baruch the scribe and Jeremiah the prophet. But the LORD had hidden them.

20–21 King Jehoiakim's reception of the message was openly hostile. Unlike Josiah, his godly father (cf. 2 Kings 22:1–23:25), Jehoiakim was not interested in spiritual reform. He was interested in an alliance with Egypt and was not favorable to Babylon (cf. 2 Kings 23:34–35). Before the officials came into the inner courtyard where the king's chambers were, they deposited the scroll in the room of Elishama for safekeeping (v.20). They may have surmised what Jehoiakim's response to it would be; so they tried to keep it out of his reach. But the king ordered the scroll read in his presence (v.21).

22–26 So startling are the events that follow that Jeremiah describes them in detail. The king was in the winter house (v.22), not a separate dwelling, but a warm apartment in a sheltered part of the palace facing the winter sun (cf. Amos 3:15). It was December, 604 B.C.; in Jerusalem fall and winter are cool because of rain and occasional light snow. A brazier (NIV, "firepot") with burning charcoal was placed in a low place in the middle of the room. Jehoiakim reacted violently to the reading. In disdain he cut and burned the scroll (v.23). The writing on the scroll was in columns (*dᵉlātôt*, lit., "doors"); in form these columns resembled doors, a usage found in Arabic and rabbinical Hebrew (so Peake). The text was, then, written on perpendicular columns on papyrus strips glued together, rolled on a small stick. The arrangement was the same as for the scrolls read in the synagogues today. In an appalling act of blasphemy and contempt for God's revelation in his written Word, Jehoiakim took a scribe's knife and cut off consecutive strips of the scroll as Jehudi read them and tossed them into the fire. Most of the court officials stood by indifferently (v.24). They shared the king's contempt for God's truth. Contrast Jehoiakim's utter irreverence for the scroll Jehudi read to him with the godly response of his father, Josiah, to the reading of the rediscovered Law (cf. 2 Kings 22:11). Three men (v.25) who opposed the king's actions are mentioned. Elnathan (cf. 26:22) is now on Jeremiah's side. In a further act, Jehoiakim compounded his sin by ordering the arrest of Baruch and Jeremiah (v.26). But the Lord intervened and used faithful friends to hide them. God knows how to protect both his message and his messengers (cf. vv.26, 32).

Notes

26 Jerahmeel was not the actual son of Jehoiakim, who at this time was only thirty years old (2 Kings 23:36). Reference is apparently to one of the princes of the dynasty.

e. The prophecies rewritten

36:27–28

> 27After the king burned the scroll containing the words that Baruch had written at Jeremiah's dictation, the word of the LORD came to Jeremiah: 28"Take another scroll and write on it all the words that were on the first scroll, which Jehoiakim king of Judah burned up."

27–28 Soon after the king's destruction of the scroll (v.27), the Lord ordered Jeremiah to write a duplicate of it (v.28). God's message was not to be lost but rewritten *in toto* with more added to it. It takes more than a king's knife to destroy God's message.

f. The condemnation of Jehoiakim

36:29–31

> 29"Also tell Jehoiakim king of Judah, 'This is what the LORD says: You burned that scroll and said, "Why did you write on it that the king of Babylon would certainly come and destroy this land and cut off both men and animals from it?" 30Therefore, this is what the LORD says about Jehoiakim king of Judah: He will have no one to sit on the throne of David; his body will be thrown out and exposed to the heat by day and the frost by night. 31I will punish him and his children and his attendants for their wickedness; I will bring on them and those living in Jerusalem and the people of Judah every disaster I pronounced against them, because they have not listened.' "

29–31 The king's anger at Babylon (v.29) may show that Jehoiakim had already decided on rebellion against Babylon (cf. 2 Kings 24:1), a rebellion that resulted in the captivity during the reign of Jehoiachin. The three-month reign of Jehoiachin (cf. 2 Kings 24:6, 8) does not contradict the prediction of v.30. Jehoiachin's succession was not a valid one but only a token one because he was immediately besieged by Nebuchadnezzar, surrendered in three months, and then went into exile, where he died after many years. No other descendant of Jehoiakim ever ascended the throne. Zedekiah was the uncle of Jehoiachin. It has been conjectured that Jehoiakim died either in a palace uprising or in an uprising of the people (v.31; cf. 22:18–19).

g. The prophecies recorded again

36:32

> 32So Jeremiah took another scroll and gave it to the scribe Baruch son of Neriah, and as Jeremiah dictated, Baruch wrote on it all the words of the scroll that Jehoiakim king of Judah had burned in the fire. And many similar words were added to them.

32 Jehoiakim's destruction of the scroll was one of many attempts through the centuries to destroy God's Word. But the Word of the Lord is indestructible. The God who inspires the Word will see to its preservation. It is certain that our present text of the Book of Jeremiah is longer than the original portions that had brief abstracts of Jeremiah's earlier prophecies. The additions doubtless included the doom of the godless king. After the Israelites broke the Ten Commandments, the Lord rewrote them and gave them to Moses (cf. Exod 31:28; 32:15–16; 34:1; also 1 Peter 1:25). Theodore Watts-Dunton wisely said, "When murdered Truth returns she comes to kill" (so Lewis).

4. Resolute Jeremiah and weak Zedekiah (37:1–21)

Chapters 37–39 are prophecies from the reign of Zedekiah, dealing with events and messages during the siege and capture of Jerusalem. Chapters 37–44 are a continuous record of the later work and experiences of Jeremiah, beginning with the accession of Zedekiah. They include the incidents from the fall of the city and from Jeremiah's sojourn in Egypt. Chapters 37–38 cover the period of the siege of Jerusalem (588–586 B.C.). In chapter 37 we have the captivity of the prophet, in chapter 39 that of Zedekiah.

a. Zedekiah's request

37:1–5

> 1Zedekiah son of Josiah was made king of Judah by Nebuchadnezzar king of Babylon; he reigned in place of Jehoiachin son of Jehoiakim. 2Neither he nor his attendants nor the people of the land paid any attention to the words the LORD had spoken through Jeremiah the prophet.
> 3King Zedekiah, however, sent Jehucal son of Shelemiah with the priest Zephaniah son of Maaseiah to Jeremiah the prophet with this message: "Please pray to the LORD our God for us."
> 4Now Jeremiah was free to come and go among the people, for he had not yet been put in prison. 5Pharaoh's army had marched out of Egypt, and when the Babylonians who were besieging Jerusalem heard the report about them, they withdrew from Jerusalem.

1 This verse shows the fulfillment of the judgment Jeremiah pronounced against the godless Jehoiakim in 36:30. Instead of Jehoiakim's son Coniah (Jehoiachin), Nebuchadnezzar put on the throne Zedekiah, who was not descended from Jehoiakim but was his brother and thus the uncle of Coniah. It has been suggested that as an uncle of Coniah, Zedekiah was probably considered to be the ruler in place of his nephew, who was deported to Babylon after three months. This may explain the unusual expression *yimlok-melek* ("reigned as king"; NIV, "was made king"; cf. 2 Kings 24:17). Eighteen years pass between chapters 36 and 37. Now the narrative centers on the last two years of the reign of Zedekiah, who was appointed king by Nebuchadnezzar after solemnly pledging his loyalty in the name of the Lord. Because of Egyptian influence at court, which he could not resist, Zedekiah decided to break his pledge. This was the immediate cause of the final siege of Jerusalem. This chapter appears to be the beginning of Zedekiah's reign, but earlier chapters have already spoken of him (cf. chs. 21, 27–29, 32, 34). He reigned for eleven years (597–586 B.C.).

2–3 The root of Judah's trouble was not political but spiritual; the people were disobedient to God (v.2). In spite of his refusal to heed the word of God, Zedekiah sent messengers to Jeremiah (v.3). It was the second time he had done this (cf. 21:1–2). The approach of the Egyptian forces (vv.5, 9) seemed to contradict the message of 34:2–7; moreover, with the withdrawal of the Babylonian army, Zedekiah may have thought that Jeremiah's predictions of doom were wrong after all (so Cundall). Also, Zedekiah may have been encouraged by his alliance with Pharaoh Hophra (c. 590–570 B.C.). At any rate, he revolted against Babylon. He may indeed have doubted his own prophets, and so he wanted to get a message from Jeremiah that would please him. Thus he asked the prophet to pray for him (v.3)—i.e., to support his actions (so Cunliffe-Jones). In other words, what Zedekiah wanted was for the Lord to make the temporary withdrawal of the Babylonians permanent. He may somehow have felt that the presence of Jeremiah, though he predicted doom, would insure God's protection against Jerusalem's capture. As for his regard for Jeremiah, it was tinged with superstition. Jehucal (cf. 38:1), one of the messengers Zedekiah sent to Jeremiah, later became an enemy of the prophet.

4–5 Though Jeremiah was not yet imprisoned (v.4), he was shortly arrested (v.13). To help understand the narrative, there is a historical note in v.5. (For the historical situation, see 34:8–11.) At the approach of Egyptian troops, Babylon temporarily raised her siege of Jerusalem. The pharaoh was Pharaoh Hophra (cf. 44:30), the Apries of Herodotus (2.161; 4.159). Soon after this, the Babylonians defeated the Egyptians and resumed the siege of Jerusalem.

Notes

4 Jeremiah uses several different words for imprisonment in this chapter: בֵּית כֶּלֶא (*bêt kele'*, "prison"; vv.4, 15, 18); בֵּית הָאֵסוּר (*bêt hāʾēsûr*, "imprisoned"; v.15); בֵּית הַבּוֹר (*bêt habbôr*) with הַחֲנֻיוֹת (*haḥᵃnuyôt*, "vaulted cell in a dungeon"; v.16); חֲצַר הַמַּטָּרָה (*hᵃṣar hammaṭṭārāh*, "courtyard of the guard"; v.21 *bis*). Already in 20:2 the prophet was put in fetters. During the siege of Jerusalem, he was incarcerated in the court of the guard (32:2), that is,

610

the quarters of the sentry guard of the palace. Finally, Jeremiah was confined in the house of Jonathan the secretary, which was taken over to serve as a prison with a dungeon and cells. Punitive confinement was apparently unknown in the ancient Near East, Greece, and Rome (cf. TWOT, 1:62–63).

5 Pharaoh Hophra (44:30) was the fourth ruler of the Twenty-Sixth Dynasty, ruling from 589–570 B.C. He was an ally of the Judean dynasty. Apries was his name (the *Ha'abre'* of the Egyptians and the Hophra of the Hebrews). He succeeded his father Psammetik II. According to v.7 he decided to avoid an encounter with the Babylonian forces. Zedekiah's appeal for help (Ezek 17:15, 17) had availed him nothing. The date of Zedekiah's rebellion against Nebuchadnezzar coincided with the accession of Apries. Hophra may have wanted to meet Nebuchadnezzar on the Euphrates as his grandfather Neco had (J.H. Breasted, *A History of Egypt,* 2d ed. [New York: Charles Scribner's Sons, 1912], p. 586). In the long run, Hophra showed that he was no match for the Babylonians.

b. *Jeremiah's reply*

37:6–10

> ⁶Then the word of the LORD came to Jeremiah the prophet: ⁷"This is what the LORD, the God of Israel, says: Tell the king of Judah, who sent you to inquire of me, 'Pharaoh's army, which has marched out to support you, will go back to its own land, to Egypt. ⁸Then the Babylonians will return and attack this city; they will capture it and burn it down.'
> ⁹"This is what the LORD says: Do not deceive yourselves, thinking, 'The Babylonians will surely leave us.' They will not! ¹⁰Even if you were to defeat the entire Babylonian army that is attacking you and only wounded men were left in their tents, they would come out and burn this city down."

6–10 Jeremiah did not waver in his fidelity to the truth. The relief of Jerusalem was, he said, only temporary and would ultimately change nothing (vv.6–8). It was only a passing incident. The Egyptian army may have been defeated (cf. Ezek 30:21; so Peake). Circumstances and appearances to the contrary, God's ultimate word about Jerusalem was that it would be taken and burned. There was no basis for a false hope. Then the prophet stated (v.9) in the strongest terms, which some have called hyperbolic, God's unchanging purpose to destroy Jerusalem. This was unquestionably the will of the Lord. Escape was out of the question. Even the "wounded" would be able to carry out the doom threatening God's people (v.10).

Notes

10 The hyperbole underscores the hopeless condition of Jerusalem before the Babylonians. מְדֻקָּר (*m*duqqār,* "wounded") is literally "thrust through," "pierced," "transfixed," thus mortally wounded men. An interesting parallel is found in the history of the Indian mutiny (so Binns): "When the British power seemed gone, a native prince sent to his astrologer to ask what would be the final issue of the mutiny. The striking reply he received was, 'If all of the Europeans save one are slain, that one will remain and fight and conquer.'"

c. *The charge of treason against Jeremiah*

37:11–15

> ¹¹After the Babylonian army had withdrawn from Jerusalem because of Pharaoh's army, ¹²Jeremiah started to leave the city to go to the territory of Benjamin to get his share of the property among the people there. ¹³But when he reached the Benjamin Gate, the captain of the guard, whose name was Irijah son of Shelemiah, the son of Hananiah, arrested him and said, "You are deserting to the Babylonians!"
> ¹⁴"That's not true!" Jeremiah said. "I am not deserting to the Babylonians." But Irijah would not listen to him; instead, he arrested Jeremiah and brought him to the officials. ¹⁵They were angry with Jeremiah and had him beaten and imprisoned in the house of Jonathan the secretary, which they had made into a prison.

11–12 This section deals with Jeremiah's imprisonment after he was charged with treason. There was no proof whatever that he meant to defect to the Babylonians when the siege was temporarily lifted (v. 11). His enemies misinterpreted his leaving the city (v. 12) and threw him into a dungeon. Some scholars have suggested that Jeremiah, convinced of the truth of his own prophecies, was fleeing for safety to Anathoth (so Lewis). But this would have been completely out of character for the prophet. Others hold that he left the city to take over the property he had bought from his cousin Hanamel (cf. ch. 32). But this is chronologically impossible because that purchase had not yet taken place (so Henderson). Besides, it had occurred while he was in prison in the courtyard of the guard.

Nor did Jeremiah leave Jerusalem to buy bread and supplies or to get his priestly share of the land at Anathoth, which he held in common with his family (so Payne Smith). What he did do was leave the city to care for certain of his property affairs in his native Anathoth. The verb *ḥālaq* in v. 12 means "divide" (NIV, "get his share"), as of property—so the Vulgate, Targum, and Syriac. Jeremiah's intention is clear; the time was opportune for settling his affairs. But he planned to remain in Judah in spite of his divinely given warnings of impending disaster.

13–15 The Benjamin Gate (v. 13) was north of the city and led to the territory of that tribe (cf. 38:7–8; Zech 14:10). Except for what is said here, we know nothing of Irijah. He accused Jeremiah, who was already suspect because of his exhortations to surrender to the invaders (cf. 21:8–10; so Cheyne), of defecting to the enemy. But Jeremiah could hardly have been deserting to the enemy, because they were already gone (v. 11). The charge was vicious and nonsensical. Some expositors have suggested that revenge for Jeremiah's prediction of the death of Irijah's grandfather Hananiah (cf. 28:16) motivated the charge (so JFB). It is not hard to understand why Jeremiah was so unpopular with the army. Many who heard him followed his advice and deserted to the Babylonians (cf. 38:2, 19; 39:9; 52:15). The officials involved in beating and arresting him were surely not those of Josiah's time (vv. 14–15; cf. 26:16; 36:19), for they were now probably captives in Babylon with Coniah. Beating Jeremiah was an indignity his sensitive spirit felt deeply (cf. 20:2). The home of Jonathan the secretary was made the prophet's prison, perhaps because he was just one of many deserters and political prisoners. It was not uncommon in the ancient East to use part of an officer's home as a prison. The treatment Jeremiah received is understandable, not excusable, on the grounds of the desperate plight of the city. Jonathan's house turned out to be a place where Jeremiah's life was endangered (v. 20).

Notes

12 מִשָּׁם לַחֲלִק (laḥªliq miššām) is a technical term, occurring only here. The Hiphil has an elision of the intervocalic ḥ. Literally the term means "to cause to divide." Jeremiah's destination was probably his native town of Anathoth (1:1; 32:8). JPS renders "to receive his portion there." The presupposition is that a relative had died in Anathoth; so it was incumbent on Jeremiah to be present in connection with the inheritance (so Freedman). The account in chapter 32 concerns a later time. Curiously, Rabbi David Kimchi (A.D. 1160–1230) translates "to escape thence into the midst of the people," because he expected to be arrested and tried to avoid it. The accusation against Jeremiah was false because he expected to transact his affairs publicly "among the people there." Bright translates "to attend to a division of property among his people there." This is essentially as Smith-Goodspeed, NIV, NASB, JB, BV, and NEB translate it (all contra KJV). Though the passage has been troublesome to expositors and translators (LXX MSS render the verb three different ways), it is clear that the verb is often employed with reference to possessions. The Vulgate, Targum, and Syriac so understand it as well.

d. Jeremiah in the dungeon

37:16–21

> ¹⁶Jeremiah was put into a vaulted cell in a dungeon, where he remained a long time. ¹⁷Then King Zedekiah sent for him and had him brought to the palace, where he asked him privately, "Is there any word from the LORD?"
> "Yes," Jeremiah replied, "you will be handed over to the king of Babylon."
> ¹⁸Then Jeremiah said to King Zedekiah, "What crime have I committed against you or your officials or this people, that you have put me in prison? ¹⁹Where are your prophets who prophesied to you, 'The king of Babylon will not attack you or this land'? ²⁰But now, my lord the king, please listen. Let me bring my petition before you: Do not send me back to the house of Jonathan the secretary, or I will die there."
> ²¹King Zedekiah then gave orders for Jeremiah to be placed in the courtyard of the guard and given bread from the street of the bakers each day until all the bread in the city was gone. So Jeremiah remained in the courtyard of the guard.

16–17 The prophet was put in "a vaulted cell in a dungeon" (lit., "the house of the cistern-pit") (v.16). The cell was a subterranean room adjoining the dungeon. The "long time" refers to the period when the Babylonians renewed their siege. So desperate was the situation for Jerusalem that Zedekiah felt he must have another message from Jeremiah even if he had to speak to him in secret (v.17). The nature of this meeting (vv.17–20) shows Jeremiah's unpopularity as well as Zedekiah's weakness in confronting his officials face to face. By this time he realized that Jeremiah was a true prophet of God. Evidently he was hoping Jeremiah would give him a more encouraging word about the Babylonian menace. But Jeremiah did not change his message; it was God's word, and the condition of Judah remained the same. Though without confidence in his advisers, Zedekiah was too weak to take a firm stand. Note the contrast between the frightened king in his palace and the resolute prophet in his prison (cf. 1:18–19)!

18–20 These verses show Jeremiah's humanity. He asked for justice, not pity. He wanted a valid accusation (v.18) because he knew he was innocent of any treasonable actions (so KD). Since his words had proved to be true, why should he be imprisoned? If he was imprisoned for telling the truth, why were the false prophets, whose predictions were unfulfilled, not given the same treatment (v.19)? They were the real traitors. Jeremiah's questions were uncomfortably fair because events had unmasked the false prophets (cf. Deut 13:1–5; 18:20–22). The situation was ironic: the false prophets who lied to the king and the nation were free; Jeremiah who told them the truth was in prison (so Habel, Bewer)! The prophet then makes a very human request. He asks not to be sent back to the house of Jonathan the secretary (v.20; cf. v.15), lest he die there.

21 Solicitous for the welfare of the prophet, Zedekiah reversed the decision of his officials and transferred Jeremiah to the guardroom, a move that doubtless gave him more security and saved him other indignities. The king also gave him a daily allotment from the rapidly failing food supply. But he did not liberate the prophet, because he still feared his officials. This verse is the only place in Scripture where the name of a street in Jerusalem appears: "the street of the bakers," i.e., Baker Street. It was a Near Eastern custom to name streets after those who worked in them.

5. Confined in a cistern (38:1–13)

The events recorded in this chapter took place near the end of the siege of Jerusalem. As tensions mounted in Judah, the anti-Babylonian group at court wanted to do away with their chief opponent, Jeremiah.

a. The accusation against Jeremiah

38:1–4

> ¹Shephatiah son of Mattan, Gedaliah son of Pashhur, Jehucal son of Shelemiah, and Pashhur son of Malkijah heard what Jeremiah was telling all the people when he said, ²"This is what the LORD says: 'Whoever stays in this city will die by the sword, famine or plague, but whoever goes over to the Babylonians will live. He will escape with his life; he will live.' ³And this is what the LORD says: 'This city will certainly be handed over to the army of the king of Babylon, who will capture it.'"
> ⁴Then the officials said to the king, "This man should be put to death. He is discouraging the soldiers who are left in this city, as well as all the people, by the things he is saying to them. This man is not seeking the good of these people but their ruin."

1–3 The officials' opposition to Jeremiah kept up to the Fall of Jerusalem. They hated him for his condemnation of their godless policies. The four mentioned (v.1) doubtless represented a larger group. Jeremiah's confinement in the courtyard of the guard (cf. 37:21) still permitted him to make his message known. With the security of the guardroom as a base, he could have had access to a good many people. Gedaliah was probably the son of the Pashhur who beat Jeremiah and placed him in the stocks (cf. 20:1–6). Jehucal is mentioned in 37:3. All were in the Egyptian party. They naturally quoted Jeremiah's words in their accusation. They considered his messages, like those in chapter 21, treasonable; and even to ordinary listeners they sounded that way. Clearly, Jeremiah spoke not as one governed by expediency but as one constrained by the Lord. His counsel was either to surrender or suffer ruin (vv. 2–3).

4 Jeremiah was charged with working against the war effort and with weakening the will of the people to resist the invaders. Since he was speaking during the final months of the siege, it is no wonder his message was judged dangerous. By weakening the morale of the soldiers with whom he was in contact in the guardroom, he infuriated his enemies. Words similar to his are found in a charge in Lachish Letter 6 against certain leaders in Jerusalem. The letter (ostracon) was from an outpost captain to Yaosh, commander at Lachish: "And behold the words of the officials are not good, but only to weaken your hands and to slacken the hands of the men who are informed about them." There was probably truth in the statement of Jeremiah's opposition (cf. v. 19) because some would have believed his words, which were, of course, God's message. The officials on whom the burden of the defense of the city rested saw him only as a traitor. They called for his death. Politicians are often obtuse to spiritual issues, and Judah's leaders never saw that the Exile was God's way of using the Babylonians to purge the nation of idolatry. The Babylonians were only his agents.

Notes

4 With pestilence, famine, and desertion, as well as the fact that some were already taken captive in Jehoiachin's reign (cf. 2 Kings 24:14–16), Jeremiah's insistence on capitulation to the Babylonian forces was indeed "discouraging" (מְרַפֵּא [*m*ᵉ*rappē᾽*, lit., "weakening the hands"]). Lachish Letter 6 (see commentary above) employs the same phraseology, i.e., "weaken the hands" (ANET, p. 322). It has been suggested that the Lachish Letter, probably written two years prior to the events of chapter 38, indicates that the king and some of his officials were willing to surrender to Babylon (so Hyatt). Some MSS read מְרַפֶּה (*m*ᵉ*rappeh*, "to slacken, loosen"). (On the interchange of forms between לֹא and לֹה, see GKG, p. 216, sec. 75rr.)

b. Jeremiah in the cistern

38:5–6

> ⁵"He is in your hands," King Zedekiah answered. "The king can do nothing to oppose you."
> ⁶So they took Jeremiah and put him into the cistern of Malkijah, the king's son, which was in the courtyard of the guard. They lowered Jeremiah by ropes into the cistern; it had no water in it, only mud, and Jeremiah sank down into the mud.

5–6 Zedekiah was too weak to withstand his officials (v. 5). His capitulation to them was a clear giveaway of his lack of moral fiber. While he did not actually sign Jeremiah's death warrant (so Freedman), neither did he do anything to prevent it. The intention of Jeremiah's enemies was plain enough: they wanted to silence him for good. To throw Jeremiah into the miry cistern (v. 6) would have surely resulted in his death had he not been rescued. This was his third and harshest imprisonment. In ancient and modern Jerusalem, there are many cisterns to catch the winter rain water for the dry summer. The depth of this cistern can be judged by the fact that ropes were used to lower Jeremiah into it. By this punishment his enemies tried to salve their consciences from the burden of having actually slain him (so KD). Restrained by the Lord, they stopped just short of executing his prophet. "Malkijah, the king's son" was not one of Zedekiah's sons but a royal prince (cf. 36:26).

c. The rescue of Jeremiah

38:7–13

7But Ebed-Melech, a Cushite, an official in the royal palace, heard that they had put Jeremiah into the cistern. While the king was sitting in the Benjamin Gate, 8Ebed-Melech went out of the palace and said to him, 9"My lord the king, these men have acted wickedly in all they have done to Jeremiah the prophet. They have thrown him into a cistern, where he will starve to death when there is no longer any bread in the city."
10Then the king commanded Ebed-Melech the Cushite, "Take thirty men from here with you and lift Jeremiah the prophet out of the cistern before he dies."
11So Ebed-Melech took the men with him and went to a room under the treasury in the palace. He took some old rags and worn-out clothes from there and let them down with ropes to Jeremiah in the cistern. 12Ebed-Melech the Cushite said to Jeremiah, "Put these old rags and worn-out clothes under your arms to pad the ropes." Jeremiah did so, 13and they pulled him up with the ropes and lifted him out of the cistern. And Jeremiah remained in the courtyard of the guard.

7–9 The abundant detail in this passage (vv.7–13) shows that it is an eyewitness account. God uses the most unlikely agents: as "a eunuch" (v.7, NIV mg.), Ebed-Melech was excluded by divine law from the congregation of God's people (cf. Deut 23:1). In ancient courts eunuchs were employed as keepers of the royal harem. Thus they had private access to the king (v.8; cf. 2 Kings 24:15). It must, however, be recognized that *saris* did not always mean a castrated person but had a broader meaning, such as "officer" or "court official." The times were surely out of joint. Only a foreigner cared enough about Jeremiah to rescue him. Evidently Zedekiah did not know how his officials had used his capitulation to them, and he was too cowardly to ask them about it. But one official, Ebed-Melech, took pity on Jeremiah and told the king of his plight (v.9). It took courage for him to oppose the prophet's enemies. Ebed-Melech did not mince matters in speaking to Zedekiah but told him that Jeremiah was in deadly peril. He boldly accused the officials and pled with the king for the prophet's life. Under the famine condition of the siege, it was unlikely that Jeremiah would get food.

10 Zedekiah was concerned and provided a rescue team of thirty men. Because the LXX and one Hebrew MS read "three" for "thirty," a number of scholars choose the lesser figure. But such slight evidence is insufficient to overrule the MT, and only a kind of hypercriticism would call in question biblical numbers on such grounds. Granted that all thirty men would not have been needed to lift Jeremiah from the cistern, they would have been a sufficient guard to discourage the officials from intervening. Apparently the king expected some opposition from them (so Cundall et al.).

11–13 In these verses the language of an eyewitness is evident. Godly Ebed-Melek knew where to get the needed manpower (v.11). He knew what the wardrobe storeroom contained. He understood how weak Jeremiah was. There is a fine touch of compassion in v.12. So Jeremiah was transferred to the guardroom (v.13). His fourth imprisonment, this was a lifesaving move from the noxious cistern.

Notes

7 Concerning the presence of a סָרִיס (*sārîs*, "official," "eunuch") in a Jewish court, Orelli says: "Lev xxii.24 and Deut xxiii.2 [Heb.; Eng.1] raise no difficulty in the case of a slave come from abroad. In a court so thoroughly worldly, where a great harem existed (v.22), heathenism would be imitated in this respect also." See also 2 Kings 9:32.

6. *Counsel to the king* (38:14–28)

a. *Zedekiah's secret interview with Jeremiah*

38:14–23

> ¹⁴Then King Zedekiah sent for Jeremiah the prophet and had him brought to the third entrance to the temple of the LORD. "I am going to ask you something," the king said to Jeremiah. "Do not hide anything from me."
>
> ¹⁵Jeremiah said to Zedekiah, "If I give you an answer, will you not kill me? Even if I did give you counsel, you would not listen to me."
>
> ¹⁶But King Zedekiah swore this oath secretly to Jeremiah: "As surely as the LORD lives, who has given us breath, I will neither kill you nor hand you over to those who are seeking your life."
>
> ¹⁷Then Jeremiah said to Zedekiah, "This is what the LORD God Almighty, the God of Israel, says: 'If you surrender to the officers of the king of Babylon, your life will be spared and this city will not be burned down; you and your family will live. ¹⁸But if you will not surrender to the officers of the king of Babylon, this city will be handed over to the Babylonians and they will burn it down; you yourself will not escape from their hands.'"
>
> ¹⁹King Zedekiah said to Jeremiah, "I am afraid of the Jews who have gone over to the Babylonians, for the Babylonians may hand me over to them and they will mistreat me."
>
> ²⁰"They will not hand you over," Jeremiah replied. "Obey the LORD by doing what I tell you. Then it will go well with you, and your life will be spared. ²¹But if you refuse to surrender, this is what the LORD has revealed to me: ²²All the women left in the palace of the king of Judah will be brought out to the officials of the king of Babylon. Those women will say to you:
>
> > " 'They misled you and overcame you—
> > those trusted friends of yours.
> > Your feet are sunk in the mud;
> > your friends have deserted you.'
>
> ²³"All your wives and children will be brought out to the Babylonians. You yourself will not escape from their hands but will be captured by the king of Babylon; and this city will be burned down."

14–16 This was Zedekiah's last meeting with Jeremiah. It is not a duplicate of 37: 17–21 because of differences of time and circumstance. The king realized that only through Jeremiah could he get the truth (v.14). Again he questions (cf. 37:17) the prophet and receives essentially the same answer (v.15). The king still hoped for a change in the Lord's message, but it remained the same. The meeting took place privately (v.16), probably in a room connecting the palace to the temple (so Streane). Apparently Jeremiah believed that Zedekiah had approved the brutal treatment he had received. He was no longer eager to warn a king who would neither protect him nor believe his message—a king who could never be trusted to keep his word. Jeremiah was under no illusions as to how his message would be received. In a highly secret oath, the king promised Jeremiah that no harm would come to him for disclosing the Lord's message.

17–19 The alternatives for Zedekiah were still the same: surrender and live (v.17) or resist and suffer the worst (v.18). Though Nebuchadnezzar himself was not at the siege, he had his headquarters at Riblah (cf. 39:5; 2 Kings 25:6). Zedekiah was afraid not only of the officials in Judah but also of the Jews who had defected to Babylon (v.19; cf. 39:9; 52:15)—a persistent fear that affected all his political decisions and showed his weakness of character and lack of faith. Somehow he could never do what he knew was right. He was afraid the Babylonians would turn him over for torture to the Jewish defectors. They had always advised submission to Babylon (so Payne Smith) and would have dealt harshly with him for not doing as they had done—a course of action that might have spared Jerusalem the agony of a long siege. What a choice he made in view of the alternatives! He feared men more than he feared God (cf. Prov 29:25). Nor would he believe the solemn assurances of his own safety that Jeremiah gave him.

20–23 As for Zedekiah's refusal to obey God (v.20), the Lord showed Jeremiah in the vision of the two baskets of figs some of its consequences (24:1–10). The picture in chapter 24 and in this chapter (vv.18, 21–23) was not overdrawn; the Babylonians usually treated rebel kings ruthlessly and often mutilated them and put them to death. So certain was the coming doom that Jeremiah even predicted what the women of the royal house, the royal harem, would say on being taken into captivity (v.22). More cutting than the ridicule of the defectors, whom Zedekiah feared, would be the ridicule the palace women would heap on him for his gullibility in trusting faithless allies. Desiring to gain favor with their Babylonian masters, the women would point out that Zedekiah's friends had impelled him to a suicidal opposition (so Freedman). In Jeremiah's times a conquering king customarily took over the harem of his defeated foe (v.23; cf. 2 Sam 16:21–22). In his hour of deepest distress, Zedekiah's so-called friends would leave him in the lurch, as his feet were sinking in the mire. Out of his own experience, Jeremiah could understand all this. But the Lord would not protect Zedekiah as he had protected the prophet. What had happened to Jeremiah physically (cf. v.6) would be the lot of the king politically and spiritually. So the blame rested where it belonged—on the shoulders of Zedekiah, who would bring indignity and defeat on himself, ruin to the nation and its capital, and lasting shame on his own family.

Notes

14–28 A few scholars (e.g., Skinner after Steuernagel et al.) claim that this portion is a duplicate of 37:17–21. With the fluctuating conditions in Judah in a time of unprecedented stress, it is entirely credible that such incidents occurred more than once.

19 The constant refusal of Zedekiah to heed the insistent warning of Jeremiah, whom he respected, may seem mystifying today. But the king's fears had a basis in fact. As the Babylonian invasion continued, numbers of Judeans, disenchanted with Zedekiah's policy, defected to the enemy. It is not hard to imagine their actions, should the king fall into their hands. The verb used is strong: הִתְעַלְּלוּ (*hit'allelû*, "they will deal ruthlessly"; NIV, "they will mistreat"). The same word is employed in the incident of the extreme abuse of the Levite's concubine by the men of Gibeah (Judg 19:25).

22 The latter part of this verse is in *qinah* (lamentation) meter, i.e., 3 to 2. Actually, Judah's allies (27:3) rejoiced over the plight of Jerusalem (probably Obad 7). Among the friends were doubtless the false prophets. If Zedekiah feared the mockery of deserters, how much more galling that of his own harem!

---

b. *The officials' inquiry*

38:24–28

> ²⁴Then Zedekiah said to Jeremiah, "Do not let anyone know about this conversation, or you may die. ²⁵If the officials hear that I talked with you, and they come to you and say, 'Tell us what you said to the king and what the king said to you; do not hide it from us or we will kill you,' ²⁶then tell them, 'I was pleading with the king not to send me back to Jonathan's house to die there.'"
>
> ²⁷All the officials did come to Jeremiah and question him, and he told them everything the king had ordered him to say. So they said no more to him, for no one had heard his conversation with the king.
>
> ²⁸And Jeremiah remained in the courtyard of the guard until the day Jerusalem was captured.

24–26 Again Zedekiah did not heed the Lord's advice that came to him through Jeremiah. Till the last moment the king remained weak and fearful. He was fearful that if news of his secret talk with Jeremiah leaked out, it would be seriously misunderstood by the officials. So he warned the prophet that the officials might kill him (v.24). Verse 27 shows that the precaution was needed. Just as suspicious of the king as he was of them, the officials had been spying on him. So Zedekiah told the prophet to reveal only his plea not to be sent back to Jonathan's house (vv.25–26; cf. 37:15, 20).

27 Jeremiah's compliance with the king's request has been severely criticized on ethical grounds. One scholar thinks he agreed to tell a lie. Though he would not compromise on the word of God, he was more compromising in lesser matters (so Frost). Jeremiah's answer has been called a "half-truth" or "a white lie" for the king's sake (so Hyatt). But another interpretation is that he told the truth, nothing but the truth, but not the whole truth (so Clarke). Still another interpretation is that for Jeremiah to tell the partial truth was misleading, but he did it to shield the king (so Bewer). We must be extremely reluctant to fault a true prophet of God like Jeremiah—a man of courage, brotherly love, patriotism, tremendous spiritual stature, and unparalleled devotion. In his defense the following facts need to be considered.

1. The precarious position of the king must be taken into account.
2. To allay suspicion was as much in the king's interest as in his own.
3. Jeremiah's answer was not a falsehood because the petition was implied in vv. 15–16 (so Laetsch).
4. At this critical time, the king did not want to occasion a break between himself and his generals (so Payne Smith).
5. Actually, the officials had no authority to question either the king or the prophet.
6. The officials wanted to use the information for evil purposes.
7. Jeremiah told only what was necessary and no more.
8. It was his way of bolstering Zedekiah's battered morale (so Cunliffe-Jones).

28 This verse shows that the capture of Jerusalem verified Jeremiah's forty years of ministry (so KD).

Notes

26–27 Hyatt asks for indulgence for Jeremiah's "half-truth" and "white lie." This language is too strong. Even if the position is taken that the prophet could not divulge the facts to the princes without betraying a confidence (so Freedman), it is not an adequate explanation. It is better to realize that, because the princes and their spies had no right to the information, Jeremiah was right in limiting himself to the one item of his not being consigned to the dungeon, which was unquestionably true (so Henderson). Moreover, if such be not the case, what of Samuel's visit to Bethlehem where God himself is involved (1 Sam 16:2–3)?

7. The Fall of Jerusalem (39:1–18)

Without doubt, the Fall of Jerusalem described in this passage dramatically authenticated Jeremiah's prophecies. The genuineness of most of the chapter has been questioned. The LXX omits vv. 4–13, but this is not conclusive negative evidence in light of the condition of the LXX text of Jeremiah (so Streane). Furthermore, the account generally agrees with those in chapter 52 and 2 Kings 25, though certain details are problematic. Some scholars suggest that the repetition of material in chapter 52 is the result of difference in authorship. But the preferable view is that these two accounts are complementary and supplementary, not contradictory (so Bright).

a. The capture of the city

39:1–3

> This is how Jerusalem was taken: [1]In the ninth year of Zedekiah king of Judah, in the tenth month, Nebuchadnezzar king of Babylon marched against Jerusalem with his whole army and laid siege to it. [2]And on the ninth day of the fourth month of Zedekiah's eleventh year, the city wall was broken through. [3]Then all the offi-

cials of the king of Babylon came and took seats in the Middle Gate: Nergal-Sharezer of Samgar, Nebo-Sarsekim a chief officer, Nergal-Sharezer a high official and all the other officials of the king of Babylon.

1–3 After the long siege, the city walls were finally breached and Jerusalem fell. The dates in vv.1–2 span the beginning and end of the siege, which lasted about eighteen months, though some scholars have suggested that the siege lasted two and one-half years (cf. ZPEB, 3:476). The consensus of expositors favors the shorter period. The time has, however, been computed differently—viz., either from January, 587 B.C. (the ninth year) to July, 586 B.C. (the eleventh year) (so Bewer) or from December, 589 B.C., to June, 587 B.C. (so Cunliffe-Jones). The fall of the city, which had been weakened by the siege without and by famine within (cf. 52:4–16; 2 Kings 25:1–12), is described more fully in chapter 52. Jeremiah gives the Babylonian names of the Babylonian high officials (v.3). Nergal-Sharezer was Nebuchadnezzar's son-in-law and succeeded him under the name Neriglissar. The "chief officer" (*rab-sārîs*) was head of the eunuchs who served as chamberlains. "A high official" is literally "chief magi" (*rab-māg*). It is unclear how many individuals are actually listed here (cf. NIV mg., cf. also KD). When these officials sat in the gate of the city, the prediction of 1:15 was fulfilled. The "Middle Gate" was probably between the upper and lower divisions of the city. The purpose of the officials' session at the Middle Gate was either to plan their military strategy or to establish their quarters there.

Notes

1–2 At this time years were reckoned from the Babylonian New Year in the spring (March/April). Thus the siege of the capital began in January, 588 B.C., and continued until July, 587 B.C. (with a probable interruption in the summer of 588; so Bright) (cf. 52:4–6).

3 The Babylonian officers formed a military government and tribunal. The two by the name of Nergal-Sharezer are the same person, whom several have equated with Nergal-šarri-uṣur ("Nergal, protect the king") or Neriglissar (560–556 B.C.), who succeeded Nebuchadnezzar's son (Evil-Merodach) on the Babylonian throne in 560, after a revolt (cf. ZPEB, 4:410).

b. *The fate of Zedekiah*

39:4–8

⁴When Zedekiah king of Judah and all the soldiers saw them, they fled; they left the city at night by way of the king's garden, through the gate between the two walls, and headed toward the Arabah.

⁵But the Babylonian army pursued them and overtook Zedekiah in the plains of Jericho. They captured him and took him to Nebuchadnezzar king of Babylon at Riblah in the land of Hamath, where he pronounced sentence on him. ⁶There at Riblah the king of Babylon slaughtered the sons of Zedekiah before his eyes and also killed all the nobles of Judah. ⁷Then he put out Zedekiah's eyes and bound him with bronze shackles to take him to Babylon.

⁸The Babylonians set fire to the royal palace and the houses of the people and broke down the walls of Jerusalem.

4–5 This passage (vv.4–8) describes the flight, capture, torture, and imprisonment of Zedekiah. The flight was at night; so the verb "saw" (v.4) is to be taken in the sense of hearing or learning that the Babylonians had taken the gate of the citadel of Zion (so Streane). Zedekiah, realizing the end of Jerusalem had come, still hoped to save his life. He and his company tried to escape by way of the Jordan Valley ("Arabah") to Gilead (so KD) or to Arabia Deserta (so Henderson) or to Egypt (so Clarke). The position of "the two walls" can only be conjectured; there may have been a gate in a double wall between Zion and Ophel. Zedekiah aimed to escape to the eastern side of the Jordan. The "king's garden" was near the Pool of Siloam (cf. Neh 3:15); the gate was probably the Fountain Gate (cf. Neh 2:14; so Harrison).

Zedekiah was taken to Riblah (v.5), where Nebuchadnezzar had his headquarters. It was a strategic site and had been the military headquarters of Pharaoh Neco in his campaign against Assyria (cf. 2 Kings 23:33). Riblah, which was on the Orontes River, was fifty miles south of Hamath (the modern Hama), some sixty-five miles north of Damascus. Here was a good vantage point for gaining control of both Syria and Palestine.

6–8 At Riblah, Nebuchadnezzar began slaying all the resisters, starting with the king's sons and going on to the nobles of Judah (v.6). Only Zedekiah was spared for captivity after he saw with his own eyes the slaughter and then was blinded. "The nobles of Judah" were those who had been so persistently and perniciously opposed to Jeremiah. By modern standards what Nebuchadnezzar did was unusually harsh, but it was in accord with ancient pagan practices and is understandable in view of the trouble that Judah and especially Zedekiah had given Babylon. This kind of punishment, especially the blinding (v.7), is mentioned in the Hammurabi Code (so Freedman). Thus two prophecies were fulfilled: (1) Zedekiah would see the king of Babylon and be taken there (cf. 32:3–4), and (2) he would die in Babylon without ever seeing it (cf. Ezek 12:13). To add to his torture, Zedekiah had to witness the slaughter of his sons and the nobles "so the last memory of this world's light might remain a grief" (so Ruskin, quoted in Elliott-Binns). This kind of punishment was very ancient (cf. Judg 16:21). Assyrian sculptures show how kings delighted to put out, often with their own hands, the eyes of captive rulers (so JFB). Verse 8 adds the finishing touches to the gruesome scene. The Fall of Jerusalem was so important that Scripture relates it four times—here, in chapter 52, in 2 Kings 25, and in 2 Chronicles 36.

c. The release of Jeremiah

39:9–14

9Nebuzaradan commander of the imperial guard carried into exile to Babylon the people who remained in the city, along with those who had gone over to him, and the rest of the people. 10But Nebuzaradan the commander of the guard left behind in the land of Judah some of the poor people, who owned nothing; and at that time he gave them vineyards and fields.

11Now Nebuchadnezzar king of Babylon had given these orders about Jeremiah through Nebuzaradan commander of the imperial guard: 12"Take him and look after him; don't harm him but do for him whatever he asks." 13So Nebuzaradan the commander of the guard, Nebushazban a chief officer, Nergal-Sharezer a high official and all the other officers of the king of Babylon 14sent and had Jeremiah taken out of the courtyard of the guard. They turned him over to Gedaliah son of Ahikam, the son of Shaphan, to take him back to his home. So he remained among his own people.

9–10 After Nebuchadnezzar had dealt with the leadership of Judah, he took the people of Judah into exile in Babylon (v.9). This final deportation of the nation (586 B.C.) came some eleven years after that in Jehoiachin's time. Nebuzaradan, commander of the imperial guard (lit., chief of the executioners), was the man who had this assignment. In order to make a new beginning and not leave the land utterly desolate, Nebuzaradan, who was authorized by Nebuchadnezzar to oversee the settlement of the conquered land, placed some of the poorest people in charge of fields and vineyards as their own (v.10), though with reclamation rights by the conqueror (cf. 52:16; 2 Kings 25:12). The Babylonians doubtless felt that gratitude would prevent the settlers from rebelling.

11–14 More interesting than the land grant to the poor were the instructions of Nebuchadnezzar about Jeremiah (v.11). Undoubtedly the Babylonians had favorable information about Jeremiah and probably considered him a sympathizer. Besides, those who had deserted Judah in the siege gave a report of him. Jeremiah's advice about submitting to Babylon even during the siege had been proclaimed over so long a time that it could not have escaped the attention of the Babylonian authorities. They realized that he was no threat to them. Paradoxically, he was treated better by foreign invaders than by his own countrymen whom he so dearly loved (v.12). So word was passed along (v.13) to release Jeremiah from the courtyard of the guard and entrust him to Gedaliah, the appointed governor, with whom he was to remain (v.14). Gedaliah was the son of Ahikam, who had been active in saving Jeremiah's life (cf. 26:24). For three generations his family had been true to the word of the Lord that came through his prophets.

Many have seen a contradiction between the account in 39:11–14 and that in 40:1–6. But the passages may be harmonized in this way: (1) at the command of Nebuchadnezzar, Jeremiah was released from prison and committed to the care of Gedaliah; (2) while captives were being transferred to Babylon, Jeremiah mingled with the people (cf. 39:14) to comfort and instruct them in their new life; (3) in the confusion of the mass deportation, Jeremiah was not recognized by the soldiers who placed him in chains with the others; and (4) at Ramah he was recognized by officials and released (40:1) (so Jensen). The discrepancy between the accounts may well arise from the brevity of the narrative. Perhaps the situation was that those who had not borne arms, among them Jeremiah, were taken by the Babylonians to Ramah as prisoners until Nebuchadnezzar decided their fate. Later, when Nebuzaradan came to Jerusalem to carry out the king's commands regarding the city, at the special order of Nebuchadnezzar, Nebuzaradan sent for Jeremiah from the prisoners taken to Ramah, freed him, and allowed him to choose his residence. In a condensed account, Jeremiah's release from his imprisonment might be spoken of as a sending for him out of prison, even though at the exact time of his liberation he was not in the courtyard of the palace guard in Jerusalem but had already been carried away to Ramah as an exile (so KD).

623

Notes

---

9 "The commander of the imperial guard" is רַב־טַבָּחִים (*raḇ-ṭabbāḥîm*), which literally is "the chief butcher," an instance where the old name remained after the function had changed entirely (cf. Gen 39:1; Dan 2:14; cf. also TWOT, 1:342).

10 Much discussion has centered on the term וִיגֵבִים *wîḡēḇîm*, "and fields") because of the uncertainty of meaning. LXX omits vv.4–10 and 11–13. A Greek translation is καὶ ὑ-δρεύματα (*kai hydreumata*, "and watering places, wells" = וְגֵבִים [*weḡēḇîm*]); Syriac and Targum have חַקְלִין (*ḥaqlîn*, "fields"); Vulgate, *cisternas* ("cisterns") from *gēḇîm*, following the Greek. KB translates strangely: *Fronleistungen*, "compulsory service." Notice the awkward end to the verse.

---

d. The commendation of Ebed-Melech

39:15–18

> ¹⁵While Jeremiah had been confined in the courtyard of the guard, the word of the LORD came to him: ¹⁶"Go and tell Ebed-Melech the Cushite, 'This is what the LORD Almighty, the God of Israel, says: I am about to fulfill my words against this city through disaster, not prosperity. At that time they will be fulfilled before your eyes. ¹⁷But I will rescue you on that day, declares the LORD; you will not be handed over to those you fear. ¹⁸I will save you; you will not fall by the sword but will escape with your life, because you trust in me, declares the LORD.'"

15–18 Verses 11–14 show how the Lord preserved his prophet; vv.15–18 show the Lord's concern for Jeremiah's rescuer. The scene goes back to Jeremiah's imprisonment in the cistern (38:1–13). This message must have come to Jeremiah soon after Ebed-Melech had rescued him (v.15). It is included here so as not to break into the chain of events (cf. 38:14–39:14). Ebed-Melech needed this message of hope, for he had doubtless incurred the wrath of Jeremiah's enemies for lifting him out of the cistern and so feared reprisals (v.16). Ebed-Melech was assured that he would escape death (vv.17–18) because his compassionate acts were motivated by his trust in the Lord.

III. Ministry of Jeremiah After the Fall of Jerusalem (40:1–45:5)

Chapters 40–44 contain prophecies and a record of events after the Fall of Jerusalem. Chapters 40–42 deal with prophecies and events in Judah; chapters 43–44 with those in Egypt.

A. Ministry to the Survivors in Judah (40:1–42:22)

1. Gedaliah the governor (40:1–16)

a. The release of Jeremiah

40:1–6

> ¹The word came to Jeremiah from the LORD after Nebuzaradan commander of the imperial guard had released him at Ramah. He had found Jeremiah bound in chains among all the captives from Jerusalem and Judah who were being carried

into exile to Babylon. ²When the commander of the guard found Jeremiah, he said to him, "The LORD your God decreed this disaster for this place. ³And now the LORD has brought it about; he has done just as he said he would. All this happened because you people sinned against the LORD and did not obey him. ⁴But today I am freeing you from the chains on your wrists. Come with me to Babylon, if you like, and I will look after you; but if you do not want to, then don't come. Look, the whole country lies before you; go wherever you please." ⁵However, before Jeremiah turned to go, Nebuzaradan added, "Go back to Gedaliah son of Ahikam, the son of Shaphan, whom the king of Babylon has appointed over the towns of Judah, and live with him among the people, or go anywhere else you please."

Then the commander gave him provisions and a present and let him go. ⁶So Jeremiah went to Gedaliah son of Ahikam at Mizpah and stayed with him among the people who were left behind in the land.

1 This passage (vv.1–6) is actually an amplification of 39:11–14. (For the discrepancy between v.1 and 39:11–14, see the comment on the latter.) Since there is no prophetic word till 42:9, "word" is to be taken in the sense of history as well as prophecy. The two were, however, related; the OT historical books are included under the heading of The Prophets. Ramah, the modern er-Ram, is about five miles north of Jerusalem. This Benjamite town was the place where the captives were questioned before being deported to Babylon. In the confusion when Jerusalem fell, Jeremiah was at first taken and placed in chains—manacles for the hands only (cf. v.4). When Jeremiah arrived at Ramah, he was released at the command of Nebuzaradan, who had evidently been told who Jeremiah was and what Nebuchadnezzar had ordered to be done with him.

2–3 Some expositors doubt whether Nebuzaradan could or would have said the words quoted in vv.2–3. Was this his own theology or does it reflect that of the writer? Some think the quotation incongruous for a Babylonian and take it as a recast by the writer in terms of his own faith. But this is not the only possible explanation. Although the words are couched in Hebrew theological terms, this is not so improbable as it at first appears. The Assyrians paid attention to the beliefs of the people whom they fought, for use in psychological warfare (cf. 2 Kings 18:22, 33–35; so WBC). The Babylonians may have been aware of certain supernatural reasons for Judah's fall; as one view proposes, Jeremiah's reputation as a prophet was evidently known to them (so Harrison). Unquestionably the words sound like those of Jeremiah himself, and this may show that Nebuzaradan had some acquaintance with the prophet's teaching. The simplest explanation may be that he knew of the content of Jeremiah's main emphasis in preaching and was simply quoting it as appropriate for the occasion.

4–5 Nebuzaradan first freed Jeremiah from his manacles (v.4) and then gave him a choice of where he would live (v.5). These actions were wholly within his authority as an official representative of Nebuchadnezzar, who was then in Riblah. Jeremiah was given the option of either going to Babylon or remaining in Judah. Nebuzaradan promised to care for him in Babylon: "I will look after you" (lit., "I will set my eye on you," i.e., "keep an eye on"). Recognizing that Jeremiah was not sure about where he would go, Nebuzaradan sent him back to Gedaliah. The book says nothing about any relationship between Jeremiah and Gedaliah, who was made puppet governor of Judea by the Babylonians. A seal dating from this time discovered at Lachish is inscribed with the name of a "Gedaliah," who was "over the House"—i.e., a palace governor (cf. Isa 36:22). The man referred to could have been the Gedaliah of Jeremiah's time. It is obvious that Nebuchadnezzar had lost all faith in the house of David (so Bewer). His dealings with the last three kings of Judah were disappointing in the extreme.

6 Nebuzaradan sent Jeremiah off with some food and a gift, the nature of which is not specified. The way he treated the prophet stands in striking contrast with what his own countrymen did to him, particularly in the last days of Jerusalem (cf. Matt 13:57). Apparently the Babylonians did not care to have the Jews remaining in Jerusalem, their former capital; so they made Mizpah the administrative center of the remnant in the land.

There are two views as to the location of Mizpah. One view (held by many) places it about two miles north of Ramah and identifies it with present-day Tell en-Nasbeh (so Bright; also favored by Kraeling, *Rand McNally Bible Atlas*). The other view places it about four miles southwest of Ramah, at present-day Nebi Samwil (so Frost; also ZPEB, 4:254–57).

Jeremiah chose to stay in the land he loved. This does not mean that he doubted his own message in 24:4–10. He loved his people in spite of their mistreatment, hatred, and threats on his life. Now he would at least be free of ungodly priests and false prophets. His devotion to the land and his conviction that it would be the scene of future blessing influenced his decision to remain in it at this critical time (so Ball).

Notes

---

1 An emotional account of the rabbis relates that when the prophet saw the file of chained prisoners, he voluntarily had himself bound to show his complete identification with the lot of his people. It could well be, for he had been thoroughly bound to their cause for a lifetime (so Freedman).

5 Gedaliah ("the LORD is great") was the son of Ahikam the son of Shaphan, a prominent official in the reigns of Josiah and Jehoiakim and protector of Jeremiah (26:24; 2 Kings 22:12, 14). Shaphan may have been the scribe in the court of Josiah at the finding of the Book of the Law (2 Kings 22:3–14). Rashi, quoting a Midrash, stated that while Jeremiah was undecided, God told him to return to Gedaliah, thus their comment on "the word . . . to Jeremiah from the LORD" (v.1) (cited in Freedman).

---

b. Gedaliah's assurances

40:7–10

7When all the army officers and their men who were still in the open country heard that the king of Babylon had appointed Gedaliah son of Ahikam as governor over the land and had put him in charge of the men, women and children who were the poorest in the land and who had not been carried into exile to Babylon, 8they came to Gedaliah at Mizpah—Ishmael son of Nethaniah, Johanan and

Jonathan the sons of Kareah, Seraiah son of Tanhumeth, the sons of Ephai the Netophathite, and Jaazaniah the son of the Maacathite, and their men. ⁹Gedaliah son of Ahikam, the son of Shaphan, took an oath to reassure them and their men. "Do not be afraid to serve the Babylonians," he said. "Settle down in the land and serve the king of Babylon, and it will go well with you. ¹⁰I myself will stay at Mizpah to represent you before the Babylonians who come to us, but you are to harvest the wine, summer fruit and oil, and put them in your storage jars, and live in the towns you have taken over."

7–8 Gedaliah's appointment by Nebuchadnezzar as governor (v.7) encouraged some of the surviving Jews who had fled to neighboring areas to return to Judah. Just as Nebuchadnezzar had confidence in Gedaliah, so did his countrymen. The land had been deprived of its leaders; so chiefs of guerrilla bands, who remained hidden while the Babylonian army was besieging, waited the turn of events after the fall of the capital. They showed their trust in Gedaliah's ability to govern by joining him at Mizpah (v.8). He was a good ruler and was doubtless supported by Jeremiah. Ishmael was, according to 41:1, a grandson of Elishama, of the house of David. Netophah was a place in Judah between Bethlehem and Tekoa; it is the modern village of Beit Nettif, about twelve miles west of Bethlehem. Maacah was southeast of Hermon.

9–10 Gedaliah tried to quiet the fears of the survivors and advocated submission to the conquering power (v.9). He sought to reestablish normal living in the land and promised to represent them before the Babylonians (v.10). To some, however, he appeared to be a collaborator with the destroyer of their nation. Since Jerusalem fell in the middle of summer (cf. 39:2), the people had time to gather the late fruits of summer to sustain them during their first bleak winter in the land (so WBC). Moreover, they would need the harvests to pay tribute to the Babylonians. Everything was being done to hasten the return to normal peaceful conditions. Notice that the invaders had shown great enlightenment in refraining from any defoliation or "scorched-earth" policy, such as in modern warfare. The clause "the towns you have taken over" indicates that the captains of the roaming bands took what towns or cities pleased them.

c. *The return of the fugitives*

40:11–12

¹¹When all the Jews in Moab, Ammon, Edom and all the other countries heard that the king of Babylon had left a remnant in Judah and had appointed Gedaliah son of Ahikam, the son of Shaphan, as governor over them, ¹²they all came back to the land of Judah, to Gedaliah at Mizpah, from all the countries where they had been scattered. And they harvested an abundance of wine and summer fruit.

11–12 With his forthright honesty, Gedaliah inspired confidence; and his orders were obeyed. Many of those returning to Judah (v.12) had fled from the Babylonians and had taken refuge in a number of neighboring countries. In God's mercy these refugees constituted a remnant. That one of their own nation was made governor gave them confidence (v.11); so they felt that the Babylonians were not wholly without compassion for them in their time of tragic need.

d. *The warning of Gedaliah*

40:13–16

> ¹³Johanan son of Kareah and all the army officers still in the open country came to Gedaliah at Mizpah ¹⁴and said to him, "Don't you know that Baalis king of the Ammonites has sent Ishmael son of Nethaniah to take your life?" But Gedaliah son of Ahikam did not believe them.
> ¹⁵Then Johanan son of Kareah said privately to Gedaliah in Mizpah, "Let me go and kill Ishmael son of Nethaniah, and no one will know it. Why should he take your life and cause all the Jews who are gathered around you to be scattered and the remnant of Judah to perish?"
> ¹⁶But Gedaliah son of Ahikam said to Johanan son of Kareah, "Don't do such a thing! What you are saying about Ishmael is not true."

13–14 Judah was still in a state of much unrest. Its ordeal had been a long one. And now a plot to assassinate Gedaliah comes to light. It was instigated by Baalis, king of Ammon, who used as his agent Ishmael son of Nethaniah. The man who told Gedaliah of the plot was the loyal Johanan son of Kareah (v.13). What occasioned the plot? In view of the complexity of human nature, we may surmise a number of factors that led to the plot. Gedaliah had apparently forgotten that Ishmael was of the house of David and thus did not appreciate being passed by in Gedaliah's favor. Or Ishmael may have considered Gedaliah a traitor for agreeing to govern under the Babylonians. Baalis may have felt that eliminating Gedaliah would make it easier to carry out his own plans to conquer Judah. The king of Ammon may have feared that Gedaliah might again make Judah a formidable nation and a potential threat to him. Also, Baalis (v.14), an ally of Zedekiah and an enemy of the Babylonians (cf. 27:3), was angry that the family of Ahikam opposed the league referred to in chapter 27. Recently an excavation in Jordan has uncovered the Siran Bottle (dated in the period of 667–580 B.C.), which bears the name of a King Ba'lay, who has been identified (so Cross) with the Baalis of Jeremiah 40:13–14 (so G.E. Wright in "Newsletter of ASOR" [April, 1974]).

15–16 A man of ability but lacking in knowledge of men and their devices, Gedaliah was too trusting and naive to believe Johanan's warning. The least he could have done was to have protected himself against the assassination he had been warned of (so Cunliffe-Jones). What Johanan feared, actually happened (41:1–3); and the remnant was scattered because of Gedaliah's death (so Freedman). Though Johanan tried earnestly to impress Gedaliah that his life was essential for the welfare of the remnant in Judah (v.15), he apparently failed to inspire confidence. Moreover, Gedaliah may have been overconfident. At any rate, he was not convinced of Johanan's veracity (v.16). Gedaliah was right in forbidding Johanan to assassinate Ishmael but wrong in his estimate of Ishmael.

Notes

---

13 "The LORD is gracious" is the meaning of the name "Johanan." There were ten men in the OT who had this name. Johanan the son of Kareah, the contemporary of Jeremiah (2 Kings 25:23), is the best known. He was a captain in Judah during the invasion of 588–586

B.C. When Gedaliah was made governor of Judah, Johanan came with others to Mizpah (Jer 40:8, 13). When his warning concerning Ishmael was unheeded, he led the soldiers against the assassin and recovered those taken captive by him (ch. 41). Fearing reprisals from Babylon for the murder of the governor, he went with a remnant to Egypt, taking Jeremiah and Baruch by force with them (43:1–7; cf. ZPEB, 3:622–23).

14 Baalis, king of the Ammonites, otherwise unknown, was determined to destroy the remnant of Judah to further his own prestige and power (cf. Jos. Antiq. X, 159–67 [ix.2–3]). Ishmael the son of Nethaniah (41:1) was of royal lineage (cf. 2 Kings 25:23). An enthusiastic member of the anti-Babylonian party, he was both jealous of and filled with hatred for Gedaliah.

---

2. The atrocities of Ishmael and the flight into Egypt (41:1–18)

The narrative in chapter 40 goes on without a break in chapter 41, which describes the havoc Ishmael wrought among the remnant in Judah.

a. The assassination of Gedaliah

41:1–3

> ¹In the seventh month Ishmael son of Nethaniah, the son of Elishama, who was of royal blood and had been one of the king's officers, came with ten men to Gedaliah son of Ahikam at Mizpah. While they were eating together there, ²Ishmael son of Nethaniah and the ten men who were with him got up and struck down Gedaliah son of Ahikam, the son of Shaphan, with the sword, killing the one whom the king of Babylon had appointed as governor over the land. ³Ishmael also killed all the Jews who were with Gedaliah at Mizpah, as well as the Babylonian soldiers who were there.

1 Because v. 1 gives only the month and not the year, two dates have been proposed for the assassination of Gedaliah: 586 B.C. and 583–582 B.C. Those who support the first date (so CHS, KD) believe that only three months elapsed from the fall of the city to the events now recorded (cf. 39:2). But a number of more recent commentators prefer the latter date. They think the text does not require that the events in chapter 41 occurred in the same year as the Fall of Jerusalem. On the basis of 52:30, they hold that the reaction of Babylon to the assassination took place after five years, so that 41:1 gives the end of Gedaliah's governorship only (so Cunliffe-Jones, Bright, Hyatt). The Jews still keep the Fast of Gedaliah in the seventh month (September/October) on the third day of the month, the first and second days being the New Year (so Freedman; cf. Zech 7:5; 8:19; see also 2 Kings 25:8, 25). Ishmael came from a collateral line of the Davidic family through Elishama, son of David (cf. 2 Sam 5:16). Moreover, he was prominent in affairs of state with Zedekiah.

2–3 The "ten men" (v. 2) should not be thought of as being alone, for they may have brought a retinue of attendants with them. In addition to the reasons already given (see comments in ch. 40), Ishmael, being violently anti-Babylonian, may have been motivated by deep resentment at the cruel treatment of Zedekiah (cf. 39:6–7). Ishmael carried out his dastardly plot while enjoying the hospitality of Gedaliah. Pretending friendship for him, he violated the sacred law of Eastern hospitality. In spite of having been warned of an assassination plot, Gedaliah had taken no precautions. Ishmael made no distinction between Jews or Babylonians; he killed all the fighting men, including Gedaliah's Babylonian bodyguard (v.3). For eleven men to kill so large a group indicates how unsuspecting the victims were. The reference to "all the Jews" does not include all that were in the land but only those who were in the house with Gedaliah. The number of Babylonian troops was apparently small.

Notes

1–2 Tradition has it, since the text indicates no day, that the assassination of Gedaliah was on the third day of the month. Later researchers claimed it took place on New Year's Day (the first of Tishri), but the Fast of Gedaliah was postponed to the third of the month (*Shulḥan 'Aruk* ["the set table"—a code of rabbinical Judaism by Joseph Caro (c. 1500) on ritual and legal questions], *Oraḥ Ḥayyim* 549.1 ["way of life"—part of the code of Jacob ben Asher (c. 1300) on worship]). The ordinances of the day are the same as those of other fast days because the Fast of Gedaliah falls within the Ten Days of Penitence, which are decreed by the rabbis for the interval between New Year's (actually, the Feast of Trumpets) and the Day of Atonement (cf. JE, 5:579–80). The governorship of Gedaliah lasted only two months (so tradition), but the historian H. Graetz (*History of the Jews*, 6 vols. [New York: George Dobsevage, 1927], 1:322) claims it continued for more than four years.

---

b. *The massacre of the pilgrims*

41:4–10

> [4]The day after Gedaliah's assassination, before anyone knew about it, [5]eighty men who had shaved off their beards, torn their clothes and cut themselves came from Shechem, Shiloh and Samaria, bringing grain offerings and incense with them to the house of the LORD. [6]Ishmael son of Nethaniah went out from Mizpah to meet them, weeping as he went. When he met them, he said, "Come to Gedaliah son of Ahikam." [7]When they went into the city, Ishmael son of Nethaniah and the men who were with him slaughtered them and threw them into a cistern. [8]But ten of them said to Ishmael, "Don't kill us! We have wheat and barley, oil and honey, hidden in a field." So he let them alone and did not kill them with the others. [9]Now the cistern where he threw all the bodies of the men he had killed along with Gedaliah was the one King Asa had made as part of his defense against Baasha king of Israel. Ishmael son of Nethaniah filled it with the dead.
> [10]Ishmael made captives of all the rest of the people who were in Mizpah—the king's daughters along with all the others who were left there, over whom Nebuzaradan commander of the imperial guard had appointed Gedaliah son of Ahikam. Ishmael son of Nethaniah took them captive and set out to cross over to the Ammonites.

4–5 For Ishmael human life was so cheap that he had no compunction in slaughtering seventy pilgrims. Such a deed could not be concealed indefinitely, but for a time it was carefully concealed (v.4). A group of men were on the way to Jerusalem to lament its desolation (v.5). Observe two things:

1. The men were from the northern kingdom. Josiah had destroyed the altar at Bethel (one of the lasting effects of Josiah's reform); so they were bringing offerings to the Jerusalem temple.

2. In spite of the destruction of the temple itself, they came to the temple site,

which was still used for worship by those who survived the fall of the city. Even the ruins were held to be sacred, just as the Western Wall of the temple in Jerusalem is sacred to this day. Also, a token shrine might have been built.

Though living among heathen colonists (cf. 2 Kings 17:24–41), the men from the northern kingdom had continued to worship the Lord in Jerusalem and to celebrate the feasts (cf. 2 Chron 34:9). The Samaritan conflict with the Jews did not surface until the return from exile (cf. Ezra 4:1–6). These eighty men were mourning for the destroyed temple as well as for the ruined city (cf. 16:6; 47:5; 48:37). They had even gashed themselves—a relapse into heathen custom forbidden in Deuteronomy 14:1. Their offerings (lit., "present" or "tribute") were bloodless sacrifices because no facilities were available for animal sacrifices (cf. Deut 12:13–14, 17–18).

6–8 Ishmael went out to meet the men, weeping hypocritically as though for the loss of the temple (v.6). Courteously he invited them to pay their respects to Gedaliah the governor before going on to Jerusalem. So he lured them into Mizpah, where he had them trapped. Just as in the assassination of Gedaliah, Ishmael used the element of surprise. Here it enabled eleven men to slaughter seventy of the eighty pilgrims. The motive for this massacre is not entirely clear. It may have been done for plunder and to intimidate the remnant in Judah. Casting them into a cistern (v.7) was senseless; it spoiled Mizpah's water supply; for the Jews, water polluted by a dead body was ceremonially unclean and unfit to drink.

Ishmael's greed had led him to spare ten of the eighty men because of their cache of food (v.8), which was probably concealed in a cistern in a field. In the Near East it is still customary to use cisterns for grain storage (so Streane).

9–10 At this point (v.9), Jeremiah inserted a historical notation, showing that King Asa of Judah (913–873 B.C.) had ordered this cistern to be made to insure ample water for Mizpah when he fortified it against King Baasha of Israel (910–887 B.C.) (cf. 1 Kings 15:22; 2 Chron 16:6). At Tell en-Nasbeh excavators have found fifty-three such cisterns (so WBC). Ishmael's next stop was to transport the remnant from Mizpah to Ammon (v.10). (According to 40:14, Ishmael was in alliance with Baalis the Ammonite king.) Ishmael's motive in transporting the remnant may have been threefold: (1) to escape punishment, (2) to find refuge with Baalis who had instigated the assassination of Gedaliah (40:14), and (3) to sell the remnant as slaves to the Ammonites (so Clarke, JFB). The king's daughters, spared through Babylonian clemency, were royal princesses, not necessarily Zedekiah's own daughters, but women related to Ishmael. Included among this remnant were probably Jeremiah and Baruch (cf. 42:2).

Notes

5 Shechem, Shiloh, and Samaria are the modern Nablus (situated in the valley between Mount Gerizim and Mount Ebal), Seilûn (7:12), and Sebastiyeh (cf. 2 Kings 17:6). These towns of the northern kingdom had been destroyed almost a century and a half before this (722–721 B.C.). The remnant of the Ten Tribes, later known as Samaritans after admixture with foreign peoples imported by the Assyrians, still kept their worship of the God of Israel according to Deuteronomy 16:16, which required pilgrimages to Jerusalem at stated seasons. Moreover, these Israelites had rejoined Judah in the reign of Josiah (2 Kings 23:15, 19).

9 There is no mention of Asa's cistern in the OT historical books (cf. 1 Kings 15:22; 2 Chron 16:6), only that to build Geba and Mizpah he used material that Baasha had used to fortify Ramah. The cistern, then, was part of Asa's defensive arrangements, probably to supply water during the siege. But there is no record of its construction and no archaeological identification thus far.

---

c. The escape of Ishmael

41:11–15

> [11]When Johanan son of Kareah and all the army officers who were with him heard about all the crimes Ishmael son of Nethaniah had committed, [12]they took all their men and went to fight Ishmael son of Nethaniah. They caught up with him near the great pool in Gibeon. [13]When all the people Ishmael had with him saw Johanan son of Kareah and the army officers who were with him, they were glad. [14]All the people Ishmael had taken captive at Mizpah turned and went over to Johanan son of Kareah. [15]But Ishmael son of Nethaniah and eight of his men escaped from Johanan and fled to the Ammonites.

11–15 Johanan, having had prior knowledge of the plot (v.11), was quick to follow Ishmael's tracks. Now Johanan acted responsibly, not as he had previously wanted to do (40:15). He and those with him overtook the assassin before he had gone far (v.12)—Gibeon is about a mile from Mizpah. Gibeon, the modern el-Jib, was the city of priests in the tribe of Benjamin (cf. Josh 18:25; 21:17). It has been suggested that "the great pool" is the same as "the pool of Gibeon" (cf. 2 Sam 2:13). It may be the large, rock-hewn cistern from the early Iron Age discovered at el-Jib (so Harrison). Ishmael may have taken a circuitous route to confuse his pursuers. Some scholars think v.12 makes Nebi Samwil, southwest of Gibeon, the more likely location of Mizpah rather than Tell en-Nasbeh (so Bright). When the people saw Johanan and his companions, they rejoiced (v.13); for they had followed Ishmael only because they had been compelled to do so (v.14). And because of the popularity of Gedaliah, they were glad to see his murder avenged (so Plumptre). Ishmael lost only two of his men and drops out of the narrative after fleeing to Ammon (v.15).

d. The flight to Egypt

41:16–18

> [16]Then Johanan son of Kareah and all the army officers who were with him led away all the survivors from Mizpah whom he had recovered from Ishmael son of Nethaniah after he had assassinated Gedaliah son of Ahikam: the soldiers, women, children and court officials he had brought from Gibeon. [17]And they went on, stopping at Geruth Kimham near Bethlehem on their way to Egypt [18]to escape the Babylonians. They were afraid of them because Ishmael son of Nethaniah had killed Gedaliah son of Ahikam, whom the king of Babylon had appointed as governor over the land.

16–18 Johanan now decided to go as quickly as possible to Egypt. He and the army officers with him (v.16) feared reprisals when the news of Gedaliah's assassination reached Babylon (v.18). Ishmael had completely frustrated any plans for peaceful settlement in the land. Geruth (*gērût*) (v.17) means "lodging-place" (so KB, s.v.; also Streane) rather than "sheepfolds" (*gidrôt*). The site is unknown. Kimham was the son of Barzillai, the wealthy Gileadite and faithful partisan of David during the revolt of Absalom (cf. 2 Sam 9:38, 41). The lodging place was a khan (caravansary) on the caravan route to Egypt. Able in military matters—he had given advice to Gedaliah—Johanan was wrong in thinking flight to Egypt was the only solution to the problems of the remnant. Actually, it created other problems, and certainly it did not place them beyond the reach of Nebuchadnezzar.

3. Warning against going to Egypt (42:1-22)

The narrative continues. Johanan overtook and routed Ishmael and his forces, the residue of which escaped to Ammon. At this point the remnant of people were afraid to remain in Judah and were equally afraid to seek safety in a foreign country. Johanan and the remnant were anxious not to make a mistake that would incur the wrath of God, which had already been poured out on Jerusalem and Judah, hence their inquiry of Jeremiah. They did not recognize that by deciding to go to Egypt they had already decided on a certain course of action (cf. 41:17).

a. The inquiry of the remnant

42:1-6

> [1]Then all the army officers, including Johanan son of Kareah and Jezaniah son of Hoshaiah, and all the people from the least to the greatest approached [2]Jeremiah the prophet and said to him, "Please hear our petition and pray to the Lord your God for this entire remnant. For as you now see, though we were once many, now only a few are left. [3]Pray that the Lord your God will tell us where we should go and what we should do."
> [4]"I have heard you," replied Jeremiah the prophet. "I will certainly pray to the Lord your God as you have requested; I will tell you everything the Lord says and will keep nothing back from you."
> [5]Then they said to Jeremiah, "May the Lord be a true and faithful witness against us if we do not act in accordance with everything the Lord your God sends you to tell us. [6]Whether it is favorable or unfavorable, we will obey the Lord our God, to whom we are sending you, so that it will go well with us, for we will obey the Lord our God."

1-3 There was an unusual unity among the remnant, all of whom were without exception concerned about what they should do and where they should go. Jezaniah (v.1) is not the Jaazaniah of 40:8 but the Azariah of 43:2. The LXX reads "Azariah" here and in 43:2. Jezaniah might well have had more than one name (cf. King Uzziah and his additional name of Azariah [2 Kings 15:1]). Hoshaiah may be the Hoshaiah whose name appears in the Lachish Letters (so Bewer). The remnant came to Jeremiah, who had apparently been a captive of Ishmael. The esteem in which they still held Jeremiah is evident in their recognition of him as a prophet of the Lord (v.2). Most expositors consider their inquiry a hypocritical one. Others, however, have suggested that, if it had been such, the Lord would not have responded as he did but would have exposed their hypocrisy. They had actually hoped that God would answer according to their desires (so KD). They earnestly wanted confirmation of their decision, not guidance from the Lord (v.3; cf. v.17; so Freedman). According to their thinking, the unrest and absence of security in Judah made resettlement there an impossibility.

4–6 Jeremiah gently reminds the remnant (v.4) that the Lord is their God as well as his. Since he is no longer restrained from praying for them, he would gladly agree to ask the Lord for guidance. Realizing the gravity of their situation, he promised not to hold back any part of the Lord's answer. At this, the people solemnly pledged to obey everything the Lord would tell Jeremiah (v.5)—i.e., they promised to obey the Lord regardless of the nature of his answer (v.6). Later on the record shows that they actually wanted approval to settle in Egypt (cf. 43:2). Even more, their request for the Lord to be "a true and faithful witness against us" implies their acceptance of his punishment for disobeying his express will.

Notes

6 אֲנוּ (*'anû,* "we") is a *hapax legomenon.* It is commonly found in postbiblical Hebrew and may have been a common expression in Jeremiah's day (so CHS).

b. *The Lord's answer to Jeremiah's question*

42:7–17

> [7]Ten days later the word of the LORD came to Jeremiah. [8]So he called together Johanan son of Kareah and all the army officers who were with him and all the people from the least to the greatest. [9]He said to them, "This is what the LORD, the God of Israel, to whom you sent me to present your petition, says: [10]'If you stay in this land, I will build you up and not tear you down; I will plant you and not uproot you, for I am grieved over the disaster I have inflicted on you. [11]Do not be afraid of the king of Babylon, whom you now fear. Do not be afraid of him, declares the LORD, for I am with you and will save you and deliver you from his hands. [12]I will show you compassion so that he will have compassion on you and restore you to your land.'
> [13]"However, if you say, 'We will not stay in this land,' and so disobey the LORD your God, [14]and if you say, 'No, we will go and live in Egypt, where we will not see war or hear the trumpet or be hungry for bread,' [15]then hear the word of the LORD, O remnant of Judah. This is what the LORD Almighty, the God of Israel, says: 'If you are determined to go to Egypt and you do go to settle there, [16]then the sword you fear will overtake you there, and the famine you dread will follow you into Egypt, and there you will die. [17]Indeed, all who are determined to go to Egypt to settle there will die by the sword, famine and plague; not one of them will survive or escape the disaster I will bring on them.'"

7 For ten days Jeremiah awaited the Lord's message. We may imagine the suspense and tension of this time. The prophet wanted to be certain of the Lord's will. Here was a matter on which the entire future of the nation might depend and one that at the least was crucial for the remnant. Perhaps God made them wait there ten days so that they would be prepared to follow his leading (so KD). Jeremiah undoubtedly spent this time in prayer. He knew that God delays or answers according to his will (so Bewer). Jeremiah was unwilling to speak until he had received the Lord's explicit word (Bright). Also, God wanted to give the Jews an opportunity to show the sincerity of their claim that they would obey his leading (Henderson) and to allow time for their anxiety that bordered on panic to be dispelled (Streane). This passage (vv.7–17) sheds light on the inspiration of the prophets. They did not confuse God's revelation with personal desires or judgments. They would not announce God's will until they knew it. Scripture always distinguishes between the subjective (the prophet's own thoughts) and the objective (the word of God) in all revelatory matters (Peake). Here the Lord's answer was that remaining in the land would bring his blessing.

8–12 Once more Jeremiah had to deliver an unpopular message (vv.8–9). Its verbs —viz., build up, tear down, plant, uproot (v.10)—are reminiscent of 1:10 and 24:6. In strong anthropopathic language (v.11) the Lord implies that the penalty given Judah will be cancelled (so KD). In other words, the Lord will change his dealings with the nation. With us, repenting involves a change of purpose. But God's purpose always remains the same; his dealings with us are according to our obeying or disobeying his will. At this point God will deal with Judah in a different way since the people are now in a different category than before the Fall of Jerusalem. During Nebuchadnezzar's siege of Jerusalem, the people had cause to fear him; now there is no occasion for them to do this. In fact, God would see that Nebuchadnezzar would show them compassion and God would turn to their favor every action of this king (v.12).

13–17 In unsparing words, Jeremiah warned of the terrifying consequences if the remnant insisted on leaving the land (vv.13–14). Trust in man would neither avail them nor bless them. They would find no safety in Egypt (v.15). In fact, going there would bring on them the very disasters they were trying to escape. Notice in v.16 the tragic triad—war ("the sword"), "famine," and death. They hoped that the farther they were from Babylon, the less they would be in danger of invasion. Although Egypt had lost the Battle of Carchemish (605 B.C.), it had not been the scene of military actions. On the other hand, Judah had from the time of the Battle of Megiddo (609 B.C.) constantly experienced the rigors of war. Thus the remaining Jews could not fail to be impressed by the contrast between peaceful Egypt and war-torn Judah. Actually, however, Judah's trials were past; Egypt's were soon to begin (so Payne Smith).

Jeremiah was quick to see that his listeners were already determined on a different course of action than the one the Lord had for them. Fleeing to Egypt would bring terrible trials (notice the addition of the plague to the triad in v.17). (Nebuchadnezzar was yet to invade Egypt; cf. 43:8–13; cf. also ANET, p. 308, for archaeological evidence.)

c. Further penalties for settling in Egypt

42:18–22

> [18]"This is what the LORD Almighty, the God of Israel, says: 'As my anger and wrath have been poured out on those who lived in Jerusalem, so will my wrath be poured out on you when you go to Egypt. You will be an object of cursing and horror, of condemnation and reproach; you will never see this place again.'
>
> [19]"O remnant of Judah, the LORD has told you, 'Do not go to Egypt.' Be sure of this: I warn you today [20]that you made a fatal mistake when you sent me to the

LORD your God and said, 'Pray to the LORD our God for us; tell us everything he says and we will do it.' [21]I have told you today, but you still have not obeyed the LORD your God in all he sent me to tell you. [22]So now, be sure of this: You will die by the sword, famine and plague in the place where you want to go to settle."

18–22 The surivors of the Fall of Jerusalem and Judah would suffer the same fate in Egypt that had overtaken them because of their disobedience (v.18). Egypt, instead of being a refuge, would be the place of their undoing, without a glimmer of hope of their returning to their native country. In an epilogue after the Lord's reply, Jeremiah adds to the admonition in vv.13–18. The Lord's message remains unchanged—stay in the land and do not settle in Egypt (v.19). He rebukes them for asking his will with no intention of following it. The warning is unmistakable; the doom is certain (v.20). Jeremiah shows the remnant their duplicity in asking for a message from God when they had no intention of following it. All the time they had intended doing their own will in the hope that God's will would coincide with theirs (v.21). So they were victims of self-deception and self-delusion. How little did they realize that in Egypt the temptation for them to worship idols—the very sin that had led to the nation's fall—would be even stronger than before! Jeremiah also reminds them it was not he that had instituted the inquiry; they themselves were responsible for provoking the Lord's severe answer. The passage closes with the threefold judgment of sword, famine, and plague ringing in their ears (v.22). The issue was clear, the warning was faithfully transmitted; but the remnant were set on having their own way.

Notes

20 "You made a fatal mistake" is literally "you are leading astray at the cost [or risk] of your own lives" (הִתְעֵתֶם בְּנַפְשׁוֹתֵיכֶם, *hit͑ēteym b͑enapšôtêkem*). BHS prefers the Qere הִתְעֵתֶם (*hit͑êtem*). The object of the verb is omitted as in Isa 3:12; 30:28 (so Laetsch). There is no basis to follow LXX, which reads ἐπονηρεύσασθε (*eponēreusasthe*, "you have done evil [harm]") against yourselves). The verb is not found elsewhere with בּ (*b*) of the person. (See Prov 10:17, which is also a Hiphil.)

B. *Ministry in Egypt* (43:1–44:30)

Chapters 43–44 relate to the remnant in Egypt. Johanan and the people disregarded the Lord's warning and went there, taking Jeremiah and Baruch, probably by force. The prophet doubtless died in Egypt.

1. *The flight to Egypt* (43:1–13)

a. *The warning flouted*

43:1–7

[1]When Jeremiah finished telling the people all the words of the LORD their God—everything the LORD had sent him to tell them— [2]Azariah son of Hoshaiah and Johanan son of Kareah and all the arrogant men said to Jeremiah, "You are lying! The LORD our God has not sent you to say, 'You must not go to Egypt to

settle there.' ³But Baruch son of Neriah is inciting you against us to hand us over to the Babylonians, so they may kill us or carry us into exile to Babylon."

⁴So Johanan son of Kareah and all the army officers and all the people disobeyed the LORD's command to stay in the land of Judah. ⁵Instead, Johanan son of Kareah and all the army officers led away all the remnant of Judah who had come back to live in the land of Judah from all the nations where they had been scattered. ⁶They also led away all the men, women and children and the king's daughters whom Nebuzaradan commander of the imperial guard had left with Gedaliah son of Ahikam, the son of Shaphan, and Jeremiah the prophet and Baruch son of Neriah. ⁷So they entered Egypt in disobedience to the LORD and went as far as Tahpanhes.

1–3 The response to Jeremiah's message from the Lord (v.1) was both immediate and negative. In no uncertain terms, Azariah and Johanan and "all the arrogant men" (v.2) who dominated the frightened remnant accused Jeremiah of lying. To divert attention from breaking their promise to obey the Lord's message, they tried to save face, not only by giving Jeremiah the lie, but also by accusing Baruch of conniving to get Jeremiah to deliver the remnant to the Babylonians (v.3). Because Jeremiah was an old man and might conceivably have been under the influence of his secretary and companion, the charge against Baruch had a superficial plausibility. But there was not a scintilla of evidence for it. The prophet who would not trim his message for the king would never have been manipulated by his secretary.

4–6 At the death of Gedaliah, Johanan, who appears in a bad light ever since his determined opposition to Jeremiah, became the rallying center for the people (v.4). His action cannot be divorced from an element of self-promotion. The remnant (v.5) was made up of the many Jews who had fled to nearby countries after the Fall of Jerusalem. Unfortunately they all agreed to follow Johanan and their other leaders instead of the Lord. Such is the perversity of fallen human nature; when people reach unanimity, too often they rebel against the will of God (cf. Gen 11:1–4). Jeremiah and Baruch were doubtless taken to Egypt against their will (v.6), for them to have gone there voluntarily would have violated Jeremiah's prophecies (cf. 32:6–15; 40:1–6; 42:13–18; so Cunliffe-Jones, Orelli et al.).

7 This verse shows the full extent of the people's disobedience. They arrived in Egypt at Tahpanhes, a fortress city on the northern border of Lower Egypt guarding the road to Syria. Pharaoh had a palace here. Located on the Pelusian branch of the Nile, Tahpanhes was known to the Greeks as Daphne (cf. 2:16). It is the modern Tell el-Defenneh. Think of it! Abraham's descendants returned to Egypt long after their liberation from it. With great suffering they had been delivered from their bondage in Egypt only to return there a defeated and hopeless remnant nearly nine hundred years later (so Morgan).

Notes

2 הָאֲנָשִׁים הַזֵּדִים (hāʾᵃnāšîm hazzēdîm, "the arrogant men") carries the thought of insolence, presumption, more than just "proud" (so KJV, ASV). The basic meaning is "boil" (TDOT, 4:46–47).

7 Tahpanhes was the Pelusian Daphne mentioned by Herodotus (2.30.107) as being garrisoned by Greek mercenaries by Pharaoh Psammetik of the Twenty-Sixth Dynasty (664–610 B.C.) to withstand invasions of Arabian and Asiatic forces (cf. ZPEB, 5:588).

---

b. *Jeremiah's prophecy in Egypt*

43:8–13

> **8**In Tahpanhes the word of the Lord came to Jeremiah: **9**"While the Jews are watching, take some large stones with you and bury them in clay in the brick pavement at the entrance to Pharaoh's palace in Tahpanhes. **10**Then say to them, 'This is what the Lord Almighty, the God of Israel, says: I will send for my servant Nebuchadnezzar king of Babylon, and I will set his throne over these stones I have buried here; he will spread his royal canopy above them. **11**He will come and attack Egypt, bringing death to those destined for death, captivity to those destined for captivity, and the sword to those destined for the sword. **12**He will set fire to the temples of the gods of Egypt; he will burn their temples and take their gods captive. As a shepherd wraps his garment around him, so will he wrap Egypt around himself and depart from there unscathed. **13**There in the temple of the sun in Egypt he will demolish the sacred pillars and will burn down the temples of the gods of Egypt.' "

The fugitives probably stopped at Tahpanhes in order to obtain permission from Pharaoh to enter the country and to assure themselves of some means of livelihood during their stay in it. We are not told how Jeremiah and Baruch fared in Egypt. The word of God is not, however, in any way bound by geographical limitations. Jeremiah's first message to the remnant in Egypt foretold the certainty of Nebuchadnezzar's victory over Egypt. Therefore, the flight of the remnant was useless (cf. the parallel in Amos 5:19). Because of the tenor of his message, Jeremiah's stay in Egypt was not a happy one. His own brethren were unsympathetic to him; and, when his political position became known, the government could hardly have favored him. There is no archaeological evidence of Nebuchadnezzar's conquest of Egypt, though there is evidence that he invaded it.

8–9 In Tahpanhes the Lord told Jeremiah to act out a message for the people (v.8). He was to hide some large stones in the mortar of the brick pavement at the entrance to Pharaoh's house at Tahpanhes (v.9). This was the place where Nebuchadnezzar would set up his throne on his invasion that was to bring death and destruction to Egypt (v.11). Excavations by Flinders Petrie at Tell Defenneh uncovered a large paved area in front of what he identified as Pharaoh's house (so WBC). But some scholars believe the reference here is not to Pharaoh's palace (his main palace having been elsewhere) but to the government building in Tahpanhes. Elephantiné Papyri locate the king's house there (so Bright).

10–11 If the Jews had gone to Egypt to escape the Babylonians, their flight was futile because the Lord was going to send Nebuchadnezzar to invade it (v.11; ch. 44). The royal "canopy" (v.10) has been understood as a covering over the throne or perhaps as a gorgeous carpet on which the throne stood. The exact meaning is difficult because the word *šapriwr* is a *hapax legomenon,* but it certainly refers to something splendid. A fragmentary text in the British Museum indicates that Nebuchadnezzar's invasion of Egypt occurred in the thirty-seventh year of his reign (568–567 B.C.). Amasis was on the Egyptian throne at the time (so ANET, p. 308). It was a punitive expedition against Egypt; after it Babylonia and Egypt had amicable relations (so Bright). Notice that the Lord called Nebuchadnezzar "my servant" (cf. 27:6)—the executor of death, captivity, and destruction for Egypt (v.11).

12 Verses 12–13 show the Lord's unalterable opposition to the idolatry of Egypt. The change in pronouns in v.12 (NIV mg.) is difficult to Western ears but intelligible in the Hebrew. Nebuchadnezzar would burn the wooden images and the temples with them and carry off the idols of gold to Babylon. In ancient times idols of defeated foes were carried in the triumphal processions of conquering kings. Not only would the temples be destroyed, but the sacred pillars—i.e., the obelisks, monuments of Egypt's idolatrous pride (cf. Deut 16:21–22; 2 Kings 23:14)—would be broken. Jeremiah likens the ease with which Nebuchadnezzar would do these things to the casual way in which a shepherd wraps himself in his garment. In fact, the conqueror will return unscathed from Egypt (so Clarke). The sacred pillars were the finest representations of Egyptian idolatry (so KD). The king of Egypt at this time was Pharaoh Hophra (cf. 44:30). The Babylonian historian Berossus confirms the conquest of Egypt by Nebuchadnezzar (so Jos. *Contra Apion* I, 132–36 [19]).

13 "The temple of the sun" is the modern Tell Husn, about six miles northeast of Cairo. The sun god was elaborately worshiped there in antiquity. The reference to "Egypt" distinguishes the Egyptian city from the Palestinian one with the same name (cf. 2 Kings 14:11). But the prophet has not spoken his last word on Egypt; more follows in chapters 44 and 46.

Notes

9 The irony of the situation is unmistakable. Contrary to Jeremiah's explicit word, Johanan and his men forcefully took the Judean remnant to Egypt, only to learn that Nebuchadnezzar could reach them there and that they would see ("are watching"—v.8) the very spot where the conqueror would set his throne. Flinders Petrie has claimed positive identification of the site. Notice how many humanly unpredictable elements Jeremiah included: (1) Nebuchadnezzar's invasion of Egypt, (2) his victory, (3) the very place he would set up his throne, (4) the decoration of his throne, (5) the lives he would destroy, (6) the temples he would demolish, and (7) the gods he would take captive. This passage vividly points out how definite and detailed biblical prophecy can be when God wills it so.

10 שַׁפְרוּר (*šapriwr*, "royal canopy") is found nowhere else in the OT. Freedman suggests that the term derives from an Assyrian root with the sense of "to spread out," hence the variety of meanings offered by scholars.

13 בֵּית שֶׁמֶשׁ (*bêt šemeš*, "Beth Shemesh"—"house [i.e., temple] of the sun"), the Greek Heliopolis ("city of the sun") and the On of the Egyptians (Gen 41:45), was the capital of the thirteenth nome of Lower Egypt. Since Heliopolis was indeed the city of obelisks ("sacred pillars"), it is clear why Jeremiah predicts their demolition. Some obelisks originally at On have been carried off to Alexandria, Rome, Istanbul, London, and New York. Only one has been left at On (cf. ZPEB, 4:535–36).

2. *Condemnation of Ishtar worship* (44:1-30)

This chapter contains Jeremiah's last message. It has been dated 580 B.C. because the dispersion implied in v.1 would have taken some years. The message reviews the Lord's dealings with Judah and emphatically reminds the Jews in Egypt that their sins have brought on them the wrath of God that had been foretold by Jeremiah.

a. *Exhortation to heed past experience*

44:1-10

> ¹This word came to Jeremiah concerning all the Jews living in Lower Egypt—in Migdol, Tahpanhes and Memphis—and in Upper Egypt: ²"This is what the LORD Almighty, the God of Israel, says: You saw the great disaster I brought on Jerusalem and on all the towns of Judah. Today they lie deserted and in ruins ³because of the evil they have done. They provoked me to anger by burning incense and by worshiping other gods that neither they nor you nor your fathers ever knew. ⁴Again and again I sent my servants the prophets, who said, 'Do not do this detestable thing that I hate!' ⁵But they did not listen or pay attention; they did not turn their wickedness or stop burning incense to other gods. ⁶Therefore, my fierce anger was poured out; it raged against the towns of Judah and the streets of Jerusalem and made them the desolate ruins they are today.
> ⁷"Now this is what the LORD God Almighty, the God of Israel, says: Why bring such great disaster on yourselves by cutting off from Judah the men and women, the children and infants, and so leave yourselves without a remnant? ⁸Why provoke me to anger with what your hands have made, burning incense to other gods in Egypt, where you have come to live? You will destroy yourselves and make yourselves an object of cursing and reproach among all the nations on earth. ⁹Have you forgotten the wickedness committed by your fathers and by the kings and queens of Judah and the wickedness committed by you and your wives in the land of Judah and the streets of Jerusalem? ¹⁰To this day they have not humbled themselves or shown reverence, nor have they followed my law and the decrees I set before you and your fathers."

1-6 This passage (vv.1-10) rebukes the Jews dispersed in Egypt. It is surprising that the Jews were practicing idolatry in Egypt; they had not yet learned from their past sins. Jeremiah mentions four places, three in Lower (northern) Egypt—Migdol, Tahpanhes, and Memphis—and Upper (southern) Egypt (lit., Pathros) (v.1). The mention of these places shows how rapidly the Jews had spread out in Egypt.

Now Jeremiah delivers his final message. The reason for this prophecy was the continued idolatry of the exiles (vv.3-5) in spite of their captivity experience (v.2). If ever a prophecy had immediacy, it was this one; for in it Jeremiah brought the light of history to bear on the very day in which he spoke (v.6). In the first six verses of the message, Jeremiah gives his hearers a history lesson that stressed human cause and divine effect.

7-10 Moving to the current hour (v.7), Jeremiah remonstrated with the people regarding the sins in which they were still steeped (v.8). Once more the nation was committing national suicide (so Bewer). All the warnings previously extended made no difference in their thinking or in their acts. It was Hegel, in the introduction to his *Philosophy of History* (1807), who rightly said: "What experience and history teach is this—that people and governments never have learned anything from history, or acted on principles deduced from it." So with these Jews in Egypt! They had become ensnared in the idolatry of that land—a sin that the Lord had foreseen and that was one of the reasons God had forbidden them to go there. But, heedless of their past, they went and served the gods of Egypt. Disheartening this must have been for Jeremiah, who had spent a lifetime preaching against idolatry in Judah; and now the Jews were practicing in Egypt the very sins that had brought about the Fall of Jerusalem. Notice the reference to their wives (v.9); they were in the forefront of the idolatrous worship the Jews carried on in Egypt. The remnant showed (v.10) that they were neither repentant nor contrite (*dukkeʾû*, "bruised"; cf. Isa 53:5).

Notes

1 Migdol, on the northeastern border of Egypt, has been identified with modern Tell el-Her, about eleven miles south of Pelusium (so WBC). It was probably the Roman Magdolo of the Antonine Itinerary and the Migdol of Sethos I (ZPEB, 4:223). Tahpanhes has already been referred to in the comments at 43:7 and 43:9. Memphis (Noph) was a city on the west bank of the Nile about thirteen miles south of Cairo, near the apex of the Nile Delta. Legend has it that it was the first capital of united Egypt under King Menes. The city is mentioned eight times in the Bible, all in the OT prophets: Hosea, Isaiah, Jeremiah, and Ezekiel. Archaeological digs have been carried out here by Flinders Petrie, C.S. Fisher, Pennsylvania University Museum, and the Egyptian Department of Antiquities (ZPEB, 4:179–83). Pathros is Upper Egypt, or the Nile Valley between Cairo and Aswan. The name appears in Assyrian inscriptions of the seventh century B.C. Besides in the Bible—Isaiah (11:11), Jeremiah (44:1, 15), and Ezekiel (29:14; 30:14) mention the area—the Elephantiné Papyri from the fifth century B.C. tell us that a Jewish colony settled there.

It is known that Jewish communities existed in parts of Egypt at an early period. In Jeremiah's day Jews had settled in two northern frontier areas (the first two sites mentioned) and in two more inland places.

b. *Warning of punishment*

44:11–14

11"Therefore, this is what the LORD Almighty, the God of Israel, says: I am determined to bring disaster on you to destroy all Judah. 12I will take away the remnant of Judah who were determined to go to Egypt to settle there. They will all perish in Egypt; they will fall by the sword or die from famine. From the least to the greatest, they will die by sword or famine. They will become an object of cursing and horror, of condemnation and reproach. 13I will punish those who live in Egypt with the sword, famine and plague, as I punished Jerusalem. 14None of the remnant of Judah who have gone to live in Egypt will escape or survive to return to the land of Judah, to which they long to return and live; none will return except a few fugitives."

11–14 Now judgment is announced (v.11). It is the same for the Jews in Egypt as it had been for those in Judah. Here the warning is fuller than in 42:17–18. The reference to "all Judah" covers all the Jews there in Egypt—with the exception of permanent Jewish settlers there and the few mentioned in vv.14b, 28 (so Streane). First of all, Jeremiah roundly rebukes them for coming to Egypt (vv.12–13). Then he dramatically specifies the troubles the remnant can expect in Egypt. He makes it clear that he is not referring to any permanent Jewish settlers in Egypt (cf. v.14) but only to the remnant who had sought refuge there in the hope of returning to the land of Judah at the earliest opportunity. Only casual fugitives will survive. For the remnant the picture is one of unrelieved gloom.

c. The stubborn persistence in idolatry

44:15–19

> 15Then all the men who knew that their wives were burning incense to other gods, along with all the women who were present—a large assembly—and all the people living in Lower and Upper Egypt, said to Jeremiah, 16"We will not listen to the message you have spoken to us in the name of the LORD! 17We will certainly do everything we said we would: We will burn incense to the Queen of Heaven and will pour out drink offerings to her just as we and our fathers, our kings and our officials did in the towns of Judah and in the streets of Jerusalem. At that time we had plenty of food and were well off and suffered no harm. 18But ever since we stopped burning incense to the Queen of Heaven and pouring out drink offerings to her, we have had nothing and have been perishing by sword and famine."
>
> 19The women added, "When we burned incense to the Queen of Heaven and poured out drink offerings to her, did not our husbands know that we were making cakes like her image and pouring out drink offerings to her?"

15–19 This passage is one of the strangest in the book. How stubborn the resistance to Jeremiah's message was! Note the key role of the women (v.15). The inclusive language—"all the men," "all the women," "all the people"—is a literary generalization used for emphasis and should not be taken literally. The people openly and unashamedly refused to forsake their idolatry; indeed, they found pragmatic justification for it. They brazenly declared that they would keep on in their idolatry (vv.16–17). The occasion here may have been an idolatrous feast in which the women had a major part (so Streane). The women were so prominent in this worship doubtless because Astarte, "the Queen of Heaven" (vv.17, 18, 19, 25), was the goddess of fertility.

The remnant—women as well as men—defied Jeremiah.

1. The people flatly refused to heed the Lord's message Jeremiah brought them (v.16).

2. They were determined to go on in idolatrous worship just as they had with their forefathers and kings in Judah in the very same vile worship of the Queen of Heaven (v.17). They admitted that they were not engaging in any new worship.

3. They affirmed a causal relationship between their idolatry and the abundance of food (v.17). (See David Noel Freedman's excellent article "The Biblical Idea of History," Int 21, no. 1 [1967]: 32–49.)

4. They also affirmed that when they stopped their idolatrous practices, food shortages and war were the result (v.18). They doubtless ascribed their troubles to the reforms of Josiah, to which they senselessly attributed the downfall of Judah. (Theological gymnasts are not restricted to the twentieth century.) In short, the remnant claimed that idolatry had done more for them than the Lord whom Jeremiah represented. Nothing is more blinding than unbelief. Not once did they connect their trials with their sins (so KD).

5. Finally, in an insolent rhetorical question that required an affirmative reply,

the women asked Jeremiah whether they had carried on their worship of the Queen of Heaven without the knowledge and approval of their husbands. (See Num 30:3, 6–7, 12, where the law says that a married woman's vows were only binding if her husband approved them [so Bewer].) Since their husbands approved, why then should Jeremiah complain about the women's actions? The cakes (v.19) had an image of Astarte on them, said to be the image of the full moon, either formed by the cake or stamped on it (so Streane).

Notes

17 In מְלֶכֶת הַשָּׁמַיִם (*m^{e}leket haššāmayim*, "Queen of Heaven"), מְלֶכֶת (*m^{e}leket*) is a strange form, which some have altered to read מְלֶאכֶת (*m^{e}le'ket*, "work" or "worship" of heaven). The reference is probably to the Assyro-Babylonian Ishtar. The Hebrew phrase occurs only in Jeremiah, once in 7:18 and four times in this chapter. It may be that her cult was merged with that of a Canaanite goddess. Dahood claims that the goddess is Shapash (cited by Bright).

Ishtar (Canaanite 'Athtart) was the goddess of war and love. She represented the female principle of fertility (so Orelli). Her popularity is confirmed by the fact that at Babylon alone there were 180 open-air shrines dedicated to her worship (ZPEB, 3:334–35). Ashtoreth is the Hebrew of which Astarte is the Greek. This ancient goddess was called Ishtar in Akkadian, Inanna in Sumerian, and 'Athtart in Ugaritic. Her counterpart in the NT is Artemis (cf. Acts 19; in Latin, Diana). The worship of this goddess was widespread in the ancient Near East. Her specific association was with sex and/or fertility in both human and animal creation. In the OT Ashtoreth (with a male deity Ashtar) had certain associations of astrological importance (cf. ZPEB, 1:341–42, 359–61).

d. Condemnation of the remnant's stubbornness

44:20–30

20Then Jeremiah said to all the people, both men and women, who were answering him, 21"Did not the LORD remember and think about the incense burned in the towns of Judah and the streets of Jerusalem by you and your fathers, your kings and your officials and the people of the land? 22When the LORD could no longer endure your wicked actions and the detestable things you did, your land became an object of cursing and a desolate waste without inhabitants, as it is today. 23Because you have burned incense and have sinned against the LORD and have not obeyed him or followed his law or his decrees or his stipulations, this disaster has come upon you, as you now see."

24Then Jeremiah said to all the people, including the women, "Hear the word of the LORD, all you people of Judah in Egypt. 25This is what the LORD Almighty, the God of Israel, says: You and your wives have shown by your actions what you promised when you said, 'We will certainly carry out the vows we made to burn incense and pour out drink offerings to the Queen of Heaven.'

"Go ahead then, do what you promised! Keep your vows! 26But hear the word of the LORD, all Jews living in Egypt: 'I swear by my great name,' says the LORD, 'that no one from Judah living anywhere in Egypt will ever again invoke my name or swear, "As surely as the Sovereign LORD lives." 27For I am watching over them for harm, not for good; the Jews in Egypt will perish by sword and famine until they are all destroyed. 28Those who escape the sword and return to the land of Judah from Egypt will be very few. Then the whole remnant of Judah who came to live in Egypt will know whose word will stand—mine or theirs.

29" 'This will be the sign to you that I will punish you in this place,' declares the LORD, 'so that you will know that my threats of harm against you will surely stand.' 30This is what the LORD says: 'I am going to hand Pharaoh Hophra king of Egypt over to his enemies who seek his life, just as I handed Zedekiah king of Judah over to Nebuchadnezzar king of Babylon, the enemy who was seeking his life.' "

20–22 Verses 20–30 constitute the very last message of Jeremiah recorded in the book. The remaining chapters contain prophecies dating from earlier years. The message abounds in contrast and confrontation. Jeremiah flatly denies the women's twisted defense of their idolatry (v.20). How obtuse they were not to realize that all the while they were engaged in their detestable practices, God knew all about what they were doing (v.21)! The plain fact was that God, now as before (v.22), could no longer abide their idolatries. This was a far cry from their claim that prosperity attended them as long as they were idolatrous.

23–25 Since the people were going ahead with their idolatrous worship (v.23), Jeremiah announces their punishment (v.24). It was tragic that corrupt rulers had so influenced the nation's womanhood. In a powerful expression of irony and revulsion (v.25), Jeremiah tells the remnant to proceed with fulfilling their godless vows. He may have been pointing to their incense and libations and to the very cakes they were carrying.

26–28 The severe prediction in v.26 has been interpreted in two ways. Some scholars take it as meaning that God was saying that he would no longer be their covenant God. Thus they would forfeit the privilege of calling on his name (so Streane). Others think that v.26 means that the remnant would not be able to name God's name because they would perish in Egypt (so Bewer, KD). Naegelsbach (CHS) suggests that the Jews later repented of their obstinacy and were spared because in the centuries before Christ there was a large Jewish population in Egypt. The death penalty (v.27) is perhaps best understood with the qualification that the remnant (cf. v.14) are excluded from this threat. Only they will survive to know the truth of Jeremiah's prophecy; they will be easily numbered because they are so few. The outcome of events will demonstrate whose word stands (v.28); God is always willing to have his word tested alongside man's.

29–30 The last verses of the chapter give the sign (v.29) of the truth of God's words. It was the fall (v.30) of Pharaoh Hophra (588–568 B.C.), the ally of Zedekiah, who sent an army to help him when Jerusalem was besieged (cf. 37:5). Even this Pharaoh whose protection the Jews had sought would succumb to his enemies. He is the Apries of Herodotus (2.161) and the Hophra of history. The text does not compel the interpretation that Pharaoh Hophra was killed in the invasion of Egypt by Babylon. The facts are otherwise. Hophra was actually overthrown by Amasis, one of his officers, who revolted against him and then shared rule with him (Herod. 2:161–63, 169). Amasis rebelled against Nebuchadnezzar in 570 B.C. and was defeated in 568 B.C. So sixteen years after the Fall of Jerusalem, Hophra was dethroned and strangled by some of his subjects. Again Jeremiah was vindicated.

Scripture is silent on what happened to Jeremiah after the events of this chapter, though tradition has been overly active. There are many legends concerning his death. One states that he was killed at Daphne. Another claims he carried away the tabernacle, hiding it in the mountain where Moses died (2 Macc 2:4–8). Yet another indicates he was alive with Enoch and Elijah, expected to return as a forerunner of the Messiah. Still another connects him with the British Israel theory and the Coronation Stone; it is claimed that fugitive Israelites under Jeremiah and Baruch landed in Ireland. The modern movement is traced to Richard Brothers (1757–1824), an officer in the British Navy, who claimed he was a "nephew of the Almighty" and a descendant of David (HERE, 1:482). We agree with the judgment that "the theory meets with no support from serious ethnologists or archaeologists" (F.L. Cross, ed., *The Oxford Dictionary of the Christian Church* [London: Oxford University Press, 1957], p. 199).

Notes

21–23 No OT passage can be made to teach God's absolute rejection of the sacrificial system, not even Isa 1:10–17; Hos 6:6; Amos 5:21–25; or Mic 6:1–8. The reason is patent: God himself instituted the system. By his prophets he constantly inveighs against sacrifices—indeed, all ritual—that do not accompany piety.

29–30 Pharaoh Hophra at one time commissioned one of his court officials, Amasis, to suppress a military revolt, only to have him proclaimed king by the soldiers. Hophra and Amasis were coregents for about three years. When a struggle broke out between them, Hophra was killed (strangled) and Amasis reigned until 526 B.C. It has been suggested that this passage is a *vaticinium ex eventu* (so Hitzig, Graf), but without convincing proof (cf. KD).

C. The Message to Baruch (45:1–5)

This brief chapter contains the message the Lord gave to Baruch. Historically it supplements 36:1–8 and can be precisely dated at 604 B.C. (cf. 36:1). This antedates sections about the remnant and Egypt. Most expositors dwell on the rebuke the chapter contains; some, however, suggest that the message to Baruch was meant not as a rebuke but as a commendation. Actually, it has both elements. Baruch was admittedly modest and reliable (so Frost). The message, then, was meant to encourage Baruch, who had become disheartened, just as Jeremiah had been.

1. Baruch's complaint

45:1–3

> [1]This is what Jeremiah the prophet told Baruch son of Neriah in the fourth year of Jehoiakim son of Josiah king of Judah, after Baruch had written on a scroll the words Jeremiah was then dictating: [2]"This is what the LORD, the God of Israel, says to you, Baruch: [3]You said, 'Woe to me! The LORD has added sorrow to my pain; I am worn out with groaning and find no rest.' "

1–3 Baruch came from an influential family of noble birth. He was the grandson of Mahseiah (cf. 32:12), governor of Jerusalem in Josiah's reign (cf. 2 Chron 34:8). His brother had been chief chamberlain in the court of Zedekiah (cf. 51:59). Jeremiah may have had other secretaries, but Baruch is the only one mentioned in the book.

He may have had hopes of attaining a high office or even of receiving the gift of prophecy. But such expectations were not to be realized. Rather, he was to spend his life in a secondary role. So he may have been depressed. "The words" (v.1) refer to the scroll (ch. 36; cf. "the fourth year of Jehoiakim"). Baruch shared Jeremiah's burdens (v.2). He grieved over what he had to record about the people's sin and their coming punishment (v.3). His sorrow, pain, and groaning wore him out, and his emotional involvement in what he wrote gave him no rest.

Notes

1 The name "Baruch" (בָּרוּךְ *bārûk*) means "Blessed" and is transliterated in the LXX, Vulgate, and Targum. His father's name, Neriah (נֵרִיָּה, *nērîyāh*), means "The LORD is my lamp." Three men besides Jeremiah's secretary bore the name Baruch in the OT (cf. Neh 3:20; 10:6; 11:5). The Book of Jeremiah has twenty-three occurrences of the name, of which sixteen are found in chapter 36. The two references in chapter 45 are the last. From all appearances Baruch was the confidant and closest friend of the prophet, a gracious gift of the Lord in view of the Lord's command to Jeremiah not to marry. Baruch took Jeremiah's dictation of his messages; even when these were destroyed by Jehoiakim, Baruch was privileged to be the penman for the redictation. The deeds of Jeremiah's property (32:12–16) were entrusted to Baruch for safekeeping. With the Fall of Jerusalem in 586 B.C., Baruch and Jeremiah were taken to Egypt. When Baruch was accused of undue influence on the prophet, he did not reply. Somehow the figure of Baruch has fired the imagination of following generations. Among the Pseudepigrapha there is an Apocalypse of Baruch; and, as a supplement to the biblical Book of Jeremiah, there exists a Book of Baruch.

3 S. Blank has cited an analogy between Jonah 4:10–11 and Jeremiah 45 to illustrate the contrast between Baruch's and Jonah's self-pity and the Lord's heartache over the judgment he must inflict.

2. The response of the Lord

45:4–5

⁴The LORD said, "Say this to him: 'This is what the LORD says: I will overthrow what I have built and uproot what I have planted, throughout the land. ⁵Should you then seek great things for yourself? Seek them not. For I will bring disaster on all people, declares the LORD, but wherever you go I will let you escape with your life.' "

4–5 These verses imply that the Lord's concern for his people is greater than any man's. The destruction of Judah is in view in v.4 (so Hyatt). On the other hand, it has been proposed (so KD) that "throughout the land" actually refers to the whole earth as seen from "on all people" (v.5). The verbs in v.4 remind us of 1:10, where they furnish the outline for Jeremiah's prophetic ministry. The reply to Baruch's complaint (v.3) was simple: Do not expect to be more than you are (v.5). Why should Baruch be so concerned about his own welfare and position? He should not be self-seeking. When the nation was suffering drastic judgment, instead of making demands, he should be satisfied that his life was spared. With this he must be content. The last clause of v.5 implies that Baruch will have to flee for his life. Short though the chapter is, it has a timeless message for the Lord's servant.

Notes

4 The complaint of Baruch in v.3 is the only place where his reactions to the tragic events around him are stated. His life was filled with strife, sorrow, and loss. Verse 4 gives us the final reiteration of the theme in 1:10 (cf. 18:7–10; 24:6; 31:4, 28, 40; 32:41; 33:7; 42:10).

5 The unusual expression וְנָתַתִּי נַפְשְׁךָ לְשָׁלָל (wᵉnātattî napšᵉkā lᵉšālāl, lit., "But I will give you your life for [as] a booty") occurs in Jer 21:9; 38:2; 39:18; and here. Obviously, the words have a military connotation. Most English translations render the words literally, but the force of the idiom is lost. KJV translates "but thy life will I give unto thee for a prey in all places whither thou goest" (so ASV). RSV has little change and not much more light. NEB has the basic concept but adds some words unnecessarily. BV (following Smith-Goodspeed) is better than the older versions but is still not too clear—e.g., "as a prize of war." The best renderings are in JB—"As for you, I will let you escape with your own life, wherever you may go"—and NIV—"but wherever you go I will let you escape with your life."

IV. Prophecies Concerning the Nations (46:1–51:64)

Except for chapter 52, the remainder of Jeremiah is made up of prophecies against foreign nations. Though some scholars have doubted that these prophecies come from Jeremiah, there is an increased tendency to credit him with the material. In the light of his commission as a prophet to the nations (cf. 1:5) and his appointment by God over nations and kingdoms (cf. 1:10; so Cunliffe-Jones, WBC), there is no valid reason to deny his authorship of this section. The LXX puts these prophecies in an entirely different place—viz., after 25:13—and arranges them in a different order. Since all the prophets had a word from God for foreign nations, so especially would Jeremiah (cf. 1:10; cf. also Isa 13–21, 23; Ezek 25–32; Amos 1:3–2:3). The prophecies against Egypt (ch. 46) and Babylon (chs. 50–51) contain promises of Israel's restoration (cf. 46:27–28; 50:19–20). Some of the messages were sent to Babylon; others were delivered in Egypt. Parts of chapters 50–51 date from the reign of Cyrus. The battle between Egypt and Babylon at Carchemish forms the background for 46:2–6. Jeremiah was a man of world vision. He was a contemporary of five kings of Judah, of the greatest monarch of the neo-Chaldean empire, and of four kings of Egypt. The latter were Psammetik I (664–609 B.C.), Neco II (609–594 B.C.), Psammetik II (594–588 B.C.), and Hophra (588–568 B.C.), all from the Twenty-Sixth Dynasty. Chapters 46–51 have been acclaimed as some of the finest poetry in all the prophetic Scriptures (so Bright).

The prophecies concern ten nations (some count nine)—Egypt, Philistia, Moab, Ammon, Edom, Syria (Damascus), Kedar, Hazor, Elam, and Babylon. They were doubtless given to Jeremiah at different times, though collected here under a common theme: judgment. The prophecies move from west to east. Unlike the prophecies against foreign nations in other books of OT prophets, the nations' sins are not specifically identified; only the judgments are singled out.

At this point it is highly important to consider certain basic principles that underlie all biblical prophecies that threaten world powers.

1. God is the God of all the nations. As the Sovereign over everything, he has the authority to speak to all peoples.

2. God is first and foremost the God of holiness and righteousness (cf. Isa 6:3).

3. God's judgments are never vindictive (revengeful) but vindicative (justifying).

4. Judgment is God's strange work (cf. Isa 28:21; Ezek 33:11). He does not delight in it; he rejoices in salvation (cf. Matt 1:21).

5. God is impartial. He judges among the nations just as he judges Israel's sin.

Caption for the Prophecies Against the Nations

46:1

¹This is the word of the LORD that came to Jeremiah the prophet concerning the nations:

1 This verse serves as the introduction and title for all the chapters that follow, except the historical one (ch. 52). That this caption appears here may well indicate that these prophecies are in the right place in the book.

Notes

1 In the LXX the oracles of the nations appear right after 25:13a. The Hebrew order tallies generally with the list in 25:19–26 and with the chronological order of the history of the nations dealt with (so Hyatt). The authenticity of these prophecies has been discussed thoroughly by scholars, but agreement is lacking. Noteworthy are the facts that (1) the prophecies touch very little on historical events, (2) no king is mentioned, and (3) the literary style differs from the rest of the book.

A. *Concerning Egypt (46:2–28)*

1. *The defeat of the Egyptian army*

46:2–6

²Concerning Egypt:

This is the message against the army of Pharaoh Neco king of Egypt, which was defeated at Carchemish on the Euphrates River by Nebuchadnezzar king of Babylon in the fourth year of Jehoiakim son of Josiah king of Judah:

³"Prepare your shields, both large and small,
    and march out for battle!
⁴Harness the horses,
    mount the steeds!
Take your positions
    with helmets on!
Polish your spears,
    put on your armor!
⁵What do I see?
    They are terrified,
they are retreating,
    their warriors are defeated.
They flee in haste
    without looking back,
    and there is terror on every side,"

declares the LORD.

> 6"The swift cannot flee
>   nor the strong escape.
> In the north by the River Euphrates
>   they stumble and fall."

2 This chapter is concerned with a prophecy against Egypt. The Pharaoh Neco referred to is the one who slew Josiah at Megiddo (609 B.C.) and thus placed Jehoahaz on the Judean throne. In three months he removed him, imprisoned him at Riblah, and set up Jehoiakim as king. It was in Jehoiakim's fourth year that Neco was defeated at Carchemish (605 B.C.). Carchemish is not at the junction of the rivers Chebar and Euphrates but farther up the Euphrates. The only great city in that region, it was the key to Syria on the east and commanded the passage of the Euphrates. It had been under the rule of the Hittites and Assyrians. The name "Carchemish" means "the fort of Chemosh," god of the Moabites (cf. 2 Kings 23:13) (so Streane). After the fall of the Assyrian Empire, Carchemish was the battleground between Egypt and Babylon. At the Battle of Carchemish, the military ambitions of Egypt were blocked. Thus it was one of the decisive battles in history. It proved that the Assyrian power could not restrain the rising might of Babylon, which Egypt opposed in favor of Assyria. Carchemish was the downfall of Neco. Nebuchadnezzar pursued him toward Egypt but was halted by the news of the death of his father, Nabopolassar. On returning to Babylon, Nebuchadnezzar was crowned king. Babylon now dominated Mesopotamia and the near eastern Mediterranean area. The times of the Gentiles had begun (cf. Luke 21:24; also Dan 2:36–38). The fourth year of Jehoiakim was the first year of Nebuchadnezzar (cf. 25:1).

3–6 In words tinged with sarcasm, Jeremiah vividly describes the preparation of the Egyptians for the battle, their march to it, and their defeat. The "shields, both large and small" (v.3) were the large shield protecting the whole body of the heavily armed soldier and the small round buckler protecting the lightly armed soldier. Horses and steeds (v.4) were always an important element of Egyptian warfare. Their helmets on, the Egyptians are told to put themselves in battle formation. Helmets were worn only in combat (so Streane). Coats of mail ("armor") were worn by light troops. An army as well accoutered as the one described here would naturally be victorious. But events take an unexpected turn. What brought defeat to such a force? Panic supernaturally induced did (v.5). In spite of the Egyptians' fleetness and power (v.6), they were conquered and destined not to return home but to fall on foreign soil. History has fully confirmed Jeremiah's predictions: Egypt's advance was halted at the Euphrates.

Notes

---

2 The Battle of Carchemish took place in 605 B.C. British archaeologists have found evidence at Carchemish in Syria that the town was destroyed about 600 B.C. The large number of Egyptian objects found there indicate an occupation of the site by an Egyptian army shortly before its fall. Some of the finds are from Psammetik I and Neco. There are still some scholars who deny the historicity of the battle. But the "battle was a turning point in the history of the ancient Near East; thereafter Babylon, under its Chaldean dynasty, was the leader in world affairs, and Egypt was in a secondary position" (Hyatt, p. 1106).

2. The humbling of Egypt's pride

46:7-12

> 7"Who is this that rises like the Nile,
>   like rivers of surging waters?
> 8Egypt rises like the Nile,
>   like rivers of surging waters.
> She says, 'I will rise and cover the earth;
>   I will destroy cities and their people.'
> 9Charge, O horses!
>   Drive furiously, O charioteers!
> March on, O warriors—
>   men of Cush and Put who carry shields,
>   men of Lydia who draw the bow.
> 10But that day belongs to the LORD, the LORD Almighty—
>   a day of vengeance, for vengeance on his foes.
> The sword will devour till it is satisfied,
>   till it has quenched its thirst with blood.
> For the Lord, the LORD Almighty, will offer sacrifice
>   in the land of the north by the River Euphrates.
>
> 11"Go up to Gilead and get balm,
>   O Virgin Daughter of Egypt.
> But you multiply remedies in vain;
>   there is no healing for you.
> 12The nations will hear of your shame;
>   your cries will fill the earth.
> One warrior will stumble over another;
>   both will fall down together."

7-9 Now the name of the nation, whose army has been defeated, is mentioned (v.8). The approach of the Egyptian army is compared to the annual flooding of the Nile (v.7). The rivers referred to are the branches of the Nile in the Delta region in Lower Egypt. Egypt's boast of world conquest (v.8) and her flight and defeat (vv.5-6) are described, and both descriptions lead to a climax. Her chariots and infantry are summoned to sally forth (v.9), and the implication is that with them will be the mercenary troops who from the time of Psammetik formed the main part of the Egyptian forces. Cush and Put are Ethiopia and Libya (or Somaliland—both descended from Ham) (cf. Gen 10:6; Ezek 30:5). The Lydians (cf. Ludites, Gen 10:13) were not from the coast of Asia Minor but an African people living west of Egypt (so Bewer). They were the lightly armed part of the army.

10 There is more to military campaigns, however, than international conflicts. Verse 10 presents the theological interpretation of the defeat of the Egyptians. It has been suggested that the vengeance here referred to was for the death of Josiah at Megiddo (so Freedman), but this is improbable in the light of Isaiah 61:2 and parallel passages. Notice that Jeremiah does not speak of the Day of the Lord but of a day that is peculiarly God's—in short, the time of God's judgment on a nation. Apparently there are no eschatological implications in v.10.

11–12 Somewhat in the manner of a taunt song, Jeremiah advises Egypt to seek a remedy for her wounds (v.11). Her defeat dealt her an irrecoverable blow; she could not heal herself. Not only was Gilead noted for its healing balm (cf. 8:22), but Homer spoke of Egypt as full of physicians. From antiquity she was famous for her medical arts (cf. Pliny). It was from Egypt and India that the knowledge of medicine came to Europe (cf. Herod. 2.116). The defeat will be publicized among the nations (v.12). In their rout, the warriors will get in each other's way.

Notes

7–8 The word יְאוֹר (*ye'ôr*) is of Egyptian origin and is a common noun meaning "ditch," "canal," "river" (cf. Job 28:11 [10 MT]; Isa 33:21). As a proper name its use is restricted to the Nile (cf. Isa 19:8; Amos 8:8; 9:5 et al.).
11 Homer spoke of Egyptian prowess in medicine (*Odyssey* 4.229). Herodotus (3.1.132) stated that both Cyrus and Darius sent to Egypt for physicians (so Streane).

3. *The coming of Nebuchadnezzar*

46:13–19

¹³This is the message the LORD spoke to Jeremiah the prophet about the coming of Nebuchadnezzar king of Babylon to attack Egypt:

> ¹⁴"Announce this in Egypt, and proclaim it in Migdol;
> proclaim it also in Memphis and Tahpanhes:
> 'Take your positions and get ready,
> for the sword devours those around you.'
> ¹⁵Why will your warriors be laid low?
> They cannot stand, for the LORD will push them down.
> ¹⁶They will stumble repeatedly;
> they will fall over each other.
> They will say, 'Get up, let us go back
> to our own people and our native lands,
> away from the sword of the oppressor.'
> ¹⁷There they will exclaim,
> 'Pharaoh king of Egypt is only a loud noise;
> he has missed his opportunity.'
>
> ¹⁸"As surely as I live," declares the King,
> whose name is the LORD Almighty,
> "one will come who is like Tabor among the mountains,
> like Carmel by the sea.
> ¹⁹Pack your belongings for exile,
> you who live in Egypt,
> for Memphis will be laid waste
> and lie in ruins without inhabitant."

13–14 Nebuchadnezzar's conquest of Egypt left it vulnerable to future attack. Not only at Carchemish, but in Egypt itself the victory would be Babylon's (cf. 43:8–13). Some scholars would date this prophecy during Jeremiah's stay in Egypt. Actually Nebuchadnezzar's invasion of Egypt (v.13) came long after the Battle of Carchemish, which had prepared the way for it. Verse 14 announces that the foe has already reached the Egyptian borders. The surrounding nations had been subdued, perhaps even Tyre; so Nebuchadnezzar moved on Egypt (so Streane). As has already been said, it was the news of the death of his father that had prevented Nebuchadnezzar from moving deeper into Egypt. He had to return to Babylon to take up his duties as king (so KD).

15–17 Instead of "Why will your warriors be laid low?" (v. 15), the LXX reads "Why is Apis fled?" There is no consonantal change in the Hebrew but just a simple division of the verb in the first clause into a noun and a verb (see Notes). Apis was the sacred bull of Egypt, the incarnation of Osiris, god of Egypt. The image of Apis was often brought into battle (cf. its influence on Israel [Exod 32:4–5] and on Jeroboam [1 Kings 12:28–29]; so Bewer, Frost, Hyatt). If this reading is correct, the thought is that the gods of Egypt could not stand in the hour of test. Some expositors, however, oppose the view that v. 15 refers to Apis because Apis was worshiped only in Memphis and was in no sense representative of the gods or power of Egypt, as the context demands (so KD). In v. 16 the speech of the soldiers is overheard, as mercenary troops decide to return to their own countries. They call Pharaoh "a noise" (i.e., a braggart) (v. 17), blaming him for ruining his chances of victory by his procrastination—probably an allusion to his inaction when Nebuchadnezzar returned to Babylon after Carchemish.

18–19 Nebuchadnezzar's return to Egypt is likened to the majesty of Tabor and Carmel (v. 18), mountains in northern Palestine on the road to Egypt. The Babylonian invasion of Egypt will be as outstanding as is Tabor among the mountains and as irresistible as impregnable Carmel (so Myers). The defeated Egyptians are exhorted to provide themselves with what they will need for exile (v. 19).

Notes

15 The MT reads מַדּוּעַ נִסְחַף (*maddûªa nisḥap*, "Why will your warriors be laid low?"). LXX reads נסחף (a verb) as two words—נָס חַף (*nās ḥap*, "Why did Haf flee?"). Haf is Apis, the bull of Egypt, a symbol of Osiris. On textual, contextual, and stylistic grounds, MT is preferable.

4. The Fall of Egypt

46:20–26

> 20"Egypt is a beautiful heifer,
>   but a gadfly is coming
>   against her from the north.
> 21The mercenaries in her ranks
>   are like fattened calves.
> They too will turn and flee together,
>   they will not stand their ground,
> for the day of disaster is coming upon them,
>   the time for them to be punished.

22Egypt will hiss like a fleeing serpent
as the enemy advances in force;
they will come against her with axes,
like men who cut down trees.
23They will chop down her forest,"
declares the LORD,
"dense though it be.
They are more numerous than locusts,
they cannot be counted.
24The Daughter of Egypt will be put to shame,
handed over to the people of the north."

25The LORD Almighty, the God of Israel, says: "I am about to bring punishment
on Amon god of Thebes, on Pharaoh, on Egypt and her gods and her kings, and
on those who rely on Pharaoh. 26I will hand them over to those who seek their
lives, to Nebuchadnezzar king of Babylon and his officers. Later, however, Egypt
will be inhabited as in times past," declares the LORD.

20–24 Jeremiah describes Egypt's doom in highly figurative language. The "beautiful heifer" (v.20) is Egypt; the "gadfly" from the north is Nebuchadnezzar. Egypt's mercenaries are like calves fattened for slaughter (v.21). The fleeing Egyptians will sound like a serpent escaping from woodsmen by slithering through underbrush (v.22). The Babylonians carried axes—a novelty to the Jews. The serpent figure is an ironic reference to one of the most noted of Egyptian deities, prominent even in royal insignia—the coiled uraeus. The devastating power of the enemy is likened to a locust plague (v.23)—a proverbial figure (cf. Joel 1:1–2:27). Returning to literal language, Jeremiah declares that Egypt will be at the mercy of the Babylonians (v.24).

25–26 In two verses in prose, Jeremiah predicts judgment on the gods and kings of Egypt (v.25). Amon (Amun) was the chief god of No (Thebes), the capital of Upper Egypt. The judgment will overtake all the people of Israel who looked to Pharaoh for help against Babylon (so KD). Yet the desolation of Egypt will not be perpetual; the Lord promises her future restoration (v.26; cf. Isa 19:24–25; Ezek 29:8–14). In messianic times Egypt will be reinhabited (so KD).

Notes

20 קֶרֶץ (*qereṣ*), a *hapax legomenon,* derives from the verb that means "to nip, bite," hence, "a stinging insect," i.e., "gadfly." The destruction of Egypt is likened to the sting that a gadfly can inflict on a heifer.

5. *Blessing on Jacob*

46:27–28

27"Do not fear, O Jacob my servant;
do not be dismayed, O Israel.
I will surely save you out of a distant place,
your descendants from the land of their exile.

Jacob will again have peace and security,
  and no one will make him afraid.
28Do not fear, O Jacob my servant,
  for I am with you," declares the LORD.
"Though I completely destroy all the nations
  among which I scatter you,
  I will not completely destroy you.
I will discipline you but only with justice;
  I will not let you go entirely unpunished."

27-28 In striking contrast with the vivid portrayal of Egypt's fall and destruction is the salvation here promised the people of Israel in words that would encourage Israel in captivity (cf. 30:10-11). Looking, as they do, beyond the captivity, vv.27-28 are indeed consoling. Notice how much is packed into these two verses. If Egypt's woes were but temporary, those of Israel would be even more so.

B. *Concerning Philistia*

47:1-7

¹This is the word of the LORD that came to Jeremiah the prophet concerning the Philistines before Pharaoh attacked Gaza:

²This is what the LORD says:

"See how the waters are rising in the north;
  they will become an overflowing torrent.
They will overflow the land and everything in it,
  the towns and those who live in them.
The people will cry out;
  all who dwell in the land will wail
³at the sound of the hoofs of galloping steeds,
  at the noise of enemy chariots
  and the rumble of their wheels.
Fathers will not turn to help their children;
  their hands will hang limp.
⁴For the day has come
  to destroy all the Philistines
and to cut off all survivors
  who could help Tyre and Sidon.
The LORD is about to destroy the Philistines,
  the remnant from the coasts of Caphtor.
⁵Gaza will shave her head in mourning;
  Ashkelon will be silenced.
O remnant on the plain,
  how long will you cut yourselves?
⁶" 'Ah, sword of the LORD,' ˌyou cryˌ
  'how long till you rest?
Return to your scabbard;
  cease and be still.'
⁷But how can it rest
  when the LORD has commanded it,
when he has ordered it
  to attack Ashkelon and the seacoast?"

The Philistines settled in the coastal region known as the Philistine plain. Their pentapolis consisted of Ekron, Ashdod, Gaza, Ashkelon, and Gath. The Philistines were greatly reduced in power by the campaigns of David against them, but during the divided kingdom they asserted their independence of Judah. Military actions against them from the Assyrian Age down through the time of Alexander the Great weakened them; finally they were conquered by the Maccabees (second century B.C.) and merged into Israel. (For other prophecies against Philistia, see Isa 14:28–31; Ezek 25:15–17; Amos 1:6–8; and Zeph 2:4–7.)

1 The somewhat indefinite historical reference in v.1 makes it difficult to date this prophecy. One view identifies the Pharaoh as Neco, who conquered Gaza about the time he defeated Josiah at Megiddo (cf. 2 Kings 23:29–30); another view sees the Pharaoh as Neco capturing Gaza on his return from his defeat at Carchemish; still another view identifies the Pharaoh as Hophra, who took Gaza in his campaign against Tyre and Sidon. The historical data are lacking; so it is difficult to make an identification as to the time or the occasion of the attack.

2–3 In a vivid metaphor (v.2), Jeremiah uses a flood to describe the Babylonian threat to Tyre and Sidon. The word "waters" is an OT figure for an army, as in 46:8 (cf. Isa 8:7, where Assyria is compared to the Euphrates). The distress from the invading Babylonians will be so great (v.3) that fathers will leave their children defenseless; limpness of hands indicates the paralyzing effect of fear. "The day" (v.4) is not the Day of the Lord (contra Welch). In her distress, Philistia will find no help in her former allies, Tyre and Sidon. These two cities were flourishing commercial centers on the coast of what is now Lebanon. Jeremiah sees Philistia as the remnant of the ancient Aegean civilization headed by Caphtor (Crete, cf. Amos 9:7; so Frost). Crete was probably the original home of the Philistines before their entrance to Palestine (cf. Deut 2:23).

5–7 Shaving the head (v.5) is a sign of deep mourning (cf. 16:6; 41:5; 48:37). It may also be a metaphor of the city's destruction. Gashing themselves was forbidden to the Jews (Deut 14:1). Herodotus (2.159) states that after the Battle of Megiddo (cf. 2 Kings 23:29), Pharaoh Neco overran Kadytis, usually equated with Gaza (so Cunliffe-Jones et al). Interpreters have found "remnant on the plain" difficult to explain. One view is that it is in apposition with Ashkelon (so Streane). Others (so RSV) prefer the reading of the LXX, "Anakim," a tall nation. Connected with the Philistines (cf. Josh 11:22), the Anakim lived near Hebron in prehistoric times (ZPEB, 1:152–53). The cry in v.6 is the cry of the Philistines—their appeal is for the divine judgments to cease. "The sword of the LORD" must first, however, accomplish its judgment on the seacoast, the Philistine plain, is Jeremiah's answer. Some expositors believe that vv.6–7 were with 48:10 the source of Judas Maccabeus's vision in which Jeremiah gave him a golden sword (cf. 2 Macc 15:15–16; so Cunliffe-Jones).

Notes

4 The mention of Tyre and Sidon indicates that there may have been a pact between Philistia and Phoenicia. Action against the former could presage danger for the latter. The Phoeni-

cian cities rebelled against Babylon in 594 B.C. (cf. 27:3), 587 B.C., and after the destruction of Jerusalem in 586 B.C. (so Bright).

Three suggestions have been advanced for the identification of Caphtor: Cappadocia, Crete, and Cyprus (so Henderson). On the basis of Deut 2:23 and Amos 9:7, Crete would appear to have the advantage (cf. ZPEB, 1:748–49). The lack of more details is indeed tantalizing throughout the passage.

5 The normal rendering of שְׁאֵרִית עִמְקָם (šeʾērît ʿimqām, lit., "remnant of their valley [plain]") seems to convey little meaning. In Ugaritic the root עמק (ʿmq) has the sense of "valley," "plain," as well as "strength," "force" (UT, p. 105, nos. 623–24). "Remainder of their strength" seems to fit the LXX reading עֲנָקִים (ʿanāqîm), Ἐνακίμ (Enakim), a reference to the giants in Canaan before the Israelite conquest (cf. Josh 11:22, where Gaza, Gath, and Ashdod are mentioned). There is insufficient evidence, however, to sustain the LXX reading here (so KD; see Bright also).

C. Concerning Moab (48:1–47)

The Moabites were descendants of Lot (cf. Gen 19:37). They lived east of the Dead Sea and were often in conflict with Israel. Moab joined in the marauding bands Nebuchadnezzar sent against Judah in 602 B.C., after Jehoiakim's revolt (cf. 2 Kings 24:2; Jer 12:7–13). They joined in a plot to revolt against Babylon early in Zedekiah's reign (cf. 27:1–11). (For Moab and Israel, see Gen 19:30–38; Num 22:24; 2 Kings 3:4–27.) The Moabites were conquered by Nebuchadnezzar and disappeared as a nation. (For other prophecies against Moab, see Deut 23:3; Ps 60:8; 83:6–7; 108:9; Isa 15–16; 25:10–12; Jer 9:26; 25:21; 27:3; Ezek 25:8–11; Amos 2:1–3; Zeph 2:8–11.)

There is no way to determine with certainty the date of the prophecy in this chapter. Its historical setting may be the Moabite invasion into Judah during Jehoiakim's reign. This prophecy against Moab is longer than any other prophecy in chapters 46–49. The length may reflect in part the extensive use of geographical names, probably for parallelism and intensity (so Frost). It is the most thorough of all the OT prophecies about Moab. As to its literary values, it has been considered the most polished of Jeremiah's writings (so Cowles).

1. Desolation of the Moabite cities

48:1–10

Concerning Moab:

This is what the LORD Almighty, the God of Israel, says:

"Woe to Nebo, for it will be ruined.
  Kiriathaim will be disgraced and captured;
  the stronghold will be disgraced and shattered.
²Moab will be praised no more;
  in Heshbon men will plot her downfall:
  'Come, let us put an end to that nation.'
You too, O Madmen, will be silenced;
  the sword will pursue you.
³Listen to the cries from Horonaim,
  cries of great havoc and destruction.
⁴Moab will be broken;
  her little ones will cry out.

⁵They go up the way to Luhith,
  weeping bitterly as they go;
on the road down to Horonaim
  anguished cries over the destruction are heard.
⁶Flee! Run for your lives;
  become like a bush in the desert.
⁷Since you trust in your deeds and riches,
  you too will be taken captive,
and Chemosh will go into exile
  together with his priests and officials.
⁸The destroyer will come against every town,
  and not a town will escape.
The valley will be ruined
  and the plateau destroyed,
  because the Lord has spoken.
⁹Put salt on Moab,
  for she will be laid waste,
her towns will become desolate,
  with no one to live in them.

¹⁰"A curse on him who is lax in doing the Lord's work!
  A curse on him who keeps his sword from bloodshed!"

1–2 More than a score of cities are mentioned in this chapter. Some of the names have been taken as common rather than proper nouns. "Nebo" (v.1) is not the mountain (cf. Deut 32:49) but the city of Reuben (cf. Num 32:38). According to the Moabite Stone, it was taken by King Mesha of Moab (c. 895 B.C.). "Kiriathaim" is, according to Eusebius, ten miles west of Medeba (so KD). Misgab may be a common noun meaning "stronghold" (NIV). The towns of Moab will be plundered. So the list continues, often with a play on words in the Hebrew. Moab will have no more basis for boasting (v.2). There is a play on words in "Heshbon" (*ḥešbôn*) and "will plot" (*ḥāšᵉbû*). Originally Moab extended from Heshbon to Bozrah (ZPEB, 1:554; 2:147). Heshbon was a Levitical city (cf. Josh 21:39) and border-town between Reuben and Gad. Here the Babylonians planned their attack on Moab. Once the capital of the Amorite kingdom of Sihon (cf. Num 21:26; Deut 2:24), Heshbon was given to Reuben (cf. Josh 13:17), then passed to the Gadites, becoming a Levitical city (cf. Josh 21:39). It was ten miles east of Jordan, opposite Jericho, almost midway between the Arnon and the Jabbok rivers. Its enemies decided on conquest and destruction. Madmen (*maḏmēn*), a play on words with "will be silenced" (*tiddōmmî*), is not referred to elsewhere; the site is unknown.

3–6 Only destruction is decreed for Horonaim (v.3)—the name is evidently used for the two Beth-horons (cf. 2 Sam 13:34). Some understand Moab in v.4 to refer not to the country generally but to the city of Ar of Moab (cf. Num 21:28; Isa 15:1) in the valley of the Arnon. This is unlikely because Jeremiah could have given the full name. The "little ones" may mean the "abject ones," made so by distress (so Streane), or, less likely, the surrounding cities of Moab (contra KD). Whether ascending or descending, the fugitives will go weeping as they flee from the enemy (v.5). Their condition is likened (v.6) to a desert bush (juniper)—a picture of destruction and forsakenness.

7 Pride was the root of Moab's trouble. Her idolatry was centered in the worship of Chemosh, a name occurring several times on the Moabite Stone (so Hyatt). Che-

657

mosh was the national deity of Moab (cf. Num 21:29; 1 Kings 11:7, 33) and is mentioned in vv.7, 13, and 46 of this chapter. The reference to trust in "deeds and riches" implies that the reason for Moab's fall was her materialism. When Chemosh went into exile, his followers accompanied him. Idols were usually taken captive with their worshipers (43:12; Isa 46:1–2).

8–10 The "valley" (v.8) is the Jordan Valley, which touched Moab on the west. All the Moabite cities will be involved in the doom. The "plateau" is the extensive region where most of the Moabite cities were located. With the towns doomed for destruction, flight would be the only hope for Moab; but she would need wings (v.9, NIV mg.) to escape the sudden onslaught of the enemy. Since the Lord has commissioned Moab's enemies to punish her, they are to be diligent (v.10) in performing their duty. Verse 10 was the favorite of Pope Hildebrand (Gregory VII) (so Cunliffe-Jones).

Notes

3 "Horonaim" appears on the Moabite stone as "Horonen." Its location is unknown.

9 נְצָא תֵצֵא ... צִיץ (ṣîṣ ... nāṣō' tēṣē', "wings ... she will fly away" [NIV mg.]) is a vivid paronomasia with the use of four sibilants. Neither BDB nor KB affirms the meaning "wings" for ṣîṣ, though in later usage this sense is found (so Freedman). This meaning appears in the Aramaic (M. Jastrow, *Dictionary of the Targumim*, 2 vols. [New York: Title, 1943], s.v.). TWOT (2:765) indicates it is a *hapax legomenon* with "meaning dubious."

2. *The proud complacency of Moab*

48:11–19

> 11"Moab has been at rest from youth,
>   like wine left on its dregs,
> not poured from one jar to another—
>   she has not gone into exile.
> So she tastes as she did,
>   and her aroma is unchanged.
> 12But days are coming,"
>   declares the LORD,
> "when I will send men who pour from jars,
>   and they will pour her out;
> they will empty her jars
>   and smash her jugs.
> 13Then Moab will be ashamed of Chemosh,
>   as the house of Israel was ashamed
>   when they trusted in Bethel.
>
> 14"How can you say, 'We are warriors,
>   men valiant in battle'?
> 15Moab will be destroyed and her towns invaded;
>   her finest young men will go down in the slaughter,"
>   declares the King, whose name is the LORD Almighty.
> 16"The fall of Moab is at hand;
>   her calamity will come quickly.

¹⁷Console her, all who live around her,
    all who know her fame;
say, 'How broken is the mighty scepter,
    how broken the glorious staff!'
¹⁸"Come down from your glory
    and sit on the parched ground,
O inhabitants of the Daughter of Dibon,
for he who destroys Moab
    will come up against you
    and ruin your fortified cities.
¹⁹Stand by the road and watch,
    you who live in Aroer.
Ask the man fleeing and the woman escaping,
    ask them, 'What has happened?' "

11–13 Moab had enjoyed a more settled life than Judah, but now she is to know upheaval and disturbances. The Moabites had been made tributary but not exiled. Now their rest would be changed to unrest. Moab had experienced a certain insulation from judgment. She had not undergone frequent invasions and deportations. As in the figure of "wine" (v.11), her flavor had continued unchanged. No longer will Moab rest quietly. Unlike an earthenware jar that is carefully tilted so as not to lose the sediment of the wine, Moab will be roughly dealt with ("pour her out") and emptied like jars and smashed like jugs (v.12). Moab's hope will be unrealized; Chemosh will be powerless to aid her (v.13). The confidence of Israel (the northern kingdom) in the Bethel sanctuary, where the bull was worshiped, was in vain. In the hour of trial, the bull did not protect the Israelites from Shalmaneser and deportation. The worship set up by Jeroboam at Bethel was a religious calamity to Israel (cf. 1 Kings 12:26–33). Whether in Moab or Israel, God is interested only in genuine faith in him.

14–17 Moreover, Moab will no longer boast of her valor (v.14). When the enemy forces march on her cities, slaughter will abound. "The LORD Almighty" vouches for the prediction (v.15); in spite of what the Moabites think, the Lord is still their Lord also, not Chemosh. And the hour of reckoning is not far off (v.16; cf. for the language, Deut 32:35). The blow will be so great that the neighboring lands will sympathize with the Moabites and mourn with them (v.17). The emblems of their rule and authority, "the scepter" and "the glorious staff," will be broken, showing that their power and national glory will pass.

18–19 Dibon (v.18) stood on two hills; so her people are commanded to come down and sit on the ground. They are about to be deported, but in their hunger and thirst they must await the pleasure of the enemy (v.19) (so Streane). Dibon is thirteen miles east of the Dead Sea near the Arnon River. The Moabite Stone (Mesha Stone) was found here in 1868. Aroer is the southernmost city of Reuben on the northern side of the Arnon River.

3. *The downfall of Moab*

    48:20–28

²⁰"Moab is disgraced for she is shattered.
    Wail and cry out!

Announce by the Arnon
    that Moab is destroyed.
21Judgment has come to the plateau—
    to Holon, Jahzah and Mephaath,
22 to Dibon, Nebo and Beth Diblathaim,
23 to Kiriathaim, Beth Gamul and Beth Meon,
24 to Kerioth and Bozrah—
    to all the towns of Moab, far and near.
25Moab's horn is cut off;
    her arm is broken,"

                        declares the LORD.

26"Make her drunk,
    for she has defied the LORD.
Let Moab wallow in her vomit;
    let her be an object of ridicule.
27Was not Israel the object of your ridicule?
    Was she caught among thieves,
that you shake your head in scorn
    whenever you speak of her?
28Abandon your towns and dwell among the rocks,
    you who live in Moab.
Be like a dove that makes its nest
    at the mouth of a cave."

20–28 If anyone in Aroer should ask why the fugitives were streaming from Moab (cf. v.19), the answer would be that the land of Moab was devastated (v.20). So Jeremiah issues the call to proclaim by the River Arnon the destruction of Moab. The Arnon is the perennial stream that flows into the Dead Sea. Thus the news that the Babylonians have utterly destroyed Moab will reach its very border. The towns involved in the destruction are named to show its extent (vv.21–24). In Joshua's time they were in the portion allotted to the Reubenites and later reconquered by the Moabites. Almost all of them except Holon appear in the Pentateuch and in Joshua. These towns are listed from north to south. According to modern scholars, most of the places are unknown (so Frost). The Bozrah of v.24 is not that of Isaiah 63:1, which belonged to Edom. The "horn" (v.25) (i.e., an animal horn) and the arm (i.e., a human one) are metaphors of strength and military power, which Moab will lose totally. The main reason for her fall was the sin of pride. Judgment will come on the Moabites because of their derisive, arrogant treatment of the Lord's people (v.27). Drunkenness from the wrath of God (v.26) is the same metaphor that appears in 25:27–29. Moab treated Israel with the contempt shown a thief caught in the act. So the Moabites are exhorted to leave their settlements (v.28) and live precariously.

4. The pride of Moab

    48:29–39

29"We have heard of Moab's pride—
    her overweening pride and conceit,
her pride and arrogance
    and the haughtiness of her heart.
30I know her insolence but it is futile,"

                        declares the LORD,

"and her boasts accomplish nothing.
31Therefore I wail over Moab,

for all Moab I cry out,
I moan for the men of Kir Hareseth.
32I weep for you, as Jazer weeps,
O vines of Sibmah.
Your branches spread as far as the sea;
they reached as far as the sea of Jazer.
The destroyer has fallen
on your ripened fruit and grapes.
33Joy and gladness are gone
from the orchards and fields of Moab.
I have stopped the flow of wine from the presses;
no one treads them with shouts of joy.
Although there are shouts,
they are not shouts of joy.

34"The sound of their cry rises
from Heshbon to Elealeh and Jahaz,
from Zoar as far as Horonaim and Eglath Shelishiyah,
for even the waters of Nimrim are dried up.
35In Moab I will put an end
to those who make offerings on the high places
and burn incense to their gods,"

declares the LORD.

36"So my heart laments for Moab like a flute;
it laments like a flute for the men of Kir Hareseth.
The wealth they acquired is gone.
37Every head is shaved
and every beard cut off;
every hand is cut
and every waist is covered with sackcloth.
38On all the housetops in Moab
and in the public squares
there is nothing but mourning,
for I have broken Moab
like a jar that no one wants,"

declares the LORD.

39"How shattered she is! How they wail!
How Moab turns her back in shame!
Moab has become an object of ridicule,
an object of horror to all those around her."

29–35 Jeremiah has already referred to Moab's pride (cf. comments on vv.7, 11), but not in the strong terms of v.29, where it is mentioned six times. The Hebrew is alliterative. Those who have heard of the sin are Jeremiah and his countrymen (cf. Isa 16:6). (In the remainder of this chapter, there are numerous affinities with Isa 15–16; see Notes.) With pride always go boastings, but they are futile (v.30). Because of the impending judgment, the Lord through his prophet expresses his compassion and sorrow for his creatures, the Moabites. "Kir Hareseth" (v.31) was the chief fortified city of Moab (cf. Isa 16:7, 11). Moab's ruin is likened to that of a vineyard because Moab was noted for its vineyards, which will be destroyed (v.32). The joy usually accompanying the vintage (v.33) will now be replaced by lamentations. The bitter cry of mourning will be carried from one place to another so as to cover the whole land (v.34). The places mentioned are in the north and south borders of Moab. Furthermore, God will cut off all the idolatrous worship of the Moabites (v.35).

36–39 In v.36 Jeremiah saw that he will lament for Moab the way her people do. Flutes were used at funerals; so they denote mourning. The usual signs of mourning —shaved heads and beards, lacerated hands, sackcloth—will be visible (v.37). Moab is no longer a useful vessel (v.38) but a shattered one (v.39). She will be a sad spectacle to all: mourning, shame, ridicule, and terror will mark her.

Notes ·

29–30 It has been suggested (so Cheyne, Freedman) that Isaiah (16:6) and Jeremiah (here) were quoting freely a proverb concerning Moab's well-known pride (cf. Isa 25:11; Zeph 2:8–10).

There are numerous parallel verses between Jeremiah and Isaiah, and this fact supports the early-date view of Isaiah.

Isaiah	Jeremiah
15:2	48:1
15:2–3	48:37
15:3	48:38
15:4	48:21, 5
15:4–6	48:5, 34
15:5	48:3
15:5; 16:7, 11	48:31
15:7	48:36
16:2	48:9
16:6	48:29
16:8–9	48:32
16:10	48:33
16:11	48:36
16:12	48:35

31–32 Jeremiah's lamentation—"I wail . . . cry out . . . moan . . . weep"—shows that prophetic denunciations were never heartless nor vindictive; because all men are creatures of God, it is with brokenheartedness that he must judge them and their sins (cf. Lam 3:33). If this truth be overlooked, there is no redeeming value to a study of the menacing predictions of the prophets or even of the Lord Jesus Christ (cf. Matt 23).

5. *The terror caused by the invader*

48:40–47

⁴⁰This is what the LORD says:

> "Look! An eagle is swooping down,
>   spreading its wings over Moab.
> ⁴¹The cities will be captured
>   and the strongholds taken.
> In that day the hearts of Moab's warriors
>   will be like the heart of a woman in labor.
> ⁴²Moab will be destroyed as a nation
>   because she defied the LORD.
> ⁴³Terror and pit and snare await you,
>   O people of Moab,"

declares the LORD.

44"Whoever flees from the terror
   will fall into a pit,
whoever climbs out of the pit
   will be caught in a snare;
for I will bring upon Moab
   the year of her punishment,"

                                      declares the LORD.

45"In the shadow of Heshbon
   the fugitives stand helpless,
for a fire has gone out from Heshbon,
   a blaze from the midst of Sihon;
it burns the foreheads of Moab,
   the skulls of the noisy boasters.
46Woe to you, O Moab!
   The people of Chemosh are destroyed;
your sons are taken into exile
   and your daughters into captivity.

47"Yet I will restore the fortunes of Moab
   in days to come,"

                                      declares the LORD.

Here ends the judgment on Moab.

40–47 Finally, Jeremiah proclaims that God's judgment still hangs over Moab. He likens the swiftness of the enemy's approach (v.40) to the flight of an eagle (vulture) —viz., Nebuchadnezzar (cf. 49:22; Ezek 17:3). The "cities" (v.41) is literally "kerioth" (*qᵉrîyôt*) in the Hebrew (cf. Amos 2:2). The strongest in Moab will be utterly helpless. The cause of her fall was her defiant pride toward God (v.42). Verse 43 contains a good example of triple assonance, which may be translated "terror and trapfall and trap" (so Bright; cf. Isa 24:17–18). For Moab there will be no escape from the calamity; it is everywhere (v.44; cf. Amos 5:19). Even fleeing for refuge to Heshbon will not avert the destruction (v.45). Balaam's prediction will be fulfilled (cf. Num 21:28; 24:17). Even the name Moab appears to have been submerged after her exile (v.46) by that of the Arabians. But God's pity knows no end. Wrath is always his strange work in which he does not delight. The Moabites will not utterly perish (cf. 46:26; 49:6, 39); they too will have a remnant. So the restoration of Moab is predicted (v.47), but without details. "Days to come" definitely refers to messianic times (so Freedman, Harrison, KD).

Notes

42 After the Moabites were exiled, they disappeared as a people, having been absorbed by neighboring nations. But see v.47 and the time indicated there.

43 פַּחַד וָפַחַת וָפָח (*paḥad wāpaḥat wāpāḥ,* "terror and pit and snare") has an unusual and striking triple assonance in the first two consonants, employing at the same time three initial explosive consonants. The device had already been employed by the master stylist Isaiah (cf. Isa 24:17–18).

Chapter 49 deals with prophecies against five (or six) nations. All had incurred God's wrath for their idolatry and for their treatment of Israel.

D. *Concerning Ammon*

49:1–6

¹Concerning the Ammonites:

This is what the LORD says:

"Has Israel no sons?
   Has she no heirs?
Why then has Molech taken possession of Gad?
   Why do his people live in its towns?
²But the days are coming,"
   declares the LORD,
"when I will sound the battle cry
   against Rabbah of the Ammonites;
it will become a mound of ruins,
   and its surrounding villages will be set on fire.
Then Israel will drive out
   those who drove her out,"

says the LORD.

³"Wail, O Heshbon, for Ai is destroyed!
   Cry out, O inhabitants of Rabbah!
Put on sackcloth and mourn;
   rush here and there inside the walls,
for Molech will go into exile,
   together with his priests and officials.
⁴Why do you boast of your valleys,
   boast of your valleys so fruitful?
O unfaithful daughter,
   you trust in your riches and say,
   'Who will attack me?'
⁵I will bring terror on you
   from all those around you,"

declares the Lord, the LORD Almighty.

"Every one of you will be driven away,
   and no one will gather the fugitives.

⁶"Yet afterward, I will restore the fortunes of the
      Ammonites,"

declares the LORD.

The Ammonites were descended from Ben-Ammi, son of Lot (cf. Gen 19:38). Their territory was north of Moab. A more migratory people than the Moabites, it seems that the Ammonites originally occupied the land in which the tribe of Gad was settled after the fall of Sihon, who had probably captured it from Ammon (so Streane). Their important city was Rabbah. The conquest of the Transjordanian tribes by Tiglath-Pileser III of Assyria in 733 B.C. (cf. 2 Kings 15:29) led the Ammonites to encroach on Gad's territory (so Cundall), which was east of the Jordan from Heshbon to the Jabbok (cf. Num 32:34–36; Josh 13:24–28), and settle between the Arnon and Jabbok rivers toward the desert.

The Ammonites were often in conflict with Israel; they opposed Judah during Jehoiakim's reign (cf. 2 Kings 24:2) and helped the downfall of the remnant after the Fall of Jerusalem (cf. 40:11–14). They joined in the invasion of Judah in 602 B.C. (cf.

2 Kings 24:2) and were among the conspirators against Babylon (cf. 27:3). They were condemned because they confiscated land from Gad during the Assyrian invasion in 733–732 B.C. The destroyer of Ammon, though not named, was probably Nebuchadnezzar. (For other prophecies about Ammon, see Ezek 21:20, 28–32; 25:1–7; Amos 1:13–15; Zeph 2:8–11.)

1–3 These rhetorical questions connote reproach. Jeremiah asks whether the tribe of Gad had no heirs (v.1) since the god of the Ammonites was inheriting their land and his people were living in Gad's cities. Although the northern tribes had been carried away by Tiglath-Pileser III, their land still belonged to them and was to be inherited by their sons. "Molech" (*malkām*, "their king") was the national god of Ammon (cf. 1 Kings 11:5, 7, 33). War and destruction will overtake Rabbah (v.2), the chief city of the Ammonites, now Amman, the capital of the Hashemite Kingdom of Jordan. Her nearby villages will be engulfed in the catastrophe. Jeremiah names (v.3) two of the more prominent Ammonite towns that the Babylonians will devastate. Five or six miles from the Ammonite border, Heshbon was under the Amorite king Sihon (cf. Num 21:25–30, 34). Later it came under Moabite control (so WBC). Ai is not the Ai captured by Joshua (cf. Josh 8:1–29) but the Ammonite Ai mentioned only here.

4–6 Living in an inaccessible country with mountains on three sides, Ammon considered herself beyond invasion. She was proud of her valleys made fertile by the Arnon waters (v.4). The rendering "flowing valley" (lit. Heb.; NIV, "valleys so fruitful") is problematic (see Notes). Everyone will flee precipitately by the shortest route with no one to rally the fugitives (v.5). Josephus (Antiq. X, 181 [ix.7]) says that Nebuchadnezzar defeated Ammon in the fifth year after the destruction of Jerusalem. The Ammonites opposed Israel even after the Exile (cf. Neh 4:1–15) and in the Maccabean era (cf. 1 Macc 5:6, 30–43; so KD). As with Moab (cf. 48:47), the Lord graciously promises restoration (v.6).

Notes

1 Molech, Malcam, and Milcom all derive from מֶלֶךְ (*melek*), the word for "king." Whereas the Hebrew has מַלְכָּם (*malkām*, "Malcam," lit., "their king"), LXX, Syriac, and Vulgate all render "Milcom." The change is only one of pointing. On the basis of 1 Kings 11:7, most scholars identify Milcom with Molech (ZPEB, 4:225). Verse 3 appears to place it beyond doubt.

3 In הִתְשׁוֹטַטְנָה (*hitšôṭaṭnāh*, "rush here and there") the normal transposition expected in the intensive stems of the ת (*t*) and the שׁ (*š*) is absent. Hitzig is doubtless correct in explaining the deviation to the force of the reduplication of the ט (*ṭ*), which necessitated, for the sake of euphony, that the *ṭ* be placed farther back, i.e., in the usual position for the Hithpolel (and, of course, the Hithpael). The reference of הִשָּׁרַטְנָה (*hiśśāraṭnāh*, "tear," "cut") in KB (p. 955) is not parallel.

4 זָב עִמְקֵךְ (*zāḇ ʿimqēk*, "flowing valley"; NIV, "valleys so fruitful") may mean either flowing with abundance or losing its inhabitants; but neither is very happy. If the word עֵמֶק (*ʿēmeq*, "valley") is taken as "strength," "might" (as in Ugaritic), then a strong and meaningful translation results: "Why boast of your strength, your ebbing strength?" (so Bright after Dahood).

E. *Concerning Edom*

49:7–22

⁷Concerning Edom:

This is what the LORD Almighty says:

> "Is there no longer wisdom in Teman?
>   Has counsel perished from the prudent?
>   Has their wisdom decayed?
> ⁸Turn and flee, hide in deep caves,
>   you who live in Dedan,
> for I will bring disaster on Esau
>   at the time I punish him.
> ⁹If grape pickers came to you,
>   would they not leave a few grapes?
> If thieves came during the night,
>   would they not steal only as much as they wanted?
> ¹⁰But I will strip Esau bare;
>   I will uncover his hiding places,
>   so that he cannot conceal himself.
> His children, relatives and neighbors will perish,
>   and he will be no more.
> ¹¹Leave your orphans; I will protect their lives.
>   Your widows too can trust in me."

¹²This is what the LORD says: "If those who do not deserve to drink the cup must drink it, why should you go unpunished? You will not go unpunished, but must drink it. ¹³I swear by myself," declares the LORD, "that Bozrah will become a ruin and an object of horror, of reproach and of cursing; and all its towns will be in ruins forever."

> ¹⁴I have heard a message from the LORD:
>   An envoy was sent to the nations to say,
>   "Assemble yourselves to attack it!
>   Rise up for battle!"
>
> ¹⁵"Now I will make you small among the nations,
>   despised among men.
> ¹⁶The terror you inspire
>   and the pride of your heart have deceived you,
> you who live in the clefts of the rocks,
>   who occupy the heights of the hill.
> Though you build your nest as high as the eagle's,
>   from there I will bring you down,"
>
> declares the LORD.
>
> ¹⁷"Edom will become an object of horror;
>   all who pass by will be appalled and will scoff
>   because of all its wounds.
> ¹⁸As Sodom and Gomorrah were overthrown,
>   along with their neighboring towns,"
>
> says the LORD,
>
> "so no one will live there;
>   no man will dwell in it.
> ¹⁹"Like a lion coming up from Jordan's thickets
>   to a rich pastureland,
> I will chase Edom from its land in an instant.
>   Who is the chosen one I will appoint for this?
> Who is like me and who can challenge me?
>   And what shepherd can stand against me?"

> ²⁰Therefore, hear what the Lord has planned against Edom,
>   what he has purposed against those who live in Teman:
> The young of the flock will be dragged away;
>   he will completely destroy their pasture because of them.
> ²¹At the sound of their fall the earth will tremble;
>   their cry will resound to the Red Sea.
> ²²Look! An eagle will soar and swoop down,
>   spreading its wings over Bozrah.
> In that day the hearts of Edom's warriors
>   will be like the heart of a woman in labor.

This prophecy is closely related to that of Obadiah, which was written after 587–586 B.C. (so Hyatt et al.). (It is only fair to say that some cogent arguments are given for an early date [estimates of scholars vary over a period of half a millennium] of the Book of Obadiah, so KD and F.E. Gaebelein.) The Edomites, whose relations with Israel were always poor, were descendants of Esau (cf. Gen 36:1–19) who lived in the mountainous region south of the Dead Sea toward the Gulf of Aqabah, until the Nabateans displaced them. Later on the Maccabees forced them to become Jews. (For prophecies about Edom, see Ezek 25:12–14; 35:1–15; Joel 3:19; Amos 9:12; Obad 1–16; and incidentally Isa 21:11–12 with 34:5–7 and 63:1–6.) The severity in all the prophecies about Edom reflects the close and stormy relationship between Esau (progenitor of the Edomites) and his twin, Jacob (progenitor of Israel). Edom's cardinal sin was its pride manifested in its unrelenting and violent hatred of Israel and its rejoicing in her misfortunes (Obad 3, 10–14). There is no prophecy of future restoration for Edom.

7–12 Teman (v.7) was in northern Edom, the home of Eliphaz (Job 2:11), and was renowned for wisdom (Ezek 25:13). The rhetorical questions (v.9) show how suddenly calamity overwhelmed the wisest in Edom. Could they not see that destruction was imminent? Dedan (v.8), a tribe living south of Edom, was known for its commerce (25:23; Ezek 25:13). The people of Dedan are warned to flee from their usual contacts with Edom, lest they be overtaken in its destruction. Contrary to the practice of grape gatherers (v.9), who left something for the poor, the enemies of Edom will leave nothing but will plunder everything (v.10). The compassionate tone of v.11, though surprising in view of the severity of the prophecy against Edom, is in keeping with the Lord's character. The sense of v.11 is that when the men of Edom have been slain in war, their widows and orphans may look to the Lord for protection. But the nation will have to drink the cup of God's wrath (v.12; cf. 25:28). If Israel had to drink of this cup, how could Edom escape? Because of the Edomites' complicity in Jerusalem's fall, they were especially guilty (cf. Obad 10–14).

13–22 Here the desolation of Edom is underscored. Bozrah (vv.13, 22) is referred to because it was the capital of Edom in Jeremiah's time. It was midway between Petra and the Dead Sea, and here it represents all the Edomite cities (cf. Isa 63:1). It is the modern el-Buseirah. The completeness of Edom's overthrow is left beyond doubt (v.15). The cause of Edom's downfall was her inveterate pride (v.16; cf. 48:7, 29; 49:4; Obad 3, 10–14). Jeremiah's message from the Lord (v.14) is that the nations have been summoned to war against Edom. Because of her fortifications and topography, Edom had convinced herself that she was impregnable. The "rock" (*sela'*;

NIV, "rocks" [v.16]) referred to was later called Sela (*Petra*, Gr.)—the capital city and chief fortress of the Edomites. The ruin of Edom will be irreversible (v.17), like that of Sodom and Gomorrah and their neighboring cities Admah and Zeboiim (v.18; cf. Gen 14:2, 8). Edom's foe will pounce like a lion scattering a flock (v.19). (Verses 19–21 are repeated in 50:44–46 where they refer to Babylon.) Dispersion, destruction, and devastation will be the lot of Edom. Its doom shows how fearful a thing it is to fall into the hands of the living God (Heb 10:31).

Notes

8 Dedan has been placed southeast of Edom in the Hejaz, probably the El-ʿulä oasis with the surrounding area (so Bright, with reference to W.F. Albright).

16 תִּפְלֶצֶת (*tipleṣet*, "terror") is a *hapax legomenon;* however, the verb root פָּלַץ (*pālaṣ*, "shudder") is found along with two derivatives besides the one under consideration here. Because מִפְלֶצֶת (*mipleṣet*, "repulsive") in 1 Kings 15:13 has reference to a horrible idol is an insufficient basis to believe that the name of the god has dropped out here (contra Bright; cf. TWOT, 2:726).

20 Here and in v.30 Jeremiah uses עֵצָה (*ʿēṣāh*) as parallel to מַחֲשָׁבָה (*maḥªšābāh*) for the "plan" and "purpose" of God in relation to the nations on whom he must pour out judgment. The plan and purpose here must not be confused with the overall program indicated in Eph 3:11. It is more limited than that because God is acting righteously as the Governor of the universe in calling to account particular nations for their moral failures.

F. Concerning Damascus

49:23–27

23Concerning Damascus:

> "Hamath and Arpad are dismayed,
>   for they have heard bad news.
> They are disheartened,
>   troubled like the restless sea.
> 24Damascus has become feeble,
>   she has turned to flee
>   and panic has gripped her;
> anguish and pain have seized her,
>   pain like that of a woman in labor.
> 25Why has the city of renown not been abandoned,
>   the town in which I delight?
> 26Surely, her young men will fall in the streets;
>   all her soldiers will be silenced in that day,"
>   declares the LORD Almighty.
> 27"I will set fire to the walls of Damascus;
>   it will consume the fortresses of Ben-Hadad."

23–27 Expositors have difficulty fitting this prophecy into any recorded event relating to Damascus. The important cities in Syria were Hamath, Zobah, and Damascus, the last being the seat of a powerful dynasty. Hamath and Arpad (v.23) had their own local kings and gods (cf. Sennacherib's boast [2 Kings 18:34; 19:13]). Word of the enemies' approach terrifies one city after another.

Hamath on the Orontes (modern Hama) is about 110 miles north of Damascus, and Arpad is about 95 miles north of Hamath. Damascus was in southern Syria. All three Syrian cities had been conquered by Assyria (Isa 10:9). Damascus was also defeated by Nebuchadnezzar in 605 B.C. (so Welch). The reference to the "sea" (v.23) must be figurative, because Syria had no seacoast in ancient times. Suggestions as to the meaning are "restlessness" (so WBC) or "trouble" (so Freedman). Damascus (v.24) was famous in antiquity because of its location in a large oasis and because of its commerce (cf. Ezek 27:18). It should have been abandoned before its conquest (v.25). The young men (v.26), soldiers, the walls (v.27), and fortresses of the city are all to be destroyed. Fire will ruin its walls and defenses. Ben-Hadad was the name of a dynasty that ruled Damascus in the ninth and eighth centuries B.C. as well as the name of individual kings (cf. 1 Kings 15:18, 20; 2 Kings 13:24). In conquering Damascus, Nebuchadnezzar vindicated Babylon's surge toward the west.

Notes

23 Hamath, the city on the Orontes River, appears in Amos 6:2 as Hamath Rabbah (Heb.; NIV, "great Hamath"). An important city, it is found frequently in the inscriptions. In the Greek period it was called Epiphania (now Hama) and was the limit to which Israelite rule reached (cf. 1 Kings 8:65; 2 Kings 14:25; Zech 9:2).

נָמֹגוּ בַיָּם דְּאָגָה (*nāmōgû bayyām deʾāgāh*, "troubled like the restless sea") is literally "They melt. In the sea is anxiety; it cannot be still." The passage is admittedly difficult. Volz (*Jeremiah*) proposed a conjectural reading: נָמֹג לִבָּם מִדְּאָגָה (*nāmōg libbām middeʾāg-āh*, "Their heart dissolves with worry; it cannot be still"). Although the reading does make sense and calls for minimal consonantal change, it must be considered only a possibility.

G. *Concerning Kedar and Hazor*

49:28–33

[28]Concerning Kedar and the kingdoms of Hazor, which Nebuchadnezzar king of Babylon attacked:

This is what the LORD says:

"Arise, and attack Kedar
  and destroy the people of the East.
[29]Their tents and their flocks will be taken;
  their shelters will be carried off
  with all their goods and camels.
Men will shout to them,
  'Terror on every side!'

[30]"Flee quickly away!
  Stay in deep caves, you who live in Hazor,"

declares the LORD.

"Nebuchadnezzar king of Babylon has plotted against you;
  he has devised a plan against you.

> 31"Arise and attack a nation at ease,
>   which lives in confidence,"
>
>   declares the LORD,
>
> "a nation that has neither gates nor bars;
>   its people live alone.
> 32Their camels will become plunder,
>   and their large herds will be booty.
> I will scatter to the winds those who are in distant places
>   and will bring disaster on them from every side,"
>   declares the LORD.
> 33"Hazor will become a haunt of jackals,
>   a desolate place forever.
> No one will live there;
>   no man will dwell in it."

28–33 Nebuchadnezzar also moved against some of the eastern tribes. Their secluded position in the Arabian desert will insure them no safety (v.31). They too will feel the might of Babylon. Kedar (v.28) was an Ishmaelite desert tribe (cf. Gen 25:13; Isa 21:13, 16; Ezek 27:21). Although these nomads, who were rich in livestock (vv.29, 32), were good at archery (Isa 21:16–17), Nebuchadnezzar conquered them. Hazor (v.30) is not the fortress Hazor in northern Palestine (cf. Josh 11:1–13) because this Hazor was in a desert region. No other reference to it is found in the Bible. Some expositors believe it was an Arab settlement in the south of Palestine (so Cowles); others take it as a collective name for villages in which half-nomadic Arabs lived (cf. Isa 42:11). The kingdoms of Hazor may have included Kedar and those named in 25:23 (so Hyatt). Little is known of the early history of the Arabs. Josephus (*Contra Apion* I, 133 [19]) quotes Berossus in reference to a conquest of Arabia by Nebuchadnezzar. Kedar (cf. 2:10) is mentioned often in Assyrian inscriptions (so Myers). Terror and destruction will strike the people of Hazor and Kedar as it has other people (cf. 6:25; 20:4; 46:5). The Lord calls the Babylonian forces to attack Hazor (v.31). Behind judgment scenes the Lord is at work carrying out his plan. As did so many others, Kedar and Hazor lived in careless self-complacency.

H. *Concerning Elam*

49:34–39

34This is the word of the LORD that came to Jeremiah the prophet concerning Elam, early in the reign of Zedekiah king of Judah:

35This is what the LORD Almighty says:

> "See, I will break the bow of Elam,
>   the mainstay of their might.
> 36I will bring against Elam the four winds
>   from the four quarters of the heavens;
> I will scatter them to the four winds,
>   and there will not be a nation
>   where Elam's exiles do not go.
> 37I will shatter Elam before their foes,
>   before those who seek their lives;
> I will bring disaster upon them,
>   even my fierce anger,"
>
>   declares the LORD.
>
> "I will pursue them with the sword
>   until I have made an end of them.

38I will set my throne in Elam
and destroy her king and officials,"

declares the LORD.

39"Yet I will restore the fortunes of Elam
in days to come,"

declares the LORD.

34-39 This prophecy dates from the beginning of Zedekiah's reign (v.34)—i.e., 598 B.C. Elam was an ancient kingdom (cf. Gen 14:1), two hundred miles east of Babylon and west of the Tigris River. Elam had been an important power but was conquered about 640 B.C., in the time of Ashurbanipal of Assyria (so Hyatt). Later it was united with Media, then Persia. Its capital, Susa, was the residence of Darius Hystaspes (so Myers) and became the nucleus of the Persian Empire (Neh 1:1; Dan 8:2). The purpose of this prophecy may have been to show that Elam would not and could not curb the Babylonian power. The reference to breaking the bow (v.35) is a pointed one because the Elamites were famous for their skill in archery (Isa 22:6); the bow was their main weapon. Nevertheless, invaders will overwhelm them from every direction (v.36). When compared with other prophecies of Jeremiah against foreign nations, this one against Elam does not mention Nebuchadnezzar but refers only to enemies in general (v.37). Verse 38 indicates that the Lord himself will sit in judgment on Elam (cf. 1:15). "In days to come" Elam is to be restored (v.39). Some have seen the fulfillment of this prophecy when Elam, with Susa as her capital, became the center of the Persian Empire. But the phrase "in days to come" shows the eschatological dimension of the prophecy.

Notes

34-36 Elam, the Elymais of the Greeks and Romans, part of ancient Susiana west of Persia, is used in Scripture of the country in general. It is about coextensive with the modern Iranian province of Khuzistan. The Assyrians and Babylonians referred to it as Elamtu (ZPEB, 2:262-64). The rabbis, who identified Elam with Persia, considered the fulfillment of the prophecy to be in the time of Haman (so Freedman). This is too restrictive an interpretation in view of the general terms used.

I. *Concerning Babylon* (50:1–51:64)

The prophecy against Babylon (chs. 50–51) is by far the longest of those against foreign nations. Some scholars (S.R. Driver, Eichhorn, Ewald, Frost, Hyatt et al.) have denied Jeremiah's authorship of these chapters on several grounds.

1. Elsewhere Jeremiah speaks well of Babylon and tells the captives to pray for her welfare; here he foretells her overthrow in drastic language.

2. The style of chapters 50–51 differs from that of Jeremiah.

3. These chapters reveal a greater knowledge of Babylon than Jeremiah could have had.

All these arguments against Jeremiah's authorship are, however, vulnerable on the following grounds.

1. To deny the prophet's authorship of these chapters is to misunderstand the very heart of his ministry. He was the Lord's messenger. When he urged Judah to submit to Nebuchadnezzar (cf. 27:6) and foretold the fall of Babylon for her pride and cruelty, he was speaking for the Lord just as much as when he declared Babylon to be the agent for executing God's judgment on Judah. Moreover, he had already spoken of the Lord's future dealings with Babylon in 25:12, 26.

2. The style in chapters 50–51 does resemble that of Jeremiah in other parts of the book; changes in style (and to some extent all writers vary their style) reflect changes in subject matter.

3. Jeremiah's knowledge of Babylon was what would be expected of a man who had personal contact with Babylonians and with those in high office in Judah.

4. The final prophecy against Babylon comes as the logical conclusion to the other prophecies against foreign nations. In these prophecies Jeremiah moved from the nations on the border of Judah and Israel, to the more remote nations, and then to the one under which the Jewish commonwealth fell in 586 B.C. (so Streane).

The chapters at hand emphatically stress the truth of Matthew 25:31–46: The criterion by which God judges the nations is their treatment of his chosen people whom he has made the vehicle of salvation (cf. John 4:22) and placed at the center of the consummation of human history (cf. Isa 2:1–4).

The only clue to the date of chapters 50–51 is 51:59–60, which mentions the fourth year of Zedekiah—i.e., 594–593 B.C. Two main emphases run throughout these chapters: the fall of Babylon and the return of the Jewish exiles to their home. This does not mean that Jeremiah was pro-Babylon or pro-Judah. He declared that Judah must be punished for her sins, and Babylon was God's agent for it. Then Babylon was to be judged for her own sins (cf. Isa 10:5–19, with reference to Assyria, and Hab 2:1–20, with reference to Babylon).

It has troubled some scholars that chapters 50–51 predict the violent destruction of Babylon, whereas its defeat by Cyrus in 539 B.C. took place without a battle and with no damage to the city. But with other predictive prophecies, if a fulfillment does not occur in one period, it is to be sought for in another and future one.

1. *Babylon's doom announced*

50:1–10

¹This is the word the LORD spoke through Jeremiah the prophet concerning Babylon and the land of the Babylonians:

> ²"Announce and proclaim among the nations,
>   lift up a banner and proclaim it;
>   keep nothing back, but say,
> 'Babylon will be captured;
>   Bel will be put to shame,
>   Marduk filled with terror.
> Her images will be put to shame
>   and her idols filled with terror.'
> ³A nation from the north will attack her
>   and lay waste her land.
> No one will live in it;
>   both men and animals will flee away.
> ⁴"In those days, at that time,"
>   declares the LORD,

"the people of Israel and the people of Judah together
  will go in tears to seek the LORD their God.
⁵They will ask the way to Zion
  and turn their faces toward it.
They will come and bind themselves to the LORD
  in an everlasting covenant
  that will not be forgotten.

⁶"My people have been lost sheep;
  their shepherds have led them astray
  and caused them to roam on the mountains.
They wandered over mountain and hill
  and forgot their own resting place.
⁷Whoever found them devoured them;
  their enemies said, 'We are not guilty,
for they sinned against the LORD, their true pasture,
  the LORD, the hope of their fathers.'

⁸"Flee out of Babylon;
  leave the land of the Babylonians,
  and be like the goats that lead the flock.
⁹For I will stir up and bring against Babylon
  an alliance of great nations from the land of the north.
They will take up their positions against her,
  and from the north she will be captured.
Their arrows will be like skilled warriors
  who do not return empty-handed.
¹⁰So Babylonia will be plundered;
  all who plunder her will have their fill,"

declares the LORD.

1–10 Since these two chapters so clearly dwell on one subject, detailed analysis of them is not necessary. Verses on common themes will be treated as units. The references to Babylon are not, as a rule, to the city but to the nation (v.1).

First of all, the idols of Babylon are discredited. Bel and Merodach (Marduk) are alternate names for the same great Babylonian deity. Jeremiah sees the future doom as already completed. The idols are contemptuously referred to (v.2) as "dung pellets" (NIV, "her idols"; see Notes).

"A nation from the north" (i.e., the Medes and Persians) will execute judgment on Babylon (vv.3, 9). The Lord exhorts his people to flee from Babylon (v.8) because of the impending invasion. Scattered (vv.6–7) and penitent Israel is given a chance to escape. Flight alone will enable her to escape Babylon's doom. The reunited nation (vv.4–5) will return to Jerusalem to join herself to the Lord, never to forget the eternal covenant.

Notes

---

2 Bel is related to the West Semitic Baal (lit., "lord," "possessor"). Enlil was the Sumerian counterpart of Bel among the pre-Semitic Sumerians. When Babylon rose to power, its chief deity, Marduk (pointed Merodach in OT), was invested with the characteristics of Enlil and accorded the title of Bel, which in time displaced Marduk in common use. Marduk occurs only in 50:2, but Bel appears in 50:2; 51:44; Isa 46:1; and Dan 5:1, 9, 22, 29,

30 (in the Daniel references, it is a constituent part of the name of Belshazzar) (cf. ZPEB, 1:511; 4:72).

גְּלוּלֶיהָ (*gillûleyhā*, "her idols") is not the usual Hebrew term for idols, one of which appears earlier in this verse. *Young's Concordance* lists ten different Hebrew words for idols but even so fails to list the noun under discussion. גִּלּוּל (*gillûl*), used many times in the OT but always in the plural, denotes "logs," "blocks," that is, shapeless things (BDB). Bright translates it "godlets." Ewald, after the rabbis, derisively renders it "dungy things."

5 The pronouncement and elaboration of בְּרִית עוֹלָם (*bᵉrît 'ôlām*, "everlasting covenant") constitutes one of the great contributions of Jeremiah to OT and, indeed, biblical theology (cf. 31:31–33; 32:40; 33:21; and here).

---

2. Babylon's sin and judgment

50:11–16

> ¹¹"Because you rejoice and are glad,
>   you who pillage my inheritance,
> because you frolic like a heifer threshing grain
>   and neigh like stallions,
> ¹²your mother will be greatly ashamed;
>   she who gave you birth will be disgraced.
> She will be the least of the nations—
>   a wilderness, a dry land, a desert.
> ¹³Because of the LORD's anger she will not be inhabited
>   but will be completely desolate.
> All who pass Babylon will be horrified and scoff
>   because of all her wounds.
>
> ¹⁴"Take up your positions around Babylon,
>   all you who draw the bow.
> Shoot at her! Spare no arrows,
>   for she has sinned against the LORD.
> ¹⁵Shout against her on every side!
>   She surrenders, her towers fall,
>   her walls are torn down.
> Since this is the vengeance of the LORD,
>   take vengeance on her;
>   do to her as she has done to others.
> ¹⁶Cut off from Babylon the sower,
>   and the reaper with his sickle at harvest.
> Because of the sword of the oppressor
>   let everyone return to his own people,
>   let everyone flee to his own land."

11–16 Judgment on Babylon will be in retaliation for her treatment of Israel. Babylon herself is addressed (vv.11–12) so that she may realize the issues involved in her visitation. No nation in ancient times influenced the fortunes of Israel in a more devastating way than Babylon did (so Bright). The desolation of Babylon is expressed in numerous ways, which reveal the brilliant literary skill of Jeremiah. Babylon's enemies are summoned to wreak destruction on her (vv.14–16). Babylon was in a fertile agricultural area. With the decline of her political power, the irrigation canals were silted up so that the country became desolate (v.13). Cyrus, who unified the Medo-Persian Empire and then overwhelmed Babylon (ZPEB, 1:1054–56), was careful to spare the country; so the references (v.16) must be to a later attack. Babylon will learn the agony the law of retaliation entails.

3. *Consolation to Israel*

    50:17–20

> ¹⁷"Israel is a scattered flock
>   that lions have chased away.
> The first to devour him
>   was the king of Assyria;
> the last to crush his bones
>   was Nebuchadnezzar king of Babylon."

¹⁸Therefore this is what the LORD Almighty, the God of Israel, says:

> "I will punish the king of Babylon and his land
>   as I punished the king of Assyria.
> ¹⁹But I will bring Israel back to his own pasture
>   and he will graze on Carmel and Bashan;
> his appetite will be satisfied
>   on the hills of Ephraim and Gilead.
> ²⁰In those days, at that time,"
>   declares the LORD,
> "search will be made for Israel's guilt,
>   but there will be none,
> and for the sins of Judah,
>   but none will be found,
> for I will forgive the remnant I spare."

17–20 This short portion summarizes the biblical interpretation of Israel's history. The sufferings of Israel are stated (v.17), then the judgment God will bring on those who inflicted such sufferings on Israel (v.18), next her return to her land in peace and plenty (v.19), and, finally, the greatest blessing of all—the pardon of Israel's iniquity (v.20). All these will be realized in messianic times, as v.20 declares.

4. *God's vengeance on Babylon*

    50:21–28

> ²¹"Attack the land of Merathaim
>   and those who live in Pekod.
> Pursue, kill and completely destroy them,"
>
>   declares the LORD.
>
>   "Do everything I have commanded you.
> ²²The noise of battle is in the land,
>   the noise of great destruction!
> ²³How broken and shattered
>   is the hammer of the whole earth!
> How desolate is Babylon
>   among the nations!
> ²⁴I set a trap for you, O Babylon,
>   and you were caught before you knew it;
> you were found and captured
>   because you opposed the LORD.
> ²⁵The LORD has opened his arsenal
>   and brought out the weapons of his wrath,
> for the Sovereign LORD Almighty has work to do
>   in the land of the Babylonians.
> ²⁶Come against her from afar.
>   Break open her granaries;
>   pile her up like heaps of grain.

Completely destroy her
and leave her no remnant.
²⁷Kill all her young bulls;
let them go down to the slaughter!
Woe to them! For their day has come,
the time for them to be punished.
²⁸Listen to the fugitives and refugees from Babylon
declaring in Zion
how the LORD our God has taken vengeance,
vengeance for his temple."

21-28 Once more God calls on the foes of Babylon to execute his wrath on her. "Merathaim" (v.21)—i.e., "double rebellion"—signifies Babylon. Southern Babylon was known as *mât marrâti* ("Land of the Bitter River"). "Pekod" means "visitation" or "punishment." An eastern Babylonian tribe was named *Puqudu* (so Hyatt). Cause and effect are indicated in the play on the place names—i.e., "double rebellion," "visitation." The unexpected nature of the visitation is pointed out (v.24). Babylon, who hammered so many nations to pieces (v.23), will know the armory of God opened against her (v.25) through her foes. There will be wholesale slaughter of Babylon's finest manhood (vv.26-27). Clearly God is reckoning with Babylon for having burned his temple in her capture of Jerusalem (v.28). The escapees from Babylon will announce in Zion that the Lord has avenged the destruction of his temple (cf. 51:11).

Notes

24 According to Herodotus (1.191), Cyrus captured Babylon by diverting the Euphrates River into a trench. The Persians attacked the Babylonians so unexpectedly that when the outer areas of the city had already been taken those in the center did not realize that they were captured (so KD).

5. Babylon's arrogance

50:29-32

²⁹"Summon archers against Babylon,
all those who draw the bow.
Encamp all around her;
let no one escape.
Repay her for her deeds;
do to her as she has done.
For she has defied the LORD,
the Holy One of Israel.
³⁰Therefore, her young men will fall in the streets;
all her soldiers will be silenced in that day,"

declares the LORD.

³¹"See, I am against you, O arrogant, one,"
declares the Lord, the LORD Almighty,
"for your day has come,
the time for you to be punished.

³²The arrogant one will stumble and fall
   and no one will help her up;
I will kindle a fire in her towns
   that will consume all who are around her."

29–32 The stress here is on Babylon's insufferable arrogance against the Lord. The fall of the proud will be complete. The exiles, as they summon archers (v.29), are seen exulting over God's retribution on Babylon. The rendering "archers" for *rabbîm* (contra "many" so LXX and other ancient translations) agrees with the following words in apposition—i.e., "all those who draw the bow"—and requires a change only in the Hebrew vowels. The call is to complete the extinction of the haughty empire. The view has been set forth (so Cunliffe-Jones) that God could not be judging Babylon for the Fall of Jerusalem, when Jeremiah had informed Zedekiah more than once that Babylon was performing the will of God (37:7–10; 38:18). Such a position, however, fails to take into account God's sovereign overruling of the innate hatred against his people ungodly men have even when cast into the role of benefactors (cf. Pharaoh and Israel in Egypt; cf. Zeph 1:15, etc.) and their accountability for their pride and cruelty. Verse 30 is practically a verbatim repetition of 49:26, where Jeremiah pronounced judgment on Damascus. It is equally appropriate. Babylon is viewed (vv.31–32) as the epitome of arrogance—pride personified! The message originally addressed to Jerusalem is directed against Babylon here, with the necessary changes. For godless Babylon (v.32) the consequences can only be fall, fire, and final consumption.

6. *Israel's Kinsman-Redeemer*

50:33–40

³³This is what the LORD Almighty says:

"The people of Israel are oppressed,
   and the people of Judah as well.
All their captors hold them fast,
   refusing to let them go.
³⁴Yet their Redeemer is strong;
   the LORD Almighty is his name.
He will vigorously defend their cause
   so that he may bring rest to their land,
   but unrest to those who live in Babylon.

³⁵"A sword against the Babylonians!"
   declares the LORD—
"against those who live in Babylon
   and against her officials and wise men!
³⁶A sword against her false prophets!
   They will become fools.
A sword against her warriors!
   They will be filled with terror.
³⁷A sword against her horses and chariots
   and all the foreigners in her ranks!
   They will become women.
A sword against her treasures!
   They will be plundered.
³⁸A drought on her waters!
   They will dry up.

For it is a land of idols,
  idols that will go mad with terror.
39"So desert creatures and hyenas will live there,
  and there the owl will dwell.
It will never again be inhabited
  or lived in from generation to generation.
40As God overthrew Sodom and Gomorrah
  along with their neighboring towns,"

                                   declares the LORD,

"so no one will live there;
  no man will dwell in it."

33–40 Few nations have ever realized that God is the Kinsman-Redeemer of Israel (v.34). The OT concept of kinsman-redeemer includes the protection of a relative's person and property. It involves avenging the murder of a relative, the purchase of his alienated property, and/or the marriage to his widow (cf. Lev 25:25; Num 35:21; Ruth 4). The Kinsman-Redeemer is voluntarily committed to champion Israel's cause. He brings peace to his own but unrest to his oppressors. In a sense, Israel is the epitome of all that Babylon enslaved. Notice in vv.35–38 the fivefold mention of the sword (cf. Ezek 21).

Notes

39 Bright attempts to render the assonance of צִיִּים אֶת־אִיִּים (ṣiyyîm 'et-'iyyîm, "desert creatures and hyenas") by "goblins and ghouls." C.C. Torrey (*The Second Isaiah: A New Interpretation* [New York: Scribner, 1928], pp. 289–90) considered them, not as animals, but probably demons of the desert (cf. KB, pp. 801, 35).

7. *The permanence of Babylon's doom*

   50:41–46

41"Look! An army is coming from the north;
  a great nation and many kings
  are being stirred up from the ends of the earth.
42They are armed with bows and spears;
  they are cruel and without mercy.
They sound like the roaring sea
  as they ride on their horses;
they come like men in battle formation
  to attack you, O Daughter of Babylon.
43The king of Babylon has heard reports about them,
  and his hands hang limp.
Anguish has gripped him,
  pain like that of a woman in labor.
44Like a lion coming up from Jordan's thickets
  to a rich pastureland,
I will chase Babylon from its land in an instant.
  Who is the chosen one I will appoint for this?
Who is like me and who can challenge me?
  And what shepherd can stand against me?"

⁴⁵Therefore, hear what the LORD has planned
    against Babylon,
what he has purposed against the land
    of the Babylonians:
The young of the flock will be dragged away;
    he will completely destroy their pasture because of them.
⁴⁶At the sound of Babylon's capture the earth will tremble;
    its cry will resound among the nations.

41–46 This section should be compared with 6:22–24 and 49:19–21. The lion (v.44) now is Cyrus; in 49:19 it was Nebuchadnezzar. The desolation of Babylon will be permanent, as was that of Sodom and Gomorrah (cf. v.40). The doom of Babylon will indeed terrify the nations who witness it (v.46). That vv.44–46 are also found in 49:19–21 shows affinity between these parts of Jeremiah's writings. In 6:22–24 Judah was warned of an unnamed northern invader. In this portion the offender is seen as Babylon, who is directly addressed with appropriate changes. The "many kings" (v.41) are those who were allied with Persia (e.g., the Medes) to bring about the defeat of Babylon. The executors of Babylon's judgment (v.42) are described as to their war paraphernalia, their vast cavalry, the deafening tumult, their military formation, and their merciless attitude toward their enemy. It is quite clear why the "king of Babylon" (v.43) is overcome with fear. Verses 44–46 are practically a verbatim repetition of the condemnation of Edom in 49:19–21. The reason is clear: since Edom's sins resemble Babylon's, God in righteousness must judge them similarly. The phrase "among the nations" (v.46) indicates a wider audience than the one in view in 49:21 because of the greater prominence of the Babylonian power.

Chapter 51, the longest in the book, continues the message of condemnation and ruin for Babylon and concludes with a word concerning an important mission sent to Babylon by Jeremiah.

8. *The Lord's vengeance on Babylon*

51:1–14

¹This is what the LORD says:

"See, I will stir up the spirit of a destroyer
    against Babylon and the people of Leb Kamai.
²I will send foreigners to Babylon
    to winnow her and to devastate her land;
they will oppose her on every side
    in the day of her disaster.
³Let not the archer string his bow,
    nor let him put on his armor.
Do not spare her young men;
    completely destroy her army.
⁴They will fall down slain in Babylon,
    fatally wounded in her streets.
⁵For Israel and Judah have not been forsaken
    by their God, the LORD Almighty,
though their land is full of guilt
    before the Holy One of Israel.

⁶"Flee from Babylon!
    Run for your lives!
Do not be destroyed because of her sins.

It is time for the LORD's vengeance;
  he will pay her what she deserves.
7Babylon was a gold cup in the LORD's hand;
  she made the whole earth drunk.
The nations drank her wine;
  therefore they have now gone mad.
8Babylon will suddenly fall and be broken.
  Wail over her!
Get balm for her pain;
  perhaps she can be healed.
9" 'We would have healed Babylon,
  but she cannot be healed;
let us leave her and each go to his own land,
  for her judgment reaches to the skies,
  it rises as high as the clouds.'

10" 'The LORD has vindicated us;
  come, let us tell in Zion
  what the LORD our God has done.'
11"Sharpen the arrows,
  take up the shields!
The LORD has stirred up the kings of the Medes,
  because his purpose is to destroy Babylon.
The LORD will take vengeance,
  vengeance for his temple.
12Lift up a banner against the walls of Babylon!
  Reinforce the guard,
station the watchmen,
  prepare an ambush!
The LORD will carry out his purpose,
  his decree against the people of Babylon.
13You who live by many waters
  and are rich in treasures,
your end has come,
  the time for you to be cut off.
14The LORD Almighty has sworn by himself:
  I will surely fill you with men, as with a swarm
    of locusts,
  and they will shout in triumph over you."

1–4 The northern enemy is dispatched against Babylon, which is to be destroyed as chaff is winnowed from grain (v.2). "Leb Kamai" (v.1) is Hebrew for "the heart of those who rise against me." It is a cipher for Chaldea (cf. comments at 25:26 on *Atbash* of Sheshach for Babylon; cf. 51:41). Why Jeremiah used these ciphers is not known, because he generally used the name Babylon. An obvious reason would be to hide the identity of the nation prophesied against. It is the enemies of Babylon who are called on to perform the will of God regarding her. Though the Babylonians with their weapons (v.3) man the walls, yet they are to be attacked and none spared (v.4).

5–10 The judgment is the vengeance of the Lord on Babylon for her treatment of Judah (vv.5–6). She that was as a cup of wrath to the nations will now be shattered herself (cf. 25:15–16). The cup was a golden one (v.7) because she intoxicated the nations with her wealth and power. And there is no healing for her mortal wound (vv.8–9). Thus will God vindicate his cause in Judah (v.10).

11–14 The aggressor (Media) is now identified (v. 11) and the work of judgment described. The Medes were allied with Babylon in the destruction of Nineveh in 612 B.C. Later they joined the Persians to defeat Babylon in 539 B.C. (so WBC; cf. Dan 5:28, 31; 8:20). Again Jeremiah specifies that the judgment is for the destruction of the temple. All Babylon's strength cannot avert her fall that has been determined by the Lord (vv. 12–13). The invaders will swarm over her like locusts (v. 14).

Notes

11 מַלְכֵי מָדַי (*malkê māday*, "kings of the Medes") may refer to the provincial governors; or, as in Isa 13:17, Medes is a general designation for the ancient Indo-European (Aryan) people of northwest Iran who were amalgamated with the Persians in the seventh century B.C. The Babylonian Empire was destroyed by a coalition under Darius the Mede and Cyrus the Persian (ZPEB, 4:148–50).

9. *The omnipotent Lord and impotent idols*

51:15–26

> [15]"He made the earth by his power;
> he founded the world by his wisdom
> and stretched out the heavens by his understanding.
> [16]When he thunders, the waters in the heavens roar;
> he makes clouds rise from the ends of the earth.
> He sends lightning with the rain
> and brings out the wind from his storehouses.
>
> [17]"Every man is senseless and without knowledge;
> every goldsmith is shamed by his idols.
> His images are a fraud;
> they have no breath in them.
> [18]They are worthless, the objects of mockery;
> when their judgment falls, they will perish.
> [19]He who is the Portion of Jacob is not like these,
> for he is the maker of all things,
> including the tribe of his inheritance—
> The LORD Almighty is his name.
>
> [20]"You are my war club,
> my weapon for battle—
> with you I shatter nations,
> with you I destroy kingdoms,
> [21]with you I shatter horse and rider,
> with you I shatter chariot and driver,
> [22]with you I shatter man and woman,
> with you I shatter old man and youth,
> with you I shatter young man and maiden,
> [23]with you I shatter shepherd and flock,
> with you I shatter farmer and oxen,
> with you I shatter governors and officials.

[24]"Before your eyes I will repay Babylon and all who live in Babylonia for all the wrong they have done in Zion," declares the LORD.

25"I am against you, O destroying mountain,
you who destroy the whole earth,"

declares the LORD.

"I will stretch out my hand against you,
roll you off the cliffs,
and make you a burned-out mountain.
26No rock will be taken from you for a cornerstone,
nor any stone for a foundation,
for you will be desolate forever,"

declares the LORD.

15–23 In chapter 10, Jeremiah showed how the house of Israel had no cause to fear the impotent idols of the pagans. Here he demonstrates to the Babylonians the uselessness of their idols (vv.17–18), who will all be destroyed before the mighty Creator and Ruler of the universe (vv.15–16, 19). The biblical doctrine of the requital is predicated on the basis of God's control over the affairs of all the nations on the ground of his creative activity (27:5) and his zeal for righteousness (Gen 18:25). The law of retaliation (lex talionis) is found in the OT (Isa 10:5–19; 37:22–29; Jer 27:4–11, esp. v.7) and in the NT (Matt 26:52; Rom 2:1). In vv.20–23, Cyrus of Persia, the Lord's "war club," shatters Babylon. This passage underscores the great power of Persia (so Hyatt et al.). Ten times the phrase "with you" falls like hammer blows (vv.21–23). The Hebrew verb *nippēṣ* indicates a violent and intensive shattering (cf. Exod 15:6; Pss 2:9; 137:9; Hos 10:14; 13:16).

24–26 Babylon was situated on a plain; so "O destroying mountain" is a metaphor for a powerful kingdom (v.25; cf. Dan 2:35, 44–45). But Babylon will become as an extinct volcano—"a burned-out mountain." She will never be rebuilt (v.26).

10. *The nations summoned*

51:27–33

27"Lift up a banner in the land!
Blow the trumpet among the nations!
Prepare the nations for battle against her;
summon against her these kingdoms:
Ararat, Minni and Ashkenaz.
Appoint a commander against her;
send up horses like a swarm of locusts.
28Prepare the nations for battle against her—
the kings of the Medes,
their governors and all their officials,
and all the countries they rule.
29The land trembles and writhes,
for the LORD's purposes against Babylon stand—
to lay waste the land of Babylon
so that no one will live there.
30Babylon's warriors have stopped fighting;
they remain in their strongholds.
Their strength is exhausted;
they have become like women.
Her dwellings are set on fire;
the bars of her gates are broken.
31One courier follows another
and messenger follows messenger

to announce to the king of Babylon
   that his entire city is captured,
³²the river crossings seized,
   the marshes set on fire,
   and the soldiers terrified."

³³This is what the LORD Almighty, the God of Israel, says:

"The Daughter of Babylon is like a threshing floor
   at the time it is trampled;
the time to harvest her will soon come."

27–33 A call summons the nations to fight against Babylon (v.27). As God's avenger, Cyrus will harvest her (v.33). The people north of Babylon, who were conquered by the Medes early in the sixth century B.C., are named: Ararat, Minni, and Ashkenaz. The first are the Urartu of the Assyrian inscriptions, practically Armenia, north of Lake Van. The second are the Mannaeans of the Assyrian records, who lived south of Lake Urmia. The last, the Ashguzai of the Assyrian inscriptions, were nomads living east of Lake Urmia (cf. Gen 10:3). These three are called to aid the Medes (v.28) against Babylon (so Hyatt).

Notes

---

27 Ararat is known from Gen 8:4. It is the Urartu (a somewhat altered form being Uruaṭri), which is attested in Assyrian records of the thirteenth century B.C., a land north of Assyria in Armenia, with its center at Lake Van. Minni (Mannaeans) resided in the area south of Lake Urmia in western Iran from the ninth to the seventh centuries B.C. The Assyrian inscriptions describe the people as warlike. In the Bible, only Jeremiah mentions them. Ashkenaz has been identified with the Scythians, who lived near Lake Urmia near Ararat. They were crude and warlike. Herodotus (4:11–12) mentions their conquest of the Cimmerians (Gomer). In time their name became synonymous with barbarian. In modern Hebrew Ashkenaz denotes Germany and Ashkenazi signifies a German Jew (ZPEB, 1: 255–57, 356, 358; 4:240–41).

---

11. *Babylon's defenses useless*

   51:34–44

³⁴"Nebuchadnezzar king of Babylon has devoured us,
   he has thrown us into confusion,
   he has made us an empty jar.
Like a serpent he has swallowed us
   and filled his stomach with our delicacies,
   and then has spewed us out.
³⁵May the violence done to our flesh be upon Babylon,"
   say the inhabitants of Zion.
"May our blood be on those who live in Babylonia,"
   says Jerusalem.
³⁶Therefore, this is what the LORD says:

"See, I will defend your cause
   and avenge you;

I will dry up her sea
    and make her springs dry.
[37]Babylon will be a heap of ruins,
    a haunt of jackals,
an object of horror and scorn,
    a place where no one lives.
[38]Her people all roar like young lions,
    they growl like lion cubs.
[39]But while they are aroused,
    I will set out a feast for them
    and make them drunk,
so that they shout with laughter—
    then sleep forever and not awake,"

                        declares the LORD.

[40]"I will bring them down
    like lambs to the slaughter,
    like rams and goats.

[41]"How Sheshach will be captured,
    the boast of the whole earth seized!
What a horror Babylon
    will be among the nations!
[42]The sea will rise over Babylon;
    its roaring waves will cover her.
[43]Her towns will be desolate,
    a dry and desert land,
a land where no one lives,
    through which no man travels.
[44]I will punish Bel in Babylon
    and make him spew out what he has swallowed.
The nations will no longer stream to him.
    And the wall of Babylon will fall."

34–44 The Lord in his judgment will answer Zion's complaint against Babylon (vv.34–36a). This will mean the end of Babylon (vv.36b–37). Babylon is compared to lions' cubs (v.38). She will be given a feast, followed not by the usual drunken sleep, but by a perpetual sleep of death (vv.39–40). In v.41 another cipher is found in the name of Sheshach (cf. comments at v.1).

Two things for which Babylon was famous were the god Bel and the great wall of the city (v.44). Bel will be compelled to disgorge the nations he has swallowed, and the great wall (admired by Herodotus [1.178–81]) will collapse.

12. *Warning to Israel to flee Babylon*

    51:45–48

[45]"Come out of her, my people!
    Run for your lives!
    Run from the fierce anger of the LORD.
[46]Do not lose heart or be afraid
    when rumors are heard in the land;
one rumor comes this year, another the next,
    rumors of violence in the land
    and of ruler against ruler.
[47]For the time will surely come
    when I will punish the idols of Babylon;

her whole land will be disgraced
and her slain will all lie fallen within her.
48Then heaven and earth and all that is in them
will shout for joy over Babylon,
for out of the north
destroyers will attack her,"

declares the LORD.

45–48 Again, the Lord's people are warned to flee the doomed city before disaster strikes (v.45). They will need faith and courage until Babylon falls (v.46). But they are not to be terrified by the rumors that will be rife, for each year will have its own rumors of tyrants against tyrants (so Welch). Heaven and earth will rejoice over Babylon's fall (v.48; cf. Rev 19).

Notes

45 There are some commentators who relate Jer 51–52 to Rev 17–18 and feel that the Revelation passages demand a rebuilding of Babylon. It must be stated at the outset that such a discussion does not touch the premillennial position in any vital area since premillennialists can be found on both sides of the issue of the rebuilding of the ancient city. Furthermore, this writer sees no way that the Revelation passages (as will be shown presently) can be determinative in the matter. The decision must ultimately be based on one's interpretation of Jer 51–52. The reason is that the apostle John is *not* speaking of literal, historical Babylon. First, he uses the word "mystery" with reference to Babylon. This conveys the force of a mystical Babylon. Second, Revelation is fond of using proper nouns figuratively: (1) Jezebel (2:20); (2) the key of David (3:7); (3) Jerusalem (the new) comes down out of heaven (21:2, 10); (4) Sodom and Egypt (11:8); (5) Gog and Magog (20:8, not the same geographical areas of Ezek 38–39); (6) Babylon (chs. 17–18, not the city of Mesopotamia, which was situated on a plain [cf. 17:9]).

The chief references to Babylon are in Genesis, the Prophets, and Revelation. The references indicate that the city of old signified spiritual confusion (Gen 11). The apostle John states that the idolatry of ancient times will be headed up in an ecclesiastical and political colossus with many commercial ramifications (Rev 17–18). It will be all anti-God systems (cults and religions) concentrated in a vast ecclesiastical system. "Rome alone answers to the description given" (H.A. Ironside, *Lectures on the Book of Revelation* [New York: Loizeaux, 1930], p. 297; cf. pp. 302, 307; cf. also the works of A.C. Gaebelein, W.R. Newell, F.W. Grant et al.)

13. *The certainty of Babylon's fall*

51:49–53

49"Babylon must fall because of Israel's slain,
just as the slain in all the earth
have fallen because of Babylon.
50You who have escaped the sword,
leave and do not linger!
Remember the LORD in a distant land,
and think on Jerusalem."

> ⁵¹"We are disgraced,
>   for we have been insulted
>   and shame covers our faces,
> because foreigners have entered
>   the holy places of the LORD's house."
>
> ⁵²"But days are coming," declares the LORD,
>   "when I will punish her idols,
> and throughout her land
>   the wounded will groan.
> ⁵³Even if Babylon reaches the sky
>   and fortifies her lofty stronghold,
>   I will send destroyers against her,"
>
>   declares the LORD.

49–53 Retribution will overtake Babylon. The remnant of Israel is ashamed when they think of Jerusalem, for they have been the cause of the temple's defilement by strangers. And Babylon's idolatry will not escape judgment.

14. *The completeness of Babylon's destruction*

51:54–58

> ⁵⁴"The sound of a cry comes from Babylon,
>   the sound of great destruction
>   from the land of the Babylonians.
> ⁵⁵The LORD will destroy Babylon;
>   he will silence her noisy din.
> Waves of enemies will rage like great waters;
>   the roar of their voices will resound.
> ⁵⁶A destroyer will come against Babylon;
>   her warriors will be captured,
>   and their bows will be broken.
> For the LORD is a God of retribution;
>   he will repay in full.
> ⁵⁷I will make her officials and wise men drunk,
>   her governors, officers and warriors as well;
> they will sleep forever and not awake,"
>   declares the King, whose name is the LORD Almighty.

⁵⁸This is what the LORD Almighty says:

> "Babylon's thick wall will be leveled
>   and her high gates set on fire;
> the peoples exhaust themselves for nothing,
>   the nations' labor is only fuel for the flames."

54–58 Jeremiah sees the destroyers of Babylon as already present (v.54). The enemy overruns the land (vv.55–56) as tidal waves sweep over a country (so Cunliffe-Jones). When most needed, Babylon's men are made drunk by God's wrath (v.57). The slave labor of many nations expended in building the wall will have been for naught (v.58).

Notes

58 The Hebrew here is חֹמוֹת בָּבֶל (*ḥōmôt bāḇel*), which is literally "walls of Babylon." Many Hebrew MSS, the LXX, and the Vulgate read *ḥômat* ("wall of "), which requires minimal consonantal change and agrees with the singular verb that follows. Babylon had a double ("thick," so NIV) wall for defense, which, according to Herodotus (1.178ff.), surrounded an area of two hundred square miles. The thickness of the wall allowed four chariots to run abreast (Nineveh's wall permitted three chariots).

15. *The mission of Seraiah*

51:59–64

[59]This is the message Jeremiah gave to the staff officer Seraiah son of Neriah, the son of Mahseiah, when he went to Babylon with Zedekiah king of Judah in the fourth year of his reign. [60]Jeremiah had written on a scroll about all the disasters that would come upon Babylon—all that had been recorded concerning Babylon. [61]He said to Seraiah, "When you get to Babylon, see that you read all these words aloud. [62]Then say, 'O LORD, you have said you will destroy this place, so that neither man nor animal will live in it; it will be desolate forever.' [63]When you finish reading this scroll, tie a stone to it and throw it into the Euphrates. [64]Then say, 'So will Babylon sink to rise no more because of the disaster I will bring upon her. And her people will fall.' "

The words of Jeremiah end here.

59–64 This is Jeremiah's word to Seraiah, the staff officer who was responsible for looking after the comfort of the king of Judah whenever he stopped for the night (v.59). He was probably the brother of Baruch (cf. 32:12). In lieu of Jeremiah, Seraiah was to perform a symbolic act. This is the only place in Scripture where this visit is recorded. The fourth year of Zedekiah (594–593 B.C.) was, it has been suggested, the year when Zedekiah attempted to clear himself of complicity in a revolt against Babylon.

Seraiah's symbolic act (vv.60–63) was a visual enactment of the fall of Babylon. This passage is an appendix to the prophecy that shows how it was taken to Babylon. It is remarkable that at the very time Jeremiah was advising submission to that city, he was also foretelling her final overthrow. This answers the objections of those expositors who feel that chapters 50–51 could not have been written by Jeremiah in view of his attitude toward Babylon expressed earlier in the book.

Verse 64 is commonly understood to be a compiler's note, added to separate chapter 51 from chapter 52, which parallels passages in 2 Kings.

V. Historical Supplement (52:1–34)

This chapter is a historical supplement to the Book of Jeremiah. It deals with the Fall of Jerusalem; tells what the Babylonians did to the temple and its vessels; describes how Nebuchadnezzar treated Zedekiah, Jehoiachin, and other officials; and lists the number of Jews taken into exile. The purpose of the chapter is to show how Jeremiah's prophecies were fulfilled in contrast to those of the false prophets. The chapter is almost identical with 2 Kings 24:18–25:30.

A. The Fall of Jerusalem

52:1–11

¹Zedekiah was twenty-one years old when he became king, and he reigned in Jerusalem eleven years. His mother's name was Hamutal daughter of Jeremiah; she was from Libnah. ²He did evil in the eyes of the LORD, just as Jehoiakim had done. ³It was because of the LORD's anger that all this happened to Jerusalem and Judah, and in the end he thrust them from his presence.

Now Zedekiah rebelled against the king of Babylon.

⁴So in the ninth year of Zedekiah's reign, on the tenth day of the tenth month, Nebuchadnezzar king of Babylon marched against Jerusalem with his whole army. They camped outside the city and built siege works all around it. ⁵The city was kept under siege until the eleventh year of King Zedekiah.

⁶By the ninth day of the fourth month the famine in the city had become so severe that there was no food for the people to eat. ⁷Then the city wall was broken through, and the whole army fled. They left the city at night through the gate between the two walls near the king's garden, though the Babylonians were surrounding the city. They fled toward the Arabah, ⁸but the Babylonian army pursued King Zedekiah and overtook him in the plains of Jericho. All his soldiers were separated from him and scattered, ⁹and he was captured.

He was taken to the king of Babylon at Riblah in the land of Hamath, where he pronounced sentence on him. ¹⁰There at Riblah the king of Babylon slaughtered the sons of Zedekiah before his eyes; he also killed all the officials of Judah. ¹¹Then he put out Zedekiah's eyes, bound him with bronze shackles and took him to Babylon, where he put him in prison till the day of his death.

1–11 Verses 1–3 give a brief summary of the reign of Zedekiah and show the proximate cause of the Fall of Jerusalem. The narrative goes on to give a vivid account of how the city fell. So crucial was this event that the OT records it four times—in 2 Kings 25; 2 Chronicles 36:11–21; Jeremiah 39:1–14; and in this passage.

Notes

11 בֵּית הַפְּקֻדֹּת (bêṯ happᵉquddōṯ, "prisonhouse"; NIV, "prison") is not the usual term (מַטָּרָה, maṭṭārāh; cf. 32:2, 8, 12; 33:1; 37:21 et al.) for "prison." Because the LXX has οἰκία μύλωνος (oikia mylōnos, "house of punishment"), Hitzig held that Zedekiah was compelled to turn the mill, as Samson did (Judg 16:21).

B. Results of the Fall

52:12–27a

¹²On the tenth day of the fifth month, in the nineteenth year of Nebuchadnezzar king of Babylon, Nebuzaradan commander of the imperial guard, who served the king of Babylon, came to Jerusalem. ¹³He set fire to the temple of the LORD, the royal palace and all the houses of Jerusalem. Every important building he burned down. ¹⁴The whole Babylonian army under the commander of the imperial guard broke down all the walls around Jerusalem. ¹⁵Nebuzaradan the commander of the guard carried into exile some of the poorest people and those who remained in the city, along with the rest of the craftsmen and those who had gone over to the king of Babylon. ¹⁶But Nebuzaradan left behind the rest of the poorest people of the land to work the vineyards and fields.

¹⁷The Babylonians broke up the bronze pillars, the movable stands and the bronze Sea that were at the temple of the LORD and they carried all the bronze to Babylon. ¹⁸They also took away the pots, shovels, wick trimmers, sprinkling bowls, ladles and all the bronze articles used in the temple service. ¹⁹The commander of the imperial guard took away the basins, censers, sprinkling bowls, pots, lampstands, ladles and bowls used for drink offerings—all that were made of gold or silver.

²⁰The bronze from the two pillars, the Sea and the twelve bronze bulls under it, and the movable stands, which King Solomon had made for the temple of the LORD, was more than could be weighed. ²¹Each of the pillars was eighteen cubits high and twelve cubits in circumference; each was four fingers thick, and hollow. ²²The bronze capital on top of the one pillar was five cubits high and was decorated with a network and pomegranates of bronze all around. The other pillar, with its pomegranates, was similar. ²³There were ninety-six pomegranates on the sides; the total number of pomegranates above the surrounding network was a hundred.

²⁴The commander of the guard took as prisoners Seraiah the chief priest, Zephaniah the priest next in rank and the three doorkeepers. ²⁵Of those still in the city, he took the officer in charge of the fighting men, and seven royal advisers. He also took the secretary who was chief officer in charge of conscripting the people of the land and sixty of his men who were found in the city. ²⁶Nebuzaradan the commander took them all and brought them to the king of Babylon at Riblah. ²⁷There at Riblah, in the land of Hamath, the king had them executed.

12–27a Here the narrative goes into detail about what happened in Jerusalem after it fell. The slight variations between this chapter and 2 Kings 24–25 are only minor. There is no contradiction between v.12 and v.29. In the former the accession year of Nebuchadnezzar has been included; in the second it has not. The account of the taking of the sacred vessels to Babylon (cf. 1 Kings 6–8) is more elaborate here than that in 2 Kings. Zedekiah's revolt surely had an effect opposite from what the priests and false prophets had wanted. Solomon's magnificent temple, one of the wonders of the ancient world, was plundered and ruined. In v.24 the three orders of the priests are referred to. Apparently the priests and false prophets had been largely responsible for inciting Zedekiah's revolt against Nebuchadnezzar. They and the chief officers of the city were captured because of their responsibility for the calamity (vv.24–27a).

C. Nebuchadnezzar's Captives

52:27b–30

So Judah went into captivity, away from her land. ²⁸This is the number of the people Nebuchadnezzar carried into exile:

in the seventh year, 3,023 Jews;
²⁹in Nebuchadnezzar's eighteenth year,
  832 people from Jerusalem;
³⁰in his twenty-third year,
  745 Jews taken into exile by Nebuzaradan
  the commander of the imperial guard.
  There were 4,600 people in all.

27b–30 The deportations to Babylon listed here (so Hyatt) occurred (1) in 598–597 B.C., (2) in 587–586 B.C., and (3) in 582–581 B.C. Under Judean kings there were three deportations: (1) under Jehoiakim (606 B.C.), which marked the beginning of the seventy years of exile; (2) under Jehoiachin (597); and (3) under Zedekiah (586) (so Jensen). If only Jews are numbered or only males reckoned in vv.28–30, the ultimate total of exiles was doubtless much higher (so Freedman). The smallness of the figures has been a chief reason why scholars of liberal persuasion tend to credit them, since they generally believe that figures are inflated with time. But this cannot be a final criterion.

Notes

28–30 Most expositors follow the list of deportations given by Hyatt, beginning with Jehoiachin (597) and concluding with an invasion in 582–581 B.C. (the twenty-third year of Nebuchadnezzar), in retaliation for the assassination of Gedaliah. Jensen's list is preferable because it takes into account Dan 1:1–3. Possibly those who do not take the first deportation as Dan 1:1–3 do so because there is no numerical reckoning of the captives given there. Cowles, commenting on this passage, says, "By this account, captives were taken from Jerusalem to Babylon at three different periods. There was still a fourth, not named here, viz., in the fourth year of Jehoiakim and the first year of Nebuchadnezzar, or, rather, just before he ascended his throne. (See 2 Kings 24:1–4, and 2 Chron. 36:5–7, and Dan. 1:1–5.)." The discrepancy of one year can be explained on the basis of accession and nonaccession years.

It is obvious at first glance that the writers of 2 Kings and Jeremiah were not in collusion concerning the numbers of deportees, else they would not have allowed so clear a discrepancy in numbers to remain. Second, no writer has yet been able to prove that either writer was in error in the enumeration. They are both explicit in their figures. Third, the records indicate that both writers were counting from different perspectives. For instance, the smaller figure may include only adult males and the larger number may give the total number of exiles. It has been suggested that one figure gives the Jews, that is, those from Judah only, whereas the other figure is more inclusive. Until further information is forthcoming, no one can be dogmatic as to what principle was followed. Least of all can anyone fault the sacred records for inaccuracies. All too often in the past such an approach has been found in sad error!

D. Evil-Merodach's Kindness to Jehoiachin

52:31–34

> [31]In the thirty-seventh year of the exile of Jehoiachin king of Judah, in the year Evil-Merodach became king of Babylon, he released Jehoiachin king of Judah and freed him from prison on the twenty-fifth day of the twelfth month. [32]He spoke kindly to him and gave him a seat of honor higher than those of the other kings who were with him in Babylon. [33]So Jehoiachin put aside his prison clothes and for the rest of his life ate regularly at the king's table. [34]Day by day the king of Babylon gave Jehoiachin a regular allowance as long as he lived, till the day of his death.

31–34 This passage agrees with 2 Kings 25:27–30. The humane treatment accorded Jehoiachin (c. 561 B.C.) is confirmed by cuneiform tablets (cf. E.F. Weidner, "Jojachin, König von Juda, in babylonischen Keilschrifttexten," *Mélanges syriens offerts* *à Monsieur René Dussaud*, II [Paris, 1939]: 923–35). These verses conclude Jeremiah's somberly beautiful book with a comforting thought—viz., that the Lord did not forget the Davidic line, even in exile.

Notes

31 אֱוִיל מְרֹדַךְ (*'ewîl merōḏaḵ*, "Evil-Merodach") is a transliteration of the Assyro-Babylonian Amel ("man of ")-Marduk ("Marduk"). He was Nebuchadnezzar's son, who reigned from 562 B.C. to 560 B.C.

נָשָׂא רֹאשׁ (*nāśā' rō'š*, "lift up the head"; NIV, "released") is first found in Gen 40:13, 20, in the Joseph account. Jewish tradition claims Evil-Merodach was imprisoned by his father for some action in the government during a period of Nebuchadnezzar's indisposition. While in prison, Evil-Merodach became a friend of Jehoiachin. On his accession to the throne, Evil-Merodach released Jehoiachin and gave him a prominent place at the royal table (so Freedman). The tradition has marks of an ad hoc explanation.

LAMENTATIONS

H. L. Ellison

LAMENTATIONS

Introduction

1. Name and Position
2. Background
3. Unity
4. Authorship
5. Date
6. Place of Origin
7. Purpose
8. Literary Form
9. Theological Values
10. Canonicity
11. Text
12. Bibliography
13. Outline

1. Name and Position

In the Talmud (*Baba Bathra* 15a), this book is called *qînôt* ("Lamentations"); this is represented in the LXX by *thrēnoi* (Vul. *Treni*). The name commonly used in Hebrew, however, is *'êkāh* ("How"), the first word of the first, second, and fourth laments. In the Hebrew canon it stands in the Writings as the third of the Megilloth, or Scrolls, between Ruth and Ecclesiastes. Although some scholars infer from Josephus (Antiq. X, 78 [v.1]) that Lamentations was in the second division of the canon, there is no real evidence that it was ever listed among the Prophets. The position in the English Bible—immediately after Jeremiah—is due to the LXX, which the Vulgate follows.

2. Background

The book consists of five laments, all but the third explicitly based on the destruction of Jerusalem by the Chaldeans in 587 B.C. and its aftermath. There are no grounds for attributing the more general language of the third to a different background. The vividness of the pictures points clearly to the work of an eyewitness. Though he was conscious of the suffering elsewhere in Judah, he concentrated on the position in Jerusalem.

3. Unity

There is such a unity in style and theological outlook, and the date of the composition falls within such a limited period, that nothing can be proved or gained by arguing for a plurality of authors—except possibly for the third lament. There is also little or no scope for claiming editorial work and interpolations. A fair case can be made for arranging the laments in the order 2,4,5,1—with 3 undatable.

4. Authorship

In Hebrew the book is anonymous. The LXX begins: "And it came to pass after Israel had been taken away into captivity and Jerusalem had been laid waste that Jeremiah sat weeping and lamented this lamentation over Jerusalem and said" (Vul. adds: "with a bitter spirit sighing and wailing"; cf. Knox, in loc.). Both Young[1] and Harrison (IOT, p. 1069) share the view that this was probably a false deduction from 2 Chronicles 35:25. It is hazardous to deduce from Josephus (Antiq. X, 78 [v.1]) that he made the same deduction.

There is general agreement among more moderate writers—both conservative and liberal—that once we abandon the LXX tradition, arguments for and against authorship by Jeremiah are fairly evenly balanced. We do well, then, to respect the seal of anonymity impressed on the book by the Holy Spirit. The claim for authorship by Jeremiah seems to be mainly sentimental. Arguments from style show no more, as is borne out by the Lachish ostraca, than that on other grounds the laments fit the period we attribute them to. Theological similarities with Jeremiah were to be expected from anyone who accepted his teaching and that of the great prophets in general. In the commentary attention will be drawn to the few passages that are hard to attribute to Jeremiah. A special discussion of the authorship of chapter 3 will be found at the beginning of the commentary there.

5. Date

Few commentators seriously suggest that any of the five laments fall outside the period 586–538 B.C. Indeed, the lack of national hope points to completion before 562 B.C., when the release of Jehoiachin from prison (2 Kings 25:27–30) must have awakened some expectation that Jeremiah's promises would be fulfilled. Such hope as is expressed in chapter 3 is for the individual rather than the nation; elsewhere national hope scarcely rises above anticipation that hostile nations will share the judgment that has befallen Zion.

6. Place of Origin

There are no a priori objections to the view that Jeremiah composed the later laments in Egypt, or that they were all written by some exile in Babylonia. Yet the impression created by the laments as a whole is that they were composed in or near the ruins of Jerusalem itself. If we could answer the question of their purpose with certainty (see section 7), it would be easier to suggest a definite answer to this question.

---

[1]E.J. Young, *Introduction to the Old Testament*, rev. ed. (Grand Rapids: Eerdmans, 1964), p. 342.

7. Purpose

Already in Zechariah 7:3, 5; 8:19, we find that the destruction of the temple on the seventh day of the fifth month (2 Kings 25:8–9) was remembered by an annual fast. (This was transferred in the second century A.D. to the ninth day of the month and has since then commemorated the two destructions of the temple and the crushing of Bar Kochba's revolt in A.D. 135. It is called Tisha b'Av.) We may be certain that this fast was observed from the first, almost certainly with ceremonies in the ruins of the temple. We see from Jeremiah 41:5 that it was still a goal for pilgrimage. For as far back as tradition reaches, Lamentations has been read on Tisha b'Av; and it is not unreasonable to assume that it was intended for this purpose from the first.

The immediate purpose of the Book of Lamentations, however, does not fully explain its presence in the canon, because, at least for the Christian, it would now have little more than historical and antiquarian interest. The Bible finds room for every element of human experience, including overwhelming human sorrow. This can come to the individual (e.g., Job) or to the nation as a whole. In such a position even the comfortable words of Scripture do not always bring solace and a ray of light. Though Jeremiah had set a limit to Babylonian rule (25:11–12) and had promised national restoration (chs. 30–31), the hearts of the survivors were too stunned to appreciate the promises, of which there is no trace in Lamentations. Even in the era of the gospel, the same thing occasionally happens; then the brokenhearted who turn to these laments discover that they are not the first to pass through thick darkness before emerging into the sunlight again. So they realize that their God is the one who puts their tears onto his scroll (Ps 56:8).

The modern reader may wonder at the extremes of sorrow expressed in the book and may be puzzled that the Jews should have continued to mourn the destruction by Nebuchadnezzar (the destruction by Titus in A.D. 70 is another matter). It is in fact hard for us to realize how complete the destruction was.

The old "City of David" lies outside the present city walls. This is only partially due to the effects of the destruction by the Romans. The Chaldeans so broke down the Jebusite and Davidic walls and terraces that restoration was impossible; and Nehemiah had to build his wall much higher up the slope, greatly reducing the area of what had been the center of the city.[2]

There is also no trace in the temple area of anything that can be linked with Solomon, certainly not the "stables" that have been given his name. Even the huge blocks of stone visible at the base of the West (Wailing) Wall are Herodian, not Solomonic.

All this means that at the return from exile, a completely new beginning was needed. Lamentations, in this sense, is a funeral dirge over an irrecoverable past.

8. Literary Form

Chapter 5 is a normal Hebrew poem of twenty-two verses. With a few exceptions, it consists of pairs of three-beat lines in which the second stands in parallelism with the first. Chapters 1–4 are predominantly in the *"Qinah* metre," a term coined by

---

[2]Cf. Winton Thomas, *Archaeology and Old Testament Study* (London: Oxford, 1967).

Budde in 1882, who claimed it was the meter used in laments generally. It consists of a long line, normally of five beats, dividing unevenly $(3+2)$ and showing much less parallelism than normal Hebrew poetry. Whether Budde was correct in linking this meter with funeral laments remains an open question, for it is used elsewhere as well; but it would certainly have suited impromptu eulogizing of the dead. In Lamentations 1–4 a high proportion of the lines fall into this pattern, but there are sufficient exceptions to show that it was used in no mere mechanical manner.

In addition, these chapters are built on the basis of an alphabetic acrostic. Chapters 1–2 each contain twenty-two verses, each verse having three lines, and the first word of each verse showing the acrostic letter. Chapter 4 is on the same pattern but has only two lines to a verse. Chapter 3, with sixty-six verses, has three verses for each letter of the alphabet, thus reminding us of Psalm 119, though there the groups are of eight verses each. A further peculiarity is that in chapters 2–4 pe comes before ayin, contrary to the usual order of the Hebrew alphabet, which seems to have been fixed already in Ugaritic.

Various explanations have been offered for the use of such an acrostic structure. In Psalm 119—apart from showing the author's virtuosity—it aids the memory, but that can hardly have been the motive here. One likely suggestion is that such a literary convention controlled the expression of profound grief. Another suggestion is that the use of the alphabet symbolizes that the completeness—"the A to Z"—of grief is being expressed.

That chapter 5 has twenty-two verses has caused some to suggest that the laments were first written in normal verse and then rewritten to include the acrostic. This idea is ingenious but unprovable.

9. Theological Values

The problem of suffering presented itself to Israel on two levels—national and personal. Jeremiah best shows that the two must be kept separate; for while he anticipated and justified the downfall of Jerusalem and the Davidic monarchy, he could not understand his personal suffering, which he as a righteous man should—according to popular theology—have avoided. The classical work on the suffering of the righteous is Job. Lamentations deals with the problem of national suffering.

While there is no effort to minimize Judah's sin, the writer is clearly overwhelmed by the greatness of her doom. Would Jeremiah have been similarly affected? This is one of the strongest arguments against his authorship. Yet there is a clear recognition that the disaster was caused by God, not his enemies. Even the mockery of Judah's enemies was caused by God (2:17). Hence, the laments are shot through with prayer; and prayer leads to hope in a situation in which hope appears meaningless. (There seems to be no memory of Jeremiah's limitation on the period of Chaldean rule, presumably because it was overshadowed by the greatness of the disaster; cf. the disciples' forgetfulness of Jesus' foretelling his resurrection.)

There is an apparent contradiction between 3:37–39, with its stress on God's sovereign rule, and 3:31–36, with its stress on his justice and covenant love. The contradiction is greater if this chapter (following the commentary) is regarded as the lament of a righteous man and not of the people as a whole who are suffering for their sin.

This is the problem of Job, where ultimately God's giving his servant into the power of Satan is never fully motivated, just as God does not answer Habakkuk's question (1:13), which raises the reverse problem of God's use of the wicked. Ultimately there are depths in God's actions that finite man cannot grasp. God's revelation in word and act consistently shows his justice and covenant love; yet there is always a residue of human experience that demands our bowing to a wisdom too high for our understanding. This finds its supreme example in the Cross and in the cry of Jesus in Mark 15:34. This is why every facile theory of the Atonement has failed to satisfy for long, for there are depths concealed in Golgotha that pass human understanding. Only when in glory we see free will and predestination reconciled will we also grasp how God's sovereign will is compatible with his justice and covenant love to his people.

10. Canonicity

There is no evidence that the canonicity of Lamentations was ever challenged. If the suggestion about its purpose (see above) is correct, Lamentations would have become part of Israel's sacred writings in the same way the Psalms did.

11. Text

The MT is well preserved, and little help for possible corrections can be obtained from the LXX or Syriac. These seem to be based on the present MT. Indeed, variants in the LXX apparently are due mainly to corruption of the Greek text rather than to a difference in the Hebrew. Annual liturgical repetition would aid accurate reproduction, but experience with hymns shows how easily changes in the text can creep in. It is significant that the extra lines in 1:7 and 2:19 add no new information, and though they intensify the anguish of these verses, have no substantial effect on the meaning.

Of the nineteen nonmetrical changes of text suggested in the notes, only one is purely conjectural, and it does not alter the sense significantly. Nine have versional and sometimes Hebrew MS support; some involve only a change in the Hebrew vowels. Where consonants are involved, they fall into the recognized categories of scribal error. In no case is there a significant change of meaning.

12. Bibliography

Albrektson, Bertil. *Studies in the Text and Theology of the Book of Lamentations*. Studia Theologica Lundensia. Vol. 21. Lund: Gleerup, 1963.

Archer, Gleason, L. *A Survey of Old Testament Introduction* (SOTI). Chicago: Moody, 1964, pp. 353–55.

Gottwald, N.K. *Studies in the Book of Lamentations*. Studies in Biblical Theology, no. 14. London: SCM, 1954.

Harrison, R.K. *Jeremiah and Lamentations*. Downers Grove, Ill.: InterVarsity, 1973.

Hillers, D.R. *Lamentations*. A.B. New York: Doubleday, 1972.

Keil, C.F. *The Prophecies of Jeremiah*. Vol. 2. KD. Grand Rapids: Eerdmans, 1949.

Peake, A.S. *Jeremiah and Lamentations*. Vol. 2. The Century Bible. Edinburgh: T.C. and E.C. Jack, 1910.

Simeon, Charles. *Expository Outlines on the Whole Bible*. 1847. Reprint. Grand Rapids: Zondervan, 1956.

Streane, A.W. *Jeremiah and Lamentations*. 2d ed. CBSC. Cambridge: Cambridge University Press, 1926.

Waltke, Bruce. "Lamentations." *Zondervan Pictorial Encyclopedia of the Bible* (ZPEB). 5 vols. Grand Rapids: Zondervan, 1975, 3:862–65.

13. Outline

I. The Desolation and Misery of Jerusalem (1:1–22)
    1. The Poet's Description (1:1–11b)
    2. The City's Plea (1:11c–16)
    3. The Poet's Lament (1:17)
    4. The City's Confession (1:18–22)

II. The Lord's Anger With His People (2:1–22)
    1. The Casting Off of People and Sanctuary (2:1–9)
    2. The Agony of the People (2:10–17)
    3. A Call to Prayer (2:18–19)
    4. The Response (2:20–22)

III. An Israelite's Complaint (3:1–66)
    1. His Personal Sufferings (3:1–20)
    2. Consolation and Hope of Grace (3:21–39)
    3. A Call to Penitence (3:40–51)
    4. The Growth of Hope (3:52–57)
    5. An Appeal for Vengeance (3:58–66)

IV. Zion, Past and Present (4:1–22)
    1. The Contrast (4:1–11)
    2. The Sin of Priests and Prophets (4:12–16)
    3. Vain Hopes (4:17–20)
    4. The Reversal of Doom (4:21–22)

V. An Appeal to the Lord (5:1–22)
    1. The Affliction of the Lord's People (5:1–18)
    2. The Lord's Abiding Power (5:19–22)

Text and Exposition

I. The Desolation and Misery of Jerusalem (1:1–22)

This lament is evidently somewhat later than chapters 2, 4, 5 (ch. 3 is undatable). The writer was no longer stunned by the utter brutality of defeat and destruction but was able to see what had happened in perspective. Jerusalem mourned by this time less for what she had suffered than for what she had become.

The lament could be interpreted as a dialogue between poet and city; but we should rather see the poet's description moving the mourning, widowed city to burst out into a plea both to God and to those strangers that would pass by and see her misery and desolation.

1. *The Poet's Description*

1:1–11b

¹How deserted lies the city,
    once so full of people!
How like a widow is she,
    who once was great among the nations!
She who was queen among the provinces
    has now become a slave.

²Bitterly she weeps at night,
    tears are upon her cheeks.
Among all her lovers
    there is none to comfort her.
All her friends have betrayed her;
    they have become her enemies.

³After affliction and harsh labor,
    Judah has gone into exile.
She dwells among the nations;
    she finds no resting place.
All who pursue her have overtaken her
    in the midst of her distress.

⁴The roads to Zion mourn,
    for no one comes to her appointed feasts.
All her gateways are desolate,
    her priests groan,
her maidens grieve,
    and she is in bitter anguish.

⁵Her foes have become her masters;
    her enemies are at ease.
The Lord has brought her grief
    because of her many sins.
Her children have gone into exile,
    captive before the foe.

⁶All the splendor has departed
    from the Daughter of Zion.
Her princes are like deer
    that find no pasture;

in weakness they have fled
before the pursuer.

[7]In the days of her affliction and wandering
Jerusalem remembers all the treasures
that were hers in days of old.
When her people fell into enemy hands,
there was no one to help her.
Her enemies looked at her
and laughed at her destruction.

[8]Jerusalem has sinned greatly
and so has become unclean.
All who honored her despise her,
for they have seen her nakedness;
she herself groans
and turns away.

[9]Her filthiness clung to her skirts;
she did not consider her future.
Her fall was astounding;
there was none to comfort her.
"Look, O LORD, on my affliction,
for the enemy has triumphed."

[10]The enemy laid hands
on all her treasures;
she saw pagan nations
enter her sanctuary—
those you had forbidden
to enter your assembly.

[11]All her people groan
as they search for bread;
they barter their treasures for food
to keep themselves alive.

1 The poet first looked at Jerusalem, the capital and representative of Judah, and contrasted what she once had been with what she then was. Even in the great days of David and Solomon, the territories of Israel never compared with those of Egypt, Assyria, and Babylonia at their height; while for buildings, riches (except perhaps in the days of Solomon), and population, Jerusalem never rivaled the great cities of the Near East. Yet we are not to take the poet's language as nationalistic or sentimental. Israel as God's land and Jerusalem as the city of God's sanctuary always held the hope of seeing Yahweh's universal kingship. So the poet was describing her potential in God's purposes. But what hope was there since the city was lying in ruins, deserted, and the land a vassal or slave?

2 In the "night" of her desolation, Jerusalem is pictured as weeping, not merely because of her sufferings, but even more because she had been betrayed by her "lovers" and "friends." These terms (cf. Jer 4:30; 30:14) are best explained by Ezekiel 23 and Hosea 8:9–10. The suggestion is not that there had been some signal act of betrayal by Judah's allies, even though Egypt, which had incited the city to rebellion against Nebuchadnezzar, had always pursued an essentially selfish policy. It is rather that, once the monarchy was firmly established, Israel was always faced with an inescapable choice. She could rely on God for her safety against external aggression, or she could turn to allies great and small. The first obvious example is found in 1 Kings 15:16–20. The prophets warned Israel that such alliances involved apostasy (cf. Hos 5:13; 8:8, 11; 14:3), but both the northern and the southern leaders would not listen. Judah had learned that such friends were a broken reed (Ezek 29:6–7), a lesson that we today have all too often had to learn as well.

3 From Jerusalem the poet turned to the people of Judah who had gone into exile, leaving the city deserted. This does not mean that the afflictions and deportations had been completely effective. The usual rendering "Judah has gone into exile because of affliction" (KJV), which suggests voluntary exile (cf. Jer 40:11; 42:4–7; 44:1), can hardly be justified. Not even 2 Samuel 15:19 and still less Ezekiel 12:3 provide evidence that *gālāh* ("to go into exile") was ever used of voluntary exile.

To "live among the nations" is used in 4:20 of national existence under the monarchy; hence to "dwell among the nations" need not have any reference to exile. The NIV's rendering is correct. The lack of "a resting place" refers to Judah's inability to guarantee peace under the monarchy.

4 Not even pilgrims came to the sanctuary. Ezra 3:2–6 shows that the temple building was not necessary for sacrifices to be brought, and Jeremiah 41:5 indicates that pilgrims came to the site even after the destruction of the temple. Apparently even that practice ceased, which suggests that this may be the latest of the laments. "Her priests" would be any surviving priests who had escaped deportation and remained as near the sacred site as possible. The linking of the "maidens" with the priests is also found in Jeremiah 31:13–14 and Joel 1:8–9, though whether this is because they had some part in the temple cultus (Ps 68:25) must remain an open question.

5 All this had been foreseen in the covenant (cf. Deut 28:44); thus there is the frank and open confession that this was the Lord's doing "because of her many sins." Though *pešaʿ* is traditionally rendered "transgression," it is essentially a secular word meaning "rebellion"—a word that brings out more fully its meaning in this type of context. Similarly, going into exile was one of the punishments foretold for a breach of the covenant (cf. Deut 28:36, 63–68). A touch of added pathos is given by "her children" paying the penalty for the sins of their parents.

6 Zion's majesty had collapsed. Her "princes" (*śārîm*, cf. Notes) had fled like famished stags before the hunters, caring nothing for the herd. Twice Jerusalem had yielded without a fight (2 Kings 24:1, 12; Dan 1:2); and at the last Zedekiah and his captains fled for their lives, abandoning the doomed city (2 Kings 25:4).

7 Jerusalem is seen as participating in the sufferings of her inhabitants. She remembered the days of "affliction and wandering," i.e., banishment in misery, when her people became the helpless prey of the conquerors. This again supports the view that this lament was composed some time after the fall of the city. Worst of all was the mocking laughter of her enemies. To this day in Bible lands laughter does not occupy the place it does in the West. Much of it would come under the condemnation of Ecclesiastes 7:6, where the laughter of fools is compared with the crackling of thorns under a pot. In the vast majority of cases, laughter is linked with scorn. Even in Genesis 17:17 and 18:12, its motive was incredulity; and in passages like

Job 8:21 and Psalm 126:2, the cause came less from happiness than from the reversal of fortune that had brought down and shamed one's enemies. The glee of Jerusalem's enemies came doubtless from the same motive that underlies some aspects of modern anti-Semitism—viz., a human reaction to Israel's claim to be God's elect. While malice still plays its part in modern laughter, the general humanizing of outward manners by Christianity has in some ways mitigated this element.

8–9 In v.5 it was recognized that Jerusalem's disasters were a result of her breach of the covenant; here she is compared to a debased, slatternly harlot, shamelessly exposing her nakedness and indifferent to the marks of menstrual blood—"filthiness"—on her garments, while "people shake their heads at her" (cf. Notes). Since harlotry is repeatedly used for Israel's idolatry and Baal worship, it is obviously implied here.

Though Israel earlier had ignored the warnings of the prophets (v.9a), the completeness of her collapse had finally brought her to her senses. We have her plea in v.9c, based on the insolence of her enemies. She knew she had no grounds for begging for a reversal of fortune, but the insolent triumphing of the enemy called for divine retribution. This is a frequent note in the OT, perhaps the most striking being in Isaiah 10:12, where the Assyrian was to be punished, not because he had smitten Judah, but because of his pride while doing it. The NEB follows the OL (cf. Notes) and renders, "Look, LORD, upon her misery," i.e., the poet, not Jerusalem, was speaking. It is much smoother, but this in itself makes the OL suspect. "The enemy has triumphed" (NIV, RSV, NEB) is literally correct but misleading. It is not the victory but the insolent boasting after it that is meant.

10 The worst feature of all was that Jerusalem had lost what she held most dear. Later sentiment had enveloped Jerusalem in a haze of earthly glory and beauty, but in fact her outstanding glory then, as later, was the temple—and even the temple derived its chief glory from its sanctity. This had been brutally violated by the conquerors.

Those who had been forbidden to enter the Lord's congregation were the Ammonites and the Moabites (Deut 23:3), descended from Lot, and so distantly related to Israel. They are not mentioned as fighting against Jerusalem at this time; so the argument seems to be that if distantly related tribes were excluded, how much more the completely unrelated Chaldeans!

11a–b The poet brings his lament to a climax. The usual renderings give an improbable anticlimax. In proportion to what Jerusalem had suffered, to say, "They barter their treasures for food," does not seem to be particularly serious. In addition, it is hard to believe that when the Chaldeans had finished plundering the city, there was much treasure left. Already Theodoret (c. 450) suggested what is probably the true meaning of the statement—viz., "They gave their darlings for food to keep alive." This use of "treasures" may be found in Hosea 9:16. It is unimportant whether we think of them eating their children (cf. 2:20; 4:10 [prophesied in Deut 28:53–57; cf. also 2 Kings 6:28–29]) or selling them into slavery. Probably both are intended.

Notes

4 The LXX and the OL presuppose נְהוּגֹת (*nᵉhûgôt*, "have been dragged away") for נוּגֹת (*nûgôt*, "have been afflicted"; NIV, "grieve"). This is unnecessary, and the MT gives a better parallelism.

6 שַׂר (*śar*) originally meant "the king's representative" and was used for his high ministers of state, chieftains, and army leaders. It does not imply membership in the royal family.

7 This verse is metrically irregular, having four *qinah* lines instead of three, something found again only in 2:19. In this type of poetry, such an irregularity is inexplicable—it does not even heighten the effect—so NEB, JB, and virtually all modern commentators omit the second line—"all the treasures that were hers in days of old"—though a few prefer the omission of the third, which is much less likely. It should be noted that if we retain the extra line, we have to translate as the NIV: "In the last days of her affliction and wandering Jerusalem remembers . . . ," though there is nothing in the MT to suggest the "in."

8 We are told in the first line that "Jerusalem has sinned greatly and so has become unclean [לְנִידָה (*lᵉnîḏāh*)]." This is the only instance where this form is found. It is normally (not KJV) assumed that it is a variant form for נִדָּה (*niddāh*, "menstrual impurity") and so is rendered by one or another suitable euphemism. If this is correct, it seems impossible to explain why a variant of a well-known technical term should have been used, or alternately how the text became corrupted. It is preferable to follow the LXX, Rashi, KJV, RV mg., which derive it from נוּד (*nûḏ*, "wander") and to translate it "she is removed." Better still, as has been done in the comments above, is to accept Ibn Ezra's view, followed by a number of recent scholars, including Hillers, who linked it with the other meaning of *nûḏ*, i.e., "shake the head." At the same time it is likely that it was intended that the hearer think of the common term *niddāh* as well.

9 The OL, followed by the Bohairic, presupposes עָנְיָהּ (*'onyāhh*, "her affliction") in place of the MT's עָנְיִי (*'onyî*, "my affliction"). In cases of this kind, it is impossible to find any purely scribal ground for preferring one reading above another. Since, however, it is normally preferable to follow the more difficult text, so long as it is not due to obvious scribal error, we shall be wise to retain the MT here.

2. The City's Plea

1:11c–16

> "Look, O LORD, and consider,
> for I am despised.
>
> 12"Is it nothing to you, all you who pass by?
> Look around and see.
> Is any suffering like my suffering
> that was inflicted on me,
> that the LORD brought on me
> in the day of his fierce anger?
>
> 13"From on high he sent fire,
> sent it down into my bones.
> He spread a net for my feet
> and turned me back.
> He made me desolate,
> faint all the day long.
>
> 14"My sins have been bound into a yoke;
> by his hands they were woven together.

> They have come upon my neck
>   and the Lord has sapped my strength.
> He has handed me over
>   to those I cannot withstand.
>
> 15"The Lord has rejected
>   all the warriors in my midst;
> he has summoned an army against me
>   to crush my young men.
> In his winepress the Lord has trampled
>   the Virgin Daughter of Judah.
>
> 16"This is why I weep
>   and my eyes overflow with tears.
> No one is near to comfort me,
>   no one to restore my spirit.
> My children are destitute
>   because the enemy has prevailed."

11c We are to think of Jerusalem's being so moved by the poet's words that she broke out in a prayer, which forms a suitable halfway stage in the poem. "Look, . . . for I am despised" (NIV, RSV) seems to miss the main point of the prayer. The NEB is probably more correct with "Look, O LORD, and see how cheap I am accounted" (cf. TWOT s.v. *zālal*, 1:244). It is not the fact of being despised but the extent to which she is looked down on that she hopes may move God to pity.

12 From God Jerusalem turns with a plea for pity to the nations round about, pictured as travelers passing along the roads of devastated Judah. "The day of his fierce anger" is the Day of the Lord. Just as in Mark 13 and parallels the Fall of Jerusalem is linked with the sufferings of the end time, so it is here (cf. also Jer 4:23–28). It would be pedantic to object to the use of the first two lines of this verse in a meditation on our Lord's passion. For all that, there is no connection; and a careless use of the verse could lead to a false theory of the Atonement.

13–14 These verses outline Jerusalem's sufferings and give the reason for them. The fire from on high continues the picture of God's burning anger, acting like a high fever with its racking pains, which brings death. Not Jerusalem's enemies, but God himself had entrapped the city, bringing it to an inescapable and ignominious end (cf. Ezek 12:13; 17:20). The result has been an example of desolation and weakness, as though from a fatal disease. There can be little doubt that the MT of v.14 is questionable (cf. Notes). The best rendering, perhaps, is that suggested by Hillers: "Watch is kept over my steps" (cf. NIV mg.). "By his hands they were woven together" then refers to "my steps," having the same force as the "net" of v.13. "They have come upon my neck" implies that Jerusalem just could not withstand her enemies when they came against her. For a position of Jerusalem's strength, the siege, which lasted only a year and a half, was surprisingly short (2 Kings 25:1–2; cf. the three years' resistance by Samaria [2 Kings 17:5–6]).

15–16 Nothing but despair was left. Our understanding of v.15 depends on our interpretation of *mô'ēd* in line 2. The NIV, NEB, and JB read *mô'ād* ("an army," "the gathering of troops"), in which case Zion's lament is no more than a repetition

707

of the complete destruction of all that was strongest and fairest in Judah. There is more likely a climax here, and we should understand *môʿēd* as a joyful harvest festival (cf. TWOT, 1:388–89), to which, not Jerusalem, but her enemies were invited. So bitter was the experience that Jerusalem did not use the name "LORD" ("Yahweh"), with its covenant associations, but "Lord" (*ʾdōnāy*). "The Lord has rejected all the warriors in my midst," treated them like chaff: "he has summoned [a festival] against me to crush my young men," not merely to thresh them; and "in his winepress the Lord has trampled the Virgin Daughter of Judah," to provide the wine of rejoicing. (Judah is mentioned to underline the fact that there was no hope of her compensating for Jerusalem's disaster.)

Jerusalem's heartbroken sob in v.16 is that "the enemy has prevailed." Defeat is bitter, but doubly so when the victors are God's enemies. Modern translations rightly follow the early versions in omitting the repetition of "mine eye" (KJV, ASV) (cf. Notes).

Notes

14 Instead of עֹל נִשְׂקַד (*niśqad ʿōl*, "bound into a yoke"), the LXX presupposes עַל נִשְׁקַד (*niśqad ʿal*, "he kept a watch over"). The reading of *š* instead of *ś* avoids a *hapax legomenon* and is supported by numerous Hebrew MSS, the LXX, Vulgate, and Syriac, while the reading *ʿal* finds support also in the Syriac.

The emendation of "steps" for "sins" involves reading פְּשָׂעַי (*peśāʿay*) for פְּשָׁעַי (*pešāʿay*) (cf. 1 Sam 20:3). The NEB's "His yoke was lifted on to my neck" implies עָלָה עֻלּוֹ צֶל צַוָּארִי (*ʾālāh ʿullô ʿal ṣawwaʾrî*) (supported by Symm.) instead of the MT's עָלוּ עַל (*ʾālû ʿal*, lit., "they go up upon"), which has the advantage of avoiding a short line.

16 A few Hebrew MSS, the LXX, Syriac, Targum, and Vulgate omit the second עֵינִי (*ʿênî*, "my eye"), which is in any case surplus to the metrical requirements.

3. The Poet's Lament

1:17

> 17Zion stretches out her hands,
>   but there is no one to comfort her.
> The LORD has decreed for Jacob
>   that his neighbors become his foes;
> Jerusalem has become
>   an unclean thing among them.

17 To prepare us for Jerusalem's final confession, the poet recorded that though Zion "stretches out her hands" in prayer, there is no comfort; for the destruction was Yahweh's command. Abandoned by him, Jerusalem had become a filthy (menstruous) thing scorned by all.

4. The City's Confession

1:18–22

> 18"The LORD is righteous,
>   yet I rebelled against his command.

Listen, all you peoples;
  look upon my suffering.
My young men and maidens
  have gone into exile.

19"I called to my allies
  but they betrayed me.
My priests and my elders
  perished in the city
while they searched for food
  to keep themselves alive.

20"See, O LORD, how distressed I am!
  I am in torment within,
and in my heart I am disturbed,
  for I have been most rebellious.
Outside, the sword bereaves;
  inside, there is only death.

21"People have heard my groaning,
  but there is no one to comfort me.
All my enemies have heard of my distress;
  they rejoice at what you have done.
May you bring the day you have announced
  so they may become like me.

22"Let all their wickedness come before you;
  deal with them
as you have dealt with me
  because of all my sins.
My groans are many
  and my heart is faint."

18–22 While the poet had been speaking, Jerusalem had had time to consider her position once more. She immediately confessed that her plight had been caused by her rebellion alone (v.18). The RSV is certainly at fault in introducing "but" in v.18b—"but hear, all you peoples"—for this would imply some measure of self-excuse, which is not present. Jerusalem's one hope is Yahweh's judgment on her enemies, though she did not expect restoration as a result. She told them that they would not suffer less than she had, the more so as "I called to my allies but they betrayed me" (v.19).

The very fact that Jerusalem's one hope and comfort (vv.20–21) was the similar fate awaiting her enemies is an almost irrefutable argument against Jeremiah's authorship, for he had foretold both the restoration of Jerusalem and the downfall of the Chaldeans after seventy years (Jer 25:12). This very hopelessness is the best testimony to the utter shock the Fall of Jerusalem caused even among the godly. It also helps explain why Jeremiah was so isolated, the optimism of many after Jehoiachin's deportation (Jer 28:1–4; 29:8–9), and the madness of Zedekiah's revolt. Those who condemn Jerusalem's attitude as representing the lower level of the OT should ponder passages like Revelation 6:9–10; 19:1–3. There are a number of minor textual problems in this section (cf. Notes), with only small bearing on the meaning.

Notes

---

20 The rendering "inside [i.e., 'at home'], there is only death" (NIV, KJV, ASV) for כַּמָּוֶת
בַּבַּיִת (*babbayit kammāwet*) can hardly be correct. The omission of כְּ (*kᵉ*, "as") in the JB,
following the Syriac, makes it easier but does not explain the MT. The NEB may be
correct with "as plague does within doors," for מָוֶת (*māwet*) does have this meaning, but
normally only where the context makes it clear (e.g., Jer 15:2; 18:21). More likely is
Hillers's emendation: כָּפָן (*kāpān*) or כַּפְנוּת (*kapnût*), i.e., "famine."

21 הֵבֵאתָ יוֹם (*hēḇēʾtā yôm*) is interpreted by the KJV and ASV as a prophetic perfect: "Thou
wilt bring the day"; some modern versions—RSV, NEB, JB—render it as an imperative:
"Bring the day" (so Syr.). The NIV renders it by a subjunctive: "May you bring the day."

II. The Lord's Anger With His People (2:1–22)

The main notes in the first lament were desertion, desolation, and shame; here
the stress is rather on destruction. One has the impression that it was composed
between the capture of the city in the fourth month (2 Kings 25:3–4) and the coming
of Nebuzaradan to mete out Nebuchadnezzar's vengeance (2 Kings 25:8–12) a month
later; for unless it is poetic license, the dead still lay on the streets unburied. This
would explain why the first lament, though the latest in time, is placed first. Initially
the sheer impact of physical disaster is overwhelming; it is only later that the shame
of it all is seen as even worse.

1. The Casting Off of People and Sanctuary

2:1–9

> ¹How the Lord has covered the Daughter of Zion
>   with the cloud of his anger!
> He has hurled down the splendor of Israel
>   from heaven to earth;
> he has not remembered his footstool
>   in the day of his anger.
>
> ²Without pity the Lord has swallowed up
>   all the dwellings of Jacob;
> in his wrath he has torn down
>   the strongholds of the Daughter of Judah.
> He has brought her kingdom and its princes
>   down to the ground in dishonor.
>
> ³In fierce anger he has cut off
>   every horn of Israel.
> He has withdrawn his right hand
>   at the approach of the enemy.
> He has burned in Jacob like a flaming fire
>   that consumes everything around it.
>
> ⁴Like an enemy he has strung his bow;
>   his right hand is ready.
> Like a foe he has slain
>   all who were pleasing to the eye;

he has poured out his wrath like fire
  on the tent of the Daughter of Zion.

⁵The Lord is like an enemy;
  he has swallowed up Israel.
He has swallowed up all her palaces
  and destroyed her strongholds.
He has multiplied mourning and lamentation
  for the Daughter of Judah.

⁶He has laid waste his dwelling like a garden;
  he has destroyed his place of meeting.
The LORD has made Zion forget
  her appointed feasts and her Sabbaths;
in his fierce anger he has spurned
  both king and priest.

⁷The Lord has rejected his altar
  and abandoned his sanctuary.
He has handed over to the enemy
  the walls of her palaces;
they have raised a shout in the house of the LORD
  as on the day of an appointed feast.

⁸The LORD determined to tear down
  the wall around the Daughter of Zion.
He stretched out a measuring line
  and did not withhold his hand from destroying.
He made ramparts and walls lament;
  together they wasted away.

⁹Her gates have sunk into the ground;
  their bars he has broken and destroyed.
Her king and her princes are exiled among the nations,
  the law is no more,
and her prophets no longer find
  visions from the LORD.

1 The storm had passed over the poet's head. As he picked himself up and gazed on the desolation around him, he declared with the voice of faith that this had been the work of the "Lord" (ᵃḏōnāy), the All-Sovereign—this title is used four times in this section—though the name "LORD" ("Yahweh") is used three times in the latter part to make it clear that God remains the God of Israel.

The sun of Jerusalem had been hidden; "the splendor of Israel," i.e., the temple, had been hurled from its high eminence ("from heaven"); and it had been spurned. "His footstool" can hardly mean the ark, as supposed by some; for Jeremiah 3:16, which must date from before the destruction of the temple, is evidence that it had vanished earlier.

2 All Judah had been devastated, and the kingdom—probably, as in the LXX, "the king"—and its rulers had lost their sacred character ("he has brought down," lit., "profaned").

3 Both actively ("he has cut off every horn," i.e., all strength) and passively ("he has withdrawn his right hand"), God had destroyed his people.

4–5 God is then depicted as a mighty, hostile warrior, armed with bow to slay at a distance and with sword for close fighting (taking "on the tent of the Daughter of Zion" with "all who were pleasing to the eye"), and finally burning up all that was left. He had behaved like an enemy.

6 Like an enemy, the Lord "has destroyed his place of meeting," i.e., the temple. The LXX reading—*kᵉgepen* ("as a vine"), followed by the NEB, instead of the MT's *kaggan* ("like a garden")—suggests a corrupted text but does not help us to the correct one; and no modern emendation carries conviction. The rest of the verse clearly refers to the destruction of the temple. "King and priest" are here linked; for, as the history of the monarchy clearly shows, the king was the supervisor of the temple cultus, even if he was excluded from many of the priestly functions.

7 The thought is here continued. "The walls of her palaces" (*armᵉnôṯêhā*) are fortified residences. *'Armôn* is nowhere else used of the temple, which the context would suggest; so its use may have been caused by the mention of "king and priest" in the previous verse. Under the monarchy, too, the temple formed part of a grandiose complex, including the royal palace and state buildings. The enemies' shouts of triumph are compared to the festal shouts of joy (cf. Pss 66:1; 81:1; 95:1 et al.).

8–9 From the temple the lament passes briefly to the city and then to the king (surely Jehoiachin is meant) and his ministers in exile. "The law is no more, and her prophets no longer find visions from the LORD" should be regarded as a unitary statement. There was no indication of God's will, either through priestly interpretation of the law or through prophetic vision. Once again it is hard to see Jeremiah as the author of the statement. (See v.14 for the prophets.)

2. The Agony of the People

2:10–17

> ¹⁰The elders of the Daughter of Zion
>   sit on the ground in silence;
> they have sprinkled dust on their heads
>   and put on sackcloth.
> The young women of Jerusalem
>   have bowed their heads to the ground.
>
> ¹¹My eyes fail from weeping,
>   I am in torment within,
> my heart is poured out on the ground
>   because my people are destroyed,
> because children and infants faint
>   in the streets of the city.
>
> ¹²They say to their mothers,
>   "Where is bread and wine?"
> as they faint like wounded men
>   in the streets of the city,
> as their lives ebb away
>   in their mothers' arms.
>
> ¹³What can I say for you?
>   With what can I compare you,
>   O Daughter of Jerusalem?

To what can I liken you,
that I may comfort you,
O Virgin Daughter of Zion?
Your wound is as deep as the sea.
Who can heal you?

¹⁴The visions of your prophets
were false and worthless;
they did not expose your sin
to ward off your captivity.
The oracles they gave you
were false and misleading.

¹⁵All who pass your way
clap their hands at you;
they scoff and shake their heads
at the Daughter of Jerusalem;
"Is this the city that was called
the perfection of beauty,
the joy of the whole earth?"

¹⁶All your enemies open their mouths
wide against you;
they scoff and gnash their teeth
and say, "We have swallowed her up.
This is the day we have waited for;
we have lived to see it."

¹⁷The LORD has done what he planned;
he has fulfilled his word,
which he decreed long ago.
He has overthrown you without pity,
he has let the enemy gloat over you,
he has exalted the horn of your foes.

10 From the bitter past the lament turns to the even more bitter present. The mention of the "elders" and "young women" is probably intended to include the whole surviving population. Sitting on the ground in sackcloth, with dust on the head, in silence, and bowing the head to the ground speak strongly of mourning.

11–12 The poet joined in the mourning in language that shows his physical participation: "My eyes fail from weeping, I am in torment within, my heart is poured out on the ground" (v.11); i.e., it joins in the mourning rites. The fall of the city and the execution of the desperate men who had defended it did not bring the starvation to an end. During the first stage of military occupation, foraging in the surrounding countryside would not have been permitted. "Bread and wine" probably refers to essentials and semiluxuries.

13 So great was the suffering that words failed: "What can I say for you [cf. Notes]? With what can I compare you . . .? Your wound is as deep as the sea." It is probable that not the extent of the sea is intended (cf. NEB) but rather that the devastation of the city was reminiscent of the chaotic sea.

14 The best commentaries on this verse are Jeremiah 23:18–22 and Ezekiel 13:10–16. Just as the majority of preachers are so obsessed with the holiness of the church that they have not been able to take the church's shortcomings seriously, so it was in Israel. It took the shock of the Babylonian exile to break the power and influence of the popular prophets and to discredit them finally.

15–17 In ancient times when each pagan city or group of cities had its own deity or deities (henotheism), there was a degree of mutual toleration in spite of rivalries. However, Israel's claim that Yahweh was the only God, that Israel was his people, and that Jerusalem was his capital caused bitter jealousy and joy at their downfall (v.16). "The Lord . . . has fulfilled his word, which he decreed long ago" (v.17) refers presumably to passages like Leviticus 26:14–46 and Deuteronomy 28:15–68.

Notes

13 The MT has אֲעִידֵךְ (ᵃʿîḏēḵ, "What can I say for you?"), but attempts to justify this (e.g., NIV, NEB) do violence to the Hebrew. The Vulgate overcomes this by reading אֶעֱרָךְ (ʾeʿᵉrōḵ, "compare").
15 The last line of this verse heavily overloads the meter and is doubtless a scribal memory of Ps 48:2.

3. *A Call to Prayer*

2:18–19

> ¹⁸The hearts of the people
>   cry out to the Lord.
> O wall of the Daughter of Zion,
>   let your tears flow like a river
>   day and night;
> give yourself no relief,
>   your eyes no rest.

> ¹⁹Arise, cry out in the night,
>   as the watches of the night begin;
> pour out your heart like water
>   in the presence of the Lord.
> Lift up your hands to him
>   for the lives of your children,
> who faint from hunger
>   at the head of every street.

18–19b Despair should drive people to God; so the poet called Zion to prayer, for we must translate, "Cry out from the heart, O wall of the Daughter of Zion" (v.18; cf. Notes). Many wish to emend "wall"; but though the expression may seem strange, it is a call for everything, including the ruins, to join in the prayer of anguish.

19c This line bears out the interpretation already given in v.12, i.e., that the lament describes the position after the capture of the city, not the sufferings during the siege. For "who faint from hunger at the head of every street" (NIV; cf. KJV, ASV), see Notes.

Notes

18 Several modern translations (e.g., RSV, NEB, NAB, JB) emend צַעַק (ṣāʿaq, "[their heart] cried"; so NIV, KJV, NASB)—with no suitable antecedent (NIV et al. supply "of the people") and separated from the second half of the line, which obviously belong to it—to צַעֲקִי (ṣaʿăqî, "cry out [from the heart]").

19 As in 1:7, this verse contains four lines; and for the reasons given there, many feel that the last line here should be deleted.

4. The Response
2:20–22

> 20"Look, O LORD, and consider:
>   Whom have you ever treated like this?
> Should women eat their offspring,
>   the children they have cared for?
> Should priest and prophet be killed
>   in the sanctuary of the Lord?
>
> 21"Young and old lie together
>   in the dust of the streets;
> my young men and maidens
>   have fallen by the sword.
> You have slain them in the day of your anger;
>   you have slaughtered them without pity.
>
> 22"As you summon to a feast day,
>   so you summoned against me terrors on every side.
> In the day of the LORD's anger
>   no one escaped or survived;
> those I cared for and reared,
>   my enemy has destroyed."

20–22 Whether the poet was composing a prayer for the survivors, whether it was meant as an ideal prayer, or whether it was a poetic expression of what was being prayed is immaterial. A similar problem is presented by Jeremiah 3:22b–25. In one way the prayer is even more hopeless than the later one in 1:20–22. It is a desperate recounting of utmost woe. It is doubtful whether the NIV, the NEB, and the JB are correct in finding a question in v.20a. It is rather a reminder—the prayer is addressed to the LORD—that there was a covenant relationship. Since the prophets had stressed the inviolability of the temple (cf. Jer 7:4), it was natural that they should gather there in its last hour. For the "solemn assembly" or "feast day" (v.22), see comments at 1:15.

III. An Israelite's Complaint (3:1–66)

Were this lament in the Psalter, it is improbable that it would have been definitely linked with the Fall of Jerusalem; for most of its language has no particular applicability to it, and that which has could come from any situation of major distress. The traditional view, strengthened by the attribution of the book as a whole to the prophet, has seen in it Jeremiah's personal lament (so ISBE, p. 1825); but the use of the first person *plural* in vv.40–47 has been held by many to militate against this. In the royal psalms there are instances of this alternation between king and people, but not in personal laments. This and other factors have led to widespread agreement among modern scholars—including E.J. Young and R.K. Harrison (cf. Introduction: Authorship)—that in this chapter personified Jerusalem or Judah is speaking. (Attempts by some to break the lament into a number of portions by various authors do not concern us here, the more so because of their intrinsic improbability, and especially because the hypothetical original sections would have had to be rewritten to fit them into the acrostic pattern.)

The difficulties in this view are insurmountable. Not only in chapters 1, 2, and 4, but in the OT generally, the personification of a people or city is feminine. In addition, such an interpretation runs counter to the open confession of sin in the other laments. These incontrovertible facts have led to a swing back to an individual interpretation. Detail may be found in Hillers's commentary (cf. Bibliography). I cannot, however, agree with him that "every man" is speaking. It would be an exceptional Israelite who could use this language, and some of his experiences could hardly be generalized.

The commentary is based on the assumption that Jeremiah is speaking—to ascribe chapter 3 to the prophet does not determine his authorship of the remainder of the book, for there is no need to assume unitary authorship—and that the introduction of the first person plural is his placing of words in the people's mouth, as he possibly did in Jeremiah 3:22b–25.

The reminiscences of many psalms is one of the arguments used against authorship by Jeremiah. Behind this lies—consciously or unconsciously—the supposition that many of these were written later than the prophet, an assumption that modern psalm-studies have almost completely dissipated. If the prophet adopted the difficult treble acrostic (cf. Introduction: Literary Form) as a curb on his anguish, the adoption of familiar phrases from the Psalms, especially from the psalms of lamentation, should create no psychological or literary difficulty in the ascription of this lament to him.

1. *His Personal Sufferings*

3:1–20

> [1]I am the man who has seen affliction
>   by the rod of his wrath.
> [2]He has driven me away and made me walk
>   in darkness rather than light;
> [3]indeed, he has turned his hand against me
>   again and again, all day long.
>
> [4]He has made my skin and my flesh grow old
>   and has broken my bones.

⁵He has besieged me and surrounded me
  with bitterness and hardship.
⁶He has made me dwell in darkness
  like those long dead.

⁷He has walled me in so I cannot escape;
  he has weighed me down with chains.
⁸Even when I call out or cry for help,
  he shuts out my prayer.
⁹He has barred my way with blocks of stone;
  he has made my paths crooked.

¹⁰Like a bear lying in wait,
  like a lion in hiding,
¹¹he dragged me from the path and mangled me
  and left me without help.
¹²He drew his bow
  and made me the target for his arrows.

¹³He pierced my heart
  with arrows from his quiver.
¹⁴I became the laughingstock of all my people;
  they mock me in song all day long.
¹⁵He has filled me with bitter herbs
  and sated me with gall.

¹⁶He has broken my teeth with gravel;
  he has trampled me in the dust.
¹⁷I have been deprived of peace;
  I have forgotten what prosperity is.
¹⁸So I say, "My splendor is gone
  and all that I had hoped from the LORD."

¹⁹I remember my affliction and my wandering,
  the bitterness and the gall.
²⁰I well remember them,
  and my soul is downcast within me.

1 In the OT "to see" frequently goes beyond the obtaining of a visual image and involves a sharing in it, as here (cf. note at 5:1). The Hebrew perfect *rāʾāh* ("see") here includes present experience. We should render most of the verbs in vv. 1–18 by present perfects or presents, for there is no suggestion that the experiences were past. The omission of the name of God is not metrically motivated; its nonappearance in vv. 1–21—except in v. 18 (see comment)—is intended to underline the poet's feelings of abandonment and separation. For "the rod of his wrath," see Job 9:34; 21:9; Psalm 89:32; and Isaiah 10:5.

2–3 *Nāhag* ("driven") is used of driving animals, never of God's gracious leading (v. 2). It was done by the rod of his anger. For God's compulsion, see Jeremiah 20:7, 9. "Indeed, he has turned his hand against me again and again, all day long" (v. 3) is a complaint of exceptional suffering.

4 The force of the Hebrew *billāh* ("grow old") is not to make old but to produce the effect of aging, i.e., to wear out. It could be that the breaking of his bones refers to fever pains (cf. comments at 1:13–14), a meaning that suits Isaiah 38:13.

5 JPS and Hillers render this verse "he has besieged and encircled me with poverty and hardship" (cf. Notes). NIV's "bitterness" [*rō'š*] speaks of the ultimate poverty—the loss of all hope.

6 "Darkness" is one of the traditional features of Sheol. The force of "those long dead"—if indeed we should not render "those dead forever"—is that they are also forgotten.

7–8 The mention of "chains" (v.7) suggests that we should think of the poet's being "walled in" in some dungeon from which his cries for help could not be heard (v.8). There may well be some link in thought with Jeremiah 38:6.

9 The poet was like a man trapped in a maze. The walls were so well built—"with blocks of stone"—that he could not glimpse the right way through any cracks in them, while side paths led to dead ends or away from escape.

10–12 Even worse, the poet found the path beset with danger. (For the bear and the lion [v.10], see Amos 5:9 and Hosea 13:8.) If somehow he managed to escape his deadly foes and God's leading astray (v.11), he found God, the grim hunter, there to shoot him, not his assailants (v.12; cf. Job 16:12–13).

13 "He pierced my heart with arrows" may simply be a reminiscence of Job 16:13. This figure shows the power of the archer's arm, which transfixed the poet with arrows. "In my back he has planted his darts" (JB) is almost certainly wrong, for it would imply that even as the poet had fled from the wild animals, he had fled from God. "Heart" (NIV, RSV) is a valid equivalent for the metaphorical meaning but misses the literal picture of "kidneys" apparently intended here.

14 RSV ("of all peoples") and the NEB ("to all nations") do not explain in a marginal note that they are not following the MT's *'ammî* ("my people"; so NIV; cf. Notes). This is a vital point in determining whether we hear the voice of an individual or of personified Israel. It is easier to see Jeremiah as the butt of popular ballads than fallen Jerusalem as a constant theme in her neighbors' taunt songs.

15 "Bitter herbs" (NIV) preserves the parallelism with *la'ănāh* ("gall"), which is traditionally rendered "wormwood." Wormwood is the name given to certain plants used for imparting a bitter flavor to some drinks; the name has no connection with either worm or wood.

16 "He has broken [*gāras*] my teeth with gravel; he has trampled [*kāpaš*] me in the dust." *Kāpaš* is a *hapax legomenon; gāras* is found only once elsewhere (Ps 119:20). There are therefore some variations in renderings. Some suggest the feeding on gravel and dust (or ashes) in mockery; some, the violent grinding of the face in the ground by others. The latter seems the more probable. Yet again it could be argued that it refers to the type of bread made from the sweepings of the granary floor that Jeremiah must have received toward the end of the siege.

17 In the parallelism of "deprived of peace [*šālôm*]" and "forgotten what prosperity [*ṭôbāh*] is," *šālôm* must carry its nuance of "success" or "prosperity" (cf. TWOT,

2:931). A reference to God—"Thou hast removed" (KJV, ASV)—is to be avoided as being premature (cf. v.18); no change of consonantal text is involved.

18 In "my splendor [*neṣaḥ*] is gone," *neṣaḥ* indicates "glory" rather than strength. Both for the prophet and for Israel, hope in the Lord was their glory; when that was gone, they were on the level of the pagans round about. The poet's mention of "the LORD" broke the spell of misery that had bound him.

19–20 The MT's "Remember my affliction" is premature; the writer first has to recall the character of the Lord (vv.22–23). The NIV follows the LXX in rendering "I remember my misery and my wandering, the bitterness and the gall [*rō'š;* cf. note at v.5]."

Notes

5 ראֹשׁ (*rō'š*) is a "bitter and poisonous herb" (BDB, p. 912). Though "gall" would seem to be unsuitable here (and in v.19), TWOT (2:826) supports that meaning. BDB adds that *rō'š* is always used figuratively. JPS and Hillers read רֵאשׁ (*rē'š*, "poverty"), a variant (Prov 6:11; 30:8) of רֵישׁ (*rêš*), which gives excellent sense.

14 A *sebir* (an ancient Jewish textual conjecture), a number of Hebrew MSS, and the Syriac read עַמִּים (*'ammîm*, "peoples")—MSS with *'ammîm* can be explained by the *sebir*. That the reading is unknown in the LXX and the Vulgate and is rejected by the MT tradition makes it highly suspect; it is probably an early attempt to make possible the personification of the speaker as Israel.

19 The MT reads זְכָר (*z^ekor*, "remember"). For the reason given above (personification of the speaker as Israel), most modern translations follow the LXX: זָכַרְתִּי (*sākartî,* "I remember").

2. Consolation and Hope of Grace

3:21–39

²¹Yet this I call to mind
  and therefore I have hope:

²²Because of the LORD's great love we are not consumed,
  for his compassions never fail.
²³They are new every morning;
  great is your faithfulness.
²⁴I say to myself, "The LORD is my portion;
  therefore I will wait for him."

²⁵The LORD is good to those whose hope is in him,
  to the one who seeks him;
²⁶it is good to wait quietly
  for the salvation of the LORD.
²⁷It is good for a man to bear the yoke
  while he is young.

²⁸Let him sit alone in silence,
  for the LORD has laid it on him.

29Let him bury his face in the dust—
  there may yet be hope.
30Let him offer his cheek to one who would strike him,
  and let him be filled with disgrace.

31For men are not cast off
  by the Lord forever.
32Though he brings grief, he will show compassion,
  so great is his unfailing love.
33For he does not willingly bring affliction
  or grief to the children of men.

34To crush underfoot
  all prisoners in the land,
35to deny a man his rights
  before the Most High,
36to deprive a man of justice—
  would not the Lord see such things?

37Who can speak and have it happen
  if the Lord has not decreed it?
38Is it not from the mouth of the Most High
  that both calamities and good things come?
39Why should any living man complain
  when punished for his sins?

21 The "hope" that the writer expressed here is not created by denying or minimizing suffering and misery. Rather, these are transformed when the mind is turned to God.

22 The vital word in this verse is *hesed* ("great love"), the covenant love and loyalty of the Lord that leads to *raḥᵃmîm* ("compassion," "mercy"), derived from *reḥem* ("womb"). The covenant had called Israel into existence, and the Lord's loving mercy to what he had created would not end.

23 The very fact of awakening to a new day is in itself a renewal of God's mercy. Man has passed safely through the night, a foreshadowing of death. So the verse ends with "faithfulness," the counterpart of *hesed*, with which the previous verse started.

24 The traditional rendering "says my soul" (KJV, ASV, RSV) is misleading, for *nepeš* is the whole of a man; indeed, "myself" (NIV) is sufficient. The poet says, in effect, that he has had so little of this world's goods and pleasures because his share has been the Lord (cf. Pss 16:5; 73:26; 119:57; 142:5).

25–27 These three verses begin with "good" (*ṭôb*). The significance of this word in Hebrew may escape the modern reader. For us it tends to mean that which conforms to our concepts, but in the OT it is above all that which expresses God's will and purpose. Here there is the acceptance of God's time and God's will (v.25), faith expressing itself in quiet hope and the learning of discipline (v.26). There is perhaps too ready a rejection of the variant reading "bear the yoke while he is young" (v.27; cf. Notes). For the usual rendering, see Hebrews 12:7–11.

28–30 This group of verses states how the principles of vv.25–27 will be worked out, especially that of bearing the yoke. The implication of "Let him sit alone in silence, for the LORD has laid it on him" (v.28) is that God's yoke of service will separate one from ordinary human life and lead him to be an outcast (cf. Job 2:8). Silence implies both an acceptance of God's will and a refusal to complain to men. With this should go the complete submission to God pictured in v.29 by the Oriental obeisance. It leads too to the willingness to be treated like a slave (v.30), for the yoke was a symbol of servitude (but cf. Jer 20:1–2). The principles formulated here will, of course, apply equally to the man called to be a prophet and to the people called to be God's private treasure (Exod 19:5–6).

31–33 These verses give reasons that will make the bearing of the yoke easier, viz., God's rejection—i.e., his failure to use—is temporary (v.31). Note that something is lacking (cf. Notes). Even if he afflicts, compassion and covenant love will again be shown (v.32); his infliction of pain and punishment is never arbitrary (v.33).

34–36 A contrast to God's gracious and loving dealing is offered in three pictures of man's inhumanity. There is the ill-treating of the prisoner just because he is a prisoner (v.34); there is no reason for thinking that Jeremiah was thinking of the Chaldeans rather than of his own people. There is also the denial of justice (v.35). God is here called the Most High (ʿelyôn) to stress that since he is the God of heaven, he is all-seeing; hence the denial of justice is a deliberate flouting of his will. There is the deliberate twisting of a man's right (v.36), as though God did not see.

37–39 This section of the lament stresses the almighty power of God, which makes the acceptance of his will necessary. He is behind both good and calamity (v.38; cf. Isa 45:7); so why should a man complain when he suffers for his sins? So long as he is alive, things can change (v.39).

Notes

---

22 The MT reads לֹא־תָמְנוּ (lōʾ-tāmᵉnû, "we are not consumed"). The Targum, probably the Syriac, and one Hebrew MS read לֹא תַמּוּ (lōʾ-tammu, "they are not at an end"; i.e., the tokens of the Lord's love are not completed). This is preferable because nothing in the context justifies the first person plural.

27 The MT reads בִּנְעוּרָיו (binʿûrāyw, "in his youth"). Numerous Hebrew MSS, some LXX MSS, the OL, and the Vulgate read מִנְּעוּרָיו (minnᵉʿûrāyw, "from his youth"). A choice is possible only on subjective grounds, and the rejected reading should appear in the margin.

31 The line is obviously short. The usual emendations are "For the LORD will not cast off his servants for ever" (NEB) and "For the LORD does not reject mankind for ever and ever" (JB; cf. NIV). One or the other is probably correct, but the choice remains subjective.

---

3. A Call to Penitence

3:40–51

40Let us examine our ways and test them,
and let us return to the LORD.
41Let us lift up our hearts and our hands
to God in heaven, and say:
42"We have sinned and rebelled
and you have not forgiven.

43"You have covered yourself with anger and pursued us;
you have slain without pity.
44You have covered yourself with a cloud
so that no prayer can get through.
45You have made us scum and refuse
among the nations.

46"All our enemies have opened their mouths
wide against us.
47We have suffered terror and pitfalls,
ruin and destruction."
48Streams of tears flow from my eyes
because my people are destroyed.

49My eyes will flow unceasingly,
without relief,
50until the LORD looks down
from heaven and sees.
51What I see brings grief to my soul
because of all the women of my city.

This section divides into two parts. In vv.40–47 the poet put a prayer into the mouth of the people. Then in vv.48–51 he added his tears to the people's plea.

40 The people agree that complaint (cf. v.39) is out of place. They must examine their ways, i.e., what they have done.

41 They lift up not merely their hands, the normal position for petition, but the whole inner man ("our hearts") to God; in other words, no mere formal prayer was involved.

42–43 There is a contrast between "we" and "you" (v.42); rebellion and disobedience were on Israel's side, a refusal to forgive on God's, with the implication that his attitude was just. The thought continues in v.43—"You have covered yourself with anger" (so also RSV, JB)—and so pursuit and slaying have been merciless.

44–46 That God is veiled from man's gaze by cloud and darkness is commonplace in the OT (cf. Exod 20:21; 40:34–35; Lev 16:2; 1 Kings 8:10, 12; Pss 18:9, 11; 97:2; Isa 6:4; Nah 1:3). But this veiling was never considered an obstacle to prayer. The JB's rendering—"You have covered yourself in a cloud too thick for prayer to pierce"— seems to best capture the idea here. The confession of complete worthlessness follows (v.45; cf. Nah 3:6 for the concept and, in a very different setting, 1 Cor 4:13). As a result of God's action, his people's enemies despise them openly (v.46). The same thought is found in 2:16 and is paralleled in Psalm 35:21 (in Ps 22:13 the concept is different). Judah could not defend her honor and had no friends to do it for her.

47 There is alliteration in both halves of the Hebrew of "we have suffered terror and pitfalls, ruin and destruction." The word translated "pitfall" (*pahat*) is not the one translated "pit" in vv.53, 55 (*bôr*). *Pahat* probably means a hunter's trap (cf. Isa 24:17–18; Jer 48:43–44).

48 On the assumption that we have personified Judah or Jerusalem throughout, it seems impossible to explain the switch back to the first person singular at this point. If it is Jeremiah speaking, the people's confession reminds him of their sufferings and then even more of his own. The verse is strongly reminiscent of Jeremiah 9:1; 14:17.

49–51 Jeremiah's tears, i.e., his pleading for Israel, would continue till God responded. The Hebrew of v.51 is literally "My eye has dealt with my soul from [more than?] the daughters of my city." The NIV, KJV, ASV, RSV, JB do not do justice to the MT. Hillers's emendation of "suffering" for "my eye" (cf. Notes) commends itself. Then the sense would be, "Till the LORD looks down from heaven and sees the suffering done to me [lit., my soul] because of the daughters of my people."

Notes

---

51 Hillers suggests reading עוֹנִי (*ʿônî*, "suffering") for עֵינִי (*ʿênî*, "my eye"). The confusion of ו (*w*, waw) and י (*y*, yod) is one of the commonest of scribal errors and would be the easier here because of *ʿênî* in v.49.

---

4. The Growth of Hope

3:52–57

> [52] Those who were my enemies without cause
> hunted me like a bird.
> [53] They tried to end my life in a pit
> and threw stones at me;
> [54] the waters closed over my head,
> and I thought I was about to be cut off.
>
> [55] I called on your name, O LORD,
> from the depths of the pit.
> [56] You heard my plea: "Do not close your ears
> to my cry for relief."
> [57] You came near when I called you,
> and you said, "Do not fear."

52–54 Agony over the fate of his people reminded the poet of his own fate. For the picture of the hunted bird, see Psalms 11:1–2; 124:7; 140:5. Jeremiah 18:18 is an example of what is meant. It is widely suggested that "they tried to end my life in a pit" (KJV; ASV, "dungeon") cannot refer to the incident in Jeremiah 38:6, where the same word *bôr* is used, because of the mention of water in v.54. The argument is hardly valid, for the mixture of literal and metaphorical is not rare in Hebrew poetry; in any case, "waters closed over my head" (v.54) is a common picture for distress (cf. Job 27:20; Pss 42:7; 66:12; 69:12; 88:7; 124:4; Isa 43:2). "And they closed it over me with a stone" (v.53, NEB) gives the sense. There is no real justification for taking *'eben* ("stone") as a collective, i.e., "stones," as do the NIV, RSV, JB, Hillers. A cistern was normally closed by a stone over its mouth.

55 Since one cistern would not be made below another, "the lowest pit" (NASB) is a meaningless rendering. "The lowest dungeon" (RV) hides this fact. We should, therefore, translate "from the depths of the pit" (NIV, RSV, NEB) or "the deep pit" (JB).

56 It is not easy to be sure of the exact force of the words. Three renderings are suggested.

1. Hillers takes the perfect *šāmā'tā* as a "precative perfect," i.e., equivalent to an imperative, and renders, "Hear my voice; do not close your ears." He gives the same interpretation to the other perfects in vv.57–61. This is perfectly possible, but it seems unlikely that this fairly rare usage would be used eight times in succession.

2. "You heard my plea: 'Do not close your ears . . . ,'" i.e., the remainder of the verse is his prayer.

3. "You heard my plea [then, so now] do not close your ear." The advantage of this rendering is that past salvation is made the basis of present hope. The second half of the verse is "to my cry for relief," but it seems better to follow some versions (cf. Notes).

Notes

56 The MT's לְשַׁוְעָתִי (*lešaw'ātî*, "cry for help") is read by the LXX and Symmachus as לִתְשׁוּעָתִי (*litšû'ātî*, "to my relief, salvation"; i.e., "to relieve, save me"), with some support from the Syriac. A number of MSS and the Vulgate delete it.

5. *An Appeal for Vengeance*

3:58–66

> 58O Lord, you took up my case;
>   you redeemed my life.
> 59You have seen, O LORD, the wrong done to me.
>   Uphold my cause!
> 60You have seen the depth of their vengeance,
>   all their plots against me.
>
> 61O LORD, you have heard their insults,
>   all their plots against me—

⁶²what my enemies whisper and mutter
    against me all day long.
⁶³Look at them! Sitting or standing,
    they mock me in their songs.

⁶⁴Pay them back what they deserve, O Lord,
    for what their hands have done.
⁶⁵Put a veil over their hearts,
    and may your curse be on them!
⁶⁶Pursue them in anger and destroy them
    from under the heavens of the Lord.

58–66 The rendering of these verses is straightforward. Unless we follow Hillers and take the perfects in vv.58–61 as imperatives (cf. comment at v.56), it would seem impossible to apply the confidence in God's intervention and punishment of his enemies to Judah at the time that Lamentations must be dated. This is one of the reasons for the tendency of some modern scholars to date chapter 3 much later than the others. If, however, we hear Jeremiah speaking, the difficulty vanishes. God's protection over him in the past is an adequate basis for confidence in the future.

Some, however, would ask whether the prophet could speak like this. Passages like Jeremiah 11:20; 12:3; 15:15; 17:18; 18:21–23 are an adequate answer. Some may suggest that the prophet had surely grown beyond such imprecations, and that in the destruction of Jerusalem he would have seen God's punishment of his enemies.

We must remember that for the sake of his people, Jeremiah had abandoned everything, even the consolations of family life and children (Jer 16:1–4). In addition, though God had given him some of the most glowing pictures of Israel's restoration, including the promise of the new covenant, there is no indication that God had given him a glimpse of life beyond the grave. How heavy then must have been the burden of rejection and ingratitude that followed him even into Egypt!

IV. Zion, Past and Present (4:1–22)

We may reasonably date this lament not very long after chapter 2. Sufficient time had elapsed for the first shock to wear off, and the poet was able to bring what had happened to a focus and so supplements chapter 2.

1. *The Contrast*

4:1–11

¹How the gold has lost its luster,
    the fine gold become dull!
The sacred gems are scattered
    at the head of every street.

²How the precious sons of Zion,
    once worth their weight in gold,
are now considered as pots of clay,
    the work of a potter's hands!

³Even jackals offer their breasts
    to nurse their young,
but my people have become heartless
    like ostriches in the desert.

⁴Because of thirst the infant's tongue
    sticks to the roof of its mouth;
the children beg for bread,
    but no one gives it to them.

⁵Those who once ate delicacies
    are destitute in the streets.
Those nurtured in purple
    now lie on ash heaps.

⁶The punishment of my people
    is greater than that of Sodom,
which was overthrown in a moment
    without a hand turned to help her.

⁷Their princes were brighter than snow
    and whiter than milk,
their bodies more ruddy than rubies,
    their appearance like sapphires.

⁸But now they are blacker than soot;
    they are not recognized in the streets.
Their skin has shriveled on their bones;
    it has become as dry as a stick.

⁹Those killed by the sword are better off
    than those who die of famine;
racked with hunger, they waste away
    for lack of food from the field.

¹⁰With their own hands compassionate women
    have cooked their own children,
who became their food
    when my people were destroyed.

¹¹The Lord has given full vent to his wrath;
    he has poured out his fierce anger.
He kindled a fire in Zion
    that consumed her foundations.

1–2 Emendations have been proposed for the first line of v.1 on the grounds that gold does not tarnish! Similar objections have been raised to Matthew 5:13. Since the second line refers to the destroyed temple, we can easily see a reference to its gold-covered panels and golden vessels so covered with dust that their value is no longer discernible. Similarly, it is no longer possible to discern the value of the enslaved survivors (v.2).

3–5 It is of little importance whether we understand "jackal" (v.3), as in most translations, or "whale" (NEB). In either case it is a mammal whose maternal care might not be expected. The ostrich was proverbial because of its apparent neglect of its eggs (Job 39:13–18), and "my people" (cf. Notes) had become like it in their neglect of their babes (v.4). Money had ceased to have meaning (v.5); so the rich women had no helpers and only such food as they could find among the garbage.

6 Whether the lament says that "the punishment" or "the iniquity" of Judah was worse than that of Sodom (cf. Ezek 16:44–52) is uncertain. Ultimately it is unimportant, for the measure of iniquity and its punishment were held to be linked.

7–9 *Nāzir* is normally rendered Nazirite, but in Genesis 49:26 and Deuteronomy 33:16 it is used of one separated by rank and qualities from his contemporaries. This is obviously the sense here, and so "princes" is a satisfactory rendering (v.7). The description is of men who were able to devote themselves to their physical appearance. (For "appearance like sapphires," see Notes.) An ignominious fate fell to these once fair nobles (v.8). So bad was their situation that death was preferable to life (v.9).

10–11 The description in v.10 is reminiscent of 2 Kings 6:25–29. Hunger drives humans to inhuman action. All this fell on the people because they had provoked the Lord to wrath (v.11).

Notes

3 בַּת־עַמִּי (*baṯ-ʿammî*) is literally "daughter of my people," but obviously individual women are intended. No emendation is called for since *baṯ* can be taken as a collective.

7 סַפִּיר (*sappîr*) is not "sapphire" as we know it but lapis lazuli (NIV mg., RSV mg., NEB), a dark blue, opaque stone.

סַפִּיר גִּזְרָתָם (*sappîr gizrāṯām*, "appearance like sapphires") is a *hapax legomenon* for which there is no etymological explanation. There is much to be said for Hillers's rendering: "their beards were lapis lazuli," with hair or eyebrows as possible alternatives for beard. There are parallels in ancient Near-Eastern literature. Very dark black with a bluish tinge is meant.

2. The Sin of Priests and Prophets

4:12–16

> 12The kings of the earth did not believe,
>   nor did any of the world's people,
>   that enemies and foes could enter
>   the gates of Jerusalem.
>
> 13But it happened because of the sins of her prophets
>   and the iniquities of her priests,
>   who shed within her
>   the blood of the righteous.
>
> 14Now they grope through the streets
>   like men who are blind.
>   They are so defiled with blood
>   that no one dares to touch their garments.
>
> 15"Go away! You are unclean!" men cry to them.
>   "Away! Away! Don't touch us!"

When they flee and wander about,
  people among the nations say,
  "They can stay here no longer."

16The Lord himself has scattered them;
  he no longer watches over them.
The priests are shown no honor,
  the elders no favor.

12 There is an obvious element of exaggeration here. Essentially it means that Jerusalem's deliverance in the time of Sennacherib showed men that, so long as the Lord's hand was over it, the city was impregnable.

13 This protection had been withdrawn because of the blood-guilt of the priests and prophets. We are here dealing with one of the fundamental concepts of prophetic ethics. Ezekiel 22:1–12 shows that the concept of bloodshed was far wider than murder or homicide; all that cut at the roots of society or that deprived men of their land and livelihood shortened their lives and so was bloodshed. Priest and prophet contributed positively and negatively—positively by advocating or condoning such behavior, negatively by failing to condemn those who wronged their fellow men.

14–16 It is usual to take these verses as the direct continuation of v.13, giving the fate of the blood-guilty priests and prophets; bearing the mark of Cain, moral lepers, they were rejected wherever they went. The difficulty is that Jeremiah 29:15–23 and the earlier chapters of Ezekiel do not support such a picture for those who had been deported with Jehoiachin, while the poet would hardly know the fate of those who had survived the Fall of Jerusalem. It may well be intended as a picture of the miserable survivors as a whole, as they were scattered abroad. This is supported by the mention of elders rather than prophets in v.16. It should be remembered that Judah was almost completely bereft of people of standing.

Notes

15–16 The MT of these verses raises a number of difficulties. Whatever conjectural emendations are made, the final interpretations are very similar (cf. modern translations); so there is little point in closer investigation. There is no doubt that both lines in v.16 are overlong, which supports the suggestion of textual corruption; but the sense is good. It is likely that we should read the singular in the second line, viz., "He showed no favour to priests" (NEB, and, by implication, NIV, RSV); this would make the Lord the subject throughout.

3. Vain Hopes

4:17–20

17Moreover, our eyes failed,
  looking in vain for help;
from our towers we watched
  for a nation that could not save us.

> 18Men stalked us at every step
>   so we could not walk in our streets.
> Our end was near, our days were numbered,
>   for our end had come.
>
> 19Our pursuers were swifter
>   than eagles in the sky;
> they chased us over the mountains
>   and lay in wait for us in the desert.
>
> 20The Lord's anointed, our very life breath,
>   was caught in their traps.
> We thought that under his shadow
>   we would live among the nations.

17–20 The blindness of those who had gone into exile was matched only by that of those who were left at home. Hoping against hope, they had looked for Egypt's help almost to the last moment (v.17; Jer 37:3–10). The use of "we" in these verses suggests that the poet had shared in these hopes. This and the manner in which Zedekiah is spoken of (v.20) are irreconcilable with authorship by Jeremiah. (For v.19, see Lev 26:8; Deut 32:30; Isa 30:16–17.) It is reasonably likely that the vivid memory of Zedekiah's last, desperate attempt to escape (Jer 52:6–9) lies behind vv.19–20. Judah's madness and blindness were due not only to faith in the inviolability of the temple but also of the Davidic dynasty. This is the obvious explanation why Jeremiah had so little to say about the messianic hope. "Our very life breath" and "under his shadow" are taken from the ancient court-language of the Near East.

4. The Reversal of Doom

4:21–22

> 21Rejoice and be glad, O Daughter of Edom,
>   you who live in the land of Uz.
> But to you also the cup will be passed;
>   you will be drunk and stripped naked.
>
> 22O Daughter of Zion, your punishment will end;
>   he will not prolong your exile.
> But, O Daughter of Edom, he will punish your sin
>   and expose your wickedness.

21–22 The vain hopes were gone, and only the stark reality remained. To Edom (v.21), who stands for all the enemies of Judah (cf. Isa 34; Ezek 35), the poet says, in effect, "Rejoice while you can, for judgment is coming to you also." The nakedness involved shame and revelation of sins, but it also implied slavery (cf. Isa 47:2–3). The consolation for Zion (v.22) was that she had received all the punishment she could (cf. Isa 40:2); there could be no more exile.

V. An Appeal to the Lord (5:1–22)

The absence of an alphabetic acrostic and of the *qinah* meter suggest that this lament may be by another hand, but all dogmatism would be out of place. The note of lamentation is reinforced by the repetitive (forty-five times) use of words ending in *û*. The only verse where this is lacking is v.19, which is one of praise. Though there are some references to incidents during the siege, the lament deals mainly with the sequel, which suggests some lapse of time.

1. *The Affliction of the Lord's People*

5:1–18

¹Remember, O Lord, what has happened to us;
  look, and see our disgrace.
²Our inheritance has been turned over to aliens,
  our homes to foreigners.
³We have become orphans and fatherless,
  our mothers like widows.
⁴We must buy the water we drink;
  our wood can be had only at a price.
⁵Those who pursue us are at our heels;
  we are weary and find no rest.
⁶We submitted to Egypt and Assyria
  to get enough bread.
⁷Our fathers sinned and are no more,
  and we bear their punishment.
⁸Slaves rule over us,
  and there is none to free us from their hands.
⁹We get our bread at the risk of our lives
  because of the sword in the desert.
¹⁰Our skin is hot as an oven,
  feverish from hunger.
¹¹Women have been ravished in Zion,
  and virgins in the towns of Judah.
¹²Princes have been hung up by their hands;
  elders are shown no respect.
¹³Young men toil at the millstones;
  boys stagger under loads of wood.
¹⁴The elders are gone from the city gate;
  the young men have stopped their music.
¹⁵Joy is gone from our hearts;
  our dancing has turned to mourning.
¹⁶The crown has fallen from our head.
  Woe to us, for we have sinned!
¹⁷Because of this our hearts are faint,
  because of these things our eyes grow dim
¹⁸for Mount Zion, which lies desolate,
  with jackals prowling over it.

1 Remembrance in the Bible is never a mere recalling. It always involves resultant action; so this is a call to God to act (cf. note at 3:1).

2 The traditional rendering of *naḥªlāh* is "inheritance" (so NIV); but, though this was its original meaning, the word normally means "possessions," however obtained. "Patrimony" (NEB) has the advantage of not unduly stressing the inheritance concept.

3 In contemporary society the fatherless orphan and the widow without grown sons were the weakest, unless they had powerful patrons. There is an implied plea to God to act.

4 Second Kings 24:14; 25:12, and Jeremiah 39:10 make it clear that most of those left in Judah were the very poor, who were expected to keep the fields and vineyards in order. No foreign settlers were brought in, though there is little doubt that this was Nebuchadnezzar's intention, overruled by God. So this verse probably refers to the very heavy taxation that had to be paid if the survivors were to live.

5 The same idea underlies this verse: "Those who pursue us are at our heels; we are weary and find no rest." Other versions have a reference to yokes on the necks of the people (so RSV; cf. Notes). This is not an allusion to slave masters, though many people had been dragged away as slaves; but it was the need to live that drove them on, and they had forfeited God's promise of rest from their enemies (cf. Deut 12:10; 25:19; 2 Sam 7:1, 11).

6–7 It is true that Nebuchadnezzar claimed to be continuing the Assyrian power, as did Cyrus later (cf. Ezra 6:22); but that can hardly be the force of "Assyria" here (v.6). The poet is referring to something "our fathers" did (v.7). It cannot refer simply to political alliances, for there is no suggestion that such alliances were motivated by famine conditions. If that had been the case, they probably would have turned to Egypt rather than to Assyria. The answer is suggested by Hosea. In Hosea 2:5, 8 he shows Israel worshiping the Baalim, the fertility gods of nature. This reduced Yahweh for them to a god among gods, and so they sought alliances with Egypt and Assyria (Hos 5:13; 7:11; 12:1). Now their descendants had reaped the bitter harvest, as Samaria had done a century and a half earlier.

8–10 Instead of their own king and ministers, the people were ruled by Babylonian officials, most of relatively low standing (v.8), who were proud of the title "slaves of the king"; there was no court of appeal against their arbitrary brutality. This showed itself in the difficulty experienced in obtaining food (vv.9–10), which involved risk to life and limb and extreme exposure (cf. Notes); "hot" skin is literally "scorched" or "blackened" skin, showing general starvation.

11–13 The brutality the people were experiencing was only a continuation of what they had experienced earlier, when the Chaldeans had captured the city. "Princes have been hung up by their hands" (v.12) suggests torture to make the rich reveal where they had hidden their treasures; however, the meaning is indicated by the second element concerning elders. "Elders are shown no respect" manifestly refers not to mere withholding of respect but to a deliberate shaming. Hence the hanging, perhaps impaling, is of the dead to dishonor their corpses. Since Nebuchadnezzar did not torture those he regarded as most guilty (Jer 52:10–11, 24–27), it is not likely that any were hung up or impaled while still alive. Now (v.13) "young men toil at the millstones" (cf. Notes). In happier days they would have been soldiers; now they had to do women's work. "Boys stagger under loads of wood"; i.e., they were treated as serfs.

14–16 Old and young had found the course of life disjointed (v.14), and all joy had gone because of past sin (vv.15–16).

731

17–18 The supreme sign of God's anger was that the temple mount had become the abode of wild animals (v.18). *Šûʿāl* is used for both jackal and fox, the former being more suitable here (NIV, RSV, NEB, JB). No great lapse of time is suggested. The temple mount remained sacred ground (cf. Jer 41:5). We cannot affirm with any certainty whether sacrifices were continued on the sacred site; but if they were (note that there is no suggestion of this in Lamentations), it would have been only on special occasions. At other times even the surviving priests would have avoided the site in their consciousness of sin and defilement. Even today most strictly orthodox Jews will not enter the temple area. The West (Wailing) Wall is outside the holy area. And jackals rapidly occupy ruins, as may still be observed.

Notes

5 The MT has עַל צַוָּארֵנוּ (*ʿal ṣawwāʾrēnû*, "on our necks"). A simple case of haplography, however, yields Symmachus's reading עֹל עַל צַוָּארֵנוּ (*ʿōl ʿal ṣawwāʾrēnû*, "yoke on our necks"), which is probably more correct. The NIV's "at our heels" is perhaps a little too idiomatic.

9 The MT has חֶרֶב הַמִּדְבָּר (*ḥereḇ hammiḏbār*, "sword in the desert"). No suitable meaning has been suggested, for it can hardly be a poetic synonym for the weapons of the Bedouin. Hillers links *miḏbār* with the root *d-b-r*, I ("to be behind," "pursue" [not in BDB, but cf. TDOT, 3:94–95]), hence the rendering "To get bread we risk our lives before the pursuer's sword."

13 The MT reads בַּחוּרִים טְחוֹן נָשָׂאוּ (*baḥûrîm ṭᵉḥôn nāśāʾû*): the rendering "Young men toil at the millstones" (NIV, KJV, RSV) implies the reading לִטְחוֹן (*liṭḥôn*, "with respect to a millstone"); so some render "the young men bare the mill" (RV, NASB mg., ASV), but this is improbable, as even smaller millstones would seldom be transported.

2. The Lord's Abiding Power

5:19–22

> ¹⁹You, O LORD, reign forever;
>   your throne endures from generation to generation.
> ²⁰Why do you always forget us?
>   Why do you forsake us so long?
> ²¹Restore us to yourself, O LORD, that we may return;
>   renew our days as of old
> ²²unless you have utterly rejected us
>   and are angry with us beyond measure.

19 The "throne" is the visible symbol of kingly rule. As might be expected, in this verse alone the lamenting *û* sound is not heard (see pp. 729–30).

20 The poet returned to the plea with which the lament began. "Remember" (v.1) is taken up by "forget"; "look and see" by "forsake."

21 Suddenly there was the overwhelming realization that true repentance is possible only as initiated by an act of God (cf. Jer 31:18, 33–34; Ezek 36:26–27). This is a foreshadowing of the NT doctrine of regeneration. Unfortunately, it was grasped by few at the time. Normative Judaism lays very great stress on the importance of repentance but has always regarded it as something essentially within man's control.

22 Translators have interpreted the opening *kî 'im* in four main ways. The "unless" of NIV and JB and the "but" of KJV would normally lead us to expect a negative expression in the preceding verse. RSV's "or hast thou utterly rejected us?" is virtually indefensible. "For hast thou . . .?" (AV mg.) drops the *'im* with the LXX, OL, and some Hebrew MSS. Probably the best rendering is NEB's "For if thou has utterly rejected us/then great indeed has been thy anger against us."

Nevertheless, whatever the cost in loss of dramatic effect, it is understandable that when Lamentations is read in the synagogue, especially on Tisha b'Av (see Introduction: Purpose), v.21 is repeated at this point so that the reading will not end on such a sad note. (This same procedure is followed in the reading of the last two verses of Ecclesiastes.)

Just as it is difficult for us to grasp why Jeremiah should have had to suffer more than his contemporaries, so it seems strange to many that one who could so pour out his heart to God should receive so little consolation. There was not even the burning hope of return and restoration that had been voiced by Jeremiah and Ezekiel. The simple fact is that the people of Israel—with few exceptions—had so failed to grasp God's revelation that an experience parallel to the bondage in Egypt and a new Exodus were needed to prepare Israel for the appearance of her Messiah and the world's Savior.

EZEKIEL

Ralph H. Alexander

EZEKIEL

Introduction

1. Background
2. Unity and Authorship
3. Date
4. Place of Origin and Destination
5. Occasion and Purpose
6. Literary Form and Structure
7. Theological Values
8. Text
9. Bibliography
10. Outline

1. Background

Israel's idolatrous abominations caused the ten northern tribes of that nation to be taken into captivity by Assyria in 722 B.C. At that time the southern kingdom of Judah was spared through the influence of righteous men like Isaiah. Judah soon experienced revival and spiritual refreshment under the leadership of young King Hezekiah. He had learned the spiritual lessons from the downfall of Israel and was encouraged by the ministry of the prophet Isaiah (2 Kings 18–19). However, Hezekiah's faith in Yahweh and zeal for the Mosaic covenant was forgotten when his son Manasseh and his grandson Amon rejected the ways of the Lord. For fifty-five years (2 Kings 21:1–18) they turned the people to all kinds of idolatry and wickedness. This so perverted the people that they repudiated the law of God and forgot that it existed.

Josiah, Amon's righteous son, brought renewed hope to Judah; but it came too late. As he was having the temple repaired, a copy of the Mosaic law was discovered (2 Kings 22). On reading it, Josiah was moved to obey it fully (2 Kings 23). He purified the temple and officially cleansed the land of the abominations of Manasseh and Amon. But among the people this reformation was only perfunctory. The idolatry of Manasseh's long reign had so corrupted the hearts of the people that there was little genuine repentance (cf. Jer 3:10). The Mosaic covenant declared that the nation of Israel would be taken captive and dispersed among the nations if the people continually disobeyed the stipulations of that covenant (Lev 26; Deut 28–29). That curse was now certain. It was the only thing that would remove the wickedness of Israel and cause the people to return to Yahweh their God.

Meanwhile, on the international scene there was a new power struggle. Assyria, the dominant nation in the ancient Near East for more than 250 years, was declining, while the Neo-Babylonian Empire was rising under the leadership of Nabopolassar. In 612 B.C. the Babylonians defeated the Assyrians; and Nineveh, their capital city, fell. The remnants of the Assyrian army under Ashuruballit II retreated westward to Haran, where, with their backs to the Egyptians, they endeavored to keep resistance alive.

In 609 B.C. Pharaoh Neco of Egypt marched to the aid of Assyria with a large force. At Megiddo, Josiah, the reformer king of Judah, tried to stop the advance of Neco, only to be killed in the ensuing battle. Neco continued on to Haran to support Ashuruballit in his attempt to retain Haran, but the strength of the Babylonians gave them a decisive victory over Assyria and Egypt.

Though Neco failed in his effort to aid Assyria at Haran, he did begin to consolidate Palestine and Syria. He removed Jehoahaz, the pro-Babylonian son of Josiah whom the people of Judah crowned as their new king, and established Jehoiakim, Josiah's eldest pro-Egyptian son, as his vassal king in Judah. Throughout this international turmoil, Jeremiah the prophet warned the people of Judah to submit to the Babylonians and not to follow the enticements of Egypt. But they would not listen.

In 605 B.C. Nebuchadnezzar, the crown prince of Babylonia, attacked the combined Assyrian and Egyptian forces at Carchemish on the Euphrates in one of the most important battles of history. In Nebuchadnezzar's overwhelming victory, two great powers of the ancient Near East fell, never again to rise to international significance. As the Babylonians pushed their conquest southward, they invaded Judah and deported a group of young nobles from there (2 Kings 24:1; 2 Chron 36:6; Dan 1:1–3, 6). This began the great Babylonian captivity of Judah that would ultimately affect every Israelite.

Jehoiakim was both a reluctant vassal of Babylon and a greedy ruler over his people, despising the Mosaic covenant and the reform of his father, Josiah (Jer 22:13–17). After three years of unwilling submission to Nebuchadnezzar, Jehoiakim refused to heed the warnings of Jeremiah and revolted against Babylon in favor of Egypt (2 Kings 24:1). The stalemate in battle between Babylon and Egypt on the frontier of Egypt in 601 B.C. encouraged him. The revolt was a mistake on Jehoiakim's part, for as soon as Nebuchadnezzar reorganized his army, he retaliated against those nations that had revolted and had refused to pay tribute to him.

In December 598 B.C., during the month that the Babylonians began to attack Judah, Jehoiakim died. His eighteen-year-old son, Jehoiachin, succeeded him (2 Kings 24:8), only to surrender the city of Jerusalem to Nebuchadnezzar three months later. Jehoiachin, his mother, his wives, his officials, and the leading men of the land (2 Kings 24:12–16), including Ezekiel, a priest (Ezek 1:1–3), were led away into exile in 597 B.C. Zedekiah (Mattaniah), Jehoiachin's uncle, was established by Nebuchadnezzar as a regent vassal over Judah. Though in exile, Jehoiachin remained the recognized king of Judah by Babylon, as demonstrated from administrative documents found in the excavations at Babylonia (Babylonian text 28122, ANET, p. 308).

Buoyed by the false prophets' messages that Nebuchadnezzar's power was soon to be broken and the exiles would triumphantly return, and seduced by the seemingly renewed strength of Pharaohs Psammetik II (594–588 B.C.) and Apries (588–568 B.C.), on whom the vacillating Zedekiah pinned his hopes of restored national independence, he was persuaded to rebel once more against Nebuchadnezzar. The response of Babylon was immediate. Early in 588 the Babylonian army laid siege to Jerusalem (2 Kings 25:1; Jer 32:1–2), having already destroyed the fortress cities of the Judean hill country (vividly described in the Lachish Letters). In the fall of 586 Jerusalem was destroyed; Zedekiah was captured and blinded after witnessing the execution of his sons; many inhabitants of Jerusalem were murdered by the Babylonians; and others were deported to Babylonia (2 Kings 25:2–21; Jer 52:5–27). Judah had fallen.

It was in this period of international turmoil and unrest, combined with the immorality and apostasy of Judah, that Ezekiel ministered. Having grown up during the reform of Josiah, and having been taken captive in the deportation of Jehoiachin in 597 B.C., Ezekiel, both a priest and a prophet, proclaimed to the exiled Jews in Babylonia the Lord's judgment and ultimate blessing.

The following outline will clarify the chronological relationship between the Judean, Egyptian, and Babylonian kings.

1. Judean kings

Josiah (640–609 B.C.)
Jehoahaz (Josiah's second son) (609 B.C.)
Jehoiakim (Josiah's eldest son) (609–597 B.C.)
Jehoiachin (Jehoiakim's son) (597 B.C.)
Zedekiah (Josiah's youngest son) (a regent) (597–586 B.C.)
Jerusalem destroyed (586 B.C.)

2. Egyptian kings

Psammetikus I (664–609 B.C.)
Neco (609–594 B.C.)
Psammetikus II (594–588 B.C.)
Apries (Hophra) (588–568 B.C.)

3. Neo-Babylonian kings

Nabopolasser (626–605 B.C.)
Nebuchadnezzar (605–562 B.C.)

2. Unity and Authorship

Till the second quarter of the twentieth century, biblical scholars considered the Book of Ezekiel an unfragmented unity, possessing orderliness and purpose of development. Those holding to the traditional unity of the book and Ezekiel's authorship use six factors to support their position: (1) balanced structure and logical arrangement, (2) autobiographical nature, (3) clear chronological sequence, (4) internal consistency of the message within the structural balance, (5) uniformity of language and style, and (6) consistency of Ezekiel's personality throughout the book.[1]

Ezekiel's authorship and the unity of the book were never seriously questioned before the second quarter of the twentieth century, though some consider Josephus's remark (Antiq. X, 79 [v.1]) that Ezekiel left behind him two books to be an early witness to disunity. Initial objections to the unity of the book were based on critical literary analysis. Ewald (1875) sought to find multiple authorship by asserting that there was within the book written material that differed from oral messages,

---

[1]For a full discussion, cf. R.K. Harrison, IOT, pp. 823–32, or H.H. Rowley, *Men of God: Studies in Old Testament History and Prophecy* (London: Nelson, 1963), pp. 169–210.

whereas Kraetzschmar (1900) argued that the book contained inconsistencies of style such as doublets, parallelisms, and the author's interchange between the first and third person. Holscher (1924), followed by Herntrich (1932), Oesterley (1934), Robinson (1934), and Irwin (1943), dissected the book between the "true Ezekiel," a poet, and other authors who wrote in prose.

C.C. Torrey (1930), arguing on historical and geographical grounds, maintained that a fictitious pseudoauthor wrote the book around 230 B.C. Torrey's mysterious author sought to disguise himself as a prophet from the time of Manasseh as he wrote the first twenty-four chapters. The chapters dealing with Jerusalem and her abominations, Torrey maintained, could not have been written after Josiah's reform. Bertholet (1936) divided the book on geographical and historical considerations, holding to a double ministry for Ezekiel: 593–586 B.C. in Jerusalem and 586 B.C. and following in Babylon. Variations of this position gained some popularity.

Cooke (1926) and Howie (1950) have guided the majority of contemporary biblical scholars back to a belief in the unity and single authorship of the book. Though Ezekiel's visions caused him to see events in Jerusalem while living in Babylon, there are less difficulties in accepting the traditional unity than in altering the text and subjectively devising stylistic, geographical, and historical objections with no real basis. The majority of contemporary scholars have followed Howie and Zimmerli (*Ezekiel I,* pp. 1–15, 41–56, 68–74) because the style and content of Ezekiel are so remarkably consistent (so Eichrodt, Greenberg, Zimmerli, Wevers), though some hold to a Palestinian locale for the composition (Auvray, Brownlee), some to later editing (Brownlee, Greenberg, Zimmerli), and some to rhetorical criticism and structural analysis (Boadt, Parunak).

3. Date

Few books in the OT place the emphasis on chronology that Ezekiel does. The first three verses of chapter 1 mark the chronological setting, dating the book by Jehoiachin's deportation to Babylon in 597 B.C. The first prophetic message is dated in "the fifth year of the exile of King Jehoiachin" (593 B.C.) and the last-dated message (29:17–30:19) was given in "the twenty-seventh year" (571 B.C.). The book contains thirteen chronological notices. Chapters 1–24, which announce judgment on Jerusalem and Judah with the basis for it, are dated 593–589 B.C. (1:1–3; 8:1; 20:1; 24:1). The prophecies against the foreign nations in chapters 25–32 are dated 587–585 B.C. (26:1; 29:1; 30:20; 31:1; 32:1; 17), with the exception of 29:17–30:19. The messages of blessing and hope in chapters 33–48 were delivered between 585 and 573 B.C. (33:21; 40:1).

The following chronology of Ezekiel, including major events and the dated messages, is substantially based on the work of Freedy and Redford.[2]

---

[2]Cf. A. Malamat, "The Last Kings of Judah and the Fall of Jerusalem," *Israel Exploration Journal* 18 (1968): 137–56; id., "Twilight of Judah: In Egyptian-Babylonian Maelstrom," VetTest Supplement 28 (1975): 123–45.

Dating in Ezekiel

	Year	Month	Day
The first year of Jehoiachin's captivity (2 Kings 24:12)	June 597	— — —
The beginning of Ezekiel's ministry and his first message (Ezek 1:1–3)	June/July 593	5 — 5
Ezekiel's second-dated message: the vision of temple abominations (Ezek 8:1)	Aug./Sept. 592	6 6 5
Ezekiel's third-dated message: response to the elders' inquiry (Ezek 20:1)	July/Aug. 591	7 5 10
Ezekiel's fourth-dated message: Jerusalem's judgment (Ezek 24:1)	Dec./Jan. 589/588	9 10 10
Beginning of the second siege (2 Kings 25:1)	Dec./Jan. 589/588	— — —
Ezekiel's fifth-dated message: judgment on Tyre (Ezek 26:1)	March/April 587–586	11 — 1
Ezekiel's sixth-dated message: judgment on Egypt (Ezek 29:1)	Dec./Jan. 588/587	10 10 12
Ezekiel's seventh-dated message: judgment on Egypt (Ezek 29:17)	March/April 571	27 1 1
Ezekiel's eighth-dated message: news of Pharaoh's defeat (Ezek 30:20)	March/April 587	11 1 7
Ezekiel's ninth-dated message: news of Pharaoh's final defeat (Ezek 31:1)	May/June 587	11 3 1
Siege of Jerusalem in progress (Jer 21:1–2)	587	— — —
Ezekiel's tenth-dated message: lament over Pharaoh (Ezek 32:1)	March 585	12 12 1
Ezekiel's eleventh-dated message: lament over Pharaoh (Ezek 32:17)	April 585	12 12 15
Destruction of Jerusalem (2 Kings 25:8)	Sept. 586	— — —
Ezekiel's twelfth-dated message: news of Jerusalem's fall (Ezek 33:21)	Dec./Jan. 586/585	12 10 5
Ezekiel's last-dated message: millennial vision (Ezek 40:1)	March/April 573	25 1 10

Though most biblical scholars accept the basic chronology set forth in Ezekiel, some critics argue for a late date by saying that a prophet cannot pronounce simultaneously the type of judgment and blessing that one finds in Ezekiel. Therefore, the book had to have been written at different times, the latter being that of the intertestamental period. Others hold a similar late date based on the geographical consideration that part of the book was written from a Palestinian viewpoint whereas the remainder was composed by a Babylonian eyewitness. Still others declare that the discrepancies between Ezekiel and the priestly code demonstrate that the date of composition must have been at least partially in the intertestamental period.[3]

On the contrary, the use of apocalyptic literature (37:1–14; 40–48), which follows the scheme of the Mesopotamian dream-vision of the seventh and sixth centuries B.C.,[4] argues against a late date and for authorship of the book during the Exile. (For a complete contemporary analysis of the date of Ezekiel, see Howie.)

4. Place of Origin and Destination

Ezekiel 1:1–3 and 3:15 clearly define the place of origin of Ezekiel's ministry as Babylonia, specifically at the site of Tel Aviv located near the Kebar River and the ancient site of Nippur. This "River" has been identified by many with the *naru kabari* (mentioned in two cuneiform texts from Nippur), a canal making a southeasterly loop, connecting at both ends with the Euphrates River.

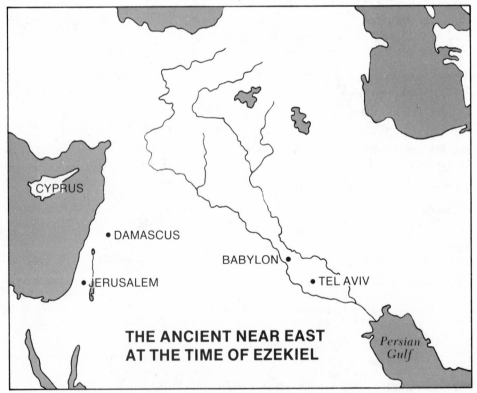

THE ANCIENT NEAR EAST
AT THE TIME OF EZEKIEL

CYPRUS

DAMASCUS

BABYLON

JERUSALEM

TEL AVIV

Persian Gulf

---

[3]For refutations of these arguments for a late date, see Harrison, IOT, pp. 822–55, and Archer, SOTIrev., pp. 368–76.

[4]Cf. A. Leo Oppenheim, *The Interpretation of Dreams in the Ancient Near East With a Translation of an Assyrian Dream-Book*, Transactions of the American Philosophical Society, New Series, vol. 46, part 3 (Philadelphia, 1956), pp. 179–373.

The conditions of the Jews in the Babylonian exile were not severe. Though placed at the specific site of Tel Aviv, it seems that they had freedom of movement within the country and the opportunity to engage in commerce. They were regarded more as colonists than slaves.

Ezekiel's messages were primarily for the exiles in Babylonia. He condemned the abominations that were leading Jerusalem and Judah to ultimate destruction. The exiles questioned the prophecies of Ezekiel; and he, in turn, answered them carefully. He played the role of a watchman to warn them of the impending judgment on Judah and to proclaim the hope of their ultimate restoration to the land of Israel. Though in some of Ezekiel's visions (chs. 8 and 11) he was carried to Jerusalem, his messages were not directly given for the benefit of the Jews in Palestine. The distance between Babylon and Jerusalem would preclude these messages being directed to Jerusalem, though certainly some of the concepts of Ezekiel may have filtered back to Palestine. Jeremiah, Ezekiel's contemporary, however, was simultaneously proclaiming a similar message of warning and judgment to those remaining in Jerusalem and Judah.

5. Occasion and Purpose

When God created the nation of Israel, he gave the people the Mosaic covenant (Exod 20–Num 9; Deut) as their constitution. As already the Lord's people, this covenant told them how to live for him. The law was not given to burden the Hebrews; it was given for their own good (Deut 10:12–13), so that they might be blessed (Deut 5:28–33).

Yet the history of Israel was marked by disobedience to this covenant. Often she followed the gods of the peoples around her. As the historical sketch in section 1 shows, the kingdoms of Israel and Judah became increasingly corrupted and ultimately forgot their constitution, the Mosaic covenant. The covenant itself had warned the Israelites that if they continued to stray from the Lord's ways revealed in the statutes and commandments of the law, the Lord would discipline them through dispersion in order to bring them back to himself.[5]

This theme fills the Book of Ezekiel. Ezekiel spoke to his contemporaries, declaring to them the faithfulness, holiness, and glory of God. Their God would bring judgment, cleansing, and ultimate blessing through which all peoples might come to know that he, the God of Israel, was the one true God. The Lord desired to turn the exiles of Israel away from their sinful ways and restore them to himself. His judgment, therefore, was exercised as an instrument of love to cause them to see their abominations and recognize the Lord's faithfulness to his covenants. He was faithful to his promises both to judge and to bless. The destruction of Jerusalem demonstrated God's faithfulness to his holy character (cf. Lev 26; Deut 28–30) as revealed in his covenants. He gave the hope that one day the true Shepherd, the Messiah, would come to lead his people, Israel. Though their contemporary rulers had ex-

---

[5]The blessings and curses formulas in the Mosaic covenant, as well as the entire Mosaic covenant, reflect the pattern of suzerain-vassal treaties from the first millennium B.C. (cf. Meredith G. Kline, *Treaty of the Great King: The Covenant Structure of Deuteronomy* [Grand Rapids: Eerdmans, 1963], for a full discussion).

ploited them and led them away from the Lord, in the future the people would be restored to the Promised Land (Gen 12:7) by a righteous leader. In that day all the covenants of the Lord would be fulfilled to his people (Ezek 37:24–28).

Ezekiel, as a watchman for Israel, warned her of the judgment that was imminent and stressed the need for individual responsibility as well as national accountability before God. Each Israelite was personally to turn to the Lord. Likewise, the whole nation must ultimately return to him.

6. Literary Form and Structure

Traditionally Ezekiel is divided into three distinct sections. Chapters 1–24 proclaim the coming judgment on Jerusalem and its causes. Chapters 25–32 announce judgment on the foreign nations, while chapters 33–48 declare the blessings of future restoration and the messianic kingdom.

The threefold division shows the logical development and unity of the book. Many, however, tend to view these three sections as distinct and isolated topics without much interrelation. On the contrary, Ezekiel tied the entire book together structurally and thematically. The prophecy began with his vision of the glory of God (chs. 1–3). Without a proper understanding of the glorious and holy character of God, the announcements of judgment would be meaningless (chs. 4–7). The Lord showed how Israel's wickedness had caused his glory to depart from her midst till she would be cleansed through the coming judgment (chs. 8–11). The announcements of this judgment are clarified as objections and are answered in chapters 12–19. Then Ezekiel summarized the nature of the impending discipline and the reasons for it (chs. 20–24). Chapters 25–32 form an integral part of the previous structural unit, for in them the Lord condemned the nations around Judah for rejoicing in her destruction. Those who cursed Israel were to be cursed (Gen 12:3). God faithfully executed that promise.

Lest the exiles in Babylonia lose all hope, the Lord promised their ultimate restoration to the land of blessing, Israel. The Lord would cleanse his people and fulfill his covenants with them so that they might dwell in the Promised Land, become his faithful people, experience the outpouring of the Spirit of the new covenant, and live under the righteous rule of the Messiah in the promised Davidic kingdom (2 Sam 7). When this had occurred, then the departed glory of the Lord would return to the new temple established in the messianic kingdom. Israel would worship God in righteousness according to his holy statutes and ordinances (Ezek 40–48).

The book is not only developed logically but is also arranged chronologically. The pivotal point historically and chronologically is the Fall of Jerusalem in 586 B.C. The messages contained in chapters 1–24 are all dated prior to the Fall of Jerusalem, preparing the exiles for the judgment that was to come on Jerusalem. Once that judgment had come, as described in chapter 24, Ezekiel turned his attention to judgment on the nations. These messages (chs. 25–33) were given during and following the siege of Jerusalem, in 586–585 B.C. One exception is the message in 29:17–30:19, included in this chronological section because of its logical relationship to the judgment on the foreign nations (cf. commentary at 29:17–30:19). Then 33: 21–39:29 was delivered on the night before the fugitive arrived in Babylon to tell the exiles that Jerusalem had fallen (Dec./Jan. 586/585 B.C.). These messages encouraged the exiles when that news came. Fourteen years later, the final section of the prophecy in chapters 40–48 was delivered, culminating the logical development of the book.

Few books of the Bible use such a wide variety of literary forms as does Ezekiel. Though most of the book is prose, some of it is poetry. Ezekiel uses almost every kind of literary device and imagery to communicate graphically the messages of judgment and blessing: dream-visions (chs. 1–3; 8–11); apocalyptic literature (37:1–14; 40–48); drama (4–5; 12); allegory, parable, proverbs (16:44; 18:2); and funeral dirges (19; 26–28; 32). The frequent rhetorical questions and repetitious phrases enhance the vitality and thrust of the oracles.

Dream-visions were common in Mesopotamia in the seventh and sixth centuries B.C.[6] This literary form had two major parts: (1) the setting of the vision, declaring the time, recipient, place of reception, and general circumstances; and (2) the description of the vision just as it was seen by the recipient. Ezekiel used this common type of literature in his book and also developed (along with Daniel and Zechariah in the OT) apocalyptic literature in the dream-vision format. This may be defined as "symbolic visionary prophetic literature, composed during oppressive conditions, consisting of visions whose events are recorded exactly as they were seen by the author and explained through a divine interpreter, and whose theological content is primarily eschatological."[7] Twice Ezekiel used this genre, which would be well known to the exiles, to encourage them during their time of oppression. Both apocalyptic visions contained messages of restoration and blessing.

7. Theological Values

Five prominent theological concepts pervade these prophetic pages: (1) the nature of God; (2) the purpose and nature of God's judgment; (3) individual responsibility; (4) the ethical, religious, and moral history of Israel and (5) the nature of Israel's restoration and the millennial worship.

God's attributes most strongly emphasized are those related to his covenant promises. A righteous and holy God set forth in the Mosaic covenant a righteous way of life for the well-being of his people, Israel. If they followed the stipulations of that covenant, they would be blessed in every spiritual and physical way (Lev 26:3–13; Deut 28:1–14). If they rebelled against the Lord's righteous ordinances and disobeyed them, the Lord—being holy, just, and righteous—would discipline the people and withhold blessing (Lev 26:14–39; Deut 28:15–68). Ezekiel demonstrated the Lord's faithfulness to these promises. He was being faithful to judge Israel and Judah because they had broken the law. Likewise he also would faithfully restore the people to the land of blessing and confer on them messianic blessings based on the Abrahamic, Davidic, and new covenants (Lev 26:40–45; Deut 30; cf. Gen 12:1–3; 2 Sam 7:12–17; Jer 31:31–34).

God's character logically reflects judgment. The Lord loved Israel and chose her as his very own people to bless the world (Gen 12:2–3; Exod 19:4–6; Deut 7:6–11). Since she strayed from his righteous ways, the Lord brought judgment on her to make her conscious of her wickedness so that she would return to him. Ezekiel

---

[6]Oppenheim, *Interpretation of Dreams*, pp. 186–225.

[7]Ralph H. Alexander, "Hermeneutics of Old Testament Apocalyptic Literature" (Th.D. diss., Dallas Theological Seminary, 1968), p. 45.

continually declared that the purpose of the Lord's judgment was to cause Israel, or the nations, to "know that I am the LORD," a phrase repeated over sixty-five times in this book. Judgment was for Israel's good because it would result in her return to the Lord and her understanding that he was the only true God.

Though the Lord often dealt with Israel nationally, Ezekiel balanced this with an emphasis on individual responsibility (cf. Deut 24:16; 29:17–21). A person was not delivered from God's curse by the righteousness of the majority of the nation or some other person's spirituality. Each person was accountable to God. Each needed to obey the statutes of God's word in order to live righteously before him. Everyone was equally responsible for his own disobedience and unrighteousness. Therefore Ezekiel exhorted the exiles individually to turn from their sinful ways and live righteously according to the Mosaic covenant (chs. 18; 23).

Along with the judgment of God announced in this prophecy, Ezekiel vindicated the Lord's righteous justice by recounting Israel's ethical, moral, and religious history. This was most vividly accomplished through the imagery of Israel as a spiritual prostitute who, having been wooed and married by God, had prostituted herself by going after the gods of other nations throughout her entire history. This idolatry and unfaithfulness had characterized her from her birth in Egypt.

In spite of Israel's consistent idolatry, the Lord gave her a message of hope through his prophet. One of the most complete descriptions of Israel's restoration to the land of Palestine in the end times was given in the hope messages (33:21–39:29). The basis, manner, and results of Israel's restoration to the Promised Land were clearly enunciated. Likewise, the most exhaustive delineation of the worship system in the Millennium was set forth in chapters 40–48. Anyone who studies eschatology must know these sections of Ezekiel.

8. Text

Many scholars feel that the text of Ezekiel that we have is in one of the worst states of preservation of any OT book. The basis for this opinion normally lies in the supposed obscurities of technical expressions (such as dates and measurements) and *hapax legomena* (words appearing only once) that have led to copyist errors. Many translators have resorted to conjecture and textual emendations to try to solve these problems and "make sense" of the text.

But textual evidence for most of the "corrections" is sparse. The issue really lies in the area of inspiration. The presupposition of many critical scholars is that the text is not inspired by God. Therefore they feel free to alter the text as they wish to. I hold an a priori position that the Scriptures are both verbally and plenarily inspired. Unless there is adequate and sufficient textual data to warrant a better reading of the MT in accord with normal textual-critical guidelines, no reason exists to alter it. Some appeal to the LXX to control the Hebrew text of Ezekiel, but the paraphrasing tendency of that textual recension along with its propensity to omit repetitions and to interpolate explanations impugn its reliability.[8] A proper understanding of the argument of the book demonstrates that the Hebrew text may be understood adequately as it stands.

---

[8]Cf. Moshe Greenberg, "The Use of the Ancient Versions for Interpreting the Hebrew Text," VetTest Supplement 29 (1976): 131–48.

9. Bibliography

Books

Alexander, Ralph H. *Ezekiel*. Chicago: Moody, 1976.
Barnett, R.D. "Ezekiel and Tyre." In W.F. Albright Volume of *Eretz Israel*, vol. 9. Jerusalem: Israel Exploration Society, 1969.
Boadt, Lawrence. *Ezekiel's Oracles Against Egypt: A Literary and Philological Study of Ezekiel 29–32*. Chicago: Loyola University Press, 1980.
Brownlee, W.H. "Ezekiel." In *The International Standard Bible Encyclopedia*. ISBE. Vol. 2, rev. ed. Edited by Geoffrey W. Bromiley. Grand Rapids: Eerdmans, 1982, pp. 250–63.
Carley, Keith W. *The Book of the Prophet Ezekiel*. Cambridge: Cambridge University Press, 1974.
Cassuto, V. "The Arrangement of the Book of Ezekiel." V. Cassuto, *Biblical and Oriental Studies*. Vol. 1. Jerusalem: Magnes, 1973, pp. 227–40.
Clements, R.E. "The Ezekiel Tradition: Prophecy in a Time of Crisis." *Israel's Prophetic Tradition: Essays in Honor of Peter Ackroyd*, edited by R. Coggins, A. Phillips, and M. Knibb. London: Cambridge University Press, 1982, pp. 119–36.
Cooke, George A. *A Critical and Exegetical Commentary on the Book of Ezekiel*. ICC. Edited by S.R. Driver, A. Plummer, and C.A. Briggs. Edinburgh: T. & T. Clark, 1936.
Craigie, Peter C. *Ezekiel*. The Daily Study Bible, edited by John C.L. Gibson. Philadelphia: Westminster, 1983.
Davidson, A.B. *The Book of Ezekiel*. Cambridge: Cambridge University Press, 1892.
Eichrodt, Walter. *Ezekiel: A Commentary*. Philadelphia: Westminster, 1970.
Ellison, Henry L. *Ezekiel: The Man and His Message*. Grand Rapids: Eerdmans, 1956.
Feinberg, Charles Lee. *The Prophecy of Ezekiel: The Glory of the Lord*. Chicago: Moody, 1969.
Gaebelein, A.C. *The Prophet Ezekiel: An Analytical Exposition*. New York: Our Hope, 1918.
Greenberg, Moshe. "The Vision of Jerusalem in Ezekiel 8–11: A Holistic Interpretation." *The Divine Helmsman: Studies on God's Control of Human Events, Presented to Lou H. Silberman*. New York: KTAV, 1980, pp. 146ff.
———. *Ezekiel 1–20*. The Anchor Bible. Garden City, N.Y.: Doubleday, 1983.
Hoekema, Anthony. *The Bible and the Future*. Grand Rapids: Eerdmans, 1979.
Ironside, H.A. *Ezekiel*. Neptune, N.J.: Loizeaux, 1949.
Irwin, William A. *The Problem of Ezekiel*. Chicago: University of Chicago Press, 1943.
Kaiser, Walter C., Jr. *Toward an Old Testament Theology*. Grand Rapids: Zondervan, 1978.
Keil, Carl F. *Biblical Commentary on the Prophecies of Ezekiel*. KD. 2 vols. Grand Rapids: Eerdmans, 1950.
Pentecost, J. Dwight. *Things to Come*. Findlay, Ohio: Dunham, 1958.
Skinner, John. *The Book of Ezekiel*. New York: A.C. Armstrong and Sons, 1901.
Taylor, John B. *Ezekiel: An Introduction and Commentary*. Downers Grove, Ill.: InterVarsity, 1969.
Unger, Merrill F. *Great Neglected Bible Prophecies*. Wheaton, Ill.: Scripture, 1955.
Van Dijk, H.J. *Ezekiel's Prophecy on Tyre*. Rome: Pontifical Biblical Institute, 1968.
Wevers, John W. *Ezekiel*. London: Nelson, 1969.
Yamauchi, Edwin M. *Foes From the Northern Frontier*. Grand Rapids: Baker, 1982.
Zimmerli, Walter. *Ezekiel I and II*. Philadelphia: Fortress, 1979.

Journals

Alexander, Ralph H. "A Fresh Look at Ezekiel 38 and 39." *Journal of the Evangelical Theological Society* 17 (Summer 1974): 157–69.
Boadt, Lawrence. "Textual Problems in Ezekiel and Poetic Analysis of Paired Words." *Journal of Biblical Literature* 97, 4 (1978): 489–99.

DeVries, S.J. "Remembrance in Ezekiel." *Interpretation* 16 (1962): 58–64.

Dressler, Harold H.P. "The Identification of the Ugaritic Dnil with the Daniel of Ezekiel." *Vetus Testamentum* 29 (1979): 152–61.

Freedmen, David N. "The Book of Ezekiel." *Interpretation*. 18 (October 1954): 446–71.

Freedy, K.S. and Redford, D.B. "The Dates in Ezekiel in Relation to Biblical, Babylonian and Egyptian Sources." *Journal of the American Oriental Society* 903 (1970): 460–85.

Good, Edwin M. "Ezekiel's Ship: Some Extended Metaphors in the Old Testament." *Semitics* (1970): 79–103.

Habel, N. "The Form and Significance of the Call Narrative." *Zeitschrift für die alttestamentliche Wissenschaft* 77 (1965): 297–323.

Howie, C.G. "The Date and Composition of Ezekiel." *Journal of Biblical Literature*, Monograph Series 4, 1950.

Lindars, Barnabas. "Ezekiel and Individual Responsibility." *Vetus Testamentum* 15 (1965): 452–67.

McRae, Allan A. "The Key to Ezekiel's First Thirty Chapters." *Bibliotheca Sacra* 122 (July–September 1965): 227–33.

Parunak, H. Van Dyke. "The Literary Architecture of Ezekiel's Mar'ot Elohim." *Journal of Biblical Literature* 99, 1 (1980): 61–74.

Saggs, H.W.F. "Branch to the Nose (Ezek. 8:17)." *Journal of Theological Studies* 11 (1980): 61–74.

_____. "External Goals in the OT (Ezek. 13:17–21)." *Journal of Semitic Studies* 19 (1974): 1–12.

Zimmerli, Walter. "The Message of the Prophet Ezekiel." *Interpretation* 23 (April 1969): 131–57.

Unpublished Works

Parunak, H. Van Dyke. "Structural Studies in Ezekiel." Ph.D. dissertation, Harvard University, 1978.

10. Outline

I. Ezekiel's Commission (1:1–3:27)
    A. The Vision of God's Glory (1:1–28)
        1. The setting of the vision (1:1–3)
        2. The description of the vision (1:4–28)
            a. The living beings (1:4–14)
            b. The wheels and their movement (1:15–21)
            c. The expanse (1:22–28)
    B. The Lord's Charge to Ezekiel (2:1–3:27)
        1. The recipients of Ezekiel's ministry (2:1–5)
        2. Ezekiel's encouragement in the ministry (2:6–7)
        3. The nature of Ezekiel's ministry (2:8–3:11)
        4. The conclusion of the vision (3:12–15)
        5. Ezekiel: a watchman to Israel (3:16–21)
        6. Ezekiel's muteness (3:22–27)
II. Judah's Iniquity and the Resulting Judgment (4:1–24:27)
    A. The Initial Warnings of the Watchman (4:1–7:27)
        1. Monodramas of the siege of Jerusalem (4:1–5:17)
            a. The brick and the plate (4:1–17)
            b. The division of hair (5:1–4)
            c. The significance of the symbolic acts (5:5–17)
        2. The coming judgment on the land of Judah (6:1–7:27)
            a. Destruction of pagan religious shrines (6:1–14)
            b. The imminency and comprehensiveness of the curse (7:1–13)
            c. The response to the curse (7:14–27)
    B. The Vision of the Exodus of God's Glory (8:1–11:25)
        1. The idolatry of the house of Israel (8:1–18)
            a. The image of jealousy (8:1–6)
            b. Idol worship of the elders (8:7–13)
            c. Tammuz worship of the women (8:14–15)
            d. Sun worship (8:16–18)
        2. Judgment on Jerusalem and the departure of God's glory (9:1–11:23)
            a. The man with the writing kit (9:1–4)
            b. The executioners' judgment (9:5–8)
            c. Vindication of God's judgment (9:9–11)
            d. Coals of fire on Jerusalem (10:1–7)
            e. Cherubim and Ichabod (10:8–22)
            f. Judgment on Jerusalem's leaders (11:1–13)
            g. The future of the remnant (11:14–21)
            h. The departure of the Lord's glory from Jerusalem (11:22–25)
    C. The Lord's Reply to the Exiles' Invalid Rationalizations of Hope (12:1–19:14)
        1. The dramatic tragedy of exile (12:1–20)
            a. Introduction (12:1–2)
            b. A picture of deportation (12:3–16)

   c. A drama of fear (12:17–20)
 2. The faithfulness of God: the present judgment
   (12:21–28)
 3. The condemnation of contemporary false prophets
   (13:1–23)
   a. Judgment on the prophets (13:1–16)
   b. Judgment on the prophetesses (13:17–23)
 4. The effect of the false prophets on the leaders (14:1–11)
 5. No deliverance apart from personal righteousness
   (14:12–23)
 6. Jerusalem, an unprofitable vine (15:1–8)
 7. Jerusalem's history as a prostitute (16:1–63)
   a. The birth of Jerusalem (16:1–5)
   b. The Lord's courtship and marriage of Jerusalem
   (16:6–14)
   c. Jerusalem's prostitution with other lands and gods
   (16:15–34)
   d. Jerusalem: judged a prostitute (16:35–43)
   e. The perversion of Jerusalem (16:44–58)
   f. Restoration: the promise of love (16:59–63)
 8. The riddle and the parable of the two eagles (17:1–24)
 9. Individual responsibility for righteousness (18:1–31)
   a. Proverb versus principle (18:1–4)
   b. Three illustrations of the principle (18:5–18)
   c. The explanation of the principle (18:19–32)
 10. A lament for the princes of Israel (19:1–14)
D. The Defective Leadership of Israel (20:1–23:49)
 1. The history of Israel's rebellion and the Lord's grace
   (20:1–44)
   a. Rebellion in Egypt (20:1–9)
   b. Rebellion in the wilderness (20:10–26)
   c. Rebellion in the conquest and settlement of the
   land (20:27–29)
   d. Rebellion of Judah in Ezekiel's day (20:30–44)
 2. Judgment on Judah's contemporary leaders (20:45–21:32)
   a. The burning of the southern forest (20:45–21:7)
   b. The slaughter of the sword (21:8–17)
   c. The imminent judgment by Babylonia (21:18–27)
   d. Postponement of judgment on Ammon (21:28–32)
 3. The cause of judgment: Judah's idolatrous rulers
   (22:1–31)
   a. Deliberate disobedience to the Mosaic covenant
   (22:1–16)
   b. The purification of judgment (22:17–22)
   c. The void of righteous leaders (22:23–31)
 4. An allegorical summary of Israel's political prostitution
   (23:1–49)
   a. Israel's sordid youth (23:1–4)
   b. Samaria's prostitution (23:5–10)

        c. Jerusalem's prostitution (23:11–35)
        d. Judgment for prostitution (23:36–49)
   E. The Execution of Jerusalem's Judgment (24:1–27)
     1. The parable of the cooking pot (24:1–14)
     2. Signs to the exiles (24:15–27)
        a. The death of Ezekiel's wife (24:15–24)
        b. The removal of Ezekiel's muteness (24:25–27)

III. Judgment on the Foreign Nations (25:1–33:20)
   A. Judgment on Judah's Closest Neighbors (25:1–17)
     1. Judgment on Ammon (25:1–7)
     2. Judgment on Moab (25:8–11)
     3. Judgment on Edom (25:12–14)
     4. Judgment on Philistia (25:15–17)
   B. Judgment on Tyre (26:1–28:19)
     1. Judgment by Babylonia (26:1–21)
        a. A judgment oracle against Tyre (26:1–14)
        b. The response of vassal nations to Tyre's fall
          (26:15–18)
        c. The Lord's concluding verdict (26:19–21)
     2. Ezekiel's funeral dirge over Tyre (27:1–36)
        a. The building of Tyre's ship of pride (27:1–11)
        b. Tyre's vast commercial relations (27:12–24)
        c. The sinking of the ship of Tyre (27:25–36)
     3. A judgment speech against the ruler of Tyre (28:1–10)
     4. A funeral dirge for the king of Tyre (28:11–19)
   C. Judgment on Sidon (28:20–24)
   D. Israel's Restoration From the Nations (28:25–26)
   E. Judgment on Egypt (29:1–32:32)
     1. The introductory prophecy of judgment on Egypt
       (29:1–16)
     2. A day of the Lord: the consummation of Egypt's
       judgment (29:17–30:19)
        a. Babylonia's compensation of Egypt for the spoilless
          siege of Tyre (29:17–21)
        b. Nebuchadnezzar's invasion of Egypt (30:1–19)
     3. Pharaoh's broken arms (30:20–26)
     4. Egypt's fall compared with Assyria's fall (31:1–18)
     5. A funeral dirge for Egypt (32:1–16)
     6. Ezekiel's summary lament over Egypt (32:17–32)
     7. Ezekiel's warning to the exiles (33:1–20)

IV. The Future Blessings of a Faithful Covenant God (33:21–48:35)
   A. Restoration to the Promised Land (33:21–39:29)
     1. Israel and the Promised Land (33:21–33)
     2. Shepherds false and true (34:1–31)
        a. The accusation against the false shepherds (34:1–6)
        b. God's verdict concerning the leadership of Israel
          (34:7–31)
     3. Preparation of the land (35:1–36:15)

a. Removal of oppressors (35:1–15)
b. A prophecy of encouragement (36:1–15)
4. The restoration to the land (36:16–37:14)
  a. The basis for Israel's dispersion (36:16–21)
  b. A description of the final restoration (36:22–32)
  c. The effects of the restoration (36:33–38)
  d. A vision of restoration (37:1–14)
5. Israel's reunion amid fulfilled covenants (37:15–28)
6. The Promised Land and foreign possession (38:1–39:29)
  a. The initial judgment speech against Gog (38:1–23)
    1) The identity of the major participants (38:1–3)
    2) The invasion of Gog into Israel (38:4–16)
    3) God's judgment on Gog (38:17–23)
  b. Reiteration and expansion of God's judgment speech against Gog (39:1–29)
    1) Invasion and judgment (39:1–8)
    2) The aftermath of judgment on Gog (39:9–20)
  c. The summary of the six night messages (39:21–29)
B. God's Glory Returns (40:1–48:35)
1. The setting of the apocalyptic vision (40:1–4)
2. The apocalyptic vision (40:5–48:35)
  a. The millennial temple (40:5–42:20)
    1) The outer court (40:5–27)
    2) The inner court (40:28–47)
    3) The house of God (40:48–41:26)
    4) The priests' buildings (42:1–14)
    5) The measurement of the temple area (42:15–20)
  b. The return of the glory of God to the temple (43:1–12)
  c. Temple ordinances (43:13–46:24)
    1) The altar of sacrifice: description and dedication (43:13–27)
    2) Regulations for the east gate (44:1–3)
    3) The priests and the service of the temple (44:4–16)
    4) Ordinances for the Zadokian priesthood (44:17–31)
    5) The sacred area of the Holy Land (45:1–8)
    6) The role of the prince in the Millenium (45:9–46:18)
      a) An exhortation to the contemporary unrighteous leaders (45:9–12)
      b) Making atonement for the people and the sanctuary (45:13–20)
      c) Leadership in worship (45:21–46:15)
      d) Inheritance (46:16–18)
    7) The priests' kitchens (46:19–24)
  d. Topographical aspects of the Millennium (47:1–48:35)

1) The temple river (47:1–12)
2) Divisions of the land (47:13–48:35)
   a) Boundaries of the land and principles for distribution (47:13–23)
   b) Tribal allotments in the north (48:1–7)
   c) The special gift of the land (48:8–22)
   d) Tribal allotments in the south (48:23–29)
   e) The city and its gates (48:30–35)

Text and Exposition

I. Ezekiel's Commission (1:1–3:27)

A. *The Vision of God's Glory* (1:1–28)

1. *The setting of the vision*

1:1–3

> ¹In the thirtieth year, in the fourth month on the fifth day, while I was among the exiles by the Kebar River, the heavens were opened and I saw visions of God. ²On the fifth of the month—it was the fifth year of the exile of King Jehoiachin— ³the word of the LORD came to Ezekiel the priest, the son of Buzi, by the Kebar River in the land of the Babylonians. There the hand of the LORD was upon him.

1–3 The setting of the Mesopotamian dream-visions—which occurred in both the Assyrian period and the Babylonian period (cf. Oppenheim, *Interpretation of Dreams*, pp. 186–87)—consisted of four elements: (1) the date, (2) the place of reception, (3) the recipient, and (4) the circumstances. Ezekiel included all four aspects in his vision.

The date of this vision is stated in two different ways: (1) "in the thirtieth year, in the fourth month on the fifth day" (v.1), and (2) "on the fifth of the month—it was the fifth year of the exile of King Jehoiachin" (v.2). The "thirtieth year" has been explained several ways. (For a survey of the explanations, see Anthony D. York, "Ezekiel I: Inaugural and Restoration Visions?" VetTest 27 [1977]: 82–98.) Some refer it to the thirtieth year following Josiah's reform. There is no evidence for such a connection between Josiah and Ezekiel nor for dating in the OT from an event unless explicit reference to that event is given. Others see the date related to Nabopolassar's reign, though without data. Some assume that the reference is to the thirtieth year of Jehoiachin and is the date of the compilation of the book (so Howie), though this would be out of harmony with v.2 and would require that verse to be an explanatory gloss (so Taylor).

Still others understand this date to relate to the age of Ezekiel. This is the most probable view for two reasons. It was not uncommon that dates were given according to a man's age when personal reminiscences were being reported (cf. Gen 8:13). Additionally, Ezekiel was a priest; and a man entered his priestly ministry at the age of thirty (Num 4:3, 23, 30, 39, 43; 1 Chron 23:3). Therefore, Ezekiel apparently received this vision and his commission in the very year he would have begun his priestly service. This date highlights the priestly atmosphere of Ezekiel's message.

The "thirtieth year" of Ezekiel was related to the fifth year of King Jehoiachin's exile by the same day of the month and probably the same month. The month is understood in v.2 from the explicit statement in v.1. Jehoiachin was deported to Babylonia in 597 B.C. Therefore Ezekiel's commission was received in 593 B.C. Jehoiachin's year of deportation became the focal point of all dating within the book.

Ezekiel saw this vision "by the Kebar River in the land of the Babylonians" (v.3). The river Kebar, a navigable canal, flowed southeast from the city of Babylon (see Introduction: Place of Origin and Destination).

Ezekiel was the stated recipient of the vision (v.3). He was a priest and the son of Buzi. Nothing is known about Buzi, though as Ezekiel's father he would also have been a priest. The notation of Ezekiel's priesthood is significant. He would have been well acquainted with the Mosaic covenant and the priestly functions of the temple, both of which pervade the entire message of this book. Ezekiel was able to describe clearly the glory of God in the temple and the temple functions. He also was prepared to evaluate accurately the rebellion of his people against the explicit commands of the law, which was the basis for the Lord's judgments that Ezekiel announced. Moreover, this priestly background enabled Ezekiel to understand the millennial temple vision concluding the entire prophecy.

The only circumstances set forth in this introduction to the subsequent vision were that "the word of the LORD came to Ezekiel" and "the hand of the LORD was upon him" (v.3). These phrases were used whenever Ezekiel was about to receive or proclaim a revelation from God (esp. a vision, 3:22; 8:1; 33:22; 37:1; 40:1; cf. 2 Kings 3:15). "The hand of the Lord was upon him" connotes the idea of God's strength on behalf of the person involved (3:14; cf. Isa 25:10; 41:10, 20), a concept inherent in the name "Ezekiel" (yᵉḥezqēʾl), which means "God strengthens." God was preparing Ezekiel to receive a vision that would provide the necessary framework for understanding the rest of the prophecy. It is important to the interpretation of this book to note the phrase "I saw visions of God" (v.1), for this immediately declared the nature of the following vision.

Notes

1 The plural form of the noun מַרְאָה (marʾāh, "vision") may imply a series of visions or a vision in process (8:3; 40:2; 43:3; cf. Gen 46:2), the latter being dominant in Ezekiel. The plural may be a plural of generalization (so Greenberg, *Ezekiel 1–20*), indicating an indetermination. Others (e.g., Zimmerli) see the plural as representing a fixed usage.

2 In order to understand a 593 B.C. date for the fifth year of Jehoiachin's exile (597 B.C.), one must use the Nisan (March/April) to Nisan calendar of the Babylonians. Jehoiachin's "first" year would be March 597 B.C. to March 596 B.C. Therefore, the fourth month of the fifth year of Jehoiachin would be June/July 593 B.C. (so Freedy and Redford).

The first person of v.1 and the third person of vv.2–3 have led some to assume a dual authorship. However, all three verses are integral to the setting of the vision, and vv.2–3 parenthetically explain the indefinite date of v.1.

3 דְבַר־יהוה אֶל־ (dᵉbar-YHWH ʾel-, "the word of the LORD came to . . .") becomes a regular technical formula to introduce divine reception of God's word by the prophet. No other prophetic book surpasses Ezekiel's fifty occurrences of this formula, which often introduces a new unit of the book. For fuller discussion, see Zimmerli, *Ezekiel 1*, pp. 144–45; TDOT, 3:111–14; TWOT, 1:180.

The term כַּשְׂדִּים (kaśdîm) may be used for either "Babylonians" or for a special group of wise men in Babylonia (cf. Dan 2:2, 4).

2. The Description of the Vision (1:4–28)

a. The living beings

● 1:4–14

⁴I looked, and I saw a windstorm coming out of the north—an immense cloud with flashing lightning and surrounded by brilliant light. The center of the fire

looked like glowing metal, [5]and in the fire was what looked like four living creatures. In appearance their form was that of a man, [6]but each of them had four
faces and four wings. [7]Their legs were straight; their feet were like those of a calf
and gleamed like burnished bronze. [8]Under their wings on their four sides they
had the hands of a man. All four of them had faces and wings, [9]and their wings
touched one another. Each one went straight ahead; they did not turn as they
moved.

[10]Their faces looked like this: Each of the four had the face of a man, and on
the right each had the face of a lion, and on the left the face of an ox; each also
had the face of an eagle. [11]Such were their faces. Their wings were spread out
upward; each had two wings, one touching the wing of another creature on either
side, and two wings covering its body. [12]Each one went straight ahead. Wherever
the spirit would go, they would go, without turning as they went. [13]The appearance of the living creatures was like burning coals of fire or like torches. Fire
moved back and forth among the creatures; it was bright, and lightning flashed
out of it. [14]The creatures sped back and forth like flashes of lightning.

N. Habel ("The Form and Significance of the Call Narrative," ZAW 77 [1965]:
297–323) has pointed out that there is a general pattern to the commission narratives
of the prophets. First, there is the divine confrontation—an introductory word that
forms the basis and background for the succeeding commission. Then the commission itself enumerates the task the prophet is called to and its importance. Third,
the objections the prophet may offer are stated, after which the "call" narrative
closes with reassurances from the Lord that answer these objections and assure the
prophet that the Lord is with him. All four elements are found in Ezekiel's commission and are noted below.

The vision of vv. 4–28 comprises the divine confrontation of Ezekiel's commission.
This vision has bewildered many and has discouraged them from continuing their
study of this prophecy. This need not be if normal grammatical-historical hermeneutics are used. Four principles of this hermeneutical system are especially
important when interpreting visionary literature.

1. Seek to understand the major idea presented through the vision and do not
dwell on minutiae. This guideline is underscored in the second principle.

2. Follow the divine interpretations normally accompanying the visions. These
divine interpretations concentrate on the overall concept rather than on details.

3. Be keenly aware of parallel passages and the harmony of Scripture, since the
prophets normally sought to apply past revelations of God to their contemporary
situations. The general prophetic message among the prophets is essentially the
same.

4. Use the same approach with the symbols and imagery of visionary literature as
used with figurative language. Thus symbols and imagery are properly understood
as figures and are not to be taken literally.

In this first vision the divine interpretation declares that God and his glory are
portrayed (vv. 1, 28). This portrayal required the use of a vision and its abundant
imagery, for the unfathomable God cannot be adequately described in human
terms. Since God can be visualized only in terms of "likeness," the vision abounds
in terms like "as" (k^e); "resembling"; "looked like" (d^{e}mût); "like" (k^{e}mar'ēh); and
"appearance" (mar'ēh).

The Lord confronted Ezekiel with this glorious vision to impress on him the
majesty, holiness, and wonder of the God who was about to execute judgment on
the people of Israel. Ezekiel was awestricken by God's holiness. The indelible im-

pression of this theophany would be a constant encouragement to Ezekiel in his difficult ministry of announcing God's judgments on his own contemporaries. The awesome holiness of God visualized in Ezekiel's commission would be a backdrop against which he could see the wickedness of Israel and thereby understand why God had to judge his sinful people. When the nations profaned the Lord by claiming that Judah was in captivity because her God was weak, Ezekiel would know that his God was greater than Babylonia's gods. Though the Lord had chosen to discipline his people then, he would be victorious over all the nations when he would restore Israel to her Promised Land.

This was the same glorious, covenant-keeping God who first revealed himself to Israel in a similar vision of splendor on Mount Sinai (Exod 19). He reappeared as the glory inhabiting the Most Holy Place in the dedication of the tabernacle (Exod 24:15–18; 29:42–46; 40:34–38). This theophany led the children of Israel through the wilderness (Num 9:15–23; 14:10; 16:19; 20:6), filled Solomon's temple (1 Kings 8:10–11; 2 Chron 5:14), and appeared at Isaiah's commission (Isa 6:3). Though some may be disturbed that the manifestation of God's glory is not always identical throughout Scripture, the variation in details is to be expected when one considers the limitlessness of God. However, the consistency of the manifestation of God's glory was such that Ezekiel, a priest and a student of the Scriptures, immediately recognized that this was a vision of the glory of the Lord (v.28).

4–14 This vision began with a common introductory formula to visions: "I looked and I saw" (v.4; cf. v.15; 2:9; 8:2, 7; 10:1, 9; 37:8; 40:4–5; 44:4). Ezekiel suddenly saw what appeared to be a raging electrical storm—dark clouds, lightning, and thunder—coming from the north (v.4). Within this storm he saw four figures resembling living beings (v.5; cf. Rev 4), which he described. Though the beings looked like men, each one had four faces and four wings (vv.6, 9, 11; 10:5, 12, 14, 21–22; Rev 4:8 describes living beings with six wings). The man's face was dominant, being on the front of each creature (v.10), while the lion's face was on the right, the ox's (or cherub's, cf. 10:14, 22) face on the left, and the eagle's face on the back.

The wings were joined together (vv.9, 23), with two covering each side of each being and the other two spread for movement, touching the wings of the other living beings (vv.11, 23). When the wings fluttered they sounded like a great thunder of rushing water, a violent rainstorm, or a noisy military encampment—like the voice of the "Almighty" God (*šadday*; v.24; cf. 3:13; 10:5). Each side of the living being had hands like a man's under its wing (v.8; cf. 10:7–8, 12, 21), straight legs, and feet like a calf (v.7).

The rapid movement of these living beings was like flashes of lightning (v.14). Their forward movement was in the direction the man's face looked. When they moved, they did not turn around (vv.9, 12–13). These creatures moved only under the control of the "spirit," which, in this context of God's glory (v.12), is most likely the Holy Spirit of God.

In addition to the general appearance of brightness, these creatures contained in their midst that which looked like coals of fire (v.13), from which lightning issued. These living beings are identified in chapter 10 as cherubim (10:15, 20). Some have found some relation to religious and mythical creations of the ancient Near East, like the genii that guarded temples. Others see the cherubim forming a throne-chariot on which the Lord rode (cf. 1:22–28). Support for this idea is found in 2 Samuel 22:11; 1 Chronicles 28:18; and Psalm 18:11. This may well be the imagery conveyed in this vision. Certainly Ezekiel was acquainted with cherubim from his training in the temple, with its many representations of these creatures (Exod 25–26; 36–37; 1 Kings 6; 2 Chron 3), as well as his knowledge of the "cherubim" imagery from Mesopotamian culture with its guardian genii before temples (cf. comments at 10:8–22; 28:11–19; cf. Greenberg, *Ezekiel 1–20*, p. 55). Cherubim often accompanied references to God's glory in the OT; yet the specific functions of cherubim are nowhere clearly delineated.

Notes

4 The evidence for the meaning of the word חַשְׁמַל (*ḥašmal*, "glowing metal") is extremely sparse. The meaning is not "amber" (KJV, RV) but more the sense of something that shines, perhaps a shining metal.

5 The term חַיָּה (*ḥāyāh*, "living creature") is feminine; yet the pronominal suffixes in these verses that refer back to this word are found both in the masculine plural—e.g., לָהֶם (*lāhem*, "of them") in v.6 and לְאַרְבַּעְתָּם (*leʾarbaʿtām*, "each of the four") in v.10—and in the feminine plural—לְאַרְבַּעְתָּן (*leʾarbaʿtān*, "each of the four"; NIV, "each"), also in v.10. The feminine forms show agreement with the predominant character of the living beings, viz., the concept of אָדָם (*ʾādām*, "man"), which is masculine (cf. v.5). Some had thought that the masculine term כְּרוּב (*kerûb*, "cherub") from ch. 10 was in Ezekiel's mind here, but that seems unlikely. The masculine gender is considered by grammarians as the "prior gender" because it sometimes designates the feminine (cf. Gen 1:27; 32:1 et al.). Likewise, confusion of gender is not unusual in Hebrew grammar. It is usual that the nearest qualifier is feminine with a feminine substantive (cf. GKC, par. 145t).

6 פָּנִים (*pānîm*, "faces") is understood as a numerical plural here and elsewhere in the chapter (e.g., vv.8–10) rather than as a plural of extension.

The dual form כְּנָפַיִם (*kenāpayim*, "wings") is used in this verse instead of the plural form, since the wings are considered in pairs (cf. v.11; 10:21; Isa 6:2). The meaning is two pairs of wings.

b. *The wheels and their movement*

1:15–21

15As I looked at the living creatures, I saw a wheel on the ground beside each creature with its four faces. 16This was the appearance and structure of the wheels: They sparkled like chrysolite, and all four looked alike. Each appeared to be made like a wheel intersecting a wheel. 17As they moved, they would go in any one of the four directions the creatures faced; the wheels did not turn about as the creatures went. 18Their rims were high and awesome, and all four rims were full of eyes all around.

19When the living creatures moved, the wheels beside them moved; and when the living creatures rose from the ground, the wheels also rose. 20Wherever the spirit would go, they would go, and the wheels would rise along with them, because the spirit of the living creatures was in the wheels. 21When the creatures moved, they also moved; when the creatures stood still, they also stood still; and when the creatures rose from the ground, the wheels rose along with them, because the spirit of the living creatures was in the wheels.

15–18 There was one high and awesome wheel beside each of the four living creatures (vv.15–17; cf. 10:9) that had the general appearance of a sparkling precious stone—"chrysolite" (*taršîš*)—with a rim full of eyes (v.18; cf. Rev 4:6).

19–21 When these wheels were functioning, they gave the impression of a wheel being in the midst of another wheel. The wheels moved in conjunction with the living beings (v.19), going in any direction, lifting up off the earth, and standing still. All the movement was under the direction of the Spirit (vv.20–21). Chapters 3 and 10 further describe the wheels as making rumbling sounds when they whirled (3:12–13; 10:5, 13).

Notes

15 The LXX renders the Hebrew פָּנָיו (*pānāyw*, "faces") as τοῖς τέσσαρσιν (*tois tessarsin*, "to the four"), understanding that there was one wheel to each living being, not one wheel for each of the four faces of each living creature, which could be implied by the third masculine singular suffix on *pānāyw*. The LXX reading is in keeping with v.16 and 10:9. However, one could understand the third masculine singular suffix of *pānāyw* as a reference to the four living beings as a singular unit with the four faces being the dominant face of each creature—the face of a man. This would then have the same meaning as the LXX citation. (The LXX has many omissions in this section of difficult Hebrew; cf. Greenberg, "Use of Ancient Versions," pp. 131–48.)

c. The expanse

1:22–28

²²Spread out above the heads of the living creatures was what looked like an expanse, sparkling like ice, and awesome. ²³Under the expanse their wings were stretched out one toward the other, and each had two wings covering its body. ²⁴When the creatures moved, I heard the sound of their wings, like the roar of rushing waters, like the voice of the Almighty, like the tumult of an army. When they stood still, they lowered their wings.

²⁵Then there came a voice from above the expanse over their heads as they stood with lowered wings. ²⁶Above the expanse over their heads was what looked like a throne of sapphire, and high above on the throne was a figure like that of a man. ²⁷I saw that from what appeared to be his waist up he looked like glowing metal, as if full of fire, and that from there down he looked like fire; and brilliant light surrounded him. ²⁸Like the appearance of a rainbow in the clouds on a rainy day, so was the radiance around him.

This was the appearance of the likeness of the glory of the LORD. When I saw it, I fell facedown, and I heard the voice of one speaking.

22–28 An awesome expanse resembling sparkling ice appeared like a platform over the heads of the four living creatures (vv.22–23; cf. Rev 4:6). The likeness of a throne made from precious lapis lazuli (NIV "sapphire") was above this expanse, and the likeness of a man was on the throne (v.26; cf. Exod 24:10; Rev 4:2). The man appeared to be surrounded by fire, which gave him a radiance similar to a rainbow (vv.27–28; cf. 8:2; Dan 10:6; Rev 4:3, 5).

The most significant phrase of the entire chapter is in the last verse: "This was the appearance of the likeness of the glory of the LORD." This reference would relate more directly to the likeness of the man on the throne, but Exodus 19, 1 Kings 6, Isaiah 6, Daniel 10, and Revelation 4 also should cause the reader to see the *entire* vision as a manifestation of God's glory (cf. v. 1). God revealed his magnificent person to Ezekiel to prepare him for ministry. The Lord would continue to appear to Ezekiel in this same fashion throughout the book to encourage him that he was a servant of almighty God (cf. 3:12, 23–24; 8:2–4; 9:3; 10:1–20; 11:22–23; 43:2–4).

Throughout the OT God's prophets were confronted with a revelation of his glory that made an indelible imprint on their ministry. When they became discouraged, they would recall the revelation of God's glory at their commission, which spurred them on in the Lord's service steadfastly.

Likewise, today if one is to minister for the Lord, that person must first have a divine confrontation and come to an understanding of God's great glory; for only in light of the knowledge of God will one have strength and perseverance to serve God humbly—no matter what the situation may be. This divine confrontation adds seriousness and purpose to the call of God's servant. He may not necessarily see a vision or have an emotional experience in this confrontation, but the Holy Spirit will impress God's character on the servant's heart as he seeks to live and minister in light of God's person revealed in God's Word. When one genuinely comes to see God's glory, he cannot help but fall prostrate in worship before the almighty God, even as Ezekiel did (v. 28).

This manifestation of the Lord's glory formed a backdrop for the announcements of judgment that Ezekiel would make. Since the glorious, holy God who gave the Mosaic covenant (Exod 19) could not tolerate disobedience to that covenant because of his righteous character, he had to execute judgment on the iniquity that his holy nature could not tolerate. Therefore, when God brought judgment on Jerusalem, his glory had to leave its residence in the temple (10:1–20; 11:22–23). However, the Lord's glory would return (cf. ch. 43) after the cleansing of God's people would be completed. Thus the revelation of God's glory became a significant theme throughout the prophecy, showing a unity of purpose within the book.

Notes

24 The name שַׁדַּי (*šadday*, "Almighty") for God probably derives from the Akkadian *šaddu* ("mountain"). It conveyed a sovereign, overpowering God.

26 Lapis lazuli—סַפִּיר (*sappîr*, "sapphire")—was a well-known precious stone of the ancient Near East, bluish in color, having the appearance of a glaze.

B. *The Lord's Charge to Ezekiel (2:1–3:27)*

1. *The recipients of Ezekiel's ministry*

2:1–5

> ¹He said to me, "Son of man, stand up on your feet and I will speak to you." ²As he spoke, the Spirit came into me and raised me to my feet, and I heard him speaking to me.

³He said: "Son of man, I am sending you to the Israelites, to a rebellious nation that has rebelled against me; they and their fathers have been in revolt against me to this very day. ⁴The people to whom I am sending you are obstinate and stubborn. Say to them, 'This is what the Sovereign LORD says.' ⁵And whether they listen or fail to listen—for they are a rebellious house—they will know that a prophet has been among them.

1–2 The voice of God speaking from the theophany addressed Ezekiel with the title "Son of man" (v.1). This became Ezekiel's normal designation throughout the remainder of the book, being used over ninety times to refer to Ezekiel, though found nowhere else in the OT except in Daniel 7:13; 8:17. This title indicates the frailty and weakness of man the creature humbled before the mighty and majestic God, who had just been revealed in the previous vision (so Eichrodt, Feinberg). By this title Ezekiel would be reminded continually that he was dependent on the Spirit's power, which enabled him to receive the message of God (v.2) and to deliver it in the power and authority of the Lord— "This is what the Sovereign LORD says" (v.4). This same name—"Son of Man"—was given Christ in the Gospels (Luke 19:10) to emphasize his relation to humanity and his voluntary dependence on the Spirit of God.

The full sense of this title in Daniel 7:13; 8:17 and in the NT in relation to deity is a complex issue. Helpful insights can be found in F.F. Bruce, "The Background to the Son of Man Sayings," in *Christ the Lord: Studies in Christology Presented to Donald Guthrie*, ed. Harold H. Rowden (Downers Grove, Ill.: Inter-Varsity, 1982), pp. 50–70, and in O. Michel and I.H. Marshall, "The Son of Man," DNTT, 3:613–34, 665.

3–4 The commission side of Ezekiel's call narrative encompasses the majority of chapters 2 and 3 (2:1–5; 2:8–3:7; 3:16–21, 24–27). God was about to commission Ezekiel for a most difficult task. He was to go to his own people in exile, the people God described as rebellious against himself, his law, and his messengers, the prophets (v.3). This was not a new condition, for this nation had transgressed the Mosaic covenant throughout her history. God's chosen people were "obstinate" and "stubborn" (v.4), literally, "hard-hearted" and "hard-faced," demonstrating a strong-willed determination to resist God and his ways. Undoubtedly a major contribution to Judah's current rebellion were the abominations of Manasseh that had stained the hearts of the people.

5 Ezekiel's message was not to be conditioned on his listeners' response. Even if the people closed their ears to Ezekiel's words, he was to speak in God's authority and not his own. Only then would the people know that a prophet had been among them. How important it is that God's spokesmen today take heed to this principle!

Notes

---

3 מֹרְדִים (*môreḏîm*, "rebellious") is a characteristic active participle used nine times in this commission and over fifteen times in the entire book to describe the persistent character of the nation Israel as bold and audaciously rebellious.

The plural noun גּוֹיִם (*gôyim*, "nations"; NIV, "nation") refers to the two separate nations of Israel and Judah, which made up the entire nation of Israel in Ezekiel's day (cf. 35:10; 36:13–15; 37:19–22). The "house of Israel" and the "house of Judah" are phrases often used interchangeably in Ezekiel (2:3; 3:4–7; 4:3; 8:1–12; 9:9; 11:15 et al.). This indicates that the reuniting of Israel and Judah had its beginning in the Babylonian captivity. The consideration of אֶל גּוֹיִם (*'el gôyim*, "to nations") as a marginal gloss (so Zimmerli) is unwarranted.

The verb פָּשַׁע (*pāša'*, "revolt") signifies an attitude of flat refusal to subject oneself to proper authority. This term conveys a breach (of trust) by a vassal and an overreaching (cf. J. Pedersen, *Israel I and II* [London: Oxford University Press, 1926], p. 417, and Rolf Knierseim, *Hauptbegriffe für Sünde im Alten Testament* [Gutersloh: Gutersloher Verlaghaus G. Mohn, 1965]).

4 אֲדֹנָי יהוה (*'adōnāy YHWH*, "The Sovereign LORD") is the name most commonly used for God in Ezekiel, over two hundred times. It emphasizes God as the covenant God of Israel and, therefore, her Lord and great King, against whom she had rebelled. It is an authoritative title. Ezekiel used this title in the introduction to his messages and frequently in their conclusions to highlight Yahweh's lordship over Israel. Although the NIV renders this compound name of God as "Sovereign LORD," a more literal translation would be "Lord Yahweh."

---

2. Ezekiel's encouragement in the ministry

2:6–7

⁶And you, son of man, do not be afraid of them or their words. Do not be afraid, though briers and thorns are all around you and you live among scorpions. Do not be afraid of what they say or terrified by them, though they are a rebellious house. ⁷You must speak my words to them, whether they listen or fail to listen, for they are rebellious.

6–7 In light of the difficult ministry Ezekiel was being called to, the Lord reassured him (v.6; cf. 3:8–11, 22–23). Regardless of how frightful the opposition may be—pricking him as thorns or stinging him as scorpions—Ezekiel was not to be afraid or become dismayed and give up. On the contrary, he was to be faithful in the proclamation of God's message, for his recipients were rebels who needed his warnings (v.7). This truth is still a source of encouragement to those called to proclaim the truth of God's Word in the midst of a perverse and wicked generation.

3. The nature of Ezekiel's ministry

2:8–3:11

⁸But you, son of man, listen to what I say to you. Do not rebel like that rebellious house; open your mouth and eat what I give you."

⁹Then I looked, and I saw a hand stretched out to me. In it was a scroll, ¹⁰which he unrolled before me. On both sides of it were written words of lament and mourning and woe.

¹And he said to me, "Son of man, eat what is before you, eat this scroll; then go and speak to the house of Israel." ²So I opened my mouth, and he gave me the scroll to eat.

³Then he said to me, "Son of man, eat this scroll I am giving you and fill your stomach with it." So I ate it, and it tasted as sweet as honey in my mouth.

⁴Then he said to me: "Son of man, go now to the house of Israel and speak my words to them. ⁵You are not being sent to a people of obscure speech and difficult language, but to the house of Israel—⁶not to many peoples of obscure

speech and difficult language, whose words you cannot understand. Surely if I had sent you to them, they would have listened to you. [7]But the house of Israel is not willing to listen to you because they are not willing to listen to me, for the whole house of Israel is hardened and obstinate. [8]But I will make you as unyielding and hardened as they are. [9]I will make your forehead like the hardest stone, harder than flint. Do not be afraid of them or terrified by them, though they are a rebellious house."

[10]And he said to me, "Son of man, listen carefully and take to heart all the words I speak to you. [11]Go now to your countrymen in exile and speak to them. Say to them, 'This is what the Sovereign LORD says,' whether they listen or fail to listen."

2:8–3:3 The Lord's charge to Ezekiel emphasized the absolute necessity of hearing, understanding, and assimilating God's message prior to going forth as a spokesman for the Lord. Ezekiel was to listen to God (2:8a) and not rebel against him as did the people of Israel, who failed to listen to his word. Ezekiel was not to let the people pull him down to their level.

Before beginning his ministry, Ezekiel was to symbolize his complete acceptance of the Lord's message by eating the scroll (2:8b–3:3). The nature of the message he would proclaim was written on the scroll: funeral dirges, mournings, and lamentations (2:9). Certainly this was not a joyous note to begin on. But even when the ministry would seem difficult and distasteful, the Lord would cause his word to be as sweet as honey (3:3; cf. Pss 19:10; 119:103; Prov 16:24; 24:13–14; Jer 15:16).

4–9 The recipients' response to Ezekiel's messages was not to govern the nature or manner of his ministry. The people rejected the divine messenger because they were first alienated from God (v.7). Though Israel was obstinate, and though it would have been easier to preach to foreign people in a foreign language (cf. Isa 28:11), Ezekiel was to be strong (as his name implies) and not respond in fear and dismay (vv.4–7). The Lord fully prepared Ezekiel for his task by making him more determined than the people of Israel (v.8)—as sharp and hard as flint (v.9; cf. comment at 1:3 for the meaning of Ezekiel's name). The Lord always prepares and reassures his messengers with the needed equipment.

10–11 The word of the Lord had to become part of Ezekiel (cf. Jer 1:9) before he could "go" and "speak" (Ezek 3:1). Ezekiel was to meditate on the Lord's message, giving continual attention to it throughout his ministry (v.10). Only then would he be able to speak repeatedly with God's authority—even to audiences who did not care to listen (v.11).

Notes

2:9 Some emend the MT by substituting הוֹי (hôy, "woe") for הִי (hî, "lament"). The LXX and the Vulgate are appealed to for support in favor of the former reading (so NIV). However, a noun rather than an interjection would fit the text better. It is certainly possible that hî demonstrates the syncope of the form נְהִי (neʰhî, "mourning").

3:5 עִמְקֵי שָׂפָה (ʿimqê śāpāh, "obscure speech"; lit., "deep of lip") implies an unintelligible language (cf. Isa 33:19), while וְכִבְדֵי לָשׁוֹן (wᵉkiḇdê lāšôn, "difficult language"; lit., "heaviness of language") denotes a dullness and sluggishness of speech.

9 שָׁמִיר (šāmîr, "stone") has not only the sense of adamant but also sharpness, both of them relevant to Ezekiel's preparation.

---

4. The conclusion of the vision

3:12–15

¹²Then the Spirit lifted me up, and I heard behind me a loud rumbling sound—May the glory of the Lᴏʀᴅ be praised in his dwelling place!—¹³the sound of the wings of the living creatures brushing against each other and the sound of the wheels beside them, a loud rumbling sound. ¹⁴The Spirit then lifted me up and took me away, and I went in bitterness and in the anger of my spirit, with the strong hand of the Lᴏʀᴅ upon me. ¹⁵I came to the exiles who lived at Tel Abib near the Kebar River. And there, where they were living, I sat among them for seven days—overwhelmed.

12–13 The vision concluded with Ezekiel's being raised up by the Spirit (v.12) and hearing a final benediction that assured him that he had witnessed a revelation of God's glory (v.13).

Ezekiel's transportation was not a case of hypnotism, autosuggestion, or the parapsychic phenomena of bodily levitation. The text demonstrates that the transportation was in a vision, experienced under the compulsion of the Holy Spirit (cf. Edward J. Young, *My Servants, the Prophets* [Grand Rapids: Eerdmans, 1952], pp. 182–87).

14–15 These verses recount Ezekiel's objection to his commission (the third element of the normal prophetic-call narrative). As Ezekiel was brought back to the exiles at Tel Abib, he struggled with the distasteful ministry he had been called to (v.14). He was anguished and angry that he must deliver a displeasing message to an unreceptive audience. This would certainly not be a successful ministry in the eyes of men.

It took Ezekiel seven days to sort out his thoughts and feelings after having seen this vision. The Lord's hand was on him to control him as he sat appalled at the wonder and horror he had experienced (v.15). Ezekiel's condition and the period of seven days were instructive to the exiles: mourning for the dead normally took seven days (Gen 50:10; Num 19:11; Job 2:13), as did the length of time for a priest's consecration (Lev 8:33). Ezekiel was being consecrated for the priesthood on his thirtieth birthday and commissioned to proclaim Judah's funeral dirge.

Notes

---

14 מַר (mar, "bitterness") includes the concepts of "distress," "heavy heart," and "anguish."

15 תֵּל אָבִיב (tēl 'āḇîḇ "Tel Abib"; Akkad. til abūbi) means "hill of rain flood," "deluge," most likely a mound that had been deserted and uninhabited on which the exiles were settled.

וָאֵשֵׁר (wā'ēšēr, untr. in NIV) probably should be read as אֲשֶׁר (ᵃšer, "which") with the LXX.

The Hiphil participle מַשְׁמִים (*mašmîm*, "overwhelmed") indicates a condition of being appalled by horror and wonder.

5. *Ezekiel: a watchman to Israel*

3:16–21

> [16]At the end of seven days the word of the LORD came to me: [17]"Son of man, I have made you a watchman for the house of Israel; so hear the word I speak and give them warning from me. [18]When I say to a wicked man, 'You will surely die,' and you do not warn him or speak out to dissuade him from his evil ways in order to save his life, that wicked man will die for his sin, and I will hold you accountable for his blood. [19]But if you do warn the wicked man and he does not turn from his wickedness or from his evil ways, he will die for his sin; but you will have saved yourself.
>
> [20]"Again, when a righteous man turns from his righteousness and does evil, and I put a stumbling block before him, he will die. Since you did not warn him, he will die for his sin. The righteous things he did will not be remembered, and I will hold you accountable for his blood. [21]But if you do warn the righteous man not to sin and he does not sin, he will surely live because he took warning, and you will have saved yourself."

16–17 Ezekiel's basic prophetic role was to be a watchman to the house of Israel (v.17; cf. chs. 18; 33). A watchman in OT times stood on the wall of the city as a sentry, watching for any threat to the city from without or within. If he saw an invading army on the horizon, or dangers within the city like fire or riots, the watchman would immediately sound the alarm to warn the people (2 Sam 18:24–27; 2 Kings 9:17–20).

18–21 Ezekiel was to listen to the Lord and then warn the people of Judah concerning the judgment on the horizon. His warning was based on the Mosaic covenant (Exod 20–Num 9; Deut), which showed those in a relationship with the Lord how to live life in the best way. The covenant's righteous stipulations, lovingly given for the good of the people (Deut 5:28–33; 6:25; 10:12–13), enabled them to enter into all the blessings God desired to pour out on them (Lev 26:1–13; Deut 16:20; 28:1–14; Mal 3:10–12). If they disobeyed these righteous ordinances and wandered from God's way of living, the Lord promised that he would lovingly discipline his people to cause them to return to the righteous life he prepared for their good (Lev 26:14–39; Deut 28:15–68). Ezekiel, therefore, was to warn Israel that God's inescapable discipline was coming.

Ezekiel's role as a watchman (cf. Isa 56:10; Jer 6:17; Hos 9:8), like that of the watchman of a city, was not reprobative and injurious but corrective and beneficial. He was to warn the wicked man that, if he did not turn from his wickedness, he would die in his unrighteousness (vv.18–19). Likewise, Ezekiel admonished the righteous man not to turn from his righteous ways—loyalty to the Mosaic code—and disobey God's commands; for if he did, he would surely die (vv.20–21). These warnings were directed to individuals.

When a righteous man turned from righteousness and did evil, God placed a "stumbling block" before him. The man had already turned from God's ways and done evil (v.20); so this stumbling block was not placed by God deliberately to cause the righteous to fall into sin. Rather, it was an obstacle set into the path of this man to see how he would continue to respond. If he fell, then physical death came. Some see the stumbling block as equivalent to a death sentence (so Greenberg, *Ezekiel 1–20*).

If a watchman saw a potential danger to a city and failed to warn its inhabitants, he was held responsible for the following destruction. So God warned Ezekiel that if he failed to warn the people of God's curse on disobedience, Ezekiel would be responsible for their death—"I will hold you accountable for his blood" (v.20; cf. Gen 9:5–6; Judg 9:24; 2 Sam 4:5–12; Acts 18:6; 20:26). Ezekiel himself would have to die for his negligence (cf. Pss 37:35–36; 55:23; Prov 10:27; 1 John 5:16). Those charged with declaring God's Word have a weighty responsibility to be faithful.

"Life" and "death" in this context are to be understood as physical, not eternal, life and death. The concept of life and death in the Mosaic covenant is primarily physical. The Mosaic covenant was given to guide those who had already entered into a relationship with God by faith (Lev 18:5; Deut 4:37–40; ch. 6; 7:6–11; 10:15–17; 30:15–20). The Hebrews could live righteously and freely by keeping these commands (Lev 18:5; Deut 16:20; cf. Jon 14:15). But if they disobeyed, physical death, resulting in a shortened life, was the normal result (Deut 30:15–20; cf. discussion of premature death in M. Tsevat, "Studies in the Book of Samuel I," HUCA 32 [1961]: 191–216). The emphasis was on living a righteous life, an emphasis certainly needed today. Eternal security was not the issue in this passage! This covenant pointed the people on to faith in the Messiah, whose work for salvation is pictured in the festive and sacrificial system (cf. Heb 9:6–10:18); but the keeping of the commandments of the law never provided salvation. Throughout the Scriptures, eternal salvation is always by faith, never by works of any kind (Rom 3:20; 4:4–5; Titus 3:5–7).

Notes

16–21 Critics argue that the watchman theme in these verses is an interpolation, having been built and developed from chs. 18 and 33 (esp. the latter). Such is not necessitated by a common theme, for each passage is used uniquely in Ezekiel's argument (cf. development in loc.). For treatment of this issue, cf. Greenberg, *Ezekiel 1–20*, pp. 90–97.

6. *Ezekiel's muteness*

3:22–27

22The hand of the LORD was upon me there, and he said to me, "Get up and go out to the plain, and there I will speak to you." 23So I got up and went out to the plain. And the glory of the LORD was standing there, like the glory I had seen by the Kebar River, and I fell facedown.
24Then the Spirit came into me and raised me to my feet. He spoke to me and said: "Go, shut yourself inside your house. 25And you, son of man, they will tie with ropes; you will be bound so that you cannot go out among the people. 26I will make your tongue stick to the roof of your mouth so that you will be silent and unable to rebuke them, though they are a rebellious house. 27But when I speak to you, I will open your mouth and you shall say to them, 'This is what the Sovereign LORD says.' Whoever will listen let him listen, and whoever will refuse let him refuse; for they are a rebellious house.

22–23 Ezekiel's commission concluded with a second glimpse of God's glory. Ezekiel, obedient to the Lord's command (v.22), went out to the plain where God's glory appeared to him (v.23), as it did in the vision of chapter 1.

24–27 As Ezekiel fell down before God in true humility and reverence, the Spirit prepared him to receive the message that he was to deliver to the exiles (cf. 4:1–7:27). Ezekiel was directed to return home and shut himself up in his house (v.24). The exiles would tie him up with rope (v.25). Then Yahweh would make Ezekiel mute so that he could not reprove the people unless God opened his mouth (vv.26–27). Whenever God would enable Ezekiel to speak, he would speak only in the Lord's authority regardless of the people's response. The phrase "Whoever will listen let him listen" (a favorite saying of Christ) stressed individual responsibility to respond inwardly to the message.

Ezekiel's muteness would last approximately seven and one-half years, till the Fall of Jerusalem (cf. dates in 1:1–3 with 33:21–22). Yet he would deliver several oral messages in the intervening period (cf. 11:25; 14:1; 20:1). The concept of muteness, therefore, was not one of total speechlessness throughout the seven and one-half years. Rather, Ezekiel was restrained from speaking publicly among the people in contrast to the normal vocal ministry of the prophets. The prophets usually moved among their people, speaking God's message as they observed the contemporary situation. But Ezekiel would remain in his home, except to dramatize God's messages (cf. 4:1–5:17). He would remain mute (v.26), *except* when God opened the prophet's mouth to deliver a divine message (v.27). Then his mouth would be closed till the next time that the Lord chose for him to speak. Instead of Ezekiel's going to the people, the people had to come to him. Though this rebellious people initially rejected Ezekiel's ministry (v.25), the elders started sneaking away to seek the Lord's message from Ezekiel as contemporary world events began vindicating his divine warnings.

Notes

22 The בִּקְעָה (biq'āh, "plain") denotes the wide open plain common in the heart of Babylonia in contrast to גַיְא (gay', "mountain valley"), נַחַל (nahal, "river bed"), and sometimes עֵמֶק ('emeq, "valley"). This would argue for the events of Ezekiel happening in Babylonia (cf. Gen 11:2; Ezek 8:4; 37:1–14).

26 Robert R. Wilson ("Interpretation of Ezekiel's Dumbness," VetTest 22 [1972]: 91–104) argues that לֹא־תִהְיֶה לְאִישׁ מוֹכִיחַ (lō'-tihyeh le'îš môkîah, "unable to rebuke") should be understood as "legal Mediator." Since this phrase qualifies Ezekiel's muteness, that muteness should be seen as God's forbidding Ezekiel to act as a legal mediator on behalf of the nation before Yahweh. Communication would move solely from Yahweh to the people as the prophet *only* delivered the sentence of the divine Judge: Jerusalem's doom. Only after the Fall of Jerusalem (cf. 24:27; 33:22) would any other prophetic function be allowed. This appears to be substantiated by Yahweh's refusal to allow the elders in exile to seek him till after the Fall of Jerusalem (cf. 8:1; 14:4–22; 20:1).

II. Judah's Iniquity and the Resulting Judgment (4:1–24:27)

Chapters 4–24 combine a series of oral messages and symbolic acts designed to warn the people of Judah that judgment was coming and to explain the reason for this imminent discipline. In chapters 4–7 Ezekiel dramatized the coming siege of Jerusalem (ch. 4) and the subsequent dispersion of the people in exile (ch. 5). He concluded the drama by declaring that this imminent judgment would destroy pagan idolatry. The exile could not be escaped through human efforts (chs. 6–7). The vision of God's glory reappeared to Ezekiel (ch. 8) to expose, by contrast, the defilement of Judah resulting from her current participation in idolatrous heathen rituals. Subsequently God's glory left Jerusalem and Judah, enabling God to pour out his wrath on Israel in accord with the Mosaic covenant (chs. 9–11). The exiles objected to this, but Ezekiel effectively answered their complaints (chs. 12–19). They were reminded that their history, characterized by unfaithfulness to their Lord and spiritual prostitution promulgated by corrupt leadership (chs. 20–23), condemned them. Chapter 24 concludes by vividly describing the Fall of Jerusalem.

A. The Initial Warnings of the Watchman (4:1–7:27)

1. Monodramas of the siege of Jerusalem (4:1–5:17)

a. The brick and the plate

4:1–17

¹"Now, son of man, take a clay tablet, put it in front of you and draw the city of Jerusalem on it. ²Then lay siege to it: Erect siege works against it, build a ramp up to it, set up camps against it and put battering rams around it. ³Then take an iron pan, place it as an iron wall between you and the city and turn your face toward it. It will be under siege, and you shall besiege it. This will be a sign to the house of Israel.

⁴"Then lie on your left side and put the sin of the house of Israel upon yourself. You are to bear their sin for the number of days you lie on your side. ⁵I have assigned you the same number of days as the years of their sin. So for 390 days you will bear the sin of the house of Israel.

⁶"After you have finished this, lie down again, this time on your right side, and bear the sin of the house of Judah. I have assigned you 40 days, a day for each year. ⁷Turn your face toward the siege of Jerusalem and with bared arm prophesy against her. ⁸I will tie you up with ropes so that you cannot turn from one side to the other until you have finished the days of your siege.

⁹"Take wheat and barley, beans and lentils, millet and spelt; put them in a container and make them into bread for yourself. You are to eat it during the 390 days you lie on your side. ¹⁰Weigh out twenty shekels of food to eat each day and eat it at set times. ¹¹Also measure out a sixth of a hin of water and drink it at set times. ¹²Eat the food as you would a barley cake; bake it in the sight of the people, using human excrement for fuel." ¹³The LORD said, "In this way the people of Israel will eat defiled food among the nations where I will drive them."

¹⁴Then I said, "Not so, Sovereign LORD! I have never defiled myself. From my youth until now I have never eaten anything found dead or torn by wild animals. No unclean meat has ever entered my mouth."

¹⁵"Very well," he said, "I will let you bake your bread over cow manure instead of human excrement."

¹⁶He then said to me: "Son of man, I will cut off the supply of food in Jerusalem. The people will eat rationed food in anxiety and drink rationed water in despair, ¹⁷for food and water will be scarce. They will be appalled at the sight of each other and will waste away because of their sin.

1–3 The Lord showed Ezekiel the methods he was to use in warning of the impending siege of Jerusalem and the resulting exile. Though Ezekiel was mute, God directed him to act out the warnings (probably just outside Ezekiel's house; cf. 3:24–25). The exiles had observed Ezekiel's unique seven-day consecration (3:15–16). Now they would wonder what strange thing he would do next. The parables Ezekiel acted out demanded an audience.

Ezekiel took a clay brick (*lᵉḇānāh*) and scratched on it a diagram of Jerusalem (v.1). Then he simulated a siege of the city with "siege works" (*dāyēq*), "ramp" (or "mounds," *sōlᵉlāh*), battering rams, and military encampments (v.2). With an iron plate between him and the city, Ezekiel played this war game with determination ("turn your face," v.3) for 430 days while prophesying against Jerusalem (vv.6–7). All this was "a sign to the house of Israel" of the coming siege of Jerusalem.

The interpretation of the "iron pan" is difficult. It was the kind of pan used only by the priests for certain offerings (Lev 2:5; 6:21; 7:9). It was placed between Ezekiel and the city inscribed on the clay brick. Some (Feinberg, Cooke) interpret this plate as a seige wall, showing the severity of the siege against Jerusalem and the impossibility of escape. Others (Taylor) see it as a picture of God's determined hostility toward Jerusalem in bringing the siege. Still others interpret it as either a symbol of the city's fortifications or a barrier of sin Israel had erected between herself and God. The "pan" was declared to be a "wall." Normally walls provided protection or containment. The Lord had warned Ezekiel of the hostile reception of his ministry (cf. 2:6). Therefore, the imagery portrays either Ezekiel's protection as he acted out the siege or the siege wall around Jerusalem erected by the Babylonians.

4–8 After acting out Jerusalem's siege, Ezekiel was directed to dramatize the length of time God's people would undergo punishment for their iniquity. He faced north first (symbolically toward Israel), lying on his left side for 390 days to represent the time for bearing the punishment for Israel's sins (vv.4–5). When the 390 days were "finished," then Ezekiel would "lie down again," this time for forty days on his right side, facing south (symbolically toward Judah), to portray the punishment for Judah's wickedness (v.6). He would be bound in each of these positions so that he could not change sides till he had completed the allotted days to portray the siege for each nation respectively (v.8). The text does not demand that Ezekiel be on his side twenty-four hours each day. The rest of chapter 4 has Ezekiel fixing meals, while in chapter 8 Ezekiel sat in his house with the exilic elders during the final days of lying on his right side. It would seem that a portion of each day would suffice to fulfill the symbolism and the text.

Though the basic meaning of this section is clear, the numbers have given rise to many explanations. Certain things are plain: each day represented a year (vv.5–6; cf. Num 14:34); and the years signified a period during which God's people would receive discipline, not the period in which they sinned. Many expositors include the 40 years in the 390 years (on the basis of v.9), seeing the time periods running concurrently. But such an interpretation seems to contradict the plain sense of vv.5–6 and v.8. Verse 9 does not demand this interpretation, since the 390 days convey only the time Ezekiel was to eat defiled food. Some amend the text to agree with the LXX readings of 190 and 150 days, taking these as round numbers to represent the 150 years from the invasion of Tiglath-pileser in 734 B.C. to Jerusalem's fall in 586 B.C. plus the 40 years of Judah's captivity in Babylon. Still others understand the numbers as symbolizing the future general discipline on Israel in terms of the Egyptian sojourn of 430 years and the wilderness wanderings of 40 years. However, there is nothing that warrants either the alteration of the text or the symbolizing of the numbers.

Normally the numbers would be taken literally as periods of time separated into two distinct and successive intervals of 390 and 40 years (vv.5–6). Ezekiel's reference point for chronological determination was Jehoiachin's deportation of 597 B.C. This, therefore, would appear to be the natural starting point for measuring the time periods in these verses. The 430 years would denote the punishment inflicted by conquering foreign powers on the children of Israel and Judah from the deportation of Jehoiachin, their recognized king, to the inception of the Maccabean rebellion in 167 B.C. During the Maccabean period the Jews once again exercised dominion over Judah. Though this is a possible solution, dogmatism concerning these numbers must be avoided.

9–17 During the 390 days Ezekiel lay on his side acting out a "siege" of Jerusalem, God placed him on a strict diet. Ezekiel was to eat bread made from a mixture of several different grains (v.9). He would be rationed to two pints (the sixth part of a hin) of water and one-half pound (twenty shekels) of bread for his daily food for over a year (vv.10–12). This meagre diet was to communicate the reality of the famine during the siege of Jerusalem. The Lord would "cut off the supply of food" (v.16) in Jerusalem as he promised in Leviticus 26:16, 20, 26, 29. There would be a scarcity of any one kind of grain for bread and also lack of water. The inhabitants of Jerusalem would rot away and look on one another in horror (v.17; cf. Lev 26:19, 35; 2 Kings 25:3; Jer 34:17–22).

In addition to his beggarly sustenance, Ezekiel was to bake his rationed bread over a fire made unclean from human dung (v.12; cf. Deut 23:12–14). Some have misconstrued the mixture of grains in v.9 as ritual defilement by misunderstanding Leviticus 19:19 and Deuteronomy 22:9. Though eating combined grains was acceptable, using human dung was defiling (v.13), since the eating of unclean food was forbidden by the Mosaic covenant (Lev 22:8; Deut 12:15–19; 14:21; Ezek 44:31). Since Ezekiel, a faithful priest, had never eaten defiled food, he cried out to the Lord, requesting not to have to eat unclean food (v.14). God graciously permitted him to use the common fuel of cow's dung instead of human excrement (v.15). This unclean manner of preparing food described the Captivity that would follow the imminent siege and fall of Jerusalem. The captives would eat the defiled foods of the foreign nations they would be banished to (v.13; cf. Dan 1:8).

God was not changing his law when he commanded Ezekiel to do all this. God temporarily caused Ezekiel to disregard the principle of eating unclean food to dramatize in an extreme way how abhorrent the Captivity would be. God used an acted parable to convey this truth in a way that would surely be understood. However, this was only symbolic; the eating of unclean food as a normal practice was not being condoned. God sovereignly protected Ezekiel against any ill effects of eating defiled food.

Notes

1–17 The literary structure of this chapter is that of a symbolic act or sign-action. A discussion of this structure can be found in Zimmerli, *Ezekiel I*, pp. 156–57, and in Craig Woodward, "The Form of Prophetic Symbolic Acts in the Old Testament" (Master's thesis, Western Conservative Baptist Seminary, 1983).

4–5,9 The LXX's substitution of 190 for the MT's 390 in vv.5, 9 and the addition of the number 150 in v.4 appear to be later interpolations attempting to make sense out of the difficult Hebrew. The close accuracy of the 190-year number in conjunction with the years between the Fall of Samaria (722 B.C.) and the restoration from Babylonia (539 B.C.) lends credence to the view that the LXX translator attempted to alter the text.

4 The term עָוֹן (*ʿawōn*, "sin") has three basic meanings: (1) "iniquity," (2) "guilt of iniquity," (3) "the punishment for iniquity." Here the context reflects the second meaning (cf. Zimmerli, *Ezekiel I*, pp. 164–65), though the third meaning can be equally argued (cf. Num 14:33–34; Zimmerli, *Ezekiel I*, pp. 166–67).

6 The repetition of the phrase יוֹם לַשָּׁנָה (*yôm lašānāh*, "a day for each year") gives emphasis to the concept of a day representing a year.

b. *The division of hair*

5:1–4

> [1]"Now, son of man, take a sharp sword and use it as a barber's razor to shave your head and your beard. Then take a set of scales and divide up the hair. [2]When the days of your siege come to an end, burn a third of the hair with fire inside the city. Take a third and strike it with the sword all around the city. And scatter a third to the wind. For I will pursue them with drawn sword. [3]But take a few strands of hair and tuck them away in the folds of your garment. [4]Again, take a few of these and throw them into the fire and burn them up. A fire will spread from there to the whole house of Israel.

1 Ezekiel completed the drama begun in chapter 4 by shaving his head and beard, weighing the hair, and dividing it equally into three groups. This final act also pictured defilement. Shaving the head and beard was a pagan ritual for the dead (27:31; cf. Isa 22:12; Jer 16:16; Amos 8:10), which the law forbade (Deut 14:1), and a sign of humiliation and disgrace (7:18; cf. 2 Sam 10:4). If an Israelite priest shaved his head, he was defiled and no longer holy to the Lord (Lev 21:5). Ezekiel defiled and humiliated himself as a symbol of the humiliation of the people of Judah who were defiled and no longer holy to the Lord. Nothing was left to do but to mourn their death as a nation.

2–4 The hair symbolized the inhabitants of Jerusalem. One-third of them would be burned when Jerusalem would be burned after the siege (v.2a; 2 Kings 25:9). Part of these people would have already died through famine and distress during the siege (v.12a). The second third of the inhabitants would die by the sword when Jerusalem fell (vv.2b, 12b; 2 Kings 25:18–21a; 2 Chron 36:17). The final third would be scattered to the wind in exile (vv.2c, 12c; 2 Kings 25:11, 21b). A portion from this last group would be judged by fire (which affected all Israel) as they left Jerusalem (v.4), while some would die by the sword in captivity (v.2d). Out of this final third, the Lord would deliver a remnant of Jerusalem's citizens, as depicted by Ezekiel's placing a few hairs from this group securely into the hem of his garment (v.3).

Notes

2–4 The terms מִשָּׁם (*miššām,* "from there"; untr. NIV), אוֹתָם (*'ōṯām,* "them"), and מֵהֶם (*mē-hem,* "from them"; NIV, "of these") in vv.3–4 have as their antecedent the last וְהַשְּׁלִשִׁית (*wᵉhaššᵉlišîṯ,* "and the [NIV, 'a'] third") in v.2.

c. *The significance of the symbolic acts*

5:5–17

> [5]"This is what the Sovereign Lᴏʀᴅ says: This is Jerusalem, which I have set in the center of the nations, with countries all around her. [6]Yet in her wickedness she has rebelled against my laws and decrees more than the nations and countries around her. She has rejected my laws and has not followed my decrees.
>
> [7]"Therefore this is what the Sovereign Lᴏʀᴅ says: You have been more unruly than the nations around you and have not followed my decrees or kept my laws. You have not even conformed to the standards of the nations around you.
>
> [8]"Therefore this is what the Sovereign Lᴏʀᴅ says: I myself am against you, Jerusalem, and I will inflict punishment on you in the sight of the nations. [9]Because of all your detestable idols, I will do to you what I have never done before and will never do again. [10]Therefore in your midst fathers will eat their children, and children will eat their fathers. I will inflict punishment on you and will scatter all your survivors to the winds. [11]Therefore as surely as I live, declares the Sovereign Lᴏʀᴅ, because you have defiled my sanctuary with all your vile images and detestable practices, I myself will withdraw my favor; I will not look on you with pity or spare you. [12]A third of your people will die of the plague or perish by famine inside you; a third will fall by the sword outside your walls; and a third I will scatter to the winds and pursue with drawn sword.
>
> [13]"Then my anger will cease and my wrath against them will subside, and I will be avenged. And when I have spent my wrath upon them, they will know that I the Lᴏʀᴅ have spoken in my zeal.
>
> [14]"I will make you a ruin and a reproach among the nations around you, in the sight of all who pass by. [15]You will be a reproach and a taunt, a warning and an object of horror to the nations around you when I inflict punishment on you in anger and in wrath and with stinging rebuke. I the Lᴏʀᴅ have spoken. [16]When I shoot at you with my deadly and destructive arrows of famine, I will shoot to destroy you. I will bring more and more famine upon you and cut off your supply of food. [17]I will send famine and wild beasts against you, and they will leave you childless. Plague and bloodshed will sweep through you, and I will bring the sword against you. I the Lᴏʀᴅ have spoken."

5 This chapter continues with an explanation of the full significance of Ezekiel's symbolic monodrama. The Lord emphasized the recipient of the siege and the coming judgments by the statement "This is Jerusalem." Immediately one's attention was brought back to the city etched on the clay brick in 4:1. Jerusalem was the object of God's love. He had established her as the center of the earth geographically and theologically. She had been greatly blessed. However, all these symbolic actions demonstrated what would happen to her.

6–7 A judgment speech—with accusations against Jerusalem enumerated and a verdict pronounced—reinforced the monodrama. The basic accusation was stated in vv.6–7: Jerusalem, this blessed city, had responded to God's blessing by rebelling against his commandments, refusing his ways, and failing to live life according to the Mosaic covenant. She had become so wicked that she did not even adhere to the common laws of the nations around her. Some of Jerusalem's inhabitants would resort to cannibalism during the coming siege (v.10a; cf. Lev 26:29; Deut 28:53; 2 Kings 6:28–29; Jer 19:9; Lam 4:10). They had already defiled his holy sanctuary with detestable idolatry (v.11a; ch. 8).

8–17 Verses 8–9 give the principal statement of God's verdict. He would execute the judgments pronounced in the Mosaic covenant on Jerusalem in the sight of the nations. Never again would God execute a judgment like this. He would withdraw himself from the sanctuary (v.11b; cf. 10:4; 11:22–23) to pour out his judgment without pity. One-third of the inhabitants of Jerusalem would die in the city through disease and famine; one-third would die by the sword. A remnant would be scattered in every direction among the nations (vv.10b, 12). Famine, wild beasts, plagues, and bloodshed would all be part of Jerusalem's judgment (vv.16–17b; Lev 26:21–26). The land of Judah would become a desolation, causing the nations to ridicule her because of what God had done to her (v.14). At the same time these nations would be struck with fear and terror at God's justice and wrath even on his very own people (v.15). Judah's judgment served as a warning to these nations of the judgments God would bring on them if they cursed Israel (cf. Gen 12:3).

As a result of this judgment, God's justice would be satisfied (v.13a) and the people of Jerusalem would know that the Lord had executed his wrath (v.13b). The punishment was certain. The Lord had spoken (v.17)!

Notes

6–7 The terms מִשְׁפָּט (mišpāṭ, "law") and חֹק (ḥōq, "decree") are synonyms, with the first word emphasizing the civil and criminal law while the latter one stresses the positive enactments of moral, ceremonial, and civil institutions. These expressions cover both the casuistic and the apodictic types of law (cf. A. Alt, "The Origins of Israelite Law," in *Essays on Old Testament History and Religion* [Garden City, N.Y.: Doubleday, 1967], pp. 101–71).

7–11 לָכֵן (lāḵēn, "therefore") appears four times in these verses, urging a climactic certainty of consequences (cf. F.J. Goldbaum, "Two Hebrew Quasi-Adverbs: lkn and ʾkn," JNES 23 [1964]: 132ff., and W.E. March, "Lāḵēn: Its Functions and Meanings," in *Rhetorical Criticism: Essays in Honor of J. Muilenburg*, edd. J. Jackson and M. Kessler [Pittsburgh: Pickwick, 1974], pp. 256–86).

2. *The coming judgment on the land of Judah* (6:1–7:27)

a. *Destruction of pagan religious shrines*

6:1–14

> ¹The word of the LORD came to me: ²"Son of man, set your face against the mountains of Israel; prophesy against them ³and say: 'O mountains of Israel, hear the word of the Sovereign LORD. This is what the Sovereign LORD says to the mountains and hills, to the ravines and valleys: I am about to bring a sword against you, and I will destroy your high places. ⁴Your altars will be demolished and your incense altars will be smashed; and I will slay your people in front of your idols. ⁵I will lay the dead bodies of the Israelites in front of their idols, and I will scatter your bones around your altars. ⁶Wherever you live, the towns will be laid waste and the high places demolished, so that your altars will be laid waste and devastated, your idols smashed and ruined, your incense altars broken down, and what you have made wiped out. ⁷Your people will fall slain among you, and you will know that I am the LORD.
>
> ⁸"'But I will spare some, for some of you will escape the sword when you are scattered among the lands and nations. ⁹Then in the nations where they have been carried captive, those who escape will remember me—how I have been grieved by their adulterous hearts, which have turned away from me, and by their eyes, which have lusted after their idols. They will loathe themselves for the evil they have done and for all their detestable practices. ¹⁰And they will know that I am the LORD; I did not threaten in vain to bring this calamity on them.
>
> ¹¹"'This is what the Sovereign LORD says: Strike your hands together and stamp your feet and cry out "Alas!" because of all the wicked and detestable practices of the house of Israel, for they will fall by the sword, famine and plague. ¹²He that is far away will die of the plague, and he that is near will fall by the sword, and he that survives and is spared will die of famine. So will I spend my wrath upon them. ¹³And they will know that I am the LORD, when their people lie slain among their idols around their altars, on every high hill and on all the mountaintops, under every spreading tree and every leafy oak—places where they offered fragrant incense to all their idols. ¹⁴And I will stretch out my hand against them and make the land a desolate waste from the desert to Diblah—wherever they live. Then they will know that I am the LORD.'"

1–7 Ezekiel began his first major judgment oracle with an introductory formula he often used throughout the book: "The word of the LORD came to me" (v.1). God interrupted Ezekiel's muteness to announce judgment on Judah's mountains, hills, ravines, and valleys (vv.2–3). Ezekiel set his face against these four geographical features of the land, for it was in them that the pagans normally established their religious shrines (cf. 2 Kings 23:10). Syncretistic Canaanite religion—with its perverted emphasis on sex, war, cults of the dead, snake worship, and idolatry—preferred high places and groves of trees for its place of worship. Manasseh, king of Judah (695–642 B.C.), had led in the resurgence of these pagan cults that had engulfed the people by Ezekiel's day.

The Lord pronounced judgment on the heathen shrines and their cultic practices that had been adopted by his people. He would remove the temptation facing his people by destroying all the "high places," "altars," "incense altars" (vv.3–4), and "idols" (v.6), thus eliminating their pagan practices. These shrines would become desecrated by the scattering of bones of the dead around them (v.5). The "scattering of bones" is a phrase used for judgment in which uncleanness and shame are conveyed (cf. Pss 53:5; 141:7). The bones would be those of the Israelites who had become engrossed in these pagan practices (v.7; cf. 2 Kings 23:20; Jer 8:1–2). The Lord was faithful to his promise in Leviticus 26:30: "I will destroy your high places, cut down your incense altars and pile your dead bones on the lifeless forms of your idols, and I will abhor you." God refused to allow anything to take his rightful place (cf. Exod 20:1–3). Through this discipline Judah would know that he was the only God (v.7; cf. v.14).

8–10 God always accompanied his pronouncements of judgment with the proclamation of a way to escape (v.8). One escaped by turning to the Lord and following his ways (cf. Jer 18:7–10). Thus within Ezekiel's judicial sentence was the Lord's assurance that some of the exiles would see the wickedness of their ways and be ashamed. They would remember the Lord and recognize that he did not speak in vain when he instructed his people to live righteously or suffer the discipline that would restore them to God's way (v.9). A remnant of the exiles would respond to God's discipline and repent of their past idolatry and spiritual fornication that had grieved and hurt him. They would come to know that he truly *is* the Lord their God (v.10). The whole purpose of God's judgment was to cause his people to return to him.

11–14 Reverting to his theme of impending judgment, the Lord instructed Ezekiel to demonstrate joy because of the coming judgment (v.11a). Clapping the hands and stamping the feet signified either joyful praise or derision over sin and judgment (21:14–17; 22:13; 25:6; cf. Lam 2:15; Nah 3:19). Here Ezekiel exhibited God's delight over the comprehensive eradication of pagan shrines and practices from the land. The entire land would become as desolate as the wilderness toward Diblah (vv.11b–12). Everyone would be touched by the judgment: the distant ones by disease, the near ones by the sword, the remainder outside and inside Jerusalem by famine. Four times Ezekiel was directed to remind the exiles that the purpose for God's judgment was to restore his hearers to an experiential knowledge of God (vv.7, 10, 13, 14). This major thrust of the book (mentioned over sixty-five times) called for an intimate relationship with the Lord rather than a destructive allegiance to impotent idols (vv.13–14).

In every generation God's judgment and discipline is misunderstood by most people. God's chief desire is to bring people to himself—or back to himself. When mankind willfully refuses to turn to him, God mercifully uses discipline and judgment to cause the people to recognize that *he is the only true God,* always faithful to what he has said in his word!

Notes

1 הָרֵי יִשְׂרָאֵל (*hārê yiśrāʾēl,* "the mountains of Israel"), frequent in Ezekiel, means the whole land of Israel in a broad sense here.

3 בָּמָה (*bāmāh,* "high place") frequently refers to cultic platforms on high places where sacrifice and other religious acts were performed (cf. 1 Sam 9:12–14). Sometimes the idea of height seems omitted and only the cultic concept remains (cf. Jer 7:31; 32:35, where a "high place" is located in the Hinnom Valley). Israel was commanded to destroy pagan high places (cf. Num 33:52), for a "high place" represented worship of competing deities

(cf. P.H. Vaughan, *The Meaning of 'BĀMĀ' in the Old Testament* [London: Cambridge University Press, 1974]; TDOT, 2: 139–45; TWOT, 1: 113).

4,5,9,13 Ezekiel's favorite word for "idol," גִּלּוּל (*gillûl*)—used more often in Ezekiel than any other book of the OT—has questionable derivations, though it is normally linked to גֵל (*gēl*, "dung pellets"). A detestable nature is associated with the word, implying the disgust of the Lord with these idols.

7, 10,13,14 The common verb יָדַע (*yāda'*, "know") involves more than mere factual knowledge; it connotes experience and an intimate relationship. When God desires judgment to bring about a knowledge of himself, it is not just a factual understanding but an experiential one.

14 The proper noun דִּבְלָתָה (*diblātāh*, "Diblah") is an unknown place name. Since the Hebrew ד (*d*) and ר (*r*) are easily confused orthographically, some conclude that the text should read רִבְלָתָה (*riblātāh*, "Riblah"), referring to the known site of Riblah, with ה (*h*) terminative suffix. Then the meaning would be that God's judgment would cause desolation from the southern wilderness toward Riblah, a city lying to the north on the Orontes River south of Kedesh. Though this is a possible solution, no substantial external evidence attests the name Riblah. It is also possible that archaeology may find a city of Diblah in the future.

---

b. *The imminency and comprehensiveness of the curse*

7:1–13

> ¹The word of the LORD came to me: ²"Son of man, this is what the Sovereign LORD says to the land of Israel: The end! The end has come upon the four corners of the land. ³The end is now upon you and I will unleash my anger against you. I will judge you according to your conduct and repay you for all your detestable practices. ⁴I will not look on you with pity or spare you; I will surely repay you for your conduct and the detestable practices among you. Then you will know that I am the LORD.
>
> ⁵"This is what the Sovereign LORD says: Disaster! An unheard-of disaster is coming. ⁶The end has come! The end has come! It has roused itself against you. It has come! ⁷Doom has come upon you—you who dwell in the land. The time has come, the day is near; there is panic, not joy, upon the mountains. ⁸I am about to pour out my wrath on you and spend my anger against you; I will judge you according to your conduct and repay you for all your detestable practices. ⁹I will not look on you with pity or spare you; I will repay you in accordance with your conduct and the detestable practices among you. Then you will know that it is I the LORD who strikes the blow.
>
> ¹⁰"The day is here! It has come! Doom has burst forth, the rod has budded, arrogance has blossomed! ¹¹Violence has grown into a rod to punish wickedness; none of the people will be left, none of that crowd—no wealth, nothing of value. ¹²The time has come, the day has arrived. Let not the buyer rejoice nor the seller grieve, for wrath is upon the whole crowd. ¹³The seller will not recover the land he has sold as long as both of them live, for the vision concerning the whole crowd will not be reversed. Because of their sins, not one of them will preserve his life.

1–4 God gave a second message to Ezekiel. Its first thirteen verses contain four brief, intensive prophetic speeches in poetic form that emphasize the imminency and comprehensiveness of the coming judgment on all Judah. Numerous short sentences and the repetition of words and phrases express the intensity of the message. The recurrence of the word "end" six times in the first six verses stresses the finality of the judgment (cf. Amos 8:2). Judgment had come! Imminency was heightened by the reiteration of the verb "coming" (seven times in vv.5–12); the repetition of "now" (vv.3, 8 [NIV, "about to"]); and the use of terms like "time," "day," and "is near" (v.7).

The first prophetic speech in this message (vv.1–4) emphasizes the extent—"the four corners of the land" (v.2)—of the judgment and its basis, while two main points summarize the reason for judgment. First, Judah would be judged according to her wicked ways. Her abominations would be brought on her (v.3). The judgment was "in kind," i.e., the Exile would bring the Judeans into countries where the same abominable practices they have taken part in were a daily occurrence (v.4). The expectation was that this would cause them to detest these wicked rituals. Second, the Lord would not have pity on anyone. He would not spare them. Though his long-suffering, forbearance, and compassion had withheld discipline, such restraint would no longer continue. God's judgment genuinely manifested his love, for its purpose was to cause Judah to know that he was God.

5–9 The second oracle in this chapter emphasizes the horror and surprise of the judgment as well as the person of the judge. The terror that would fill the land is stressed by the repetition of the words "disaster" and "end" (vv.5–6), in addition to the announcement that the judgment would be a time of panic, not joy like that experienced at harvest festivals (v.7; cf. Isa 16:10; Jer 25:30). The unexpectedness (chs. 12–19) of judgment is reflected by the play on words in "the end has come" and "roused itself" (*haqqēṣ hēqîṣ*) in v.6 as well as by phrases such as "Doom has come," "time has come," and "the day is near" (v.7). Verses 8–9 give the basis for the judgment stated in vv.3–4. The message closed by stunning the exiles with a new name for God: "The LORD who strikes the blow" (*YHWH makkeh*), the one who would now judge Judah (v.9b).

10–11 The third oracle focuses on the imminency, comprehensiveness, and readiness of judgment. The five-line poem (v.10) underscores the nearness of the judgment: "The day is here! It has come! Doom has burst forth, the rod has budded, arrogance has blossomed!" The dawn of the judgment day had arrived. It had suddenly budded and blossomed. The "rod" in v.10 has generally been understood to refer either to Nebuchadnezzar as the instrument of judgment used by the Lord or to the insolence of the kings of Israel. The only passage in Scripture referring to a "budded rod" is Numbers 17, where God used such a rod to denote his choice. But since judgment on Judah is described here, it would seem best to understand the "rod" as an instrument of judgment that had been divinely chosen and was ready for use (viz., fully blossomed). The concept of the budding rod stands in parallelism with the previous line of the poem indicating imminency and with the following line describing the nature of the rod God would use to discipline Judah—a rod of arrogance. Nebuchadnezzar fit the description of this rod as an instrument of judgment.

Many have distinguished between the "rod" of v.10 and the "rod" of v.11. Contextually this is problematical. It seems that v.11 elaborates on the nature of the instrument of judgment. The violence of Babylonia (cf. v.21) had risen to become a rod against wickedness. God would use this weapon to devastate the land so that nothing of value would be left (v.11). Feinberg (p. 45), preferring "lament" over "value" for *nōah*, says, "So great would be the slaughter that no one would survive to lament the dead." The judgment would indeed be comprehensive!

12–13 The last oracle emphasized the permanency and quickness of the judgment. The suddenness of the judgment was illustrated by one unable to regain what he had sold due to the rapidity of the coming discipline. Most likely this example was given with the law of the sabbatical year (Deut 15:1–2) or the Year of Jubilee in mind (Lev 25:13–16). According to the law, if one sold his land in payment for a debt, that land reverted to him on the sabbatical year or the Year of Jubilee, whichever came first. Ezekiel maintained that if one sold land under this arrangement, he would not realize its return since neither he nor the buyer would be in the land of Judah seven years hence. Though the buyer might rejoice over the fact that he would never have to return the land, it would not be a time of rejoicing for either party. When judgment came, neither would own the property. Babylon would possess it!

The vision of judgment was certain! God would not repeal it! No one would be able to continue to live in his iniquity, for all wickedness would be judged.

Notes

5 The participle in the phrase הִנֵּה בָאָה (*hinnēh bā'āh*, "behold it is coming") normally requires an expressed subject (NIV has "disaster"); but since indefiniteness is to be conveyed, the feminine participle is used. It is a general indefinite phrase of imminency.

7,10 צְפִרָה (*ṣᵉpirāh*, "doom") has been rendered in various ways due to scant etymological data and usage (only three times in the MT—twice in this chapter, vv.7, 10, and in Isa 28:5). Some translate the word as "diadem" on the basis of synonymous parallelism in the Isaiah verse. Others render it "doom" on little basis at all. Still others explain it as "mourning" based on the Aramaic cognate *ṣaprāh*. This latter rendering best fits all passages, especially the emphasis of this verse.

11 The noun מַטֶּה (*maṭṭēh*, "rod") may mean either "weapon" (Isa 10:5, 24; 30:32) or be used in the figurative sense of a ruler's "scepter" (Ps 110:2; Jer 48:17). Both senses are present here.

The term נֹה (*nōah*, "value"), a *hapax legomenon*, is rendered "wailing" in KJV, as if derived from נָהָה (*nāhāh*). Others understand it as "eminency" from נוה (*nwh*) and the Arabian *n'aha* (cf. Bd, s.v.; KD 1:103).

c. *The response to the curse*

7:14–27

^{14}Though they blow the trumpet and get everything ready, no one will go into battle, for my wrath is upon the whole crowd.

^{15}"Outside is the sword, inside are plague and famine; those in the country will die by the sword, and those in the city will be devoured by famine and plague. ^{16}All who survive and escape will be in the mountains, moaning like doves of the valleys, each because of his sins. ^{17}Every hand will go limp, and every knee will become as weak as water. ^{18}They will put on sackcloth and be clothed with terror. Their faces will be covered with shame and their heads will be shaved. ^{19}They will throw their silver into the streets, and their gold will be an unclean thing. Their silver and gold will not be able to save them in the day of the Lord's wrath. They will not satisfy their hunger or fill their stomachs with it, for it has made them stumble into sin. ^{20}They were proud of their beautiful jewelry and used it to make their detestable idols and vile images. Therefore I will turn these into an unclean thing for them. ²¹I will hand it all over as plunder to foreigners and as loot to the wicked of the earth, and they will defile it. ²²I will turn my face away from them, and they will desecrate my treasured place; robbers will enter it and desecrate it.

²³"Prepare chains, because the land is full of bloodshed and the city is full of violence. ²⁴I will bring the most wicked of the nations to take possession of their houses; I will put an end to the pride of the mighty, and their sanctuaries will be desecrated. ²⁵When terror comes, they will seek peace, but there will be none. ²⁶Calamity upon calamity will come, and rumor upon rumor. They will try to get a vision from the prophet; the teaching of the law by the priest will be lost, as will the counsel of the elders. ²⁷The king will mourn, the prince will be clothed with despair, and the hands of the people of the land will tremble. I will deal with them according to their conduct, and by their own standards I will judge them. Then they will know that I am the Lᴏʀᴅ."

14–18 The last half of this chapter vividly describes the reactions of the Judeans to this swift and violent judgment. Moral dissipation, famine, and disease had so decimated the nation that she was unable to muster an army when the trumpet sounded for battle (v.14). Therefore the Babylonians easily approached Jerusalem for the siege (cf. Lev 26:7).

Disease and hunger would slay those within Jerusalem, and the sword would catch by surprise those working outside the walls in their fields (v.15). Those who were fortunate enough to escape the initial invasion fled to the hills (v.16). There, shuddering in fear (v.18), weak and dismayed—"Every hand will go limp, and every knee will become as weak as water" (v.17)—they would be ashamed and humiliated by their sins that brought this destruction. They would put on sackcloth in mourning, shave their heads in humiliation (v.18; cf. Gen 37:34; 1 Kings 20:31; Isa 15:2–3; Jer 16:6; 48:37) and moan like doves (v.16).

19 Nothing could deliver the Israelites from God's awesome wrath demonstrated in Jerusalem and Judah's destruction in 586 ʙ.ᴄ. Many of the inhabitants had lived for wealth so long that material gain had become an obsession to them. Yet in the judgment these riches would mean nothing. Idolatry, wickedness, and materialism had robbed them of everything and led them into judgment. Money would be thrown away like something sexually unclean (Lev 20–21).

20–22 Judah had profaned her sanctuary (v.20). The "beautiful jewelry" (ṣᵉbî'edyô) referred to Jerusalem and her temple, for both Hebrew terms were used by the prophets to represent Jerusalem and the temple (16:11; 23:40; cf. Isa 49:18; Jer 4:30; Dan 8:9; 11:16, 41, 45). "My treasured place" (v.22) likewise referred to the temple when connected with the full discussion of Jerusalem's fall in 24:21, 25. The Judeans had taken ornaments and treasures from the temple and had defiled God's temple by using them to make idols. Ironically, God would allow foreigners to profane the temple, plundering its treasures. Everything would become spoil for Babylon.

23–24 The "chains" (v.23) were prepared to bind the captives for deportation to Babylonia. This was their due for the violent crimes they had committed. As the Judeans were leaving, the worst foreigners among the nations would enter and possess the land (v.24), profaning their holy places. The land would come under Babylonian dominion.

779

25–27 The last response for some was to seek help (v.25). People would run to the prophet in hope of a visionary revelation of deliverance or to the priest for messages from the law that might help, or to the elders for counsel in this time of distress (v.26; cf. Jer 18:18). None could offer help. They had no answers at all! The leadership had failed in its responsibility to lead the people in God's ways. It was too late! The anguish of judgment had come! If the people had sought peace earlier, it would have been available; but now there was no peace. Kings and princes would be horrified and mourn (v.27). God had judged Israel by her own judgments—by the Mosaic covenant they should have known and followed. The only redeeming factor was that they would learn that the Lord truly was God and that his covenants were to be obeyed!

Notes

19–20 נִדָּה (niddāh, "unclean thing") refers frequently to the uncleanness that comes from a women's menstrual flow (18:6; 22:10; cf. Lev 12:2; 15:19–26; 18:19; 20:21). It denotes a severe impurity that is to be avoided, such as defilement by a corpse (cf. Num 19:9–21; 31:23). Israel was to loathe and abhor "impure things."

20 The third masculine singular suffix וֹ (ô) on עֶדְיוֹ (ʿedyô, "his jewelry") is a collective—"their"—contextually (cf. "their silver and gold" of v.19).

27 The difference between הַמֶּלֶךְ (hammelek, "the king") and נָשִׂיא (nāśîʾ, "prince") may be explained by Jehoiachin being the legitimate king (in Babylonia) while Zedekiah was the "prince," or "leader," in Judah (cf. discussion at 12:12–14). Some take the two titles to be synonymous, as "king-chief." For other alternatives, see Greenberg, *Ezekiel 1–20*, pp. 156–57.

B. The Vision of the Exodus of God's Glory (8:1–11:25)

1. The idolatry of the house of Israel (8:1–18)

a. The image of jealousy

8:1–6

> ¹In the sixth year, in the sixth month on the fifth day, while I was sitting in my house and the elders of Judah were sitting before me, the hand of the sovereign LORD came upon me there. ²I looked, and I saw a figure like that of a man. From what appeared to be his waist down he was like fire, and from there up his appearance was as bright as glowing metal. ³He stretched out what looked like a hand and took me by the hair of my head. The Spirit lifted me up between earth and heaven and in visions of God he took me to Jerusalem, to the entrance to the north gate of the inner court, where the idol that provokes to jealousy stood. ⁴And there before me was the glory of the God of Israel, as in the vision I had seen in the plain.
>
> ⁵Then he said to me, "Son of man, look toward the north." So I looked, and in the entrance north of the gate of the altar I saw this idol of jealousy.
>
> ⁶And he said to me, "Son of man, do you see what they are doing—the utterly detestable things the house of Israel is doing here, things that will drive me far from my sanctuary? But you will see things that are even more detestable."

1–6 Verse 1 describes the single vision of chapters 8–11. The date was "in the sixth year, in the sixth month on the fifth day" (Aug./Sept.) 592 B.C. (v.1). The recipient was Ezekiel, in light of the context and the pronoun "I." He received the vision while sitting in his house with the elders of Judah sitting before him.

God's hand came on Ezekiel, causing him to be caught up into the vision (v.2). When the chronological notices of 1:1–3 and 8:1 are compared, it is seen that Ezekiel received this vision about fourteen months (approx. 420 days) into his symbolic siege of Jerusalem (cf. comments at 4:4–8; cf. also Introduction: Date). He was still lying daily on his right side, bearing the iniquity of Judah (cf. 4:6). Most likely the elders had been watching this performance, wondering whether anything new would happen. It was fitting for Ezekiel to be on his right side when this vision of Judah's judgment appeared to him.

These elders were not contemporary elders in Judah who had come from Judah to Babylonia to seek counsel from Ezekiel. This would be most unlikely in light of the distance and time involved. Moreover, the depraved character of the Judean elders revealed in this vision would not have led them to take such an arduous journey to Babylonia for genuine spiritual reasons. The elders sitting before Ezekiel were the leaders of the Judean exiles in Babylonia who had already been deported from Judah in the captivities of Daniel (605 B.C.) and Jehoiachin (597 B.C.).

Some have sought to alter the text of the date in v.1, for they cannot think of Ezekiel acting out the siege of Jerusalem and receiving a vision at the same time. But there is nothing to hinder both events from happening simultaneously. In fact, since Ezekiel was dramatizing the judgment on Jerusalem, it would also have been appropriate that he communicate the reasons for this judgment. These reasons were revealed in the vision and then transmitted to the elders.

The vision's primary thrust was to make known the cause of the coming judgment on Jerusalem, the political and the religious capital of Judah and the center of all activity in the nation. The political rulers, the prophets, and the priests were to lead Judah in her holy ways. In this vision Ezekiel saw the contrast between God's glory in the sanctuary (vv.2–3) and the extreme moral and spiritual corruption of the nation's leadership. The latter was the main cause for God's judgment on Jerusalem. In chapter 8 the abominable idolatry practiced by Judah's leaders in the temple precinct was exposed. Chapters 9–11 depict the judgment of a holy God on the unholy perversion described in chapter 8. Progressively God's glory was removed from Jerusalem and Judah. Appointed men were sent to pour out fiery judgment on this wicked idolatry and its proponents. The Judean leaders were singled out for special condemnation in 11:14–21, but the faithful remnant who repented of their sinful ways were marked for protection (9:4) and reassured of ultimate restoration and cleansing (11:14–21).

The vision began in vv.1–6 with Ezekiel seeing the same manifestation of God's glory that he had seen on the river Kebar in chapters 1–3. In the vision of chapter 8, the likeness of a man of the same appearance as the one in the vision of chapter 1 (v.4; cf. 1:27) caught Ezekiel by his hair and transported him by the Spirit to Jerusalem in the vision (v.3). (For a discussion concerning transportation in a vision, see comments at 3:12–15.) In Jerusalem Ezekiel saw God's glory in the temple. Such glorious splendor stood in stark contrast to the religious perversion being practiced in the temple area.

Ezekiel found himself standing at the entrance of the inner court's north gate (v.3), known also as the altar gate because the altar of sacrifice was located just inside that gate (v.5; cf. Lev 1:11). He stood in the outer court at the gate's entrance, not in the inner court. As he looked northward into the outer court, he saw the "idol of jealousy." This idol provoked the Lord to jealousy, for he had declared in the Mosaic covenant that he alone was God (Exod 20:1–3) and that all idolatry was forbidden (Deut 4:16; 32:16, 21; cf. 1 Kings 14:22; Ps 78:58). The idol's description was vague. Therefore it cannot be identified with certainty. Many expositors interpret it as a reestablishment of the idol of Asherah, the mother-goddess of the Canaanite pantheon, which Manasseh had erected in the temple (2 Kings 21:7; 2 Chron 33:7) but later removed (2 Chron 33:15). This image of Asherah certainly had its attraction, for Josiah also had had to remove it in his reformation (2 Kings 23:6). Jeremiah's denunciation of the worship of the Queen of Heaven may also relate to this image (Jer 7:18; 44:17–30). The fact that the image's identity seems to be assumed in the context may also argue for this identification.

The statement "But you will see things that are even more detestable" (v.6) concludes this brief examination of the "idol of jealousy." This conclusion emphasizes the progressing severity of Judah's idolatry (vv.6, 13, 15).

Notes

2 The MT reads אֵשׁ (*'ēš*, "fire") in the phrase דְּמוּת כְּמַרְאֵה־אֵשׁ (*dᵉmût kᵉmar'ēh-'ēš*, "a figure like that of a fire"). The better reading (so NIV)—in agreement with both the LXX and the context (cf. מָתְנָיו [*māṯᵉnāyw*, "his waist"])—is אִישׁ (*'îš*, "man"). It is not uncommon to find the internal *matres lexionis* yod missing orthographically.

5–6 Zimmerli (*Ezekiel I*, p. 239) argues that the "idol" of Ezekiel cannot be identical to the Asherah idol because the Asherah idol was in the inner court and Ezekiel's idol was a guardian figure that was part of the north gate (as found in Mesopotamia). For an alternate view, see H. Torczyner, "Semel Ha-Qinah Ha-Maqneh (Ezek 8:3, 5)" JBL 65 (1946): 293–302.

b. *Idol worship of the elders*

8:7–13

⁷Then he brought me to the entrance to the court. I looked, and I saw a hole in the wall. ⁸He said to me, "Son of man, now dig into the wall." So I dug into the wall and saw a doorway there.

⁹And he said to me, "Go in and see the wicked and detestable things they are doing here." ¹⁰So I went in and looked, and I saw portrayed all over the walls all kinds of crawling things and detestable animals and all the idols of the house of Israel. ¹¹In front of them stood seventy elders of the house of Israel, and Jaazaniah son of Shaphan was standing among them. Each had a censer in his hand, and a fragrant cloud of incense was rising.

¹²He said to me, "Son of man, have you seen what the elders of the house of Israel are doing in the darkness, each at the shrine of his own idol? They say, 'The Lord does not see us; the Lord has forsaken the land.'" ¹³Again, he said, "You will see them doing things that are even more detestable."

7–9 Ezekiel was brought into the north entry gate. There he saw a hole in the wall and was told to dig through the wall, enter, and observe what the elders of Israel were doing secretly in the inner court (vv. 7–9). These seventy elders were not the Sanhedrin of NT times. That institution had not yet begun. They were most likely the leaders of the nation who based their traditional position on Moses' appointment of the seventy elders to assist him in governing God's people (Exod 24:1, 9; Num 11:16–25).

10–11 Jaazaniah, the son of Shaphan, was leading these men in burning incense (v. 10) to all sorts of sculptured animals, reptiles, and detestable things (v. 11; cf. zoomorphic representations of gods in Egypt). Perhaps the detestable things were the animals declared unclean in Leviticus 11. Some understood this Jaazaniah to be the son of Josiah's secretary of state named Shaphan (2 Kings 22:8–14; 2 Chron 34:15–21; Jer 26:24; 29:3; 36:10; 40:5, 9, 11; 41:2; 43:6). If so, this would certainly show the rapid degradation of leadership in Judah.

12–13 The Judean leaders were practicing their corrupt worship of these idols (perhaps foreign motifs) in the dark, each in his own room. This individual chamber of each elder is difficult to explain. Were these chambers built into the wall that separated the inner and outer courts, or were these rooms the private homes of each elder, indicating that each was engaged in this perverse ritual privately as well as publicly? Contextually, the former is preferable, since the entire discussion concerns events in the inner court. However, no such chambers were known to have existed within the inner court of Solomon's temple. Sparse information about the courts of Solomon's temple preclude any definitive conclusion.

These leaders rationalized their activities by declaring that God did not see them nor was he present anymore. He had forsaken the land as demonstrated by the deportations of 605 B.C. and 597 B.C. (v. 12). They denied the existence of God in direct opposition to his name: "the one who always is." They negated his omnipresence and omniscience, choosing to exchange "the glory of the immortal God for images made to look like . . . birds and animals and reptiles" (Rom 1:23). In saying that God had forsaken the land, the elders repudiated his faithfulness to the Abrahamic covenant, his love for his chosen people, and his immutability. With this kind of rationalization, they permitted themselves to do anything they desired. If God did not exist, then no one need care about him. It is tragic that the same attitude exists today among so many people. They have no concept of a glorious, holy God. Romans 1:18–31 succinctly describes the consequence.

c. Tammuz worship of the women

8:14–15

> ¹⁴Then he brought me to the entrance to the north gate of the house of the LORD, and I saw women sitting there, mourning for Tammuz. ¹⁵He said to me, "Do you see this, son of man? You will see things that are even more detestable than this."

14–15 Leaving the inner court and the iniquity of the elders, Ezekiel returned to the entry way of the inner court's north gate (v. 14), where he observed women worshiping Tammuz, an ancient Akkadian deity, the husband and brother of Ishtar. Tammuz, later linked to Adonis and Aphrodite by name, was a god of fertility and rain, similar to Hadad and Baal. In the seasonal mythological cycle, he died early in the fall when vegetation withered. His revival, by the wailing of Ishtar, was marked by the buds of spring and the fertility of the land. Such renewal was encouraged and celebrated by licentious fertility festivals.

Tammuz is normally traced back to the annual death and descent into the netherworld of the Sumerian god Dumuzi, a symbol of plenty (cf. T. Jacobsen, *The Treasures of Darkness* [New Haven: Yale University Press, 1976], pp. 25–73). Recent studies question the validity of the resurrection theme in Tammuz worship (cf. Edwin Yamauchi, "Tammuz and the Bible," JBL 84 [1965]: 283–90).

The date of this vision was in the months of August/September when Tammuz "died." This month later became known in the Hebrew calendar as the month of Tammuz. At the time of this vision, the land of Palestine would have been parched from the summer sun; and the women would have been lamenting Tammuz's death. They perhaps were also following the ritual of Ishtar, wailing for the revival of Tammuz. But there were still greater abominations, declared the Lord (v.15; cf. vv.6, 13).

d. Sun worship

8:16–18

16He then brought me into the inner court of the house of the LORD, and there at the entrance to the temple, between the portico and the altar, were about twenty-five men. With their backs toward the temple of the LORD and their faces toward the east, they were bowing down to the sun in the east.

17He said to me, "Have you seen this, son of man? Is it a trivial matter for the house of Judah to do the detestable things they are doing here? Must they also fill the land with violence and continually provoke me to anger? Look at them putting the branch to their nose! 18Therefore I will deal with them in anger; I will not look on them with pity or spare them. Although they shout in my ears, I will not listen to them."

16 Ezekiel returned to the temple's inner court, where he noticed twenty-five men with their backs to the temple, facing east in sun worship. The identity of these men is unsure. Many interpreters assume that they were priests, since only priests were permitted access into the inner court (2 Chron 4:9; Joel 2:17). It has, however, just been observed that the seventy elders of Israel were practicing their idolatry within the inner court; so these strict regulations were not being followed. On the contrary, it would seem strange that only a portion of the seventy would have been engaged in the sun worship. The specific numbers of seventy (v.11) and twenty-five (v.16) were probably given to aid in distinguishing the two groups. Therefore, it is more likely that these twenty-five men were priests, though one cannot be dogmatic about it. If they were priests, perhaps the number is twenty-five because there was a representative of each of the twenty-four courses of the priests plus the high priest (cf. 1 Chron 23). Regardless of the identity of these men, sun worship was strictly forbidden by the Mosaic covenant (Deut 4:19); and both Hezekiah and Josiah had had to remove this pagan practice from Judah during their reigns (2 Kings 23:5, 11; 2 Chron 29:6–7).

17–18 These verses summarize this chapter of perverse idolatry by declaring that this wickedness of Judah's leaders had allowed violence to fill the land. All this had repeatedly provoked God. They were even "putting the branch to their nose" (v.17).

This latter phrase is problematic. Some (e.g., Taylor), along with early Jewish commentators, render the word $z^e m \hat{o} r \bar{a} h$ ("branch") as "stench." However, the word's normal reading is "twig." H.W.F. Saggs ("Notes and Studies: The Branch to the Nose," JTS [October 1960]: 318–29) holds that putting the twig to the nose was part of the ritual practice of sun worship, a concept that fits this context well. Whether Saggs is correct or not, the context implies that the act was offensive to God. (For a discussion of the Sopherim's emendation and a survey of various interpretations of "putting the branch to their nose," cf. Greenberg, *Ezekiel 1–20*, pp. 172–73.)

All these abominable, idolatrous rituals brought the wrath of a holy God. He would judge without compassion. He would refuse to listen to the people's cries for mercy, even though they shouted with a very loud voice. Judgment would come! The remainder of the vision would continue to emphasize that point.

Notes

16 ב (k^e, "as") is rendered "about" by Greenberg (*Ezekiel 1–20*, p. 172) so that the number "twenty-five" may be viewed as a round number (so NIV).

2. Judgment on Jerusalem and the departure of God's glory (9:1–11:23)

a. The man with the writing kit

9:1–4

¹Then I heard him call out in a loud voice, "Bring the guards of the city here, each with a weapon in his hand." ²And I saw six men coming from the direction of the upper gate, which faces north, each with a deadly weapon in his hand. With them was a man clothed in linen who had a writing kit at his side. They came in and stood beside the bronze altar.

³Now the glory of the God of Israel went up from above the cherubim, where it had been, and moved to the threshold of the temple. Then the LORD called to the man clothed in linen who had the writing kit at his side ⁴and said to him, "Go throughout the city of Jerusalem and put a mark on the foreheads of those who grieve and lament over all the detestable things that are done in it."

1–2 As Ezekiel stood in the temple's inner courtyard, aghast by the abominations being practiced, the Lord announced the coming of the city's executioners (v.1). Ezekiel saw them enter the "upper gate" (v.2), equivalent to the inner court's north gate (cf. 2 Kings 15:35; 2 Chron 27:3; Jer 20:2; 36:10). Each executioner carried a lethal weapon in his hand. They gathered together and stood beside the bronze altar (v.2). Among them was a man clothed in linen and carrying a writing kit.

Ezekiel 8:18 provides a transition in the vision. In the verse God announced judgment on Jerusalem because of the heathen worship practiced in the temple. The Lord would execute his discipline through these seven men (six executioners and the man in linen). A holy and righteous God would not allow idolatry to rob him of his rightful place as Israel's true God. The basis of the judgment was God's glory and holiness as seen in the theophany of glory and the linen clothing of the man with the writing kit. Linen was often worn by divine messengers (cf. Dan 10:5; 12:6–7; Rev 15:6) and was used for the priestly garment (Exod 28:42; 1 Sam 2:18; 22:18). In this sense linen portrayed the purity and holiness of God. On the other hand, judgment was stressed by these men gathering at the bronze altar, the altar of sacrificial judgment, ready to execute their assigned task.

3 The glorious God prepared to delegate the execution of this judgment to these men as he arose from above the cherub (the singular is to be understood collectively; so NIV) and proceeded to the temple's threshold. Some understand this to mean that God's glory arose from its historic position over the cherubim of the ark of the covenant and began a progressive departure from the temple. Leaving the Most Holy Place, it came first to the temple's entry. Others believe that God's glory, as seen in the visionary likeness of the man in 8:2, departed from a cherubim throne-chariot and moved directly to the temple threshold. The latter position argues that the "glory" and the cherubim are separated in 10:3–5, 18 and that it is unlikely that God's glory had been dwelling in the Most Holy Place during the pagan worship practices in the courtyard. However, since the following context (chs. 9–11) shows the progressive departure of God's glory from the temple, Jerusalem, and Judah, it seems better to understand this action as a combination of both concepts.

Most likely God's glory, envisioned in the man of 8:2, had separated from the cherubim throne-chariot in the vision and moved from the Most Holy Place (cf. 8:4) to the temple threshold. From there the picture of God's departure from his people in preparation for judgment began. With judgment imminent, God's glory could not be present over the ark of the covenant in the Most Holy Place or in the presence of the divine Judge. Therefore, the Lord vividly demonstrated his readiness to judge by withdrawing his glory from his people. God's glory moved from the Most Holy Place to the entry of the temple to assign the tasks of judgment.

4 The Lord commanded the man clothed with linen and carrying the scribal implements to go throughout Jerusalem and mark everyone who had genuine remorse and concern for the sins of the city, those who saw that the heathen ways of Jerusalem were contrary to the Mosaic covenant and desired to see that covenant properly instituted in the city. This man marked them on their forehead with a mark of protection as the impending judgment drew near (cf. Rev 7:3; 9:4; 14:1). These people had a righteous heart attitude.

Notes

1 The term פְּקֻדָּה (pᵉquddāh, "guards") may mean "oversight" or "visitation." The concept of "visitation" may connote the bringing of blessing, though normally it relates to the visitation of punishment on a given place or people. The latter concept is used in this verse (cf. Num 16:19; Isa 10:3; Hos 9:7; Mic 7:4).

2 The word קֶסֶת (qeset, "kit") is used only in this context in the OT. Some take it to be an

Egyptian loan word (from the form *qst*) for a writing case with all the necessary implements, or a scribal palette (so Cooke, Taylor).

The term בְּתוֹכָם (*beṯôḵām*) normally means "in the midst of them" or "among them" (NIV, "with them"). The word is the basis for determining whether the man with the writing equipment is one of the six men or whether he is an additional person. Either view could be correct, though the seventh-person view seems more likely in light of this term.

4 The word for "mark" is the Hebrew letter תָו (*tāw*), the last letter of the Hebrew alphabet. The orthography of the letter in Ezekiel's day was X, a cross, which some have construed to be prophetic of Christ's crucifixion. It is doubtful that such was meant to be conveyed by the normal word for "mark."

---

b. *The executioners' judgment*

9:5–8

> [5]As I listened, he said to the others, "Follow him through the city and kill, without showing pity or compassion. [6]Slaughter old men, young men and maidens, women and children, but do not touch anyone who has the mark. Begin at my sanctuary." So they began with the elders who were in front of the temple.
> [7]Then he said to them, "Defile the temple and fill the courts with the slain. Go!" So they went out and began killing throughout the city. [8]While they were killing and I was left alone, I fell facedown, crying out, "Ah, Sovereign LORD! Are you going to destroy the entire remnant of Israel in this outpouring of your wrath on Jerusalem?"

5–7 God commanded the six men to follow the man with the scribal kit throughout Jerusalem and to exercise individual judgment on everyone who did not have the mark of protection, regardless of sex or age (vv.5–6). They were to spare none. They began with the seventy elders polluting the temple with their secret worship of sculptured animals in the inner court. This was where God was to be worshiped, but instead it had been polluted. Judgment started in the temple (cf. 1 Peter 4:17) in Jerusalem, the center from which religious leadership should come. However, Judah's leadership was corrupt. Therefore, the temple courtyards would be defiled by the blood of these worshipers of heathen deities (v.7; cf. Num 19:11; 2 Kings 23:16).

8 As Ezekiel found himself the only inner-court survivor of the judgment, he became alarmed at the mass of people destroyed by these executioners. Although his forehead was hard, his heart throbbed with love for God and man. He pleaded with God not to eradicate the entire remnant of Judah. The remnant in this context referred to Judah as the remnant of God's people. She was the only tribe left, and some of that tribe had gone into exile to Babylonia already (605 B.C. and 597 B.C.). The present judgment, illustrated by these six men, looked as if it would consume the remainder of Judah.

God has sovereignly elected by his grace a faithful remnant of Israel (Rom 11:4–5). There is a remnant in Israel in all ages. A remnant of Israel will ultimately be saved (Rom 9:27–29).

c. Vindication of God's judgment

9:9–11

> ⁹He answered me, "The sin of the house of Israel and Judah is exceedingly great; the land is full of bloodshed and the city is full of injustice. They say, 'The LORD has forsaken the land; the LORD does not see.' ¹⁰So I will not look on them with pity or spare them, but I will bring down on their own heads what they have done."
> ¹¹Then the man in linen with the writing kit at his side brought back word, saying, "I have done as you commanded."

9–10 The Lord's response to Ezekiel's concern for the nation was to remind him that the iniquity of Judah was extremely great (v.9). Violence and spiritual perversion had filled the land because the people had forgotten God's character, assuming that he did not see what they were doing because he had deserted them. They denied God's omniscience, omnipresence, and faithfulness. The Lord had not left, because he presently was judging Judah for her iniquity and would not spare anyone. He *did* know the wickedness of the people, for he would recompense them for it (v.10; cf. 1 Peter 4:17).

11 As an encouragement to Ezekiel that all Judah had not strayed from God, the man with the writing kit reported, "I have done as you commanded." In other words, the righteous ones had been marked.

d. Coals of fire on Jerusalem

10:1–7

> ¹I looked, and I saw the likeness of a throne of sapphire above the expanse that was over the heads of the cherubim. ²The LORD said to the man clothed in linen, "Go in among the wheels beneath the cherubim. Fill your hands with burning coals from among the cherubim and scatter them over the city." And as I watched, he went in.
> ³Now the cherubim were standing on the south side of the temple when the man went in, and a cloud filled the inner court. ⁴Then the glory of the LORD rose from above the cherubim and moved to the threshold of the temple. The cloud filled the temple, and the court was full of the radiance of the glory of the LORD. ⁵The sound of the wings of the cherubim could be heard as far away as the outer court, like the voice of God Almighty when he speaks.
> ⁶When the LORD commanded the man in linen, "Take fire from among the wheels, from among the cherubim," the man went in and stood beside a wheel. ⁷Then one of the cherubim reached out his hand to the fire that was among them. He took up some of it and put it into the hands of the man in linen, who took it and went out.

1–2 God instructed the man clothed in linen to take fire coals from the center of the cherubim throne-chariot (cf. ch. 1) and to pour them out in judgment on the city to purify it. Coals of fire were often symbolic of cleansing in the OT (cf. Isa 6).

3–5 This parenthesis clarifies the setting. The cherubim throne-chariot was in the inner courtyard to the south of the temple (v.3). The temple precinct had been cleansed by the six men, and God's glory had moved to the temple door. From there it filled the temple and the courts (vv.4–5).

6–7 The man in linen faithfully responded to the Lord's command to take coals from the cherubim (v.6). The cherub of v.7 was probably the living being with a face like a "cherub" (v.14). This living being handed the live coals to the man in linen.

Notes

3 This verse begins with a waw disjunctive, which indicates that a parenthetical expression follows. The consecutive sequence of events is not resumed till the waw consecutive at the beginning of v.6.

e. *Cherubim and Ichabod*

10:8–22

⁸(Under the wings of the cherubim could be seen what looked like the hands of a man.)

⁹I looked, and I saw beside the cherubim four wheels, one beside each of the cherubim; the wheels sparkled like chrysolite. ¹⁰As for their appearance, the four of them looked alike; each was like a wheel intersecting a wheel. ¹¹As they moved, they would go in any one of the four directions the cherubim faced; the wheels did not turn about as the cherubim went. The cherubim went in whatever direction the head faced, without turning as they went. ¹²Their entire bodies, including their backs, their hands and their wings, were completely full of eyes, as were their four wheels. ¹³I heard the wheels being called "the whirling wheels." ¹⁴Each of the cherubim had four faces: One face was that of a cherub, the second the face of a man, the third the face of a lion, and the fourth the face of an eagle.

¹⁵Then the cherubim rose upward. These were the living creatures I had seen by the Kebar River. ¹⁶When the cherubim moved, the wheels beside them moved; and when the cherubim spread their wings to rise from the ground, the wheels did not leave their side. ¹⁷When the cherubim stood still, they also stood still; and when the cherubim rose, they rose with them, because the spirit of the living creatures was in them.

¹⁸Then the glory of the Lᴏʀᴅ departed from over the threshold of the temple and stopped above the cherubim. ¹⁹While I watched, the cherubim spread their wings and rose from the ground, and as they went, the wheels went with them. They stopped at the entrance to the east gate of the Lᴏʀᴅ's house, and the glory of the God of Israel was above them.

²⁰These were the living creatures I had seen beneath the God of Israel by the Kebar River, and I realized that they were cherubim. ²¹Each had four faces and four wings, and under their wings was what looked like the hands of a man. ²²Their faces had the same appearance as those I had seen by the Kebar River. Each one went straight ahead.

8–17, 20–22 The living beings of chapter 1 are identified as cherubim in this passage, especially in vv.15, 20, 22. Cherubim appear elsewhere in the Scriptures, though they were new to the discussion in Ezekiel. Some scholars question why Ezekiel did not recognize these living creatures as cherubim in chapter 1. Maybe it was because he now observed them more closely; or perhaps now in the temple

789

setting, he related their likeness to the cherubim designs common to the temple decor (1 Kings 6–7).

In the ancient Near East, a winged sphinx with a human head and a lion's or bull's body was often identified as a "cherub." The OT cherubim are primarily represented as guardians and protectors (cf. Gen 3:24), though they also continually performed worship on the mercy seat of the ark of the covenant (Exod 25:18–20). The concept of cherubim forming a throne-chariot for God's glory is founded on several OT passages (cf. 1 Sam 4:4; 2 Sam 6:2; 2 Kings 19:15; 1 Chron 13:6; 1 Chron 28:18; Pss 18:10; 80:1; 99:1). Perhaps as a throne-chariot, they were protectors and guardians of God's glory.

This passage does not add much additional information about the living beings of chapter 1 except for their identity as cherubim. But the "ox" face of the cherubim in chapter 1 is described as a cherub's face in v. 14. This may be in keeping with the form of the cherubim in ancient Near Eastern sculpture as described in the previous paragraph. Perhaps a "cherub" had the look of a bull or an ox. Apart from this detail, the material in this section reiterates the cherubim descriptions of chapter 1.

18–19 A principal theme in this vision and in the book is the departure and return of God's glory. God's glory departed from the temple because of the corruption within Jerusalem and Judah, but it would return in the end time when the nation had been fully cleansed (cf. 43:1–9). The gradual departure of God's glory began in 9:3 and 10:4, when the glory of God left the Most Holy Place and moved to the temple's entrance. God's glory departed from the temple's threshold and assumed its place on the cherubim throne-chariot. Together they went to the temple's east gate (v. 19), from where they finally departed (cf. 11:22–23). Deuteronomy 31:17 and Hosea 9:12 had declared that this departure would occur if the people strayed from God's ways. In 1 Samuel 4 a similar example of the departure of God's glory at a time of judgment was memorialized by the name of Eli's grandson "Ichabod" (v. 21), which means "inglorious." Once again, in Ezekiel's day God wrote "Ichabod" over Jerusalem and Judah.

Notes

20 Little can be gained from the etymology of the Hebrew word כְּרוּב (*k^erûb*, "cherub"). The Akkadian verb *karābu* means "to pray, bless," and *kāribu* connotes "intercession." The cultural background and the usage of the Hebrew word within contexts provide a better basis for determining the meaning of "cherub."

f. *Judgment on Jerusalem's leaders*

11:1–13

¹Then the Spirit lifted me up and brought me to the gate of the house of the Lᴏʀᴅ that faces east. There at the entrance to the gate were twenty-five men, and I saw among them Jaazaniah son of Azzur and Pelatiah son of Benaiah, leaders of the people. ²The Lᴏʀᴅ said to me, "Son of man, these are the men who are plotting evil and giving wicked advice in this city. ³They say, 'Will it not soon be

time to build houses? This city is a cooking pot, and we are the meat.' ⁴Therefore prophesy against them; prophesy, son of man."

⁵Then the Spirit of the LORD came upon me, and he told me to say: "This is what the LORD says: That is what you are saying, O house of Israel, but I know what is going through your mind. ⁶You have killed many people in this city and filled its streets with the dead.

⁷"Therefore this is what the Sovereign LORD says: The bodies you have thrown there are the meat and this city is the pot, but I will drive you out of it. ⁸You fear the sword, and the sword is what I will bring against you, declares the Sovereign LORD. ⁹I will drive you out of the city and hand you over to foreigners and inflict punishment on you. ¹⁰You will fall by the sword, and I will execute judgment on you at the borders of Israel. Then you will know that I am the LORD. ¹¹This city will not be a pot for you, nor will you be the meat in it; I will execute judgment on you at the borders of Israel. ¹²And you will know that I am the LORD, for you have not followed my decrees or kept my laws but have conformed to the standards of the nations around you."

¹³Now as I was prophesying, Pelatiah son of Benaiah died. Then I fell face-down and cried out in a loud voice, "Ah, Sovereign LORD! Will you completely destroy the remnant of Israel?"

1 The extended vision of 8:1–11:24 continues. As Ezekiel watched God's glory move to the east gate of the temple complex, the Spirit brought him to that gate. Here God showed Ezekiel more of the perversion of the nation's leadership. Twenty-five men were gathered together, led by Jaazaniah, the son of Azzur, and Pelatiah, the son of Benaiah, leaders of the people. These twenty-five political leaders were not the twenty-five sun-worshipers of 8:16. Similar numbers do not make the groups identical. Likewise, Jaazaniah son of Azzur should not be identified with Jaazaniah son of Shaphan in 8:11. Though the name is the same, the fathers had different names; and there is no evidence to show that a man at that time had both the name Shaphan and the name Azzur. Though this may have been true, it seems best to understand these as two different people till we know more.

2–3 These leaders had given the people false and evil counsel (v.2). They had planned evil things, deceiving the inhabitants of Jerusalem and Judah by encouraging them to build homes at a time when the prophets were continually warning of the impending Babylonian destruction (v.3). These leaders were complacent and apathetic, believing that there was no imminent danger (cf. 7:7–8). They declared that Jerusalem's inhabitants were secure inside Jerusalem's walls by promulgating the proverb: "This city is a cooking pot, and we are the meat" (v.3). Jerusalem, "the pot," provided security to its inhabitants, "the meat," just as a pot protected the meat within it. Prophets, like Ezekiel, were declared to be misguided men using scare tactics.

4–6 Ezekiel prophesied to these twenty-five men. Some, finding this difficult to accept, have understood vv.1–21 as a later interpolation. But nothing in the context prevents Ezekiel from prophesying within the vision (cf. 37:1–4). Ezekiel's prophecy was a judgment oracle with the accusation stated in vv.5–6 and the verdict declared in vv.7–12. Ezekiel reminded these leaders that their actions were not hidden from God's omniscience; he knew exactly what they were thinking, saying, and doing (v.5). God knew they had rejected the prophets' warnings, exchanged the righteous statutes of the law for idolatry, and murdered the inhabitants of Jerusalem with their devious schemes (v.6).

7-12 The verdict was expressed in the same imagery as the people's proverbial statements in v.3. The "pot" of Jerusalem would protect only the righteous whom these wicked leaders had already slain (v.7). These corrupt leaders and their followers would be brought outside the "pot" of Jerusalem and struck down by the dreaded sword of foreigners (vv.8–11). Babylonia would execute this judgment, slaying the Judeans throughout the land (cf. 2 Kings 25:18–21). With the Fall of Jerusalem to Nebuchadnezzar in 586 B.C., the Judean leaders and their subjects would know that the Lord was truly *the* Lord (v.12). They would observe that he faithfully executed the righteous judgment he had declared would come on a people who failed to live according to the Mosaic statutes. If Israel would obey, she would live (Lev 18:5). But she had chosen rather to live by the idolatrous ways of the nations around her and to receive the law's curse instead of its blessing.

13 While Ezekiel was prophesying this message to the leaders, Pelatiah died. He did not actually hear Ezekiel's prophecy, but news of Pelatiah's death would confirm Ezekiel as a prophet. This stunning result of his prophecy caused Ezekiel to fear once again that God would destroy all the remnant of Israel (v.13).

Notes

1 שָׂרֵי הָעָם (*śārê hā'ām,* "leaders of the people") is a phrase used only in later OT texts (cf. 1 Chron 21:2; 2 Chron 24:23; Neh 11:1). A similar, though more precise, term used by Jeremiah is שָׂרֵי יְהוּדָה (*śārê yᵉhûḏāh,* "Leaders of Judah"; cf. Jer 26:10; 29:2; 34:19; 52:10). These titles designated men as state officials with public responsibility among the people, often possessing judicial power. They seemed to have been ministers of the king. Lists of such "leaders" included military commanders, heralds, and royal secretaries (cf. 2 Sam 8:16–18; 20:23–26; 1 Chron 18:14–17; cf. Roland de Vaux, *Ancient Israel* [New York: McGraw-Hill, 1961], p. 127).

3 לֹא בְקָרוֹב בְּנוֹת בָּתִּים (*lōʾ bᵉqārôḇ bᵉnôṯ bāttîm,* "not time to build houses") is a phrase used both literally and metaphorically. Metaphorically it denotes the sense of establishing a family (cf. Deut 25:9; Ruth 4:11; Prov 24:27), though this sense does not seem to apply in the present context. A literal interpretation fits best. Alternate views can be found in Greenberg, *Ezekiel 1–20,* p. 157.

סִיר (*sîr,* "cooking pot"), though a word used for various types of pottery, like "washing pot," "water jar," etc., most commonly designates a widemouth "cooking pot" that was broad and shallow. Originally it was without handles, but two handles were later attached.

g. *The future of the remnant*

11:14–21

¹⁴The word of the LORD came to me: ¹⁵"Son of man, your brothers—your brothers who are your blood relatives and the whole house of Israel—are those of whom the people of Jerusalem have said, 'They are far away from the LORD; this land was given to us as our possession.'

¹⁶"Therefore say: 'This is what the Sovereign LORD says: Although I sent them far away among the nations and scattered them among the countries, yet for a little while I have been a sanctuary for them in the countries where they have gone.'

¹⁷"Therefore say: 'This is what the Sovereign Lᴏʀᴅ says: I will gather you from the nations and bring you back from the countries where you have been scattered, and I will give you back the land of Israel again.'

¹⁸"They will return to it and remove all its vile images and detestable idols. ¹⁹I will give them an undivided heart and put a new spirit in them; I will remove from them their heart of stone and give them a heart of flesh. ²⁰Then they will follow my decrees and be careful to keep my laws. They will be my people, and I will be their God. ²¹But as for those whose hearts are devoted to their vile images and detestable idols, I will bring down on their own heads what they have done, declares the Sovereign Lᴏʀᴅ."

14–15 Ezekiel's great concern for the remnant of Judah had not gone unnoticed by the Lord (v.14). God encouraged Ezekiel in this message that he and a remnant, his kindred, were purposely being kept by God through the Captivity. The citizens of Judah had looked on the exiles as the unclean and sinful part of the nation. Was not God judging them by their deportation? The Judeans encouraged the exiles to get as far away from the land of Israel as possible, because God had given it to those still in Judah, not to the sinful exiles (v.15).

16–20 On the contrary, God showed that it was the remnant he had deported that he cared for; and he showed his care by promising to regather the exiles to the Promised Land (vv.16–20). This is the first mention of a future restoration in Ezekiel. The prophets held out restoration as a continual hope to the righteous. On the basis of the Mosaic covenant, judgment was all the prophets could offer Judah for her sins. The promise of restoration to the land, though declared in the blessings of the Mosaic covenant (Lev 26:40–45; Deut 30:1–10), was based on the eternal covenants to Abraham (Gen 12:1–3), David (2 Sam 7:12–16), and Jeremiah (Jer 31:31–34).

In exile the Lord would continue to be an ever-present sanctuary (refuge) for his people, making provisions for them no matter where they were scattered. This is the same ever-present God who today meets the needs of those who trust him, regardless of their circumstances. God promised that when he had finished disciplining the remnant of Israel, he would (1) regather them (v.17a), (2) restore them to the land of Israel (v.17b), (3) cleanse the land of its abominations (v.18), and (4) fulfill the new covenant with them (vv.19–20).

The new covenant promised in Jeremiah 31:31–34 provided for (1) a change of heart and (2) a new spirit. This new spirit would be the outpouring of the Spirit promised by the prophets (Deut 30:6; Jer 31:33; Joel 2:28–29), further developed in Ezekiel 36:26–27, and initially instituted in Acts 2. The new heart and spirit would replace Israel's old heart of stone (Zech 7:12), which had become hardened against the Lord and his ways. The people would be empowered to live in the godly manner set forth in the stipulations of the Mosaic covenant (v.20). Finally they would truly reflect the Mosaic covenant formula: they would be God's people, and he would be their God.

Through his death for sin, once for all, Christ, the Mediator of the new covenant (Heb 8:6), made it possible for all believers to receive the Spirit's divine enablement so that they too might live according to God's righteous standards revealed in the Mosaic covenant. This is available to all today who place their faith in the resurrected Messiah, Jesus Christ.

21 However, God warned those who did not repent and follow him that they would be held accountable and would be judged.

Notes

---

15 גְּאֻלָּתֶךָ (geʾullāteka, "kindred," "relatives") is a term used to describe a close relationship that existed in a family that necessitated that possessions return to that "family" under the law of the jubilee year (Lev 25). Tribal solidarity is stressed. In this context the word refers to land being usurped from absent original owners. Leviticus 25 was not being followed (cf. TDOT, 2: 350–55).

16 In the מִקְדָּשׁ (miqdāš, "sanctuary"), the divine Presence was established among the covenant people. Though they were temporarily separated from the land and the temple sanctuary, God himself would be their "sanctuary." They would worship and serve him without the temple building till they were restored and the temple rebuilt. Yahweh would graciously accept their limited forms of worship.

19 אֶחָד (ʾeḥād, "undivided") stresses the undividedness and singleness of the heart that would be received. In Jer 32:39 "one heart" is complemented and explained by singleness of mind and constancy of conduct.

---

h. *The departure of the Lord's glory from Jerusalem*

11:22–25

> 22Then the cherubim, with the wheels beside them, spread their wings, and the glory of the God of Israel was above them. 23The glory of the LORD went up from within the city and stopped above the mountain east of it. 24The Spirit lifted me up and brought me to the exiles in Babylonia in the vision given by the Spirit of God.
> Then the vision I had seen went up from me, 25and I told the exiles everything the LORD had shown me.

22–25 After God had encouraged Ezekiel about the future restoration of the Judean remnant, God's glory departed east from Jerusalem to the Mount of Olives (vv.22–23). His presence among Israel was hereafter pictured as removed (till his return in 43:1–4). Judgment was now certain! Ezekiel was brought back to Babylonia in the vision, and the vision stopped (v.24). He recounted the entire vision to the exiles who had been observing his symbolic siege and had seen him caught up in the vision (v.25).

C. *The Lord's Reply to the Exiles' Invalid Rationalizations of Hope* (12:1–19:14)

1. *The dramatic tragedy of exile* (12:1–20)

a. *Introduction*

12:1–2

> 1The word of the LORD came to me: 2"Son of man, you are living among a rebellious people. They have eyes to see but do not see and ears to hear but do not hear, for they are a rebellious people.

1–2 The introductory phrase—"The word of the LORD came to me" (v.1)—indicates the beginning of a new series of messages. Ezekiel always gave specific dates for new visions or oracles. Since no new chronological notice was given, and since the speeches of chapters 12–19 were closely related thematically to the foregoing vision, it can be assumed that these messages were uttered shortly after Ezekiel's explanation of the vision in chapters 8–11.

God immediately reminded Ezekiel that he lived among "a rebellious people" (v.2). Ezekiel had been warned of this in his commission (2:3–8), but now he would experience the reality of that truth. The exiles had been watching his symbolic acts and hearing his judgment oracles for over a year. He had communicated the imminency of the judgment, its severity, and its basis (chs. 4–11) through every possible means. Though the elders had ears and eyes, they had neither heard his messages nor seen his visual signs in chapters 8–11. The people were blind and deaf to God's truth (cf. Isa 6:9–10; Jer 5:21). Regrettably, such hardness of heart and blindness of eye had characterized Israel's history. Ezekiel had to speak to this rebellion.

The exiles had not grasped the serious consequences of Ezekiel's warnings. They still hoped for an early return to Palestine, for they viewed the continued preservation of Jerusalem and Judah as signs of security. After all, Jerusalem was the eternal city. They presented several reasons for their hope and security—as well as their objections to Ezekiel's warning—in chapters 12–19.

First, if judgment was to come, it would not be in their lifetime, as Ezekiel had declared (ch. 12). Second, Ezekiel was only one of many prophets. Most prophets and prophetesses announced hope and reasons for optimism. Why should the people listen to Ezekiel (ch. 13)? Third, the leaders in Judah were ultimately responsible. If there was to be any judgment, it would be on them, not the exiles (ch. 14). Fourth, if real danger of judgment should exist, then they would only have to find some righteous man to intercede for them before God. Thus they would be delivered (ch. 14). Fifth, how could Ezekiel possibly believe that God would judge his own chosen people? He would not do that (chs. 15–16). Sixth, it would not be fair for God to judge anyone for his forefathers' sins. The people thought Ezekiel was saying that God did judge one for his forefathers' sins (ch. 17). Seventh, if judgment was really coming, then there was nothing they could do to stop it; for they would be paying for their fathers' sins. It would not make any difference if they repented (ch. 18). Eighth, Zedekiah, the contemporary ruler of Judah, could be trusted. He would throw off the yoke of Babylonia (ch. 19).

Ezekiel patiently, systematically, and adamantly (cf. 3:8–9) challenged the naive reasoning of the exiles, undermining each source of their optimistic rejection to his warnings of judgment. When Ezekiel had finished his challenges, no excuses remained.

A basic pattern is noticeable in the structure of Ezekiel's prophecy: each vision is followed by a message that expands and develops the concepts in the vision. The vision of Ezekiel's commission (chs. 1–3) was followed by the announcements of judgment on Jerusalem. The vision of Jerusalem's iniquity and judgment (chs. 8–11) was elaborated in chapters 12–19. The vision of chapters 8–11 chiefly dealt with religious corruption in the temple, whereas chapters 12–19 will develop the wickedness of all leaders in Judah (kings, prophets, and priests) as the core of the nation's iniquity. Emphasis in these chapters will rest on corrupt leadership and reasons for the coming judgment.

b. A picture of deportation

12:3–16

3"Therefore, son of man, pack your belongings for exile and in the daytime, as they watch, set out and go from where you are to another place. Perhaps they will understand, though they are a rebellious house. 4During the daytime, while they watch, bring out your belongings packed for exile. Then in the evening, while they are watching, go out like those who go into exile. 5While they watch, dig through the wall and take your belongings out through it. 6Put them on your shoulder as they are watching and carry them out at dusk. Cover your face so that you cannot see the land, for I have made you a sign to the house of Israel."

7So I did as I was commanded. During the day I brought out my things packed for exile. Then in the evening I dug through the wall with my hands. I took my belongings out at dusk, carrying them on my shoulders while they watched.

8In the morning the word of the LORD came to me: 9"Son of man, did not that rebellious house of Israel ask you, 'What are you doing?'

10"Say to them, 'This is what the Sovereign LORD says: This oracle concerns the prince in Jerusalem and the whole house of Israel who are there.' 11Say to them, 'I am a sign to you.'

"As I have done, so it will be done to them. They will go into exile as captives. 12"The prince among them will put his things on his shoulder at dusk and leave, and a hole will be dug in the wall for him to go through. He will cover his face, so that he cannot see the land. 13I will spread my net for him, and he will be caught in my snare; I will bring him to Babylonia, the land of the Chaldeans, but he will not see it, and there he will die. 14I will scatter to the winds all those around him—his staff and all his troops—and I will pursue them with drawn sword.

15"They will know that I am the LORD when I disperse them among the nations and scatter them through the countries. 16But I will spare a few of them from the sword, famine and plague, so that in the nations where they go they may acknowledge all their detestable practices. Then they will know that I am the LORD."

3–7 All of Ezekiel's symbolic acts had undoubtedly drawn curious spectators who continually came to see what act he might do next. Even though the exiles had failed to grasp the significance of Ezekiel's previous messages, once again God graciously sought to convey his warnings to them. Maybe they would understand this time. The Lord repeatedly encouraged Ezekiel to perform a new drama for everyone to see. Ezekiel would be a "sign" to them (vv.6, 11).

Therefore, Ezekiel would act out something familiar to everyone watching: the process of deportation. During the day he would gather the small amount of belongings a deportee could take with him (cf. J.B. Pritchard, ed., *Ancient Near East in Pictures* [Princeton: Princeton University Press, 1954], plates 10, 311, 363–64, 366, 373) and bring them out where everyone could see them (vv.3–4a). In the evening he would dig a hole through the mud-brick wall of his house. Leaving through the hole, Ezekiel carried his bag like an exile (vv.4b–6a). Next he would cover his face (v.6b) and go to another place while all the people watched. Ezekiel's act was a sign that God would bring additional exiles to Babylon (v.6c).

8–16 Since all the exiles had participated in a deportation themselves (either in 605 B.C. or 597 B.C.), they should have understood clearly Ezekiel's picture of deportation. God reminded Ezekiel that many had not understood the drama, for they were asking, "What are you doing?" (vv.8–9). Therefore, Ezekiel explained his dramatization so none would miss its meaning.

Ezekiel prophesied deportation of a remnant from Jerusalem in 586 B.C., especially as it related to Zedekiah, the current Judean ruler (v.10). Ezekiel told the captives that he was a "sign" to them of the exile that the current inhabitants of Jerusalem would soon experience (v.11). His message probably shattered any hope that they might have had that he was portraying their imminent departure from Babylonia.

Verses 12–14 related specifically to Zedekiah, the prince. He was called "the prince" (v.12) because he was not the legitimate king. That right belonged to Jehoiachin who was in Babylonia. Zedekiah would load his bags at night (2 Kings 25:4; Jer 39:4; 52:7), escape with difficulty through the gates of the king's garden in southeast Jerusalem, and flee toward the Jordan where he would be caught by Nebuchadnezzar's army like an animal on the hunt—"spread my net for him" (v.13a; cf. 2 Kings 25:5–6; Jer 39:5; 52:7–8). The figure of a conqueror catching enemies in a net is from the imagery of the fowler or hunter in the ancient Near East. Deities in this culture are also pictured as hunting and seizing their enemies (cf. Pritchard, *Ancient Pictures*, plate 298). Zedekiah's troops would be scattered, and he would be brought before Nebuchadnezzar at Riblah (v.13b). There his sons and the nobles would be slaughtered before his eyes, after which he would be blinded. Therefore Zedekiah would never see the land of Babylonia, though he would die there as a captive (vv.13c–14; 2 Kings 25:5, 7; Jer 39:6–7; 52:8, 10–11). Ezekiel's covering of his face in the dramatization most likely indicated that Zedekiah would seek to disguise himself in his flight from the city. The fact that in fleeing he "will not see" the land with his eyes would correlate with Zedekiah's blinding and deportation.

Moreover, God wanted to make clear the purpose of the Exile. The deportations were designed to show the deportees that the Lord was the faithful, loving, and powerful God over Israel they should return to. Lest the foreign nations misunderstand Judah's dispersion, God had the exiles testify that their abominations precipitated the deportations. In this way the nations would realize that the Lord was holy, righteous, and cared for his people, Israel. He was not one who allowed them to be conquered because he did not care. This latter notion was very common in the ancient Near East. Each nation was uniquely related to its patron deity. If a nation was defeated in battle or decimated by famine and disease, this meant its god was weak and incapable of protecting and caring for its people. To prevent such a misconception, the Lord would send a remnant of Jews among the nations to witness that they were in exile only because of *their own* iniquity, not because of the Lord's failure. Then perhaps the nations would come to know that the Lord was the only true God (vv.15–16).

Notes

5 Ezekiel dug through a קִיר (qîr, "house wall"), not through a חוֹמָה (ḥômāh, "city wall"). Most likely Tel Abib would not have had a city wall. Therefore Ezekiel had to make his illustration in the best manner possible—by digging through the wall of his own mudbrick house.

12 E.A. Speiser ("Background and Function of the Biblical Nāsi'," CBQ 25 [1963]: 111–17) argues that נָשִׂיא (nāśî', "prince") would be understood best by the English word "leader."

c. A drama of fear

12:17–20

> 17The word of the LORD came to me: 18"Son of man, tremble as you eat your food, and shudder in fear as you drink your water. 19Say to the people of the land: 'This is what the Sovereign LORD says about those living in Jerusalem and in the land of Israel: They will eat their food in anxiety and drink their water in despair, for their land will be stripped of everything in it because of the violence of all who live there. 20The inhabited towns will be laid waste and the land will be desolate. Then you will know that I am the LORD.'"

17–20 In another brief act Ezekiel was to quiver and tremble while he ate and drank (vv.17–18). This displayed the fear and horror that would come on the citizens of Jerusalem and all the cities of Judah when their towns were destroyed and lay in ruins. The land would be emptied of its fruitfulness because of the violence that had been done in it (v.19). The violence they had done to others would return on their own heads, reflecting the principle of lex talionis.

This terrible judgment was designed to cause the Judeans to know that the Lord was real and that he was faithful to his promises (v.20). Those things they had refused to learn in times of blessing, God would teach them through the horrors of judgment. But his judgment was still a manifestation of his love; for if he had not cared for them, he would never have disciplined them. That same principle is just as true today (cf. Heb 12:5–11).

Notes

---

19 עַם הָאָרֶץ (ʿam hāʾāreṣ, "the people of the land") appears to represent the Judean community in exile, the audience of Ezekiel. Ezekiel uses the phrase in various ways: (1) mostly of the inhabitants of the land of Israel; (2) the people of a hypothetical land (33:2); (3) the commoners, in contrast to a king or the higher classes (7:27; 22:29; 45:16, 22); and (4) the Judeans in exile.

---

2. The faithfulness of God: the present judgment

12:21–28

> 21The word of the LORD came to me: 22"Son of man, what is this proverb you have in the land of Israel: 'The days go by and every vision comes to nothing'? 23Say to them, 'This is what the Sovereign LORD says: I am going to put an end to this proverb, and they will no longer quote it in Israel.' Say to them, 'The days are near when every vision will be fulfilled. 24For there will be no more false visions or flattering divinations among the people of Israel. 25But I the LORD will speak what I will, and it shall be fulfilled without delay. For in your days, you rebellious house, I will fulfill whatever I say, declares the Sovereign LORD.'"
> 26The word of the LORD came to me: 27"Son of man, the house of Israel is saying, 'The vision he sees is for many years from now, and he prophesies about the distant future.'
> 28"Therefore say to them, 'This is what the Sovereign LORD says: None of my words will be delayed any longer; whatever I say will be fulfilled, declares the Sovereign LORD.'"

21–25 Ezekiel confronted the exiles' rationalizations of his messages. It had become obvious that the apathy of his audiences had blunted their understanding of his symbolic acts and oracles (12:2).

These Jewish exiles did not think that Ezekiel's prophecies were valid. Through the proverb—"The days go by and every vision comes to nothing" (v.22)—the captives asserted that they believed all the previous judgments proclaimed by Isaiah, Micah et al. were not true, for they had not come to pass. Why should they now accept Ezekiel's prophecies as valid? Their outlook presumed on God's grace, long-suffering and forbearance. It showed an unbelief in God's immutability and the trustworthiness of his word as revealed in the Scriptures. It was only because of his grace that God had not disciplined Israel sooner. He had waited so Israel might change her mind and return to him. Instead, the people had strayed further, living in the fantasy of security when judgment was imminent (cf. 2 Peter 3:4). The people falsely believed that there would be a long time of peace ahead (v.22).

God declared that the exiles' proverb would be heard no more, for judgment was imminent. On the contrary, the Lord created a new proverb: "The days are near when every vision will be fulfilled" (v.23). The judgments that the Lord had promised both in the Law and the Prophets would be executed during the Exile. What God had said, he would do (v.25). It is tragic that mankind often learns this truth only through the experience of judgment or discipline. Judgment on Jerusalem would bring the false visions and deceptive divinations, by which the false prophets continually sought to encourage unscriptural ways, to an abrupt halt (v.24).

26–28 Others had believed Ezekiel's warning of judgment yet thought it would come, not in their lifetime, but in the distant future (vv.26–27). This attitude is always present, for even today no one wants to consider the idea that God might soon judge them or their nation. The same attitude relates to the second coming of Christ (cf. 2 Peter 3:4).

God's response to Judah was brief and to the point: Judgment would no longer be delayed! What God had said, he would do—and he would do it soon (v.28)!

3. The condemnation of contemporary false prophets (13:1–23)

a. Judgment on the prophets

13:1–16

> ¹The word of the LORD came to me: ²"Son of man, prophesy against the prophets of Israel who are now prophesying. Say to those who prophesy out of their own imagination: 'Hear the word of the LORD! ³This is what the Sovereign LORD says: Woe to the foolish prophets who follow their own spirit and have seen nothing! ⁴Your prophets, O Israel, are like jackals among ruins. ⁵You have not gone up to the breaks in the wall to repair it for the house of Israel so that it will stand firm in the battle on the day of the LORD. ⁶Their visions are false and their divinations a lie. They say, "The LORD declares," when the LORD has not sent them; yet they expect their words to be fulfilled. ⁷Have you not seen false visions and uttered lying divinations when you say, "The LORD declares," though I have not spoken?
>
> ⁸" 'Therefore this is what the Sovereign LORD says: Because of your false words and lying visions, I am against you, declares the Sovereign LORD. ⁹My hand will be against the prophets who see false visions and utter lying divinations. They will not belong to the council of my people or be listed in the records of the house of

Israel, nor will they enter the land of Israel. Then you will know that I am the Sovereign LORD.

¹⁰" 'Because they lead my people astray, saying, "Peace," when there is no peace, and because, when a flimsy wall is built, they cover it with whitewash, ¹¹therefore tell those who cover it with whitewash that it is going to fall. Rain will come in torrents, and I will send hailstones hurtling down, and violent winds will burst forth. ¹²When the wall collapses, will people not ask you, "Where is the whitewash you covered it with?"

¹³" 'Therefore this is what the Sovereign LORD says: In my wrath I will unleash a violent wind, and in my anger hailstones and torrents of rain will fall with destructive fury. ¹⁴I will tear down the wall you have covered with whitewash and will level it to the ground so that its foundation will be laid bare. When it falls, you will be destroyed in it; and you will know that I am the LORD. ¹⁵So I will spend my wrath against the wall and against those who covered it with whitewash. I will say to you, "The wall is gone and so are those who whitewashed it, ¹⁶those prophets of Israel who prophesied to Jerusalem and saw visions of peace for her when there was no peace, declares the Sovereign LORD.' "

1–7 In 12:21–28 Ezekiel spoke against the exiles' false security that led them to think that judgment was not imminent. They had received encouragement in this position by the visions and divinations of the many false prophets. Now Ezekiel would deliver God's denunciation on these prophets. Ezekiel was instructed to charge the prophets to listen to the Lord's word, not to their own hearts; for judgment ("woe") was about to be delivered against them for their foolish ways (vv.2–3).

Before the judgment verdict was delivered (vv.8–16), God clearly delineated the characteristics of the prophets that had brought this judgment on them (vv.4–7). The prophets were summarized as "foolish." The word "foolish" (*nābāl*) implied more than our concept of stupidity. It was a broad term that encompassed spiritual and moral insensitivity contrary to the nature of a wise man. The word was used to describe people who blasphemed (Ps 74:18), who were arrogant (1 Sam 25:25), who were atheistic (Ps 14:1), and who lacked self-discipline and humility. Ezekiel described the basic cause of their foolishness as their reliance on their own hearts and failure to seek God's revelation (cf. Jer 23:16–22; ch. 29).

These prophets had misled those who relied on them. The prophets followed their own desires, failing to care for the people and seeing the perversions of their own hearts as God's revelation. As prophets they saw visions, but these visions were false and full of lies (vv.6, 8; cf. 10, 16) because the prophets had really not seen anything at all (v.3). They used pagan practices of divination for every means (except God's revelation) to seek a message from God: watching the movement of stars, studying animals' internal organs, casting lots, etc. This only resulted in counterfeit statements that were deceitfully prefaced with the prophetic formula of divine authority: "The LORD declares." Yet the Lord had not spoken, nor had he sent them (vv.6–7). They were only speaking from their own perverse hearts (v.2; cf. Jer 17:9), hoping for a word of confirmation (v.6c) that never came. God emphatically denied that he had spoken through these men (v.7b).

These prophets followed their own spirit, not the Spirit of God (v.3). The desires of their fleshly spirits caused them to behave like "jackals among ruins" (v.4). Jackals loved to play among rubble, seeking dens for themselves. They did not care about the ruins. Neither did these prophets care about the people of Judah but made dens in their own self-interest. They played their own games of false prophecy that destroyed the people and the land. So they failed to prepare the people for the difficult times ahead or for the intense times in which they lived. Judah faced judgment and deportation unless the people turned to the Lord.

The prophets were to step in and repair the "breaks in the wall" (v.5) caused by violations of the Mosaic covenant. They were to exhort the people concerning the truths of that covenant in order to repair the breaks and protect the people from judgment. But they were negligent of their responsibilities. No one could be found to repair the "breaks" for God's people (22:30; cf. Ps 106:23). Moreover, they failed to secure the sanctuary with holiness so that it might stand in the battles of the "day of the LORD," viz., Nebuchadnezzar's invasion and siege of Jerusalem in which the temple would fall. Sinful abominations had been permitted in the temple due in part to the failure of these prophets to speak the truth and warn the people of the statutes and ordinances of the Mosaic covenant. In this context the "day of the LORD" did not imply the future eschatological judgment. The context of the passage argues that "the day of the LORD" was the immediate judgment by Babylon and the battles that would result from that punishment on contemporary Judah.

This, then, was the character of the prophets who had abused their gifts and offices and dulled the people's ears to the true message of Ezekiel and the other true prophets. Today there are also many "false prophets" ministering in religious places, leading people into judgment rather than turning them to Christ and the security of a life of peace with God and eternity with him (cf. 2 Cor 11:13–15).

8–16 The false prophets had failed as "watchmen" (cf. 3:16–21) over the nation of Judah, crying "peace" (v.10) when judgment was on the horizon. These prophets had an empty word to speak and had seen lies (vv.8–10, 16). God's verdict was simple and clear: "I am against you" (v.8). Ezekiel repeated the reasons for the judgment in repetitive statements.

These false prophets would be cut off from the people and have no part with the nation of Israel (v.9) because they had misled the people of Judah (v.10a). As prophets they had been in the hierarchy of the nation and in influential places, but they would no longer be in the council of God's people (cf. Jer 23:22). Instead, their names would be eliminated from the citizenry of Israel. They would not reenter the land of Israel when Israel would be restored from the Babylonian captivity (c. 539 B.C.). The purpose of this judgment was to cause the prophets to turn to the Lord and know that he existed as the only true God. The implication was that they still had an opportunity to repent and come to the Messiah in eternal salvation.

The judgment of the prophets was described in terms of their participation in "whitewashing" (vv.10b–16). The prophets had implemented their proclamations of peace through helping the people remodel their homes and decorate them in this time of false security. Some expositors look on the "walls" in this passage as symbolic, referring to the outer deception of the prophets. The "flimsy wall" (ḥayiṣ) may be seen as a metaphor for the prophets' flimsy prophecies of "peace," whitewashed over to make them look strong and substantial. This, however, would equate the two clauses in v.10 that lead to the conclusion of v.11. Moreover, a nonliteral interpretation is not required. If the prophets were declaring a time of peace and prosperity, it was not out of line for them to encourage home building. Consequently they had gone around plastering walls and helping people decorate the thin partitions of their homes. It was the confirmation of a "settle down and live" philosophy. However, God declared that these walls and their decorative plaster would fall beneath the raging rains of his anger and the hail and violent wind of his wrath.

When the walls would be destroyed, so also would the prophets be consumed in the destruction (vv. 10c–11, 13–14). No one would be concerned about house decorations then (v. 12). God would establish another new proverb: "The wall is gone and so are those who whitewashed it" (v. 15).

Many still are deceived by the false security of material prosperity that leads to obsession with house decorations, building, etc. Material prosperity is not the central issue of life. Christ alone and total obedience to all his commands—these are the central issues of life (Matt 28:18–20).

Notes

---

1 The contest between true and false prophets surfaces in Isa 28:7–10; 30:10–11; Jer 5:31; 6:13–14; 8:10–11; 14:13–15; 20:6; Amos 7:14; Mic 2:11; 3:5–7; and in the NT (cf. Jesus, Paul, Peter, and Jude).

2 The Hebrew מִלִּבָּם (*millibbām*, "imagination") has the basic meaning "heart," the inner man with its seat of emotion and decision.

5 יוֹם יהוה (*yôm YHWH*, "day of the LORD") is a day in which the Lord is in control, usually demonstrative of his power in victory over enemies. A good summary of interpretations is found in Elmer A. Martens, *God's Design* (Grand Rapids: Baker, 1981), pp. 125–30.

9 כְּתָב (*ketāb*, "listed") in this text has confused some. They interpret this word and its context to mean the "book of life" (Rev 3:5; 20:15), with its eternal implications. Others understand this term to refer to the citizen register of the nation of Israel as discussed in Ezra 2:62 and Neh 7:64 (cf. Isa 4:3). The latter position seems the best in light of the context about the prophets' loss of their influential role and their failure to return to the land after the Captivity. Thus part of the judgment on these prophets was their excommunication from citizenship in Israel. They probably did not participate in the "eternal book of life," but this text does not support the notion.

An intimate circle of trusted friends where one can receive counsel is conveyed by סוֹד (*sôd*, "council"). In this context Israel, God's people is depicted as that intimate circle from which the false prophets will be excluded (cf. Gen 49:6).

---

b. Judgment on the prophetesses

13:17–23

[17]"Now, son of man, set your face against the daughters of your people who prophesy out of their own imagination. Prophesy against them [18]and say, 'This is what the Sovereign LORD says: Woe to the women who sew magic charms on all their wrists and make veils of various lengths for their heads in order to ensnare people. Will you ensnare the lives of my people but preserve your own? [19]You have profaned me among my people for a few handfuls of barley and scraps of bread. By lying to my people, who listen to lies, you have killed those who should not have died and have spared those who should not live.

[20]"'Therefore this is what the Sovereign LORD says: I am against your magic charms with which you ensnare people like birds and I will tear them from your arms; I will set free the people that you ensnare like birds. [21]I will tear off your veils and save my people from your hands, and they will no longer fall prey to your power. Then you will know that I am the LORD. [22]Because you disheartened the righteous with your lies, when I had brought them no grief, and because you encouraged the wicked not to turn from their evil ways and so save their lives, [23]therefore you will no longer see false visions or practice divination. I will save my people from your hands. And then you will know that I am the LORD.'"

17-19 The Lord exhorted Ezekiel to turn and prophesy against the prophetesses who, like the false prophets, also had prophesied from their own hearts (v.17). These women were involved in divination and sorcery. Their practice of witchcraft was common in the ancient Near East—especially Babylonia and Egypt. But witchcraft was forbidden in the Mosaic covenant (Lev 19:26). The practice of the false prophetesses was to tie bands of cloth to their wrists and place veils over their heads as they cast spells over people's lives in order to bind them and hunt them down. These women caused the righteous to die and kept the wicked alive (v.18).

Barley and bread were also instruments of sorcery (v.19). Some have understood the bread and barley to represent the cheap payment these prophetesses would accept in return for their occult practices; but Hittite practices and later Syrian rituals demonstrate that divination was carried out with barley bread either as part of the pagan sacrificial ritual or as a means of determining whether the victim would live or die. The prophetesses, therefore, profaned God by misrepresentation. Though appearing to be God's prophetesses, they polluted his name when they used occult practices (cf. H.W.F. Saggs, "External Souls in the Old Testament [Ezk 13:17-21]," JSS [1974]:1-12).

These women not only had the power to kill people through their incantations, but they also lied to God's people. Because the Judeans listened to these lies, many died unnecessarily. This is not to say that the ultimate authority over life and death rested with these prophetesses, for that authority rests only with almighty God who alone grants permission for men to die (cf. Job 1-2).

20-23 These verses contain the judgment verdict Ezekiel announced against these prophetesses. God would tear off their cloth bands and their veils with which they hunted people and bound them. In doing so he would free the righteous in Judah from the grip of these witches and sorceresses (vv.20-21).

The Lord reasserted the reasons for the punishment that would come on these prophetesses (v.22). They had used deceptive and counterfeit means to dishearten the righteous, pulling them into their cultic snare and influence. At the same time they encouraged the wicked to disobey God's ways. When the righteous turned from his righteous ways, and when the wicked stayed in his wicked ways, both would die physically. This is what was happening.

Therefore, God would cause the false visions and cultic divinations of these false prophetesses to cease, delivering his people from their wicked hands (v.23). Regrettably many of God's people had followed them. But God would judge these women and free his righteous people. When he would do that, then these prophetesses would know that he was the ever-present one, the Lord, faithful and immutable. Again, judgment was designed to bring people to a knowledge of God.

Notes

18 יָדַי (yāḏay, "my hands"; NIV, "their wrists") presents a difficult textual problem. Two basic approaches are taken: (1) read יָד (yāḏ, "hand") with the LXX, Vulgate, Symmachus et al., understanding the final י (y, yod) as dittography for the following ו (w, waw); or (2) read יָדַיִם (yāḏayim, "hands") with a paucity of MSS from the collection of Kennicott and de Rossi, the Syriac, and the Targum, in which the final ם (m, mem) would have been

dropped in the MT due to scribal error. The former position has stronger MS evidence and seems preferable, with the singular noun viewed as generic.

Some understand כְּסָתוֹת (kᵉsātôt, "magic charms") to be derived from the Akkadian kasû ("to bind," "ban") (so Zimmerli). The noun form would mean "bandages" or "cords." Others interpret the term as "cushions" (so Greenberg). The exact meaning of the term is still obscure, though occult practices are clearly in view.

20 Similar magical charms are observed in execration texts of Egypt and cultic figurines found near Beit Jibrin in Palestine. The word לִפְרְחוֹת (lᵉpōrᵉhôt) is problematic. Most expositors have rendered the term as "like birds" (NIV) or "flying things." Three meanings may be used to translate this form: (1) "to bud or blossom" (Gen 40:10; Hos 14:8); (2) "to break out" (used with disease) (Exod 9:9–10; Lev 13:20; 14:43); or (3) "to fly." The normal rendering of the term is either "to bud" or "to break out" in disease. Therefore it seems best in this context to understand the term in the sense of seeking persons to inflict them with diseases, a practice in harmony with pagan witchcraft rituals. The prophetesses had sought people on whom they would inflict diseases that would result in death to some, cure for others.

---

4. The effect of the false prophets on the leaders

14:1–11

> ¹Some of the elders of Israel came to me and sat down in front of me. ²Then the word of the LORD came to me: ³"Son of man, these men have set up idols in their hearts and put wicked stumbling blocks before their faces. Should I let them inquire of me at all? ⁴Therefore speak to them and tell them, 'This is what the Sovereign LORD says: When any Israelite sets up idols in his heart and puts a wicked stumbling block before his face and then goes to a prophet, I the LORD will answer him myself in keeping with his great idolatry. ⁵I will do this to recapture the hearts of the people of Israel, who have all deserted me for their idols.'
>
> ⁶"Therefore say to the house of Israel, 'This is what the Sovereign LORD says: Repent! Turn from your idols and renounce all your detestable practices!
>
> ⁷" 'When any Israelite or any alien living in Israel separates himself from me and sets up idols in his heart and puts a wicked stumbling block before his face and then goes to a prophet to inquire of me, I the LORD will answer him myself. ⁸I will set my face against that man and make him an example and a byword. I will cut him off from my people. Then you will know that I am the LORD.
>
> ⁹" 'And if the prophet is enticed to utter a prophecy, I the LORD have enticed that prophet, and I will stretch out my hand against him and destroy him from among my people Israel. ¹⁰They will bear their guilt—the prophet will be as guilty as the one who consults him. ¹¹Then the people of Israel will no longer stray from me, nor will they defile themselves anymore with all their sins. They will be my people, and I will be their God, declares the Sovereign LORD.' "

1–2 Some of the Judean elders in the exile came before Ezekiel (v.1). These "responsible" leaders of the people came to seek clarification from Ezekiel about his denunciation of the prophets and to inquire from him what God's ways for them should be (cf. vv.3–4, 7, 9). Their lives and attitudes showed they had followed the false prophets and prophetesses (v.3).

3 These leaders of the people outwardly sought God's will by coming to Ezekiel, a true spokesman for the Lord, to inquire about his messages. At the same time, however, they inwardly were exalting idols on the throne of their hearts as the real gods of their lives (vv.3–4, 7). Theirs was a fickle, twofold allegiance. Their lust for

idols led to the elders' stumbling into sin. Their outward rebellion against God, their practice of pagan rituals, and their refusal to keep the Mosaic covenant showed their inward worship of these false gods. This verse is important for those who come to Scripture seeking guidance. No true direction can be given to those who have erected idols in their hearts.

How, asked the Lord, could these elders honestly consider consulting the true God when they were inwardly worshiping idols (cf. Ps 66:18)? How, in turn, should God respond to those who desire to serve both "God and Money" (Matt 6:24)?

4–11 The reply was in the form of a verdict introduced by "therefore" (*lākēn*, v.4). The Lord broadened his answer to include any person in Israel who may have harbored this dual allegiance; phrases like "any Israelite" and "house of Israel" (vv.4, 6–7) unmasked this hypocrisy. The elders represented the entire nation that had followed their leadership.

The Lord's reply was threefold: two portions related to the elders and the nation at large, while one was directed at the false prophets. In response to the elders, the Lord first declared that he would give them over to the many idols in their hearts (v.4). God did not do this out of vindictiveness but out of love, for he knew that satiation with idolatry was the only way for Israel to repent of her sin. The people would become nauseated with the emptiness and perversion of idolatry. God wanted to "recapture" their hearts that had become alienated from him through lust for these idolatrous practices (v.5). He wanted to convict them of sin so that they would heed his invitation to repent.

God not only purposes to convict sinners of their sin but also to bring them to his Messiah. Therefore the Lord lovingly exhorted these double-minded elders and their followers to "repent" and to turn from their idols and abominations to him (v.6). Instead of heart allegiance to idols, a heart allegiance to God was necessary.

The Lord's second response was directed toward those who had refused his invitation to repent (vv.7–8). If they did not heed this, God himself would answer their empty inquiry with action, not words. In fulfillment of the "curse" stipulations of the Mosaic covenant, God would set his face against these people, cut them off as citizens of Israel (cf. 13:9; Lev 20:3, 5–6), and make them "examples" and "bywords" for all nations to see his faithfulness in executing his covenant judgments (Deut 28:37). If they rejected the offer to repent, then the Lord would use judgments to cause them to know that he truly was the ever-present God of Israel.

Finally, the Lord turned to the prophets whose false visions and deceptive proclamations had misled the elders and people. If these false prophets were enticed to prophesy in any way other than that which God had given through Ezekiel, it would only be because God had permitted it (v.9a). God ultimately controls all things, even false prophets. He used them to condemn themselves and their listeners through their apostate proclamations (cf. v.6; 1 Kings 22:18–23). These prophets would receive the same punishment God would mete out to the fickle inquirers, for the iniquity of each was the same: idolatry (vv.9b–10; cf. v.8; 13:9). The Lord was never fickle. He consistently brought judgment on the idol worshipers in order to restore them to himself. Likewise, this judgment on the prophets was given so that the Israelites might no longer wander away from their Lord and defile themselves but that they might come into the relationship God had always desired them to have with him as his people. This relationship was continually expressed in the OT through the covenant formula: "They will be my people, and I will be their God" (v.11; cf. Exod 19:5–6; Lev 26:12; Jer 7:23; 31:33; Ezek 11:20; 37:28). God would remove the false prophets and leaders so that his people might be those who truly followed his ways as revealed in the Mosaic covenant.

Notes

---

5 As the verb תָּפַשׂ (*tepōś*, "recapture") conveys the forceful seizing of prisoners (1 Sam 15:8; 1 Kings 13:4) or an animal (Ezek 19:4, 8) and the conquest of a city (Deut 20:19; Josh 8:8) or parents seizing a rebellious son (Deut 21:19), so the Lord's heart for Israel to return to him is seen in his laying hold of those who have gone astray in idolatry.

6 The Hiphil form of the verb שׁוּב (*šûb*, "turn") is used twice in this verse (NIV has "renounce" the second time) to emphasize the initiative that is needed for a person to repent.

7 The inclusion of גֵּר (*gēr*, "alien") shows that the warning applied not only to the Israelite but also to all who came to live in Israel. Aliens were subject to the holy demands of the Mosaic covenant and were to submit to Yahweh as their God (cf. Lev 17:8–16; 20:2–7; 22:17–25).

---

5. *No deliverance apart from personal righteousness*

14:12–23

> ¹²The word of the LORD came to me: ¹³"Son of man, if a country sins against me by being unfaithful and I stretch out my hand against it to cut off its food supply and send famine upon it and kill its men and their animals, ¹⁴even if these three men—Noah, Daniel and Job—were in it, they could save only themselves by their righteousness, declares the Sovereign LORD.
>
> ¹⁵"Or if I send wild beasts through that country and they leave it childless and it becomes desolate so that no one can pass through it because of the beasts, ¹⁶as surely as I live, declares the Sovereign LORD, even if these three men were in it, they could not save their own sons or daughters. They alone would be saved, but the land would be desolate.
>
> ¹⁷"Or if I bring a sword against that country and say, 'Let the sword pass throughout the land,' and I kill its men and their animals, ¹⁸as surely as I live, declares the Sovereign LORD, even if these three men were in it, they could not save their own sons or daughters. They alone would be saved.
>
> ¹⁹"Or if I send a plague into that land and pour out my wrath upon it through bloodshed, killing its men and their animals, ²⁰as surely as I live, declares the Sovereign LORD, even if Noah, Daniel and Job were in it, they could save neither son nor daughter. They would save only themselves by their righteousness.
>
> ²¹"For this is what the Sovereign LORD says: How much worse will it be when I send against Jerusalem my four dreadful judgments—sword and famine and wild beasts and plague—to kill its men and their animals! ²²Yet there will be some survivors—sons and daughters who will be brought out of it. They will come to you, and when you see their conduct and their actions, you will be consoled regarding the disaster I have brought upon Jerusalem—every disaster I have brought upon it. ²³You will be consoled when you see their conduct and their actions, for you will know that I have done nothing in it without cause, declares the Sovereign LORD."

12–14 As the elders listened to Ezekiel's call to repentance (vv.1–11), some might have thought of Abraham's request (Gen 18) that God deliver Sodom if a sufficient number of righteous people were found there. Perhaps the Lord would do the same now for Jerusalem. Could his impending judgment on Jerusalem be diverted if some well-known righteous man or men could be found? Some immediately thought of Daniel, their contemporary, who was ministering before Nebuchadnezzar in the city of Babylon.

God's reply was negative. Jerusalem was more culpable than Sodom. A few righteous men would have delivered Sodom. Here none could turn away the wrath. God reminded the elders that any nation that was unfaithful to him and turned to other gods, such as they and the people of Israel had done with their idols (v.13; cf. vv.1–11), would be punished, since God was faithful to his covenant curses as well as to his covenant promises (Lev 26:22–26). Each individual and each land was responsible for its own standing before God. Only the personal righteous deeds of each individual would deliver him in a time of judgment (v.14).

15–20 Ezekiel illustrated his point through four common vehicles of judgment: beasts, the sword, disease, and famine. If any one of these judgments were to come on the land—and they *would* according to Leviticus 26:22–26—not even the personal righteousness of a Noah, a Daniel, or a Job would be able to deliver another person from judgment (vv.15–20). They would not even be able to deliver members of their own families. These three men were used as illustrations because of their righteous character. The righteousness of Noah (Gen 6:9), Job (Job 1:1, 8; 2:3), and Daniel (Dan 6:4–5, 22) delivered each of them respectively out of the dangers they faced; but each had little effect on his contemporary situation. They delivered no one else but themselves. Seldom were righteous men able to turn away God's wrath from a nation (cf. 22:30; Ps 106:23). A vicarious deliverance from individual sin, however, is impossible, except for the singular *eternal* vicarious deliverance provided by Jesus the Messiah in his substitutionary death for all sins (cf. John 14:6; Acts 4:12; 2 Cor 5:21). He alone can deliver others because of his death for their sin and his resurrection from the dead.

21–23 Judah's current situation was no exception (v.21). God would send his four severe judgments (sword, famine, beasts, and diseases) against Jerusalem. But to vindicate his justice before the exiles, the Lord would spare a small remnant of unrepentant Hebrews and send them into exile in Babylonia (v.22). Some commentators view this remnant as a righteous remnant, but the context and the consistent use of the term "actions" (*ᵃlîlāh*) in an evil sense throughout the OT when referring to mankind argues for an unrighteous remnant. This was strictly a manifestation of God's grace. When these unrighteous people would go into exile in Babylonia, the exiles already in Babylonia would observe their deeds and see how wicked the Judeans had become. Through this the exiles would be consoled that God was perfectly just in his judgment on Jerusalem (vv.22–23). As the exiles saw that the Judge of all the earth did right (Gen 18:25), they would be comforted in their sorrow over what had happened to Jerusalem.

Notes

14 Some commentators reject any reference to the historical, biblical Daniel of the Book of Daniel in the term דָנִאֵל (*dāni'ēl*, "Daniel"). They argue that the word in the Book of Daniel (Dan 1:6) is written דָנִיֵּאל (*dāniyē'l*, "Daniel") whereas this different term probably refers to the Danel of the Ugaritic mythological material excavated at Ras Shamra (so Taylor). The OT, however, never refers to this mythological "Danel," nor would the referral to a pagan character as a display of God's righteousness along with Noah and Job be at all in harmony with the work of a true prophet nor with the nature of the righteousness of the Mosaic covenant, which is relevant. H.H.P. Dressler ("The Identification of the Ugaritic Dnil with the Daniel of Ezekiel," VetTest 29 [1979]: 152–61) argues well that the Ugaritic Dnil is not portrayed in the Aqhat Text as wise, righteous, a king, or able to save his son(s) or daughter(s). In addition Dnil was a worshiper of pagan deities, which would be opposed to the "antiidolatry" righteousness of this chapter (cf. contra John Day, "The Daniel of Ugarit and Ezekiel and the Hero of the Book of Daniel," VetTest 30 [1980]: 174–84). Moreover, an orthographical difference between the name as represented in this passage and that in the Book of Daniel is common: viz., the omission of the internal letter yod. However, the doubling of the yod (as found in the Book of Daniel) lacks explanation. E. Lipiski, in his review of Andre Lacocque's *Le Livre de Daniel* (in the book review section of VetTest 28 [1978]: 233–39), points out that the Masoretic pointing and the Greek transcription Δανιὴλ (*Daniēl*) demonstrate that the West Semitic name was vocalized "Daniel," not "Danel," as early as the eighteenth century B.C.

22 When the OT uses עֲלִילָה (*ᵃlîlāh*, "action"), it consistently has an evil connotation in reference to mankind. However, it retains a nuance of good when referring to God. The term is used more in Ezekiel than in any other OT book. Elsewhere in Ezekiel the word is in a definite context of evil. Therefore it should be taken in the same sense in this verse.

6. *Jerusalem, an unprofitable vine*

15:1–8

¹The word of the LORD came to me: ²"Son of man, how is the wood of a vine better than that of a branch on any of the trees in the forest? ³Is wood ever taken from it to make anything useful? Do they make pegs from it to hang things on? ⁴And after it is thrown on the fire as fuel and the fire burns both ends and chars the middle, is it then useful for anything? ⁵If it was not useful for anything when it was whole, how much less can it be made into something useful when the fire has burned it and it is charred?

⁶"Therefore this is what the Sovereign LORD says: As I have given the wood of the vine among the trees of the forest as fuel for the fire, so will I treat the people living in Jerusalem. ⁷I will set my face against them. Although they have come out of the fire, the fire will yet consume them. And when I set my face against them, you will know that I am the LORD. ⁸I will make the land desolate because they have been unfaithful, declares the Sovereign LORD."

1–5 This parable implies that the exiles had asked about God's consistency. They understood that they were his chosen people, his choice vine. How could he destroy them? They had been through the fire of two invasions and deportations by the Babylonians, but each time they had endured and sprouted up again. They did not believe that God's judgments would destroy Judah as Ezekiel had proclaimed.

The parable shows the worthlessness of a vine except for bearing fruit. Its wood was too soft, weak, and crooked for building. It was not even fit for making a peg to hang some utensil or clothing on (vv.2–3). If a vine was naturally of so little value, it certainly could not be expected to be useful when charred by fire (vv.4–5).

6–8 These verses provide the interpretation of this parable, centering, as was normal, on its major concepts. In the parable the inhabitants of Jerusalem were likened to the vine, a common OT symbol for the nation of Israel (v.6; Gen 49:22; Ps 80; Isa 5:1–7; Jer 2:21; Hos 10:1). Just as the vine was profitable only for fruit bearing, so Judah and Jerusalem were to be fruitful. The nation never was like other nations (trees) in military strength and riches except when they were trusting in the Lord (cf. David's reign). God had chosen Israel to be a blessing to the nations (Gen 12:1–3), though throughout her history she never had been very fruitful in this respect. Israel had been as unproductive as an uncultivated vine. Now, having experienced the fire of God's judgment through the Babylonian invasions and deportations of 605 B.C. and 597 B.C., her value was entirely gone. She was worthless as a fruit bearer (a blessing to the nations). She was fit only as fuel for fire. The Lord would return her to the fire of his discipline when Nebuchadnezzar would burn Jerusalem in 586 B.C. (v.7). The inhabitants of Jerusalem would be devoured (v.6), and the land would then lie desolate (v.8; cf. 2 Kings 25:9; Ps 66:12).

The reason for this fiery judgment was once more made clear: Judah had been unfaithful to the Lord and his covenant. They had failed to be a blessing to the world. They had disobeyed God's ordinances and had sinned. They were worthless and useless because of their idolatry. Graciously, the exiles could still be useful and fruitful for God, but only if they remained faithful to him. This principle still applies. In order to cause them to return to himself, the Lord brought this ruin on those living in Jerusalem. Through this judgment the exiles would know that he was their ever-present God (v.7). It was this gracious, loving purpose of God's judgments that the exiles had failed to understand in questioning his consistency. So he disciplined his chosen people to make them fruitful instead of unproductive (cf. John 15:1–16).

Notes

2 גֶּפֶן (gepen, "vine") is the normal term used throughout the OT for a fruit-bearing vine. Some commentators seek to distinguish the vine in this passage from the normal symbol of a vine used to depict Israel, but neither the word nor its OT context warrants this differentiation. Another term sometimes used to represent Israel as a "choice fruitful vine" is שׂוֹרֵק (śôrēq), but this in no way conflicts with gepen.

זְמוֹרָה (zᵉmôrāh, "branch") is commonly used in the OT to indicate a twig or branch pruned from a tree or vine. The comparison of the uselessness of the vine to a pruned branch enhances the worthlessness of the vine.

3 The term יָתֵד (yāṯēḏ, "peg") is used for a tent peg or a wall peg. Sometimes it is used figuratively of a person who is reliable (Isa 22:23–25; Zech 10:4).

7. *Jerusalem's history as a prostitute* (16:1–63)

a. *The birth of Jerusalem*

16:1–5

> ¹The word of the LORD came to me: ²"Son of man, confront Jerusalem with her detestable practices ³and say, 'This is what the Sovereign LORD says to Jerusalem: Your ancestry and birth were in the land of the Canaanites; your father was an Amorite and your mother a Hittite. ⁴On the day you were born your cord was not cut, nor were you washed with water to make you clean, nor were you rubbed with salt or wrapped in cloths. ⁵No one looked on you with pity or had compassion enough to do any of these things for you. Rather, you were thrown out into the open field, for on the day you were born you were despised.

1–2 The exiles were unconvinced by the parable of the vine (ch. 15). They were not persuaded that Judah was as worthless and useless as the parable implied. Ezekiel must be mistaken. Certainly, they thought, the vine of Israel may have done a few things wrong in her past; but she was chosen of God and could not be as worthy of judgment as Ezekiel implied. Therefore, the Lord instructed him to "confront Jerusalem with her detestable practices" (v.2). Ezekiel would show just how corrupt Israel's history was by tracing Jerusalem's history. Verse 2 is strategic in interpreting this chapter; it emphasizes that God was dealing with Jerusalem. Though Jerusalem was the capital of the nation, the passage does not warrant an interpretation that sees this chapter discussing only the history of the nation as a whole. The history given was that of Jerusalem, which became the capital of Israel and the symbol of the nation (as Washington is metonymy for the United States). The concept that must be remembered is that this is not strictly a history of Israel. Likewise, every facet of the allegory need not be interpreted for allegories, like parables, seek to communicate a basic truth. It was the purpose of this allegory to show to the exilic leaders all the terrible abominations that had brought the impending judgment on their capital, Jerusalem. Needless to say, the abominations of Jerusalem pervaded the nation, and the judgments she would experience would likewise affect all Judah.

Some people are offended by the stark realism of this chapter. However, God is always straightforward about life. The realism of Israel's history demands an accurate and vivid analogy (cf. Hosea).

3 Jerusalem was conceived by the Amorites and the Hittites in the land of Canaan. This was not a spiritual birth (so Feinberg) but a physical one. The city was not founded by the Hebrews but by the heathen peoples of Canaan. The reference to Jerusalem's father as an Amorite and her mother as a Hittite has stirred much debate among expositors. However, the thrust of the passage is to show how the city came into being. This was accomplished by the Amorites and the Hittites, for the land of Canaan was also known biblically as the land of the Amorites and the land of the Hittites, especially when the discussion concerned the hill country of Judah and the city of Jerusalem (Gen 10:16; 15:16; Num 13:29; Josh 1:4; 5:1; 7:7; 24:15, 18; Amos 2:10). Jerusalem was a Jebusite city when the children of Israel entered the land under Joshua (Josh 15:8, 63) and a member of the Amorite league joined together against the Hebrews at Gibeon (Josh 5:1).

4–5 Jerusalem had been treated in a manner similar to a child left to exposure on birth. It was the custom in the ancient Near East to wash a newborn child, rub it with salt for antiseptic reasons, and wrap it in cloths, changing these twice by the fortieth day after the umbilical cord was cut. Such common treatment was not given to Jerusalem, by analogy, in her beginning. She was a foundering city, uncared for by the people of Canaan or by Israel in the conquest of the land, for the Hebrews failed to conquer the city of Jebus (Josh 15:63). In fact, they allowed this city to lie as an unwanted child throughout the period of the Judges (vv.4–5). It was a widespread custom in the ancient Near East to eliminate unwanted children (esp. girls) by exposing them (cf. ANET, p. 119).

Notes

---

4 The term לְמָשְׁעִי (*lᵉmišʿî*, "to make clean") is a *hapax legomenon,* and therefore its meaning is questionable. Most Semiticists relate the word to the Assyrian *mišu,* meaning "to cleanse, wash," and would point to a similar Arabic root and the rendering in the Targum that have the same sense.

5 תֻּשְׁלְכִי (*tušlᵉkî*, "thrown out") is argued to mean "expose" by M. Cogan, "Technical Term for Exposure," JNES 27 (1968): 133ff.

---

b. *The Lord's courtship and marriage to Jerusalem*

16:6–14

> ⁶"Then I passed by and saw you kicking about in your blood, and as you lay there in your blood I said to you, "Live!" ⁷I made you grow like a plant of the field. You grew up and developed and became the most beautiful of jewels. Your breasts were formed and your hair grew, you who were naked and bare.
>
> ⁸' 'Later I passed by, and when I looked at you and saw that you were old enough for love, I spread the corner of my garment over you and covered your nakedness. I gave you my solemn oath and entered into a covenant with you, declares the Sovereign Lᴏʀᴅ, and you became mine.
>
> ⁹' 'I bathed you with water, and washed the blood from you and put ointments on you. ¹⁰I clothed you with an embroidered dress and put leather sandals on you. I dressed you in fine linen and covered you with costly garments. ¹¹I adorned you with jewelry: I put bracelets on your arms and a necklace around your neck, ¹²and I put a ring on your nose, earrings on your ears and a beautiful crown on your head. ¹³So you were adorned with gold and silver; your clothes were of fine linen and costly fabric and embroidered cloth. Your food was fine flour, honey and olive oil. You became very beautiful and rose to be a queen. ¹⁴And your fame spread among the nations on account of your beauty, because the splendor I had given you made your beauty perfect, declares the Sovereign Lᴏʀᴅ.

6 The Lord saw Jerusalem in her ignoble condition and sent David, the newly anointed king over Israel (2 Sam 5:6–10), to rescue her from the Jebusites and her maltreatment. God determined Jerusalem's destiny when he found her and stressed that she would live!

7 Once delivered, Jerusalem received the blessings and benefits of the Lord, her lover. He promised to increase her population like the plants of the field. Under his gracious care Jerusalem grew to full maturity (puberty) as a city. Though she had reached marriageable age, she was still "naked and bare."

8–14 The Lord visited Jerusalem and claimed her in marriage by spreading his garment over her (v.8; cf. Ruth 3:9). He entered into a marriage covenant with Jerusalem (cf. Prov 2:17; Mal 2:14) as described in Psalm 132:13–17. She became the Lord's city where he dwelt when David brought the ark of the covenant to Jerusalem and purchased the threshing floor of Arunah, the Jebusite (2 Sam 6; 24), in preparation for the temple's construction. As a groom to his bride, God lavished marriage gifts on Jerusalem (vv.10–13; cf. Gen 24:53; Ps 45:13–15; Isa 61:10): ornaments, cleansing, anointing, costly garments, jewelry, a crown, and fine foods. She was made exceedingly beautiful and advanced to royalty under the reigns of David and Solomon. Her fame and beauty became renowned throughout the ancient Near East as the capital of the leading nation of that day (v.14; 1 Kings 10; Lam 2:15). Some maintain that this "rags-to-riches" motif was a popular oriental tale (so Taylor), but this view lacks supporting evidence.

Notes

---

7 Some commentators emend the opening words of this verse to make it read, with the LXX, "Live and grow up; like a plant of the field I have made you." The MT makes good sense without following this conjecture.

10 שַׁחַת (*tāḥaš*, "leather sandals") seems to be related to the Egyptian *tḥs* ("to stretch hide, leather"). It portrays a fine leather of the kind used in the tabernacle (Exod 26:14; Num 4:25). In the present context the finest of clothing is being stressed.

---

c. *Jerusalem's prostitution with other lands and gods*

16:15–34

15" 'But you trusted in your beauty and used your fame to become a prostitute. You lavished your favors on anyone who passed by and your beauty became his. 16You took some of your garments to make gaudy high places, where you carried on your prostitution. Such things should not happen, nor should they ever occur. 17You also took the fine jewelry I gave you, the jewelry made of my gold and silver, and you made for yourself male idols and engaged in prostitution with them. 18And you took your embroidered clothes to put on them, and you offered my oil and incense before them. 19Also the food I provided for you—the fine flour, olive oil and honey I gave you to eat—you offered as fragrant incense before them. That is what happened, declares the Sovereign LORD.

20" 'And you took your sons and daughters whom you bore to me and sacrificed them as food to the idols. Was your prostitution not enough? 21You slaughtered my children and sacrificed them to the idols. 22In all your detestable practices and your prostitution you did not remember the days of your youth, when you were naked and bare, kicking about in your blood.

23" 'Woe! Woe to you, declares the Sovereign LORD. In addition to all your other wickedness, 24you built a mound for yourself and made a lofty shrine in every public square. 25At the head of every street you built your lofty shrines and degraded your beauty, offering your body with increasing promiscuity to anyone who passed by. ²⁶You engaged in prostitution with the Egyptians, your lustful neighbors, and provoked me to anger with your increasing promiscuity. ²⁷So I stretched out my hand against you and reduced your territory; I gave you over to the greed of your enemies, the daughters of the Philistines, who were shocked by your lewd conduct. ²⁸You engaged in prostitution with the Assyrians too, because you were insatiable; and even after that, you still were not satisfied. ²⁹Then you increased your promiscuity to include Babylonia, a land of merchants, but even with this you were not satisfied.

³⁰" 'How weak-willed you are, declares the Sovereign LORD, when you do all these things, acting like a brazen prostitute! ³¹When you built your mounds at the head of every street and made your lofty shrines in every public square, you were unlike a prostitute, because you scorned payment.

³²" 'You adulterous wife! You prefer strangers to your own husband! ³³Every prostitute receives a fee, but you give gifts to all your lovers, bribing them to come to you from everywhere for your illicit favors. ³⁴So in your prostitution you are the opposite of others; no one runs after you for your favors. You are the very opposite, for you give payment and none is given to you.

15 God had warned Israel not to forget him when she came into all the benefits that he would give her in the Promised Land (Deut 6:10–12). This exhortation was soon forgotten by the nation's leaders. No sooner had the Lord crowned Jerusalem with beauty and fame as his bride than she began to trust in her beauty rather than in God who gave it to her. She began to commit spiritual adultery with every nation. Solomon led Israel, the dominant nation of her day, contrary to God's way of faith by making treaties with many nations (cf. Deut 17:14–20; 1 Kings 11:1–13). It was customary to seal international treaties with a marriage. Solomon's many foreign wives attested to his reliance on these treaties rather than on the Lord. This led to his worship of the foreign gods of his wives. The emphasis came to be on externals and material objects. The very gifts God had given to Jerusalem had become the means of her downfall, for she loved the gifts rather than the giver.

16–22 From rebellion under Solomon, when Jerusalem's eyes turned away from God to the world's things, Jerusalem, as the capital of Israel, gradually led her nation down the path of corruption. The gifts of God were not inherently evil. However, Jerusalem became married to the gifts rather than to the Lord. She constructed pagan high places for worship and decorated them with her garments and committed adultery against God on them (v.16; 2 Kings 23:7). She formed male images from her precious metals and clothed them with her exquisite textiles. She fornicated by worshiping them with incense, libations, and offerings (vv.17–19; Jer 10:9). Such pagan rituals were practiced in Mesopotamia (cf. Helmer Ringgren, *Religions of the Ancient Near East* [Philadelphia: Westminster, 1973], pp. 81–89) and in Egypt (cf. J. Cerny, *Ancient Egyptian Religion* [London: Hutchinson's University Library, 1952], pp. 101–2).

Worst of all, Jerusalem offered her children in sacrifice to these idols, as was common in the worship of the pagan deity Molech (2 Kings 16:3; 21:6; 23:10; Jer 32:35). This was contrary to the Mosaic covenant (Lev 18:21)! She entered into every kind of religious abomination practiced among the heathen peoples (vv.20–21). She had forgotten what God had done for her in her youth when she had nothing and deserved nothing. She forgot that he rescued her from a despicable state and elevated her to royalty and beauty (v.22). This commentary on the perversion of Jerusalem is both heartbreaking and convicting. Many believers today tend to forget what Christ has done for them on the cross and all the blessings he has poured out on them (Eph 1:3).

23–25 It would have been enough if Jerusalem had simply entered into the abominatons of the pagan religions, but she became a militant advocate of these heathen practices. Jerusalem established pagan high places and mounds for abominable worship in every street. She took the initiative to offer herself lewdly as a prostitute by inviting every false religious ritual to come and have an intimate part of her syncretistic spiritual adultery. In doing so she made her God-given beauty detestable (vv.23–25). So God began to declare his "woe" on Jerusalem as she broke his heart with her prostitution (v.23).

26–30 Jerusalem also began to play the prostitute with Egypt. Egypt had lusted after Israel throughout the united kingdom period. Then Jeroboam I and others prostituted themselves with Egypt (v.26; 2 Kings 17:4; 18:21; Isa 30:7; 36:2), though prophets like Hosea and Isaiah condemned this spiritual and political adultery. Jerusalem sought political relations with foreign nations rather than security in her God. This angered the Lord so that he delivered Jerusalem into the hands of the Philistines and caused Jerusalem to lose portions of the territory she had ruled over (v.27; cf. Jehoram et al., 2 Chron 21:16–17; 28:18; Isa 1:7–8). Though this should have caused Jerusalem to reevaluate her sinful ways, she blatantly continued her harlotry, having political "relations" with Assyria and Babylonia. Yet her desires were never satisfied (vv.28–29). Ahaz sought relations with Assyria (2 Kings 15:19–20; 16:7–18); and overtures to Babylonia were made even during the reign of Hezekiah (2 Kings 20:12–19), though Isaiah rebuked the leaders for these political desires (Isa 20:5–6; 30:1–5; 31:1). Political relations with Assyria and Babylonia normally brought also the demand to worship their gods.

30–34 The Lord cried out to Jerusalem, condemning their weakness in soliciting suitors in his place (vv.30–34). Because of the weakness of her heart relationship with God, she, as an unfaithful wife, had sought out strangers (nations) with whom she would have her "relations" instead of with the Lord, her husband (v.32). Instead of the normal practice of receiving gifts, or pay, for her services as a prostitute, Jerusalem was different in that she solicited these strangers (nations) (v.34). She bribed or paid them in order to secure intimate relationships with them (cf. Hos 8:9). God summarized: Jerusalem has a rebellious and disobedient heart of infidelity (v.30). She is without excuse!

Notes

25 תְּפַשְּׂקִי אֶת־רַגְלַיִךְ (tᵉpaśśᵉqî 'et-raglayik, "offering your body") literally means "you spread apart your feet," the opening of something that is usually closed. This is only one of many graphic expressions that show how utterly despicable was Jerusalem's conduct.

29 The term כְּנַעַן (kᵉna'an, "merchant") is not used in the geographical sense but as an appelative noun in the commercial nuance of "merchant," e.g., 17:4; Zeph 1:11. The appositional relation of this word to כַּשְׂדִּימָה (kaśdîmāh, "Chaldea") likewise argues for use of kᵉna'an in this way, since the Babylonians were known as merchants.

30 Jerusalem is characterized by the figure of a prostitute who is שַׁלֶּטֶת (*šallāṭet*, "brazen"). This term normally has the sense of "headstrong," "domineering," though the Arabic *salîtat* is rendered "loud-tongued."

33 The gifts Jerusalem gave to solicit her lovers are called נְדָנַיִךְ (*nᵉḏānayik*, "your gifts"), which is probably a loanword from the Akkadian *nudunnu*. This Akkadian term means "gift," especially the marriage gift from a husband (maybe dowry). The Talmud renders this term as a bridal outfit given to a daughter by her father. Jerusalem appears to be giving away her bridal gifts from the Lord in order to seduce lovers to have relations with her.

---

d. Jerusalem: judged a prostitute

16:35–43

35" 'Therefore, you prostitute, hear the word of the Lord! 36This is what the Sovereign Lord says: Because you poured out your wealth and exposed your nakedness in your promiscuity with your lovers, and because of all your detestable idols, and because you gave them your children's blood, 37therefore I am going to gather all your lovers, with whom you found pleasure, those you loved as well as those you hated. I will gather them against you from all around and will strip you in front of them, and they will see all your nakedness. 38I will sentence you to the punishment of women who commit adultery and who shed blood; I will bring upon you the blood vengeance of my wrath and jealous anger. 39Then I will hand you over to your lovers, and they will tear down your mounds and destroy your lofty shrines. They will strip you of your clothes and take your fine jewelry and leave you naked and bare. 40They will bring a mob against you, who will stone you and hack you to pieces with their swords. 41They will burn down your houses and inflict punishment on you in the sight of many women. I will put a stop to your prostitution, and you will no longer pay your lovers. 42Then my wrath against you will subside and my jealous anger will turn away from you; I will be calm and no longer angry.

43" 'Because you did not remember the days of your youth but enraged me with all these things, I will surely bring down on your head what you have done, declares the Sovereign Lord. Did you not add lewdness to all your other detestable practices?

35–41 Judgment was declared on Jerusalem (v.35). She had indulged in obscene, spiritual adultery with the nations and their perverse idols (v.36). The Lord would now use these very nations she had played the harlot with as instruments to discipline her (v.37; cf. ch. 25). Those nations Jerusalem had truly loved in fornication and those she had hated God would use to strip her bare of all her riches and blessings so that all might see the barrenness and nakedness of Jerusalem and Judah without God's blessing (vv.37–39). These foreign nations would judge her and make her pay the penalty for adultery and infanticide as set forth in the Mosaic covenant: death (v.38; Exod 21:12; stoning, Lev 20:10). They would mockingly destroy her brothels (places of idolatry), tear off her clothes (cf. Hos 2:12; Nah 3:5), and spoil her garments so that she stood naked for all to see (v.39). Then she would be tried, stoned, and cut in pieces (v.40). Her houses would be burned (v.41) as these nations executed God's justice on her as one who practiced idolatry in contradiction to the law (Deut 13:12–18). This would not be a private discipline but rather a public one, executed before many women, or "nations," in harmony with the figure at hand.

42–43 This punishment would ultimately be accomplished by the Babylonian invasion of 586 B.C. under Nebuchadnezzar. Thereby Jerusalem's idolatrous abominations would cease. She would lie in burned ruins. The remnant of her population would be taken captive into Babylonia. There the Israelites would turn from idolatry to monotheism, learning the lesson God's judgment was designed to teach. At that time God's wrath would also cease against Jerusalem, for his justice would have been satisfied (v. 42). Jerusalem had forgotten God. In order that she might remember him once again, God would bring this discipline on her. Though mankind may forget God, his love prevents him from forgetting his own (v. 43). God takes his commitments in personal relationships seriously.

e. The perversion of Jerusalem

16:44–58

44" 'Everyone who quotes proverbs will quote this proverb about you: "Like mother, like daughter." 45You are a true daughter of your mother, who despised her husband and her children; and you are a true sister of your sisters, who despised their husbands and their children. Your mother was a Hittite and your father an Amorite. 46Your older sister was Samaria, who lived to the north of you with her daughters; and your younger sister, who lived to the south of you with her daughters, was Sodom. 47You not only walked in their ways and copied their detestable practices, but in all your ways you soon became more depraved than they. 48As surely as I live, declares the Sovereign LORD, your sister Sodom and her daughters never did what you and your daughters have done.

49" 'Now this was the sin of your sister Sodom: She and her daughters were arrogant, overfed and unconcerned; they did not help the poor and needy. 50They were haughty and did detestable things before me. Therefore I did away with them as you have seen. 51Samaria did not commit half the sins you did. You have done more detestable things than they, and have made your sisters seem righteous by all these things you have done. 52Bear your disgrace, for you have furnished some justification for your sisters. Because your sins were more vile than theirs, they appear more righteous than you. So then, be ashamed and bear your disgrace, for you have made your sisters appear righteous.

53" 'However, I will restore the fortunes of Sodom and her daughters and of Samaria and her daughters, and your fortunes along with them, 54so that you may bear your disgrace and be ashamed of all you have done in giving them comfort. 55And your sisters, Sodom with her daughters and Samaria with her daughters, will return to what they were before; and you and your daughters will return to what you were before. 56You would not even mention your sister Sodom in the day of your pride, 57before your wickedness was uncovered. Even so, you are now scorned by the daughters of Edom and all her neighbors and the daughters of the Philistines—all those around you who despise you. 58You will bear the consequences of your lewdness and your detestable practices, declares the LORD.

44–48 Ezekiel changed the figure slightly at this point to make a comparison between Jerusalem, Sodom, and Samaria. These three cities were likened to three sisters. All were the offspring of their Hittite mother and Amorite father (cf. comment at vv. 1–5). In what manner their mother, the Hittites, despised her husband and children is not clear. It may be that she too had rejected the Lord and had sacrificed her children to idols. However, the emphasis of the allegory was to demonstrate the abominable degradation of sin that characterized the land of Canaan, for Canaan was renowned for her religious syncretism in which she experimented with every kind of idolatry and religious perversion.

A common proverb applied to these three cities: "Like mother, like daughter" (v.44). This saying was equivalent to our "Like father, like son." Jerusalem, Sodom, and Samaria had all been nourished in the perverted religious systems of the land of Canaan, and now they were characterized by their parents' wickedness. However, Jerusalem became the preeminent sister in spiritual abominations and wickedness (v.45). Though Samaria was Jerusalem's "older" (greater) sister to the north in greatness in strength and military might and Sodom (Gen 10:19) was Jerusalem's "younger" (smaller) sister to the south in prestige and strength, Jerusalem had outstripped them both in her depravity and rebellion against God (v.46). Though both sisters were known for their wickedness, Jerusalem had become more corrupt than either of them (vv.47–48).

49–50 Sodom's chief sin had been pride and self-exaltation. This stemmed from her abundant materialism (food), given to her from God (Gen 13:10), which had resulted in false security, apathy, a luxurious life of ease, and the corollary disdain and neglect of the poor and needy (v.49). This material ease fostered sexual perversion (Gen 13:13; 18:20; 19:4–5). This passage stands as both an exhortation and a warning against such wickedness and life styles today. As evil as Sodom was, she did not begin to do evil like Jerusalem. (Jeremiah described how the prophets of Jerusalem committed adultery, lied, and encouraged evildoers so that none turned from their wickedness, just like Sodom [Jer 23:14; cf. 2 Kings 15:37; 16:6; 24:2; 2 Chron 28:18–19; Isa 3:9; Ezek 22:15].) If God removed Sodom in judgment, as he did, certainly Jerusalem would receive greater punishment (vv.48, 50; Lam 4:6; cf. Matt 11:23–24).

51–52 Jerusalem had sinned twice as much as Samaria, the wicked capital of the northern kingdom, which had already gone into captivity because of her abominations before God (v.51; 1 Kings 12:25–33; 15:30; 16:20, 26, 31–34). Jerusalem's wickedness was so perverse that she caused Sodom and Samaria with all their evil to appear righteous by comparison (v.52).

53–58 Judgment would come on Jerusalem. Just as haughty Jerusalem abhorred Sodom when she was a byword among the nations because of her corruption, so Jerusalem would be a similar byword in her day to Edom (or Aram) and Philistia. They, and other nations, would despise her (vv.56–57). Jerusalem's only hope as she bore this reproach for her abominations (v.58) was the promise that God would restore her from her captivity in the future. God would not only restore Jerusalem, but he would also restore Sodom and Samaria in that day when he brings restoration to the land of Canaan (vv.53–54; cf. ch. 36). Their restoration, along with Jerusalem, would humble Jerusalem and humiliate her for all her wickedness.

Notes

45 The construction אֲחוֹת אֲחוֹתֵךְ (*'ăḥôt 'ăḥôtēk*, "sister of your sisters") indicates the superlative genitive in the bound construction. The construction signifies that Jerusalem is the preeminent sister among the sister-cities when it comes to participation in corrupt abominations.

46 The phrases אֲחוֹתֵךְ הַגְּדוֹלָה (*ʾăḥôṯēḵ haggᵉḏôlāh*, "your older sister") and אֲחוֹתֵךְ הַקְּטַנָּה (*ʾăḥôṯēḵ haqqᵉṭannāh*, "your younger sister") mean literally "your great sister" and "your small sister," respectively. Though these two constructions are idiomatic for "older" (greater) and "younger" (smaller), Ezekiel used the idioms properly within the figure, but with an emphasis on the literal meaning of the words. The play on the idioms stresses that Samaria was greater than Jerusalem and Sodom smaller than Jerusalem.

57 The MT reads אֲרָם (*ʾărām*, "Aram" or "Syria"), though many translate the word as אֱדֹם (*ʾᵉḏōm*, "Edom") following the Syriac and the multiplicity of MSS. Those who accept the reading as "Edom" point to the ease of a copyist's error in writing ר (*r*) or ד (*d*) and to the fact that the Arameans were no longer in existence as a threatening nation at Ezekiel's time. This presumes that the reproach of Jerusalem by the nation mentioned in this term was to occur either simultaneously with or subsequent to Ezekiel's ministry. This, then, would argue against maintaining the MT reading of "Aram" in preference to Edom (cf. 25:15).

---

f. Restoration: the promise of love

16:59–63

> 59 " 'This is what the Sovereign LORD says: I will deal with you as you deserve, because you have despised my oath by breaking the covenant. 60Yet I will remember the covenant I made with you in the days of your youth, and I will establish an everlasting covenant with you. 61Then you will remember your ways and be ashamed when you receive your sisters, both those who are older than you and those who are younger. I will give them to you as daughters, but not on the basis of my covenant with you. 62So I will establish my covenant with you, and you will know that I am the LORD. 63Then, when I make atonement for you for all you have done, you will remember and be ashamed and never again open your mouth because of your humiliation, declares the Sovereign LORD.' "

59 The Lord concluded this allegory by affirming his immutable faithfulness to his covenants. He would discipline Jerusalem (and Israel) as the Mosaic covenant promised, because they had failed to be faithful to him and had broken their covenant with him. The covenant broken by their spiritual adultery (cf. v.8) was the Mosaic covenant, the only one Israel entered through an oath (Exod 24:7–8). Deuteronomy 29:10–21 describes that oath, reaffirmed on the plains of Moab, in which Israel agreed to obey the Mosaic covenant or suffer its curses (Lev 26:14–39; Deut 28:14–68). But Judah, represented by her capital, Jerusalem, had broken that covenant exactly as described in Deuteronomy 29. God would faithfully execute the justice of that covenant on them—viz., the curses.

The word "oath" (*ʾālāh*) can also mean "curse" and was used both ways throughout the OT. God purposely used this term to communicate both the idea of Jerusalem's despising of the oath of Exodus 24 and Deuteronomy 29 and the concept of her disregard for the promise of the curse.

60 Nevertheless, when the Lord would complete his judgments on Jerusalem, he promised that he would continue to be faithful by remembering his everlasting covenant that he made with the nation in her youth. In the Mosaic covenant, in Leviticus 26:40–45, the Lord promised that, after his future and final judgment on Israel, he would remember the covenant that he had made with Abraham. In the Abrahamic covenant God promised to give the land of Canaan to Israel as an eternal possession (cf. Gen 17:7–8; Lev 26:42). This was an everlasting covenant, and God would graciously and lovingly remember to do what he had promised. The unfaithfulness of men does not alter the faithfulness of God (cf. 2 Tim 2:13).

61–63 When God would remember his covenant with Abraham and restore Jerusalem and Judah to the land of Canaan, then Jerusalem would remember her evil ways that forced her into exile and would be ashamed (vv.61, 63a). Jerusalem would be reestablished in the future kingdom (cf. ch. 48) in a place of preeminence. Though she had been more wicked than either Sodom or Samaria and would receive greater judgment, the Lord would sovereignly exalt her over them by giving them to her as "daughters" (20:43; 36:31). As "daughters" these cities would no longer be thought of as "sisters" (city/nation) but as cities with their suburbs under the jurisdiction of Jerusalem (cf. v.46; Judg 1:27). The Lord's return of Sodom and Samaria to Jerusalem as daughters is not based on the Mosaic covenant, however, but on the grace of God (cf. M.H. Woudstra, "The Everlasting Covenant in Ezekiel 16:59–63," *Calvin Theological Journal* 6 [1971]: 22–48).

This restoration would cause Jerusalem to know that the Lord was her everpresent, always faithful God (v.62), who chose her of his own accord in the past and will save her in the future. Never again would Jerusalem and Judah mention their past sins after they are restored; God would make atonement for their sins and forget all their iniquity (v.63). This, of course, would be accomplished by Jesus Christ's death on the cross, by which he paid the penalty for all sin, once and for all, as promised in the new covenant (Jer 31:34).

Notes

60 The term אוֹתָךְ (*ʾ ôtāk*, "you"), the objective personal pronoun, should be rendered אִתָּךְ (*ʾittāk*, "with you"). This would make better sense grammatically since the verb זָכַר (*zākar*, "remember") already has an object in בְּרִיתִי (*berîtî*, "covenant"), and it would be in harmony with the parallel usage in v.62. The orthographical difference of the insertion of a waw rather than a yod was a common scribal error.

The waw prefix on וַהֲקִמֹתִי (*wahaqimôtî*, "when I establish") should be rendered "when," introducing a temporal clause. The causative form of the verb underscores the initiative of God in the original establishment of the everlasting covenant with his people.

8. The riddle and the parable of the two eagles

17:1–24

[1]The word of the LORD came to me: [2]"Son of man, set forth an allegory and tell the house of Israel a parable. [3]Say to them, 'This is what the Sovereign LORD says: A great eagle with powerful wings, long feathers and full plumage of varied colors came to Lebanon. Taking hold of the top of a cedar, [4]he broke off its topmost shoot and carried it away to a land of merchants, where he planted it in a city of traders.

[5]"'He took some of the seed of your land and put it in fertile soil. He planted it like a willow by abundant water, [6]and it sprouted and became a low, spreading vine. Its branches turned toward him, but its roots remained under it. So it became a vine and produced branches and put out leafy boughs.

7" 'But there was another great eagle with powerful wings and full plumage. The vine now sent out its roots toward him from the plot where it was planted and stretched out its branches to him for water. ⁸It had been planted in good soil by abundant water so that it would produce branches, bear fruit and become a splendid vine.'

⁹"Say to them, 'This is what the Sovereign LORD says: Will it thrive? Will it not be uprooted and stripped of its fruit so that it withers? All its new growth will wither. It will not take a strong arm or many people to pull it up by the roots. ¹⁰Even if it is transplanted, will it thrive? Will it not wither completely when the east wind strikes it—wither away in the plot where it grew?' "

¹¹Then the word of the LORD came to me: ¹²"Say to this rebellious house, 'Do you not know what these things mean?' Say to them: 'The king of Babylon went to Jerusalem and carried off her king and her nobles, bringing them back with him to Babylon. ¹³Then he took a member of the royal family and made a treaty with him, putting him under oath. He also carried away the leading men of the land, ¹⁴so that the kingdom would be brought low, unable to rise again, surviving only by keeping his treaty. ¹⁵But the king rebelled against him by sending his envoys to Egypt to get horses and a large army. Will he succeed? Will he who does such things escape? Will he break the treaty and yet escape?

¹⁶" 'As surely as I live, declares the Sovereign LORD, he shall die in Babylon, in the land of the king who put him on the throne, whose oath he despised and whose treaty he broke. ¹⁷Pharaoh with his mighty army and great horde will be of no help to him in war, when ramps are built and siege works erected to destroy many lives. ¹⁸He despised the oath by breaking the covenant. Because he had given his hand in pledge and yet did all these things, he shall not escape.

¹⁹" 'Therefore this is what the Sovereign LORD says: As surely as I live, I will bring down on his head my oath that he despised and my covenant that he broke. ²⁰I will spread my net for him, and he will be caught in my snare. I will bring him to Babylon and execute judgment upon him there because he was unfaithful to me. ²¹All his fleeing troops will fall by the sword, and the survivors will be scattered to the winds. Then you will know that I the LORD have spoken.

²²" 'This is what the Sovereign LORD says: I myself will take a shoot from the top of a cedar and plant it; I will break off a tender sprig from its topmost shoots and plant it on a high and lofty mountain. ²³On the mountain heights of Israel I will plant it; it will produce branches and bear fruit and become a splendid cedar. Birds of every kind will nest in it; they will find shelter in the shade of its branches. ²⁴All the trees of the field will know that I the LORD bring down the tall tree and make the low tree grow tall. I dry up the green tree and make the dry tree flourish.

" 'I the LORD have spoken, and I will do it.' "

1-10 As the exiles listened to Ezekiel's long allegory of Jersulam's history of spiritual infidelity to the Lord, some began to raise questions. Why were they being judged for all the past sins of their nation? It was not fair! Ezekiel would respond, declaring that they would be judged for the contemporary lack of trust in the Lord, which they had shown by their tendency to rely on Egypt for security and by the corruption of their regent, Zedekiah.

In this chapter Ezekiel used a riddle to communicate this message. A "riddle" (*ḥîḏāh;* NIV, "allegory") was commonly used in international politics between kings (cf. Harry Torczyner, "The Riddle in the Bible," HUCA 1 [1924]: 125–49). If one failed to answer the riddle of the other, he might be called on to submit to him as a vassal. In some cases he might even be put to death. In the use of this riddle, the two kings were God and Zedekiah. The Lord was giving the riddle; if Zedekiah failed to understand it, he and his people would either submit as vassals to the Lord or die. Most of Judah would die.

The riddle was also classified as a *māšāl* ("parable," "allegory," or "proverb"). All three words are used of this term. The basic meaning inherent in the root is that of comparison. It is a comparison between two items. In this case the comparison in the riddle was clarified in the interpretation section.

The historical background for this riddle is found in 2 Kings 24:6–20; 2 Chronicles 36:8–16, and Jeremiah 37; 52:1–7. Judah's kings were fickle in failing to follow the prophets' warnings and in yielding to the Babylonians, God's instrument of discipline. On the contrary, the kings continued to seek security and aid from Egypt. This issue was at the heart of this chapter.

The structure of this chapter is simple. Verses 1–10 set forth the riddle, vv.11–21 declare the interpretation, while vv.22–24 conclude with an epilogue. It is important to remember that every detail of a riddle does not have a meaning. Rather one should look for the major concepts. Likewise, it would be prudent to follow the divine interpretation given in vv.11–21.

The riddle was set forth in two parts. Verses 1–6 describe an eagle that was extremely glorious and multicolored (v.3). This bird flew to Lebanon (the land of Canaan; cf. Josh 1:4; 2 Kings 14:9) and took the top of a cedar and the topmost young twigs (v.4) and brought them to the land of merchants (Babylonia; cf. 16:29). Then the eagle took some seeds from Canaan and planted them in a land of fertile soil (v.5; cf. Deut 8:7; 11:11). The seed grew into a low spreading vine that sent out shoots and branches toward the eagle (v.6).

The second part of the riddle (vv.7–10) portrays another great eagle (v.7)—not quite as glorious as the first—which caused the transplanted vine to turn its branches and roots toward it. Though the vine was initially planted in good soil so that it would yield abundant produce (v.8), it would no longer thrive; for it would be uprooted and its fruit cut off by the east wind (vv.9–10). No man would be able to restore it.

11–14 The interpretation section was structured in the form of the common prophetic-judgment speech to an individual (cf. Claus Westermann, *Basic Forms of Prophetic Speech* [Philadelphia: Westminster, 1967], pp. 169–94). Verses 11–12a give the summons to listen; vv.12b–18 give the charges; and vv.19–21 announce God's intervention in judgment with the word "therefore."

It is interesting to note that often the eagle was used symbolically in the OT to represent God's punitive power (Deut 28:49) and the speed with which a conqueror advanced (Isa 46:11; Jer 48:40; 49:22). In this chapter each eagle represented a conquering king whom, in part, God used as an instrument of his punitive wrath on Judah.

The first eagle was Nebuchadnezzar, the king of Babylonia (v.12), who would take King Jehoiachin (crest of the cedar) and his young princes and nobles (topmost young twigs) into exile in Babylonia, a land of merchants (cf. 1 Kings 10:27; 2 Kings 24:10–12; Jer 22:15, 23). The cedar has messianic overtones (cf. Isa 10:33–11:1). It represents the line of David that culminates in *the* Messiah, Jesus Christ. Jehoiachin was of the Davidic line. The "seed" (v.5) was defined as one from the royal seed (v.13) whom Nebuchadnezzar would take and place in the field of Canaan. This member of the royal seed was Zedekiah (or Mattaniah; cf. 2 Kings 24:17; Jer 37:1), Jehoiachin's uncle, whom Nebuchadnezzar established as regent over the remnant in Judah by entering into a binding covenant with Zedekiah. Jehoiachin still remained the legitimate king though he was in exile in Babylonia. Zedekiah and the Hebrews remaining in the land with him were to become a flourishing vine, but instead they became a worthless and useless vine like the one already described in chapter 15. It was low and spreading because Nebuchadnezzar never allowed it to exalt itself (v.14).

15–21 The second eagle represented the king of Egypt (vv.15–21) to whom Zedekiah sent for military aid when he rebelled against Nebuchadnezzar (v.7— "stretched out its branches" toward the second eagle) in 588 B.C. and broke the covenant he had made with Nebuchadnezzar (vv.15–16; cf. 2 Chron 36:13). This act of trust in Egypt had been opposed rigorously by both Isaiah (Isa 30:1–2) and Jeremiah (Jer 37:7). God rhetorically asked whether the vine (Zedekiah and the small nation of Judah) would prosper. The emphatic answer was no! On the contrary, Zedekiah and Judah would suffer God's judgment through Nebuchadnezzar when he would attack Judah, because Zedekiah had despised the covenant with him (and Yahweh) and had broken it by turning to Egypt (2 Chron 36:13; cf. Ezek 5:7).

Because of his disobedience both to his covenant with Nebuchadnezzar (sworn in God's name; cf. 2 Chron 36:13) and to his covenant with God (v.18), judgment was pronounced on Zedekiah (v.19). He would experience the judgments promised in the Mosaic covenant he had also broken, for God would spread a net and seize him with the Babylonian army and bring him to Babylonia in exile (v.20). Egypt would be of no help when Jerusalem was besieged by Nebuchadnezzar (v.17), for Zedekiah's army would fall by the sword (v.21a), the remaining population would be scattered throughout the land (v.21b), and Zedekiah would ultimately die in Babylonia (v.16; cf. 12:13–14). Yet all this was a manifestation of God's grace, for he faithfully executed his justice in order that Zedekiah might come to know that the Lord, the only true God, had spoken in these judgments (v.21c).

22–24 This epilogue provided an oracle of salvation. Wherever God pronounced judgment, he normally declared hope as well. Judah had failed to remain "planted" and "fruitful." In the future, however, after God had cleansed Judah through his discipline, *he* would take a "tender sprig" from the topmost shoots of the cedar and "plant it on a high and lofty mountain" (v.22). This cutting of the cedar was not from the first cutting made by Nebuchadnezzar in vv.4, 12, for Jeremiah 22:28–30 declared that the physical line of Jehoiachin (Coniah) would not continue to sit on the Davidic throne. Rather, the line would continue through other descendants of David. This new cutting was, however, from the "cedar," the messianic line. It was the "tender one," a concept that had messianic implications (Isa 11:1; Jer 23:5–6; 33:14–16; Zech 3:8; 6:12–13). This was *the* Messiah whom God would establish as King over Israel in the messianic kingdom. The high and lofty mountain may have reference to Mount Zion and the temple complex (cf. 20:40; Ps 2:6; Mic 4:1), but this is only conjecture. This messianic kingdom would be great and fruitful as a stately cedar tree (v.23). All the birds would nest in its branches—perhaps a figure of the nations of the world (cf. Dan 4:17, 32, 34–37; Matt 13:31–32). All the trees (or nations according to the immediate context) would submit to the Messiah and his rule (v.24). God had spoken; he would do it!

Notes

8,10 The term שְׁתוּלָה (*šᵉṯûlāh*, "transplanted," "planted") must be understood by the context to refer to Judah being weakened by turning to Egypt. The stronger and more fruitful place was the one where Babylonia originally had planted her for prosperity.

19 The apparent discord between the masculine suffix נְתַתִּיו (*niṯattîw*, "I will bring down") and the seemingly feminine antecedents בְּרִית (*bᵉrîṯ*, "covenant") and אָלָה (*'ālāh*, "oath") is resolved if one understands the masculine suffix as a general reference to the entire offense rather than to the "covenant" or "oath" specifically.

---

9. *Individual responsibility for righteousness* (18:1–31)

a. *Proverb versus principle*

18:1–4

¹The word of the LORD came to me: ²"What do you people mean by quoting this proverb about the land of Israel:

> " 'The fathers eat sour grapes,
>   and the children's teeth are set on edge'?

³"As surely as I live, declares the Sovereign LORD, you will no longer quote this proverb in Israel. ⁴For every living soul belongs to me, the father as well as the son—both alike belong to me. The soul who sins is the one who will die.

1–4 In chapter 16 Ezekiel set forth the proverb "Like mother, like daughter" (v.44) to show Israel had taken on herself the heathen character of the land of Canaan. Israel had given in to her environment. Ezekiel's hearers perhaps grasped that proverbial concept but misapplied it in their fatalistic perspective toward judgment. They reasoned that the present generation was being judged because of the past wickedness of their forefathers. It really did not make any difference, then, what the contemporary Israelites did. If Ezekiel was right in pronouncing judgment, then the people would simply be the unfortunate recipients of the ancient principle in the Decalogue: "I, the LORD your God, am a jealous God, punishing the children for the sin of the fathers to the third and fourth generations of those who hate me" (Exod 20:5).

The exiles who received Ezekiel's message misunderstood the message of Exodus 20:5 and Deuteronomy 5:9. This principle of the Decalogue teaches that children would be affected by their father's sin. Parents model for their children. The sinful behavior of parents is readily followed by their children. Regrettably, therefore, children frequently found themselves practicing the same sinful acts as their father. Likewise, they must accept the same just punishment for such actions. However, each child is still individually responsible. He can abort the "sin-punishment-inheritance" progression at any time. But he must repent and do what is right.

The misunderstanding of the exiles, which could lead to irresponsibility and fatalism, was expressed in the contemporary proverb in Judah: "The fathers eat sour grapes, and the children's teeth are set on edge" (v.2); i.e., what the father did affected his children. The people believed (cf. Jer 31:27–30; Lam 5:7) that righteousness and wickedness were hereditary; therefore, there was no reason to change one's ways.

The Lord's response to this new proverb was that the hereditary principle would cease immediately (v.3), for it had been erroneously applied to righteousness and unrighteousness. Each man was righteous or unrighteous, lived or died, according to his own actions. God solemnly declared that "every living soul belongs to me" (v.4); for he is the Creator of everyone, and all had equality before him. They were free to make a decision to walk in his ways or not; they were *not bound* by heredity. The principle of individual responsibility had always been true (cf. Gen 2:17; 4:7; Deut 24:16; 2 Kings 14:6; Ezek 3:16–21; 14:12–20; 33:1–20). A son was not bound to be like his father, though that was the concept among Ezekiel's contemporaries, as it often is today.

A basic principle is set forth at the conclusion of v.4: "The soul who sins is the one who will die." Life and death in this context were not eternal but physical. One enters into eternal life by faith in the Messiah, Jesus Christ, whether by looking forward in faith to his work on the cross, as did the OT saint, or in looking back in faith, as does the believer today. Doing the works of the Mosaic covenant never saved anyone, whether in the OT, NT, or today. Eternal salvation was always by faith alone (cf. Gen 15:6; Rom 4:5; Eph 2:8–9). The stipulations of the Mosaic covenant were given to a people who were already in a trusting relationship with God. These stipulations provided a concrete, practical outworking of faith in the God who redeemed Israel from Egypt and gave the people his law. Trust in him entailed the ritual of blood sacrifice as well as obedience to his commands. If they obeyed these commands, they would show their righteousness, receive God's blessings, and live. But if they failed to live according to God's ways as revealed in the law, the Mosaic covenant declared that even those who had believed in the Messiah would die physically (cf. Deut 28:58–66; 30:15–20). If, however, they had never trusted in their Messiah, portrayed in the sacrifices, then they would also die eternally.

Notes

2 The meaning of תִּקְהֶינָה (*tiqheynāh*, "are set on edge") is literally "to become blunt or dull." Ecclesiastes 10:10 uses the term to portray a blunt iron tool. In later Hebrew the concept of being "numb" or "senseless" is expressed. A derived sense in the Hebrew and Aramaic root pictures grapes becoming sour. Specific implications are not clear. The concept of a father's act affecting his child in some way is plain.

b. *Three illustrations of the principle*

18:5–18

> 5"Suppose there is a righteous man
> who does what is just and right.
> 6He does not eat at the mountain shrines
> or look to the idols of the house of Israel.
> He does not defile his neighbor's wife
> or lie with a woman during her period.
> 7He does not oppress anyone,
> but returns what he took in pledge for a loan.

He does not commit robbery
　but gives his food to the hungry
　and provides clothing for the naked.
[8]He does not lend at usury
　or take excessive interest.
He withholds his hand from doing wrong.
　and judges fairly between man and man.
[9]He follows my decrees
　and faithfully keeps my laws.
That man is righteous;
　he will surely live,

declares the Sovereign LORD.

[10]"Suppose he has a violent son, who sheds blood or does any of these other things [11](though the father has done none of them):

"He eats at the mountain shrines.
He defiles his neighbor's wife.
[12]He oppresses the poor and needy.
He commits robbery.
He does not return what he took in pledge.
He looks to the idols.
He does detestable things.
[13]He lends at usury and takes excessive interest.

Will such a man live? He will not! Because he has done all these detestable things, he will surely be put to death and his blood will be on his own head.
[14]"But suppose this son has a son who sees all the sins his father commits, and though he sees them, he does not do such things:

[15]"He does not eat at the mountain shrines
　or look to the idols of the house of Israel.
He does not defile his neighbor's wife.
[16]He does not oppress anyone
　or require a pledge for a loan.
He does not commit robbery,
　but gives his food to the hungry
　and provides clothing for the naked.
[17]He withholds his hand from sin
　and takes no usury or excessive interest.
He keeps my laws and follows my decrees.

He will not die for his father's sin; he will surely live. [18]But his father will die for his own sin, because he practiced extortion, robbed his brother and did what was wrong among his people.

5–9 Ezekiel used three examples—viz., a righteous father, an unrighteous son, and a righteous grandson. Certainly many exiles had observed vivid illustrations of the principle of individual responsibility in the lives of righteous King Hezekiah; his wicked son, Manasseh; and his righteous great-grandson, Josiah.

The principle of individual responsibility shows that a righteous man, one in a trusting relationship with the Lord and who practiced righteousness and justice, would live physically and eternally. First, however, the Lord must define righteousness according to the Mosaic covenant (v.9a). Five legal areas differentiate righteous acts from unrighteous deeds. First, the righteous man refrained from pagan sacrificial meals at the heathen high mountain shrines and from the prevalent idolatry found in the northern kingdom of Israel (vv.5–6a; forbidden in Deut 12:2–4).

Second, he refused to defile his neighbor's wife or to have relations with a woman during her menstrual period (v.6b; stipulated in Exod 20:14; Lev 15:24; 18:19; 20:- 10, 18; Deut 22:22). Third, he did not oppress people through maltreatment and extortion but rather restored the pledge of a poor person's debt (v.7a; commanded in Exod 22:26–27; Deut 24:6; Amos 2:8). The wealthy took advantage of the poor, especially finding orphans, widows, and strangers easy prey for their extortion schemes. Fourth, the righteous man did not steal (v.7b; forbidden in Exod 20:15; Lev 19:13) but fed and clothed the destitute (Deut 15:11; 24:19–22; Isa 58:7). Finally, refusing to take interest from his fellow Israelites (v.8a; forbidden in Exod 22:25; Deut 23:19–20; Ps 15:5; Isa 24:2), the righteous man practiced only justice among them (v.8b; Lev 19:15–16, 35–36; Deut 25:13–16). Interest could be charged foreigners in commercial relations, but it was contrary to the principle of love and concern for one of the covenant people to profit from a poor fellow Hebrew by extorting interest on charitable loans. Verse 9 summed up the definition of a righteous person—viz., one who lived by the Mosaic statutes was righteous and would surely live physically and eternally to enjoy the blessings of life as God had planned (cf. Lev 18:1–5; Deut 11; 26:16–19; 30:15–20). This list of examples clearly demonstrates that a man's attitude and acts toward others provide a true index of his faith and attitude toward God.

10–13 The second example deals with the unrighteous son of the righteous son. The son demonstated his unrighteousness and lack of faith by a lifestyle opposite that of his father. Whatever his father did in righteousness, the son did not do; and whatever his father refrained from in righteousness, that the unrighteous son did (vv.10b –13a). He also committed murder (v.10a). Verse 18 summarizes his wicked deeds as "extortion, robbed his brother and did what was wrong among his people." Since he failed to live according to the righteous stipulations of the law, he would not live physically or eternally at all (v.13b). This type of man was certainly manifested by the life of Manasseh.

14–18 Would an unrighteous man necessarily have an unrighteous son? The third illustration shows that this did not have to be so. If the grandson did all the righteous deeds of the Mosaic covenant, like his godly grandfather (vv.15–17; cf. vv.5–9), and refused to follow his wicked father's unrighteous acts (v.14), then he would not die because of his father's wickedness, according to the hereditary principle, but would surely live (v.17b). But his father would die because of his own iniquity (v.18).

Notes

6 Most of the things forbidden in vv.6–8 would be forbidden by most people today. However, the prohibition from sexual relations with a menstruous woman would more likely be ignored today, though Leviticus and Ezekiel consider such to be a serious act that pollutes the land (cf. H.L. Ellison, *Ezekiel: The Man and His Message* [Grand Rapids: Eerdmans, 1956], p. 72). Perhaps this prohibition should still be followed unless clear justification can be found in Scripture to do otherwise (cf. R.J. Rushdoony, *The Institutes of Biblical Law*

[Oklahoma City: Presbyterian and Reformed Renewal Ministries, 1973], pp. 427–30), as is true with the other prohibitions in these verses.

8 Many have taken the combination of the terms נֶשֶׁךְ (nešek, "usury," "interest") and תַּרְבִּית (tarbît, "excessive interest") as a hendiadys. But this view has never been without question. Other positions include (1) the two terms show the two sides of interest; it bites the debtor and increases the lender; (2) the lender takes a bite (nešek) when the loan is made and then demands the full amount (tarbît) in repayment; and (3) nešek is interest on a monetary loan whereas tarbît is interest on a loan of victuals (cf. Samuel E. Loewenstamm, "נשׁך and מ/תרתת," JBL 88 [1969]: 78–80). Distinction between the two words is still not clear.

---

c. The explanation of the principle

18:19–32

19"Yet you ask, 'Why does the son not share the guilt of his father?' Since the son has done what is just and right and has been careful to keep all my decrees, he will surely live. 20The sould who sins is the one who will die. The son will not share the guilt of the father, nor will the father share the guilt of the son. The righteousness of the righteous man will be credited to him, and the wickedness of the wicked will be charged against him.

21"But if a wicked man turns away from all the sins he has committed and keeps all my decrees and does what is just and right, he will surely live; he will not die. 22None of the offenses he has committed will be remembered against him. Because of the righteous things he has done, he will live. 23Do I take any pleasure in the death of the wicked? declares the Sovereign LORD. Rather, am I not pleased when they turn from their ways and live?

24"But if a righteous man turns from his righteousness and commits sin and does the same detestable things the wicked man does, will he live? None of the righteous things he has done will be remembered. Because of the unfaithfulness he is guilty of and because of the sins he has committed, he will die.

25"Yet you say, 'The way of the Lord is not just.' Hear, O house of Israel: Is my way unjust? Is it not your ways that are unjust? 26If a righteous man turns from his righteousness and commits sin, he will die for it; because of the sin he has committed he will die. 27But if a wicked man turns away from the wickedness he has committed and does what is just and right, he will save his life. 28Because he considers all the offenses he has committed and turns away from them, he will surely live; he will not die. 29Yet the house of Israel says, 'The way of the Lord is not just.' Are my ways unjust, O house of Israel? Is it not your ways that are unjust?

30"Therefore, O house of Israel, I will judge you, each one according to his ways, declares the Sovereign LORD. Repent! Turn away from all your offenses; then sin will not be your downfall. 31Rid yourselves of all the offenses you have committed, and get a new heart and a new spirit. Why will you die, O house of Israel? 32For I take no pleasure in the death of anyone, declares the Sovereign LORD. Repent and live!

19–24 Having stated the basic principle of individual responsibility in vv.1–4 and illustrated it in vv.5–18, Ezekiel then elaborated aspects of this principle. The discussion was initiated by the exiles' rhetorical question: "Why does the son not share the guilt of his father?" (v.19a). God answered the question by a series of subprinciples. First, whenever anyone—even the son of an unrighteous man—lived righteously according to the stipulations of the Mosaic covenant, he would live physically and ultimately eternally (v.20a). Second, the unrighteous sinner who disobeyed God's righteous way for living revealed in the law would die physically and ultimately eternally (v.20a). Third, a son would not bear the penalty for a father's sins, nor would a father bear the punishment for his son's sins (v.20b). Fourth, a righteous person lived because of his righteousness (cf. Lev 18:5), but the wicked would die because of his sin (v.20c; Deut 30:17–18). Fifth, a wicked person could live physically and ultimately eternally if he trusted in the Messiah, if he would turn from his sinful rebellion and obey the righteous commandments. His past sins would not be remembered because of his righteous acts by which he now lived (vv.21–22). Only God's marvelous grace had kept that wicked person from dying previously. Sixth, God did not rejoice when a wicked man died. Rather, God was delighted when a wicked man turned to him in obedience and lived (v.23; cf. v.31; 2 Peter 3:9). Sinful mankind normally sees judgment as God's delight. Nothing could be further from God's desire, else he would not have sent his only Son to be judged on the cross for the sin of the whole world (1 John 2:1–2). Finally, there was never a time or place where the righteous man, who had trusted in the Messiah, could feel free to sin; for if he turned away from living by God's righteous stipulations and sinned, then he too would surely die physically (but not eternally) (v.24). He would die because of his unfaithfulness to God and the unrighteous acts he did. God never condones sin nor grants anyone a license to disobey his holy commands.

25–29 Ezekiel again raised a rhetorical statement that expressed the mind of the exiles: "The way of the Lord is not just" (vv.25a, 29b). God replied that it was Israel's ways, not his, that were inequitable and unrighteous. They sought to apply the principle of heredity incorrectly to righteousness and unrighteousness (vv.25b, 29b). The principle was repeated that the righteous man was righteous only because he had practiced righteousness and justice according to the Mosaic covenant, and the wicked was unrighteous because he had turned from the righteous demands of the law. God's grace, in harmony with his law, always allowed the wicked to become righteous by turning from his wickedness and practicing the righteous ordinances of the Mosaic covenant. Likewise, the righteous would die physically if he failed to walk in God's holy ways (vv.26–28). Righteousness or unrighteousness was not inherited. Righteousness was reckoned to the individual when he did the righteous acts of God revealed in the Scriptures. Likewise, unrighteousness was credited to the individual who failed to practice God's righteous ways. The decision was up to the individual, not heredity.

30–32 The Lord concluded this message by pleading with the people to repent individually from their sins (vv.30–31). This was a strong invitation to live. Why die when they could live? Later Ezekiel would develop how a new heart and spirit would ultimately be appropriated by Israel (36:26). Repentance was available to the people of Israel in Ezekiel's day. The Lord does not delight in the death of one person who dies because of his sin (v.32). Therefore the Lord exhorted the people to "repent and live!"

10. A lament for the princes of Israel

19:1–14

> [1]"Take up a lament concerning the princes of Israel [2]and say:
>
>> " 'What a lioness was your mother
>> among the lions!

She lay down among the young lions
and reared her cubs.
³She brought up one of her cubs,
and he became a strong lion.
He learned to tear the prey
and he devoured men.
⁴The nations heard about him.
and he was trapped in their pit.
They led him with hooks
to the land of Egypt.

⁵" 'When she saw her hope unfulfilled,
her expectation gone,
she took another of her cubs
and made him a strong lion.
⁶He prowled among the lions,
for he was now a strong lion.
He learned to tear the prey
and he devoured men.
⁷He broke down their strongholds
and devastated their towns.
The land and all who were in it
were terrified by his roaring.
⁸Then the nations came against him,
those from regions round about.
They spread their net for him,
and he was trapped in their pit.
⁹With hooks they pulled him into a cage
and brought him to the king of Babylon.
They put him in prison,
so his roar was heard no longer
on the mountains of Israel.

¹⁰" 'Your mother was like a vine in your vineyard
planted by the water;
it was fruitful and full of branches
because of abundant water.
¹¹Its branches were strong,
fit for a ruler's scepter.
It towered high
above the thick foliage,
conspicuous for its height
and for its many branches.
¹²But it was uprooted in fury
and thrown to the ground.
The east wind made it shrivel,
it was stripped of its fruit;
its strong branches withered
and fire consumed them.
¹³Now it is planted in the desert,
in a dry and thirsty land.
¹⁴Fire spread from one of its main branches
and consumed its fruit.
No strong branch is left on it
fit for a ruler's scepter.'

This is a lament and is to be used as a lament."

1–9 The final question raised by the recipients of Ezekiel's messages concerned the trustworthiness of the contemporary rulers of Judah to lead the nation back to prominence. Should they trust in their present rulers?

Ezekiel responded with a funeral dirge for Judah's princes. The contemporary rulers were not worthy of anyone's trust. They were examples of the wicked man whom Ezekiel described in chapter 18. These rulers had been responsible for Judah's present condition. They would die. No true rulers would be left in Judah.

A dirge was normally sung, or chanted, by professional mourners after the death of the deceased and during his funeral. Ezekiel expressed the Lord's sadness over the Judean leadership's failure by chanting this elegy over her final rulers prior to their deaths (v.1).

The lament centered first around the imagery of a lioness and her whelps. The figurative use of a lion was not uncommon in the OT and normally had royal overtones, especially in reference to those of the Davidic line (cf. Gen 49:9; Num 23:24; 1 Kings 10:19–20; Mic 5:8; Rev 5:5). Contextually the lioness must be identified as the nation of Israel (v.2). Israel had taken her place among the nations. The young whelps represented given kings of Israel, and in historical and biblical context they signified certain latter rulers in the kingdom of Judah. The portrayal of nations and kings as lions being captured can be seen in the famous lion-hunting bas-reliefs of Ashurbannipal and Esarhaddon (cf. ANET, p. 300; Pritchard, *Ancient Pictures*, plate 447). The symbol of the lion was also found at Megiddo on the royal seal of Shema, a servant of Jeroboam II (ZPEB, 5:323).

The first whelp was Jehoahaz (vv.3–4), who had been placed on the throne by the Judeans following the death of his father, Josiah (2 Kings 23:31). Jehoahaz learned, as a young lion, to tear and devour mankind, doing evil in the sight of the Lord (v.3; 2 Kings 23:32). Becoming world renowned for the violence in his reign of three months, he was seized in 609 B.C. like a hunted lion and brought bound to Egypt where he ultimately died (v.4; 2 Kings 23:33–34; 2 Chron 36:1–4; Jer 22:10–12).

The second whelp was Jehoiakim's son, Jehoiachin, (vv.5–9; cf. 2 Kings 24:8–17; 2 Chron 36:8–10); Jehoiakim was bypassed. Judah's hope had perished with the nation's decline under Jehoiakim's pro-Egyptian leadership. Hope was renewed as the young eighteen-year-old prince Jehoiachin became king (vv.5–6). However, his reign was not substantially different from his father's, for Jehoiachin too learned to devour mankind.

Jehoiachin destroyed cities and desolated the land (v.7). Yet he also did not escape the snare of the "lion-hunting" nations that trapped him in their "pit" and brought him to Nebuchadnezzar in a "cage" in 597 B.C. Later he was released (2 Kings 25:27–30; 2 Chron 36:9–11). No longer would he "roar" in Judah.

10–14 In v.10 the imagery changes to that of a "vine." The figure is as common as that of a lion in the OT. It often typified the nation of Israel (15:1–6; 17:1–10; cf. Ps 80:8–16; Isa 5:1–7; 27:2–6). The imagery probably changed from the specific Davidic figure of a lion to the figure of a vine since Zedekiah was not the legitimate legal king of Judah, as were Jehoahaz and Jehoiachin.

The vine referred to the historic nation of Israel. It had been planted beside abundant water in the land of Canaan (Deut 8:7–8), where it had grown large and fruitful during the kingdom period with many branches for ruling scepters (or kings) (vv.10b–11). Yet this vine was finally plucked up and cast to the ground, where its exposed roots withered under the blasts of the east wind (Babylonia) (cf. 17:6–10,

15). The vine (or nation) was transplanted into a desert place—into captivity (v. 13). The "fire" that "spread from one of its main branches" was the destruction that Zedekiah, Judah's current ruler, had brought on Judah ("consumed its fruit") (v. 14a). Judah's present condition was the responsibility, in part, of Zedekiah. Ezekiel had answered the exiles' question (in this chapter) by demonstrating the foolishness of trusting in Zedekiah, for he was partially responsible for the imminent judgment. In fact, there was not a "strong branch" in Judah at all—no one "fit for a ruler's scepter" (v. 14b), not even Zedekiah, who would be deported in 586 B.C. There was no hope! Judgment was coming!

Notes

1 A קִינָה (*qînāh*, "lament," "dirge") is a funeral chant with a mournful rhythm (3:2). Though it may be sung by anyone at a funeral, it was regularly used by professional women mourners and wailers.

The term נָשִׂיא (*nāśî*', "prince") is used frequently throughout Ezekiel in place of the term מֶלֶה (*melek*, "king"; cf. 7:27; 12:10; 21:17[12 EV]; 30[25 EV]; 27:21 et al.). *Nāśî*' basically means "ruler" or "leader." *Melek* is normally reserved for the legitimate king by Ezekiel.

7 The first two words in this verse have been rendered in various ways. Many find scribal errors in the two words. They change the וַיֵּדַע (*wayyēḏaʿ*, "he knew") to וַיָּרַע (*wayyārōaʿ*, "he broke"). This change is most certainly possible, since the error of writing ד (*d*) for ר (*r*) was one of the more common orthographical mistakes made by copyists. The second term presents greater difficulty, for the rendering of אַרְמְנוֹתֵיהֶם (*'armᵉnôṯêhem*, "their strongholds") for the MT's אַלְמְנוֹתָיו (*'almᵉnôṯāyw*, "his widows") demands writing an ר (*r*) instead of an ל (*l*), which would not be likely in early orthography. Commentators normally appeal to the seeming confusion of these two terms in Isa 13:22 and to the parallelism of the poetry in the Ezekiel context as strong arguments in favor of "strongholds." Certainly a synonymous parallelism in the Ezekiel context would best be satisfied with this translation. However, the Isaiah passage does not require an interchange of terms. Moreover, there is an Assyrian term *almattu* rendered "fortress." It would seem more likely that this term would be used in Ezek 19:7 rather than amending the text. On the strength of the parallelism of the first line of v.7, the possibility of *'almᵉnôṯāyw* being derived from the Assyrian *almattu* and the common scribal error of writing *r* for *d* (supported by the LXX) (understanding יָרַע [*yārōaʿ*, "broke"] in place of יֵדַע [*yēḏaʿ*, "knew"]), the writer would read the text as follows: "And he broke down their fortresses and devastated their cities."

9 The term סוּגַר (*sûgar*, "cage") is probably a loanword from the Akkadian *sigaru*, which can mean an animal cage or a neckband for prisoners. It is very likely that Ezekiel played on the word, using it literally for a neckband for Jehoiachin and at the same time using the sense of "animal cage" in the imagery of the passage (cf. I. Gelb, "Prisoners of War in Early Mesopotamia," JNES 32 [1973]: 86).

10 Many seek to find some other root for the term בְּדָמֵךְ (*bᵉḏāmkā*, "in your blood") than דָּם (*dām*, "blood"). The basis for their quest is the difficulty of the meaning conveyed by the phrase "in your blood." However, in the context the nuance of the kingdom of Judah (the vine) carrying the life flow of the kings (especially in light of the Davidic covenant) is perfectly acceptable as the interpretation of this term. The NIV reads בְּכַרְמֵךְ (*bᵉkarmekā*, "in your vineyard") with two Hebrew MSS and the LXX.

D. The Defective Leadership of Israel (20:1–23:49)

1. The history of Israel's rebellion and the Lord's grace (20:1–44)

a. Rebellion in Egypt

20:1–9

[1]In the seventh year, in the fifth month on the tenth day, some of the elders of Israel came to inquire of the LORD, and they sat down in front of me.

[2]Then the word of the LORD came to me: [3]"Son of man, speak to the elders of Israel and say to them, "This is what the Sovereign LORD says: Have you come to inquire of me? As surely as I live, I will not let you inquire of me, declares the Sovereign LORD.'

[4]"Will you judge them? Will you judge them, son of man? Then confront them with the detestable practices of their fathers[5] and say to them: 'This is what the Sovereign LORD says: On the day I chose Israel, I swore with uplifted hand to the descendants of the house of Jacob and revealed myself to them in Egypt. With uplifted hand I said to them, "I am the LORD your God." [6]On that day I swore to them that I would bring them out of Egypt into a land I had searched out for them, a land flowing with milk and honey, the most beautiful of all lands. [7]And I said to them, "Each of you, get rid of the vile images you have set your eyes on, and do not defile yourselves with the idols of Egypt. I am the LORD your God."

[8]"But they rebelled against me and would not listen to me; they did not get rid of the vile images they had set their eyes on, nor did they forsake the idols of Egypt. So I said I would pour out my wrath on them and spend my anger against them in Egypt. [9]But for the sake of my name I did what would keep it from being profaned in the eyes of the nations they lived among and in whose sight I had revealed myself to the Israelites by bringing them out of Egypt.

1 The chronological notice (July/August 591 B.C.; cf. Introduction: Date) in v.1 indicates the beginning of a new segment of the book and a new series of messages. Eleven months had passed since Ezekiel had delivered the previous revelations from God (cf. 8:1). The exact time lapse between Ezekiel's completion of the last funeral dirge in chapter 19 and the beginning of this new oracle is unknown. During this time, however, the Jewish leaders in Babylonia had given thought to Ezekiel's response to their arguments against his prophecies. It still appeared that they had some hope that Judah would be able to find deliverance from her present state.

In the late summer of 591 B.C., the news of Egypt's victory in the Sudan reached the remnant of Judeans at Tel Abib. Rumors also indicated that Psammetik II would make a triumphal conquest of Palestine. The exiles' expectations were most certainly heightened as they hoped that Egypt would prove to be the redeemer to free them from Nebuchadnezzar. Zedekiah had foolishly shared the same dream when he revolted from Babylonian rule and placed his confidence in Egypt's strength somewhere between the end of 591 and 589 B.C. Such a move was ill-timed; for the Pharaoh soon became ill, and the potential might of Egypt never materialized.

Though the text is silent concerning the exact nature of the elders' inquiry as they came to Ezekiel, it was probably conceived in this contemporary context. "Would Zedekiah's current diplomacy with Egypt succeed in bringing freedom for the exiles from the tyranny of Nebuchadnezzar?" "Would the Hebrew captives soon return to the Promised Land?"

Ezekiel's messages in chapters 20–23 set forth the Lord's response to this unspoken query. God would not even listen to such a foolish question, for had the nation not seen the issue yet? Israel's history had been one of persistent rebellion against her God (vv. 1–44). In the face of such rebellion, God had demonstrated his unending grace toward his people with great longsufferance. The time had come for the nation to prepare herself for judgment, for the Lord was going to soon bring Nebuchadnezzar against Jerusalem to destroy the city and to take additional captives to Babylonia (20:45–21:32). Why would God do this? Because Judah's wickedness—especially that of her leaders—was full (chs. 22–23).

The elders in exile sought an audience with Ezekiel. "To inquire of the LORD" was a popular idiom indicating that a prophetic audience was being requested for the purpose of securing an interpretation of a certain event (1 Kings 14:5–18; 22:7–28; 2 Kings 8:8–15; 22:13–20; Jer 21:2–14; 37:7–10). It was probable that the elders were seeking a prediction concerning the outcome of Zedekiah's overtures of Egypt.

2–6 The Lord outlined a summary of his response to the silent inquiry: (1) God refused to give them an audience (emphasized by an emphatic oath) for such a question (v. 3); (2) he refused because of the abominations of Judah (v. 4b); and (3) the nation of Judah must be judged for her iniquity (v. 4a). These aspects of his response would be enlarged as Ezekiel would recount the history of Israel's rebellion against God and God's undying forbearance and grace toward his wicked people.

A basic literary pattern was followed in the passage: God's benevolence was stated, followed by an assertion of Israel's rebellion, an announcement of God's judgment, and the declaration of God's grace. The latter two elements are characteristically repeated in a given historical period.

Israel's history as a nation began in Egypt where God chose her. He made himself known to Israel and swore that he would be her God (v. 5; Deut 7:6–11). He took an oath to bring his people into the fruitful and glorious land he had promised Abraham (v. 6; Gen 12:7; Exod 3:8, 13–18; 6:1–8; Jer 3:19; Dan 8:9; 11:16, 42, 45). In the Abrahamic covenant God had stated that he would take one man (Abraham), create a nation from that man, and use that nation to be an instrument of blessing to the entire world (Gen 12:1–3). In order to bring a nation into being, three elements were essential: (1) a people, (2) a government, and (3) a homeland. The people of Israel came into being in Egypt (the thrust of v. 5), the government (Mosaic covenant) was received at Mount Sinai, and the homeland was acquired through Joshua's conquest of Canaan.

7–9 Some have questioned why Jacob's descendants had to undergo the prolonged discipline in Egypt. Ezekiel declared that the reason lay in their detestable worship of Egyptian idols (v. 7). God's benevolent love was not only shown to Israel in her special calling and promises but also in his warning to remove her pagan deities so that he alone would be her God (cf. 23:3, 8; Lev 17:7; 18:3; 26:30; Deut 29:16–17; Josh 24:14). The Lord did not want his people to develop incorrect worship patterns.

However, as Israel's history continued, she did not heed God's gracious warnings. She rebelled against him by continuing to worship the Egyptian idols (v. 8a). Therefore, the Lord determined to pour out his wrath on Israel in the 430-year captivity in Egypt (v. 8b). Yet, when the captivity was completed, God graciously brought his people out of Egypt (as promised in Gen 15:13–16) so that his name would not be profaned among the nations (v. 9). The Lord's name embodied all he was. He was the ever-present, eternal, covenant God of Israel.

It was common in the ancient Near East for nations to have patron deities. If a given nation was subdued by another nation, decimated by a plague, or in any manner lowered in the sight of other nations, the patron deity of that besieged nation was looked on as being unable to protect his nation. He became weak in the eyes of the world (cf. the Mesha Stela). The Lord did not want the Egyptian bondage to be misconstrued as a demonstration of his inadequacies, for the truth was just the opposite. It was because of his immutable faithfulness to his promises that he disciplined his people. But the name of the Lord was holy, and the Israelites were to bear continually a proper witness to that holy name (Exod 19:5–6). Though Israel had failed to sanctify the name of the Lord among the nations, the Lord himself would do so by his deliverance of Israel from Egypt. Then all the nations would know that he was the Lord, the true, faithful, and powerful God of Israel (Exod 7:5; Ps 106:8–12).

Notes

---

4 The interrogative הֲ (*hᵃ*) associated with הֲתִשְׁפֹּט (*hᵃṭišpōṭ*, "Will you judge") carries the sense of an impassioned or indignant affirmation (cf. BDB, p. 210, 1.c). The repetition of the phrase conveys emphasis.

5 בְּיוֹם (*bᵉyôm*, "on the day") is perhaps overtranslated in the NIV. It means simply "when." The use of בָּחֳרִי (*boḥᵒrî*, "I chose") is the only use of this term in Ezekiel. The root implies a choice of something out of a group, chosen to perform a task. It gives the idea of God's loving, gracious, eternal choice (election) of Israel by oath to become a unique nation out of the nations of the world in order to be God's instrument of blessing to the world (cf. the Abrahamic covenant). Such election by Yahweh required a response of loyal obedience on Israel's part.

The unique use of בֵּית יַעֲקֹב (*bêt yaʿᵃqōb*, "house of Jacob") in this context highlights the formative period of the nation of Israel, when God created the nation from the house (i.e., sons) of Jacob.

---

b. Rebellion in the wilderness

20:10–26

¹⁰Therefore I led them out of Egypt and brought them into the desert. ¹¹I gave them my decrees and made known to them my laws, for the man who obeys them will live by them. ¹²Also I gave them my Sabbaths as a sign between us, so they would know that I the LORD made them holy.

¹³"Yet the people of Israel rebelled against me in the desert. They did not follow my decrees but rejected my laws—although the man who obeys them will live by them—and they utterly desecrated my Sabbaths. So I said I would pour out my wrath on them and destroy them in the desert. ¹⁴But for the sake of my name I did what would keep it from being profaned in the eyes of the nations in whose sight I had brought them out. ¹⁵Also with uplifted hand I swore to them in the desert that I would not bring them into the land I had given them—a land flowing with milk and honey, most beautiful of all lands—¹⁶because they rejected my laws and did not follow my decrees and desecrated my Sabbaths. For their hearts were devoted to their idols. ¹⁷Yet I looked on them with pity and did not destroy them or put an end to them in the desert. ¹⁸I said to their children in the desert, "Do not follow the statutes of your fathers or keep their laws or defile

yourselves with their idols. [19]I am the LORD your God; follow my decrees and be careful to keep my laws. [20]Keep my Sabbaths holy, that they may be a sign between us. Then you will know that I am the LORD your God."

[21]"'But the children rebelled against me: They did not follow my decrees, they were not careful to keep my laws—although the man who obeys them will live by them—and they desecrated my Sabbaths. So I said I would pour out my wrath on them and spend my anger against them in the desert. [22]But I withheld my hand, and for the sake of my name I did what would keep it from being profaned in the eyes of the nations in whose sight I had brought them out. [23]Also with uplifted hand I swore to them in the desert that I would disperse them among the nations and scatter them through the countries, [24]because they had not obeyed my laws but had rejected my decrees and desecrated my Sabbaths, and their eyes lusted after their fathers' idols. [25]I also gave them over to statutes that were not good and laws they could not live by, [26]I let them become defiled through their gifts—the sacrifice of every firstborn—that I might fill them with horror so they would know that I am the LORD.'

10–12 As in vv.5–10, Ezekiel followed his basic pattern in this chapter: God's blessing (vv.10–12); Israel's rebellion (vv.13, 21); and God's sanctification of his name through limited judgment (vv.14–20, 22–26), the latter two items being repeated.

Ezekiel turned from Israel's corrupt beginning to the generation that God brought out of Egypt by his great power (v.10; Exod 12–15). God's kindness and grace were manifested in the Exodus and in the giving of the covenant through Moses (cf. "my decrees," "my laws," v.11; cf. Exod 19–Num 9; Deut). This covenant was given to a people who were to be in a covenant relationship with God. It explained the godly principles that enabled one to live life at its best. God, as the Creator of life, knew how life was to be lived. Therefore, the Israelites were to observe all the commandments of the law, practicing them in daily life (Lev 18:5; Deut 10:12–13).

The Mosaic covenant followed the pattern of the international suzerain-vassal treaties of the second millennium B.C. A great king would enter into a covenant with a lesser power in order to provide blessings and protection to that vassal. The subject nation would, in turn, follow the stipulations laid down by the great king. God chose to reveal Israel's constitution in this familiar literary form. God was the great king, and Israel had become his vassal. The Lord had been benevolent to Israel by bringing her out of Egyptian servitude. Israel, in turn, was to be a witness for God in the world, living according to God's righteous stipulations of the Mosaic covenant. The great king would seal this covenant by placing his "sign" in the midst of the legal policy. The sign was a portrait of himself in some manner. The Lord placed his sign-seal of the Mosaic covenant in the midst of the Decalogue (cf. Kline, *Great King*, pp. 18–19). He represented himself as the Creator in the sign of the Sabbath (Exod 20:8–11; 31:13, 17). By continually observing the weekly Sabbath, Israel would be reminded that God graciously set her apart as an instrument of blessing to the world and as a witness against the pagans who had exchanged the worship of the Creator for the worship of his creation (v.12; Neh 9:14; Rom 1:25).

13–17 The phrase "the man who obeys them will live by them" (v.13) reflects Leviticus 18:5. It is not a reference to eternal salvation by works. As the background of Leviticus 18:5 was idolatry, so rebellion of this kind sets the context of this phrase in Ezekiel. Obeying God's laws showed Israel's faith in the Lord; disobedience showed Israel's unbelief. Those who received life by faith in God were to live that life by keeping his commandments—then and now (cf. Rom 10:4–5; Gal 3:10–25; see Walter C. Kaiser, Jr., "Leviticus 18:5 and Paul: Do This and You Shall Live (Eternally?)," JETS 14 [1971]: 19–28).

In spite of the gracious blessings of God, this generation of Israelites rebelled against their Lord in the wilderness by rejecting the commands of the Mosaic covenant and profaning the Sabbaths (v.13a; cf. Num 11–14). Therefore, the Lord resolved to destroy Israel (v.13b; Num 14:11–12); yet he would not, because his name would be profaned before the nations if he destroyed his people. The nations would think that he was unable to protect Israel in the wilderness once he brought them forth from Egypt (v.14). Moses interceded in this manner on behalf of God's people (Num 14:13–19; Deut 1:26–40; Ps 106:23–25) so that the Lord spared them. Instead God declared that he would not bring that generation into the Promised Land because they had rejected his ways in their idolatrous hearts (vv.15–17; cf. Num 14:32). It was only because of the Lord's holy name that he graciously spared the nation from destruction.

18–26 All members of Israel twenty years and under had the prospect of entering the land of Canaan. This was a benevolent act of God toward this second generation. God, knowing the nation's past attraction to idolatry, warned this new generation not to follow their father's idolatrous and rebellious ways. They were to live God's ways and observe the weekly Sabbath as a sign of the Mosaic covenant. Thereby they would realize that the Lord was their God (vv.18–20). However, as in the cycle of their fathers, this generation also rebelled against the Lord, failing to live by the law and profaning the Sabbaths. Once again God resolved to destroy his people (v.21). Yet, as before, God's holiness restrained his wrath so that his name might not be desecrated among the nations (v.22; cf. Num 16:21–22; 25:1–9). Instead, God swore that he would disperse his people among the nations (vv.23–24; Lev 26:33; Deut 28:64; Ps 106:26–27), give them over to statutes they could not live by (v.25), and pronounce their sacrifices unclean. Then he would make them desolate and thereby cause them to know that he was the Lord their God (v.26). That God would give Israel "statutes that were not good" (v.25) means that Israel would choose to live according to the world's ordinances that brought misery and death (cf. 11:12; Lev 26; Deut 28:15–29:19; 2 Kings 17:26–41).. The "gifts" in v.26 referred to religious sacrifices (cf. Exod 28:38; Lev 23:38). The specific offerings in this context were the child-sacrifices of their firstborn to their pagan deities (Exod 13:12; Lev 18:21; Deut 18:10). This practice was especially common in the worship of Molech (2 Kings 21:6; 2 Chron 28:3).

Notes

11 חֹק (ḥōq, "decree") and מִשְׁפָּט (mišpāṭ, "law") may give emphasis to apodictic and casuistic law respectively, since ḥōq is derived from חָקַק (ḥāqaq, "to engrave") and mišpāṭ from שָׁפַט (šāpaṭ, "to judge"). However, efforts to make clear distinctions between these two terms have not been completely successful. When the two words are used coordinately, they often designate the whole of God's law (a hendiadys). In the present context the stipulations of the Mosaic covenant seem to be described by these coordinate words.

20 קַדֵּשׁוּ (qaddēšû, "keep holy") implies that one keep something in the sacred, holy sphere separated from the common and profane. In the Piel the verb describes the act of consecration. The Sabbaths of the Lord were to be kept sacred and holy (cf. TWOT, 2: 786–87).

c. Rebellion in the conquest and settlement of the land

20:27–29

> 27"Therefore, son of man, speak to the people of Israel and say to them, 'This is what the Sovereign LORD says: In this also your fathers blasphemed me by forsaking me: 28When I brought them into the land I had sworn to give them and they saw any high hill or any leafy tree, there they offered their sacrifices, made offerings that provoked me to anger, presented their fragrant incense and poured out their drink offerings. 29Then I said to them: What is this high place you go to?' " (It is called Bamah to this day.)

27–29 The Lord described the sin of Israel's first generations as blasphemy and unfaithfulness (v.27; Num 15:30–31). When a person (in any age) despises God's word, he slanders (or blasphemes) God. Such a one fails to live according to God's way and gives a poor testimony of God's character to others. This was as true in Ezekiel's day as it is today.

Israel had not learned by her forefathers' mistakes. The generation of Hebrews who entered Canaan began practicing the Canaanites' heathen rituals they saw (vv.28–29). The meaning of the term *bāmāh* ("high place") is uncertain (cf. TWOT, 1: 113). It is used in this context as a proper noun, designating a place. Perhaps the place that became known as the "high place" was at the site of Gibeon. This city had played a significant religious role in Israel's early history in Canaan (cf. 1 Sam 9; 1 Kings 3:4; 11:7; 1 Chron 16:39; 21:29; 2 Chron 1:3, 13). However, there is insufficient data to confirm this interpretation.

Notes

27 The translation of מָעַל (*māʿal*, "transgress") by "forsake" appears somewhat weak. This verb is used to designate "the breaking or violation of religious law as a conscious act of treachery" (TWOT, 1: 520). In the OT the normal victim against whom the act is perpetrated by Israel is Yahweh, Israel's Suzerain.

d. Rebellion of Judah in Ezekiel's day

20:30–44

> 30"Therefore say to the house of Israel: 'This is what the Sovereign LORD says: Will you defile yourselves the way your fathers did and lust after their vile images? 31When you offer your gifts—the sacrifice of your sons in the fire—you continue to defile yourselves with all your idols to this day. Am I to let you inquire of me, O house of Israel? As surely as I live, declares the Sovereign LORD, I will not let you inquire of me.
> 32" 'You say, "We want to be like the nations, like the peoples of the world, who serve wood and stone." But what you have in mind will never happen. 33As surely as I live, declares the Sovereign LORD, I will rule over you with a mighty hand and

an outstretched arm and with outpoured wrath. ³⁴I will bring you from the nations and gather you from the countries where you have been scattered—with a mighty hand and an outstretched arm and with outpoured wrath. ³⁵I will bring you into the desert of the nations and there, face to face, I will execute judgment upon you. ³⁶As I judged your fathers in the desert of the land of Egypt, so I will judge you, declares the Sovereign LORD. ³⁷I will take note of you as you pass under my rod, and I will bring you into the bond of the covenant. ³⁸I will purge you of those who revolt and rebel against me. Although I will bring them out of the land where they are living, yet they will not enter the land of Israel. Then you will know that I am the LORD.

³⁹" 'As for you, O house of Israel, this is what the Sovereign LORD says: Go and serve your idols, every one of you! But afterward you will surely listen to me and no longer profane my holy name with your gifts and idols. ⁴⁰For on my holy mountain, the high mountain of Israel, declares the Sovereign LORD, there in the land the entire house of Israel will serve me, and there I will accept them. There I will require your offerings and your choice gifts, along with all your holy sacrifices. ⁴¹I will accept you as fragrant incense when I bring you out from the nations and gather you from the countries where you have been scattered, and I will show myself holy among you in the sight of the nations. ⁴²Then you will know that I am the LORD, when I bring you into the land of Israel, the land I had sworn with uplifted hand to give to your fathers. ⁴³There you will remember your conduct and all the actions by which you have defiled yourselves, and you will loathe yourselves for all the evil you have done. ⁴⁴You will know that I am the LORD, when I deal with you for my name's sake and not according to your evil ways and your corrupt practices, O house of Israel, declares the Sovereign LORD.' "

30–31 God suddenly brought the cyclic pattern of his benevolence, Israel's rebellion, his judgment, and his grace to bear on the contemporary scene (*ʿad hayyôm*). He challenged the current elders, as representatives of the exiles and Judah, with a question: Are you not rebelling like your fathers? Were they not defiling themselves —playing the harlot with Canaan's detestable idols and offering their sons as sacrifices to idols (vv.30–31)? Contemporary Israel was as rebellious as her ancestors had been. So the Lord turned to the immediate issue of the people's inquiry. He emphatically replied that he would not give an audience to anyone who disobeyed his ways yet said that they wanted to know his will.

32–37 Because he loved her, God rejected Israel's desire to be like other idolatrous nations (v.32). In doing so he carried the cycle of judgment and grace into Israel's future history. In his judgment he would rule over her now (v.33); yet he would restore Judah at the end of the Babylonian captivity (v.34). However, there would be a second dispersion of the Israelites in which God would judge Israel and bring the people "into the desert of the nations" as he had done during Israel's Egyptian sojourn (vv.35–36). This dispersion is most likely the one that happened in the first century A.D.

Yet, as God's grace followed judgment, so he would ultimately bring Israel into the bond of the covenant as his special possession (v.37; cf. Hos 2:14–15). When a sheep passed under his shepherd's rod, it indicated that that sheep belonged to the shepherd (cf. Lev 27:32; Mic 7:14). "Shepherd" was a common ancient Near Eastern metaphor for king. A rod could also have the connotation of wrath and discipline (Ps 89:32; Lam 3:1). However, since "passing under my rod" is parallel with "bring you into the bond of the covenant," the idea of shepherd possession seems the basic idea expressed by this phrase.

38 The covenant was described in terms of a cleansing that would result in the knowledge of God. This is the heart issue of the new covenant promise (36:25–38; Jer 31:31–34). Israel would ultimately become a cleansed flock of the Lord through the new covenant. The process of cleansing would purge out sinners from Israel in that they would not return to the land of blessing when the Lord would ultimately restore his people to that land (cf. Dan 12:10; Jer 31:34). The future cycle of God's alternating judgment and grace would be similar to that displayed in the "first" wilderness wandering after Israel came forth from Egypt.

39–44 The brief résumé of Israel's history of rebellion concluded with an application to Ezekiel's contemporaries. God had delivered them over to their idols since they too had refused to listen to him (v.39a; cf. Rom 1:24–25). The Lord also encouraged them by reminding them of his ultimate grace to Israel at the end time ("afterward" in v.39b). Once Israel was cleansed through the final judgment, God would make sure that she did not allow his holy name to be profaned among the nations again. God would accomplish this by bringing back all Israel of that day to worship on his holy mountain. There he would accept them and their sacrificial worship (vv.40–41; cf. chs. 40–48). The Israelites would see his faithfulness and come to know him ultimately through their restoration (v.42). The Israelites would have a contrite heart that loathed their past sins (v.43). They would come to see that God's grace had been poured out on them throughout the millennia, because the Lord refused to allow his holy name to be defiled (v.44). God had continually dealt with them on the basis of his grace rather than on what they deserved. The same principle holds true today!

Notes

---

30 The continual sinning of Israel is stressed by the use of the participles נִטְמָאִים (niṭmeʾîm, "defiling") and זֹנִים (zōnîm, "lusting").

40 הַר מְרוֹם (har merôm, "high mountain") of Israel most likely refers to the place of worship in the millennial kingdom (cf. 43:12). Though this future place of worship is often referred to as "Zion" (Isa 35:10; 59:20; Joel 3:17, 21; Mic 4:7), this does not necessarily mean that Mount Zion, as it is geographically known in the OT, will be the exact place mentioned in this verse. Geographical changes will take place in Palestine at the beginning of the Millennium (cf. ch. 47; Zech 14). Also, the term "Zion" is used to refer to the city of Jerusalem. The mountain in this verse should be understood in keeping with 43:12.

44 The chapter division in the MT is between v.44 and v.45 in the English text. This division best follows the argument of the book at this point.

---

2. Judgment on Judah's contemporary leaders (20:45–21:32)

a. The burning of the southern forest

20:45–21:7

⁴⁵The word of the LORD came to me: ⁴⁶"Son of man, set your face toward the south; preach against the south and prophesy against the forest of the southland. ⁴⁷Say to the southern forest: 'Hear the word of the LORD. This is what the Sover-

eign LORD says: I am about to set fire to you, and it will consume all your trees, both green and dry. The blazing flame will not be quenched, and every face from south to north will be scorched by it. ⁴⁸Everyone will see that I the LORD have kindled it; it will not be quenched.' "

⁴⁹Then I said, "Ah, Sovereign LORD! They are saying of me, 'Isn't he just telling parables?' "

²¹:¹The word of the LORD came to me: ²"Son of man, set your face against Jerusalem and preach against the sanctuary. Prophesy against the land of Israel ³and say to her: 'This is what the LORD says: I am against you. I will draw my sword from its scabbard and cut off from you both the righteous and the wicked. ⁴Because I am going to cut off the righteous and the wicked, my sword will be unsheathed against everyone from south to north. ⁵Then all people will know that I the LORD have drawn my sword from its scabbard; it will not return again.'

⁶"Therefore groan, son of man! Groan before them with broken heart and bitter grief. ⁷And when they ask you, 'Why are you groaning?' you shall say, 'Because of the news that is coming. Every heart will melt and every hand go limp; every spirit will become faint and every knee become as weak as water.' It is coming! It will surely take place, declares the Sovereign LORD."

45–49 Having surveyed the history of Israel's rebellion and found the nation deserving of judgment in Ezekiel's day, God announced and described the judgment that he was about to bring on Judah. Four messages described God's judgment by Babylonia (cf. vv.45; 21:1, 8, 18). The first message consists of a parable (vv.45–49) and its explicit interpretation (21:1–7). The parable described a forest fire in the southern forests that burned every tree, whether green or dry (vv.46–47). Each person would see that God kindled the unquenchable fire (v.48). The parable emphasized the "south" by using the three most common Hebrew terms for that direction (cf. Notes). The southern forest referred to the southern kingdom of Judah, a forested area in biblical times, even into the upper Negev.

Verse 49 provides a transition between the parable and its interpretation. Ezekiel's hearers were frustrated. Ezekiel, the old parabolic speaker, was at it again. This was another one of those parables they did not understand. Therefore, God would give the interpretation.

1–5 The parable's interpretation was revealed in these verses. Ezekiel was instructed to "set [his] face toward the south" (20:46). The south was defined as Jerusalem, its sanctuaries, and all the land of Israel (which was then Judah) (v.2). The fire in the parable (20:47) represented a sword of judgment (v.3), i.e., the sword of Nebuchadnezzar and his armies (cf. vv.18–27). The green and dry trees symbolize the righteous and the wicked, respectively. God's judgment would be comprehensive. When God would pour out his wrath on the sinner, the effects would cover the entire land from north to south. Each person would be touched by the sword of his fury (vv.4–5; cf. 20:47). Both the righteous and the wicked would experience the land's devastation. Everyone would know that the Lord was the one who brought the judgment (v.5; cf. 20:48).

6–7 The effects of God's wrath on Judah would also be devastating. The people would lose strength. Ezekiel communicated these emotional responses to the people by groaning as one who was in emotional distress and in bitter anguish. When the exiles inquired as to the cause of his grief, he would tell them that he was a sign of the emotional distress they would have when God's judgment would come.

At that time their hearts would melt, their spirits would faint, and their hands and knees would become weak like water (vv. 6–7). This would happen. This was not just a scare tactic. God declared that this judgment would "surely take place."

Notes

46 The MT versification shows the unity of 20:45–49 (MT 21:1–5) with 21:1–7 (MT 21:6–12). The three words used for "south" in this verse are (1) תֵּימָנָה (*têmānāh*), which basically means "right," so that when facing east in the normal orientation of that day, the "right" would be "south"; (2) דָּרוֹם (*dārôm*) is Ezekiel's normal designation for "south," used only for geographical directions in all OT occurrences; and (3) נֶגֶב (*negeḇ*), a term that denotes a "dried-up land," normally the region south of the Judean hill country from Beersheba south, though it is also used for geographical direction (especially here combined with the word "forest"). The LXX incorrectly understood all three expressions as place names. That these three words are uniquely connected and interpreted as Jerusalem, the sanctuary, and the land of Israel, respectively, cannot be substantiated without question. That the "south" in this context encompasses Jerusalem, the sanctuary, and the land of Israel is supported by the interpretation of 21:2.

47 פָּנִים (*pānîm*) has been translated by some as "surface" and by others in the more normal sense of "face." Contextually the latter seems the better rendering, in light of the "everyone" of 20:48 and "all people" of 21:5 and the judgment's comprehensiveness.

6 שִׁבְרוֹן מָתְנַיִם (*šiḇrôn moṯnayim*, "broken heart") literally means "breaking of loins." "Loins" in the OT are viewed as the center of physical strength and the seat of emotions. When they are "broken," the strength is gone and one is helpless. The emotions are shattered.

b. The slaughter of the sword

21:8–17

[8]The word of the LORD came to me: [9]"Son of man, prophesy and say, 'This is what the LORD says:

" 'A sword, a sword,
  sharpened and polished—
[10]sharpened for the slaughter,
  polished to flash like lightning!

" 'Shall we rejoice in the scepter of my son ⌞Judah⌟? The sword despises every such stick.

[11]" 'The sword is appointed to be polished,
  to be grasped with the hand;
it is sharpened and polished,
  made ready for the hand of the slayer.
[12]Cry out and wail, son of man,
  for it is against my people;
it is against all the princes of Israel.
They are thrown to the sword
  along with my people.
Therefore beat your breast.

13" 'Testing will surely come. And what if the scepter of Judah, which the sword despises, does not continue? declares the Sovereign LORD.'

14"So then, son of man, prophesy
and strike your hands together
Let the sword strike twice,
even three times.
It is a sword for slaughter—
a sword for great slaughter.
closing in on them from every side.
15So that hearts may melt
and the fallen be many,
I have stationed the sword for slaughter
at all their gates.
Oh! It is made to flash like lightning,
it is grasped for slaughter.
16O sword, slash to the right,
then to the left,
wherever your blade is turned.
17I too will strike my hands together,
and my wrath will subside.
I the LORD have spoken."

8–13 Ezekiel was instructed to sing a song (poem) about a sword, sharpened, polished, and ready for the slaughter, with the speed of lightning (vv.9–10a). The sword is pictured as ready to be taken by the hand of the slayer (v.11—identified as Nebuchadnezzar in vv.18–23).

Therefore, Ezekiel would weep and wail; for the Babylonian sword of judgment was against Judah, God's people, especially her leaders (v.12a). Ezekiel would strike his breast (or, better, "thigh"), a gesture of remorse, grief, and despair over this heartbreaking verdict (v.12b; cf. Jer 31:19). The people of Judah had been tested and found wanting. In v.13 the masculine gender of the verb *bōḥan* ("testing") cannot, as some desire, refer to the feminine *ḥereḇ* ("sword") but must refer contextually to the near masculine singular antecedent *ʿām* ("people"). Since the nation had failed the testing, the solemn question was whether Judah and her ruler ("the scepter," cf. v.10) would continue to exist? Would God's judgment be final?

Judah (and the exiles) was rejoicing and still hoping in the promise of the royal messianic line through the tribe of Judah. In Genesis 49:10 both "scepter" and "my son" are used to describe the promise. The messianic overtones of Genesis 49:9–10, together with the promises of the Davidic covenant (2 Sam 7), were foundational to Judah's hope. She was certain that God's messianic promises ("scepter of my son") (cf. Gen 49:9–10; 2 Sam 7) would preserve her as a nation forever. She need not fear Ezekiel's pronouncements of judgment (by Babylonia; cf. vv.18–23). However, the people had forgotten the stipulation of discipline even in the Davidic covenant (2 Sam 7:14) as well as the cursing formula of the Mosaic covenant (Deut 28–29).

There was no immediate hope for contemporary Judah in the promises of Genesis 49 (cf. v.27), for God would be faithful to exercise his justice in discipline on Judah and her current ruler in order to purify her. But the ultimate "scepter of Judah," the Messiah, would not be extinguished (cf. v.13). This was Judah's only hope in the midst of their current judgment. When Judah would ultimately be purified, then *the* "scepter" (Messiah) would rule over his people (cf. v.27).

14–17 Ezekiel clapped his hands in approval of the judgment but with scorn and contempt for the iniquity that had precipitated God's wrath (v.14a; cf. 6:11; 22:13; 25:6; Num 24:10; 2 Kings 11:12; Job 27:23; Ps 47:1; Isa 55:12). By this act Ezekiel demonstrated the Lord's attitude of justice toward Judah's sin and encouraged the sword's greater effectiveness. The intensity of the judgment was emphasized by the doubling and tripling of the sword; it became three times more effective than it normally would be. Two and three swords were not present; rather, the sword's swiftness and intensity manifested in God's wrath produced two to three times the normal slaughter. The sword totally encompassed the people; their hearts melted, and many fell in their gates in the lightning fast invasion (vv.14–15). Ultimately the sword seemed to be in God's hand (v.11; cf. vv.15, 17). The judgment was comprehensive (cf. vv.4–5, 7, 47). The song (poem) builds to a climax. The sword's devastation covered the entire country from right (or south) to left (or north), a play on words depicting the sharpening of the sword blade back and forth as well as the comprehensiveness of the judgment from north to south (v.16). The Lord gave his approval by clapping. But he also declared that his wrath would cease when this judgment was complete (v.17).

Notes

10 Interpretations of "the scepter of my son" vary. Some find its meaning in Ps 2, but nothing in that context has any direct relationship to this passage. A scepter of discipline by foreigners is sometimes set forth as the meaning, but support is insufficient.

14 שְׁלִישָׁתָה (šᵉlîšitāh, "three times") is a *hapax legomenon* and has been conjecturally amended in numerous translations. The form, taken as rendered in the MT, is an adjective with the ה (h) terminative affixed, giving a directional emphasis to the meaning of "third." KD renders it adverbially as "three-fold." The sense is that the word has been doubled and is moving toward a third sword.

c. *The imminent judgment by Babylonia*

21:18–27

¹⁸The word of the Lord came to me: ¹⁹"Son of man, mark out two roads for the sword of the king of Babylon to take, both starting from the same country. Make a signpost where the road branches off to the city. ²⁰Mark out one road for the sword to come against Rabbah of the Ammonites and another against Judah and fortified Jerusalem. ²¹For the king of Babylon will stop at the fork in the road, at the junction of the two roads, to seek an omen: He will cast lots with arrows, he will consult his idols, he will examine the liver. ²²Into his right hand will come the lot for Jerusalem, where he is to set up battering rams, to give the command to slaughter, to sound the battle cry, to set battering rams against the gates, to build a ramp and to erect siege works. ²³It will seem like a false omen to those who have sworn allegiance to him, but he will remind them of their guilt and take them captive.

²⁴"Therefore this is what the Sovereign Lord says: 'Because you people have brought to mind your guilt by your open rebellion, revealing your sins in all that you do—because you have done this, you will be taken captive.

²⁵" 'O profane and wicked prince of Israel, whose day has come, whose time of punishment has reached its climax, ²⁶this is what the Sovereign Lord says: Take off the turban, remove the crown. It will not be as it was: The lowly will be exalted

and the exalted will be brought low. [27]A ruin! A ruin! I will make it a ruin! It will not be restored until he comes to whom it rightfully belongs; to him I will give it.'

18-21 The prophetic "sword song" is now integrated and reinforced by symbolic action. Ezekiel drew a map, perhaps in the dirt or on a brick, on which he made a road from Babylonia toward Canaan. He placed a signpost in the road where it forked, one branch leading toward Rabbath-Ammon, the capital of Ammon, and the other branch descending to Jerusalem (vv. 18-20). Damascus was the normal junction where the road divided. The king of Babylonia, Nebuchadnezzar, was shown standing at the fork in the road, using all manner of magic and divination in order to determine which nation he should attack first (v. 21). The combined conspiracy of Judah and Ammon against Babylonia in 589 B.C. undoubtedly precipitated this coming of the Babylonian army. Shaking arrows inscribed with personal or place names (belomancy) was a form of casting lots. Each arrow was marked with a name, the arrows placed in the quiver, the quiver whirled about, and the first arrow to fall out was the gods' decision. Household idols were intimately related to ancestral inheritance. Perhaps also they were consulted as mediums, representatives for their forefathers, who were supposed to give guidance (necromancy). The liver, being the seat of the life, was commonly examined with a decision of divination being determined from its color or markings (hepatoscopy). Nebuchadnezzar used all three means of divination with the same result. Though God did not condone divination in any form, he was the sovereign God who controlled all things. He could control these pagan practices to accomplish his will (cf. Jer 27:6).

22-23 The unanimous decision of this divining was to pursue the path to Jerusalem (v. 22) and to lay siege to that city (cf. 4:2). The inhabitants of Judah responded in unbelief. They were convinced that this was false divination and continued to place confidence in their covenant treaties with Nebuchadnezzar or their Mosaic covenant with God ("sworn allegiance," v. 23). The phrase "sworn allegiance" has led to two basic interpretations. Some maintain that the oaths were involved in the Mosaic covenant, for Judah had already broken her agreements with Nebuchadnezzar and would not be relying on them. Others maintain that the treaty-oaths were those made with Babylonia, for contextually the two participants are Babylonia and Judah. One could argue that the Mosaic covenant had already been broken; so Judah would not be relying on it. Perhaps the argument of the entire passage and the prophet's earlier invective against breaking political treaties (cf. 17:16-18) lends greater weight to the treaty concept with Babylonia. Regardless of which view we accept, Judah was placing unfounded confidence in treaties she had broken. This provided no security at all. Judah was deluded. On the contrary, Nebuchadnezzar ("he") would bring Judah's iniquity to remembrance when he, as God's instrument of wrath, destroyed the nation.

24-27 This message was concluded with a judicial sentence. Since Judah's sins had become manifest (v. 24), Jerusalem would be seized; and the wicked prince of Israel, Zedekiah, would be cut off in this time of final ("climax") punishment (in 586 B.C.) (v. 25). The removal of the priesthood and the kingship from Judah were pictured, respectively, in the removal of the high priest's turban (Exod 28:4, 37, 39; 29:6; 39:28, 31; Lev 8:9; 16:4) and the king's crown (v. 26). These would not be rightly worn again till "he comes to whom it rightfully belongs" (v.27), a definite reference to Genesis 49:10 and the king-priest Messiah (cf. Heb 5–7). "Until Shiloh comes" in Genesis 49:10 (NIV mg.) shows that the rule (scepter) would remain in the tribe of Judah till Messiah (Shiloh as a proper name; cf. ZPEB, 5:402–4) came. Ezekiel used this reference with its messianic overtones to stress also in this context that the kingship (and priesthood) would be removed in judgment but returned ultimately in the Messiah's coming in accord with Genesis 49:10. God's judgment would be so complete that everything would be "topsy-turvy" socially ("the low will be exalted and the exalted will be brought low"). The threefold repetition of "ruin" stresses the intensity of God's wrath and its destruction administered by Babylonia.

Notes

21 תְּרָפִים (terāpîm, "idols") were household gods, probably of Hittite origin, primarily associated with divination (cf. TWOT, 2: 980).

23 שְׁבֻעוֹת לָהֶם (šebu'ê šebu'ôt lāhem, lit., "to those who have sworn allegiances") supports the political treaties view, since "allegiances" (pl.) are involved.

d. Postponement of judgment on Ammon

21:28–32

28"And you, son of man, prophesy and say, 'This is what the Sovereign LORD says about the Ammonites and their insults:

" 'A sword, a sword,
    drawn for the slaughter,
polished to consume
    and to flash like lightning!
29Despite false visions concerning you
    and lying divinations about you,
it will be laid on the necks
    of the wicked who are to be slain,
whose day has come,
    whose time of punishment has reached its climax.
30Return the sword to its scabbard.
    In the place where you were created,
in the land of your ancestry,
    I will judge you.
31I will pour out my wrath upon you
    and breathe out my fiery anger against you;
I will hand you over to brutal men,
    men skilled in destruction.
32You will be fuel for the fire,
    your blood will be shed in your land,
you will be remembered no more;
    for I the LORD have spoken.' "

28–32 The other route that Nebuchadnezzar could have taken at the fork in the road was the road to Ammon (cf. v.20). Since Ammon would mock and mistreat

Judah in her collapse before Babylonia, Ezekiel sang the same "sword song" to Ammon (v.28). The Ammonites had seen empty visions and divined lies that would lead them to fall on Judah, "on the necks of the wicked who are to be slain," at their time of punishment for iniquity (v.29).

God, however, stayed Ammon's terrorizing of Judah by calling for the sword to be placed back into the sheath (v.30a). Why this was done, we do not know. God would judge Ammon by the sword in their own land (v.30b; cf. 25:1–7), where he would pour out indignation on them with the fire of his wrath, delivering them to men skilled in destruction who would devour them (vv.31–32). This judgment on Ammon was not forgotten just because Babylonia chose to attack Jerusalem first. It was certain! The time element of this judgment was not certain, though it seemed related to the judgment soon to be executed by Babylonia (cf. 25:1–7). Ammon would be remembered no more.

3. The cause of judgment: Judah's idolatrous rulers (22:1–31)

a. Deliberate disobedience to the Mosaic covenant

22:1–16

¹The word of the LORD came to me: ²"Son of man, will you judge her? Will you judge this city of bloodshed? Then confront her with all her detestable practices ³and say: 'This is what the Sovereign LORD says: O city that brings on herself doom by shedding blood in her midst and defiles herself by making idols, ⁴you have become guilty because of the blood you have shed and have become defiled by the idols you have made. You have brought your days to a close, and the end of your years has come. Therefore I will make you an object of scorn to the nations and a laughingstock to all the countries. ⁵Those who are near and those who are far away will mock you, O infamous city, full of turmoil.

⁶" 'See how each of the princes of Israel who are in you uses his power to shed blood. ⁷In you they have treated father and mother with contempt; in you they have oppressed the alien and mistreated the fatherless and the widow. ⁸You have despised my holy things and desecrated my Sabbaths. ⁹In you are slanderous men bent on shedding blood; in you are those who eat at the mountain shrines and commit lewd acts. ¹⁰In you are those who dishonor their fathers' bed; in you are those who violate women during their period, when they are ceremonially unclean. ¹¹In you one man commits a detestable offense with his neighbor's wife, another shamefully defiles his daughter-in-law, and another violates his sister, his own father's daughter. ¹²In you men accept bribes to shed blood; you take usury and excessive interest and make unjust gain from your neighbors by extortion. And you have forgotten me, declares the Sovereign LORD.

¹³" 'I will surely strike my hands together at the unjust gain you have made and at the blood you have shed in your midst. ¹⁴Will your courage endure or your hands be strong in the day I deal with you? I the LORD have spoken, and I will do it. ¹⁵I will disperse you among the nations and scatter you through the countries; and I will put an end to your uncleanness. ¹⁶When you have been defiled in the eyes of the nations, you will know that I am the LORD.' "

1–2 Though Israel's history of wickedness demanded discipline (chs. 20–21), it was the abominations of contemporary Israel and her rulers that had ignited the punishment. Since the people had failed to see this fact, God directed Ezekiel to deliver three judgment messages to make this clear once more. The first detailed the manner in which the nation, led by her leaders in the capital city, Jerusalem, had broken the Mosaic covenant (vv.1–16). The second emphasized God's burning judgment that would display the people's impurity (vv.17–22). The third message stressed the failure of every aspect of Judah's society—especially her leadership—to follow God's ways (vv.23–31).

Ezekiel would act as a prosecutor of the nation (v.2), thus causing the "city of bloodshed" to become conscious of all her abominations that were the bases of the coming judgment. Jerusalem's chief characteristic was her bloodguiltiness, the taking of lives (cf. the repetition of "blood" in vv.3–4, 6, 9, 12–13). This perversion resulted from her disobedience to God's law.

3–5 The accusation was stated in two parts: (1) the abominations of Jerusalem (vv.3–5) and (2) the abominations of Judah's rulers (vv.6–12).

Jerusalem had committed murder in various ways. These would be itemized in the elaboration of the leaders' wickedness (vv.6–12; cf. 18:15–17). But the underlying cause of this bloodshed was the idolatry in the capital city. Her inhabitants had covered the city with idols that were contrary to her divine calling and that, in turn, defiled her (Exod 20:3–7). Since pagan religious practices did not restrict human sacrifice and wicked ways, the influence of idolatry had fostered indiscriminate murder that had, in turn, brought guilt (vv.3–4a). The acts of idolatry and bloodshed had brought God's judgment near. Jerusalem had come of age for judgment. She would become a reproach to the surrounding nations, both far and near. They would laugh at her miserable state and her infamous reputation (vv.4b–5). When a righteous people follow the world's ways, as Judah had done, the world ends up laughing at her.

6 The chief cause of Jerusalem's wickedness had been her evil rulers, especially her recent kings (e.g., Manasseh and Jehoiakim) and prince (Zedekiah). Each one had acted in his own strength to shed blood through the misuse of his power (cf. 2 Kings 21:16; 24:4). Each went as far as his power enabled him. Each broke the explicit prohibitions of the Mosaic covenant (Exod 20:13).

7–12 These verses list the many ways these rulers committed murder with their basic reasons for this. Each act violated the Mosaic covenant. The rulers ignored the rightful place and authority of parents, thus destroying the home (v.7a; prohibited in Exod 20:12; Lev 19:3). Socially these leaders were taking advantage of the helpless (v.7b; prohibited in Exod 22:21–24; 23:9; Lev 19:33; Deut 24:17). The indifference of the rulers to those they ruled over was directly related to their indifference to the holy things of God. They profaned the Sabbaths by ignoring them and thereby demonstrated their rejection of the Mosaic covenant, its divine ways, and their great God (v.8; prohibited in Exod 20:8; Lev 19:3).

On the contrary, the rulers engaged in heathen religious rituals (v.9b; prohibited in Deut 12:1–2; 16:21–22). Using informers ("slanderous men") these leaders carried out premeditated murders (v.9a; prohibited in Lev 19:16; cf. 1 Kings 21; Jer 6:28; 9:3). These same officials engaged in sexual sins (vv.9c–11; cf. note at 18:6; cf. Lev 18:6–23; 20:10–21). They prospered through illegitimate gain (v.12; cf. note at 18:8; prohibited in Exod 23:8; Deut 24:6, 10–12; 23:19–20; 27:25; cf. Isa 1:23; Amos 5:12; Mic 3:11). But at the heart of all these outward displays of wickedness was the main cause: "You have forgotten me, declares the Sovereign LORD." When one forgets God and leaves his ways, the path into every kind of abomination opens before him.

13–16 Ezekiel concluded this judgment speech with God's verdict of scorn for Jerusalem's dishonest gain and murder. God struck his hands (v.13) in a gesture of disapproval, venting his fury and expressing his triumph in judgment (so Zimmerli). He even questioned Jerusalem concerning her ability to stand through the days of judgment. Would her heart and hands be able to stand God's discipline (v.14)? The judgment would be threefold: (1) dispersion among the nations (v.15a), (2) cleansing of Jerusalem's impurity (v.15b), and (3) Jerusalem's desecration before all the nations by the Babylonians (v.16a). God's primary purpose in judgment, however, was to cause his people to know that he was the Lord, the only true God (v.16b).

Notes

16 Some render וְנִחַלְתְּ (weniḥalte, "you have been defiled") by the first person form וְנִחַלְתִּי (weniḥalti, "I have been defiled"), as found in many MSS. However, the MT makes good sense, for Jerusalem will profane herself before the nations when she is laid in ruins by the Babylonians and taken captive among the nations. It is not necessary that God be directly stated in the context as the initiator of her desecration.

b. The purification of judgment

22:17–22

> 17Then the word of the Lord came to me: 18"Son of man, the house of Israel has become dross to me; all of them are the copper, tin, iron and lead left inside a furnace. They are but the dross of silver. 19Therefore this is what the Sovereign Lord says: 'Because you have all become dross, I will gather you into Jerusalem. 20As men gather silver, copper, iron, lead and tin into a furnace to melt it with a fiery blast, so will I gather you in my anger and my wrath and put you inside the city and melt you. 21I will gather you and I will blow on you with my fiery wrath, and you will be melted inside her. 22As silver is melted in a furnace, so you will be melted inside her, and you will know that I the Lord have poured out my wrath upon you.' "

17–22 The imagery of the smelting process is at the heart of this second judgment speech. Israel was shown to be worthless as dross already, as if from a previous smelting (vv.18–19a). Now she would once again be melted by the heat of God's wrath in the furnace of Jerusalem (vv.19b–22a). This fire of God's wrath would literally be executed by the Babylonians when they would burn and sack Jerusalem. Even with this fiery trial, God desired to make himself and his justice known (vv.22b.).

c. The void of righteous leaders

22:23–31

> 23Again the word of the Lord came to me: 24"Son of man, say to the land, 'You are a land that has had no rain or showers in the day of wrath.' 25There is a conspiracy of her princes within her like a roaring lion tearing its prey; they devour people, take treasures and precious things and make many widows within her. 26Her priests do violence to my law and profane my holy things; they do not

distinguish between the holy and the common; they teach that there is no difference between the unclean and the clean; and they shut their eyes to the keeping
of my Sabbaths, so that I am profaned among them. ²⁷Her officials within her are
like wolves tearing their prey; they shed blood and kill people to make unjust gain.
²⁸Her prophets whitewash these deeds for them by false visions and lying divina-
tions. They say, 'This is what the Sovereign LORD says'—when the LORD has not
spoken. ²⁹The people of the land practice extortion and commit robbery; they
oppress the poor and needy and mistreat the alien, denying them justice.
³⁰"I looked for a man among them who would build up the wall and stand
before me in the gap on behalf of the land so I would not have to destroy it, but
I found none. ³¹So I will pour out my wrath on them and consume them with my
fiery anger, bringing down on their own heads all they have done, declares the
Sovereign LORD."

23–29 Verse 24 summarizes God's accusation and verdict: the land of Judah was
unclean and would therefore receive no "rain" of blessing in the day of judgment
("wrath"; cf. Deut 28:24). Judah was an impure nation mainly because the people
had failed in their responsibilities, especially those appointed as leaders.

Three categories of leaders are given, along with their failures. The princes
(prophets? cf. note at v.25) had conspired against the people for the purpose of
personal prosperity. The people had been blindly led by these false princes (false
prophets?) into situations (e.g., battle, rebellion, etc.) that had brought death to
many, increasing the number of widows in the nation (v.25). These leaders were
devouring lives like vicious lions.

The priests, who should have been leading the people into the knowledge of God
in the Mosaic covenant, had done violence to that covenant by polluting God's holy
statutes (v.26). They had failed to observe or to teach the distinction between the
holy and profane, the clean and the unclean. They disregarded the observance of
the Sabbath and profaned God through their pagan ritual practices. They gave poor
instruction in the things of the Lord. What instruction they did give was only for
monetary gain (cf. Mic 3:11).

The political "officials" (śārîm, "nobles") in the land had acted like ravenous
wolves, using violence to destroy people for personal gain (v.27; cf. vv.6–7, 9, 12).

Through their false visions and lying divinations, the prophets had whitewashed
their own impure motives and led the people astray by falsely claiming to have
God's authority—"This is what the Sovereign LORD says" (v.28; cf. 13:10).

Finally, God condemned the people for following this corrupt leadership and
maltreating one another. They had practiced extortion, robbery, and oppression of
the poor, needy, and stranger through unjust avenues (v.29). It was every man for
himself, each doing what was for his own profit (cf. Judg 21:25).

30–31 The Lord was unable to find anyone who would stand defensively, through
spiritual leadership and intercession, for the nation against the impending judgment
(v.30; cf. the previous oracle, in which *all* were dross [v.19]). Moses had stood in the
breach of the wall before the Lord in his day, to intercede for his people and to
instruct them in the ways of the Lord as a leader (Ps 106:23). But now God could
find no one to step to the front and lead Judah to repentance and to a godly walk
according to the stipulations of the Mosaic covenant.

Some have maintained that v.30 is contradictory to chapter 14, in which Ezekiel
argued that no righteous leader or man could deliver the nation from the impending

judgment because of his own personal righteousness. The current context argues that there was no person to take the lead and lead the nation into confession and a resulting righteous life among the people that would turn away God's wrath. There was no ruler who would intercede for the people. They were all corrupt! Therefore, the Lord concluded this last message with a judgment verdict. He would consume the people with the fire of his wrath. They were responsible for the coming judgment (v.31)!

Notes

24 The NIV has read מָטְרָה (*muṭṭārāh*, "has had rain") with the LXX against מְטֹהָרָה (*mᵉṭōhārāh*, "has been cleansed") of the MT. The LXX's rendering creates redundancy with גֻּשְׁמָה (*gušmāh*, "rain"; cf. discussion below). The MT's concept of uncleanness would seem to fit the context best.

גֻּשְׁמָה (*gušmāh*, "rain") is a *hapax legomenon* and therefore has presented translation problems. It is a noun with a third feminine feminine suffix. Some see the form without the mappiq in the ה (*h*), rendering it as a third feminine singular Pual perfect. Either way the root idea is "rain." It is possible to render the MT's לֹא גֻשְׁמָה (*lō᾽ gušmāh*, "no rain") as "[There will be] no rain for her," understanding the pronominal suffix as an objective genitive (cf. GKC, par. 135m).

25 נְבִיאֶיהָ (*nᵉbî᾽eyhā*, "her prophets") has been amended by some scholars to נְשִׂיאֶיהָ (*nᵉśî᾽eyhā*, "her princes") in harmony with the LXX. Those who read "princes" argue that it makes better sense to have four categories (princes, priests, officials, and prophets) rather than to repeat "prophets." Moreover, they declare, it is more logical to have "princes," rather than "prophets," "devouring lives" as "roaring lions." However, it would be perfectly satisfactory to repeat the term "prophets" (MT) in the context and to elaborate on their wicked ways.

28 The third masculine plural pronoun לָהֶם (*lāhem*, "for them") may have its antecedent in the immediate subject of the clause, נְבִיאֶיהָ (*nᵉbî᾽eyhā*, "her prophets"). Then it would be understood reflexively. Or the antecedent may be שָׂרֶיהָ (*śāreyhā*, "her officials"), in which case the pronoun would be rendered as an indirect object. In the first instance the reflexive sense would imply that the prophets were "whitewashing" for their own ends, whereas the use of the pronoun as an indirect object would mean that the prophets were aiding the officials with their heathen divining practices, through which they tried to whitewash the murder of the officials by giving them divine sanction. Normally the pronoun would be reflexive when restricted to the same person as the subject of the verb to its clause, which is probably so here.

29 עַם הָאָרֶץ (*῾am hā᾽āreṣ*, "the people of the land") refers to the commoners in contrast to the leadership of the nation (cf. note at 12:19).

4. An allegorical summary of Israel's political prostitution (23:1–49)

a. Israel's sordid youth

23:1–4

¹The word of the Lᴏʀᴅ came to me: ²"Son of man, there were two women, daughters of the same mother. ³They became prostitutes in Egypt, engaging in prostitution from their youth. In that land their breasts were fondled and their virgin

bosoms caressed. ⁴The older was named Oholah, and her sister was Oholibah.
They were mine and gave birth to sons and daughters. Oholah is Samaria, and
Oholibah is Jerusalem.

1–4 Ezekiel concluded the discussion of Israel's defective leadership with a summary allegory of the political adultery into which Israel's corrupt rulers had led her
(vv. 1–49). Though chapters 16 and 23 liken Israel to a prostitute, the emphasis of
each allegory is different. Chapter 16 stressed the history of Israel's spiritual adultery with pagan idols and heathen religions in likeness to the religions of Canaan,
the "mother" of the two 'daughters (16:44). Chapter 23 emphasizes Israel's political
adultery in which she sought security in political alliances with foreign powers.
Chapter 16 tended to stress the beginnings of Israel's history, whereas chapter 23
places more emphasis on her later history.

Several distinct speeches comprise the whole allegory. Before specific oracles
were addressed to Samaria and Jerusalem, Ezekiel briefly discussed the family background of these "two sisters" (vv. 2–4). They were both "born" of the same
"mother," an emphasis on their common origin from the united nation of Israel that
existed from the time of Egypt to Solomon. It was during their stay in Egypt as
youths that they had learned the trade of prostitution (v. 3; cf. 16:26; 20:7–8; Num
25:3–9; Josh 24:14; 2 Kings 21:15; Hos 1:2). Though the straightforward language of
Israel's perverted "sexual relations" with other countries may be morally and cultur-
ally offensive to many today, God did not hedge in clearly and concisely describing
the crudeness and perversion of wickedness and sin.

The two sisters of this chapter are named (v. 4). Samaria, the oldest (or lit. "greatest") in the sense of initiating perverted relations with other nations and in receiving
her punishment first, was named Oholah, which means "her tent." The significance
of this name is not clear, unless it refers to her propensity for heathen tent-shrines,
which are well attested (e.g., a recently excavated platform for a tent-shrine on
Mount Gerizim). Jerusalem, the younger of the two sisters, was called Oholibah,
meaning "my tent is in her." Perhaps this name had reference to God's temple
("tent" or "tabernacle") that dwelt in the city of Jerusalem (cf. 2 Sam 6:17; 1 Kings
8:4; 1 Chron 15:1; 16:1 et al.), in contrast to Samaria having "her own tent." Both
cities belonged to the Lord as his possession, specifically as his nations. Whether
this statement of possession was meant to convey "marriage" or "parenthood" is not
indicated within the text. It is best not to make explicit interpretations in an allegory
where the text and the context fail to delimit such a meaning. Both cities bore
children. These children most likely referred to their inhabitants and satellite
towns.

Notes

4 The lack of the mappiq in the ה (h) at the end of the two names for the sisters has raised
questions among some scholars as to the accuracy of translating these names as if they
conclude with a third feminine singular pronominal suffix. However, such a practice of
omitting the mappiq is used elsewhere in the OT when constructions such as these are
used as proper names.

וַתִּהְיֶינָה לִי (*wattihyeynāh lî*, "and they were mine") is better translated "and they became mine."

---

b. *Samaria's prostitution*

23:5–10

> 5"Oholah engaged in prostitution while she was still mine; and she lusted after her lovers, the Assyrians—warriors 6clothed in blue, governors and commanders, all of them handsome young men, and mounted horsemen. 7She gave herself as a prostitute to all the elite of the Assyrians and defiled herself with all the idols of everyone she lusted after. 8She did not give up the prostitution she began in Egypt, when during her youth men slept with her, caressed her virgin bosom and poured out their lust upon her.
>
> 9"Therefore I handed her over to her lovers, the Assyrians, for whom she lusted. 10They stripped her naked, took away her sons and daughters and killed her with the sword. She became a byword among women, and punishment was inflicted on her.

5–8 Samaria (Oholah), the eldest of the sisters, was the first to be accused of being unfaithful to the Lord by seeking security in the strength of other nations rather than in God's omnipotent protection (v.5). Samaria, the capital of the northern kingdom of Israel, had particularly sought "relations" with Assyria as her "lover." She had seduced the governors, officials, and military leaders of Assyria to enter into relations with her, which they willingly did (vv.6–7a; cf. 2 Kings 15:19–20; 17:3–4; Hos 5:13; 7:11; 8:9; 12:1–2; Amos 5:26). The Black Obelisk of Shalmaneser III shows Jehu, Israel's king, bowing in submission to Shalmaneser III and giving tribute to him as was the custom. Not only did Israel submit to political alliances with Assyria, but she likewise defiled herself by going after the idols and gods of Assyria (v.7b). This spiritual and political prostitution was not a new trend in Israel. Such perversion had characterized this nation since she began to practice this type of adultery in Egypt. What she had learned in her youth had regrettably affected her whole life. It had created a habit pattern that she had found increasingly difficult to break.

9–10 Therefore, the Lord announced his verdict. He would give Samaria into the hands of her lovers, the Assyrians, who would strip her bare of her inhabitants by either taking them into captivity or slaying them with the sword (vv.9–10). This occurred in 722 B.C. Assyria, the object of Israel's sinful lusts, became the instrument of Israel's judgment. God often allowed a nation or an individual to receive his fill of the perversion into which he had entered (cf. Jacob with Laban; Prov 1:31; Rom 1:24–32). Samaria's prostitution was so perverse that her name became a "byword" for an immoral woman (nation) among women (nations; cf. the use of the name "Jezebel" today).

Notes

5 קְרוֹבִים (*qᵉrôḇîm*, "warriors") normally means "near ones." The word initially appears ambiguous in this verse, though v.12 shows that the term is used to represent some sort of an official, perhaps one who is near to the king. Contextually the word does not refer to other nations near to Israel. Others (e.g., Zimmerli) have pointed to the closeness with the word קְרָב ($q^erāḇ$, "war") and the Akkadian *qur(ru)būti* ("body guards," "guardsmen"). It appears that the NIV translates the term with these similar words in view.

c. *Jerusalem's prostitution*

23:11–35

[11]"Her sister Oholibah saw this, yet in her lust and prostitution she was more depraved than her sister. [12]She too lusted after the Assyrians—governors and commanders, warriors in full dress, mounted horsemen, all handsome young men. [13]I saw that she too defiled herself; both of them went the same way.

[14]"But she carried her prostitution still further. She saw men portrayed on a wall, figures of Chaldeans portrayed in red, [15]with belts around their waists and flowing turbans on their heads; all of them looked like Babylonian chariot officers, natives of Chaldea. [16]As soon as she saw them, she lusted after them and sent messengers to them in Chaldea. [17]Then the Babylonians came to her, to the bed of love, and in their lust they defiled her. After she had been defiled by them, she turned away from them in disgust. [18]When she carried on her prostitution openly and exposed her nakedness, I turned away from her in disgust, just as I had turned away from her sister. [19]Yet she became more and more promiscuous as she recalled the days of her youth, when she was a prostitute in Egypt. [20]There she lusted after her lovers, whose genitals were like those of donkeys and whose emission was like that of horses. [21]So you longed for the lewdness of your youth, when in Egypt your bosom was caressed and your young breasts fondled.

[22]"Therefore, Oholibah, this is what the Sovereign LORD says: I will stir up your lovers against you, those you turned away from in disgust, and I will bring them against you from every side—[23]the Babylonians and all the Chaldeans, the men of Pekod and Shoa and Koa, and all the Assyrians with them, handsome young men, all of them governors and commanders, chariot officers and men of high rank, all mounted on horses. [24]They will come against you with weapons, chariots and wagons and with a throng of people; they will take up positions against you on every side with large and small shields and with helmets. I will turn you over to them for punishment, and they will punish you according to their standards. [25]I will direct my jealous anger against you, and they will deal with you in fury. They will cut off your noses and your ears, and those of you who are left will fall by the sword. They will take away your sons and daughters, and those of you who are left will be consumed by fire. [26]They will also strip you of your clothes and take your fine jewelry. [27]So I will put a stop to the lewdness and prostitution you began in Egypt. You will not look on these things with longing or remember Egypt anymore.

[28]"For this is what the Sovereign LORD says: I am about to hand you over to those you hate, to those you turned away from in disgust. [29]They will deal with you in hatred and take away everything you have worked for. They will leave you naked and bare, and the shame of your prostitution will be exposed. Your lewdness and promiscuity [30]have brought this upon you, because you lusted after the nations and defiled yourself with their idols. [31]You have gone the way of your sister; so I will put her cup into your hand.

[32]"This is what the Sovereign LORD says:

> "You will drink your sister's cup,
> a cup large and deep;
> it will bring scorn and derision,
> for it holds so much.
> [33]You will be filled wtih drunkenness and sorrow,
> the cup of ruin and desolation,
> the cup of your sister Samaria.

34You will drink it and drain it dry;
you will dash it to pieces
and tear your breasts.

I have spoken, declares the Sovereign LORD.

35"Therefore this is what the Sovereign LORD says: Since you have forgotten me and thrust me behind your back, you must bear the consequences of your lewdness and prostitution."

11–21 God turned to deliver his accusation against Samaria's younger sister, Jerusalem. Though Jerusalem, the capital of the southern kingdom of Judah, observed the consequences of Samaria's prostitution (in Samaria's fall to Assyria in 722 B.C.), she did not learn from Samaria's experience. Instead, Jerusalem proceeded to engage in more lustful and corrupt fornication than that of Samaria (v. 11). Rather than seeing her mission to be a servant of the Lord bringing salvation to the nations, like a prostitute Jerusalem cleverly used the nations for her own advantage.

Jerusalem's first major "lover" was Assyria, after whom she lusted in the same manner as did Samaria (v. 12; cf. v. 5; Ahaz in 2 Kings 16:8; Isa 7:7–9). Judah, having become defiled by the Assyrian idols (v. 13), then extended her prostitution to the Babylonians. She had inordinate affections for the Babylonian rulers (cf. Jer 22:21), seeing images of them on walls. Bas-reliefs were common decorations in Mesopotamian palaces and temples. Perhaps this statement was an allusion to some Judean envoys who were sent to Babylonia and saw the witness of her great power demonstrated on such walls. Judah did send messengers to woo Babylonia into "relations" with her, and Babylonia complied by entering into such "relations" with Jerusalem (vv. 14–16; cf. Jehoahaz and Jehoiakim, 2 Kings 23:32, 37). Judah became defiled through her political alliance with Babylonia. She had trusted in the human security of world powers rather than in God's perfect security. It appeared that Jerusalem realized her error in part after she became a vassal of Babylonia. She became disgusted with the Babylonians after she was debased (v. 17) and turned away (in pro-Egyptian policy). The relationship with Babylonia did not turn out to be all that she hoped for. But it was too late! God, in turn, announced that he also had become disgusted (alienated) with Jerusalem, which would be demonstrated by her fall in 586 B.C. to Nebuchadnezzar (v. 18).

As if Jerusalem had not learned her lesson, she turned away from Babylonia only to turn to Egypt for aid through "relations" with that nation (vv. 19–21; cf. Jer 2:18; 6:8; 37:5–7; Lam 4:17). It was like striking up an old relationship. Jerusalem failed to learn from the distasteful relationship with Babylonia that security lay, not in men, but in the Lord. Egypt, of course, was extremely anxious to enter into "relations" with Judah; for the Pharaohs were planning intervention in Asia. Such desire on Egypt's part was portrayed by the figure of lustful donkeys and horses (cf. Jer 2:24; 5:8; 13:27), while Jerusalem equally desired to renew the sexual perversion of her youth with Egypt.

22–27 Having accused Jerusalem of crass prostitution with the nations, the Lord announced his judgment verdict in four short speeches. The first speech stresses the fact that he would use Jerusalem's "lovers" to execute judgment on her (v. 22). The Babylonians whom Jerusalem then hated would be commissioned by God to judge Jerusalem through military aggression. Babylonia with all her entourage of vassal nations (including the eastern tribal groups of Pekod, Shoa, and Koa along with the Assyrians) would assault Jerusalem with a hatred stirred by God's jealousy against Jerusalem (vv.23–25a).

The "Chaldeans" initially referred to the people living immediately north of the Persian Gulf. With the rise of the Neo-Babylonian Empire, the term was used to describe the entire Babylonian Empire. The mention of "Babylonians" and "all the Chaldeans" shows that "Chaldean" was a broader term for the empire.

The details of the Babylonian judgment on Jerusalem are described in terms of ancient Near Eastern punishment for an adulteress: her "nose" and "ears" would be cut off (cf. ANET, p. 181). This figure was symbolized by the deportation of Judah's sons and daughters to Babylon (v.25b; cf. 2 Kings 24:10–16; 25:11; Dan 1:1). The remainder of Jerusalem's inhabitants would die by the sword and fire (cf. 2 Kings 25:18–21). Babylonia would strip Jerusalem of all her garments, leaving her disgraced as a prostitute (v.26). Jerusalem's "clothes" were her beautiful jewels, most likely a reference to her wealth and possessions (cf. v.46), though perhaps a reference to the temple treasures (cf. 2 Kings 25:13–17; 2 Chron 36:18). The severity of Babylonian judgment and deportation would terminate Jerusalem's adulterous relationship with Egypt. Judah would forget Egypt and never seek aid from her again (v.27). Such has been the case ever since the Babylonian captivity in 586 B.C.

28–31 The second judgment message is somewhat repetitious of the first one (cf. vv.28–29 with vv.22–26). Two additional factors are emphasized in this message. First, Babylonia's judgment on Jerusalem would demonstrate before all the nations the severity of Jerusalem's wicked adulterous ways (v.29). When Jerusalem would be left desolate, then the nations would understand that Judah had erred greatly to receive such punishment. Second, the specific reasons for Jerusalem's discipline were enumerated. She had committed political and spiritual adultery with the nations and their idols rather than trusting in the Lord for security and remaining faithful to him and his ways (v.30; cf. Exod 20:1–7 and Deut 17:14–20, which warn against such mistrust). Jerusalem had also erred by following Samaria's example and walking in her adulterous ways (v.31a). Therefore Jerusalem would share in the "cup" of Samaria's punishment (v.31b).

32–34 The third message among these four short judgment oracles was a poem, perhaps a song. It spoke of the "cup" of Samaria that Jerusalem must drink. The term "cup" was often used by the prophets to refer to God's wrath (cf. Matt 20:22; 26:39; Rev 14:10). This "cup song" concentrated on the theme of judgment like the "sword song" (21:8–17). Jerusalem's "cup" of judgment would include ridicule and mocking (v.32). She would be drunken, sorrowful, horrified, and devastated (v.33). Jerusalem would drain the entire contents of God's wrath, shatter the pottery cup by casting it down, and tear her breasts in utter agony (v.34). The horror of her punishment was sobering.

35 The final message of these four judgment oracles is but one verse in length, but it is perhaps the most significant of all. The chief reason for Jerusalem's impending judgment was that she had forgotten the Lord ("thrust me behind your back"). When a nation (or an individual) discards God, there is no other road to follow but that which leads to perversion and utter degradation.

Notes

18 וַתֵּקַע נַפְשִׁי מֵעָלֶיהָ (*wattēqaʿ napšî mēʿāleyhā*, "I turned away from her in disgust") is literally "my soul was torn away from her." "Soul" often refers to appetites, tastes, and passions, frequently used in connection with emotional states of joy, bliss, and love. The word is used here to show God's passionate displeasure with Jerusalem (Judah).

21 The NIV, following the Syriac and the Vulgate, has לְמַעַךְ (*lᵉmaʿēk*, "fondle") in analogy with v.3 over against the MT's לְמַעַן (*lᵉmaʿan*, "because"). Both words make sense in the context; but the MT is perhaps to be preferred since the Syriac may represent an attempt to coordinate v.21 with v.3.

23 The names Pekod, Shoa, and Koa are taken by most scholars to refer to tribes located on the eastern borders of the Babylonian Empire. פְּקוֹד (*pᵉqôd*, "Pekod") is believed to be equivalent to the Assyrian *pukudu*, the name of a tribe in southeastern Babylonia. שׁוֹעַ (*šôaʿ*, "Shoa") is equated with the Assyrian *sutû* or *sutî*, a term used by nomads east of the Tigris River. Originally these nomads lived in the Syrian desert according to the Amarna letters, but in the eleventh century B.C. they entered the eastern territory of Babylonia. קוֹעַ (*qôaʿ*, "Koa") finds its parallel in the Assyrian term *kutu*, a tribal group east of the Tigris River on the border of Elam and Media, appearing in Assyrian inscriptions during the eleventh century B.C. and mentioned as part of Babylonia when conquered by Cyrus.

24 הָצֶן (*hōṣen*, "weapons") is unclear. Some amend the text to חֹצֶן (*hōṣen*, "bosom"), but this creates more confusion. Some look at the Arabic *ḥiṣān* ("stallion") as a possible solution. The meaning has not yet been clarified.

32–33 The earliest evidence known for the cup to represent the destiny in store for men is in UT, II, AB, III, 14–16 (see G.R. Driver, *Canaanite Myths and Legends* [Edinburgh: T. & T. Clark, 1956], pp. 95ff.). The cup represents one's portion in life fixed by God for good (Prov 16:5 et al.) or evil. Jeremiah applied the imagery for evil to the heathen nations; Ezekiel applied it to Israel; our Lord applied it to himself!

---

d. Judgment for prostitution

23:36–49

³⁶The Lᴏʀᴅ said to me: "Son of man, will you judge Oholah and Oholibah? Then confront them with their detestable practices, ³⁷for they have committed adultery and blood is on their hands. They committed adultery with their idols; they even sacrificed their children, whom they bore to me, as food for them. ³⁸They have also done this to me: At that same time they defiled my sanctuary and desecrated my Sabbaths. ³⁹On the very day they sacrificed their children to their idols, they entered my sanctuary and desecrated it. That is what they did in my house.

⁴⁰"They even sent messengers for men who came from far away, and when they arrived you bathed yourself for them, painted your eyes and put on your jewelry. ⁴¹You sat on an elegant couch, with a table spread before it on which you had placed the incense and oil that belonged to me.

⁴²"The noise of a carefree crowd was around her; Sabeans were brought from the desert along with men from the rabble, and they put bracelets on the arms of the woman and her sister and beautiful crowns on their heads. ⁴³Then I said about the one worn out by adultery, 'Now let them use her as a prostitute, for that is all she is.' ⁴⁴And they slept with her. As men sleep with a prostitute, so they slept with those lewd women, Oholah and Oholibah. ⁴⁵But righteous men will sentence them to the punishment of women who commit adultery and shed blood, because they are adulterous and blood is on their hands.

⁴⁶"This is what the Sovereign Lᴏʀᴅ says: Bring a mob against them and give them over to terror and plunder. ⁴⁷The mob will stone them and cut them down

with their swords; they will kill their sons and daughters and burn down their houses.

^{48}"So I will put an end to lewdness in the land, that all women may take warning and not imitate you. ^{49}You will suffer the penalty for your lewdness and bear the consequences of your sins of idolatry. Then you will know that I am the Sovereign LORD."

36–39 This final message of the entire section summarizes chapters 20–23. Though each city had been treated separately in the immediately preceeding messages, now the two sisters are combined. Ezekiel was exhorted to "judge" both women—to prosecute, exposing their abominations (v.36). The sinfulness of their adulterous religious worship was first outlined. They had committed spiritual adultery by worshiping idols rather than the Lord (v.37a; cf. the prohibition in Exod 22:20; 23:13; Deut 4:15–24; 12:24–32). Part of this worship had involved child sacrifice (often to Molech) and, therefore, murder ("blood is on their hands," v.37b; forbidden in Exod 20:13; Lev 18:21; 20:1–5). The combination of idolatry and child sacrifice was performed in the Lord's sanctuary and thereby defiled it (v.38a; cf. the prohibition in Exod 20:24–26). The implication was that these perversions were also performed on the Sabbaths. Thus the Sabbaths were profaned (v.38b; forbidden in Exod 20:8–11; Lev 19:3, 30). In addition the prophets had asserted that the Sabbath was neglected during most of the period of the divided kingdoms.

Samaria was equally condemned for defiling the temple (v.39). This may have meant that she defiled the temple by her absence from proper worship in it and by her construction of heathen shrines. It may have meant that the remnant of Israelites in the northern kingdom were participating in the pagan rituals in the temple. Perhaps both actions were true.

40–42 These two "cities" were both condemned for their adulterous political desires in which they had sought out relationships with foreign nations for security alliances. Such alliances were forbidden in Deuteronomy 17:14–20. These two cities seduced foreign nations as a harlot would lure lovers with her cosmetics and clothing, even offering them a feast in which they used the incense and oil of the Lord's sanctuary (vv.40–41). All sorts of sordid "men" responded to the wooing, even drunkards from the desert—most likely a reference to the Arabians, Moabites, Edomites, or Sabeans (cf. note at v.42). These "lovers" gave Judah the hire of harlots—bracelets, crowns, etc. (v.42).

43–47 God's indictment culminated in a summary verdict on "the one worn out by adultery" (v.43). The use of the singular feminine form here and in vv.40–42 was either for the sake of discussing the work of *a* harlot in the illustration or perhaps specifically to narrow the discussion to Jerusalem by way of a final application. It was tragic that Jerusalem and/or Samaria would be known by this epithet, but they had been characterized by a history of political prostitution with many nations.

Those whom Jerusalem and Samaria lured into "relations" would now judge these two cities (vv.43–45). Contextually the nations who would judge Jerusalem and Samaria (essentially Assyria and Babylonia respectively) were called "righteous men." Certainly this did not mean that they were righteous in God's sight with respect to eternal salvation. Rather, it implied that these "men," or nations, were acting righteously in judging Samaria and Jerusalem (cf. Cyrus's performing God's righteous purpose in Isa 41). Assyria and Babylonia would judge Samaria and Jerusalem with the judgment prescribed for an adulteress and murderer in the Mosaic covenant: death, normally by stoning (cf. Exod 21:2; Lev 20:10; Deut 22:22). The "sisters" would be tossed about, robbed, stoned, and cut down with the sword; and their children would be murdered and their houses burned (v.47).

48–49 God's purpose in this judgment is fourfold. Such discipline would put an end to wickedness in the Promised Land (v.48a). In addition, this judgment would instruct all other nations ("women") in the fruitlessness of following this same manner of unrighteousness (v.48b). It was necessary, however, that these two cities and their respective nations bear the punishment for the sin of their idolatry (v.49a). Finally, God must execute this punishment in order to bring Israel and Judah into a correct and proper knowledge of himself (v.49b).

Notes

42 The translation "Sabeans" comes from סְבָאִים (s^eḇā'îm). The root may also mean "drunkards," in accord with the Qere reading of סוֹבְאִים (sôḇ^e'îm).

E. The Execution of Jerusalem's Judgment (24:1–27)

1. The parable of the cooking pot

24:1–14

¹In the ninth year, in the tenth month on the tenth day, the word of the LORD came to me: ²"Son of man, record this date, this very date, because the king of Babylon has laid siege to Jerusalem this very day. ³Tell this rebellious house a parable and say to them: 'This is what the Sovereign LORD says:

" 'Put on the cooking pot; put it on
and pour water into it.
⁴Put into it the pieces of meat,
all the choice pieces—the leg and the shoulder.
Fill it with the best of these bones;
5   take the pick of the flock.
Pile wood beneath it for the bones;
bring it to a boil
and cook the bones in it.

6" 'For this is what the Sovereign LORD says:

" 'Woe to the city of bloodshed,
to the pot now encrusted,
whose deposit will not go away!
Empty it piece by piece
without casting lots for them.

7" 'For the blood she shed is in her midst:
She poured it on the bare rock;
she did not pour it on the ground,
where the dust would cover it.

858

⁸To stir up wrath and take revenge
I put her blood on the bare rock,
so that it would not be covered.

⁹" 'Therefore this is what the Sovereign LORD says:

" 'Woe to the city of bloodshed!
I, too, will pile the wood high.
¹⁰So heap on the wood
and kindle the fire.
Cook the meat well,
mixing in the spices;
and let the bones be charred.
¹¹Then set the empty pot on the coals
till it becomes hot and its copper glows
so its impurities may be melted
and its deposit burned away.
¹²It has frustrated all efforts;
its heavy deposit has not been removed,
not even by fire.

¹³" 'Now your impurity is lewdness. Because I tried to cleanse you but you would not be cleansed from your impurity, you will not be clean again until my wrath against you has subsided.

¹⁴" 'I the LORD have spoken. The time has come for me to act. I will not hold back; I will not have pity, nor will I relent. You will be judged according to your conduct and your actions, declares the Sovereign LORD.' "

1-2 The normal introductory formula of a message (cf. 6:1-7) combined with a specific chronological notice introduce this new series of messages. The date was a momentous one! It was the very day Nebuchadnezzar's siege of Jerusalem began (v.2): December/January 589/588 B.C. (cf. Introduction: Date). Through divine revelation Ezekiel understood that the fulfillment of his prophecies had begun, two years and five months from the date of his last series of messages (cf. 20:1). This chronological notice, based on the years of Jehoiachin's exile, is corroborated by similar notices in 2 Kings 25:1 and Jeremiah 39:1; 52:4, which were based on Zedekiah's regnal years. The years of Zedekiah's reign and the years of Jehoiachin's captivity were synchronous.

This is a pivotal chapter in the development of the book. Till now Ezekiel has variously proclaimed the Lord's coming judgment on Jerusalem and Judah. He has systematically answered each argument against the impending judgment. Nothing remained except for the enactment of that discipline recorded in this chapter. The beginning of Babylonia's siege of Jerusalem was described. Then Ezekiel prophesied against the foreign nations who had abused Judah and mocked her during her judgments (25:1-33:20). These foreign nations would be judged for their wicked attitude and actions toward Judah. However, the hope of future restoration and blessing would be promised to Judah.

The importance of this day is seen in the repetition of the phrase "this very date [or 'day']" in v.2. In addition the Lord commanded that Ezekiel "record the date" in the sense of permanently noting it. This affirmed the validity of his prophecies so that the exiles would surely know that a prophet had been in their midst. In addition, this specific day became a memorial day in Israel's history, being remembered by an annual fast (cf. Zech 8:19).

859

Chapters 24–25 contain the three messages delivered on the date given in 24:1. The first two (in ch. 24) stress the beginning of the siege of Jerusalem. Verses 3–4 describe the siege with a parable and its interpretation. The features of God's judgment, previously discussed in Ezekiel's warning, are renewed. The second message emphasizes the response that the exiles and the Judeans should have had to this siege (vv.15–27). Ezekiel was instructed to restrain his emotions after the death of his wife. This was a picture lesson to the people that they should not mourn over Jerusalem's destruction. After all, they had continually defiled God's sanctuary and had been warned of the imminent judgment, which came as no surprise. Finally, Ezekiel declared that the scorn of Judah's neighbors would not go unnoticed. Judah was reminded of the Lord's perfect justice in executing judgment on these nations as well as Judah.

3–8 Ezekiel's parable of the boiling pot was given to "the rebellious house," the people of Israel (v.3; cf. 2:3, 6–8; 3:9). The key to the proper interpretation of the parable is the explicit contextual statement given in v.2: "The king of Babylon has laid siege to Jerusalem this very day." The parable was given in light of this siege of Jerusalem.

Ezekiel once again concentrated his message in a song, here in the "cooking pot song" (cf. the "sword song," 21:8–17; the "cup song," 23:32–34). The parable (vv.4–5) describes a pot being placed on burning bones. Water would be poured into the pot and pieces of choice mutton boiled vigorously.

Two interpretative speeches follow the parable. Each interprets and expands the parable and then announces a verdict. The first verdict-speech (vv.6–8) identifies the pot and stresses the reasons for Jerusalem's present judgment. The "pot" represented Jerusalem, "the city of bloodshed" (v.6; cf. v.2; 22:2–12, 27). The pieces of meat, choice members of the flock, were nowhere explicitly identified. Since the "pot" was Jerusalem, the context was one of a "siege" judgment; and the term "flock" was used elsewhere by Ezekiel almost entirely to represent the people of Israel (cf. ch. 34). The pieces of meat most likely pictured Jerusalem's inhabitants who would be "boiled" in the judgment fire of Nebuchadnezzar's siege. The parable portrayed the siege of Jerusalem as her people boiling in the pot of God's wrath.

This first interpretative speech added a new dimension of encrusted deposits (v.6) on the pot. Verses 7–8 imply that these "deposits" represented the violent bloodshed of this "bloody city," which was like blood poured on a bare rock and not covered with dirt. Jerusalem had done nothing to cover (or to atone) for her bloodshed as required by the Mosaic covenant (Lev 17:13). Uncovered blood evoked God's vengeance (cf. Gen 4:10; Isa 26:21). The Lord declared that he had put Jerusalem's blood on the bare rock and would not allow it to be covered so that his wrath might be poured out on her.

Another new feature was that after the cooking the pieces would be removed from the pot without favoritism. The concept of "casting lots" (v.6) is that a "lot" would not fall on any person (piece of flesh) so that he would be granted favor to be removed to exile over against someone else. From man's perspective it is arbitrary and at random, but God is sovereign in all his doings.

9–14 The second verdict-speech continued the interpretation and expansion by emphasizing Jerusalem's purification through the judgment. Through the intense heat of the fire, the meat boiled till only the bones remained and were charred (vv.9–10).

On completion of this intense boiling (the siege), the contents were removed (deportation into exile) and the empty "pot" placed on the fire till it became red hot and "its heavy deposits" (Filthiness of bloodshed) were melted and consumed (vv. 11 –12). God would cleanse his holy city Jerusalem. He had previously cleansed her (most likely in reference to the deportation of 605 B.C. and 597 B.C.), but she was still unclean. She had become dirty and rusty again with the filthiness of her bloodshed (v. 13a). But the Lord's fire of judgment would now accomplish a complete work so that Jerusalem would be purified, but not till God caused his wrath on Jerusalem to cease (v. 13b). Ezekiel's entire prophecy implies that God's wrath will cease and Israel will be cleansed completely when God begins to restore Israel to the land of Canaan in the end time (cf. 36:22–32).

This message was certain. God had spoken; he would do what he had said. He would not neglect this righteous judgment, for he was just. He spared no one in pity nor would he be sorry for anyone, for Jerusalem would receive the just due of her wicked deeds (v. 14).

Notes

5 דּוּר הָעֲצָמִים תַּחְתֶּיהָ (dûr hā‘ăṣāmîm taḥteyhā) is a difficult phrase. Many translations read הָעֵצִים (hā‘ēṣîm, "wood") rather than the MT's הָעֲצָמִים (hā‘ăṣāmîm, "bones"). There is no textual basis for any alteration of the text. The change is made purely on the basis of sense and the use of "wood" in v. 10. However, "bones" were used along with wood in ancient times for fuel; so it is best to let the MT remain as it is. Thus the NIV has "pile wood beneath it for the bones."

2. Signs to the exiles (24:15–27)

a. The death of Ezekiel's wife

24:15–24

15The word of the LORD came to me: 16"Son of man, with one blow I am about to take away from you the delight of your eyes. Yet do not lament or weep or shed any tears. 17Groan quietly; do not mourn for the dead. Keep your turban fastened and your sandals on your feet; do not cover the lower part of your face or eat the customary food ,of mourners,."

18So I spoke to the people in the morning, and in the evening my wife died. The next morning, I did as I had been commanded.

19Then the people asked me, "Won't you tell us what these things have to do with us?"

20So I said to them, "The word of the LORD came to me; 21Say to the house of Israel, 'This is what the Sovereign LORD says: I am about to desecrate my sanctuary—the stronghold in which you take pride, the delight of your eyes, the object of your affection. The sons and daughters you left behind will fall by the sword. 22And you will do as I have done. You will not cover the lower part of your face or eat the customary food ,of mourners,. 23You will keep your turbans on your heads and your sandals on your feet. You will not mourn or weep but will waste away because of your sins and groan among yourselves. 24Ezekiel will be a sign to you; you will do just as he has done. When this happens, you will know that I am the Sovereign LORD.'

15–17 The Lord informed Ezekiel that shortly he would take Ezekiel's wife from him "with one blow," a phrase that normally referred to a plague or disease (vv.15–16a; cf. Exod 9:14). This predicted death of Ezekiel's wife was heightened when it was emphasized that she was "the delight of [his] eyes" (see note at v.25).

In the funeral rites of the ancient Near East, the mourner normally would tear his garments and put on sackcloth (2 Sam 3:31). He would remove his shoes and head-dress (2 Sam 15:30; Mic 1:8), shave his head, and put earth on his head (1 Sam 4:12). The lower part of the face (from the mustache down) would be covered with a veil of some sort (2 Sam 15:30; 19:4). The mourner would roll his head or his whole body in dust and then lie, or sit, among a heap of ashes (Isa 58:5; Mic 1:10). He would fast for a day (2 Sam 1:12; 3:35), after which friends would bring "mourning bread" (Jer 16:7). Funeral lamentations—repeated shrill cries—would be made by the family, relatives, and professional mourners (2 Sam 1:17; 11:26; Mic 1:8).

In vv.16b–17 the Lord instructed Ezekiel not to use any of these normal procedures to mourn the loss of his wife. In fact, he was not to mourn at all, not even to shed a tear. He was only to groan silently. This was certainly an unnatural response to death, especially in the culture of Ezekiel's day. Priests mourned the death of a family member (Lev 21:1–3), but Ezekiel would not even be allowed that privilege.

18–19 Ezekiel probably shared this message with the people in the morning; in that evening his wife died. He faithfully responded to her death according to God's command, though undoubtedly this was one of the most difficult things he ever did (v.18). Only through the Lord's strength was he able to obey. Such an unnatural response to death immediately arrested the attention of his audience, and they readily inquired as to the meaning of his actions (v.19). Ezekiel's entire life was a testimony to the exiles. Likewise, this should be the case with all who are the children of God by faith in Christ Jesus.

20–24 Ezekiel's reply to the people's inquiry was an explanation of this picture lesson (v.20). The delight of the exiled people's eyes was the pride (2 Chron 36:19; Lam 1:10–11) and affection that they had in the temple at Jerusalem (v.21; cf. v.25). However, the Lord would defile the temple and slay the Judean children in the Babylonian siege of Jerusalem (v.21b). Ezekiel was to be a sign to them (v.24a). They were to respond to the destruction of the temple and the death of their children in the same manner that Ezekiel responded to the death of his wife (vv.22–23). Just as the delight of his eyes (his wife) was taken, so the delight of their eyes (the temple and their children) would be taken. Why should they not mourn? Because Jerusalem's fall had been foretold by many of the prophets, especially Ezekiel. This judgment should have been expected! Jerusalem's destruction would surely confirm Ezekiel's prophetic gift (v.24b).

Notes

16 מַגֵּפָה (*maggēpāh*, "one blow," "plague") is frequently used, along with its cognates, to indicate the wrath of God (cf. Num 16:46), as is surely conveyed in this verse.

17 שָׂפָם (*śāpām*, "lower part of your face") is normally rendered "moustache" (BDB, s.v.). The NIV's "mourners" is actually the normal Hebrew word for "men" (אֲנָשִׁים, *ᵃnāšîm*),

but the context shows that "mourners" are in view. Some have amended the word to אוֹנִים
(ʾônîm, "mourners") with the Targum and the Vulgate, though textual support is weak.
21 "Object of your affection" is a debated translation of מַחְמַל נַפְשְׁכֶם (maḥmal napšᵉkem).
Maḥmal is a hapax legomenon in the OT. The variation of similar expressions in this verse
and in v.25 would argue against emending the text to מַחְמַד (maḥmad, "desire"). The root
idea of חָמַל (ḥāmal) stresses the feeling of compassion. Therefore, this onetime use of
maḥmal napšᵉkem is considered to be the "object of affection." For נֶפֶשׁ (nepeš, "soul,"
"life") having the meaning of "affection," see TWOT (s.v.).

---

b. The removal of Ezekiel's muteness

24:25–27

> 25"And you, son of man, on the day I take away their stronghold, their joy and
> glory, the delight of their eyes, their heart's desire, and their sons and daughters
> as well—26on that day a fugitive will come to tell you the news. 27At that time your
> mouth will be opened; you will speak with him and will no longer be silent. So you
> will be a sign to them, and they will know that I am the LORD."

25–27 These verses were not a separate message but another part of the Lord's
reply to the exiles in vv.20–24. This part, however, was directed specifically to
Ezekiel.

In 3:25–27 Ezekiel had been made mute (cf. comment in loc.). Now the Lord was
announcing that Ezekiel's muteness would be removed when the siege of Jerusalem
was completed. On the day Jerusalem fell, a fugitive would escape to bring the news
of Jerusalem's collapse to Ezekiel in Babylon (vv.25–26). On the day that the fugitive would arrive in Babylon, approximately three months following the destruction
of Jerusalem, Ezekiel's mouth would be opened; and he would have the freedom to
move among his people and proclaim continually the message of hope for the future
(v.27a). He would once again intercede before the Lord on their behalf. This fulfillment would be described in 33:21–22 (cf. 2 Kings 25:8) in the very night on which
Ezekiel would deliver his great message of hope for Israel (33:31–39:29). The removal of his muteness would be another affirmation of Ezekiel's prophetic gift to the
exiles. When they saw the fulfillment of the Lord's messages through his prophets,
then the exiles would know that the Lord was the God of Israel (v.27b).

III. Judgment on the Foreign Nations (25:1–33:20)

A. Judgment on Judah's Closest Neighbors (25:1–17)

1. Judgment on Ammon

25:1–7

> 1The word of the LORD came to me: 2"Son of man, set your face against the
> Ammonites and prophesy against them. 3Say to them, 'Hear the word of the
> Sovereign LORD. This is what the Sovereign LORD says: Because you said "Aha!"
> over my sanctuary when it was desecrated and over the land of Israel when it was
> laid waste and over the people of Judah when they went into exile, 4therefore I
> am going to give you to the people of the East as a possession. They will set up
> their camps and pitch their tents among you; they will eat your fruit and drink your
> milk. 5I will turn Rabbah into a pasture for camels and Ammon into a resting place

for sheep. Then you will know that I am the LORD. [6]For this is what the Sovereign LORD says: Because you have clapped your hands and stamped your feet, rejoicing with all the malice of your heart against the land of Israel, [7]therefore I will stretch out my hand against you and give you as plunder to the nations. I will cut you off from the nations and exterminate you from the countries. I will destroy you, and you will know that I am the LORD.' "

1–7 In 25:1–33:20 the prophet thematically grouped all the oracles against foreign nations that he received from the Lord (cf. Isa 13–23; Jer 46–51). Though these messages were delivered at different times (see date of each message in its order—Introduction: Date), topically they were formed into a singular unit and significantly placed together at this point in the book. It is significant because it shows that heathenism can never triumph over God's revelation through Israel. Ezekiel had warned Judah of judgment in the first twenty-three chapters. Chapter 24 climaxed these warnings with the announcement of the beginning of Judah's foretold punishment. With the fall of Judah and Jerusalem, Ezekiel turned to announce judgment on the foreign nations that had in some manner cursed Israel (cf. 25:1–33:20; cf. Gen 12:3). By inserting these judgment oracles against the nations here, he concluded the book decisively and constructively with promise. Receiving a renewed commission in 33:1–20, Ezekiel closed his prophecy with the encouraging announcement that Israel would be brought back safely to her promised land (33:21–48:35).

The above outline of the book gives its thematic development. However, because of the larger thematic arrangement, the development of the immediate context of chapters 25–32 has often been overlooked. Chapter 25 does not start a new series of messages according to the book's literary structure. The four short oracles against Judah's immediate neighbors are a continuation of Ezekiel's dated judgment message that began at 24:1 and concludes at 25:17. This, therefore, was originally a singular series of messages, all delivered at the same time according to Ezekiel's normal chronological notices. The messages in this series announce judgment on Judah and then turn to denounce the surrounding nations that had rejoiced over Judah's downfall and had hoped for personal spoil and gain. God announced judgment on these nations lest their gleeful taunts continue and the exiles question his faithfulness to his promises (cf. Gen 12:3).

The oracles of chapter 25 cannot be separated structurally from Ezekiel's other messages delivered at the date given in 24:1. Though the speeches in chapter 25 were used as the beginning of the "foreign nation judgment section," there is nothing that literarily warrants a major break between chapter 24 and chapter 25 any more than one would expect a break between chapter 23 and chapter 24.

The judgment announced on these nations did not come as a surprise. It had already been predicted several times by Jeremiah (Jer 9:25–26; 25:1–26; 27:1–11; 48:1–49:22). Nebuchadnezzar and his Babylonian armies would be the instrument of judgment on these nations as well as on Judah. These nations would also experience captivity in Babylonia for seventy years (Jer 25:11). God promised that those who cursed Israel would be cursed (Gen 12:3). Now he would bring that "cursing" on these nations through the instrumentality of Babylonia. Judgment would continue on these nations till the second coming of Christ, when the Lord will reign over them (cf. Isa 11:14; Dan 11:41; Joel 3:1–4). Thus God's perspective of judgment extended from the immediate judgment by Babylonia to the end times.

A basic literary pattern is followed by all four judgment speeches in this chapter:

introduction, accusation, and verdict. The specific judgment oracle against Ammon is in vv.2–7. The introduction for this message is in vv.2–3a: Ezekiel was to prophesy against the children of Ammon, exhorting them to listen to God's word and not the message of their own gods. Judgment on Ammon has already been briefly discussed in 21:20, 28–32; but at that point in Ezekiel's argument Ammon's judgment was deferred till the prior discipline of Jerusalem was executed.

The accusation and verdict against Ammon are stated in two mini-speeches (vv.3–5 and vv.6–7), the content of each being essentially the same. Ammon was accused of expressing satisfaction over the misfortune of Judah, her enemy and rival (v.3b). This was clearly shown by the interjection *he'āḥ* ("Aha!" cf. 26:2; 36:2). The Ammonites had clapped their hands and stamped their feet in joyous contempt (v.6; cf. comments at 6:11) over the temple's defilement (cf. 24:21), the desolation of the land of Judah, and the captivity of the Judean people by Babylonia (v.3b); cf. 2 Kings 24:2; Jer 49:1; Zeph 2:8–10).

Ezekiel announced the verdict with his customary particle "therefore" (*lākēn*; vv.4, 7). God was ready to give the Ammonites as a possession to the "people of the East," who would exploit the land of Ammon by settling down in it and eating the produce of that country (vv.4, 7a). The desolation of the land would be symbolized by the use of Rabbah, their capital, as a pasture for camels and the use of the land of the children of Ammon for a resting place of flocks (v.7b). The "people of the East" are not identified specifically anywhere in Scripture. The phrase was used to refer to any peoples living east of another people. However, the immediate context, parallel passages (mentioned above), and ancient history all argue for the designation of "Babylonia" as Ezekiel's contemporary "people of the East." Moreover, Josephus (Antiq., X, 180–81 [ix.7]) recorded that Nebuchadnezzar brought Ammon and Moab into subjection in the fifth year after the Fall of Jerusalem (c. 582/581 B.C.).

Ezekiel's proclamation of God's continuing purpose for judgment was not changed in his announcement of judgment on Ammon. God desired that this discipline would cause the Ammonites to know that he was the Lord, the God of Israel, the only true God (vv.5, 7).

Notes

2 The Ammonites descended from Lot's incestuous relationship with his youngest daughter (Gen 19:30–38). They settled in the Transjordan area south of Gilead, around their later capital, Rabbah (modern Amman).

2. Judgment on Moab

25:8–11

> [8]"This is what the Sovereign LORD says: 'Because Moab and Seir said, "Look, the house of Judah has become like all the other nations," [9]therefore I will expose the flank of Moab, beginning at its frontier towns—Beth Jeshimoth, Baal Meon and Kiriathaim—the glory of that land. [10]I will give Moab along with the Ammonites to the people of the East as a possession, so that the Ammonites will not be remembered among the nations; [11]and I will inflict punishment on Moab. Then they will know that I am the LORD.'"

8–11 Moab had cursed the people of Israel (cf. Gen 12:3), being disrespectful of Judah's divine election as an instrument of blessing to the world (cf. Gen 12:1–3; Exod 19:5–6; Deut 7:6–8). Moab had likened Judah to all other nations because she had fallen to Babylonia. Such a defeat indicated to Moab and other nations that Judah's God was weak. Therefore, any special calling of Judah by that God would be considered a joke. So Moab laughed at Judah's defeat in light of her professed election (Jer 48:27; Zeph 2:8–9).

Seir was said to have this same disrespectful attitude toward Judah (v.8). Many see the word "Seir" as a later addition to the text. However, there is no clear support for such a conclusion. The text is simply declaring that Edom, known elsewhere in the OT as Seir (cf. Gen 32:3; 36:30; Ezek 35), shared with Moab this same disdain of Judah. However, a more complete accusation of Edom follows in the next judgment speech (v.12).

The verdict on Moab (vv.9–11) was a manifestation of God's promise to curse those who curse Israel (cf. Gen 12:3). The Lord would expose Moab's northwest flank (the mountain plateau overlooking the Jordan rift, an almost inaccessible cliff that constituted her strongest defense and is therefore likened to a shoulder) to the invasion of the people of the East. The attack would begin on this shoulder of the land of Moab, along a line drawn from north to south between the cities of Beth Jeshimoth (in the Jordan Valley), Baal Meon (about five miles southwest of Madebah), and Kiriathaim (location uncertain), "the glory of the land" (the best part; cf. an atlas). Again, the "people of the East" most likely refers to the Babylonians who attacked Moab in 583/582 B.C. (cf. v.4), though some (e.g., Taylor) argue that they were Nabatean tribesmen who invaded this area not long after this time. The people of Moab would be given as a possession to these "people of the East" along with the children of Ammon, implying that the same invasion was involved (i.e., Babylonia; cf. vv.4, 7). Moab would be exiled and laid desolate (Jer 48:7–9). Neither Moab nor Ammon would "be remembered among the nations" till the end times (v.10b; cf. Isa 11:14). This judgment was to begin with Nebuchadnezzar and conclude with the second coming of the Lord. God's consistent purpose in judgment was stated again: he desired through this judgment that Moab would come to know that he was the Lord, the only true God (v.11).

Notes

8 The Mesha Stone recounts the king of Moab's boast that his god Chemosh had vanquished Israel (ANET, pp. 320–21).

The Moabites descended from Lot's incestuous union with his eldest daughter (Gen 19:30–38). They normally inhabited the area on the Transjordan plateau between Wadi Arnon on the north and Wadi Zered on the south, though they often pushed north of Wadi Arnon.

3. *Judgment on Edom*

25:12–14

12"This is what the Sovereign LORD says: 'Because Edom took revenge on the house of Judah and became very guilty by doing so, 13therefore this is what the

Sovereign LORD says: I will stretch out my hand against Edom and kill its men and their animals. I will lay it waste, and from Teman to Dedan they will fall by the sword. ¹⁴I will take vengeance on Edom by the hand of my people Israel, and they will deal with Edom in accordance with my anger and my wrath; they will know my vengeance, declares the Sovereign LORD.' "

12–14 The accusation against Edom centered on her perpetual attitude of vengeance against Judah (v. 12), an attitude that began with the conflict between Jacob (Israel) and Esau (Edom) (Gen 25:30; 27:41–46; 32:4). This resentful and vindictive spirit had characterized Edom's relations with Israel throughout history (36:1–7; Lam 4:21–22; Amos 1:11–12). Edom had desired to possess Israel and Judah (35:10) and had joined Ammon and Moab in degrading Judah (cf. v.8; 36:5; Ps 137:1, 7–9). She had committed grievous acts against Judah. Edom's behavior was inexcusable because he was a twin brother! Israel respected this solidarity, but Edom spurned it.

Therefore, God announced his verdict on Edom, a judgment that would be expanded in 35:1–36:15. Edom would become a desolation as the Lord cut off both mankind and cattle from that land. This devastation of Edom would be comprehensive from Teman even to Dedan. The specific identification of these two place names is not yet known, though most commentators see them as the extremities of the country in light of the context of v.13 (cf. Joel 3:19). (The Edomites normally inhabited the Transjordan region south of Wadi Zered.) Other passages in the OT indicate that this punishment would be executed by Nebuchadnezzar (Jer 9:26; 25:21; 27:1–11). Certainly Ezekiel 32:29 and Malachi 1:2–5 assume that Edom's desolation was past. However, God also declared that he would execute his vengeance on Edom in return for its vengeance on Judah and would do so through the instrumentality of Israel. The historical context of Ezekiel's day precluded this event from happening at that time. However, Ezekiel and other prophets declared that Israel would possess Edom in the end time as well (cf. 35:1–36:15; Isa 11:14; Dan 11:41; Amos 9:12; Obad 18).

The purpose of God's judgment on Edom was stated differently than the norm. Edom would know God's vengeance in his judgment (v.14). They would understand that he was the faithful God of Israel who would curse those who cursed his people. In turn Edom would observe that he was the true God.

Notes

12 The infinitive absolute אָשׁוֹם (*'āšôm*, "be guilty") follows the finite verb and in such a position normally indicates continuous action or repetition. The nuance in this verse implies that Edom continually committed criminal acts against Judah. The infinitive absolute rarely expresses emphasis when it follows the finite verb.

4. Judgment on Philistia

25:15–17

¹⁵"This is what the Sovereign LORD says: 'Because the Philistines acted in vengeance and took revenge with malice in their hearts, and with ancient hostility

sought to destroy Judah, [16]therefore this is what the Sovereign LORD says: I am about to stretch out my hand against the Philistines, and I will cut off the Kerethites and destroy those remaining along the seacoast. [17]I will carry out great vengeance on them and punish them in my wrath. Then they will know that I am the LORD, when I take vengeance on them.' "

15–17 Ezekiel moved geographically clockwise as he announced judgment on Judah's closest neighbors. The Philistines also were accused of responding with vengeance against Judah, especially with contempt and perpetual enmity. Their purpose was to destroy Judah (v. 15). Such continual hostility against Israel by Philistia had been demonstrated in its interaction with Samson (Judg 13–16), Eli (1 Sam 4), Saul (1 Sam 13; 31), David (2 Sam 5), Hezekiah (2 Kings 18:8), Jehoram (2 Chron 21: 16–17), and Ahaz (2 Chron 28:18).

God's judgment verdict (vv.16–17) declared that he would "cut off the Kerethites," a synecdoche for "Philistines" or a portion of them (1 Sam 30:14; Zeph 2:5). God's great vengeance against the Philistines was a judgment "in kind" for their revengeful attitude and actions against Judah. His destruction of Philistia would be complete, even consuming the remnant of them that were on the coast. His wrath, however, was for correction so that Philistia would come to know through this act on them that he was the only true God (v.17b).

Though the time of this punishment on Philistia was not stated, the context assumes time in harmony with the three verdicts executed on Ammon, Moab, and Edom by Babylon (cf. Jer 25:20; 47:1–7). The ultimate fruition of this judgment would be realized when Israel possesses Philistia in the end time (cf. Isa 11:14; Joel 3:1–4; Obad 19; Zeph 2:4–7).

Notes

15 The three repetitions of the root נָקַם (nāqam, "acted in vengeance," "took revenge") emphasize the intensity of Philistia's revengeful acts against Judah.
16 The Philistines of that day were probably descended from the "sea peoples" who migrated from the Aegean area. Biblically the Philistines came from Caphtor (Jer 47:4; Amos 9:7 et al.), generally thought to be Crete. In turn this Cretan origin is underscored by the term "Kerethites," a name that is thought to mean "Cretans" and is used in this verse in reference to the Philistines or a portion of them.

כְּרֵתִים (kerētîm, "Kerethites") is also most likely used here for wordplay with חִכְרַתִּי (hikrattî, "I will cut off").

B. Judgment on Tyre (26:1–28:19)

1. Judgment by Babylon (26:1–21)

a. A judgment oracle against Tyre

26:1–14

[1]In the eleventh year, on the first day of the month, the word of the LORD came to me: [2]"Son of man, because Tyre has said of Jerusalem, 'Aha! The gate to the

nations is broken, and its doors have swung open to me; now that she lies in ruins I will prosper,' ³therefore this is what the Sovereign LORD says: I am against you, O Tyre, and I will bring many nations against you, like the sea casting up its waves. ⁴They will destroy the walls of Tyre and pull down her towers; I will scrape away her rubble and make her a bare rock. ⁵Out in the sea she will become a place to spread fishnets, for I have spoken, declares the Sovereign LORD. She will become plunder for the nations, ⁶and her settlements on the mainland will be ravaged by the sword. Then they will know that I am the LORD.

⁷"For this is what the Sovereign LORD says: From the north I am going to bring against Tyre Nebuchadnezzar king of Babylon, king of kings, with horses and chariots, with horsemen and a great army. ⁸He will ravage your settlements on the mainland with the sword; he will set up siege works against you, build a ramp up to your walls and raise his shields against you. ⁹He will direct the blows of his battering rams against your walls and demolish your towers with his weapons. ¹⁰His horses will be so many that they will cover you with dust. Your walls will tremble at the noise of the war horses, wagons and chariots when he enters your gates as men enter a city whose walls have been broken through. ¹¹The hoofs of his horses will trample all your streets; he will kill your people with the sword, and your strong pillars will fall to the ground. ¹²They will plunder your wealth and loot your merchandise, they will break down your walls and demolish your fine houses and throw your stones, timber and rubble into the sea. ¹³I will put an end to your noisy songs, and the music of your harps will be heard no more. ¹⁴I will make you a bare rock, and you will become a place to spread fishnets. You will never be rebuilt, for I the LORD have spoken, declares the Sovereign LORD.

1–6 Ezekiel turned toward the north to announce judgment on the city of Tyre and its environs. The length of this oracle suggests the political and religious significance of this city (cf. ch. 28). His indictment of Tyre was set forth in a series of four messages: (1) a judgment speech with explanatory appendixes (vv. 1–21); (2) a funeral dirge over the fall of the city (27:1–36); (3) a judgment speech against the prince of Tyre (28:1–10); and (4) a funeral dirge over the fall of the king of Tyre (28:11–19). This section on Tyre alternates judgment speeches with funeral laments.

The date for these four oracles is given in v. 1: "the eleventh year, on the first day of the month." The specific month was not stated, and this has led to disagreements over the accuracy of this chronological notice. Without the month being declared, one can be no more specific concerning this date than to say that the oracles occurred on the first day of one of the months during the year 587/586 B.C. (which began in March/April 587 B.C.). Some argue that the "eleventh" year is incorrect since v. 2 implies that the Fall of Jerusalem was past. Appeal is made to the LXX for reading "twelfth" year. However, the entire context of these oracles is future (cf. vv. 7–14 and their specific detail concerning Babylonia's invasion), and there is no reason why the verbs in v. 2 cannot be rendered as "prophetic perfects" in the same manner as in vv. 3–21. Therefore, it seems that these oracles were pronounced against Tyre while the siege of Jerusalem was in process in the "eleventh" year.

The historical data concerning Tyre is sparse. The biblical record first mentions the city as a strong, fortified town that formed part of the boundary of the inheritance of the tribe of Asher (Josh 19:29). Tyre was prominent in the days of David and Solomon and throughout the remainder of OT history. Hiram, Solomon's contemporary, enlarged and beautified the city. Tyre became an important maritime city of the ancient Near East, being involved in great commercial and colonial enterprises throughout the Mediterranean area, the Red Sea, and the Indian Ocean. With the rise of Assyria to power, Tyre periodically submitted to Assyria's lordship, paying tribute out of the abundance of her wealth (as in the cases of Esarhaddon and Ashurbanipal). Whenever possible, however, Tyre rebelled against the Assyrian power and withstood the Assyrian retribution in the security of its island fortress (as in the case of Sennacherib). As Assyria began to decline in strength, Tyre exerted her complete independence. Tyre was in this latter condition when these oracles were delivered.

Verses 1b–6 compose the basic judgment speech against Tyre with the accusation (introduced by "because") stated in v.2 and the verdict (introduced by "therefore") delivered in vv.3–6. Tyre was accused of delighting in the prospects of Jerusalem's downfall so that she might obtain the spoils of the city and the advantages of its fall (e.g., Jerusalem controlled the trade routes connecting Egypt and Arabia with the north). The interjection "Aha!" (*he'āḥ*) (v.2) expresses Tyre's satisfaction over Jerusalem's misfortune (cf. 25:3; 36:2). Tyre looked forward to the "gate to the nations" being broken down. The term "doors" is plural and normally refers to doors of a house or a gate. In this passage reference is to the gates of Jerusalem, which would be broken for the access to the nations. Though commentators have sought to see commercial freedom or political accessibility in this phrase, it seems best to understand it as the Fall of Jerusalem. Her gates would be broken by Babylonia and opened to Tyre.

Tyre's major desire was to be filled with the spoils of Jerusalem and with the opportunities that would then be hers in western Asia, since Jerusalem "lies in ruins." The Babylonians had taken the city, leaving it open for Tyre to take advantage of the spoils of Jerusalem. It was this incessant desire for wealth and riches, now expressed toward God's holy city and its people, that brought God's wrath on Tyre in fulfillment of his promise in Genesis 12:3.

Proverbs 17:5b declares that "whoever gloats over disaster will not go unpunished." This was the theme of the verdict (vv.3–6). God, who personally would be against Tyre, would bring many nations successively, like the waves of the sea, to destroy Tyre and make her like a bare rock, useful only for drying nets (vv.3–5a). "Out in the sea" (v.5; cf. 27:4; 28:2 et al.) describes Tyre's almost impregnable situation. The cliffs of Moab, the heights of Edom, and the island fortress of Tyre were no defense against the sovereign Lord. Tyre would become spoil for all nations, just as she sought to spoil Jerusalem (v.5b). Even Tyre's outlying coastal settlements (lit., "daughters") would be destroyed (v.6a). But even through this prolonged judgment, God's purpose would be that Tyre would too come to know that he was the Lord, the only true God (v.6b).

The siege of Tyre by Nebuchadnezzar lasted for thirteen years (c. 586–573 B.C.). Under King Ba'ali II, Tyre accepted Babylonian suzerainty and was ruled by "judges." However, when Babylonia declined in power, Tyre regained her independence once again. This brief freedom lasted till the second "wave" of destruction brought her into submission to the Persians around 525 B.C. Tyre's remaining history demonstrated the continuing "waves" of conquerors: the resistance to Alexander the Great, eventuating in her collapse; her initial resistance to the Seleucid kingdom of Antiochus III, terminating in her becoming part of that kingdom; her submission to Rome; and her fall to the Saracens in the fourteenth century A.D., after which she never again regained any importance. God was faithful to bring the "many nations" against Tyre in successive "waves" of conquest. The Lord Jesus did bring his preaching and healing ministry to this heathen city (Matt 15:21; Mark 7:24–31; Luke 6:17). Her responsibility and judgment would be less than that of the

Galileans who rejected Christ's constant ministry to them (Matt 11:21–22; Luke 10:13–14).

7–14 Ezekiel gave an explanatory appendix to this first judgment speech in these verses: Babylonia under her contemporary ruler, Nebuchadnezzar, would be the initiator of this long series of judgments on Tyre by many nations (cf. v.3).

Nebuchadnezzar and his great army are identified in v.7. The process of his siege of Tyre is fully described, with siege works, ramps, shields, battering rams, and other implements of war, including cavalry (vv.8–10). The city's destruction and the slaying of its inhabitants are described, followed by the taking of spoils and the demolition of the remaining glories of Tyre (vv.11–12). The change from the singular pronoun "he" to the plural "they" in v.12 may demonstrate a broadening of the instrument of judgment from Babylonia to the many future nations that would plunder Tyre. Certainly Alexander the Great literally threw Tyre's "stones, timber and rubble into the sea" when he built a one-half mile causeway out to the island fortress to conquer the city.

Tyre's desolation is emphasized by the lack of any song in the city (an indication of cessation of normal social activities) and the town's bareness portrayed by the figure of a bare rock used only for spreading fishing nets to dry (vv.13–14).

Notes

2 The subject of the three verbs in this verse is דַּלְתוֹת (*daltôt*, "doors"), which is plural whereas the verbs are all feminine singular. In this case the agreement is *ad sensum*, in which the "doors" are looked on as a singular unity.

The phrase נָסֵבָּה אֵלָי (*nāsēbbāh 'ēlāy*, "have swung open to me") may be rendered passively or reflexively. The subject of all the verbs in this verse is "doors," which are treated as singular in the sense that the entire city was in view. Therefore this phrase might be rendered "she [doors of Jerusalem] will turn herself to me," or "she will be turned to me." Since the first phrase of the accusation—"the gate . . . is broken" (lit., "doors . . . are broken")—implies that Babylonia had taken the city, this second phrase would seem to imply that the doors of the city were then opened (or "were turned") to Tyre (in the passive sense). It is unlikely that Jerusalem would be turning herself (reflexively) to Tyre in the sense of seeking aid, if Jerusalem had already fallen.

7 The spelling of Nebuchadnezzar in this verse is נְבוּכַדְרֶאצַּר (*neḇûkadre'ṣṣar*, "Nebuchadrezzar"). The name is spelled both ways in the MT. The Babylonian form was *Nabu-kudurriuṣur*, meaning most likely "Nebo protects the crown." Therefore, in the light of the Babylonian spelling, Nebuchadrezzar is thought to be the more correct rendering, being closer to the Babylonian, while Nebuchadnezzar may have been the popular, western Aramaic form (cf. Dan 1:1; 2:1).

14 The fact that there is a modern Tyre causes one to question the phrase "You will never be rebuilt." One explanation could be that the modern town has not been rebuilt over the majority of the ancient ruins. More likely, however, is the explanation that the city would never again reach the grandeur and importance of Tyre in the biblical period—which has been the case.

b. *The response of vassal nations to Tyre's fall*

26:15-18

15"This is what the Sovereign LORD says to Tyre: Will not the coastlands tremble at the sound of your fall, when the wounded groan and the slaughter takes place in you? 16Then all the princes of the coast will step down from their thrones and lay aside their robes and take off their embroidered garments. Clothed with terror, they will sit on the ground, trembling every moment, appalled at you. 17Then they will take up a lament concerning you and say to you:

> " 'How you are destroyed, O city of renown,
>   peopled by men of the sea!
> You were a power on the seas,
>   you and your citizens;
> you put your terror
>   on all who lived there.
> 18Now the coastlands tremble
>   on the day of your fall;
> the islands in the sea
>   are terrified at your collapse.'

15–18 Tyre had many vassals along the coast and among the islands who had depended on her as their protector. Ezekiel prophesied that when the news of Tyre's fall to Babylonia would be received by these peoples, they would be terribly frightened (v.15). What would happen to them? Their princes would abdicate their thrones—perhaps in an act of surrender and submission to Babylonia before she attacked them (v.16). As mourners they would not sing a lament song in luxurious dress. They were stunned and stood in amazement as to how Tyre could fall. In fright and astonishment these vassal rulers sang a funeral dirge (vv.17–18) over the deceased Tyre (cf. 27:30). Since they had depended on Tyre for protection, what would happen to them? Ironically, Tyre had the poor sense to rejoice over Jerusalem's fall. These cities, however, had the good sense to realize that Tyre's fall spelled the same for them.

Notes

17–18 The major feature of a funeral in the ancient Near East was the קִינָה (*qînāh*, "dirge," "lament"). Its full expression contained a eulogy, praising the dead person's qualitites (as in v.17), and a bewailing of the deceased's fate (as in v.18) (see deVaux, *Ancient Israel*, pp. 60–61).

c. *The Lord's concluding verdict*

26:19-21

19"This is what the Sovereign LORD says: When I make you a desolate city, like cities no longer inhabited, and when I bring the ocean depths over you and its vast waters cover you, 20then I will bring you down with those who go down to the pit, to the people of long ago. I will make you dwell in the earth below, as in ancient ruins, with those who go down to the pit, and you will not return or take your place in the land of the living. ²¹I will bring you to a horrible end and you will be no more. You will be sought, but you will never again be found, declares the Sovereign LORD."

19–21 A prophecy of Tyre's eternal death was certainly an appropriate response to the funeral dirge of the nations. Further poetic elaboration of the verdict given in vv.3–6 is set forth in vv.19–21. Ezekiel made reference to the imagery of vv.3–6 in order to pinpoint the aspect of the previous message that he wanted to expand. At the time that Tyre would be made a ruin by the great waves of nations (v.3) and left as a barren rock (v.4), God would make sure that she never again regained her place of prominence on this earth (vv.19–21). Two additional factors were added in this brief elaboration. First, Tyre would die. She would "go down to the pit" (v.20a) as had those in the past who had already died. In her ruined state she would be as if she dwelt in Sheol in the earth below. Descent into the pit is a frequent concept for death in Ezekiel and in other prophets (cf. 31:14–16; 32:18, 23–25; Isa 14:15; 38:18). Second, Tyre would never again exist and play an important role in history as she had in the past (vv.20b–21). Though some might look for her, she would not be found.

Notes

19 תְּהוֹם (*tᵉhôm*, "ocean depths") probably refers to primeval waters of chaos. Tyre's geography explains the way her destruction is seen.

20 Some render תֵשֵׁבִי (*tēšēḇî*, "dwell") as *tāšuḇî* ("return"), but there is no need to do so. The context is perfectly clear with the reading of the MT. Tyre will not dwell again in the land of the living. She will die. She will not exist.

וְנָתַתִּי צְבִי (*wᵉnātattî ṣᵉḇî*, "and I will give glory") is a difficult phrase. The LXX reads ἀνασταθῇς (*anastathēs*, "take your place"), the equivalent of the Hebrew word וְתִתְיַצְּבִי (*wᵉtityaṣṣᵉḇî*, "take your stand"). Since the letters are the same with the exception of the nun, and since the immediate context concerns Tyre's failure to exist again and to carry on her previously prominent role on earth, the reading of the Hebrew behind the LXX text is probably the best. Likewise, the reading "and I will give glory in the land of the living" would be very difficult to understand in the context.

2. Ezekiel's funeral dirge over Tyre (27:1–36)

a. The building of Tyre's ship of pride

27:1–11

¹The word of the LORD came to me: ²"Son of man, take up a lament concerning Tyre. ³Say to Tyre, situated at the gateway to the sea, merchant of peoples on many coasts, 'This is what the Sovereign LORD says:

" 'You say, O Tyre,
"I am perfect in beauty."
⁴Your domain was on the high seas;
your builders brought your beauty to perfection.

⁵They made all your timbers
   of pine trees from Senir;
they took a cedar from Lebanon
   to make a mast for you.
⁶Of oaks from Bashan
   they made your oars;
of cypress wood from the coasts of Cyprus
   they made your deck, inlaid with ivory.
⁷Fine embroidered linen from Egypt was your sail
   and served as your banner;
your awnings were of blue and purple
   from the coasts of Elishah.
⁸Men of Sidon and Arvad were your oarsmen;
   your skilled men, O Tyre, were aboard as your seamen.
⁹Veteran craftsmen of Gebal were on board
   as shipwrights to caulk your seams.
All the ships of the sea and their sailors
   came alongside to trade for your wares.

¹⁰ "Men of Persia, Lydia and Put
   served as soldiers in your army.
They hung their shields and helmets on your walls,
   bringing you splendor.
¹¹Men of Arvad and Helech
   manned your walls on every side;
men of Gammad
   were in your towers.
They hung their shields around your walls;
   they brought your beauty to perfection.

1–3 A previous dirge had been sung by neighboring kings (26:15–18). This new message was another funeral lament, but one that Ezekiel would sing at Tyre's death (v.2). The chief cause for this major maritime power's collapse was her pride (v.3). Tyre thought she had the best of everything. As a result she became full of self-conceit, presuming herself to be "perfect" in all her grandeur, wealth, and material goods, which she had acquired through trade with the nations. The Lord hates pride (Prov 8:13). Pride comes before destruction (Prov 16:18) and keeps one from seeking God (Ps 10:4). This was the state of the city of Tyre.

4–11 The destruction of Tyre would be lamented as the wreck of a magnificent ship. The imagery is sustained through the poem and climaxes in the wreckage (see Edwin M. Good, "Ezekiel's Ship: Some Extended Metaphors in the Old Testament," *Semitics* 1 [1970]: 79–103). Some have suggested that the imagery of a ship came from the likeness of one of the island-city's ships. In typical dirge style the deceased's former splendor was first accented. Ezekiel used the imagery of a ship being constructed and equipped to show Tyre's pride and her development of prominence and dominion as a maritime empire.

Tyre's domain (lit., "borders") was in the heart of the sea (v.4). She was one of the greatest maritime leaders of her day (see comments at 26:1–6). Her sea traffic extended throughout the ancient Near East. The imagery in these verses demonstrated how Tyre built her empire and fame. She obtained the finest materials of each geographical area through maritime trade. She used her dominion over other nations to build and beautify her own "ship" (Tyre).

The construction of the "ship" of Tyre is portrayed in vv.5–7. The wood for her frame came from the pine (or fir) in the district of Mount Hermon (Senir), while her "mast" was made from choice cedars of Lebanon (v.5). The ship's "oars" were made from the oaks of Bashan; and her "deck," inlaid with ivory, was made from cypress wood from Cyprus (v.6). Her "sail" and "banner" were made of Egypt's fine linen, while her "awnings" were made of purple and blue textiles of Elishah (v.7). The thrust of these verses conveys the idea that Tyre's development into a beautiful and great maritime city-state came through acquiring the finest materials of her day from the areas that produced them. She obtained these materials through the prominence and power of her sea merchants.

Those that engineered the development and expansion of Tyre's merchant activity were native Phoenicians (vv.8–9). Tyre secured the best-trained veteran sea merchants from the Phoenician cities of Sidon, Arvad, and Gebal (Byblos) to be her "crew" and "shipwrights." Phoenicians were experienced in maritime trade. However, the intelligentsia of Tyre itself actually "sailed" the ship. She was so adept at sea trade that soon everyone traded with her. In turn this necessitated armed protection of her city and ships. She was then able to attract military mercenaries from far off Persia, Lydia, and Put (in Africa), as well as more local soldiers from Arvad, Helech, and Gammad (vv.10–11). Tyre's ability to allure these mercenaries came undoubtedly from her splendor, wealth, and power. In turn, the presence of these foreigners enhanced Tyre's significance. Truly Tyre became a magnificient maritime empire that attracted nations from all over the ancient Near East to trade with her and to come and experience her greatness as a city. In light of this Tyre could say, "I am perfect in beauty" (v.3).

Notes

5 שְׂנִיר (śᵉnîr, "Senir") is identified in Deut 3:9 and S of Sol 4:8 as Mount Hermon or Sirion. First Chronicles 5:23 relates Senir with Mount Hermon and Baal Hermon on the east of the Jordan rift.

בְּרוֹשׁ (bᵉrôš, "pine") is a debated term as to what type of wood is actually meant. BDB (s.v.) renders the word "cypress" or "fir." William L. Holladay, ed. (A Concise Hebrew and Aramaic Lexicon of the Old Testament [Grand Rapids: Eerdmans, 1971], s.v.), translates the term "juniper."

6 בַּת־אֲשֻׁרִים (bat-ᵃšurîm, "daughter of Ashurim") would read better in the context with the consonants arranged as בִּתְאַשֻּׁרִים (bit'aššurîm, "of cypress wood"). תְּאַשּׁוּר (tᵉ'aššûr, "cypress wood") makes more sense in the context and is supported in the Targum. The same consonants are used but with a different division. "Cypress wood" is argued by Holladay (Concise Hebrew and Aramaic Lexicon, s.v.), while BDB (s.v.) translates "box-tree; a small evergreen tree c. 20 ft high growing in Lebanon." Cooke (p. 297) says the meaning is uncertain.

כִּתִּים (kittîyim, "Cyprus") is also a debated term. Genesis 10:4 uses the word to refer to one of the sons of יָוָן (yāvān, "Greece"), along with Elishah, Tarshish, and Dodanim. Jeremiah 2:10 uses the phrase אִיֵּי כִתִּיִּים ('iyê kittîyîm), meaning either "coasts" or "islands of Kittim." This verse implies that the location borders the sea. Most translations and scholars take the word to refer to Cyprus. Kition was a city of Cyprus, and the name was later extended to include southern Cyprus.

7 אֱלִישָׁה ('ᵉlîšāh, "Elishah") is unknown except for its reference at Genesis 10:4 as one of the sons of Greece. Some have conjectured Italy, Sicily, or Carthage.

10–11 לוּד (lûḏ, "Lydia") and פּוּט (pûṭ, "Put") are taken by most scholars to refer respectively to Lydia in western Asia Minor and to a country on the African coast of the Red Sea. חִילֵךְ (ḥêlēḵ, "Helech") and גַּמָּדִים (gammāḏîm, "men of Gamad") are unidentified place names.

---

b. *Tyre's vast commercial relations*

27:12–24

12" 'Tarshish did business with you because of your great wealth of goods; they exchanged silver, iron, tin and lead for your merchandise.
13" 'Greece, Tubal and Meshech traded with you; they exchanged slaves and articles of bronze for your wares.
14" 'Men of Beth Togarmah exchanged work horses, war horses and mules for your merchandise.
15" 'The men of Rhodes traded with you, and many coastlands were your customers; they paid you with ivory tusks and ebony.
16" 'Aram did business with you because of your many products; they exchanged turquoise, purple fabric, embroidered work, fine linen, coral and rubies for your merchandise.
17" 'Judah and Israel traded with you; they exchanged wheat from Minnith and confections, honey, oil and balm for your wares.
18" 'Damascus, because of your many products and great wealth of goods, did business with you in wine from Helbon and wool from Zahar.
19" 'Danites and Greeks from Uzal bought your merchandise; they exchanged wrought iron, cassia and calamus for your wares.
20" 'Dedan traded in saddle blankets with you.
21" 'Arabia and all the princes of Kedar were your customers; they did business with you in lambs, rams and goats.
22" 'The merchants of Sheba and Raamah traded with you; for your merchandise they exchanged the finest of all kinds of spices and precious stones, and gold.
23" 'Haran, Canneh and Eden and merchants of Sheba, Asshur and Kilmad traded with you. 24In your market place they traded with you beautiful garments, blue fabric, embroidered work and multicolored rugs with cords twisted and tightly knotted.

12–24 Ezekiel's lament sets forth the many trade relations that Tyre had throughout the ancient Near East. Not only do these verses develop the extensiveness of her commercial enterprise, but they are also valuable for gaining an understanding of the geography, natural resources, and trade relations of the Near East during this historical period.

The emphasis of this part of the dirge was that the nations desired to trade with Tyre because of the abundance of goods she had to trade. The list of geographic locations and the major items that each nation had to trade show the extent, abundance, and variety of Tyre's trade (vv. 12–23). When these various places are located on a map of the ancient Near East, it can be seen that Tyre traded with almost every region: from Tarshish (Spain) to northeast Anatolia (Tubal, Beth Togarmah) on an east-west axis (through the Aegean), and from Arabia through Syria and Palestine on a north-south axis. Each area brought the products of its land to trade with Tyre. Certainly the commercial operations of Tyre were vast!

Notes

Many of the place names in this section are difficult to identify. Suggestions and problems will be dealt with below.

12 תַּרְשִׁישׁ (taršîš, "Tarshish") is listed as one of the sons of Greece ("Javan") in Gen 10:4. It is commonly thought to be located in southern Spain. An inscription from Esarhaddon's reign implies that it is located at the west end of the Mediterranean Sea.

13–14 תּוּבָל (tûḇal, "Tubal") and מֶשֶׁךְ (mešeḵ, "Meshech") are found together in Gen 10:2 and are recognized by many scholars to be located in the eastern part of Asia Minor, on either side of the anti-Tarsus mountains, i.e., in present eastern Turkey. בֵּית תּוֹגַרְמָה (bêṯ tôḡ armāh, "Beth Togarmah") is likewise mentioned in Gen 10:3 and is normally identified as ancient Armenia, east of the area of Tubal and Meshech.

15 The Hebrew בְּנֵי דְדָן (bᵉnê dᵉḏān, "men of Dedan") is rendered in the LXX as υἱοι Ῥοδιων (huioi Rhodiōn, "men of Rhodes"). The ד (d) in Hebrew is easily confused with the ר (r), and such is perhaps the case here. Some argue for the LXX reading on the basis that Dedan is mentioned in v.20 and would not be expected to appear twice. Also, the term here is mentioned along with many coastlands. However, Sheba is mentioned twice (vv.22–23) and is not normally rendered as two separate identities. Though we may not understand the exact geographical significance and relation, it seems best to stay with the MT till stronger evidence points otherwise.

17 מִנִּית (minnîṯ, "Minnith") is a place in the area of Ammon (Judg 11:33). Yohanan Aharoni (*The Land of the Bible, a Historical Geography*, trs. A.F. Rainey [Philadelphia: Westminster, 1967], p. 243) locates Minnith in the area west of Rabbath-Ammon.

The term פַּנַּג (pannag, "confections") is agreed on by most scholars to be a kind of food, but the exact type is uncertain.

18 חֶלְבּוֹן (ḥelbôn, "Helbon") is thought by some to be located north of Damascus, while the site of צָחַר (ṣāḥar, "Zahar") is unknown.

19 וְדָן (wᵉḏān, "and Danites") has also been rendered "Vedan" (NASB). This shows that there is no agreement as how to understand the Hebrew term in light of the context.

אוּזָּל (ʾûzzāl, "Uzal") appears to be a place in Arabia (cf. Gen 10:27; 1 Chron 1:21). BDB (s.v.) suggests that it may be an old capital of Yemen. Alan Millard ("Ezekiel XXVII.19: The Wine Trade of Damascus," JSS [1962]: 201–3) amends the text and links the initial phrase of v.19 to v.18. He then understands this to represent the wine trade of Damascus.

20 דְּדָן (dᵉḏān, "Dedan"; cf. v.15) is normally thought to be a south Arabian tribal area on the Persian Gulf (cf. Gen 10:7).

21 קֵדָר (qēḏār, "Kedar") is usually located in Arabia as a nomadic people.

22 As descendants of Ham in Genesis 10:6–7, שְׁבָא (šᵉḇāʾ, "Sheba") and רַעְמָה (raʿmāh, "Raamah") are normally placed in the area of Arabia.

23 עֶדֶן (ʿeden, "Eden") is located south of Haran by some, whereas כַּנֵּה (kannēh, "Canneh") and כִּלְמַד (kilmaḏ, "Kilmad") are unknown.

---

c. The sinking of the ship of Tyre

27:25–36

> 25" 'The ships of Tarshish serve
>   as carriers for your wares.
> You are filled with heavy cargo
>   in the heart of the sea.
> 26Your oarsmen take you
>   out to the high seas.

But the east wind will break you to pieces
in the heart of the sea.
27Your wealth, merchandise and wares,
your manners, seamen and shipwrights,
your merchants and all your soldiers,
and everyone else on board
will sink into the heart of the sea
on the day of your shipwreck.
28The shorelands will quake
when your seamen cry out.
29All who handle the oars
will abandon their ships;
the mariners and all the seamen
will stand on the shore.
30They will raise their voice
and cry bitterly over you;
they will sprinkle dust on their heads
and roll in ashes.
31They will shave their heads because of you
and will put on sackcloth.
They will weep over you with anguish of soul
and with bitter mourning.
32As they wail and mourn over you,
they will take up a lament concerning you:
"Who was ever silenced like Tyre,
surrounded by the sea?"
33When your merchandise went out on the seas,
you satisfied many nations;
with your great wealth and your wares
you enriched the kings of the earth.
34Now you are shattered by the sea
in the depths of the waters;
your wares and all your company
have gone down with you.
35All who live in the coastlands
are appalled at you;
their kings shudder with horror
and their faces are distorted with fear.
36The merchants among the nations hiss at you;
you have come to a horrible end
and will be no more.' "

25–27 This last section of Ezekiel's funeral lament over Tyre gives God's verdict and the nation's response. The imagery of a sinking ship continued the metaphor and portrayed Tyre's demise. Laden with all the wealth of the nations and her resulting pride in materialism, the "ship" of Tyre became extremely vulnerable to the "seas" (v.25). Led out on the high seas of commercial adventure by her obsession for more wealth, Tyre quickly succumbed to the strong "east wind" of Babylonia (v.26). (In the light of the judgment verdict of ch. 26, the imagery of the east wind surely must portray the nation of Babylonia.) All Tyre's "cargo" of wealth, materialism, and pride, along with those serving her (v.27; cf. vv.8–24), sank suddenly into the sea.

28–36 Those who had traded with Tyre (cf. vv.12–24) quickly "abandoned their ships," i.e., their work for Tyre, and stood stunned and shocked on the shore (vv.28 –29). They bitterly mourned for Tyre in her death by putting on sackcloth, shaving their heads, placing dust on their heads, and rolling in ashes—all normal conduct at a funeral (vv. 30–32a). They loudly lamented Tyre's demise in vv. 32b–36. They had never seen anyone collapse as quickly as Tyre. She had been supreme in the maritime world, constantly satisfying others with her wares, but now nothing was left. It had all sunk into the sea. Tyre was nonexistent (vv. 32b–34).

These nations and their kings who had traded with Tyre became afraid that they too would have the same thing happen to them (cf. 26:17–18). In fear and self-protection, they quickly turned from being ones who adored Tyre to ones who totally disowned her. They hissed at her in a derogatory manner. Perhaps they felt that such actions would gain them favor with the Babylonians (vv. 35–36).

How quickly the proud fall! Materialism and wealth, which seem so attractive, often make men prominent in the eyes of others. But God hates pride and materialism. Those who think of themselves as important will quickly fall before the judgment of God. Tyre found this out. She would exist no more!

3. A judgment speech against the ruler of Tyre

28:1–10

¹The word of the Lord came to me: ²"Son of man, say to the ruler of Tyre, This is what the Sovereign Lord says:

> " 'In the pride of your heart
>   you say, "I am a god;
> I sit on the throne of a god
>   in the heart of the seas."
> But you are a man and not a god,
>   though you think you are as wise as a god.
> ³Are you wiser than Daniel?
>   Is no secret hidden from you?
> ⁴By your wisdom and understanding
>   you have gained wealth for yourself
> and amassed gold and silver
>   in your treasuries.
> ⁵By your great skill in trading
>   you have increased your wealth,
> and because of your wealth
>   your heart has grown proud.

⁶" 'Therefore this is what the Sovereign Lord says:

> " 'Because you think you are wise,
>   as wise as a god,
> ⁷I am going to bring foreigners against you,
>   the most ruthless of nations;
> they will draw their swords against your beauty
>   and wisdom
>   and pierce your shining splendor.
> ⁸They will bring you down to the pit,
>   and you will die a violent death
>   in the heart of the seas.
> ⁹Will you then say, "I am a god,"
>   in the presence of those who kill you?
> You will be but a man, not a god,
>   in the hands of those who slay you.
> ¹⁰You will die the death of the uncircumcised
>   at the hands of foreigners.

I have spoken, declares the Sovereign Lord.' "

1–5 Having announced judgment on the city of Tyre in chapter 26 and sung a funeral lament over the city in chapter 27, likening it to an overloaded ship that was sunk by the east wind of Babylonia, God commanded Ezekiel to deliver a final judgment speech against the ruler of Tyre—perhaps Ittobaal II—of those days, though the speech is in many ways not against any one particular king but Tyre's kings per se.

With the normal introduction in vv.1–2, Ezekiel proclaimed the accusation in vv.2b–5. Tyre's king is described as a very wise man. Through his wisdom and insight in commercial sea-trade, he was able to amass Tyre's great abundance of wealth (vv.4–5; cf. ch. 27). However, the accumulation of riches and its accompanying splendor and importance created a haughty pride in this ruler (v.5b; cf. 27:3). He was so impressed with himself that he actually began to think that he was a god—perhaps even El, the chief deity of the Canaanite pantheon (v.2). Ancient Near Eastern thought often viewed the king as the embodiment of the god(s) (cf. John Gray, "Canaanite Kingship in Theory and Practice," VetTest 2 [1952]: 193–200). He was sitting on the "throne of a god in the heart of the seas." Most likely Tyre's well-known, magnificent temple of Melkart, Tyre's patron deity, was in the prophet's mind. It was not uncommon for a city or a temple to be called the throne of a god, even in the OT (cf. Ps 132:13–14; Jer 3:17 et al.). On ancient bas-reliefs of Tyre, the city and its temple are seen projecting high out of the surrounding sea.

It was this arrogant pride and self-exaltation as a god that brought God's accusation against Tyre's ruler. In rebuke God charged that Tyre's ruler was not a god but merely a man, even though he had thought of himself as having the character of a pagan deity. He thought he possessed a god's wisdom. However, God questioned whether Tyre's ruler was as wise as Daniel (v.3a), the prophet who had revealed secrets to Nebuchadnezzar. The implied answer was no! Did Tyre's ruler know all secrets (v.3b)? No! At least Daniel knew some. No, Tyre's ruler was not a god but only a man. Though we may not blatantly exalt ourselves in this manner today, we actually do deify ourselves whenever we think we know better than God how things ought to be done.

6–10 Ezekiel announced the verdict against Tyre's ruler in vv.7–10a, summarizing the accusation in v.6. God would humble him by bringing him to a horrible death (v.8), the death of the uncircumcised at the hand of ruthless foreigners (vv.7, 10). No longer would he have beauty and splendor (v.7). Strangers' swords would cut off his wealth and grandeur. A disgraceful death is conveyed by the phrase "the death of the uncircumcised" (v.10). Phoenicians practiced circumcision; so to be slain as an uncircumcised male would be to die a barbarian's death. God mocked the ruler's claim to divinity by declaring that the ruler would not claim deity before his slayers but would obviously be a mere mortal in their hands.

Notes

2 נָגִיד (*nāgîd*, "prince") is used only here in Ezekiel. Frequently the term is used in the OT for a charismatic "ruler." Prominent leadership in various areas (i.e., the "man at the top") is conveyed by this more general term. "King" would be more specific.

Tyre's ruler asserted, "I am a god." The word for "god" is אֵל (*'ēl*, "divinity"). El, a pagan deity, was the chief god of the Canaanite pantheon. Therefore, it is uncertain whether he was claiming only divinity or whether he was claiming to be El. Probably the former in light of the context.

3 Many take the term דָּנִאֵל (dāni'ēl, "Daniel") to be the mythological character Danel in Ugaritic religious literature. The claim is based on the variant writing of the name in this text. Elsewhere in the OT the name Daniel is spelled דָּנִיֵּאל (dāniyē'l, "Daniel"). However, the mythological character Danel is not particularly noted for great wisdom, whereas the prophet Daniel is. Also the spelling of this word in our text is not the proper spelling of Danel. The variant between the reading in the text of Ezekiel and that of Daniel involves the addition of only a י (y, yod). The yod, as a *matres lexionis*, would easily explain its addition in Daniel and lack in Ezekiel. These are simply variant spellings of the same name (cf. note at 14:14).

7 עָרִיצֵי גוֹיִם (ārîṣê gôyim, "the most ruthless of nations") is plural, most likely referring to all the military hordes from subject nations that were part of the Babylonian army (cf. 30:11; 31:12; 32:12; with 23:23).

10 Some argue that in light of 1 Sam 18:25, 27, עֲרֵלִים (ʿᵃrēlîm, "uncircumcision") may also be rendered "castration." Such would be a disgraceful death, though this meaning is not needed here to convey the idea of a dishonorable death.

---

4. A funeral dirge for the king of Tyre

28:11–19

[11]The word of the LORD came to me: [12]"Son of man, take up a lament concerning the king of Tyre and say to him: 'This is what the Sovereign LORD says:

" 'You were the model of perfection,
full of wisdom and perfect in beauty.
[13]You were in Eden,
the garden of God;
every precious stone adorned you;
ruby, topaz and emerald,
chrysolite, onyx and jasper,
sapphire, turquoise and beryl.
Your settings and mountings were made of gold;
on the day you were created they were prepared.
[14]You were anointed as a guardian cherub,
for so I ordained you.
You were on the holy mount of God;
you walked among the fiery stones.
[15]You were blameless in your ways
from the day you were created
till wickedness was found in you.
[16]Through your widespread trade
you were filled with violence,
and you sinned.
So I drove you in disgrace from the mount of God,
and I expelled you, O guardian cherub,
from among the fiery stones.
[17]Your heart became proud
on account of your beauty,
and you corrupted your wisdom
because of your splendor.
So I threw you to the earth;
I made a spectacle of you before kings.
[18]By your many sins and dishonest trade
you have desecrated your sanctuaries.

> So I made a fire come out from you,
>   and it consumed you,
> and I reduced you to ashes on the ground
>   in the sight of all who were watching.
> ¹⁹All the nations who knew you
>   are appalled at you;
> you have come to a horrible end
>   and will be no more.' "

This is one of the more difficult passages in the Book of Ezekiel—if not in the whole Bible! The reason for the difficulty lies mainly in the lack of sufficient data to reach precise conclusions. There are many terms and phrases that are only used in these verses in the OT. There are no parallels or other contexts from which to gain clues to the understanding of this lament. Therefore any interpretation of this section must be constantly open to reevaluation in light of new data from ancient languages and cultural concepts.

The most logical and expected understanding of this section is to see it as Ezekiel's funeral lament for Tyre's king. The progression of the prophecies against Tyre have alternated judgment speeches with funeral laments. Chapter 26 presented a judgment speech against the city, and chapter 27 followed with the funeral dirge over the city. Chapter 28:1–10 set forth a judgment speech against Tyre's ruler, and one would expect that 28:11–19 would be the corresponding funeral dirge for this king. Therefore, one should start with the most natural and logical understanding of these verses, i.e., that the human king of Tyre (the same as the ruler of Tyre in vv. 1–10) was the person under discussion.

Many, however, have interpreted the passage in other ways. Some have understood the king of Tyre to be Satan. Others have seen ancient mythology as the basis of the passage. Ancient mythology should be kept in mind, for it shows the Phoenicians' religious thinking and provides cultural aid in interpreting the passage. However, to interpret the passage as a myth is unwarranted. To understand the king of Tyre to be Satan also has its difficulties, as will be noted below. No interpretation is without problems, but the most natural and seemingly easier position is to take Tyre's king to be the human ruler of that city in Ezekiel's day.

11–12 The difficulty in the passage lies in explaining the description that was given for this king. He was said to be full of wisdom and perfect in beauty (v. 12), concepts already conveyed about Tyre's ruler (vv. 2–5) and his city (27:3). He was also "the model of perfection" or, more literally, "the one sealing a plan." As Tyre's king and the mastermind of the city's commercial sea traffic, it is certainly easy to understand how he would be known as the one who established and approved the function of affixing a seal—a plan that enabled the city to become the maritime leader of its day.

13a This individual was also declared to have been in "Eden, the garden of God." Of course, the word "God" could refer either to the true God or to a god (cf. v. 2). "Eden" is used often in the Scriptures to refer to the Paradise described in Genesis 1–3. "Eden" clearly is used also as a simile to portray the splendor of a given geographical area, like the Jordan Valley viewed by Lot in Genesis 13:10. "Eden" is used figuratively by Ezekiel in 31:9, based on a literal understanding of "Eden." It is impossible to conceive that Tyre's contemporary king was in the Garden of Eden at the time of creation; so many argue that Tyre's king was Satan, since he was in

Eden in Genesis 3. However, as will be noted below, there are elements that must be conjectured about Satan in this passage if one chooses to take this interpretation.

The concept of the Garden of Eden presents one of the major difficulties in interpreting this section as Tyre's literal human king. A possible solution may be found in understanding ancient Near Eastern temples. These ancient temples normally encompassed a large enclosure with a garden, not just a building (cf. van Dijk, p. 117). If the term for "God" in this phrase is understood as "god," then perhaps "Eden, a garden of a god," was an expression used metaphorically to describe the splendor of the temple complex of Melkart, the "king of the city" (which was the meaning of the god's name), with whom Tyre's human king was seeking identity. Though this interpretation is a hypothesis (as are all others), normal cultural hermeneutics may aid in the explanation of the text and should not be ignored. It is readily admitted that this phrase "you were in Eden, the garden of God" is the most difficult obstacle to the interpretation of the king of Tyre as the literal king of the city. The above, however, is certainly a plausible understanding of the phrase.

13b–14a The remainder of v. 13 and the first half of v. 14 picture Tyre's king as a cherub. In the ancient Near East a cherub was understood to be a sphinxlike creature with an animal body (normally that of a bull or lion), wings, and a human head (cf. comments at 1:13; 10:8–22). These statutory creatures normally guarded the entrances to pagan temples. The cherubim of God guarded the ark of the covenant, the Garden of Eden, and formed the throne-chariot of God. It seems as if Tyre's king was identifying himself with the patron deity of Tyre, Melkart, directly or symbolically, as the god's guardian sphinx. The Phoenician male-sphinx (or cherub) was normally bejeweled and sometimes had the head of the priest-king (cf. Barnett, p. 13). The sphinx was considered to be all-wise. Such a description fits well the verses under discussion, for the king is called a guardian cherub (sphinx) and the many jewels listed in v. 13 as his covering befit the many jewels that adorned the Phoenician sphinx (cherub). The passage would then be declaring that the king of Tyre had become as the guardian cherub for the god Melkart and was bejeweled with his riches as cherub-sphinx normally was. The term "created" would be used in the sense of bringing the king to the throne. God was always the Creator; so this would demonstrate that it was the true God who had sovereignly placed this contemporary king on the throne of Tyre (cf. Deut 4:19; 32:8, which confirm God's sovereignty over pagan nations and religions).

To assume that the stones were the garment of Satan in the Garden of Eden and that Satan was a guardian cherub of Eden would be purely hypotheses without any exegetical basis elsewhere in Scripture. In fact, neither Michael nor Gabriel are described as cherubim, and one might expect that Satan was on the same level as these before his fall.

14b "The holy mount of God [or 'god']" may have at least two possible identities. The phrase "holy mount" is consistently used in the OT to describe Jerusalem and/or Zion as the central place of worship and the dwelling place of the Lord (Ps 99:9; Isa 56:7). It is to "my holy mountain" that the children of Israel will be regathered in the millennial kingdom (Isa 11:9; 65:25). If, therefore, the specific phrase "the holy mount of God" (which is only used in this passage in the OT) was taken to refer to Jerusalem, then this would mean that the king of Tyre was in (not on) the city of Jerusalem walking amid fiery stones. In the light of 26:1–6, which described the desire of Tyre to gather the spoils of Jerusalem after its fall to the Babylonians, the latter part of v. 14 would speak of the entrance into Jerusalem by Tyre's king to gather the spoils of that city even while its stones were still smoldering. On the other hand, the concept of "the mount of god" was used in Canaanite mythology to refer to the seat of the gods, normally in the recesses of the north. Perhaps this phrase then implied that Tyre's king was in the domain of the pagan deities since he himself claimed to be a god and was perhaps a guardian cherub of the god Melkart.

If the latter position concerning the meaning of the phrase "the holy mount of god" is taken, then one must explain the meaning of walking "among the fiery stones." The ritual of burning a god has been discovered on a bowl from Sidon and is recorded in the cult of Melkart at Tyre (cf. Barnett, pp. 9–10). Melkart's resurrection was celebrated by a "burning in effigy," from which he would then be revitalized through the fire and the smelling of the burnt offering. Again, in keeping with the Phoenician religious-cultural background with which the passage is so closely tied by the king's claim of deity, perhaps the explanation of walking among the fiery stones is a reference to the king's self-exaltation of himself even as the god Melkart —even to the extent of his claiming resurrection after burning by fire.

It should be observed at this point that the "holy mount of God" is never used in Scripture to mean heaven. Such would have to be its interpretation if the king of Tyre was identified with Satan. Likewise, walking among the fiery stones would be an enigma if Satan was the person described here. One of the two explanations above for the phrase "holy mount of God [god]" would appear to be more plausible.

15–19 Last, this king was declared to be perfect in his ways from the day he was created till he sinned (v. 15). The word "perfect" does not imply "sinless perfection." It was used to show that one was blameless or unobjectionable in a given area. This would then mean that the king of Tyre was a good king against whom objections were not raised from the moment of his coronation till pride possessed him and he sinned.

The sin of the king of Tyre was pride that arose from the splendor he achieved through his vast commercial traffic (vv. 15–17; cf. vv. 2–5). The king's obsession for material gain opened the city to all the evils prevalent amid those involved in commercial traffic. He became filled with violence (v. 16). His wisdom was dulled by the glitter of wealth and splendor. He became proud (v. 17). He also profaned his sanctuaries, a reference most likely to the idolatries practiced in the temple of Melkart (v. 18). Such a description of the sin of the king of Tyre is totally unfitting for Satan. Contextually these descriptions relate to Tyre's human king and his city as described repeatedly in chapters 26–28. Only by seeing Satan as the force behind Tyre's king and the spirit working in him can one even begin to relate these verses to Satan. But, as demonstrated above, there are many difficulties with identifying Satan as the king of Tyre when examining the characteristics of that king.

This funeral lament concluded with a description of the fall of this king under God's judgment (vv. 16–19). God would bring him down in disgrace from his self-deification, from "the mount of god." As a cherub he would be eliminated from the area of the fiery stones, i.e., his professed immortality by fiery resurrection would be destroyed when he died (or he would be removed from taking spoils from Jerusalem). God would cast him to the ground before all the world's kings and cause fire to come forth from him to devour him. Just what is meant by the fire coming out from the king is not clear. His death would be sudden and horrible, and he would exist no more. Certainly this description of the fall and judgment on Tyre's king is befitting a human, but it does not coincide with what we know of Satan's fall and ultimate destruction as revealed elsewhere in Scripture.

Therefore, it is concluded that Tyre's king is best understood as the literal human contemporary king of that city in Ezekiel's day. Each characteristic given about him in these verses can be explained in light of the cultural and religious context of that day. Contrarily, the identification of the king as Satan must be done to a large extent on a presupposition that the descriptions here refer to Satan. Most of these descriptions—if they do in fact relate to Satan—are revealed nowhere else in Scripture. In light of the logical flow of the context and the explanations of the king's character given above, it is concluded that a human king is described herein.

However, let it be stated again that the data for a clear interpretation of this passage is sparse indeed. Therefore one must always be open to reevaluate and reexamine his position on this text.

Notes

---

12 The phrase תׇכְנִית חֹותֵם (ḥôṯēm toḵnîṯ, "sealing a plan") is difficult. The specific form ḥôṯēm is found only in this verse in the OT. Many equate it with the noun ḥôṯām ("seal"). Though the form is that of the Qal active participle, some argue that the holem-waw normally is not found in the participle; therefore this probably is not a participial form. However, it seems best to understand the form as a Qal active participle, for the plene writing often is found in the participle elsewhere in the OT. Therefore the word should be translated as "sealer" or "sealing" rather than as a noun. Toḵnîṯ is usually translated "plan" or "pattern," as in 43:10, its only other use in this book, where the context clearly conveys that meaning. Holladay (Concise Hebrew and Aramaic Lexicon, s.v.) translates it "perfect example." This agrees with the NIV's "model of perfection" (see also BDB on both words). The clear usage of the word in 43:10 should be a guiding factor in understanding the word here. Otherwise one must conjecture in a passage already full of difficult terms and unsure meanings.

13 The phrase גַּן־אֱלֹהִים (gan-'elōhîm, "the garden of God [god]") is only found in this chapter and in 31:9 in the OT. The phrase is related to Eden in both passages. The phrases גַּן־יהוה (gan-YHWH, "garden of Yahweh") and גַּן־עֵדֶן (gan-'ēḏen, "Garden of Eden") are found several times in the OT. They are both used to describe the paradise in Gen 1–3. All these phrases are used as figures of speech (especially similes) in the OT by which some land area is said to be extraordinarily beautiful and pleasant.

The word מְסֻכָתֶךָ (mᵉsukāṯeḵā, "adorned") is also a hapax legomenon. If it is derived from the verbal root סוּךְ (sûḵ, "to fence or hedge"), then the noun would mean "hedge" or "fence" as in Mic 7:4. If this is correct, then perhaps the passage is speaking about some fence of precious stones that surrounded "Eden, the garden of God." This is unknown from the rest of Scripture. However, the "settings and mounting" (which are not without their own problems) mentioned later in the verse would imply jewelry perhaps more than fasteners of a fence. If the noun is derived from the verbal root סָכַךְ (sākaḵ, "overshadow," "screen," "cover"), then the noun has the usual meaning of a "covering," often in reference to garments. In this sense the noun would tend to refer to the clothing of the "king."

The stones listed in this verse are similar to those on the high priest's breastplate in Exod 28:17–20. The order is different here in Ezekiel, which includes only nine of the twelve stones of Exod 28:17–20. The LXX inserts all twelve stones from Exod 28 into

Ezek 28:13. However, there is no substantial reason for assuming any relation to Exod 28:17–20 on Ezekiel's part.

תֻּפֶּיךָ (tuppeykā, "your settings") is considered by most lexicographers to be the noun תֹף (tōp, "timbrel," "tambourine," "drum"). None of these words fit the context. Tōp is derived from the verb תָּפַף (tāpap, "beat"); so perhaps this noun has another meaning that only appears in the OT at this one place. It may have something to do with beating jewelry into its shape. נְקָבֶיךָ (neqābeykā, "your mountings") comes from the root נָקַב (nāqab, "pierce") and is again most likely a jeweler's technical term. Since both words are preceded by מְלֶאכֶת (mele'ket, "workmanship"), it seems more probable that the entire phrase is speaking about the mounting and setting of the many precious stones mentioned in the verse. The MT places the heavy accent (Atnah) under the word "gold." The Masoretes considered gold to be in the list of precious metals and stones and not considered as the metal from which the settings and mountings are made.

When בָּרָא (bārā', "create") is used to denote creation, God is always the subject. Though not used in the OT in the sense of "ordain," the word is used to convey the idea of one being brought into being for a specific task; and that appears to be the meaning in this verse.

14 מִמְשַׁח (mimšah, "anointed") is a hapax legomenon, though most likely derived from the verbal root מָשַׁח (māšah, "anoint"). Some say the term is unexplainable (Holladay, Concise Hebrew and Aramaic Lexicon, s.v.).

The phrase הַר קֹדֶשׁ אֱלֹהִים (har qōdeš 'elōhîm, "the holy mountain of God") is only used in this construction in the OT in this verse. The phrase "my holy mount" is common in the OT, which, whether stated or indirectly implied through the context, normally refers to Jerusalem and Zion. In ch. 28 this may be the meaning of "the holy mount of God," or the understanding may need to be obtained from the Phoenician concept of their gods inhabiting the holy mountain.

אַבְנֵי־אֵשׁ ('abnê-'ēš, "fiery stones") is also a hapax legomenon phrase and therefore difficult to interpret.

15 תָמִים (tāmîm, "perfect") does not imply perfection from all defects but normally implies blamelessness in a given area. Often it conveys the idea of "blamelessness in a moral sense," but that is likely not the idea here.

16 מָלוּ (mālû, "they filled") is probably a defective form of the verb מָלֵא (mālē', "fill"). A few MSS read מָלְאוּ (māl'û, "they filled"). The LXX and the Syriac read מִלֵּאתָ (mille'ta, "you filled") (so NIV).

The word אַבֶּדְךָ ('abbedkā, "I will let you perish") connotes destruction and perishing. Since it is syntactically related to "from the midst of the fiery stones," some render it in the sense of "expel" (e.g., NIV, RSV, NAB), but this is probably not the best meaning. Likewise with אֲחַלֶּלְךָ ('ehallelkā, "I will profane, pollute, or disgrace"), the idea is not "to cast down" (KJV, RSV, NASB) or "drive out" (NIV).

18 The plural form מִקְדָּשֶׁיךָ (miqdāšeykā, "your sanctuaries") very likely stands for a single temple, syntactically being a plural of extension. This is the way the form is used in 21:7 and by Jeremiah in Jer 51:51.

C. Judgment on Sidon

28:20–24

20The word of the LORD came to me: 21"Son of man, set your face against Sidon; prophesy against her 22and say: 'This is what the Sovereign LORD says:

" 'I am against you, O Sidon,
and I will gain glory within you.
They will know that I am the LORD,
when I inflict punishment on her
and show myself holy within her.

> ²³I will send a plague upon her
> and make blood flow in her streets.
> The slain will fall within her,
> with the sword against her on every side
> Then they will know that I am the LORD.

> ²⁴" 'No longer will the people of Israel have malicious neighbors who are painful briers and sharp thorns. Then they will know that I am the Sovereign LORD.

20–24 Sidon, a sister city of Tyre, lay in the shadow of Tyre's maritime leadership in Ezekiel's day. Equally, Sidon's judgment was very brief following that of Tyre.

God's judgment on Sidon would consist of a plague and death by the sword (v.23). Bloodshed would be rampant. But God's judgment was for good, not evil. It was a manifestation of God's grace, for therein the Lord was glorified when the Sidonians realized that he was truly the Lord and God (v.22). God's judgment is his last effort, so to speak, to bring people to himself. This was effective among the Sidonians as well as other nations. Likewise, the Lord was shown to be holy, unique, and distinct from sinful humanity and all who might claim deity. God's holiness demands that he be just and execute judgment on sin. This holiness was demonstrated in his judgment on sinful Sidon.

Verse 24 summarizes the previous judgment oracles against the nations (chs. 25–28). When these judgments would be completed, then Israel would be free from these despising and harassing nations' constant pricking and pain that she had received for so long. Israel would observe that God had been faithful to his promises to eliminate her oppressors. Then she would also recognize and know that the Lord truly is her God.

D. Israel's Restoration From the Nations

28:25–26

> ²⁵" 'This is what the Sovereign LORD says: When I gather the people of Israel from the nations where they have been scattered, I will show myself holy among them in the sight of the nations. Then they will live in their own land, which I gave to my servant Jacob. ²⁶They will live there in safety and will build houses and plant vineyards; they will live in safety when I inflict punishment on all their neighbors who maligned them. Then they will know that I am the LORD their God.' "

25–26 The judgment of the nations around Israel was given to encourage the exiles that God would faithfully exercise his righteousness against the nations as well as Judah. Ezekiel encouraged the Judeans further with a reminder that the Lord would regather them from among all the nations where they had been scattered by God's judgment. This restoration to Palestine would take place when God executed his judgments on the nations, judgments that would not be completed fully till the end times. By regathering Israel God would demonstrate to all nations that he was the holy God, unique and distinct. None of man's proposed deities had ever been able to accomplish a restoration such as this, and they never would; for the Lord alone was God and none other.

When the Lord would restore Israel to Canaan, he would show his immutable character of faithfulness. He promised this land to Abraham (Gen 12:7), Isaac (Gen

26:3), and Jacob (Gen 35:12) in the Abrahamic covenant. The Lord would cause his people to live in that land in security and prosperity. At that time they would know without doubt that he was the Lord their God.

This brief message would be a source of encouragement to the exiles. Moreover, it was only a preview of the fuller development of the restoration message that would be given in chapters 33–39.

E. *Judgment on Egypt* (29:1–32:32)

Ezekiel concluded his prophecies against the nations with a series of six judgment messages against Egypt. Egypt had played a very significant role in the final days of the Judean kingdom. From 609 B.C. till her fall to Babylonia in 605 B.C., Egypt had dominated Judah. With the momentous victory over Egypt at Carchemish, Babylonia began to rule Judah. Nevertheless Egypt continued to try to regain the Judean allegiance, frequently encouraging Judah to rebel against Babylonia. The Egyptian Pharaoh Hophra tried unsuccessfully to interrupt the Babylonians' siege of Jerusalem.

Since Ezekiel's prophecies against Egypt are so intricately interwoven into the history of his day, a brief historical chronology is supplied to help the reader understand the relation between Ezekiel's messages and the contemporary historical events. (For a detailed treatment of the chronology of this period and its difficulties, see Freedy and Redford, pp. 462–85.)

Dec./Jan.	589/588 B.C.	2 Kings 25:1; Ezek 24:1
	Beginning of the second siege of Jerusalem	
(12 months)	588 B.C.	Jer 37:5–11
	Pharaoh Hophra's interruption of the siege of Jerusalem	
Dec./Jan.	588/587 B.C.	Ezek 29:1–16
(3 months)	Ezekiel's introductory prophecy against Egypt	
Mar./Apr.	587 B.C.	Ezek 30:20–26
(2 months)	Ezekiel's description of the initial defeat of Hophra and the ultimate desolation of Egypt by Babylonia	
May/June	587 B.C.	Ezek 31:1–18
	Egypt's complete fall likened to Assyria's collapse	
(13 months)	587 B.C.	Jer 32:1–5
	Siege of Jerusalem in progress	
June/July	586 B.C.	2 Kings 25:7
(1 month)	End of Zedekiah's regency	
July/Aug.	586 B.C.	2 Kings 25:8
(5 months)	Jerusalem's destruction	

Dec./Jan.	586/585 B.C.	Ezek 33:21
(2 months)	The exiles' reception of the report of Jerusalem's fall	
Feb./Mar.	585 B.C.	Ezek 32:1–16
(½ month)	Egypt's funeral dirge sung by Ezekiel	
Mar.	585 B.C.	Ezek 32:17–33:20
(14 years)	Ezekiel's lament of Egypt's fall and warning to the Judean exiles to turn to the Lord	
Mar./Apr.	571 B.C.	Ezek 29:17–30:19
	Prophecy of Egypt as Babylonia's spoils in Egypt's day of the Lord	

From the above chronological survey, it becomes evident that Ezekiel's prophecies reflected his historical and chronological orientation as he dated his messages against Egypt. It appears that the advancement of Egyptian forces into Palestine under Hophra during Nebuchadnezzar's siege of Jerusalem must have precipitated this series of oracles. Ezekiel's first message was a general prophecy of Egypt's complete desolation because of her pride and her unreliable support of Judah (29:1–16). In his third prophecy (30:20–26), Ezekiel referred to the defeats of Pharaoh Hophra by the Babylonian forces. This was only the beginning of God's judgments on Egypt. There would also be a full destruction on the entire nation because of Egypt's arrogant pride, a haughtiness that Ezekiel likened to that of Assyria at her height of power. But as Assyria was brought down by God, so also Egypt would fall, announced Ezekiel in his fourth message (31:1–18). As in previous prophecies against foreign nations, Ezekiel followed his judgment messages with a lament over Egypt's demise (32:1–16). A summary of his oracles of judgment against Egypt and a warning to the Judean exiles to turn to the Lord and live while there was still opportunity concluded Ezekiel's prophecies (32:17–33:20).

Two observations are important. Ezekiel not only followed historical and chronological development in these prophecies, but he also developed them logically and thematically. This combination of chronological and thematic development characterizes the Book of Ezekiel. Second, the prophecy in 29:17–30:19 was chronologically out of place. Here Ezekiel's thematic concern overweighed his chronological concern. By placing this chronologically final message immediately after the introductory prophecy of December/January 588/587 B.C. (29:1–16), Ezekiel provided for his readers an immediate and a full understanding that Egypt's ultimate and complete destruction foretold in that first message would come through the Babylonians after 571 B.C. Everything prior to that time was only preliminary. Likewise, the placement of the 571 B.C. message (29:17–30:19) after the introductory prophecy against Egypt provided a transition from the judgments on Tyre to those on Egypt. Nebuchadnezzar was the instrument of judgment on Tyre; but since he did not secure the spoils of war from that city due to Egypt's intervention, God would give Egypt as spoils to Babylonia instead. Finally, with the knowledge of ultimate judgment on Egypt acquired, each succeeding prophecy in this series of six messages could be better understood.

1. The introductory prophecy of judgment on Egypt

29:1-16

[1]In the tenth year, in the tenth month on the twelfth day, the word of the LORD came to me: [2]"Son of man, set your face against Pharaoh king of Egypt and prophesy against him and against all Egypt. [3]Speak to him and say: 'This is what the Sovereign LORD says:

" 'I am against you, Pharaoh king of Egypt,
 you great monster lying among your streams.
You say, "The Nile is mine;
 I made it for myself."
[4]But I will put hooks in your jaws
 and make the fish of your streams stick to your scales.
I will pull you out from among your streams,
 with all the fish sticking to your scales.
[5]I will leave you in the desert,
 you and all the fish of your streams.
You will fall on the open field
 and not be gathered or picked up.
I will give you as food
 to the beasts of the earth and the birds of the air.

[6]Then all who live in Egypt will know that I am the LORD.

" 'You have been a staff of reed for the house of Israel. [7]When they grasped you with their hands, you splintered and you tore open their shoulders; when they leaned on you, you broke and their backs were wrenched.

[8]"Therefore this is what the Sovereign LORD says: I will bring a sword against you and kill your men and their animals. [9]Egypt will become a desolate wasteland. Then they will know that I am the LORD.

" 'Because you said, "The Nile is mine; I made it," [10]therefore I am against you and against your streams, and I will make the land of Egypt a ruin and a desolate waste from Migdol to Aswan, as far as the border of Cush. [11]No foot of man or animal will pass through it; no one will live there for forty years. [12]I will make the land of Egypt desolate among devastated lands, and her cities will lie desolate forty years among ruined cities. And I will disperse the Egyptians among the nations and scatter them through the countries.

[13]" 'Yet this is what the Sovereign LORD says: At the end of forty years I will gather the Egyptians from the nations where they were scattered. [14]I will bring them back from captivity and return them to Upper Egypt, the land of their ancestry. There they will be a lowly kingdom. [15]It will be the lowliest of kingdoms and will never again exalt itself above the other nations. I will make it so weak that it will never again rule over the nations. [16]Egypt will no longer be a source of confidence for the people of Israel but will be a reminder of their sin in turning to her for help. Then they will know that I am the Sovereign LORD.' "

1-7 Pharaoh was likened to a crocodile ("monster," v.3) in the midst of the Nile that the Lord would catch, pull from the Nile, and leave on the dry land to die. Though *tannîm* may be translated either "monster" or "crocodile," it seems best in light of Egyptian culture and religion to use the imagery most fitting to the Egyptians. The "crocodile" was common as a fearful creature of the Nile; the "monster" was not. The crocodile normally was caught with hooks in the jaws and then pulled on dry land where it would be slaughtered (cf. Herodotus 2.70). This is the figure used in these verses. The crocodile god, Sebek, was very important to the Egyptians in the Nile delta area. He was considered Egypt's protector and at times was identified with the solar deity, Re (cf. Diodorus 1.35). Even the biblical references frequently use this term in imagery of Egypt (32:2; cf. Ps 74:13; Isa 51:9).

In the imagery the crocodile represented the Pharaoh, the protector of Egypt, who dominated the Nile (metonymy for the entire country of Egypt). This was Hophra's (Apries') arrogant self-image. Herodotus implied that Pharaoh Apries was so strong in his position that he felt no god could dislodge him. In his reign he sent an expedition against Cyprus, besieged and took Gaza (cf. Jer 47:1) and the city of Sidon, was victorious against Tyre by sea, and considered himself master over Palestine and Phoenicia. Such pride was consistent with the denunciation in this message (v.3), for the Pharaoh felt that the Nile (Egypt) belonged to him and that he had created it for himself. This arrogance had also shown itself in an attempt to interrupt Babylonia's siege of Jerusalem—an attempt thwarted by God.

The imagery of catching a crocodile beautifully expressed God's judgment on Pharaoh. He would be pulled from his position of dominance and pride and left as carnage for the birds and animals. He would not even be afforded the royal burial so important to the Pharaohs. The tombs in the Valley of the Kings at Thebes demonstrate how important proper royal burial was to the Pharaohs' successful journey through the Egyptian afterlife. Lack of such burial would have been a horrible fate. The indictment was broadened to include all Egyptians (fish?) (vv.4–5), for as a nation they had failed to be of political support to Israel. Rather they were as a staff made of reeds (a second imagery) that shattered when Israel leaned on it, seriously wounding her (vv.6–7; cf. Isa 36:6). Egypt never was a reliable support for Israel.

8–16 The imagery in vv.3–7 was interpreted and expanded in this latter portion of the message. The Pharaoh stood as metonymy for Egypt. Both the Pharaoh and all Egypt would perish, and the land would become desolate when God would bring the sword against that land because of their pride (vv.8–9). The desolation would affect the entire country from Migdol in the northeast delta (generally identified with Tel el Her, about twelve and one-half miles northeast of modern Qantara) to Seveneh (Syene, located at modern Aswan opposite Elephantine Island on the east bank near the first cataract). These sites were effectively ancient Egypt's northern and southern boundaries. The judgment would also extend into Cush, modern Ethiopia (ancient Nubia) between the Nile's second and third cataracts. The streams or canals in the Nile's delta would be affected also, as indicated in a later message (v.10; cf. 30:12; 32:13–14).

While Egypt was desolate for forty years (v.11), her inhabitants would be scattered among the nations (v.12). Though no specific data is available from Egypt's ancient literature concerning this dispersion, such a scattering most certainly took place at the hands of the Babylonians (cf. later messages). Egypt's fate was like a repetition of Judah's (cf. the forty years parallel in 4:6). If Egypt fell to the Babylonians about 568 B.C., as implied in the chronicles of the Babylonian kings, then a forty-year "captivity" of Egypt would end under the Persians. Since it was the Persians' practice to return many peoples displaced by the Babylonians, this very well may be the case. Sources for Egyptian and Babylonian history of this period are sparse. In addition, kings of the ancient Near East did not normally admit failure. Just because there is no direct statement in ancient history concerning this dispersion does not mean that it did not occur. God's word is more valid than our conjectures or ignorance.

When Egypt would be restored to her land after forty years (v.13), she would inhabit the area of Pathros or "Upper Egypt," the land area essentially between modern Cairo and Aswan. Never again would Egypt be a great kingdom over other nations. It would always be a lowly kingdom, for God would make Egypt weak (vv. 14–15). No longer would Israel look with confidence toward Egypt. Every time she would look to Egypt in the future, Israel would be reminded of her sin in turning to Egypt for help in the past (v. 16).

The purpose of God's judgment messages was always the same. He desired that those judged would recognize through the discipline that he was the Lord, the only true God, the God of Israel. This was the purpose in Egypt's judgment (vv. 9b, 16b).

Notes

3 The meaning of the Hebrew word תַנִּים (tannîm) is disputed. The normal rendering is תַנִּין (tannîn) rather than tannîm. The term may have become confused with the plural תַנִּינִם (tannînim, "monsters," "crocodiles") or with the plural תַן (tan, "jackal"). Moreover the מ (m) and the נ (n) are sometimes interchanged in Semitic languages. There is insufficient data for a definitive answer. The word's meanings and its cognates range from "jackal" to "serpent," "dragon," "sea-monster," "monster," "crocodile." In all OT contexts where the term is used, a fearful creature is imagined. Some interpret the term as a mythological creature of the deep, but there is no basis for such in most passages, especially in Ezekiel. Since "crocodile" is most fitting in light of Egyptian culture and religion, that interpretation has been used in this commentary.

7 The NIV has rendered בְכַפְּךְ (ḇakkapḵ, "with your hand") as "with their hands," following the LXX and the Syriac. The NIV's reading seems to fit the context best. Singular "hand" can be understood as a collective. The difficulty lies with the variance in the suffix.

2. A day of the Lord: the consummation of Egypt's judgment (29:17–30:19)

a. Babylonia's compensation of Egypt for the spoilless siege of Tyre

29:17–21

> [17]In the twenty-seventh year, in the first month on the first day, the word of the LORD came to me: [18]"Son of man, Nebuchadnezzar king of Babylon drove his army in a hard campaign against Tyre; every head was rubbed bare and every shoulder made raw. Yet he and his army got no reward from the campaign he led against Tyre. [19]Therefore this is what the Sovereign LORD says: I am going to give Egypt to Nebuchadnezzar king of Babylon, and he will carry off its wealth. He will loot and plunder the land as pay for his army. [20]I have given him Egypt as a reward for his efforts because he and his army did it for me, declares the Sovereign LORD.
> [21]"On that day, I will make a horn grow for the house of Israel, and I will open your mouth among them. Then they will know that I am the LORD."

17–21 As a fulfillment of God's judgment on Tyre, Nebuchadnezzar and the Babylonian army laid siege to Tyre for thirteen years (cf. Jos. Antiq. X, 228 [xi.1]). The scant historical data indicates that Egypt and Tyre became allies under Pharaoh Hophra (Apries). The extended siege of Tyre was perhaps due to the aid Tyre received from the Egyptians. In such an act Hophra was going contrary to God's purposes. Not only was the siege prolonged by Egyptian support, but some also surmise that Egypt's maritime aid enabled Tyre to send away her wealth for security during the siege. When Tyre surrendered about 573 B.C. (J.D. Newsome, *By the Waters of Babylon* [Atlanta: John Knox, 1979]. p. 159), Babylonia gained almost no spoils from the long siege (v.18). Therefore God promised in this latest-dated oracle of Ezekiel (v.17; cf. chronological discussion at intro. to 29:1–32:32) that Nebuchadnezzar would receive Egypt as compensation for the spoils he failed to receive from Tyre (v.19). "Every head was rubbed bare and every shoulder made raw" indicates that they were carrying heavy loads on their heads and shoulders during the siege (so Wevers) and perhaps the chafing of helmets (so Taylor). Nebuchadnezzar would carry off Egypt's superior wealth as pay for his army and as a belated "reward" for his execution of God's judgment against Tyre (v.20).

Though some perceive that this passage demonstrates the incomplete fulfillment of Ezekiel's prophecies against Tyre, such a position rests on silence. On the contrary, these verses demonstrate that God faithfully executed his word against Tyre through Babylonia as he promised. The Scriptures do not demand that complete fulfillment lay in this one siege alone.

These verses also indicate for the first time that the instrument of God's judgment on Egypt will be Babylonia under Nebuchadnezzar's leadership (cf. Jer 43:8–13). Since Nebuchadnezzar died in 562 B.C., this predicted desolation of Egypt by Nebuchadnezzar's army would have to have occurred before then. One fragmentary Babylonian text from the chronicles of the Chaldean king (B.M. 33041) implies that Babylonia invaded Egypt about 568/567 B.C. This is corroborated by Josephus (Antiq. X, 180–82 [ix.7]).

God used Babylonia's conquest of Egypt to strengthen and encourage Israel in exile (v.21). The phrase "make a horn grow" can be understood when two aspects of the horn symbolism are grasped: (1) strength and (2) a leader or ruler. Some think "horn" refers here to the Messiah because of comparison with Psalm 132:17. However, the context of Ezekiel 29 argues against the messianic interpretation. The passage treats the judgment on Egypt and states that at the time of Nebuchadnezzar's invasion "a horn" will grow for Israel. No Messiah—or any other ruler—came in Israel around 586 B.C. The symbol must refer to the strength and encouragement that Israel was to receive when she observed God's faithfulness to execute his judgment on her enemy, Egypt, in accord with both these prophecies and the Abrahamic covenant (Gen 12:3). At this time Ezekiel's mouth would be opened among the exiles to proclaim God's purposes and workings more freely, since the exiles would be more ready to listen. Through these events the Israelites who had not yet understood would perceive that the God who was accomplishing these mighty acts in faithfulness was the Lord their God (v.21).

b. *Nebuchadnezzar's invasion of Egypt*

30:1–19

¹The word of the LORD came to me: ²"Son of man, prophesy and say: 'This is what the Sovereign LORD says:

" 'Wail and say,
   Alas for that day!"
³For the day is near,
   the day of the LORD is near—
a day of clouds,
   a time of doom for the nations.

⁴A sword will come against Egypt,
and anguish will come upon Cush.
When the slain fall in Egypt,
her wealth will be carried away
and her foundations torn down.

⁵Cush and Put, Lydia and all Arabia, Libya and the people of the covenant land will fall by the sword along with Egypt.
⁶" 'This is what the LORD says:

" 'The allies of Egypt will fall
and her proud strength will fail.
From Migdol to Aswan
they will fall by the sword within her,
declares the Sovereign LORD.

⁷" 'They will be desolate
among desolate lands,
and their cities will lie
among ruined cities.
⁸Then they will know that I am the LORD,
when I set fire to Egypt
and all her helpers are crushed.

⁹" 'On that day messengers will go out from me in ships to frighten Cush out of her complacency. Anguish will take hold of them on the day of Egypt's doom, for it is sure to come.

¹⁰" 'This is what the Sovereign LORD says:

" 'I will put an end to the hordes of Egypt
by the hand of Nebuchadnezzar king of Babylon.
¹¹He and his army—the most ruthless of nations—
will be brought in to destroy the land.
They will draw their swords against Egypt
and fill the land with the slain.
¹²I will dry up the streams of the Nile
and sell the land to evil men;
by the hand of foreigners
I will lay waste the land and everything in it.

I the LORD have spoken.

¹³" 'This is what the Sovereign LORD says:

" 'I will destroy the idols
and put an end to the images in Memphis.
No longer will there be a prince in Egypt,
and I will spread fear throughout the land.
¹⁴I will lay waste Upper Egypt
set fire to Zoan
and inflict punishment on Thebes.
¹⁵I will pour out my wrath on Pelusium,
the stronghold of Egypt,
and cut off the hordes of Thebes.
¹⁶I will set fire to Egypt;
Pelusium will writhe in agony,
Thebes will be taken by storm;
Memphis will be in constant distress.
¹⁷The young men of Heliopolis and Bubastis
will fall by the sword,
and the cities themselves will go into captivity.
¹⁸Dark will be the day at Tahpanhes

when I break the yoke of Egypt;
there her proud strength will come to an end.
She will be covered with clouds,
    and her villages will go into captivity.
[19]So I will inflict punishment on Egypt,
    and they will know that I am the Lord.' "

1–19 There is a tendency to take the phrase "the day of the Lord" and make it a technical theological phrase with a single meaning. This idiom and the phrase "a day of clouds" often refer to the Day of the Lord at history's end, when God will execute final judgment and blessing on Israel and the nations. However, "a day of the Lord" may be any specific time period when God is doing a special work. Such appears the case in this passage. The context demonstrates that this "day of the Lord" (v.3) relates specifically to God's judgment on Egypt through the instrumentality of Babylonia. The specific geographical terminology from Ezekiel's day was used, and Nebuchadnezzar was declared to be the agent of judgment. In addition, the event is called a "day of Egypt" (v.9), limiting the judgment to Egypt and her satellites alone. It does occur during the "time of doom for the nations" (v.3), when Babylonia would bring God's wrath on those nations that had in some manner "cursed" Israel (cf. Gen 12:3; Ezek 25:32; Jer 25, 27, 45–48).

Egypt's day of the Lord, a day of doom (v.9), would be a dark day in her history ("a day of clouds," v.3). The masses would fear as Egypt's proud strength ceased before Nebuchadnezzar's sword. Many would be slain (vv.6, 10–11, 13, 18). Egypt's great riches would be carried off to Babylonia along with many people (vv.4, 17–18; cf. Jos. Antiq. X, 182 [ix. 7]). Not even a prince (leader) would be left in the country (v.13). Many idolatrous statues of the Egyptian gods would be destroyed in the Babylonian quest for complete victory and wealth.

The entire land would lie desolate from Migdol in the north to Syene in the south (v.6; cf. comment at 29:10). Pathros, that major portion of Upper Egypt between modern Cairo and Aswan, would be laid waste. Egypt's major cities would bear the punishment of Babylon: Zoan in the northeastern delta; Thebes, Egypt's perennial southern capital; Pelusium, or Sais, the residence of the ruling Twenty-Sixth Dynasty of Ezekiel's day located on the northeast border; Heliopolis, a major religious center; Bubastis; and Tahpanhes, a frontier fortress perhaps identical with modern Tell Deferneh, ten miles west of Qantara (vv.14–18). The Nile's streams would be dried up (v.12; cf. 32:13–14).

Egypt's allies would fall also to Babylonia's sword: Cush, or Ethiopia; Lydia in western Anatolia (modern Turkey); Arabia to the east; and Libya to the west (vv.5–7). Even the Judeans ("people of the covenant land"), who probably had fled to Egypt following Gedaliah's assassination (2 Kings 25:23–26), would suffer under the Babylonian invasion (v.5b). The judgment would be comprehensive and awful, though God's purpose would be accomplished. This judgment was a manifestation of God's grace; for through it he would finally cause the Egyptians to understand that he, the Lord God of Israel, is the only true God (vv.8, 19).

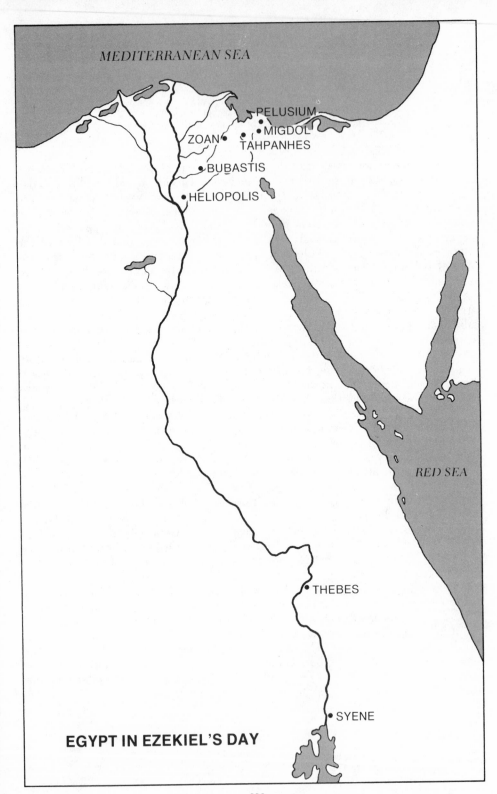

MEDITERRANEAN SEA

PELUSIUM

MIGDOL

ZOAN
TAHPANHES

BUBASTIS

HELIOPOLIS

RED SEA

THEBES

SYENE

EGYPT IN EZEKIEL'S DAY

Notes

3 יוֹם לַיהוה (*yôm laYHWH,* "a day of the LORD") is not a construct state and therefore is not properly translated "the day of the LORD," literally, "a day [belonging] to the LORD." The word יוֹם (*yôm,* "day") is indefinite twice in this verse.

Those who see the "day of the LORD" here as an earnest of the eschatological Day of the Lord (cf. Joel), keeping it as a technical expression, generally link together the near and distant future into a singular meaning with multiple fulfillments. For a summary of proposals for the origin of this phrase, see A. Joseph Everson, "The Days of Yahweh," JBL 93 (1974): 329–37.

5 The translation "Arabia" is based on a revocalization of הָעֶרֶב (*hā'ereb,* "Arabia"?) to עֶרָב (*'arāb,* "Arabia") with the Syriac. However, some prefer to read *'ēreb* ("mixed company") since the term is modified by כָּל (*kol,* "all") (so Wevers). The exact meaning is still unclear.

The LXX reads לוּב (*lûb,* "Libians"?) for כּוּב (*kûb,* "Libians"?). Many accept this view (NIV). However, the LXX's Λίβυες (*Libues*) normally means "Put," and the LXX has a different list of countries. The exact meaning of *kûb* remains unknown.

3. *Pharaoh's broken arms*

30:20–26

[20]In the eleventh year, in the first month on the seventh day, the word of the LORD came to me: [21]"Son of man, I have broken the arm of Pharaoh king of Egypt. It has not been bound up for healing or put in a splint so as to become strong enough to hold a sword. [22]Therefore this is what the Sovereign LORD says: I am against Pharaoh king of Egypt. I will break both his arms, the good arm as well as the broken one, and make the sword fall from his hand. [23]I will disperse the Egyptians among the nations and scatter them through the countries. [24]I will strengthen the arms of the king of Babylon and put my sword in his hand, but I will break the arms of Pharaoh, and he will groan before him like a mortally wounded man. [25]I will strengthen the arms of the king of Babylon, but the arms of Pharaoh will fall limp. Then they will know that I am the LORD, when I put my sword into the hand of the king of Babylon and he brandishes it against Egypt. [26]I will disperse the Egyptians among the nations and scatter them through the countries. Then they will know that I am the LORD."

20–26 Ezekiel returned to his chronological sequence of messages (v.1). Pharaoh Hophra had sought to interrupt Babylonia's siege of Jerusalem at some point during the year 588 B.C. (Jer 34:1, 21:22; 37:5, 9). The Judeans' hopes were raised in expectation of deliverance from the siege. However, Hophra was not successful. The Babylonians defeated Hophra and his army and sent them back to Egypt, after which Nebuchadnezzar renewed his siege of Jerusalem. The prophetic message in these verses followed Hophra's abortive intervention by a few months (Mar./Apr. 587 B.C.). God declared that he had shattered Hophra's arm (v.21). The flexed arm was a common Egyptian symbol for the Pharaoh's strength. Often statues or images of the Pharaoh have this arm flexed, wielding a sword in battle. A king with great biceps was especially a popular concept under the Saites Dynasty of Ezekiel's day. In addition Hophra took a second formal title that meant "possessed of a muscular arm" or "strong-armed" (Freedy and Redford, pp. 482–83). Therefore Hophra's defeat was most suitably represented by "breaking his arm." Ezekiel then takes the imagery further by declaring that Hophra's arm had not been splinted so that it might heal. Hophra's strength had been broken, and he had not regained that strength. He was unable to wield the sword.

This initial defeat of the Egyptian Pharaoh was only a prelude of the complete devastation that God would bring on Egypt by Babylonia. In contrast God would strengthen Nebuchadnezzar's arms and place the Lord's sword in his hand to enable him to bring complete disability to Egypt. Nebuchadnezzar would symbolically break both arms of the Pharaoh. Hophra would be unable to hold a sword at all (vv.22, 24–25). This would occur about 568 B.C., according to Ezekiel's prophecy delivered in 571 B.C. (29:17–30:19). Once again God reminded Egypt of her dispersion among the nations at that final destruction (vv.23, 26; cf. 29:12; 30:17–18). The result was equally reinforced: the Egyptians would realize that it was the Lord who brought this judgment (v.26).

4. Egypt's fall compared with Assyria's fall

31:1–18

¹In the eleventh year, in the third month on the first day, the word of the LORD came to me: ²"Son of man, say to Pharaoh king of Egypt and to his hordes:

" 'Who can be compared with you in majesty?
³Consider Assyria, once a cedar in Lebanon,
    with beautiful branches overshadowing the forest;
it towered on high,
    its top above the thick foliage.
⁴The waters nourished it,
    deep springs made it grow tall;
their streams flowed
    all around its base
and sent their channels
    to all the trees of the field.
⁵So it towered higher
    than all the trees of the field;
its boughs increased
    and its branches grew long,
    spreading because of abundant waters.
⁶all the birds of the air
    nested in its boughs,
all the beasts of the field
    gave birth under its branches;
all the great nations
    lived in its shade.
⁷it was majestic in beauty,
    with its spreading boughs,
for its roots went down
    to abundant waters.
⁸The cedars in the garden of God
    could not rival it,
nor could the pine trees
    equal in boughs,
nor could the plane trees
    compare with its branches—
no tree in the garden of God
    could match its beauty.
⁹I made it beautiful
    with abundant branches,

the envy of all the trees of Eden
in the garden of God.

¹⁰" 'Therefore this is what the Sovereign LORD says: Because it towered on high, lifting its top above the thick foliage, and because it was proud of its height, ¹¹I handed it over to the ruler of the nations, for him to deal with according to its wickedness. I cast it aside, ¹²and the most ruthless of foreign nations cut it down and left it. Its boughs fell on the mountains and in all the valleys; its branches lay broken in all the ravines of the land. All the nations of the earth came out from under its shade and left it. ¹³All the birds of the air settled on the fallen tree, and all the beasts of the field were among its branches. ¹⁴Therefore no other trees by the waters are ever to tower proudly on high, lifting their tops above the thick foliage. No other trees so well-watered are ever to reach such a height, they are all destined for death, for the earth below, among mortal men, with those who go down to the pit.

¹⁵" 'This is what the Sovereign LORD says: On the day it was brought down to the grave I covered the deep springs with mourning for it; I held back its streams, and its abundant waters were restrained. Because of it I clothed Lebanon with gloom, and all the trees of the field withered away. ¹⁶I made the nations tremble at the sound of its fall when I brought it down to the grave with those who go down to the pit. Then all the trees of Eden, the choicest and best of Lebanon, all the trees that were well-watered, were consoled in the earth below. ¹⁷Those who lived in its shade, its allies among the nations, had also gone down to the grave with it, joining those killed by the sword.

¹⁸" 'Which of the trees of Eden can be compared with you in splendor and majesty? Yet you, too, will be brought down with the trees of Eden to the earth below; you will lie among the uncircumcised, with those killed by the sword.

" 'This is Pharaoh and all his hordes, declares the Sovereign LORD.' "

1–9 This beautiful poetic message was delivered two months after the previous prophecy concerning the shattering of Egypt's strength (May/June 587 B.C.). The implication was that Egypt was still proud.

Ezekiel used the imagery of a great cedar of Lebanon, the tallest of the known trees, to represent Assyria, which had recently fallen (612 B.C.). Egypt, in turn, would be compared with Assyria (v.2). The great cedar, Assyria (v.3), was well-watered, perhaps an indirect reference to her great water sources in the Tigris and Euphrates rivers (v.4). Egypt, of course, equally prided herself in her unending supply of Nile water. The cedar (Assyria) had been higher than all other trees (or nations) (v.5); and she was more beautiful than any other tree, even every original variety of beautiful tree in the Garden of Eden (vv.3, 7–9). Every bird nested in her boughs, and every beast bore its young and was shaded under her branches (v.6). These birds and beasts represented the nations under Assyria's control and in her service (cf. Dan 4:10–12, 19–22; Matt 13:31–32). Assyria was perhaps the greatest nation known to that point in history.

10–17 "Pride goes before destruction" (Prov 16:18) aptly describes the continued imagery. Assyria became proud of her greatness ("height," v.10). For this cause the cedar (Assyria) was handed over to the ruler of nations (Nebuchadnezzar) to treat her as she had treated other nations—ruthlessly (v.11). She was cut down and cast aside by the most ruthless of foreign nations (a phrase frequently used in these chapters to denote Babylon) (v.12). God restrained Assyria's water source (v.15). She was worthless after her fall. All nations (other trees, birds, and beasts) mourned and trembled at the cedar's (Assyria's) demise; they too were equally destined for the pit of Sheol (vv.12–14, 16–17). No other nation of that day would ever reach the height that Assyria had reached (v.14).

18 If Egypt thought she was more majestic and had greater splendor than other nations of her day, the Lord reminded her that she too would descend to Sheol. She would "die" disgracefully as an uncircumcised foreigner without a decent burial—a horrible thought for proud Egyptian royalty that cherished its royal burial and despised foreigners (cf. comment at 29:5). If God brought Assyria down, Egypt could be certain that she, who had never come close to Assyria's greatness, would also fall.

Notes

3 Many reject the word אַשּׁוּר (*aššûr*, "Assyria") from the text on the basis of critical conjecture. There is no MS evidence for such an omission.

10 The verb גָּבַהְתָּ (*gābahtā*, "it towered") is properly a second person form ("you towered") rather than a third person verbal form. Only the Syriac text represents the word as a third person verbal form. This is not sufficient reason to alter the text. The second person is best understood as a statement of direct address that is not out of order in a statement of accusation.

5. A funeral dirge for Egypt

32:1–16

¹In the twelfth year, in the twelfth month on the first day, the word of the Lᴏʀᴅ came to me: ²"Son of man, take up a lament concerning Pharaoh king of Egypt and say to him:

> " 'You are like a lion among the nations;
> you are like a monster in the seas
> thrashing about in your streams,
> churning the water with your feet
> and muddying the streams.

³" 'This is what the Sovereign Lᴏʀᴅ says:

> " 'With a great throng of people
> I will cast my net over you,
> and they will haul you up in my net.
> ⁴I will throw you on the land
> and hurl you on the open field.
> I will let all the birds of the air settle on you
> and all the beasts of the earth gorge themselves on you.
> ⁵I will spread your flesh on the mountains
> and fill the valleys with your remains.
> ⁶I will drench the land with your flowing blood
> all the way to the mountains,
> and the ravines will be filled with your flesh.
> ⁷When I snuff you out, I will cover the heavens
> and darken their stars;
> I will cover the sun with a cloud,
> and the moon will not give its light.

8All the shining lights in the heavens
   I will darken over you;
   I will bring darkness over your land,
             declares the Sovereign Lord.
9I will trouble the hearts of many peoples
   when I bring about your destruction among the nations,
   among lands you have not known.
10I will cause many peoples to be appalled at you,
   and their kings will shudder with horror because of you
   when I brandish my sword before them.
On the day of your downfall
   each of them will tremble
   every moment for his life.

11" 'For this is what the Sovereign Lord says:

" 'The sword of the king of Babylon
   will come against you.
12I will cause your hordes to fall
   by the swords of mighty men—
   the most ruthless of all nations.
They will shatter the pride of Egypt,
   and all her hordes will be overthrown,
13I will destroy all her cattle
   from beside abundant waters
no longer to be stirred by the foot of man
   or muddied by the hoofs of cattle.
14Then I will let her waters settle
   and make her streams flow like oil,
             declares the Sovereign Lord.
15When I make Egypt desolate
   and strip the land of everything in it,
when I strike down all who live there,
   then they will know that I am the Lord.'

16"This is the lament they will chant for her. The daughters of the nations will chant it; for Egypt and all her hordes they will chant it, declares the Sovereign Lord."

1–10 Two months had passed since the exiles in Babylonia had learned of Jerusalem's fall seven months earlier. As they began to comprehend that the Lord did exist and had been faithful to destroy Jerusalem even as he had said, they perhaps wondered whether God would be faithful to punish the heathen nations as he had declared. Conversely Egypt had seen the collapse of Jerusalem and Judah, and Egypt may have begun to gloat in pride over her own survival and power. Lest, on the one hand, the Egyptians think that God would not follow through to judge them and, on the other hand, the exiles begin questioning their new understanding of God's faithfulness to his word, Ezekiel delivered this funeral dirge for Egypt in March 585 B.C.

In the previous judgment prophecies against nations, Ezekiel often followed a judgment message with a lament over that nation. So, having delivered three oracles of condemnation, Ezekiel composed a funeral dirge (v.2). He portrayed Egypt as dead, and so the funeral dirge was to be sung. It would be sung by the "daughters of the nations" as they watched Egypt expire (v.16; see comment and note at 19:1).

The lament over Egypt was principally a recapitulation of the judgment messages, emphasizing Egypt's false pride and bewailing the fate of judgment. Once again the double imagery portrayed the Pharaoh's energetic pride but ineffective strength. Hophra was likened to a young lion and a thrashing crocodile that only muddied the streams of the Nile (v.2; cf. 29:3). The crocodile (Pharaoh) would be captured with a net (v.3) and hurled on the open field as food for the birds and animals (v.4). The carnage would be so great that it would fill every ravine and mountain (vv.5–6). It would be as if a great darkness covered the land (vv.7–8), demonstrating that Egypt's great sun gods were impotent to help. Cosmic collapse is a common image with earth-shaking events (cf. Joel 2:28; Acts 2). The nations who sang this funeral dirge would be stunned and horrified that Egypt had fallen in their midst (vv.9–10).

11–16 These verses help interpret the imagery just described. The slaughter of Egypt would occur at the hands of the Babylonians, the most ruthless of all peoples (vv.11–12). Everyone and every place would be touched, including the great Nile. When all life had disappeared, then the Nile would cease to be stirred up and would flow as smoothly as oil (vv.13–14). Only then would Egypt's pride be shattered (v.12). Pride is a terrible plague in anyone's life. So much did God care for Egypt that in his grace he brought this severe judgment so that they might finally realize that the Lord was the only true God and would turn to him (v.15).

Notes

1 The MT reads בִּשְׁתֵּי עֶשְׂרֵה שָׁנָה (*bištê 'eśrēh šānāh*, "in the twelfth year"). This is unacceptable to some since it would postdate Jerusalem's fall and the prophecy in vv.3–16 and they appeal to a reading in the LXX and in thirteen Hebrew MSS: בְּעַשְׁתֵּי עֶשְׂרֵה שָׁנָה (*be'aštê 'eśrēh šānāh*, "in the eleventh year"). This reading, they argue, was altered to the present MT reading by a scribal omission of the ע ('). This scant textual evidence is insufficient to change this chronological notice.

5 רָמוּתֶךָ (*rāmûtekā*, "your remains") is a difficult word because of the lack of sufficient evidence of its derivation. Though "remains" makes good sense in the context, there is no lexical cognate of its root to lend support to this conjecture. A more likely rendering might be "highness" or "lofty (stature)" as a derivation from the root רוּם (*rûm*, "to be high, exalted," "to rise").

6. *Ezekiel's summary lament over Egypt*

32:17–32

> [17]In the twelfth year, on the fifteenth day of the month, the word of the Lord came to me: [18]"Son of man, wail for the hordes of Egypt and consign to the earth below both her and the daughters of mighty nations, with those who go down to the pit. [19]Say to them, 'Are you more favored than others? Go down and be laid among the uncircumcised.' [20]They will fall among those killed by the sword. The sword is drawn; let her be dragged off with all her hordes. [21]From within the grave the mighty leaders will say of Egypt and her allies, 'They have come down and they lie with the uncircumcised with those killed by the sword.'
> [22]"Assyria is there with her whole army; she is surrounded by the graves of all her slain, all who have fallen by the sword. [23]Their graves are in the depths of the pit and her army lies around her grave. All who had spread terror in the land of the living and slain, fallen by the sword.
> [24]"Elam is there, with all her hordes around her grave. All of them are slain,

fallen by the sword. All who had spread terror in the land of the living went down uncircumcised to the earth below. They bear their shame with those who go down to the pit. ²⁵A bed is made for her among the slain, with all her hordes around her grave. All of them are uncircumcised, killed by the sword. Because their terror had spread in the land of the living, they bear their shame with those who go down to the pit; they are laid among the slain.

²⁶"Meshech and Tubal are there, with all their hordes around their graves. All of them are uncircumcised, killed by the sword because they spread their terror in the land of the living. ²⁷Do they not lie with the other uncircumcised warriors who have fallen, who went down to the grave with their weapons of war, whose swords were placed under their heads? The punishment for their sins rested on their bones, though the terror of these warriors had stalked through the land of the living.

²⁸"You too, O Pharaoh, will be broken and will lie among the uncircumcised, with those killed by the sword.

²⁹"Edom is there, her kings and all her princes; despite their power, they are laid with those killed by the sword. They lie with the uncircumcised with those who go down to the pit.

³⁰"All the princes of the north and all the Sidonians are there; they went down with the slain in disgrace despite the terror caused by their power. They lie uncircumcised with those killed by the sword and bear their shame with those who go down to the pit.

³¹"Pharaoh—he and all his army—will see them and he will be consoled for all his hordes that were killed by the sword, declares the Sovereign LORD. ³²Although I had him spread terror in the land of the living, Pharaoh and all his hordes will be laid among the uncircumcised, with those killed by the sword, declares the Sovereign LORD."

17–32 This was Ezekiel's final prophecy against Egypt. It was given in April 585 B.C., and concluded his oracles against the nations (chs. 25–32). Ezekiel was to wail for the Egyptians because they too would descend into the pit of death, as had all other mighty nations ("daughters of mighty nations") that had preceded them (vv.18, 28, 31–32). Egypt would not be favored over the uncircumcised (without honor) nations she had proudly disdained (v.19). She too would die a shameful, barbarian's death like all the other countries (vv.20–21). Assyria (vv.22–23), Elam (to the southeast of Assyria) (vv.24–25), Meshech and Tubal (in eastern Anatolia, modern Turkey) (vv.26–27), Edom (v.29), all the princes of the north countries, and all the Sidonians (v.30) had wrought some terror on the earth. For this cause they all had descended to Sheol. God had wrought his terror on them, and he would continue to bring his terror on any nation that dealt violently with others in this world. That is why God quickly brought his terror through the Babylonians against Egypt (vv.31–32).

Notes

18, 23–25, 29–30 בּוֹר (*bôr*, "pit") is frequently a synonym for "Sheol." The idea of the place of the deceased as a "pit" most likely arose from the normal burial practice of digging a "pit," or a large hole, in the earth for a burial place. Each country here is pictured in her grave with her hordes of armies strewn about her even as bones of the dead were normally scattered around the family tombs of the ancient Near East.

7. Ezekiel's warning to the exiles

33:1–20

¹The word of the LORD came to me: ²"Son of man, speak to your countrymen and say to them: 'When I bring the sword against a land and the people of the land choose one of their men and make him their watchman, ³and he sees the sword coming against the land and blows the trumpet to warn the people, ⁴then if anyone hears the trumpet but does not take warning and the sword comes and takes his life, his blood will be on his own head. ⁵Since he heard the sound of the trumpet but did not take warning, his blood will be on his own head. If he had taken warning, he would have saved himself. ⁶But if the watchman sees the sword coming and does not blow the trumpet to warn the people and the sword comes and takes the life of one of them, that man will be taken away because of his sin, but I will hold the watchman accountable for his blood.'

⁷"Son of man, I have made you a watchman for the house of Israel; so hear the word I speak and give them warning from me. ⁸When I say to the wicked, 'O wicked man, you will surely die,' and you do not speak out to dissuade him from his ways, that wicked man will die for his sin, and I will hold you accountable for his blood. ⁹But if you do warn the wicked man to turn from his ways and he does not do so, he will die for his sin, but you will have saved yourself.

¹⁰"Son of man, say to the house of Israel, 'This is what you are saying: "Our offenses and sins weigh us down, and we are wasting away because of them. How can we live?"' ¹¹Say to them, 'As surely as I live, declares the Sovereign LORD, I take no pleasure in the death of the wicked, but rather that they turn from their ways and live. Turn! Turn from your evil ways! Why will you die, O house of Israel?'

¹²"Therefore, son of man, say to your countrymen, 'The righteousness of the righteous man will not save him when he disobeys, and the wickedness of the wicked man will not cause him to fall when he turns from it. The righteous man, if he sins, will not be allowed to live because of his former righteousness.' ¹³If I tell the righteous man that he will surely live, but then he trusts in his righteousness and does evil, none of the righteous things he has done will be remembered; he will die for the evil he has done. ¹⁴And if I say to the wicked man, 'You will surely die,' but he then turns away from his sin and does what is just and right—¹⁵if he gives back what he took in pledge for a loan, returns what he has stolen, follows the decrees that give life, and does no evil, he will surely live, he will not die. ¹⁶None of the sins he has committed will be remembered against him. He has done what is just and right; he will surely live.

¹⁷"Yet your countrymen say, 'The way of the Lord is not just.' But it is their way that is not just. ¹⁸If a righteous man turns from his righteousness and does evil, he will die for it. ¹⁹And if a wicked man turns away from his wickedness and does what is just and right, he will live by doing so. ²⁰Yet, O house of Israel, you say, 'The way of the Lord is not just.' But I will judge each of you according to his own ways."

1–20 This latter half of Ezekiel's concluding prophecy against Egypt echoes two previous messages: Ezekiel's commission as a watchman (v. 7; ch. 3) and his exhortation to individual responsibility (v. 8; chs. 3; 18). Ezekiel had faithfully performed his responsibility as a watchman for Israel (v. 9). He had warned her of God's impending judgment that was on the horizon (chs. 4–24). Three to four months prior to this present message, Ezekiel had equally encouraged the people with messages of hope concerning their ultimate restoration to the land (33:21–39:29). They had not heeded his warning concerning judgment and consequently found themselves in captivity, with Jerusalem and Judah in ashes. Ezekiel was exonerated from guilt for the destruction and captivity because he had been God's responsible watchman. The Judeans could only blame themselves for failing to heed the warning.

Therefore, Ezekiel gave one final warning to the exiles: Turn now to the Lord! Why die? (v.11). At least the exiles had come to recognize that God's judgment had come because of their sin (v.10). Previously (ch. 18) the people had blamed their parents' sin for any coming judgment. Now they recognized fully their own wickedness was causing them to waste away.

Ezekiel sought to encourage the exiles. God did not find pleasure in death because of wickedness. Conversely God delighted in those who turned from sin (v.11), followed his ways in the Mosaic covenant, and lived! Each individual was personally responsible and could not blame anyone else for his righteousness or his wickedness. If he were declared to be righteous, it was because he had decided personally to follow the Lord and his covenant. If he were judged to be wicked, it was because he personally had decided to reject the Lord and his law and to live according to his own desires (vv.12–20). To some Judeans it did not seem that God's ways were fair and just (v.17). They still wanted to put the godless on the same level as the righteous. However, God's ways are always fair and just, for he does not blame one person for another person's sin. The Lord fairly judges every person according to his own actions (v.20).

Each Israelite in Babylonia, as he pondered God's fulfillment of judgment on Jerusalem and Judah and the promised destruction of the heathen nations, had a decision to make. Would he personally turn from sin to God and physically live (cf. comments at chs. 3; 18) or would he not? That is the question that confronts each of us today as well. The warnings are over.

Notes

17,20 יִתָּכֵן (*yittāḵēn*, "be just") denotes both an "adjustment to ordinary standards" as well as "gauging" or "estimating by comparison with a standard." The former concept is more appropriate to Ezekiel's argument since the Israelites did not feel that the Lord's way was adjusted to their ordinary standards (cf. TWOT, 2:970).

IV. The Future Blessings of a Faithful Covenant God (33:21–48:35)

The majority of evangelical interpreters maintain that they use a literal grammatical-historical hermeneutic. However, that hermeneutic seems to be viewed differently by different groups within Evangelicalism. Three basic definitions are given (for a full discussion of the variant hermeneutical positions, cf. standard textbooks on hermeneutics; e.g., Bernard Ramm, *Protestant Biblical Interpretation* [Grand Rapids: Baker, 1970], or A. Berkeley Mickelsen, *Interpreting the Bible* [Grand Rapids: Eerdmans, 1963].) First, some hold "literal" to mean "literalistic." This latter term is variously understood, being used to describe "letterism" as well as "a straightforward reading of the text," usually excluding figures of speech. Second, some understand "literal" interpretation to be the normal reading of the text that allows for figures of speech, historical perspective, contextual study, progressive revelation, analogy of faith, etc. Third, others understand "literal" as reading Scripture in a normal literal manner with most prophetic material seen as symbolic and figurative —the reality of which is to be interpreted predominantly by NT concepts of the church. Some here would also see additional facets of the Prophets as yet unfulfilled.

Those who hold the first and third positions normally maintain that they are also holding the second position. In turn, those holding the first and third positions would tend to argue that the other does not hold the second position. In other words, almost all Evangelicals maintain that they consistently use a normal literal hermeneutic and that others do not. Therefore, the approach taken in this commentary—as well as that of other Evangelicals—will be briefly outlined.

The present commentary is approached from a normal literal hermeneutic as described in position two above, though those holding the third position may argue that the commentator holds the first position described. Ezekiel 33–48 is approached with a straightforward reading of the text in the light of history, context, figures of speech, the analogy of faith, progressive revelation, etc. The flow of the argument of the book is emphasized within the context of the entire canon of Scripture and its themes. Apocalyptic visions are viewed as containing considerable symbolism as well as much reality. The interpretation of divine interpreters within visions are followed. These interpreters interpret symbols (cf. ch. 37) but allow to be taken as reality what may be understood in a straightforward reading of the text (e.g., the temple in chs. 40–42) (cf. Alexander, "Hermeneutics of Apocalyptic Literature"). Spiritual lessons may be learned from the realities, even as the future temple of Ezekiel 40–48, with its sacrifices, conveys spiritual lessons as described by the divine interpreter (e.g., the importance of holiness).

Various facets of chapters 33–48 may be used as analogies, illustrations, and object lessons in the NT; but such does not demand that the NT is necessarily giving a "fulfillment" of these chapters. For example, there are various uses of the imagery of the temple in the NT: the church (1 Cor 3:9–12); individual believers (1 Cor 6:14–20); and a literal temple with eschatological significance (2 Thess 2:3–4). Which imagery would be the "fulfillment" or "reality" of Ezekiel's temple? One observes how the various facets and truths conveyed by the OT presentation of the temple (or any other OT item or event) may be used in comparative imagery to teach similar truths in the NT. But such use by NT writers does not mean that these comparisons are necessarily tantamount to "fulfillments" or "realities" of the OT "shadows" by taking many aspects of the OT to be metaphorical or "shadow" only.

However, as observed above, there are those who approach Ezekiel 33–48 with a hermeneutic that views much of the OT prophetic material as symbolic and figurative. In this sense they modify their hermeneutic somewhat when approaching prophetic material. Stress is placed on the NT writers' use of the OT as a dominant interpretive tool. The OT prophetic sections (or its entirety, for some) serve as a metaphor and physical "type" of the "antitype" church. It is argued that the spiritual interpretation of the NT writers looks at the church as the "fulfillment" of these OT expectations (cf. Acts 3:24–25; 1 Peter 1:10–12). The NT writers used a different hermeneutic, in some ways, than the OT writers. This, they would argue, is observed in Paul's statements that we are at the end of the age; the discussion of OT shadows and realities in Christ by the writer of Hebrews; and John's use of the temple as Christ's body (John 2), the new birth by the Spirit (John 3), spiritual water (John 4), and streams of water for the Spirit (John 7). Apocalyptic is viewed as always symbolic, a literary representation of some reality. Nothing can be taken literally within apocalyptic literature, many maintain. Those things that seem improbable or difficult, if literally fulfilled, should be taken as metaphor or symbol. This approach, however, could be devastating to much of Scripture.

Those who hold to the above-described approach to prophetic passages would approach Ezekiel 33–48 as follows. The restoration described in chapters 34, 36–37 is normally interpreted as Israel's return from the Babylonian captivity with the reappointment of a member of David's house as leader. The Messianic Age of Davidic ruling finds fulfillment by some in Jesus' ruling today, though such is not yet perfect—but will be in the future new earth. This, therefore, sees several "realities" of this "metaphor" of restoration. The cleansing of God's people would be through the Messiah's (Christ's) blood, and the Spirit would be given at Pentecost. Prosperity is viewed as current and yet to be fulfilled completely in the future kingdom (the latter concept held by some). Chapters 38–39 appear to be difficult to interpret from this approach since few have much to say about the contents of these prophecies. Patrick Fairbairn (*Ezekiel and the Book of His Prophecy* [Edinburgh: T. & T. Clark, 1963], in loc.) understands these chapters to be portraying a "sure and final victory over all sources of evil." Chapters 40–48 generally describe "the glorious future of the people of God in the age to come in terms which the Jews of that day would understand" (Hoekema, p. 205).

Some from this perspective understand Ezekiel 40–48 as entirely fulfilled in the church today, while others in this approach see in the descriptions of these chapters a picture of the final state on the new earth as well; i.e., some have "already" been inaugurated by Christ and some have "not yet" taken place (so Hoekema, p. ix). Specifically the temple symbolizes the NT "reality" of the heavenly temple (the church, Heb 12:22?) where Christ ministers today (cf. R.J. McKelvey, *The New Temple* [London: Oxford University Press, 1981], p. 10).

For some there also remains a future fulfillment for the people of God. This "heavenly reality" is *rarely* described by those holding this position, nor is this "reality" related to the detailed "symbols" in Ezekiel 40–48. The sacrifices symbolize worship. Here Hoekema (p. 204) seeks support from the *New Scofield Bible* (p. 888): "The reference to sacrifices is not to be taken literally, in view of the putting away of such offerings, but is rather to be regarded as a presentation of the worship of redeemed Israel, in her own land and in the millennial temple, using the terms with which the Jews were familiar in Ezekiel's day." This quote is used to substantiate that even dispensationalists recognize a nonliteral approach to portions of Ezekiel 40–48. In defense of the *New Scofield Bible*, this is only one of two ways that it declares the sacrifices could be interpreted.

The river flowing from the temple in Ezekiel 47 is likened to the Spirit as found in John 7:37–39. Other aspects of these nine chapters seem to remain quite vague. The many details of these chapters would be difficult to comment on if one took the approach just described, for such an approach can only deal in generalities. The details would have little or no meaning.

Therefore, following a normal literal hermeneutic, this commentary will present a view of Israel's future restoration to the land after which she will be cleansed, receive a new heart, and live in security and prosperity under the Messiah's rule in the future millennial kingdom. A literal temple will be constructed according to detailed plans in order to display God's holiness. Sacrifices will be instituted as memorials of the soteriological work of Christ on the cross. A real river will flow from the temple to heal the land. A completely new geographical setting will be established.

A. *Restoration to the Promised Land* (33:21–39:29)

God desires to bless; he does not delight in cursing. However, both blessing and cursing are very much a part of God's covenant program. Ezekiel's entire prophecy is given in light of God's covenants with Israel. To perceive the unity and development of Ezekiel, it is necessary to understand God's covenants.

The Abrahamic covenant is God's basic program for blessing the world (Gen 12:1–3). In this covenant God declared that he would choose one man, Abram; from that one man he would create the nation Israel; and through that nation he would bless the world. The creation of Israel is a major thrust of Genesis through Joshua. For a nation to exist three elements are needed: (1) a people, (2) a government, and (3) a homeland. The people of Israel came into being in Egypt from the twelve sons of Jacob (Israel). Israel's government was received on Mount Sinai in the form of the Mosaic covenant. The land was acquired through the conquest of Canaan under Joshua.

The Mosaic covenant (Exod 20–Num 9, Deut), which was closely related to the Abrahamic covenant, provided Israel's constitution that governed all aspects of life. As Israel kept the Mosaic covenant, she would appropriate the blessings of the Abrahamic covenant; e.g., being in the land of blessing and being a blessing to the nations (cf. Gen 12:3, 7). However, at any point in history when Israel disobeyed the Mosaic covenant, she would find also that she did not benefit from Abrahamic covenant blessings; e.g., she would find herself outside the land of blessing and, in turn, would not be a blessing to the nations. Israel's failure to follow the Mosaic covenant was exactly what had caused her to be exiled in Babylonia. Israel found that her God was faithful to bring the judgments of Deuteronomy 27–28 on her.

In the Davidic covenant (2 Sam 7:12–16) God promised that David's descendants would always sit on his throne: an eternal throne over an eternal kingdom. The concept of the Messiah is based on this covenant, for each king of Israel was a messiah, an "anointed one." This covenant promised that someday the final son of David would rule on David's throne—the Messiah who would rule over the messianic kingdom.

Jeremiah announced a new covenant that God would make with his people, a covenant that would replace the functions of the Mosaic covenant. It would incorporate the Mosaic covenant in that the Mosaic covenant would be written on the hearts of those who believed in the Messiah under the new covenant. The new covenant would improve on the old covenant. Under the provisions of the new covenant, all sin would be forgiven once and for all (by the Messiah); and the Spirit of God would be poured out on all who believed (cf. ch. 36; 2 Cor 3).

All these covenants provided the backdrop for Ezekiel's messages. After receiving his commission (chs. 1–3), Ezekiel warned Israel that the Lord would judge (curse) her in accord with the Mosaic covenant: she would be dispersed among the nations, and Jerusalem and Judah would become desolate (chs. 4–23). In chapter 24 Ezekiel declared that the siege of Jerusalem, the execution of God's prophesied judgment on his people, had begun. Then as a reminder of God's faithfulness to the Abrahamic covenant, Ezekiel announced judgment on those nations that had oppressed Israel (vv.25:1–33:30; cf. Gen 12:3).

The Fall of Jerusalem forms the pivotal point of Ezekiel's prophecy. The warnings had been consummated with the Fall of Jerusalem. God would also deal with the foreign nations. But now there was the need to encourage the exiles that the Lord was as faithful to his promises to bless as he was to those to curse. The remainder of this book (33:21–48:35) emphasizes the blessings of the covenants. God would restore Israel to her land (Mosaic covenant, specifically Deut 30) and place within her a new heart and a new Spirit (new covenant). She would dwell in peace and security as her Lord, the Messiah, would reign over her (Davidic covenant). All God's promises of blessing would be consummated in the fulfillment of each covenant, including the peace covenant. The Messiah would reign over Israel forever, and no one would ever again dispossess Israel from her land.

The concept of the land is particularly significant to the six messages delivered in that one night before the news of Jerusalem's fall reached the exiles in Babylonia. Since Jerusalem had fallen, would the land be lost to Israel (33:21–33)? It was the false "shepherds" of Israel who had lost the land for Israel by leading the people astray from the truth. But the true "shepherd," the Messiah, would ultimately restore the land to Israel (ch. 34). Those foreigners who had possessed the land of Israel and had oppressed her people would be judged and removed so that Israel might again possess her own land (35:1–36:15). Then God would restore Israel to her promised land (36:16–37:14) and reunite the nation in fulfillment of God's covenants with her (37:15–28). Never again would a foreign power have dominion over Israel in her land (chs. 38–39).

1. *Israel and the Promised Land*

33:21–33

²¹In the twelfth year of our exile, in the tenth month on the fifth day, a man who had escaped from Jerusalem came to me and said, "The city has fallen!" ²²Now the evening before the man arrived, the hand of the LORD was upon me, and he opened my mouth before the man came to me in the morning. So my mouth was opened and I was no longer silent.

²³Then the word of the LORD came to me: ²⁴"Son of man, the people living in those ruins in the land of Israel are saying, 'Abraham was only one man, yet he possessed the land. But we are many; surely the land has been given to us as our possession.' ²⁵Therefore say to them, 'This is what the Sovereign LORD says, Since you eat meat with the blood still in it and look to your idols and shed blood, should you then possess the land? ²⁶You rely on your sword, you do detestable things, and each of you defiles his neighbor's wife. Should you then possess the land?'

²⁷"Say this to them: 'This is what the Sovereign LORD says: As surely as I live, those who are left in the ruins will fall by the sword, those out in the country I will give to the wild animals to be devoured, and those in strongholds and caves will die of a plague. ²⁸I will make the land a desolate waste, and her proud strength will come to an end, and the mountains of Israel will become desolate so that no one will cross them. ²⁹Then they will know that I am the LORD, when I have made the land a desolate waste because of all the detestable things they have done.'

³⁰"As for you, son of man, your countrymen are talking together about you by the walls and at the doors of the houses, saying to each other, 'Come and hear the message that has come from the LORD.' ³¹My people come to you, as they usually do, and sit before you to listen to your words, but they do not put them into practice. With their mouths they express devotion, but their hearts are greedy for unjust gain. ³²Indeed, to them you are nothing more than one who sings love

songs with a beautiful voice and plays an instrument well, for they hear your words but do not put them into practice.

³³"When all this comes true—and it surely will—then they will know that a prophet has been among them."

21–22 The date and setting of the six messages in 33:21–39:29 are given in these two verses. Ezekiel had closed chapter 24 (vv. 26–27) by prophesying that a fugitive would escape Jerusalem's destruction and come and report the city's fall to the Babylonian exiles. The fulfillment of that prophecy is in these verses. The siege of Jerusalem had begun in December/January 589/588 B.C. (24:1; 2 Kings 25:1). Two years and seven months later, Jerusalem fell (Sept. 586 B.C.) (2 Kings 25:8). As the city fell, an unknown fugitive escaped—or was brought by the Babylonians—and came to report Jerusalem's destruction to the exiles. Five months later (Dec./Jan. 586/585 B.C.), on the morning after Ezekiel delivered all six messages, that report was received by the exiles (v. 21). Ezekiel's muteness, which had lasted for seven and one-half years (3:24–27), ended as God opened Ezekiel's mouth to speak these six messages of encouragement to the exiles immediately prior to their reception of the tragic news of Jerusalem's fall (v. 22; cf. comments at 3:24–27 for a discussion of the problem of Ezekiel's muteness).

23–29 The first of Ezekiel's six messages has two aspects: (1) a question by the Judean remnant concerning the land (vv. 23–29) and (2) the manner in which the Israelites in Canaan and in Babylonia had responded to Ezekiel's ministry (vv. 30–33). Jerusalem had fallen! Would Israel lose the land? The remnant in the ruins of Jerusalem were questioning the fate of the land promised to Abraham. Was not that land theirs according to the promise to Abraham (cf. Gen 12:7)? Why were they, Abraham's descendants, now to be separated from the land given to their forefathers (v. 24)? Was not the Abrahamic covenant still valid? Did not the Abrahamic promises pertain to them as survivors of the destruction?

The Lord answered that the hope of keeping the Promised Land lay on an incorrect understanding of the covenants. If Israel disobeyed the Mosaic covenant stipulations, she would not receive the Abrahamic covenant blessings, one of which was being in the Promised Land. Ezekiel pointed out to these false and pretentious claimants to the land that they had violated the Mosaic covenant statutes (vv. 25–26): they had eaten blood (cf. Lev 17:10–14; 19:26), worshiped idols (18:6; cf. Exod 20:4–5), made detestable things, shed blood with the sword (18:10; cf. Exod 20:13), and defiled one another's wife (18:6; 22:11; cf. Exod 20:14). In light of these violations, did they really think they should possess the land?

God's verdict was no! The judgments of the Mosaic covenant (Deut 27:28; 29:25–29) were being executed: those left in Judah would die by the sword, by disease, or fall prey to animals (v. 27). Their arrogant pride would cease (v. 28). The land *would* become a desolation and waste (vv. 27–28). Most important, God's purpose for judgment on his people would be accomplished: they would come to know that he was their God when these judgments were executed (v. 29).

30–33 The Israelites in exile and the remnant in Palestine had looked on Ezekiel's ministry in mockery. They would gossip that they should go and hear God's word (v. 30). Yet when they came to Ezekiel, or heard his message, they would listen; but they would not act in accord with his warnings (v. 31). They orally expressed devotion, but their hearts were greedy for material gain. They were "playing games" with God. To them Ezekiel was no more than a good entertainer. He was amusing to listen to and to watch, with all his symbolic acts and prophecies. But just as an entertainer demands no response, so they did not sense a need to respond to Ezekiel's messages (v.32; cf. 2 Tim 4:3). However, as Ezekiel's prophecies became reality —and such had already begun in the Fall of Jerusalem—then Israel would realize that a true prophet had been among them (v.33). Oh the importance of listening to men of God and acting on God's word that they proclaim!

Notes

---

21 Initial cursory comparison of the dates of 2 Kings 25:8; Jer 39:2; 52:6–12, and Ezekiel's dates for the interval between the Fall of Jerusalem and the arrival of the fugitive's report have been estimated to be as much as seventeen months. However, since 2 Kings and Jeremiah used the autumn (Tishri) calendar and Ezekiel used the spring (Nisan) calendar, the period of time is reduced to about five months (for a full discussion, see Freedy and Redford, pp. 466–68).

26 עֲמַדְתֶּם עַל־חַרְבְּכֶם (*ᵃmadtem᷉ al-ḥarbᵉkem*, "You rely on your sword") is literally "you stand on your sword," an idea first mentioned here in Ezekiel. It refers to living by violence, perhaps as observed in oppression of the needy, robbery, child sacrifice, etc. (cf. ch. 18).

---

2. Shepherds false and true (34:1–31)

a. The accusation against the false shepherds

34:1–6

> [1]The word of the LORD came to me: [2]"Son of man, prophesy against the shepherds of Israel; prophesy and say to them: 'This is what the Sovereign LORD says: Woe to the shepherds of Israel who only take care of themselves! Should not shepherds take care of the flock? [3]You eat the curds, clothe yourselves with the wool and slaughter the choice animals, but you do not take care of the flock. [4]You have not strengthened the weak or healed the sick or bound up the injured. You have not brought back the strays or searched for the lost. You have ruled them harshly and brutally. [5]So they were scattered because there was no shepherd, and when they were scattered they became food for all the wild animals. [6]My sheep wandered over all the mountains and on every high hill. They were scattered over the whole earth, and no one searched or looked for them.

1–6 In the previous message Ezekiel explained that Palestine had been lost to Israel because she had violated the Mosaic covenant. Therefore she would not now experience the blessing of being in the Promised Land, a blessing of the Abrahamic covenant only experienced when the nation obeyed the Mosaic covenant stipulations. But the more severe indictment belonged to Israel's leaders, depicted in this new message as "shepherds," a common metaphor in the ancient Near East for a ruler (cf. also Ps 23; John 10).

First, this judgment speech sets forth the reason for God's judgment on Israel's past "shepherds" (v.2). Israel's leaders had thought only of themselves and material gain. They had not cared for the "flock" (v.3). Instead of feeding the flock, they fed on the flock, taking food and clothing for themselves instead of providing for the people. They had failed to provide for the needy—those weak and sick. They had not sought for sheep that had been lost. They did not care what happened to the people as long as they as leaders had all their own personal needs met. They were harsh and brutal in their rule (v.4). God makes it clear that a leader has a primary responsibility to care for those he leads, even at the sacrifice of his own desires. Would that political and spiritual leaders both then and now would recognize this heart attitude of leadership!

Because of the de facto lack of a shepherd to lead them, the flock of Israel was lead astray and ended up being scattered among the nations (vv.5–6; cf. Jer 23:9–10). Since they no longer had a shepherd's protection, they became as food for wild beasts. There was no shepherd to search them out and care for them (cf. Matt 9:36). Lack of leadership always leads to the disintegration of God's people and personal and corporate heartache and injury. Leadership carries an awesome responsibility.

b. *God's verdict concerning the leadership of Israel*

34:7–31

> 7" 'Therefore, you shepherds, hear the word of the LORD: 8As surely as I live, declares the Sovereign LORD, because my flock lacks a shepherd and so has been plundered and has become food for all the wild animals, and because my shepherds did not search for my flock but cared for themselves rather than for my flock, 9therefore, O shepherds, hear the word of the LORD: 10This is what the Sovereign LORD says: I am against the shepherds and will hold them accountable for my flock. I will remove them from tending the flock so that the shepherds can no longer feed themselves. I will rescue my flock from their mouths, and it will no longer be food for them.
>
> 11" 'For this is what the Sovereign LORD says: I myself will search for my sheep and look after them. 12As a shepherd looks after his scattered flock when he is with them, so will I look after my sheep. I will rescue them from all the places where they were scattered on a day of clouds and darkness. 13I will bring them out from the nations and gather them from the countries, and I will bring them into their own land. I will pasture them on the mountains of Israel, in the ravines and in all the settlements in the land. 14I will tend them in a good pasture, and the mountain heights of Israel will be their grazing land. There they will lie down in good grazing land, and there they will feed in a rich pasture on the mountains of Israel. 15I myself will tend my sheep and have them lie down, declares the Sovereign LORD. 16I will search for the lost and bring back the strays. I will bind up the injured and strengthen the weak, but the sleek and the strong I will destroy. I will shepherd the flock with justice.
>
> 17" 'As for you, my flock, this is what the Sovereign LORD says: I will judge between one sheep and another, and between rams and goats. 18Is it not enough for you to feed on the good pasture? Must you also trample the rest of your pasture with your feet? Is it not enough for you to drink clear water? Must you also muddy the rest with your feet? 19Must my flock feed on what you have trampled and drink what you have muddied with your feet?
>
> 20" 'Therefore this is what the Sovereign LORD says to them: See, I myself will judge between the fat sheep and the lean sheep. 21Because you shove with flank and shoulder, butting all the weak sheep with your horns until you have driven them away, 22I will save my flock, and they will no longer be plundered. I will judge between one sheep and another. 23I will place over them one shepherd, my servant David, and he will tend them; he will tend them and be their shepherd. 24I the LORD will be their God, and my servant David will be prince among them. I the LORD have spoken.
>
> 25" 'I will make a covenant of peace with them and rid the land of wild beasts so that they may live in the desert and sleep in the forests in safety. 26I will bless

them and the places surrounding my hill. I will send down showers in season; there will be showers of blessing. ²⁷The trees of the field will yield their fruit and the ground will yield its crops; the people will be secure in their land. They will know that I am the Lᴏʀᴅ, when I break the bars of their yoke and rescue them from the hands of those who enslaved them. ²⁸They will no longer be plundered by the nations, nor will wild animals devour them. They will live in safety, and no one will make them afraid. ²⁹I will provide for them a land renowned for its crops, and they will no longer be victims of famine in the land or bear the scorn of the nations. ³⁰Then they will know that I, the Lᴏʀᴅ their God, am with them and that they, the house of Israel, are my people, declares the Sovereign Lᴏʀᴅ. ³¹You my sheep, the sheep of my pasture, are people, and I am your God, declares the Sovereign Lᴏʀᴅ.' "

7–10 The accusation against Israel's "shepherds" has been given. The normal judicial procedure was to repeat the accusation immediately before announcing the verdict. Therefore, the first matter of this judicial sentence was to review the charge so that it might be clear: Israel's "shepherds" had been selfish, insensitive leaders who had plundered the flock for personal gain and had allowed the people to become prey for other nations (vv.7–8).

On the basis of this indictment, God promised to remove the leaders from their position so that the flock of Israel might no longer be devoured by these wolves in shepherds' clothes. The Lord would hold each "false shepherd" accountable for his shepherding (vv.9–10).

11–16b The Lord also desired to encourage his flock, the people of Israel. Though they were responsible for their own actions, they had been led astray by these brutal leaders. The Lord encouraged them by declaring that he would personally assume the responsibility for "shepherding" the flock of Israel. Whereas Israel's recent rulers had failed to protect the people and to search for those who had strayed, the Lord promised that he would search, rescue, and regather the flock of Israel from the nations; then he would care for them as a loving shepherd (vv.11–13a; contra v.6). He would restore Israel to her own land and feed her on the lush pastures of Israel's own mountains and ravines (vv.13b–15; cf. vv.25, 27a, 29; contra vv.4–6). Individual needs would finally be met; those lost would be sought and found. The injured would be healed; the weak would be strengthened. The Lord would care for every need of his flock (v.16a; contra v.4).

16c–24 God would shepherd his people in justice (v.16c; contra v.4). Those who had taken advantage of the flock through their position as shepherds would be treated like all other sheep or goats. Previous shepherds were likened to fat, sleek, and strong sheep because they had fed on the best pasture and drank the clear water. Out of lack of concern for the flock's other members, they arrogantly had trampled the rest of the pasture and muddied the clear drinking water (vv.17–19). They had abused their positions of strength and "bullied" the other sheep, driving them away (vv.20–21). These "shepherds" would be judged and destroyed (vv.16b–17, 20), for there was no place for such irresponsible behavior among leaders.

The Lord would deliver Israel from all distress, whether from poor leadership or from the predatory nations (v.22; cf. vv.28–29b). He would do so by appointing one true and responsible Shepherd for his people: the Messiah, his servant David (vv.23–24). The Lord would be Israel's God; his servant David, the Messiah, would be

913

Israel's Ruler on earth after he restored Israel to her land. Two members of the Godhead were clearly discerned with varying functions. The phrase "my servant David" regularly referred to the Messiah. Jeremiah equated the Messiah to the true Shepherd from the line of David, calling him "a righteous Branch," "the LORD Our Righteousness" (Jer 23:5–6). The identity is also implied elsewhere in the Prophets (Jer 30:9; Ezek 37:24–25; Hos 3:5).

In John 10 Jesus declared, "I am the good shepherd" (v.14). In addition to describing the pastoral aspects of his ministry, it certainly appears that he had Ezekiel 34 in mind. He was declaring to those discerning Jews that he was the true and righteous Shepherd of whom Ezekiel spoke—the Messiah. He would lay down his life for the sheep, not exploit them.

25–31 Finally, the Lord encouraged Israel with the establishment of another covenant with them: the "covenant of peace" (vv.25–31; cf. 37:26–28; 38:11–13; 39:25–29). This covenant was not the new covenant. This peace covenant would be inaugurated in the future when the Lord had fulfilled all his other covenants with Israel. First, this covenant guaranteed the ultimate removal of all foreign nations ("wild beasts") from Israel's land so that she might live securely (v.25; cf. vv.13–15; 35:1–36:15; 38–39). Second, God would bless Israel and her land with "showers of blessings." The result would be full satisfaction from the land's abundant produce (vv.26–27a, 29a; cf. 36:16–37:28). Third, Israel would live in complete security (vv.27b–29; cf. chs. 38–39). No longer would she be plundered or scorned by the nations. Never again would she experience famine. Fourth, when God delivers Israel from all her captors and restores her safely to her land, then she will have realized that he truly is the Lord her God (v.27c). Fifth, the Mosaic formula of relationship between Israel and the Lord would become a reality. The Lord would truly become their God, and they would finally be his people, following his ways at every turn (vv.30–31; cf. Exod 6:7; Deut 29:12–15). According to Jeremiah, this relationship will be entered when Israel accepts the new covenant (Jer 31:31–34) instituted by the Mediator of that covenant, the Messiah (cf. Heb 8:6).

This announcement of the peace covenant provides a transition to the following messages delivered in this series of six oracles. Each of the next four speeches elaborates an aspect of the peace covenant. Ezekiel 35:1–36:15 describes how the foreign plundering nations would be removed and judged in preparation for Israel's return to her own land. The message in 36:16–37:14 provides a beautiful and descriptive account of God's restoration of Israel to her land. Ezekiel 37:15–28 stresses the full reunion of the nation and the fulfillment of her covenants when this peace covenant is established. Finally, Ezekiel 38–39 develops the concept of Israel's permanent and complete security in the Lord, for he would thwart the final attempt by a foreign power (Gog) to possess Israel's land and to plunder God's people.

Israel could rejoice; for though she had experienced the cruel and incompetent leadership of recent rulers, she now was assured that God would provide perfect leadership through the Good Shepherd, the Messiah, who would care for her as a shepherd should. There was hope!

Notes

11, 15, 23–24 The Lord stressed his personal involvement in shepherding Israel by using the personal pronoun אֲנִי (*'ᵃnî*, "I"). It is he and none other who will be the Shepherd. This is further seen in v.23, where the personal pronoun הוּא (*hû'*, "he") emphasizes that the Messiah will be the Shepherd.

12 "A day of clouds and darkness" describes the judgment aspects of the eschatological Day of the Lord (cf. Joel 2:2, 10; Zeph 1:15). Ezekiel foretells the time when the Messiah will deliver Israel, regathering his dispersed people (36:16–37; cf. Ps 97:1–6).

16 The LXX, Syriac, and Vulgate read אֶשְׁמֹר (*'ešmōr*, "I will guard, watch over") over against the MT's אַשְׁמִיד (*'ašmîd*, "I will destroy"). Contextually the Lord's aid to the helpless is being contrasted with his judgment of the strong who have oppressed his sheep. Therefore the MT reading should be retained.

23–24 הֲקִמֹתִי (*haqimōṯî*, "I will place") points back to the Davidic covenant in 2 Sam 7:12–16, where the Lord promised to establish David's line on the throne of the everlasting Davidic kingdom. Here that "one shepherd," "servant," and "prince," the descendant of David, is established.

עֶבֶד (*'eḇeḏ*, "servant") is a term used to describe the expected character of Israel's kings. A king was to be a servant who always obeyed his master (Yahweh), sought first his master's desire, and lived by faith in his master's every provision for him. Jesus, the Messiah, was the perfect Servant to his heavenly Father.

נָשִׂיא (*nāśî'*, "prince") shows that the Messiah, David's descendant, would become *the* "leader" ("prince") over Israel, in contrast to the past "leaders."

25–27 These verses do not conflict with Isa 11:6–9, for the fullness of millennial redemption of this earth will not of necessity be instantaneous when the restoration begins.

26 גִּבְעָתִי (*giḇ'āṯî*, "my hill") most likely refers to Mount Zion, the place of the temple and of the Lord's special meeting with his people Israel.

29 מַטָּע לְשֵׁם (*maṭṭā' lᵉšēm*, "a land renowned"; lit., "a renown planting") is a singular phrase used collectively (cf. Mic 1:6) to refer to the revitalized land of Israel when the Lord restores his people. The לְ (*l*) is an emphatic lamed (cf. M. Dahood, "Emphatic Lamedh in Jer 14:21 and Ezek 34:29," CBQ 37 [1975]:341–42).

3. *Preparation of the land* (35:1–36:15)

a. *Removal of oppressors*

35:1–15

> [1]The word of the LORD came to me: [2]"Son of man, set your face against Mount Seir; prophesy against it [3]and say: 'This is what the Sovereign LORD says: I am against you, Mount Seir, and I will stretch out my hand against you and make you a desolate waste. [4]I will turn your towns into ruins and you will be desolate. Then you will know that I am the LORD.
>
> [5]"'Because you harbored an ancient hostility and delivered the Israelites over to the sword at the time of their calamity, the time their punishment reached its climax, [6]therefore as surely as I live, declares the Sovereign LORD, I will give you over to bloodshed and it will pursue you. Since you did not hate bloodshed, bloodshed will pursue you. [7]I will make Mount Seir a desolate waste and cut off from it all who come and go. [8]I will fill your mountains with the slain; those killed by the sword will fall on your hills and in your valleys and in all your ravines. [9]I will make you desolate forever; your towns will not be inhabited. Then you wil know that I am the LORD.
>
> [10]"'Because you have said, "These two nations and countries will be ours and

we will take possession of them," even though I the LORD was there, ¹¹therefore as surely as I live, declares the Sovereign LORD, I will treat you in accordance with the anger and jealousy you showed in your hatred of them and I will make myself known among them when I judge you. ¹²Then you will know that I the LORD have heard all the contemptible things you have said against the mountains of Israel. You said, "They have been laid waste and have been given over to us to devour." ¹³You boasted against me and spoke against me without restraint, and I heard it. ¹⁴This is what the Sovereign LORD says: While the whole earth rejoices, I will make you desolate. ¹⁵Because you rejoiced when the inheritance of the house of Israel became desolate, that is how I will treat you. You will be desolate, O Mount Seir, you and all of Edom. Then they will know that I am the LORD.' "

1–9 Ezekiel had encouraged the Babylonian exiles that they would no longer be governed by predatory rulers. Instead the Lord would establish his Messiah as their "shepherd."

But what about the land of Israel? Did it not lay desolate? Were there not foreign oppressors presently ruling that country? How would the Messiah govern his people in a land ravaged by foreigners? These questions very likely came to the captives' minds as they listened to Ezekiel. The Lord understood these concerns and desired to ease their fears by announcing that he would personally remove all foreign oppressors from Israel and prepare that land to receive her people.

Edom (Mount Seir; cf. v.15; Gen 36:30; 2 Chron 20:10; 25:11) was most likely chosen as a representative of those nations that had sought to occupy Israel's land and exert dominion over her (vv.2–3). Edom, perhaps more than any other nation, had continually detested and resented Israel. It started with the conflict between Jacob (Israel) and Esau (Edom) (Gen 25:22–34; 27; 36:1). Edom had sought to block Israel's first entrance into the Promised Land (Num 20:14–21; 24:15–19), though Edom would not do so again. There were conflicts during the times of Saul (1 Sam 14:47), Solomon (1 Kings 11:14–22), Jehoshaphat (2 Chron 20:1–23), Jehoram (2 Kings 8:21), and Ahaz (2 Chron 28:17). The prophets regularly made reference to Edom's antagonism toward Israel and the resulting judgment they would receive (Isa 11:11–16; Dan 11:41; Amos 2:1). Malachi demonstrated that the hatred between these nations was still common in his day (Mal 1:2–5). Therefore, it was fitting that Ezekiel used Edom as the epitome of nations that sought to overrun and acquire Israel's land for themselves.

Two brief accusations (vv.5, 10) against Edom were followed by respective verdicts (vv.6:9; 11–15). First, Edom was indicted on two charges: (1) Edom had harbored hostility against Israel throughout her history (cf. 25:12), and (2) Edom was the accomplice of other nations and had delivered Israel over to them whenever possible. Psalm 137:7 and Lamentations 4:21–22 imply that Edom gladly aided the Babylonian invasion of Judah in 589–586 B.C. Obadiah 10–14 also denounces Edom for her betrayal of Israel in time of need. The implication of Ezekiel's accusation is that in the future Edom would again be Israel's antagonist.

God would punish Edom. Since Edom had not refrained from bloodshed in her hatred of Israel, the Lord also would bring unbridled bloodshed on Edom (v.6; cf. Isa 34:6–8; 63:1–6). Edom's land would be filled with inhabitants slain by the sword (v.8). As Edom had been continually hostile toward Israel, so God would bring an unending desolation throughout Mount Seir (vv.7, 9a; cf. 25:12–14; Jer 49:13, 17; Obad 18). Cities would be uninhabited. No one would carry on normal relations with Edom, for she would not exist. As a result of this judgment, however, Edom would know that the one who brought this discipline was the God of Israel, the only true God (vv. 4, 9b).

10–15 The second reason for judgment on Edom was threefold (v. 10; cf. vv. 12–13): (1) Edom desired to control the two countries of Israel and Judah; (2) Edom, in her desire to devour Israel, had defamed her with contempt and had spoken boastfully against the Lord; and (3) Edom had failed to recognize the God of Israel as the only true God. Edom felt that the Lord did not care what she did nor hear what she said.

As Edom had done to Israel out of her anger, jealousy, and hatred, so God would do to Edom (v. 11a). Such a display of God's vindication against Edom would cause Israel to recognize that truly this was her God who was intervening on her behalf (v. 11b). Likewise, since Edom had rejoiced when Israel became desolate, so the Lord would make Edom desolate when all the earth is happy (vv. 14–15a). The implication is that Edom would not exist in the end time when God brings unparalleled joy to this earth. However, God's desired result of this judgment on Edom was a recognition on her part that the God of Israel did exist and was the only true God (v. 15b).

Notes

5 The specific hostility against Israel discussed in Obad 10–14 is uncertain. There is a long-standing debate over the date of this prophetic book. One's date of Obadiah bears greatly on the date of this invasion of Israel.

בְּעֵת עֲוֹן קֵץ ($b^e\dot{e}t$ $^{a}w\bar{o}n$ $q\bar{e}\d{s}$) may be rendered "the time their punishment reaches its climax," or perhaps it would be better translated "the time of their final iniquity." $Q\bar{e}\d{s}$ ("end") has the normal sense of termination rather than climax. The phrase refers best to a future iniquity of Israel in addition to the past ones mentioned in this context.

10 The reference to two nations is without specific identity. Since the context concerns Israel, and since Israel has been divided into the north kingdom of Israel and the southern kingdom of Judah during Edom's most recent dealings with her, it would appear that the two nations refer to Israel and Judah. This is also supported by the reunion of those two divisions of God's people described in 37:15–28.

b. A prophecy of encouragement

36:1–15

¹"Son of man, prophesy to the mountains of Israel and say, 'O mountains of Israel, hear the word of the LORD. ²This is what the Sovereign LORD says: The enemy said of you, 'Aha! The ancient heights have become our possession.'' ³Therefore prophesy and say, 'This is what the Sovereign LORD says: Because they ravaged and hounded you from every side so that you became the possession of the rest of the nations and the object of people's malicious talk and slander, ⁴therefore, O mountains of Israel, hear the word of the Sovereign LORD: This is what the Sovereign LORD says to the mountains and hills, to the ravines and valleys, to the desolate ruins and the deserted towns that have been plundered and ridiculed by the rest of the nations around you—⁵this is what the Sovereign LORD says: In my burning zeal I have spoken against the rest of the nations, and against all Edom, for with glee and with malice in their hearts they made my land their own possession so that they might plunder its pastureland.' ⁶Therefore

prophesy concerning the land of Israel and say to the mountains and hills, to the ravines and valleys: 'This is what the Sovereign LORD says: I speak in my jealous wrath because you have suffered the scorn of the nations. ⁷Therefore this is what the Sovereign LORD says: I swear with uplifted hand that the nations around you will will also suffer scorn.

⁸" 'But you, O mountains of Israel, will produce branches and fruit for my people Israel, for they will soon come home. ⁹I am concerned for you and will look on you with favor; you will be plowed and sown, ¹⁰and I will multiply the number of people upon you, even the whole house of Israel. The towns will be inhabited and the ruins rebuilt. ¹¹I will increase the number of men and animals upon you, and they will be fruitful and become numerous. I will settle people on you as in the past and will make you prosper more than before. Then you will know that I am the LORD. ¹²I will cause people, my people Israel, to walk upon you. They will possess you, and you will be their inheritance; you will never again deprive them of their children.

¹³" 'This is what the Sovereign LORD says: Because people say to you, "You devour men and deprive your nation of its children," ¹⁴therefore you will no longer devour men or make your nation childless, declares the Sovereign LORD. ¹⁵No longer will I make you hear the taunts of the nations, and no longer will you suffer the scorn of the peoples or cause your nation to fall, declares the Sovereign LORD.' "

1–12 This prophecy of encouragement interestingly took the form of a judgment speech. The accusations provided the basis on which God would encourage the "land" of Israel. The land of Israel could make the following charges against foreign nations: (1) many nations had claimed the right of ownership of Israel (vv.2–3), including her ancient religious sites; (2) the nations surrounding Israel had brought desolation to Palestine as they trampled through the land in conquest (v.3). The land of Israel had become a mockery of evil rumors and gossip among the nations (vv.2–4).

The Lord vindicates his righteousness and his people. He had declared in the Abrahamic covenant that he would bless those who bless Israel, but he also would curse those who curse his people (Gen 12:3). Therefore God declared that Israel had borne enough scorn and shame from the nations. His fiery jealousy would come against those who had joyously and scornfully invaded Israel for spoils (vv.5–6). As the nations had brought shame on Israel, so he would cause them to bear shame and disgrace. The Lord emphatically "lifted up his hand" against the nations in a symbol of strength and wrath (v.7). He would exonerate his people.

Blessing normally follows judgment in God's scheme. So, having pronounced judgment on the scornful nations (following the principle of lex talionis), the Lord turned to encourage Israel by describing his preparation of her land for her return in the end time. He stresses that this would be *his* work.

The mountains of Israel were contrasted with Mount Seir. After Israel's destruction one might have expected Mount Seir to triumph over the mountains of Israel. Though the land of Israel lay desolate in Ezekiel's day, God looked with favor on it and promised that he would prepare that land for Israel's return by making it productive and fruitful once again (vv.8–9, 34). The land would be encouraged by receiving its own people back. All Israel would return. The people and the cattle would be more plentiful than ever before. Her cities would again be inhabited and every waste place rebuilt (vv.10–11; cf. v.33). In demonstration of God's faithfulness to the Abrahamic covenant (Gen 12:7), Israel would finally possess her land as the inheritance promised by God but never before fully realized (v.12). When God restores his people, the condition of the land would surpass any previous state of the land (v.11). But would the land be deprived of its children (the Israelites) again and become desolate? The Lord reassured the land of Israel and the exiles that when God regathers his people to the Promised Land in that last regathering of the end times, the land will never again be deprived of its children (v.12). All will recognize that the Lord has done this great thing (v.11).

13–15 The second charge (v.13) brought against the land was that she had devoured people and, in turn, had become "childless" among the nations (v.14). This conclusion arose from observing the many horrible misfortunes Israel had experienced. This was a false accusation. God refuted this charge, for he would restore his people to that land. Then Israel would no longer hear taunts of scorn and shame from the nations. She would never again bear such reproach (v.15) and would never again cease to be a nation. God encouraged the exiles by declaring that he would give them the Messiah as their ruler and would remove the oppressive nations from the land of Israel to prepare the way for the restoration of his people.

Notes

3 The term שָׁאָף (šāʾōp, "hounded") may also be translated "trampled," which possibly fits the context better.

5 The transition from judgment on Edom to that of the nations is especially noted in the announcement of judgment against the nations *and* Edom in this verse. From this point forward the statements are addressed to the nations as a whole rather than only to Edom as in ch. 35. Chapter 36 broadens the model of Edom into the whole picture of all oppressive nations.

5, 12 אַרְצִי (ʾarṣî, "my land," v.5) and עַמִּי (ʿammî, "my people," v.12) emphasize that the land and this people were God's unique possession (cf. v.20; Gen 12:1, 7; 15:7; 18; Exod 19:5–6; Lev 25:23; Deut 32:43; Ps 78:54; Jer 2:7). Any worldly designs on his people or land were proved wrong when pitted against the divine plan for Israel. God's land and people were not the nations' to claim, especially with contempt.

4. The restoration to the land (36:16–37:14)

Ezekiel's previous message concluded with a description of the Lord's preparation of the land of Canaan for the return of his people (36:1–15). This provided the natural transition from God's removal of foreign oppressors from the land (35:1–15) to the subject of this new message: Israel's restoration to her land. This prophecy emphasizes the *people's* return and contains four distinct parts. So that the Lord's grace and mercy in regathering his people might be fully understood, the reason for their scattering among the nations is outlined by contrast (36:16–21). This is followed by a beautifully detailed portrayal of how the Lord would restore the people to the land (36:22–32) followed by the effective results of that return (36:33–38). As an encouragement to the Babylonian exiles, Ezekiel would conclude this oracle with an apocalyptic vision, illustrating the return of God's nation to the land promised to their forefathers (37:1–14).

a. *The basis for Israel's dispersion*

36:16–21

> ¹⁶Again the word of the LORD came to me: ¹⁷"Son of man, when the people of Israel were living in their own land, they defiled it by their conduct and their actions. Their conduct was like a woman's monthly uncleanness in my sight. ¹⁸So I poured out my wrath on them because they had shed blood in the land and because they had defiled it with their idols. ¹⁹I dispersed them among the nations, and they were scattered through the countries; I judged them according to their conduct and their actions. ²⁰And wherever they went among the nations they profaned my holy name, for it was said of them, 'These are the LORD's people, and yet they had to leave his land.' ²¹I had concern for my holy name, which the house of Israel profaned among the nations where they had gone.

16–21 Why was it necessary for the Lord to restore his people to the land he had promised to them? Why were they not in that land? To highlight the importance of Israel's reestablishment on the land of their forefathers, Ezekiel summarized Israel's past history that had brought her dispersion among the nations. By her disobedience to the Mosaic covenant stipulations, Israel had defiled her sacred land (v.17). Israel's two major crimes were (1) bloodshed, which was brought among her own people through infanticide, intrigue, violence, and selfishness, and (2) idolatry, which pervaded the people's lives and drew them continually away from the Lord (v.18). Their actions were so abominable that that Lord regarded their defilement as impure as that of a woman during her menstrual cycle (v.17; cf. 18:6; 22:10; Lev 12:2–5; 15:19–30). God had set forth in Israel's constitution, the Mosaic covenant, that if she persisted in disobeying the lifestyle given to her in that covenant, he would scatter her people among the nations in discipline (cf. Deut 29:1–30:10). The Lord had been faithful to his word and had sown Israel like seed throughout the countries of that day (v.19).

God was so concerned that Israel be restored to a proper relationship with him that he sent his people out of the Promised Land so that they might learn the importance of following his ways. God's ways are always best; for he, the Creator of life, knows how life can best be lived. But in disciplining Israel in this manner, the Lord risked his own reputation in the world. A nation was unique tied to its land in the ancient Near East. If a people were forced off their land, whether by conquest, famine, disease, or any other reason, this was a demonstration that their god was not sufficiently strong to protect and care for them. Therefore, when God scattered Israel among the nations, they perceived that Israel's God was weak; thereby the name of the Lord was profaned among them.

It was so important to God that Israel learn his ways and obey them, however, that he allowed his name to be defiled among foreign nations. But the Lord would not allow his name to be defiled forever. Israel's return to her land would be based on the Lord's compassion for his own holy name that had been profaned (cf. the Lord's Prayer: "hallowed be your name," Matt 6:9; Luke 11:2). Through Israel's restoration to her own land, God would demonstrate to the nations that he was the only true God. His name would be set apart in holiness, as it should be. Therefore, in order that his name might be vindicated, the Lord would restore Israel to her land, and not because of any great thing she had done (vv.20–21; cf. vv.22–23). What a contrast between God's holiness and grace and man's sin! Sin never deserves mercy; yet the Lord always deals graciously and mercifully as well as justly.

Notes

17 The verb טָמֵא (*ṭimmēʾ*, "defile") is frequently used in the Mosaic covenant for defiling God's holiness by breaking his commandments. Such disobedience had made Israel's land unclean.

18 גִּלּוּלִים (*gillûlîm*) is Ezekiel's favorite expression for "idols." It is used as a mocking polemic against them, perhaps being derived from גֵּל (*gel* "dung"), thus the meaning of "dung things" or "dung idols" (cf. TDOT, 3:1–5).

20 שֵׁם (*šēm*, "name"), especially when referring to Yahweh, is "inextricably bound up with the being of God" (TWOT, 2:934), conveying the whole person of God in his holiness (cf. TWOT, 2:934–35).

b. *A description of the final restoration*

36:22–32

²²"Therefore say to the house of Israel, 'This is what the Sovereign LORD says: It is not for your sake, O house of Israel, that I am going to do these things, but for the sake of my holy name, which you have profaned among the nations where you have gone. ²³I will show the holiness of my great name, which has been profaned among the nations, the name you have profaned among them. Then the nations will know that I am the LORD, declares the Sovereign LORD, when I show myself holy through you before their eyes.

²⁴"'For I will take you out of the nations, I will gather you from all the countries and bring you back into your own land. ²⁵I will sprinkle clean water on you, and you will be clean; I will cleanse you from all your impurities and from all your idols. ²⁶I will give you a new heart and put a new spirit in you; I will remove from you your heart of stone and give you a heart of flesh. ²⁷And I will put my Spirit in you and move you to follow my decrees and be careful to keep my laws. ²⁸You will live in the land I gave your forefathers; you will be my people, and I will be your God. ²⁹I will save you from all your uncleanness. I will call for the grain and make it plentiful and will not bring famine upon you. ³⁰I will increase the fruit of the trees and the crops of the field, so that you will no longer suffer disgrace among the nations because of famine. ³¹Then you will remember your evil ways and wicked deeds, and you will loathe yourselves for your sins and detestable practices. ³²I want you to know that I am not doing this for your sake, declares the Sovereign LORD. Be ashamed and disgraced for your conduct, O house of Israel!

22–23 In OT times one's name and person were equivalent; a name represented the person (cf. TWOT, 2:934–35). Through Israel's rebellion against God, the people had defamed God's person. Therefore, not only would his covenant faithfulness be displayed when he restored Israel to her land, but he would also bring honor and sanctity to his name and person throughout the nations, through his supernatural regathering of Israel. Then the nations would know that the righteous and loving God of Israel was the only true God (vv.22–23).

24–32 The reestablishment of Israel on her land is wonderfully described in these verses (cf. 11:14–21). God foretold Israel's restoration after the Exile when Moses restated the Mosaic covenant on the plains of Moab (Deut 29:1–30:10). The pattern of restoration was (1) return, (2) cleansing from sin, (3) enablement of the Spirit, and (4) prosperity.

First, the Lord would remove his people from the nations where they had been scattered. He would gather them and bring them back to the land of Canaan, which had been promised to their forefathers in the Abrahamic covenant (v.24; cf. 11:17).

Second, the Lord would cleanse Israel in her land from all sin and idolatry that had defiled her (v.25; cf. v.17; 11:18). "Sprinkling with clean water" symbolizes cleansing through divine forgiveness by blood (cf. Exod 12:22; Lev 14:4–7; 49:53; Ps 51:7; 1 Cor 6:11). For ceremonial cleansing to be more than a ritual, it was essential that the people repent and acknowledge their past iniquity about which God would remind them. As they would loath their former transgressions with their shame and disgrace, they would understand how gracious was their cleansing (vv.31–32a). Likewise, if ceremonial cleansing was to be meaningful, actual cleansing and forgiveness of sin must be made. This would be through the new covenant (Jer 31:31–34); for Israel's return to the land, the people would accept the Messiah as their Savior, through whose death all sin was once and for all forgiven. Iniquity would be remembered no more. They would exchange their old rebellious hearts of stone for sensitive hearts of flesh (v.26; cf. 11:19; 18:31; 2 Cor 3:3–6).

Third, in the new covenant the people would also receive a new spirit, God's Holy Spirit (vv.26–27; cf. 11:19–20; 18:31; 37:14; 39:29; Joel 2:28–29; Acts 2:17–18; 2 Cor 3:6–18), who would enable them to live God's way, strengthening them to follow the Mosaic covenant's commandments (v.27; cf. Rom 7:7–8:4; Heb 8:6–10:-39). The old Mosaic covenant would be written on the heart of those living under the new covenant (Jer 31:33). Therefore, the new covenant replaced the Mosaic covenant by adding those things that made it better, but not by eliminating the good, righteous, and godly Mosaic stipulations that described how to live a godly life. The new covenant provided forgiveness of sin once and for all and the Holy Spirit's indwelling.

Fourth, a cleansed Israel would return permanently to a productive and plentiful land that would be more than "flowing with milk and honey" (vv.1–15). Never again would the land allow Israel to be disgraced among the nations through famine (vv.28a–30; 34:29). Likewise, the epitome of the Mosaic covenant for Israel and the Lord was expressed in a formula that now would become a reality: Israel would be God's people and he will be her God (v.28b). The nations would observe this marvelous transformation in Israel and see the Lord as the only gracious and loving God, for Israel was not deserving of restoration (v.32b).

This context and that of similar accounts of God's restoration of Israel to her land, along with the historical perspective, make it clear that the return mentioned in this passage does not refer to the return to Canaan under Zerubbabel but to a final and complete restoration under the Messiah in the end times. The details of Israel's reestablishment on her land set forth above simply did not occur in the returns under Zerubbabel, Ezra, and Nehemiah.

Notes

24–32 Some would view the return as the restoration of Israel from Babylon, the cleansing as that provided through Jesus' shed blood, the coming of the Spirit at Pentecost, but prosperity as not yet fully occurring. This is opposed to a future, end-time return as set forth in the commentary.

c. The effects of the restoration

36:33–38

³³ 'This is what the Sovereign LORD says: On the day I cleanse you from all your sins, I will resettle your towns, and the ruins will be rebuilt. ³⁴The desolate land will be cultivated instead of lying desolate in the sight of all who pass through it. ³⁵They will say, "This land that was laid waste has become like the garden of Eden; the cities that were lying in ruins, desolate and destroyed, are now fortified and inhabited." ³⁶Then the nations around you that remain will know that I the LORD have rebuilt what was destroyed and have replanted what was desolate. I the LORD have spoken, and I will do it.'

³⁷"This is what the Sovereign LORD says: Once again I will yield to the plea of the house of Israel and do this for them: I will make their people as numerous as sheep, ³⁸as numerous as the flocks for offerings at Jerusalem during her appointed feasts. So will the ruined cities be filled with flocks of people. Then they will know that I am the LORD."

33–38 The effects of Israel's restoration would be great. The land would produce like the Garden of Eden. It would be Paradise regained (cf. Isa 51:3; Rom 8:19–22; 2 Peter 3:13; Rev 21:1–4, 23–27). Ruined cities would be rebuilt and fortified for the many inhabitants (vv.33–35). The people of Israel would increase so in number that they would constitute a large flock for the Shepherd, Messiah. They would be numerous like the flocks kept for the many offerings in Jerusalem during Israel's appointed feasts (vv.37–38). The most important consequence of Israel's restoration would be the spread of the knowledge of the Lord throughout the world. The nations would unequivocally know that Israel's God had accomplished this great restoration. They would know that he was not a weak god but the only God who does exactly what he says (v.36). Israel herself will humbly acknowledge that the one who restored her was the Lord her God (v.38).

Notes

35 גַּן־עֵדֶן (gan-ʿēḏen, "the garden of Eden") is used here as a simile to picture the "Paradise regained" condition of the land of Israel in the Messianic Age (contra 28:13).

d. A vision of restoration

37:1–14

¹The hand of the LORD was upon me, and he brought me out by the Spirit of the LORD and set me in the middle of a valley; it was full of bones. ²He led me back and forth among them, and I saw a great many bones on the floor of the valley, bones that were very dry. ³He asked me, "Son of man, can these bones live?"

I said, "O Sovereign LORD, you alone know."

⁴Then he said to me, "Prophesy to these bones and say to them, 'Dry bones, hear the word of the LORD! ⁵This is what the Sovereign LORD says to these bones: I will make breath enter you, and you will come to life. ⁶I will attach tendons to you and make flesh come upon you and cover you with skin; I will put breath in you, and you will come to life. Then you will know that I am the LORD.' "

⁷So I prophesied as I was commanded. And as I was prophesying, there was a

noise, a rattling sound, and the bones came together, bone to bone. ⁸I looked, and tendons and flesh appeared on them and skin covered them, but there was no breath in them.

⁹Then he said to me, "Prophesy to the breath; prophesy, son of man, and say to it, 'This is what the Sovereign Lᴏʀᴅ says: Come from the four winds, O breath, and breathe into these slain, that they may live.'" ¹⁰So I prophesied as he commanded me, and breath entered them; they came to life and stood up on their feet—a vast army.

¹¹Then he said to me: "Son of man, these bones are the whole house of Israel. They say, 'Our bones are dried up and our hope is gone; we are cut off.' ¹²Therefore, prophesy and say to them: 'This is what the Sovereign Lᴏʀᴅ says: O my people, I am going to open your graves and bring you up from them; I will bring you back to the land of Israel. ¹³Then you, my people, will know that I am the Lᴏʀᴅ, when I open your graves and bring you up from them. ¹⁴I will put my Spirit in you and you will live, and I will settle you in your own land. Then you will know that I the Lᴏʀᴅ have spoken, and I have done it, declares the Lᴏʀᴅ.'"

1–2 This section provides the concluding illustration of this oracle on restoration that began at 36:16. Chapter 37 began without any transition, simply revealing the apocalyptic vision that concluded Ezekiel's message on Israel's future restoration. This vision pictures the manner in which the Lord would restore his people.

Apocalyptic literature is not familiar to most people. In Ezekiel's day the exiles would have been acquainted with the Mesopotamian dream-visions and their literary form. It seems that the Lord adapted this specific type of literature that was in vogue in the seventh and sixth centuries B.C. in Mesopotamia and developed a new type of biblical literature known as apocalyptic (cf. Introduction: Literary Form and Structure). This literature is a symbolic visionary-prophetic literature, consisting of visions whose events are recorded exactly as they were seen by the author and are explained through a divine interpreter. The theological content is primarily eschatological. It is equally interesting that this type of biblical literature was normally composed during times when its recipients experienced oppressive conditions. All these elements are observed in the passage before us. Symbols were used, such as the bones. Ezekiel actually recounted what he saw in the vision. Certainly the vision was part of the prophetic message of Ezekiel. The theological emphasis of the vision was on future things that were to encourage the Judean exiles who were in oppressive conditions. A divine interpretation was supplied. Therefore Ezekiel used an apocalyptic vision to illustrate how God would restore Israel.

Apocalyptic literature has a simple twofold form: (1) the setting of the vision in which the recipient and the geographical location are identified, and (2) the vision per se with its divine interpretation. The setting is expressed in vv. 1–2. Ezekiel was brought by the Lord into the valley (or plain), perhaps the same valley mentioned in chapter 1 where Ezekiel saw the visions of God. Ezekiel, as the recipient, saw the valley filled with innumerable bones that were extremely dry. The Spirit of the Lord led him around the valley, and he passed among these bones.

3–10 This apocalyptic vision has two distinct sections in the vision itself. First, Ezekiel recounted what he saw and did in vv. 3–10. Then the vision closes with the interpretation in vv. 11–14. As one reads an apocalyptic vision, he feels as if he is there, for the details are given in the first person by the recipient. The Lord asked Ezekiel whether these bones would live (v. 3a). Ezekiel, acknowledging his lack of omniscience, replied that only the Lord knew (v. 3b).

A prophecy was then given to Ezekiel for the dry bones. The Lord would cause them to live. Tendons, flesh, skin, and breath would come on the bones so that live people would be formed. Then this "resurrected" people would know that God was the Lord (vv.4–6). So Ezekiel did exactly as the Lord commanded and proclaimed the Lord's words to the dead, dry bones. While he was speaking, all the bones came together and took on themselves tendons, flesh, and skin. But no breath was found in them (vv.7–8).

Ezekiel was instructed to prophesy again, this time to the breath to come from the four winds—probably indicating the full power of the entering breath (i.e., from every direction) to renew the bodies—and to breathe on these slain ones so that they might live (v.9). On doing so, Ezekiel saw this army of people come alive! Such was the vision itself.

The recovery of the bones to form bodies pictured Israel's ultimate national restoration (vv.4–8). Breath (wind or Spirit) entering these restored bodies portrayed spiritual renewal (vv.9–10). This imitated the sequence in chapter 36 (cf. John 3).

11–14 In interpreting apocalyptic visions, certain basic principles should be followed. The divine interpretation given within the vision should be followed carefully, neither adding to it nor elaborating on aspects of it. Apocalyptic visions were never meant to have every detail interpreted, only the major thrust of the vision was to be grasped.

As one examines the vision and its divine interpretation, several factors are noteworthy. The bones are identified as the whole house of Israel, the slain ones of v.9 (v.11; cf. 36:10). The bones (or entire house of Israel in that day) would declare three things about themselves (v.11; cf. Ps 6:2). First, they were dry, an obvious condition of bones from people who have been dead for a very long time. Though quantitative time may be implied by the dryness of the bones, the emphasis of the interpretation was on qualitative spiritual deadness—"our hope is gone" and "we are cut off" (v.11). Second, the bones (Israel) declared that their hope had perished. The people of Israel, having been deceased as a nation for so long, had lost all hope of becoming a nation again or of seeing God's covenants fulfilled. Third, the bones (Israel) said that they were separated from one another, i.e., the people would be separated and dispersed from one another immediately before their restoration. That was their current condition.

The vision itself is rather self-evident and needs no interpretation once the bones are identified. The vision clearly demonstrated the restoration to life of a people who had been dead for some time. It was in two stages: first physical (or national) restoration and then spiritual renewal (keeping in mind that the word for breath, wind, and spirit is the same in Hebrew). The creation of man followed a similar pattern: the body formed first, then the breath received (cf. Gen 2:7). This national and spiritual restoration is elaborated in the interpretation section through another figure, that of a resurrection from graves. Both the imagery of dry bones becoming live people and the figure of resurrection from a grave illustrate the same truth. Israel, who had been nonexistent as a people on their own land and scattered throughout the nations, would be brought back to life physically as a nation in their own land. Just as these events in the vision would be miraculous, so will be Israel's restoration. Once in the land they would be renewed spiritually when God placed his Spirit (identity of the breath or spirit in the vision) within them in keeping with the new covenant and the message just delivered in chapter 36 (v.14; cf. vv.9–10; 36:22–32; 37:15–28).

The entire context of these six messages was future. The context of chapters 36–37, before and following this apocalyptic vision, indicates that Israel's national restoration in the end time was in view. It was not to be just a physical restoration nor only a spiritual restoration. A national regathering of Israel from among the nations in the end time (as seen from the context), a spiritual conversion of Israel, and a reestablishment of the nation in the land of promise are in view both in 36:16–38 and in this apocalyptic vision (vv.13–14). This is *not* a resurrection of *all* the descendants of Israel.

This could genuinely be termed a "rebirth" of the nation. Just as the necessary elements of a nation were essential to the initial formation of Israel in Genesis through Joshua—a people, a government, and a land—so God would provide all three essentials once again in this rebirth of Israel in the future. The people of that day are brought together through restoration in 36:16–37:28. The land is provided in the prophecy of 35:1–36:15. The government of renewed Israel would be given in Ezekiel's apocalyptic vision revealed in chapters 40–48. When Israel would be restored and become a nation once again, then the people would definitely know that the Lord did it and that he and none other was their God (vv.13–14).

Notes

1–2 The definite article ‏הָ‎ (*ha,* "the") is used with the word "valley" in ‏הַבִּקְעָה‎ (*habbiqʿāh,* "the valley") and refers to a specific valley, perhaps the one mentioned in ch. 1, where Ezekiel saw the visions of God.

5 ‏רוּחַ‎ (*rûaḥ,* "wind," "breath," "spirit") has all three meanings in this chapter (cf. vv.9, 14), which is appropriate for the symbolic apocalyptic vision. The symbol of "wind" or "breath" is interpreted as "Spirit" (cf. TWOT, 2:836–37).

11 ‏נִגְזַרְנוּ לָנוּ‎ (*nigzarnû lānû,* "we are cut off") conveys the idea of the division of God's people into parts. The prepositional phrase *lānû* is a reflexive (ethical or *commodi*) dative that stresses the significance of the action in question *for* the subject (cf. GKC, par. 119s). In this verse the emphasis is on the division of the plural subject, Israel, into many parts.

5. *Israel's reunion amid fulfilled covenants*

37:15–28

¹⁵The word of the LORD came to me: ¹⁶"Son of man, take a stick of wood and write on it, 'Belonging to Judah and the Israelites associated with him.' Then take another stick of wood, and write on it, 'Ephraim's stick, belonging to Joseph and all the house of Israel associated with him.' ¹⁷Join them together into one stick so that they will become one in your hand.

¹⁸"When your countrymen ask you, 'Won't you tell us what you mean by this?' ¹⁹say to them, 'This is what the Sovereign LORD says: I am going to take the stick of Joseph—which is in Ephraim's hand—and of the Israelite tribes associated with him, and join it to Judah's stick, making them a single stick of wood, and they will become one in my hand.' ²⁰Hold before their eyes the sticks you have written on ²¹and say to them, 'This is what the Sovereign LORD says: I will take the Israelites out of the nations where they have gone. I will gather them from all around and bring them back into their own land. ²²I will make them one nation in the land, on the mountains of Israel. There will be one king over all of them and

they will never again be two nations or be divided into two kingdoms. ²³They will no longer defile themselves with their idols and vile images or with any of their offenses, for I will save them from all their sinful backsliding, and I will cleanse them. They will be my people, and I will be their God.

²⁴" 'My servant David will be king over them, and they will all have one shepherd. They will follow my laws and be careful to keep my decrees. ²⁵They will live in the land I gave to my servant Jacob, the land where your fathers lived. They and their children and their children's children will live there forever, and David my servant will be their prince forever. ²⁶I will make a covenant of peace with them; it will be an everlasting covenant. I will establish them and increase their numbers, and I will put my sanctuary among them forever. ²⁷My dwelling place will be with them; I will be their God, and they will be my people. ²⁸Then the nations will know that I the Lord make Israel holy, when my sanctuary is among them forever.' "

15–17 Ezekiel used a symbolic act to demonstrate that the two previously divided kingdoms of Israel and Judah would once again be reunited into one nation when God brings his people back into their land. Israel would then be complete with all her covenants fulfilled.

Ezekiel took two sticks of wood (v.16). He wrote the names of Judah and her companions on one stick and those of Ephraim and her companions on the other, one stick representing the former kingdom of Judah, the other the previous kingdom of Israel. When Ezekiel put these two sticks together in his hand, they became one stick (v.17).

18–28 These verses give the interpretation of the symbolic act (v.18). The union of the two sticks into one portrayed the reunion of the nations of Judah and Israel into a united kingdom in the land promised in the Abrahamic covenant (vv.19, 22–25; Gen 12:1–3, 7; 16:10; 17:7–9; 22:17–18; 28:4, 13–15). Never again would the nation be divided. The Messiah, David's greater Son, would be the only King, Shepherd, and Prince that Israel would ever have in accord with the Davidic covenant (vv.22b, 24a, 25b; cf. 34:10b–31; 2 Sam 7:13, 16). This united people of God would be cleansed from their former idolatry and transgressions through the complete forgiveness provided by the Messiah's death and the ministry of the Spirit promised in the new covenant (v.23a; 36:16–32; Jer 31:31–34). By accepting the new covenant, Israel would be enabled through the Holy Spirit to follow the righteous stipulations of the Mosaic covenant and to live by them (v.24b). Then Israel would finally be the unique, choice people that God had created for himself; and he would be their God—finally fulfilling the ideal of the Mosaic covenant (vv.23b, 27; cf. Exod 19:5–6; Lev 26:12; Deut 7:6; 14:2, 21; 26:18–19; 27:9; Jer 30:22; 31:33; 32:38).

The Lord would enact his peace covenant (cf. 34:25–29) with Israel at the time of her restoration to the land, when all her other covenants with God would be fulfilled (v.26). Under this peace covenant Israel would be established in her land, her numbers would increase (cf. Gen 22:17–18), and the Lord would place his sanctuary —his dwelling place—among his people forever (vv.26–27; cf. 40:5–43:9). Then all nations would see that it was the Lord who made Israel holy. She would be set apart from all nations as God's special possession. No other nation would have the Lord dwelling in its sanctuary uniquely in its midst as would Israel (v.28; cf. chs. 40–48).

When all Israel's covenants have been consummated, then the Lord will enact his peace covenant with Israel. She will dwell in peace forever under the rule of her king, the Messiah (34:25–29; 37:26; cf. 38:11).

Notes

23 The MT's מוֹשְׁבֹתֵיהֶם (*môšĕbōtêhem*, "their dwellings") is changed to מְשׁוּבֹתֵיהֶם (*mĕšûbōtêhem*, "their backsliding") in the LXX and in Symmachus (so NIV). The metathesis of the letters וּ (*w*) and שׁ (*š*) could likely be a scribal error. The context favors "their backsliding."

6. *The Promised Land and foreign possession* (38:1–39:29)

These two chapters may be viewed as isolated from the previous messages delivered on the night prior to the arrival of the fugitive from Jerusalem to announce Jerusalem's fall (cf. 33:21–22). Others would see these two chapters integrally related to chapters 40–48. However, Ezekiel's chronological scheme argues against the latter position, for he normally kept his themes and messages within the chronological framework of what preceded, not what followed. Ezekiel 40:1 supplies a major chronological notice that would separate the messages before it from those after by approximately twelve and one-half years (cf. 33:21).

The message in Ezekiel 38–39 was the sixth and last in his series of messages delivered that night before the news came of Jerusalem's destruction. A major subject of the five previous messages had been the land of Israel. First, there was the concern expressed over its loss by the remnant in Palestine (33:21–33). The cause for its loss was Israel's disobedience as she followed corrupt leadership. The Lord reassured Israel that he would remove her arrogant and cruel rulers and establish the Messiah, David's descendant, as the eternal Shepherd over Israel in the end time (ch. 34). God would remove those nations that had devoured the land and made it desolate through oppression and dominance (ch. 35), and he would prepare the land for the return of Israel (36:1–15). The restoration of the *people* of Israel to the Promised Land was described in 36:16–38 and beautifully illustrated in the apocalyptic vision of 37:1–14. Israel would return united with the Messiah as her singular ruler, with all God's covenants with her fulfilled. Then the Lord would inaugurate his peace covenant with Israel as she dwelt peacefully in her land (37:15–28; cf. 34:25–29).

The message in Ezekiel 38–39 initially describes the entire nation of Israel peacefully dwelling in their land in security. They had entered into their peace covenant with God and were living without walls, bars, or doors (38:7). The remainder of the message describes a final. attempt by foreigners to possess the land of Israel. The endeavor would fail because God, faithful to the peace covenant and his name, would defend Israel. He would not permit his holy name to be profaned again by a conquest and dispersal of Israel (36:20; 39:7). What an encouragement this should have been to the exiles!

The events and details of Ezekiel 38–39 are relatively easy to understand. One must keep in mind that 39:1–8 is essentially a restatement of 38:1–23 with some expansion. Such reiteration was common in the judgment-speech literature during the sixth and fifth centuries B.C.—the time of Ezekiel. The major interpretative difficulties in these two chapters are the identity of characters and places, as well as the time when these events occur.

a. The initial judgment speech against Gog (38:1–23)

1) The identity of the major participants

38:1–3

> ¹The word of the LORD came to me: ²"Son of man, set your face against Gog, of the land of Magog, the chief prince of Meschech and Tubal; prophesy against him ³and say: 'This is what the Sovereign LORD says: I am against you, O Gog, chief prince of Meshech and Tubal.

1–3 Ezekiel prophesied against Gog of the land of Magog, the chief prince of Meshech and Tubal (v.2). The exact identity of each proper name has occupied many expositors and spawned many and varied interpretations of this text. The data will be examined in order to determine what one can and cannot understand about these terms (cf. Edwin M. Yamauchi, *Foes From the Northern Frontier* [Grand Rapids: Baker, 1982]).

The major term is Gog. Normally Gog is considered to be a person. A significant difficulty in the identification of this term is that the term is only used twice in the OT: in 1 Chronicles 5:4 and in the passage under discussion. Gog in 1 Chronicles 5:4 was a Reubenite prince, but there appears to be no basis for associating this Reubenite prince with the Gog in Ezekiel.

Various solutions have been offered. First, some would identify Gog with Gugu, or Gyges, the king of Lydia who reigned approximately a century before Ezekiel (so S.H. Hooke, "Gog and Magog," ExpT 26 [1914]: 317; and Taylor, p. 244). Second, Gog has been related to the Sumerian *gug* ("darkness") (so W.F. Albright, "Gog and Magog," JBL 43 [1924]: 378–85). Third, Gagu, the ruler of the land of Sakhi, an area north of Assyria, has been mentioned as a possible identity (so Hooke). Fourth, a mountainous district north of Melitene has been suggested (so Albright). Fifth, the term could be understood as an official title because the LXX uses the word "Gog" in place of a usual title for several kings in the OT (cf. Num 24:7; Deut 3:1, 13; 4:47; Amos 7:1). However, there are those who think that the LXX used the term "Gog" as a general name for any enemy of God's people. Last, some understand "Gog" to be derived from the associate term in the context, "Magog" (so Fairbairn, *Ezekiel*, p. 415).

None of the proposed solutions have sufficient support to warrant their acceptance as the identity of the term "Gog." It does seem that Gog was a person, whether mentioned in this context by name or by title. Further identification does not seem wise in light of the paucity of data, nor is the specific identity of Gog necessary in order to interpret the significance of this passage. Further discussion of the time of these events will aid in a more general identification of the person of Gog.

Magog, a Japhetic descendant (Gen 10:2) in the table of nations, is identified by Josephus (Antiq. I, 123 [vi. 1]) as the land of the Scythians, a mountainous region around the Black and Caspian seas. This position is generally accepted.

The phrase "chief prince of Meshech and Tubal" has been interpreted variously.

The word *rōʾš* presents the major difficulty in the phrase. The term's normal meaning was "head" or "chief." Some understand the word as a proper noun, the name of a geographical area, viz., "Rosh." Such a country is unknown elsewhere in biblical or extrabiblical literature. Meshech and Tubal, normally mentioned together in the Scriptures (cf. 27:13; 32:26) and the two geographical place names immediately associated with the term *rōʾš*, do not occur in connection with a country by the name of Rosh either inside or outside Scripture. There is no evidence from the ancient Near East that a country named Rosh ever existed. Some would understand *rōʾš* as modern Russia. Proponents of this view usually appeal to etymology based on similar sounds (to the hearing) between the two words. Such etymological procedures are not linguistically sound, nor is etymology alone a sound hermeneutical basis on which to interpret a word. The word "Russia" is a late eleventh-century A.D. term. Therefore, the data does not seem to support an interpretation of *rōʾš* as a proper name of a geographical region or country.

The accentual system and syntactical constructions of the Hebrew language strongly indicate an appositional relationship between the words "prince" and "chief." Both terms are related equally, then, to the two geographical words Meshech and Tubal. Grammatically it would seem best to render the phrase as "the prince, the chief ['head' or 'ruler'] of Meshech and Tubal." Meshech is the name of a son of Japheth in Genesis 10:2 and 1 Chronicles 1:5. The name is normally connected with the word Tubal (cf. 27:13; 32:26). The biblical and extrabiblical data, though sparse, would imply that Meshech and Tubal refer to geographical areas or countries in eastern modern Turkey, southwest of Russia and northwest of Iran. This, however, gives no basis for identifying these place names with any modern country. Some would see in Meshech and Tubal references to the modern Russian cities of Moscow and Tobolsk. However, there is no etymological, grammatical, historical, or literary data in support of such a position.

It can be concluded that Gog is a person from the region of Magog who is the prince, the chief ruler, over the geographical areas, or countries, Meshech and Tubal. These land areas or countries appear to be located generally toward the south of the Black and Caspian seas in the modern countries of Turkey, Russia, and Iran.

Notes

2–3 The syntactical relationship of נְשִׂיא (*nᵉśîʾ*, "prince") and רֹאשׁ (*rōʾš*, "chief") to each other is appositional according to the accentual system in the MT. The accent on *nᵉśîʾ* is a *zaqep magnum*, a strong disjunctive accent. The accent on הַמָּגוֹג (*hammāgôg*, "Magog") is a *zaqep parvum*, another strong disjunctive accent. These two accents set apart the word "prince." *Rōʾš* has a conjunctive accent (*majela*) that joins it accentually with מֶשֶׁךְ (*mešek*, "Meshech"). Syntactically, *rōʾš mešek* is a construct state—"chief of Meshech." Since *nᵉśîʾ* and *rōʾš* are appositionally related, and since *rōʾš* is in a construct relationship with Meshech and Tubal, the term "prince" should also be in a construct relationship with the place names Meshech and Tubal (cf. 39:1). This type of syntactical relationship of appositional nouns both in construct with the same absolute noun is not uncommon in Hebrew (cf. 1 Sam 28:7; Isa 23:12; 37:22; Jer 14:17; 46:9; and *GKC*, par. 130e).

2) *The invasion of Gog into Israel*

38:4-16

4I will turn you around, put hooks in your jaws and bring you out with your whole army—your horses, your horsemen fully armed, and a great horde with large and small shields, all of them brandishing their swords. 5Persia, Cush and Put will be with them, all with shields and helmets, 6also Gomer with all its troops, and Beth Togarmah from the far north with all its troops—the many nations with you.

7" 'Get ready; be prepared, you and all the hordes gathered about you, and take command of them. 8After many days you will be called to arms. In future years you will invade a land that has recovered from war, whose people were gathered from many nations to the mountains of Israel, which had long been desolate. They had been brought out from the nations, and now all of them live in safety. 9You and all your troops and the many nations with you will go up, advancing like a storm; you will be like a cloud covering the land.

10" 'This is what the Sovereign LORD says: On that day thoughts will come into your mind and you will devise an evil scheme. 11You will say, "I will invade a land of unwalled villages; I will attack a peaceful and unsuspecting people—all of them living without walls and without gates and bars. 12I will plunder and loot and turn my hand against the resettled ruins and the people gathered from the nations, rich in livestock and goods, living at the center of the land." 13Sheba and Dedan and the merchants of Tarshish and all her villages will say to you, "Have you come to plunder? Have you gathered your hordes to loot, to carry off silver and gold, to take away livestock and goods and to seize much plunder?" '

14"Therefore, son of man, prophesy and say to Gog: 'This is what the Sovereign LORD says: In that day, when my people Israel are living in safety, will you not take notice of it? 15You will come from your place in the far north, you and many nations with you, all of them riding on horses, a great horde, a mighty army. 16You will advance against my people Israel like a cloud that covers the land. In days to come, O Gog, I will bring you against my land, so that the nations may know me when I show myself holy through you before their eyes.

4–16 This section portrays Israel lying peacefully and securely in her land following her restoration by God (v.8b cf. 36:16–37:14). God had fulfilled his covenants with his people, and they were basking in the land's fruitfulness and the unquestioned security that they possessed in the strength of God's faithfulness to his word. Unexpectedly their safety was in grave jeopardy. Like a storm cloud's sudden darkness, disaster loomed on the northern horizon as an awesome horde of nations from every corner of the earth appeared. Gog, the chief prince of Meshech and Tubal, was their mastermind and commander (vv.4b, 9). Peoples had joined him from every direction of the compass; Persia from the east; Cush (Ethiopia/Nubia) from the southwest; Put (normally identified as Libya or some African country) from the west or southwest; and Gomer (probably the ancient Cimmerians) and Beth Togarmah (possibly the ancient Til-garimmu southeast of the Black Sea; cf. note at 27:12) from the north (vv.5–6). They were ready to invade Israel.

Gog had devised an evil plan. He intended to attack defenseless Israel who so naively trusted in her God. She had not protected herself: no city walls and no gates with doors and bars (v.11). What a "ripe plum" these unsuspecting people were for the vicious Gog. He would plunder their land and gather all their possessions for his spoils (v.12). Other nations like Sheba and Dedan, along with merchants from Tarshish, would be shocked and question Gog's design to plunder and loot Israel (v.13).

God, however, made it perfectly clear that he sovereignly brought Gog on the land of Israel (vv.4a, 14–17), though Gog thought it was his idea. God would cause

Gog to come on Israel by figuratively putting hooks in his jaws and leading him there (vv.4a, 14). Though this may seem incongruous with God's restoration of his people and the security promised in the peace covenant, God would cause this invasion to be initiated by Gog so that all the world might know once and for all that the Lord was a faithful God. He would defeat Gog before Gog brought any harm to Israel and her land, even as God had promised (cf. 34:22, 28–29; 36:1–15). All would see that God was holy, right, and immutably faithful; and he would not permit his name to be profaned again.

The time of this invasion was indicated by the temporal statements in these verses and the context of this message. The phrase *mîyāmîm rabbîm* ("after many days," v.8) was normally used to express an indefinite time period—a long time. It was, however, used sometimes to reach as far as the end times (cf. Jer 32:14; Dan 8:26; Hos 3:4). The expression *bᵉ'aḥᵃrît haššānîm* ("in future years," v.8) is found only in this verse in the OT. Since, however, this phrase is in the same verse and context as "after many days," one should understand its meaning in light of its context. The phrase *bᵉ'aḥᵃrît hayyāmîm* ("in days to come," v.16) tends to fix this invasion at the end times, for this phrase was normally used in reference to Israel's final restoration to the messianic kingdom and Messiah's reign (cf. Gen 49:1; Isa 2:2; Jer 23:20; 30:24; Hos 3:5; Mic 4:1). Verses 8 and 12 indicate that this invasion was planned at a time when Israel had been restored from the sword, having been regathered from among the nations. This regathering was followed by a peace and security that Israel would know in the restoration to her land (described in 36:22–37:14). She felt so safe that she did not even seek to fortify herself (v.11). Israel historically has never enjoyed such an idyllic situation since she returned from Babylon in 539 B.C. It seems plausible, therefore, to suggest that Ezekiel here has in view the future golden age, at the end of which time this invasion will occur. The phrase *yāšbû lābeṭaḥ* ("live in safety," v.8; also vv.11, 14; cf. 39:26) was used in Ezekiel as a description of messianic security after Israel's restoration. This is seen in the context of these night messages (cf. 34:25–29) as well as in other prophetic oracles concerning the end times and the Davidic, messianic kingdom (28:26; cf. Jer 23:6; 33:16; Zech 14:11). Finally, the entire context of these six messages deals with the future restoration of Israel to her homeland by the Messiah.

The combination of temporal notices that point to the messianic period as well as the general context of this passage clearly establish that the time of this invasion is the end times, after the people of Israel have been restored to the Promised Land and are living securely under Messiah's protection. Further delineation of this time within the eschatological timetable will be discussed at chapter 39.

Notes

8, 11, 14 יָשַׁב לָבֶטַח (*yāšab lābeṭaḥ*, "live in safety") is significant. בֶּטַח (*beṭaḥ*, "security") expresses "that sense of well-being and security which results from having something or someone in whom to place confidence" (TWOT, 1:101). One in such a state feels secure and is unconcerned about harm. The noun is used in two basic ways: "the promise that those who are rightly related to God will dwell securely (Lev 25:18; Ps 16:9); and indication of the transitory nature of any security other than God's (Judg 18:7; Isa 47:8; Ezek 30:9)" (TWOT, 1:102). False security is portrayed in Scripture of those who were unconcerned in their gullibility and unfound faith, e.g., Shechemites (cf. Gen 34:25), a neighbor (Prov 3:29), people of Laish (Judg 18:7, 10, 27), Cush (Ezek 30:9), wicked Israel (Amos 6:1), and inhabitants of Kedar and Hazor who all suffered from the consequences of such false hope. In the OT false security was held only by pagans or the Israelite who was not trusting in the Lord. However, when Israel was found trusting in the Lord for security, that security was *always* sure and genuine (cf. Lev 26:5; Deut 33:12; Jer 32:37; 33:16; Hos 2:18). Such was the nature of Israel in this chapter. She had been brought back to the land by the Lord, cleansed with a new heart and the Spirit, and guaranteed security by the Lord (cf. Jer 23:6; Zech 14:11). If the security in this chapter is false, then the Lord's character has been profaned (cf. TDOT, 2:88–94).

12 The MT reads יָדְךָ (*yādka*, "your hand") rather than the LXX's—all MSS but one—χεῖρά μου (*cheira mou*, "my hand"). The infinitives that begin v.12 may be understood as indicating the purpose of the verbs אֶעֱלֶה (*ʾeʿeleh*, "I will invade") and אָבוֹא (*ʾābôʾ*, "I will attack") in v.11. In this case the LXX's rendering ("my hand") would be preferred, for Gog would still be speaking. If, however, the Lord is speaking in v.11a and the main verb is assumed as "you will do this," then the infinitives would state the purpose of this verbal ellipsis and "your hand" (in reference to Gog) would be fitting. Both are valid options syntactically. Perhaps it would be best, then, to prefer the MT.

13 The MT's כָּל־כְּפִרֶיהָ (*kol kepireyhā*, "all her young lions") is rendered in the LXX, Theodotion, and the Syriac as πᾶσαι αἱ κῶμαι αὐτῶν (*pasai ai kōmai autōn*, "all their villages"). Young lions are often used as figures of energetic rulers. Such would most likely be the case if this translation were used in this text. "Villages" would certainly make sense in the geographical context of Sheba, Dedan, and Tarshish. Either rendering would fit. Again, perhaps it would be best to remain with the MT (a somewhat harder rendering, though sensible).

16 God's sovereign working is highlighted grammatically by the Hiphil stem in the verb וַהֲבִאוֹתִיךָ (*wahaḇiʾôtîkā*, "and I will cause to bring you").

---

3) God's judgment on Gog

38:17–23

> [17]" 'This is what the Sovereign Lᴏʀᴅ says: Are you not the one I spoke of in former days by my servants the prophets of Israel? At that time they prophesied for years that I would bring you against them. [18]This is what will happen in that day: When Gog attacks the land of Israel, my hot anger will be aroused, declares the Sovereign Lᴏʀᴅ. [19]In my zeal and fiery wrath I declare that at that time there shall be a great earthquake in the land of Israel. [20]The fish of the sea, the birds of the air, the beasts of the field, every creature that moves along the ground, and all the people on the face of the earth will tremble at my presence. The mountains will be overturned, the cliffs will crumble and every wall will fall to the ground. [21]I will summon a sword against Gog on all my mountains, declares the Sovereign Lᴏʀᴅ. Every man's sword will be against his brother. [22]I will execute judgment upon him with plague and bloodshed; I will pour down torrents of rain, hailstones and burning sulfur on him and on his troops and on the many nations with him. [23]And so I will show my greatness and my holiness, and I will make myself known in the sight of many nations. Then they will know that I am the Lᴏʀᴅ.'

17–23 In his judgment God reminded Gog that the Lord's servants, the prophets, had formerly foretold this end-time invasion (v.17). Though there are no specific references to Gog in any of the other prophets, there are general references to the final destruction of the enemies of God's people (cf. Deut 30:7; Isa 26:20–21; Jer 30:18–24).

Israel's dependence on God was not in vain. At the very moment that Gog would come against the land of Israel, God's burning wrath would arise against Gog (v.18). The Lord was a jealous God and faithful to protect his own. God's fiery fury would break forth suddenly against Gog and his horde. The entire earth would be jolted with an enormous earthquake that would topple mountains, cliffs, and every wall. Every creature on the earth, within the sea and within the air, would shutter in awe and fear at the presence of almighty God who had come to annihilate Gog and his followers (vv.19–20). Gog's armies and the nations following him would become so confused that they would slay one another in suicidal strife (v.21; cf. Judg 7:22; 1 Sam 14:20; Hag 2:22; Zech 14:13), while the Lord supernaturally destroyed them with diseases, bloodshed, and catastrophic torrents of rain, hailstones, and burning sulphur (v.22). God would vindicate his holy name and magnify himself as the only true God in the eyes of all nations with this annihilation of Gog (v.23). The purpose of all God's judgments is only to make himself known in all his greatness and holiness to those who can come to know him in no other way.

Notes

---

19 קָנָא (*qānā'*, "be jealous, zealous") "expresses a very strong emotion whereby some quality or possession of the object is desired by the subject" (TWOT, 2:802). The Lord is a jealous God (Exod 20:5) who would ultimately turn his jealous wrath against any nation or enemy of his chosen people in order to vindicate his name (cf. 36:5–6; 39:25) (TWOT, 2:802–3).

22 וְנִשְׁפַּטְתִּי (*wᵉnišpaṭṭî*, "and I will execute judgment") is in the Niphal. The stress should be on the middle idea of judging for oneself.

---

b. *Reiteration and expansion of God's judgment speech against Gog* (39:1–29)

1) *Invasion and judgment*

39:1–8

> [1]"Son of man, prophesy against Gog and say: 'This is what the Sovereign LORD says: I am against you, O Gog, chief prince of Meshech and Tubal. [2]I will turn you around and drag you along. I will bring you from the far north and send you against the mountains of Israel. [3]Then I will strike your bow from your left hand and make your arrows drop from your right hand. [4]On the mountains of Israel you will fall, you and all your troops and the nations with you. I will give you as food to all kinds of carrion birds and to the wild animals. [5]You will fall in the open field, for I have spoken, declares the Sovereign LORD. [6]I will send fire on Magog and on those who live in safety in the coastlands, and they will know that I am the LORD.
> [7]" 'I will make known my holy name among my people Israel. I will no longer let my holy name be profaned, and the nations will know that I the LORD am the Holy One in Israel. [8]It is coming! It will surely take place, declares the Sovereign LORD. This is the day I have spoken of.

1–2 These verses give a summary restatement of 38:1–16. God would sovereignly coerce Gog to invade Israel, but at the same time God would defeat Gog in a display of his faithfulness to Israel.

3–8 Ezekiel 38:17–23 described God supernaturally using the elements of nature to destroy Gog. Earthquakes, disease, and hailstones would decimate Gog and his hordes. This judgment on Gog is further developed in chapter 39. Gog would be completely disarmed. No battle appears to have ensued with Israel (v.3; cf. 38:21). Gog's armies would fall throughout the land—on the mountains and in the open field (vv.4a, 5). The slaughter of Gog's hordes would provide food for every bird of prey and wild beast (v.4b; cf. vv.17–20). In addition God would bring a fiery judgment on the territory of Magog and on her allies who felt secure in their coastlands and/or islands (v.6a). God would use Gog's defeat as a demonstration to the nations that he, the Holy One of Israel, was the only true God. He was faithful to his covenant people to whom he had promised eternal peace and security in the peace covenant (cf. 34:25–31; 37:24–28). He would not permit his holy name to be profaned again through the conquest and dispersion of Israel. Israel, in turn, would make the Lord's name holy in her midst; for she would see his immutable faithfulness through his protection of her in this final attempt to invade Israel's land (vv.6b–7). As encouragement to the Jewish exiles, the Lord stressed again that Gog's destruction would most certainly occur (v.8). God's intrinsic holiness is strongly stressed in vv.7–8 in contrast to the evil and profane nature of Gog and his hordes. The "Holy One in Israel" (v.7) expresses God's absolute separation from evil. He maintains his holiness and that of his land by judging Gog. His holiness is also demonstrated in his keeping his promises (TWOT, 2:786–89).

2) The aftermath of judgment on Gog

39:9–20

9" 'Then those who live in the towns of Israel will go out and use the weapons for fuel and burn them up—the small and large shields, the bows and arrows, the war clubs and spears. For seven years they will use them for fuel. 10They will not need to gather wood from the fields or cut it from the forests, because they will use the weapons for fuel. And they will plunder those who plundered them and loot those who looted them, declares the Sovereign Lord.

11" 'On that day I will give Gog a burial place in Israel, in the valley of those who travel east toward the Sea. It will block the way of travelers, because Gog and all his hordes will be buried there. So it will be called the Valley of Hamon Gog.

12" 'For seven months the house of Israel will be burying them in order to cleanse the land. 13All the people of the land will bury them, and the day I am glorified will be a memorable day for them, declares the Sovereign Lord.

14" 'Men will be regularly employed to cleanse the land. Some will go throughout the land and, in addition to them, others will bury those that remain on the ground. At the end of the seven months they will begin their search. 15As they go through the land and one of them sees a human bone, he will set up a marker beside it until the gravediggers have buried it in the Valley of Hamon Gog. 16(Also a town called Hamonah will be there.) And so they will cleanse the land.'

17"Son of man, this is what the Sovereign Lord says: Call out to every kind of bird and all the wild animals: 'Assemble and come together from all around to the sacrifice I am preparing for you, the great sacrifice on the mountains of Israel. There you will eat flesh and drink blood. 18You will eat the flesh of mighty men and drink the blood of the princes of the earth as if they were rams and lambs, goats and bulls—all of them fattened animals from Bashan. 19At the sacrifice I am preparing for you, you will eat fat till you are glutted and drink blood till you are drunk. 20At my table you will eat your fill of horses and riders, mighty men and soldiers of every kind,' declares the Sovereign Lord.

9–10 God totally disarmed Gog's armies (cf. v.3). So great was the resulting assemblage of weapons that it would take the Israelites seven years to burn them all. These weapons would provide fuel for Israel during these seven years so that she would not need to use any of her own fuel resources (vv.9–10a). Likewise, though Gog and his entourage had sought to take spoils from Israel, it would be Israel who would take spoils from them. Again, judgment "in kind" is observed (v.10b).

11–16 The magnitude of Gog's armies created a staggering problem with their death. All of them needed to be buried in order to cleanse the land of Israel. A specific valley known as the "valley of those who travel east toward [or 'of'] the Sea" was designated as the burial place (v.11). Whether the proper rendering is "toward" or "of" could make a distinct difference as to which sea is involved. If the sea was the Dead Sea, then the valley would either be east of that sea—and therefore out of the normal boundaries of Israel—or a valley that led travelers east toward the Dead Sea. The only valley to fit remotely this description would be the Esdraelon Valley in lower Galilee. One would then still need to travel south to the Dead Sea. If the sea was understood as the Mediterranean, then the specific valley could be any valley in the land of Israel east "of" that sea. Though one might see the Esdraelon Valley as an essential east-west valley that was well traveled throughout history and would fit the text well, none of the theories of identification of this valley can be substantiated without question because of the sparse data. The text does make it clear that the massive burial of Gog and his hordes in this valley would cause a major obstacle to travel. For this reason the valley would be named the Valley of Hamon Gog (the hordes of Gog) (v.11).

The multitude of carcasses would require more than seven months to bury in order to cleanse the land (v.12; cf. Lev 5:2; 21:1; Deut 21:1–9). Every person in Israel would be involved. For seven months they would bury the easily observed bodies lying on the ground. After seven months overseers, "men regularly employed" (v.14), would designate two groups to carry out a "mopping up" operation. One group would search throughout the land to find any remnant of a body—even a bone—and mark it. These would be collected and taken to the Valley of Hamon Gog for burial by the second group (vv.13–15). A city named Hamonah (horde) would be located in the Valley of Hamon Gog (v.16), perhaps viewed as a city of the dead. The city's exact nature is unclear. Gog's burial would be a memorable day for the Lord, for the death of this enemy demonstrates God's faithfulness to protect his people forever and brings glory to the Lord's name (v.13b).

17–20 The search throughout the land for bones of the deceased enemy may have arisen due to the great feast on the dead by the carrion-eating birds and animals of prey invited to feed on the carnage of Gog and his followers (vv.17–20; cf. v.4). This great slaughter was called a "sacrifice" (v.17) that the Lord prepared for these birds and animals on Israel's mountains (cf. similar imagery in Isa 34:6 and Jer 46:10). The flesh and fat of princes, warriors, and their animals would be consumed; and their blood would be drunk till these fowls and beasts were glutted and drunk. Rams, lambs, goats, and bulls of Bashan were always well-fed and strong. The parallel of this imagery to the defeated princes emphasizes that these were not weaklings but the strong and mighty of the earth (cf. v.18).

Excursus

There is a formidable allusion to the great feast in vv.17–20 in Revelation 19:17–21. Revelation 19:11–16 presents a heavenly scene of the Second Advent. The Lord comes on a white horse with his armies to judge and make war in righteousness. The sword that proceeds out of his mouth smites the nations as he treads out the winepress of his great wrath. Revelation 19:17–21 is a distinctly different section (beginning with the familiar phrase *eidon* ["I saw"]), in which an angel invites all the birds to a "great supper of God," a feast on the mighty leaders of the nations who had gathered against the Lord and who would be slain by the sword of his mouth (cf. Isa 11:4; 49:2). The beast and the false prophet would be seized and cast into the lake of fire. The birds would fill themselves on the carnage of the others.

In his "great supper of God," John appears to allude explicitly to the feast on the carnage of Gog's hordes in Ezekiel 39:17–20. Most commentators cite the cross-reference of Ezekiel 39:17–20 in comments on Revelation 19. Nowhere else in the entirety of Scripture is there any other likeness to this event. Either John had reference to Ezekiel 39 or he had reference to no known event in biblical prophecy. Yet it was part of John's literary artistry to use OT imagery to communicate his message. It would appear difficult to disassociate these two passages.

Why would John directly link Ezekiel 39 to Revelation 19 in his argument? The restoration and messianic context of Ezekiel's message is also that of John. Revelation 19:11–16 presents a heavenly glimpse of the Messiah at his second coming (futuristic interpretation) after Israel has been restored to her land (cf. Rev 7). The beast and the kings of the earth with their armies (Rev 19:19) are certainly similar to the nations assembled with Gog in Ezekiel (Ezek 38:4–7, 9, 15, 22; 39:4, 11; Rev 19:15, 18–19, 21). The Lord's judgment in Ezekiel 38–39 finds parallel features in the Messiah's treading out God's winepress of wrath in Revelation 19. The Lord calls for a sword against Gog, and the sword out of the Lord's mouth smites the nations that come against him in Revelation (cf. Ezek 38:21; Rev 19:15, 20).

An explicit chronology is not set forth in the Revelation. Therefore it is difficult to know the exact time of Revelation 19, though the second coming of the Messiah is in view. It appears that Messiah comes to defeat all nations and perhaps conclude the Battle of Armageddon. Yet the context of Ezekiel 38–39 would see Israel already at peace, dwelling in security, having been restored from the sword. Such would not be in harmony with the Battle of Armageddon. Since this battle is not mentioned in Revelation 19 explicitly, perhaps the events of Revelation 19 do not relate to Armageddon but specifically to the demise of the beast as foretold in Ezekiel 38–39. Armageddon had already been treated in Revelation 14 and 16. Therefore, though the Messiah may conclude the events of Armageddon with his return, the next event in a possible transition period between the conclusion of the Tribulation and the beginning of the Millennium would be this defeat of the beast who sought to make one final attempt to secure Israel's land.

Biblical scholars admit that there is no explicit scriptural statement about a transitional period between the Tribulation and the Millennium, though such seems plausible. There was a transition period between the Mosaic covenant and the full institution of the new covenant (cf. the time from Christ's death to Pentecost). Likewise, there may be a transitional period between the rapture of the church and the beginning of the tribulation period, since there is no explicit Scripture to identify the Rapture as simultaneous with the beginning of the Tribulation. A transitional period between the Tribulation and the Millennium may not be out of place, though this hypothesis is admittedly weak, being based on silence.

Why would John not mention Gog in Revelation 19 if this passage is a fulfillment of Ezekiel 38–39? Perhaps John wanted to identify the demise of the beast and his hordes with Ezekiel 38–39 without confusing his readers. The last mention of the beast by John had been in Revelation 17. If John used the name Gog (which may only be a person's title, u.s.) in Revelation 19, the readers would probably not have associated that name with the beast. Rather they would have been unaware of who this "Gog" was in the Revelation 19 context. By using the name "beast" and at the same time making expicit allusion to Ezekiel's Gog invasion in the unique feast of the birds, John apparently sought to equate the beast with Gog for his readers. Then his readers would see the events of Revelation 19:17–21 as a fulfillment of the Gog prophecy. This interpretation of Revelation 19:17–21, then, helps establish the exact time when Ezekiel 38–39 will occur (q.v. further discussion infra.).

It is important to observe that in addition to the specific allusion between Revelation 19 and Ezekiel 39 found in the "bird supper," none of the details of Ezekiel 38–39 is violated in the Revelation 19 context. One may ask how Gog (the beast) could escape from Armageddon in order to return later. Others may inquire as to which nations would be present at the invasion of Gog to observe his destruction as recounted in Ezekiel. Some might question the seeming disparity between Gog's burial in Ezekiel and the casting of the beast into the lake of fire. Still others might wonder how Israel could be living securely in her land so quickly after the Battle of Armageddon. Some plausible answers are suggested.

1. Nothing in the biblical text would preclude the absence of the beast from Armageddon or would not permit his escape if he were present.

2. The accounts of the Battle of Armageddon do not require *all* people on the earth to be present. For example, the nations in Matthew 25 must survive to be judged. Therefore, nations could remain to view Gog's (the beast's) fall.

3. The term "Gog" in Ezekiel 38–39 is used in a collective sense to refer to Gog's entire entourage (cf. 38:9, 15–16, 21; 39:4). In addition "Gog" and "his horde" in 39:11 most likely were appositional so that Gog's burial is really the burial of the hordes, a concept that would be in agreement with the name given to the valley of burial, Hamon-Gog (Gog's horde).

4. There is nothing in the context of Revelation 19–20 and the statement of these events that would require that each event occur immediately after the previous one. If a transitional period is assumed, time would be provided for Israel to become secure and peaceful in her land following the Battle of Armageddon.

Though the Revelation 19 passage aids in determining the fulfillment and the time of Gog's invasion and defeat in Ezekiel 38–39, other factors are involved in seeking to gain a complete perspective of these issues. It is recognized that interpreting the time of these events in the prophetic program of the end times is a most difficult issue, with which many have seriously and prayerfully grappled, resulting in different positions. It is important to briefly consider the major interpretations of the time element of Ezekiel 38–39 in order to see the issues.

Some (e.g., David L. Cooper, *When Gog's Armies Meet the Almighty* [Los Angeles: The Biblical Research Society, 1940], pp. 80–81) would place the events of Ezekiel 38–39 prior to the tribulation period since Israel's secure dwelling could only be explained if the Tribulation had not yet begun. However, the context of restoration in Ezekiel is messianic, at the end times; and the phrase "live securely" likewise stresses millennial security in the context of Ezekiel 38–39. Israel is said to have been freed already "from the sword," an event that would not occur till the Tribulation's end. Ezekiel 39:7, 22 declares that the Lord's name would never be profaned again, a fact that is hardly possible with the Tribulation forthcoming. Moreover, the concept of the nations "knowing the Lord" by recognizing his sovereignty would fit best at the time of his second coming rather than before the Tribulation (cf. 38:16, 22–23; 39:7, 21–24). Therefore, it would seem that this position would not adequately fit the details of Ezekiel 38–39.

Proponents (e.g., Pentecost, pp. 350–352) in favor of these events occurring in the middle of the Tribulation argue that Gog's invasion should be equated with the king of the north's invasion in Daniel 11:40–41, which, in turn, precipitates the Antichrist's breaking his covenant with Israel in the middle of the Tribulation. These maintain that the invasion would occur when Israel is dwelling in her own land, enjoying *false* security of relative peace provided through her pact with the Antichrist (cf. 38:8; Dan 9:27). Gog's invasion and destruction is believed to become a sign to the nations and to Israel that would cause them to "know" the Lord in the midst of the Tribulation, supposedly agreeing with the Revelation, which declares that many will be saved at that time. It is also reasoned that since Gog was the king of the north, and since he was not mentioned in Revelation 19:20 along with the destruction of the beast and false prophet, of necessity he must have already been destroyed. That fall, of course, is said to have occurred in the middle of the Tribulation.

In examining these arguments for a mid-tribulation fulfillment of Ezekiel 38–39, the following observations are noted.

1. There is no specific basis in the biblical text for equating Gog with the king of the north.

2. A concept of "false security" and prosperity (38:11–12) are both inconsistent with the purpose of the Tribulation (a time of Israel's chastisement and punishment) and contrary to the usual meaning of the phrase "live safely" in Ezekiel 38–39 (a millennial concept).

3. The cleansing of the land through burning weapons and burying bodies for seven years and seven months respectively would seem inconceivable during the abomination of desolation, when judgment is at its height.

4. Ezekiel 38:8, 16 declares that Israel has been restored from the sword into messianic blessing; yet this would be incongruous with the tribulation period.

5. Ezekiel 38–39 clearly points out that it is God who destroys Gog, not the Antichrist.

6. Ezekiel's assertions (39:7, 22, 25) that the Lord's name would never again be profaned among the nations seem antithetical with the tribulation period. Therefore, it seems questionable that the events of Ezekiel 38–39 transpire in the middle of the Tribulation.

Several (e.g., Feinberg, pp. 218, 230–31; Ironside, p. 265) place the time of these events at the end of the tribulation period. Gog's armies are viewed as among those gathered together against the Messiah in Zechariah 12 and 14:1–14. Some holding this position would identify Gog with the personage in Daniel 11:40 while others would disassociate Gog from the Armageddon battle. The latter would postulate that Ezekiel 38–39 describes a battle at the end of the Tribulation prior to the judgment of Matthew 25 and the Millennium. These adherents maintain that the "living safely" is a false security based on Israel's wealth (cf. 38:11–12).

In response to those who would identify Gog with the person in Daniel 11:40, many of the responses to the mid-tribulational view given above would be valid here, since this position essentially becomes a mid-tribulational interpretation. Whether the battle begins in the middle or at the end of the Tribulation makes little difference. The time of Armageddon certainly does not provide a time for Israel to be "living safely." A false security (cf. notes at 38:8, 11, 14), based on

Israel's wealth, seems contrary to Ezekiel's argument that the security rested on Israel's restoration, the Messiah's presence, and the absence of any oppression under the Lord's protection. Some holding this position come very close to a time in a transitional period between the end of the Tribulation and the beginning of the Millennium, as outlined above in the discussion of Revelation 19 and its relation to Ezekiel 39. Such would seem a better position.

The majority of expositors (e.g., Ellison, p. 133; Davidson, p. 301) see these events of Ezekiel 38–39 taking place after the Millennium as described in Revelation 20:7–10. The strong argument for this position is the explicit reference to Gog and Magog in Revelation 20:8. The use of these terms must be explained. The context of the Millennium would surely satisfy Israel's peaceful, prosperous, and safe dwelling. Restoration would have already been accomplished. Nations would be present to observe "Gog's" rebellion. Time would surely be available for the burial of bodies and the burning of weapons.

Objections, however, have been raised against this view.

1. It is argued that Gog is a northern coalition while in Revelation the armies come from the four corners of the earth. In response it should be noticed that Gog brings with him nations from every point of the compass (38:5–6).

2. It is maintained that Ezekiel says nothing of Jerusalem whereas John states that the nations encompassed the beloved city. In answer it should be observed that John's mention of the "beloved city" does not conflict with Ezekiel, for he states that Gog comes on the mountains of Israel which most certainly would include Jerusalem.

3. It is believed that the burning of the weapons and disposal of the bodies would militate against this event at the end of the Millennium, since the great white throne judgment immediately follows. However, it has been observed above that the chronology of the Revelation does not demand immediate sequence of events, especially in Revelation 19–20. A transition period here is equally plausible.

Therefore, it would seem that Revelation 20:7–10 is also a fulfillment of Ezekiel 38–39. Such is a valid hermeneutical principle. In this case the fulfillment would be seen in two far moments: one in Revelation 19:17–21 and one in Revelation 20:7–10. The connection between Ezekiel 38–39 and Revelation 19:17–21; 20:7–10 lies in the singular concept of God's defeat of the great final attempt of the Evil One to once again possess the land of Israel. Revelation 19 finds the attempt thwarted in the destruction of the beast and his armies (Satan's major representative on earth), whereas Revelation 20 sets forth Satan's fall as the completion of this theme. Both are the last and greatest enemies of Israel. John only summarized the events in each case since the full description was recounted in Ezekiel 38–39. The allusion to the great feast in Revelation 19 was used by John to bring to his readers' attention the events of Ezekiel 38–39, with which they would have been familiar. The term "Gog" was not used so as *not* to confuse the identity of the beast. On the contrary, in Revelation 20 the explicit equation is made between Satan and Gog so that the readers also would identify Satan's rebellion with the events of Ezekiel 38–39. Both passages describe attempts by Israel's greatest enemies, the beast and Satan, to possess the land of Israel and to nullify God's promise. This is the singularity of meaning of Ezekiel 38–39 and Revelation 19–20, giving corporate wholeness to this theme throughout Scripture. The Lord demonstrated himself as the immutable God who faithfully protects Israel in accord with his word.

Notes

9, 12, 14 Some critics see a conflict between the seven years of v.9 and the seven months of vv.12, 14. However, the two time periods refer to different times. Nothing here argues for the lack of literalness in the text.

11 קִדְמַת הַיָּם (qidmat hayyām, "east toward the Sea") is a construct relationship. קִדְמָה (qidmāh) normally has the sense of "east," "in front of," or "over against." In construct with the absolute form hayyām, the phrase would best be rendered "east of the Sea." Construct forms are not normally translated adverbially. To render the phrase adverbially, the word קֶדֶם (qedem, "east") with a he locative suffix usually would be used. However, qidmāh is not used adverbially in the construct form.

14 The verb יַבְדִּילוּ (yabdîlû, "employed" or "divide," "set apart") has as its subject אַנְשֵׁי תָמִיד ('anšê tāmîd, "men . . . regularly" or "men of continual [service]") instead of the pronoun הֵם (hem, "they") in v.13. The verb בָּדַל (bādal, "divide") may take the participle as its object (BDB, s.v.). The sense then is that these men of continual service would be a group of overseers who divide the people into two groups: those who went and marked the bones and those who buried them. The uses of two אֵת ('et, "with," or the sign of the definite direct object) should be understood as follows: the first 'et is the preposition "with" and the second is the sign of the definite direct object of the participle מְקַבְּרִים (meqabberîm, "burying").

17-20 In seeking to determine the time element of the events of this great sacrificial feast and Gog's invasion, the following hermeneutical principles should govern the procedure: (1) a normal grammatical-historical hermeneutic; (2) a priority of the Ezekiel 38-39 text, not overlooking any facet of these chapters for the sake of a position; (3) permitting the basic time reference to come from the Ezekiel passage; (4) allowing the NT to help interpret the OT; and (5) keeping hypotheses to a minimum.

c. The summary of the six night messages

39:21-29

21"I will display my glory among the nations, and all the nations will see the punishment I inflict and the hand I lay upon them. 22From that day forward the house of Israel will know that I am the LORD their God. 23And the nations will know that the people of Israel went into exile for their sin, because they were unfaithful to me. So I hid my face from them and handed them over to their enemies, and they all fell by the sword. 24I dealt with them according to their uncleanness and their offenses, and I hid my face from them.

25"Therefore this is what the Sovereign LORD says: I will now bring Jacob back from captivity and will have compassion on all the people of Israel, and I will be zealous for my holy name. 26They will forget their shame and all the unfaithfulness they showed toward me when they lived in safety in their land with no one to make them afraid. 27When I have brought them back from the nations and have gathered them from the countries of their enemies, I will show myself holy through them in the sight of many nations. 28Then they will know that I am the LORD their God, for though I sent them into exile among the nations, I will gather them to their own land, not leaving any behind. 29I will no longer hide my face from them, for I will pour out my Spirit on the house of Israel, declares the Sovereign LORD."

21-29 Gog's destruction provided the climax of Ezekiel's six messages of encouragement delivered to the exiles the night prior to the fugitive's arrival with the news that Jerusalem had fallen. Gog's defeat would be the Lord's final display of his glory among the nations as he restored Israel to her promised land. All other nations would stand in awe at God's punishment on Gog (v.21).

These six messages have stressed God's covenant promises to Israel, especially those concerning the land. When Israel experiences God's marvelous faithfulness in restoration and protection against Gog, she would know without question from that day forward that the Lord was her God, the only true God, and there was none other (vv.22, 25, 28). In turn the nations would know that the Lord had not been a weak God when he sent Israel into exile, rather they would observe that he cared enough to set his face against Israel because of her sin of unfaithfulness to him (vv.23–24). Likewise, the nations would observe that it was God's grace and faithfulness that brought Israel back from among the nations, gave her her promised land, and enabled her to live safely on that land without fear of oppression. In this way the Lord would show himself holy in the eyes of the nations (v.27). He was jealous for his name not to be profaned as when the nations construed him to be as other gods (v.25). The Lord would never again turn his face from Israel and allow someone to oppress her! No one would bring terror on Israel again (vv.26, 29a)! God would cleanse Israel, removing her shame and sin and then pouring out his Spirit on her in accord with the new covenant (vv.26, 29b). All Israel's covenants would be fulfilled. She would live secure forever under the peace covenant administered by her king, the Messiah!

Notes

25 שְׁבִית (*šᵉḇyyṯ*) (vocalization unsure) has been rendered two ways: "captivity" (NIV) and "fortunes" (NASB). The Hebrew derivation is uncertain (BDB, s.v.). The noun is used in the sense of returning from captivity (cf. Jer 29:14; 30:3) and restoring fortunes (cf. Deut 30:3; Jer 30:18; Ezek 16:53). The meaning in this verse is not clear.

26 The infinitive construction בְּשִׁבְתָּם (*bᵉšiḇtām*, "when they lived") must determine its time framework from the context. The future context as well as the entire preceding context of six messages argue that it would be best to render the phrase "when they live" rather than in the past tense.

B. *God's Glory Returns* (40:1–48:35)

Excursus

The description in these nine chapters of a temple, the filling of that temple with God's glory, a sacrificial system for worship in that temple, priestly functions, and the tribal and priestly allotment of land is rather evident and clear to the reader. The question that has puzzled interpreters is What does it all mean? Should these chapters be interpreted literally or figuratively? Does this section refer to a historical situation (past, present) or to the future? If to the future, does it concern the Millennium or the eternal state? Is there not a retrogression to OT modes of worship; and, if so, how does this fit with the NT teaching of the finished and complete work of Christ? Surely this portion of the book contains some very puzzling and difficult concepts that cannot be ignored. Therefore it seems wise to examine some basic interpretative issues in order to determine as accurate an understanding of the text as possible using a normal grammatical-historical hermeneutic. (See also the excursus at the introduction to 33:21–48:35, pp. 905–8.)

Is Ezekiel 40–48 Historical or Future?

These chapters have been interpreted as referring to Solomon's temple, the temple of Zerubbabel (either real or proposed), Herod's temple, or a future temple in the Millennium or in the eternal state. Some, having difficulty understanding the passage when taken literally, interpret the section allegorically as teaching about the church and its earthly blessings and glories, while others understand the passage to symbolize the reality of the heavenly temple where Christ ministers today.

The historical fulfillments do not fit the details of the passage. The temples of Solomon, Zerubbabel, or Herod do not share the design and dimensions of the temple described in Ezekiel 40–42. The worship procedure set forth in chapters 43–46, though Mosaic in nature, has not been followed in history in exactly the manner described in these chapters. The river that flows forth from the temple in 47:1–12 has never flowed from any of the three historical temples mentioned above. The only comparisons to this river are seen in Genesis 2:8–14 and Revelation 22:1–2 (cf. Isa 35:6–7; Joel 3:18; Zech 14:8). The geographical dimensions and tribal allotments of the land are certainly not feasible today, nor have they ever been followed in times past. Geographical changes will be necessary prior to the fulfillment of chapters 45, 47–48. Therefore one would not look to historical (past or present) fulfillments of these chapters but to the future.

The figurative or "spiritualizing" interpretative approach does not seem to solve any of the problems of Ezekiel 40–48; it tends to create new ones. When the interpreter abandons a normal grammatical-historical hermeneutic because the passage does not seem to make sense taken that way and opts for an interpretative procedure by which he can allegorize, symbolize, or "spiritualize," the interpretations become subjective. Different aspects of a passage mean whatever the interpreter desires. There are no governing interpretative principles except the interpreter's mind (though there is appeal to the NT understanding of the OT). Even apocalyptic visions such as found in these chapters require a normal grammatical-historical hermeneutic. To interpret these chapters in any manner other than a normal, literal approach would appear to contradict the interpretative guide in the vision who warns Ezekiel that he is to write down all the minute details concerning the plan for the temple and its regulations so that these details might be considered carefully and followed in every aspect (40:4; 43:10–11; 44:5; cf. Exod 25:9; 1 Chron 28:19). Therefore a figurative approach does not adequately treat the issues of Ezekiel 40–48.

In order to determine the general time-frame of these chapters, they will be examined in light of the development and flow of Ezekiel's argument in the entire book. He has shown the presence of God's glory in the historical Jerusalem temple and its departure from that temple because of Israel's sin of breaking the Mosaic covenant. The Fall of Jerusalem and the Captivity in Babylon were the consequence (chs. 4–24). After declaring how the nations would also be judged (25:1–33:20), Ezekiel encouraged the Jewish captives through six night messages of hope (33:21–39:29). In these he informed them that the Messiah would restore them to their Promised Land in the future and become a true shepherd to them. They would be cleansed and all their covenants would be fulfilled. Even in the end times, after the land prospers and Israel dwells securely in it, some will try to take the Promised Land away from Israel and profane the Lord's name; but the Lord will not permit it (chs. 38–39). It would seem logical, therefore, that Ezekiel would conclude the logical and chronological development of his prophecy by describing the messianic kingdom and the return of God's glory to govern his people (chs. 40–48) rather than suddenly reverting back to some historical period, whether immediately following the Captivity or during Herod's temple, or to describe an idealistic temple.

Ezekiel appears to have been contrasting the past and contemporary desecration of the temple and its regulations with the future holiness and righteousness of the temple and its functions. Ezekiel also used this format in chapters 33–39. The correct future procedure would bring shame and conviction on Ezekiel's contemporaries (43:6–12; 44:5–16; 45:9–12). This would again point to a future fulfillment of these chapters.

God's glory is a most important feature of Ezekiel's prophecy. The return of God's glory to the new temple in 43:1–12 is the climax of the book. The context implies that this could only occur after Israel has been restored to her Promised Land and cleansed. The stress is on holiness. Holiness had not characterized Israel as a people heretofore; and, according to Ezekiel 36, Israel would not be a holy people in accord with God's standard till after they had been restored to the Promised Land and cleansed in the Messianic Age. When God's glory returns, it will remain in Israel's midst forever (43:6–7). The development of this unifying factor in Ezekiel's prophecy would argue strongly for a future fulfillment of chapters 40–48.

Finally, the entire context and argument of the Scriptures concerning God's outworking of his redemptive plan in history would seem to place these chapters and the aspects mentioned above in the time of the consummation of all history. This is perhaps best seen in the river of life that flows from the temple to bring healing to the land (47:1–12). This concept is first seen in Genesis 2:8–14 in the Garden of Eden, the perfect environment of God's holiness. With sin, this garden and its river were removed. When God concludes his redemptive program and brings full salvation to mankind with eternal life through the passion of Jesus Christ, his Son, it is most appropriate that the river of eternal life would again flow to demonstrate full healing on the earth. This conclusion to the full circle of God's redemptive program is also shown in Revelation 22:1–6 in God's description of the eternal state. Such is also conveyed by other OT prophets (cf. Isa 35:5–6; Joel 3:18; Zech 14:8).

Therefore, the context and argument of the Book of Ezekiel as well as the development of God's redemptive program argue strongly for a future fulfillment of the events of Ezekiel 40–48 in the end times.

Does Ezekiel 40–48 Relate to the Millennium or to the Eternal State?

It is first necessary to understand the prophetic perspective of the OT prophets. We must see the prophetic message from their viewpoint initially, not from our contemporary perspective in light of the NT. The predictive revelations of the OT prophets concerned two main issues: (1) the time of the judgment and discipline that was to come on Israel because of her perennial sin and breaking of the Mosaic covenant; and (2) the ultimate period of blessing, following Israel's future judgment, when Israel would be restored to the Promised Land, cleansed of her sin, and brought into the messianic kingdom. At that time all of Israel's covenants would be fulfilled, and she would live in perfect security under the divine rule of the Messiah.

The OT prophets tended not to make distinctions within the period of discipline and judgment. Rather they portrayed near and far aspects of this time in the same passage. The discipline would begin with the Babylonian captivity and would continue till the end time. Some distinctions were observed, but chronological relations were seldom delineated.

Likewise the prophets did not make distinctions between the Millennium and the eternal state when describing the period of messianic blessing. Further distinctions are primarily the result of progressive revelation disclosed in the NT, especially in the Revelation, though some distinctions are implied in the OT prophets (e.g., Dan 9–12).

Ezekiel, like his contemporaries, intermixed these various elements in his prophecies of judgment and the future kingdom. Undoubtedly this contributes to the difficulty in distinguishing the Millennium and the eternal state in these chapters.

In light of the whole Scripture, it appears that the Millennium is like a "firstfruits" of the eternal state. The Millennium will be like a preview of the eternal messianic kingdom that will be revealed fully in the eternal state. Therefore, because the two are alike in nature, they share distinct similarities. Yet because they are both different revealed time periods, they would likewise reflect some dissimilarities. Since the OT prophets, like Ezekiel, frequently failed to see distinctions, one should be careful about stating that Ezekiel 40–48 is describing only the Millennium or only the eternal state. One must look to the NT for any further clues for delineation, whenever such are given.

Many OT prophetic concepts and imageries are used by John in the Revelation, as observed already in his allusion to the "bird supper" of Ezekiel 38–39. Revelation 21–22 speaks of the eternal state. There are definite allusions to Ezekiel 40–48 in this portion of the Revelation, with striking similarities. Both writers receive apocalyptic visions on a high mountain with an intercepting messenger present, holding a measuring rod to measure various structures (Ezek 40:2–5; Rev 21:2, 10, 15). Both visions portray waters flowing forth toward the east, with trees alongside and leaves for healing (Ezek 47:1–7, 12; Rev 22:1–2). The names of Israel's twelve tribes are written on the city's twelve gates in both visions (Ezek 48:31–34; Rev 21:12), and three gates each are found on the east, south, north, and west sides of the city respectively (Ezek 48:30–34; Rev 21:13).

In addition, however, there are equally clear dissimilarities between the two passages. The city's dimensions are different (Ezek 48:30–35; Rev 21:15–17). The waters that flow toward the east have different sources: the temple in Ezekiel (43:7; 47:1–5) and God's throne in the Revelation (22:1, 3). It might appear that these sources are really similar since Ezekiel maintains that God's throne is the temple; but John, in his vision, declares that God's throne is in Jerusalem. The temple and the city of Jerusalem are distinctly different entities in Ezekiel (45:2–4; 48:10, 15–17), and in the Revelation vision there is no temple structure (21:22; 22:3). Since a major aspect of Ezekiel 40–48 is the temple and its regulations, perhaps this would argue for Ezekiel's discussion to reflect the Millennium more than the eternal state. The tribal allotments of Ezekiel include the sea as the western boundary (47:15–20), whereas in the Revelation John declares that the sea no longer exists (Rev 21:1). Therefore, Ezekiel's tribal boundaries could not exist in the eternal state if the sea no longer existed. Items are discussed in each passage that are not mentioned in the other. These, of course, neither argue for similarity or dissimilarity. But the dissimilarities discussed above indicate that Ezekiel's vision is more concerned with millennial concepts than the eternal state, whereas the Revelation vision is focused on the eternal state.

The river flowing east from the temple would likewise appear to be millennial since the source is different from the Revelation passage. But here the similar nature of the two passages is perhaps best observed. Ezekiel may very well give a glimpse of the eternal state with this similar facet. Perhaps what is seen in the

Millennium will also be seen in the eternal state though with slight modification. Since the Lord will take the place of the temple in the eternal state, the river could flow out of the millennial temple as the throne of God in Ezekiel 47 and out of the throne of God, distinct from a temple, in Revelation 22.

It seems, therefore, that Ezekiel 40–48 may be primarily describing the millennial temple, its regulations for worship, and the tribal allotments. The Millennium is only a beginning, sort of a microcosm, of the eternal state and a transition into it. Consequently, to observe reflections of Ezekiel 40–48 in the picture of the eternal state revealed in Revelation 21–22 should be expected and should not surprise the reader.

Is Not the Existence of a Temple, Priests, and a Sacrificial System a Retrogression to OT Modes of Worship?

As previously stated, a normal grammatical-historical hermeneutic should be used when interpreting the Book of Ezekiel. In doing so, a real temple, real sacrifices, and real priests are observed functioning in the millennial context. When the sacrifices and priestly functions are closely examined, it becomes evident that they are Mosaic in nature, though omissions and modifications are present. Such an observation may cause concern since the reinstitution of a Mosaic worship system may seem contrary to NT teaching. The NT states that Jesus Christ died once and for all on the cross for all sin. There is no need for a further sacrifice for sin. Likewise, the Lord's Table is designed to bring remembrance of the Lord's death to the worshipers. Why go back to OT modes of worship set forth under the old covenant when the new covenant has been instituted?

An examination of Ezekiel's purpose, especially in this section, combined with a comparison of the Levitical worship concepts with that of Ezekiel and of the NT will help us solve some of these dilemmas. Ezekiel was a priest; thus he frequently looked on issues in his prophecy from a priestly perspective. He would be expected to view the new worship principles from his vantage point with a temple, sacrifices, and priests involved. Likewise, God normally reveals himself in terms of the culture and perspective of those receiving his revelation. Such could be expected here.

The recipients of this vision are described as "the house of Israel." This terminology is used by Ezekiel to describe Israel at any time in her existence—past, present, or future. Old Testament apocalyptic literature, as found in these chapters, was to be a source of hope and encouragement in a time of discouragement. Revelation that a temple would be rebuilt in the messianic kindgom to which God's glory would return and in which the nation would worship the Lord as he had commanded would surely be an encouragement of hope. Should not the description of worship in the messianic kingdom be in terms both understandable to Israel as well as in keeping with the covenant worship of her God?

In Ezekiel 37:15–28 all the covenants given to Israel would be fulfilled at the time of her restoration to the Promised Land and the institution of the messianic kingdom. This includes the Abrahamic covenant, Davidic covenant, new covenant, peace covenant, *and the Mosaic covenant*. The covenant formula of the Mosaic covenant—"they will be my people, and I will be their God"—will be operative as Israel walks in the stipulations of the Mosaic covenant, cleansed under the new covenant, and experiencing the eternal reign of her king, the Messiah, under the Davidic covenant (37:23–26; cf. Exod 19:5–6; Lev 26:12; Deut 26:18–19; Jer 30:18–22; 31:33; 32:36–40). Because Israel was in a relationship with God through the Abrahamic and Mosaic covenants, she had always been expected to worship the Lord in holiness. Her entire worship procedure was designed to point her to God's holiness and to her need to be holy before him (cf. Lev). The basic emphasis throughout Ezekiel 40–48 is on God's holiness. The holiness of the Lord's temple and the worship of him are contrasted with the profaning of his name and his temple in Israel's past worship. Israel would have a final opportunity to worship God correctly—in the purity of holiness. Such worship would demonstrate that Israel had truly been redeemed and cleansed.

Ezekiel 40–48 presents only the Hebrew perspective of millennial worship. This does not preclude other worship forms from also existing and being carried out (cf. Luke 22:18). The manifestations and functions of all God's covenants do not contradict but rather complement one another. Therefore Israel will finally be a people of God, living and worshiping in the holiness revealed in the Mosaic stipulations. The omissions and modifications from the Mosaic system observed in Ezekiel 40–48 are undoubtedly present to enable the various aspects of the different covenants to harmonize.

One difficulty sensed by many is the need for and the purpose of a temple. Is not the presence of a temple anachronistic? However, the existence of a temple as a place of worship would be the normal concept from an OT perspective (cf. 2 Sam 7:12–16; 1 Kings 9:3; 2 Chron 6:14–7:16; 29:1–30:27; Ps 132). Likewise, without a temple complex sacrifices could not be offered properly. Therefore the temple would be necessary for worship (Ezek 43–46).

Ezekiel sets forth two major purposes for the millennial temple. First, the temple will provide a throne for God among his people (43:6–7), the residency of his glory (43:1–12) from which he will rule over his people. Second, the temple complex will reflect God's holiness by its walls of separation, various courts, and temple divisions (40:5; 42:14–20). The design of the structure will cause the people of that day to be ashamed of their iniquities. Therefore a temple structure should not prevent or hinder other worship forms that may exist in the Millennium (e.g., the Lord's Table) unless one divides the periods of God's working so that only certain architectural forms can be used for the worship of God at a given time, which does not seem biblical. There have been a variety of structures in which Christians worship in the church age. There seems to be no scriptural concept that would forbid a Christian from worshiping in a temple built to almighty God. A temple, in and of itself, does not appear to be anachronistic.

A second major difficulty is the relationship between Ezekiel's sacrificial system and the NT teaching of Christ's death as a finished and complete work for sin. Can the two be harmonized, or are they contradictory? In order to understand the issues, Ezekiel's millennial sacrificial system must be described. In doing so, a comparison will be made to the Mosaic system. It will be observed that almost all aspects of the Ezekiel system are identical with Mosaic procedure. It is primarily the omissions, with some modifications in keeping with the purpose of Ezekiel's worship, that compose the differences.

Though the general phrase "all the appointed feasts of the house of Israel" is used in 45:17, only three festivals are explicitly mentioned in these chapters: Passover and the Feast of Unleavened Bread, the Feast of Tabernacles, and, by implication, the Feast of Firstfruits. Passover (45:21–24) began on the fourteenth day of the first month (Nisan), and the people were to eat unleavened bread for seven days (cf. Exod 12:1–30; Num 28:16–25). The "leader" (*nāśîʾ*) offered a sin offering each day along with a grain offering for himself and for the people of the land (cf. Num 28:22–24). Daily the leader also offered a burnt offering with its grain offering (cf. Num 28:19–21, 23–24). These items parallel those in the Levitical system. Likewise, Ezekiel declared that the same offerings as those made for Passover would be made for the Feast of Tabernacles for a similar length of time (Ezek 45:25). Numbers 29:12–38 only differs by adding a daily drink offering. This festival began on the fifteenth day of the seventh month and lasted for seven days, as prescribed in the Mosaic system. In addition, Ezekiel 44:30 states that "the best of all of the firstfruits . . . will belong to the priests." This does not necessarily imply a Feast of Firstfruits but is the only mention of the idea of firstfruits in the Ezekiel system.

The offerings and sacrifices to be used in worship and consecration of the temple make up most of the Ezekiel system. In addition to the offerings of the various festivals, the Israelites would be required to offer daily to God burnt offerings with their accompanying grain offering in the morning (cf. Exod 29:38–42; Lev 6:12; Num 28:3–7). The Mosaic procedure required this offering daily, both in the morning *and* in the evening, along with a drink offering. Offerings on the Sabbaths, new moons, and all appointed festivals would include the burnt offering, grain offering, and drink offering in Ezekiel's worship (45:17; cf. Lev 23:37; Num 28:9–15). Only on the observance of new moons did the Mosaic list add the sin offering. Ezekiel also declared that the priests were to sacrifice for the leader a burnt offering and a fellowship offering on both the Sabbath and the new moon (46:2–7; Num 29:39). The leader may also offer a freewill burnt offering and fellowship offerings on the Sabbath (46:12).

Ezekiel's temple is purified ("atoned for") on the first and seventh days of the first month (of each year?) with a sin offering (45:18–20). Similar procedures are outlined in the Mosaic system but with the addition of burnt offerings and fellowship offerings (cf. Num 7:87–89; 2 Chron 7:1–10; 29:20–24). When the altar of burnt sacrifice is built, it would be cleansed, consecrated, and dedicated for seven days with both burnt offerings and sin offerings (43:18–25; cf. Exod 29:36–37; Lev 7:14). After the seven days, the altar may be used for regular offerings (43:27). This passage is silent concerning whether the altar's cleansing and consecration are to be repeated. Finally, Israel will make a special contribution of grains, oil, and animals for the leader to use in the regular atonement for the house of Israel (45:15–17; cf. Lev 9:17–24). The atonement offerings are the sin offering, grain offering, burnt offering, and fellowship offering. No time is specified as to how often or when such atonement is to be made.

The priesthood in Ezekiel is composed of the Levites as helpers in the maintenance, administration, and function of temple worship; but those of the Zadok line will be the only ones permitted to minister before the Lord with the most holy things (44:5–16). The other Levites are denied this privilege due to their past unfaithfulness in carrying out the duties of the sanctuary. There is no high priest. The only stated priestly functions are the slaughter, washing, cooking, and eating of various sacrifices (40:38–42; 42:13; 44:29; 46:20; cf. Lev 7:7; Num 18:8–10).

Therefore, most stated aspects of the worship procedure in Ezekiel are like those of the Mosaic system. The major distinctions include the absence of a Day of Atonement, an ark of the covenant, the Feast of Weeks (or Pentecost), a high priest, and a full, ministering Levitical priesthood. These are, of course, distinctive omissions. The absence of the Day of Atonement and the ark of the covenant where the atoning blood was sprinkled may stress the fact that the work of propitiation has already been accomplished. Being an argument from silence, however, it is difficult to be certain or to make any significant argument. It would seem that if these items were to have been included in the millennial system of Ezekiel, they would have been mentioned since they were extremely important factors in the Mosaic system. The lack of a high priest may point to the high priesthood of Jesus Christ, who will be ruling in the Millennium (Heb 4:14–5:10; 7:11–8:13).

Therefore, the millennial worship system is distinctly different from the Mosaic system only in that certain Mosaic elements are omitted or modified, most likely because of Christ's finished work on the cross. It is important to observe that millennial sacrifices are discussed elsewhere in the OT prophets (Isa 56:5–7; 60:7, 13; 66:20–23; Jer 33:15–22; Zech 14:16–21). The concept is not unique to Ezekiel.

The question whether these sacrifices are efficacious is crucial. It is important to remember that the Mosaic covenant was given to a people who had already entered into a relationship with the Lord in the Abrahamic covenant. The Mosaic covenant was not given to bring one into a relationship with God but to demonstrate how one in that relationship was to live holy before him. True worship grows out of a personal relationship with God.

The Mosaic worship system, therefore, was to be used by those in a relationship with God. Never did the sacrifices and offerings deliver one from sin. They were never efficacious for the Israelite or anyone else. Rather, the sacrifices were picture lessons and types of the Messiah's work whereby he would atone for all sin in a propitious manner through the sacrifice of his own blood once and for all. The sin and guilt (compensation) offerings were reminders of one's personal inherent sin and the need for cleansing from that sinfulness by the shedding of innocent blood. These offerings were observed much in the sense in which a believer today confesses his sin (1 John 1:9) in light of the finished work of Christ for sin. The believers' confession is not efficacious. It is only Christ's finished work that provides forgiveness of sin. Confession, however, reminds the believer that he has sinned and that the sin has been forgiven by Christ's blood. The sin and guilt offerings, therefore, reminded the Israelite that he was sinful and that he needed the Messiah's innocent blood, typified in the animal, to cleanse him of his sin and to bring forgiveness from God.

The burnt offering pictured the offerers' commitment to the Lord. It was voluntary, even as commitment is today. The burnt offerings required daily and at other festivals were constant reminders that the Israelites needed to be totally committed to their Lord.

The fellowship offerings reflected the offerers' thanksgiving to God and the peace that existed between them and God. Certainly believers today are to express their thankfulness to God for the various blessings bestowed on them because of their relationship with the Lord.

The sacrifices of the Mosaic system were never efficacious. Only the sacrifice of Jesus Christ was efficacious. The offerings of the Levitical system were continual picture lessons and types of the work the Messiah would accomplish and the holy manner in which the Israelites were to walk.

The concept of atonement creates a major problem for many with the sacrificial system in Ezekiel. The etymology of "atonement" and its original meaning are uncertain. Either the verb derives from a root similar to the Assyrian verb *kuppuru* ("to cleanse," "wipe away"), or it comes from the Hebrew and Arabic root *kōper* ("paying a ransom," "to cover"). The Hebrew verb means "to atone by offering a substitute," which is "always used in connection with the removal of sin or defilement" (TWOT, 1:452–53). When a sacrifice for atonement was brought in the Mosaic system, it was brought because God required it, not because of the initiative of the offerer (Lev 10). It was God alone who gave forgiveness and cleansing, not the act of sacrifice. The basis for forgiveness and cleansing was the ultimate work of the Messiah's innocent blood that was the ransom for the penalty of death owed by the sinner. The sacrificial animal could not offer an efficacious ransom; rather, the atonement sacrifice was only a picture lesson of Christ's finished work (cf. Kaiser, *OT Theology*, pp. 117–18).

All mentions of "atonement" in Ezekiel 40–48 relate to the concept of purification or consecration of the temple or altar with the exception of two references. Exodus 29:44–45a and 40:9–16 recount the anointing and consecration of the temple, the altar, and the priests after the construction of the temple (cf. Lev 8; 9:7–24). The Solomonic dedication is observed in 1 Kings 8:62–66. Most of the occurrences of the word *kāpar* ("to atone") in Ezekiel 40–48 refer to such dedications, consecrations, and purification of the millennial temple and altar. The atonement of the people is mentioned in only 45:15–17. There the concept would be the same as that in the Mosaic system: a picture lesson of the ultimate atoning work of Christ when he would pay the ransom price of his blood to atone for sin and provide forgiveness of sin once and for all.

The Mosaic Day of Atonement for sin (cf. Lev 16:21–22, 30, 34) occurred annually in OT times, but it would not be observed in the Millennium. However, sin would still occur in the Millennium among the house of Israel, people who had natural bodies with a sin nature. Therefore the atonement offerings for the leader and the people would be a marvelous picture lesson and reminder of the work that the Messiah accomplished on the cross to enable their sin to be forgiven. It would also remind them that they were sinful people who needed that redemption provided through the innocent blood of Christ. But the sacrifices in Ezekiel are memorials of Christ's work even as the Mosaic sacrifices were picture lessons and types of the work he would do. Neither is efficacious.

The writer of Hebrews in chapters 7–10 discusses the relationship between the Mosaic sacrifices and the work of Christ. It is instructive to examine these chapters for they confirm the argument stated above. The law required that nearly everything be cleansed with blood, and without the shedding of blood there was no forgiveness (Heb 9:21–22). This is observed in both the Mosaic and the Ezekiel systems of atonement. But the elements of the tabernacle (temple) and its furnishings were only copies of heavenly things (Heb 9:23); and though they needed to be purified with sacrifices, the real need of purification would be made by Christ's sacrifice, of which these things were only copies (Heb 9:24–28). These aspects of the Mosaic covenant were only a shadow (a picture) of the things that were coming. They were not the reality itself (Heb 10:1). Because the Mosaic covenant dealt here in shadows, the Mosaic system could never make its worshipers perfect through the repeated sacrifices that never could take away sin (Heb 10:2–4, 11). The sacrifices cleansed only outwardly as a picture (Heb 9:11–14). Jesus inwardly cleanses our consciences from the sinful acts that lead to death (Heb 10:8–14). If the Mosaic sacrifices could have cleansed its worshipers and made them perfect, those sacrifices would have stopped once and for all. But they could not cleanse (Heb 10:2). Therefore they were continued as regular reminders of sin, because it was impossible for the blood of animals to take away sin. Jesus offered himself once for the sins of mankind. The reality of the pictures had come, even as promised in the new covenant (Heb 7:27).

The writer of Hebrews goes on to say that where sins have been forgiven, there is no longer any sacrifice for sin. Understood in the context of Hebrews described above, there is no longer the need for the picture lessons and reminders now that the reality of Christ's efficacious blood sacrifice has been offered once and for all. No other efficacious sacrifice could be offered because only Christ's sacrifice of himself is efficacious. However, the writer of Hebrews does not declare that pictorial sacrifices and festivals absolutely can no longer be observed as reminders and picture lessons of what Christ did after his singularly efficacious sacrifice has been completed. Since the sacrifices and festivals in the OT system were only pictures, they could never conflict with the sacrifice of the Messiah. They never were and never could be efficacious.

Likewise, the sacrifices in the millennial system described by Ezekiel are only picture lessons and reminders of the sin of man and of the only efficacious sacrifice for sin once and for all made by Christ. The millennial sacrifices will be both reminders to believers in millennial worship and picture lessons to unbelievers born in the Millennium. (These "unbelievers" could be born from the Jews who enter the Millennium from the tribulation period.) On the basis of the OT role of the sacrifices and the argument of the writer of Hebrews, it does not appear that the pictorial sacrifices of the Mosaic system nor the memorial sacrifices of the millennial worship conflict with the finished and complete work of Jesus' sacrifice for all sins once and for all on the cross.

Consequently, the sacrifices in the millennial sacrificial system of Ezekiel appear to be only memorials of Christ's finished work and pictorial reminders that mankind by nature is sinful and in need of redemption from sin. Not only is this view substantiated by comparison with the Mosaic covenant in which the sacrifices were picture lessons and types, but it is also confirmed by the writer of Hebrews as observed above.

In addition, the very observances of the Lord's Table is an argument in favor of this memorial view. The Lord's Table is itself a memorial of Christ's death. The observance of the Lord's Table is not a substitute for Christ's death and does not in that sense conflict with the finished work of Christ. As a memorial, the Lord's Table will apparently be celebrated with Christ present in the messianic kingdom (Millennium) when Christ returns (Matt 26:29; Mark 14:25; Luke 22:18). If the Lord's Table is a memorial and the sacrifices of the Ezekiel system are memorials, the two should not in any way conflict with each other but should be able to coexist. One, of course, may ask why both need to be observed if they perform the same role. It would seem that the Lord's Table is the primary memorial to those believers of the church age while the sacrifices in Ezekiel would be the primary commemoration of the Jews, though nothing would certainly prohibit *any* of the singular people of God—Jews or Gentiles—from participating in the worship of either memorial.

Therefore, the purposes of the sacrificial system in Ezekiel's worship procedure can be stated. The sacrificial system will be used as picture lessons to demonstrate the need for holiness in the consecration and purifying of the temple and the altar. They will be visual reminders of man's sinfulness and his need for redemption while at the same time being pictorial memorials of the finished and completed sacrifice of the Messiah who provided atonement for mankind once and for all. The pictures of a holy life and the need for continual commitment to the Messiah's lordship will be demonstrated in the regular burnt offerings. Thanksgiving to God will be visually expressed in the fellowship offerings. In addition, the sacrifices will provide food for the millennial priests even as it did for the Mosaic priests (44:29–31).

Priests will be necessary in the millennial worship-system to conduct the sacrifices for the leader and the people. In addition priests will carry out all the necessary ministries of the temple. The main role of the priests, however, will be to demonstrate to everyone in the Millennium the distinction between the holy and the profane (Ezek 44).

How will the Gentiles and the church relate to this worship system with its OT modes? As noted above, nothing prohibits a Gentile or a church believer from joining the worship in commemoration of Christ's finished work. In addition, the church will also celebrate the Lord's Table. All these reminders of Christ's great work of redemption will be a constant avenue of worship for all the people of God who desire to worship the Lord (cf. Eph 2:14–16). Even in our day we see the spiritual value and great avenue of worship for church believers as they celebrate the Passover service (cf. Rom 15:14; 1 Cor 10:1–12). It does not enter their minds that they are saved by the observance of this service; but the celebration is an extremely instructive, vivid picture lesson of the death of the Lamb of God. Likewise, those who have witnessed the slaughter of lambs for the Samaritan Passover in Israel could never again look lightly on the death of the Lamb of God. As believers, they would not in any way today think that one of those slaughtered lambs was the efficacious provision for their sins, but they would go away praising and glorifying God with thanksgiving for the marvelous sacrifice of the Messiah as a substitute for themselves. That is what will occur in the millennial worship as these memorial sacrifices and the Lord's Table are observed.

A Summary of the Argument of Ezekiel 40–48

Thirteen years had past since Ezekiel had encouraged the exiles with the six messages of restoration hope (33:21–39:29). Then, through an apocalyptic vision, Ezekiel would give a final encouragement by describing the nature of the messianic kingdom. This vision would be the culmination of the book and reveal the climax of God's working with Israel throughout history. God would establish Israel as a holy nation to worship him and demonstrate his person. When God originally created Israel, three elements were essential for her existence: a people, a government, and a homeland. When God reestablishes Israel as a nation in the messianic kingdom, these same three elements must exist. God would regather the people through the great restoration described in chapters 34–37. Then he would give Israel her new government (guidelines for living) and establish her in her Promised Land forever (chs. 40–48).

The reestablishment of Israel's government is described in chapters 40–46. The center of her new life would be the Lord himself who would return in glory to rule in her midst (43:1–9). The need for a residence for God's glory would be fulfilled in the construction of the millennial temple described in detail in chapters 40–42. Here God would reign with the temple as his throne (43:7), just as he had done previously in the tabernacle and then the temple. The regulations in 43:13–46:24 describe how the priests, leaders, and the people were to live holy lives. Requirements and functions were outlined; and Israel was charged to perform these regulations in an unerring manner, thereby demonstrating God's holiness (43:10–11; 44:5–8).

The description of Israel's restoration to her Promised Land is given in chapter 36. Then in chapter 47–48 the Lord demonstrates how he would continually heal, bless, and refresh the land in its perfect state through the river of life (47:1–12; cf. Gen 2:8–10; Rev 22:1–3). Tribal borders would be established; and land would be set aside for the priests, leader, city, and the sanctuary. With Israel reestablished in the land of blessing, the Lord would reaffirm his eternal presence with them in a new name for the city (Jerusalem): *Yahweh šāmmāh* ("THE LORD IS THERE") (48:35). The Lord would be there forever!

1. The setting of the apocalyptic vision

40:1–4

¹In the twenty-fifth year of our exile, at the beginning of the year, on the tenth of the month, in the fourteenth year after the fall of the city—on that very day the hand of the LORD was upon me and he took me there. ²In visions of God he took me to the land of Israel and set me on a very high mountain, on whose south side were some buildings that looked like a city. ³He took me there, and I saw a man

whose appearance was like bronze; he was standing in the gateway with a linen cord and a measuring rod in his hand. ⁴The man said to me, "Son of man, look with your eyes and hear with your ears and pay attention to everything I am going to show you, for that is why you have been brought here. Tell the house of Israel everything you see."

1–4 There are four essential elements in the literary setting of an apocalyptic vision: the date, the identity of the vision's recipient, the location of the vision's recipient, and noteworthy circumstances under which the vision was received.

The date of this apocalyptic vision has four aspects. First, Ezekiel expressed the date in terms of his normal calendrical system (v. 1). Ezekiel has dated all the major sections of the book in reference to Jehoiachin's deportation into Babylonian exile: 597 B.C. (cf. chronological discussions at 1:1–3). This vision was received in the twenty-fifth year of Jehoiachin's captivity, or in 573 B.C.

Second, the vision was received in the first of the year, or the first month of the year. Israel had two different annual calendars. The civil calendar began in the fall month of Tishri (September/October). The religious calendar began in the spring month of Nisan (March/April). Some expositors prefer the civil calendar while others accept the religious calendar. Though the text is not explicit in this matter, the religious calendar would seem preferable since Ezekiel was a priest and the concerns of the apocalyptic vision relate to religious matters. If so, the date would be more explicitly March/April 573 B.C.

The vision was received on the tenth day of the month. If it is correct to designate the month as Nisan, then this apocalyptic vision would have been received on the tenth day of Nisan, the very day the people may have begun to prepare for the Passover four days later. Whether they actually observed the Passover or not in exile, surely they would be contemplating Israel's redemption out of Egypt and the creation of their nation. This vision, then, would be an encouragement that the Lord would complete his purposes for the nation in the messianic kingdom.

Finally, the vision was received in the fourteenth year after Jerusalem fell to the Babylonians, in 586 B.C. This also would corroborate the date of 573 B.C.

The second major element of the setting of an apocalyptic vision is the identity of the vision's recipient. Though Ezekiel's name is not given in these verses, the copious use of the first person pronoun in light of the context of the entire book would certainly argue strongly that the recipient was Ezekiel.

The third aspect of the setting of this vision is the location in which it was received. Ezekiel saw the vision from a very high mountain in Israel (v.2). From that mountain he could see a city to the south. Neither the mountain nor the city is identified in the passage. However, Ezekiel was taken into the city where he then saw the temple's construction in detail. In light of the geography of Ezekiel's day, one would conceive that the city was most likely Jerusalem. To identify a very high mountain to the north of Jerusalem, however, would not be possible in light of the geography of Ezekiel's day or ours. Perhaps it would be best to leave the city and the mountain unidentified.

The final aspect of a literary setting of an apocalyptic vision is the noteworthy circumstances under which the vision was received (vv.3–4). A divine messenger with the appearance of bronze was present. He was carrying both a measuring rod and a linen measuring cord. He exhorted Ezekiel to pay careful attention to all that he would be shown, because this vision was being given to him so that he might tell it in detail to the "house of Israel."

Notes

2 מִנֶּגֶב (*minnegeb*, "on the south") is rendered in the LXX by ἀπέναντι (*apenanti*, "opposite"). This rendering would assume a Hebrew text of נֶגֶד (*neged*, "opposite"). The Hebrew letters ב (*b*) and ד (*d*) have reflected similar orthography throughout much of the history of the Hebrew language. This might account for a copyist's error. It would seem best to keep the MT form.

2. The apocalyptic vision (40:5–48:35)

The vision has four basic segments that are primarily noted by the differences of subject matter: (1) the description of the millennial temple (40:5–42:20); (2) the return of God's glory to the temple (43:1–9); (3) the temple regulations (43:10–46:24); and (4) the topographical aspects of the Millennium (47:1–48:35).

a. The millennial temple (40:5–42:20)

A divine messenger guided Ezekiel through the temple complex, beginning on the outside and working gradually inward through the outer and inner courts to the temple sanctuary. He provided an abundance of details, especially dimensions. These plans and specific dimensions are accurate enough to enable plans to be drawn and models to be constructed with a fair degree of accuracy. First, floor plans were revealed. Any superstructure must be conjectured to a great degree. Such specific details and plans do argue for the literalness of this temple and its proposed construction. It would be helpful to the reader to refer constantly to the enclosed diagrams of the temple complex, the outer gate system, the plan of the sanctuary, and the design of the altar of sacrifice as the text is read.

1) The outer court

40:5–27

> [5]I saw a wall completely surrounding the temple area. The length of the measuring rod in the man's hand was six long cubits, each of which was a cubit and a handbreadth. He measured the wall; it was one measuring rod thick and one rod high.
> [6]Then he went to the gate facing east. He climbed its steps and measured the threshold of the gate; it was one rod deep. [7]The alcoves for the guards were one rod long and one rod wide, and the projecting walls between the alcoves were five cubits thick. And the threshold of the gate next to the portico facing the temple was one rod deep.
> [8]Then he measured the portico of the gateway; [9]it was eight cubits deep and its jambs were two cubits thick. The portico of the gateway faced the temple.
> [10]Inside the east gate were three alcoves on each side; the three had the same measurements, and the faces of the projecting walls on each side had the same measurements. [11]Then he measured the width of the entrance to the gateway; it was ten cubits and its length was thirteen cubits. [12]In front of each alcove was a wall one cubit high, and the alcoves were six cubits square. [13]Then he measured

the gateway from the top of the rear wall of one alcove to the top of the opposite one; the distance was twenty-five cubits from one parapet opening to the opposite one. [14]He measured along the faces of the projecting walls all around the inside of the gateway—sixty cubits. The measurement was up to the portico facing the courtyard. [15]The distance from the entrance of the gateway to the far end of its portico was fifty cubits. [16]The alcoves and the projecting walls inside the gateway were surmounted by narrow parapet openings all around, as was the portico; the openings all around faced inward. The faces of the projecting wall were decorated with palm trees.

[17]Then he brought me into the outer court. There I saw some rooms and a pavement that had been constructed all around the court; there were thirty rooms along the pavement. [18]It abutted the sides of the gateways and was as wide as they were long; this was the lower pavement. [19]Then he measured the distance from the inside of the lower gateway to the outside of the inner court; it was a hundred cubits on the east side as well as on the north.

[20]Then he measured the length and width of the gate facing north, leading into the outer court. [21]Its alcoves—three on each side—its projecting walls and its portico had the same measurements as those of the first gateway. It was fifty cubits long and twenty-five cubits wide. [22]Its openings, its portico and its palm tree decorations had the same measurements as those of the gate facing east. Seven steps led up to it, with its portico opposite them. [23]There was a gate to the inner court facing the north gate, just as there was on the east. He measured from one gate to the opposite one; it was a hundred cubits.

[24]Then he led me to the south side and I saw a gate facing south. He measured its jambs and its portico, and they had the same measurements as the others. [25]The gateway and its portico had narrow openings all around, like the openings of the others. It was fifty cubits long and twenty-five cubits wide. [26]Seven steps led up to it, with its portico opposite them; it had palm tree decorations on the faces of the projecting walls on each side. [27]The inner court also had a gate facing south, and he measured from this gate to the outer gate on the south side; it was a hundred cubits.

5 As the temple was measured, many dimensions were given in chapters 40–42. The cubit was the standard of measurement, but the length of the cubit was not as exact as one might prefer. Many have sought to determine more accurately the linear measurements of the Scripture. Archaeological data, however, has been sparse. Moreover, the linear measurements of the ancient Near East were based on the parts of the body that, of course, vary from person to person. The normal cubit was the distance between the tip of the middle finger to the tip of the elbow. On the average person this distance was approximately eighteen inches. The handbreadth was the measurement of the hand's width at the base of the fingers. This normally measured about three inches. In addition there were long cubit measurements and short cubit measurements in different countries and in the same country at different time periods in the ancient Near East. Precision, therefore, is impossible in light of the nature of the measurement and the limitation of the data. For the purposes of measurement in chapters 40–42, it seems best to take the *normal* cubit length of approximately eighteen inches.

The divine messenger who guided Ezekiel carried a measuring rod six cubits long. The long cubit was composed of one normal cubit plus a handbreadth, or eighteen plus three inches. Therefore, since the measurements in this portion of Ezekiel were made with this measuring rod, it will be assumed that the "cubit" in Ezekiel was normally the "long cubit" of twenty-one inches. A table of measurement equivalents follows.

Measurement Equivalents

(Based on a cubit of approximately 21 inches)
1 palm   c. 3 inches (equals 1/6 cubit)
1 cubit   c. 1.75 feet (21 inches)
1 rod   c. 10.50 feet (or 6 cubits)

The examination of the temple complex began on the outside where the messenger showed Ezekiel a wall that completely surrounded the complex. The wall was one rod high and one rod wide, or six long cubits for each dimension—approximately ten and one-half feet.

6–16 Ezekiel was taken to the eastern outer gate of the temple complex (v.6). The divine messenger explained the gate's design and its dimensions in detail. The description began from the outside of the gate and worked inward. All the terminology is not clear in the Hebrew language since some words are used only in this context. Therefore, the exact meaning of each item and the corresponding relationship of each dimension cannot always be certain. However, there is sufficient clarity to give a fairly good account of the plan of the gate system and to enable a basic diagram (cf. fig. 1). It will aid the student to look at the attached diagram while reading this portion of the text. The capital letters following an item in the description below refer to the corresponding item in the diagram.

The gate was composed of seven steps (E) that led up to the gate from the outside. Perhaps these steps were the equivalent of the "entrance" mentioned in v.11. If so, the entrance steps measured ten cubits wide and thirteen cubits long. The north and south outer gates have the identical dimensions of the east gate (cf. vv.20–27).

The gate's outer threshold (OT) measured ten cubits wide (v.11) and six cubits deep (v.6). The entire gate system resembled the multiple entry gates archaeologists discovered from the Solomonic period. There were several guard rooms (cf. 1 Kings 24:28; 2 Chron 12:11), or alcoves, on either side of the inner part of the Solomonic gate. In this gate there were three alcoves (A) on either side of the inside of the gate, each six cubits square (vv.7a, 10, 12b) with a wall (FW) one cubit high in front of each (v.12a). The dimension of the walls (S) separating the three inner alcoves was five cubits (v.7b). The gate's inner threshold (IT) was one rod deep (six cubits) like the outer threshold (v.7c).

A portico (P), or vestibule, on the inside of the gate faced the courtyard. It was eight cubits wide with a two-cubit door jamb facing the temple (vv.8–9). Verse 14 could be understood to give the total dimensions of the portico if all sides (both widths and both lengths) were measured. There would be a total of sixty cubits (eight cubits wide by twenty-two cubits long). On the other hand, if *'êlîm* ("projecting walls," "porticoes") be taken to mean door jambs or pilasters, the sixty cubits could be the height of each door jamb of each gate. There were windows, or parapet openings (O), in each alcove and in the portico; but the number and exact location of each is uncertain (v.16). The diagram only gives an example. The only decoration mentioned were palm tree designs that were found on the inner walls of the alcoves and/or on the door jambs of the portico.

The overall dimensions of the gate system were twenty-five cubits wide by fifty cubits long (vv.13, 15).

Figure 1

Gate Systems for all Gates
of the Outer Court

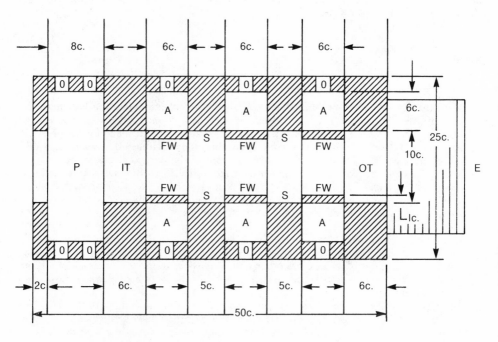

Key:

FW Wall (barriers, borders, space) (Ezek 40:12a)
A   Alcoves (side rooms, guard rooms) (Ezek 40:7a, 10a, 12b)
P   Portico (porch, vestibule) (Ezek 40:7c, 8–9, 14)
S   Walls separating alcoves (Ezek 40:7b, 10b)
OT Outer threshold of the gate (Ezek 40:6, 11)
IT Inner threshold of the porch (Ezek 40:7c)
O   Windows (parapet openings) (Ezek 40:16)
E   Steps (Ezek 40:6b, 22b, 26a)

Overall height, length, and width of the gate (Ezek 40:13–15)

17–19 As the reader examines the outer courtyard, compare figure 2. The courtyard had a pavement strip (LP) the width of the east gate's length: fifty cubits. The pavement formed a border all around the outside edges of the outer court and was known as the lower pavement. Thirty rooms (R) were on this pavement around the outer court. The diagram only places these rooms equally on all three sides, but the actual arrangement is not given in the text (vv. 17–18). The dimension of the outer courtyard from the inside of the outer eastern gate to the inner eastern gate was said to be one hundred cubits (v. 19). The same dimension separated the north and south outer gate systems from their corresponding inner gates (40:23, 27).

20–27 The outer northern and southern gate systems were exactly identical with the outer eastern gate (cf. vv. 6–16).

Notes

8 More than twenty Hebrew MSS, the Syriac, and the Vulgate delete the last three Hebrew words—מֵהַבַּיִת קָנֶה אֶחָד (mēhabbayit qāneh 'eḥād, "from the house," "one rod")—from this verse. Most feel that this is a case of dittography from the end of v. 7 (where NIV has "one rod deep"). If the MT is allowed to stand, the six-cubit rod measurement does not make sense in light of the other measurements of the portico given in v. 9.

14 The meaning of this entire verse is uncertain due primarily to the uncertain meaning of the word אַיִל ('ayil, "projecting wall"). In v. 9 it appears to mean "door jamb," but in vv. 10, 16 it seems to mean "a face of a projecting wall." In addition, it is not clear which specific wall or jamb would be meant when the dimension of sixty cubits is given in this verse. As implied in the commentary, perhaps the term אֵילִים ('êlîm, "projecting walls"?) in this verse refers to the total dimensions of the portico or to the height of the door jambs (pilasters). This is primarily conjectured due to the sum of the wall sides in the portico equaling the number sixty whereas other wall dimensions in the gate system do not total sixty. If the meaning "door jamb" (pilasters) is held, the sixty cubits would most likely indicate the height.

15 The term הָיָאתוֹן (hāy'itôn, "entrance") is obscure. The Qere reading is אִיתוֹן ('itôn, "entrance"; BDB, s.v.), which is derived from rearranging the letters and which makes good sense in the verse. In addition, more than twenty Hebrew MSS, the Vulgate, and the LXX would agree with the Qere reading.

2) The inner court

40:28–47

28Then he brought me into the inner court through the south gate, and he measured the south gate; it had the same measurements as the others. 29Its alcoves, its projecting walls and its portico had the same measurements as the others. The gateway and its portico had openings all around. It was fifty cubits long and twenty-five cubits wide. 30(The porticoes of the gateways around the inner court were twenty-five cubits wide and five cubits deep.) 31Its portico faced the outer court; palm trees decorated its jambs, and eight steps led up to it.

32Then he brought me to the inner court on the east side, and he measured the gateway; it had the same measurements as the others. 33Its alcoves, its projecting walls and its portico had the same measurements as the others. The gateway and its portico had openings all around. It was fifty cubits long and twenty-five cubits wide. [34]Its portico faced the inner court; palm trees decorated the jambs on either side, and eight steps led up to it.

[35]Then he brought me to the north gate and measured it. It had the same measurements as the others, [36]as did its alcoves, its projecting walls and its portico, and it had openings all around. It was fifty cubits long and twenty-five cubits wide. [37]Its portico faced the outer court; palm trees decorated the jambs on either side, and eight steps led up to it.

[38]A room with a doorway was by the portico in each of the inner gateways, where the burnt offerings were washed. [39]In the portico of the gateway were two tables on each side, on which the burnt offerings, sin offerings and guilt offerings were slaughtered. [40]By the outside wall of the portico of the gateway, near the steps at the entrance to the north gateway were two tables, and on the other side of the steps were two tables. [41]So there were four tables on one side of the gateway and four on the other—eight tables in all—on which the sacrifices were slaughtered. [42]There were also four tables of dressed stone for the burnt offerings, each a cubit and a half long, a cubit and a half wide and a cubit high. On them were placed the utensils for slaughtering the burnt offerings and the other sacrifices. [43]And double-pronged hooks, each a hand-breadth long, were attached to the wall all around. The tables were for the flesh of the offerings.

[44]Outside the inner gate, within the inner court, were two rooms, one at the side of the north gate and facing south, and another at the side of the south gate and facing north. [45]He said to me, "The room facing south is for the priests who have charge of the temple, [46]and the room facing north is for the priests who have charge of the altar. These are the sons of Zadok, who are the only Levites who may draw near to the Lord to minister before him."

[47]Then he measured the court: It was square—a hundred cubits long and a hundred cubits wide. And the altar was in front of the temple.

28–37 In the examination of the inner court, the guide first discussed the gates, then the rooms for preparation of the sacrifices, next the rooms for the ministering priests, and last the general dimension and character of the inner court.

The guide showed the three gates to the inner court to Ezekiel in a counterclockwise direction, beginning at the south gate. Each of these gates was identical in its dimensions and basic design with the three gates of the outer court (cf. vv.28–29, 32–33, 35–36). Two distinct alterations were made in the inner gate design over that of the outer gate. All inner gates had their porticoes facing outward toward the outer court rather than on the inside (vv.31, 34, 37). In addition, each stairway leading up to an inner gate system had eight steps rather than seven. Verse 30 indicates that the portico dimensions of the inner gates was five cubits by twenty-five cubits. However, this dimension does not harmonize with the dimensions of the porticoes in the outer gates (cf. vv.8–9, 14); and the text states that the dimensions were the same between the inner and outer gate systems, excluding the two exceptions just mentioned. Perhaps the best solution is to say that the dimensions of the portico of the inner gates varies slightly with that of the outer gates as a third modification.

38–43 As Ezekiel and the divine messenger were standing beside the northern inner gate system, the messenger described the rooms (W) and tables (T) to be used for the preparation of the sacrifices. There was a room located beside the door jamb outside each inner court gate. This means each room (W) was in the outer courtyard beside the stairs leading up to the portico of the inner gate. Here the burnt offerings were to be washed for ceremonial cleansing (v.38). Though the word for gate is plural in v.38, it is singular in v.39. The implication would be that the two tables on either side of each inner gate portico would be for the slaughter of offerings. This is supported, in part, by the use of all three gates for entrance to offer sacrifices by the prince and the people (cf. 46:1–2, 9). On these four tables (T) in each portico, the burnt offerings, sin offerings, and guilt offerings—the only sacrifices requiring an animal or bird to be killed—would be slaughtered. The significance of the offerings is discussed above in the introduction to this section and below where these sacrifices are mentioned in the worship ritual.

The northern inner gate had some furniture unique only to it (vv.40–43). Two additional tables (T) for slaughter of sacrifices were placed on either side of the stairs outside the north inner gate in the outer courtyard. This made a total of eight tables both outside and inside the north inner gate: four inside and four outside. Four additional small tables of dressed stone, one and one-half cubits square and one cubit high, on which the utensils for slaughtering the sacrifices would be laid, were distributed around the northern inner gate (v.42). Double-pronged hooks were placed around the portico's wall (v.43).

44–46 Inside the northern and eastern inner gates were rooms (PS) for the priests of the sons of Zadok. They were the only ones of the Levitical priesthood permitted to minister directly to the Lord. The exclusion of Levi's other descendants from this ministry is explained in chapter 44. The MT states that the rooms were specifically for singers. Though other functions are mentioned for the priests who resided in these rooms (vv.45–46), singing was a priestly function in OT temple worship (cf. 1 Chron 16:4–6; 23:5; 2 Chron 29). The rooms that faced south on the inside of the north inner gate housed the priests who ministered in the temple. The room that faced north on the inside of the east gate housed those priests who ministered primarily at the altar of sacrifice.

47 The inner court courtyard was one hundred cubits square. The altar of sacrifice, described in chapter 43, was in front of the temple (TEM) (see fig. 2).

Notes

---

30 Though it might be attractive to delete this verse, only a paucity of Hebrew MSS and the LXX do so. The LXX is not a strong witness in the prophetic books, especially Ezekiel. The rationale for this deletion is the argument of dittography from v.29. Though it is most difficult to harmonize this verse with the dimensions of the porticoes in vv.8–9, 14 (the latter itself a problem verse), it would appear best to let the MT stand.

37 The difficulty in determining the meaning "portico" over against "door jamb" comes from the various forms of words with the consonants אלם ('lm; cf. vv.31, 34). In v.8 'ulām ("portico") is clear. The problem of אַיִל ('ayil, "door jamb"?) and אֵילִים ('ēlîm, "projecting walls"?) was discussed in the note at v.14. Here in v.37 the form אֵילָו ('ēlāw, "its jamb") would be better understood with the LXX as "portico" in parallel with אֵלַמּוֹ ('ēlammāw, "its portico") in vv.31, 34.

38–40 The LXX and the Syriac read the singular בְּאוּלָם הַשַּׁעַר (bᵉ'ûlām haššaʿar, "the portico of the gate"), instead of the plural of the MT בְּאֵילִים הַשְּׁעָרִים (bᵉ'ēlîm haššᵉʿārîm, "the porticoes of the gates"). This is based on the understanding that bᵉ'ēlîm, is a corruption of bᵉ'ûlām. However, the support from the MSS evidence is not strong, nor is the alteration necessitated by the context. Since 46:1–2, 9 indicates that all three gates are used for entrance for sacrifice, the plural of "gates" would be fitting. The placing of the rooms

Figure 2
Temple Complex

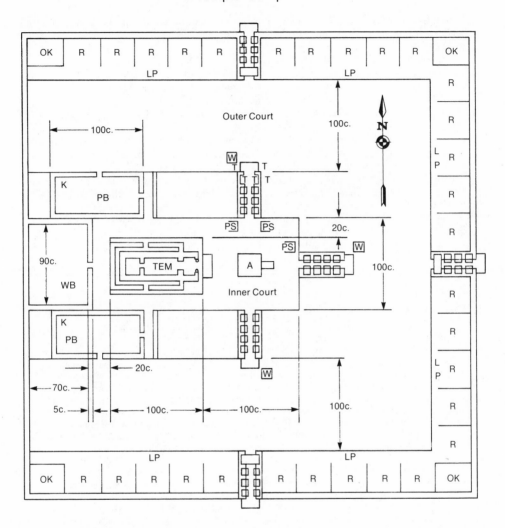

Key:

A   Altar (Ezek 40:47b)

WB   Building of the separation yard (Ezek 41:12, 13b, 15)

K   Kitchen for priests to boil sacrifices (Ezek 46:19–20)

OK   Kitchens for priests to boil people's sacrifices (Ezek 46:21–24)

LP   Pavement strip (Ezek 40:17–18)

PB   Priests' chambers (Ezek 42:1–14)

R   Rooms in outer court for storage or priests' quarters (Ezek 40:17)

PS   Rooms for singers (priests) (Ezek 40:44–46)

T   Tables for slaughter of sacrifices (two at each point) (Ezek 40:39–43)

TEM   Temple proper (Ezek 40:48–41:11, 13a, 14, 16, 23–26)

W   Rooms for washing offerings (Ezek 40:38)

       Inner court (Ezek 40:44–47a)

       Outer court (Ezek 40:17–19, 23, 27, 39–43)

       Width from outer gates to inner gates (Ezek 40:19, 23, 27)

beside the door jambs would be even more fitting than beside the portico, though either reading would imply the same location. Therefore, it seems best to accept the MT reading.

One could, however, take the singular "gate" in v.39 together with the instructions in vv.40–43 and understand v.39 to refer only to the northern inner gate. The reference only to the "north gate" in v.40 would distinguish the information relating to the northern gate from the previous data relating to all three inner gates.

44 The LXX reads δύο ἐξέδραι (*duo exedrai*, "two rooms"). The MT reads לִשְׁכוֹת שָׁרִים (*liškôt šārîm*, "rooms for singers"). Verse 44 indicates more than one room on the inside of the north gate even without changing the word *šārîm* to שְׁתַּיִם (*šetayim*, "two"). The alteration would not conflict, but neither is it necessary. It would seem better to accept the MT rather than the lone voice of the LXX.

In addition, the אֶחָד (*'eḥād*, "one") indicates only one room beside the east gate whereas the plural פְּנֵיהֶם (*penêhem*, "their faces"; NIV, "facing") implies two or more beside the north gate.

The LXX reads πρὸς νότον (*pros noton*, "to the south") in place of the MT's הַקָּדִים (*haqqādîm*, "the east"). Again it would seem best to accept the MT (contra NIV), which consistently has the better readings than the LXX since there is no other argument to alter the MT reading.

---

3) *The house of God*

40:48–41:26

[48]He brought me to the portico of the temple and measured the jambs of the portico; they were five cubits wide on either side. The width of the entrance was fourteen cubits and its projecting walls were three cubits wide on either side. [49]The portico was twenty cubits wide, and twelve cubits from front to back. It was reached by a flight of stairs, and there were pillars on each side of the jambs.

[41:1]Then the man brought me to the outer sanctuary and measured the jambs; the width of the jambs was six cubits on each side. [2]The entrance was ten cubits wide, and projecting walls on each side of it were five cubits wide. He also measured the outer sanctuary; it was forty cubits long and twenty cubits wide.

[3]Then he went into the inner sanctuary and measured the jambs of the entrance; each was two cubits wide. The entrance was six cubits wide, and the projecting walls on each side of it were seven cubits wide. [4]And he measured the length of the inner sanctuary; it was twenty cubits, and its width was twenty cubits across the end of the outer sanctuary. He said to me, "This is the Most Holy Place."

[5]Then he measured the wall of the temple; it was six cubits thick, and each side room around the temple was four cubits wide. [6]The side rooms were on three levels, one above another, thirty on each level. There were ledges all around the wall of the temple to serve as supports for the side rooms, so that the supports were not inserted into the wall of the temple. [7]The side rooms all around the temple were wider at each successive level. The structure surrounding the temple was built in ascending stages, so that the rooms widened as one went upward. A stairway went up from the lowest floor to the top floor through the middle floor.

[8]I saw that the temple had a raised base all around it, forming the foundation of the side rooms. It was the length of the rod, six long cubits. [9]The outer wall of the side rooms was five cubits thick. The open area between the side rooms of the temple [10]and the ‚priests'‚ rooms was twenty cubits wide all around the temple. [11]There were entrances to the side rooms from the open area, one on the north and another on the south; and the base adjoining the open area was five cubits wide all around.

[12]The building facing the temple courtyard on the west side was seventy cubits

wide. The wall of the building was five cubits thick all around, and its length was ninety cubits.

¹³Then he measured the temple; it was a hundred cubits long, and the temple courtyard and the building with its walls were also a hundred cubits long. ¹⁴The width of the temple courtyard on the east, including the front of the temple, was a hundred cubits.

¹⁵Then he measured the length of the building facing the courtyard at the rear of the temple, including its galleries on each side; it was a hundred cubits.

The outer sanctuary, the inner sanctuary and the portico facing the court, ¹⁶as well as the thresholds and the narrow windows and galleries around the three of them—everything beyond and including the threshold was covered with wood. The floor, the wall up to the windows, and the windows were covered. ¹⁷In the space above the outside of the entrance to the inner sanctuary and on the walls at regular intervals all around the inner and outer sanctuary ¹⁸were carved cherubim and palm trees. Palm trees alternated with cherubim. Each cherub had two faces: ¹⁹the face of a man toward the palm tree on one side and the face of a lion toward the palm tree on the other. They were carved all around the whole temple. ²⁰From the floor to the area above the entrance, cherubim and palm trees were carved on the wall of the outer sanctuary.

²¹The outer sanctuary had a rectangular doorframe, and the one at the front of the Most Holy Place was similar. ²²There was a wooden altar three cubits high and two cubits square; its corners, its base and its sides were of wood. The man said to me, "This is the table that is before the Lᴏʀᴅ." ²³Both the outer sanctuary and the Most Holy Place had double doors. ²⁴Each door had two leaves—two hinged leaves for each door. ²⁵And on the doors of the outer sanctuary were carved cherubim and palm trees like those carved on the walls, and there was a wooden overhang on the front of the portico. ²⁶On the sidewalls of the portico were narrow windows with palm trees carved on each side. The side rooms of the temple also had overhangs.

48–49 The divine messenger moved next to the temple structure (cf. fig. 3). The fourteen-cubit-wide entrance of the sanctuary (v.48) was reached by a flight of stairs (v.49). Facing the entrance (EP) Ezekiel observed five-cubit-wide door jambs (PJ) protruding three cubits from the inside of the temple wall on either side. Pillars (PL), perhaps similar to Joachin and Boaz of the Solomonic and Herodian temples, stood in front of the door jambs one on either side. As Ezekiel stepped into the temple's portico (EP) (vestibule), he saw a room twenty cubits wide by eleven cubits deep.

1–2 The outer sanctuary (OS), or Holy Place, consisted of a room twenty cubits wide by forty cubits long. Its ten-cubit-wide entrance (ET) was bounded on either side with six-cubit-wide door jambs (TJ) on walls that protruded from the side walls of the chamber by five cubits on each side.

3–4 Ezekiel moved into the inner sanctuary (IS) through a six-cubit-wide entrance (EH) with two-cubit-wide door jambs (HJ) on walls seven cubits wide. As Ezekiel viewed the twenty-cubit-square room, he was told that this room was "the Most Holy Place." By narrowing the entrance ways to the portico (40:48), to the outer sanctuary (41:2), and to the inner sanctuary (41:3) from fourteen cubits, to ten cubits, to six cubits, respectively, the architect focused the worshiper's eyes on the Most Holy Place, the center of worship.

5–11 A six-cubit-thick wall (v.5a) surrounded the entire temple. Next to this wall, but not attached to it, were ninety side rooms (SR), four cubits wide and constructed on three stories. The thirty rooms on each level became wider as one moved higher up through each story (vv.5b–7). Stairs joined the three stories from bottom to top. These side rooms (SR) had an outer wall five cubits thick (v.9), and they all rested on a six-cubit-high foundation on either side of the temple proper (v.8). This foundation extended an additional five cubits beyond the temple's outer wall to the edge of the foundation (v.11b). Entrances to these side rooms were only on the north and south sides of the temple structure (v.11a). One entered from the inner court into the singular entrance on each side. Twenty cubits separated these side rooms from the priests' chambers (cf. 42:1–14; cf. also fig. 2) at the side of the inner court on both the north and the south (vv.9–10).

12–26 A separate building (WB) was west of the temple proper (fig. 2), seemingly next to the western wall of the entire temple complex (vv.12, 13b). Its function is unknown. The structure was seventy cubits wide by ninety cubits long with a five-cubit-thick wall all around. With its five-cubit wall on either side plus its ninety-cubit length, the building was exactly one hundred cubits across from north to south, exactly the same width as the inner courtyard and the inner court to the east of the temple proper (vv.13–15).

The decorations of the temple structure (vv.15–20) consisted of windows all around the portico, the outer sanctuary, and the inner sanctuary. All the inside walls of each aspect of the temple structure were covered with a wood wainscoating up to the windows, and the windows were covered, too. These wooden inner walls, as well as the outer walls, were carved with cherubim interspersed with palm trees. Each cherub had two faces, one each facing the palm tree on either side of it. The faces were those of a man and a lion. Though the cherubim may symbolize the guardianship of God's holiness, any significance of the palm trees is uncertain.

The only furniture in the temple was a wooden altar, three cubits high by two cubits square (v.22). The divine messenger called it "the table that is before the LORD." This altar was much smaller than the altar of sacrifice (cf. 43:13–17). Some have suggested that this was the altar of incense that sat before the veil of the Most Holy Place in the Mosaic system. The altar of incense symbolized the saints' prayers in the tabernacle.

Both the entrance to the outer sanctuary (ET) and the entrance to the inner sanctuary (EH) had rectangular doors. These were double doors, hinged with two leaves for each door. The doors to the outer sanctuary were carved with cherubim interspersed with palm trees in the same manner as the outer walls (v.25).

The entire temple complex was of great beauty and symmetry.

Notes

48 The LXX insertion of πηχῶν δέκα τεσσάρων, καί ἐπωμίδες τῆς θύρας (pēchōn deka tessarōn, kai epōmides tēs thyras, "fourteen cubits, and the projecting walls of the door") is unwarranted and redundant since the MT may be clearly understood as three cubits on either side of the entrance itself. Verse 49 shows the entire portico to be twenty cubits wide.

49 The depth of the portico is עַשְׁתֵּי עֶשְׂרֵה (ʿaštê ʿeśrēh, "eleven") cubits in the MT. The LXX reads δώδεκα (dōdeka, "twelve") cubits. Since all the dimensions of the temple structure

Figure 3
The Temple Sanctuary

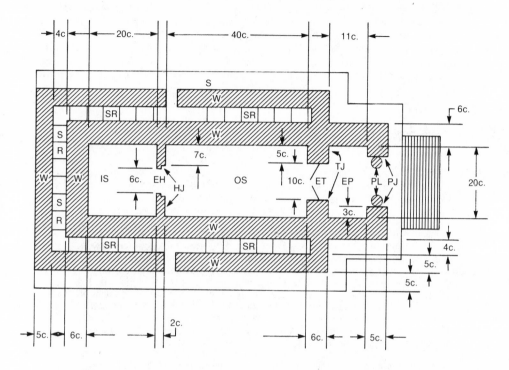

Key:

ET   Entry to the temple (outer sanctuary) (Ezek 41:2a; cf. 41:23–25)
EH   Entry to the Most Holy Place (inner sanctuary) (Ezek 41:3;
          cf. 41:23–25)
OS   Holy Place (outer sanctuary) (Ezek 41:2b, 21b)
IS   Most Holy Place (inner sanctuary((Ezek 41:4)
EP   Portico (porch, vestibule) (Ezek 40:48–49)
PL   Pillars (Ezek 40:49)
HJ   Projecting wall (jamb, post) of the entry to the Most Holy Place
          (Ezek 41:3)
PJ   Projecting wall (jamb, post) of the porch (Ezek 40:48)
TJ   Projecting wall (jamb, post) of the temple proper (Ezek 41:1)
SR   Side rooms of the temple sanctuary (Ezek 41:5b–11a)
S   Space left around the temple (platform) (Ezek 41:11b)
W   Wall of the temple (Ezek 41:5a)
       Overall dimensions of the temple with yard on either side
          (Ezek 41:13a, 14)
       Windows (Ezek 41:16, 26) on the porch, side chambers, and
          decoration (Ezek 41:16–20)

are not certain (e.g., the length of the side rooms), all the detail dimensions cannot be added together to see whether they match the one hundred cubits given as the structure's overall length. If that were possible, one could perhaps know whether the text should read eleven or twelve. But since this is not possible, and the data in support of the number "twelve" is only the LXX, it would seem best to accept the MT reading.

41:1 The LXX (NIV) probably deleted the MT's רֹחַב הָאֹהֶל (*rōḥab hāʾōhel*, "the width of the tent") because of its awkwardness in the flow of the text. However, the phrase could be stating that the width of the jamb walls is the same as the width of the wall of the entire sanctuary, i.e., six cubits (cf. v.5).

---

4) *The priests' buildings*

42:1–14

> ¹Then the man led me northward into the outer court and brought me to the rooms opposite the temple courtyard and opposite the outer wall on the north side. ²The building whose door faced north was a hundred cubits long and fifty cubits wide. ³Both in the section twenty cubits from the inner court and in the section opposite the pavement of the outer court, gallery faced gallery at the three levels. ⁴In front of the rooms was an inner passageway ten cubits wide and a hundred cubits long. Their doors were on the north. ⁵Now the upper rooms were narrower, for the galleries took more space from them than from the rooms on the lower and middle floors of the building. ⁶The rooms on the third floor had no pillars, as the courts had; so they were smaller in floor space than those on the lower and middle floors. ⁷There was an outer wall parallel to the rooms and the outer court; it extended in front of the rooms for fifty cubits. ⁸While the row of rooms on the side next to the outer court was fifty cubits long, the row on the side nearest the sanctuary was a hundred cubits long. ⁹The lower rooms had an entrance on the east side as one enters them from the outer court.
>
> ¹⁰On the south side along the length of the wall of the outer court, adjoining the temple courtyard and opposite the outer wall, were rooms ¹¹with a passageway in front of them. These were like the rooms on the north; they had the same length and width, with similar exits and dimensions. Similar to the doorways on the north ¹²were the doorways of the rooms on the south. There was a doorway at the beginning of the passageway that was parallel to the corresponding wall extending eastward, by which one enters the rooms.
>
> ¹³Then he said to me, "The north and south rooms facing the temple courtyard are the priests' rooms, where the priests who approach the LORD will eat the most holy offerings. There they will put the most holy offerings—the grain offerings, the sin offerings and the guilt offerings—for the place is holy. ¹⁴Once the priests enter the holy precincts, they are not to go into the outer court until they leave behind the garments in which they minister, for these are holy. They are to put on other clothes before they go near the places that are for the people."

1–9 There were two buildings (PB) in the outer court just outside the inner court on the north and on the south (vv.1, 3, 10, 13; cf. fig. 2). The northern building was described in detail while the southern building was likened to the northern one. The building was one hundred cubits long, east to west, and fifty cubits wide, north to south (vv.2b, 8). It lay parallel to both the outer court pavement to the north (v.3) and the inner court's north wall that it abuts (cf. 41:10). The northern building was three-storied with many rooms and galleries on each floor (v.3c). The two lower stories had pillars as structural supports (v.6). The rooms on the third floor were smaller, though the third floor had larger galleries than the middle and ground floors (v.5). All rooms appeared to have doors on the north side (v.4b). The lower floor had an entrance on the north (v.2a) with a ten-cubit wide and one-cubit long step in front of it (v.4a; cf. vv.11–12). The building's lower floor also had an eastern entrance (v.9). In front of this eastern entrance was a wall parallel to the east end of the building (vv.7–8a). Perhaps this wall provided a separation from the rest of the activity of the outer court, giving privacy.

10–12 The southern building was similar to the northern building in every facet, providing perfect symmetry, which was a hallmark of the overall design. The singular problem found in these verses is the reading of the word "south" rather than the word "Eastward" in the MT of v.10. The LXX reads "south," which, in this case, is most likely the better reading. This is supported by the explicit statement in vv.12–13 that this was a building on the south. Likewise, the parallel to the northern building along with the symmetry of the entire complex would argue for the building to be on the south.

13–14 These two buildings provided a holy place where the ministering Zadokian priests could eat the holy offerings and change from their holy ministering garments to everyday clothes. The priests were to eat portions of the grain offerings, the sin offerings, and the guilt offerings. This building also provided a place to store these portions of the sacrifices. The priests would leave the priestly garments in these buildings. In doing so they would continue to distinguish between the holy and the profane.

Notes

4 The use of מַהֲלָךְ (mahᵃlak, "inner passageway") and the assertion that this "passage," or "step," is ten cubits wide but only *one* cubit long is a difficult problem. Since there is no textual question concerning mahᵃlak, a common solution is to accept the LXX and the Syriac readings that would change the אֶחָת (*'eḥāt*, "one") to one hundred cubits, the length of the north side of the building. Though this is an option, the term mahᵃlak can be rendered "step." By continuing to accept the MT, one could understand the phrase as a singular step that is ten cubits wide and one cubit long.

5) *The measurement of the temple area*

42:15–20

[15]When he had finished measuring what was inside the temple area, he led me out by the east gate and measured the area all around: [16]He measured the east side with the measuring rod; it was five hundred cubits. [17]He measured the north side; it was five hundred cubits by the measuring rod. [18]He measured the south side; it was five hundred cubits by the measuring rod. [19]Then he turned to the west side and measured; it was five hundred cubits by the measuring rod. [20]So he measured the area on all four sides. It had a wall around it, five hundred cubits long and five hundred cubits wide, to separate the holy from the common.

15–20 The divine messenger brought Ezekiel outside the entire temple complex through the east gate (v.15). Ezekiel was shown the vast area that would be set aside for the sanctuary. It measured five hundred rods square (cf. NIV mg.), almost a square mile. Some immediately reject the term "rod" and replace it with "cubit," the standard of measure in these verses. As support, the deletion of "rods" in the LXX is cited. However, such an alteration is contrary to 45:2. That verse declares the temple environs to be five hundred square. Neither the term "rod" nor "cubit" is stated. Ezekiel 45:2 does state that a border of fifty *cubits* provides an open space around the five hundred square area. Ezekiel's explicit use of the term "cubit" seems to have been to distinguish cubits from the rods of the five hundred square area as already revealed in 42:15–20. Some argue that an area five hundred rods square would be too large and not fit the topography well. But such an argument is not persuasive when Zechariah and other prophets demonstrate that the whole Palestinian topography will undergo geographical modifications at the beginning of the Millennium. No good reason appears to reject the term "rod" in these verses.

This large area provided a separation space between the holy (the temple complex and its worship) and the common (or profane) terrain of everyday life (v.20b). Israel had frequently forgotten to make this distinction in her past history.

Notes

16 The MT reads אֲמוֹת (*'ēmôt*, "cubits") instead of מֵאוֹת (*mē'ôt*, "one hundred"). A large number of Hebrew MSS along with the Qere reading and the unquestionable parallel readings in vv.17–19 argue strongly that the text should read *mē'ôt*.

For the problem of קָנִים (*qānîm*, "rods"), see the commentary.

b. *The return of the glory of God to the temple*

43:1–12

¹Then the man brought me to the gate facing east, ²and I saw the glory of the God of Israel coming from the east. His voice was like the roar of rushing waters, and the land was radiant with his glory. ³The vision I saw was like the vision I had seen when he came to destroy the city and like the visions I had seen by the Kebar River, and I fell facedown. ⁴The glory of the LORD entered the temple through the gate facing east. ⁵Then the Spirit lifted me up and brought me into the inner court, and the glory of the LORD filled the temple.

⁶While the man was standing beside me, I heard someone speaking to me from inside the temple. ⁷He said: "Son of man, this is the place of my throne and the place for the soles of my feet. This is where I will live among the Israelites forever. The house of Israel will never again defile my holy name—neither they nor their kings—by their prostitution and the lifeless idols of their kings at their high places. ⁸When they placed their threshold next to my threshold and their doorposts beside my doorposts, with only a wall between me and them, they defiled my holy name by their detestable practices. So I destroyed them in my anger. ⁹Now let them put away from me their prostitution and the lifeless idols of their kings, and I will live among them forever.

¹⁰"Son of man, describe the temple to the people of Israel, that they may be ashamed of their sins. Let them consider the plan, ¹¹and if they are ashamed of all they have done, make known to them the design of the temple—its arrangement, its exits and entrances—its whole design and all its regulations and laws. Write these down before them so that they may be faithful to its design and follow all its regulations.

¹²"This is the law of the temple: All the surroundings area on top of the mountain will be most holy. Such is the law of the temple.

1–5 Ezekiel was brought to the outer court's east gate where he looked out toward the east (v.1). Here Ezekiel would see the most important aspect of this entire apocalyptic vision: God's glory returning to the temple!

The glory that Ezekiel saw had the same likeness of God's glory that he had seen in his inaugural visions on the river Kebar (chs. 1, 3) and that which had departed from the temple during his announcement of destruction on Jerusalem (chs. 8, 10, 11). Since Jerusalem's destruction, God's glory had not been present in Jerusalem nor among his people. Israel had been under discipline in Babylonia and would remain under discipline till the end times. Then she would be cleansed and restored to her promised land by the Messiah. God's glory would not even fill Zerubbabel's temple nor the temple of Herod (cf. Hag 2:7).

The recipients of Ezekiel's messages and visions would be encouraged and take heart by this vision. Some would remember the glory of Solomon's temple, and this temple would be vastly superior to Solomon's (cf. Hag 2:3). This vision made it very clear that God's glory *would* return after Israel was cleansed and after the millennial temple had been constructed according to the divine plan given in chapters 40–42. It would be similar to the dedication of the tabernacle (Exod 40:34–35) and the Solomonic temple (1 Kings 8:10–11; 2 Chron 5:13–14; 7:1–3) when God's glory filled them. What a glorious climax to God's good and wonderful plan for Israel! Ezekiel saw the marvelous glory of God coming from the east (v.2), entering the east gate (v.4), and completely filling the temple (v.5). It caused the entire land to become radiant with God's glory. The sound of its coming and its presence were just like the sound of rushing water Ezekiel had heard coming from the cherubim's wings in the previous visions of God's glory (cf. 1:24). God had indeed returned to dwell among his people!

6–12 The significance of this vision of God's glory was so important that the Lord himself interpreted it to Ezekiel (v.6). The temple was to be God's throne and residence among Israel forever (v.7). The promises of chapters 33–37 would be fulfilled when God's glory returned. The glory of God would fill the temple, and God's holiness would permeate the entire temple complex. This, in turn, would be instructive both for Ezekiel's contemporaries and for the house of Israel living in the Messianic Age. When God's glory returned, Israel would never again defile the Lord's holy name (cf. 39:7) through her religious prostitution in the temple precinct (cf. 2 Kings 23:7) and the burial of the corpses of kings in their high places (v.7). The indication is that these burial high places of Ezekiel's day might have been located within the temple area, though there is no explicit mention of such in the Scriptures. The kings had also placed their palaces right next to the temple on the south and thereby defiled God's name with their detestable practices (v.8). Israel had religiously defiled the Lord's name through her idolatrous practices on high places. Therefore the Lord used this vision to exhort Israel's day to put away these practices of defilement (v.9).

Ezekiel's contemporaries would be ashamed of their sins when they heard of this vision and saw the new temple design with the promised return of God's glory (vv.10–11). Likewise, millennial Israel would be ashamed for all her past sins as she reflected on the holiness of God's glory and the perfection of the new temple design in contrast to Israel's past unfaithfulness and defilement. The Lord instructed Israel in the vision's interpretation to follow carefully the detailed plan of the millennial temple in its construction so that God's glory might fill it.

There was only one basic law for the temple area: all the area on the temple mountain would be holy. The stress would be on God's holiness and his place of rule and residency. Holiness would be the emphasis in the Millennium. All worship structures and regulations were to demonstrate God's holiness. A continual contrast would be observed between the holy and the profane. The Messiah would judge unholiness with the rod of iron (cf. Ps 2:8–9; Rev 2:27; 12:5; 19:15)!

Notes

3 The MT reads בְּבֹאִי (b⁰bō'î, "when I came"), whereas a paucity of Hebrew MSS, Theodotion, and the Vulgate read בְּבֹאוֹ (b⁰bō'ô, "when he came"). The difference between the two pronominal suffixes means the differences between either the Lord coming to destroy (third masc. sing.) or Ezekiel coming to destroy (first common sing.). Since the textual MSS evidence is relatively weak, it would seem best to accept the MT reading. In doing so this would mean that the prophet was so strongly tied to the divine message that he announced that he was viewed as bringing God's destruction in his prophetic announcements.

7 The last phrase of this verse (also cf. v.9) presents some difficulties in translation. The term פֶּגֶר (peger, "corpse," "carcass") is perhaps used in Lev 26:30 metaphorically of "lifeless idols," though in the same verse the term is understood literally as "corpse." It would seem best to take this term in Ezekiel in its normal meaning rather than to take a metaphorical use (which is used only once and is accompanied with the word for idol). The MT reads בָּמוֹתָם (bāmôtām, "in their high places"). Some MSS, Theodotion, and the Targum read b⁰môtām ("in their death"). Though the latter seems easier, the MT reading could equally make sense in this context of religious pollution of the temple area.

c. Temple ordinances (43:13–46:24)

The Lord gave directives for the maintenance of holiness as the temple functions were performed. Instructions were given for the construction and consecration of the altar of sacrifice (43:13–27) as well as regulations to govern the proper use of the temple (44:1–9). Ezekiel 44:10–31 sets forth ordinances for priestly conduct. The land's sacred district was marked out in 45:1–8. A historical exhortation to Ezekiel's contemporary leaders interrupted the discussion of temple regulations (45:9–12). The duties of the prince (leader) in worship are delineated in 45:13–46:18, followed by the manner in which the priestly kitchens in the temple are to function (46:19–24).

1) The altar of sacrifice: description and dedication

43:13–27

13"These are the measurements of the altar in long cubits, that cubit being a cubit and a handbreadth: Its gutter is a cubit deep and a cubit wide, with a rim of one span around the edge. And this is the height of the altar: 14From the gutter on the ground up to the lower ledge it is two cubits high and a cubit wide, and from the smaller ledge up to the larger ledge it is four cubits high and a cubit wide. [15]The altar hearth is four cubits high, and four horns project upward from the hearth. [16]The altar hearth is square, twelve cubits long and twelve cubits wide. [17]The upper ledge also is square, fourteen cubits long and fourteen cubits wide, with a rim of half a cubit and a gutter of a cubit all around. The steps of the altar face east."

[18]Then he said to me, "Son of man, this is what the Sovereign LORD says: These will be the regulations for sacrificing burnt offerings and sprinkling blood upon the altar when it is built: [19]You are to give a young bull as a sin offering to the priests, who are Levites, of the family of Zadok, who come near to minister before me, declares the Sovereign LORD. [20]You are to take some of its blood and put it on the four horns of the altar and on the four corners of the upper ledge and all around the rim, and so purify the altar and make atonement for it. [21]You are to take the bull for the sin offering and burn it in the designated part of the temple area outside the sanctuary.

[22]On the second day you are to offer a male goat without defect for a sin offering, and the altar is to be purified as it was purified with the bull. [23]When you have finished purifying it, you are to offer a young bull and a ram from the flock, both without defect. [24]You are to offer them before the LORD, and the priests are to sprinkle salt on them and sacrifice them as a burnt offering to the LORD.

[25]"For seven days you are to provide a male goat daily for a sin offering; you are also to provide a young bull and a ram from the flock, both without defect. [26]For seven days they are to make atonement for the altar and cleanse it; thus they will dedicate it. [27]At the end of these days, from the eighth day on, the priests are to present your burnt offerings and fellowship offerings on the altar. Then I will accept you, declares the Sovereign LORD."

13–17 Though not all the terms used to describe the altar of sacrifice have certain meanings, the basic design is sufficiently clear (cf. fig. 4). The altar was to be located in front of the sanctuary in the inner court (cf. fig. 2, A).

The altar was described from the bottom to the top. The bottom portion (B) of the altar was composed of a one-cubit-high base with a one-cubit-wide gutter around the altar (v. 13). The gutter had a rim of one span length (approx. nine inches) (v. 13c). On top of this base were three sections of the altar (vv. 14–17a). Next to the base (B) was a two-cubit-high section (I), sixteen cubits square, with a one-cubit ledge around it. This ledge formed a gutter one cubit wide with a one-half-cubit-high rim. The middle section (E) was four cubits high, fourteen cubits square, including a one-cubit-wide ledge around it. The hearth (H), four cubits high and twelve cubits square, formed the altar's top portion. One horn (HA) projected from each of the four corners. Steps (S) led to the top on the east side, but the dimensions of the stairs were not given. These steps were in contrast to the altar of sacrifice under the Mosaic system, where it was forbidden to go up by steps on the altar (Exod 20:24–26). This millennial altar was very large: approximately thirty-one and one-half feet square at the base by approximately nineteen and one-quarter feet high!

18–27 After the altar of sacrifice was constructed, it would be necessary to cleanse and dedicate it (v. 18). Cleansing was needed because everything associated with man partook of sin and therefore needed to be cleansed, especially if it was to be used in the worship of the Lord. A similar cleansing and dedication took place with the altar of sacrifice of the tabernacle (Exod 29:36–37; Lev 8:14–17) and the altar of Solomon's temple (2 Chron 7:9).

The ritual cleansing and atonement for the altar took seven days (vv. 25–27). On

Figure 4
Altar of Sacrifice

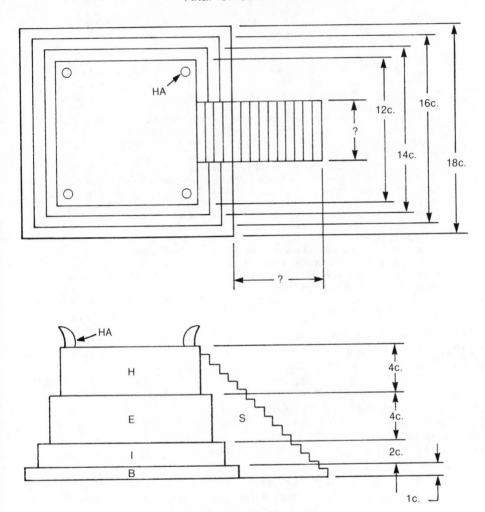

Key:

H	Altar hearth (Ezek 43:15–16)
E	Enclosure (Ezek 43:14, 17)
I	Interior (Ezek 43:14, 17)
B	Bottom (Ezek 43:13)
HA	Horns of the altar (Ezek 43:20)
S	Steps (Ezek 43:17b; cf. Ezek 40:47b)

the first day a special sin offering of a young bull was made by the Zadokian priests. They were to take some of the blood of the sacrifice and put it on the four horns of the altar, the four corners of the altar's upper ledge, and all around the rim (vv. 19–20a). This sin offering, which J. Milgrom ("Sin-Offering or Purification-Offering?" VetTest 21 [1971]: 237–39) clarifies as a purification offering, would cleanse, or purify, the altar from its sinfulness, thereby making atonement for the altar. Atonement here has the idea of wiping away or cleansing, after which the altar would be holy (v. 20b; cf. Lev 8:14–15). The remainder of the sin offering was burned in a designated part of the temple area (cf. 42:20) but outside the sanctuary precinct per se (v. 21; Lev 8:17).

On the second and succeeding five days, the priests offered a sin offering of a male goat without defect, in order to continue to purify the altar (vv. 22, 25a). After this ceremonial cleansing with the sin offering, the priests symbolized the altar's consecration by offering a young bull and a ram, both without defect and sprinkled with salt, as a burnt offering before the Lord (vv. 23–24, 25b). With these offerings each day for the prescribed seven days, the altar would be atoned and cleansed in dedication (v. 26; cf. Exod 29:36–37).

After the seven-day ceremonial cleansing and dedication of the altar of sacrifice, the priests would begin to present the burnt offerings and fellowship offerings on the altar for the people (v. 27a). Not only would the Lord then accept their offerings because they had properly consecrated the altar, but he also would accept the worshipers. What a glorious truth! Because of the Messiah's sacrifice, all who believe are accepted!

Notes

20, 26 Three verbs used in these verses connote cleansing and purification. חָטֵא (ḥiṭṭē', "purify") conveys the idea of "cleansing from sin." כִּפֶּר (kippēr, "atone") has the sense of "wiping away sin" or "cleansing." טָהֵר (ṭāhēr) is the normal Hebrew verb for "cleanse" in a general sense.

In v. 26 מִלְאוּ יָדָו (mil'û yāḏāw, "dedicate") literally means "they filled his hands." This idiom most likely originates from a similar Babylonian expression that depicted an installment in which the person was conferred with dignity.

2) Regulations for the east gate

44:1–3

> [1]Then the man brought me back to the outer gate of the sanctuary, the one facing east, and it was shut. [2]The LORD said to me, "This gate is to remain shut. It must not be opened; no one may enter through it. It is to remain shut because the LORD, the God of Israel, has entered through it. [3]The prince himself is the only one who may sit inside the gateway to eat in the presence of the LORD. He is to enter by way of the portico of the gateway and go out the same way."

1–2 The outer east gate (cf. 40:6–16) was to remain closed permanently. This was done because of reverence for the gate's special sanctity, for it was the gate through which the Lord entered into the millennial precinct in his glory (vv. 1–2; cf. 43:1–4). This gate is not the "golden gate" located in the old city of Jerusalem today, because the dimensions of the two temple areas are vastly different. The structures of the current "temple area" will not exist in the millennial period.

3 Only the "prince" was permitted to enter this gate. He must enter and leave by way of the portico from the outer court only. His only function within that gate was to eat bread in the presence of the Lord, but exactly which meal or for what purpose is not stated.

The identity of this "prince" has been a puzzle to many. The meaning of the Hebrew word *nāśî'* has in itself contributed to the problem. The English word "prince" connotes royalty. However, the word *nāśî'* would best be translated "leader" (cf. E.A. Speiser, "Background and Function of the Biblical *Nāśî'*," CBQ 25 [1963]: 111–17). This leader was not the Messiah, because the leader made a sin offering for himself (cf. 45:22). If the "leader" were Jesus Christ, then he, the Messiah, would need cleansing from sin. Such was not possible (cf. Heb 4:15). In addition, this leader had natural children (46:16), another impossibility for the Messiah. The leader was a man. Some have identified him with David, citing 34:23–24 and 37:24 as support. However, these passages have been shown above to apply to the Messiah, not David.

The identity of the leader is unknown. He functions as the people's leader in their millennial worship, almost like a high priest, but not having the same role and function.

3) The priests and the service of the temple

44:4–16

> ⁴Then the man brought me by way of the north gate to the front of the temple. I looked and saw the glory of the Lᴏʀᴅ filling the temple of the Lᴏʀᴅ, and I fell facedown.
>
> ⁵The Lᴏʀᴅ said to me, "Son of man, look carefully, listen closely and give attention to everything I tell you concerning all the regulations regarding the temple of the Lᴏʀᴅ. Give attention to the entrance to the temple and all the exits of the sanctuary. ⁶Say to the rebellious house of Israel, "This is what the Sovereign Lᴏʀᴅ says: Enough of your detestable practices, O house of Israel! ⁷In addition to all your other detestable practices, you brought foreigners uncircumcised in heart and flesh into my sanctuary, desecrating my temple while you offered me food, fat and blood and you broke my covenant. ⁸Instead of carrying out your duty in regard to my holy things, you put others in charge of my sanctuary. ⁹This is what the Sovereign Lᴏʀᴅ says: No foreigner uncircumcised in heart and flesh is to enter my sanctuary, not even the foreigners who live among the Israelites.
>
> ¹⁰ 'The Levites who went far from me when Israel went astray and who wandered from me after their idols must bear the consequences of their sin. ¹¹They may serve in my sanctuary, having charge of the gates of the temple and serving in it; they may slaughter the burnt offerings and sacrifices for the people and stand before the people and serve them. ¹²But because they served them in the presence of their idols and made the house of Israel fall into sin, therefore I have sworn with uplifted hand that they must bear the consequences of their sin, declares the Sovereign Lᴏʀᴅ. ¹³They are not to come near to serve me as priests or come near any of my holy things or my most holy offerings; they must bear the shame of their detestable practices. ¹⁴Yet I will put them in charge of the duties of the temple and all the work that is to be done in it.
>
> ¹⁵ 'But the priests, who are Levites and descendants of Zadok and who faithfully carried out the duties of my sanctuary when the Israelites went astray from

me, are to come near to minister before me; they are to stand before me to offer sacrifices of fat and blood, declares the Sovereign LORD. [16]They alone are to enter my sanctuary; they alone are to come near my table to minister before me and perform my service.

4–5 The emphasis in this vision had been on God's glory and the resulting holiness that was required in all aspects of millennial worship. Ezekiel was brought again to see the Lord's glory filling the temple, and his immediate response was reverence and awe as he fell prostrate in worship (v.4). The Lord undoubtedly used this experience to impress again on Ezekiel the importance of holiness, for holiness must characterize the priests and their actions.

The priests would instruct the rest of the people in holiness, teaching holiness by their lives, their priestly function, and their word. For this reason Ezekiel was exhorted to watch and listen carefully to all the temple regulations, especially those concerning the entrances and exits (v.5). There the priests would contact both the common life in the people and the holiness of the temple's inner court and sanctuary. There they would meet and serve the people.

6–9 The religions of the ancient Near East frequently used foreign captives as temple servants to aid the priests. The Lord's rebuke of Israel in these verses reflected ancient Israel's adoption of this practice. This custom was first observed in Israel when Joshua made the Gibeonites temple servants (Josh 9:23, 27). Israel seems to have continued this practice through the time of Ezra (Ezra 8:20). However, the Mosaic covenant expressed that foreigners who were uncircumcised in flesh and heart were not to minister in the temple as priests, along with all other Israelites not of the Aaronic line (cf. Num 3:10). Perhaps originally some of these foreigners had been circumcised both in the flesh and in the heart so that they could enter the temple area lawfully and make an offering (cf. Num 15:14). Certainly Isaiah 56:3, 6 indicates that such would be possible in the messianic kingdom (cf. Zech 14:21). But Israel had broken the Mosaic covenant with the detestable practice of having foreign temple-servants not only entering the sanctuary but also taking charge of the temple duties. By their handling priestly functions related to the holy things (vv.6–8), they had desecrated the temple. If these foreigners had been circumcised in flesh and heart, they could have assisted the priests. But foreigners should never have been permitted to take over the priests' functions. This showed a great disregard for God's covenant on the part of the priests.

The Mosaic covenant called for all to be circumcised in their hearts as well as in the flesh, the sign of the Abrahamic covenant (cf. Lev 26:41; Deut 10:16; 30:6; Jer 4:4; 9:25). There must be a change of heart toward the Lord and his ways, a true circumcising of the hardness of the heart's foreskin. This was necessary for the Israelite and the foreigner if they were to enter into a proper relationship with the Lord.

Therefore, an explicit command was given: No foreigner, uncircumcised of heart and flesh, could enter the temple, not even those living among Israel (v.9). However, the implication was that the foreigner circumcised in heart and flesh could enter as any other person, but he could not function in any manner as a priest.

10–14 The Lord clarified who could minister in the millennial temple and in what manner. The Levites would be in charge of the temple gates, where they would slaughter the burnt offerings and other sacrifices for the people and assist them in their worship (v. 11). The Levites would also be responsible for all work done in the temple, perhaps those duties previously handled by foreigners (v. 14).

Limitations were placed on Levites' ministry. They would not be permitted to serve the Lord as priests; nor would they be allowed to come near any of the Lord's holy things, especially his most holy offerings (v. 13a). They would serve neither in the inner court nor in the temple itself. The reason for this restriction was explicit (vv. 10, 12, 13b). As a group they had strayed from the Lord in the past and had pursued idolatry. In so doing they had also led the nation into this sin (cf. ch. 8). To name a particular Levitical apostasy would only lead to speculation. But they were to be held accountable for these past transgressions even as they were warned in Numbers 18:23. They must bear sin's consequences and shame, which are always difficult to hide.

15–16 The descendants of Zadok in the Levitical line were placed into major priestly functions under Solomon first (1 Kings 2:26–35), though this had been been foretold in 1 Samuel 2:35 (cf. 2 Sam 8:17; 15:24–29; 1 Chron 6:7–8). They alone had remained faithful to their duties in the Lord's temple when all the rest of Israel had gone away from the Lord (v. 15a). Because of their faithfulness then, the Lord would give to them that singularly unique ministry before him in the millennial sanctuary. They alone would stand before the Lord to offer sacrifices (v. 15). They alone would be permitted to enter the temple and come near the Lord's table to perform his service of worship (v. 16). Exactly which "table" is meant is not certain, though the only "table" within the temple that has been mentioned is the altar within the temple's outer sanctuary (41:22). However, the altar of sacrifice was not called a table in Ezekiel 40–48, though this term was of the altar of sacrifice in the Mosaic system. It is certain from chapters 45–46 that the sons of Zadok would bring the sacrifices for the prince and the people daily, on the Sabbaths, and at the appointed festivals. What a great privilege and blessing would be theirs because of their past faithfulness to God's commands!

Notes

15 Zadok was the son of Ahitub of Eleazer's line, a descendant of Aaron (cf. 1 Chron 6:50–53). He was a priest alongside Abiathar during David's reign (cf. 2 Sam 8:17), showing loyalty to David during Absalom's rebellion (cf. 2 Sam 9:11–13; 15:24–29). When the house of Abiathar (cf. Eli) was deposed by Solomon (cf. 1 Sam 2:27–36; 1 Kings 2:27, the Zadokite priesthood remained. The Zadokite line remained till Antiochus IV, a Gentile, inappropriately appointed Menelaus to the high priesthood in 171 B.C. Interestingly the Qumran community looked forward to the restoration of the Zadokite priesthood.

15–16 Isaiah 66:21 would seem to contradict the exclusive priestly ministry of the Zadokite Levitical line during the Millennium. Isaiah 66, however, primarily reflects the conditions of the eternal state, whereas Ezekiel 44 seems to be discussing primarily millennial worship (see discussion on Ezekiel 40–48's relationship to the Millennium and the eternal state in the excursus in loc.). Perhaps these separate emphases might explain the differences, with a broader priestly ministry in the eternal state, though the close relationship between the Millennium and the eternal state seems to always exist in the prophets.

4) Ordinances for the Zadokian priesthood

44:17–31

> [17] 'When they enter the gates of the inner court, they are to wear linen clothes; they must not wear any woolen garment while ministering at the gates of the inner court or inside the temple. [18]They are to wear linen turbans on their heads and linen undergarments around their waists. They must not wear anything that makes them perspire. [19]When they go out into the outer court where the people are, they are to take off the clothes they have been ministering in and are to leave them in the sacred rooms, and put on other clothes, so that they do not consecrate the people by means of their garments.
>
> [20] 'They must not shave their heads or let their hair grow long, but they are to keep the hair of their heads trimmed. [21]No priest is to drink wine when he enters the inner court. [22]They must not marry widows or divorced women; they may marry only virgins of Israelite descent or widows of priests. [23]They are to teach my people the difference between the holy and the common and show them how to distinguish between the unclean and the clean.
>
> [24] 'In any dispute, the priests are to serve as judges and decide it according to my ordinances. They are to keep my laws and my decrees for all my appointed feasts, and they are to keep my Sabbaths holy.
>
> [25] 'A priest must not defile himself by going near a dead person; however, if the dead person was his father or mother, son or daughter, brother or unmarried sister, then he may defile himself. [26]After he is cleansed, he must wait seven days. [27]On the day he goes into the inner court of the sanctuary to minister in the sanctuary, he is to offer a sin offering for himself, declares the Sovereign LORD.
>
> [28] 'I am to be the only inheritance the priests have. You are to give them no possession in Israel; I will be their possession. [29]They will eat the grain offerings, the sin offerings and the guilt offerings; and everything in Israel devoted to the LORD will belong to them. [30]The best of all the firstfruits and of all your special gifts will belong to the priests. You are to give them the first portion of your ground meal so that a blessing may rest on your household. [31]The priests must not eat anything, bird or animal, found dead or torn by wild animals.

17–19 Various regulations and functions for the Zadokian priests are spelled out in the remainder of this chapter. The clothing worn when ministering highlights the holiness of their ministry. Linen was to be worn when these priests entered the inner court to serve (vv. 17–18; cf. Exod 28:42; Lev 16:4). The linen not only depicted purity by its whiteness, but its coolness kept the priests from perspiring and thereby becoming unclean. In addition to the outer linen garment, the priests wore linen undergarments and a linen turban. Woolen clothes, or those made of material that would tend to make the priests hot and thereby perspire, were forbidden.

When the priests left the inner court to go out among the common people, they were required to change their clothes (cf. Lev 6:11), leaving their linen garments in the sacred rooms so designated (42:1–14). In this way they would not improperly make the people holy with their ministering clothes (v. 19). Contact with a holy thing would consecrate. The Levitical concept of transmission of holiness concerned the transmitting of the state of holiness (Exod 29:37; 30:29; Lev 6:27). A person or object would enter into the state of holiness in the sense of becoming subject to restrictions of holiness to which other holy people or objects were subject (cf. TWOT, 2:786–87). Haggai 2:12 demonstrates that such holy objects only consecrate that which they have touched but nothing else (i.e., they did not communicate holiness to the third degree), while defilement spreads. Ezekiel prohibited the wearing of the consecrated priestly garments in everyday situations (i.e., outside the inner court) to avoid diffusion of the state of holy restriction of the priesthood (cf. Lev 21:1–8). This would aid in maintaining a clear distinction between the holy and the profane.

20–22 The Zadokian priests were to keep several additional regulations. They were not to shave their heads nor allow their hair to grow long. It was to be trimmed properly (v.20). Shaving the head was often associated with pagan religion in which hair was offered to the gods in order to establish a relationship. Perhaps this was at least one of the reasons for forbidding the shaving of the head. Long hair could depict mourning. Priests were not to practice idolatry or pagan mourning rites (cf. Lev 10:6; 21:5, 10). As this hair regulation was a sign of holiness for the priests in the Mosaic system (Lev 21:6), so it must be in the millennial system.

No priest was to drink wine while ministering (v.21; cf. Lev 10:9). He was to make sure that he had full control of himself when performing the Lord's service. This was holiness.

A Zadokian priest was permitted to marry an Israelite virgin or the widow of a priest. This would maintain the holiness of marriage. He could not marry any other widow or a divorced woman (v.22). This restriction, which had been true for the high priest in the Mosaic system, would now be applied to all priests (cf. Lev 21:7, 14).

23–24 The reason for the above regulations for the Zadokian priests were stated. The regulations would enable the priests to teach the Israelites the difference between something holy and something common through the visual lessons of their priestly lives. The above regulations (vv.17–22) show the people *how* to distinguish between clean and unclean acts and objects (v.23; cf. Lev 10:10–11; 11:47; Deut 33:10; contra Ezek 22:26). In addition, these priests would serve as judges for any dispute, making their decision according to God's ordinances (v.24a; cf. Deut 17:9; 19:17; 21:5). They were always to keep God's laws and every decree concerning the appointed feasts and the Sabbaths, the sign of the Mosaic covenant (v.24b).

25–27 There would be individuals entering the Millennium with natural bodies from the tribulation period. These, of course, would ultimately die physically, though physical life would be much longer during the Millennium (cf. Isa 65:20). A priest was defiled by coming near a dead person, and so this was forbidden, except in a case of a member of his immediate family (v.25; Lev 21:1–3). Though the priest could care for a dead family member, he would be defiled; and it would be necessary for him to be cleansed according to biblical guidelines (cf. Num 19:11–19) and wait seven days, the period of cleansing (v.26). When a priest returned to minister in the inner court after defilement and cleansing, it would be necessary for him to offer a sin offering as a purification offering for himself (v.27).

28–31 All provisions for the priests would be made by the Lord. He would be their inheritance and their possession. No other possessions were to be given to them except those specified in these verses (v.28). The priests' food would be provided by the Lord through the people's offerings. The priests would eat from the grain offer-

ings, the sin offerings, and the guilt offerings. They would also partake of everything
devoted to the Lord by the Israelites, the best of all the firstfruits, all special gifts,
and the ground meal of the people (vv.29–30a; cf. Num 18:10–13). A "devoted"
thing (*ḥerem*) was that given by an Israelite that in no way could be regained or
redeemed (cf. Lev 27:21, 28; Num 18:14). However, the priests were not allowed to
eat anything that had been torn by a wild animal or was found dead (v.31; cf. Lev
17:5; 22:8; Deut 14:21).

The Israelites were promised blessing for their faithful giving to the priests in this
way (v.30b; cf. Mal 3:8–12). There is always blessing in giving to the Lord!

Notes

28 The NIV's "I am to be the only inheritance the priests have" is certainly a free rendering
of the MT's וְהָיְתָה לָהֶם לְנַחֲלָה אֲנִי נַחֲלָתָם (*wᵉhāyᵉtāh lāhem lᵉnaḥᵃlāh ʾᵃnî naḥᵃlātām*, "And
it will be for their inheritance [that] I am their inheritance"), though it may be considered
a dynamic equivalent.

5) *The sacred area of the Holy Land*

45:1–8

¹" 'When you allot the land as an inheritance, you are to present to the Lord a
portion of the land as a sacred district, 25,000 cubits long and 20,000 cubits wide;
the entire area will be holy. ²Of this, a section 500 cubits square is to be for the
sanctuary, with 50 cubits around it for open land. ³In the sacred district, measure
off a section 25,000 cubits long and 10,000 cubits wide. In it will be the sanctuary,
the Most Holy Place. ⁴It will be the sacred portion of the priests, who minister in
the sanctuary and who draw near to minister before the Lord. It will be a place for
their houses as well as a holy place for the sanctuary. ⁵An area 25,000 cubits
long and 10,000 cubits wide will belong to the Levites, who serve in the temple, as
their possession for towns to live in.

⁶" 'You are to give the city as its property an area 5,000 cubits wide and 25,000
cubits long, adjoining the sacred portion; it will belong to the whole house of
Israel.

⁷" 'The prince will have the land bordering each side of the area formed by the
sacred district and the property of the city. It will extend westward from the west
side and eastward from the east side, running lengthwise from the western to the
eastern border parallel to one of the tribal portions. ⁸This land will be his possession in Israel. And my princes will no longer oppress my people but will allow the
house of Israel to possess the land according to their tribes.

1–8 A specific portion of Israel's land in the Millennium would be set aside for a
sacred area for the priests and the sanctuary (cf. fig. 5, items C, L, P, S, Z, F). The
entire area would be a contribution to the Lord by Israel. That land would not really
belong to the priests but to the Lord. In this sense, also, the Lord would continue
to be the priests' inheritance.

This contribution to the Lord for a holy area would measure twenty-five thousand
rods by twenty thousand rods. The NIV translates "cubits" rather than "rods" as the
standard of measure. Actually no word for a standard is given in the text. This is

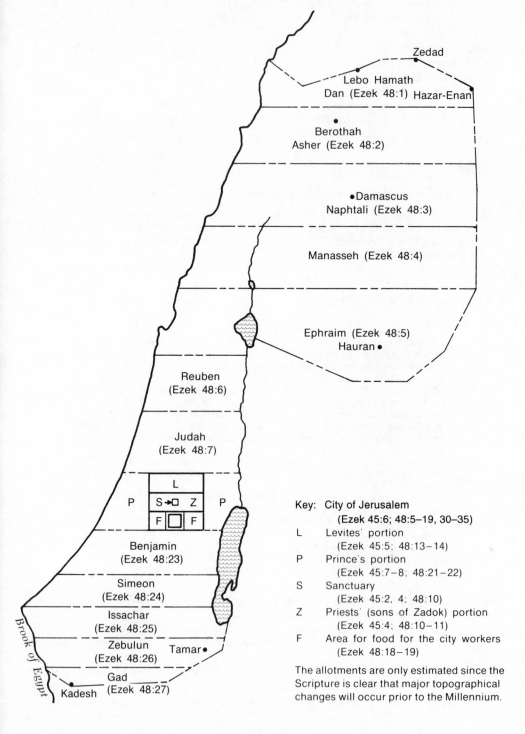

Figure 5
Land Allotment in the Millennium
(Ezek 45:1–8; 47:13–48:35)

Zedad

Lebo Hamath
Dan (Ezek 48:1) Hazar-Enan

Berothah
Asher (Ezek 48:2)

•Damascus
Naphtali (Ezek 48:3)

Manasseh (Ezek 48:4)

Ephraim (Ezek 48:5)
Hauran •

Reuben
(Ezek 48:6)

Judah
(Ezek 48:7)

L
P   S→□ Z   P
F □ F

Benjamin
(Ezek 48:23)

Simeon
(Ezek 48:24)

Issachar
(Ezek 48:25)

Zebulun   Tamar •
(Ezek 48:26)

Gad
Kadesh (Ezek 48:27)

Brook of Egypt

Key: City of Jerusalem
       (Ezek 45:6; 48:5–19, 30–35)
L   Levites' portion
       (Ezek 45:5; 48:13–14)
P   Prince's portion
       (Ezek 45:7–8; 48:21–22)
S   Sanctuary
       (Ezek 45:2, 4; 48:10)
Z   Priests' (sons of Zadok) portion
       (Ezek 45:4; 48:10–11)
F   Area for food for the city workers
       (Ezek 48:18–19)

The allotments are only estimated since the
Scripture is clear that major topographical
changes will occur prior to the Millennium.

because a standard had already been given in 42:15–20: rods (see comments in loc.). Ezekiel continued to assume that this measurement was understood and only notes the exception to it in the measurement of a fifty-cubit-wide open area around the five hundred-square-rod sanctuary area. The explicit use of cubit for the open area plus the explicit use of rods for the five-hundred-rod-square sanctuary area in 42:15–20 make it clear that the standard of measure for the sanctuary area should be rods, not cubits. Only the open area border around the sanctuary area would be measured in cubits.

This twenty-five thousand rods by twenty thousand rods area was further subdivided into two equal areas twenty-five thousand rods by ten thousand rods (vv.3–5). One was a sacred portion (Z) for the Zadokian priests who were to minister to the Lord in the temple (v.4; cf. 44:15–16; 48:9–12). Here they would place their houses. In the center of this area would be the five-hundred-rod-square area for the sanctuary, the Most Holy Place (v.3). This five-hundred-rod-square area would have a fifty-cubit-wide border of open land all around it as a barrier to separate it from all else. This would stress the holiness of the sanctuary area.

The other twenty-five thousand rod by ten thousand rod area (L) would belong to the Levites who would assist the Zadokian priests in the temple (v.5; cf. 44:10–14; 48:13–14). They would use the area for their towns. This entire area would run parallel to the portion for the Zadokian priests, immediately to the north (cf. 48:8, 21).

Another area of twenty-five thousand rods by five thousand rods, adjoining the Zadokian sacred area to the south, would provide for the city (C and F) (v.6; cf. 48:15–19, 30–35). This city was most likely Jerusalem, though no name was given. The city area would belong to the entire house of Israel.

Finally, an area was allotted to the "prince" (vv.7–8). His portion was the land immediately to the east and west of the entire sacred area composed of the Levites' portion, the Zadokian priests' portion, and the city area (cf. 48:21–22). It would parallel the tribal boundaries of Judah and Benjamin. See figure 5 for the relationship of these areas.

Ezekiel concluded this section by declaring that Israel's millennial leaders would no longer oppress God's people as leaders had done in the past (cf. 11:1–13; 14:1–11; 20:1–23:49; 34:1–10). They would allow the people to possess their own land according to their tribes without any attempts to confiscate land (cf. 48:1–29).

Notes

1 The MT's עֲשָׂרָה (ʿᵃśārāh, "ten") would be read better as עֶשְׂרִים (ʿeśrîm, "twenty") with the LXX, Syriac, and Vulgate. Verses 3, 5, and 48:13 show that this sacred area was to encompass both the ten-thousand-rod Levitical area and the ten-thousand-rod Zadokite area—the total being twenty thousand rods.

5 The LXX has read עָרִים לָשֶׁבֶת (ʿārîm lāšābet, "towns to live [in]") over againt the MT's ת עֶשְׂרִים לְשָׁכֹ (ʿeśrîm lešākōt, "twenty chambers"). The variants could easily be attributed to mental error of the scribes. The LXX reading fits the context best and should be preferred.

6) The role of the prince in the Millennium (45:9–46:18)

a) An exhortation to the contemporary unrighteous leaders

45:9–12

> ⁹ 'This is what the Sovereign LORD says: You have gone far enough, O princes of Israel! Give up your violence and oppression and do what is just and right. Stop dispossessing my people, declares the Sovereign LORD. ¹⁰You are to use accurate scales, an accurate ephah and an accurate bath. ¹¹The ephah and the bath are to be the same size, the bath containing a tenth of a homer and the ephah a tenth of a homer; the homer is to be the standard measure for both. ¹²The shekel is to consist of twenty gerahs. Twenty shekels plus twenty-five shekels plus fifteen shekels equal one mina.

9–12 The concluding verse of the preceding section implied that the leaders in Israel's past and in Ezekiel's day had seized property that was not theirs (cf. 46:18). Therefore, Ezekiel exhorted his contemporary princes (leaders) concerning their violence and oppression in which they used unjust and inaccurate scales and standards of measure. This kind of unrighteous conduct must stop in Ezekiel's day (v.9). It would not exist in the messianic kingdom.

The proper standards of measure were given. It was observed above (40:5) that linear measurements of the ancient Near East were not as accurate as those of today. This is also true of volume measurements. Ezekiel delineated the proper standard of volume measure in the terms of his day. An ephah (approx. one bushel) was a dry measure equivalent to a bath (approx. nine gallons), a liquid measure. Both were equivalent to one-tenth of an homer (approx. ninety gallons or eleven bushels), which was the basic standard of volume measure (v.11). Ezekiel also exhorted his contemporaries to make sure that their scales and measures were accurate according to this standard (v.10).

Likewise, Ezekiel clarified the proper standard for weights. One shekel weight (approx. two-fifths of an ounce) consisted of twenty gerahs (approx. one-fiftieth of an ounce). Sixty shekels comprised one mina (approx. twenty-four ounces) (v.12). It was very important that the leaders of the people be just in all their business dealings!

b) Making atonement for the people and the sanctuary

45:13–20

> ¹³ 'This is the special gift you are to offer: a sixth of an ephah from each homer of wheat and a sixth of an ephah from each homer of barley. ¹⁴The prescribed portion of oil, measured by the bath, is a tenth of a bath from each cor (which consists of ten baths or one homer, for ten baths are equivalent to a homer). ¹⁵Also one sheep is to be taken from every flock of two hundred from the well-watered pastures of Israel. These will be used for the grain offerings, burnt offerings and leadership offerings to make atonement for the people, declares the Sovereign LORD. ¹⁶All the people of the land will participate in this special gift for the use of the prince in Israel. ¹⁷It will be the duty of the prince to provide the burnt offerings, grain offerings and drink offerings at the festivals, the New Moons and the Sabbaths—at all the appointed feasts of the house of Israel. He will provide the sin offerings, grain offerings, burnt offerings and fellowship offerings to make atonement for the house of Israel.
> ¹⁸ 'This is what the Sovereign LORD says: In the first month on the first day you

are to take a young bull without defect and purify the sanctuary. ¹⁹The priest is to take some of the blood of the sin offering and put it on the doorposts of the temple, on the four corners of the upper ledge of the altar and on the gateposts of the inner court. ²⁰You are to do the same on the seventh day of the month for anyone who sins unintentionally or through ignorance; so you are to make atonement for the temple.

13–17 Contrary to the unrighteous behavior of Israel's past leaders, Israel's prince (leader) in the Millennium would be faithful to the Lord's righteous requirements. One of the prince's duties would be to make atonement for the people.

Atonement is a word that carries many connotations. Most view this term theologically with a sense of expiation for sin of a person or a people. Such was the picture lesson of the Day of Atonement in the Mosaic system (cf. Lev 16). It has also been observed that the concept of atonement may stress purification, especially when atonement was made for things. In either case, the atonement rituals of the Mosaic system and those of the millennial system described in these chapters were picture lessons and reminders of mankind's sinfulness and their need for a complete cleansing from sin and forgiveness through the efficacious atoning sacrifice of the Messiah, Jesus Christ. No other sacrifice ever provided efficacious atonement, and no other sacrifice ever would. The full and complete provision for forgiveness of man's sin was provided once and for all by Jesus Christ's shed blood, when he delivered mankind from all sin by the substitute of his life for ours (cf. comments at the introductory section to chs. 40–48).

The Israelites had made a special contribution of materials for the tabernacle's construction (cf. Exod 25:2–7; 35:5, 21, 24; 36:3, 6). In a similar manner Israel in the messianic kingdom would make a special contribution of grain, oil, and sheep to the prince from which he would, in turn, make atonement for them (vv. 13–16; cf. Exod 30:13–15; Lev 1:4). The contribution from each Israelite was one-sixth ephah (about one-sixth bushel) out of each homer (approx. eleven bushels) of wheat or barley that was harvested (v. 13), one-tenth of a bath (about one gallon) of oil from each cor (or liquid homer—approx. ninety gallons) of oil each would have (v. 14), and one sheep from every flock of two hundred that had been fed on Israel's well-watered pastures (v. 15a).

From this contribution the prince would provide grain offerings, burnt offerings, and fellowship offerings for the people's atonement (v. 15b; cf. Lev 9:7; 10:17). The general statement of v. 15 was further specified in v. 17. The prince (or leader) would bring burnt offerings, grain offerings, fellowship offerings, sin offerings, and drink offerings to make atonement for Israel at each of her festivals, her new moon celebrations, and her Sabbaths (v. 17). These rituals of atonement were commemorative of the complete and finished work of Christ for sin through the sacrifice of himself. They were in no way efficacious. They were picture-lessons and reminders to the people of their Messiah's marvelous saving work. What praise and worship they would give to the Lord for his gracious provision for sin as they viewed these sacrificial reminders in worship (cf. Rev 5:7–14)!

These acts of commemoration of atonement were limited to the weekly Sabbath, the celebration of the new moons, and all appointed festivals of Israel (cf. Lev 23:1–44; Num 28:1–29, 40). There is no special Day of Atonement in the Millennium. That special day had its full fruition in the special day of efficacious atonement provided by Christ on the cross. The people also were not asked to contribute any bulls, goats, or rams that would later be specified as the animals for sin and burnt offerings (cf. 45:21–25; 46:2–8, 11–12), in addition to the daily burnt offering (46:13–14). Though data is insufficient, perhaps these animals for the atoning sin and burnt offerings were provided by the prince (cf. vv.18, 22; 2 Chron 31:3) and not by the people in order to symbolize that God alone could make that provision; the people could not. The offerer in the Mosaic system was reminded of the substitute death for his own sins when he brought his own animal for his sin offering, except on the Day of Atonement, when all the sins of the nation were atoned for symbolically. In the Millennium the stress seemed to be that God provided the substitute, as the prince provided from his own resources the bulls, rams, and male goats.

18–20 It was also the millennial prince's annual duty to purify the temple sanctuary. On the first day of the first month (Nisan) of the ecclesiastical year, the prince ("you"), as leader, would bring a sin offering of a young bull without defect in order to purify the temple sanctuary (v.18; cf. Lev 16:16, 33; 22:20). This was necessary because of mankind's sin that would defile the temple's holiness (v.20b). Even the Zadokian priests, being human, could sin. Therefore the temple sanctuary had to be cleansed annually through this atoning (purifying) sacrifice as a reminder to all of the holiness of God and his sanctuary (v.20c; cf. 2 Chron 7:1–10; 29:20–24). In the ceremony the priest would take blood from the sacrificial bull and place it on the temple's doorposts (cf. 41:21—where the priests enter), on the four corners of the upper ledge of the altar of sacrifice, and on the gateposts of the inner court (v.19). This would be repeated on the seventh day of the month (v.20a). Through this ceremony the temple was purified symbolically for the coming year so that all might continue to worship the Lord in holiness and purity.

Notes

13 The term תְּרוּמָה (terûmāh, "special gift") is best rendered "contribution." In the Mosaic system the word was used for any special offering or gift that an Israelite would contribute to the Lord of his own free will. These contributions always went to the priests (cf. Lev 7:14; Deut 12:6, 11, 17). In the Millennium the people would contribute supplies for offerings in the worship services. They would also contribute land for the sacred area (v.1). תָּרִימוּ (tārîmû, "you are to offer") is in the plural, which indicates that the people were to make this contribution (cf. v.16).

18,20 In both verses the main verbs are in the second person singular, with the exception of כִּפַּרְתֶּם (kippartem, "you are to make atonement"), which is second person plural. This clarifies that it is the prince who actually makes the offering, though in doing so he represents all the people. When he makes atonement for the temple, the people also purify the temple through his representation.

20 The NIV's translation of שֹׁגֶה וּמִפֶּתִי (šōgeh ûmippetî, "going astray and naive") as "sins unintentionally or through ignorance" confuses the issue and creates theological perplexity concerning the concept of "unintentional sin" (cf. Kaiser, *OT Theology*, pp. 117–18).

c) *Leadership in worship*

45:21–46:15

²¹" 'In the first month on the fourteenth day you are to observe the Passover, a feast lasting seven days, during which you shall eat bread made without yeast.

²²On that day the prince is to provide a bull as a sin offering for himself and for all the people of the land. ²³Every day during the seven days of the Feast he is to provide seven bulls and seven rams without defect as a burnt offering to the LORD, and a male goat for a sin offering. ²⁴He is to provide as a grain offering an ephah for each bull and an ephah for each ram, along with a hin of oil for each ephah.

²⁵" 'During the seven days of the Feast, which begins in the seventh month on the fifteenth day, he is to make the same provision for sin offerings, burnt offerings, grain offerings, and oil.

⁴⁶:¹" 'This is what the Sovereign LORD says: The gate of the inner court facing east is to be shut on the six working days, but on the Sabbath day and on the day of the New Moon it is to be opened. ²The prince is to enter from the outside through the portico of the gateway and stand by the gatepost. The priests are to sacrifice his burnt offering and his fellowship offerings. He is to worship at the threshold of the gateway and then go out, but the gate will not be shut until evening. ³On the Sabbaths and New Moons the people of the land are to worship in the presence of the LORD at the entrance to that gateway. ⁴The burnt offering the prince brings to the LORD on the Sabbath day is to be six male lambs and a ram, all without defect. ⁵The grain offering given with the ram is to be an ephah, and the grain offering with the lambs is to be as much as he pleases, along with a hin of oil for each ephah. ⁶On the day of the New Moon he is to offer a young bull, six lambs and a ram, all without defect. ⁷He is to provide as a grain offering one ephah with the bull, one ephah with the ram, and with the lambs as much as he wants to give, along with a hin of oil with each ephah. ⁸When the prince enters, he is to go in through the portico of the gateway, and he is to come out the same way.

⁹" 'When the people of the land come before the LORD at the appointed feasts, whoever enters by the north gate to worship is to go out the south gate; and whoever enters by the south gate is to go out the north gate. No one is to return through the gate by which he entered, but each is to go out the opposite gate. ¹⁰The prince is to be among them, going in when they go in and going out when they go out.

¹¹" 'At the festivals and the appointed feasts, the grain offering is to be an ephah with a bull, an ephah with a ram, and with the lambs as much as one pleases, along with a hin of oil for each ephah. ¹²When the prince provides a freewill offering to the LORD—whether a burnt offering or fellowship offerings—the gate facing east is to be opened for him. He shall offer his burnt offering or his fellowship offerings as he does on the Sabbath day. Then he shall go out, and after he has gone out, the gate will be shut.

¹³" 'Every day you are to provide a year-old lamb without defect for a burnt offering to the LORD; morning by morning you shall provide it. ¹⁴You are also to provide with it morning by morning a grain offering, consisting of a sixth of an ephah with a third of a hin of oil to moisten the flour. The presenting of this grain offering to the LORD is a lasting ordinance. ¹⁵So the lamb and the grain offering and the oil shall be provided morning by morning for a regular burnt offering.

21–25 The prince led in the observance of the Passover and the Feast of Tabernacles. These were the only two feasts specifically mentioned in the worship procedure of Ezekiel.

The Passover (v.21; cf. Exod 12:1–14; Lev 23:5–8; Num 28:16–25) was observed in a manner similar to its observance under the Mosaic system. The Day of Passover would be celebrated on the fourteenth day of the first month (Nisan). The prince would provide a sin offering for himself and the people in commemoration of Christ's work (v.22). The Feast of Unleavened Bread would then continue for seven days. During these seven days no one was to eat unleavened bread. Each day the prince would make a daily sacrifice of seven bulls and seven rams, all without defect, as a burnt offering (commitment) to the Lord. In addition the prince would offer daily a male goat as a sin offering for the whole nation (v.23; cf. Num 28:19–24). A grain offering of one ephah mixed with one hin (approx. twelve pints) of oil would accompany each burnt offering (v.24). These procedures followed closely those of the Mosaic system.

The Feast of Tabernacles began on the fifteenth day of the seventh month (Tishri) and lasted for seven days (v.25; cf. Lev 23:33–43; Num 29:12–38, where minor variations are observed). The same daily sacrifices made for Passover would be made also for the Feast of Tabernacles. This observance provided a continual reminder of God's gracious fulfillment of his promise to bring Israel securely and permanently into the Promised Land. Surely the Israelites will give praise and thanksgiving continually to God for this!

46:1–8 The Sabbath and the observance of the new moon would be part of the worship ritual during the Millennium. It may seem incongruous that the Sabbath, the sign of the Mosaic covenant (cf. Exod 31:13, 16–17), would be observed in the millennial kingdom when it is not observed during the church age under the new covenant. Is this a retrogression in God's purposes? Not if it is understood that all God's covenants would be fulfilled and operating in the messianic kingdom (cf. 37:15–28). The Mosaic covenant would find its fruition in the messianic kingdom in that Israel finally would be God's people and he would be their God in a relationship that was to exist under the Mosaic covenant. That the pictorial sacrifices had their reality in the work of Christ does not nullify the relationship of Mosaic covenant that is a holy one. The Mosaic covenant showed Israel how to live a holy life in a relationship with God, and that type of life is still valid under the new covenant (cf. Jer 31:33–34; Rom 8:4). Therefore, for the Mosaic covenant and the new covenant to be fulfilled side by side is not incongruous. Ezekiel, however, was looking at the situation only from his perspective under the Mosaic covenant.

Just as work was to be done for six days and on the Sabbath the Israelite was to rest, so for six days the inner court's east gate would remain closed but on the Sabbath it would be open for worship (vv.1, 2c). On the Sabbath the prince would lead again his people in worship. He would enter the inner court's east gate and stand by the gate post, enjoying a position not possessed by the people (v.2a). Though the specific post was not clear, it would seem likely that it would be the doorjamb of the portico since the tables for the slaughter of offerings were in the portico. Here the prince would bring his burnt offerings and fellowship offerings that would be sacrificed by the priests, since he could not enter into the inner court (v.2b; cf. Num 29:38). The burnt offering would consist of six male lambs and a ram, all without defect, and each accompanied by a grain offering composed of one ephah of flour for the ram but as much as desired for the lambs. One hin of oil was to be mixed with each ephah of flour (v.5; cf. Num 28:9–10). The makeup of the fellowship (thanksgiving) offering was not stated, since it was normally a freewill offering of whatever the offerer chose to bring. The prince would worship at the gate's inner threshold and then return in the same way that he entered (vv.2c, 8). He would not enter the inner court. The people would worship at the east gate in the Lord's presence as the prince performed these sacrifices and worshiped within the gate (v.3).

The procedure for worship on the new moons was exactly the same for worship on the Sabbath except that the makeup of the burnt offering added a young bull along with the animals offered on the Sabbath (vv.6–7; cf. Num 28:11–15).

9–12 When Israel came to worship at the time of the appointed feasts (v.9; cf. Lev 23:37), the prince participated with the people, going in to worship and leaving whenever they did (v.10). The people entered through either the north or the south gate when they worshiped. They were not to return through the gate that they had entered but were to exit through the gate opposite from where they had entered (v.9). By entering one gate and leaving through its opposite, the flow of the festive crowd was regulated and confusion eliminated (cf. 1 Cor 14:33). Whether these gates were the outer or inner temple gates is not stated, though it would seem to be the inner court gates since the people had normal access to the temple's outer court. If so, this was the first instance of others besides the priests entering the inner court. However, if the outer gates were in view, the arrangement of entering by one gate and leaving by its opposite would pertain only to these special days, probably because of the masses.

The sacrifices offered on these appointed feasts and festivals were specifically enumerated when each festival, like Passover and Tabernacles, was discussed, or they were not specified. It was stressed that a grain offering of one ephah of flour must accompany each bull or ram offered, and as much flour as desired would make up the grain offering that accompanied the sacrifice of a lamb (v.11). If the prince desired to make a freewill offering of a burnt offering of consecration or a fellowship offering of thanksgiving, the east gate was to be opened specially for this act of worship and then closed when he finished. This was the only exception to that gate remaining closed throughout the normal six days (v.12). The prince was to present his freewill offerings in the same manner as he made offerings on the Sabbath.

13–15 There were, therefore, three occasions for sacrifice: (1) major festivals, (2) freewill offerings of the priest, (3) daily offerings. In the daily offerings the prince also led the people. Each morning he would present a burnt offering of a one-year-old lamb without defect accompanied by a grain offering of one-sixth ephah of flour and one-third hin of oil (v.13). Under the Mosaic system the daily burnt offering was offered both in the morning and in the evening. Here the offering was to be made only in the morning. The reason was not stated. This daily burnt offering, which demonstrated the commitment of God's people to him, was to be a daily reminder of that commitment. The grain offering as an accompaniment with any animal sacrifice was also to be a lasting ordinance among God's people, being a constant reminder of God's provision (v.14).

d) *Inheritance*

46:16–18

> 16" 'This is what the Sovereign LORD says: If the prince makes a gift from his inheritance to one of his sons, it will also belong to his descendants; it is to be their property by inheritance. 17If, however, he makes a gift from his inheritance to one of his servants, the servant may keep it until the year of freedom; then it will revert to the prince. His inheritance belongs to his sons only; it is theirs. 18The prince must not take any of the inheritance of the people, driving them off their property. He is to give his sons their inheritance out of his own property, so that none of my people will be separated from his property.' "

16–18 Inheritance was extremely important to the Israelite. Many laws were established to guarantee that an Israelite retained family property. This concept contin-ues in the messianic kingdom, at least in the case of the prince. Any inheritance given to one of his sons would remain with that son's descendants (v. 16). Anything given to one of his servants would revert to the prince in the jubilee year, or the year of freedom (v. 17a; cf. Lev 25:10; 27:24). The emphasis was that the prince's inheritance belonged solely to his sons (v. 17b). Ezekiel stressed, in addition, that the prince was not permitted to take other people's property and make it part of his inheritance as Israel's past leaders had so often done (v. 18a; cf. 34:3-4; 1 Kings 21:19; Mic 2:1-2). No one was ever to be separated from his property (v. 18b). The fact that the prince has sons argues against his identity as the Messiah.

7) The priests' kitchens

46:19-24

> [19]Then the man brought me through the entrance at the side of the gate to the sacred rooms facing north, which belonged to the priests, and showed me a place at the western end. [20]He said to me, "This is the place where the priests will cook the guilt offering and the sin offering and bake the grain offering, to avoid bringing them into the outer court and consecrating the people."
>
> [21]He then brought me to the outer court and led me around to its four corners, and I saw in each corner another court. [22]In the four corners of the outer court were enclosed courts, forty cubits long and thirty cubits wide; each of the courts in the four corners was the same size. [23]Around the inside of each of the four courts was a ledge of stone, with places for fire built all around under the ledge. [24]He said to me, "These are the kitchens where those who minister at the temple will cook the sacrifices of the people."

19-24 Ezekiel was brought out of the inner court to the north side of the outer court (v. 19). He was led to the entrance of the building (PB, in fig. 2) that contained the rooms where the priests ate the most holy offerings and changed their garments (cf. 42:13-14). The rooms in this building faced north (42:1-5). Here the divine messenger showed Ezekiel the place at the end of these sacred rooms where the priests would cook guilt offerings and sin offerings (v. 20). Here they also baked the grain offerings and ate all the offerings. This way the priests would not have to take these offerings into the outer court to cook them and thereby consecrate the people (cf. 44:19).

There were four kitchens (OK) in the four corners of the outer court, each forming a court in itself. Each of these kitchens was forty by thirty cubits. There was a stone ledge around the inside of each room under which fireplaces were built (vv. 21-23). These ample kitchen facilities enabled the priests (probably the Levites, cf. 44:10-14) to cook the people's sacrificial meals (v. 24).

d. Topographical aspects of the Millennium (47:1-48:35)

It is appropriate to conclude this prophetic book with a discussion of the land of Israel during the Millennium. The land has played a significant role in the history of God's people. In the Abrahamic covenant God promised to give Canaan to Abraham and the descendants as their national land (Gen 12:7). As God created the nation, he gave the people a constitution in the Mosaic covenant and a homeland in Canaan. The acquisition of the land was accomplished through Joshua's conquest. In the nation's constitution, the Mosaic covenant, God promised that Israel would appropriate the Abrahamic covenant blessings as the people obeyed the Mosaic covenant stipulations (Deut 7:12; 8:2). One of those blessings was to be in the land of Canaan. However, throughout her history Israel consistently broke the Mosaic covenant to the extent that as discipline the people were removed from the Promised Land and scattered among the nations, especially Babylonia. Ezekiel has prophesied of God's future promise to restore the people of Israel to their Promised Land, cleanse them from their wickedness, and give them a new heart, followed by salvation bliss in the land (36:24–30). Never again would Israel lose possession of her land (ch. 39).

A fitting climax to the book, therefore, is to have Ezekiel describe the character of Israel's land during the Millennium with, perhaps, glimpses into the eternal state. The divine messenger would show Ezekiel the river that would heal the land. Then he would clarify Israel's boundaries and tribal allotments during the Millennium (cf. fig. 5, p. 979).

1) The temple river

47:1–12

> ¹The man brought me back to the entrance to the temple, and I saw water coming out from under the threshold of the temple toward the east (for the temple faced east). The water was coming down from under the south side of the temple, south of the altar. ²He then brought me out through the north gate and led me around the outside to the outer gate facing east, and the water was flowing from the south side.
>
> ³As the man went eastward with a measuring line in his hand, he measured off a thousand cubits and then led me through water that was ankle-deep. ⁴He measured off another thousand cubits and led me through water that was knee-deep. He measured off another thousand and led me through water that was up to the waist. ⁵He measured off another thousand, but now it was a river that I could not cross, because the water had risen and was deep enough to swim in—a river that no one could cross. ⁶He asked me, "Son of man, do you see this?"
>
> Then he led me back to the bank of the river. ⁷When I arrived there, I saw a great number of trees on each side of the river. ⁸He said to me, "This water flows toward the eastern region and goes down into the Arabah, where it enters the Sea. When it empties into the Sea, the water there becomes fresh. ⁹Swarms of living creatures will live wherever the river flows. There will be large numbers of fish, because this water flows there and makes the salt water fresh; so where the river flows everything will live. ¹⁰Fishermen will stand along the shore; from En Gedi to En Eglaim there will be places for spreading nets. The fish will be of many kinds—like the fish of the Great Sea. ¹¹But the swamps and marshes will not become fresh; they will be left for salt. ¹²Fruit trees of all kinds will grow on both banks of the river. Their leaves will not wither, nor will their fruit fail. Every month they will bear, because the water from the sanctuary flows to them. Their fruit will serve for food and their leaves for healing."

1–12 Ezekiel was brought in the apocalyptic vision to the temple's entrance, where he saw water streaming eastward from under the south side of the temple-entrance threshold (41:2). The stream passed by the south side of the altar of sacrifice in the inner court, through the outer court, and out the temple complex along the south side of the outer eastern gate (vv. 1–2). The divine messenger took Ezekiel to explore the extent of this stream. The messenger used a measuring line to mark off four one-thousand cubit intervals (approx. one-third of a mile each) (vv. 3–5). At each one-thousand-cubit interval, the messenger took Ezekiel out into the stream to examine its depth. The depth increased at each interval from ankle deep, to knee deep, to waist deep, and finally to a depth in which one must swim. At the four-thousand-cubit mark, the stream had become a river of such magnitude that it could not be crossed. The river appeared so torrential and/or so wide that it was not possible to swim across it. This river continued to flow southeasterly toward the Arabah, the desolate Jordan Valley rift that extends south to the Red Sea (modern Gulf of Aqabah). The river flowed into the Dead Sea and caused that sea to become alive (vv.8–9).

The basic purpose of this divine river was to bring life. Many trees lined its sides (v.7). Every kind of fruit tree grew on both sides. Their leaves never withered and their fruit was perennial, bearing every month of the year because the divine river watered these trees. Their fruit provided food, and their leaves provided healing (v.12). The entire Dead Sea and the Arabah were healed by these waters, causing the Dead Sea to swarm with marine life to the extent that fishermen fished its entire length from En Gedi to En Eglaim, catching a great variety of fish (vv.9–10). The Arabah bloomed (cf. Isa 35:1–2, 6–7; Joel 3:18). Only the swamps and marshes were not healed. They were left to provide salt for the people (v.11). Everywhere else the river brought its life-giving power (v.9).

This river is similar to the rivers in the Garden of Eden and the eternal state. In Genesis 2:8–10 God provided a river that gave life to the land in that perfect environment. That life-giving river dried up with the fall of man. Now, in Ezekiel and the Revelation, the full redemption of the land would be completed (cf. Rom 8:19–22). Once again the divine life-giving waters would flow from the source of God's residence, the temple, and heal the land.

The river in Revelation 22:1–2 (cf. Zech 14:8) is extremely similar to the one described in Ezekiel 47. Though Revelation 22:2 only mentions the tree of life on either side of the river, it seems that the word "tree" in that context is most likely used in a collective sense. No variance would then exist with the trees in Ezekiel, only further clarification. As the tree of life was beside the river in the Garden of Eden, so the tree of life in abundance will be beside the life-giving river in the eternal state, if not in the Millennium. The variance between Ezekiel's account of this river and that of John in the Revelation centers on the river's source. God is the source of both rivers; but Ezekiel saw the river issuing from the temple, whereas John saw the river coming from the throne of God and of the Lamb (a temple not existing according to Rev 21:22). The river in Revelation 22:2 also flowed down the city's street, which seems difficult, but not impossible, in the Ezekiel account. Whether the visions of Ezekiel and John speak of the same river that was seen in both the Millennium and the eternal state, or whether the two rivers are different, one in the Millennium and one in the eternal state, both were similar in purpose. The source of the land's redemption and healing came from God and his throne. He would heal the land in the Millennium and also in the eternal state. After all, the Millennium is the doorway to the eternal state.

Notes

1–6 Commentators on John 7:37–39 struggle to identify which passages Jesus had in mind when he said, "As the Scripture has said," concerning the "streams of water" in their relationship to the Spirit. Usually the commentators see the reference to the general tenor of the OT. That Ezek 47:1–12 is being "fulfilled" by John 7:37–39 is problematic in the least. "Fulfillment and interpretation must be distinguished from "comparison and analogies" and other uses of the OT by the NT.

10 The location of En Eglaim is not certain. Some place it on the tongue of the Dead Sea, in which case the passage would mean that fishermen fished on both sides of the Dead Sea (cf. *Student Map Manual: Historical Geography of the Bible Lands* [Grand Rapids: Zondervan, n.d.], regional map, sec. 1–15). Others have conjectured that the site is more to the east of the Dead Sea. No one knows for sure.

---

2) *Divisions of the land* (47:13–48:35)

a) *Boundaries of the land and principles for distribution*

47:13–23

¹³This is what the Sovereign Lord says: "These are the boundaries by which you are to divide the land for an inheritance among the twelve tribes of Israel, with two portions for Joseph. ¹⁴You are to divide it equally among them. Because I swore with uplifted hand to give it to your forefathers, this land will become your inheritance.

¹⁵"This is to be the boundary of the land:

"On the north side it will run from the Great Sea by the Hethlon road past Lebo Hamath to Zedad, ¹⁶Berothah and Sibraim (which lies on the border between Damascus and Hamath), as far as Hazer Hatticon, which is on the border of Hauran. ¹⁷The boundary will extend from the sea to Hazar Enan, along the northern border of Damascus, with the border of Hamath to the north. This will be the north boundary.
¹⁸"On the east side the boundary will run between Hauran and Damascus, along the Jordan between Gilead and the land of Israel, to the eastern sea and as far as Tamar. This will be the east boundary.
¹⁹"On the south side it will run from Tamar as far as the waters of Meribah Kadesh, then along the Wadi of Egypt to the Great Sea. This will be the south boundary.
²⁰"On the west side, the Great Sea will be the boundary to a point opposite Lebo Hamath. This will be the west boundary.

²¹"You are to distribute this land among yourselves according to the tribes of Israel. ²²You are to allot it as an inheritance for yourselves and for the aliens who have settled among you and who have children. You are to consider them as native-born Israelites; along with you they are to be allotted an inheritance among the tribes of Israel. ²³In whatever tribe the alien settles, there you are to give him his inheritance," declares the Sovereign Lord.

13–14 Ezekiel first set forth the manner in which the land would be distributed (cf. fig. 5). The land would be divided equally (lit., "each like his brother") among Israel's twelve tribes (vv. 13–14a). Two portions would go to Joseph in the form of tribal allotments for his two sons: Manasseh and Ephraim (cf. the promise in Gen 48:5–6, 22). The tribe of Joseph had been divided into two tribes to replace Levi. Therefore there were only twelve tribal land divisions of equal proportions. The tribe of Levi had become the priestly tribe, and in the Millennium they would have a special land for their residence (cf. 45:1–8; 48:8–14). The principle of equality would prevail. Any past abuses of inequity would be remedied.

The Lord reminded Israel that the reception of any portion of the Promised Land by a tribe was strictly on the basis of God's promise (v.14). None of them had done anything to deserve an allotment. God had promised the inheritance of this land in his covenant with Abraham (cf. Gen 12:7; 15:7, 18–21; 17:8).

15–20 Israel's national boundaries in the Millennium were similar to those of ancient Israel (cf. Num 34:3–12). The borders followed known place names from Ezekiel's day and were given in such detail that they were without question to be taken literally. (Follow fig. 5 as this portion is studied.)

The boundary started at the north, and each side was described in order clockwise. The north border (vv.15–17; cf. Num 34:7–9) started at an unspecified point on the Great (Mediterranean) Sea, though the remainder of the description would imply that that point might be around the mouth of the present-day Litanni River (on Lebo Hamath, cf. note at v.15). This border followed an easterly direction in between the unknown boundaries of Damascus on the south and Hamath on the north to the site of Hazar Enan. The sites of Berothah, Sibraim, and Hazer Hatticon have not been located. Hamath and Zedad (perhaps modern Sadad southeast of Homs) as well as the area of Hauran have each received at least tentative identification. The general scope of this border can be seen in figure 5.

The land's eastern border ran between the Hauran and Damascus districts to the Jordan River, where it followed the river south of the eastern (or Dead) sea (v.18; Num 34:10–12). The southern border extended from Tamar (southwest of the Dead Sea) through Meriboth Kadesh (or Kadesh-barnea, cf. Num 20:13, 24; 27:14), to the wadi of Egypt (present day Wadi el-Arish), which it followed to the Great (Mediterranean) Sea (v.19; cf. Num 34:3–5). The western boundary was the Great Sea (v.20; cf. Num 34:6). In contrast the land of God's people in the eternal state will have no sea, since the sea will no longer exist (Rev 21:1). Old Testament Israelite boundaries included two and one-half tribes in the Transjordan.

21–23 Further guidelines for the distribution of the land were given in order to treat the question of allotment as it related to aliens in Israel's midst. Aliens who had settled within Israel in a given tribe and had borne children (indicating their permanency) were to be included in that given tribe when the land was distributed. These aliens were to be treated as if they were native Israelites (v.22). In this Israel would obey the Mosaic convenant (cf. Lev 19:34).

Notes

15 The term לְבוֹא (lᵉḇôʾ, "Lebo") is best rendered as a verb ("to enter") in this verse due to the word order. Rearrangement of the word order is not warranted. In v.20 the term appears to be part of a combination place name, Lebo Hamath.

18 Some would read תָּמָרָה (tāmārāh, "towards Tamar") in place of the MT's תָּמֹדּוּ (tāmōddû, "to measure"). Though the LXX and the Syriac support the first reading, it appears to be influenced by the place name Tamar, mentioned in v.19, that starts the southern border. It would be best to accept the MT's reading.

19 Though the place מְרִיבוֹת קָדֵשׁ (mᵉrîḇôt qāḏēš, "Meriboth Kadesh") has a plural afformative rather than the singular afformative of מְרִיבַת קָדֵשׁ (mᵉrîḇat qāḏēš, "Meribah Kadesh"), the geographical context and the parallel in Num 34:3–5 would argue for the sites being identical.

---

b) *Tribal allotments in the north*

48:1–7

> ¹"These are the tribes, listed by name: At the northern frontier, Dan will have one portion; it will follow the Hethlon road to Lebo Hamath; Hazar Enan and the northern border of Damascus next to Hamath will be part of its border from the east side to the west side.
> ²"Asher will have one portion; it will border the territory of Dan from east to west.
> ³"Naphtali will have one portion; it will border the territory of Asher from east to west.
> ⁴"Manasseh will have one portion; it will border the territory of Naphtali from east to west.
> ⁵"Ephraim will have one portion; it will border the territory of Manasseh from east to west.
> ⁶"Reuben will have one portion; it will border the territory of Ephraim from east to west.
> ⁷"Judah will have one portion; it will border the territory of Reuben from east to west.

1–7 Each tribal area was declared to be equal according to 47:14. Each would have parallel borders on the north and south and would stretch from the west boundary to the east boundary, in equal sizes, one next to the other. (Note that fig. 5 only approximates the land areas since exact dimensions are not given. The areas will be equal, however, though they may not be equal in fig. 5 except for the north-south dimension.)

The allotments were listed for the tribes beginning at the north and progressing south. The order has no conformity to any other in Israel's history. The tribes that originated through Jacob's wives' handmaids were placed on the outer extremities, whereas the tribes from Jacob's wives, Rachel and Leah, were in the center of the land (cf. Gen 35:23–26). The faithful tribes of the southern kingdom of Judah—Judah and Benjamin—would have the privileged positions next to the land's special sacred portion. The order of the tribes from the north to the special sacred portion of the land were Dan (v.1), Asher (v.2), Naphtali (v.3), Manasseh (v.4), Ephraim (v.5), Reuben (v.6), and Judah (v.7).

c) *The special gift of the land*

48:8–22

> ⁸"Bordering the territory of Judah from east to west will be the portion you are to present as a special gift. It will be 25,000 cubits wide, and its length from east to west will equal one of the tribal portions; the sanctuary will be in the center of it.
> ⁹"The special portion you are to offer to the LORD; will be 25,000 cubits long and 10,000 cubits wide. ¹⁰This will be the sacred portion for the priests. It will be 25,000 cubits long on the north side, 10,000 cubits wide on the west side, 10,000 cubits wide on the east side and 25,000 cubits long on the south side. In the center of it will be the sanctuary of the LORD. ¹¹This will be for the consecrated priests, the Zadokites, who were faithful in serving me and did not go astray as

the Levites did when the Israelites went astray. ¹²It will be a special gift to them from the sacred portion of the land, a most holy portion, bordering the territory of the Levites.

¹³"Alongside the territory of the priests, the Levites will have an allotment 25,000 cubits long and 10,000 cubits wide. Its total length will be 25,000 cubits and its width 10,000 cubits. ¹⁴They must not sell or exchange any of it. This is the best of the land and must not pass into other hands, because it is holy to the LORD.

¹⁵"The remaining area, 5,000 cubits wide and 25,000 cubits long, will be for the common use of the city, for houses and for pastureland. The city will be in the center of it ¹⁶and will have these measurements: the north side 4,500 cubits, the south side 4,500 cubits, the east side 4,500 cubits, and the west side 4,500 cubits. ¹⁷The pastureland for the city will be 250 cubits on the north, 250 cubits on the south, 250 cubits on the east, and 250 cubits on the west. ¹⁸What remains of the area, bordering on the sacred portion and running the length of it, will be 10,000 cubits on the east side and 10,000 cubits on the west side. Its produce will supply food for the workers of the city. ¹⁹The workers from the city who farm it will come from all the tribes of Israel. ²⁰The entire portion will be a square, 25,000 cubits on each side. As a special gift you will set aside the sacred portion, along with the property of the city.

²¹"What remains on both sides of the area formed by the sacred portion and the city property will belong to the prince. It will extend eastward from the 25,000 cubits of the sacred portion to the eastern border, and westward from the 25,000 cubits to the western border. Both these areas running the length of the tribal portions will belong to the prince, and the sacred portion with the temple sanctuary will be in the center of them. ²²So the property of the Levites and the property of the city will lie in the center of the area that belongs to the prince. The area belonging to the prince will lie between the border of Judah and the border of Benjamin.

8–14 A portion of the land—25,000 rods wide and having the same length as the tribal allotments from east to west—was set aside by the people as a special contribution to the Lord (v.8; cf. 45:1–8). (It seems best to understand "rods" here rather than "cubits," as explained in the comments at 42:15–20 and 45:1–8.) This special portion was composed of four distinct parts (cf. fig. 5): (1) the sacred area given to the Zadokian priests (vv.9–12), (2) the Levites' land (vv.13–14), (3) the city land (vv.15–20), and (4) the prince's land (vv.21–22).

The special contribution to the Lord for the sacred area of the Zadokian priests (Z, fig. 5) (vv.9–12; cf. 45:2–5) was 25,000 rods long on its north and south sides and 10,000 rods long on its east and west sides. The Lord's sanctuary (S) would be in the center of this territory (v.10b; cf. 45:4c).

To the north of this Zadokian portion would lie the Levites' land (L, fig. 5) (vv.13–14). This territory would have the same dimensions as that of the Zadokian priests mentioned above. The Lord did exhort the Levites to make sure that they did not sell, exchange, or in any way allow this land to pass to others because it belonged to the Lord (v.14). It was holy to him.

15–20 Land set aside for the city would be 25,000 rods long on the north and south sides and 5,000 rods long on the east and west sides (v.15a). This land would be used for the city, houses, and pasture (v.15b). The city (C, fig. 5) would be in the exact center of this portion (v.15c). The city would be 4,500 rods square with a strip of land 250 rods wide all around it on each side (vv.16–17). This land strip would be used for the city's pastureland. The city's total dimensions with its border would be 5,000 rods square (cf. v.15; 45:6). The remainder of the land on either side (F) of the city would be used for growing food for the workers in the city (v.18). These two equal segments would be 5,000 rods long on the east and west sides and 10,000 rods long on their north and south sides. Workers from every tribe who lived in the city would farm this land (v.19).

The entire area that included the Levites' land, the Zadokian land, and the city land would form a combined area 25,000 rods square (v.20).

21–22 The land on either side of this 25,000-rod-square sacred area would be given to the prince (P, fig. 5) (v.21; cf. 45:7–46:18). His land areas to the east and west of the sacred portion would extend to the national boundaries, east and west, as did all the tribal areas. The property of the Levites and priests, along with that of the city, would lie in the center of the prince's land. The entire sacred area and the prince's land would lie between the tribal allotments of Judah to the north and Benjamin to the south (v.22).

d) Tribal allotments in the south

48:23–29

²³"As for the rest of the tribes: Benjamin will have one portion; it will extend from the east side to the west side.
²⁴"Simeon will have one portion; it will border the territory of Benjamin from east to west.
²⁵"Issachar will have one portion; it will border the territory of Simeon from east to west.
²⁶"Zebulun will have one portion; it will border the territory of Issachar from east to west.
²⁷"Gad will have one portion; it will border the territory of Zebulun from east to west.
²⁸"The southern boundary of Gad will run south from Tamar to the waters of Meribah Kadesh, then along the Wadi of Egypt to the Great Sea.
²⁹"This is the land you are to allot as an inheritance to the tribes of Israel, and these will be their portions," declares the Sovereign LORD.

23–29 The tribal allotments of Israel's land south of the land's special portion are stated in these verses. Receiving the equal allotments, in order, from Benjamin south, were Benjamin (vv.23–24), Simeon (v.25), Issachar (v.26), Zebulun (v.27), and Gad (v.28). A summary is given in v.29.

e) The city and its gates

48:30–35

³⁰"These will be the exits of the city: Beginning on the north side, which is 4,500 cubits long, ³¹the gates of the city will be named after the tribes of Israel. The three gates on the north side will be the gate of Reuben, the gate of Judah and the gate of Levi.
³²"On the east side, which is 4,500 cubits long, will be three gates: the gate of Joseph, the gate of Benjamin and the gate of Dan.
³³"On the south side, which measures 4,500 cubits, will be three gates: the gate of Simeon, the gate of Issachar and the gate of Zebulun.
³⁴"On the west side, which is 4,500 cubits long, will be three gates: the gate of Gad, the gate of Asher and the gate of Naphtali.

35"The distance all around will be 18,000 cubits.
"And the name of the city from that time on will be:
THE LORD IS THERE."

30–35 The city in the center of the 10,000 by 5,000 rod section south of the priests' sacred area is not named (cf. vv.15–19). Most likely it was Jerusalem (cf. Zech 14:8). In keeping with the dimensions given in vv.15–19, Ezekiel declared that the distance around the city, minus its pasture strip, would be 18,000 rods (v.35a). The main emphasis in this section is on the city's twelve gates, each named after one of Israel's tribes (vv.30–34). Similarly, Jerusalem in the eternal state would have three gates on each side, each gate being named after one of Israel's tribes (cf. Rev 21:12–13). There were three gates on each side of the city in Ezekiel's vision. The descendants of Leah were on the north and south sides. On the north the three gates were named Reuben (the first born), Judah (tribe of David), and Levi (tribe of priests) (v.31). On the south the three gates were named Simeon, Issachar, and Zebulun (v.33). The three gates on the east were named after Rachel's two sons, Joseph and Benjamin, plus Dan, the son of Bilhah, Rachel's handmaid (v.32). The three gates on the west were named after the descendants of the two handmaids, Zilpah and Bilhah: Gad, Asher, and Naphtali (v.34).

Ths city was square, and the city in the Revelation also is square (actually, it is a cube; cf. Rev 21:16). These likenesses between the city in Ezekiel and that in the Revelation have caused some to identify them with each other. However, additional data in the Revelation should cause some hesitancy about a quick decision. If the two are not identical, they certainly demonstrate that the characteristics of the Millennium and those of the eternal state are similar.

Ezekiel concluded his great prophecy by giving the city a name, a name that the city would have from that day forward: "The LORD is there" (*YHWH šāmmāh*). The Lord would reside forever with his people. Never again would they be separated from him through discipline. Forever Israel would live as God's people and he as their God! This name would characterize God's city just as in Hebrew thought any new name gave a new character to its recipient.